THE
JANUARY
6TH
REPORT

Published by Celadon Books in collaboration with

THE NEW YORKER

THE
JANUARY
6TH
REPORT

The Report of the Select Committee to
Investigate the January 6th Attack on
the United States Capitol

Preface by
DAVID REMNICK

Epilogue by
CONGRESSMAN JAMIE RASKIN

CELADON
BOOKS

NEW YORK

CELADON
BOOKS

Founded in 2017, Celadon Books, a division of
Macmillan Publishers, publishes a highly curated list
of twenty to twenty-five new titles a year. The list of
both fiction and nonfiction is eclectic and focuses
on publishing commercial and literary books and
discovering and nurturing talent.

———————

www.celadonbooks.com

The Library of Congress Cataloging-in-Publication
Data is available upon request.

ISBN 978-1-250-87752-9 (paperback)
ISBN 978-1-250-87795-6 (ebook)

Our books may be purchased in bulk for promotional, educational,
or business use. Please contact your local bookseller or the Macmillan Corporate
and Premium Sales Department at 1-800-221-7945, extension 5442,
or by email at MacmillanSpecialMarkets@macmillan.com.

First Edition: 2022

CONTENTS

NOTE TO THE READER:

All page numbers below refer to running page numbers in this book. The page numbers within The January 6th Report have been left intact and unaltered.

Scan the code or go to bit.ly/january-6th-report
to access the January 6th Report's appendices,
transcripts, and additional content.

PREFACE

By David Remnick

In the weeks while the House select committee to investigate the insurrection at the Capitol was finishing its report, Donald Trump, the focus of its inquiry, betrayed no sense of alarm or self-awareness. At his country-club exile in Palm Beach, Trump ignored the failures of his favored candidates in the midterm elections and announced that he was running again for President. He dined cheerfully and unapologetically with a spiralling Kanye West and a young neo-fascist named Nick Fuentes. He mocked the government's insistence that he turn over all the classified documents that he'd hoarded as personal property. Finally, he declared that he had a "major announcement," only to unveil the latest in a lifetime of grifts. In the old days, it was Trump University, Trump Steaks, Trump Ice. This time, he was hawking "limited edition" digital trading cards at ninety-nine dollars apiece, illustrated portraits of himself as an astronaut, a sheriff, a superhero. The pitch began with the usual hokum: "Hello everyone, this is Donald Trump, hopefully your favorite President of all time, better than Lincoln, better than Washington."

In his career as a New York real-estate shyster and tabloid denizen, then as the forty-fifth President of the United States, Trump has been the most transparent of public figures. He does little to conceal his most distinctive characteristics: his racism, misogyny, dishonesty, narcissism, incompetence, cruelty, instability, and corruption. And yet what has kept Trump afloat for so long, what has helped him evade ruin and prosecution, is perhaps his most salient quality: he is shameless. That is the never-apologize-never-explain core of him. Trump is hardly the first dishonest President, the first incurious President, the first liar. But he is the most shameless. His contrition is impossible to conceive. He is insensible to disgrace.

On December 19, 2022, the committee spelled out a devastating set of accusations against Trump: obstruction of an official proceeding; conspiracy to defraud the nation; conspiracy to make false statements; and, most grave of all, inciting, assisting, aiding, or comforting an insurrection. For the first time in the history of the United States, Congress referred a former President to the Department of Justice for criminal prosecution. The criminal referrals have no formal authority, though they could play some role in pushing Jack Smith, the special counsel appointed by Attorney General Merrick Garland, to issue indictments. The report certainly adds immeasurably to the wealth of evidence describing Trump's actions and intentions. One telling example: The committee learned that Hope Hicks, the epitome of a loyal adviser, told Trump more than once in the days leading up to the protest to urge the demonstrators to keep things peaceful. "I suggested it several times Monday and Tuesday and he refused," she wrote in a text to another adviser. When Hicks questioned Trump's behavior concerning the insurrection and the consequences for his legacy, he made his priorities clear: "Nobody will care about my legacy if I lose. So, that won't matter. The only thing that matters is winning."

Trump has been similarly dismissive of the committee's work, going on the radio to tell Dan Bongino, the host of "The Dan Bongino Show," that he had been the victim of a "kangaroo court." On Truth

Social, his social-media platform, he appealed to the loyalty of his supporters: "Republicans and Patriots all over the land must stand strong and united against the Thugs and Scoundrels of the Unselect Committee…. These folks don't get it that when they come after me, the people who love freedom rally around me. It strengthens me. What doesn't kill me makes me stronger."

Experience makes it plain that Trump will just keep going on like this, deflecting, denying, lashing out at his accusers, even if it means that he will end his days howling in a bare and echoing room. It matters little that the report shows that even members of his innermost circle, from his Attorney General to his daughter, know the depths of his vainglorious delusions. He will not repent. He will not change. But the importance of the committee's report has far less to do with the spectacle of Trump's unravelling. Its importance resides in the establishment of a historical record, the depth of its evidence, the story it tells of a deliberate, coördinated assault on American democracy that could easily have ended with the kidnapping or assassination of senior elected officials, the emboldenment of extremist groups and militias, and, above all, a stolen election, a coup.

The committee was not alone in its investigation. Many journalists contributed to the steady accretion of facts. But, with the power of subpoena, the committee was able to uncover countless new illuminating details. One example: In mid-December, 2020, the Supreme Court threw out a lawsuit filed by the State of Texas that would have challenged the counting of millions of ballots. Trump, of course, supported the suit. He was furious when it, like dozens of similar suits, was dismissed. According to Cassidy Hutchinson, who worked directly for Mark Meadows, the White House chief of staff, Trump was "raging" about the decision: "He had said something to the effect of, 'I don't want people to know we lost, Mark. This is embarrassing. Figure it out. We need to figure it out. I don't want people to know that we lost.'"

In large measure, this report is the story of how Trump, humiliated by his loss to Joe Biden, conspired to obstruct Congress, defraud the country he was pledged to serve, and incite an insurrection to keep himself in power.

The origins of the committee and its work are plain: On January 6, 2021, thousands marched on the Capitol in support of Trump and his conspiratorial and wholly fabricated charge that the Presidential election the previous November had been stolen from him. Demonstrators breached police barricades, broke through windows and doors, and ran through the halls of Congress threatening to exact vengeance on the Vice-President, the Speaker of the House, and other officeholders. Seven people died as a result of the insurrection. About a hundred and fourteen law-enforcement officers were injured.

Half a year later, the House of Representatives voted to establish a panel charged with investigating every aspect of the insurrection—including the role of the former President. An earlier attempt in the Senate to convene an investigative panel had met with firm resistance from the Minority Leader, Mitch McConnell, who called it an "extraneous" project; despite support from six Republican senators, it failed to get the sixty votes required. It was left to the Democratic leadership in the House to form a committee. The vote, held on June 30, 2021, was largely along party lines, but the U.S. House Select Committee to Investigate the January 6th Attack on the United States Capitol officially came into existence.

Speaker Nancy Pelosi then asked the Republicans to name G.O.P. members to join the panel. The House Minority Leader, Kevin McCarthy, responded by proposing some of the most prominent election deniers in his caucus, including Jim Jordan, of Ohio, who had attended "Stop the Steal" demonstrations and was sure to behave as an ardent obstructionist. Pelosi, who had named Liz Cheney, of

Wyoming, to the panel, rejected two of McCarthy's five recommendations, saying, "The unprecedented nature of January 6th demands this unprecedented decision." After conferring with Trump, McCarthy refused to provide alternatives, and abruptly withdrew all of his proposals, gambling that doing so would derail or discredit the initiative. Pelosi, in turn, asked a second Republican who had, with Cheney, voted to impeach the President on a vote held on January 13th—Adam Kinzinger, of Illinois—to serve on the committee. Both Cheney and Kinzinger accepted.

Cheney, a firm conservative and the daughter of former Vice-President Dick Cheney, had made her judgment of Trump well known. "The President of the United States summoned this mob, assembled the mob, and lit the flame of this attack," she said not long after the insurrection. "Everything that followed was his doing." She knew that by opposing Trump and joining Kinzinger and the Democrats on the committee she was almost sure to lose her seat in Congress. She didn't care, she said later, declaring her work on the panel, on which she served as vice-chair, the "most important" of her career. The G.O.P. leadership was unimpressed with this declaration of principle. In February, 2022, the Republican National Committee censured both Cheney and Kinzinger.

In deciding how to proceed with its investigation, the committee's chairman, Bennie G. Thompson, of Mississippi, along with Liz Cheney and the seven other members, looked to a range of similarly high-profile investigative panels of the past, including the so-called Kefauver Committee, which investigated organized crime, in 1950-51; the President's Commission on the Assassination of President John F. Kennedy, known as the Warren Commission, in 1963-64; the Senate Watergate hearings, in 1973; the Iran-Contra hearings, in 1987; and, particularly, the 9/11 Commission, in 2002-04. The committee hired staff investigators who had worked in the Department of Justice and in law enforcement, and they conducted more than a thousand interviews. Teams were color-coded and tasked with making "deep dives" into various aspects of January 6th. The division of labor included a "blue team," which examined the preparation for and the reaction to events by law enforcement; a "green team," which examined the financial backing for the plot; a "purple team," which conducted an analysis of the extremist groups involved in the storming of the Capitol; a "red team," which studied the rally on the Ellipse and the Stop the Steal movement; and a "gold team," which looked specifically at Trump's role in the insurrection.

Committee members also insisted on inquiring into whether Trump planned to use emergency powers to overturn the vote, call out the National Guard, and invoke the Insurrection Act. Was Trump's inaction during the rioting on Capitol Hill merely a matter of miserable leadership, or was it a deliberate strategy of fomenting chaos in order to stay in the White House? "That dereliction of duty causes us real concern," Thompson said. In this way, an inquiry into a specific episode broadened to encompass a topic of still greater significance: Had the President sought to undermine and circumvent the American system of electoral democracy?

The political urgency of the committee's work was geared to the calendar. Members had initially hoped to complete and publish a report before the 2022 midterm elections. But that proved impossible, such was the volume of evidence. Still, the committee members knew they could not go on indefinitely. The Republicans were likely to win back a majority in the House, in November, and McCarthy, who was the most likely to succeed Nancy Pelosi as Speaker, would almost certainly choose not to reauthorize the committee, effectively shutting it down; it was also quite possible, they knew, that McCarthy and the Republicans might generate "counter" hearings as an act of retribution.

As the committee began its work, it was soon clear that the Republican leadership in the House had made a tactical error in refusing to appoint any members to the panel. Even Republicans less vociferous than Jordan would have had the power to slow down the investigations, debate points with Democratic members, and appoint less aggressive staff members. Instead, the committee, with its seven Democrats and two anti-Trump Republicans, worked in relative harmony, taking full advantage of a sense of common purpose and the capacities of a congressional committee.

Still, they faced predictable obstacles. Not only did many Trump loyalists refuse to testify; much of the American public was, after so many previous investigations, impeachments, scandals, and news alerts, weary of hearing about the unending saga of Donald Trump. Who would pay attention? What more was there to learn? In a polarized America, who was left to be persuaded? Committee members such as Jamie Raskin, of Maryland, insisted that the real purpose of the investigation was to establish the truth. What prosecutors and the electorate make of those facts is beyond the committee's authority.

The committee members determined that they could not go about the hearings in the old way, with day after day of interminable questioning of witnesses. Instead, they needed to produce discrete, well-produced, briskly paced multimedia "episodes" designed to highlight various aspects of the insurrection: its origins, its funding, the behavior of the President, the level of involvement by white nationalists, militias, and other menacing groups. The members agreed that, in an age of peak TV, they needed to present a kind of series, one that was dramatic, accessible, accurate, evidence-rich, and convincing. Ideally, they would provide a narrative that did not merely preach to the converted but reached the millions of Americans who were indifferent to or confused by the unending stream of noise, indirection, hysteria, lying, and chaos that had characterized the hyperpolarized era. The committee also recognized that only a minority would watch the full hearings, much less read every word of a long narrative report months later. They needed to produce the hearings in a way that could also be transmitted effectively in bits on social media and go viral. They needed memorable moments and characters. In the words of one staffer, "We needed to bring things to life."

To help with that effort, the committee hired an adviser, the British-born television producer James Goldston, who had been a foreign correspondent for the BBC in Northern Ireland and Kosovo. Goldston had also covered the impeachment of Bill Clinton. In 2004, he moved to New York and went to work at ABC, where he ran "Good Morning America" and "Nightline"; between 2014 and 2021, he served as president of ABC News. The committee decided to videotape its depositions, and Goldston was among those who helped to select brief and particularly vivid moments from those long interviews, the way a journalist uses quotations or scenes to enliven a piece of narrative prose. The committee's presentations also employed everything from surveillance video to police radio traffic to the e-mails and tweets of government officials, right-wing media personalities, militia leaders, and the insurrectionists on Capitol Hill.

"We live in an era where, no matter how important the subject, it's competing for attention," Goldston told a reporter for TheWrap. "People are distracted, people have got a lot going on. And so, the hope was, by bringing these new techniques to this format, that we could engage people in a way that perhaps they wouldn't otherwise have been." The second prime-time hearing brought in nearly eighteen million viewers, an audience comparable to NBC's "Sunday Night Football." The Republican House leadership was predictably unimpressed with the committee's commitment to narrative, prompting Kevin McCarthy to say that the Democrats had hired Goldston to "choreograph their Jan. 6 political theater."

The committee's published report does not have a single authorial voice. Rather, it is a collaborative effort written mainly by a team of investigators and staffers, with input from members of the committee. And, while it lacks a mediating, consistent voice, it is a startlingly rich narrative, thick with details of malevolent intent, political conspiracy, sickening violence, and human folly. There is no question that historians will feast on these pages; what the Department of Justice does with this evidence remains to be seen.

At times, there's comedy embedded in this tragic narrative. A figure such as Eric Herschmann, a Trump adviser, holds the stage long enough to recount telling the Trump lawyer John Eastman that his plan to overturn the election is "completely crazy": "Are you out of your effing mind?" And: "Get a great effing criminal defense lawyer. You're gonna need it." Viewers of Herschmann's deliciously profane taped testimony were transfixed by at least two artifacts on the wall behind him: a baseball bat with the word "Justice" written on it and a print of "Wild Thing," Rob Pruitt's image of a panda, which also makes an appearance in the erotic thriller "Fifty Shades of Grey."

Anyone who watched the hearings and who now reads this report will dwell at times on the outsized figures who emerge, either in their own testimony or as described by others: the neo-fascistic campaign strategist and onetime White House aide Steve Bannon; the blandly ambitious Mark Meadows, the chief of staff in the final year of the Trump Administration; and, of course, the oft-inebriated Rudy Giuliani, the onetime New York City mayor and Trump's personal lawyer.

Time and again, senior figures in the drama refused to testify, hiding behind claims of executive privilege. The report includes many comical instances of would-be witnesses claiming their Fifth Amendment rights and refusing to answer questions as benign as where they went to college. And so it was often the junior staffers in the Administration, with far less to spend on legal fees and with their futures at risk, who stepped forward to describe what they had seen and heard. The most memorable such episode came on June 28th, when Cassidy Hutchinson, the earnest young aide to Meadows, testified live before the committee. Hutchinson had already been deposed four times, for a total of more than twenty hours. Liz Cheney, as the vice-chair, began the session by announcing that Hutchinson had received an ominous phone call from someone in Trump's circle saying, "He wants me to let you know he's thinking about you. He knows you're loyal. And you're going to do the right thing when you go in for your deposition." Cheney bluntly referred to this as tantamount to witness tampering. When the report and its accompanying materials were finally released, we learned that Hutchinson told the committee that a former Trump White House lawyer named Stefan Passantino, who represented her early in the process, had instructed her to feign a faulty memory and "focus on protecting the President." She said Passantino made it plain that he would help find her "a really good job in Trump world" so long as she protected "the family." Hutchinson also testified that an aide to Meadows, Ben Williamson, had passed along a message from Meadows that he "knows that you'll do the right thing tomorrow and that you're going to protect him and the boss."

But Hutchinson, who had been a loyal staffer in the Trump White House, privy to countless conversations in and around the offices of the President and the chief of staff, would not be intimidated. She found new counsel and thwarted the thuggish attempts to gain her silence, delivering some of the most damning testimony of the investigation. She described conversations, some secondhand, that made it plain that Trump knew full well that he had lost the election but would stop at nothing to keep power. Because of her preternatural calm before the microphone, the uninflected, more-in-sadness-than-in-anger tone of her delivery, Hutchinson was often compared to John Dean, the White House counsel under Richard Nixon, who emerged from the Watergate hearings as the most memorable and decisive witness.

But the nature of Hutchinson's testimony, in keeping with the era, was distinctly more lurid than Dean's. She recalled how Trump hurled his lunch against the wall, splattering ketchup everywhere, when he learned that Attorney General William Barr had publicly declared that there was, in fact, no evidence of election fraud. On other occasions, she said, the President pulled out "the tablecloth to let all the contents of the table go onto the floor and likely break or go everywhere." She recounted the names of the many Trumpists—including Meadows, Giuliani, Matt Gaetz, and Louie Gohmert—who had requested that Trump grant them pardons in connection with the Capitol attack. She said that, three days before the insurrection, the White House counsel, Pat Cipollone, told Trump that, if he carried out his plan to march to the Capitol with the crowds, "we're going to get charged with every crime imaginable." Hutchinson testified that on January 6th Cipollone told Meadows, "They're literally calling for the Vice President to be effing hung." As she recalled, "Mark had responded something to the effect of 'You heard him, Pat. He thinks Mike deserves it. He doesn't think they're doing anything wrong.' "

Finally, Hutchinson made it clear just how much Trump had wanted to join the insurrectionists on Capitol Hill. Trump was so incensed with his Secret Service detail for refusing to take him there, she testified, that he lunged at the agent driving his car and struggled for the wheel. The report corroborates Hutchinson's testimony, saying that the "vast majority" of its law-enforcement sources described a "furious interaction" between the President and his security contingent in his S.U.V. The sources said that Trump was "furious," "insistent," "profane," and "heated." The committee concluded that Trump had hoped to lead the effort to overturn the election either from inside the House chamber or from a stage outside the building.

Hutchinson was equally forthright about Trump's disregard for public safety. Despite being told that many of the supporters who came out to see him speak on January 6th were armed, she said, Trump insisted that the Secret Service remove the "mags"—the metal detectors.

He was not terribly concerned that someone might be killed or injured, so long as it wasn't him. "I don't fucking care that they have weapons," he said, according to Hutchinson. "They're not here to hurt me."

The insurrection at the Capitol was of such grave consequence for liberal democracy and the rule of law that commentators have struggled ever since to find some historical precedent to provide context and understanding to a nation in a state of continuing crisis. Some thought immediately of the sack of the Capitol, in 1814, though the perpetrators then were foreign, soldiers of the British crown. Others have pointed to contested Presidential elections of the past—1824, 1876, 1960, 2000—but those ballots were certified, peacefully and lawfully, by Congress. None of the losers sought to foment an uprising or create a national insurgency. Compare Trump's self-absorption and rage with Al Gore's graceful acceptance of the Supreme Court's decision handing the election to George W. Bush: "Tonight, for the sake of our unity as a people and the strength of our democracy, I offer my concession."

Still, there have been efforts to overturn the constitutional order, notably in the "secession winter" of 1860-61, when seven slaveholding states, having warned that they would never accept the election of Abraham Lincoln, declared themselves in opposition to the United States itself. As Lincoln prepared for his inauguration, to be held in March, he received a series of warnings that an army raised in Virginia might invade Washington, D.C. So prevalent were the rumors of a Confederate conspiracy that Congress assembled a committee to "inquire whether a secret organization hostile to the government of the United States exists in the District of Columbia." Lincoln was particularly concerned about a potential plot to undermine the counting of electors, an event scheduled for February. In the end, John Breckinridge, James Buchanan's Vice-President and a loser in the 1860 Presidential race, obeyed the law. Although Breckinridge was sympathetic to the secessionist cause, he presided with "Roman fidelity" at the certification vote, according to Representative Henry Dawes, of Massachusetts, "and the nation was saved." But only temporarily. On April 12, 1861, the South Carolina militia opened fire on the Union garrison at Fort Sumter and the Civil War began.

A civil war, in the nineteenth-century understanding of the term, is not at hand. But what makes the events of January 6, 2021, so alarming is that they were inspired and incited by the President of the United States, Donald Trump, who remains popular among so many Republicans and a contender to return to the White House.

The events of January 6th were the culmination of a long campaign that Trump and members of his circle have led against the legitimacy of American elections. The campaign's most powerful weapon was the undermining of truth itself, the insidious deployment of conspiracy theories and "alternative facts."

Trump first announced his emergence from the worlds of New York real estate and reality-show television by declaring that Barack Obama, the first Black President, had been born in Kenya, not Hawaii, and was, therefore, ineligible to hold office. After joining the 2016 Presidential race, Trump continued to traffic in casual accusations and unfounded conspiracy theories: Ted Cruz's father was an associate of Lee Harvey Oswald. Antonin Scalia might have been murdered. Obama and Joe Biden might have staged the killing of Osama bin Laden with a body double. Trump welcomed the endorsement of the professional conspiracy theorist Alex Jones, who had earlier claimed that Hillary Clinton had "personally murdered and chopped up and raped" children, and that the mass murder at Sandy Hook had been "staged." The most consequential conspiracy theory of Trump's political career, however, charged that American elections were rigged.

In 2016, Trump, once he had a hold on the Republican Party nomination, began the process of undermining confidence in the entire electoral system. The reporter Jonathan Lemire, in his book,

"The Big Lie," recalls attending a rally, in Columbus, Ohio, at which Trump told his followers, weeks before the nominating Convention, "I'm afraid the election is going to be rigged, I have to be honest." On Fox News, talking with Sean Hannity, Trump again expressed his doubts: "I hope the Republicans are watching closely, or it's going to be taken away from us." Trump began to warn that he was not necessarily prepared to accede to the election results. At one of the Presidential debates, the moderator, Chris Wallace, asked Trump if he would make a commitment to accept the outcome, no matter what. Trump refused: "I will look at it at the time. What I've seen is so bad."

Clinton won the popular vote by a margin of more than two per cent, but, because she fell well short in the Electoral College, there was no compulsion on Trump's part to consider extralegal action. But four years later, as Trump lagged behind Joe Biden in the polls, he revived the theme. "MILLIONS OF MAIL-IN BALLOTS WILL BE PRINTED BY FOREIGN COUNTRIES, AND OTHERS," he tweeted. "IT WILL BE THE SCANDAL OF OUR TIMES!" Once more, Trump refused to promise a peaceful transfer of power. A month and a half before the election, he said, "Get rid of the ballots and you'll have a very peaceful—there won't be a transfer, frankly. There will be a continuation."

This kind of rhetoric was of grave concern to Democrats, including Speaker Pelosi, who privately told confidants, "He's going to try to steal it." And, not long after the voting ended, the tweets from Trump began:

> Last night I was leading, often solidly, in many key States, in almost all instances Democrat run & controlled. Then, one by one, they started to magically disappear as surprise ballot dumps were counted. VERY STRANGE, and the pollsters got it completely & historically wrong!

> They are finding Biden votes all over the place—in Pennsylva-
> nia, Wisconsin, and Michigan. So bad for our Country!

On November 7th, the Associated Press, Fox News, and, soon, all the other major news outlets called Pennsylvania, and the election, for Biden. The battleground states—Pennsylvania, Michigan, Georgia, Arizona, and Wisconsin—all went Biden's way, and, in the end, he won 306 electoral votes to Trump's 232. In his victory speech, the President-elect said, "It's time to put away the harsh rhetoric. To lower the temperature."

This was a vain hope. As the Trump White House emptied, a motley assemblage of satraps and third-raters—Giuliani; a former federal prosecutor, Sidney Powell; the MyPillow C.E.O., Mike Lindell; the former law professor and Federalist Society leader John Eastman—stayed behind to encourage Trump in his most conspiratorial fantasies and schemes. In their effort to challenge election results in various states, Trump's lawyers filed sixty-two federal and state lawsuits. They lost sixty-one of those suits, winning only on an inconsequential technical matter in Pennsylvania. By mid-December, even Mitch McConnell began referring to "President-elect Joe Biden." When Trump called to berate him for conceding the ballot, McConnell, for once, stood up to him. "The Electoral College has spoken," he said. "You lost the election."

The only option Trump had left was to challenge the certification of the vote. With Eastman in the lead, his team concocted a plan that called on Vice-President Pence to declare that voting in seven states was still in dispute and to eliminate those electors. If the remaining forty-three states put forward their electors, Trump would win the election, 232–222. As part of that plan—what Chairman Thompson called, from the first day of the hearings, "an attempted coup"—Trump pressured government and election officials to coöperate. Former Deputy Attorney General Richard Donoghue testified that

Trump did not conceal his intent, telling Donoghue, "What I'm asking you to do is just say it was corrupt and leave the rest to me and the Republican congressmen." Once Trump unleashed his campaign of intimidation against local election officials, the death threats against those officials came from all directions. Ruby Freeman, an election worker in Georgia, testified, "There is nowhere I feel safe. Nowhere. Do you know how it feels to have the President of the United States target you?"

Another version of the plan had Pence calling for a ten-day-long recess and sending the slates back to the so-called "disputed" states. Eastman himself conceded that this plan would be rejected unanimously by the Supreme Court. Even so, the White House could surely be retained if Trump could convince Pence to "do the right thing."

On the night of January 5th, the President met with Pence at the White House and tried to pressure him into adopting the scheme that Eastman had devised. For years, Pence had been the most loyal of deputies, never daring to challenge the falsehoods or the cruelties of his master. Trump, after all, had rescued him from political oblivion. But Pence would not go along with the plot. His job on January 6th, he told the President, was ceremonial. He was only there "to open envelopes."

Trump was outraged. "You've betrayed us," he told Pence. "I made you. You were nothing."

The committee's report is not a work of scholarship removed from its era. It was compiled by politicians and staff members and published at a moment of continuing peril and uncertainty. And the committee was formed in the contrails of the terrifying episode it was charged with investigating.

Although an abundance of new details has surfaced, the contours of what happened have never been in doubt. The events on January

6, 2021, began with a well-planned rally on the Ellipse, the fifty-two-acre park south of the White House. Trump had tweeted in advance, "Be there, will be wild!" Katrina Pierson, a spokeswoman for Trump's 2016 campaign and one of the organizers of the rally, had texted another organizer saying that Trump "likes the crazies," and wanted Alex Jones to be among the speakers. Jones did not speak, but Trump himself supplied the inflammatory rhetoric. In the seventy-minute-long speech he gave on the Ellipse, he told his followers they would "save our democracy" by rejecting "a fake election," and warned them that "if you don't fight like hell, you're not going to have a country anymore." He taunted his Vice-President: "Mike Pence, I hope you're going to stand up for the good of our Constitution and for the good of our country. And if you're not, I'm going to be very disappointed in you." He set a tone of combativeness, defiance, and eternal resistance. And he put the life of his own Vice-President in jeopardy. As Chairman Thompson put it at one hearing, "Donald Trump turned the mob on him."

Even though senior officials around Trump had told him that it was long past time to step aside—William Barr informed congressional investigators that he told Trump that reports of voting fraud were "bullshit"—Trump refused to listen. ("I thought, boy, if he really believes this stuff, he has, you know, lost contact with, he's become detached from reality," Barr recalled.) Trump was unrelenting. "We will never give up," he told the crowd on the Ellipse. "We will never concede. It doesn't happen. You don't concede when there's theft involved. Our country has had enough. We will not take it anymore." After listening to the President's repeated calls to fight, and to march to the Capitol building—"you'll never take back our country with weakness"—thousands of his followers, some of them armed, some of them carrying Confederate symbols, some deploying flagpoles as spears, headed toward Capitol Hill.

As the march began, at around 1 p.m., Representative Paul Gosar, of Arizona, and Senator Ted Cruz, of Texas, both conservative Republicans, rose in Congress to object to the counting of the electoral ballots from Arizona. But Pence had already told Trump he would not go along with his plot, and there was no sign that Gosar, Cruz, and Trump's loyalists in Congress had the numbers to succeed. McConnell, at that time the Senate Majority Leader, said, "Voters, the courts, and the states have all spoken—they've all spoken. If we overrule them all, it would damage our republic forever."

By 2 p.m., demonstrators began to overrun the Capitol Police, sometimes using improvised weapons. Caroline Edwards, of the Capitol Police, testified to the committee that there was "carnage" in the halls: "I was slipping in people's blood." The insurrectionists kept coming, breaking through windows and doors, assaulting police officers, and, once inside, they went hunting for the Vice-President, the Speaker of the House, and other officials who refused to participate in the President's scheme to overturn the election. At around 2:20 p.m., the Senate, and then the House, went into emergency recess, as Capitol Police officers rushed members of both chambers to safety. The two Democratic congressional leaders, Nancy Pelosi and Charles Schumer, fearing for their lives and the lives of their colleagues, were reduced to sequestering in a safe location. In the final session of the committee's investigation, we saw footage of Pelosi, enraged yet composed, deploying her cell phone to get someone to come to the aid of the legislative branch.

Trump watched these events on television at the White House with scant sense of alarm. He refused to send additional police or troops to quell the violence. At 2:24 p.m., he tweeted, "Mike Pence didn't have the courage to do what should have been done to protect our Country and our Constitution." By 3 p.m., insurrectionists, some of them in cosplay battle gear, had swarmed into the Senate chamber. Trump's passivity was not passivity at all. As Adam Kinzinger put it, "President Trump did not fail to act. He chose not to act." Liz

Cheney was no less blunt. "He refused to defend our nation and our Constitution," she said during the hearings. "I say this to my Republican colleagues who are defending the indefensible, there will come a day when Donald Trump is gone. But your dishonor will remain."

For Trump, the choice was simple. The insurrectionists were his people, his shock troops, there to do his bidding. Nothing about the spectacle seemed to disturb him: not the gallows erected outside the building, not the savage beatings, not threats to Pence and Pelosi, not graffiti like "Murder the Media," not the chants of "1776! 1776!" And so he ignored calls to action even from his own party. At 3:11 p.m., Mike Gallagher, a Republican from Wisconsin, tweeted, "We are witnessing absolute banana republic crap in the United States Capitol right now. @realdonaldtrump you need to call this off." Trump would not tell his supporters to go home until the early evening, when the damage had been done.

And though Trump and the insurrectionists failed to halt the certification of the ballot, they did get substantial support: a hundred and forty-seven Republicans in Congress voted to overturn the election results. At 3:42 a.m. on January 7th, Vice-President Pence, speaking to a joint session of Congress, certified the election of Joe Biden as the forty-sixth President of the United States. When, however, the midterms were held, two years later, dozens of Republican candidates continued to claim that his election was fraudulent. Those few Republicans, like Liz Cheney, who took a stand against Trump were swept out of office.

January 6th was a phenomenon rooted both in the degraded era of Trump and in the radicalization of a major political party during the past generation. The very power of these developments explains why many people may approach this congressional report with a sense of fatigue, even denial. Part of Trump's dark achievement has been to bludgeon the political attention of the country into submission.

When a nation has been subjected to that degree of cynicism—what is politely called "divisiveness"—it can lose its ability to experience outrage. As a result, the prospect of engaging with this congressional inquiry into Trump's attempt to delegitimatize the machinery of electoral democracy is sometimes a challenge to the spirit. That is both understandable and a public danger. And yet a citizenry that can no longer bring itself to pay attention to such an investigation or to absorb its astonishing findings risks moving even farther toward a disturbing "new normal": a post-truth, post-democratic America.

A republic is predicated on faith—not religious faith but a faith in the fundamental legitimacy of its political institutions and the decisions they issue. To concede the legitimacy of statutes, rulings, and election returns is not necessarily to favor them. It's simply to participate in the basic system that gives them form and force; citizens can, through democratic machinery, seek to defeat or contest candidates they deplore, initiatives that offend them, court opinions they consider misguided. By contrast, the campaign that culminated in the Capitol attack of January 6th was, fatefully, against democracy itself. It sought to instill profound mistrust in the process of voting—the mechanism through which, even in highly imperfect democracies, accountability is ultimately secured.

The committee and its work were far from apolitical, and yet to dismiss the report as *merely* political would be a perilous act of resignation and defeatism. The questions that hovered over the inquiry from the start—what more is there to learn? who is really listening?—persisted and loomed over the midterm elections. When the hearings began, the polling outfit FiveThirtyEight reported that Trump's approval rating was 41.9 per cent; when the hearings ended, it was 40.4 per cent, a minuscule dip. As Susan B. Glasser, of *The New Yorker*, wrote, "All that damning evidence, and the polls were basically unchanged. The straight line in the former President's approval rating is the literal representation of the crisis in American democracy.

There is an essentially immovable forty per cent of the country whose loyalty to Donald Trump cannot be shaken by anything." And yet the Republicans failed in their promise to produce a "red wave" in the midterms. The Democrats maintained their slender hold on the Senate and lost far fewer seats in the House than was expected. And while the reasons behind the Republican failure were many, ranging from the imperilment of abortion rights to the dismal quality of so many of the Party's candidates, it was clear that one of the principal reasons was a deep concern about the future of democracy.

The most urgent thing to learn is whether a two-and-a-half-century-old republic will resist future efforts to undercut its foundations—to steal, through concerted deception, the essential legitimacy of its constitutional order. The contents of the report insist that complacency is not an option. The report also insists on accountability, though that will ultimately be the responsibility of the Department of Justice and the American public. The report has provided the evidence, the truth. Now it remains to be seen if it will be acted upon.

The violation of January 6th was ultimately so brazen that many of Trump's own loyalists could not, in the end, bring themselves to defend him. Even some on the radical right have come to recognize the insurrection's implications for the future. Jason van Tatenhove was once the media spokesman for the militia group known as the Oath Keepers, which played a crucial role in the uprising. He left the group well before January 6th, but he remained well connected enough to know that the Oath Keepers were eager to take part in an "armed revolution." Testifying before the committee, he expressed his sense of betrayal by Donald Trump, and a growing sense of alarm: "If a President that's willing to try to instill and encourage, to whip up, a civil war among his followers uses lies and deceit and snake oil, regardless of the human impact, what else is he going to do?"

Trump is running again for President. Perhaps his decline is irreversible. But it would be foolish to count on that. Should he win back the White House, he will come to office with no sense of restraint. He will inevitably be an even more radical, more resentful, more chaotic, more authoritarian version of his earlier self. And he would hardly be an isolated figure in the capital. Following the results of the midterm elections, Congress is now populated with dozens of election deniers and many more who still dare not defy Trump. The stakes could not be higher. If you are reaching for optimism—and despair is not an option—the existence and the depth of the committee's project represents a kind of hope. It represents an insistence on truth and democratic principle. In the words of the man who tried and failed to overturn a Presidential election, you don't concede when there's theft involved.

Union Calendar No. XXX

117th Congress
2d Session

HOUSE OF REPRESENTATIVES

Report
117-000

FINAL REPORT

OF THE

SELECT COMMITTEE TO INVESTIGATE THE JANUARY 6TH ATTACK ON THE UNITED STATES CAPITOL

December X, 2022
Committed to the Committee of the Whole House on the
State of the Union and ordered to be printed

U.S. GOVERNMENT PUBLISHING OFFICE
WASHINGTON : 2022

49-937

For sale by the Superintendent of Documents, U.S. Government Publishing Office
Internet: bookstore.gpo.gov Phone: toll free (866) 512-1800; DC area (202) 512-1800
Fax: (202) 512-2104 Mail: Stop IDCC, Washington, DC 20402-0001

DAVID B. BUCKLEY *Staff Director*
KRISTIN L. AMERLING *Deputy Staff Director and Chief Counsel*
HOPE GOINS *Senior Counsel to the Chairman*
JOSEPH B. MAHER *Senior Counsel to the Vice Chair*
TIMOTHY J. HEAPHY *Chief Investigative Counsel*
JAMIE FLEET *Senior Advisor*
TIMOTHY R. MULVEY *Communications Director*
CANDYCE PHOENIX *Senior Counsel and Senior Advisor*
JOHN F. WOOD *Senior Investigative Counsel and Of Counsel to the Vice Chair*

KATHERINE B. ABRAMS, *Staff Associate*
TEMIDAYO AGANGA-WILLIAMS, *Senior Investigative Counsel*
ALEJANDRA APECECHEA, *Investigative Counsel*
LISA A. BIANCO, *Director of Member Services and Security Manager*
JEROME P. BJELOPERA, *Investigator*
BRYAN BONNER, *Investigative Counsel*
RICHARD R. BRUNO, *Senior Administrative Assistant*
MARCUS CHILDRESS, *Investigative Counsel*
JOHN MARCUS CLARK, *Security Director*
JACQUELINE N. COLVETT, *Digital Director*
HEATHER I. CONNELLY, *Professional Staff Member*
MEGHAN E. CONROY, *Investigator*
HEATHER L. CROWELL, *Printer Proofreader*
WILLIAM C. DANVERS, *Senior Researcher*
SOUMYALATHA O. DAYANANDA, *Senior Investigative Counsel*
STEPHEN W. DEVINE, *Senior Counsel*
LAWRENCE J. EAGLEBURGER, *Professional Staff Member*
KEVIN S. ELLIKER, *Investigative Counsel*
MARGARET E. EMAMZADEH, *Staff Associate*
SADALLAH A. FARAH, *Professional Staff Member*
DANIEL GEORGE, *Senior Investigative Counsel*
JACOB H. GLICK, *Investigative Counsel*
AARON S. GREENE, *Clerk*
MARC S. HARRIS, *Senior Investigative Counsel*
ALICE K. HAYES, *Clerk*
QUINCY T. HENDERSON, *Staff Assistant*
JENNA HOPKINS, *Professional Staff Member*
CAMISHA L. JOHNSON, *Professional Staff Member*

THOMAS E. JOSCELYN, *Senior Professional Staff Member*
REBECCA L. KNOOIHUIZEN, *Financial Investigator*
CASEY E. LUCIER, *Investigative Counsel*
DAMON M. MARX, *Professional Staff Member*
EVAN B. MAULDIN, *Chief Clerk*
YONATAN L. MOSKOWITZ, *Senior Counsel*
HANNAH G. MULDAVIN, *Deputy Communications Director*
JONATHAN D. MURRAY, *Professional Staff Member*
JACOB A. NELSON, *Professional Staff Member*
ELIZABETH OBRAND, *Staff Associate*
RAYMOND O'MARA, *Director of External Affairs*
ELYES OUECHTATI, *Technology Partner*
ROBIN M. PEGUERO, *Investigative Counsel*
SANDEEP A. PRASANNA, *Investigative Counsel*
BARRY PUMP, *Parliamentarian*
SEAN M. QUINN, *Investigative Counsel*
BRITTANY M. J. RECORD, *Senior Counsel*
DENVER RIGGLEMAN, *Senior Technical Advisor*
JOSHUA D. ROSELMAN, *Investigative Counsel*
JAMES N. SASSO, *Senior Investigative Counsel*
GRANT H. SAUNDERS, *Professional Staff Member*
SAMANTHA O. STILES, *Chief Administrative Officer*
SEAN P. TONOLLI, *Senior Investigative Counsel*
DAVID A. WEINBERG, *Senior Professional Staff Member*
AMANDA S. WICK, *Senior Investigative Counsel*
DARRIN L. WILLIAMS, JR., *Staff Assistant*
ZACHARY S. WOOD, *Clerk*

CONTRACTORS & CONSULTANTS

Rawaa Alobaidi
Melinda Arons
Steve Baker
Elizabeth Bisbee
David Canady
John Coughlin
Aaron Dietzen
Gina Ferrise
Angel Goldsborough
James Goldston
Polly Grube
L. Christine Healey
Danny Holladay
Percy Howard
Dean Jackson
Stephanie J. Jones
Hyatt Mamoun
Mary Marsh
Todd Mason
Ryan Mayers
Jeff McBride
Fred Muram
Alex Newhouse
John Norton
Orlando Pinder
Owen Pratt
Dan Pryzgoda
Brian Sasser
William Scherer
Driss Sekkat
Chris Stuart
Preston Sullivan
Brian Young

Innovative Driven

HOUSE OF REPRESENTATIVES,
SELECT COMMITTEE TO
INVESTIGATE THE
JANUARY 6TH ATTACK ON THE
UNITED STATES CAPITOL,
Washington, DC,
December 00, 2022.

Hon. CHERYL L. JOHNSON,
Clerk, U.S. House of Representatives,
Washington, DC.

DEAR MS. JOHNSON: By direction of the Select
Committee to Investigate the January 6th Attack on the
United States Capitol, I hereby transmit its final report
pursuant to section 4(a) of House Resolution 503, 117th
Congress.

Sincerely,

BENNIE G. THOMPSON,
Chairman.

"THE LAST BEST HOPE OF EARTH"

"I do solemnly swear that I will support and defend the Constitution of the United States against all enemies, foreign and domestic; that I will bear true faith and allegiance to the same; that I take this obligation freely, without any mental reservation or purpose of evasion; and that I will well and faithfully discharge the duties of the office on which I am about to enter: So help me God."

All Members of the United States Congress take this sacred oath. On January 6, 2021, Democrats and Republicans agreed that we would fulfill this oath—and that we had an obligation to signal to the world that American Democracy would prevail.

In furtherance of fulfilling this duty, the Select Committee to Investigate the January 6th Attack on the United States Capitol was charged with investigating the facts, circumstances and causes that led to this domestic terror attack on the Capitol, the Congress and the Constitution.

We owe a debt of gratitude to Chairman Bennie Thompson, Vice Chair Liz Cheney, the patriotic Members of Congress and dedicated staff—who devoted themselves to this investigation, to uncovering the truth and to writing a report that is a "Roadmap for Justice."

The Select Committee to Investigate the January 6th Attack has succeeded in bringing clarity and demonstrating with painstaking detail the fragility of our Democracy. Above all, the work of the Select Committee underscores that our democratic institutions are only as strong as the commitment of those who are entrusted with their care.

As the Select Committee concludes its work, their words must be a

clarion call to all Americans: to vigilantly guard our Democracy and to give our vote only to those dutiful in their defense of our Constitution.

Let us always honor our oath to, as Abraham Lincoln said, "nobly save, or meanly lose, the last best hope of earth." So help us God.

Nancy Pelosi

NANCY PELOSI
Speaker of the House

We were told to remove our lapel pins. At the start of every new Congress, House Members are presented with lapel pins. They are about the size of a quarter and carry a seal of a bald eagle.

On a routine day in the Capitol, there are thousands of tourists, advocates, and workers. Typically, the pins are an easy way to spot House Members.

However, on January 6, 2021, the pin that once was a badge of honor and distinction turned into a bullseye.

On that day, tear gas fogged the air as gunfire rang out, and a violent mob crashed against the sealed doors. Concerned for our safety, Capitol Police officers told us that our lapel pins would make us a target for rioters.

As the Capitol Police rushed Members of Congress and staff to safety, that simple and, in context, sensible warning stuck with me. On January 6, 2021, my colleagues and I came to work with the intent of fulfilling our oaths of office and constitutional duty to carry out the peaceful transfer of power. We were the people's representatives in the people's House doing the people's business. Sadly, on that day, the danger was too great for our work to continue and for us to remain in the Capitol. It was too dangerous to be identified as a representative of the American people.

I've been a Member of the House for nearly 30 years. In that time, there's not a day that goes by that I don't feel a profound sense of duty and responsibility to the men and women who sent me to Congress to be their voice. After all, I'm from a part of the country where, in my lifetime, Black people were excluded entirely from political processes. Jim Crow laws prevented my father from registering to vote, and tragically during his life, he never cast a vote.

For generations, the people in communities I represent have struggled to have their voices heard by their government. Therefore, I take my duties and responsibilities seriously, advocating for greater economic opportunity, robust infrastructure, better schools, and safer housing for my constituents.

However, that long struggle to overcome oppression and secure basic civil and human rights continues to be my highest priority. I am always mindful of the journey that brought me to Washington as a member of Congress to be the voice of the women and men of Mississippi. As a violent mob stormed the Capitol trying to take away people's votes, rioters carried the battle flag from a failed rebellion of confederate states. This moment resonated deeply with me because of my personal history. Additionally, I continually think about the ongoing struggle to ensure justice and equality for all Americans.

The Capitol building itself is a fixture in our country's history, of both good and bad. After all, this structure is among the most recognizable symbols of American democracy. The Capitol's shining dome, topped with the statue of goddess Freedom, was built partially by the labor of enslaved people in the 18th and 19th centuries. Dark chapters of America's history are written into the building's marble, sandstone, and mortar. And yet in the halls and chambers of this building, leaders of courage passed amendments to our Constitution and enacted the laws that banned slavery, guaranteed equal rights under the law, expanded the vote, promoted equality, and moved our country, and her people, forward. The Capitol Building itself is a symbol of our journey toward a more perfect union. It is a temple to our democracy.

Those great moments in our history have come when men and women put loyalty to our country and Constitution ahead of politics and party. They did the right thing. The work of the Select Committee certainly originates from the same tradition. Our bipartisan membership has moved politics to the side and focused on the facts, circumstances, and causes of January 6th.

When I think back to January 6th, after nearly a year and a half of investigation, I am frightened about the peril our democracy faced. Specifically, I think about what that mob was there to do: to block the peaceful transfer of power from one president to another based on a lie that the election was rigged and tainted with widespread fraud.

I also think about why the rioters were there, besieging the legislative branch of our government. The rioters were inside the halls of Congress because the head of the executive branch of our government, the then-President of the United States, told them to attack. Donald Trump summoned that mob to Washington, DC. Afterward, he sent them to the Capitol to try to prevent my colleagues and me from doing our Constitutional duty to certify the election. They put our very democracy to the test.

Trump's mob came dangerously close to succeeding. Courageous law enforcement officers put their lives on the line for hours while Trump sat in the White House, refusing to tell the rioters to go home, while watching the assault on our republic unfold live on television.

When it was clear the insurrection would fail, Trump finally called off the mob, telling them, "We love you." Afterward, Congress was able to return to this Capitol Building and finish the job of counting the Electoral College votes and certifying the election.

This is the key conclusion of the Select Committee, all nine of us, Republicans and Democrats alike.

But who knows what would have happened if Trump's mob had succeeded in stopping us from doing our job? Who knows what sort of constitutional grey zone our country would have slid into? Who would have been
left to correct that wrong?

As required by House Resolution 503, which established the Select
Committee, we've explored in great detail the facts, circumstances, and
causes of the attack. This report will provide new details that supplement
those findings the committee already presented during our hearings.

But there are some questions for which there are still no clear answers,
even if all the facts, circumstances, and causes are brought to bear. The
"What If?" questions. For the good of American democracy, those questions
must never again be put to the test. So, while it's important that this report
lays out what happened, it's just as important to focus on how to make sure
that January 6th was a one-time event—to identify the ongoing threats
that could lead us down that dangerous path again—with hopes and
humble prayers that the committee's work is carried on through corrective
action.

This report will provide greater detail about the multistep effort devised
and driven by Donald Trump to overturn the 2020 election and block the
transfer of power. Building on the information presented in our hearings
earlier this year, we will present new findings about Trump's pressure
campaign on officials from the local level all the way up to his Vice President, orchestrated and designed solely to throw out the will of the voters
and keep him in office past the end of his elected term.

As we've shown previously, this plan faltered at several points because
of the courage of officials (nearly all of them Republicans) who refused to
go along with it. Donald Trump appeared to believe that anyone who shared
his partisan affiliation would also share the same callous disregard for his
or her oath to uphold the rule of law. Fortunately, he was wrong.

The failure of Trump's plan was not assured. To the contrary, Trump's
plan was successful at several turns. When his scheme to stay in power
through political pressure hit roadblocks, he relentlessly pushed ahead with
a parallel plan: summoning a mob to gather in Washington, DC on January
6th, promising things "will be wild!"

That mob showed up. They were armed. They were angry. They believed
the "Big Lie" that the election had been stolen. And when Donald Trump
pointed them toward the Capitol and told them to "fight like hell," that's
exactly what they did.

Donald Trump lit that fire. But in the weeks beforehand, the kindling he
ultimately ignited was amassed in plain sight.

That's why as part of the Select Committee's investigation, we took a hard look at whether enough was done to mitigate that risk. Our investigative teams focused on the way intelligence was gathered, shared, and assessed. We probed preparations by law enforcement agencies and security responses on the day of the attack. We followed the money, to determine who paid for a number of events in the run-up to the attack and to gain a clearer understanding of the way the former President's campaign apparatus cashed in on the big lie. And we pulled back the curtain at certain major social media companies to determine if their policies and protocols were up to the challenge when the President spread a message of violence and his supporters began to plan and coordinate their descent on Washington.

The Select Committee's conclusion on these matters—particularly dealing with intelligence and law enforcement—is consistent with our broader findings about the causes of January 6th. Were agencies perfect in their preparations for January 6th and their responses as the violence unfolded? Of course not. Relevant oversight committees and watchdogs should continue to find efficiencies and improvements, some of which are laid out in Committee's recommendations.

But the shortfall of communications, intelligence and law enforcement around January 6th was much less about what they did or did not know. It was more about what they could not know. The President of the United States inciting a mob to march on the Capitol and impede the work of Congress is not a scenario our intelligence and law enforcement communities envisioned for this country. Prior to January 6th, it was unimaginable. Whatever weaknesses existed in the policies, procedures, or institutions, they were not to blame for what happened on that day.

And so, when I think about the ongoing threats—when I think about how to avoid having to confront those "What-Ifs?" in the future—my concerns are less with the mechanics of intelligence gathering and security posture, as important as those questions are. My concerns remain first and foremost with those who continue to seek power at the expense of American democracy.

What if those election officials had given in to Donald Trump's pressure? What if the Justice Department had gone along with Trump's scheme to declare the 2020 election fraudulent? What if the Vice President had tried to throw out electoral votes? What if the rioters bent on stopping the peaceful transfer of power hadn't been repelled?

To cast a vote in the United States of America is an act of both hope and faith. When you drop that ballot in the ballot box, you do so with the confidence that every person named on that ballot will hold up their end of the bargain. The person who wins must swear an oath and live up to it. The

people who come up short must accept the ultimate results and abide by the
will of the voters and the rule of law. This faith in our institutions and laws
is what upholds our democracy.

If that faith is broken—if those who seek power accept only the results
of elections that they win—then American democracy, only a few centuries
old, comes tumbling down.

That's the danger.

What's the solution?

The Committee believes a good starting point is the set of recommendations we set forth in our report, pursuant to House Resolution 503.
Driven by our investigative findings, these recommendations will help
strengthen the guardrails of our democracy.

Beyond what we recommend, in my view and as I said during our hearings, the best way to prevent another January 6th is to ensure accountability for January 6th. Accountability at all levels.

I have confidence in our Department of Justice and institutions at the
state and local level to ensure accountability under the law. As this report is
released, we see those processes moving forward.

But preventing another January 6th will require a broader sort of
accountability. Ultimately, the American people chart the course for our
country's future. The American people decide whom to give the reins of
power. If this Select Committee has accomplished one thing, I hope it has
shed light on how dangerous it would be to empower anyone whose desire
for authority comes before their commitment to American democracy and
the Constitution.

I believe most Americans will turn their backs on those enemies of
democracy.

But some will rally to the side of the election deniers, and when I think
about who some of those people are, it troubles me deep inside. White
supremacists. Violent extremists. Groups that subscribe to racism, anti-
Semitism, and violent conspiracy theories; those who would march through
the halls of the Capitol waving the Confederate battle flag.

These are people who want to take America backward, not toward some
imagined prior greatness, but toward repression. These are people who
want to roll back what we've accomplished. I believe that those who aligned
with the scheme to overturn the election heeded Donald Trump's call to
march on the Capitol because they thought taking up Donald Trump's cause
was a way to advance their vile ambitions.

That is why I did not remove my lapel pin on January 6th.

Our country has come too far to allow a defeated President to turn himself into a successful tyrant by upending our democratic institutions,

fomenting violence, and, as I saw it, opening the door to those in our country whose hatred and bigotry threaten equality and justice for all Americans.

We can never surrender to democracy's enemies. We can never allow America to be defined by forces of division and hatred. We can never go backward in the progress we have made through the sacrifice and dedication of true patriots. We can never and will never relent in our pursuit of a more perfect union, with liberty and justice for all Americans.

I pray that God continues to bless the United States of America.

BENNIE G. THOMPSON
Chairman

In April 1861, when Abraham Lincoln issued the first call for volunteers for the Union Army, my great-great grandfather, Samuel Fletcher Cheney, joined the 21st Ohio Volunteer Infantry. He fought through all four years of the Civil War, from Chickamauga to Stones River to Atlanta. He marched with his unit in the Grand Review of Troops up Pennsylvania Avenue in May 1865, past a reviewing stand where President Johnson and General Grant were seated.

Silas Canfield, the regimental historian of the 21st OVI, described the men in the unit this way:

> *Industry had taught them perseverance, and they had learned to turn aside for no obstacle. Their intelligence gave them a just appreciation of the value and advantage of free government, and the necessity of defending and maintaining it, and they enlisted prepared to accept all the necessary labors, fatigues, exposures, dangers, and even death for the unity of our Nation, and the perpetuity of our institutions.*[1]

I have found myself thinking often, especially since January 6th, of my great-great grandfather, and all those in every generation who have sacrificed so much for "the unity of our Nation and the perpetuity of our institutions."

At the heart of our Republic is the guarantee of the peaceful transfer of power. Members of Congress are reminded of this every day as we pass through the Capitol Rotunda. There, eight magnificent paintings detail the earliest days of our Republic. Four were painted by John Trumbull, including one depicting the moment in 1793 when George Washington resigned his commission, handing control of the Continental Army back to Congress. Trumbull called this, "one of the highest moral lessons ever given the world." With this noble act, George Washington established the indispensable example of the peaceful transfer of power in our nation.

Standing on the West Front of the Capitol in 1981, President Ronald Reagan described it this way:

> *To a few of us here today, this is a solemn and most momentous occasion, and yet in the history of our nation it is a commonplace occurrence. The orderly transfer of authority as called for in the Constitution routinely takes place, as it has for almost two centuries, and few of us stop to think how unique we really are. In the eyes of many in the world, this every-4-year ceremony we accept as normal is nothing less than a miracle.*

Every President in our history has defended this orderly transfer of authority, except one. January 6, 2021 was the first time one American President refused his Constitutional duty to transfer power peacefully to the next.

In our work over the last 18 months, the Select Committee has recognized our obligation to do everything we can to ensure this never happens again. At the outset of our investigation, we recognized that tens of millions of Americans had been persuaded by President Trump that the 2020 Presidential election was stolen by overwhelming fraud. We also knew this was flatly false, and that dozens of state and federal judges had addressed and resolved all manner of allegations about the election. Our legal system functioned as it should, but our President would not accept the outcome.

What most of the public did not know before our investigation is this: Donald Trump's own campaign officials told him early on that his claims of fraud were false. Donald Trump's senior Justice Department officials—each appointed by Donald Trump himself—investigated the allegations and told him repeatedly that his fraud claims were false. Donald Trump's White House lawyers also told him his fraud claims were false. From the beginning, Donald Trump's fraud allegations were concocted nonsense, designed to prey upon the patriotism of millions of men and women who love our country.

Most Americans also did not know exactly how Donald Trump, along with a handful of others, planned to defeat the transfer of Presidential power on January 6th. This was not a simple plan, but it was a corrupt one. This report lays that plan out in detail—a plan that ultimately had seven parts, anticipating that Vice President Pence, serving in his role as President of the Senate, would refuse to count official Biden electoral slates from multiple states. We understood from the beginning that explaining all the planning and machinations would be complex and would require many hours of public presentations and testimony. We also understood that our presentations needed to be organized into a series of hearings that presented the key evidence for the American public to watch live or streamed over a reasonable time period, rather than rely on second-hand accounts as reported by media organizations with their own editorial biases. We organized our hearings in segments to meet that goal. Tens of millions of Americans watched.

Among the most shameful findings from our hearings was this: President Trump sat in the dining room off the Oval Office watching the violent riot at the Capitol on television. For hours, he would not issue a public statement instructing his supporters to disperse and leave the Capitol, despite urgent pleas from his White House staff and dozens of others to do so. Members of his family, his White House lawyers, virtually all those around him knew that this simple act was critical. For hours, he would not do it. During this time, law enforcement agents were attacked and seriously injured, the Capitol was invaded, the electoral count was halted and the lives of those in the Capitol were put at risk. In addition to being unlawful, as described in this report, this was an utter moral failure—and a clear dereliction of duty. Evidence of this can be seen in the testimony of his White House Counsel and several other White House witnesses. No man who would behave that way at that moment in time can ever serve in any position of authority in our nation again. He is unfit for any office.

$$* \quad * \quad * \quad * \quad *$$

In presenting all of the information in our hearings, we decided that the vast majority of our witnesses needed to be Republicans. They were. We presented evidence from two former Trump Administration Attorneys General, a former White House Counsel, many former Trump-appointed White House, Justice Department, and Trump Campaign staff, a respected former conservative judge, the former Secretary of Labor, and many others.

Like our hearings, this report is designed to deliver our findings in detail in a format that is accessible for all Americans. We do so in an executive summary, while also providing immense detail for historians and others. We are also releasing transcripts and evidence for the public to review, consistent with a small number of security and privacy concerns. A section of this report also explains the legal conclusions we draw from the evidence, and our concerns about efforts to obstruct our investigation.

The Committee recognizes that this investigation is just a beginning; it is only an initial step in addressing President Trump's effort to remain in office illegally. Prosecutors are considering the implications of the conduct we describe in this report. As are voters. John Adams wrote in 1761, "The very ground of our liberties is the freedom of elections." Faith in our elections and the rule of law are paramount to our Republic. Election-deniers— those who refuse to accept lawful election results—purposely attack the rule of law and the foundation of our country.

As you read this report, please consider this: Vice President Pence, along with many of the appointed officials who surrounded Donald Trump, worked to defeat many of the worst parts of Trump's plan to overturn the election. This was not a certainty. It is comforting to assume that the institutions of our Republic will always withstand those who try to defeat our Constitution from within. But our institutions are only strong when those who hold office are faithful to our Constitution. We do not know what would have happened if the leadership of the Department of Justice declared, as Donald Trump requested, that the election was "corrupt," if Jeff Clark's letters to State Legislatures had been sent, if Pat Cipollone, Jeff Rosen, Richard Donoghue, Steve Engel and others were not serving as guardrails on Donald Trump's abuses.

Part of the tragedy of January 6th is the conduct of those who knew that what happened was profoundly wrong, but nevertheless tried to downplay it, minimize it or defend those responsible. That effort continues every day. Today, I am perhaps most disappointed in many of my fellow conservatives who know better, those who stood against the threats of communism and Islamic terrorism but concluded that it was easier to appease Donald Trump, or keep their heads down. I had hoped for more from them.

The late Charles Krauthammer wrote, "The lesson of our history is that the task of merely maintaining strong and sturdy the structures of a constitutional order is unending, the continuing and ceaseless work of every generation." This task is unending because democracy can be fragile and our institutions do not defend themselves.

The history of our time will show that the bravery of a handful of Americans, doing their duty, saved us from an even more grave Constitutional crisis. Elected officials, election workers, and public servants stood against Donald Trump's corrupt pressure. Many of our witnesses showed selfless patriotism and their words and courage will be remembered.

The brave men and women of the Capitol Police, Metropolitan Police and all the other law enforcement officers who fought to defend us that day undoubtedly saved lives and our democracy.

Finally, I wish to thank all who honorably contributed to the work of the Committee and to this Report. We accomplished much over a relatively short period of time, and many of you sacrificed for the good of your nation. You have helped make history and, I hope, helped right the ship.

LIZ CHENEY
Vice Chair

ENDNOTE

1. Silas S. Canfield, *History of the 21st Regiment Ohio Volunteer Infantry in the War of the Rebellion* (Vrooman, Anderson & Bateman, printers, 1893), p. 10.

TABLE OF CONTENTS

Contents.. Page

Contents .... Page

Contents . . . . Page

On October 31, 2022, in a Federal courthouse in Washington, DC, Graydon Young testified against Stewart Rhodes and other members of the Oath Keepers militia group. The defendants had been charged with seditious conspiracy against the United States and other crimes related to the January 6, 2021, attack on Congress.[1]

In his testimony that day, Young explained to the jury how he and other Oath Keepers were provoked to travel to Washington by President Donald Trump's tweets and by Trump's false claims that the 2020 Presidential election was "stolen" from him.[2] And, in emotional testimony, Young acknowledged what he and others believed they were doing on January 6th: attacking Congress in the manner the French had attacked the Bastille at the outset of the French Revolution.[3] Reflecting on that day more than a year and half later, Young testified:

> Prosecutor: And so how do you feel about the fact that you were pushing towards a line of police officers?
>
> Young: Today I feel extremely ashamed and embarrassed. . . .
>
> Prosecutor: How did you feel at the time?
>
> Young: I felt like, again, we were continuing in some kind of historical event to achieve a goal.
>
> * * *
>
> Prosecutor: Looking back now almost two years later, what would that make you as someone who was coming to D.C. to fight against the government?
>
> Young: I guess I was [acting] like a traitor, somebody against my own government.[4]

Young's testimony was dramatic, but not unique. Many participants in the attack on the Capitol acknowledged that they had betrayed their own country:

- Reimler: "And I'm sorry to the people of this country for threatening the democracy that makes this country so great . . . My participation in the events that day were part of an attack on the rule of law." [5]
- Pert: "I know that the peaceful transition of power is to ensure the common good for our nation and that it is critical in protecting our country's security needs. I am truly sorry for my part and accept full responsibility for my actions." [6]
- Markofski: "My actions put me on the other side of the line from my

Protestors gather at the Capitol.

(Photo by Samuel Corum/Getty Images)

brothers in the Army. The wrong side. Had I lived in the area, I would have been called up to defend the Capitol and restore order . . . My actions brought dishonor to my beloved U.S. Army National Guard." [7]

- Witcher: "Every member—every male member of my family has served in the military, in the Marine Corps, and most have saw combat. And I cast a shadow and cast embarrassment upon my family name and that legacy." [8]

- Edwards: "I am ashamed to be for the first time in my 68 years, standing before a judge, having pleaded guilty to committing a crime, ashamed to be associated with an attack on the United States Capitol, a symbol of American democracy and greatness that means a great deal to me." [9]

Hundreds of other participants in the January 6th attack have pleaded guilty, been convicted, or await trial for crimes related to their actions that day. And, like Young, hundreds of others have acknowledged exactly what provoked them to travel to Washington, and to engage in violence. For example:

- Ronald Sandlin, who threatened police officers in the Capitol saying, "[y]ou're going to die," posted on December 23, 2020: "I'm going to be there to show support for our president and to do my part to stop the steal and stand behind Trump when he decides to cross the rubicon. If you are a patriot I believe it's your duty to be there. I see it as my civic responsibility." [10]

- Garret Miller, who brought a gun to the Capitol on January 6th, explained: "I was in Washington, D.C. on January 6, 2021, because I believed I was following the instructions of former President Trump and he was my president and the commander-in-chief. His statements also had me believing the election was stolen from him." [11]

- John Douglas Wright explained that he brought busloads of people to Washington, DC, on January 6th "because [Trump] called me there, and he laid out what is happening in our government." [12]

- Lewis Cantwell testified: If "the President of the United States . . . [is] out on TV telling the world that it was stolen, what else would I believe, as a patriotic American who voted for him and wants to continue to see the country thrive as I thought it was?" [13]

- Likewise, Stephen Ayres testified that "with everything the President was putting out" ahead of January 6th that "the election was rigged . . . the votes were wrong and stuff . . . it just got into my head." "The President [was] calling on us to come" to Washington, DC. [14] Ayres "was hanging on every word he [President Trump] was saying" [15] Ayres posted that "Civil War will ensue" if President Trump did not stay in power after January 6th.[16]

The Committee has compiled hundreds of similar statements from participants in the January 6th attack.[17]

House Resolution 503 instructed the Select Committee to "investigate and report upon the facts, circumstances, and causes relating to the January 6, 2021, domestic terrorist attack upon the United States Capitol Complex" and to "issue a final report" containing "findings, conclusions, and recommendations for corrective measures." The Select Committee has conducted nine public hearings, presenting testimony from more than 70 witnesses. In structuring our investigation and hearings, we began with President Trump's contentions that the election was stolen and took testimony from nearly all of the President's principal advisors on this topic. We focused on the rulings of more than 60 Federal and State courts rejecting President Trump's and his supporters' efforts to reverse the electoral outcome.

Despite the rulings of these courts, we understood that millions of Americans still lack the information necessary to understand and evaluate what President Trump has told them about the election. For that reason, our hearings featured a number of members of President Trump's inner circle refuting his fraud claims and testifying that the election was not in fact stolen. In all, the Committee displayed the testimony of more than four

dozen Republicans—by far the majority of witnesses in our hearings—
including two of President Trump's former Attorneys General, his former
White House Counsel, numerous members of his White House staff, and the
highest-ranking members of his 2020 election campaign, including his
campaign manager and his campaign general counsel. Even key individuals
who worked closely with President Trump to try to overturn the 2020 election on January 6th ultimately *admitted* that they lacked actual evidence
sufficient to change the election result, and they *admitted* that what they
were attempting was unlawful.[18]

   This Report supplies an immense volume of information and testimony
assembled through the Select Committee's investigation, including information obtained following litigation in Federal district and appellate courts, as
well as in the U.S. Supreme Court. Based upon this assembled evidence, the
Committee has reached a series of specific findings,[19] including the following:

1. Beginning election night and continuing through January 6th and
   thereafter, Donald Trump purposely disseminated false allegations of
   fraud related to the 2020 Presidential election in order to aid his effort
   to overturn the election and for purposes of soliciting contributions.
   These false claims provoked his supporters to violence on January 6th.
2. Knowing that he and his supporters had lost dozens of election lawsuits, and despite his own senior advisors refuting his election fraud
   claims and urging him to concede his election loss, Donald Trump
   refused to accept the lawful result of the 2020 election. Rather than
   honor his constitutional obligation to "take Care that the Laws be
   faithfully executed," President Trump instead plotted to overturn the
   election outcome.
3. Despite knowing that such an action would be illegal, and that no
   State had or would submit an altered electoral slate, Donald Trump
   corruptly pressured Vice President Mike Pence to refuse to count
   electoral votes during Congress's joint session on January 6th.
4. Donald Trump sought to corrupt the U.S. Department of Justice by
   attempting to enlist Department officials to make purposely false
   statements and thereby aid his effort to overturn the Presidential
   election. After that effort failed, Donald Trump offered the position of
   Acting Attorney General to Jeff Clark knowing that Clark intended to
   disseminate false information aimed at overturning the election.
5. Without any evidentiary basis and contrary to State and Federal law,
   Donald Trump unlawfully pressured State officials and legislators to
   change the results of the election in their States.
6. Donald Trump oversaw an effort to obtain and transmit false electoral
   certificates to Congress and the National Archives.

7. Donald Trump pressured Members of Congress to object to valid slates of electors from several States.

8. Donald Trump purposely verified false information filed in Federal court.

9. Based on false allegations that the election was stolen, Donald Trump summoned tens of thousands of supporters to Washington for January 6th. Although these supporters were angry and some were armed, Donald Trump instructed them to march to the Capitol on January 6th to "take back" their country.

10. Knowing that a violent attack on the Capitol was underway and knowing that his words would incite further violence, Donald Trump purposely sent a social media message publicly condemning Vice President Pence at 2:24 p.m. on January 6th.

11. Knowing that violence was underway at the Capitol, and despite his duty to ensure that the laws are faithfully executed, Donald Trump refused repeated requests over a multiple hour period that he instruct his violent supporters to disperse and leave the Capitol, and instead watched the violent attack unfold on television. This failure to act perpetuated the violence at the Capitol and obstructed Congress's proceeding to count electoral votes.

12. Each of these actions by Donald Trump was taken in support of a multi-part conspiracy to overturn the lawful results of the 2020 Presidential election.

13. The intelligence community and law enforcement agencies did successfully detect the planning for potential violence on January 6th, including planning specifically by the Proud Boys and Oath Keeper militia groups who ultimately led the attack on the Capitol. As January 6th approached, the intelligence specifically identified the potential for violence at the U.S. Capitol. This intelligence was shared within the executive branch, including with the Secret Service and the President's National Security Council.

14. Intelligence gathered in advance of January 6th did not support a conclusion that Antifa or other left-wing groups would likely engage in a violent counter-demonstration, or attack Trump supporters on January 6th. Indeed, intelligence from January 5th indicated that some left-wing groups were instructing their members to "stay at home" and not attend on January 6th.[20] Ultimately, none of these groups was involved to any material extent with the attack on the Capitol on January 6th.

15. Neither the intelligence community nor law enforcement obtained intelligence in advance of January 6th on the full extent of the ongoing planning by President Trump, John Eastman, Rudolph Giuliani and their associates to overturn the certified election results. Such agencies apparently did not (and potentially could not) anticipate the provocation President Trump would offer the crowd in his Ellipse speech, that President Trump would "spontaneously" instruct the crowd to march to the Capitol, that President Trump would exacerbate the violent riot by sending his 2:24 p.m. tweet condemning Vice President Pence, or the full scale of the violence and lawlessness that would ensue. Nor did law enforcement anticipate that President Trump would refuse to direct his supporters to leave the Capitol once violence began. No intelligence community advance analysis predicted exactly how President Trump would behave; no such analysis recognized the full scale and extent of the threat to the Capitol on January 6th.

16. Hundreds of Capitol and DC Metropolitan police officers performed their duties bravely on January 6th, and America owes those individuals immense gratitude for their courage in the defense of Congress and our Constitution. Without their bravery, January 6th would have been far worse. Although certain members of the Capitol Police leadership regarded their approach to January 6th as "all hands on deck," the Capitol Police leadership did not have sufficient assets in place to address the violent and lawless crowd.[21] Capitol Police leadership did not anticipate the scale of the violence that would ensue after President Trump instructed tens of thousands of his supporters in the Ellipse crowd to march to the Capitol, and then tweeted at 2:24 p.m. Although Chief Steven Sund raised the idea of National Guard support, the Capitol Police Board did not request Guard assistance prior to January 6th. The Metropolitan Police took an even more proactive approach to January 6th, and deployed roughly 800 officers, including responding to the emergency calls for help at the Capitol. Rioters still managed to break their line in certain locations, when the crowd surged forward in the immediate aftermath of Donald Trump's 2:24 p.m. tweet. The Department of Justice readied a group of Federal agents at Quantico and in the District of Columbia, anticipating that January 6th could become violent, and then deployed those agents once it became clear that police at the Capitol were overwhelmed. Agents from the Department of Homeland Security were also deployed to assist.

17. President Trump had authority and responsibility to direct deployment of the National Guard in the District of Columbia, but never gave

any order to deploy the National Guard on January 6th or on any other day. Nor did he instruct any Federal law enforcement agency to assist. Because the authority to deploy the National Guard had been delegated to the Department of Defense, the Secretary of Defense could, and ultimately did deploy the Guard. Although evidence identifies a likely miscommunication between members of the civilian leadership in the Department of Defense impacting the timing of deployment, the Committee has found no evidence that the Department of Defense intentionally delayed deployment of the National Guard. The Select Committee recognizes that some at the Department had genuine concerns, counseling caution, that President Trump might give an illegal order to use the military in support of his efforts to overturn the election.

* * *

This Report begins with a factual overview framing each of these conclusions and summarizing what our investigation found. That overview is in turn supported by eight chapters identifying the very specific evidence of each of the principal elements of President Trump's multi-part plan to overturn the election, along with evidence regarding intelligence gathered before January 6th and security shortfalls that day.

Although the Committee's hearings were viewed live by tens of millions of Americans and widely publicized in nearly every major news source,[77] the Committee also recognizes that other news outlets and commentators have actively discouraged viewers from watching, and that millions of other Americans have not yet seen the actual evidence addressed by this Report. Accordingly, the Committee is also releasing video summaries of relevant evidence on each major topic investigated.

This Report also examines the legal implications of Donald Trump and his co-conspirators' conduct and includes criminal referrals to the Department of Justice regarding President Trump and certain other individuals. The criminal referrals build upon three relevant rulings issued by a Federal district court and explain in detail how the facts found support further evaluation by the Department of Justice of specific criminal charges. To assist the public in understanding the nature and importance of this material, this Report also contains sections identifying how the Committee has evaluated the credibility of its witnesses and suggests that the Department of Justice further examine possible efforts to obstruct our investigation. We also note that more than 30 witnesses invoked their Fifth Amendment privilege against self-incrimination, others invoked Executive Privilege or categorically refused to appear (including Steve Bannon, who has since been convicted of contempt of Congress).

Finally, this report identifies a series of legislative recommendations, including the Presidential Election Reform Act, which has already passed the House of Representatives.

EXECUTIVE SUMMARY: OVERVIEW OF THE EVIDENCE DEVELOPED

In the Committee's hearings, we presented evidence of what ultimately became a multi-part plan to overturn the 2020 Presidential election. That evidence has led to an overriding and straight forward conclusion: the central cause of January 6th was one man, former President Donald Trump, whom many others followed. None of the events of January 6th would have happened without him.

THE BIG LIE

In the weeks before election day 2020, Donald Trump's campaign experts, including his campaign manager Bill Stepien, advised him that the election results would not be fully known on election night.[23] This was because certain States would not begin to count absentee and other mail-in votes until election day or after election-day polls had closed.[24] Because Republican voters tend to vote in greater numbers on election day and Democratic voters tend to vote in greater numbers in advance of election day, it was widely anticipated that Donald Trump could initially appear to have a lead, but that the continued counting of mail-in, absentee and other votes beginning election night would erode and could overcome that perceived lead.[25] Thus, as President Trump's campaign manager cautioned, understanding the results of the 2020 election would be a lengthy "process," and an initial appearance of a Trump lead could be a "red mirage."[26] This was not unique to the 2020 election; similar scenarios had played out in prior elections as well.[27]

Prior to the 2020 election, Donald Trump's campaign manager Bill Stepien, along with House Republican Leader Kevin McCarthy, urged President Trump to embrace mail-in voting as potentially beneficial to the Trump Campaign.[28] Presidential advisor and son-in-law Jared Kushner recounted others giving Donald Trump the same advice: "[M]ail in ballots could be a good thing for us if we looked at it correctly."[29] Multiple States, including Florida, had successfully utilized mail-in voting in prior elections, and in 2020.[30] Trump White House Counselor Hope Hicks testified: "I think he [President Trump] understood that a lot of people vote via absentee ballot in places like Florida and have for a long time and that it's worked fine."[31] Donald Trump won in numerous States that allowed no-excuse absentee voting in 2020, including Alaska, Florida, Idaho, Iowa, Kansas, Montana, North Carolina, North Dakota, Ohio, Oklahoma, South Dakota, and Wyoming.[32]

On election night 2020, the election returns were reported in almost exactly the way that Stepien and other Trump Campaign experts predicted, with the counting of mail-in and absentee ballots gradually diminishing President Trump's perceived lead. As the evening progressed, President Trump called in his campaign team to discuss the results. Stepien and other campaign experts advised him that the results of the election would not be known for some time, and that he could not truthfully declare victory.[33] "It was far too early to be making any calls like that. Ballots—ballots were still being counted. Ballots were still going to be counted for days."[34]

Campaign Senior Advisor Jason Miller told the Select Committee that he argued against declaring victory at that time as well, because "it was too early to say one way [or] the other" who had won.[35] Stepien advised Trump to say that "votes were still being counted. It's too early to tell, too early to call the race but, you know, we are proud of the race we run—we ran and we, you know, think we're—think we're in a good position" and would say more in the coming days.[36]

President Trump refused, and instead said this in his public remarks that evening: "This is a fraud on the American public. This is an embarrassment to our country. We were getting ready to win this election. Frankly, we did win this election. We did win this election . . . . We want all voting to stop."[37] And on the morning of November 5th, he tweeted "STOP THE COUNT!"[38] Halting the counting of votes at that point would have violated both State and Federal laws.[39]

According to testimony received by the Select Committee, the only advisor present who supported President Trump's inclination to declare victory was Rudolph Giuliani, who appeared to be inebriated.[40] President Trump's Attorney General, William Barr, who had earlier left the election night gathering, perceived the President's statement this way:

> [R]ight out of the box on election night, the President claimed that there was major fraud underway. I mean, this happened, as far as I could tell, before there was actually any potential of looking at evidence. He claimed there was major fraud. And it seemed to be based on the dynamic that, at the end of the evening, a lot of Democratic votes came in which changed the vote counts in certain States, and that seemed to be the basis for this broad claim that there was major fraud. And I didn't think much of that, because people had been talking for weeks and everyone understood for weeks that that was going to be what happened on election night . . . .[41]

President Trump's decision to declare victory falsely on election night and, unlawfully, to call for the vote counting to stop, was not a spontaneous decision. It was premeditated. The Committee has assembled a range of

President Trump declares victory in a speech at an election night party.
(Photo by Chip Somodevilla/Getty Images)

evidence of President Trump's preplanning for a false declaration of victory. This includes multiple written communications on October 31 and November 3, 2020, to the White House by Judicial Watch President Tom Fitton.[42] This evidence demonstrates that Fitton was in direct contact with President Trump and understood that President Trump would falsely declare victory on election night and call for vote counting to stop. The evidence also includes an audio recording of President Trump's advisor Steve Bannon, who said this on October 31, 2020, to a group of his associates from China:

> And what Trump's gonna do is just declare victory, right? He's gonna declare victory. But that doesn't mean he's a winner. He's just gonna say he's a winner . . . The Democrats—more of our people vote early that count. Theirs vote in mail. And so they're gonna have a natural disadvantage, and Trump's going to take advantage of it—that's our strategy. He's gonna declare himself a winner. So when you wake up Wednesday morning, it's going to be a firestorm . . . . Also, if Trump, if Trump is losing, by 10 or 11 o'clock at night, it's going to be even crazier. No, because he's gonna sit right there and say "They stole it. I'm directing the Attorney General to shut down all ballot places in all 50 states." It's

going to be, no, he's not going out easy. If Trump—if Biden's winning, Trump is going to do some crazy shit.[43]

Also in advance of the election, Roger Stone, another outside advisor to President Trump, made this statement:

I really do suspect it will still be up in the air. When that happens, the key thing to do is to claim victory. Possession is nine-tenths of the law. No, we won. Fuck you, Sorry. Over. We won. You're wrong. Fuck you.[44]

On election day, Vice President Pence's staff, including his Chief of Staff and Counsel, became concerned that President Trump might falsely claim victory that evening. The Vice President's Counsel, Greg Jacob, testified about their concern that the Vice President might be asked improperly to echo such a false statement.[45] Jacob drafted a memorandum with this specific recommendation: "[I]t is essential that the Vice President not be perceived by the public as having decided questions concerning disputed electoral votes prior to the full development of all relevant facts."[46]

Millions of Americans believed that President Trump was telling the truth on election night—that President Trump actually had proof the election was stolen and that the ongoing counting of votes was an act of fraud.

As votes were being counted in the days after the election, President Trump's senior campaign advisors informed him that his chances of success were almost zero.

Former Trump Campaign Manager Bill Stepien testified that he had come to this conclusion by November 7th, and told President Trump:

Committee Staff: What was your view on the state of the election at that point?

Stepien: You know, very, very, very bleak. You know, I—we told him—the group that went over there outlined, you know, my belief and chances for success at this point. And then we pegged that at, you know, 5, maybe 10 percent based on recounts that were—that, you know, either were automatically initiated or could be—could be initiated based on, you know, realistic legal challenges, not all the legal challenges that eventually were pursued. But, you know, it was—you know, my belief is that it was a very, very—5 to 10 percent is not a very good optimistic outlook.[47]

Trump Campaign Senior Advisor Jason Miller testified to the Committee about this exchange:

> Miller: I was in the Oval Office. And at some point in the conversation Matt Oczkowski, who was the lead data person, was brought on, and I remember he delivered to the President in pretty blunt terms that he was going to lose.
>
> Committee Staff: And that was based, Mr. Miller, on Matt and the data team's assessment of this sort of county-by-county, State-by-State results as reported?
>
> Miller: Correct.[48]

In one of the Select Committee's hearings, former Fox News political editor Chris Stirewalt was asked what the chance President Trump had of winning the election after November 7th, when the votes were tallied and every news organization had called the race for now-President Biden. His response: "None." [49]

As the Committee's hearings demonstrated, President Trump made a series of statements to White House staff and others during this time period indicating his understanding that he had lost.[50] President Trump also took consequential actions reflecting his understanding that he would be leaving office on January 20th. For example, President Trump personally signed a Memorandum and Order instructing his Department of Defense to withdraw all military forces from Somalia by December 31, 2020, and from Afghanistan by January 15, 2021.[51] General Keith Kellogg (ret.), who had been appointed by President Trump as Chief of Staff for the National Security Council and was Vice President Pence's National Security Advisor on January 6th, told the Select Committee that "[a]n immediate departure that that memo said would have been catastrophic. It's the same thing what President Biden went through. It would have been a debacle." [52]

In the weeks that followed the election, President Trump's campaign experts and his senior Justice Department officials were informing him and others in the White House that there was no genuine evidence of fraud sufficient to change the results of the election. For example, former Attorney General Barr testified:

> And I repeatedly told the President in no uncertain terms that I did not see evidence of fraud, you know, that would have affected the outcome of the election. And, frankly, a year and a half later, I haven't seen anything to change my mind on that.[53]

Former Trump Campaign lawyer Alex Cannon, who was asked to oversee incoming information about voter fraud and set up a voter fraud tip line, told the Select Committee about a pertinent call with White House Chief of Staff Mark Meadows in November 2020:

> Cannon: So I remember a call with Mr. Meadows where Mr. Meadows was asking me what I was finding and if I was finding anything. And I remember sharing with him that we weren't finding anything that would be sufficient to change the results in any of the key States.
>
> Committee Staff: When was that conversation?
>
> Cannon: Probably in November. Mid- to late November . . . .
>
> Committee Staff: And what was Mr. Meadows's reaction to that information?
>
> Cannon: I believe the words he used were: "So there is no there there?" [54]

President Trump's Campaign Manager Bill Stepien recalled that President Trump was being told "wild allegations" and that it was the Campaign's job to "track [the allegations] down":

> Committee Staff: You said that you were very confident that you were telling the President the truth in your dealings with [him]. And had your team been able to verify any of these allegations of fraud, would you have reported those to the President?
>
> Stepien: Sure.
>
> Committee Staff: Did you ever have to report that—
>
> Stepien: One of my frustrations would be that, you know, people would throw out, you know, these reports, these allegations, these things that they heard or saw in a State, and they'd tell President Trump. And, you know, it would be the campaign's job to track down the information, the facts. And, you know, President Trump, you know—if someone's saying, hey, you know, all these votes aren't counted or were miscounted, you know, if you're down in a State like Arizona, you liked hearing that. It would be our job to track it down and come up dry because the allegation didn't prove to be true. And we'd have to, you know, relay the news that, yeah, that tip that someone told you about those votes or that fraud or, you know, nothing came of it.
>
> That would be our job as, you know, the truth telling squad and, you know, not—not a fun job to be, you know, much—it's an easier job to

be telling the President about, you know, wild allegations. It's a harder job to be telling him on the back end that, yeah, that wasn't true.

Committee Staff: How did he react to those types of conversations where you [told] him that an allegation or another wasn't true?

Stepien: He was—he had—usually he had pretty clear eyes. Like, he understood, you know—you know, we told him where we thought the race was, and I think he was pretty realistic with our viewpoint, in agreement with our viewpoint of kind of the forecast and the uphill climb we thought he had.[55]

Trump Campaign Senior Advisor Jason Miller told the Committee that he informed President Trump "several" times that "specific to election day fraud and irregularities, there were not enough to overturn the election."[56]

Vice President Pence has also said publicly that he told President Trump there was no basis to allege that the election was stolen. When a reporter recently asked "Did you ever point blank say to the President [that] we lost this election?," Pence responded that "I did . . . Many times."[57] Pence has also explained:

There was never evidence of widespread fraud. I don't believe fraud changed the outcome of the election. But the President and the Campaign had every right to have those examined in court. But I told the President that, once those legal challenges played out, he should simply accept the outcome of the election and move on.[58]

The General Counsel of President Trump's campaign, Matthew Morgan, informed members of the White House staff, and likely many others, of the Campaign's conclusion that none of the allegations of fraud and irregularities could be sufficient to change the outcome of the election:

What was generally discussed on that topic was whether the fraud, maladministration, abuse, or irregularities, if aggregated and read most favorably to the campaign, would that be outcome determinative. And I think everyone's assessment in the room, at least amongst the staff, Marc Short, myself, and Greg Jacob, was that it was not sufficient to be outcome determinative.[59]

In a meeting on November 23rd, Barr told President Trump that the Justice Department was doing its duty by investigating every fraud allegation "if it's specific, credible, and could've affected the outcome," but that "they're just not meritorious. They're not panning out."[60]

Barr then told the Associated Press on December 1st that the Department had "not seen fraud on a scale that could have effected a different outcome in the election."[61] Next, he reiterated this point in private meetings with the President both that afternoon and on December 14th, as well as in his final press conference as Attorney General later that month.[62] The Department of Homeland Security had reached a similar determination two weeks earlier: "**There is no evidence that any voting system deleted or lost votes, changed votes, or was in any way compromised.**"[63]

In addition, multiple other high ranking Justice Department personnel appointed by President Trump also informed him repeatedly that the allegations were false. As January 6th drew closer, Acting Attorney General Rosen and Acting Deputy Attorney General Donoghue had calls with President Trump on almost a daily basis explaining in detail what the Department's investigations showed.[64] Acting Deputy Attorney General Richard Donoghue told the Select Committee that he and Acting Attorney General Rosen tried "to put it in very clear terms to the President. And I said something to the effect of 'Sir, we've done dozens of investigations, hundreds of interviews. The major allegations are not supported by the evidence developed. We've looked in Georgia, Pennsylvania, Michigan, Nevada. We're doing our job.'"[65] On December 31st, Donoghue recalls telling the President that "people keep telling you these things and they turn out not to be true."[66] And then on January 3rd, Donoghue reiterated this point with the President:

> [A]s in previous conservations, we would say to him, you know, "We checked that out, and there's nothing to it."[67]

Acting Attorney General Rosen testified before the Select Committee that "the common element" of all of his communications with President Trump was President Trump urging the Department to find widespread fraud that did not actually exist. None of the Department's investigations identified any genuine fraud sufficient to impact the election outcome:

> During my tenure as the Acting Attorney General, which began on December 24 of [2020], the Department of Justice maintained the position, publicly announced by former Attorney General William Barr, that the Department had been presented with no evidence of widespread voter fraud in a scale sufficient to change the outcome of the 2020 election.[68]

As President Trump was hearing from his campaign and his Justice Department that the allegations of widespread fraud were not supported by the evidence, his White House legal staff also reached the same conclusions, and agreed specifically with what Barr told President Trump. Both White House Counsel Pat Cipollone and White House Senior Advisor Eric Herschmann reinforced to President Trump that the Justice Department was doing its duty to investigate allegations of supposed voter fraud.[69]

Cipollone told the Select Committee that he "had seen no evidence of massive fraud in the election" and that he "forcefully" made this point "over and over again." For example, during a late-night group meeting with President Trump on December 18th, at which he and Herschmann urged Trump not to heed the advice of several election conspiracists at the meeting:

> Cipollone: They didn't think that we were, you know—they didn't think we believed this, you know, that there had been massive fraud in the election, and the reason they didn't think we believed it is because we didn't.

> Committee Staff: And you articulated that forcefully to them during the meeting?

> Cipollone: I did, yeah. I had seen no evidence of massive fraud in the election. . . . At some point, you have to deliver with the evidence. And I—again, I just to go back to what [Barr] said, he had not seen and I was not aware of any evidence of fraud to the extent that it would change the results of the election. That was made clear to them, okay, over and over again.[70]

Similarly, White House Attorney Eric Herschmann was also very clear about his views:

> [T]hey never proved the allegations that they were making, and they were trying to develop.[71]

In short, President Trump was informed over and over again, by his senior appointees, campaign experts and those who had served him for years, that his election fraud allegations were nonsense.

How did President Trump continue to make false allegations despite all of this unequivocal information? President Trump sought out those who were not scrupulous with the facts, and were willing to be dishonest. He found a new legal team to assert claims that his existing advisors and the Justice Department had specifically informed him were false. President Trump's new legal team, headed by Rudolph Giuliani, and their allies ultimately lost dozens of election lawsuits in Federal and State courts.

The testimony of Trump Campaign Manager Bill Stepien helps to put this series of events in perspective. Stepien described his interaction with Giuliani as an intentional "self-demotion," with Stepien stepping aside once it became clear that President Trump intended to spread falsehoods.

Stepien knew the President's new team was relying on unsupportable accusations, and he refused to be associated with their approach:

There were two groups of family. We called them kind of my team and Rudy's team. I didn't mind being characterized as being part of "team normal," as reporters, you know, kind of started to do around that point in time. [72]

Having worked for Republican campaigns for over two decades, Stepien said, "I think along the way I've built up a pretty good -- I hope a good reputation for being honest and professional, and I didn't think what was happening was necessarily honest or professional at that point in time." [73]

As Giuliani visited Campaign headquarters to discuss election litigation, the Trump Campaign's professional staff began to view him as unhinged. [74] In addition, multiple law firms previously engaged to work for the Trump Campaign decided that they could not participate in the strategy being instituted by Giuliani. They quit. Campaign General Counsel Matthew Morgan explained that he had conversations with "probably all of our counsel who [we]re signed up to assist on election day as they disengaged with the campaign." [75] The "general consensus was that the law firms were not comfortable making the arguments that Rudy Giuliani was making publicly." [76] When asked how many outside firms expressed this concern, Morgan recalled having "a similar conversation with most all of them." [77]

Stepien grew so wary of the new team that he locked Giuliani out of his office:

Committee Staff: Yeah. I'm getting the sense from listening to you here for few hours that you sort of chose to pull back, that you were uncomfortable with what Mr. Giuliani and others were saying and doing and, therefore, you were purposefully stepping back from a day-to-day role as the leader of the campaign. Is that—I don't want to put words in your mouth. Is that accurate?

Stepien: That's accurate. That's accurate. You know, I had my assistant -- it was a big glass kind of wall office in our headquarters, and I had my assistant lock my door. I told her, don't let anyone in. You know, I'll be around when I need to be around. You know, tell me what I need to know. Tell me what's going on here, but, you know, you're going to see less of me.

And, you know, sure enough, you know, Mayor Giuliani tried to, you know, get in my office and ordered her to unlock the door, and she didn't do that, you know. She's, you know, smart about that. But your words are ones I agree with. [78]

Over the weeks that followed, dozens of judges across the country specifically rejected the allegations of fraud and irregularities being advanced

by the Trump team and their allies. For example, courts described the arguments as "an amalgamation of theories, conjecture, and speculation,"
"allegations ... sorely wanting of relevant or reliable evidence," "strained
legal arguments without merit," assertions that "did not prove by any
standard of proof that any illegal votes were cast and counted," and even a
"fundamental and obvious misreading of the Constitution." [79]

Reflecting back on this period, Trump Campaign Communications
Director Tim Murtaugh texted colleagues in January 2021 about a news
report that the New York State Bar was considering expelling Rudolph Giuliani over the Ellipse rally: "Why wouldn't they expel him based solely on
the outrageous lies he told for 2 1/2 months?" [80]

This is exactly what ultimately came to pass. When suspending his
license, a New York court said that Giuliani "communicated demonstrably
false and misleading statements to courts, lawmakers and the public at
large in his capacity as lawyer for former President Donald J. Trump and the
Trump campaign in connection with Trump's failed effort at reelection in
2020." [81] The court added that "[t]he seriousness of [Giuliani's] uncontro-
verted misconduct cannot be overstated." [82]

Other Trump lawyers were sanctioned for making outlandish claims of
election fraud without the evidence to back them up, including Sidney Powell, Lin Wood and seven other pro-Trump lawyers in a case that a Federal
judge described as "a historic and profound abuse of the judicial process":

> It is one thing to take on the charge of vindicating rights associated
> with an allegedly fraudulent election. It is another to take on the
> charge of deceiving a federal court and the American people into
> believing that rights were infringed, without regard to whether any
> laws or rights were in fact violated. This is what happened here.[83]

A group of prominent Republicans have more recently issued a report—
titled *Lost, Not Stolen*—examining "every count of every case brought in
these six battleground states" by President Trump and his allies. The report
concludes "that Donald Trump and his supporters had their day in court
and failed to produce substantive evidence to make their case." [84] President
Trump and his legal allies "failed because of a lack of evidence and not
because of erroneous rulings or unfair judges . . . . In many cases, after
making extravagant claims of wrongdoing, Trump's legal representatives
showed up in court or state proceedings empty-handed, and then returned
to their rallies and media campaigns to repeat the same unsupported
claims." [85]

There is no reasonable basis for the allegation that these dozens of rulings by State and Federal courts were somehow politically motivated.[86] The
outcome of these suits was uniform regardless of who appointed the judges.

One of the authors of *Lost, Not Stolen*, longtime Republican election lawyer Benjamin Ginsberg, testified before the Select Committee that "in no instance did a court find that the charges of fraud were real," without variation based on the judges involved.[87] Indeed, eleven of the judges who ruled against Donald Trump and his supporters were appointed by Donald Trump himself.

One of those Trump nominees, Judge Stephanos Bibas of the U.S. Court of Appeals for the Third Circuit, rejected an appeal by the Trump Campaign claiming that Pennsylvania officials "did not undertake any meaningful effort" to fight illegal absentee ballots and uneven treatment of voters across counties.[88] Judge Bibas wrote in his decision that "calling an election unfair does not make it so. Charges require specific allegations and then proof. We have neither here." [89] Another Trump nominee, Judge Brett Ludwig of the Eastern District of Wisconsin, ruled against President Trump's lawsuit alleging that the result was skewed by illegal procedures that governed drop boxes, ballot address information, and individuals who claimed "indefinitely confined" status to vote from home.[90] Judge Ludwig wrote in his decision, that "[t]his Court has allowed plaintiff the chance to make his case and he has lost on the merits" because the procedures used "do not remotely rise to the level" of breaking Wisconsin's election rules.[91]

Nor is it true that these rulings focused solely on standing, or procedural issues. As Ginsberg confirmed in his testimony to the Select Committee, President Trump's team "did have their day in court." [92] Indeed, he and his co-authors determined in their report that 30 of these post-election cases were dismissed by a judge after an evidentiary hearing had been held, and many of these judges explicitly indicated in their decisions that the evidence presented by the plaintiffs was wholly insufficient on the merits.[93]

Ultimately, even Rudolph Giuliani and his legal team acknowledged that they had no definitive evidence of election fraud sufficient to change the election outcome. For example, although Giuliani repeatedly had claimed in public that Dominion voting machines stole the election, he admitted during his Select Committee deposition that "I do not think the machines stole the election." [94] An attorney representing his lead investigator, Bernard Kerik, declared in a letter to the Select Committee that "it was impossible for Kerik and his team to determine conclusively whether there was widespread fraud or whether that widespread fraud would have altered the outcome of the election." [95] Kerik also emailed President Trump's chief of staff on December 28, 2020, writing: "We can do all the investigations we want later, but if the president plans on winning, it's the legislators that have to be moved and this will do just that." [96] Other Trump lawyers and supporters, Jenna Ellis, John Eastman, Phil Waldron, and Michael Flynn, all invoked their Fifth Amendment privilege against self-incrimination when

Rudolph Giuliani, Bernard Kerik, and other hold a press conference at Four Seasons Total Landscaping on November 7, 2020 falsely claiming Donald Trump had won the state of Pennsylvania.

(Photo by Chris McGrath/Getty Images)

asked by the Select Committee what supposed proof they uncovered that the election was stolen.[97] Not a single witness--nor any combination of witnesses--provided the Select Committee with evidence demonstrating that fraud occurred on a scale even remotely close to changing the outcome in any State.[98]

By mid-December 2020, Donald Trump had come to what most of his staff believed was the end of the line. The Supreme Court rejected a lawsuit he supported filed by the State of Texas in the Supreme Court, and Donald Trump had this exchange, according to Special Assistant to the President Cassidy Hutchinson:

> The President was fired up about the Supreme Court decision. And so I was standing next to [Chief of Staff Mark] Meadows, but I had stepped back . . . The President [was] just raging about the decision and how it's wrong, and why didn't we make more calls, and just this typical anger outburst at this decision . . . And the President said I think—so he had said something to the effect of, "I don't want people to know we lost, Mark. This is embarrassing. Figure it out. We need to figure it out. I don't want people to know that we lost." [99]

On December 14, 2020, the Electoral College met to cast and certify each State's electoral votes. By this time, many of President Trump's senior staff, and certain members of his family, were urging him to concede that he had lost.

Labor Secretary Gene Scalia told the Committee that he called President Trump around this time and gave him such feedback quite directly:

> [S]o, I had put a call in to the President—I might have called on the 13th; we spoke, I believe, on the 14th—in which I conveyed to him that I thought that it was time for him to acknowledge that President Biden had prevailed in the election . . . . But I communicated to the President that when that legal process is exhausted and when the electors have voted, that that's the point at which that outcome needs to be expected . . . . And I told him that I did believe, yes, that once those legal processes were run, if fraud had not been established that had affected the outcome of the election, that, unfortunately, I believed that what had to be done was concede the outcome.[100]

Deputy White House Press Secretary Judd Deere also told President Trump that he should concede. He recalled other staffers advising President Trump at some point to concede and that he "encouraged him to do it at least once after the electoral college met in mid-December." [101] White House Counsel Pat Cipollone also believed that President Trump should concede: "[I]f your question is did I believe he should concede the election at a point in time, yes, I did." [102]

Attorney General Barr told the Select Committee this: "And in my view, that [the December 14 electoral college vote] was the end of the matter. I didn't see—you know, I thought that this would lead inexorably to a new administration. I was not aware at that time of any theory, you know, why this could be reversed. And so I felt that the die was cast . . . ." [103]

Barr also told the Committee that he suggested several weeks earlier that the President's efforts in this regard needed to come to an end soon, in conversation with several White House officials after his meeting with Trump on November 23rd:

> [A]s I walked out of the Oval Office, Jared was there with Dan Scavino, who ran the President's social media and who I thought was a reasonable guy and believe is a reasonable guy. And I said, how long is he going to carry on with this 'stolen election' stuff? Where is this going to go?
>
> And by that time, Meadows had caught up with me and—leaving the office, and caught up to me and said that—he said, look, I think that he's becoming more realistic and knows that there's a limit to how far he can take this. And then Jared said, you know, yeah, we're working on this, we're working on it.[104]

Despite all that Donald Trump was being told, he continued to purposely and maliciously make false claims. To understand the very stark differences between what he was being told and what he said publicly and in fundraising solicitations, the Committee has assembled the following examples.

Then–Deputy Attorney General Jeffrey Rosen (12/15/20):	*President Trump one week later (12/22/20):*
"And so he said, 'Well, what about this? I saw it on the videotape, somebody delivering a suitcase of ballots.' And we said, 'It wasn't a suitcase. It was a bin. That's what they use when they're counting ballots. It's benign.'" [105]	"There is even security camera footage from Georgia that shows officials telling poll watchers to leave the room before pulling suitcases of ballots out from under the tables and continuing to count for hours." [106]
Acting Deputy Attorney General Richard Donoghue (12/27 & 12/31/20):	*President Trump later that week (1/2/21):*
"I told the President myself that several times, in several conversations, that these allegations about ballots being smuggled in in a suitcase and run through the machine several times, it was not true, that we looked at it, we looked at the video, we interviewed the witnesses, that it was not true . . . . I believe it was in the phone call on December 27th. It was also in a meeting in the Oval Office on December 31st." [107]	"[S]he stuffed the machine. She stuffed the ballot. Each ballot went three times, they were showing: Here's ballot number one. Here it is a second time, third time, next ballot." [108]
GA Sec. State Brad Raffensperger (1/2/21):	*President Trump one day later (1/3/21):*
"You're talking about the State Farm video. And I think it's extremely unfortunate that Rudy Giuliani or his people, they sliced and diced that video and took it out of context." . . . "[W]e did an audit of that and we proved conclusively that they were not scanned three times. . . . Yes, Mr. President, we'll send you the link from WSB." [Trump]: "I don't care about a link. I don't need it." [109]	"I spoke to Secretary of State Brad Raffensperger yesterday about Fulton County and voter fraud in Georgia. He was unwilling, or unable, to answer questions such as the 'ballots under table' scam, ballot destruction, out of state 'voters', dead voters, and more. He has no clue!" [110]

Attorney General Barr (12/1/20):	*President Trump one day later (12/2/20):*
"Then he raised the 'big vote dump,' as he called it, in Detroit. And, you know, he said, people saw boxes coming into the counting station at all hours of the morning and so forth.... I said, 'Mr. President, there are 630 precincts in Detroit, and unlike elsewhere in the State, they centralize the counting process, so they're not counted in each precinct, they're moved to counting stations, and so the normal process would involve boxes coming in at all different hours.' And I said, 'Did anyone point out to you—did all the people complaining about it point out to you, you actually did better in Detroit than you did last time? I mean, there's no indication of fraud in Detroit.'" [111]	"I'll tell you what's wrong, voter fraud. Here's an example. This is Michigan. At 6:31 in the morning, a vote dump of 149,772 votes came in unexpectedly. We were winning by a lot. That batch was received in horror. . . . In Detroit everybody saw the tremendous conflict . . . there were more votes than there were voters." [112]
Acting Deputy Attorney General Richard Donoghue (12/27/20):	*President Trump ten days later (1/6/21):*
"The President then continued, there are 'more votes than voters...'. But I was aware of that allegation, and I said, you know, that was just a matter of them 'comparing the 2020 votes cast to 2016 registration numbers.' That is 'not a valid complaint.'" [113]	"More votes than they had voters. And many other States also." [114]
Acting Deputy Attorney General Richard Donoghue (1/3/21):	*President Trump three days later (1/6/21):*
"[W]e would say to him, you know, 'We checked that out, and there's nothing to it. . . . And we would cite to certain allegations. And so—like such as Pennsylvania, right. 'No, there were not 250,000 more votes reported than were actually cast. That's not true.' So we would say things like that." [115]	"In Pennsylvania, you had 205,000 more votes than you had voters. And the number is actually much greater than that now. That was as of a week ago. And this is a mathematical impossibility unless you want to say it's a total fraud." [116]

GA Sec. State Brad Raffensperger (1/2/21):	President Trump two days later (1/4/21):
[Trump]: "[I]t's 4,502 who voted, but they weren't on the voter registration roll, which they had to be. You had 18,325 vacant address voters. The address was vacant, and they're not allowed to be counted. That's 18,325." . . . [Raffensperger]: "Well, Mr. President, the challenge that you have is the data you have is wrong." [117]	"4,502 illegal ballots were cast by individuals who do not appear on the state's voter rolls. Well, that's sort of strange. 18,325 illegal ballots were cast by individuals who registered to vote using an address listed as vacant according to the postal service." [118]
GA Sec. of State Brad Raffensperger (1/2/21):	President Trump four days later (1/6/21):
[Trump]: "So dead people voted, and I think the number is close to 5,000 people. And they went to obituaries. They went to all sorts of methods to come up with an accurate number, and a minimum is close to about 5,000 voters." . . . [Raffensperger]: "The actual number were two. Two. Two people that were dead that voted. So that's wrong." [119]	"[T]he number of fraudulent ballots that we've identified across the state is staggering. Over 10,300 ballots in Georgia were cast by individuals whose names and dates of birth match Georgia residents who died in 2020 and prior to the election." [120]
GA Sec. State General Counsel Ryan Germany (1/2/21):	President Trump four days later (1/6/21):
[Trump]: "You had out-of-state voters. They voted in Georgia, but they were from out of state, of 4,925." . . . [Germany]: "Every one we've been through are people that lived in Georgia, moved to a different state, but then moved back to Georgia legitimately." . . . "They moved back in years ago. This was not like something just before the election. So there's something about that data that, it's just not accurate." [121]	"And at least 15,000 ballots were cast by individuals who moved out of the state prior to November 3rd election. They say they moved right back." [122]

White House Press Secretary Kayleigh McEnany (n.d.): "[T]he one specific I remember referencing was I don't agree with the Dominion track." . . . "I specifically referenced waving him off of the Dominion theory earlier in my testimony." . . . [Q] "Are you saying you think he still continued to tweet that after you waved him off of it?" [A] "Yeah . . ."[123]	***President Trump:*** Between mid-November and January 5, 2021, President Trump tweeted or retweeted conspiracy theories about Dominion nearly three dozen times.[124]
Trump Campaign Senior Advisor Jason Miller: "...the international allegations for Dominion were not valid." [Q] "Okay. Did anybody communicate that to the President?" [A]: "I know that that was—I know that was communicated. I know I communicated it"[125]	***President Trump:*** "You have Dominion, which is very, very suspect to start off with. Nobody knows the ownership. People say the votes are counted in foreign countries and much worse..."[126]
Attorney General Barr (11/23/20): "I specifically raised the Dominion voting machines, which I found to be one of the most disturbing allegations— 'disturbing' in the sense that I saw absolutely zero basis for the allegations . . . I told him that it was crazy stuff and they were wasting their time on that and it was doing great, great disservice to the country."[127]	***President Trump three days later (11/26/20):*** "[T]hose machines are fixed, they're rigged. You can press Trump and the vote goes to Biden. . . . All you have to do is play with a chip, and they played with a chip, especially in Wayne County and Detroit."[128]
Attorney General Barr (12/1/20): "I explained, I said, look, if you have a machine and it counts 500 votes for Biden and 500 votes for Trump, and then you go back later and you have a—you will have the 1,000 pieces of paper put through that machine, and you can see if there's any discrepancy...there has been no discrepancy."[129]	***President Trump one day later (12/2/20):*** "In one Michigan County, as an example, that used Dominion systems, they found that nearly 6,000 votes had been wrongly switched from Trump to Biden, and this is just the tip of the iceberg. This is what we caught. How many didn't we catch?"[130]

Attorney General Barr (12/14/20): "'I will, Mr. President. But there are a couple of things,' I responded. 'My understanding is that our experts have looked at the Antrim situation and are sure it was a human error that did not occur anywhere else. And, in any event, Antrim is doing a hand recount of the paper ballots, so we should know in a couple of days whether there is any real problem with the machines.' "[131]	*President Trump one day later (12/15/20):* "This is BIG NEWS. Dominion Voting Machines are a disaster all over the Country. Changed the results of a landslide election. Can't let this happen. . . ."[132]
Then-Deputy Attorney General Jeffrey Rosen (12/15/20): "[O]ther people were telling him there was fraud, you know, corruption in the election. The voting machines were no good. And we were telling him that is inconsistent, by 'we,' I mean Richard Donoghue and myself, that that was not what we were seeing." . . . "There was this open issue as to the Michigan report. And—I think it was Mr. Cuccinelli, not certain, but had indicated that there was a hand recount. And I think he said, 'That's the gold standard.' "[133]	*President Trump one day later (12/16/20):* "'Study: Dominion Machines shifted 2-3% of Trump Votes to Biden. Far more votes than needed to sway election.' Florida, Ohio, Texas and many other states were won by even greater margins than pro-jected. Did just as well with Swing States, but bad things happened. @OANN"[134]
National Security Adviser Robert O'Brien (12/18/20): "I got a call from, I think, Molly Michael in outer oval, the President's assistant, and she said, 'I'm connect-ing you to the Oval' . . . somebody asked me, was there—did I have any evidence of election fraud in the vot-ing machines or foreign interference in our voting machines. And I said, no, we've looked into that and there's no evidence of it."[135]	*President Trump one day later (12/19/20):* ". . . There could also have been a hit on our ridiculous voting machines during the election, which is now obvious that I won big, making it an even more corrupted embar-rassment for the USA. @DNI-_Ratcliffe @SecPompeo"[136]

Acting Deputy AG Richard Donoghue (12/31/20):	*President Trump two days later (1/2/21):*
"We definitely talked about Antrim County again. That was sort of done at that point, because the hand recount had been done and all of that. But we cited back to that to say, you know, this is an example of what people are telling you and what's being filed in some of these court filings that are just not supported by the evidence."[137]	"Well, Brad. Not that there's not an issue, because we have a big issue with Dominion in other states and perhaps in yours. . . . in other states, we think we found tremendous corruption with Dominion machines, but we'll have to see." . . . "I won't give Dominion a pass because we found too many bad things."[138]
GA Sec. State Brad Raffensperger (1/2/21):	*President Trump four days later (1/6/21):*
"I don't believe that you're really questioning the Dominion machines. Because we did a hand re-tally, a 100 percent re-tally of all the ballots, and compared them to what the machines said and came up with virtually the same result. Then we did the recount, and we got virtually the same result."[139]	"In addition, there is the highly troubling matter of Dominion Voting Systems. In one Michigan county alone, 6,000 votes were switched from Trump to Biden and the same systems are used in the majority of states in our country." . . . "There is clear evidence that tens of thousands of votes were switched from President Trump to former Vice President Biden in several counties in Georgia."[140]

Evidence gathered by the Committee indicates that President Trump raised roughly one quarter of a billion dollars in fundraising efforts between the election and January 6th.[141] Those solicitations persistently claimed and referred to election fraud that did not exist. For example, the Trump Campaign, along with the Republican National Committee, sent millions of emails to their supporters, with messaging claiming that the election was "rigged," that their donations could stop Democrats from

Taped footage of William Barr speaking to the January 6th Select Committee is shown at one of its hearings.

(Photo by Mandel Ngan-Pool/Getty Images)

"trying to steal the election," and that Vice President Biden would be an "illegitimate president" if he took office.

Ultimately, Attorney General Barr suggested that the Department of Justice's investigations disproving President Trump's fraud claims may have prevented an even more serious series of events:

> [F]rankly, I think the fact that I put myself in the position that I could say that we had looked at this and didn't think there was fraud was really important to moving things forward. And I sort of shudder to think what the situation would have been if the position of the Department was, "We're not even looking at this until after Biden's in office." I'm not sure we would've had a transition at all.[142]

RATHER THAN CONCEDE, DONALD TRUMP CHOOSES TO OBSTRUCT THE JANUARY 6TH PROCEEDING

President Trump disregarded the rulings of the courts and rejected the findings and conclusions and advice from his Justice Department, his campaign experts, and his White House and Cabinet advisors. He chose instead to try to overturn the election on January 6th and took a series of very specific steps to attempt to achieve that result.

A central element of Donald Trump's plan to overturn the election relied upon Vice President Mike Pence. As Vice President, Pence served as the President of the Senate, the presiding officer for the joint session of Congress on January 6th. Beginning in December, and with greater frequency as January 6th approached, Trump repeatedly and unlawfully pressured Pence in private and public to prevent Congress from counting lawful electoral votes from several States.

To understand the plan President Trump devised with attorney and law professor John Eastman, it is necessary to understand the constitutional structure for selecting our President.

At the Constitutional Convention 233 years ago, the framers considered but rejected multiple proposals that Congress itself vote to select the President of the United States.[143] Indeed the Framers voiced very specific concerns with Congress selecting the President. They viewed it as important that the electors, chosen for the specific purpose of selecting the President, should make the determination rather than Congress:

> It was desireable, that the sense of the people should operate in the choice of the person to whom so important a trust was to be confided. This end will be answered by committing the right of making it, not to any pre-established body, but to men, chosen by the people for the special purpose, and at the particular conjuncture.[144]

The Framers understood that a thoughtful structure for the appointment of the President was necessary to avoid certain evils: "Nothing was more to be desired, than that every practicable obstacle should be opposed to cabal, intrigue and corruption."[145] They were careful to ensure that "those who from situation might be suspected of too great devotion to the president in office" "were not among those that chose the president."[146] For that reason, "[n]o senator, representative, or other person holding a place of trust or profit under the United States, can be of the number of the electors."[147]

Article II of our Constitution, as modified by the Twelfth Amendment, governs election of the President. Article II created the electoral college, providing that the States would select electors in the manner provided by State legislatures, and those electors would in turn vote for the President. Today, every State selects Presidential electors by popular vote, and each State's laws provide for procedures to resolve election disputes, including through lawsuits if necessary. After any election issues are resolved in State or Federal court, each State's government transmits a certificate of the ascertainment of the appointed electors to Congress and the National Archives.

The electoral college meets in mid-December to cast their votes, and all of these electoral votes are then ultimately counted by Congress on January 6th. The Vice President, as President of the Senate, presides over the joint session of Congress to count votes. The Twelfth Amendment provides this straight forward instruction: "The president of the Senate shall, in the presence of the Senate and House of Representatives, open all the certificates and the votes shall then be counted; The person having the greatest number of votes for President shall be the President..." The Vice President has only a ministerial role, opening the envelopes and ensuring that the votes are counted. Likewise, the Electoral Count Act of 1887 provides no substantive role for the Vice President in counting votes, reinforcing that he or she can only act in a ministerial fashion—the Vice President may not choose, for example, to decline to count particular votes. In most cases (*e.g.*, when one candidate has a majority of votes submitted by the States) Congress has only a ministerial role, as well. It simply counts electoral college votes provided by each State's governor. Congress is not a court and cannot overrule State and Federal court rulings in election challenges.

As January 6th approached, John Eastman and others devised a plan whereby Vice President Pence would, as the presiding officer, declare that certain electoral votes from certain States *could not* be counted at the joint session.[148] John Eastman knew before proposing this plan that it was not legal. Indeed, in a pre-election document discussing Congress's counting of electoral votes, Dr. Eastman specifically disagreed with a colleague's proposed argument that the Vice President had the power to choose which envelopes to "open" and which votes to "count." Dr. Eastman wrote:

> I don't agree with this. The 12th Amendment only says that the President of the Senate opens the ballots in the joint session then, in the passive voice, that the votes shall then be counted. 3 USC § 12 [of the Electoral Count Act] says merely that he is the presiding officer, and then it spells out specific procedures, presumptions, and default rules for which slates will be counted. Nowhere does it suggest that the president of the Senate gets to make the determination on his own. § 15 [of the Electoral Count Act] doesn't either.[149]

Despite recognizing prior to the 2020 election that the Vice President had no power to refuse to count certain electoral votes, Eastman nevertheless drafted memoranda two months later proposing that Pence could do exactly that on January 6th—refuse to count certified electoral votes from Arizona, Georgia, Michigan, Nevada, New Mexico, Pennsylvania and Wisconsin.[150]

Eastman's theory was related to other efforts overseen by President Trump (described in detail below, *see infra*) to create and transmit fake electoral slates to Congress and the National Archives, and to pressure States to change the election outcome and issue new electoral slates. Eastman supported these ideas despite writing two months earlier that:

> Article II [of the Constitution] says the electors are appointed "in such manner as the Legislature thereof may direct," but I don't think that entitles the Legislature to change the rules after the election and appoint a different slate of electors in a manner different than what was in place on election day. And 3 U.S.C. §15 [of the Electoral Count Act] gives dispositive weight to the slate of electors that was certified by the Governor in accord with 3 U.S.C. §5.[151]

Even after Eastman proposed the theories in his December and January memoranda, he acknowledged in conversations with Vice President Pence's counsel Greg Jacob that Pence could not lawfully do what his own memoranda proposed.[152] Eastman admitted that the U.S. Supreme Court would unanimously reject his legal theory. "He [Eastman] had acknowledged that he would lose 9-0 at the Supreme Court." [153] Moreover, Eastman acknowledged to Jacob that he didn't think Vice President Al Gore had that power in 2001, nor did he think Vice President Kamala Harris should have that power in 2025.[154]

In testimony before the Select Committee, Jacob described in detail why the Trump plan for Pence was illegal:

> [T]he Vice President's first instinct, when he heard this theory, was that there was no way that our Framers, who abhorred concentrated power, who had broken away from the tyranny of George III, would ever have put one person—particularly not a person who had a direct interest in the outcome because they were on the ticket for the election—in a role to have decisive impact on the outcome of the election. And our review of text, history, and, frankly, just common sense, all confirmed the Vice President's first instinct on that point. There is no justifiable basis to conclude that the Vice President has that kind of authority.[155]

This is how the Vice President later described his views in a public speech:

> I had no right to overturn the election. The Presidency belongs to the American people, and the American people alone. And frankly,

there is no idea more un-American than the notion that any one person could choose the American President. Under the Constitution, I had no right to change the outcome of our election.[156]

But as January 6th approached, President Trump nevertheless embraced the new Eastman theories, and attempted to implement them. In a series of meetings and calls, President Trump attempted to pressure Pence to intervene on January 6th to prevent Congress from counting multiple States' electoral votes for Joe Biden. At several points in the days before January 6th, President Trump was told directly that Vice President Pence could not legally do what Trump was asking. For example, at a January 4th meeting in the Oval Office, Eastman acknowledged that any variation of his proposal—whether rejecting electoral votes outright or delaying certification to send them back to the States—would violate several provisions of the Electoral Count Act. According to Greg Jacob:

> In the conversation in the Oval Office on the 4th, I had raised the fact that . . . [Eastman's] preferred course had issues with the Electoral Count Act, which he had acknowledged was the case, that there would be an inconsistency with the Electoral Count Act[ ][157]

Jacob recorded Eastman's admission in an internal memo he drafted for Vice President Pence on the evening of January 4th: "Professor Eastman acknowledges that his proposal violates several provisions of statutory law." [158] And, during a phone call with President Trump and Eastman on the evening of January 5, 2021, Eastman *again* acknowledged that his proposal also would violate several provisions of the Electoral Count Act.

> [W]e did have an in-depth discussion about [the Electoral Count Act] in the subsequent phone calls as I walked him through provision after provision on the recess and on the fact that . . . Congressmen and Senators are supposed to get to object and debate. And he acknowledged, one after another, that those provisions would—in order for us to send it back to the States, we couldn't do those things as well. We can't do a 10-day, send it back to the States, and honor an Electoral Count Act provision that says you can't recess for more than one day and, once you get to the 5th, you have to stay continuously in session.[159]

As Pence's Chief of Staff, Marc Short, testified that the Vice President also repeatedly informed President Trump that the Vice President's role on January 6th was only ministerial.

Committee Staff: But just to pick up on that, Mr. Short, was it your impression that the Vice President had directly conveyed his position on these issues to the President, not just to the world through a Dear Colleague Letter, but directly to President Trump?

Marc Short: Many times.

Committee Staff: And had been consistent in conveying his position to the President?

Short: Very consistent.[160]

As the situation grew increasingly acrimonious, Vice President Pence's private counsel Richard Cullen contacted former Fourth Circuit Judge Michael Luttig, a renowned conservative judge for whom Eastman had previously clerked, and asked Luttig to make a public statement. On January 5th, Luttig wrote the following on Twitter: "The only responsibility and power of the Vice President under the Constitution is to faithfully count the electoral college votes as they have been cast."[161] As Judge Luttig testified in the Committee's hearings, "there was no basis in the Constitution or laws of the United States at all for the theory espoused by Eastman—at all. None."[162] Judge Luttig completely rejected Eastman's "blueprint to overturn the 2020 election" as "constitutional mischief" and 'the most reckless, insidious, and calamitous failure[ ] in both legal and political judgment in American history."[163]

Contemporaneous written correspondence also confirms both that: (1) Eastman himself recognized Pence could not lawfully refuse to count electoral votes, and (2) President Trump also knew this. While sheltering in a loading dock with the Vice President during the violent January 6th attack, Greg Jacob asked Eastman in an email, "Did you advise the President that in your professional judgment the Vice President DOES NOT have the power to decide things unilaterally?" Eastman's response stated that the President had "been so advised," but then indicated that President Trump continued to pressure the Vice President to act illegally: "But you know him—once he gets something in his head, it is hard to get him to change course."[164]

To be absolutely clear, no White House lawyer believed Pence could lawfully refuse to count electoral votes. White House Counsel Pat Cipollone told the Select Committee this:

I thought that the Vice President did not have the authority to do what was being suggested under a proper reading of the law. I conveyed that, ok? I think I actually told somebody, you know, in the Vice President's—"Just blame me." You know this is—I'm not a politician, you know . . . but, you know, I just said, "I'm a lawyer. This is my legal opinion."[165]

Greg Jacob and Judge Michael Luttig testify at January 6th Select Committee hearing.
(Photo by House Creative Services)

Cipollone also testified that he was "sure [he] conveyed" his views.[166] Indeed, other testimony from Cipollone indicates that Trump knew of Cipollone's view and suggests that Trump purposely excluded Cipollone from the meeting with Pence and Pence's General Counsel on January 4th.[167] Indeed, at one point, Cipollone confronted Eastman in the hallway outside the Oval Office and expressed his disapproval of and anger with Eastman's position. According to Jason Miller, "Pat Cipollone thought the idea was nutty and had at one point confronted Eastman basically with the same sentiment" outside the Oval Office.[168] Pat Cipollone did not deny having an angry confrontation with Eastman outside of the Oval Office—though he said he didn't have a specific recollection, he had no reason to contradict what Jason Miller said and, moreover, said that Eastman was aware of his views.[169]

Likewise, Eric Herschmann, another White House lawyer, expressed the same understanding that Eastman's plan "obviously made no sense" and "had no practical ability to work."[170] Herschmann also recounted telling Eastman directly that his plan was "completely crazy":

And I said to [Eastman], hold on a second, I want to understand what you're saying. You're saying you believe the Vice President, acting as President of the Senate, can be the sole decisionmaker as to, under your theory, who becomes the next President of the

United States? And he said, yes. And I said, are you out of your F'ing mind, right. And that was pretty blunt. I said, you're completely crazy.[171]

Deputy White House Counsel Pat Philbin also had the same understanding.[172] Indeed, as Herschmann testified, even Rudolph Giuliani doubted that Vice President Mike Pence had any legal ability to do what Eastman had proposed.[173]

Despite all this opposition from all White House lawyers, Trump nevertheless continued to exert immense pressure on Pence to refuse to count electoral votes.

The pressure began before the January 4th Oval Office meeting with Pence, Eastman, Jacob, Short and Trump, but became even more intense thereafter. On the evening of January 5, 2021, the New York Times published an article reporting that "Vice President Mike Pence told President Trump on Tuesday that he did not believe he had the power to block congressional certification of Joseph R. Biden, Jr.'s victory in the Presidential election despite President Trump's baseless insistence that he did."[174] This reporting was correct—both as to the Vice President's power and as to Vice President Pence having informed President Trump that he did not have the authority to change the outcome of the election. But in response to that story, late in the evening before the January 6th joint session, President Trump dictated to Jason Miller a statement falsely asserting, "The Vice President and I are in *total agreement* that the Vice President has the power to act."[175] This statement was released at President Trump's direction and was false.[176]

Thereafter, Trump continued to apply public pressure in a series of tweets. At 1:00 a.m. on January 6th, "[i]f Vice President @Mike_Pence comes through for us, we will win the Presidency. Many States want to decertify the mistake they made in certifying incorrect & even fraudulent numbers in a process NOT approved by their State Legislatures (which it must be). Mike can send it back!"[177] At 8:17 a.m. on January 6th, he tweeted again: "States want to correct their votes, which they now know were based on irregularities and fraud, plus corrupt process never received legislative approval. All Mike Pence has to do is send them back to the States, AND WE WIN. Do it Mike, this is a time for extreme courage!"[178]

President Trump tried to reach the Vice President early in the morning of January 6th, but the Vice President did not take the call. The President finally reached the Vice President later that morning, shouting from the Oval Office to his assistants to "get the Vice President on the phone."[179] After again telling the Vice President that he had "the legal authority to send [electoral votes] back to the respective states," President Trump grew very heated.[180] Witnesses in the Oval Office during this call told the Select

President Trump speaks with Vice President Pence over the phone in the Oval Office on the morning of January 6th.
(Photo provided to the Select Committee by the National Archives and Records Administration)

Committee that the President called Vice President Pence a "wimp," [181] told him it would be "a political career killer" to certify the lawful electoral votes electing President Biden,[182] and accused him of "not [being] tough enough to make the call." [183] As Ivanka Trump would recount to her chief of staff moments later, her father called the Vice President "the p-word" for refusing to overturn the election.[184]

In response, Vice President Pence again refused to take any action other than counting the lawfully certified electoral votes of the States. But President Trump was angry and undeterred. After the conclusion of this call, he edited his speech for the Ellipse to insert language to which his lawyers objected—targeting Vice President Pence directly.[185]

Earlier that morning, Eric Herschmann had tried to remove the reference to Vice President Pence from the speech. As he told speechwriter Stephen Miller, he "didn't concur with the legal analysis" that John Eastman had advanced and believed it "wouldn't advance the ball" to discuss it publicly.[186] But after the call with Vice President Pence, speechwriters were instructed to reinsert the line. Although the final written draft of his speech referred to Pence just once—a line President Trump didn't end up reading[187]—the President went off-script five different times to pressure the Vice President:

"I hope Mike is going to do the right thing. I hope so. Because if Mike Pence does the right thing, we win the election," Trump first told the crowd.[188]

"Mike Pence is going to have to come through for us," Trump later said, "and if he doesn't, that will be a, a sad day for our country because you're sworn to uphold our Constitution."[189]

Addressing Pence directly, Trump told the assembled crowd: "Mike Pence, I hope you're going to stand up for the good of our Constitution and for the good of our country." Trump said at another point, "And if you're not, I'm going to be very disappointed in you. I will tell you right now. I'm not hearing good stories."[190]

"So I hope Mike has the courage to do what he has to do. And I hope he doesn't listen to the RINOs and the stupid people that he's listening to," Trump said.[191]

These statements to the assembled crowd at the Ellipse had Trump's intended effect—they produced substantial anger against Pence. When Pence released a statement confirming that he would not act to prevent Congress from counting electoral votes, the crowd's reaction was harshly negative.

"I'm telling you what, I'm hearing that Pence—hearing the Pence just caved. No. Is that true? I didn't hear it. I'm hear — I'm hearing reports that Pence caved. No way. I'm telling you, if Pence caved, we're going to drag motherfuckers through the streets. You fucking politicians are going to get fucking drug through the streets."[192]

Pence voted against Trump. [Interviewer: "Ok. And that's when all this started?"] Yup. That's when we marched on the Capitol.[193]

"We just heard that Mike Pence is not going to reject any fraudulent electoral votes. [Other speaker: "Boo. You're a traitor!"] That's right. You've heard it here first. Mike Pence has betrayed the United States of America. [Other speaker: "Fuck you, Mike Pence!"] Mike Pence has betrayed this President and he has betrayed the people of the United States and we will never, ever forget." [Cheers][194]

"This woman cames [sic] up to the side of us and she says Pence folded. So it was kind of, like, Ok, well — in my mind I was thinking, well that's it. You know. Well, my son-in-law looks at me and he says I want to go in."[195]

"[Q] "What percentage of the crowd is going to the Capitol?" [A] [Oath Keeper Jessica Watkins]: "One hundred percent. It has, it has spread like wildfire that Pence has betrayed us, and everybody's marching on the Capitol. All million of us. it's insane."[196]

"Bring him out. Bring out Pence. Bring him out. Bring out Pence. Bring him out. Bring out Pence. Bring him out. Bring out Pence."[197]

"Hang Mike Pence. Hang Mike Pence. Hang Mike Pence. Hang Mike Pence. Hang Mike Pence."[198]

Once Trump returned to the White House, he was informed almost immediately that violence and lawlessness had broken out at the Capitol among his supporters.[199] At 2:24 p.m., President Trump applied yet further pressure to Pence (*see infra*), posting a tweet accusing Vice President Mike Pence of cowardice for not using his role as President of the Senate to change the outcome of the election: "Mike Pence didn't have the courage to do what should have been done to protect our Country and our Constitution, giving States a chance to certify a corrected set of facts, not the fraudulent or inaccurate ones which they were asked to previously certify. USA demands the truth!"[200] Almost immediately thereafter, the crowd around the Capitol surged, and more individuals joined the effort to confront police and break further into the building.

The sentiment expressed in President Trump's 2:24 p.m. tweet, already present in the crowd, only grew more powerful as the President's words spread. Timothy Hale-Cusanelli—a white supremacist who expressed Nazi sympathies—heard about the tweet while in the Crypt around 2:25 p.m., and he, according to the Department of Justice, "knew what that meant." Vice President Pence had decided not to keep President Trump in power.[201] Other rioters described what happened next as follows:

Once we found out Pence turned on us and that they had stolen the election, like officially, the crowd went crazy. I mean, it became a mob. We crossed the gate.[202]

Then we heard the news on [P]ence . . . And lost it . . . So we stormed.[203]

They're making an announcement right now saying if Pence betrays us you better get your mind right because we're storming that building.[204]

Minutes after the tweet—at 2:35 p.m.—rioters continued their surge and broke a security line of the DC Metropolitan Police Department, resulting in the first fighting withdrawal in the history of that force.[205]

President Trump issued this tweet after he had falsely claimed to the angry crowd that Vice President Mike Pence could "do the right thing" and ensure a second Trump term, after that angry crowd had turned into a violent mob assaulting the Capitol while chanting, "Hang Mike Pence!"[206] and after the U.S. Secret Service had evacuated the Vice President from the Senate floor.[207] One minute after the President's tweet, at 2:25 p.m., the Secret Service determined they could no longer protect the Vice President in his ceremonial office near the Senate Chamber, and evacuated the Vice President and his family to a secure location, missing the violent mob by a mere 40 feet.[208]

Further evidence presented at our hearing shows the violent reaction following President Trump's 2:24 p.m. tweet and the efforts to protect Vice President Pence in the time that followed.[209]

The day after the attack on the Capitol, Eastman called Eric Herschmann to talk about continuing litigation on behalf of the Trump Presidential Campaign in Georgia. Herschmann described his reaction to Eastman this way:

> And I said to him, are you out of your F'ing mind? Right? I said, because I only want to hear two words coming out of your mouth from now on: Orderly transition. I said, I don't want to hear any other F'ing words coming out of your mouth, no matter what, other than orderly transition. Repeat those words to me." [210]

Herschmann concluded the call by telling Eastman: "Now I'm going to give you the best free legal advice you're ever getting in your life. Get a great F'ing criminal defense lawyer, you're going to need it," and hanging up the phone.[211]

In the course of investigating this series of facts, the Select Committee subpoenaed Eastman's emails from his employer, Chapman University.[212] Eastman sued to prevent Chapman from producing the emails, arguing that the emails were attorney-client privileged. Federal District Court Judge David Carter reviewed Eastman's emails *in camera* to determine, among other things, whether the emails had to be produced because they likely furthered a crime committed by one of Eastman's clients or by Eastman himself. In addition to reviewing the emails themselves, Judge Carter reviewed substantial additional evidence presented by the Select Committee and by Eastman.

After reciting a series of factual findings regarding President Trump's multi-part plan to overturn the election, Judge Carter concluded that President Trump likely violated two criminal statutes: 18 U.S.C. § 1512(c) (corruptly obstructing, impeding or influencing Congress's official proceeding to count electoral votes); and 18 U.S.C. § 371 (conspiring to defraud the United States). The Court also concluded that John Eastman likely violated at least one of these criminal laws. As to §1512(c), Judge Carter explained:

> Taken together, this evidence demonstrates that President Trump likely knew the electoral count plan had no factual justification.
>
> The plan not only lacked factual basis but also legal justification. . . .

The illegality of the plan was obvious. Our nation was founded on the peaceful transition of power, epitomized by George Washington laying down his sword to make way for democratic elections. Ignoring this history, President Trump vigorously campaigned for the Vice President to single-handedly determine the results of the 2020 election. . . . Every American—and certainly the President of the United States—knows that in a democracy, leaders are elected, not installed. With a plan this "BOLD," President Trump knowingly tried to subvert this fundamental principle. Based on the evidence, the Court finds it more likely than not that President Trump corruptly attempted to obstruct the Joint Session of Congress on January 6, 2021.[213]

As to 18 U.S.C. § 371, Judge Carter identified evidence demonstrating that both President Trump and John Eastman knew their electoral count plan was illegal, and knew it could not "survive judicial scrutiny" in any of its iterations:

Dr. Eastman himself repeatedly recognized that his plan had no legal support. . . . Dr. Eastman likely acted deceitfully and dishonestly each time he pushed an outcome-driven plan that he knew was unsupported by the law.[214]

Finally, Judge Carter concluded:

Dr. Eastman and President Trump launched a campaign to overturn a democratic election, an action unprecedented in American history. Their campaign was not confined to the ivory tower—it was a coup in search of a legal theory. The plan spurred violent attacks on the seat of our nation's government, led to the deaths of several law enforcement officers, and deepened public distrust in our political process.[215]

Judge Luttig reached similar conclusions during his live hearing testimony: "I have written, as you said, Chairman Thompson, that, today, almost two years after that fateful day in January 2021, that, still, Donald Trump and his allies and supporters are a clear and present danger to American democracy."[216]

During the hearing, Judge Luttig took issue with certain of Greg Jacob's characterizations of the 12th Amendment's text, explaining that the applicable text was not ambiguous in any way. The Committee agrees with Judge Luttig: the application of the Twelfth Amendment's text is plain in this context; it does not authorize Congress to second-guess State and Federal courts and refuse to count State electoral votes based on concerns about fraud. *See infra*. Although Jacob did not discuss his position in great detail during the hearing, his private testimony gives more insight on his actual views:

> In my view, a lot has been said about the fact that the role of the Vice President in the electoral count on January 6th is purely ministerial, and that is a correct conclusion. But if you look at the constitutional text, the role of Congress is purely ministerial as well. You open the certificates and you count them. Those are the only things provided for in the Constitution.[217]

EFFORTS TO PRESSURE STATES TO CHANGE THE ELECTION OUTCOME, AND TO CREATE AND TRANSMIT FAKE ELECTION CERTIFICATES

Anticipating that the Eastman strategy for January 6th would be implemented, President Trump worked with a handful of others to prepare a series of false Trump electoral slates for seven States Biden actually won. President Trump personally conducted a teleconference with Eastman and Republican National Committee Chair Ronna McDaniel "a few days before December 14" and solicited the RNC's assistance with the scheme.[218] McDaniel agreed to provide that assistance.[219]

A series of contemporaneous documents demonstrate what President Trump and his allies, including attorney Kenneth Chesebro, were attempting to accomplish: they anticipated that the President of the Senate (which, under the Constitution, is the Vice President) could rely upon these false slates of electors on January 6th to justify refusing to count genuine electoral votes.[220]

The false slates were created by fake Republican electors on December 14th, at the same time the actual, certified electors in those States were meeting to cast their States' Electoral College votes for President Biden. By that point in time, election-related litigation was over in all or nearly all of the subject States, and Trump Campaign election lawyers realized that the fake slates could not be lawful or justifiable on any grounds. Justin Clark, the Trump Campaign Deputy Campaign Manager and Senior Counsel told the Select Committee that he "had real problems with the process." [221] Clark warned his colleagues, "unless we have litigation pending like in these States, like, I don't think this is appropriate or, you know, this isn't the right thing to do. I don't remember how I phrased it, but I got into a little bit of a back and forth and I think it was with Ken Chesebro, where I said, 'Alright, you know, you just get after it, like, I'm out.' " [222]

Matthew Morgan, the Trump Campaign General Counsel, told the Select Committee that without an official State certificate of ascertainment,[223] "the [fake] electors were, for lack of a better way of saying it, no good or not—not valid." [224]

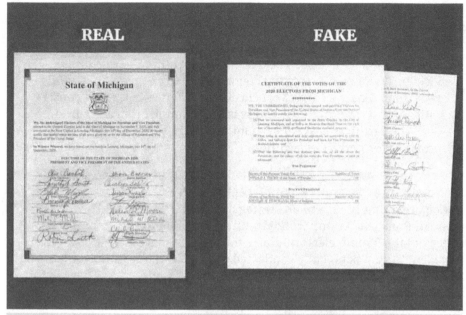

REAL

FAKE

Graphic depicting the difference between the real and the fake elector certificates.

The Office of White House Counsel also appears to have expressed concerns with this fake elector plan. In his interview by the Select Committee, White House Counsel Pat Cipollone acknowledged his view that by mid-December, the process was "done" and that his deputy, Pat Philbin, may have advised against the fake elector strategy.[225] In an informal Committee interview, Philbin described the fake elector scheme as one of the "bad theories" that were like "Whac-A-Mole" in the White House during this period.[226] Cipollone agreed with this characterization.[227]

In her testimony, Cassidy Hutchinson testified that she heard at least one member of the White House Counsel's Office say that the plan was not legal:

> Committee Staff: [T]o be clear, did you hear the White House Counsel's Office say that this plan to have alternate electors meet and cast votes for Donald Trump in States that he had lost was not legally sound?
>
> Hutchinson: Yes, sir.[228]

Multiple Republicans who were persuaded to sign the fake certificates also testified that they felt misled or betrayed, and would not have done so had they known that the fake votes would be used on January 6th without an intervening court ruling. One elector told the Select Committee that he thought his vote would be strictly contingent: "[I]t was a very consistent message that we were told throughout all of that, is this is the only reason why we're doing this, is to preserve the integrity of being able to have a challenge."[229]

The "Chairperson" of the Wisconsin fake electors, who was also at the time Chairman of the Wisconsin Republican Party, insisted in testimony to the Select Committee that he "was told that these would only count if a court ruled in our favor" and that he wouldn't have supported anyone using the Trump electors' votes without a court ruling.[230]

Despite the fact that all major election lawsuits thus far had failed, President Trump and his co-conspirators in this effort, including John Eastman and Kenneth Chesebro, pressed forward with the fake elector scheme. Ultimately, these false electoral slates, five of which purported to represent the "duly elected" electoral college votes of their States, were transmitted to Executive Branch officials at the National Archives, and to the Legislative Branch, including to the Office of the President of the Senate, Vice President Mike Pence.[231]

The fake electors followed Chesebro's step-by-step instructions for completing and mailing the fake certificates to multiple officials in the U.S. Government,[232] complete with registered mail stickers and return address labels identifying senders like the "Arizona Republican Party" and the "Georgia Republican Party."[233] The Wisconsin Republican Party's fake certificates apparently weren't properly delivered, however, so the Trump Campaign arranged to fly them to Washington just before the joint session on January 6th, and try to deliver them to the Vice President via Senator Ron Johnson and Representative Mike Kelly's offices.[234] Both Johnson and Kelly's offices attempted to do so, but Vice President Pence's aide refused the delivery.[235]

Despite pressure from President Trump, Vice President Pence and the Senate parliamentarian refused to recognize or count the unofficial fake electoral votes. Greg Jacob testified that he advised Vice President Pence on January 2nd that "none of the slates that had been sent in would qualify as an alternate slate" under the law and that the Senate Parliamentarian "was in agreement" with this conclusion.[236]

* * *

In addition to this plan to create and transmit fake electoral slates, Donald Trump was also personally and substantially involved in multiple efforts to pressure State election officials and State legislatures to alter official lawful election results. As U.S. District Judge Carter stated in his June 7, 2022, opinion:

Dr. Eastman's actions in these few weeks [in December 2020] indicate that his and President Trump's pressure campaign to stop the electoral count did not end with Vice President Pence—it targeted every tier of federal and state elected officials. Convincing state legislatures to certify competing electors was essential to stop the count and ensure President Trump's reelection.[237]

Judge Carter also explained that "Dr. Eastman and President Trump's plan to disrupt the Joint Session was fully formed and actionable as early as December 7, 2020."[238]

Chapter 2 of this report provides substantial detail on many of President Trump's specific efforts to apply pressure to State officials and legislators. We provide a few examples here:

During a January 2, 2021, call, President Trump pressured Georgia's Republican Secretary of State Brad Raffensperger to "find 11,780 votes." During that call, President Trump asserted conspiracy theories about the election that Department of Justice officials had already debunked. President Trump also made a thinly veiled threat to Raffensperger and his attorney about his failure to respond to President Trump's demands: "That's a criminal, that's a criminal offense . . . That's a big risk to you and to Ryan, your lawyer . . . I'm notifying you that you're letting it happen."[239]

Judge Carter drew these conclusions:

Mr. Raffensperger debunked the President's allegations "point by point" and explained that "the data you have is wrong;" however, President Trump still told him, "I just want to find 11,780 votes."[240]

* * *

President Trump's repeated pleas for Georgia Secretary of State Raffensperger clearly demonstrate that his justification was not to investigate fraud, but to win the election. . . . Taken together, this evidence demonstrates that President Trump likely knew the electoral count plan had no factual justification. The plan not only lacked factual basis but also legal justification.[241]

That call to Raffensperger came on the heels of President Trump's repeated attacks on Raffensperger, election workers, and other public servants about President Trump's loss in the election. A month earlier, the Georgia Secretary of State's Chief Operating Officer, Gabriel Sterling, had given this explicit public warning to President Trump and his team, a warning that the Select Committee has determined President Trump apparently saw and disregarded:[242]

[I]t has all gone too far. All of it. . . .

A 20-something tech in Gwinnett County today has death threats and a noose put out, saying he should be hung for treason because he was transferring a report on batches from an EMS to a county computer so he could read it.

It has to stop.

Mr. President, you have not condemned these actions or this language. Senators, you have not condemned this language or these actions. This has to stop. We need you to step up. And if you're going to take a position of leadership, show some.

My boss, Secretary Raffensperger—his address is out there. They have people doing caravans in front of their house, they've had people come onto their property. Tricia, his wife of 40 years, is getting sexualized threats through her cellphone.

It has to stop.

This is elections, this is the backbone of democracy, and all of you who have not said a damn word are complicit in this. It's too much....

What you don't have the ability to do—and you need to step up and say this—is stop inspiring people to commit potential acts of violence. Someone's going to get hurt. Someone's going to get shot. Someone's going to get killed.[243]

The stark warning was entirely appropriate, and prescient. In addition to the examples Sterling identified, President Trump and his team were also fixated on Georgia election workers Ruby Freeman and Wandrea "Shaye" Moss. He and Giuliani mentioned Freeman repeatedly in meetings with State legislators, at public rallies, and in the January 2nd call with Raffensperger. Referring to a video clip, Giuliani even accused Freeman and Moss of trading USB drives to affect votes "as if they [were] vials of heroin or cocaine."[244] This was completely bogus: it was not a USB drive; it was a ginger mint.[245]

After their contact information was published, Trump supporters sent hundreds of threats to the women and even showed up at Freeman's home.[246] As Freeman testified to the Select Committee, Trump and his followers' conduct had a profound impact on her life. She left her home based on advice from the FBI, and wouldn't move back for months.[247] And she explained, "I've lost my sense of security—all because a group of people, starting with Number 45 [Donald Trump] and his ally Rudy Giuliani, decided to scapegoat me and my daughter Shaye to push their own lies

Gabriel Sterling at a press conference on November 6, 2020 in Atlanta, Georgia.
(Photo by Jessica McGowan/Getty Images)

about how the Presidential election was stolen." [248] The treatment of Freeman and Moss was callous, inhumane, and inexcusable. Rudolph Giuliani and others with responsibility should be held accountable.

In Arizona, a primary target of President Trump's pressure, and ire, was House Speaker Russell "Rusty" Bowers, a longtime Republican who had served 17 years in the State legislature. Throughout November and December, Bowers spoke to President Trump, Giuliani, and members of Giuliani's legal team, in person or on the phone. During these calls, President Trump and others alleged that the results in Arizona were affected by fraud and asked that Bowers consider replacing Presidential electors for Biden with electors for President Trump.[249] Bowers demanded proof for the claims of fraud, but never got it. At one point, after Bowers pressed Giuliani on the claims of fraud, Giuliani responded, "we've got lots of theories, we just don't have the evidence." [250] Bowers explained to Giuliani: "You are asking me do something against my oath, and I will not break my oath." [251]

President Trump and his supporters' intimidation tactics affected Bowers, too. Bowers's personal cell phone and home address were doxed,[252] leading demonstrators to show up at his home and shout insults until police arrived. One protestor who showed up at his home was armed and believed to be a member of an extremist militia.[253] Another hired a truck with a defamatory and profane allegation that Bowers, a deeply religious man, was a pedophile, and drove it through Bowers's neighborhood.[254] This, again, is the conduct of thugs and criminals, each of whom should be held accountable.

In Michigan, President Trump focused on Republican Senate Majority Leader Mike Shirkey and Republican House Speaker Lee Chatfield. He invited them to the White House for a November 20, 2020, meeting during which President Trump and Giuliani, who joined by phone, went through a "litany" of false allegations about supposed fraud in Michigan's election.[255] Chatfield recalled President Trump's more generic directive for the group to "have some backbone and do the right thing," which he understood to mean overturning the election by naming Michigan's Electoral College electors for President Trump.[256] Shirkey told President Trump that he wouldn't do anything that would violate Michigan law,[257] and after the meeting ended, issued a joint statement with Chatfield: "We have not yet been made aware of any information that would change the outcome of the election in Michigan and as legislative leaders, we will follow the law and follow the normal process regarding Michigan's electors, just as we have said throughout this election."[258]

When President Trump couldn't convince Shirkey and Chatfield to change the outcome of the election in Michigan during that meeting or in calls after, he or his team maliciously tweeted out Shirkey's personal cell phone number and a number for Chatfield that turned out to be wrong.[259] Shirkey received nearly 4,000 text messages after that, and another private citizen reported being inundated with calls and texts intended for Chatfield.[260]

None of Donald Trump's efforts ultimately succeeded in changing the official results in any State. That these efforts had failed was apparent to Donald Trump and his co-conspirators well before January 6th. By January 6th, there was no evidence at all that a majority of any State legislature would even attempt to change its electoral votes.[261]

This past October, U.S. District Court Judge David Carter issued a further ruling relating to one of President Trump's lawsuits in Georgia. Judge Carter applied the crime-fraud exception to attorney-client privilege again, and identified potential criminal activity related to a knowingly false representation by Donald Trump to a Federal court. He wrote:

> The emails show that President Trump knew that the specific numbers of voter fraud were wrong but continued to tout those numbers, both in court and in public.[262]

Steven Engel, Jeffrey Rosen and Richard Donoghue at a Select Committee hearing on June 23, 2022.

(Photo by House Creative Services)

As John Eastman wrote in an email on December 31, 2020, President Trump was "made aware that some of the allegations (and evidence proffered by the experts)" in a verified State court complaint was "inaccurate." [263] Dr. Eastman noted that "with that knowledge" President Trump could not accurately verify a Federal court complaint that incorporated by reference the "inaccurate" State court complaint: "I have no doubt that an aggressive DA or US Atty someplace will go after both the President and his lawyers once all the dust settles on this." [264] Despite this specific warning, "President Trump and his attorneys ultimately filed the complaint with the same inaccurate numbers without rectifying, clarifying, or otherwise changing them." [265] And President Trump personally "signed a verification swearing under oath that the incorporated, inaccurate numbers 'are true and correct' or 'believed to be true and correct' to the best of his knowledge and belief." [266] The numbers were not correct, and President Trump and his legal team knew it.

EFFORTS TO CORRUPT THE DEPARTMENT OF JUSTICE

In the weeks after the 2020 election, Attorney General Barr advised President Trump that the Department of Justice had not seen any evidence to support Trump's theory that the election was stolen by fraud. Acting Attorney General Jeffrey Rosen and his Deputy repeatedly reinforced to President Trump that his claims of election fraud were false when they took over in mid-December. Also in mid-December 2020, Attorney General Barr announced his plans to resign. Between that time and January 6th, Trump spoke with Acting Attorney General Jeff Rosen and Acting Deputy Richard Donoghue repeatedly, attempting to persuade them and the Department of Justice to find factual support for his stolen election claims and thereby to assist his efforts to reverse election results.

As Rosen publicly testified, ". . . between December 23rd and January 3rd, the President either called me or met with me virtually every day, with one or two exceptions, like Christmas Day." [267] As discussed earlier, Justice Department investigations had demonstrated that the stolen election claims were false; both Rosen and Donoghue told President Trump this comprehensively and repeatedly.

One of those conversations occurred on December 27th, when President Trump called Rosen to go through a "stream of allegations" about the election.[268] Donoghue described that call as an "escalation of the earlier conversations" they had.[269] Initially, President Trump called Rosen directly. When Donoghue joined the call, he sought to "make it clear to the President [that] these allegations were simply not true." [270]

> So [the President] went through [the allegations]—in what for me was a 90-minute conversation or so, and what for the former Acting AG was a 2-hour conversation—as the President went through them I went piece by piece to say "no, that's false, that is not true," and to correct him really in a serial fashion as he moved from one theory to another.[271]

The President raised, among others, debunked claims about voting machines in Michigan, a truck driver who allegedly moved ballots from New York to Pennsylvania, and a purported election fraud at the State Farm Arena in Georgia.[272] None of the allegations were credible, and Rosen and Donoghue said so to the President.[273]

At one point during the December 27th call in which Donoghue refuted President Trump's fraud allegations, Donoghue recorded in handwritten notes a request President Trump made specifically to him and Acting Attorney General Rosen: "Just say the election was corrupt and leave the rest to me and the Republican Congressmen." [274] Donoghue explained: "[T]he Department had zero involvement in anyone's political strategy," and "he wanted us to say that it was corrupt." [275] "We told him we were not going to do that." [276] At the time, neither Rosen nor Donoghue knew the full extent to which Republican Congressmen, including Representative Scott Perry, were attempting to assist President Trump to overturn the election results.

The Committee's investigation has shown that Congressman Perry was working with one Department of Justice official, Jeffrey Clark, regarding the stolen election claims. Perry was working with Clark and with President Trump and Chief of Staff Mark Meadows with this goal: to enlist Clark to reverse the Department of Justice's findings regarding the election and help overturn the election outcome.[277]

After introducing Clark to the President, Perry sent multiple text messages to Meadows between December 26th and December 28th, pressing that Clark be elevated within the Department. Perry reminded Meadows that there are only "11 days to 1/6 . . . We gotta get going!," and, as the days went on, one asking, "Did you call Jeff Clark?"[278]

Acting Attorney General Rosen first learned about Clark's contact with President Trump in a call on Christmas Eve. On that call, President Trump mentioned Clark to Rosen, who was surprised to learn that Trump knew Clark and had met with him. Rosen later confronted Clark about the contact: "Jeff, anything going on that you think I should know about?"[279] Clark didn't "immediately volunteer" the fact that he had met with the President, but ultimately "acknowledged that he had been at a meeting with the President in the Oval Office, not alone, with other people."[280] Clark was "kind of defensive" and "somewhat apologetic," "casting it as that he had had a meeting with Congressman Perry from Pennsylvania and that, to his surprise, or, you know, he hadn't anticipated it, that they somehow wound up at a meeting in the Oval Office."[281] Clark's contact with President Trump violated both Justice Department and White House policies designed to prevent political pressure on the Department.[282]

While Clark initially appeared apologetic and assured Rosen that "[i]t won't happen again,"[283] he nevertheless continued to work and meet secretly with President Trump and Congressman Perry. Less than five days after assuring Rosen that he would comply with the Department's White House contacts policy, Clark told Rosen and Donoghue that he had again violated that policy. Donoghue confronted him: "I reminded him that I was his boss and that I had directed him to do otherwise."[284]

Around the same time, Representative Perry called Acting Deputy Attorney General Donoghue, criticized the FBI, and suggested that the Department hadn't been doing its job. Perry told Donoghue that Clark "would do something about this."[285]

On December 28th, Clark worked with a Department employee named Kenneth Klukowski—a political appointee who had earlier worked with John Eastman—to produce a draft letter from the Justice Department to the

State legislature of Georgia.[286] That letter mirrored a number of the positions President Trump and Eastman were taking at the time.[287] (Although both Clark and Eastman refused to answer questions by asserting their Fifth Amendment right against self-incrimination, evidence shows that Clark and Eastman were in communication in this period leading up to January 6th.[288] The draft letter to Georgia was intended to be one of several Department letters to State legislatures in swing States that had voted for Biden.[289]

The letter read: "The Department of Justice is investigating various irregularities in the 2020 election for President of the United States."[290] Clark continued: "The Department will update you as we are able on investigatory progress, but at this time we have identified significant concerns that may have impacted the outcome of the election in multiple States, including the State of Georgia."[291] This was *affirmatively untrue.* The Department had conducted many investigations of election fraud allegations by that point, but it absolutely did not have "significant concerns" that fraud "may have impacted the outcome of the election" in any State. Jeff Clark knew this; Donoghue confirmed it again in an email responding to Clark's letter: "[W]e simply do not currently have a basis to make such a statement. Despite dramatic claims to the contrary, we have not seen the type of fraud that calls into question the reported (and certified) results of the election."[292]

The letter also explicitly recommended that Georgia's State legislature should call a special session to evaluate potential election fraud. "In light of these developments, the Department recommends that the Georgia General Assembly should convene in special session so that its legislators are in a special position to take additional testimony, receive new evidence, and deliberate on the matter consistent with its duties under the U.S. Constitution."[293]

Clark's draft letter also referenced the fake electors that President Trump and his campaign organized—arguing falsely that there were currently two competing slates of legitimate Presidential electors in Georgia:[294]

> The Department believes that in Georgia and several other States, both a slate of electors supporting Joseph R. Biden, Jr., and a separate slate of electors supporting Donald J. Trump, gathered on [December 14, 2020] at the proper location to cast their ballots, and that both sets of those ballots have been transmitted to Washington, D.C., to be opened by Vice President Pence.[295]

This, of course, was part of Donald Trump and John Eastman's plan for January 6th. This letter reflects an effort to use the Department of Justice to help overturn the election outcome in Georgia and elsewhere. Rosen and Donoghue reacted immediately to this draft letter:

"[T]here's no chance that I would sign this letter or anything remotely like this," Donoghue wrote.[296] The plan set forth by Clark was "not even within the realm of possibility,"[297] and Donoghue warned that if they sent Clark's letter, it "would be a grave step for the Department to take and it could have tremendous Constitutional, political and social ramifications for the country."[298]

As Richard Donoghue testified when describing his response to Clark's proposed letter:

> Well, I had to read both the email and the attached letter twice to make sure I really understood what he was proposing because it was so extreme to me I had a hard time getting my head around it initially.
>
> But I read it, and I did understand it for what he intended, and I had to sit down and sort of compose what I thought was an appropriate response . . . .
>
> In my response I explained a number of reasons this is not the Department's role to suggest or dictate to State legislatures how they should select their electors. But more importantly, this was not based on fact. This was actually contrary to the facts as developed by Department investigations over the last several weeks and months.
>
> So, I respond to that. And for the department to insert itself into the political process this way I think would have had grave consequences for the country. It may very well have spiraled us into a constitutional crisis.[299]

Rosen and Donoghue also met with Clark about the letter. Their conversation "was a very difficult and contentious" one, according to Donoghue.[300] "What you're proposing is nothing less than the United States Justice Department meddling in the outcome of a Presidential election," Donoghue admonished Clark, to which Clark indignantly responded, "I think a lot of people have meddled in this election."[301]

Both Rosen and Donoghue refused to sign the letter, and confronted Clark with the actual results of the Department's investigations.[302] They also permitted Clark access to a classified briefing from the Office of the Director of National Intelligence ("ODNI") showing Clark that allegations he made to Rosen and Donoghue about foreign interference with voting machines were not true. According to Rosen, the decision to give Clark the briefing at that point "was a difficult question because, if he's going to brief the President, I reluctantly think it's probably better that he's heard from Director Ratcliffe than that he not, even if—I don't think he should brief the President. But, at this point, he's telling me that this is happening whether I agree with it or not. So, so I let him have that briefing." [303]

After Clark received the ODNI briefing, "he acknowledged [to Donoghue] that there was nothing in that briefing that would have supported his earlier suspicion about foreign involvement." [304] While Clark then dropped his claims about foreign interference, he continued to press to send the letter to Georgia and other States, despite being told that the Department of Justice investigations had found no fraud sufficient to overturn the election outcome in Georgia or any other States. This was an intentional choice by Jeff Clark to contradict specific Department findings on election fraud, and purposely insert the Department into the Presidential election on President Trump's behalf and risk creating or exacerbating a constitutional crisis.

By this point, President Trump recognized that neither Rosen nor Donoghue would sign the letter or support his false election claims. President Trump and his team then communicated further with Clark and offered him the job of Acting Attorney General. On January 2nd, Clark told Rosen that he "would turn down the President's offer if [Rosen] reversed [his] position and signed the letter" that he and Klukowski had drafted. [305] The next day, Clark decided to accept and informed Rosen, who then called White House Counsel to seek a meeting directly with President Trump. As Rosen put it, "I wasn't going to accept being fired by my subordinate, so I wanted to talk to the President directly." [306]

On January 3rd, that meeting was convened. Although contemporaneous White House documents suggest that Clark had *already* been appointed as the Acting Attorney General, [307] all the participants in the meeting other than Clark and President Trump aggressively opposed Clark's appointment.

At that point, Rosen decided to "broaden the circle" and ask that his subordinates inform all the other Assistant Attorneys General (AAGs) what was afoot. [308] Rosen wanted to know how the AAGs would respond if Jeff Clark was installed as the Acting Attorney General. Pat Hovakimian, who worked for Rosen, then set up a conference call. The AAGs almost immediately agreed that they would resign if Rosen was removed from office. [309]

Rosen, Donoghue, and Steve Engel, the Assistant Attorney General for the Office of Legal Counsel, attended the meeting. White House lawyers Pat Cipollone, Eric Herschmann and Pat Philbin joined as well.

When the meeting started, Clark attempted to defend his appointment. Clark declared that this was the "last opportunity to sort of set things straight with this defective election," and he had the "intelligence," the "will," and "desire" to "pursue these matters in the way that the President thought most appropriate." [310] Everyone else present disagreed that Clark could conceivably accomplish these things.

White House Counsel Pat Cipollone threatened to resign as well, describing Clark's letter as a "murder–suicide pact." [311] Cipollone warned that the letter would "damage everyone who touches it" and no one should have anything to do with it. [312]

President Trump asked Donoghue and Engel what they would do if Clark took office. Both confirmed they would resign. [313] Steve Engel recalled that the President next asked if he would resign:

> At some point, [] I believe Rich Donoghue said that senior Department officials would all resign if Mr. Clark were put in, and the President turned to me and said, "Steve, you wouldn't resign, would you?" I said, "Well, Mr. President, I've been with you through four Attorneys General, including two Acting Attorneys General, and I just couldn't be part of this if Mr. Clark were here." And I said, "And I believe that the other senior Department officials would resign as well. And Mr. Clark would be here by himself with a hostile building, those folks who remained, and nothing would get done." [314]

Donoghue added that they would not be the only ones to resign. "You should understand that your entire Department leadership will resign," Donoghue recalled saying. This included every Assistant Attorney General. "Mr. President, these aren't bureaucratic leftovers from another administration," Donoghue reminded Trump, "You picked them. This is your leadership team." Donoghue added, "And what happens if, within 48 hours, we have hundreds of resignations from your Justice Department because of your actions? What does that say about your leadership?" [315] Steve Engel then reinforced Donoghue's point, saying that Clark would be leading a "graveyard."

Faced with mass resignations and recognizing that the "breakage" could be too severe, Donald Trump decided to rescind his offer to Clark and drop his plans to use the Justice Department to aid in his efforts to overturn the election outcome. [316] The President looked at Clark and said, "I appreciate your willingness to do it. I appreciate you being willing to suffer the abuse. But the reality is, you're not going to get anything done. These guys are going to quit. Everyone else is going to resign. It's going to be a disaster. The bureaucracy will eat you alive. And no matter how much you want to get things done in the next few weeks, you won't be able to get it done, and it's not going to be worth the breakage." [317]

* * *

Evidence gathered by the Committee also suggests that President Trump offered Sidney Powell the position of Special Counsel for election

related matters during a highly charged White House meeting on December 18, 2020.[318] White House lawyers vehemently opposed Powell's appointment, and it also was not ultimately made formal.

SUMMONING A MOB TO WASHINGTON, AND KNOWING THEY WERE ANGRY AND ARMED, INSTRUCTING THEM TO MARCH TO THE CAPITOL

In the early morning hours of December 19th, shortly after the contentious December 18th White House meeting with Sidney Powell and others, Donald Trump sent a tweet urging his supporters to travel to Washington for January 6th. In that tweet, President Trump attached false allegations that the election was stolen and promised a "wild" time on January 6th.[319] This Twitter invitation was followed by over a dozen other instances in which he used Twitter to encourage supporters to rally for him in Washington, DC on January 6th.[320]

The Committee has assembled detailed material demonstrating the effects of these communications on members of far-right extremist groups, like the Proud Boys, Oath Keepers, Three Percenters, and others, and on individuals looking to respond to their president's call to action. President Trump's supporters believed the election was stolen because they listened to his words,[321] and they knew what he had called them to do; stop the certification of the electoral count.[322]

For example, one supporter, Charles Bradford Smith, noted on December 22, 2020, that "Trump is asking everyone to go" to Washington, DC on

January 6th "to fill the streets" on the "day Pence counts up the votes."[323] Derek Sulenta posted to Facebook on December 23, 2020, that "I'll be there Jan 6th to support the president no matter what happens" because "That's the day he called for patriots to show up."[324] By December 31, 2020, Robert Morss believed January 6th stood for the moment when "1776 Will Commence Again" because President Trump asked them to "Be there, Will be Wild."[325] Kenneth Grayson predicted what would eventually happen on January 6th, when on December 23, 2020, he wrote on Facebook that President Trump called people to Washington, DC through his December 19th tweet and then added "IF TRUMP TELLS US TO STORM THE FUKIN CAPITAL IMA DO THAT THEN!"[326] Some demonstrated their inspiration for January 6th by circulating flyers, which proclaimed "#OccupyCongress" over images of the United States Capitol.[327] Robert Gieswein, a Coloradan affiliated with Three Percenters who was among the first to breach the Capitol, said that he came to Washington, DC "to keep President Trump in."[328]

Chapter 8 of this report documents how the Proud Boys led the attack, penetrated the Capitol, and led hundreds of others inside. Multiple Proud Boys reacted immediately to President Trump's December 19th tweet and began their planning. Immediately, Proud Boys leaders reorganized their hierarchy, with Enrique Tarrio, Joseph Biggs, and Ethan Nordean messaging groups of Proud Boys about what to expect on January 6th.[329] Tarrio created a group chat known as the Ministry of Self-Defense for hand-selected Proud Boys whom he wanted to "organize and direct" plans for January 6th.[330] On social media, Tarrio referenced "revolt" and "[r]evolution," and conspicuously asked "What if we invade it?" on Telegram.[331] As of December 29, 2020, Tarrio told the group the events on January 6th would be "centered around the Capitol."[332]

At the time of publication of this report, prosecutions of certain Proud Boys are ongoing. To date, one Proud Boy has pled guilty to seditious conspiracy and other Proud Boys have pled guilty to other crimes, including conspiracy to obstruct Congress.[333] Jeremy Bertino, a Proud Boy who pled guilty to seditious conspiracy, admitted that he:

> understood from internal discussions among the Proud Boys that in the leadup to January 6, the willingness to resort to unlawful conduct increasingly included a willingness to use and promote violence to achieve political objectives.[334]

Moreover,

> Bertino believed that the 2020 election had been "stolen" and, as January 6, 2021, approached, believed that drastic measures,

including violence, were necessary to prevent Congress from certifying the Electoral College Vote on January 6, 2021. Bertino made his views in this regard known publicly, as well as in private discussions with MOSD leadership. Bertino understood from his discussions with MOSD leadership that they agreed that the election had been stolen, that the purpose of traveling to Washington, D.C., on January 6, 2021, was to stop the certification of the Electoral College Vote, and that the MOSD leaders were willing to do whatever it would take, including using force against police and others, to achieve that objective.[335]

As set out in Bertino's plea agreement, members of MOSD:

> openly discussed plans for potential violence at the Capitol [. . . and] members of MOSD leadership were discussing the possibility of storming the Capitol. Bertino believed that storming the Capitol would achieve the group's goal of stopping Congress from certifying the Electoral College Vote. Bertino understood that storming the Capitol or its grounds would be illegal and would require using force against police or other government officials.[336]

Another Proud Boy who has pled guilty to conspiracy and assault charges, Charles Donohoe, understood that the Proud Boys planned to storm the Capitol. Donohoe, a Proud Boys local chapter leader from North Carolina:

> was aware [as early as January 4, 2021] that members of MOSD leadership were discussing the possibility of storming the Capitol. Donohoe believed that storming the Capitol would achieve the group's goal of stopping the government from carrying out the transfer of presidential power.[337]

The Department of Justice has charged a number of Oath Keepers with seditious conspiracy. Specifically, the government alleges that "[a]fter the Presidential Election, Elmer Stewart Rhodes III conspired with his co-defendants, introduced below, and other co-conspirators, known and unknown to the Grand Jury, to oppose by force the lawful transfer of presidential power."[338] A jury agreed, convicting Stewart Rhodes and Kelly Meggs—the leader of the Florida Oath Keepers chapter—of seditious conspiracy. The jury also convicted Rhodes and Meggs, as well as fellow Oath Keepers Jessica Watkins, Kenneth Harrelson, and Thomas Caldwell,[339] of other serious felonies for their actions on January 6th.[340]

Meggs celebrated the December 19th tweet, sending an encrypted Signal message to Florida Oath Keepers that President Trump "wants us to make it WILD that's what he's saying. He called us all to the Capitol and wants us to make it wild!!! . . . Gentlemen we are heading to DC pack your shit!!"[341] Similarly, Oath Keeper Joshua James—who pleaded guilty to seditious conspiracy—told Oath Keepers that there was now a "NATIONAL CALL TO ACTION FOR DC JAN 6TH" following President Trump's words.[342]

Stewart Rhodes, the Oath Keepers' founder, felt that "the time for peaceful protest is over" after December 19th and, according to the government, "urged President Trump to use military force to stop the lawful transfer of presidential power, describing January 6, 2021, as "a hard constitutional deadline" to do so.[343] Rhodes created a "an invitation-only Signal group chat titled, 'DC OP: Jan 6 21'" on December 30, 2020, which he and other Oath Keepers, like Meggs and James, used to plan for January 6th, including by creating a "quick reaction force" of firearms to be stashed in Virginia.[344]

Multiple members of the Oath Keepers have pleaded guilty to seditious conspiracy. Brian Ulrich started planning for January 6th right after President Trump sent out his December 19th tweet. The Department of Justice summarized Ulrich's communications, as follows:

> Ulrich messaged the "Oath Keepers of Georgia" Signal group chat, "Trump acts now maybe a few hundred radicals die trying to burn down cities . . . Trump sits on his hands Biden wins . . . millions die resisting the death of the 1st and 2nd amendment." On December 20, 2020, an individual in the "Oath Keepers of Georgia" Signal group chat, who later traveled with Ulrich to Washington, D.C., and breached the Capitol grounds with Ulrich on January 6, 2021, messaged, "January 6th. The great reset. America or not."[345]

The Justice Department's Statement of Offense for Oath Keeper Joshua James provided these details:

> In advance of and on January 6, 2021, James and others agreed to take part in the plan developed by Rhodes to use any means necessary, up to and including the use of force, to stop the lawful transfer of presidential power. In the weeks leading up to January 6, 2021, Rhodes instructed James and other coconspirators to be prepared, if called upon, to report to the White House grounds to secure the perimeter and use lethal force if necessary against anyone who tried to remove President Trump from the White House, including the National Guard or other government actors who might be sent to remove President Trump as a result of the Presidential Election.[346]

The former President's call also galvanized Three Percenters to act. A group known as The Three Percenters Original sent a message to its members on December 16, 2020, noting they "stand ready and are standing by to answer the call from our President should the need arise" to combat the "pure evil that is conspiring to steal our country away from the american people" through the "2020 presidential election." [347] After President Trump's tweet, the group put out another letter instructing "any member who can attend . . . to participate" on January 6th because "[t]he President of the United States has put out a general call for the patriots of this Nation to gather" in Washington, DC.[348]

Other Three Percenter groups also responded. Alan Hostetter and Russell Taylor led a group of Three Percenters calling themselves the California Patriots–DC Brigade, who have been charged with conspiracy to obstruct Congress because they organized to fight to keep President Trump in power on January 6th after President Trump's December 19th tweet inspired them to come to Washington, DC.[349] On December 19th, Hostetter posted on Instagram:

> President Trump tweeted that all patriots should descend on Washington DC on Wednesday 1/6/2021. This is the date of the Joint Session of Congress in which they will either accept or reject the fake/phony/stolen electoral college votes.[350]

Between December 19th and January 6th, Hostetter, Taylor, and other members of the California Patriots–DC Brigade exchanged messages and posted to social media about bringing gear, including "weaponry," like "hatchet[s]," "bat[s]," or "[l]arge metal flashlights," and possibly "firearms," and, about being "ready and willing to fight" like it was "1776." Taylor even spoke in front of the Supreme Court on January 5, 2021, explaining that "[p]atriots" would "not return to our peaceful way of life until this election is made right . . . ." [351] On December 29, 2020, Taylor exclaimed "I personally want to be on the front steps and be one of the first ones to breach the doors!" [352]

Similarly, members of the Florida Guardians of Freedom, Three Percent sent around a flyer on December 24, 2020, saying they were "responding to the call from President Donald J. Trump to assist in the security, protection, and support of the people as we all protest the fraudulent election and re-establish liberty for our nation." [353] Their leader, Jeremy Liggett, posted a meme to Facebook stating that "3% Will Show In Record Numbers In DC" [354] and put out a "safety video" instructing people that they could bring "an expandable metal baton, a walking cane and a folding knife" [355] to Washington, DC on January 6th. Several have been arrested for participating in the violence around the tunnel on January 6th.[356]

When interviewed by the FBI on March 31, 2021, Danny Rodriguez—a Three Percenter from California who tased Officer Michael Fanone in the neck as rioters tried to break through a door on the west side of the Capitol—reflected on his decision to go to Washington, DC[357]:

Trump called us to D.C. . . . and he's calling for help—I thought he was calling for help. I thought he was—I thought we were doing the right thing. . . . [W]e thought we were going to hit it like a civil war. There was going to be a big battle. . . . I thought that the main fight, the main battle, was going to be in D.C. because Trump called everyone there.[358]

These groups were not operating in silos. Meggs bragged on Facebook that following President Trump's December 19th tweet he had formed an alliance between the Oath Keepers, the Florida Three Percenters, and the Proud Boys "to work together to shut this shit down."[359] On December 19th, Meggs called Enrique Tarrio and they spoke for more than three minutes.[360] Three days later, Meggs messaged Liggett, echoing his excitement about the December 19th tweet and specifically referencing the seat of Congress: "He called us all to the Capitol and wants us to make it wild!!!"[361] Liggett said "I will have a ton of men with me" and Meggs replied that "we have made Contact [sic] with PB [Proud Boys] and they always have a big group. Force multiplier. . . . I figure we could splinter off the main group of PB and come up behind them. Fucking crush them for good."[362] Aside from Meggs, Stewart Rhodes brought in at least one local militia leader[363] and Three Percenters into the Oath Keepers January 6th planning chats that came about following President Trump's tweet.[364]

Even on January 6th, rioters referenced the tweet. An unknown rioter was caught on video as they ascended the Capitol steps saying "He said it was gonna be wild. He didn't lie."[365] MPD body-worn cameras captured Cale Clayton around 3:15 p.m. as he taunted officers from under the scaffolding: "Your fucking president told us to be here. You should be on this side, right here, going with us. You are an American citizen. Your fucking President told you to do that. You too. You too. You. All of you guys. That Tweet was for you guys. For us. For you."[366]

As January 6th neared, intelligence emerged indicating that January 6th was likely to be violent, and specifically that the Capitol was a target. On January 3rd, an intelligence summary informed Department of Justice officials of plans to "occupy the Capitol" and "invade" the Capitol on January 6th. This summarized a "SITE Intelligence Group" report about the "online rhetoric focused on the 6 Jan event." Some of the reporting includes: "Calls to occupy federal buildings." "intimidating Congress and invading the capitol building." The email also quoted WUSA9 local reporting: "one of the websites used for organizing the event was encouraging attendees to bring guns."

Acting Deputy Attorney General Richard Donoghue testified:

And we knew that if you have tens of thousands of very upset people showing up in Washington, DC, that there was potential for violence.[368]

At the same time, a Defense Department official predicted on a White House National Security Council call that violence could be targeted at the Capitol on January 6th. According to Chairman of the Joint Chiefs of Staff Gen. Mark Milley:

> So during these calls, I—I only remember in hindsight because he was almost like clairvoyant. [Deputy Secretary of Defense David] Norquist says during one of these calls, the greatest threat is a direct assault on the Capitol. I'll never forget it.[369]

Likewise, documentation received by the Committee from the Secret Service demonstrates a growing number of warnings both that January 6th was likely to be violent, and specifically that the Capitol would likely be the target, including intelligence directly regarding the Proud Boys and Oath Keepers militia groups.

Even two weeks ahead of January 6th, the intelligence started to show what could happen. On December 22, 2020, the FBI received a screenshot of an online chat among Oath Keepers, seemingly referring to the State capitols besieged by protesters across the country earlier that year: "if they were going to go in, then they should have went all the way." [370] "There is only one way. It is not signs. It's not rallies. It's fucking bullets," one user replied.[371]

A public source emailed the Secret Service a document titled "Armed and Ready, Mr. President," on December 24th, which summarized online comments responding to President Trump's December 19th tweet.[372] Protestors should "start marching into the chambers," one user wrote.[373] Trump "can't exactly openly tell you to revolt," another replied. "This is the closest he'll ever get." [374] "I read [the President's tweet] as armed," someone said.[375] "[T]here is not enough cops in DC to stop what is coming," replied yet another.[376] "[B]e already in place when Congress tries to get to their meeting," the comments continued, and "make sure they know who to fear.'" [377] "[W]aiting for Trump to say the word," a person said, and "this is what Trump expects," exclaimed another.[378] Capitol Police's head of intelligence, Jack Donohue, got the same compilation from a former colleague at the New York Police Department on December 28, 2020.[379]

On December 26, 2020, the Secret Service received a tip about the Proud Boys detailing plans to have "a large enough group to march into DC armed [that] will outnumber the police so they can't be stopped." [380] "Their plan is to literally kill people," the informant stated. "Please please take this tip seriously . . . " [381] On December 29, 2020, Secret Service forwarded related warnings to Capitol Police that pro-Trump demonstrators were being urged to "occupy federal building[s]," including "march[ing] into the capital building and mak[ing] them quake in their shoes by our mere presence." [382]

Civilians also tipped off Capitol Police about people bringing weapons to besiege the Capitol. One tipster, who had "track[ed] online far right extremism for years," emailed Capitol Police warning "I've seen countless tweets from Trump supporters saying they will be armed," and "I[']ve also seen tweets from people organizing to 'storm the Capitol' on January 6th." [383]

On December 29, 2020, Secret Service forwarded related warnings to Capitol Police that pro-Trump demonstrators were being urged to "occupy federal building," including "march[ing] into the capital building and mak-[ing] them quake in their shoes by our mere presence." [384] Indeed, a Secret Service intelligence briefing on December 30th entitled "March for Trump," highlighted the President's "Will be wild!" tweet alongside hashtags #WeAreTheStorm, #1776Rebel, and #OccupyCapitols, writing "President Trump supporters have proposed a movement to occupy Capitol Hill." [385]

On January 1, 2021, a lieutenant in the intelligence branch at DC Police forwarded a civilian tip about "a website planning terroristic behavior on Jan 6th, during the rally" to Capitol Police intelligence. [386] "There are detailed plans to storm federal buildings," including "the capitol in DC on Jan 6th," the tipster reported, linking to thedonald.win. [387]

On January 2, 2021, the FBI discovered a social media posting that read, "This is not a rally and it's no longer a protest. This is a final stand . . . many are ready to die to take back #USA . . . . And don't be surprised if we take the #capital building." [388]

On January 3, 2021, a Parler user's post—under the name 1776(2.0) Minuteman— noting "after weds we are going to need a new congress" and "Jan 6 may actually be their [Members of Congress] last day in office" reached the FBI and Capitol Police. [389]

The FBI field office in Norfolk, Virginia issued an alert to law enforcement agencies on January 5th tiled "Potential for Violence in Washington, D.C. Area in Connection with Planned 'StopTheSteal' Protest on 6 January 2021," which noted:

> An online thread discussed specific calls for violence to include stating, "Be ready to fight. Congress needs to hear glass breaking, doors being kicked in, and blood . . . being spilled. Get violent . . . stop calling this a march, or rally, or a protest. Go there ready for war. We get our President or we die. NOTHING else will achieve this goal." [390]

In addition, the alert copied "perimeter maps [of the Capitol] and caravan pictures [that] were posted" on thedonald.win, particularly worrying that the "caravans . . . had the same colors as the sections of the perimeter" of the Capitol.[391] Secret Service also knew about caravans planning to come to DC to "Occupy the Capitol." [392]

That same day, representatives from DHS, FBI, DC's Homeland Security and Emergency Management Agency, Secret Service, DC Police, and Capitol Police shared a website, Red State Secession, which had a post titled "Why the Second American Revolution Starts Jan 6." A user asked visitors to post where they could find the home addresses of Democratic congressmen and "political enemies" and asked if "any of our enemies [will] be working in offices in DC that afternoon." [393] "What are their routes to and from the event?" the post continued.[394] "[T]he crowd will be looking for enemies." [395]

A Secret Service open-source unit flagged an account on thedonald.win that threatened to bring a sniper rifle to a rally on January 6th. The user also posted a picture of a handgun and rifle with the caption, "Sunday Gun Day Providing Overwatch January 6th Will be Wild." [396]

The Secret Service learned from the FBI on January 5th about right-wing groups establishing armed quick reaction forces in Virginia, where they could amass firearms illegal in DC[397] Trump supporters staged there waiting across the river "to respond to 'calls for help.'" [398] The Oath Keepers were such a group.[399]

President Trump's closest aides knew about the political power of sites like thedonald.win, which is where much of this violent rhetoric and planning happened. On December 30, 2020, Jason Miller—a Senior Adviser to and former spokesman for the former President—texted Chief of Staff Mark Meadows a link to the thedonald.win, adding "I got the base FIRED UP." [400] The link connected to a page with comments like "Gallows don't require electricity," "if the filthy commie maggots try to push their fraud through, there will be hell to pay," and Congress can certify Trump the winner or leave "in a bodybag." [401] Symbolic gallows were constructed on January 6th at the foot of the Capitol.[402]

After President Trump's signal, his supporters did not hide their plans for violence at the Capitol, and those threats made their way to national and local law enforcement agencies. As described in this report, the intelligence agencies did detect this planning, and they shared it with the White House and with the U.S. Secret Service.

Noose set up outside of the Capitol on January 6th.

Testimony from White House staff also suggests real concerns about the risk of violence as January 6th approached. Cassidy Hutchinson, for example, testified about a conversation she had with her boss, Mark Meadows, on January 2nd:

> I went into Mark's office, and he was still on his phone . . . . I said to Mark, "Rudy [Giuliani] said these things to me. What's going on here? Anything I should know about?"
>
> This was—he was, like, looking at his phone. He was like, "Oh, it's all about the rally on Wednesday. Isn't that what he was talking to you about?"
>
> I said, "Yeah. Yeah, sounds like we're going to the Capitol."
>
> He said, "Yeah. Are you talking with Tony?"
>
> "I'm having a conversation, sir."
>
> He said—still looking at his phone. I remember he was scrolling. He was like, "Yeah. You know, things might get real, real bad on the 6th."
>
> And I remember saying to him, "What do you mean?"

Mark Meadows walks along the South Lawn on October 30, 2020.
(Photo by Sarah Silbiger/Getty Images)

He was like, "I don't know. There's just going to be a lot of people here, and there's a lot of different ideas right now. I'm not really sure of everything that's going on. Let's just make sure we keep tabs on it." [403]

Hutchinson also testified about a conversation she had with Director of National Intelligence, Ratcliffe:

He had expressed to me that he was concerned that it could spiral out of control and potentially be dangerous, either for our democracy or the way that things were going for the 6th. [404]

Hope Hicks texted Trump Campaign spokesperson Hogan Gidley in the midst of the January 6th violence, explaining that she had "suggested . . . several times" on the preceding days (January 4th and January 5th) that President Trump publicly state that January 6th must remain peaceful and that he had refused her advice to do so. [405] Her recollection was that Herschmann earlier advised President Trump to make a preemptive public statement in advance of January 6th calling for no violence that day. [406] No such statement was made.

The District of Columbia Homeland Security office explicitly warned that groups were planning to "occupy the [Capitol] to halt the vote." [407]

> [W]e got derogatory information from OSINT suggesting that some
> very, very violent individuals were organizing to come to DC, and
> not only were they organized to come to DC, but they were—these
> groups, these nonaligned groups were aligning. And so all the red
> flags went up at that point, you know, when you have armed militia,
> you know, collaborating with White supremacy groups, collaborat-
> ing with conspiracy theory groups online all toward a common goal,
> you start seeing what we call in, you know, terrorism, a blended
> ideology, and that's a very, very bad sign. . . . [T]hen when they
> were clearly across—not just across one platform but across mul-
> tiple platforms of these groups coordinating, not just like chatting,
> "Hey, how's it going, what's the weather like where you're at," but
> like, "what are you bringing, what are you wearing, you know,
> where do we meet up, do you have plans for the Capitol." That's
> operational—that's like preoperational intelligence, right, and that
> is something that's clearly alarming.[408]

Again, this type of intelligence was shared, including obvious warnings
about potential violence prior to January 6th.[409] What was not shared, and
was not fully understood by intelligence and law enforcement entities, is
what role President Trump would play on January 6th in exacerbating the
violence, and later refusing for multiple hours to instruct his supporters to
stand down and leave the Capitol. No intelligence collection was apparently
performed on President Trump's plans for January 6th, nor was there any
analysis performed on what he might do to exacerbate potential violence.
Certain Republican members of Congress who were working with Trump
and the Giuliani team may have had insight on this particular risk, but none
appear to have alerted the Capitol Police or any other law enforcement
authority.

On January 2, 2021, Katrina Pierson wrote in an email to fellow rally
organizers, "POTUS expectations are to have something intimate at the
[E]llipse, and call on everyone to march to the Capitol."[410] And, on January
4, 2021, another rally organizer texted Mike Lindell, the MyPillow CEO, that
President Trump would "unexpectedly" call on his supporters to march to
the Capitol:

> This stays only between us . . . . It can also not get out about the
> march because I will be in trouble with the national park service and
> all the agencies but POTUS is going to just call for it "unexpect-
> edly." [411]

Testimony obtained by the Committee also indicates that President
Trump was specifically aware that the crowd he had called to Washington
was fired up and angry on the evening of January 5th. Judd Deere, a deputy

White House press secretary recalled a conversation with President Trump in the Oval Office on the evening of January 5th:

> Judd Deere: I said he should focus on policy accomplishments. I didn't mention the 2020 election.
>
> Committee Staff: Okay. What was his response?
>
> Deere: He acknowledged that and said, "We've had a lot," something along those lines, but didn't—he fairly quickly moved to how fired up the crowd is, or was going to be.
>
> Committee Staff: Okay. What did he say about it?
>
> Deere: Just that they were—they were fired up. They were angry. They feel like the election's been stolen, that the election was rigged, that—he went on and on about that for a little bit.[412]

Testimony indicated that President Trump was briefed on the risk of violence on the morning of the 6th before he left the White House. Cassidy Hutchinson provided this testimony:

> Vice Chair Cheney: So, Ms. Hutchinson, is it your understanding that Mr. Ornato told the President about weapons at the rally on the morning of January 6th?
>
> Hutchinson: That is what Mr. Ornato relayed to me.[413]

The head of President Trump's security detail, Bobby Engel, told the Select Committee that when he shared critical information with White House Deputy Chief of Staff Anthony Ornato, it was a means of conveying that information with the Oval Office: "So, when it came to passing information to Mr. Ornato, I—my assumption was that it would get to the chief [of staff, Mark Meadows], or that he was sharing the information with the chief. I don't—and the filtering process, or if the chief thinks it needs to get to the President, then he would share it with the President."[414] Also, Engel confirmed that if "information would come to my attention, whether it was a protective intelligence issue or a concern or—primarily, I would—I would make sure that the information got filtered up through the appropriate chain usually through Mr. Ornato. So if I received a report on something that was happening in the DC area, I'd either forward that information to Mr. Ornato, or call him about that information or communicate in some way."[415]

The Select Committee also queried Deputy Chief of Staff Ornato this November about what he generally would have done in this sort of situation, asking him the following: "Generally you receive information about things like the groups that are coming, the stuff that we talked earlier. You would bring that to Mr. Meadows and likely did here, although you don't have a specific recollection?"[416] Ornato responded: "That is correct, sir."[417] Ornato also explained to the Committee that "... in my normal daily functions, in my general functions as my job, I would've had a conversation with him about all the groups coming in and what was expected from the secret service."[418] As for the morning of January 6th itself, he had the following answer:

> Committee Staff: Do you remember talking to Chief of Staff Mark Meadows about any of your concerns about the threat landscape going into January 6th?

> Ornato: I don't recall; however, in my position I would've made sure he was tracking the demos, which he received a daily brief, Presidential briefing. So he most likely was getting all this in his daily brief as well. I wouldn't know what was in his intelligence brief that day, but I would've made sure that he was tracking these things and just mentioned, "Hey, are you tracking the demos?" If he gave me a "yeah", I don't recall it today, but I'm sure that was something that took place.[419]

Ornato had access to intelligence that suggested violence at the Capitol on January 6th, and it was his job to inform Meadows and President Trump of that. Although Ornato told us that he did not recall doing so, the Select Committee found multiple parts of Ornato's testimony questionable. The Select Committee finds it difficult to believe that neither Meadows nor Ornato told President Trump, as was their job, about the intelligence that was emerging as the January 6th rally approached.

Hours before the Ellipse rally on January 6th, the fact that the assembled crowd was prepared for potential violence was widely known. In addition to intelligence reports indicating potential violence at the Capitol, weapons and other prohibited items were being seized by police on the streets and by Secret Service at the magnetometers for the Ellipse speech. Secret Service confiscated a haul of weapons from the 28,000 spectators who did pass through the magnetometers: 242 cannisters of pepper spray, 269 knives or blades, 18 brass knuckles, 18 tasers, 6 pieces of body armor, 3 gas masks, 30 batons or blunt instruments, and 17 miscellaneous items like scissors, needles, or screwdrivers.[420] And thousands of others purposely remained outside the magnetometers, or left their packs outside.[421]

Others brought firearms. Three men in fatigues from Broward County, Florida brandished AR-15s in front of Metropolitan police officers on 14th Street and Independence Avenue on the morning of January 6th.[422] MPD advised over the radio that one individual was possibly armed with a "Glock" at 14th and Constitution Avenue, and another was possibly armed

President Trump looks backstage at the crowd gathered at the Ellipse.
(Photo provided to the Select Committee by the National Archives and Records Administration)

with a "rifle" at 15th and Constitution Avenue around 11:23 a.m.[423] The National Park Service detained an individual with a rifle between 12 and 1 p.m.[424] Almost all of this was known before Donald Trump took the stage at the Ellipse.

By the time President Trump was preparing to give his speech, he and his advisors knew enough to cancel the rally. And he certainly knew enough to cancel any plans for a march to the Capitol. According to testimony obtained by the Select Committee, President Trump knew that elements of the crowd were armed, and had prohibited items, and that many thousands would not pass through the magnetometers for that reason. Testimony indicates that the President had received an earlier security briefing, and testimony indicates that the Secret Service mentioned the prohibited items again as they drove President Trump to the Ellipse.

Cassidy Hutchinson was with the President backstage. Her contemporaneous text messages indicate that President Trump was "effing furious" about the fact that a large number of his supporters would not go through the magnetometers:

Cassidy Hutchinson: But the crowd looks good from this vanish [sic] point. As long as we get the shot. He was fucking furious

Tony Ornato: He doesn't get it that the people on the monument side don't want to come in. They can see from there and don't want to come in. They can see from there and don't have to go through mags. With 30k magged inside.

Cassidy Hutchinson: That's what was relayed several times and in different iterations

Cassidy Hutchinson: Poor max got chewed out

Cassidy Hutchinson: He also kept mentioning [an off the record trip] to Capitol before he took the stage

Tony Ornato: Bobby will tell him no. It's not safe to do. No assets available to safely do it.[425]

And Hutchinson described what President Trump said as he prepared to take the stage:

When we were in the off-stage announce area tent behind the stage, he was very concerned about the shot. Meaning the photograph that we would get because the rally space wasn't full. One of the reasons, which I've previously stated, was because he wanted it to be full and for people to not feel excluded because they had come far to watch him at the rally. And he felt the mags were at fault for not letting everybody in, but another leading reason and likely the primary reasons is because he wanted it full and he was angry that we weren't letting people through the mags with weapons—what the Secret Service deemed as weapons, and are, are weapons. But when we were in the off-stage announce tent, I was a part of a conversation, I was in the vicinity of a conversation where I overheard the President say something to the effect of, "I don't F'ing care that they have weapons. They're not here to hurt me. Take the F'ing mags away. Let my people in. They can march to the Capitol from here. Let the people in. Take the F'ing mags away."[426]

The Secret Service special agent who drove the President after his speech told the Select Committee that Trump made a similar remark in the vehicle when his demand to go to the Capitol was refused—essentially that Trump did not believe his supporters posed a security risk to him personally.[427]

Minutes after the exchange that Hutchinson described—when President Trump took the stage—he pointedly expressed his concern about the thousands of attendees who would not enter the rally area and instructed Secret Service to allow that part of the crowd to enter anyway:

. . . I'd love to have if those tens of thousands of people would be allowed. The military, the secret service. And we want to thank you and the police law enforcement. Great. You're doing a great job. But I'd love it if they could be allowed to come up here with us. Is that possible? Can you just let [them] come up, please?[428]

Although President Trump and his advisors knew of the risk of violence, and knew specifically that elements of the crowd were angry and some were armed, from intelligence and law enforcement reports that morning, President Trump nevertheless went forward with the rally, and then specifically instructed the crowd to march to the Capitol: "Because you'll never take back our country with weakness. You have to show strength and you have to be strong. We have come to demand that Congress do the right thing and only count the electors who have been lawfully slated, lawfully slated." [429] Much of President Trump's speech was improvised. Even before his improvisation, during the review of President Trump's prepared remarks, White House lawyer Eric Herschmann specifically requested that "if there were any factual allegations, someone needed to independently validate or verify the statements." [430] And in the days just before January 6th, Herschmann "chewed out" John Eastman and told him he was "out of [his] F'ing mind" to argue that the Vice President could be the sole decision-maker as to who becomes the next President.[431] Herschmann told us, "I so berated him that I believed that theory would not go forward." [432] But President Trump made that very argument during his speech at the Ellipse and made many false statements. Herschmann attended that speech, but walked out during the middle of it.[433]

President Trump's speech to the crowd that day lasted more than an hour. The speech walked through dozens of known falsehoods about purported election fraud. And Trump again made false and malicious claims about Dominion voting systems.[434] As discussed earlier, he again pressured Mike Pence to refuse to count lawful electoral votes, going off script repeatedly, leading the crowd to believe falsely that Pence could and would alter the election outcome:

And I actually, I just spoke to Mike. I said: "Mike, that doesn't take courage. What takes courage is to do nothing. That takes courage." And then we're stuck with a president who lost the election by a lot and we have to live with that for four more years. We're just not going to let that happen . . . .

When you catch somebody in a fraud, you're allowed to go by very different rules.

So I hope Mike has the courage to do what he has to do. And I hope he doesn't listen to the RINOs and the stupid people that he's listening to." [435]

This characterization of Vice President Pence's decision had a direct impact on those who marched to and approached the Capitol, as illustrated by this testimony from a person convicted of crimes committed on January 6th:

So this woman came up to the side of us, and she, says, Pence folded. So it was kind of, like, okay. Well, in my mind I was thinking, "Well, that's it, you know." Well, my son-in-law looks at me, and he says, "I want to go in."[436]

Trump used the word "peacefully," written by speech writers, one time. But he delivered many other scripted and unscripted comments that conveyed a very different message:

Because you'll never take back our country with weakness. You have to show strength and you have to be strong. We have come to demand that Congress do the right thing and only count the electors who have been lawfully slated, lawfully slated. . . .

And we fight. We fight like hell. And if you don't fight like hell, you're not going to have a country anymore . . . .[437]

Trump also was not the only rally speaker to do these things. Giuliani, for instance, also said, "Let's have trial by combat." [438] Likewise, Eastman used his two minutes on the Ellipse stage to make a claim already known to be false—that corrupted voted machines stole the election.[439]

The best indication of the impact of President Trump's words, both during the Ellipse speech and beforehand, are the comments from those supporters who attended the Ellipse rally and their conduct immediately thereafter. Videoclips show several of the attendees on their way to the Capitol or shortly after they arrived:

I'm telling you what, I'm hearing that Pence—hearing the Pence just caved. No. Is that true? I didn't hear it. I'm hear—I'm hearing reports that Pence caved. No way. I'm telling you, if Pence caved, we're going to drag motherfuckers through the streets. You fucking politicians are going to get fucking drug through the streets.[440]

Yes. I guess the hope is that there's such a show of force here that Pence will decide do the right thing, according to Trump.[441]

Pence voted against Trump. [Interviewer: Ok. And that's when all this started?] Yup. That's when we marched on the Capitol.[442]

We just heard that Mike Pence is not going to reject any fraudulent electoral votes. [Other speaker: Boo. You're a traitor! Boo!] That's right. You've heard it here first. Mike Pence has betrayed the United States of America. [Other speaker: Boo! Fuck you, Mike Pence!] Mike Pence has betrayed this President and he has betrayed the people of the United States and we will never, ever forget. [Cheers][443]

[Q] What percentage of the crowd is going to the Capitol? [A] [Oath Keeper Jessica Watkins]: One hundred percent. It has, it has spread like wildfire that Pence has betrayed us, and everybody's marching on the Capitol. All million of us. It's insane.[444]

Another criminal defendant—charged with assaulting an officer with a flagpole and other crimes—explained in an interview why he went to the Capitol and fought:

Dale Huttle: We were not there illegally, we were invited there by the President himself. . . . Trump's backers had been told that the election had been stolen. . . .

Reporter Megan Hickey: But do you think he encouraged violence?

Dale Huttle: Well, I sat there, or stood there, with half a million people listening to his speech. And in that speech, both Giuliani and [Trump] said we were going to have to fight like hell to save our country. Now, whether it was a figure of speech or not—it wasn't taken that way.

Reporter Megan Hickey: You didn't take it as a figure of speech?

Dale Huttle: No.[445]

President Trump concluded his speech at 1:10 p.m.

Among other statements from the Ellipse podium, President Trump informed the crowd that he would be marching to the Capitol with them:

Now, it is up to Congress to confront this egregious assault on our democracy. And after this, we're going to walk down, **and I'll be there with you**, we're going to walk down, we're going to walk down. Anyone you want, but I think right here, **we're going to walk down to the Capitol**, and we're going to cheer on our brave senators and congressmen and women, and we're probably not going to be cheering so much for some of them.[446]

Hutchinson testified that she first became aware of President Trump's plans to attend Congress's session to count votes on or about January 2nd. She learned this from a conversation with Giuliani: "It's going to be great.

The President's going to be there. He's going to look powerful. He's—he's going to be with the members. He's going to be with the Senators." [447] Evidence also indicates that multiple members of the White House staff, including White House lawyers, were concerned about the President's apparent intentions to go to the Capitol. [448]

After he exited the stage, President Trump entered the Presidential SUV and forcefully expressed his intention that Bobby Engel, the head of his Secret Service detail, direct the motorcade to the Capitol. The Committee has now obtained evidence from several sources about a "furious interaction" in the SUV. The vast majority of witnesses who have testified before the Select Committee about this topic, including multiple members of the Secret Service, a member of the Metropolitan police, and national security and military officials in the White House, described President Trump's behavior as "irate," "furious," "insistent," "profane" and "heated." Hutchinson heard about the exchange second-hand and related what she heard in our June 28, 2022, hearing from Ornato (as did another witness, a White House employee with national security responsibilities, who shared that Ornato also recounted to him President Trump's "irate" behavior in the Presidential vehicle). Other members of the White House staff and Secret Service also heard about the exchange after the fact. The White House employee with national security responsibilities gave this testimony:

> Committee Staff: But it sounds like you recall some rumor or some discussion around the West Wing about the President's anger about being told that he couldn't go to the Capitol. Is that right?
>
> Employee: So Mr. Ornato said that he was angry that he couldn't go right away. In the days following that, I do remember, you know, again, hearing again how angry the President was when, you know, they were in the limo. But beyond specifics of that, that's pretty much the extent of the cooler talk. [449]

The Committee has regarded both Hutchinson and the corroborating testimony by the White House employee with national security responsibilities as earnest and has no reason to conclude that either had a reason to invent their accounts. A Secret Service agent who worked on one of the details in the White House and was present in the Ellipse motorcade had this comment:

> Committee Staff: Ms. Hutchinson has suggested to the committee that you sympathized with her after her testimony, and believed her account. Is that accurate?
>
> Special Agent: I have no—yeah, that's accurate. I have no reason—I mean, we—we became friends. We worked—I worked every day

with her for 6 months. Yeah, she became a friend of mine. We had a good working relationship. I have no reason—she's never done me wrong. She's never lied that I know of.[450]

The Committee's principal concern was that the President actually intended to participate personally in the January 6th efforts at the Capitol, leading the attempt to overturn the election either from inside the House Chamber, from a stage outside the Capitol, or otherwise. The Committee regarded those facts as important because they are relevant to President Trump's intent on January 6th. There is no question from all the evidence assembled that President Trump *did have that intent.*[451]

As it became clear that Donald Trump desired to travel to the Capitol on January 6th, a White House Security Official in the White House complex became very concerned about his intentions:

> To be completely honest, we were all in a state of shock. . . . it just—one, I think the actual physical feasibility of doing it, and then also we all knew what that implicated and what that meant, that this was no longer a rally, that this was going to move to something else if he physically walked to the Capitol. I—I don't know if you want to use the word "insurrection," "coup," whatever. We all knew that this would move from a normal, democratic, you know, public event into something else.[452]

President Trump continued to push to travel to the Capitol even after his return to the White House, despite knowing that a riot was underway. Kayleigh McEnany, the White House press secretary, spoke with President Trump about his desire to go to the Capitol after he returned to the White House from the Ellipse. "So to the best of my recollection, I recall him being—wanting to—saying that he wanted to physically walk and be a part of the march and then saying that he would ride the Beast if he needed to, ride in the Presidential limo."[453]

Later in the afternoon, Mark Meadows relayed to Cassidy Hutchinson that President Trump was still upset that he would not be able to go to the Capitol that day. As he told Hutchinson, "the President wasn't happy that Bobby [Engel] didn't pull it off for him and that Mark didn't work hard enough to get the movement on the books."[454]

187 MINUTES: TRUMP'S DERELICTION OF DUTY

Just after 1:00 p.m., Vice President Pence, serving as President of the Senate under Article I of the Constitution, gaveled the Congress into its Joint Session. President Trump was giving a speech at the Ellipse, which he concluded at 1:10 pm. For the next few hours, an attack on our Capitol occurred, perpetrated by Trump supporters many of whom were present at the Ellipse for President Trump's speech. More than 140 Capitol and Metropolitan police were injured, some very seriously.[455] A perimeter security line of Metropolitan Police intended to secure the Capitol against intrusion broke in the face of thousands of armed rioters—more than 2,000 of whom gained access to the interior of the Capitol building.[456] A woman who attempted to forcibly enter the Chamber of the House of Representatives through a broken window while the House was in session was shot and killed by police guarding the chamber. Vice President Pence and his family were at risk, as were those Secret Service professionals protecting him. Congressional proceedings were halted, and legislators were rushed to secure locations.

From the outset of the violence and for several hours that followed, people at the Capitol, people inside President Trump's Administration, elected officials of both parties, members of President Trump's family, and Fox News commentators sympathetic to President Trump all tried to contact him to urge him to do one singular thing—one thing that all of these people immediately understood was required: Instruct his supporters to stand down and disperse—to leave the Capitol.

As the evidence overwhelmingly demonstrates, President Trump specifically and repeatedly refused to do so—for multiple hours—while the mayhem ensued. Chapter 8 of this report explains in meticulous detail the horrific nature of the violence taking place, that was directed at law enforcement officers at the Capitol and that put the lives of American lawmakers at risk. Yet in spite of this, President Trump watched the violence on television from a dining room adjacent to the Oval Office, calling Senators to urge them to help him delay the electoral count, but refusing to supply the specific help that everyone knew was unequivocally required. As this report shows, when Trump finally did make such a statement at 4:17 p.m.— after hours of violence—the statement immediately had the expected effect; the rioters began to disperse immediately and leave the Capitol.[457]

To fully understand the President's behavior during those hours—now commonly known as the "187 minutes"—it is important to understand the context in which it occurred. As outlined in this report, by the afternoon of January 6th, virtually all of President Trump's efforts to overturn the outcome of the 2020 election had failed. Virtually all the lawsuits had already been lost. Vice President Mike Pence had refused Trump's pressure to stop the count of certain electoral votes. State officials and legislators had refused to reverse the election outcomes in every State where Trump and his team applied pressure. The Justice Department's investigations of alleged election fraud had all contradicted Trump's allegations.

The only factor working in Trump's favor that might succeed in materially delaying the counting of electoral votes for President-elect Biden was the violent crowd at the Capitol. And for much of the afternoon of January 6th, it appeared that the crowd had accomplished that purpose. Congressional leaders were advised by Capitol Police at one or more points during the attack that it would likely take several days before the Capitol could safely be reopened.[458]

By the time the President's speech concluded, the lawlessness at the United States Capitol had already begun, but the situation was about to get much worse.

By 1:25 p.m., President Trump was informed that the Capitol was under attack.

Minutes after arriving back at the White House, the President ran into a member of the White House staff and asked if they had watched his speech on television. "Sir, they cut it off because they're rioting down at the Capitol," the employee said. The President asked what they meant by that. "[T]hey're rioting down there at the Capitol," the employee repeated. "Oh really?" the President asked. "All right, let's go see."[459] A photograph taken by the White House photographer—the last one permitted until later in the day—captures the moment the President was made aware of the violent uprising at the Capitol.[460]

Not long thereafter, as thousands of Trump supporters from the Ellipse speech continued to arrive at the Capitol, the DC Metropolitan Police Department declared a riot at the Capitol at 1:49 p.m., the same time Capitol Police Chief Steven Sund informed the DC National Guard "that there was a dire emergency on Capitol Hill and requested the immediate assistance" of as many national guard troops as possible.[461]

No photographs exist of the President for the remainder of the afternoon until after 4 p.m. President Trump appears to have instructed that the White House photographer was not to take any photographs.[462] The Select Committee also was unable to locate any official records of President Trump's telephone calls that afternoon.[463] And the President's official Daily Diary contains no information for this afternoon between the hours of 1:19 p.m. and 4:03 p.m., at the height of the worst attack on the seat of the United States Congress in over two centuries.[464]

The Select Committee did, however, obtain records from non-official sources that contained data of some phone calls President Trump made that afternoon. Even though "he was placing lots of calls" that afternoon, according to his personal assistant,[465] the Select Committee was given no records of any calls from the President to security or law enforcement officials that afternoon, and that absence of data is consistent with testimony of witnesses who would have knowledge of any such calls, who said that he did not do so.[466] Based on testimony from President Trump's close aides, we know that President Trump remained in the Dining Room adjacent to the Oval Office for the rest of the afternoon until after 4:03 p.m.[467]

In fact, from cellular telephone records, it appears that at 1:39 p.m. and 2:03 p.m., after being informed of the riot at the Capitol, President Trump called his lawyer, Rudolph Giuliani. These calls lasted approximately four minutes and eight minutes, respectively.[468] And Press Secretary Kayleigh McEnany testified that President Trump also called a number of Senators.[469] The number or names of all such Members of Congress is unknown, although Senator Mike Lee (R–UT) received one such outgoing call from the President within the hour that followed.[470]

At 1:49 p.m., just as the DC Metropolitan Police officially declared a riot and the Capitol Police were calling for help from the National Guard to address the crisis, President Trump sent a tweet with a link to a recording of his speech at the Ellipse.[471]

At about that point, White House Counsel Pat Cipollone became aware of the Capitol riot. The Committee collected sworn testimony from several White House officials, each with similar accounts. The President's White House Counsel Pat Cipollone testified that he raced downstairs, and went to the Oval Office Dining Room as soon as he learned about the violence at the Capitol—likely just around or just after 2 p.m. Cipollone knew immediately that the President had to deliver a message to the rioters—asking them to leave the Capitol.

Here is how he described this series of events:

> . . . the first time I remember going downstairs was when people had breached the Capitol... But I went down with [Deputy White House Counsel] Pat [Philbin], and I remember we were both very upset about what was happening. And we both wanted, you know, action to be taken related to that . . . But we went down to the Oval Office, we went through the Oval office, and we went to the back where the President was. . . . I think he was already in the dining room . . . I can't talk about conversations [with the President]. I think I was pretty clear there needed to be an immediate and forceful response, statement, public statement, that people need to leave the Capitol now.[472]

Cipollone also left little doubt that virtually everyone among senior White House staff had the same view:

> There were a lot of people in the White House that day . . . Senior people who, you know, felt the same way that I did and who were working very hard to achieve that result. There were—I think

Ivanka was one of them. And Eric Herschmann was there, Pat Philbin was there, and a number of other people . . . . many people suggested it. . . . Many people felt the same way. I'm sure I had conversations with Mark [Meadows] about this during the course of the day and expressed my opinion very forcefully that this needs to be done.[473]

Likewise, senior staff cooperated to produce a message for the President on a notecard, which read:

ANYONE WHO ENTERED THE CAPITOL ILLEGALLY WITHOUT PROPER AUTHORITY SHOULD LEAVE IMMEDIATELY.[474]

The President declined to make the statement. Cipollone also made it clear that the advice they were giving to the President never changed throughout this three-hour period. Trump refused to do what was necessary.

Committee Staff: [I]t sounds like you from the very onset of violence at the Capitol right around 2 o'clock were pushing for a strong statement that people should leave the Capitol. Is that right?

Cipollone: I was, and others were as well.[475]

Cassidy Hutchinson, who worked closely with Mark Meadows and sat directly outside his office, confirmed this account and described several additional details:

I see Pat Cipollone barreling down the hallway towards our office. And he rushed right in, looked at me, said, "Is Mark in his office?" And I said, "Yes." And on a normal day he would've said, "Can I pop in," or, "Is he talking to anyone," or, "Is it an appropriate time for me to go chat with him," and myself or Eliza would go let him in or tell him no. But after I had said yes, he just looked at me and started shaking his head and went over, opened Mark's office door, stood there with the door propped open, and said something to the—Mark was still sitting on his phone. I remember, like, glancing in. He was still sitting on his phone.

And I remember Pat saying to him something to the effect of, "The rioters have gotten to the Capitol, Mark. We need to go down and see the President now." And Mark looked up at him and said, "He doesn't want to do anything, Pat." And Pat said something to the effect of—and very clearly said this to Mark—something to the effect of, "Mark, something needs to be done, or people are going to die and the blood's gonna be on your F'ing hands. This is getting out of control. I'm going down there.[476]

The Select Committee believes that the entire White House senior staff was in favor of a Presidential statement specifically instructing the violent rioters to leave. But President Trump refused. White House Counsel Pat Cipollone answered certain questions from the Select Committee on this subject as follows:

> Vice Chair Cheney: And when you talk about others on the staff thinking more should be done, or thinking that the President needed to tell people to go home, who would you put in that category?
>
> Cipollone: Well, I would put . . . Pat Philbin, Eric Herschmann. Overall, Mark Meadows, Ivanka. Once Jared got there, Jared. General Kellogg. I'm probably missing some, but those are—Kayleigh I think was there. But I don't—Dan Scavino.
>
> Vice Chair Cheney: And who on the staff did not want people to leave the Capitol?"
>
> Cipollone: On the staff?
>
> Vice Chair Cheney: In the White House?
>
> Cipollone: I can't think of anybody on that day who didn't want people to get out of the Capitol once the—particularly once the violence started. No. I mean—
>
> Mr. Schiff: What about the President?
>
> Vice Chair Cheney: Yeah.
>
> . . .
>
> [Consultation between Mr. Cipollone and his counsel.]
>
> Cipollone: Yeah. I can't reveal communications. But obviously I think, you know—yeah.[477]

The testimony of a White House employee with national security responsibilities also corroborated these facts. This employee testified about a conversation between Pat Cipollone and Eric Herschmann in which Herschmann indicated that the President did not want to do anything to halt the violence. That employee told the Select Committee that he overheard Herschmann saying something to the effect of "the President didn't want anything done."[478]

Deputy Press Secretary Judd Deere also testified to the Select Committee that as soon as it was clear that the Capitol's outer perimeter had been breached, he urged that the President make a statement telling the rioters to go home:

Committee Staff: And so what did you do at that point?

Judd Deere: If I recall, I went back up to [Press Secretary] Kayleigh [McEnany]'s office and indicated that we now likely needed to say something.

Committee Staff: Okay. And why did you think it was necessary to say something?

Deere: Well, I mean, it appears that individuals are storming the U.S. Capitol building. They also appear to be supporters of Donald Trump, who may have been in attendance at the rally. We're going to need to say something.

Committee Staff: And did you have a view as to what should be said by the White House?

Deere: If I recall, I told Kayleigh that I thought that we needed to encourage individuals to stop, to respect law enforcement, and to go home. . . . And it was—it was incumbent upon us to encourage those individuals, should they be supporters of ours, to stop.[479]

Testimony from both Deputy Press Secretary Matthews and White House Counsel Cipollone indicated that it would have been easy, and nearly instantaneous, for Trump to make a public statement insisting that the crowd disperse. As Matthews explained, he could have done so in under a minute:

. . . it would take probably less than 60 seconds from the Oval Office dining room over to the Press Briefing Room. And, for folks that might not know, the Briefing Room is the room that you see the White House Press Secretary do briefings from with the podium and the blue backdrop. And there is a camera that is on in there at all times. And so, if the President had wanted to make a statement and address the American people, he could have been on camera almost instantly.[480]

Cipollone also shared that assessment:

Committee Staff: Would it have been possible at any moment for the President to walk down to the podium in the briefing room and talk to the nation at any time between when you first gave him that advice at 2 o'clock and 4:17 when the video statement went out? Would that have been possible?

Cipollone: Would it have been possible?"

Committee Staff: Yes.

Cipollone: Yes, it would have been possible.[481]

At 2:13 p.m., rioters broke into the Capitol and flooded the building.[482]

As the violence began to escalate, many Trump supporters and others outside the White House began urgently seeking his intervention. Mark Meadows's phone was flooded with text messages. These are just some of them:

2:32 p.m. from Fox News anchor Laura Ingraham: "Hey Mark, The president needs to tell people in the Capitol to go home."[483]

2:35 p.m. from Mick Mulvaney: "Mark: he needs to stop this, now. Can I do anything to help?"[484]

2:46 p.m. from Rep. William Timmons (R–SC): "The president needs to stop this ASAP"[485]

2:53 p.m. from Donald Trump, Jr.: "He's got to condem [sic] this shit. Asap. The captiol [sic] police tweet is not enough."[486]

3:04 p.m. from Rep. Jeff Duncan (R–SC): "POTUS needs to calm this shit down"[487]

3:09 p.m. from former White House Chief of Staff Reince Priebus: "TELL THEM TO GO HOME !!!"[488]

3:13 p.m. from Alyssa Farah Griffin: "Potus has to come out firmly and tell protestors to dissipate. Someone is going to get killed."[489]

3:15 p.m. from Rep. Chip Roy (R–TX): "Fix this now."[490]

3:31 p.m. from Fox News anchor Sean Hannity: "Can he make a statement. I saw the tweet. Ask people to peacefully leave the capital [sic]"[491]

3:58 p.m. from Fox News anchor Brian Kilmeade: "Please get him on tv. Destroying every thing you guys have accomplished"[492]

Others on Capitol Hill appeared in the media, or otherwise appeared via internet. Representative Mike Gallagher (R–WI) issued a video appealing directly to the President:

Mr. President, you have got to stop this. You are the only person who can call this off. Call it off. The election is over. Call it off![493]

Some Members of Congress sent texts to President Trump's immediate staff or took to Twitter, where they knew the President spent time:

Sen. Bill Cassidy (R–LA) issued a tweet: @realDonaldTrump please appear on TV, condemn the violence and tell people to disband.[494]

Rep. Jaime Herrera Beutler (R–WA) sent a text to Mark Meadows: We need to hear from the president. On TV. I hate that Biden jumped him on it.[495]

Republican Leader Kevin McCarthy tried repeatedly to reach President Trump, and did at least once. He also reached out for help to multiple members of President Trump's family, including Ivanka Trump and Jared Kushner.[496] Kushner characterized Leader McCarthy's demeanor on the call as "scared":

Kushner: I could hear in his voice that he really was nervous, and so, obviously, I took that seriously. And, you know, I didn't know if I'd be able to have any impact, but I said, you know, it's better to at least try. And so I—like I said, I turned the shower off, threw on a suit, and, you know, and rushed into the White House as quickly as I could.

Committee Staff: Yeah. What did he ask you to do? When you say have an impact, what is it specifically that he needed your help with?

Kushner: I don't recall a specific ask, just anything you could do. Again, I got the sense that, you know, they were—they were—you know, they were scared.

Committee Staff: "They" meaning Leader McCarthy and people on the Hill because of the violence?

Kushner: That he was scared, yes.[497]

Kevin McCarthy told Fox News at 3:09 p.m. about his call with the President[498] and elaborated about its contents in a conversation with CBS News's Norah O'Donnell at around 3:30 p.m.:

O'Donnell: Have you spoken with the President and asked him to perhaps come to the Capitol and tell his supporters it's time to leave?

Leader McCarthy: I have spoken to the President. I asked him to talk to the nation and tell them to stop this. . . .

* * *

O'Donnell: The President invited tens of thousands of people to quote unquote stop the steal. I don't know if you heard his more-than-hour-long remarks or the remarks of his son, who was the wind-up. It was some heated stuff, Leader McCarthy. I just wonder whether someone is going to accurately call a spade a spade, and I am giving you the opportunity right now that your precious and beloved United States Capitol and our democracy is witnessing this. Call a spade a spade.

Leader McCarthy: I was very clear with the President when I called him. This has to stop. And he has to, he's gotta go to the American public and tell them to stop this.

* * *

O'Donnell: Leader McCarthy, the President of the United States has a briefing room steps from the Oval Office. It is, the cameras are hot 24/7, as you know. Why hasn't he walked down and said that, now?

Leader McCarthy: I conveyed to the President what I think is best to do, and I'm hopeful the President will do it.[499]

The Committee has evidence from multiple sources regarding the content of Kevin McCarthy's direct conversation with Donald Trump during the violence.

Rep. Jaime Herrera Beutler (R–WA), to whom McCarthy spoke soon after, relayed more of the conversation between McCarthy and President Trump:

And he said [to President Trump], "You have got to get on TV. You've got to get on Twitter. You've got to call these people off." You know what the President said to him? This is as it's happening. He said, "Well Kevin, these aren't my people. You know, these are Antifa. And Kevin responded and said, "No, they're your people. They literally just came through my office windows and my staff are running for cover. I mean they're running for their lives. You need to call them off." And the President's response to Kevin to me was chilling. He said, "Well Kevin, I guess they're just more upset about the election, you know, theft than you are".[500]

Rep. Herrera Beutler's account of the incident was also corroborated by former Acting White House Chief of Staff Mick Mulvaney, who testified that Leader McCarthy told him several days later that President Trump had said during their call: "Kevin, maybe these people are just more angry about this than you are. Maybe they're more upset."[501]

Mulvaney was also trying to reach administration officials to urge President Trump to instruct his supporters to leave the Capitol.[502] As were many elected officials in both parties, including Nancy Pelosi and Chuck Schumer, and several Republican Members of Congress.[503]

As already noted, Cipollone and others in the White House repeatedly urged President Trump to tell his supporters to leave the Capitol. Cipollone described his conversations with Meadows after they failed to convince President Trump to deliver the necessary message:

> Committee Staff: Do you remember any discussion with Mark Meadows with respect to his view that the President didn't want to do anything or was somehow resistant to wanting to say something along the lines that you suggested.
>
> Pat Cipollone: Not just—just to be clear, many people suggested it.
>
> Committee Staff: Yeah.
>
> Cipollone: Not just me. Many people felt the same way. I'm sure I had conversations with Mark about this during the course of the day and expressed my opinion very forcefully that this needs to be done.[504]

* * *

> Committee Staff: So your advice was tell people to leave the Capitol, and that took over 2 hours when there were subsequent statements made, tweets put forth, that in your view were insufficient. Did you continue, Mr. Cipollone, throughout the period of time up until 4:17, continue, you and others, to push for a stronger statement?
>
> Cipollone: Yes.[505]

* * *

> Committee Staff: . . . at the onset of the violence when you first notice on television or wherever that rioters have actually breached the Capitol, did you have a conversation with Mark Meadows in which Meadows indicated he doesn't want to do anything, "he" meaning the President?
>
> Cipollone: I don't—I had a conversation I'm sure with Mark Meadows, I'm sure with other people, of what I thought should be done. Did Mark say that to me? I don't have a recollection of him saying that to me, but he may have said something along the lines.[506]

At 2:16 p.m., security records indicate that the Vice President was "being pulled" to a safer location.[507]

In an interview with the Select Committee, a White House Security Official on duty at the White House explained his observations as he listened to Secret Service communications and made contemporaneous entries into a security log. In particular, he explained an entry he made at 2:24 p.m.:

> Committee Staff: Ok. That last entry on this page is: "Service at the Capitol does not sound good right now."

Official: Correct.

Committee Staff: What does that mean?

Official: The members of the VP detail at this time were starting to fear for their own lives. There were a lot of—there was a lot of yelling, a lot of—I don't know—a lot [of] very personal calls over the radio. So—it was disturbing. I don't like talking about it, but there were calls to say good-bye to family members, so on and so forth. It was getting—for whatever the reason was on the ground, the VP detail thought that this was about to get very ugly.

Committee Staff: And did you hear that over the radio?

Official: Correct.

. . .

Committee Staff: ... obviously, you've conveyed that's disturbing, but what prompted you to put it into an entry as it states there, "Service at the Capitol—"

Official: That they're running out of options, and they're getting nervous. It sounds like that we came very close to either Service having to use lethal options or worse. At that point, I don't know. Is the VP compromised? Is the detail—like, I don't know. Like, we didn't have visibility, but it doesn't—if they're screaming and saying things, like, say good-bye to the family, like, the floor needs to know this is going to a whole another level soon.[508]

Also at 2:24 p.m., knowing the riot was underway and that Vice President Pence was at the Capitol, President Trump sent this tweet:

Mike Pence didn't have the courage to do what should have been done to protect our Country and our Constitution, giving States a chance to certify a corrected set of facts, not the fraudulent or inaccurate ones which they were asked to previously certify. USA demands the truth![509]

Evidence shows that the 2:24 p.m. tweet immediately precipitated further violence at the Capitol. Immediately after this tweet, the crowds both inside and outside of the Capitol building violently surged forward.[510] Outside the building, within ten minutes thousands of rioters overran the line on the west side of the Capitol that was being held by the Metropolitan Police Force's Civil Disturbance Unit, the first time in history of the DC Metro Police that such a security line had ever been broken.[511]

Virtually everyone on the White House staff the Select Committee interviewed condemned the 2:24 p.m. tweet in the strongest terms.

Police officers attempt to clear rioters inside the Capitol building.
(Photo by Brent Stirton/Getty Images)

Deputy National Security Adviser Matthew Pottinger told the Select Committee that the 2:24 p.m. tweet was so destructive that it convinced him to resign as soon as possible:

> One of my aides handed me a sheet of paper that contained the tweet that you just read. I read it and was quite disturbed by it. I was disturbed and worried to see that the President was attacking Vice President Pence for doing his constitutional duty.

> So the tweet looked to me like the opposite of what we really needed at that moment, which was a de-escalation. And that is why I had said earlier that it looked like fuel being poured on the fire.

> So that was the moment that I decided that I was going to resign, that that would be my last day at the White House. I simply didn't want to be associated with the events with the events that were unfolding at the Capitol.[512]

Deputy Press Secretary Sarah Matthews had a similar reaction:

> So it was obvious that the situation at the Capitol was violent and escalating quickly. And so I thought that the tweet about the Vice President was the last thing that was needed in that moment.

And I remember thinking that this was going to be bad for him to tweet this, because it was essentially him giving the green light to these people, telling them that what they were doing at the steps of the Capitol and entering the Capitol was okay, that they were justified in their anger.

And he shouldn't have been doing that. He should have been telling these people to go home and to leave and to condemn the violence that we were seeing.

And I am someone who has worked with him, you know, I worked on the campaign, traveled all around the country, going to countless rallies with him, and I have seen the impact that his words have on his supporters. They truly latch onto every word and every tweet that he says.

And so, I think that in that moment for him to tweet out the message about Mike Pence, it was him pouring gasoline on the fire and making it much worse.[513]

Deputy Press Secretary Judd Deere stated the following:

Committee Staff: What was your reaction when you saw that tweet?

Deere: Extremely unhelpful.

Committee Staff: Why?

Deere: It wasn't the message that we needed at that time. It wasn't going to—the scenes at the U.S. Capitol were only getting worse at that point. This was not going to help that.[514]

White House Counsel Pat Cipollone told the Select Committee, "I don't remember when exactly I heard about that tweet, but my reaction to it is that's a terrible tweet, and I disagreed with the sentiment. And I thought it was wrong." [515]

Likewise, Counselor to the President Hope Hicks texted a colleague that evening: "Attacking the VP? Wtf is wrong with him."[516]

At 2:26 p.m., Vice President Pence was again moved to a different location.[517]

President Trump had the TV on in the dining room.[518] At 2:38 p.m., Fox News was showing video of the chaos and attack, with tear gas filling the air in the Capitol Rotunda. And a newscaster reported, "[T]his is a very dangerous situation." [519] This is the context in which Trump sent the tweet.

Testimony obtained by the Committee indicates that President Trump knew about the rioters' anger at Vice President Pence and indicated something to the effect that the Vice President "deserves it." [520] As Cassidy Hutchinson explained:

> I remember Pat saying something to the effect of, "Mark, we need to do something more. They're literally calling for the Vice President to be f'ing hung." And Mark had responded something to the effect of, "You heard him, Pat. He thinks Mike deserves it. He doesn't think they're doing anything wrong." To which Pat said something, "[t]his is f'ing crazy, we need to be doing something more," briefly stepped into Mark's office, and when Mark had said something—when Mark had said something to the effect of, "He doesn't think they're doing anything wrong," knowing what I had heard briefly in the dining room coupled with Pat discussing the hanging Mike Pence chants in the lobby of our office and then Mark's response, I understood "they're" to be the rioters in the Capitol that were chanting for the Vice President to be hung. [521]

Although White House Counsel Pat Cipollone was limited in what he would discuss because of privilege concerns, he stated the following:

> Committee Staff: Do you remember any discussion at any point during the day about rioters at the Capitol chanting 'hang Mike Pence?'
>
> Cipollone: Yes. I remember—I remember hearing that—about that. Yes.
>
> Committee Staff: Yeah. And—
>
> Cipollone: I don't know if I observed that myself on TV. I don't remember.
>
> Committee Staff: I'm just curious, I understand the privilege line you've drawn, but do you remember what you can share with us about the discussion about those chants, the 'hang Mike Pence' chants?
>
> Cipollone: I could tell you my view of that.
>
> Committee Staff: Yeah. Please.
>
> Cipollone: My view of that is that is outrageous.
>
> Committee Staff: Uh-huh.
>
> Cipollone: And for anyone to suggest such a thing as the Vice President of the United States, for people in that crowd to be chanting

that I thought was terrible. I thought it was outrageous and wrong. And I expressed that very clearly to people. [522]

Almost immediately after the 2:24 p.m. tweet, Eric Herschmann went upstairs in the West Wing to try to enlist Ivanka Trump's assistance to persuade her father to do the right thing.[523] Ivanka rushed down to the Oval Office dining room. Although no one could convince President Trump to call for the violent rioters to leave the Capitol, Ivanka persuaded President Trump that a tweet could be issued to discourage violence against the police.

At 2:38 p.m., President Trump sent this tweet:

"Please support our Capitol Police and Law Enforcement. They are truly on the side of our Country. Stay peaceful!" [524]

While some in the meeting invoked executive privilege, or failed to recall the specifics, others told us what happened at that point. Sarah Matthews, the White House Deputy Press Secretary, had urged her boss, Kayleigh McEnany, to have the President make a stronger statement. But she informed us that President Trump resisted using the word "peaceful" in his message:

Committee Staff: Ms. Matthews, Ms. McEnany told us she came right back to the press office after meeting with the President about this particular tweet. What did she tell you about what happened in that dining room?

Sarah Matthews: When she got back, she told me that a tweet had been sent out. And I told her that I thought the tweet did not go far enough, that I thought there needed to be a call to action and he needed to condemn the violence. And we were in a room full of people, but people weren't paying attention. And so, she looked directly at me and in a hushed tone shared with me that the President did not want to include any sort of mention of peace in that tweet and that it took some convincing on their part, those who were in the room. And she said that there was a back and forth going over different phrases to find something that he was comfortable with. And it wasn't until Ivanka Trump suggested the phrase 'stay peaceful' that he finally agreed to include it.[525]

At 3:13 p.m., President Trump sent another tweet, but again declined to tell people to go home:

"I am asking for everyone at the U.S. Capitol to remain peaceful. No violence! Remember, WE are the Party of Law & Order—respect the Law and our great men and women in Blue. Thank you!" [526]

Almost everyone, including staff in the White House also found the President's 2:38 p.m. and 3:13 p.m. tweets to be insufficient because they did not instruct the rioters to leave the Capitol. As mentioned, President Trump's son, Donald Trump Jr., texted Meadows:

He's got to condem [sic] this shit. Asap. The captiol [sic] police tweet is not enough. [527]

Sean Hannity also texted Mark Meadows:

Can he make a statement. I saw the tweet. Ask people to peacefully leave the capital [sic].[528]

None of these efforts resulted in President Trump immediately issuing the message that was needed. White House staff had these comments:

Pottinger: Yeah. It was insufficient. I think what—you could count me among those who was hoping to see an unequivocal strong statement clearing out the Capitol, telling people to stand down, leave, go home. I think that's what we were hoping for. [529]

. . .

Matthews: Yeah. So a conversation started in the press office after the President sent out those two tweets that I deemed were insufficient. . . . I thought that we should condemn the violence and condemn it unequivocally. And I thought that he needed to include a call to action and to tell these people to go home. [530]

And they were right. Evidence showed that neither of these tweets had any appreciable impact on the violent rioters. Unlike the video-message tweet that did not come until 4:17 finally instructing rioters to leave, neither the 2:38 nor the 3:13 tweets made any difference.

At some point after 3:05 p.m. that afternoon, President Trump's Chief of Staff—and President Trump himself—were informed that someone had been shot.[531] That person was Ashli Babbitt, who was fatally shot at 2:44 p.m. as she and other rioters tried to gain access to the House chamber.[532] There is no indication that this affected the President's state of mind that day, and we found no evidence that the President expressed any remorse that day.

Meanwhile, leaders in Congress—including Speaker Pelosi, Senator Schumer, Senator McConnell—and the Vice President, were taking action. They called the Secretary of Defense, the Attorney General, governors and officials in Virginia, Maryland, and the District of Columbia, begging for assistance.[533]

President-elect Biden also broadcast a video calling on President Trump to take action:

I call on President Trump to go on national television now to fulfill his oath and defend the Constitution and demand an end to this siege.[534]

President Trump could have done this, of course, anytime after he learned of the violence at the Capitol. At 4:17 p.m., 187 minutes after finishing his speech (and even longer after the attack began), President Trump finally broadcast a video message in which he asked those attacking the Capitol to leave:

I know your pain. I know you're hurt. We had an election that was stolen from us. It was a landslide election, and everyone knows it, especially the other side, but you have to go home now. We have to have peace.[535]

President Trump's Deputy Press Secretary, Sarah Matthews testified about her reaction to this video message:

[H]e told the people who we had just watched storm our nation's Capitol with the intent on overthrowing our democracy, violently attack police officers, and chant heinous things like, "Hang Mike Pence," "We love you. You're very special." As a spokesperson for him, I knew that I would be asked to defend that. And to me, his refusal to act and call off the mob that day and his refusal to condemn the violence was indefensible. And so, I knew that I would be resigning that evening.[536]

By this time, the National Guard and other additional law enforcement had begun to arrive in force and started to turn the tide of the violence. Many of those attackers in the Capitol saw or received word of President Trump's 4:17 p.m. message, and they understood this message as an instruction to leave:[537]

- Stephen Ayres testified in front of the Select Committee that: "Well, we were there. As soon as that come out, everybody started talking about it, and it seemed like it started to disperse, you know, some of the crowd. Obviously, you know, once we got back to the hotel room, we seen that it was still going on, but it definitely dispersed a lot of the crowd."[538]
- Jacob Chansley, also known as the QAnon-Shaman answered President Trump's directive: "I'm here delivering the President's message. Donald Trump has asked everybody to go home." Another responded to Chansley: "That's our order."[539]
- Other unknown individuals also listened to President Trump's message while outside the Capitol, and responded: "He says, go home. He says, go home." And "Yeah. Here. He said to go home."[540]

At 6:01 p.m., President Trump sent his last tweet of the day, not condemning the violence, but instead attempting to justify it:

These are the things and events that happen when a sacred election landslide victory is so unceremoniously & viciously stripped away from great patriots who have been badly & unfairly treated for so long. Go home with love & in peace. Remember this day forever![541]

Staff in President Trump's own White House and campaign had a strong reaction to this message:

Sarah Matthews: At that point I had already made the decision to resign and this tweet just further cemented my decision. I thought that January 6, 2021, was one of the darkest days in our Nation's history and President Trump was treating it as a celebratory occasion with that tweet. And so, it just further cemented my decision to resign.[542]

Tim Murtaugh: I don't think it's a patriotic act to attack the Capitol. But I have no idea how to characterize the people other than they trespassed, destroyed property, and assaulted the U.S. Capitol. I think calling them patriots is a, let's say, a stretch, to say the least. . . . I don't think it's a patriotic act to attack the U.S. Capitol.[543]

Pat Cipollone: [W]hat happened at the Capitol cannot be justified in any form or fashion. It was wrong, and it was tragic. And a lot—and it was a terrible day. It was a terrible day for this country.[544]

Greg Jacob: I thought it was inappropriate. . . . To my mind, it was a day that should live in infamy.[545]

At 6:27 p.m., President Trump retired to his residence for the night. As he did, he had one final comment to an employee who accompanied him to the residence. The one takeaway that the President expressed in that moment, following a horrific afternoon of violence and the worst attack against the U.S. Capitol building in over two centuries, was this: "Mike Pence let me down." [546]

President Trump's inner circle was still trying to delay the counting of electoral votes into the evening, even after the violence had been quelled. Rudolph Giuliani tried calling numerous Members of Congress in the hour before the joint session resumed, including Rep. Jim Jordan (R–OH) and Senators Marsha Blackburn (R–TN), Tommy Tuberville (R–AL), Bill Hagerty (R–TN), Lindsey Graham (R–SC), Josh Hawley (R–MO), and Ted Cruz (R–TX).[547] His voicemail intended for Senator Tuberville at 7:02 p.m. that evening eventually was made public:

A Trump sign with Vice President Mike Pence's name removed.
(Photo by Michael Ciaglo/Getty Images)

> Guiliani: Sen. Tuberville? Or I should say Coach Tuberville. This is Rudy Guiliani, the President's lawyer. I'm calling you because I want to discuss with you how they're trying to rush this hearing and how we need you, our Republican friends, to try to just slow it down so we can get these legislatures to get more information to you.[548]

Reflecting on President Trump's conduct that day, Vice President Pence noted that President Trump "had made no effort to contact me in the midst of the rioting or any point afterward."[549] He wrote that President Trump's "reckless words had endangered my family and all those serving at the Capitol."[550]

President Trump did not contact a single top national security official during the day. Not at the Pentagon, nor at the Department of Homeland Security, the Department of Justice, the F.B.I., the Capitol Police Department, or the D.C. Mayor's office.[551] As Vice President Pence has confirmed, President Trump didn't even try to reach his own Vice President to make sure that Pence was safe.[552] President Trump did not order any of his staff to facilitate a law enforcement response of any sort.[553] His Chairman of the Joint Chiefs of Staff—who is by statute the primary military advisor to the President—had this reaction:

General Milley: You know, you're the Commander in Chief. You've got an assault going on on the Capitol of the United States of America. And there's nothing? No call? Nothing? Zero?[554]

General Milley did, however, receive a call from President Trump's Chief of Staff Mark Meadows that day. Here is how he described that call:

He said, "We have to kill the narrative that the Vice President is making all the decisions. We need to establish the narrative, you know, that the President is still in charge and that things are steady or stable," or words to that effect. I immediately interpreted that as politics, politics, politics. Red flag for me, personally. No action. But I remember it distinctly. And I don't do political narratives.[555]

Some have suggested that President Trump gave an order to have 10,000 troops ready for January 6th.[556] The Select Committee found no evidence of this. In fact, President Trump's Acting Secretary of Defense Christopher Miller directly refuted this when he testified under oath:

Committee Staff: To be crystal clear, there was no direct order from President Trump to put 10,000 troops to be on the ready for January 6th, correct?

Miller: No. Yeah. That's correct. There was no direct—there was no order from the President.[557]

Later, on the evening of January 6th, President Trump's former campaign manager, Brad Parscale, texted Katrina Pierson, one of President Trump's rally organizers, that the events of the day were the result of a "sitting president asking for civil war" and that "This week I feel guilty for helping him win" now that ". . . a woman is dead." Pierson answered: "You do realize this was going to happen." Parscale replied: "Yeah. If I was Trump and knew my rhetoric killed someone." "It wasn't the rhetoric," Pierson suggested. But Parscale insisted: "Yes it was."[558]

THE IMMEDIATE AFTERMATH OF JANUARY 6TH
In days following January 6th, President Trump's family and staff attempted repeatedly to persuade him not to repeat his election fraud allegations, to concede defeat, and to allow the transition to President Biden to proceed. Trump did make two video recordings, which initially appeared contrite. But evidence suggests that these statements were designed at least in part to ward off other potential consequences of January 6th, such as invocation of the 25th Amendment or impeachment.

In fact, Minority Leader Kevin McCarthy indicated after the attack, in a discussion with House Republican leaders, that he would ask President Trump to resign:

Rep. Cheney: I guess there's a question when we were talking about the 25th Amendment resolution, and you asked what would happen after he's gone? Is there any chance? Are you hearing that he might resign? Is there any reason to think that might happen?

Leader McCarthy: I've had a few discussions. My gut tells me no. I'm seriously thinking of having that discussion with him tonight. I haven't talked to him in a couple of days. From what I know of him, I mean, you guys all know him too, do you think he'd ever back away? But what I think I'm going to do is I'm going to call him. This is what I think. We know [the 25th Amendment resolution] will pass the House. I think there's a chance it will pass the Senate, even when he's gone. And I think there's a lot of different ramifications for that. . . . Again, the only discussion I would have with him is that I think this will pass, and it would be my recommendation you should resign.[559]

Before January 6th, Fox News personality Sean Hannity warned that January 6th could be disastrous:

Dec. 31, 2020 text from Sean Hannity to Mark Meadows: "We can't lose the entire WH counsels office. I do NOT see January 6 happening the way he is being told. After the 6 th [sic]. He should announce will lead the nationwide effort to reform voting integrity. Go to Fl and watch Joe mess up daily. Stay engaged. When he speaks people will listen." [560]

January 5, 2021 texts from Sean Hannity to Mark Meadows:

"Im very worried about the next 48 hours"

"Pence pressure. WH counsel will leave."

"Sorry, I can't talk right now."

"On with boss"[561]

A member of the Republican Freedom caucus also warned, on December 31, 2020, and on January 1, 2021:

The President should call everyone off. It's the only path. If we substitute the will of states through electors with a vote by Congress every 4 years . . . we have destroyed the electoral college . . . Respectfully.[562] If POTUS allows this to occur . . . we're driving a stake in the heart of the federal republic . . . [563]

After January 6th, Hannity worked to persuade President Trump to stop talking about election fraud, proposed that Trump pardon Hunter Biden, and discussed attending the Inauguration:

1. No more stolen election talk.
2. Yes, impeachment and 25th amendment are real, and many people will quit.
3. He was intrigued by the Pardon idea!! (Hunter)
4. Resistant but listened to Pence thoughts, to make it right.
5. Seemed to like attending Inauguration talk.[564]

Ultimately, President Trump took little of the advice from Hannity and his White House staff. A few days later, Hannity wrote again to Meadows and Jim Jordan:

Guys, we have a clear path to land the plane in 9 days. He can't mention the election again. Ever. I did not have a good call with him today. And worse, I'm not sure what is left to do or say, and I don t like not knowing if it's truly understood. Ideas?[565]

Likewise, despite her many contrary public statements, Republican Congresswoman Marjorie Taylor Greene privately texted her concerns on January 6th about a continuing and real threat of violence.

Mark I was just told there is an active shooter on the first floor of the Capitol Please tell the President to calm people This isn't the way to solve anything[566]

Donald Trump was impeached on January 13th. In a speech that day, Republican Leader Kevin McCarthy made this statement from the House floor, but voted against impeachment:

The President bears responsibility for Wednesday's attack on Congress by mob rioters. He should have immediately denounced the mob when he saw what was unfolding. These facts require immediate action by President Trump, accept his share of responsibility, quell the brewing unrest and ensure President-elect Biden is able to successfully begin his term. The President's immediate action also deserves congressional action, which is why I think a fact-finding commission and a censure resolution would be prudent.[567]

Later, McCarthy told members of the House Republican conference that Trump had acknowledged that he was at least partially responsible for the January 6th attack.

Kevin McCarthy speaks at a press conference at the Capitol building on August 27, 2021.
(Photo by Anna Moneymaker/Getty Images)

> I asked him personally today, does he hold responsibility for what happened? Does he feel bad about what happened? He told me he does have some responsibility for what happened. And he need to acknowledge that.[568]

Since January 6th, President Trump has continued to claim falsely that the 2020 Presidential election was stolen. Not only that, he has urged other politicians to push this argument as well. Representative Mo Brooks has issued a public statement appearing to represent Trump's private views and intentions:

> President Trump asked me to rescind the 2020 elections, immediately remove Joe Biden from the White House, immediately put President Trump back in the White House, and hold a new special election for the presidency.[569]

REFERRALS TO THE U.S. DEPARTMENT OF JUSTICE SPECIAL COUNSEL AND HOUSE ETHICS COMMITTEE

The Committee's work has produced a substantial body of new information. We know far more about the President's plans and actions to overturn the election than almost all Members of Congress did when President Trump was impeached on January 13, 2021, or when he was tried by the Senate in February of that year. Fifty-seven of 100 Senators voted to convict President Trump at that time, and more than 20 others condemned the President's conduct and said they were voting against conviction because the President's term had already expired.[570] At the time, the Republican Leader of the U.S. Senate said this about Donald Trump: "A mob was assaulting the Capitol in his name. These criminals were carrying his banners, hanging his flags, and screaming their loyalty to him. It was obvious that only President Trump could end this. He was the only one who could."[571] House Republican Leader Kevin McCarthy, who spoke directly with President Trump during the violence of January 6th, expressed similar views both in private and in public. Privately, Leader McCarthy stated: "But let me be very clear to you and I have been very clear to the President. He bears responsibility for his words and actions. No if, ands or buts."[572] In public, Leader McCarthy concluded: "The President bears responsibility for Wednesday's attack on Congress by mob rioters."[573]

Today we know that the planning to overturn the election on January 6th was substantially more extensive, and involved many other players, and many other efforts over a longer time period. Indeed, the violent attack and invasion of the Capitol, and what provoked it, are only a part of the story.

From the outset of its hearings, the Committee has explained that President Trump and a number of other individuals made a series of very specific plans, ultimately with multiple separate elements, but all with one overriding objective: to corruptly obstruct, impede, or influence the counting of electoral votes on January 6th, and thereby overturn the lawful results of the election. The underlying and fundamental feature of that planning was the effort to get one man, Vice President Mike Pence, to assert and then exercise unprecedented and lawless powers to unilaterally alter the actual election outcome on January 6th. Evidence obtained by the Committee demonstrates that John Eastman, who worked with President Trump to put that and other elements of the plan in place, knew even before the 2020 Presidential election that Vice President Pence could not lawfully refuse to count official, certified electoral slates submitted by the Governors of the States.[574] Testimony and contemporaneous documentary evidence also indicate that President Trump knew that the plan was unlawful before January 6th.[575] When the Vice President's counsel wrote to Eastman on January 6th to ask whether the latter had informed the President that the Vice President did not have authority to decide the election unilaterally, Eastman responded: "He's been so advised," and added, "[b]ut you know him—once he gets something in his head, it is hard to get him to change course."[576]

Many of the other elements of President Trump's plans were specifically designed to create a set of circumstances on January 6th to assist
President Trump in overturning the lawful election outcome during Congress's joint session that day. For example, President Trump pressured
State legislatures to adopt new electoral slates that Vice President Pence
could, unlawfully, count. Trump solicited State officials to "find" a sufficient number of votes to alter the final count, and instructed the Department of Justice to "just say that the election was was [sic] corrupt + leave
the rest to me and the R[epublican] Congressmen." [577] President Trump
offered the job of Acting Attorney General to Jeffrey Clark. As our evidence
has unequivocally demonstrated, Clark intended to use that position to send
a series of letters from the Department of Justice to multiple States falsely
asserting that the Department had found fraud and urging those States to
convene their legislatures to alter their official electoral slates.[578] And
President Trump, with the help of the Republican National Committee and
others, oversaw an effort to create and transmit to Government officials a
series of intentionally false electoral slates for Vice President Pence to utilize on January 6th to alter or delay the count of lawful votes.[579]

Of course, other elements of the plan complemented these efforts too.
As this Report documents, President Trump was advised by his own experts
and the Justice Department that his election fraud allegations were false,
and he knew he had lost virtually all the legal challenges to the election, but
he nevertheless engaged in a successful but fraudulent effort to persuade
tens of millions of Americans that the election was stolen from him. This
effort was designed to convince Americans that President Trump's actions
to overturn the election were justified. President Trump then urged his
supporters to travel to Washington on January 6th to apply pressure to
Congress to halt the count and change the election outcome, explaining to
those who were coming to Washington that they needed to "take back"
their country and "stop the steal." [580]

It is helpful in understanding these facts to focus on specific moments
in time when President Trump made corrupt, dishonest, and unlawful
choices to pursue his plans. For example, by December 14th when the electoral college met and certified Joe Biden's victory, President Trump knew
that he had failed in all the relevant litigation; he had been advised by his
own experts and the Justice Department that his election fraud claims were
false; and he had been told by numerous advisors that he had lost and
should concede. But despite his duty as President to take care that the laws
are faithfully executed, he chose instead to ignore all of the judicial rulings
and the facts before him and push forward to overturn the election. Likewise, in the days and hours before the violence of January 6th, President
Trump knew that no State had issued any changed electoral slate. Indeed,

neither President Trump nor his co-conspirators had any evidence that any majority of any State legislature was willing to do so. President Trump also knew that Vice President Pence could not lawfully refuse to count legitimate votes. Despite all of these facts, President Trump nevertheless proceeded to instruct Vice President Pence to execute a plan he already knew was illegal. And then knowing that a violent riot was underway, President Trump breached his oath of office; our Commander in Chief refused for hours to take the one simple step that his advisors were begging him to take—to instruct his supporters to disperse, stand down, and leave the Capitol. Instead, fully understanding what had unfolded at the Capitol, President Trump exacerbated the violence with a tweet attacking Vice President Pence.[581] Any rational person who had watched the events that day knew that President Trump's 2:24 p.m. tweet would lead to further violence. It did. And, at almost exactly the same time, President Trump continued to lobby Congress to delay the electoral count.

As the evidence demonstrates, the rioters at the Capitol had invaded the building and halted the electoral count. They did not begin to relent until President Trump finally issued a video statement instructing his supporters to leave the Capitol at 4:17 p.m., which had an immediate and helpful effect: rioters began to disperse[582]—but not before the Capitol was invaded, the election count was halted, feces were smeared in the Capitol, the Vice President and his family and many others were put in danger, and more than 140 law enforcement officers were attacked and seriously injured by mob rioters. Even if it were true that President Trump genuinely believed the election was stolen, *this is no defense.* No President can ignore the courts and purposely violate the law no matter what supposed "justification" he or she presents.

These conclusions are not the Committee's alone. In the course of its investigation, the Committee had occasion to present evidence to Federal District Court Judge David Carter, who weighed that evidence against submissions from President Trump's lawyer, John Eastman. Judge Carter considered this evidence in the context of a discovery dispute—specifically whether the Committee could obtain certain of Eastman's documents pursuant to the "crime-fraud" exception to the attorney-client privilege. That exception provides that otherwise privileged documents may lose their privilege if they were part of an effort to commit a crime or a fraud, in this case by President Trump. Judge Carter set out his factual findings, discussing multiple elements of President Trump's multi-part plan to overturn the election,[583] and then addressed whether the evidence, including Eastman's email communications, demonstrated that Trump and Eastman committed crimes. "Based on the evidence," Judge Carter explained, "the Court finds it more likely than not that President Trump corruptly attempted to obstruct the Joint Session of Congress on January 6, 2021," and "more likely than not that President Trump and Dr. Eastman dishonestly conspired to obstruct the Joint Session of Congress on January 6th." [584] Judge Carter also concluded that President Trump's and Eastman's "pressure campaign to stop the electoral count did not end with Vice President Pence—it targeted every tier of federal and state elected officials" [585] and was "a coup in search of a legal theory." [586] "The plan spurred violent attacks on the seat of our nation's government," Judge Carter wrote, and it threatened to "permanently end[] the peaceful transition of power. . . ." [587]

The U.S. Department of Justice has been investigating and prosecuting persons who invaded the Capitol, engaged in violence, and planned violence on that day. The Department has charged more than 900 individuals, and nearly 500 have already been convicted or pleaded guilty as we write. [588] As the Committee's investigation progressed through its hearings, public reporting emerged suggesting that the Department of Justice had also begun to investigate several others specifically involved in the events being examined by the Committee. Such reports indicated that search warrants had been issued, based on findings of probable cause, for the cell phones of John Eastman, Jeffrey Clark, and Representative Scott Perry. [589] Other reports suggested that the Department had empaneled one or more grand juries and was pursuing a ruling compelling several of this Committee's witnesses, including Pat Cipollone and Greg Jacob, to give testimony on topics for which President Trump had apparently asserted executive privilege. Recent reporting suggests that a Federal district court judge has now rejected President Trump's executive privilege claims in that context. [590]

Criminal referrals from a congressional committee are often made in circumstances where prosecutors are not yet known to be pursuing some of the same facts and evidence. That is not the case here. During the course of our investigation, both the U.S. Department of Justice and at least one local prosecutor's office (Fulton County, Georgia) have been actively conducting criminal investigations concurrently with this congressional investigation. [591] In fact, the U.S. Department of Justice has recently taken the extraordinary step of appointing a Special Counsel to investigate the former President's conduct. [592]

The Committee recognizes that the Department of Justice and other prosecutorial authorities may be in a position to utilize investigative tools, including search warrants and grand juries, superior to the means the Committee has for obtaining relevant information and testimony. Indeed, both the Department of Justice and the Fulton County District Attorney may now have access to witness testimony and records that have been unavailable to the Committee, including testimony from President Trump's Chief of Staff Mark Meadows, and others who either asserted privileges or invoked their Fifth Amendment rights.[593] The Department may also be able to access, via grand jury subpoena or otherwise, the testimony of Republican Leader Kevin McCarthy, Representative Scott Perry, Representative Jim Jordan and others, each of whom appears to have had materially relevant communications with Donald Trump or others in the White House but who failed to comply with the Select Committee's subpoenas.

Taking all of these facts into account, and based on the breadth of the evidence it has accumulated, the Committee makes the following criminal referrals to the Department of Justice's Special Counsel.

I. Obstruction of an Official Proceeding (18 U.S.C. § 1512(c))

Section 1512(c)(2) of Title 18 of the United States Code makes it a crime to "corruptly" "obstruct[], influence[], or impede[] any official proceeding, or attempt[] to do so." [594] Sufficient evidence exists of one or more potential violations of this statute for a criminal referral of President Trump and others.[595]

First, there should be no question that Congress's joint session to count electoral votes on January 6th was an "official proceeding" under section 1512(c). Many Federal judges have already reached that specific conclusion.[596]

Second, there should be no doubt that President Trump knew that his actions were likely to "obstruct, influence or impede" that proceeding. Based on the evidence developed, President Trump was attempting to prevent or delay the counting of lawful certified electoral college votes from multiple States.[597] President Trump was directly and personally involved in this effort, personally pressuring Vice President Pence relentlessly as the joint session on January 6th approached.[598]

Third, President Trump acted with a "corrupt" purpose. Vice President Pence, Greg Jacob, and others repeatedly told the President that the Vice President had no unilateral authority to prevent certification of the election.[599] Indeed, in an email exchange during the violence of January 6th, Eastman admitted that President Trump had been "advised" that Vice President Pence could not lawfully refuse to count votes under the Electoral Count Act, but "once he gets something in his head, it's hard to get him to change course." [600] In addition, President Trump knew that he had lost dozens of State and Federal lawsuits, and that the Justice Department, his campaign and his other advisors concluded that there was insufficient fraud to alter the outcome. President Trump also knew that no majority of any State legislature had taken or manifested any intention to take any official action that could change a State's electoral college votes.[601] But President Trump pushed forward anyway. As Judge Carter explained, "[b]ecause

President Trump likely knew that the plan to disrupt the electoral count was wrongful, his mindset exceeds the threshold for acting 'corruptly' under § 1512(c)." [602]

Sufficient evidence exists of one or more potential violations of 18 U.S.C. § 1512(c) for a criminal referral of President Trump based solely on his plan to get Vice President Pence to prevent certification of the election at the joint session of Congress. Those facts standing alone are sufficient. But such a charge under that statute can also be based on the plan to create and transmit to the executive and legislative branches fraudulent electoral slates, which were ultimately intended to facilitate an unlawful action by Vice President Pence, to refuse to count legitimate, certified electoral votes during Congress's official January 6th proceeding. [603] Additionally, evidence developed about the many other elements of President Trump's plans to overturn the election, including soliciting State legislatures, State officials, and others to alter official electoral outcomes, provides further evidence that President Trump was attempting through multiple means to corruptly obstruct, impede, or influence the counting of electoral votes on January 6th. This is also true of President Trump's personal directive to the Department of Justice to "just say that the election was was [sic] corrupt + leave the rest to me and the R[epublican] Congressmen." [604]

We also stress in particular the draft letter to the Georgia legislature authored by Jeffrey Clark and another Trump political appointee at the Department of Justice. The draft letter embraces many of the same theories that John Eastman and others were asserting in President Trump's effort to lobby State legislatures. White House Counsel Pat Cipollone described that letter as "a murder-suicide pact," and other White House and Justice Department officials offered similar descriptions. [605] As described herein, that draft letter was intended to help persuade a State legislature to change its certified slate of electoral college electors based on false allegations of fraud, so Vice President Pence could unilaterally and unlawfully decide to count a different slate on January 6th. [606] The letter was transparently false, improper, and illegal. President Trump had multiple communications with Clark in the days before January 6th, and there is no basis to doubt that President Trump offered Clark the position of Acting Attorney General knowing that Clark would send the letter and others like it. [607]

Of course, President Trump is also responsible for recruiting tens of thousands of his supporters to Washington for January 6th, and knowing they were angry and some were armed, instructing them to march to the Capitol and "fight like hell." [608] And then, while knowing a violent riot was underway, he refused for multiple hours to take the single step his advisors and supporters were begging him to take to halt the violence: to make a

public statement instructing his supporters to disperse and leave the Capitol.[609] Through action and inaction, President Trump corruptly obstructed,
delayed, and impeded the vote count.

In addition, the Committee believes sufficient evidence exists for a
criminal referral of John Eastman and certain other Trump associates under
18 U.S.C. §1512(c). The evidence shows that Eastman knew in advance of the
2020 election that Vice President Pence could not refuse to count electoral
votes on January 6th.[610] In the days before January 6th, Eastman was
warned repeatedly that his plan was illegal and "completely crazy," and
would "cause riots in the streets." [611] Nonetheless, Eastman continued to
assist President Trump's pressure campaign in public and in private,
including in meetings with the Vice President and in his own speech at the
Ellipse on January 6th. And even as the violence was playing out at the
Capitol, Eastman admitted in writing that his plan violated the law but
pressed for Pence to do it anyway.[612] In the immediate aftermath of January
6th, White House lawyer Eric Herschmann told Eastman that he should
"[g]et a great F'ing criminal defense lawyer, you're going to need it." [613]
Others working with Eastman likely share in Eastman's culpability. For
example, Kenneth Chesebro was a central player in the scheme to submit
fake electors to the Congress and the National Archives.

The Committee notes that multiple Republican Members of Congress,
including Representative Scott Perry, likely have material facts regarding
President Trump's plans to overturn the election. For example, many Members of Congress attended a White House meeting on December 21, 2020, in
which the plan to have the Vice President affect the outcome of the election
was disclosed and discussed. Evidence indicates that certain of those Members unsuccessfully sought Presidential pardons from President Trump
after January 6th,[614] as did Eastman,[615] revealing their own clear con-
sciousness of guilt.

II. Conspiracy to Defraud the United States (18 U.S.C. § 371)

Section 371 of Title 18 of the U.S. Code provides that "[i]f two or more persons conspire either to commit any offense against the United States, or to
defraud the United States, or any agency thereof in any manner or for any
purpose, and one or more of such persons do any act to effect the object of
the conspiracy, each shall be fined under this title or imprisoned not more
than five years, or both." The Committee believes sufficient evidence exists
for a criminal referral of President Trump and others under this statute.[616]

First, President Trump entered into an agreement with individuals to
obstruct a lawful function of the government (the certification of the election). The evidence of this element overlaps greatly with the evidence of the
section 1512(c)(2) violations, so we will not repeat it at length here. President Trump engaged in a multi-part plan described in this Report to

obstruct a lawful certification of the election. Judge Carter focused his opinions largely on John Eastman's role, as Eastman's documents were at issue in that case, concluding that "the evidence shows that an agreement to enact the electoral count plan likely existed between President Trump and Eastman." [617] But President Trump entered into agreements—whether formal or informal[618]—with several other individuals who assisted with the multi-part plan. With regard to the Department of Justice, Jeffrey Clark stands out as a participant in the conspiracy, as the evidence suggests that Clark entered into an agreement with President Trump that if appointed Acting Attorney General, he would send a letter to State officials falsely stating that the Department of Justice believed that State legislatures had a sufficient factual basis to convene to select new electors. This was false—the Department of Justice had reached the conclusion that there was no factual basis to contend that the election was stolen. Again, as with section 1512(c), the conspiracy under section 371 appears to have also included other individuals such as Chesebro, Rudolph Giuliani, and Mark Meadows, but this Committee does not attempt to determine all of the participants of the conspiracy, many of whom refused to answer this Committee's questions.

Second, there are several bases for finding that the conspirators used "deceitful or dishonest means." For example, President Trump repeatedly lied about the election, after he had been told by his advisors that there was no evidence of fraud sufficient to change the results of the election.[619] In addition, the plot to get the Vice President to unilaterally prevent certification of the election was manifestly (and admittedly) illegal, as discussed above. Eastman and others told President Trump that it would violate the Electoral Count Act if the Vice President unilaterally rejected electors. Thus Judge Carter once again had little trouble finding that the intent requirement ("deceitful or dishonest means") was met, stating that "President Trump continuing to push that plan despite being aware of its illegality constituted obstruction by 'dishonest' means under § 371." [620] Judge Carter rejected the notion that Eastman's plan—which the President adopted and actualized—was a "good faith interpretation" of the law, finding instead that it was "a partisan distortion of the democratic process." [621] Similarly, both President Trump and Clark had been told repeatedly that the Department of Justice had found no evidence of significant fraud in any of its investigations, but they nonetheless pushed the Department of Justice to send a letter to State officials stating that the Department had found such fraud. And Georgia Secretary of State Brad Raffensperger and others made clear to President Trump that they had no authority to "find" him 11,780 votes, but the President relentlessly insisted that they do exactly that, even to the point of suggesting there could be criminal consequences if they refused.[622]

Third, there were numerous overt acts in furtherance of the agreement, including each of the parts of the President's effort to overturn the election. As Judge Carter concluded, President Trump and Eastman participated in "numerous overt acts in furtherance of their shared plan."[623] These included, but certainly were not limited to, direct pleas to the Vice President to reject electors or delay certification, including in Oval Office meetings and the President's vulgar comments to the Vice President on the morning of January 6th. Judge Carter also addressed evidence that President Trump knowingly made false representations to a court. Judge Carter concluded that Eastman's emails showed "that President Trump knew that the specific numbers of voter fraud" cited in a complaint on behalf of President Trump "were wrong but continued to tout those numbers, both in court and to the public." Judge Carter found that the emails in question were related to and in furtherance of a conspiracy to defraud the United States.[624]

In finding that President Trump, Eastman, and others engaged in conspiracy to defraud the United States under section 371, Judge Carter relied on the documents at issue (largely consisting of Eastman's own emails) and evidence presented to the court by this Committee. This Committee's investigation has progressed significantly since Judge Carter issued his first crime-fraud ruling in March 2022. The evidence found by this Committee and discussed in detail in this Report further documents that the conspiracy to defraud the United States under section 371 extended far beyond the effort to pressure the Vice President to prevent certification of the election. The Committee believes there is sufficient evidence for a criminal referral of the multi-part plan described in this Report under section 371, as the very purpose of the plan was to prevent the lawful certification of Joe Biden's election as President.

III. Conspiracy to Make a False Statement (18 U.S.C. §§ 371, 1001)

President Trump, through others acting at his behest, submitted slates of fake electors to Congress and the National Archives. Section 1001 of Title 18 of the United States Code applies, in relevant part, to "whoever, in any matter within the jurisdiction of the executive, legislative, or judicial branch of the Government of the United States, knowingly and willfully—

(1) falsifies, conceals, or covers up by any trick, scheme, or device a material fact;

(2) makes any materially false, fictitious, or fraudulent statement or representation; or

(3) makes or uses any false writing or document knowing the same to contain any materially false, fictitious, or fraudulent statement or entry."

According to the Department of Justice, whether a false statement is criminal under section 1001 "depends on whether there is an affirmative response to each of the following questions:

1. Was the act or statement material?
2. Was the act within the jurisdiction of a department or agency of the United States?
3. Was the act done knowingly and willfully?" [625]

In addition, and as explained above, 18 U.S.C. § 371 makes it a crime to conspire to "commit any offense against the United States." [626]

The evidence suggests President Trump conspired with others to submit slates of fake electors to Congress and the National Archives. Sufficient evidence exists of a violation of 18 U.S.C. §§ 371 and 1001 for a criminal referral of President Trump and others.

As explained earlier and in Chapter 3 of this Report, the certifications signed by Trump electors in multiple States were patently false. Vice President Biden won each of those States, and the relevant State authorities had so certified. It can hardly be disputed that the false slates of electors were material, as nothing can be more material to the joint session of Congress to certify the election than the question of which candidate won which States. Indeed, evidence obtained by the Committee suggests that those attempting to submit certain of the electoral votes regarded the need to provide that material to Vice President Pence as urgent. [627]

There should be no question that section 1001 applies here. The false electoral slates were provided both to the executive branch (the National Archives) and the legislative branch. [628] The statute applies to "any matter within the jurisdiction of the executive, legislative, or judicial branch of the Government of the United States." [629] It is well established that false statements to Congress can constitute violations of section 1001. [630]

Finally, the false statement was made knowingly and willfully. There is some evidence suggesting that some signatories of the fake certificates believed that the certificates were contingent, to be used only in the event that President Trump prevailed in litigation challenging the election results in their States. That may be relevant to the question whether those electors knowingly and willfully signed a false statement at the time they signed the certificates. But it is of no moment to President Trump's conduct, as President Trump (including acting through co-conspirators such as John Eastman and Kenneth Chesebro) relied on the existence of those fake electors as a basis for asserting that the Vice President could reject or delay certification of the Biden electors. In fact, as explained earlier and in Chapter 5 of this Report, Eastman's memorandum setting out a six-step plan for overturning the election on January 6th begins by stating that "7 states have transmitted dual slates of electors to the President of the Senate."

The remaining question is who engaged in this conspiracy to make the false statement to Congress under section 1001. The evidence is clear that President Trump personally participated in a scheme to have the Trump electors meet, cast votes, and send their votes to the joint session of Congress in several States that Vice President Biden won, and then his supporters relied on the existence of these fake electors as part of their effort to obstruct the joint session. Republican National Committee (RNC) Chairwoman Ronna McDaniel testified before this Committee that President Trump and Eastman directly requested that the RNC organize the effort to have these fake (i.e., Trump) electors meet and cast their votes.[631] Thus, the Committee believes that sufficient evidence exists for a criminal referral of President Trump for illegally engaging in a conspiracy to violate section 1001; the evidence indicates that he entered into an agreement with Eastman and others to make the false statement (the fake electoral certificates), by deceitful or dishonest means, and at least one member of the conspiracy engaged in at least one overt act in furtherance of the conspiracy (e.g., President Trump and Eastman's call to Ronna McDaniel).

IV. "Incite," "Assist" or "Aid and Comfort" an Insurrection (18 U.S.C. § 2383)

Section 2383 of Title 18 of the United States Code applies to anyone who "incites, sets on foot, assists, or engages in any rebellion or insurrection against the authority of the United States or the laws thereof, or gives aid or comfort thereto."[632] The Committee recognizes that section 2383 does not require evidence of an "agreement" between President Trump and the violent rioters to establish a violation of that provision; instead, the President need only have incited, assisted, or aided and comforted those engaged in violence or other lawless activity in an effort to prevent the peaceful transition of the Presidency under our Constitution. A Federal court has already concluded that President Trump's statements during his Ellipse speech were "plausibly words of incitement not protected by the First Amendment."[633] Moreover, President Trump was impeached for "Incitement of Insurrection," and a majority of the Senate voted to convict, with many more suggesting they might have voted to convict had President Trump still been in office at the time.[634]

As explained throughout this Report and in this Committee's hearings, President Trump was directly responsible for summoning what became a violent mob to Washington, DC, urging them to march to the Capitol, and then further provoking the already violent and lawless crowd with his 2:24 p.m. tweet about the Vice President. Even though President Trump had repeatedly been told that Vice President Pence had no legal authority to stop the certification of the election, he asserted in his speech on January 6th that if the Vice President "comes through for us" that he could deliver victory to Trump: "[I]f Mike Pence does the right thing, we win the election." This created a desperate and false expectation in President Trump's mob that ended up putting the Vice President and his entourage and many others at the Capitol in physical danger. When President Trump tweeted at 2:24 p.m., he knew violence was underway. His tweet exacerbated that violence.[635]

During the ensuing riot, the President refused to condemn the violence or encourage the crowd to disperse despite repeated pleas from his staff and family that he do so. The Committee has evidence from multiple sources establishing these facts, including testimony from former White House Counsel Pat Cipollone. Although Cipollone's testimony did not disclose a number of direct communications with President Trump in light of concerns about executive privilege, the Department now appears to have obtained a ruling that Cipollone can testify before a grand jury about these communications. Based on the information it has obtained, the Committee believes that Cipollone and others can provide direct testimony establishing that President Trump refused repeatedly, for multiple hours, to make a public statement directing his violent and lawless supporters to leave the Capitol. President Trump did not want his supporters (who had effectively halted the vote counting) to disperse. Evidence obtained by the Committee also indicates that President Trump did not want to provide security assistance to the Capitol during that violent period.[636] This appalling behavior by our Commander in Chief occurred despite his affirmative constitutional duty to act to ensure that the laws are faithfully executed.[637]

The Committee believes that sufficient evidence exists for a criminal referral of President Trump for "assist[ing]" or "ai[ding] and comfort-[ing]" those at the Capitol who engaged in a violent attack on the United States. The Committee has developed significant evidence that President Trump intended to disrupt the peaceful transition of power and believes that the Department of Justice can likely elicit testimony relevant to an investigation under section 2383.

For example, Chief of Staff Mark Meadows told White House Counsel Pat Cipollone that the President "doesn't want to do anything" to stop the violence.[638] Worse, at 2:24 p.m., the President inflamed and exacerbated the mob violence by sending a tweet stating that the Vice President "didn't have the courage to do what should have been done."[639] The President threw gasoline on the fire despite knowing that there was a violent riot underway at the Capitol. Indeed, video and audio footage from the attack shows that many of the rioters specifically mentioned Vice President

Pence.[640] And immediately after President Trump sent his tweet, the violence escalated. Between 2:25 p.m. and 2:28 p.m., rioters breached the East Rotunda doors, other rioters breached the police line in the Capitol Crypt, Vice President Pence had to be evacuated from his Senate office, and Leader McCarthy was evacuated from his Capitol office.[641]

Evidence developed in the Committee's investigation showed that the President, when told that the crowd was chanting "Hang Mike Pence," responded that perhaps the Vice President deserved to be hanged.[642] And President Trump rebuffed pleas from Leader McCarthy to ask that his supporters leave the Capitol stating, "Well, Kevin, I guess these people are more upset about the election than you are." After hours of deadly riot, President Trump eventually released a videotaped statement encouraging the crowd to disperse, though openly professing his "love" for the members of the mob and empathizing with their frustration at the "stolen" election. President Trump has since expressed a desire to pardon those involved in the attack.[643]

Both the purpose and the effect of the President's actions were to mobilize a large crowd to descend on the Capitol. Several defendants in pending criminal cases identified the President's allegations about the "stolen election" as the key motivation for their activities at the Capitol. Many of them specifically cited the President's tweets asking his supporters to come to Washington, DC, on January 6th. For example, one defendant who later pleaded guilty to threatening House Speaker Nancy Pelosi texted a family member on January 6th to say: "[Trump] wants heads and I'm going to deliver."[644] Another defendant released a statement through his attorney stating: "I was in Washington, DC on January 6, 2021, because I believed I was following the instructions of former President Trump and he was my President and the commander-in-chief. His statements also had me believing the election was stolen from him."[645]

As the violence began to subside and law enforcement continued to secure the Capitol, President Trump tweeted again, at 6:01 pm to justify the actions of the rioters: "These are the things and events that happen," he wrote, when his so-called victory was "so unceremoniously & viciously stripped away. . . ."[646] When he wrote those words, he knew exactly what he was doing. Before President Trump issued the tweet, a White House staffer cautioned him that the statement would imply that he "had something to do with the events that happened at the Capitol"—but he tweeted it anyway.[647] The final words of that tweet leave little doubt about President Trump's sentiments toward those who invaded the Capitol: "Remember this day forever!"[648]

V. Other Conspiracy Statutes (18 U.S.C. §§ 372 and 2384)

Depending on evidence developed by the Department of Justice, the President's actions with the knowledge of the risk of violence could also constitute a violation of 18 U.S.C. § 372 and § 2384, both of which require proof of a conspiracy. Section 372 prohibits a conspiracy between two or more persons "to prevent, by force, intimidation, or threat, any person from accepting or holding any office, trust, or place of confidence under the United States, or from discharging any duties thereof, or to induce by like means any officer of the United States to leave the place, where his duties as an officer are required to be performed, or to injure him in the discharge of his official duties." [649] Oath Keepers Kelly Meggs, Kenneth Harrelson, and Jessica Watkins were convicted of violating 18 U.S.C. § 372 in connection with the January 6th attack on the Capitol. [650] The Committee believes that former Chief of Staff Mark Meadows (who refused to testify and was held in contempt of Congress) could have specific evidence relevant to such charges, as may witnesses who invoked their Fifth Amendment rights against self-incrimination before this Committee.

Section 2384, the seditious conspiracy statute, prohibits "conspir[acy] to overthrow, put down, or to destroy by force the Government of the United States . . . or to oppose by force the authority thereof, or by force to prevent, hinder or delay the execution of any law of the United States . . . ." [651] A jury has already determined beyond a reasonable doubt that a conspiracy existed under section 2384, as the leader of the Oath Keepers and at least one other individual were convicted of seditious conspiracy under section 2384 for their actions related to the attack on the Capitol. [652] A trial regarding a series of other "Proud Boy" defendants may also address similar issues. [653]

The Department of Justice, through its investigative tools that exceed those of this Committee, may have evidence sufficient to prosecute President Trump under sections 372 and 2384. Accordingly, we believe sufficient evidence exists for a criminal referral of President Trump under these two statutes.

VI. The Committee's Concerns Regarding Possible Obstruction of its Investigation

The Committee has substantial concerns regarding potential efforts to obstruct its investigation, including by certain counsel (some paid by groups connected to the former President) who may have advised clients to provide false or misleading testimony to the Committee. [654] Such actions could violate 18 U.S.C. §§ 1505, 1512. The Committee is aware that both the U.S. Department of Justice and the Fulton County District Attorney's Office have already obtained information relevant to these matters, including from the Committee directly. We urge the Department of Justice to examine the facts to discern whether prosecution is warranted. The Committee's broad concerns regarding obstruction and witness credibility are addressed in the Executive Summary to this Report.

VII. ACCOUNTABILITY FOR THOSE WHO PLOTTED UNLAWFULLY TO OVERTURN THE ELECTION IS CRITICAL.

To date, the Justice Department has pursued prosecution of hundreds of individuals who planned and participated in the January 6th invasion of and attack on our Capitol. But the Department has not yet charged individuals who engaged in the broader plan to overturn the election through the means discussed in this Report. The Committee has concluded that it is critical to hold those individuals accountable as well, including those who worked with President Trump to create and effectuate these plans.

In his speech from the Ellipse on January 6th, President Trump recited a host of election fraud allegations he knew to be false, and then told tens of thousands of his angry supporters this:

> And fraud breaks up everything, doesn't it? When you catch some- body in a fraud, you're allowed to go by very different rules. So I hope Mike has the courage to do what he has to do. And I hope he doesn't listen to the RINOs and the stupid people that he's listening to. [655]

The meaning of President Trump's comments was sufficiently clear then, but he recently gave America an even more detailed understanding of his state of mind. Trump wrote that allegations of "massive fraud" related to the 2020 election "allow[] for the termination of all rules, regulations and articles, even those found in the Constitution." [656] And President Trump considered pardoning those involved in the attack and has since expressed a desire to pardon them—and even give them an apology—if he returns to the Oval Office.[657]

In the Committee's judgment, based on all the evidence developed, President Trump believed then, and continues to believe now, that he is above the law, not bound by our Constitution and its explicit checks on Presidential authority. This recent Trump statement only heightens our concern about accountability. If President Trump and the associates who assisted him in an effort to overturn the lawful outcome of the 2020 elec- tion are not ultimately held accountable under the law, their behavior may become a precedent, and invitation to danger, for future elections. A failure to hold them accountable now may ultimately lead to future unlawful efforts to overturn our elections, thereby threatening the security and viability of our Republic.

VIII. REFERRAL OF MEMBERS TO THE HOUSE ETHICS COMMITTEE FOR FAILURE TO COMPLY WITH SUBPOENAS

During the course of the Select Committee's investigation of President Trump's efforts to subvert the election, the Committee learned that various Members of Congress had information relevant to the investigation. Accordingly, the Committee wrote letters to a number of Members involved in that activity inviting them to participate voluntarily in the Select Committee's investigation. None of the members was willing to provide information, which forced the Select Committee to consider alternative means of securing evidence about the conduct of these Members and the information they might have. On May 12, 2022, the Select Committee subpoenaed several members of Congress—including House Minority Leader Kevin McCarthy, Representative Jim Jordan, Representative Scott Perry, and Representative Andy Biggs—to obtain information related to the Committee's investigation.

This was a significant step, but it was one that was warranted by the certain volume of information these Members possessed that was relevant to the Select Committee's investigation, as well as the centrality of their efforts to President Trump's multi-part plan to remain in power.

Representative McCarthy, among other things, had multiple communications with President Trump, Vice President Pence, and others on and related to January 6th. For example, during the attack on the Capitol, Representative McCarthy urgently requested that the former President issue a statement calling off the rioters, to which President Trump responded by "push[ing] back" and said: "Well, Kevin, I guess these people are more upset about the election than you are." [658] And, after the attack, Representative McCarthy spoke on the House floor and said that, "[t]here is absolutely no evidence" that Antifa caused the attack on the Capitol and instead called on President Trump to "accept his share of responsibility" for the violence. [659] As noted above, Representative McCarthy privately confided in colleagues that President Trump accepted some responsibility for the attack on the Capitol. [660]

Representative Jordan was a significant player in President Trump's efforts. He participated in numerous post-election meetings in which senior White House officials, Rudolph Giuliani, and others, discussed strategies for challenging the election, chief among them claims that the election had been tainted by fraud. On January 2, 2021, Representative Jordan led a conference call in which he, President Trump, and other Members of Congress discussed strategies for delaying the January 6th joint session. During that call, the group also discussed issuing social media posts encouraging President Trump's supporters to "march to the Capitol" on the 6th. [661] An hour and a half later, President Trump and Representative

Jordan spoke by phone for 18 minutes.[662] The day before January 6th, Representative Jordan texted Mark Meadows, passing along advice that Vice President Pence should "call out all the electoral votes that he believes are unconstitutional as no electoral votes at all." [663] He spoke with President Trump by phone at least twice on January 6th, though he has provided inconsistent public statements about how many times they spoke and what they discussed.[664] He also received five calls from Rudolph Giuliani that evening, and the two connected at least twice, at 7:33 p.m. and 7:49 p.m.[665] During that time, Giuliani has testified, he was attempting to reach Members of Congress after the joint session resumed to encourage them to continue objecting to Joe Biden's electoral votes.[666] And, in the days following January 6th, Representative Jordan spoke with White House staff about the prospect of Presidential pardons for Members of Congress.[667]

Like Representative Jordan, Representative Perry was also involved in early post-election messaging strategy. Both Representative Jordan and Representative Perry were involved in discussions with White House officials about Vice President Pence's role on January 6th as early as November 2020.[668] Representative Perry was present for conversations in which the White House Counsel's Office informed him and others that President Trump's efforts to submit fake electoral votes were not legally sound.[669] But perhaps most pivotally, he was involved in President Trump's efforts to install Jeffrey Clark as the Acting Attorney General in December 2020 and January 2021. Beginning in early December 2020, Representative Perry suggested Clark as a candidate to Mark Meadows,[670] then introduced Clark to President Trump.[671] In the days before January 6th, Representative Perry advocated for President Trump to speak at the Capitol during the joint session, speaking to Mark Meadows on at least one occasion about it.[672] He was also a participant in the January 2, 2021, call in which Representative Jordan, President Trump, and others discussed issuing social media posts to encourage Trump supporters to march to the Capitol on January 6th.[673] After January 6th, Representative Perry reached out to White House staff asking to receive a Presidential pardon.[674]

Representative Biggs was involved in numerous elements of President Trump's efforts to contest the election results. As early as November 6, 2020, Representative Biggs texted Mark Meadows, urging him to "encourage the state legislatures to appoint [electors]." [675] In the following days, Representative Biggs told Meadows not to let President Trump concede his loss.[676] Between then and January 6th, Representative Biggs coordinated with Arizona State Representative Mark Finchem to gather signatures from Arizona lawmakers endorsing fake Trump electors.[677] He also contacted fake Trump electors in at least one State seeking evidence related to voter fraud.[678]

To date, none of the subpoenaed Members has complied with either voluntary or compulsory requests for participation.

Representative McCarthy initially responded to the Select Committee's subpoena in two letters on May 27 and May 30, 2022, in which he objected to the Select Committee's composition and validity of the subpoena and offered to submit written interrogatories in lieu of deposition testimony. Although the Select Committee did not release Representative McCarthy from his subpoena obligations, Representative McCarthy failed to appear for his scheduled deposition on May 31, 2022. The Select Committee responded to Representative McCarthy's letters this same day, rejecting his proposal to participate via written interrogatories and compelling his appearance for deposition testimony no later than June 11, 2022. Although Representative McCarthy again responded via letter on June 9, 2022, he did not appear for deposition testimony on or before the specified June 11, 2022, deadline.

Representative Jordan also responded to the Select Committee's subpoena just before his scheduled deposition in a letter on May 25, 2022, containing a variety of objections. Representative Jordan also requested material from the Select Committee, including all materials referencing him in the Select Committee's possession and all internal legal analysis related to the constitutionality of Member subpoenas. Although the Select Committee did not release Representative Jordan from his subpoena obligations, Representative Jordan failed to appear for his scheduled deposition on May 27, 2022. On May 31, 2022, the Select Committee responded to the substance of Representative Jordan's May 25th letter and indicated that Representative Jordan should appear for deposition testimony no later than June 11, 2022. On June 9, 2022, Representative Jordan again wrote to reiterate the points from his May 25th letter. That same day, Representative Jordan sent out a fundraising email with the subject line: "I'VE BEEN SUBPOENED." [679] Representative Jordan did not appear before the Select Committee on or before the June 11, 2022, deadline.

Representative Perry likewise responded to the Select Committee's subpoena on May 24, 2022, in a letter, "declin[ing] to appear for deposition" and requesting that the subpoena be "immediately withdrawn." [680] Although the Select Committee did not release Representative Perry from his subpoena obligations, Representative Perry failed to appear on May 26, 2022, for his scheduled deposition. Representative Perry sent a second letter to the Select Committee on May 31, 2022, with additional objections. That same day, the Select Committee responded to Representative Perry's letters and stated that he should appear before the Select Committee no later than June 11, 2022, for deposition testimony. Representative Perry responded via letter on June 10, 2022, maintaining his objections. He did not appear before the June 11, 2022, deadline.

Representative Biggs issued a press release on the day the Select Committee issued its subpoena, calling the subpoena "illegitimate" and "pure political theater." The day before his scheduled deposition, Representative Biggs sent a letter to the Select Committee with a series of objections and an invocation of Speech or Debate immunity. Although the Select Committee did not release Representative Biggs from his subpoena obligations, Representative Biggs did not appear for his scheduled deposition on May 26, 2022. On May 31, 2022, the Select Committee responded to the substance of Representative Biggs' May 25th letter and indicated that Representative Biggs should appear for deposition testimony no later than June 11, 2022. Although Representative Biggs responded with another letter on June 9th, he did not appear before the June 11, 2022, deadline.

Despite the Select Committee's repeated attempts to obtain information from these Members and the issuance of subpoenas, each has refused to cooperate and failed to comply with a lawfully issued subpoena. Accordingly, the Select Committee is referring their failure to comply with the subpoenas issued to them to the Ethics Committee for further action. To be clear, this referral is only for failure to comply with lawfully issued subpoenas.

The Rules of the House of Representatives make clear that their willful noncompliance violates multiple standards of conduct and subjects them to discipline. Willful non-compliance with compulsory congressional committee subpoenas by House Members violates the spirit and letter of House rule XXIII, clause 1, which requires House Members to conduct themselves "at all times in a manner that shall reflect creditably on the House." As a previous version of the House Ethics Manual explained, this catchall provision encompasses "'flagrant' violations of the law that reflect on 'Congress as a whole,' and that might otherwise go unpunished."[681] The subpoenaed House Members' refusal to comply with their subpoena obligations satisfies these criteria. A House Member's willful failure to comply with a congressional subpoena also reflects discredit on Congress. If left unpunished, such behavior undermines Congress's longstanding power to investigate in support of its lawmaking authority and suggests that Members of Congress may disregard legal obligations that apply to ordinary citizens.

For these reasons, the Select Committee refers Leader McCarthy and Representatives Jordan, Perry, and Biggs for sanction by the House Ethics Committee for failure to comply with subpoenas. The Committee also believes that each of these individuals, along with other Members who attended the December 21st planning meeting with President Trump at the

White House,[682] should be questioned in a public forum about their advance knowledge of and role in President Trump's plan to prevent the peaceful transition of power.

EFFORTS TO AVOID TESTIFYING, EVIDENCE OF OBSTRUCTION, AND ASSESSMENTS OF WITNESS CREDIBILITY

More than 30 witnesses before the Select Committee exercised their Fifth Amendment privilege against self-incrimination and refused on that basis to provide testimony. They included individuals central to the investigation, such as John Eastman, Jeffrey Clark, Roger Stone, Michael Flynn, Kenneth Chesebro, and others.[683] The law allows a civil litigant to rely upon an "adverse inference" when a witness invokes the Fifth Amendment. "[T]he Fifth Amendment does not forbid adverse inferences against parties to civil actions . . .."[684] The Committee has not chosen to rely on any such inference in this Report or in its hearings.

We do note that certain witness assertions of the Fifth Amendment were particularly troubling, including this:

> Vice Chair Cheney: General Flynn, do you believe the violence on January 6th was justified?
>
> Counsel for the Witness: Can I get clarification, is that a moral question or are you asking a legal question?
>
> Vice Chair Cheney: I'm asking both.
>
> General Flynn: The Fifth.
>
> Vice Chair Cheney: Do you believe the violence on January 6th was justified morally?
>
> General Flynn: Take the Fifth.
>
> Vice Chair Cheney: Do you believe the violence on January 6th was justified legally?
>
> General Flynn: Fifth.
>
> Vice Chair Cheney: General Flynn, do you believe in the peaceful transition of power in the United States of America?
>
> General Flynn: The Fifth.[685]

President Trump refused to comply with the Committee's subpoena, and also filed suit to block the National Archives from supplying the Committee with White House records. The Committee litigated the National Archives case in Federal District Court, in the Federal Appellate Court for the District of Columbia, and before the Supreme Court. The Select Committee was successful in this litigation. The opinion of the D.C. Circuit explained:

> On January 6, 2021, a mob professing support for then-President Trump violently attacked the United States Capitol in an effort to prevent a Joint Session of Congress from certifying the electoral college votes designating Joseph R. Biden the 46th President of the United States. The rampage left multiple people dead, injured more than 140 people, and inflicted millions of dollars in damage to the Capitol. Then-Vice President Pence, Senators, and Representatives were all forced to halt their constitutional duties and flee the House and Senate chambers for safety.[686]

> Benjamin Franklin said, at the founding, that we have "[a] Republic"—"if [we] can keep it." The events of January 6th exposed the fragility of those democratic institutions and traditions that we had perhaps come to take for granted. In response, the President of the United States and Congress have each made the judgment that access to this subset of presidential communication records is necessary to address a matter of great constitutional moment for the Republic. Former President Trump has given this court no legal reason to cast aside President Biden's assessment of the Executive Branch interests at stake, or to create a separation of powers conflict that the Political Branches have avoided.[687]

Several other witnesses have also avoided testifying in whole or in part by asserting Executive Privilege or Absolute Immunity from any obligation to appear before Congress. For example, the President's Chief of Staff Mark Meadows invoked both, and categorically refused to testify, even about text messages he provided to the Committee. The House of Representatives voted to hold him in criminal contempt.[688] Although the Justice Department has taken the position in litigation that a former high level White House staffer for a former President is not entitled to absolute immunity,[689] and that any interests in the confidentiality of his communications with President Trump and others are overcome in this case, the Justice Department declined to prosecute Meadows for criminal contempt. The reasons for Justice's refusal to do so are not apparent to the Committee.[690] Commentators have speculated that Meadows may be cooperating in the Justice Department's January 6th investigation.[691] The same may be true for Daniel Scavino, President Trump's White House Deputy Chief of Staff for Communications and Director of Social Media, whom the House also voted to hold in contempt.[692]

Steve Bannon also chose not to cooperate with the Committee, and the Justice Department prosecuted him for contempt of Congress.[693] Bannon has been sentenced and is currently appealing his conviction. Peter Navarro, another White House Staffer who refused to testify, is currently awaiting his criminal trial.[694]

Although the Committee issued letters and subpoenas to seven Republican members of Congress who have unique knowledge of certain developments on or in relation to January 6th, none agreed to participate in the investigation; none considered themselves obligated to comply with the subpoenas. A number of these same individuals were aware well in advance of January 6th of the plotting by Donald Trump, John Eastman, and others to overturn the election, and certain of them had an active role in that activity.[695] None seem to have alerted law enforcement of this activity, or of the known risk of violence. On January 5th, after promoting unfounded objections to election results, Rep. Debbie Lesko appears to have recognized the danger in a call with her colleagues:

> I also ask leadership to come up with a safety plan for Members [of Congress]. . . . We also have, quite honestly, Trump supporters who actually believe that we are going to overturn the election, and when that doesn't happen—most likely will not happen—they are going to go nuts.[696]

During our hearings, the Committee presented the testimony of numerous White House witnesses who testified about efforts by certain Republican Members of Congress to obtain Presidential pardons for their conduct in connection with January 6th.[697] Cassidy Hutchinson provided extensive detail in this regard:

> Vice Chair Cheney: And are you aware of any members of Congress seeking pardons?
>
> Hutchinson: I guess Mr. Gaetz and Mr. Brooks, I know, have both advocated for there'd be a blanket pardon for members involved in that meeting, and a — a handful of other members that weren't at the December 21st meeting as the presumptive pardons. Mr. Gaetz was personally pushing for a pardon, and he was doing so since early December.
>
> I'm not sure why Mr. Gaetz would reach out to me to ask if he could have a meeting with Mr. Meadows about receiving a presidential pardon.
>
> Vice Chair Cheney: Did they all contact you?
>
> Hutchinson: Not all of them, but several of them did.

Vice Chair Cheney: So, you mentioned Mr. Gaetz, Mr. Brooks.

Hutchinson: Mr. Biggs did. Mr. Jordan talked about Congressional pardons, but he never asked me for one. It was more for an update on whether the White House was going to pardon members of Congress. Mr. Gohmert asked for one as well. Mr. Perry asked for a pardon, too. I'm sorry.

Vice Chair Cheney: Mr. Perry? Did he talk to you directly?

Hutchinson: Yes, he did.

Vice Chair Cheney: Did Marjorie Taylor Greene contact you?

Hutchinson: No, she didn't contact me about it. I heard that she had asked White House Counsel's Office for a pardon from Mr. Philbin, but I didn't frequently communicate with Ms. Greene.[698]

Many of these details were also corroborated by other sources. President Personnel Director Johnny McEntee confirmed that he was personally asked for a pardon by Representative Matt Gaetz (R-FL).[699] Eric Herschmann recalled that Representative Gaetz ". . . asked for a very, very broad pardon. . . . And I said Nixon's pardon was never nearly that broad." [700] When asked about reporting that Representatives Mo Brooks and Andy Biggs also requested pardons, Herschmann did not reject either possibility out of hand, instead answering: "It's possible that Representative Brooks or Biggs, but I don't remember." [701] The National Archives produced to the Select Committee an email from Representative Mo Brooks to the President's executive assistant stating that "President Trump asked me to send you this letter" and "... pursuant to a request from Matt Gaetz" that recommended blanket Presidential pardons to every Member of Congress who objected to the electoral college votes on January 6th.[702]

These requests for pardons suggest that the Members identified above were conscious of the potential legal jeopardy arising from their conduct. As noted *infra* 136, the Committee has referred a number of these individuals to the House Ethics Committee for their failure to comply with subpoenas, and believes that they each owe the American people their direct and unvarnished testimony.

The Select Committee has also received a range of evidence suggesting specific efforts to obstruct the Committee's investigation. Much of this evidence is already known by the Department of Justice and by other prosecutorial authorities. For example:

1. The Committee received testimony from a witness about her decision to terminate a lawyer who was receiving payments for the representation from a group allied with President Trump. Among other concerns expressed by the witness:

- The lawyer had advised the witness that the witness could, in certain circumstances, tell the Committee that she did not recall facts when she actually did recall them.
- During a break in the Select Committee's interview, the witness expressed concerns to her lawyer that an aspect of her testimony was not truthful. The lawyer did not advise her to clarify the specific testimony that the witness believed was not complete and accurate, and instead conveyed that, "They don't know what you know, [witness]. They don't know that you can recall some of these things. So you saying 'I don't recall' is an entirely acceptable response to this."
- The lawyer instructed the client about a particular issue that would cast a bad light on President Trump: "No, no, no, no, no. We don't want to go there. We don't want to talk about that."
- The lawyer refused directions from the client not to share her testimony before the Committee with other lawyers representing other witnesses. The lawyer shared such information over the client's objection.
- The lawyer refused directions from the client not to share information regarding her testimony with at least one and possibly more than one member of the press. The lawyer shared the information with the press over her objection.
- The lawyer did not disclose who was paying for the lawyers' representation of the client, despite questions from the client seeking that information, and told her, "we're not telling people where funding is coming from right now."
- The client was offered potential employment that would make her "financially very comfortable" as the date of her testimony approached by entities apparently linked to Donald Trump and his associates. Such offers were withdrawn or did not materialize as reports of the content of her testimony circulated. The client believed this was an effort to impact her testimony.

Further details regarding these instances will be available to the public when transcripts are released.

2. Similarly, the witness testified that multiple persons affiliated with President Trump contacted her in advance of the witness's testimony and made the following statements:

What they said to me is, as long as I continue to be a team player, they know that I am on the right team. I am doing the right thing. I am protecting who I need to protect. You know, I will continue to stay in good graces in Trump World. And they have reminded me a couple of times that Trump does read transcripts and just keep that in mind as I proceed through my interviews with the committee.

Here is another sample in a different context. This is a call received by one of our witnesses:

[A person] let me know you have your deposition tomorrow. He wants me to let you know he's thinking about you. He knows you're a team player, you're loyal, and you're going do the right thing when you go in for your deposition.[703]

3. The Select Committee is aware of multiple efforts by President Trump to contact Select Committee witnesses. The Department of Justice is aware of at least one of those circumstances.

4. Rather than relying on representation by Secret Service lawyers at no cost, a small number of Secret Service agents engaged private counsel for their interviews before the Committee. [704] During one such witness's transcribed interview, a retained private counsel was observed writing notes to the witness regarding the content of the witness's testimony while the questioning was underway. The witness's counsel admitted on the record that he had done so.[705]

Recently, published accounts of the Justice Department's Mar-a-Lago investigation suggest that the Department is investigating the conduct of counsel for certain witnesses whose fees are being paid by President Trump's Save America Political Action Committee.[706] The public report implies the Department is concerned that such individuals are seeking to influence the testimony of the witnesses they represent.[707] This Committee also has these concerns, including that lawyers who are receiving such payments have specific incentives to defend President Trump rather than zealously represent their own clients. The Department of Justice and the Fulton County District Attorney have been provided with certain information related to this topic.

The Select Committee recognizes of course that most of the testimony we have gathered was given more than a year after January 6th. Recollections are not perfect, and the Committee expects that different accounts of the same events will naturally vary. Indeed, the lack of any inconsistencies in witness accounts would itself be suspicious. And many witnesses may simply recall different things than others.

Many of the witnesses before this Committee had nothing at all to gain from their testimony, gave straightforward responses to the questions posted, and made no effort to downplay, deflect, or rationalize. Trump Administration Justice Department officials such as Attorney General Barr,

Acting Attorney General Rosen, and Acting Deputy Attorney General Dono-
ghue are good examples. Multiple members of President Trump's White
House staff were also suitably forthcoming, including Sarah Matthews,
Matthew Pottinger, Greg Jacob, and Pat Philbin, as were multiple career
White House, military and agency personnel whose names the Committee
agreed not to disclose publicly; as were former Secretary of Labor Eugene
Scalia, Bill Stepien, and certain other members of the Trump Campaign.
The Committee very much appreciates the earnestness and bravery of
Cassidy Hutchinson, Rusty Bowers, Shaye Moss, Ruby Freeman, Brad
Raffensperger, Gabriel Sterling, Al Schmidt, and many others who provided
important live testimony during the Committees hearings.[708]

The Committee, along with our nation, offers particular thanks to Officers Caroline Edwards, Michael Fanone, Harry Dunn, Aquilino Gonell, and
Daniel Hodges, along with hundreds of other members of law enforcement
who defended the Capitol on that fateful day, all of whom should be commended for their bravery and sacrifice. We especially thank the families of
Officer Brian Sicknick, Howard Liebengood and Jeffrey Smith, whose loss
can never be repaid.

The Committee very much appreciates the invaluable testimony of General Milley and other members of our military, Judge J. Michael Luttig, and
the important contributions of Benjamin Ginsberg and Chris Stirewalt.
This, of course is only a partial list, and the Committee is indebted to many
others, as well.

The Committee believes that White House Counsel Pat Cipollone gave a
particularly important account of the events of January 6th, as did White
House lawyer, Eric Herschmann. For multiple months, Cipollone resisted
giving any testimony at all, asserting concerns about executive privilege
and other issues, until after the Committee's hearing with Hutchinson.
When he did testify, Cipollone corroborated key elements of testimony
given by several White House staff, including Hutchinson—most importantly, regarding what happened in the White House during the violence of
January 6th—but also frankly recognized the limits on what he could say
due to privilege: "Again, I'm not going to get into either my legal advice on
matters, and the other thing I don't want to do is, again, other witnesses
have their own recollections of things." Cipollone also told the Committee
that, to the extent that other witnesses recall communications attributable
to White House counsel that he does not, the communications might have
been with his deputy Pat Philbin, or with Eric Herschmann, who had strong
feelings and was particularly animated about certain issues.[709]

Of course, that is not to say that all witnesses were entirely frank or
forthcoming. Other witnesses, including certain witnesses from the Trump
White House, displayed a lack of full recollection of certain issues, or were

not otherwise as frank or direct as Cipollone. We cite two examples here, both relating to testimony played during the hearings.

Kayleigh McEnany was President Trump's Press Secretary on January 6th. Her deposition was taken early in the investigation. McEnany seemed to acknowledge that President Trump: (1) should have instructed his violent supporters to leave the Capitol earlier than he ultimately did on January 6th;[710] (2) should have respected the rulings of the courts;[711] and (3) was wrong to publicly allege that Dominion voting machines stole the election.[712] But a segment of McEnany's testimony seemed evasive, as if she was testifying from pre-prepared talking points. In multiple instances, McEnany's testimony did not seem nearly as forthright as that of her press office staff, who testified about what McEnany said.

For example, McEnany disputed suggestions that President Trump was resistant to condemning the violence and urging the crowd at the Capitol to act peacefully when they crafted his tweet at 2:38 p.m. on January 6th.[713] Yet one of her deputies, Sarah Matthews, told the Select Committee that McEnany informed her otherwise: that McEnany and other advisors in the dining room with President Trump persuaded him to send the tweet, but that ". . . she said that he did not want to put that in and that they went through different phrasing of that, of the mention of peace, in order to get him to agree to include it, and that it was Ivanka Trump who came up with 'stay peaceful' and that he agreed to that phrasing to include in the tweet, but he was initially resistant to mentioning peace of any sort." [714] When the Select Committee asked "Did Ms. McEnany describe in any way how resistant the President was to including something about being peaceful," Matthews answered: "Just that he didn't want to include it, but they got him to agree on the phrasing 'stay peaceful.'" [715]

The Committee invites the public to compare McEnany's testimony with the testimony of Pat Cipollone, Sarah Matthews, Judd Deere, and others.

Ivanka Trump is another example. Among other things, Ivanka Trump acknowledged to the Committee that: (1) she agreed with Attorney General Barr's statements that there was no evidence of sufficient fraud to overturn the election; (2) the President and others are bound by the rulings of the courts and the rule of law; (3) President Trump pressured Vice President Pence on the morning of January 6th regarding his authorities at the joint session of Congress that day to count electoral votes; and (4) President Trump watched the violence on television as it was occurring.[716] But again, Ivanka Trump was not as forthcoming as Cipollone and others about President Trump's conduct.

Indeed, Ivanka Trump's Chief of Staff Julie Radford had a more specific recollection of Ivanka Trump's actions and statements. For example, Ivanka

Trump had the following exchange with the Committee about her attendance at her father's speech on January 6th that was at odds with what the
Committee learned from Radford:

> Committee Staff: It's been reported that you ultimately decided to
> attend the rally because you hoped that you would calm the Presi-
> dent and keep the event on an even keel. Is that accurate?
>
> Ivanka Trump: No. I don't know who said that or where that came
> from.[717]

However, this is what Radford said about her boss's decision:

> Committee Staff: What did she share with you about why it was
> concerning that her father was upset or agitated after that call with
> Vice President Pence in relation to the Ellipse rally? Why did that
> matter? Why did he have to be calmed down, I should say.
>
> Radford: Well, she shared that he had called the Vice President a
> not—an expletive word. I think that bothered her. And I think she
> could tell based on the conversations and what was going on in the
> office that he was angry and upset and people were providing mis-
> information. And she felt like she might be able to help calm the
> situation down, at least before he went on stage.
>
> Committee Staff: And the word that she relayed to you that the
> President called the Vice President—apologize for being impolite—
> but do you remember what she said her father called him?
>
> Radford: The "P" word.[718]

When the Committee asked Ivanka Trump whether there were "[a]ny
particular words that you recall your father using during the conversation"
that morning with Vice President Pence, she answered simply: "No." [719]

In several circumstances, the Committee has found that less senior
White House aides had significantly better recollection of events than
senior staff purported to have.

The Select Committee also has concerns regarding certain other witnesses, including those who still rely for their income or employment on
organizations linked to President Trump, such as the America First Policy
Institute. Certain witnesses and lawyers were unnecessarily combative,
answered hundreds of questions with variants of "I do not recall" in circumstances where that answer seemed unbelievable, appeared to testify
from lawyer-written talking points rather than their own recollections,
provided highly questionable rationalizations or otherwise resisted telling
the truth. The public can ultimately make its own assessment of these

issues when it reviews the Committee transcripts and can compare the accounts of different witnesses and the conduct of counsel.

One particular concern arose from what the Committee realized early on were a number of intentional falsehoods in former White House Chief of Staff Mark Meadows's December 7, 2021 book, *The Chief's Chief.* [720] Here is one of several examples: Meadows wrote, "When he got offstage, President Trump let me know that he had been speaking metaphorically about going to the Capitol." [721] Meadows goes on in his book to claim that it "was clear the whole time" President Trump didn't intend to go to the Capitol. [722] This appeared to be an intentional effort to conceal the facts. Multiple witnesses directly contradicted Meadows's account about President Trump's desire to travel to the Capitol, including Kayleigh McEnany, Cassidy Hutchinson, multiple Secret Service agents, a White House employee with national security responsibilities and other staff in the White House, a member of the Metropolitan Police and others. This and several other statements in the Meadows book were false, and the Select Committee was concerned that multiple witnesses might attempt to repeat elements of these false accounts, as if they were the party line. Most witnesses did not, but a few did.

President Trump's desire to travel to the Capitol was particularly important for the Committee to evaluate because it bears on President Trump's intent on January 6th. One witness account suggests that President Trump even wished to participate in the electoral vote count from the House floor, standing with Republican Congressmen, perhaps in an effort to apply further pressure to Vice President Mike Pence and others. [723]

Mark Meadows's former Deputy Chief of Staff for Operations Anthony Ornato gave testimony consistent with the false account in Meadows book. In particular, Ornato told the Committee that he was not aware of a genuine push by the President to go to the Capitol, suggesting instead that "it was one of those hypotheticals from the good idea fairy . . . [b]ecause it's ridiculous to think that a President of the United States can travel especially with, you know, people around just on the street up to the Capitol and peacefully protest outside the Capitol. . . ." [724] He told the Select Committee that the only conversation he had about the possibility of the President traveling to the Capitol was in a single meeting officials from the President's advance team, [725] and his understanding is that this idea "wasn't from the President." [726] Two witnesses before the Committee, including a White House employee with national security responsibilities and Hutchinson, testified that Ornato related an account of President Trump's "irate" behavior when he was told in the Presidential SUV on January 6th that he would not be driven to the Capitol. [727] Both accounts recall Ornato doing so from his office in the White House, with another member of the Secret Service pres-ent.[728] Multiple other witness accounts indicate that the President genu-inely was "irate," "heated," "angry," and "insistent" in the Presidential vehicle.[729] But Ornato professed that he did not recall either communica-tion, and that he had no knowledge at all about the President's anger.[730]

Likewise, despite a significant and increasing volume of intelligence information in the days before January 6th showing that violence at the Capitol was indeed possible or likely, and despite other intelligence and law enforcement agencies similar conclusions,[731] Ornato claimed never to have reviewed or had any knowledge of that specific information[732] He testified that he was only aware of warnings that opposing groups might "clash on the Washington Monument" and that is what he "would have briefed to [Chief of Staff] Meadows."[733] The Committee has significant concerns about the credibility of this testimony, including because it was Ornato's responsibility to be aware of this information and convey it to decision-makers.[734] The Committee will release Ornato's November Transcript so the public can review his testimony on these topics.

SUMMARY: CREATION OF THE SELECT COMMITTEE; PURPOSES.

In the week after January 6th, House Republican Leader Kevin McCarthy initially supported legislation to create a bipartisan commission to investi-gate the January 6th attack on the United States Capitol, stating that "the President bears responsibility for Wednesday's attack on Congress by mob rioters" and calling for creation of a "fact-finding commission."[735] Leader McCarthy repeated his support for a bipartisan commission during a press conference on January 21st: "The only way you will be able to answer these questions is through a bipartisan commission."[736]

On February 15th, House Speaker Nancy Pelosi announced in a letter to the House Democratic Caucus her intent to establish the type of indepen-dent commission McCarthy had supported, to "investigate and report on the facts and causes relating to the January 6, 2021 domestic terrorist attack upon the United States Capitol Complex."[737] A few days thereafter, Leader McCarthy provided the Speaker a wish list that mirrored "suggestions from the Co-Chairs of the 9/11 Commission" that he and House Republicans hoped would be included in the House's legislation to establish the Com-mission.[738]

In particular, Leader McCarthy requested an equal ratio of Democratic and Republican nominations, equal subpoena power for the Democratic Chair and Republican Vice Chair of the Commission, and the exclusion of predetermined findings or outcomes that the Commission itself would pro-duce. Closing his letter, Leader McCarthy quoted the 9/11 Commission

Co-Chairs, writing that a "bipartisan independent investigation will earn credibility with the American public." [739] He again repeated his confidence in achieving that goal.[740] In April 2021, Speaker Pelosi agreed to make the number of Republican and Democratic Members of the Commission equal, and to provide both parties with an equal say in subpoenas, as McCarthy had requested.[741]

In May 2021, House Homeland Security Committee Chairman Bennie G. Thompson began to negotiate more of the details for the Commission with his Republican counterpart, Ranking Member John Katko.[742] On May 14th, Chairman Thompson announced that he and Ranking Member Katko had reached an agreement on legislation to "form a bipartisan, independent Commission to investigate the January 6th domestic terrorism attack on the United States Capitol and recommend changes to further protect the Capitol, the citadel of our democracy." [743]

On May 18th, the day before the House's consideration of the Thompson-Katko agreement, Leader McCarthy released a statement in opposition to the legislation.[744] Speaker Pelosi responded to that statement, saying: "Leader McCarthy won't take yes for an answer." [745] The Speaker referred to Leader McCarthy's February 22nd letter where "he made three requests to be addressed in Democrats' discussion draft." [746] She noted that "every single one was granted by Democrats, yet he still says no." [747]

In the days that followed, Republican Ranking Member Katko defended the bipartisan nature of the bill to create the Commission:

> As I have called for since the days just after the attack, an independent, 9/11-style review is critical for removing the politics around January 6 and focusing solely on the facts and circumstances of the security breach at the Capitol, as well as other instances of violence relevant to such a review. Make no mistake about it, Mr. Thompson and I know this is about facts. It's not partisan politics. We would have never gotten to this point if it was about partisan politics.[748]

That evening, the House passed the legislation to establish a National Commission to Investigate the January 6th Attack on the United States Capitol Complex in a bipartisan fashion, with 35 Republicans joining 217 Democrats voting in favor and 175 Republicans voting against.[749] In the days thereafter, however, only six Senate Republicans joined Senate Democrats in supporting the legislation, killing the bill in the Senate.[750]

On June 24th, Speaker Pelosi announced her intent to create a House select committee to investigate the attack.[751] On June 25th, Leader McCarthy met with DC Metropolitan Police Officer Michael Fanone, who was seriously injured on January 6th.[752] Officer Fanone pressed Leader McCarthy "for a commitment not to put obstructionists and the wrong people in that position."[753]

On June 30th, the House voted on H. Res. 503 to establish a 13-Member Select Committee to Investigate the January 6th Attack on the United States Capitol by a vote of 222 Yeas and 190 Nays with just two Republicans supporting the measure: Representative Liz Cheney and Representative Adam Kinzinger.[754] On July 1st, Speaker Pelosi named eight initial Members to the Select Committee, including one Republican: Representative Cheney.[755]

On July 17th, Leader McCarthy proposed his selection of five members:

Representative Jim Jordan, Ranking Member of the House Judiciary Committee;

Representative Kelly Armstrong of North Dakota; House Energy and Commerce Committee;

Representative Troy Nehls, House Transportation & Infrastructure and Veterans' Affairs Committees.

Representative Jim Banks, Armed Services, Veterans' Affairs and Education and Labor Committees;

Representative Rodney Davis, Ranking Member of the Committee on House Administration.[756]

Jordan was personally involved in the acts and circumstances of January 6th, and would be one of the targets of the investigation. By that point, Banks had made public statements indicating that he had already reached his own conclusions and had no intention of cooperating in any objective investigation of January 6th, proclaiming, for example, that the Select Committee was created ". . . solely to malign conservatives and to justify the Left's authoritarian agenda."[757]

On July 21st, Speaker Nancy Pelosi exercised her power under H. Res. 503 not to approve the appointments of Representatives Jordan or Banks, expressing "concern about statements made and actions taken by these Members" and "the impact their appointments may have on the integrity of the investigation."[758] However, she also stated that she had informed Leader McCarthy ". . . that I was prepared to appoint Representatives Rodney Davis, Kelly Armstrong and Troy Nehls, and requested that he recommend two other Members."[759]

In response, Leader McCarthy elected to remove all five of his Republican appointments, refusing to allow Representatives Armstrong, Davis and Nehls to participate on the Select Committee.[760] On July 26, 2021, Speaker Pelosi then appointed Republican Representative Adam Kinzinger.[761] In resisting the Committee's subpoenas, certain litigants attempted to argue that the Commission's Select Committee's composition violated House Rules or H. Res. 503, but those arguments failed in court.[762]

SELECT COMMITTEE WITNESSES WERE ALMOST ENTIRELY REPUBLICAN

In its ten hearings or business meetings, the Select Committee called live testimony or played video for several dozen witnesses, the vast majority of whom were Republicans. A full list is set forth below.

Republicans:

- **John McEntee** (served as Director of the White House Presidential Personnel Office in Trump Administration)
- **Judd Deere** (served as Deputy Assistant to the President and White House Deputy Press Secretary in the Trump Administration)
- **Jared Kushner** (served as a Senior Advisor to President Donald Trump)
- **Pat Cipollone** (served as White House Counsel for President Donald Trump)
- **Eric Herschmann** (served as a Senior Advisor to President Donald Trump)
- **Kayleigh McEnany** (served as White House Press Secretary in Trump Administration)
- **Derek Lyons** (served as White House Staff Secretary and Counselor to the President in the Trump Administration)
- **Cassidy Hutchinson** (served as Assistant to Chief of Staff Mark Meadows in the Trump Administration)
- **Matt Pottinger** (served as Deputy National Security Advisor in the Trump Administration)
- **Ben Williamson** (served as Senior Advisor to Chief of Staff Mark Meadows)
- **Sarah Matthews** (served as Deputy Press Secretary in the Trump Administration)
- **William Barr** (served as Attorney General in the Trump Administration)
- **Mike Pompeo** (served as Director of the Central Intelligence Agency and Secretary of State in the Trump Administration)
- **Ivanka Trump** (served as a Senior Advisor and Director of the Office of Economic Initiatives and Entrepreneurship in the Trump Administration)
- **Donald Trump Jr.** (eldest child of Donald Trump)
- **Molly Michael** (served as Deputy Assistant to the President and Executive Assistant to the President)
- **Tim Murtaugh** (served as Director of Communications for the Trump 2020 Presidential campaign)

- **Richard Donoghue** (served as Acting Deputy Attorney General in the Trump Administration)
- **Jeffrey Rosen** (served as Acting Attorney General in the Trump Administration)
- **Steven Engel** (served as Assistant Attorney General for the Office of Legal Counsel in the Trump Administration)
- **Marc Short** (served as Chief of Staff to Vice President Mike Pence)
- **Greg Jacob** (served as Counsel to Vice President Mike Pence)
- **Keith Kellogg** (served as National Security Advisor to Vice President Mike Pence)
- **Chris Hodgson** (served as Director of Legislative Affairs for Vice President Mike Pence)
- **Douglas Macgregor** (served as advisor to the Secretary of Defense in the Trump Administration)
- **Jason Miller** (served as spokesman for the Donald Trump 2016 Presidential Campaign and was a Senior Adviser to the Trump 2020 Presidential Campaign)
- **Alex Cannon** (Counsel for the Trump 2020 Presidential Campaign)
- **Bill Stepien** (served as the Campaign Manager for the Trump 2020 Presidential Campaign and was the White House Director of Political Affairs in the Trump Administration from 2017 to 2018)
- **Rudolph Giuliani** (an attorney for Donald Trump)
- **John Eastman** (an attorney for Donald Trump)
- **Michael Flynn** (served as National Security Advisor in the Trump Administration)
- **Eugene Scalia** (served as the Secretary of Labor in the Trump Administration)
- **Matthew Morgan** (General Counsel for the Trump 2020 Presidential Campaign)
- **Sidney Powell** (an attorney and advisor to Donald Trump)
- **Jeffrey Clark** (served as Acting Assistant Attorney General for the Civil Division in the Trump Administration)
- **Cleta Mitchell** (an attorney working with the Trump 2020 Presidential Campaign)
- **Ronna Romney McDaniel** (Chair of the Republican National Committee)
- **Justin Clark** (served as Deputy Campaign Manager for the Trump 2020 Presidential Campaign)
- **Robert Sinners** (Georgia State Director of Election Day Operations for the Trump 2020 Presidential Campaign)
- **Andrew Hitt** (Wisconsin Republican Party Chair)
- **Laura Cox** (Michigan Republican Party Chair)

- **Mike Shirkey** (Majority Leader, Michigan State Senate)
- **Bryan Cutler** (Speaker, Pennsylvania House of Representatives)
- **Rusty Bowers** (Speaker, Arizona House of Representatives)
- **Brad Raffensperger** (Georgia Secretary of State)
- **Gabriel Sterling** (Georgia Secretary of State, Chief Operating Officer)
- **BJay Pak** (served as United States Attorney for the Northern District of Georgia in the Trump Administration)
- **Al Schmidt** (City Commissioner of Philadelphia)
- **Chris Stirewalt** (Fox News Political Editor)
- **Benjamin Ginsberg** (Election Attorney)
- **J. Michael Luttig** (Retired judge for the U.S. Court of Appeals for the Fourth Circuit and informal advisor to Vice President Mike Pence)
- **Katrina Pierson** (served as a liaison for the White House and organizers at Donald Trump's "Save America" rally on January 6)
- **Nicholas Luna** (served as Personal Aide to President Trump)
- **Stephen Miller** (served as Senior Advisor to President Trump)
- **Vincent Haley** (served as Deputy Assistant to the President and Advisor for Policy, Strategy and Speechwriting in the Trump Administration)
- **Julie Radford** (Chief of Staff to Ivanka Trump in the Trump Administration)
- **Mick Mulvaney** (former Acting Chief of Staff and Special Envoy for Northern Ireland in the Trump Administration)
- **Elaine Chao** (Secretary of Transportation in the Trump Administration)
- **Roger Stone** (Trump associate)

Democrats:

- **Jocelyn Benson** (Michigan Secretary of State)

Other:

- **U.S. Capitol Police Officer Harry Dunn**
- **DC Metropolitan Police Officer Michael Fanone**
- **U.S. Capitol Police Sgt. Aquilino Gonell**
- **DC Metropolitan Police Officer Daniel Hodges**
- **General Mark Milley** (Chairman of the Joint Chiefs of Staff)
- **U.S. Capitol Police Officer Caroline Edwards**
- **Nick Quested** (award-winning British filmmaker)
- **Robert Schornack** (sentenced to 36 months' probation)
- **Eric Barber** (charged with theft and unlawful demonstration in the Capitol)
- **John Wright** (awaiting trial for felony civil disorder and other charges)
- **George Meza** (Proud Boy)

- **Daniel Herendeen** (sentenced to 36 months' probation for role in Capitol attack)
- **Matthew Walter** (Proud Boy)
- **Wandrea ArShaye "Shaye" Moss** (Georgia election worker)
- **Ruby Freeman** (Georgia election worker)
- **Anika Collier Navaroli** (former Twitter employee)
- **White House Security Official**
- **Jim Watkins** (Founder and owner, 8kun)
- **Jody Williams** (former owner of TheDonald.win)
- **Dr. Donell Harvin** (Chief of Homeland Security and Intelligence for the government of the District of Columbia)
- **Kellye SoRelle** (attorney for Oath Keepers)
- **Shealah Craighead** (White House Photographer)
- **Jason Van Tatenhove** (former Oath Keepers spokesperson)
- **Stephen Ayres** (plead guilty to disorderly and disruptive conduct related to Capitol attack)
- **Sgt. Mark Robinson** (Ret.) (Metropolitan Police Department)
- **Janet Buhler** (plead guilty to charges related to the Capitol attack)

ENDNOTES

1. A few weeks later, Rhodes and his associate Kelly Meggs were found guilty of seditious conspiracy, and other Oath Keepers were found guilty on numerous charges for obstructing the electoral count. Trial Transcript at 10502-508, *United States v. Rhodes et al.*, No. 1:22-cr-15 (D.D.C. Nov. 29, 2022); Alan Feuer and Zach Montague, "Oath Keepers Leader Convicted of Sedition in Landmark Jan. 6 Case," *New York Times*, (Nov. 29, 2022), available at https://www.nytimes.com/2022/11/29/us/politics/oath-keepers-trial-verdict-jan-6.html.

2. Trial Transcript at 5698, 5759, *United States v. Rhodes et al.*, No. 1:22-cr-15 (D.D.C. Oct. 31, 2022).

3. Trial Transcript at 5775, *United States v. Rhodes et al.*, No. 1:22-cr-15 (D.D.C. Oct. 31, 2022) ("for me at the time, it meant I felt it was like a Bastille type moment in history where in the French Revolution it was that big turning point moment where the population made their presence felt. I thought it was going to be a similar type of event for us").

4. Trial Transcript at 5783, 5866, *United States v. Rhodes et al.*, No. 1:22-cr-15 (D.D.C. Oct. 31, 2022).

5. Sentencing Transcript at 15-17, *United States v. Reimler*, No. 1:21-cr-239 (D.D.C. Jan. 11, 2022), ECF No. 37.

6. Sentencing Transcript at 33, *United States v. Pert*, No. 1:21-cr-139 (D.D.C. Feb. 11, 2022), ECF No. 64.

7. Sentencing Memorandum by Abram Markofski, Exhibit B, *United States v. Markofski*, No. 1:21-cr-344 (D.D.C. Dec. 2, 2021), ECF No. 44-2.

8. Sentencing Transcript at 49, *United States v. Witcher*, No. 1:21-cr-235 (D.D.C. Feb. 24, 2022), ECF No. 53.

9. Sentencing Transcript at 19–20, *United States v. Edwards*, No. 1:21-cr-366 (D.D.C. Jan. 21, 2022), ECF No. 33. *See also*, Sentencing Memorandum by Brandon Nelson, Exhibit B, *United States v. Nelson*, No. 1:21-cr-344 (D.D.C. Dec. 6, 2021), ECF No. 51-2; Sentencing Transcript at 65–66, *United States v. Griffith*, No. 1:21-cr-204 (D.D.C. Oct. 30, 2021), ECF No. 137; Sentencing

Transcript at 45, *United States v. Schornak*, 1:21-cr-278 (D.D.C. May 11, 2022), ECF No. 90; Sentencing Transcript at 35, *United States v. Wilkerson*, No. 1:21-cr-302 (D.D.C. Nov. 22, 2021), ECF No. 31; Select Committee to Investigate the January 6th Attack on the United States Capitol, Transcribed Interview of Eric Barber, (Mar. 16, 2022), pp. 50–51.

10. Statement of Facts at 5, *United States v. Sandlin*, No. 1:21-cr-88 (D.D.C. Jan. 20, 2021), ECF No. 1-1; Ryan J. Reily (@ryanjreily), Twitter Oct. 1, 2022 3:33 p.m. ET, available at https://twitter.com/ryanjreilly/status/1576295667412017157; Ryan J. Reily (@ryanjreily), Twitter, Oct. 1, 2022 3:40 p.m. ET, available at https://twitter.com/ryanjreilly/status/1576296016512692225; Government's Sentencing Memorandum at 2, 16, *United States v. Sandlin*, No. 1:21-cr-88 (D.D.C. Dec. 2, 2022), ECF No. 92.

11. Government's Opposition to Defendant's Motion to Revoke Magistrate Judge's Detention Order at 4, *United States v. Miller*, No. 1:21-cr-119 (D.D.C. Mar. 29, 2021), ECF No 16; Dan Mangan, "Capitol Rioter Garret Miller Says He Was Following Trump's Orders, Apologizes to AOC for Threat," CNBC, (Jan. 25, 2021), available at https://www.cnbc.com/2021/01/25/capitol-riots-garret-miller-says-he-was-following-trumps-orders-apologizes-to-aoc.html.

12. Select Committee to Investigate the January 6th Attack on the United States Capitol, Transcribed Interview of John Douglas Wright, (Mar. 31, 2022), pp. 22, 63.

13. Select Committee to Investigate the January 6th Attack on the United States Capitol, Transcribed Interview of Lewis Cantwell, (Apr. 26, 2022), p. 54.

14. Select Committee to Investigate the January 6th Attack on the United States Capitol, Transcribed Interview of Stephen Ayres, (June 22, 2022), p. 8.

15. Select Committee to Investigate the January 6th Attack on the United States Capitol, *Hearing on the January 6th Investigation*, 117th Cong., 2d sess., (July 12, 2022), available at https://www.govinfo.gov/committee/house-january6th.

16. Affidavit at 8, *United States v. Ayres*, No. 1:21-cr-156 (D.D.C. Jan. 22, 2021), ECF No. 5-1.

17. *See infra*, Chapter 6. See also Documents on file with the Select Committee to Investigate the January 6th Attack on the United States Capitol (Select Committee Chart Compiling Defendant Statements). The Select Committee Chart Compiling Defendant Statements identifies hundreds of examples of such testimony. Select Committee staff tracked cases filed by the Department of Justice against defendants who committed crimes related to the attack on the United States Capitol. Through Department of Justice criminal filings, through public reporting, through social media research, and through court hearings, staff collected a range of statements by these defendants about why they came to Washington, DC, on January 6th. Almost always, it was because President Trump had called upon them to support his big lie. Those defendants also discussed plans for violence at the Capitol, against law enforcement, against other American citizens, and against elected officials in the days leading up to January 6th. In the days immediately following the attack, defendants also bragged about their conduct. Some defendants later reflected on their actions at sentencing. The Select Committee Chart Compiling Defendant Statements is not meant to be comprehensive or polished; it is a small sampling of the tremendous work the Department of Justice has done tracking down and prosecuting criminal activity during the attempted insurrection.
Moreover, the trial of multiple members of the Proud Boys on seditious conspiracy and other charges is set to begin on December 19, 2022, and may provide additional information directly relevant to this topic. See Court Calendar: December 9, 2022–December 31, 2022, United States District Court for the District of Columbia, available at https://media.dcd.uscourts.gov/datepicker/index.html (last accessed Dec. 9, 2022); Alan Feuer, "Outcome in Oath Keepers Trial Could Hold Lessons for Coming Jan. 6 Cases," New York Times, (Nov. 30, 2022), available at https://www.nytimes.com/2022/11/30/us/politics/oath-keepers-stewart-rhodes.html.

18. Documents on file with the Select Committee to Investigate the January 6th Attack on the United States Capitol (National Archives Production), 076P-R000001890_00001 (December 28, 2020, email from Bernard Kerik to Mark Meadows explaining that "[w]e can do all the investigations we want later"); Documents on file with the Select Committee to Investigate

the January 6th Attack on the United States Capitol (National Archives Production), 076P-R000005090_0001 (January. 6, 2021, email from John Eastman to Gregory Jacob acknowledging that President Trump had "been so advised" that Vice President Pence "DOES NOT have the power to decide things unilaterally"); Select Committee to Investigate the January 6th Attack on the United States Capitol, *Hearing on the January 6th Investigation*, 117th Cong., 2d sess., (June 21, 2022), available at https://www.govinfo.gov/committee/house-january6th (Russell "Rusty" Bowers testimony recalling Rudolph Giuliani stating that "[w]e've got lots of theories; we just don't have the evidence"); *see also* Select Committee to Investigate the January 6th Attack on the United States Capitol, Transcribed Interview of Eric Herschmann (Apr. 6, 2022), p. 128 ("Whether Rudy was at this stage of his life in the same abilities to manage things at this level or not, I mean, obviously, I think Bernie Kerik publicly said it, they never proved the allegations that they were making, and they were trying to develop.") *Note:* Some documents cited in this report show timestamps based on a time zone other than Eastern Time—such as Greenwich Mean Time—because that is how they were produced to the Committee.

19. The Committee notes that a number of these findings are similar to those Federal Judge David Carter reached after reviewing the evidence presented by the Committee. Order Re Privilege of Documents Dated January 4-7, 2021 at 31-40, *Eastman v. Thompson et al.*, 594 F. Supp. 3d 1156 (C.D. Cal. Mar. 28, 2022) (No. 8:22-cv-99-DOC-DFM); Order Re Privilege of 599 Documents Dated November 3, 2020 - January 20, 2021 at 23-24, *Eastman v. Thompson et al.*, No. 8:22-cv-99 (C.D. Cal. June 7, 2022), ECF No. 356; Order Re Privilege of Remaining Documents at 13-17, *Eastman v. Thompson et al.*, No. 8:22-cv-99 (C.D. Cal. Oct. 19, 2022), ECF No. 372.

20. *See* Documents on file with the Select Committee to Investigate the January 6th Attack on the United States Capitol (Secret Service Production), CTRL0000091086 (United States Secret Service: Protective Intelligence Division communication noting left wing groups telling members to "stay at home" on January 6th).

21. Committee on House Administration, *Oversight of the United States Capitol Police and Preparations for and Response to the Attack of January 6th: Part I*, 117th Cong., 1st sess., (Apr. 21, 2021), available at https://cha.house.gov/committee-activity/hearings/oversight-united-states-capitol-police-and-preparations-and-response; Committee on House Administration, *Oversight of the United States Capitol Police and Preparations for and Response to the Attack of January 6th: Part II*, 117th Cong., 1st sess., (May 10, 2021), available at https://cha.house.gov/committee-activity/hearings/oversight-january-6th-attack-united-states-capitol-police-threat; Committee on House Administration, *Oversight of the January 6th Attack: Review of the Architect of the Capitol's Emergency Preparedness*, 117th Cong., 1st sess., (May 12, 2021), available at https://cha.house.gov/committee-activity/hearings/oversight-january-6th-attack-review-architect-capitol-s-emergency; Committee on House Administration, *Reforming the Capitol Police and Improving Accountability for the Capitol Police Board*, 117th Cong., 1st sess., (May 19, 2021), available at https://cha.house.gov/committee-activity/hearings/reforming-capitol-police-and-improving-accountability-capitol-police; Committee on House Administration, *Oversight of the January 6th Attack: United States Capitol Police Containment Emergency Response Team and First Responders Unit*, 117th Cong., 1st sess., (June 15, 2021), available at https://cha.house.gov/committee-activity/hearings/oversight-january-6th-attack-united-states-capitol-police-containment; Committee on House Administration, *Oversight of the January 6th Capitol Attack: Ongoing Review of the United States Capitol Police Inspector General Flash Reports*, 117th Cong., 2d sess., (Feb. 17, 2022), available at https://cha.house.gov/committee-activity/hearings/oversight-january-6th-capitol-attack-ongoing-review-united-states.

22. John Koblin, "At Least 20 Million Watched Jan. 6 Hearing," *New York Times*, (June 10, 2022), available at https://www.nytimes.com/2022/06/10/business/media/jan-6-hearing-ratings.html. Their findings were also widely noted by major media outlets, including conservative ones. "Editorial: What the Jan. 6 Hearings Accomplished," *Wall Street Journal*, (Oct. 14, 2022), available at https://www.wsj.com/articles/what-the-jan-6-inquiry-accomplished-donald-trump-liz-cheney-subpoena-congress-11665699321; "Editorial: The Jan. 6 Hearings are Over. Time to Vote.," *Washington Post*, (Oct. 13, 2022), available at

https://www.washingtonpost.com/opinions/2022/10/13/jan-6-hearings-are-over-time-vote/; "Editorial: The President Who Stood Still on Jan. 6," *Wall Street Journal*, (July 22, 2022), available at https://www.wsj.com/articles/the-president-who-stood-still-donald-trump-jan-6-committee-mike-pence-capitol-riot-11658528548; "Editorial: 'We All have a Duty to Ensure that What Happened on Jan. 6 Never Happens Again'," *New York Times*, (June 10, 2022), available at https://www.nytimes.com/2022/06/10/opinion/january-6-hearing-trump.html; "Editorial: Trump's Silence on Jan. 6 is Damning," *New York Post*, (July 22, 2022), available at https://nypost.com/2022/07/22/trumps-jan-6-silence-renders-him-unworthy-for-2024-reelection/

23. Select Committee to Investigate the January 6th Attack on the United States Capitol, Transcribed Interview of William Stepien, (Feb. 10, 2022), p. 45 ("And I told him it was going to be a process. It was going to be, you know–you know, we're going to have to wait and see how this turned out. So I, just like I did in 2016, I did the same thing in 2020.").

24. "When States Can Begin Processing and Counting Absentee/Mail-In Ballots, 2020," Ballotpedia (accessed on Dec. 5, 2022), available at https://ballotpedia.org/When_states_can_begin_processing_and_counting_absentee/mail-in_ballots,_2020.

25. *See* Select Committee to Investigate the January 6th Attack on the United States Capitol, *Hearing on the January 6th Investigation*, 117th Cong., 2d sess., (June 13, 2022), available at https://www.govinfo.gov/committee/house-january6th.

26. Select Committee to Investigate the January 6th Attack on the United States Capitol, Transcribed Interview of William Stepien, (Feb. 10, 2022), p. 45; Select Committee to Investigate the January 6th Attack on the United States Capitol, *Hearing on the January 6th Investigation*, 117th Cong., 2d sess., (June 13, 2022), available at https://www.govinfo.gov/committee/house-january6th.

27. Select Committee to Investigate the January 6th Attack on the United States Capitol, *Hearing on the January 6th Investigation*, 117th Cong., 2d sess., (June 13, 2022), available at https://www.govinfo.gov/committee/house-january6th.

28. Select Committee to Investigate the January 6th Attack on the United States Capitol, Transcribed Interview of William Stepien, (Feb. 10, 2022), p. 36.

29. Select Committee to Investigate the January 6th Attack on the United States Capitol, Transcribed Interview of Jared Kushner, (Mar. 31, 2022), p. 21.

30. John J. Martin, *Mail-in Ballots and Constraints on Federal Power under the Electors Clause*, 107 Va. L. Rev. Online 84, 86 (Apr. 2021) (noting that 45 States and DC permitted voters to request a mail-in ballot or automatically receive one in the 2020 election); Nathanial Rakich and Jasmine Mithani, "What Absentee Voting Looked Like In All 50 States," FiveThirtyEight, (Feb. 9, 2021), available at https://fivethirtyeight.com/features/what-absentee-voting-looked-like-in-all-50-states/; Lisa Danetz, "Mail Ballot Security Features: A Primer," Brennan Center for Justice, (Oct. 16, 2020), available at https://www.brennancenter.org/our-work/research-reports/mail-ballot-security-features-primer.

31. Select Committee to Investigate the January 6th Attack on the United States Capitol, Transcribed Interview of Hope Hicks, (Oct. 25, 2022), p. 24.

32. He also won in Utah, which mailed absentee ballots to all active voters, and won one or more electoral votes in both Maine and Nebraska, which allowed no-excuse absentee voting and assign their electoral votes proportionally. *See* "Table 1: States with No-Excuse Absentee Voting," National Conference of State Legislatures, (July 12, 2022), available at http://web.archive.org/web/20201004185006/https://www.ncsl.org/research/elections-and-campaigns/vopp-table-1-states-with-no-excuse-absentee-voting.aspx (archived); "Voting Outside the Polling Place: Absentee, All-Mail and Other Voting at Home Options," National Conference of State Legislatures, (Sep. 24, 2020), available at http://web.archive.org/web/20201103175057/https://www.ncsl.org/research/elections-and-campaigns/absentee-and-early-voting.aspx (archived); Federal Election Commission, "Federal Elections 2020 – Election Results for the U.S. President, the U.S. Senate and the U.S. House of Representatives," (Oct. 2022), p. 12, available at https://www.fec.gov/resources/cms-content/documents/federalelections2020.pdf.

33. *See, e.g.*, Select Committee to Investigate the January 6th Attack on the United States Capitol, Transcribed Interview of William Stepien, (Feb. 10, 2022), p. 66; Select Committee to Investigate the January 6th Attack on the United States Capitol, Deposition of Jason Miller, (Feb. 3, 2022), pp. 75-76.

34. Select Committee to Investigate the January 6th Attack on the United States Capitol, Transcribed Interview of William Stepien, (Feb. 10, 2022), pp. 54, 66.

35. Select Committee to Investigate the January 6th Attack on the United States Capitol, Deposition of Jason Miller, (Feb. 3, 2022), pp. 74-77.

36. Select Committee to Investigate the January 6th Attack on the United States Capitol, Transcribed Interview of William Stepien, (Feb. 10, 2022), pp. 60-61.

37. "Donald Trump 2020 Election Night Speech Transcript," Rev, (Nov. 4, 2020), available at https://www.rev.com/blog/transcripts/donald-trump-2020-election-night-speech-transcript.

38. Donald J. Trump (@realDonaldTrump), Twitter, Nov. 5, 2020 9:12 a.m. ET, available at http://web.archive.org/web/20201105170250/https://twitter.com/realdonaldtrump/status/1324353932022480896 (archived). *Note:* Citations in this report that refer to an archived tweet may list a timestamp that is several hours earlier or later than the one shown on the suggested webpage because tweets are archived from various time zones.

39. *See, e.g.*, 52 U.S.C. § 10307; Ariz. Rev. Stat. § 16-1010.

40. Select Committee to Investigate the January 6th Attack on the United States Capitol, Deposition of Jason Miller, (Feb. 3, 2022), pp. 77-78.

41. Select Committee to Investigate the January 6th Attack on the United States Capitol, Transcribed Interview of William Barr, (June 2, 2022), p. 8.

42. Documents on file with the Select Committee to Investigate the January 6th Attack on the United States Capitol (National Archives Production), 076P-R000010020_0001 (November 3, 2020, email exchange between Tom Fitton and Molly Michael copying proposed election day victory statement).

43. Dan Friedman, "Leaked Audio: Before Election Day, Bannon Said Trump Planned to Falsely Claim Victory," *Mother Jones*, (July 12, 2022), available at https://www.motherjones.com/politics/2022/07/leaked-audio-steve-bannon-trump-2020-election-declare-victory. We note that Mr. Bannon refused to testify and has been convicted of criminal contempt by a jury of his peers. "Stephen K. Bannon Sentenced to Four Months in Prison on Two counts of Contempt of Congress," Department of Justice, (Oct. 21, 2022), available at https://www.justice.gov/usao-dc/pr/stephen-k-bannon-sentenced-four-months-prison-two-counts-contempt-congress.

44. At his interview, Stone invoked his Fifth Amendment right not to incriminate himself in response to over 70 questions, including questions regarding his direct communications with Donald Trump and his role in January 6th. Select Committee to Investigate the January 6th Attack on the United States Capitol, Deposition of Roger Stone (Dec. 17, 2021). *See also* Documents on file with the Select Committee to Investigate the January 6th Attack on the United States Capitol (Christoffer Guldbrandsen Production), Video file 201101_1 (November 1, 2020, footage of Roger Stone speaking to associates).

45. Select Committee to Investigate the January 6th Attack on the United States Capitol, Deposition of Greg Jacob, (Feb. 1, 2022), pp. 12-13.

46. Documents on file with the Select Committee to Investigate the January 6th Attack on the United States Capitol (National Archives Production), 79VP-R000011578_0001, 079VP-R000011579_0001, 079VP-R000011579_0002 (November 3, 2020, email and memorandum from Gregory Jacob to Marc Short regarding electoral vote count).

47. Select Committee to Investigate the January 6th Attack on the United States Capitol, Transcribed Interview of William Stepien, (Feb. 10, 2022), pp. 117-18.

48. Select Committee to Investigate the January 6th Attack on the United States Capitol, Deposition of Jason Miller, (Feb. 3, 2022), p. 91.

49. Select Committee to Investigate the January 6th Attack on the United States Capitol, *Hearing on the January 6th Investigation*, 117th Cong., 2d sess., (June 13, 2022), available at https://www.govinfo.gov/committee/house-january6th.

50. *See, e.g.*, Select Committee to Investigate the January 6th Attack on the United States Capitol, Transcribed Interview of General Mark A. Milley, (Nov. 17, 2021), p. 121; Select Committee to Investigate the January 6th Attack on the United States Capitol, Transcribed Interview of Alyssa Farah Griffin, (Apr. 15, 2022), p. 62; Select Committee to Investigate the January 6th Attack on the United States Capitol, Continued Interview of Cassidy Hutchinson, (Sep. 14, 2022), p. 113; Select Committee to Investigate the January 6th Attack on the United States Capitol, Transcribed Interview of Kellyanne Conway, (Nov. 28, 2022), pp. 79-84.

51. *See* Select Committee to Investigate the January 6th Attack on the United States Capitol, Deposition of Keith Kellogg, Jr., (Dec. 14, 2021), pp. 212-21; Select Committee to Investigate the January 6th Attack on the United States Capitol, Transcribed Interview of General Mark A. Milley, (Nov. 17, 2021), pp. 108-10; Select Committee to Investigate the January 6th Attack on the United States Capitol, Deposition of John McEntee, (Mar. 28, 2022), pp. 44, 46, 48-51; Select Committee to Investigate the January 6th Attack on the United States Capitol, Transcribed Interview of Douglas Macgregor, (June 7, 2022), pp. 27-41.

52. Select Committee to Investigate the January 6th Attack on the United States Capitol, Deposition of Keith Kellogg, Jr., (Dec. 14, 2021), p. 215.

53. Select Committee to Investigate the January 6th Attack on the United States Capitol, Transcribed Interview of William Barr, (June 2, 2022), p. 6.

54. Select Committee to Investigate the January 6th Attack on the United States Capitol, Transcribed Interview of Alex Cannon, (Apr. 13, 2022), pp. 22, 33-34.

55. Select Committee to Investigate the January 6th Attack on the United States Capitol, Transcribed Interview of William Stepien, (Feb. 10, 2022), pp. 111-12.

56. Select Committee to Investigate the January 6th Attack on the United States Capitol, Deposition of Jason Miller, (Feb. 3, 2022), p. 119.

57. ABC News, "Pence Opens Up with David Muir on Jan. 6: Exclusive," YouTube, at 2:13, Nov. 14, 2022, available at https://youtu.be/-AAyKAoPFQs?t=133.

58. "CNN Townhall: Former Vice President Mike Pence," CNN, (Nov. 16, 2022), available at https://transcripts.cnn.com/show/se/date/2022-11-16/segment/01.

59. Select Committee to Investigate the January 6th Attack on the United States Capitol, Transcribed Interview of Matthew Morgan, (Apr. 25, 2022), p. 118.

60. *Select Committee to Investigate the January 6th Attack on the United States Capitol, Transcribed Interview of William Barr, (June 2, 2022), p. 18.*

61. Michael Balsamo, "Disputing Trump, Barr Says No Widespread Election Fraud," Associated Press, (Dec. 1, 2020, updated June 28, 2022), available at https://apnews.com/article/barr-no-widespread-election-fraud-b1f1488796c9a98c4b1a9061a6c7f49d.

62. Select Committee to Investigate the January 6th Attack on the United States Capitol, Transcribed Interview of William Barr, (June 2, 2022), pp. 24-30; "Bill Barr Press Conference Transcript: No Special Counsels Needed to Investigate Election or Hunter Biden," Rev, (Dec. 21, 2020), available at https://www.rev.com/blog/transcripts/bill-barr-press-conference-transcript-no-special-counsels-needed-to-investigate-election-or-hunter-biden.

63. "Joint Statement from Elections Infrastructure Government Coordinating Council & the Election Infrastructure Sector Coordinating Executive Committees," Cybersecurity and Infrastructure Security Agency, (Nov. 12, 2020), available at https://www.cisa.gov/news/2020/11/12/joint-statement-elections-infrastructure-government-coordinating-council-election (emphasis in original).

64. Select Committee to Investigate the January 6th Attack on the United States Capitol, *Hearing on the January 6th Investigation*, 117th Cong., 2d sess., (June 23, 2022), available at https://www.govinfo.gov/committee/house-january6th.

65. Select Committee to Investigate the January 6th Attack on the United States Capitol, Transcribed Interview of Richard Peter Donoghue, (Oct. 21, 2021), pp. 59-60.

66. Select Committee to Investigate the January 6th Attack on the United States Capitol, Transcribed Interview of Richard Peter Donoghue, (Oct. 21, 2021), pp. 108-09.

67. Senate Committee on the Judiciary, Transcribed Interview of Richard Donoghue, (Aug. 6, 2021), p. 156, available at https://www.judiciary.senate.gov/imo/media/doc/Donoghue%20Transcript.pdf.

68. Select Committee to Investigate the January 6th Attack on the United States Capitol, Transcribed Interview of Jeffrey Rosen, (Oct. 13, 2021), pp. 18-19.

69. Select Committee to Investigate the January 6th Attack on the United States Capitol, Transcribed Interview of Pasquale Anthony "Pat" Cipollone, (July 8, 2022), pp. 50, 123; Select Committee to Investigate the January 6th Attack on the United States Capitol, Transcribed Interview of Eric Herschmann, (Apr. 6, 2022), pp. 168-69, 184, 187.

70. Select Committee to Investigate the January 6th Attack on the United States Capitol, Transcribed Interview of Pasquale Anthony "Pat" Cipollone, (July 8, 2022), p. 50.

71. Select Committee to Investigate the January 6th Attack on the United States Capitol, Transcribed Interview of Eric Herschmann, (April 6, 2022), p. 128.

72. Select Committee to Investigate the January 6th Attack on the United States Capitol, Transcribed Interview of William Stepien, (Feb. 10, 2022), pp. 172-73.

73. Select Committee to Investigate the January 6th Attack on the United States Capitol, Transcribed Interview of William Stepien, (Feb. 10, 2022), p. 174.

74. Select Committee to Investigate the January 6th Attack on the United States Capitol, Transcribed Interview of Justin Clark, (May 17, 2022), pp. 63-70; Select Committee to Investigate the January 6th Attack on the United States Capitol, Transcribed Interview of Matthew Morgan, (Apr. 25, 2022), pp. 57-62; Select Committee to Investigate the January 6th Attack on the United States Capitol, Transcribed Interview of Timothy Murtaugh, (May 19, 2022), pp, 66-68; Select Committee to Investigate the January 6th Attack on the United States Capitol, Transcribed Interview of Alex Cannon, (Apr. 19, 2022), pp. 37-38; Documents on file with the Select Committee to Investigate the January 6th Attack on the United States Capitol (Tim Murtaugh production), XXM-0021349 (text chain with Giuliani, Ellis, Epshteyn, Ryan, Bobb, and Herschmann).

75. Select Committee to Investigate the January 6th Attack on the United States Capitol, Transcribed Interview of Matthew Morgan, (Apr. 25, 2022), p. 58.

76. Select Committee to Investigate the January 6th Attack on the United States Capitol, Transcribed Interview of Matthew Morgan, (Apr. 25, 2022), p. 58.

77. Select Committee to Investigate the January 6th Attack on the United States Capitol, Transcribed Interview of Matthew Morgan, (Apr. 25, 2022), p. 58.

78. Select Committee to Investigate the January 6th Attack on the United States Capitol, Transcribed Interview of William Stepien, (Feb. 10, 2022), p. 173.

79. *King v. Whitmer*, 505 F. Supp. 3d 720, 738 (E.D. Mich. 2020), also available at https://electioncases.osu.edu/wp-content/uploads/2020/11/King-v-Whitmer-Doc62.pdf; *Bowyer v. Ducey*, 506 F. Supp. 3d 699, 706 (D. Ariz. 2020), also available at https://storage.courtlistener.com/recap/gov.uscourts.azd.1255923/gov.uscourts.azd.1255923.84.0_2.pdf; *Donald J. Trump for President v. Boockvar*, 502 F. Supp. 3d 899, 906 (M.D. Pa. 2020), also available at https://storage.courtlistener.com/recap/gov.uscourts.pamd.127057/gov.uscourts.pamd.127057.202.0_1.pdf; *Law v. Whitmer*, No. 10 OC 00163 1B, 2020 Nev. Unpub. LEXIS 1160, at *1, 29-31, 33, 48-49, 52, 54 (Nev. Dec. 8, 2020), available at https://casetext.com/case/law-v-whitmer-1 (attaching and affirming lower

court decision), also available at https://election.conservative.org/files/2020/12/20-OC-00163-Order-Granting-Motion-to-Dismiss-Statement-of-Contest.pdf; *Wisconsin Voters Alliance v. Pence*, 514 F. Supp. 3d 117, 119 (D.D.C. 2021), also available at https://electioncases.osu.edu/wp-content/uploads/2020/12/WVA-v-Pence-Doc10.pdf.

80. Documents on file with the Select Committee to Investigate the January 6th Attack on the United States Capitol (Zach Parkinson Production), Parkinson0620 (text message between Tim Murtaugh, Zach Parkinson, and "Matt").

81. *In the Matter of Rudolph W. Giuliani*, No. 2021-00506, slip op at *2, 22 (N.Y. App. Div. May 3, 2021), available at https://int.nyt.com/data/documenttools/giuliani-law-license-suspension/1ae5ad6007c0ebfa/full.pdf.

82. *In the Matter of Rudolph W. Giuliani*, No. 2021-00506, slip op at *2, 22 (N.Y. App. Div. May 3, 2021), available at https://int.nyt.com/data/documenttools/giuliani-law-license-suspension/1ae5ad6007c0ebfa/full.pdf.

83. Opinion and Order at 1, *King v. Whitmer*, 505 F. Supp. 3d 720 (E.D. Mich. Aug. 25, 2020) (No. 20-13134), ECF No. 172.

84. Senator John Danforth, Benjamin Ginsberg, The Honorable Thomas B. Griffith, et al., *Lost, Not Stolen: The Conservative Case that Trump Lost and Biden Won the 2020 Presidential Election*, (July 2022), p. 3, available at https://lostnotstolen.org/download/378/.

85. Senator John Danforth, Benjamin Ginsberg, The Honorable Thomas B. Griffith, et al., *Lost, Not Stolen: The Conservative Case that Trump Lost and Biden Won the 2020 Presidential Election*, (July 2022), pp. 3-4, available at https://lostnotstolen.org/download/378/. We also note this: The authors of *Lost, Not Stolen* also conclude that one of the pieces of supposed evidence that President Trump and his allies have pointed to since January 6, 2021, to try to bolster their allegations that the 2020 election was stolen shows nothing of the sort. *Lost, Not Stolen* explains that Dinesh D'Souza's "2000 Mules" tries to establish widespread voter fraud in the 2020 election using phone-tracking data. "Yet the film, heartily endorsed by Trump at its Mar-a-Lago premiere, has subsequently been thoroughly debunked in analysis. What the film claims to portray is simply not supported by the evidence invoked by the film." *Id.*, at 6. Likewise, former Attorney General Bill Barr told the Select Committee: "... I haven't seen anything since the election that changes my mind [that fraud determined the outcome] including, the 2000 Mules movie." Select Committee to Investigate the January 6th Attack on the United States Capitol, Transcribed Interview of William Barr, (June 2, 2022), p. 37. He called its cell phone tracking data "singularly unimpressive" because "... in a big city like Atlanta or wherever, just by definition you're going to find many hundreds of them have passed by and spent time in the vicinity of these boxes" for submitting ballots, and to argue that those people must be "mules" delivering fraudulent ballots was "just indefensible." *Id.*, at 37–38.

86. White House Senior Advisor Eric Herschmann told the Committee that when he disputed allegations of election fraud in a December 18th Oval Office meeting, Sidney Powell fired back that "the judges are corrupt. And I was like, every one? Every single case that you've done in the country you guys lost every one of them is corrupt, even the ones we appointed?" Select Committee to Investigate the January 6th Attack on the United States Capitol, Transcribed Interview of Eric Herschmann, (Apr. 6, 2022), p. 171.

87. Select Committee to Investigate the January 6th Attack on the United States Capitol, *Hearing on the January 6th Investigation*, 117th Cong., 2d sess., (June 13, 2022), at 1:53:10-1:53:20, available at https://january6th.house.gov/legislation/hearings/06132022-select-committee-hearing.

88. Verified Complaint for Declaratory and Injunctive Relief at 46-47, *Donald J. Trump for President, Inc. v. Boockvar*, No. 4:20-cv-02078 (M.D. Pa. Nov. 9, 2020), available at https://cdn.donaldjtrump.com/public-files/press_assets/2020-11-09-complaint-as-filed.pdf.

89. Opinion at 2, 3, 16, *Donald J. Trump for President, Inc. v. Boockvar*, No. 20-3371 (3d Cir. Nov. 27, 2020), available at https://electioncases.osu.edu/wp-content/uploads/2020/11/Donald-J.-Trump-for-President-v-Boockvar-3rd-Cir-Doc91.pdf.

90. Complaint for Expedited Declaratory and Injunctive Relief Pursuant to Article II of the United States Constitution, *Trump v. Wisconsin Elections Commission*, No. 2:20-cv-01785 (E.D. Wis. Dec. 2, 2020), available at https://electioncases.osu.edu/wp-content/uploads/2020/12/Trump-v-WEC-Doc1.pdf.

91. *Trump v. Wisconsin Elections Commission*, 506 F. Supp. 3d 620, 21, 22 (E.D. Wis. 2020), available at https://electioncases.osu.edu/wp-content/uploads/2020/12/Trump-v-WEC-Doc134.pdf.

92. Select Committee to Investigate the January 6th Attack on the United States Capitol, *Hearing on the January 6th Investigation*, 117th Cong., 2d sess., (June 13, 2022), at 1:52:45 to 1:53:20, available at https://january6th.house.gov/legislation/hearings/06132022-select-committee-hearing.

93. The authors determined that thirty cases were dismissed by a judge after an evidentiary hearing had been held, compared to twenty cases that were dismissed by a judge beforehand, while the remaining fourteen were withdrawn voluntarily by plaintiffs. *See* Senator John Danforth, Benjamin Ginsberg, The Honorable Thomas B. Griffith, et al, *Lost, Not Stolen: The Conservative Case that Trump Lost and Biden Won the 2020 Presidential Election*, (July 2022), p. 3, available at https://lostnotstolen.org/download/378/.

94. Select Committee to Investigate the January 6th Attack on the United States Capitol, Deposition of Rudolph Giuliani, (May 20, 2022), p. 111.

95. Letter from Timothy C. Parlatore to Chairman Bennie G. Thompson on "Re: Subpoena to Bernard B. Kerik," (Dec. 31, 2021).

96. Documents on file with the Select Committee to Investigate the January 6th Attack on the United States Capitol (National Archives Production), 076P-R000004125_0001 (December 28, 2020, email from Kerik to Meadows).

97. When our courts weigh evidence to determine facts, they often infer that disputed facts do not favor a witness who refuses to testify by invoking his Fifth Amendment right against incriminating himself. *See Baxter v. Palmigiano*, 425 U.S. 308, 318 (1976) (the Fifth Amendment allows for "adverse inferences against parties to civil actions when they refuse to testify to probative evidence offered against them").

98. Nor was there such evidence of widespread fraud in any of the documents produced in response to Select Committee subpoenas issued to the proponents of the claims, including Rudy Giuliani and his team members and investigators Bernard Kerik and Christina Bobb, or other proponents of election fraud claims such as Pennsylvania Senator Doug Mastriano, Arizona legislator Mark Finchem, disbarred attorney Phill Kline, and attorneys Sidney Powell, Cleta Mitchell, and John Eastman. Not one of them provided evidence raising genuine questions about the election outcome. In short, it was a big scam.

99. Select Committee to Investigate the January 6th Attack on the United States Capitol, *Business Meeting on the January 6th Investigation*, 117th Cong., 2d sess., (Oct. 19, 2022), at 56:30 to 58:10, available at https://january6th.house.gov/legislation/hearings/101322-select-committee-hearing.

100. Select Committee to Investigate the January 6th Attack on the United States Capitol, Transcribed Interview of Eugene Scalia (June 30, 2022), pp. 11-13. Then-Secretary Scalia also sent a memorandum to President Trump on January 8, 2021. In that memorandum, he requested that the President "convene an immediate meeting of the Cabinet." He told the President that he was "concerned by certain statements you made since the election . . . of further actions you may be considering," and he "concluded that [his] responsibilities as a Cabinet Secretary obligate[d] [him] to take further steps to address those concerns." The Select Committee will make this memorandum available to the public. Documents on file with the Select Committee to Investigate the January 6th Attack on the United States Capitol (Department of Labor Production), CTRL0000087637, (January 8, 2021, Memorandum for The President of the United States from Secretary of Labor Eugene Scalia, regarding Request for Cabinet Meeting).

101. Select Committee to Investigate the January 6th Attack on the United States Capitol, Deposition of Judson Deere, (Mar. 3, 2022), pp. 23-25.

102. Select Committee to Investigate the January 6th Attack on the United States Capitol, Transcribed Interview of Pasquale Anthony "Pat" Cipollone (July 8, 2022), p. 12.

103. Select Committee to Investigate the January 6th Attack on the United States Capitol, Transcribed Interview of William Barr, (June 3, 2022), p. 62.

104. Select Committee to Investigate the January 6th Attack on the United States Capitol, Transcribed Interview of William Barr, (June 3, 2022), pp. 19-20.

105. Senate Committee on the Judiciary, Transcribed Interview of Jeffrey Rosen, (Aug. 7, 2021), pp. 30-31, available at https://www.judiciary.senate.gov/imo/media/doc/Rosen%20Transcript.pdf; Select Committee to Investigate the January 6th Attack on the United States Capitol, Transcribed Interview of Jeffrey Rosen, (Oct. 13, 2021), pp. 14-15 (in which Rosen confirms the general accuracy of the transcription of his Senate testimony and then is asked and agrees to the following question: [Committee staff]: "And we are going to – the select committee is going to essentially incorporate those transcripts as part of our record and rely upon your testimony there for our purposes going forward, as long as you're comfortable with that?" [Rosen]: "Yes.")

106. "Donald Trump Vlog: Contesting Election Results – December 22, 2020," Factba.se, at 9:11-9:25 (Dec. 22, 2020), available at https://factba.se/transcript/donald-trump-vlog-contesting-election-results-december-22-2020.

107. Select Committee to Investigate the January 6th Attack on the United States Capitol, Transcribed Interview of Richard Peter Donoghue, (Oct. 1, 2021), p. 43.

108. Brad Raffensperger, *Integrity Counts* (New York: Simon & Schuster, 2021), p. 191 (reproducing the call transcript); Amy Gardner and Paulina Firozi, "Here's the Full Transcript and Audio of the Call Between Trump and Raffensperger," *Washington Post*, (Jan. 5, 2021), available at https://www.washingtonpost.com/politics/trump-raffensperger-call-transcript-georgia-vote/2021/01/03/2768e0cc-4ddd-11eb-83e3-322644d82356_story.html

109. Brad Raffensperger, *Integrity Counts* (New York: Simon & Schuster, 2021), p. 191 (reproducing the call transcript); Amy Gardner and Paulina Firozi, "Here's the Full Transcript and Audio of the Call Between Trump and Raffensperger," *Washington Post*, (Jan. 5, 2021), available at https://www.washingtonpost.com/politics/trump-raffensperger-call-transcript-georgia-vote/2021/01/03/2768e0cc-4ddd-11eb-83e3-322644d82356_story.html

110. Donald J. Trump (@realDonaldTrump), Twitter, Jan. 3, 2021 8:57 a.m. ET, available at http://web.archive.org/web/20210103135742/https://twitter.com/realdonaldtrump/status/1345731043861659650 (archived).

111. Select Committee to Investigate the January 6th Attack on the United States Capitol, Transcribed Interview of William Barr, (June 2, 2022), pp. 25-26.

112. "Donald Trump Speech on Election Fraud Claims Transcript December 2," Rev, at 15:12-15:44, (Dec. 2, 2020), available at https://www.rev.com/blog/transcripts/donald-trump-speech-on-election-fraud-claims-transcript-december-2.

113. Select Committee to Investigate the January 6th Attack on the United States Capitol, Transcribed Interview of Richard Peter Donoghue, (Oct. 1, 2021), p. 64.

114. PBS NewsHour, "WATCH LIVE: Trump Speaks as Congress Prepares to Count Electoral College Votes in Biden Win," YouTube, at 1:42:58-1:43:02, Jan. 6, 2021, available at https://youtu.be/pa9sT4efsqY?t=6178.

115. Senate Committee on the Judiciary, Interview of Richard Donoghue, (Aug. 6, 2021), p. 156, available at https://www.judiciary.senate.gov/imo/media/doc/Donoghue%20Transcript.pdf.

116. PBS NewsHour, "WATCH LIVE: Trump Speaks as Congress Prepares to Count Electoral College Votes in Biden Win," YouTube, at 1:15:19-1:15:39, Jan. 6, 2021, available at https://youtu.be/pa9sT4efsqY?t=4519.

117. Brad Raffensperger, Integrity Counts (New York: Simon & Schuster, 2021), p. 191 (reproducing the call transcript); Amy Gardner and Paulina Firozi, "Here's the Full Transcript and Audio of the Call Between Trump and Raffensperger," *Washington Post*, (Jan. 5, 2021), available at https://www.washingtonpost.com/politics/trump-raffensperger-call-transcript-georgia-vote/2021/01/03/2768e0cc-4ddd-11eb-83e3-322644d82356_story.html

118. "Donald Trump Rally Speech Transcript Dalton, Georgia: Senate Runoff Election," Rev, at 51:38-52:01, (Jan. 4, 2021), available at https://www.rev.com/blog/transcripts/donald-trump-rally-speech-transcript-dalton-georgia-senate-runoff-election.

119. Brad Raffensperger, *Integrity Counts* (New York: Simon & Schuster, 2021), p. 191 (reproducing the call transcript); Amy Gardner and Paulina Firozi, "Here's the Full Transcript and Audio of the Call Between Trump and Raffensperger," *Washington Post*, (Jan. 5, 2021), available at https://www.washingtonpost.com/politics/trump-raffensperger-call-transcript-georgia-vote/2021/01/03/2768e0cc-4ddd-11eb-83e3-322644d82356_story.html

120. PBS NewsHour, "WATCH LIVE: Trump Speaks as Congress Prepares to Count Electoral College Votes in Biden Win," YouTube, at 1:32:25-1:32:43, Jan. 6, 2021, available at https://youtu.be/pa9sT4efsqY?t=5545.

121. Brad Raffensperger, *Integrity Counts* (New York: Simon & Schuster, 2021), p. 191 (reproducing the call transcript); Amy Gardner and Paulina Firozi, "Here's the Full Transcript and Audio of the Call Between Trump and Raffensperger," *Washington Post*, (Jan. 5, 2021), available at https://www.washingtonpost.com/politics/trump-raffensperger-call-transcript-georgia-vote/2021/01/03/2768e0cc-4ddd-11eb-83e3-322644d82356_story.html

122. PBS NewsHour, "WATCH LIVE: Trump Speaks as Congress Prepares to Count Electoral College Votes in Biden Win," YouTube, at 1:33:35-1:33:44, Jan. 6, 2021, available at https://youtu.be/pa9sT4efsqY?t=5615.

123. Select Committee to Investigate the January 6th Attack on the United States Capitol, Deposition of Kayleigh McEnany, (Jan. 12, 2022), pp. 143, 290-91.

124. Search results for "dominion", Trump Twitter Archive v2, (accessed Sep. 20, 2022), https://www.thetrumparchive.com/?searchbox=%22dominion%22&results=1.

125. Select Committee to Investigate the January 6th Attack on the United States Capitol, Deposition of Jason Miller (Feb. 3, 2022), pp. 117, 133.

126. "Donald Trump Thanksgiving Call to Troops Transcript 2020: Addresses Possibility of Conceding Election," Rev, at 23:35-23:46, (Nov. 26, 2020), available at https://www.rev.com/blog/transcripts/donald-trump-thanksgiving-call-to-troops-transcript-2020-addresses-possibility-of-conceding-election.

127. Select Committee to Investigate the January 6th Attack on the United States Capitol, Transcribed Interview of William Barr, (Jun. 2, 2022), p. 19.

128. "Donald Trump Thanksgiving Call to Troops Transcript 2020: Addresses Possibility of Conceding Election," Rev, at 24:16-24:35 (Nov. 26, 2020), available at https://www.rev.com/blog/transcripts/donald-trump-thanksgiving-call-to-troops-transcript-2020-addresses-possibility-of-conceding-election.

129. Select Committee to Investigate the January 6th Attack on the United States Capitol, Transcribed Interview of William Barr, (Jun. 2, 2022), p. 27.

130. "Donald Trump Speech on Election Fraud Claims Transcript December 2," Rev, at 10:46-11:06, (Dec. 2, 2020), available at https://www.rev.com/blog/transcripts/donald-trump-speech-on-election-fraud-claims-transcript-december-2.

131. William P. Barr, *One Damn Thing After Another: Memoirs of an Attorney General*, (New York: HarperCollins, 2022), at p. 554.

132. Donald J. Trump (@realDonaldTrump), Twitter, Nov. 15, 2020 12:21 a.m. ET, available at https://media-cdn.factba.se/realdonaldtrump-twitter/1338715842931023873.jpg (archived).

133. Senate Committee on the Judiciary, Transcribed Interview of Jeffrey Rosen, (Aug. 7, 2021), pp. 25, 31, available at https://www.judiciary.senate.gov/imo/media/doc/Rosen%20Transcript.pdf.

134. Donald J. Trump (@realDonaldTrump), Twitter, Dec. 16, 2020 1:09 a.m. ET, available at https://media-cdn.factba.se/realdonaldtrump-twitter/1339090279429775363.jpg (archived).

135. Select Committee to Investigate the January 6th Attack on the United States Capitol, Transcribed Interview of Robert O'Brien, (Aug. 23, 2022), pp. 164-65.

136. Donald J. Trump (@realDonaldTrump), Twitter, Dec. 19, 2020 11:30 a.m. ET, available at https://media-cdn.factba.se/realdonaldtrump-twitter/1340333619299147781.jpg (archived).

137. Select Committee to Investigate the January 6th Attack on the United States Capitol, Transcribed Interview of Richard Peter Donoghue, (Oct. 1, 2021), p. 109.

138. Brad Raffensperger, *Integrity Counts* (New York: Simon & Schuster, 2021), p. 191 (reproducing the call transcript); Amy Gardner and Paulina Firozi, "Here's the Full Transcript and Audio of the Call Between Trump and Raffensperger," *Washington Post,* (Jan. 5, 2021), available at https://www.washingtonpost.com/politics/trump-raffensperger-call-transcript-georgia-vote/2021/01/03/2768e0cc-4ddd-11eb-83e3-322644d82356_story.html

139. Brad Raffensperger, Integrity Counts (New York: Simon & Schuster, 2021), p. 191 (reproducing the call transcript); Amy Gardner and Paulina Firozi, "Here's the Full Transcript and Audio of the Call Between Trump and Raffensperger," *Washington Post,* (Jan. 5, 2021), available at https://www.washingtonpost.com/politics/trump-raffensperger-call-transcript-georgia-vote/2021/01/03/2768e0cc-4ddd-11eb-83e3-322644d82356_story.html

140. PBS NewsHour, "WATCH LIVE: Trump Speaks as Congress Prepares to Count Electoral College Votes in Biden Win," YouTube, at 1:39:09 to 1:39:27 and 1:40:51 to 1:41:01, Jan. 6, 2021, available at https://youtu.be/pa9sT4efsqY?t=5949.

141. Select Committee to Investigate the January 6th Attack on the United States Capitol, *Hearing on the January 6th Investigation,* 117th Cong., 2d sess., (June 13, 2022), available at https://www.govinfo.gov/committee/house-january6th

142. Select Committee to Investigate the January 6th Attack on the United States Capitol, Transcribed Interview of William Barr, (June 2, 2022), p. 15.

143. The framers specifically considered and rejected two constitutional plans that would have given Congress the power to select the Executive. Under both the Virginia and New Jersey Plans, the national executive would have been chosen by the national legislature. *See* Curtis A. Bradley & Martin S. Flaherty, *Executive Power Essentialism and Foreign Affairs,* 102 Mich. L. Rev. 545, 592, 595 (2004); *see also* 1 The Records of the Federal Convention of 1787, at 21, 244 (Max Farrand ed., 1911) (introducing Virginia and New Jersey Plans), available at https://oll.libertyfund.org/title/farrand-the-records-of-the-federal-convention-of-1787-vol-1; James Madison, *Notes of the Constitutional Convention* (Sep. 4, 1787) (Gov. Morris warning of "the danger of intrigue & faction" if Congress selected the President), available at https://www.consource.org/document/james-madisons-notes-of-the-constitutional-convention-1787-9-4/.

144. The Federalist No. 68, at 458 (Alexander Hamilton) (Jacob E. Cooke ed., 1961).

145. The Federalist No. 68, at 459 (Alexander Hamilton) (Jacob E. Cooke ed., 1961).

146. The Federalist No. 68, at 459 (Alexander Hamilton) (Jacob E. Cooke ed., 1961).

147. The Federalist No. 68, at 459 (Alexander Hamilton) (Jacob E. Cooke ed., 1961). *See also* U.S. Const. art. II, § 1, cl. 2 ("but no Senator or Representative, or Person holding an Office of Trust or Profit under the United States, shall be appointed an Elector").

148. Documents on file with the Select Committee to Investigate the January 6th Attack on the United States Capitol (Chapman University Production), Chapman052976 (Eastman Jan 6 scenario dual slates of electors memo); Documents on file with the Select Committee to Investigate the January 6th Attack on the United States Capitol (Chapman University Production), CTRL0000923171 (Eastman Jan. 6 scenario conduct by elected officials memo).

149. Documents on file with the Select Committee to Investigate the January 6th Attack on the United States Capitol (Chapman University Production), Chapman003228 (Eastman memo to President Trump).

150. *See Eastman v. Thompson et al.* at 6-8, 594 F. Supp. 3d 1156, (C.D. Cal. Mar. 28, 2022) (No. 8:22-cv-99-DOC-DFM).

151. Documents on file with the Select Committee to Investigate the January 6th Attack on the United States Capitol (Chapman University Production), Chapman003228 (Eastman memo to President Trump).

152. Select Committee to Investigate the January 6th Attack on the United States Capitol, Deposition of Greg Jacob (Feb. 1, 2022), p. 118.

153. Select Committee to Investigate the January 6th Attack on the United States Capitol, Deposition of Greg Jacob (Feb. 1, 2022), pp. 110, 117.

154. Select Committee to Investigate the January 6th Attack on the United States Capitol, Deposition of Greg Jacob (Feb. 1, 2022), pp. 109-10; Select Committee to Investigate the January 6th Attack on the United States Capitol, *Hearing on the January 6th Investigation*, 117th Cong., 2d sess., (June 16, 2022), available at https://www.govinfo.gov/committee/house-january6th.

155. Select Committee to Investigate the January 6th Attack on the United States Capitol, *Hearing on the January 6th Investigation*, 117th Cong., 2d sess., (June 16), available at https://www.govinfo.gov/committee/house-january6th.

156. "Former Vice President Pence Remarks at Federalist Society Conference," C-SPAN (Feb. 4, 2022), available at https://www.c-span.org/video/?517647-2/vice-president-pence-remarks-federalist-society-conference.

157. Select Committee to Investigate the January 6th Attack on the United States Capitol, Deposition of Greg Jacob, (Feb. 1, 2022), p. 122.

158. Document on file with the Select Committee (National Archives Production), VP-R0000107 (January 5, 2021, Greg Jacob memo to Vice President); *see also* Select Committee to Investigate the January 6th Attack on the United States Capitol, Deposition of Greg Jacob, (Feb. 1, 2022), pp. 127-28 (discussing memorandum).

159. Select Committee to Investigate the January 6th Attack on the United States Capitol, Deposition of Greg Jacob, (Feb. 1, 2022), pp. 122-23.

160. Select Committee to Investigate the January 6th Attack on the United States Capitol, Deposition of Marc Short, (Jan. 26, 2022), pp. 26-27.

161. Judge Luttig (@judgeluttig), Twitter, Jan. 5, 2021 9:53 a.m. ET available at https://twitter.com/judgeluttig/status/1346469787329646592.

162. Select Committee to Investigate the January 6th Attack on the United States Capitol, *Hearing on the January 6th Investigation*, 117th Cong., 2d sess., (June 16, 2022), available at https://www.govinfo.gov/committee/house-january6th.

163. Select Committee to Investigate the January 6th Attack on the United States Capitol, *Hearing on the January 6th Investigation*, 117th Cong., 2d sess., (June 16, 2022), available at https://www.govinfo.gov/committee/house-january6th.

164. Documents on file with the Select Committee, (Chapman University Production), Chapman005442 (Eastman emails with Greg Jacob).

165. Select Committee to Investigate the January 6th Attack on the United States Capitol, Transcribed Interview of Pasquale Anthony "Pat" Cipollone, (July 8, 2022), p. 88.

166. Select Committee to Investigate the January 6th Attack on the United States Capitol, Transcribed Interview of Pasquale Anthony "Pat" Cipollone, (July 8, 2022), p. 85.

167. Select Committee to Investigate the January 6th Attack on the United States Capitol, Transcribed Interview of Pasquale Anthony "Pat" Cipollone, (July 8, 2022), pp. 85-86.

168. Select Committee to Investigate the January 6th Attack on the United States Capitol, Deposition of Jason Miller, (Feb. 3, 2022), p. 157.

169. Select Committee to Investigate the January 6th Attack on the United States Capitol, Transcribed Interview of Pasquale Anthony "Pat" Cipollone, (July 8, 2022), pp. 86-87.

170. Select Committee to Investigate the January 6th Attack on the United States Capitol, Transcribed Interview of Eric Herschmann, (Apr. 6, 2022), p. 34.

171. Select Committee to Investigate the January 6th Attack on the United States Capitol, Transcribed Interview of Eric Herschmann, (Apr. 6, 2022), p. 26.

172. Select Committee to Investigate the January 6th Attack on the United States Capitol, Transcribed Interview of Pasquale Anthony "Pat" Cipollone, (July 8, 2022), p. 85.

173. Select Committee to Investigate the January 6th Attack on the United States Capitol, Transcribed Interview of Eric Herschmann, (Apr. 6, 2022), p. 40.

174. Maggie Haberman and Annie Karni, "Pence Said to Have Told Trump He Lacks Power to Change Election Result," *New York Times*, (Jan. 5, 2021), available at https://www.nytimes.com/2021/01/05/us/politics/pence-trump-election-results.html.

175. Meredith Lee (@meredithllee), Twitter, Jan. 5, 2021 9:58 p.m. ET, available at https://twitter.com/meredithllee/status/1346652403605647367; Select Committee to Investigate the January 6th Attack on the United States Capitol, Deposition of Jason Miller, (Feb. 3, 2022), p. 174-76; Greg Jacob testified that the President's statement was "categorically untrue." Select Committee to Investigate the January 6th Attack on the United States Capitol, *Hearing on the January 6th Investigation*, 117th Cong., 2d sess., (June 16, 2022), available at https://www.govinfo.gov/committee/house-january6th; Marc Short testified that the statement was "incorrect" and "false." Select Committee to Investigate the January 6th Attack on the United States Capitol, Deposition of Marc Short, (Jan. 26, 2022), p. 224; Chris Hodgson testified that it was not an accurate statement. Select Committee to Investigate the January 6th Attack on the United States Capitol, Deposition of Chris Hodgson, (Mar. 30, 2022), pp. 184-85.

176. Select Committee to Investigate the January 6th Attack on the United States Capitol, Deposition of Jason Miller, (Feb. 3, 2022), pp. 175-77 (acknowledging that Miller normally would have called the Vice President's office before issuing a public statement describing the Vice President's views but stating "I don't think that ultimately -- don't know if it ultimately would have changed anything as the President was very adamant that this is where they both were" and acknowledging that "the way this [statement] came out was the way that [Trump] wanted [it] to.").

177. Donald J. Trump (@realDonaldTrump), Twitter, Jan. 6, 2021 1:00 a.m. ET, available at http://web.archive.org/web/20210106072109/https://twitter.com/realDonaldTrump/status/1346698217304584192 (archived).

178. Donald J. Trump (@realDonaldTrump), Twitter, Jan. 6, 2021 8:17 a.m. ET, available at http://web.archive.org/web/20210106175200/https://twitter.com/realDonaldTrump/status/1346808075626426371 (archived).

179. Select Committee to Investigate the January 6th Attack on the United States Capitol, Transcribed Interview of Eric Herschmann, (Apr. 6, 2022), p. 47; Select Committee to Investigate the January 6th Attack on the United States Capitol, Deposition of Nicholas Luna, (Mar. 21, 2022), p. 126.

180. Select Committee to Investigate the January 6th Attack on the United States Capitol, Deposition of General Keith Kellogg, Jr., (Dec. 14, 2021), p. 90; *See also,* Select Committee to Investigate the January 6th Attack on the United States Capitol, Transcribed Interview of Donald John Trump Jr., (May 3, 2022), p. 84; Select Committee to Investigate the January 6th Attack on the United States Capitol, Transcribed Interview of Eric Herschmann, (Apr. 6, 2022), p. 49; Select Committee to Investigate the January 6th Attack on the United States Capitol, Transcribed Interview of White House Employee, (June 10, 2022), pp. 21-22. The Select Committee is not revealing the identity of this witness to guard against the risk of retaliation.

181. Select Committee to Investigate the January 6th Attack on the United States Capitol, Deposition of Nicholas Luna, (Mar. 21, 2022), p. 127.

182. Select Committee to Investigate the January 6th Attack on the United States Capitol, Transcribed Interview of White House Employee (June 10, 2022), p. 20. The Select Committee is not revealing the identity of this witness to guard against the risk of retaliation.

183. Select Committee to Investigate the January 6th Attack on the United States Capitol, Deposition of General Keith Kellogg, Jr., (Dec. 14, 2021), p. 92.

184. Select Committee to Investigate the January 6th Attack on the United States Capitol, Transcribed Interview of Julie Radford, (May 24, 2022), p. 19. *See also* Peter Baker, Maggie Haberman, and Annie Karni, "Pence Reached His Limit with Trump. It Wasn't Pretty," *New York Times*, (Jan. 12, 2021), available at https://www.nytimes.com/2021/01/12/us/politics/mike-pence-trump.html; Jonathan Karl, *Betrayal: The Final Act of the Trump Show*, (New York: Dutton, 2021), at pp. 273-74.

185. At 11:33 a.m., Stephen Miller's assistant, Robert Gabriel, emailed the speechwriting team with the line: "REINSERT THE MIKE PENCE LINES." Documents on file with the Select Committee to Investigate the January 6th Attack on the United States Capitol (National Archives Production), 076P-R000007531_0001 (January 6, 2021, Robert Gabriel email to Trump speechwriting team at 11:33 a.m.).

186. Select Committee to Investigate the January 6th Attack on the United States Capitol, Deposition of Stephen Miller (Apr. 14, 2022), p. 153.

187. Document on file with the Select Committee (Ross Worthington Production), RW_0002341-2351 (S. Miller Jan. 6 Speech Edits Native File), pp. 2-3.

188. "Transcript of Trump's Speech at Rally Before US Capitol Riot," *Associated Press*, (Jan. 13, 2021), available at https://apnews.com/article/election-2020-joe-biden-donald-trump-capitol-siege-media-e79eb5164613d6718e9f4502eb471f27; Documents on file with the Select Committee to Investigate the January 6th Attack on the United States Capitol (Ross Worthington Production), CTRL0000924249, (changes in speech between draft and as delivered), pp. 2, 5, 12, 16, 22.

189. "Transcript of Trump's Speech at Rally Before US Capitol Riot," *Associated Press*, (Jan. 13, 2021), available at https://apnews.com/article/election-2020-joe-biden-donald-trump-capitol-siege-media-e79eb5164613d6718e9f4502eb471f27.

190. "Transcript of Trump's Speech at Rally Before US Capitol Riot," *Associated Press*, (Jan. 13, 2021), available at https://apnews.com/article/election-2020-joe-biden-donald-trump-capitol-siege-media-e79eb5164613d6718e9f4502eb471f27.

191. "Transcript of Trump's Speech at Rally Before US Capitol Riot," *Associated Press*, (Jan. 13, 2021), available at https://apnews.com/article/election-2020-joe-biden-donald-trump-capitol-siege-media-e79eb5164613d6718e9f4502eb471f27.

192. Select Committee to Investigate the January 6th Attack on the United States Capitol, *Hearing on the January 6th Investigation*, 117th Cong., 2d sess., (June 16, 2022), at 0:14:11-0:14:29, available at https://youtu.be/vBjUWVKuDj0?t=851.

193. Select Committee to Investigate the January 6th Attack on the United States Capitol, *Hearing on the January 6th Investigation*, 117th Cong., 2d sess., (June 16, 2022), at 2:07:02-2:07:07, available at https://youtu.be/vBjUWVKuDj0?t=7609.

194. Select Committee to Investigate the January 6th Attack on the United States Capitol, *Hearing on the January 6th Investigation*, 117th Cong., 2d sess., (June 16, 2022), at 2:07:02-2:07:07, available at https://youtu.be/vBjUWVKuDj0?t=7609.

195. Select Committee to Investigate the January 6th Attack on the United States Capitol, *Hearing on the January 6th Investigation*, 117th Cong., 2d sess., (July 21, 2022), at 1:00:46-1:01:12, available at https://youtu.be/pbRVqWbHGuo?t=3645.

196. Select Committee to Investigate the January 6th Attack on the United States Capitol, *Hearing on the January 6th Investigation*, 117th Cong., 2d sess., (July 21, 2022), at 1:01:13-1:01:26, available at https://youtu.be/pbRVqWbHGuo?t=3645.

197. Select Committee to Investigate the January 6th Attack on the United States Capitol, *Hearing on the January 6th Investigation*, 117th Cong., 2d sess., (June 16, 2022), at 0:14:37-0:14:46, available at https://youtu.be/vBjUWVKuDj0?t=851.

198. Select Committee to Investigate the January 6th Attack on the United States Capitol, *Hearing on the January 6th Investigation*, 117th Cong., 2d sess., (June 16, 2022), at 0:14:47-0:14:55, available at https://youtu.be/vBjUWVKuDj0?t=851.

199. Select Committee to Investigate the January 6th Attack on the United States Capitol, Transcribed Interview of White House Employee, (June 10, 2022), pp. 26-27 (establishing time as 1:21 p.m. based on time stamp of a photograph recognized and described).

200. Donald J. Trump (@realDonaldTrump), Twitter, Jan. 6, 2021 2:24 p.m. ET, available at https://web.archive.org/web/20210106192450/https://twitter.com/realdonaldtrump/status/1346900434540240897 (archived).

201. Government's Sentencing Memorandum at 32-33, *United States v. Cusanelli*, No. 1:21-cr-37 (D.D.C. Sept. 15, 2022), ECF No. 110.

202. *See* Affidavit in Support of Criminal Complaint and Arrest Warrant at 5, *United States v. Black*, No. 1:21-cr-127 (D.D.C. Jan. 13, 2021), ECF No. 1-1, available at https://www.justice.gov/opa/page/file/1354806/download.

203. Indictment at 9, *United States v. Neefe*, No. 1:21-cr-567 (D.D.C. Sept. 8, 2021), ECF No. 1, available at https://www.justice.gov/usao-dc/case-multi-defendant/file/1432686/download.

204. Affidavit in Support of Criminal Complaint and Arrest Warrant at 8, *United States v. Evans*, No. 1:21-cr-337 (D.D.C. Jan. 8, 2021), ECF No. 1-1, available at https://www.justice.gov/usao-dc/press-release/file/1351946/download.

205. Select Committee to Investigate the January 6th Attack on the United States Capitol, *Business Meeting on the January 6th Investigation*, 117th Cong., 2d sess., (Oct. 13, 2022), at 2:26:06-2:26:26, available at https://youtu.be/IQvuBoLBuCO?t=8766; Sentencing Transcript at 19, United States v. Young, *No. 1:21-cr-291* (D.D.C. Sept. 27, 2022), ECF No. 170 (testifying for a victim impact statement, Officer Michael Fanone said: "At approximately 1435 hours, with rapidly mounting injuries and most of the MPD less than lethal munitions expended, the defending officers were forced to conduct a fighting withdrawal back towards the United States Capitol Building entrance. This is the first fighting withdrawal in the history of the Metropolitan Police Department").

206. *See* Transcript of Trump's Speech at Rally Before US Capitol Riot," *Associated Press*, (Jan. 13, 2021), available at https://apnews.com/article/election-2020-joe-biden-donald-trump-capitol-siege-media-e79eb5164613d6718e9f4502eb471f27.

207. United States Secret Service Radio Tango Frequency at 14:16.

208. United States Secret Service Radio Tango Frequency at 14:25; *see also* Spencer S. Hsu, "Pence Spent Jan. 6 at Underground Senate Loading Dock, Secret Service Confirms," *Washington Post*, (Mar. 21, 2022), available at https://www.washingtonpost.com/dc-md-va/2022/03/21/couy-griffin-cowboys-trump-jan6/.

209. Select Committee to Investigate the January 6th Attack on the United States Capitol, *Hearing on the January 6th Investigation*, 117th Cong., 2d sess., (June 16, 2022), at 2:11:22-2:13:55, available at https://youtu.be/vBjUWVKuDj0?t=7882.

210. Select Committee to Investigate the January 6th Attack on the United States Capitol, Transcribed Interview of Eric Herschmann, (Apr. 6, 2022), pp. 43-44.

211. Select Committee to Investigate the January 6th Attack on the United States Capitol, Transcribed Interview of Eric Herschmann, (Apr. 6, 2022), p. 44.

212. Complaint, Exhibit 2 (Select Committee to Investigate the January 6th Attack on the United States Capitol subpoena to Chapman University, dated Jan. 21, 2022), *Eastman v. Thompson et al. et al.*, No. 8:22-cv-99, (C.D. Cal. Jan. 20, 2022) ECF No. 1-2.

213. Order Re Privilege of Documents Dated January 4-7, 2021 at 51-52, Eastman v. Thompson et al., 594 F. Supp. 3d 1156, (C.D. Cal. Mar. 28, 2022) (No. 8:22-cv-99-DOC-DFM).

214. Order Re Privilege of Documents Dated January 4-7, 2021 at 56-57, Eastman v. Thompson et al., 594 F. Supp. 3d 1156 (C.D. Cal. Mar. 28, 2022) (No. 8:22-cv-99-DOC-DFM).

215. Order Re Privilege of Documents Dated January 4-7, 2021 at 63-64, Eastman v. Thompson et al., 594 F. Supp. 3d 1156 (C.D. Cal. Mar. 28, 2022) (No. 8:22-cv-99-DOC-DFM).

216. Select Committee to Investigate the January 6th Attack on the United States Capitol, *Hearing on the January 6th Investigation*, 117th Cong., 2d sess., (June 16, 2022), available at https://www.govinfo.gov/committee/house-january6th.

217. Select Committee to Investigate the January 6th Attack on the United States Capitol, Deposition of Greg Jacob, (Feb. 1, 2022), p. 223.

218. Select Committee to Investigate the January 6th Attack on the U.S. Capitol, Transcribed Interview of Ronna Romney McDaniel, (June 1, 2022), pp. 7-8.

219. Select Committee to Investigate the January 6th Attack on the U.S. Capitol, Transcribed Interview of Ronna Romney McDaniel, (June 1, 2022), pp. 9-11.

220. On December 13th, Chesebro memorialized the strategy in an email he sent Rudy Giuliani with the subject line: "PRIVILEGED AND CONFIDENTIAL – Brief notes on 'President of the Senate strategy." Documents on file with the Select Committee to Investigate the January 6th Attack on the United States Capitol (Chapman UniversityProduction), Chapman004708 (Dec. 13, 2020, Kenneth Chesebro email to Rudy Giuliani). Chesebro argued that the Trump team could use the fake slates of electors to complicate the joint session on January 6th if the President of the Senate "firmly t[ook] the position that he, and he alone, is charged with the constitutional responsibility not just to open the votes, but to count them— including making judgments about what to do if thereare conflicting votes." *Id.* In the weeks that followed, Chesebro and John Eastman would build upon that framework and write two memos asserting that Joe Biden's certification could be derailed on January 6th if Vice President Pence acted as the "ultimate arbiter" when opening the real and fake Electoral College votes during the joint session of Congress. Documents on file with the Select Committee to Investigate the January 6th Attack on the United States Capitol (Chapman University Production), Chapman053476 (December 23, 2020, Eastman memo titled "PRIVILEGED AND CONFIDENTIAL – Dec 23 memo on Jan 6 scenario.docx"); *see also* Documents on file with the Select Committee to Investigate the January 6th Attack on the United States Capitol (Chapman University Production), Chapman061863 (January 1, 2021, Chesebro email to Eastman).

221. Select Committee to Investigate the January 6th Attack on the U.S. Capitol, Transcribed Interview of Justin Clark, (May 17, 2022), pp. 114, 116.

222. Select Committee to Investigate the January 6th Attack on the U.S. Capitol, Transcribed Interview of Justin Clark, (May 17, 2022), pp. 116.

223. The "certificate of ascertainment" is a State executive's official documentation announcing the official electors appointed pursuant to State law. *See* 3 U.S.C. § 6.

224. Select Committee to Investigate the January 6th Attack on the U.S. Capitol, Transcribed Interview of Matthew Morgan, (Apr. 25, 2022), p. 70.

225. Select Committee to Investigate the January 6th Attack on the U.S. Capitol, Transcribed Interview of Pasquale Anthony "Pat" Cipollone (July 8, 2022), pp. 70-72.

226. Select Committee to Investigate the January 6th Attack on the U.S. Capitol, Informal Interview of Patrick Philbin (Apr. 13, 2022).

227. Select Committee to Investigate the January 6th Attack on the U.S. Capitol, Transcribed Interview of Pasquale Anthony "Pat" Cipollone (July 8, 2022), p. 75.

228. Select Committee to Investigate the January 6th Attack on the United States Capitol, Continued Interview of Cassidy Hutchinson, (Mar. 7, 2022), p. 64.

229. Select Committee to Investigate the January 6th Attack on the United States Capitol, Deposition of Shawn Still, (Feb. 25, 2022), p. 24.

230. Select Committee to Investigate the January 6th Attack on the United States Capitol, Deposition of Andrew Hitt, (Feb. 28, 2022), pp. 50–51.

231. The National Archives produced copies of the seven slates of electoral votes they received from Trump electors in States that President Trump lost. *See* Documents on file with the Select Committee to Investigate the January 6th Attack on the United States Capitol (National Archives Production), CTRL0000037568, CTRL0000037944, CTRL0000037945, CTRL0000037946, CTRL0000037947, CTRL0000037948, CTRL0000037949 (December 14, 2020, memoranda from slates of purported electors in Arizona, Georgia, Michigan, New Mexico, Nevada, Pennsylvania, and Wisconsin); Documents on file with the Select Committee to Investigate the January 6th Attack on the United States Capitol (National Archives Production), VP-R0000323_0001 (Senate Parliamentarian office tracking receipt and attaching copies of the seven slates); *See also* Documents on file with the Select Committee to Investigate the January 6th Attack on the United States Capitol (Robert Sinners Production), CTRL0000083893 (Trump campaign staffers emailing regarding submission); Documents on file with the Select Committee to Investigate the January 6th Attack on the United States Capitol (Bill Stepien Production), WS 00096 – WS 00097 (Trump campaign staffers emailing regarding submission).

232. Documents on file with the Select Committee to Investigate the January 6th Attack on the United States Capitol (David Shafer Production), 108751.0001 000004 (December 10, 2020, Kenneth Chesebro email to David Shafer).

233. Documents on file with the Select Committee to Investigate the January 6th Attack on the United States Capitol (National Archives Production), CTRL0000037944 (December 14, 2020, certificate and mailing envelope from Georgia); Documents on file with the Select Committee to Investigate the January 6th Attack on the United States Capitol (National Archives Production), CTRL0000037941 (December 14, 2020, certificate and mailing envelope from Arizona), Documents on file with the Select Committee to Investigate the January 6th Attack on the United States Capitol (National Archives Production), CTRL0000037945 (December 14, 2020, certificate and mailing envelope from Michigan).

234. Documents on file with the Select Committee to Investigate the January 6th Attack on the United States Capitol (Andrew Hitt Production), Hitt000080 (January 4, 2021, Hitt text message with Mark Jefferson); Documents on file with the Select Committee to Investigate the January 6th Attack on the United States Capitol (Angela McCallum Production), McCallum_01_001576 - McCallum_01_001577 (January 5, 2021, McCallum text messages with G. Michael Brown); Documents on file with the Select Committee to Investigate the January 6th Attack on the United States Capitol (Chris Hodgson Production) CTRL0000056548_00007 (January 6, 2021, Hodgson text messages with Matt Stroia); Documents on file with the Select Committee to Investigate the January 6th Attack on the United States Capitol (Chris Hodgson Production), CTRL0000056548_00035 (January 6, 2021, text messages from Senator Johnson's Chief of Staff, Sean Riley, to Chris Hodgson around 12:37 p.m.).

235. Select Committee to Investigate the January 6th Attack on the United States Capitol, Deposition of Chris Hodgson (Mar. 30, 2022), pp. 206–07; Documents on file with the Select Committee to Investigate the January 6th Attack on the United States Capitol (Chris Hodgson Production) CTRL0000056548_00007 (January 6, 2021, text message from Rep. Kelly's Chief of Staff, Matt Stroia, to Chris Hodgson at 8:41 a.m.), CTRL0000056548_00035 (January 6, 2021, text messages from Senator Johnson's Chief of Staff, Sean Riley, to Chris Hodgson around 12:37 p.m.); Jason Lennon, "Johnson Says Involvement with 1/6 Fake Electors Plan Only 'Lasted Seconds'," *Newsweek*, (Aug. 21, 2022), available at https:// www.newsweek.com/johnson-says-involvement-1-6-fake-electors-plan-only-lasted-seconds-1735486.

236. Select Committee to Investigate the January 6th Attack on the United States Capitol, Deposition of Greg Jacob, (Feb. 1, 2022), pp. 52–54.

237. Order Re Privilege of 599 Documents Dated November 3, 2020 - January 20, 2021 at 6, *Eastman v. Thompson et al.*, No. 8:22-cv-99 (C.D. Cal June 7, 2022), ECF No. 356.

238. Order Re Privilege of 599 Documents Dated November 3, 2020 - January 20, 2021 at 20, *Eastman v. Thompson et al..*, No. 8:22-cv-99 (C.D. Cal June 7, 2022), ECF No. 356.

239. Brad Raffensperger, *Integrity Counts* (New York: Simon & Schuster, 2021), p. 191 (reproducing the call transcript); Amy Gardner and Paulina Firozi, "Here's the Full Transcript and Audio of the Call Between Trump and Raffensperger," *Washington Post*, (Jan. 5, 2021), available at https://www.washingtonpost.com/politics/trump-raffensperger-call-transcript-georgia-vote/2021/01/03/2768e0cc-4ddd-11eb-83e3-322644d82356_story.html.

240. Order Re Privilege of Documents Dated January 4-7, 2021 at 5, *Eastman v. Thompson et al.*, 594 F. Supp. 3d 1156 (C.D. Cal. Mar. 28, 2022) (No. 8:22-cv-99-DOC-DFM), also available at https://www.cacd.uscourts.gov/sites/default/files/documents/Dkt%20260%2C%20Order%20RE%20Privilege%20of%20Jan.%204-7%2C%202021%20Documents_0.pdf. .

241. Order Re Privilege of Documents Dated January 4-7, 2021 at 35, *Eastman v. Thompson et al.*, 594 F. Supp. 3d 1156 (C.D. Cal. Mar. 28, 2022) (No. 8:22-cv-99-DOC-DFM), also available at https://www.cacd.uscourts.gov/sites/default/files/documents/Dkt%20260%2C%20Order%20RE%20Privilege%20of%20Jan.%204-7%2C%202021%20Documents_0.pdf.

242. After a journalist tweeted a video clip of key remarks from Gabriel Sterling's warning addressed to President Trump, President Trump responded by quote-tweeting that post, along with a comment that doubled down on demonizing Georgia election workers in spite of Sterling's stark and detailed warning. *See* Donald J. Trump (@realDonaldTrump), Twitter, Dec. 1, 2020 10:27 p.m. ET, available at http://web.archive.org/web/20201203173245/https://mobile.twitter.com/realDonaldTrump/status/1333975991518187521 (archived) ("Rigged Election. Show signatures and envelopes. Expose the massive voter fraud in Georgia. What is Secretary of State and @BrianKempGA afraid of. They know what we'll find!!! [linking to] twitter.com/BrendanKeefe/status/1333884246277189633"); Brendan Keefe (@BrendanKeefe), Twitter, Dec. 1, 2020 4:22 p.m. ET, available at https://twitter.com/BrendanKeefe/status/1333884246277189633 ("'It. Has. All. Gone. Too. Far," says @GabrielSterling with Georgia Sec of State after a Dominion tech's life was threatened with a noose. "Mr. President, you have not condemned these actions or this language....all of you who have not said a damn word are complicit in this.'" with embedded video of Gabriel Sterling's remarks); Select Committee to Investigate the January 6th Attack on the United States Capitol, *Hearing on the January 6th Investigation*, 117th Cong., 2d sess., (June 21, 2022), available at https://www.govinfo.gov/committee/house-january6th.

243. Stephen Fowler, "'Someone's Going to Get Killed': Election Official Blasts GOP Silence on Threats," GPB News, (Dec. 1, 2020, updated Dec. 2, 2020), available at https://www.gpb.org/news/2020/12/01/someones-going-get-killed-election-official-blasts-gop-silence-on-threats.

244. House Governmental Affairs Committee, Georgia House of Representatives, Public Hearing (Dec. 10, 2020), YouTube, at 1:55:10-1:59:10, available at https://youtu.be/9EfgETUKfsI?t=6910.

245. Select Committee to Investigate the January 6th Attack on the United States Capitol, *Hearing on the January 6th Investigation*, 117th Cong., 2d sess., (June 21, 2022), at 2:25:45 to 2:26:00, available at https://youtu.be/xa43_z_82Og?t=8745.

246. Jason Szep and Linda So, "A Reuters Special Report: Trump Campaign Demonized Two Georgia Election Workers – and Death Threats Followed," *Reuters* (Dec. 1, 2021), available at https://www.reuters.com/investigates/special-report/usa-election-threats-georgia/.

247. Amended Complaint at 52, *Freeman v. Giuliani*, No. 21-cv-03354-BAH (D.D.C. filed May 10, 2022), ECF No. 22, available at https://www.courtlistener.com/docket/61642105/22/freeman-v-herring-networks-inc.

248. Select Committee to Investigate the January 6th Attack on the United States Capitol, Transcribed Interview of Ruby Freeman, (May 31, 2022), pp. 7-8.

249. Select Committee to Investigate the January 6th Attack on the United States Capitol, *Hearing on the January 6th Investigation*, 117th Cong., 2d sess., (June 21, 2022), at 41:30-46:35,
available at https://www.youtube.com/watch?v=xa43_z_82Og; Yvonne Wingett Sanchez and
Ronald J. Hansen, "White House Phone Calls, Baseless Fraud Charges: The Origins of the
Arizona Election Review," *Arizona Republic*, (Nov. 17, 2021), available at https://
www.azcentral.com/in-depth/news/politics/elections/2021/11/17/arizona-audit-trump-
allies-pushed-to-undermine-2020-election/6045151001/; Yvonne Wingett Sanchez and
Ronald J. Hansen, "'Asked to do Something Huge': An Audacious Pitch to Reserve Arizona's
Election Results," *Arizona Republic*, (Nov. 18, 2021, updated Dec. 2, 2021), available at
https://www.azcentral.com/in-depth/news/politics/elections/2021/11/18/arizona-audit-
rudy-giuliani-failed-effort-replace-electors/6349795001/.

250. Select Committee to Investigate the January 6th Attack on the United States Capitol, *Hearing on the January 6th Investigation*, 117th Cong., 2d sess., (June 21, 2022), at 53:00-53:40,
available at https://www.youtube.com/watch?v=xa43_z_82Og.

251. Select Committee to Investigate the January 6th Attack on the United States Capitol, *Hearing on the January 6th Investigation*, 117th Cong., 2d sess., (June 21, 2022), at 41:30-46:35,
available at https://www.youtube.com/watch?v=xa43_z_82Og.

252. Dennis Welch (@dennis_welch), Twitter, Dec. 8, 2020 11:23 p.m. ET, available at https://
twitter.com/dennis_welch/status/1336526978640302080 (retweeting people who were posting Bowers's personal information); Dennis Welch (@dennis_welch), Twitter, Dec. 8, 2020
11:28 p.m. ET, available at https://twitter.com/dennis_welch/status/1336528029791604737.

253. Select Committee to Investigate the January 6th Attack on the U.S. Capitol, Transcribed
Interview of Russel "Rusty" Bowers, (June 19, 2022), pp. 50-52; Kelly Weill, "Arizona GOP Civil
War Somehow Keeps Getting Weirder," *Daily Beast*, (Dec. 11, 2020), available at https://
www.thedailybeast.com/arizona-republican-party-civil-war-somehow-keeps-getting-
weirder; Yvonne Wingett Sanchez and Ronald J. Hansen, "'Asked to do Something Huge': An
Audacious Pitch to Reserve Arizona's Election Results," *Arizona Republic*, (Nov. 18, 2021,
updated Dec. 2, 2021), available at https://www.azcentral.com/in-depth/news/politics/
elections/2021/11/18/arizona-audit-rudy-giuliani-failed-effort-replace-electors/
6349795001/.

254. Select Committee to Investigate the January 6th Attack on the United States Capitol, *Hearing on the January 6th Investigation*, 117th Cong., 2d sess., (June 21, 2022), available at
https://www.govinfo.gov/committee/house-january6th.

255. Select Committee to Investigate the January 6th Attack on the United States Capitol, Transcribed Interview of Michael Shirkey, (June 8, 2022), pp. 16-22.

256. Select Committee to Investigate the January 6th Attack on the United States Capitol, Informal Interview of Lee Chatfield, (Oct. 15, 2021).

257. Select Committee to Investigate the January 6th Attack on the United States Capitol, Transcribed Interview of Michael Shirkey, (June 8, 2022), p. 57.

258. "Legislative Leaders Meet with President Trump," State Senator Mike Shirkey, (Nov. 20,
2020), available at https://www.senatormikeshirkey.com/legislative-leaders-meet-with-
president-trump/.

259. Team Trump (Text TRUMP to 88022) (@TeamTrump), Twitter, Jan. 3, 2021 9:00 a.m. ET, available at http://web.archive.org/web/20210103170109/https://twitter.com/TeamTrump/
status/1345776940196659201 (archived); Beth LeBlanc, "Trump Campaign Lists Lawmakers'
Cells, Misdirects Calls for Chatfield to Former Petoskey Resident," *Detroit News*, (Jan. 4,
2021), available at https://www.detroitnews.com/story/news/politics/2021/01/04/trump-
campaign-lists-michigan-lawmakers-cell-numbers-misdirects-private-citizen/4130279001/;
Jaclyn Peiser, "Trump Shared the Wrong Number for a Michigan Lawmaker: A 28-Year-Old
Has Gotten Thousands of Angry Calls," *Washington Post*, (Jan. 5, 2021), available at https://
www.washingtonpost.com/nation/2021/01/05/michigan-trump-wrong-number-chatfield/.

EXECUTIVE SUMMARY

260. Select Committee to Investigate the January 6th Attack on the United States Capitol, Transcribed Interview of Michael Shirkey, (June 8, 2022), p. 52; Aaron Parseghian, "Former Michigan Resident Slammed with Calls After Trump Campaign Mistakenly Posts Number on Social Media," Fox 17 West Michigan, (Jan. 4, 2021), available at https://www.fox17online.com/news/politics/former-michigan-resident-slammed-with-calls-after-trump-campaign-mistakenly-posts-number-on-social-media.

261. Nor would any State legislature have had such authority.

262. Order Re Privilege of Remaining Documents at 16-17, *Eastman v. Thompson et al.*, No. 8:22-cv-99 (C.D. Cal Oct. 19, 2022), ECF No. 372, available at https://www.cacd.uscourts.gov/sites/default/files/documents/Dkt.%20372%2C%20Order%20Re%20Privilege%20of%20Remaining%20Documents.pdf.

263. Documents on file with the Select Committee to Investigate the January 6th Attack on the United States Capitol (Chapman University Production), Chapman060742, (December 31, 2020, from John Eastman to Alex Kaufman and Kurt Hilbert)

264. Documents on file with the Select Committee to Investigate the January 6th Attack on the United States Capitol (Chapman University Production), Chapman060742, (December 31, 2020, from John Eastman to Alex Kaufman and Kurt Hilbert).

265. Order Re Privilege of Remaining Documents at 17, *Eastman v. Thompson et al.*, No. 8:22-cv-99 (C.D. Cal Oct. 19, 2022), ECF No. 372, available at https://www.cacd.uscourts.gov/sites/default/files/documents/Dkt.%20372%2C%20Order%20Re%20Privilege%20of%20Remaining%20Documents.pdf..

266. Order Re Privilege of Remaining Documents at 17, *Eastman v. Thompson et al.*, No. 8:22-cv-099 (C.D. Cal Oct. 19, 2022), ECF No. 372, available at https://www.cacd.uscourts.gov/sites/default/files/documents/Dkt.%20372%2C%20Order%20Re%20Privilege%20of%20Remaining%20Documents.pdf.

267. Select Committee to Investigate the January 6th Attack on the United States Capitol, *Hearing on the January 6th Investigation*, 117th Cong., 2d sess., (June 23, 2022), available at https://www.govinfo.gov/committee/house-january6th.

268. Select Committee to Investigate the January 6th Attack on the United States Capitol, Transcribed Interview of Richard Peter Donoghue, (Oct. 1, 2021), p. 53.

269. Select Committee to Investigate the January 6th Attack on the United States Capitol, Transcribed Interview of Richard Peter Donoghue, (Oct. 1, 2021), pp. 47-48, 53; Select Committee to Investigate the January 6th Attack on the United States Capitol, *Hearing on the January 6th Investigation*, 117th Cong., 2d sess., (June 23, 2022), available at https://www.govinfo.gov/committee/house-january6th.

270. Select Committee to Investigate the January 6th Attack on the United States Capitol, *Hearing on the January 6th Investigation*, 117th Cong., 2d sess., (June 23, 2022), available at https://www.govinfo.gov/committee/house-january6th.

271. Select Committee to Investigate the January 6th Attack on the United States Capitol, *Hearing on the January 6th Investigation*, 117th Cong., 2d sess., (June 23, 2022), available at https://www.govinfo.gov/committee/house-january6th.

272. Select Committee to Investigate the January 6th Attack on the United States Capitol, *Hearing on the January 6th Investigation*, 117th Cong., 2d sess., (June 23, 2022), available at https://www.govinfo.gov/committee/house-january6th.

273. Select Committee to Investigate the January 6th Attack on the United States Capitol, *Hearing on the January 6th Investigation*, 117th Cong., 2d sess., (June 23, 2022), available at https://www.govinfo.gov/committee/house-january6th .

274. Select Committee to Investigate the January 6th Attack on the United States Capitol, Transcribed Interview of Richard Peter Donoghue, (Oct. 1, 2021), p. 58; Documents on file with the Select Committee to Investigate the January 6th Attack on the United States Capitol (Department of Justice Production), HCOR-Pre-Certification-Events-07282021-000738, HCOR-Pre-Certification-Events-07282021-000739 (December 27, 2020, handwritten notes from Richard Donoghue about call with President Trump).

275. Select Committee to Investigate the January 6th Attack on the United States Capitol, Transcribed Interview of Richard Peter Donoghue, (Oct. 1, 2021), p. 59.

276. Select Committee to Investigate the January 6th Attack on the United States Capitol, Transcribed Interview of Richard Peter Donoghue, (Oct. 1, 2021), p. 59.

277. Documents on file with the Select Committee to Investigate the January 6th Attack on the United States Capitol (Mark Meadows Production), MM014099 (December 26, 2020, message from Representative Perry to Meadows stating: "Mark, just checking in as time continues to count down. 11 days to 1/6 and 25 days to inauguration. We gotta get going!"), MM014100 (December 26, 2020, message from Representative Perry to Meadows stating: "Mark, you should call Jeff. I just got off the phone with him and he explained to me why the principal deputy won't work especially with the FBI. They will view it as as [sic] not having the authority to enforce what needs to be done."), MM014101 (Dec. 26, 2020 Message from Meadows to Rep. Perry stating: "I got it. I think I understand. Let me work on the deputy position"), MM014102 (Dec. 26, 2020 Message from Rep. Perry to Meadows stating: "Roger. Just sent you something on Signal"), MM014162 (December 27, 2020, message from Rep. Perry to Meadows stating: "Can you call me when you get a chance? I just want to talk to you for a few moments before I return the presidents [sic] call as requested."), MM014178 (December 28, 2020, message from Rep. Perry to Meadows stating: "Did you call Jeff Clark?"), MM014208 (December 29, 2020, message from Representative Perry to Meadows stating: "Mark, I sent you a note on signal"), MM014586 (January 2, 2021, message from Representative Perry to Meadows stating: "Please call me the instant you get off the phone with Jeff."). President Trump, Mark Meadows, and Representative Perry refused to testify before the Select Committee, and Jeffrey Clark asserted his Fifth Amendment rights in refusing to answer questions from the Select Committee. "Thompson & Cheney Statement on Donald Trump's Defiance of Select Committee Subpoena," Select Committee to Investigate the January 6th Attack on the United States Capitol, (Nov. 14, 2022), available at https://january6th.house.gov/news/press-releases/thompson-cheney-statement-donald-trump-s-defiance-select-committee-subpoena; Luke Broadwater, "Trump Sues to Block Subpoena from Jan. 6 Committee," *New York Times*, (Nov. 11, 2022), available at https://www.nytimes.com/2022/11/11/us/politics/trump-subpoena-jan-6-committee.html; H. Rept. 117-216, Resolution Recommending that the House of Representatives Find Mark Randall Meadows in Contempt of Congress for Refusal to Comply with a Subpoena Duly Issued by the Select Committee to Investigate the January 6th Attack on the United States Capitol, 117th Cong., 1st Sess. (2021), available at https://www.congress.gov/117/crpt/hrpt216/CRPT-117hrpt216.pdf; Letter from John P. Rowley III to the Honorable Bennie G. Thompson, re: Subpoena to Representative Scott Perry, May 24, 2022, available at https://keystonenewsroom.com/wp-content/uploads/sites/6/2022/05/575876667-Rep-perry-Ltr-SelectComm.pdf; Select Committee to Investigate the January 6th Attack on the United States Capitol, Deposition of Jeffrey Clark, (Nov. 5, 2021); Select Committee to Investigate the January 6th Attack on the United States Capitol, Continued Deposition of Jeffrey Clark, (Feb. 2, 2022). See also Jonathan Tamari and Chris Brennan, "Pa. Congressman Scott Perry Acknowledges Introducing Trump to Lawyer at the Center of Election Plot," *Philadelphia Inquirer*, (Jan. 25, 2021), available at https://www.inquirer.com/politics/pennsylvania/scott-perry-trump-georgia-election-results-20210125.html .

278. Documents on file with the Select Committee to Investigate the January 6th Attack on the United States Capitol (Mark Meadows Production), MM014099-014103, MM014178.

279. Select Committee to Investigate the January 6th Attack on the United States Capitol, Transcribed Interview of Jeffrey Rosen, (Oct. 13, 2021), pp. 54-55.

280. Select Committee to Investigate the January 6th Attack at the United States Capitol, Transcribed Interview of Jeffrey Rosen, (Oct. 13, 2021), p. 55.

281. Select Committee to Investigate the January 6th Attack at the United States Capitol, Transcribed Interview of Jeffrey Rosen, (Oct. 13, 2021), p. 56.

282. Select Committee to Investigate the January 6th Attack on the United States Capitol, Transcribed Interview of Richard Peter Donoghue, (Oct. 1, 2021), p. 114; Documents on file with the Select Committee to Investigate the January 6th Attack on the United States Capitol (Department of Justice Production), HCOR-Pre-CertificationEvents-07262021-000681 (Department of Justice policy), HCOR-Pre-CertificationEvents-07262021-000685 (White House policy).

283. Select Committee to Investigate the January 6th Attack at the United States Capitol, Transcribed Interview of Jeffrey Rosen, (Oct. 13, 2021), p. 56.

284. Select Committee to Investigate the January 6th Attack on the United States Capitol, Transcribed Interview of Richard Peter Donoghue, (Oct. 1, 2021), p. 82.

285. Select Committee to Investigate the January 6th Attack on the United States Capitol, Transcribed Interview of Richard Peter Donoghue, (Oct. 1, 2021), pp. 72-73; Documents on file with the Select Committee to Investigate the January 6th Attack on the United States Capitol (Department of Justice Production), HCOR-Pre-CertificationEvents-07262021-000698, (December 27, 2020, handwritten notes from Richard Donoghue about call with Congressman Perry).

286. Select Committee to Investigate the January 6th Attack on the United States Capitol, Deposition of Kenneth Klukowski, (Dec. 15, 2021), pp. 15-17, 64-80, 179-191; Documents on file with the Select Committee to Investigate the January 6th Attack on the United States Capitol (Department of Justice Production), HCOR-Pre-CertificationEvents-07262021-000697, HCOR-Pre-CertificationEvents-07262021-000698 (email with draft letter attached to December 28, 2020, email from Jeffrey Clark to Jeffrey Rosen and Richard Donoghue).

287. Select Committee to Investigate the January 6th Attack on the United States Capitol, Deposition of Kenneth Klukowski, (Dec. 15, 2021), pp. 184-88; Documents on file with the Select Committee to Investigate the January 6th Attack on the United States Capitol (Department of Justice Production), HCOR-Pre-CertificationEvents-07262021-000697, HCOR-Pre-CertificationEvents-07262021-000698 (email with draft letter attached to Dec. 28 email from Jeffrey Clark to Jeffrey Rosen and Richard Donoghue). As further discussed in Chapter 4 of this report, Klukowski, a lawyer, joined DOJ's Civil Division with just weeks remaining in President Trump's term and helped Clark on issues related to the 2020 election, despite the fact that "election-related matters are not part of the Civil portfolio." Select Committee to Investigate the January 6th Attack on the United States Capitol, Deposition of Kenneth Klukowski (Dec. 15, 2021), p. 66-67. Although Klukowski told the Select Committee that the Trump Campaign was his client before joining DOJ, *id.* at p. 190, and despite the fact that he had sent John Eastman draft talking points titled "TRUMP RE-ELECTION" that encouraged Republican State legislatures to "summon" new Electoral College electors for the 2020 election less than a week before starting at DOJ, Klukowski nevertheless helped Clark draft the December 28th letter described in this Report that, if sent, would have encouraged one or more State legislatures to take actions that could have changed the outcome of the 2020 election. *See* Documents on file with the Select Committee to Investigate the January 6th Attack on the United States Capitol (Chapman University Production), Chapman028219, Chapman028220 (December 9, 2020, email from Klukowski to Eastman with attached memo). The Select Committee has concerns about whether Klukowski's actions at DOJ, and his continued contacts with those working for, or to benefit, the Trump Campaign, may have presented a conflict of interest to the detriment of DOJ's mission. In addition, the Select Committee has concerns about many of the "privilege" claims Klukowski used to withhold information responsive to his subpoena, as well as concerns about some of his testimony, including his testimony about contacts with, among others,

John Eastman. The Committee has learned that their communications included at least four known calls between December 22, 2020, and January 2, 2021. Documents on file with the Select Committee to Investigate the January 6th Attack on the United States Capitol (Verizon Production, July 1, 2022) (showing that Klukowski called Eastman on 12/22 at 7:38 a.m. EST for 22.8 min, that Klukowski called Eastman on 12/22 at 7:09 p.m. EST for 6.4 min, that Eastman called Klukowski on 12/30 at 9:11 p.m. EST for 31.9 min, and that Klukowski called Eastman on 1/02 at 6:59 p.m. EST for 6.4 min).

288. Documents on file with the Select Committee to Investigate the January 6th Attack on the United States Capitol (Chapman University Production), Chapman061893 (Jan. 1, 2021, emails between Jeffrey Clark and John Eastman); *see* Documents on file with the Select Committee to Investigate the January 6th Attack on the United States Capitol (Verizon Production, July 1, 2022) (showing five calls between John Eastman and Jeffrey Clark from January 1, 2021, through January 8, 2021).

289. Documents on file with the Select Committee to Investigate the January 6th Attack on the United States Capitol (Department of Justice Production), HCOR-Pre-CertificationEvents-07262021-000697 (Dec. 28 email from Jeffrey Clark to Jeffrey Rosen and Richard Donoghue titled "Two Urgent Action Items") ("The concept is to send it to the Governor, Speaker, and President pro temp of each relevant state..."); Select Committee to Investigate the January 6th Attack on the United States Capitol, Deposition of Kenneth Klukowski, (Dec. 15, 2021), pp. 68-69, 79.

290. Documents on file with the Select Committee to Investigate the January 6th Attack on the United States Capitol (Department of Justice Production), HCOR-Pre-CertificationEvents-07262021-000697 (draft letter attached to December 28, 2020, email from Jeffrey Clark to Jeffrey Rosen and Richard Donoghue).

291. Documents on file with the Select Committee to Investigate the January 6th Attack on the United States Capitol (Department of Justice Production), HCOR-Pre-CertificationEvents-07262021-000697 (draft letter attached to December 28, 2020, email from Jeffrey Clark to Jeffrey Rosen and Richard Donoghue).

292. Documents on file with the Select Committee to Investigate the January 6th Attack on the United States Capitol (Department of Justice Production), HCOR-Pre-CertificationEvents-07262021-000703.

293. Documents on file with the Select Committee to Investigate the January 6th Attack on the United States Capitol (Department of Justice Production), HCOR-Pre-CertificationEvents-07262021-000697 (draft letter attached to December 28, 2020, email from Jeffrey Clark to Jeffrey Rosen and Richard Donoghue).

294. Documents on file with the Select Committee to Investigate the January 6th Attack on the United States Capitol (Department of Justice Production), HCOR-Pre-CertificationEvents-07262021-000697 (draft letter attached to December 28, 2020, email from Jeffrey Clark to Jeffrey Rosen and Richard Donoghue).

295. Documents on file with the Select Committee to Investigate the January 6th Attack on the United States Capitol (Department of Justice Production), HCOR-Pre-CertificationEvents-07262021-000697 (draft letter attached to December 28, 2020, email from Jeffrey Clark to Jeffrey Rosen and Richard Donoghue).

296. Documents on file with the Select Committee to Investigate the January 6th Attack on the United States Capitol (Department of Justice Production), HCOR-Pre-CertificationEvents-06032021-000200 (January 2, 2021, email from Jeffrey Rosen to Richard Donoghue titled "RE: Two Urgent Action Items").

297. Documents on file with the Select Committee to Investigate the January 6th Attack on the United States Capitol (Department of Justice Production), HCOR-Pre-CertificationEvents-06032021-000200 (January 2, 2021, email from Jeffrey Rosen to Richard Donoghue titled "RE: Two Urgent Action Items").

298. Documents on file with the Select Committee to Investigate the January 6th Attack on the United States Capitol (Department of Justice Production), HCOR-Pre-CertificationEvents-06032021-000200 (January 2, 2021, email from Jeffrey Rosen to Richard Donoghue titled "RE: Two Urgent Action Items").

299. Select Committee to Investigate the January 6th Attack on the United States Capitol, *Hearing on the January 6th Investigation*, 117th Cong., 2d sess., (June 23, 2022), available at https://www.govinfo.gov/committee/house-january6th.

300. Select Committee to Investigate the January 6th Attack on the United States Capitol, Transcribed Interview of Richard Peter Donoghue, (Oct. 1, 2021), p. 82.

301. Select Committee to Investigate the January 6th Attack on the United States Capitol, Transcribed Interview of Richard Peter Donoghue, (Oct. 1, 2021), p. 82.

302. Select Committee to Investigate the January 6th Attack on the United States Capitol, *Hearing on the January 6th Investigation*, 117th Cong., 2d sess., (June 23, 2022), available at https://www.govinfo.gov/committee/house-january6th; Select Committee to Investigate the January 6th Attack on the United States Capitol, Transcribed Interview of Richard Peter Donoghue, (Oct. 1, 2021), pp. 79-82; Documents on file with the Select Committee to Investigate the January 6th Attack on the United States Capitol (Department of Justice Production), HCOR-Pre-CertificationEvents-07262021-000703 (December 28, 2020, email from Richard Donoghue to Jeffrey Clark, cc'ing Jeffrey Rosen re: Two Urgent Action Items in which Donoghue writes: "there is no chance that I would sign this letter or anything remotely like this.").

303. Select Committee to Investigate the January 6th Attack at the United States Capitol, Transcribed Interview of Jeffrey Rosen, (Oct. 13, 2021), p. 73; Documents on file with the Select Committee to Investigate the January 6th Attack on the United States Capitol (Department of Justice Production), HCOR-Pre-CertificationEvents-07262021-000703 (December 28, 2020, email from Richard Donoghue to Jeffrey Clark, cc'ing Jeffrey Rosen re: Two Urgent Action Items in which Donoghue writes: "there is no chance that I would sign this letter or anything remotely like this."); Senate Committee on the Judiciary, Interview of Richard Donoghue, (August 6, 2021), at p. 99, available at https://www.judiciary.senate.gov/imo/media/doc/Donoghue%20Transcript.pdf.

304. Select Committee to Investigate the January 6th Attack on the United States Capitol, Transcribed Interview of Richard Peter Donoghue, (Oct. 1, 2021), p. 113.

305. Select Committee to Investigate the January 6th Attack on the United States Capitol, *Hearing on the January 6th Investigation*, 117th Cong., 2d sess., (June 23, 2022), available at https://www.govinfo.gov/committee/house-january6th.

306. Select Committee to Investigate the January 6th Attack on the United States Capitol, *Hearing on the January 6th Investigation*, 117th Cong., 2d sess., (June 23, 2022), available at https://www.govinfo.gov/committee/house-january6th.

307. Documents on file with the Select Committee to Investigate the January 6th Attack on the United States Capitol (National Archives Production), CTRL0000083040 (January 3, 2021, White House Presidential Call Log).

308. Select Committee to Investigate the January 6th Attack on the United States Capitol, Transcribed Interview of Richard Peter Donoghue, (Oct. 1, 2021), p. 119.

309. Select Committee to Investigate the January 6th Attack on the United States Capitol, Transcribed Interview of Richard Peter Donoghue, (Oct. 1, 2021), p. 119-20. ("And so it was unanimous; everyone was going to resign if Jeff Rosen was removed from the seat." The only exception was John Demers, the Assistant Attorney General for the National Security Division. Donoghue encouraged Demers to stay on because he didn't want to further jeopardize national security.)

310. Select Committee to Investigate the January 6th Attack on the United States Capitol, Transcribed Interview of Richard Peter Donoghue, (Oct. 1, 2021), p. 124.

311. Select Committee to Investigate the January 6th Attack on the United States Capitol, Transcribed Interview of Richard Peter Donoghue, (Oct. 1, 2021), pp. 126-28; Select Committee to Investigate the January 6th Attack on the United States Capitol, Transcribed Interview of Pasquale Anthony "Pat" Cipollone, (July 8, 2022), p. 120.

312. Select Committee to Investigate the January 6th Attack on the United States Capitol, Transcribed Interview of Richard Peter Donoghue, (Oct. 1, 2021), p. 126.

313. Select Committee to Investigate the January 6th Attack on the United States Capitol, Transcribed Interview of Richard Peter Donoghue, (Oct. 1, 2021), p. 125.

314. Select Committee to Investigate the January 6th Attack on the United States Capitol, Transcribed Interview of Steven A. Engel, (Jan. 13, 2022), p. 64.

315. Select Committee to Investigate the January 6th Attack on the United States Capitol, Transcribed Interview of Richard Peter Donoghue, (Oct. 1, 2021), p. 125.

316. Select Committee to Investigate the January 6th Attack on the United States Capitol, Transcribed Interview of Richard Peter Donoghue, (Oct. 1, 2021), pp. 131-132.

317. Select Committee to Investigate the January 6th Attack on the United States Capitol, Transcribed Interview of Richard Peter Donoghue, (Oct. 1, 2021), pp. 131-32.

318. Select Committee to Investigate the January 6th Attack on the United States Capitol, Deposition of Sidney Powell, (May 7, 2022), pp. 75, 84.

319. Donald J. Trump (@realDonaldTrump), Twitter, Dec. 19, 2020 1:42 a.m. ET, available at http://web.archive.org/web/20201219064257/https://twitter.com/realDonaldTrump/status/1340185773220515840 (archived).

320. Donald J. Trump (@realDonaldTrump), Twitter, Dec. 26, 2020 8:14 a.m. ET, available at https://twitter.com/realDonaldTrump/status/1342821189077622792; Donald J. Trump (@realDonaldTrump), Twitter, Dec. 27, 2020 5:51 p.m. ET, available at https://twitter.com/realDonaldTrump/status/1343328708963299338; Donald J. Trump (@realDonaldTrump), Twitter, Dec. 30, 2020 2:06 p.m. ET, available at https://twitter.com/realDonaldTrump/status/1344359312878149634; Donald J. Trump (@realDonaldTrump), Twitter, Jan. 1, 2021 12:52 p.m. ET, available at https://www.thetrumparchive.com/?searchbox=%22RT+%40KylieJaneKremer%22 (archived) (retweeting @KylieJaneKremer, Dec. 19, 2020 3:50 p.m. ET, available at https://twitter.com/KylieJaneKremer/status/1340399063875895296)); Donald J. Trump (@realDonaldTrump), Twitter, Jan. 1, 2021 2:53 p.m. ET, available at https://twitter.com/realDonaldTrump/status/1345095714687377418; Donald J. Trump (@realDonaldTrump), Twitter, Jan. 1, 2021 3:34 p.m. ET, available at https://twitter.com/realDonaldTrump/status/1345106078141394944; Donald J. Trump (@realDonaldTrump), Twitter, Jan. 1, 2021 6:38 p.m. ET, available at https://twitter.com/realDonaldTrump/status/1345152408591204352; Donald J. Trump (@realDonaldTrump), Twitter, Jan. 2, 2021 9:04 p.m. ET, available at https://twitter.com/realDonaldTrump/status/1345551634907209730; Donald J. Trump (@realDonaldTrump), Twitter, Jan. 3, 2021 1:29 a.m. ET, available at https://www.thetrumparchive.com/?searchbox=%22RT+%40realDonaldTrump%3A+https%3A%2F%2Ft.co%2FnslWcFwkCj%22 (archived) (retweeting Donald J. Trump (@realDonaldTrump), Jan. 2, 2021 9:04 p.m. ET, available at https://twitter.com/realDonaldTrump/status/1345551634907209730)); Donald J. Trump (@realDonaldTrump), Twitter, Jan. 3, 2021 10:15 a.m. ET, available at https://www.thetrumparchive.com/?searchbox=%22RT+%40JenLawrence21%22 (archived) (retweeting Jennifer Lynn Lawrence (@JenLawrence21)), Jan. 3, 2021 12:17 a.m. ET, available at https://twitter.com/JenLawrence21/status/1345600194826686464); Donald J. Trump (@realDonaldTrump), Twitter, Jan. 3, 2021 10:17 a.m. ET, available at https://www.thetrumparchive.com/?searchbox=%22RT+%40CodeMonkeyZ+if%22 (archived) (retweeting Ron Watkins (@CodeMonkeyZ) Jan. 2, 2021 9:14 p.m. ET, available at http://web.archive.org/web/20210103151826/https://twitter.com/CodeMonkeyZ/status/1345599512560078849 (archived)); Donald J. Trump, (@realDonaldTrump), Twitter, Jan. 3,

2021 10:24 a.m. ET, available at https://www.thetrumparchive.com/?searchbox=
%22RT+%40realMikeLindell%22 (archived) (retweeting Mike Lindell (@realMikeLindell), Jan.
2, 2021 5:47 p.m. ET, available at http://web.archive.org/web/20210103152421/https://
twitter.com/realMikeLindell/status/1345547185836978176 (archived)); Donald J. Trump
(@realDonaldTrump), Twitter, Jan. 3, 2021 10:27 a.m. ET, available at https://twitter.com/
realDonaldTrump/status/1345753534168506370; Donald J. Trump (@realDonaldTrump), Twitter, Jan. 3, 2021 10:28 a.m. ET, available at https://www.thetrumparchive.com/?searchbox=
%22RT+%40AmyKremer+we%22 (archived) (retweeting Amy Kremer (@AmyKremer), Jan. 2,
2021 2:58 p.m. ET, available at https://twitter.com/AmyKremer/status/
1345459488107749386); Donald J. Trump (@realDonaldTrump), Twitter, Jan. 4, 2021 9:46 a.m.
ET, available at https://www.thetrumparchive.com/?searchbox=
%22RT+%40realDonaldTrump+I+will+be+there.+Historic+day%21%22 (retweeting Donald J.
Trump (@realDonaldTrump), Jan. 3, 2021 10:27 a.m. ET, available at https://twitter.com/
realDonaldTrump/status/1345753534168506370); Donald J. Trump (@realDonaldTrump),
Twitter, Jan. 5, 2021 10:27 a.m. ET, available at https://twitter.com/realDonaldTrump/
status/1346478482105069568; Donald J. Trump (@realDonaldTrump), Twitter, Jan. 5, 2021
5:43 p.m. ET, available at https://twitter.com/realDonaldTrump/status/
1346588064026685443.

321. *See, e.g.,* Sentencing Memorandum of Daniel Johnson at 5, *United States v. Johnson,* No.
1:21-cr-407 (D.D.C. May 25, 2022), ECF No. 56 ("Mr. Johnson believed what he read on the
internet and heard from the President himself - that the election had been stolen.");
Select Committee to Investigate the January 6th Attack on the United States Capitol, Transcribed Interview of Zac Martin, (Mar. 9, 2022), p. 20 (answering that he believed President
Trump wanted "patriots to show up in Washington, DC on January 6th" because "we felt
like our rights were being taken away from us" given the election results).

322. *See, e.g.,* Trial Transcript at 4106-08, *United States v. Rhodes et al.,* No. 1:22-cr-15 (D.D.C.
Oct. 18, 2022) (Oath Keeper Jason Dolan testified that the Oath Keepers came to Washington, DC "to stop the certification of the election. ... [b]y any means necessary. That's why
we brought our firearms."); Motion to Suppress, Exhibit A at 34, 85-86, *United States v.
Rodriguez,* No. 1:21-cr-246 (D.D.C. Oct. 15, 2021), ECF No. 38-1 ("Trump called us. Trump
called us to DC ... and he's calling for help -- I thought he was calling for help. I thought he
was -- I thought we were doing the right thing."); Statement of Facts at 2, *United States v.
Martin,* No. 1:21-cr-394 (D.D.C. Apr. 20, 2021) ("MARTIN reported that he decided to travel to
Washington, D.C. after reading then-President Donald Trump's tweets regarding the election being stolen and a protest on January 6, 2021, flying to D.C. on January 5, 2021, and
attending the rallies on January 6, 2021, and then heading to the U.S. Capitol where he
entered along with a crowd of other individuals."); Statement of Facts at 9-10, *United
States v. Denney,* No. 1:22-cr-70 (D.D.C. Dec. 7, 2021) ("So Trump has called this himself. For
everyone to come. It's the day the electoral college is suppose [sic] to be certified by congress to officially elect Biden."); Select Committee to Investigate the January 6thth Attack
on the United States Capitol, Transcribed Interview of Dustin Thompson (Nov. 16, 2022), pp.
34, 44, 70-71 (noting that he went to the Capitol at President Trump's direction and that he
"figured [stopping the certification of the vote] was [President Trump's] plan"; *see also,*
Documents on file with the Select Committee to Investigate the January 6th Attack on the
United States Capitol (Select Committee Chart Compiling Defendant Statements).

323. Indictment at 6, *United States v. Smith,* No. 1:21-cr-567 (D.D.C. Sept. 9, 2021), ECF No. 1.

324. Statement of Facts at 3, *United States v. Sulenta,* No. 1:22-mj-00129-ZMF (D.D.C. June 6,
2022), ECF No. 1-1.

325. Stipulated Statement of Facts at 7, *United States v. Morss,* No. 1:21-cr-40 (D.D.C. August 23,
2022), ECF No. 430.

326. Statement of Facts at 9, *United States v. Grayson,* No. 1:21-cr-224 (D.D.C. Jan. 25, 2021), ECF
No. 1-1.

327. Statement of Facts at 11, *United States v. Denney,* No. 1:21-mj-00686-RMM-ZMF (D.D.C. Dec.
7, 2021), ECF No. 1-1.

328. Gieswein denies that he was a Three Percenter as of January 6, 2021, even though he affiliated with an apparent Three Percenter group at previous times. *See* Gieswein's Motion for Hearing & Revocation of Detention Order at 2-3, 18-19, 25, *United States v. Gieswein*, No. 1:21-cr-24 (D.D.C. June 8, 2021), ECF No. 18. When the FBI arrested Gieswein, the criminal complaint noted that he "appears to be affiliated with the radical militia group known as the Three Percenters." Criminal Complaint at 5, *United States v. Gieswein*, No. 1:21-cr-24 (D.D.C. Jan. 16, 2021), available at https://www.justice.gov/opa/page/file/1360831/download. *See also* Adam Rawnsley (@arawnsley), Twitter, Jan. 17, 2021 9:13 p.m. ET, available at https://twitter.com/arawnsley/status/1350989535954530315 (highlighting photos of Gieswein flashing a Three Percenter symbol).

329. Second Superseding Indictment at 9-10, *United States v. Nordean et al.*, No. 1:21-cr-175 (D.D.C. March 7, 2022), ECF No. 305.

330. Statement of Offense at 5, *United States v. Bertino*, No. 1:22-cr-329 (D.D.C. Oct. 6, 2022), ECF No. 5; Third Superseding Indictment at 6, *United States v. Nordean, et al.*, No. 1:21-cr-175 (D.D.C. June 6, 2022), ECF No. 380; Statement of Offense at 3, *United States v. Donohoe*, No. 1:21-cr-175 (D.D.C. Apr. 8, 2022), ECF No. 336.

331. Third Superseding Indictment at 13, *United States v. Nordean, et al.*, No. 1:21-cr-175 (D.D.C. June 6, 2022), ECF No. 380; Georgia Wells, Rebecca Ballhaus, and Keach Hagey, "Proud Boys, Seizing Trump's Call to Washington, Helped Lead Capitol Attack," *Wall Street Journal*, (Jan.17, 2021), available at https://www.wsj.com/articles/proud-boys-seizing-trumps-call-to-washington-helped-lead-capitol-attack-11610911596.

332. Documents on file with the Select Committee to Investigate the January 6th Attack on the United States Capitol (Jay Thaxton Production), CTRL0000070865, (December 29, 2020, Telegram chat at 11:09 a.m. from Enrique Tarrio under the name "HEIKA NOBLELEAD.").

333. "Former Leader of Proud Boys Pleads Guilty to Seditious Conspiracy for Efforts to Stop Transfer of Power Following 2020 Presidential Election," Department of Justice, (Oct. 6, 2022), available at https://www.justice.gov/opa/pr/former-leader-proud-boys-pleads-guilty-seditious-conspiracy-efforts-stop-transfer-power; "Leader of North Carolina Chapter of Proud Boys Pleads Guilty to Conspiracy and Assault Charges in Jan. 6 Capitol Breach," Department of Justice, (Apr. 8, 2022), available at https://www.justice.gov/opa/pr/leader-north-carolina-chapter-proud-boys-pleads-guilty-conspiracy-and-assault-charges-jan-6.

334. Statement of Offense at 2, *United States v. Bertino*, No. 1:22-cr-329 (D.D.C. Oct. 6, 2022), ECF No. 5.

335. Statement of Offense at 4, *United States v. Bertino*, No. 1:22-cr-329 (D.D.C. Oct. 6, 2022), ECF No. 5.

336. Statement of Offense at 4-5, *United States v. Bertino*, No. 1:22-cr-329 (D.D.C. Oct. 6, 2022), ECF No. 5.

337. Statement of Offense at 4, *United States v. Donohoe*, No. 1:21-cr-175 (D.D.C. Apr. 8, 2022), ECF No. 336. Indeed, Proud Boys leaders Biggs and Nordean told MOSD on January 5th about a plan they had discussed with Tarrio for January 6th. Although Biggs and Nordean did not share the plan's precise details, Proud Boys like Bertino and Donohoe nonetheless understood the "objective in Washington, D.C., on January 6, 2021, was to obstruct, impede, or interfere with the certification of the Electoral College vote, including by force if necessary," and that the Proud Boys "would accomplish this through the use of force and violence, which could include storming the Capitol through police lines and barricades if necessary." Statement of Offense at 8, *United States v. Bertino*, No. 1:22-cr-329 (D.D.C. Oct. 6, 2022), ECF No. 5; Statement of Offense at 6, *United States v. Donohoe*, No. 1:21-cr-175 (D.D.C. Apr. 8, 2022), ECF No. 336.

338. Superseding Indictment at 2-3, *United States v. Rhodes et al*, No. 1:22-cr-15 (D.D.C. June 22, 2022), ECF No. 167.

339. Caldwell testified that he was not an Oath Keeper. *See* Trial Transcript at 8778-79, *United States v. Rhodes et al.*, No. 1:22-cr-15 (D.D.C. Nov. 15, 2022); Hannah Rabinowitz and Holmes Lybrand, "Capitol Riot Defendant Calls Himself a 'Little Bit of a Goof' Regarding Pelosi and Pence Comments," CNN, (Nov. 15, 2022), available at https://www.cnn.com/2022/11/15/

politics/thomas-caldwell-testifies-oath-keeper-trial. Because the government tried Caldwell in a conspiracy case with known Oath Keepers, the Select Committee has referred to him as an Oath Keeper.

340.   See Trial Transcript at 10502-08, *United States v. Rhodes et al.*, No. 1:22-cr-15 (D.D.C. Nov. 29, 2022).

341.   Trial Exhibit 6860 (1.S.656.9328 - 9396), *United States v. Rhodes*, No. 1:22-cr-15 (D.D.C. Oct. 13, 2022).

342.   Superseding Indictment at 13, *United States v. Rhodes, III, et al.*, No. 22-cr-15 (D.D.C. June 22, 2022), ECF No 167.

343.   Superseding Indictment at 13-14, *United States v. Rhodes, et al.*, No. 1:22-cr-15 (D.D.C. June 22, 2022), ECF No. 167.

344.   Superseding Indictment at 15-17, *United States v. Rhodes, et al.*, No. 22-cr-15 (D.D.C. June 22, 2022), ECF No 167.

345.   Statement of Offense at 5, *United States v. Ulrich*, No. 1:22-cr-15 (D.D.C. Apr. 29, 2022), ECF No. 117.

346.   Statement of Offense at 5, *United States v. James*, No. 1:22-cr-15 (D.D.C. Mar. 2, 2022), ECF No. 60.

347.   "TTPO Stance on Election Fraud," The Three Percenters - Original, available at https://archive.ph/YemCC#selection-289.0-289.29 (archived).

348.   Statement of Facts at 7-8, *United States v. Buxton*, No. 1:21-cr-739 (D.D.C. Dec. 8, 2021), ECF No. 1-1; Post: "Oath Keepers claim to stand for the constitution yet will not call up its 30k membership to attend the 6th. I thought you guys stood for the constitution? It's your only job as an organization...now or never boys," Patriots.win, Dec. 29, 2020, available at https://patriots.win/p/11RO2hdyR2/x/c/4DrwV8RcV1s.

349.   Indictment at 1, 7, *United States v. Hostetter et al.*, No. 1:21-cr-392 (D.D.C. June 9, 2021), ECF No. 1.

350.   Indictment at 7, *United States v. Hostetter et al.*, No. 1:21-cr-392 (D.D.C. June 9, 2021), ECF No. 1.

351.   Indictment at 8-13, *United States v. Hostetter et al.*, No. 1:21-cr-392 (D.D.C. June 9, 2021), ECF No. 1.

352.   Indictment at 9, *United States v. Hostetter et al.*, No. 1:21-cr-392 (D.D.C. June 9, 2021), ECF No. 1.

353.   Statement of Facts at 4, *United States v. Cole et al.*, No. 1:22-mj-184, (D.D.C. Aug. 29, 2022), ECF No. 5-1.

354.   Statement of Facts at 5, *United States v. Cole et al.*, No. 1:22-mj-184, (D.D.C. Aug. 29, 2022), ECF No. 5-1. When the Select Committee asked about this post to the leader of the Florida Guardians of Freedom, Liggett downplayed any significance or any knowledge about other Three Percenter groups that might "show in record numbers." Select Committee to Investigate the January 6th Attack on the United States Capitol, Deposition of Jeremy Liggett, (May 17, 2022), pp. 51-52.

355.   Statement of Facts at 5-6, *United States v. Cole et al.*, No. 1:22-mj-184, (D.D.C. Aug. 29, 2022), ECF No. 5-1; #SeditionHunters (@SeditionHunters), Twitter, June 7, 2021 2:11 p.m. ET, available at https://twitter.com/SeditionHunters/status/1401965056980627458.

356.   Statement of Facts at 15-17, *United States v. Cole et al.*, No. 1:22-mj-184, (D.D.C. Aug. 29, 2022), ECF No. 5-1. The "tunnel" is actually a flight of stairs leading to a doorway from which the President emerges on Inauguration Day to take the oath of office. When the inauguration stage is present, the stairs leading to the doorway are converted into a "10-foot-wide, slightly sloped, short tunnel that was approximately 15 feet long." Government's Sentencing Memorandum at 5-6, *United States v. Young*, No. 1:21-cr-291-3 (D.D.C. Sept. 13, 2022), ECF No. 140. For other examples of how extremist groups responded to President Trump's call to action, *see* Chapter 6.

357. Indictment at 11, *United States v. Rodriguez et al.*, No. 1:21-cr-246 (D.D.C. Nov. 19, 2021), ECF No. 65; Motion to Suppress, Exhibit A at 70, *United States v. Rodriguez*, No. 1:21-cr-246 (D.D.C. Oct. 15, 2021), ECF No. 38-1.

358. Motion to Suppress, Exhibit A at 34, 85-86, *United States v. Rodriguez*, No. 1:21-cr-246 (D.D.C. Oct. 15, 2021), ECF No. 38-1.

359. Government's Opposition to Defendant's Renewed Request for Pretrial Release at 7, *United States v. Meggs*, No. 1:21-cr-28 (D.D.C Mar. 23, 2021), ECF No. 98.

360. Documents on file with the Select Committee to Investigate the January 6th Attack on the United States Capitol (Documents on file with the Select Committee to Investigate the January 6th Attack on the United States Capitol (Google Voice Production, Feb. 25, 2022).

361. Trial Exhibit 6868 (2000.T.420), *United States v. Rhodes et al.*, No. 1:22-cr-15 (D.D.C. Oct. 13, 2022).

362. Trial Exhibit 6868 (2000.T.420), *United States v. Rhodes et al.*, No. 1:22-cr-15 (D.D.C. Oct. 13, 2022).

363. Trial Exhibit 9221, *United States v. Rhodes et al.*, No.1:22-cr-15 (D.D.C. Nov. 9, 2022).

364. Motion for Bond, Exhibit 1 at 125-26, *United States v. Vallejo*, No. 1:22-cr-15 (D.D.C. Apr. 18, 2022), ECF No. 102-1 (Collection of redacted text messages, labeled as Exhibit 8, showing Rhodes adding "a CA Oath Keeper who is in with a four man team, followed by that person announcing his identifiable radio frequency) Ryan J. Reilly, "New Evidence Reveals Coordination Between Oath Keepers, Three Percenters on Jan. 6," NBC News, (May 28, 2022), available at https://www.nbcnews.com/politics/justice-department/new-evidence-reveals-coordination-oath-keepers-three-percenters-jan-6-rcna30355 (noting how public source investigators linked the identifiable radio frequency to Derek Kinnison, who is one of the California Three Percenters indicted on conspiracy charges for their conduct on January 6th. *See* Indictment, *United States v. Hostetter et al.*, No. 1:21-cr-392 (D.D.C. June 9, 2021), ECF No. 1).

365. Documents on file with the Select Committee to Investigate the January 6th Attack on the United States Capitol (Department of Justice Production), CTRL 0000010471, at 7:01 (January 6, 2021, video footage recorded by Samuel Montoya at the U.S. Capitol).

366. Documents on file with the Select Committee to Investigate the January 6th Attack on the United States Capitol, (District of Columbia Production), Axon Body 3 X6039BKH5 13.53.47 20210106-FELONYRIOT-FIRSTSTSE, at 15:28:13 (MPD body camera footage); Statement of Facts at 3, *United States v. Cale*, No. 1:22-cr-139 (D.D.C. Mar. 28, 2022), ECF No. 1-1.

367. Documents on file with the Select Committee to Investigate the January 6th Attack on the United States Capitol (Department of Justice Production), HCOR-Jan6-07222021-000603.

368. Select Committee to Investigate the January 6th Attack on the United States Capitol, Transcribed Interview of Richard Peter Donoghue, (Oct. 1, 2021), p. 143.

369. Select Committee to Investigate the January 6th Attack on the United States Capitol, Transcribed Interview of General Mark A. Milley, (Nov. 17, 2021), p. 199.

370. Documents on file with the Select Committee to Investigate the January 6th Attack on the United States Capitol (Mary McCord Production), CTRL0000930476 (December 22, 2020, email to the FBI noting troubling Oath Keepers chats),

371. Documents on file with the Select Committee to Investigate the January 6th Attack on the United States Capitol (Mary McCord Production), CTRL0000930476 (December 22, 2020, email to the FBI noting troubling Oath Keepers chats).

372. Documents on file with the Select Committee to Investigate the January 6th Attack on the United States Capitol (Secret Service Production), USSS0000038637, (December 25, 2020, email chain from PIOC on January 6th intelligence).

373. Documents on file with the Select Committee to Investigate the January 6th Attack on the United States Capitol (Secret Service Production), USSS0000038637, (December 25, 2020, email chain from PIOC on January 6th intelligence).

374. Documents on file with the Select Committee to Investigate the January 6th Attack on the United States Capitol (Secret Service Production), USSS0000038637, (December 25, 2020, email chain from PIOC on January 6th intelligence).

375. Documents on file with the Select Committee to Investigate the January 6th Attack on the United States Capitol (Secret Service Production), USSS0000038637, (December 25, 2020, email chain from PIOC on January 6th intelligence).

376. Documents on file with the Select Committee to Investigate the January 6th Attack on the United States Capitol (Secret Service Production), USSS0000038637, (December 25, 2020, email chain from PIOC on January 6th intelligence).

377. Documents on file with the Select Committee to Investigate the January 6th Attack on the United States Capitol (Secret Service Production), USSS0000038637, (December 25, 2020, email chain from PIOC on January 6th intelligence).

378. Documents on file with the Select Committee to Investigate the January 6th Attack on the United States Capitol (Secret Service Production), USSS0000038637, (December 25, 2020, email chain from PIOC on January 6th intelligence).

379. Documents on file with the Select Committee to Investigate the January 6th Attack on the United States Capitol (Capitol Police Production), CTRL0000000080 (December 28, 2020, email to John Donohue re: (LES) Armed and Ready SITE.pdf.); Select Committee to Investigate the January 6th Attack on the United States Capitol, Transcribed Interview of Jack Donohue, (Jan. 31, 2022), p. 8; Select Committee to Investigate the January 6th Attack on the United States Capitol, Informal Interview of Jack Donohue, (Jan. 7, 2022).

380. Documents on file with the Select Committee to Investigate the January 6th Attack on the United States Capitol (Secret Service Production), USSS0000067420 (December 26, 2020, email to PIOC regarding possible Proud Boys plan for January 6, 2021).

381. Documents on file with the Select Committee to Investigate the January 6th Attack on the United States Capitol (Secret Service Production), USSS0000067420 (December 26, 2020, email to PIOC regarding possible Proud Boys plan for January 6, 2021).

382. Documents on file with the Select Committee to Investigate the January 6th Attack on the United States Capitol (Capitol Police Production), CTRL0000001473 (December 29, 2020, email from PIOC-ONDUTY to THREAT ASSESSMENT re: FW: [EXTERNAL EMAIL] - Neo-Nazi Calls on D.C. Pro-Trump Protesters to Occupy Federal Building.).

383. Documents on file with the Select Committee to Investigate the January 6th Attack on the United States Capitol (Capitol Police Production), CTRL0000000087 (December 28, 2020, email re: 1/6 warning.).

384. Documents on file with the Select Committee to Investigate the January 6th Attack on the United States Capitol (Capitol Police Production), CTRL0000001473 (December 29, 2020, email from PIOC-ONDUTY@USSS.DHS.GOV to THREATS@uscp.gov titled "FW: [EXTERNAL EMAIL] - Neo-Nazi Calls on D.C. Pro-Trump Protesters to Occupy Federal Building.").

385. Documents on file with the Select Committee to Investigate the January 6th Attack on the United States Capitol (Secret Service Production), CTRL0000101135.0001, pp. 1, 3 (December 30, 2020, Protective Intelligence Brief titled "Wild Protest").

386. See Documents on file with the Select Committee to Investigate the January 6th Attack on the United States Capitol (Capitol Police Production), CTRL0000001527 (Email titled "Fwd: MPD MMS Text Tip.").

387. See Documents on file with the Select Committee to Investigate the January 6th Attack on the United States Capitol (Capitol Police Production), CTRL0000001527 (Email titled "Fwd: MPD MMS Text Tip.").

388. Documents on file with the Select Committee to Investigate the January 6th Attack on the United States Capitol, (Parler Production) PARLER_00000013 (January 2, 2021, email from Parler to the FBI re: Another to check out, attaching Parler posts).

389. Documents on file with the Select Committee to Investigate the January 6th Attack on the United States Capitol (Capitol Police Production), CTRL0000001487 (January 2, 2021, email to Capitol Police and Department of Justice with screenshots of Parler posts); Documents on file with the Select Committee to Investigate the January 6th Attack on the United States Capitol (Capitol Police Production), CTRL0000000116, CTRL0000000116.0001 (January 4, 2021, email from U.S. Capitol Police re: Comments of concern for Jan 6 rally, collecting Parler posts).

390. Documents on file with the Select Committee to Investigate the January 6th Attack on the United States Capitol (Capitol Police Production), CTRL0000001532.0001, p.2 (January 5, 2021, FBI Situational Information Report).

391. Documents on file with the Select Committee to Investigate the January 6th Attack on the United States Capitol (Capitol Police Production), CTRL0000001532.0001, p.2 (January 5, 2021, FBI Situational Information Report).

392. Documents on file with the Select Committee to Investigate the January 6th Attack on the United States Capitol (Secret Service Production), CTRL0000293417 (December 30, 2020, email to OSU-ALL titled "Discovery of Event Website- MAGA Drag the Interstate & Occupy the Capitol").

393. Documents on file with the Select Committee to Investigate the January 6th Attack on the United States Capitol (Capitol Police Production), CTRL0000000083, CTRL0000000083.0001 (January 5, 2021, email re: (U//FOUO//LES) OSINT Post of Concern.).

394. Documents on file with the Select Committee to Investigate the January 6th Attack on the United States Capitol (Capitol Police Production), CTRL0000000083, CTRL0000000083.0001 (January 5, 2021, email al re: (U//FOUO//LES) OSINT Post of Concern.).

395. Documents on file with the Select Committee to Investigate the January 6th Attack on the United States Capitol (Capitol Police Production), CTRL0000000083, CTRL0000000083.0001 (January 5, 2021, email Deleted for privacy concerns. et. al re: (U//FOUO//LES) OSINT Post of Concern.).

396. Documents on file with the Select Committee to Investigate the January 6th Attack on the United States Capitol (Secret Service Production), USSS0000066986, USSS0000066986.0001 (January 5, 2021, Secret Service email noting social media user threatening to bring a firearm to Washington, D.C. on January 6th).

397. Documents on file with the Select Committee to Investigate the January 6th Attack on the United States Capitol (Department of Interior Production), DOI_46000114_00000238, DOI_46000114_00000239 (January 5, 2021, Situational Information Report Federal Bureau of Investigation. "Potential for Violence in Washington, D.C. Area in Connection with Planned 'StopTheSteal' Protest on 6 January 2021.").

398. See Documents on file with the Select Committee to Investigate the January 6th Attack on the United States Capitol (Department of Interior Production), DOI_46000114_00000238, DOI_46000114_00000239 (January 5, 2021, Situational Information Report Federal Bureau of Investigation. "Potential for Violence in Washington, D.C. Area in Connection with Planned 'StopTheSteal' Protest on 6 January 2021.").

399. Trial Exhibit 6923 (1.S.159.817, 955), United States v. Rhodes et al., No. 22-cr-15 (D.D.C. Oct. 14, 2022) (Rhodes sent an encrypted message to Oath Keeper leadership on January 5, 2021, stating: "We will have several well equipped QRFs outside DC. And there are many, many others, from other groups, who will be watching and waiting on the outside in case of worst case scenarios.").

400. Documents on file with the Select Committee to Investigate the January 6th Attack on the United States Capitol (Mark Meadows Production), MM014441-MM01442 (December 30, 2020, 6:05 p.m. ET text from Jason Miller to Mark Meadows).

401. Select Committee to Investigate the January 6th Attack on the United States Capitol, Deposition of Jason Miller, (Feb. 3, 2022), Exhibit 45, pp. 4, 13. Miller claimed he had no idea about the comments and would have "flag[ged]" them for "Secret Service" had he seen

them. Select Committee to Investigate the January 6th Attack on the United States Capitol, Deposition of Jason Miller, (Feb. 3, 2022), pp. 210-12.

402. On his way to the Capitol, Proud Boy David Nicholas Dempsey stopped on the National Mall in front of an erected gallows, fitted with a noose, to tell the world what he hoped would happen: "Them worthless shitholes like Jerry Nadler, fuckin Pelosi ... They don't need a jail cell. They need to hang from these motherfuckers [pointing to gallows]. They need to get the point across that the time for peace is over. ... For four, or five years really, they've been fucking demonizing us, belittling us, ... doing everything they can to stop what this is, and people are sick of that shit .... Hopefully one day soon we really have someone hanging from one of these motherfuckers ... ." Statement of Facts at 2-3, *United States v. Dempsey*, No. 1:21-cr-566 (D.D.C. Aug. 25, 2021); #SeditionHunters (@SeditionHunters), Twitter, Mar. 11, 2021 8:12 p.m. ET, available at https://twitter.com/SeditionHunters/status/1370180789770588163.

403. Select Committee to Investigate the January 6th Attack on the United States Capitol, Continued Interview of Cassidy Hutchinson, (June 20, 2022), p. 49.

404. Select Committee to Investigate the January 6th Attack on the United States Capitol, Continued Interview of Cassidy Hutchinson, (May 17, 2022), p. 92.

405. Documents on file with the Select Committee to Investigate the January 6th Attack on the United States Capitol (Hope Hicks Production), SC_HH_035, SC_HH_036 (January 6, 2021, text messages with Hogan Gidley).

406. Select Committee to Investigate the January 6th Attack on the United States Capitol, Transcribed Interview of Hope Hicks, (Oct. 25, 2022), pp. 109-10.

407. Documents on file with the Select Committee to Investigate the January 6th Attack on the United States Capitol (Homeland Security and Emergency Management Agency, DC Production), CTRL0000926794 (Talking points put together by Dr. Christopher Rodriguez, Director of HSEMA, for a briefing with Mayor Muriel Bowers on December 30, 2020).

408. Select Committee to Investigate the January 6th Attack on the United States Capitol, *Hearing on the January 6th Investigation*, 117th Cong., 2d sess., (July 12, 2022), available at https://www.govinfo.gov/committee/house-january6th; Select Committee to Investigate the January 6th Attack on the United States Capitol, Transcribed Interview of Donnell Harvin, (Jan. 24, 2022), pp. 22-23.

409. Given the timing of receipt of much of this intelligence immediately in advance of January 6th, it is unclear that any comprehensive intelligence community analytical product could have been reasonably expected. But it is clear that the information itself was communicated.

410. Documents on file with the Select Committee to Investigate the January 6th Attack on the United States Capitol (Caroline Wren Production), REVU_000181 (January 2, 2021, email from Katrina Pierson to Caroline Wren and Taylor Budowich re: 1/6 Speaker Schedule).

411. Documents on file with the Select Committee to Investigate the January 6th Attack on the United States Capitol (Kylie Kremer Production), KKremer5449; Select Committee to Investigate the January 6th Attack on the United States Capitol, *Hearing on the January 6th Investigation*, 117th Cong., 2d sess., (July 12, 2022), available at https://www.govinfo.gov/committee/house-january6th.

412. Select Committee to Investigate the January 6th Attack on the United States Capitol, Deposition of Judson P. Deere, (Mar. 3, 2022), pp. 83, 86.

413. Select Committee to Investigate the January 6th Attack on the United States Capitol, *Hearing on the January 6th Investigation*, 117th Cong., 2d sess., (June 28, 2022), available at https://www.govinfo.gov/committee/house-january6th.

414. Select Committee to Investigate the January 6th Attack on the United States Capitol, Transcribed Interview of Robert "Bobby" Engel, (Nov. 17, 2022), p. 64.

415. Select Committee to Investigate the January 6th Attack on the United States Capitol, Continued Interview of Robert Engel, (Nov. 17, 2022), p. 21.

416. Select Committee to Investigate the January 6th Attack on the United States Capitol, Continued Interview of Anthony Ornato, (Nov. 29, 2022), p. 152.

417. Select Committee to Investigate the January 6th Attack on the United States Capitol, Continued Interview of Anthony Ornato, (Nov. 29, 2022), p. 152.

418. Select Committee to Investigate the January 6th Attack on the United States Capitol, Continued Interview of Anthony Ornato, (Nov. 29, 2022), p. 152.

419. Select Committee to Investigate the January 6th Attack on the United States Capitol, Continued Interview of Anthony Ornato, (Mar. 29, 2022), p. 16.

420. Documents on file with the Select Committee to Investigate the January 6th Attack on the United States Capitol (Capitol Police Production), CTRL0000086772, p. 4 (November 18, 2021, document titled: United States Secret Service - Coordinated Response to a Request for Information from the Select Committee to Investigate the January 6th Attack on the United States Capitol).

421. Documents on file with the Select Committee to Investigate the January 6th Attack on the United States Capitol (Nick Quested Production), Video file ML_DC_20210106_Sony_FS7-GC_1935.mov; Documents on file with the Select Committee to Investigate the January 6th Attack on the United States Capitol (Secret Service Production), CTRL0000882478 (Summary of updates from January 6, 2021); Select Committee to Investigate the January 6th Attack on the United States Capitol, Transcribed Interview of Dustin Thompson, (Nov. 16, 2022), pp. 30-31 ("I was seeing these, like, piles of backpacks and flagpoles [outside the magnetometers]. And some people were watching that for other people. And I just -- there were lots of piles all over the place of stuff like that.").

422. Tom Jackman, Rachel Weiner, and Spencer S. Hsu, "Evidence of Firearms in Jan. 6 Crowd Grows as Arrests and Trials Mount," *Washington Post*, (July 8, 2022), https://www.washingtonpost.com/dc-md-va/2022/07/08/jan6-defendants-guns/.

423. Documents on file with the Select Committee to Investigate the January 6th Attack on the United States Capitol (Secret Service Production), CTRL0000882478 (summary of radio traffic on January 6, 2021).

424. Documents on file with the Select Committee to Investigate the January 6th Attack on the United States Capitol (District of Columbia Production), MPD 73-78 (District of Columbia, Metropolitan Police Department, Transcript of Radio Calls, January 6, 2021); Documents on file with the Select Committee to Investigate the January 6th Attack on the United States Capitol (District of Columbia Production), CTRL0000070375, at 3:40 (District of Columbia, Metropolitan Police Department, audio file of radio traffic from January 6, 2021, from 12:00 - 13:00).

425. Documents on file with the Select Committee to Investigate the January 6th Attack on the United States Capitol (Cassidy Hutchinson Production), CH-CTRL0000000069.

426. Select Committee to Investigate the January 6th Attack on the United States Capitol, *Hearing on the January 6th Investigation*, 117th Cong., 2d sess., (June 28, 2022), available at https://www.govinfo.gov/committee/house-january6th.

427. Select Committee to Investigate the January 6th Attack on the United States Capitol, Transcribed Interview of United States Secret Service Employee, (Nov. 7, 2022), p. 77 ("The most--the thing that sticks out most was he kept asking why we couldn't go, why we couldn't go, and that he wasn't concerned about the people that were there or referenced them being Trump people or Trump supporters.").

428. "Transcript of Trump's Speech at Rally before US Capitol Riot," *Associated Press*, (Jan. 13, 2021), available at https://apnews.com/article/election-2020-joe-biden-donald-trump-capitol-siege-media-e79eb5164613d6718e9f4502eb471f27.

429. "Transcript of Trump's Speech at Rally before US Capitol Riot," *Associated Press*, (Jan. 13, 2021), available at https://apnews.com/article/election-2020-joe-biden-donald-trump-capitol-siege-media-e79eb5164613d6718e9f4502eb471f27.

430. Select Committee to Investigate the January 6th Attack on the United States Capitol, Transcribed Interview of Eric Herschmann, (Apr. 6, 2022), pp. 20-21.

431. Select Committee to Investigate the January 6th Attack on the United States Capitol, Transcribed Interview of Eric Herschmann, (Apr. 6, 2022), pp. 24, 26.

432. Select Committee to Investigate the January 6th Attack on the United States Capitol, Transcribed Interview of Eric Herschmann, (Apr. 6, 2022), pp. 26.

433. Select Committee to Investigate the January 6th Attack on the United States Capitol, Transcribed Interview of Eric Herschmann, (Apr. 6, 2022), pp. 23.

434. *See* "Donald Trump Speech 'Save America' Rally Transcript January 6," Rev, (Jan. 6, 2021), at 1:00:00 – 1:02:31, available at https://www.rev.com/blog/transcripts/donald-trump-speech-save-america-rally-transcript-january-6 (timestamping the speech).

435. "Transcript of Trump's Speech at Rally before US Capitol Riot," *Associated Press*, (Jan. 13, 2021), available at https://apnews.com/article/election-2020-joe-biden-donald-trump-capitol-siege-media-e79eb5164613d6718e9f4502eb471f27.

436. Select Committee to Investigate the January 6th Attack on the United States Capitol, *Hearing on the January 6th Investigation*, 117th Cong., 2d sess., (July 21, 2022), at 1:00:45-1:01:12, available at https://youtu.be/pbRVqWbHGuo?t=3645; Select Committee to Investigate the January 6th Attack on the United States Capitol, Transcribed Interview of Janet West Buhler, (Feb. 28, 2022), p. 40.

437. "Transcript of Trump's Speech at Rally before US Capitol Riot," *Associated Press*, (Jan. 13, 2021), available at https://apnews.com/article/election-2020-joe-biden-donald-trump-capitol-siege-media-e79eb5164613d6718e9f4502eb471f27.

438. "Transcript of Trump's Speech at Rally before US Capitol Riot," *Associated Press*, (Jan. 13, 2021), available at https://apnews.com/article/election-2020-joe-biden-donald-trump-capitol-siege-media-e79eb5164613d6718e9f4502eb471f27.

439. "Transcript of Trump's Speech at Rally before US Capitol Riot," *Associated Press*, (Jan. 13, 2021), available at https://apnews.com/article/election-2020-joe-biden-donald-trump-capitol-siege-media-e79eb5164613d6718e9f4502eb471f27.

440. Select Committee to Investigate the January 6th Attack on the United States Capitol, *Hearing on the January 6th Investigation*, 117th Cong., 2d sess., (June 16, 2022), at 0:14:11-0:15:00, available at https://youtu.be/vBjUWVKuDj0?t=851; Hearing on Motion to Modify Conditions of Release, Exhibit 07 at 7:43 - 8:00, *United States v. Nichols*, No. 1:21-cr-117 (D.D.C. Dec. 20, 2021).

441. Unframe of Mind, "Unframe of Mind in DC #stopthesteal Rally," YouTube, at 9:40 – 9:47, Jan. 6, 2021, available at https://www.youtube.com/watch?v=OFbvpBu_7ws&t=579s; Select Committee to Investigate the January 6th Attack on the United States Capitol, *Hearing on the January 6th Investigation*, 117th Cong., 2d sess., (June 16, 2022), at, at 0:14:11-0:15:00, available at https://youtu.be/vBjUWVKuDj0?t=851.

442. Walter Masterson, "Live from the Trump Rally in Washington, D.C.," YouTube, at 17:32 – 17:50, Jan. 11, 2021, available at https://www.youtube.com/watch?v=OFbvpBu_7ws&t=579s; Select Committee to Investigate the January 6th Attack on the United States Capitol, *Hearing on the January 6th Investigation*, 117th Cong., 2d sess., (June 16, 2022), at, at 2:07:02-2:07:07, available at https://youtu.be/vBjUWVKuDj0?t=7609.

443. Select Committee to Investigate the January 6th Attack on the United States Capitol, *Hearing on the January 6th Investigation*, 117th Cong., 2d sess., (June 16, 2022) at, at 2:07:13-2:07:47, available at https://youtu.be/vBjUWVKuDj0?t=7609.

444. Select Committee to Investigate the January 6th Attack on the United States Capitol, *Hearing on the January 6th Investigation*, 117th Cong., 2d sess., (July 21, 2022), at 1:00:45-1:01:12, available at https://youtu.be/pbRVqWbHGuo?t=3645; On the Media, "Jessica Watkins on 'Stop the Steal J6' Zello Channel (Unedited)," Soundcloud, at 4:00-4:18, available at https://soundcloud.com/user-403747081/jessica-watkins-on-stop-the-steal-j6-zello-channel-unedited .

445. For a video of the interview, *see* "Crown Point, Indiana Man Charged in Jan. 6 Capitol Riot Says He Has 'No Regrets'," CBS Chicago, Nov. 29, 2022, available at https://www.cbsnews.com/chicago/video/crown-point-indiana-man-charged-in-jan-6-capitol-riot-says-he-has-no-regrets/#x.

446. "Transcript of Trump's Speech at Rally before US Capitol Riot," *Associated Press*, (Jan. 13, 2021), available at https://apnews.com/article/election-2020-joe-biden-donald-trump-capitol-siege-media-e79eb5164613d6718e9f4502eb471f27 (emphasis added).

447. Select Committee to Investigate the January 6th Attack on the United States Capitol, *Hearing on the January 6th Investigation*, 117th Cong., 2d sess., (June 28, 2022), available at https://www.govinfo.gov/committee/house-january6th; Select Committee to Investigate the January 6th Attack on the United States Capitol, Continued Interview of Cassidy Hutchinson, (June 20, 2022), p. 49.

448. Select Committee to Investigate the January 6th Attack on the United States Capitol, Transcribed Interview of Pasquale Anthony "Pat" Cipollone, (July 8, 2022), p. 131 ("I just didn't think it would be, you know, a good idea for the President to go up to the Capitol."). While Cipollone did not specifically recall talking with Cassidy Hutchinson about this topic, he informed the Select Committee that he was sure that he did express his view to some people. *Id.* Hutchinson believes it was Pat Cipollone, but also testified that it may have been a different lawyer. *See* Select Committee to Investigate the January 6th Attack on the United States Capitol, Transcribed Interview of Cassidy Hutchinson, (Feb. 23, 2022), pp. 113-16.

449. For security reasons, the Select Committee is not releasing the name of this employee. Select Committee to Investigate the January 6th Attack on the United States Capitol, Transcribed Interview of White House employee with national security responsibilities, (July 19, 2022) at p. 73. *See also* Chapter 7, which discusses this topic in greater detail.

450. Select Committee to Investigate the January 6th Attack on the United States Capitol, Transcribed Interview of United States Secret Service Agent, (Nov. 21, 2022), pp. 22-23. The Select Committee has agreed to keep confidential the identity of this witness due to their sensitive national security responsibilities.

451. A book written by Chief of Staff Mark Meadows in December 2021 made the categorical claim that the President never intended to travel to the Capitol that day. *See* Mark Meadows, *The Chief's Chief* (St. Petersburg, FL: All Seasons Press, 2021), p. 250. The Committee's evidence demonstrates that Meadows's claim is categorically false. Because the Meadows book conflicted sharply with information that was being received by the Select Committee, the Committee became increasingly wary that other witnesses might intentionally conceal what happened. That appeared to be the case with Ornato. Ornato does not recall that he conveyed the information to Cassidy Hutchinson regarding the SUV, and also does not recall that he conveyed similar information to a White House employee with national security responsibilities who testified that Ornato recalled a similar account to him. The Committee is skeptical of Ornato's account.

452. Select Committee to Investigate the January 6th Attack on the United States Capitol, Transcribed Interview of White House Security Official, (July 11, 2022), p. 45. The Select Committee has agreed to keep confidential the identity of this witness due to their sensitive national security responsibilities.

453. Select Committee to Investigate the January 6th Attack on the United States Capitol, Deposition of Kayleigh McEnany, (Jan. 12, 2022), p. 159.

454. Select Committee to Investigate the January 6th Attack on the United States Capitol, Continued Interview of Cassidy Hutchinson, (June 20, 2022), p. 8.

455. Government's Sentencing Memorandum at 2-9, *United States v. Young*, No. 1:21-cr-291 (D.D.C. Sept. 13, 2022), ECF No. 140; 167 Cong. Rec. S619 (daily ed. Feb. 10, 2021), available at https://www.congress.gov/117/crec/2021/02/10/CREC-2021-02-10-pt1-PgS615-4.pdf; Michael S. Schmidt and Luke Broadwater, "Officers' Injuries, Including Concussions, Show Scope of Violence at Capitol Riot," *New York Times*, (Feb. 11, 2021), available at https://www.nytimes.com/2021/02/11/us/politics/capitol-riot-police-officer-injuries.html.

456. *See* Sentencing Transcript at 35, *United States v. Griffith*, No. 1:21-cr-204 (D.D.C. Oct. 30, 2021), ECF No. 137; Kyle Cheney and Josh Gerstein, "Where Jan. 6 Prosecutions Stand, 18 Months after the Attack," *Politico*, (July 7, 2022), available at https://www.politico.com/news/2022/07/07/jan-6-prosecutions-months-later-00044354.

457. Select Committee to Investigate the January 6th Attack on the United States Capitol, *Hearing on the January 6th Investigation*, 117th Cong., 2d sess., (July 12, 2022), at 2:36:58-2:37:30, 2:44:00-2:45:05, available at https://www.youtube.com/watch?v=rrUa0hfG6Lo ("[W]hen President Trump put his tweet out, we literally left right after that come out . . . As soon as that come out, everybody started talking about it . . . it definitely dispersed a lot of the crowd. . . . We left."); Select Committee to Investigate the January 6th Attack on the United States Capitol, *Hearing on the January 6th Investigation*, 117th Cong., 2d sess., (July 21, 2022), at 1:58:00, available at https://www.youtube.com/watch?v=pbRVqWbHGuo ("I'm here delivering the President's message. Donald Trump has asked everybody to go home. ... That's our order.").

458. Select Committee to Investigate the January 6th Attack on the United States Capitol, *Hearing on the January 6th Investigation*, 117th Cong., 2d sess., (July 21, 2022), at 1:50:59-1:52:19, available at https://youtu.be/pbRVqWbHGuo?t=6659; Select Committee to Investigate the January 6th Attack on the United States Capitol, *Business Meeting on the January 6th Investigation*, 117th Cong., 2d sess., (Oct. 13, 2022), at 2:15:45-2:17:12, available at https://youtu.be/IQvuBoLBuC0?t=8145; CBS News, "Former Vice President Mike Pence on 'Face the Nation with Margaret Brennan' | Full Interview," YouTube, at 16:23-19:01, Nov. 21, 2022, available at https://youtu.be/U9GbkPhG1Lo?t=983; Select Committee to Investigate the January 6th Attack on the United States Capitol, Transcribed Interview of Steven Andrew Sund, (Apr. 20, 2022), p. 173.

459. Select Committee to Investigate the January 6th Attack on the United States Capitol, Transcribed Interview of White House Employee, (June 10, 2022), p. 27. The Select Committee is not revealing the identity of this witness to guard against the risk of retaliation; *See* "Donald Trump Speech 'Save America' Rally Transcript January 6," Rev, (Jan. 6, 2021), available at https://www.rev.com/blog/transcripts/donald-trump-speech-save-america-rally-transcript-january-6 (timestamping the speech).

460. Documents on file with the Select Committee to Investigate the January 6th Attack on the United States Capitol (National Archives Production), Photo file 40a8_hi_j0087_0bea; Select Committee to Investigate the January 6th Attack on the United States Capitol, *Hearing on the January 6th Investigation*, 117th Cong., 2d sess., (July 21, 2022), at 34:18, available at https://youtu.be/pbRVqWbHGuo?t=2058.

461. Washington Post, "D.C. Police requested backup at least 17 times in 78 minutes during Capitol riot | Visual Forensics," YouTube, at 7:58 to 8:45, Apr. 15, 2021, available at https://youtu.be/rsQTY9083r8?t=478; Senate Committee on Homeland Security and Governmental Affairs and Senate Committee on Rules and Administration, Public Hearing, (Mar. 3, 2021), Written Testimony of William J. Walker, Commanding General District of Columbia National Guard, p. 3, available at https://www.hsgac.senate.gov/imo/media/doc/Testimony-Walker-2021-03-03.pdf.

462. Select Committee to Investigate the January 6th Attack on the United States Capitol, Transcribed Interview of Shealah Craighead, (June 8, 2022), pp. 42, 46.

463. Documents on file with the Select Committee to Investigate the January 6th Attack on the United States Capitol (National Archives Production), P-R000261; Select Committee to Investigate the January 6th Attack on the United States Capitol, *Hearing on the January 6th Investigation*, 117th Cong., 2d sess., (July 21, 2022), available at https://www.govinfo.gov/committee/house-january6th

464. Documents on file with the Select Committee to Investigate the January 6th Attack on the United States Capitol (National Archives Production), P-R000257; Select Committee to Investigate the January 6th Attack on the United States Capitol, *Hearing on the January 6th Investigation*, 117th Cong., 2d sess., (July 21, 2022), available at https://www.govinfo.gov/committee/house-january6th

465. Select Committee to Investigate the January 6th Attack on the United States Capitol, Deposition of Molly Michael, (Mar. 24, 2022), p. 138.

466. Select Committee to Investigate the January 6th Attack on the United States Capitol, Transcribed Interview of Pasquale Anthony "Pat" Cipollone, (Jul. 8, 2022), p. 174; Select Committee to Investigate the January 6th Attack on the United States Capitol, Deposition of Keith Kellogg Jr., (Dec. 14, 2021), pp. 126–27; Select Committee to Investigate the January 6th Attack on the United States Capitol, Deposition of Nicholas Luna, (Mar. 21, 2022), pp. 151-52; Select Committee to Investigate the January 6th Attack on the United States Capitol, Transcribed Interview of Christopher Charles Miller, (Jan. 14, 2022), pp. 124-26; Select Committee to Investigate the January 6th Attack on the United States Capitol, Transcribed Interview of General Mark A. Milley, (Nov. 17, 2021), pp. 80-82; Select Committee to Investigate the January 6th Attack on the United States Capitol, *Hearing on the January 6th Investigation*, 117th Cong., 2d sess., (June 23, 2022), available at https://www.govinfo.gov/committee/house-january6th; Select Committee to Investigate the January 6th Attack on the United States Capitol, Transcribed Interview of Richard Peter Donoghue, (Oct. 1, 2021), pp. 186-90.

467. Select Committee to Investigate the January 6th Attack on the United States Capitol, Deposition of Molly Michael, (Mar. 24, 2022), pp. 127, 129, 131-32, 137, 141, 143-44, 148-49, 159.

468. Documents on file with the Select Committee to Investigate the January 6th Attack on the United States Capitol (AT&T Production, Feb. 9, 2022).

469. Select Committee to Investigate the January 6th Attack on the United States Capitol, Deposition of Kayleigh McEnany, (Jan. 12, 2022), pp. 163-64; Select Committee to Investigate the January 6th Attack on the United States Capitol, *Hearing on the January 6th Investigation*, 117th Cong., 2d sess., (July 21, 2022), available at https://www.govinfo.gov/committee/house-january6th.

470. Senator Lee wrote to a reporter that he received a call from the President moments after the Senate halted its proceedings and that the President claimed he had dialed Sen. Tommy Tuberville (R-AL), so Lee let Tuberville talk to the President on his phone for 5 or 10 minutes until they were ordered to evacuate. Bryan Schott, "What Sen. Mike Lee Told Me about Trump's Call the Day of the Capitol Riot," *Salt Lake Tribune*, (Feb. 10, 2021), updated Feb. 11, 2021), available at https://www.sltrib.com/news/politics/2021/02/11/what-sen-mike-lee-told-me/; *see also* Kyle Cheney, "Tuberville Says He Informed Trump of Pence's Evacuation before Rioters Reached Senate," *Politico*, (Feb. 11, 2021), available at https://www.politico.com/news/2021/02/11/tuberville-pences-evacuation-trump-impeachment-468572.

471. 167 Cong. Rec. S634 (daily ed. Feb. 10, 2021), available at https://www.congress.gov/117/crec/2021/02/10/CREC-2021-02-10-pt1-PgS615-4.pdf; Donald J. Trump (@realDonaldTrump), Twitter, Jan. 6, 2021 1:49 p.m. ET, available at http://web.archive.org/web/20210107235835/https://twitter.com/realDonaldTrump/status/1346891760174329859 (archived).

472. Select Committee to Investigate the January 6th Attack on the United States Capitol, Transcribed Interview of Pasquale Anthony "Pat" Cipollone, (July 8, 2022), pp. 149-50.

473. Select Committee to Investigate the January 6th Attack on the United States Capitol, Transcribed Interview of Pasquale Anthony "Pat" Cipollone, (July 8, 2022), pp. 150-51.

474. Select Committee to Investigate the January 6th Attack on the United States Capitol, *Hearing on the January 6th Investigation*, 117th Cong., 2d sess., (June 28, 2022), at 1:39:03-1:40:42, available at https://youtu.be/HeQNV-aQ_jU?t=5943. Two witnesses recall writing this note: Cassidy Hutchinson and Eric Herschmann, although Hutchinson recalls that Herschmann was responsible for the revision made to the note. The Committee's review of Hutchinson's handwriting was consistent with the script of the note. Select Committee to Investigate the January 6th Attack on the United States Capitol, Transcribed Interview of Cassidy Hutchinson, (Feb. 23, 2022), p. 167; Select Committee to Investigate the January 6th Attack on the United States Capitol, Transcribed Interview of Eric Herschmann (Apr. 6, 2022), pp. 67-68. Who wrote the note is not material to the Select Committee—the important point is that it was prepared for the President.

475. Select Committee to Investigate the January 6th Attack on the United States Capitol, Transcribed Interview of Pasquale Anthony "Pat" Cipollone, (July 8, 2022), p. 162.

476. Select Committee to Investigate the January 6th Attack on the United States Capitol, *Hearing on the January 6th Investigation*, 117th Cong., 2d sess., (June 28, 2022), at 1:27:52-1:28:53, available at https://youtu.be/HeQNV-aQ_jU?t=5272; Select Committee to Investigate the January 6th Attack on the United States Capitol, Continued Interview of Cassidy Hutchinson, (June 20, 2022), pp. 25-26.

477. Select Committee to Investigate the January 6th Attack on the United States Capitol, Transcribed Interview of Pasquale Anthony "Pat" Cipollone, (July 8, 2022), p. 161; Select Committee to Investigate the January 6th Attack on the United States Capitol, *Hearing on the January 6th Investigation*, 117th Cong., 2d sess., (July 21, 2022), at 1:29:30 - 1:31:51, available at https://www.youtube.com/watch?v=pbRVqWbHGuo.

478. Select Committee to Investigate the January 6th Attack on the United States Capitol, Transcribed Interview of White House employee with national security responsibilities, (July 19, 2022), pp. 12-15, 98-99; Select Committee to Investigate the January 6th Attack on the United States Capitol, *Hearing on the January 6th Investigation*, 117th Cong., 2d sess., (July 21, 2022), at 38:02-38:44, available at https://youtu.be/pbRVqWbHGuo?t=2283.

479. Select Committee to Investigate the January 6th Attack on the United States Capitol, Deposition of Judson P. Deere, (Mar. 3, 2022), pp. 108-09.

480. Select Committee to Investigate the January 6th Attack on the United States Capitol, *Hearing on the January 6th Investigation*, 117th Cong., 2d sess., (July 21, 2022), available at https://www.govinfo.gov/committee/house-january6th.

481. Select Committee to Investigate the January 6th Attack on the United States Capitol, Transcribed Interview of Pasquale Anthony "Pat" Cipollone, (July 8, 2022), p. 163.

482. Third Superseding Indictment at 21, *United States v. Nordean et al.*, No. 1:21-cr-175 (D.D.C. June 6, 2022), ECF No. 380 (noting that Dominic Pezzola "used [a] riot shield … to break a window of the Capitol" at "2:13 p.m." and that "[t]he first members of the mob entered the Capitol through this broken window."); 167 Cong. Rec. S634 (daily ed. Feb. 10, 2021), available at https://www.congress.gov/117/crec/2021/02/10/CREC-2021-02-10-pt1-PgS615-4.pdf.

483. Documents on file with the Select Committee to Investigate the January 6th Attack on the United States Capitol (Mark Meadows Production), MM014907.

484. Documents on file with the Select Committee to Investigate the January 6th Attack on the United States Capitol (Mark Meadows Production), MM014912.

485. Documents on file with the Select Committee to Investigate the January 6th Attack on the United States Capitol (Mark Meadows Production), MM014919.

486. Documents on file with the Select Committee to Investigate the January 6th Attack on the United States Capitol (Mark Meadows Production), MM014925.

487. Documents on file with the Select Committee to Investigate the January 6th Attack on the United States Capitol (Mark Meadows Production), MM014933.

488. Documents on file with the Select Committee to Investigate the January 6th Attack on the United States Capitol (Mark Meadows Production), MM014935.

489. Documents on file with the Select Committee to Investigate the January 6th Attack on the United States Capitol (Mark Meadows Production), MM014937.

490. Documents on file with the Select Committee to Investigate the January 6th Attack on the United States Capitol (Mark Meadows Production), MM014939.

491. Documents on file with the Select Committee to Investigate the January 6th Attack on the United States Capitol (Mark Meadows Production), MM014944.

492. Documents on file with the Select Committee to Investigate the January 6th Attack on the United States Capitol (Mark Meadows Production), MM014961.

493. Select Committee to Investigate the January 6th Attack on the United States Capitol, *Hearing on the January 6th Investigation*, 117th Cong., 2d sess., (July 21, 2022), available at https://www.govinfo.gov/committee/house-january6th.

494. U.S. Senator Bill Cassidy, M.D. (@SenBillCassidy), Twitter, Jan. 6, 2021 4:03 p.m. ET, available at https://twitter.com/SenBillCassidy/status/1346925444189327361.

495. Documents on file with the Select Committee to Investigate the January 6th Attack on the United States Capitol (Mark Meadows Production), MM014971.

496. Select Committee to Investigate the January 6th Attack on the United States Capitol, Transcribed Interview of Jared Kushner, (Mar. 31, 2022), pp. 149-50; Select Committee to Investigate the January 6th Attack on the United States Capitol, Transcribed Interview of Julie Radford, (May 25, 2022), p. 37.

497. Select Committee to Investigate the January 6th Attack on the United States Capitol, Transcribed Interview of Jared Kushner, (Mar. 31, 2022), pp. 145, 150.

498. Leader McCarthy spoke on the air to Fox News starting at 3:05 p.m. ET and told the network that "I've already talked to the President. I called him. I think we need to make a statement, make sure that we can calm individuals down." Fox News (FoxNews), "LISTEN: Rep. Kevin McCarthy on protesters storming Capitol," Facebook, at 3:27-3:40, Jan. 6, 2021 (uploaded to Facebook at 3:35 p.m. ET), available at https://www.facebook.com/FoxNews/videos/listen-rep-kevin-mccarthy-on-protesters-storming-capitol/232725075039919/.

499. CBS News, "Live coverage: Protesters Swarm Capitol, Abruptly Halting Electoral Vote Count," YouTube, at 3:29:02-3:29:15, 3:29:43-3:30:03, 3:31:28-3:32:07, 3:33:52-3:34:12, Jan. 6, 2021, available at https://youtu.be/3Fsf4aWudJk?t=12542.

500. Rep. Herrera Beutler Describes Efforts to Get Trump to Intervene in Stopping Jan. 6 riot," WTHR (Feb. 13, 2021), at 1:20 - 1:50, available at https://www.wthr.com/video/news/nation-world/capitol-riot-herrera-beutler-trump-mccarthy-call/507-477fa84f-1277-444a-aad6-716c5ec9f66f.

501. Select Committee to Investigate the January 6th Attack on the United States Capitol, Transcribed Interview of John Michael "Mick" Mulvaney, (July 28, 2022), p. 43. CNN's Jamie Gangel related that she also confirmed the account with multiple other sources, reporting that "I've spoken to multiple Republican Members of the House who have knowledge of that call, who tell us that after Trump tried to say to Kevin, 'these are not my people, it's Antifa,' Kevin McCarthy said to Trump, 'no, it's not Antifa. These are your people'.... We're also told by several other Republican Members that Kevin McCarthy wasn't shy about this heated exchange with Trump, that he wanted his Members to know about it." CNN, "New Details Emerge in McCarthy's Call with Trump on January 6," YouTube, at 0:25 - 1:50, Feb. 12, 2021, available at https://www.youtube.com/watch?v=Gy1FPNluoOE.

502. Committee to Investigate the January 6th Attack on the United States Capitol, Transcribed Interview of John Michael "Mick" Mulvaney, (July 28, 2022), pp. 10-12 (describing calls and text messages to Dan Scavino and Mark Meadows).

503. *See, e.g.*, Documents on file with the Select Committee to Investigate the January 6th Attack on the United States Capitol (HBO Productions), Video file Reel_204I - All Clips Compilation.mp4 at 5:32–5:55 (January 6, 2021 footage from HBO of Nancy Pelosi and Chuck Schumer on phone call with Jeffrey Rosen); Documents on file with the Select Committee to Investigate the January 6th Attack on the United States Capitol (Mark Meadows Production), MM014906 (January 6, 2021 text message from Marjorie Taylor Greene to Mark Meadows), MM014919 (January 6, 2021 text message from William Timmons to Mark Meadows), MM014939 (January 6, 2021 text message from Chip Roy to Mark Meadows).

504. Select Committee to Investigate the January 6th Attack on the United States Capitol, Transcribed Interview of Pasquale Anthony "Pat" Cipollone, (July 8, 2022), p. 151.

505. Select Committee to Investigate the January 6th Attack on the United States Capitol, Transcribed Interview of Pasquale Anthony "Pat" Cipollone, (July 8, 2022), p. 162.

506. Select Committee to Investigate the January 6th Attack on the United States Capitol, Transcribed Interview of Pasquale Anthony "Pat" Cipollone, (July 8, 2022), p. 152.

507. Select Committee to Investigate the January 6th Attack on the United States Capitol, *Hearing on the January 6th Investigation*, 117th Cong., 2d sess., (July 21, 2022), at 0:57:48 - 0:58:19, available at https://youtu.be/pbRVqWbHGuo?t=3468.

508. Select Committee to Investigate the January 6th Attack on the United States Capitol, Transcribed Interview of White House Security Official, (July 11, 2022), pp. 81-83; Select Committee to Investigate the January 6th Attack on the United States Capitol, *Hearing on the January 6th Investigation*, 117th Cong., 2d sess., (July 21, 2022), available at https://www.govinfo.gov/committee/house-january6th. The Select Committee is not revealing the identity of this witness because of national security concerns as well as to guard against the risk of retaliation.

509. Donald J. Trump (@realDonaldTrump), Twitter, Jan. 6, 2021 2:24 p.m. ET, available at https://media-cdn.factba.se/realdonaldtrump-twitter/1346900434540240897.jpg (archived).

510. Select Committee to Investigate the January 6th Attack on the United States Capitol, *Hearing on the January 6th Investigation*, 117th Cong., 2d sess., (June 16, 2022), at 2:11:22-2:13:55, available at https://youtu.be/vBjUWVKuDj0?t=7882.

511. Select Committee to Investigate the January 6th Attack on the United States Capitol, *Hearing on the January 6th Investigation*, 117th Cong., 2d sess., (June 16, 2022), at 2:26:06-2:26:26, available at https://youtu.be/IQvuBoLBuC0?t=8766; Sentencing Transcript at 19, *United States v. Young*, No. 1:21-cr-291 (D.D.C. Sept. 27, 2022), ECF No. 170 (testifying for a victim impact statement, Officer Michael Fanone said: "At approximately 1435 hours, with rapidly mounting injuries and most of the MPD less than lethal munitions expended, the defending officers were forced to conduct a fighting withdrawal back towards the United States Capitol Building entrance. This is the first fighting withdrawal in the history of the Metropolitan Police Department.").

512. Select Committee to Investigate the January 6th Attack on the United States Capitol, *Hearing on the January 6th Investigation*, 117th Cong., 2d sess., (July 21, 2022), available at https://www.govinfo.gov/committee/house-january6th.

513. Select Committee to Investigate the January 6th Attack on the United States Capitol, *Hearing on the January 6th Investigation*, 117th Cong., 2d sess., (July 21, 2022), available at https://www.govinfo.gov/committee/house-january6th.

514. Select Committee to Investigate the January 6th Attack on the United States Capitol, Deposition of Judson P. Deere, (Mar. 3, 2022), p. 113.

515. Select Committee to Investigate the January 6th Attack on the United States Capitol, Transcribed Interview of Pasquale Anthony "Pat" Cipollone, (July 8, 2022), p. 160.

516. Documents on file with the Select Committee to Investigate the January 6th Attack on the United States Capitol (Hope Hicks Production), SC_HH_043-044 (January 6, 2021, text message from Hope Hicks to Julie Radford at 7:18 p.m.).

517. 167 Cong. Rec. S635 (daily ed. Feb. 10, 2021), available at https://www.congress.gov/117/crec/2021/02/10/CREC-2021-02-10-pt1-PgS615-4.pdf; Spencer S. Hsu, "Pence Spent Jan. 6 at Underground Senate Loading Dock, Secret Service Confirms," *Washington Post*, (Mar. 21, 2022), available at https://www.washingtonpost.com/dc-md-va/2022/03/21/couy-griffin-cowboys-trump-jan6/.

518. Select Committee to Investigate the January 6th Attack on the United States Capitol, Deposition of Molly Michael, (Mar. 24, 2022), p. 137.

519. Select Committee to Investigate the January 6th Attack on the United States Capitol, *Hearing on the January 6th Investigation*, 117th Cong., 2d sess., (July 21, 2022), available at https://www.govinfo.gov/committee/house-january6th.

520. Select Committee to Investigate the January 6th Attack on the United States Capitol, Continued Interview of Cassidy Hutchinson, (June 20, 2022), p. 27.

521. Select Committee to Investigate the January 6th Attack on the United States Capitol, *Hearing on the January 6th Investigation*, 117th Cong., 2d sess., (June 28, 2022), at 1:31:25 –

1:32:22, available at https://youtu.be/HeQNV-aQ_jU?t=5359; Select Committee to Investigate the January 6th Attack on the United States Capitol, Continued Interview of Cassidy Hutchinson, (June 20, 2022), pp. 27-28.

522. Select Committee to Investigate the January 6th Attack on the United States Capitol, Transcribed Interview of Pasquale Anthony "Pat" Cipollone, (July 8, 2022), p. 182.

523. Select Committee to Investigate the January 6th Attack on the United States Capitol, Transcribed Interview of Eric Herschmann, (Apr. 6, 2022), pp. 68-69, 71.

524. Donald J. Trump (@realDonaldTrump), Twitter, Jan. 6, 2021 2:38 p.m. ET, available at https://media-cdn.factba.se/realdonaldtrump-twitter/1346904110969315332.jpg (archived).

525. Select Committee to Investigate the January 6th Attack on the United States Capitol, *Hearing on the January 6th Investigation*, 117th Cong., 2d sess., (July 21, 2022), available at https://www.govinfo.gov/committee/house-january6th.

526. Donald J. Trump (@realDonaldTrump), Twitter, Jan. 6, 2021 3:13 p.m. ET, available at https://media-cdn.factba.se/realdonaldtrump-twitter/1346912780700577792.jpg (archived).

527. Documents on file with the Select Committee to Investigate the January 6th Attack on the United States Capitol (Mark Meadows Production), MM014925.

528. Documents on file with the Select Committee to Investigate the January 6th Attack on the United States Capitol (Mark Meadows Production), MM014944.

529. Select Committee to Investigate the January 6th Attack on the United States Capitol, *Hearing on the January 6th Investigation*, 117th Cong., 2d sess., (July 21, 2022), available at https://www.govinfo.gov/committee/house-january6th.

530. Select Committee to Investigate the January 6th Attack on the United States Capitol, *Hearing on the January 6th Investigation*, 117th Cong., 2d sess., (July 21, 2022), available at https://www.govinfo.gov/committee/house-january6th].

531. Documents on file with the Select Committee to Investigate the January 6th Attack on the United States Capitol (National Archives Production), 076P-R000004112_0001 (January 6, 2021 email at 3:05 p.m. notifying Beau Harrison of Ashli Babbitt shooting); Select Committee to Investigate the January 6th Attack on the United States Capitol, Transcribed Interview of William Beau Harrison (Aug. 18, 2022), pp. 73–76 (describing writing note and passing it to Mark Meadows or Tony Ornato); Documents on file with the Select Committee to Investigate the January 6th Attack on the United States Capitol (National Archives Production), P-R000241 (January 6, 2021 pocket card written by Beau Harrison with the message, "1x CIVILIAN GUNSHOT WOUND TO CHEST @ DOOR OF HOUSE CHABER [sic]"); Select Committee to Investigate the January 6th Attack on the United States Capitol, Transcribed Interview of White House Employee, (June 10, 2022), pp. 46–47 ("I remember seeing that [note] in front of [President Trump], yeah."). The Select Committee is not revealing the identity of this witness to guard against the risk of retaliation. *See also* Select Committee to Investigate the January 6th Attack on the United States Capitol, Transcribed Interview of Anthony Ornato, (January 28, 2022), p. 115; Select Committee to Investigate the January 6th Attack on the United States Capitol, Transcribed Interview of Eric Herschmann, (Apr. 6, 2022), p. 87 (recalling announcing during the afternoon that a Trump supporter had been killed).

532. "Department of Justice Closes Investigation into the Death of Ashli Babbitt," Department of Justice, (Apr. 14, 2021), available at https://www.justice.gov/usao-dc/pr/department-justice-closes-investigation-death-ashli-babbitt.

533. Select Committee to Investigate the January 6th Attack on the United States Capitol, *Hearing on the January 6th Investigation*, 117th Cong., 2d sess., (July 21, 2022), available at https://www.govinfo.gov/committee/house-january6th; Select Committee to Investigate the January 6th Attack on the United States Capitol, *Business Meeting on the January 6th Investigation*, 117th Cong., 2d sess., (Oct. 13, 2022), available at https://www.govinfo.gov/committee/house-january6th; ABC News, "Mike Pence Opens Up with David Muir on Jan. 6: Exclusive," YouTube, at 9:27-10:00, Nov. 14, 2022, available at https://youtu.be/-AAyKAoPFQs?t=567; Select Committee to Investigate the January 6th Attack on the United

States Capitol, Transcribed Interview of General Mark A. Milley (Nov. 17, 2021), pp. 80-81; Select Committee to Investigate the January 6th Attack on the United States Capitol, Transcribed Interview of Christopher Charles Miller (Jan. 14, 2022), pp. 124-25; Select Committee to Investigate the January 6th Attack on the United States Capitol, Transcribed Interview of Jeffrey Rosen, (Oct. 13, 2021), pp. 172-73, 182-84; Select Committee to Investigate the January 6th Attack on the United States Capitol, Transcribed Interview of Richard Peter Donoghue, (Oct. 1, 2021), p. 186.

534. NBC News, "Biden Condemns Chaos at the Capitol as 'Insurrection,'" YouTube, Jan. 6, 2021, available at https://www.youtube.com/watch?v=FBCWTqJT7M4; Select Committee to Investigate the January 6th Attack on the United States Capitol, *Hearing on the January 6th Investigation*, 117th Cong., 2d sess., (July 21, 2022), available at https://www.govinfo.gov/committee/house-january6th.

535. "Trump Video Telling Protesters at Capitol Building to Go Home: Transcript," Rev, (Jan. 6, 2021), available at https://www.rev.com/blog/transcripts/trump-video-telling-protesters-at-capitol-building-to-go-home-transcript.

536. Select Committee to Investigate the January 6th Attack on the United States Capitol, *Hearing on the January 6th Investigation*, 117th Cong., 2d sess., (July 21, 2022), available at https://www.govinfo.gov/committee/house-january6th.

537. Select Committee to Investigate the January 6th Attack on the United States Capitol, *Hearing on the January 6th Investigation*, 117th Cong., 2d sess., (July 21, 2022), available at https://www.govinfo.gov/committee/house-january6th

538. Select Committee to Investigate the January 6th Attack on the United States Capitol, *Hearing on the January 6th Investigation*, 117th Cong., 2d sess., (July 12, 2022), at 2:36:58-2:37:30, 2:44:00-2:45:05, available at https://www.youtube.com/watch?v=rrUa0hfG6Lo ("[W]hen President Trump put his tweet out, we literally left right after that come out . . . As soon as that come out, everybody started talking about it . . . it definitely dispersed a lot of the crowd. . . . We left.").

539. Select Committee to Investigate the January 6th Attack on the United States Capitol, *Hearing on the January 6th Investigation*, 117th Cong., 2d sess., (July 12, 2022), at 1:58:00, available at https://www.youtube.com/watch?v=pbRVqWbHGuo.

540. Select Committee to Investigate the January 6th Attack on the United States Capitol, *Hearing on the January 6th Investigation*, 117th Cong., 2d sess., (July 12, 2022), at 1:58:00, available at https://www.youtube.com/watch?v=pbRVqWbHGuo.

541. Donald J. Trump (@realDonaldTrump), Twitter, Jan. 6, 2021 at 6:01 p.m. ET, available at http://web.archive.org/web/20210106232133/https://twitter.com/realdonaldtrump/status/1346954970910707712 (archived).

542. Select Committee to Investigate the January 6th Attack on the United States Capitol, *Hearing on the January 6th Investigation*, 117th Cong., 2d sess., (July 21, 2022), available at https://www.govinfo.gov/committee/house-january6th.

543. Select Committee to Investigate the January 6th Attack on the United States Capitol, Transcribed Interview of Timothy Murtaugh, (May 19, 2022), p. 175; Select Committee to Investigate the January 6th Attack on the United States Capitol, *Hearing on the January 6th Investigation*, 117th Cong., 2d sess., (July 21, 2022), available at https://www.govinfo.gov/committee/house-january6th.

544. Select Committee to Investigate the January 6th Attack on the United States Capitol, Transcribed Interview of Pasquale Anthony "Pat" Cipollone, (July 8, 2022), p. 194; Select Committee to Investigate the January 6th Attack on the United States Capitol, *Hearing on the January 6th Investigation*, 117th Cong., 2d sess., (July 21, 2022), available at https://www.govinfo.gov/committee/house-january6th.

545. Select Committee to Investigate the January 6th Attack on the United States Capitol, Deposition of Greg Jacob, (Feb. 1, 2022), p. 192.

546. Select Committee to Investigate the January 6th Attack on the United States Capitol, Tran-scribed Interview of White House Employee, (June 10, 2022), p. 53. The Select Committee is not revealing the identity of this witness to guard against the risk of retaliation.

547. Documents on file with the Select Committee to Investigate the January 6th Attack on the United States Capitol, (Rudolph Giuliani Production, Mar. 11, 2022); Documents on file with the Select Committee to Investigate the January 6th Attack on the United States Capitol, (AT&T Production, Feb. 9, 2022).

548. Select Committee to Investigate the January 6th Attack on the United States Capitol, Depo-sition of Rudolph Giuliani, (May 20, 2022), pp. 205-07; Sunlen Serfaty, Devan Cole, and Alex Rogers, "As Riot Raged at Capitol, Trump Tried to Call Senators to Overturn Election," CNN, (Jan. 8, 2021), available at https://www.cnn.com/2021/01/08/politics/mike-lee-tommy-tuberville-trump-misdialed-capitol-riot; Documents on file with the Select Committee to Investigate the January 6th Attack on the United States Capitol, (Rudolph Giuliani Produc-tion, Mar. 11, 2022); Documents on file with the Select Committee to Investigate the January 6th Attack on the United States Capitol, (AT&T Production, Feb. 9, 2022).

549. Mike Pence, *So Help Me God* (New York: Simon & Schuster, 2022), p. 475.

550. Mike Pence, *So Help Me God* (New York: Simon & Schuster, 2022), p. 474.

551. Select Committee to Investigate the January 6th Attack on the United States Capitol, Tran-scribed Interview of Steven Andrew Sund, (Apr. 20, 2022), pp. 170-71; Select Committee to Investigate the January 6th Attack on the United States Capitol, Transcribed Interview of Pasquale Anthony "Pat" Cipollone, (Jul. 8, 2022), p. 174; Select Committee to Investigate the January 6th Attack on the United States Capitol, Deposition of Keith Kellogg Jr., (Dec. 14, 2021), pp. 126–27; Select Committee to Investigate the January 6th Attack on the United States Capitol, Deposition of Nicholas Luna, (Mar. 21, 2022), pp. 151-52; Select Committee to Investigate the January 6th Attack on the United States Capitol, Transcribed Interview of Christopher Charles Miller, (Jan. 14, 2022), pp. 124-26; Select Committee to Investigate the January 6th Attack on the United States Capitol, Transcribed Interview of General Mark A. Milley, (Nov. 17, 2021), pp. 80-82; Select Committee to Investigate the January 6th Attack on the United States Capitol, Transcribed Interview of Richard Peter Donoghue, (Oct. 1, 2021), pp. 186-89; Select Committee to Investigate the January 6th Attack on the United States Capitol, Transcribed Interview of Muriel Bowser, (Jan. 12, 2022), pp. 21-22.

552. ABC News, "Pence Opens Up with David Muir on Jan. 6: Exclusive," YouTube, at 10:45-11:02, Nov. 14, 2022, available at https://www.youtube.com/watch?v=-AAyKAoPFQs.

553. Select Committee to Investigate the January 6th Attack on the United States Capitol, Tran-scribed Interview of Steven Andrew Sund, (Apr. 20, 2022), pp. 170-71; Select Committee to Investigate the January 6th Attack on the United States Capitol, Transcribed Interview of Pasquale Anthony "Pat" Cipollone, (Jul. 8, 2022), p. 174; Select Committee to Investigate the January 6th Attack on the United States Capitol, Deposition of Keith Kellogg Jr., (Dec. 14, 2021), pp. 126–27; Select Committee to Investigate the January 6th Attack on the United States Capitol, Deposition of Nicholas Luna, (Mar. 21, 2022), pp. 151-52; Select Committee to Investigate the January 6th Attack on the United States Capitol, Transcribed Interview of Christopher Charles Miller, (Jan. 14, 2022), pp. 124-26; Select Committee to Investigate the January 6th Attack on the United States Capitol, Transcribed Interview of General Mark A. Milley, (Nov. 17, 2021), pp. 80-82; Select Committee to Investigate the January 6th Attack on the United States Capitol, Transcribed Interview of Richard Peter Donoghue, (Oct. 1, 2021), pp. 186-89; Select Committee to Investigate the January 6th Attack on the United States Capitol, Transcribed Interview of Muriel Bowser, (Jan. 12, 2022), pp. 21-22.

554. Select Committee to Investigate the January 6th Attack on the United States Capitol, Tran-scribed Interview of General Mark A. Milley (Nov. 17, 2021), pp. 17, 268.

555. Select Committee to Investigate the January 6th Attack on the United States Capitol, Tran-scribed Interview of General Mark A. Milley (Nov. 17, 2021), p. 296; Select Committee to Investigate the January 6th Attack on the United States Capitol, *Hearing on the January 6th Investigation*, 117th Cong., 2d sess., (July 21, 2022), available at https://www.govinfo.gov/committee/house-january6th.

556. Glenn Kessler, "Trump Falsely Claims He 'Requested' 10,000 Troops Rejected by Pelosi," *Washington Post*, (Mar. 2, 2021), available at https://www.washingtonpost.com/politics/ 2021/03/02/trump-falsely-claims-he-requested-10000-troops-rejected-by-pelosi/; "Mark Meadows: Biden Administration Policies Put 'America Last'," Fox News, (Feb. 7, 2021), available at https://www.foxnews.com/transcript/mark-meadows-biden-administration-policies-put-america-last.

557. Select Committee to Investigate the January 6th Attack on the United States Capitol, Transcribed Interview of Christopher Charles Miller (Jan. 14, 2022), pp. 100-01. On January 4, 2021, Max Miller and Katrina Pierson exchanged text messages discussing their planning activities for the 6th. In those messages, Max Miller stated: "Just glad we killed the national guard and a procession" and that "... chief [Mark Meadows] already had said no for days!". Documents on file with the Select Committee to Investigate the January 6th Attack on the United States Capitol (Max Miller Production), Miller Production 0001 (January 4, 2021, text messages between Max Miller and Katrina Pierson).

558. Select Committee to Investigate the January 6th Attack on the United States Capitol, *Hearing on the January 6th Investigation*, 117th Cong., 2d sess., (July 12, 2022), at 2:22:45-2:23:22, available at https://youtu.be/rrUa0hfG6Lo?t=8565; Documents on file with the Select Committee to Investigate the January 6th Attack on the United States Capitol (Katrina Pierson Production), KPierson0717-719.

559. "House Republican Leader Kevin McCarthy on Asking President Trump for his Resignation," ed. Alex Burns and Jonathan Martin, ThisWillNotPass.com, (Jan. 8, 2021), available at https://www.thiswillnotpass.com/bookresources.

560. Documents on file with the Select Committee to Investigate the January 6th Attack on the United States Capitol (Mark Meadows Production), MM014456.

561. Documents on file with the Select Committee to Investigate the January 6th Attack on the United States Capitol (Mark Meadows Production), MM014858 - MM014861.

562. Documents on file with the Select Committee to Investigate the January 6th Attack on the United States Capitol (Mark Meadows Production), MM014467 (December 31, 2020, text message from telephone number assigned to Carrah Jo Roy, wife of Rep. Chip Roy. to Mark Meadows). The Select Committee believes that Rep. Chip Roy sent this message.

563. Documents on file with the Select Committee to Investigate the January 6th Attack on the United States Capitol (Mark Meadows Production), MM014503 (January 1, 2021, text message from telephone number assigned to Carrah Jo Roy, wife of Rep. Chip Roy. to Mark Meadows). The Select Committee believes that Rep. Chip Roy sent this message.

564. Documents on file with the Select Committee to Investigate the January 6th Attack on the United States Capitol (Kayleigh McEnany Production), CTRL0000925383, p. 3 (January 7, 2021, text message from Sean Hannity to Kayleigh McEnany)

565. Documents on file with the Select Committee to Investigate the January 6th Attack on the United States Capitol (Mark Meadows Production), MM015209 (January 10, 2021, text message Sean Hannity to Mark Meadows and Jim Jordan).

566. Documents on file with the Select Committee to Investigate the January 6th Attack on the United States Capitol (Mark Meadows Production), MM014906.

567. "U.S. House Impeaches President Trump for Second Time, 232-197," C-SPAN, at 4:14:56 - 4:15:31, Jan. 13, 2021, available at https://www.c-span.org/video/?507879-101/house-impeaches-president-trump-time-232-197&live=.

568. "Republican Leader Kevin McCarthy says Pres. Trump Admitted He Bears Some Responsibility for the January 6 Insurrection at the U.S. Capitol," ed. Alex Burns and Jonathan Martin, ThisWillNotPass.com, (Jan. 11, 2021), available at https://www.thiswillnotpass.com/bookresources.

569. "Statement by Mo Brooks," Mo Brooks for U.S. Senate, available at https://mobrooks.com/ statement-by-mo-brooks/; Joe Walsh, "GOP Rep. Mo Brooks Claims Trump Asked Him to Reinstate Trump Presidency," *Forbes*, (Mar. 23, 2022), available at https://www.forbes.com/

sites/joewalsh/2022/03/23/gop-rep-mo-brooks-claims-trump-asked-him-to-reinstate-trump-presidency/?sh=7264e1d91edd (noting that Rep. Mo Brooks issued this statement on Wednesday, March 23, 2022).

570. *See* Ryan Goodman and Josh Asabor, "In Their Own Words: The 43 Republicans' Explanations of Their Votes Not to Convict Trump in Impeachment Trial," Just Security, (Feb. 15, 2021), *available at* https://www.justsecurity.org/74725/in-their-own-words-the-43-republicans-explanations-of-their-votes-not-to-convict-trump-in-impeachment-trial/.

571. C-SPAN, "Senate Minority Leader Mitch McConnell Remarks Following Senate Impeachment Vote," YouTube, at 5:10 – 5:46, (Feb. 13, 2021), available at https://www.youtube.com/watch?v=yxRMoqNnfvw.

572. "Republican Leader Kevin McCarthy Says Pres. Trump Admitted He Bears Some Responsibility for the January 6 Insurrection at the U.S. Capitol," Alex Burns and Jonathan Martin, eds., ThisWillNotPass.com, (Jan. 11, 2021), available at https://www.thiswillnotpass.com/bookresources; Melanie Zanona, "New Audio Reveals McCarthy said Trump Admitted Bearing Some Responsibility for Capitol Attack," CNN, (April 22, 2022), available at https://www.cnn.com/2022/04/22/politics/trump-january-6-responsibility-book/index.html. Leader McCarthy also relayed this conversation with President Trump to his Republican colleagues: "I asked him [Trump] personally today, does he hold responsibility for what happened. And he needs to acknowledge that." *Id.* The Committee believes that House Republican Leader McCarthy's testimony would be material to any criminal investigation of Donald Trump, not just to probe this apparent Trump acknowledgement of culpability, but also because Leader McCarthy spoke directly to Donald Trump and others who were in the White House on January 6th and unsuccessfully pleaded for the President's immediate assistance to halt the violence. Leader McCarthy did not comply with the Select Committee's subpoena.

573. "U.S. House Impeaches President Trump for Second Time, 232-197," C-SPAN, at 4:14:56 - 4:15:31, (Jan. 13, 2021), available at https://www.c-span.org/video/?507879-101/house-impeaches-president-trump-time-232-197&live=; 167 Cong. Rec. H172 (daily ed. Jan. 13, 2021), available at https://www.congress.gov/117/crec/2021/01/13/CREC-2021-01-13-pt1-PgH165.pdf.

574. *See supra*, Executive Summary.

575. *See supra*, Executive Summary.

576. Documents on file with the Select Committee (National Archives Production), VP-R0000156_0001 (January 6, 2021, email chain between John Eastman and Greg Jacob re: Pennsylvania letter).

577. Documents on file with Select Committee (Department of Justice Production), HCOR-Pre-Certification-Events-07282021-000738—HCOR-Pre-Certification-Events-07282021-000739 (December 27, 2020, handwritten notes from Richard Donoghue).

578. *See supra*, Executive Summary. The State legislatures lacked authority to change the lawful outcome of the State elections at that point. Nevertheless Eastman, Trump, and others nevertheless pushed for such action.

579. *See supra*, Executive Summary.

580. *See Supra,* Executive Summary; Donald J. Trump (@realDonaldTrump), Twitter, Dec. 19, 2020 1:42 a.m. ET, available at http://web.archive.org/web/20201219064257/https://twitter.com/realDonaldTrump/status/1340185773220515840 (archived); *see also, e.g.,* Donald J. Trump (@realDonaldTrump), Twitter, Dec. 26, 2020 8:14 a.m. ET, available at https://twitter.com/realDonaldTrump/status/1342821189077622792; Donald J. Trump (@realDonaldTrump), Twitter, Dec. 27, 2020 5:51 p.m. ET, available at https://twitter.com/realDonaldTrump/status/1343328708963299338; Donald J. Trump (@realDonaldTrump), Twitter, Dec. 30, 2020 2:06 p.m. ET, available at https://twitter.com/realDonaldTrump/status/1344359312878149634; Donald J. Trump (@realDonaldTrump), Twitter, Jan. 1, 2021 12:52 p.m. ET, available at https://www.thetrumparchive.com/?searchbox=%22RT+%40KylieJaneKremer%22 (retweeting @KylieJaneKremer, Dec. 19, 2020 3:50 p.m. ET, available at https://twitter.com/KylieJaneKremer/status/1340399063875895296); Donald J. Trump (@realDonaldTrump),

Twitter, Jan. 1, 2021 2:53 p.m. ET, available at https://twitter.com/realDonaldTrump/status/1345095714687377418; Donald J. Trump (@realDonaldTrump), Twitter, Jan. 1, 2021 3:34 p.m. ET, available at https://twitter.com/realDonaldTrump/status/1345106078141394944; Donald J. Trump (@realDonaldTrump), Twitter, Jan. 1, 2021 6:38 p.m. ET, available at https://twitter.com/realDonaldTrump/status/1345152408591204352; Donald J. Trump (@realDonaldTrump), Twitter, Jan. 2, 2021 9:04 p.m. ET, available at https://twitter.com/realDonaldTrump/status/1345551634907209730; Donald J. Trump (@realDonaldTrump), Twitter, Jan. 3, 2021 1:29 a.m. ET, available at https://www.thetrumparchive.com/?searchbox=%22RT+%40realDonaldTrump%3A+https%3A%2F%2Ft.co%2FnslWcFwkCj%22 (retweeting Donald J. Trump (@realDonaldTrump), Jan. 2, 2021 9:04 p.m. ET, available at https://twitter.com/realDonaldTrump/status/1345551634907209730); Donald J. Trump (@realDonaldTrump), Twitter, Jan. 3, 2021 10:15 a.m. ET, available at https://www.thetrumparchive.com/?searchbox=%22RT+%40JenLawrence21%22 (retweeting Jennifer Lynn Lawrence (@JenLawrence21), Jan. 3, 2021 12:17 a.m. ET, available at https://twitter.com/JenLawrence21/status/1345600194826686464); Donald J. Trump (@realDonaldTrump), Twitter, Jan. 3, 2021 10:17 a.m. ET, available at https://www.thetrumparchive.com/?searchbox=%22RT+%40CodeMonkeyZ+if%22 (retweeting Ron Watkins (@CodeMonkeyZ) Jan. 2, 2021 9:14 p.m. ET, available at http://web.archive.org/web/20210103151826/https://twitter.com/CodeMonkeyZ/status/1345599512560078849 (archived)); Donald J. Trump, (@realDonaldTrump), Twitter, Jan. 3, 2021 10:24 a.m. ET, available at https://www.thetrumparchive.com/?searchbox=%22RT+%40realMikeLindell%22 (retweeting Mike Lindell (@realMikeLindell), Jan. 2, 2021 5:47 p.m. ET, available at http://web.archive.org/web/20210103152421/https://twitter.com/realMikeLindell/status/1345547185836978176 (archived)); Donald J. Trump (@realDonaldTrump), Twitter, Jan. 3, 2021 10:27 a.m. ET, available at https://twitter.com/realDonaldTrump/status/1345753534168506370; Donald J. Trump (@realDonaldTrump), Twitter, Jan. 3, 2021 10:28 a.m. ET, available at https://www.thetrumparchive.com/?searchbox=%22RT+%40AmyKremer+we%22 (retweeting Amy Kremer (@AmyKremer), Jan. 2, 2021 2:58 p.m. ET, available at https://twitter.com/AmyKremer/status/1345459488107749386); Donald J. Trump (@realDonaldTrump), Twitter, Jan. 4, 2021 9:46 a.m. ET, available at https://www.thetrumparchive.com/?searchbox=%22RT+%40realDonaldTrump+I+will+be+there.+Historic+day%21%22 (retweeting Donald J. Trump (@realDonaldTrump), Jan. 3, 2021 10:27 a.m. ET, available at https://twitter.com/realDonaldTrump/status/1345753534168506370); Donald J. Trump (@realDonaldTrump), Twitter, Jan. 5, 2021 10:27 a.m. ET, available at https://twitter.com/realDonaldTrump/status/1346478482105069568; Donald J. Trump (@realDonaldTrump), Twitter, Jan. 5, 2021 5:43 p.m. ET, available at https://twitter.com/realDonaldTrump/status/1346588064026685443.

581. Donald J. Trump (@realDonldTrump), Twitter, Jan. 6, 2021 2:24 p.m. ET, available at https://www.thetrumparchive.com/?searchbox=%22mike+pence+%22&results=1 (archived) ("Mike Pence didn't have the courage to do what should have been done to protect our Country and our Constitution, giving States a chance to certify a corrected set of facts, not the fraudulent or inaccurate ones which they were asked to previously certify. USA demands the truth!"); USA Today Graphics (@usatgraphics), Twitter, Jan. 7, 2021 9:56 p.m. ET, available at https://twitter.com/usatgraphics/status/1347376642956603392 (screenshotting the since-deleted tweet).

582. "Trump Video Telling Protesters at Capitol Building to Go Home: Transcript," Rev, (Jan. 6, 2021), available at https://www.rev.com/blog/transcripts/trump-video-telling-protesters-at-capitol-building-to-go-home-transcript; Select Committee to Investigate the January 6th Attack on the United States Capitol, *Hearing on the January 6th Investigation*, 117th Cong., 2d sess., (July 12, 2022), at 2:36:58-2:37:30 and 2:44:00-2:45:05, available at https://www.youtube.com/watch?v=rrUa0hfG6Lo ("[W]hen President Trump put his tweet out, we literally left right after that come out . . . As soon as that come out, everybody started talking about it . . . it definitely dispersed a lot of the crowd. . . . We left.").

583. Order Re Privilege of Documents Dated January 4-7, 2021 at 3-16, *Eastman v. Thompson et al.*, 594 F. Supp. 3d 1156, (C.D. Cal. March 28, 2022) (No. 8:22-cv-99-DOC-DFM).

584. Order Re Privilege of Documents Dated January 4-7, 2021 at 53–53, 58, *Eastman v. Thompson et al.*, 594 F. Supp. 3d 1156, (C.D. Cal. March 28, 2022) (No. 8:22-cv-99-DOC-DFM) (referring to two Federal criminal statutes).

585. Order Re Privilege of 599 Documents Dated November 3, 2020 – January 20, 2021 at 24, *Eastman v. Thompson et al.*, No. 8:22-cv-99-DOC-DFM, (C.D. Cal. June 7, 2022), ECF No. 24.

586. Order Re Privilege of Documents Dated January 4-7, 2021 at 63–64, *Eastman v. Thompson et al.*, 594 F. Supp. 3d 1156, (C.D. Cal. March 28, 2022) (No. 8:22-cv-99-DOC-DFM).

587. Order Re Privilege of Documents Dated January 4-7, 2021 at 64, *Eastman v. Thompson et al.*, 594 F. Supp. 3d 1156, (C.D. Cal. March 28, 2022) (No. 8:22-cv-99-DOC-DFM).

588. *See* "23 Months Since the January 6th Attack on the Capitol," Department of Justice, (Dec. 8, 2022), available at https://www.justice.gov/usao-dc/23-months-january-6-attack-capitol.

589. Kyle Cheney, "Rep. Scott Perry Suing to Block DOJ Access to His Cell Phone," Politico, (Aug. 24, 2022), available at https://www.politico.com/news/2022/08/24/rep-scott-perry-suing-to-block-doj-access-to-his-cell-phone-00053486; Betsy Woodruff Swan, Josh Gerstein, and Kyle Cheney, "DOJ Searches Home of Former Official Who Aided Alleged Pro-Trump 'Coup'," Politico, (June 23, 2022), available at https://www.politico.com/news/2022/06/23/law-enforcement-trump-official-coup-00041767.

590. *See, e.g.,* Sarah Murray, Evan Perez, and Katelyn Polantz, "Federal Judge Orders Former Top Lawyers in Trump's White House to Testify in Criminal Grand Jury Probe," CNN, (Dec. 1, 2022), available at https://www.cnn.com/2022/12/01/politics/cipollone-philbin-trump-lawyers-testify.

591. Sara Murray and Jason Morris, "Fulton County Prosecutor Investigating Trump Aims for Indictments as Soon as December," CNN, (Oct. 6, 2022), available at https://www.cnn.com/2022/10/06/politics/fani-willis-georgia-prosecutor-trump-indictments-december/index.html.

592. The Special Counsel is to oversee the Department's ongoing investigation "into whether any person or entity unlawfully interfered with the transfer of power following the 2020 Presidential election or the certification of the Electoral College vote held on or about January 6, 2021." "Appointment of a Special Counsel," Department of Justice, (Nov. 18, 2022), available at https://www.justice.gov/opa/pr/appointment-special-counsel-0. In addition, the Special Counsel is to oversee the Department's "ongoing investigation involving classified documents and other Presidential records, as well as the possible obstruction of that investigation. . . ." *Id.*

593. The House of Representatives held Meadows in contempt for refusing to testify before the Committee, 167 Cong. Rec. H7814-7815 (daily ed. Dec. 14, 2021), but DOJ declined to prosecute him. *See* Josh Gerstein, Kyle Cheny, and Nicholas Wu, "DOJ Declines to Charge Meadows, Scavino with Contempt of Congress for Defying Jan. 6 Committee," *Politico*, (June 3, 2022), available at https://www.politico.com/news/2022/06/03/doj-declines-to-charge-meadows-scavino-with-contempt-of-congress-for-defying-jan-6-committee-00037230.

594. 18 U.S.C. § 1512(c)(2).

595. According to DOJ, "[a] conviction under Section 1512(c)(2) requires proof that": (1) "the natural and probable effect of the defendant's actions were to obstruct [influence or impede] the official proceeding;" (2) "that [defendant] knew that his actions were likely to obstruct [influence or impede] that proceeding;" and (3) "that he acted with the wrongful or improper purpose of delaying or stopping the official proceeding." *United States v. Andries*, No. 21-93 (RC), 2022 U.S. Dist. LEXIS 44794 at *37 n.8 (D.D.C. Mar. 14, 2022) (quoting Government's Response to Defendant's Second Supplemental Brief at 6); *see United States v. Aguilar*, 515 U.S. 593, 616 (1995) (Scalia, J., concurring in part, dissenting in part) (describing the "longstanding and well-accepted meaning" of "corruptly" as denoting "an act done with an intent to give some advantage inconsistent with official duty and the rights of others" (quoting *United States v. Ogle*, 613 F.2d 233, 238 (10th Cir. 1979))).

596. *See, e.g., United States v. Gillespie*, No. 22-CR-60 (BAH), 2022 U.S. Dist. LEXIS 214833, at *7-8 (D.D.C. Nov. 29, 2022); *United States v. Seefried*, No. 1:21-cr-287 (TNM), 2022 U.S. Dist. LEXIS

196980, at *2-3 (D.D.C. Oct. 29, 2022); *United States v. Miller*, 589 F. Supp. 3d 60, 67 (D.D.C. 2022), *reconsideration denied*, No. 1:21-CR-119 (CJN), 589 F. Supp. 3d 60 (D.D.C. May 27, 2022); *United States v. Puma*, No. 1:21-CR-454 (PLF), 2022 U.S. Dist. LEXIS 48875, at *10 (D.D.C. Mar. 19, 2022); *United States v. McHugh*, 583 F. Supp. 3d 1, 14-15 (D.D.C. 2022). *See also* T. Kanefield, "January 6 Defendants Are Raising a Creative Defense. It Isn't Working," *Washington Post*, (Feb. 15, 2022), available at https://www.washingtonpost.com/outlook/2022/02/15/jan-6-official-proceeding/.

597. *See supra*, Executive Summary.

598. *See supra*, Executive Summary.

599. *See supra*, Executive Summary.

600. Documents on file with the Select Committee (National Archives Production), VP-R0000156_0001 (January 6, 2021, email chain between John Eastman and Greg Jacob re: Pennsylvania letter). One judge on the U.S. District Court for the District of Columbia, in the course of concluding that section 1512(c) is not void for vagueness, interpreted the "corruptly" element as meaning "contrary to law, statute, or established rule." *United States v. Sandlin*, 575 F. Supp. 3d. 15-16, (D.D.C. 2021). As explained above, President Trump attempted to cause the Vice President to violate the Electoral Count Act, and even Dr. Eastman advised President Trump that the proposed course of action would violate the Act. We believe this satisfies the "corruptly" element of the offense under the *Sandlin* opinion.

601. Indeed, it would not have been legally possible for a State to have done so in the days before January 6th.

602. Order Re Privilege of Documents Dated January 4-7, 2021 at 49-50, *Eastman v. Thompson et al.*, 594 F. Supp. 3d 1156, (C.D. Cal. March 28, 2022) (No. 8:22-cv-99-DOC-DFM).

603. *See supra*, Executive Summary.

604. Documents on file with Select Committee (Department of Justice Production), HCOR-Pre-Certification-Events-07282021-000738 - COR-Pre-Certification-Events-07282021-000739 (December 27, 2020, handwritten notes from Richard Donoghue).

605. *See supra*, Executive Summary.

606. *See supra*, Executive Summary.

607. *See supra*, Executive Summary. Jeffrey Clark invoked his Fifth Amendment privilege against self-incrimination in response to questions regarding this letter. As already noted, the political appointee who assisted in drafting the letter was hired at the Justice Department on December 15, 2020, but had worked on behalf of President Trump on election challenges in the weeks beforehand (including, apparently, while simultaneously serving as Special Counsel for the White House Office of Management and Budget).

608. *See supra*, Executive Summary.

609. *See supra*, Executive Summary.

610. *See supra*, Executive Summary.

611. Select Committee to Investigate the January 6th Attack on the United States Capitol, Transcribed Interview of Eric Herschmann, (Apr. 6, 2022), p. 26.

612. Documents on file with the Select Committee (National Archives Production), VP-R0000156_0001 (January 6, 2021, email chain between John Eastman and Greg Jacob re: Pennsylvania letter).

613. Select Committee to Investigate the January 6th Attack on the United States Capitol, Transcribed Interview of Eric Herschmann, (Apr. 6, 2022), p. 44. Although Eastman invoked his Fifth Amendment rights as a reason not to answer any of this Committee's substantive questions during his deposition, he has recently suggested in public that he only wished to delay the count of votes by multiple days. As the evidence developed by this Committee demonstrates, Eastman knew that such an effort to delay the count would also be illegal. *See* Select Committee to Investigate the January 6th Attack on the United States Capitol,

Hearing on the January 6th Investigation, 117th Cong., 2d sess., (June 16, 2022), at 1:32:00-1:35:13, available at https://www.youtube.com/watch?v=vBjUWVKuDj0 ("[D]id Dr. Eastman seem to admit that both of these theories suffered from similar legal flaws? [T]his new theory, as I was pointing out to him, or the procedural theory, still violates several provisions of the Electoral Count Act, as he acknowledged.... So, he acknowledged in those conversations that the underlying legal theory was the same...."). In addition, neither Eastman nor any other co-conspirator had information establishing that any delay in counting votes would or could have changed the outcome of the election in any State.

614. *See supra,* Executive Summary. We also note that these Republican Members of Congress, who had more knowledge of Trump's planning for January 6th than any other Members of Congress, were also likely in a far superior position than any other Members to warn the Capitol Police of the risks of violence at the Capitol on January 6th.

615. *See* Select Committee to Investigate the January 6th Attack on the U.S. Capitol, *Hearing on the January 6th Investigation*, 117th Cong., 2d sess., (June 16, 2022), at 2:29:50, available at https://www.youtube.com/watch?v=vBjUWVKuDj0 ("I've decided that I should be on the pardon list, if that is still in the works.").

616. The elements of a section 371 conspiracy to defraud the United States are: (1) at least two people entered into an agreement to obstruct a lawful function of the government, (2) by deceitful or dishonest means, and (3) a member of the conspiracy engaged in at least one overt act in furtherance of the agreement. Order Re Privilege of Documents Dated January 4-7, 2021 at 53, *Eastman v. Thompson et al.,* 594 F. Supp. 3d 1156, (C.D. Cal. Mar. 28, 2022) (No. 8:22-cv-99-DOC-DFM). Put similarly, to prove a violation section 371's "defraud" provision, the Government must prove that the defendant: (1) agreed with at least one other person to defraud the United States, (2) knowingly participated in the conspiracy with the intent to defraud the United States, and (3) that at least one overt act was taken in furtherance of the conspiracy. *See United States v. Dean,* 55 F.3d 640, 647 (D.C. Cir. 1995) (citing *United States v. Treadwell,* 760 F.2d 327, 333 (D.C. Cir. 1985)); *see also United States v. Mellen,* 158, 393 F.3d 175, 181 (D.C. Cir. 2004). An individual "defrauds" the Government for purposes of section 371 if he "interfere[s] with or obstruct[s] one of its lawful governmental functions by deceit, craft or trickery, or at least by means that are dishonest." *Hammerschmidt v. United States,* 265 U.S. 182, 188 (1924); *see also United States v. Haldeman,* 559 F.2d 31, 122 n.255 (D.C. Cir. 1976) (upholding jury verdict on instruction defining "defrauding the United States" as: "depriv[ing] the Government of its right to have the officials of its departments and agencies transact their official business honestly and impartially, free from corruption, fraud, improper and undue influence, dishonesty and obstruction").

617. Order Re Privilege of Documents Dated January 4-7, 2021 at 54-55, *Eastman v. Thompson et al.,* 594 F. Supp. 3d 1156, (C.D. Cal. Mar. 28, 2022) (No. 8:22-cv-99-DOC-DFM).

618. *See* Order Re Privilege of Documents Dated January 4-7, 2021 at 53, *Eastman v. Thompson et al.,* 594 F. Supp. 3d 1156, (C.D. Cal. Mar. 28, 2022) (No. 8:22-cv-99-DOC-DFM). ("An 'agreement' between co-conspirators need not be express and can be inferred from the conspirators' conduct.").

619. *See infra,* Chapter 1.

620. Order Re Privilege of Documents Dated January 4-7, 2021 at 55, *Eastman v. Thompson et al.,* 594 F. Supp. 3d 1156, (C.D. Cal. Mar. 28, 2022) (No. 8:22-cv-99-DOC-DFM).

621. Order Re Privilege of Documents Dated January 4-7, 2021 at 57, *Eastman v. Thompson et al.,* 594 F. Supp. 3d 1156, (C.D. Cal. Mar. 28, 2022) (No. 8:22-cv-99-DOC-DFM).

622. *See infra,* Chapter 2. President Trump's call with Secretary Raffensperger may have violated several provisions of both Federal and Georgia law. We do not attempt to catalogue all the possible violations here.

623. Order Re Privilege of Documents Dated January 4-7, 2021 at 57, *Eastman v. Thompson et al.,* 594 F. Supp. 3d 1156, (C.D. Cal. Mar. 28, 2022) (No. 8:22-cv-99-DOC-DFM).

624. Order Re Privilege of Documents Dated January 4-7, 2021 at 59, *Eastman v. Thompson et al.,* 594 F. Supp. 3d 1156, (C.D. Cal. Mar. 28, 2022) (No. 8:22-cv-99-DOC-DFM).

EXECUTIVE SUMMARY

625. "908. ELEMENTS OF 18 U.S.C. § 1001," Department of Justice, (last accessed on Dec. 13, 2022), available at https://www.justice.gov/archives/jm/criminal-resource-manual-908-elements-18-usc-1001.

626. The elements of a section 371 conspiracy are discussed above.

627. As explained in Chapter 5, staffers for Rep. Mike Kelly (R-PA) and Sen. Ron Johnson (R-WI) reached out to Vice President Pence's director of legislative affairs, apparently seeking to deliver fake certificates on January 6. Documents on file with the Select Committee to Investigate the January 6th Attack on the United States Capitol (Chris Hodgson Production), 00012 (January 6, 2021, text message from Rep. Kelly's Chief of Staff, Matt Stroia, to Chris Hodgson on January at 8:41 a.m.), 00058 (January 6, 2021, text messages from Senator Johnson's Chief of Staff, Sean Riley, to Chris Hodgson around 12:37 p.m.).

628. *See infra,* Chapter 3.

629. 18 U.S.C. § 1001 (emphasis added).

630. *See, e.g., United States v. Bowser*, 964 F.3d 26, 31 (D.C. Cir. 2020), *cert. denied*, 141 S. Ct. 1390 (2021) ("[T]he False Statements Act applies to 'any investigation or review, conducted pursuant to the authority of any committee, subcommittee, commission *or office of the Congress.*' 18 U.S.C. § 1001(c)(2) (emphasis added)."); *United States v. Stone*, 394 F. Supp. 3d 1, 10 (D.D.C. 2019).

631. *See* Select Committee to Investigate the January 6th Attack on the United States Capitol, *Business Meeting on the January 6th Investigation*, 117th Cong., 2d sess., (Oct. 13, 2022), at 1:14:59-1:15:22 available at https://www.youtube.com/watch?v=IQvuBoLBuC0 ("[President Trump] turned the call over to Mr. Eastman, who then proceeded to talk about the importance of the RNC helping the campaign gather these contingent electors, in case any of the legal challenges that were ongoing changed the result of any of the states.").

632. 18 U.S.C. § 2383.

633. *Thompson v. Trump*, 590 F. Supp. 3d 46, 115 (D.D.C. 2022), appeal pending, No. 22-5069 (D.C. Cir. Mar. 18, 2022).

634. *See* Ryan Goodman and Josh Asabor, "In Their Own Words: The 43 Republicans' Explanations of Their Votes Not to Convict Trump in Impeachment Trial," Just Security, (Feb. 15, 2021), available at https://www.justsecurity.org/74725/in-their-own-words-the-43-republicans-explanations-of-their-votes-not-to-convict-trump-in-impeachment-trial/.

635. *See supra,* Executive Summary.

636. *See supra,* Executive Summary. The evidence suggests that the Vice President and certain members of President Trump's staff urged DOD to deploy the National Guard notwithstanding the President's wishes.

637. A prominent U.S. professor of criminal law has opined that President Trump can be held criminally responsible under section 2383 for his failure to act, when he had a duty to act given his constitutional obligation under Article II section 3 of the Constitution to "take Care that the Laws be faithfully executed." *See* Albert W. Alschuler, "Trump and the Insurrection Act: The Legal Framework," Just Security, (Aug. 16, 2022), available at https://www.justsecurity.org/82696/trump-and-the-insurrection-act-the-true-legal-framework/. Professor Albert Alschuler, the Julius Kreeger Professor Emeritus at the University of Chicago Law School, taught criminal law for over 50 years at many of our Nation's leading law schools. He has published a number of analytical pieces applying the "assists" and "aid and comfort" clauses of that provisions (which he analogizes to "aiding and abetting" accomplice liability) to the evidence presented at the Committee's hearings. In any event, as described above, President Trump *did* act, including through his 2:24 p.m. tweet about the Vice President that inflamed the crowd attacking the Capitol.

638. Select Committee to Investigate the January 6th Attack on the United States Capitol, Continued Interview of Cassidy Hutchinson, (June 20, 2022) p. 26.

639. Select Committee to Investigate the January 6th Attack on the United States Capitol, *Hearing on the January 6th Investigation*, 117th Cong., 2d sess., (July 21, 2022), at 1:02:53, available at https://www.youtube.com/watch?v=pbRVqWbHGuo; Donald J. Trump

(@realDonaldTrump), Twitter, Jan. 6, 2021 2:24 p.m. ET, available at https:// www.thetrumparchive.com/?searchbox= "didn't+have+the+courage+to+do+what+should+have+been+done" (archived).

640. See *infra*, Chapter 8.

641. *See supra*, Executive Summary

642. Select Committee to Investigate the January 6th Attack on the United States Capitol, Continued Interview of Cassidy Hutchinson, (June 20, 2022), p. 27.

643. *See* Mariana Alfaro, "Trump Vows Pardons, Government Apology to Capitol Rioters if Elected," *Washington Post*, (Sept. 1, 2022), available at https://www.washingtonpost.com/ national-security/2022/09/01/trump-jan-6-rioters-pardon/.

644. Jordan Fischer, Eric Flack, and Stephanie Wilson, "Georgia Man Who Wanted to 'Remove Some Craniums' on January 6 Sentenced to More than 2 Years in Prison," WUSA9, (Dec. 14, 2021), available at https://perma.cc/RSY2-J3RU.

645. Dan Mangan, "Capitol Rioter Garret Miller Says He Was Following Trump's Orders, Apologizes to AOC for Threat," CNBC, (Jan. 25, 2021), available at https://www.cnbc.com/2021/01/ 25/capitol-riots-garret-miller-says-he-was-following-trumps-orders-apologizes-to-aoc.html.

646. Donald J. Trump (@realDonaldTrump), Twitter, Jan. 6, 2021 6:01 p.m. ET, available at https://www.thetrumparchive.com/?searchbox=%22these+are+the+things+and+events%22 (archived).

647. Select Committee to Investigate the January 6th Attack on the United States Capitol, Deposition of Nicholas Luna, (Mar. 21, 2022), pp. 166–67.

648. Donald J. Trump (@realDonaldTrump), Twitter, Jan. 6, 2021 6:01 p.m. ET, available at https://www.thetrumparchive.com/?searchbox=%22these+are+the+things+and+events%22 (archived).

649. 18 U.S.C. § 372.

650. *See* "Leader of Oath Keepers and Oath Keepers Member Found Guilty of Seditious Conspiracy and Other Charges Related to U.S. Capitol Breach," Department of Justice, (Nov. 29, 2022), available at https://www.justice.gov/opa/pr/leader-oath-keepers-and-oath-keepers-member-found-guilty-seditious-conspiracy-and-other.

651. 18 U.S.C. § 2384. To establish a violation of section 2384, the government must establish (1) a conspiracy, (2) to overthrow, put down, or destroy by force the Government of the United States, or to levy war against them, or to oppose by force the authority thereof, or by force to prevent, hinder or delay the execution of any law of the United States, or by force to seize, take, or possess any property of the United States contrary to the authority thereof. *See United States v. Khan*, 461 F.3d 477, 487 (4th Cir. 2006).

652. "Leader of Oath Keepers and Oath Keepers Member Found Guilty of Seditious Conspiracy and Other Charges Related to U.S. Capitol Breach," Department of Justice, (Nov. 29, 2022), available at https://www.justice.gov/opa/pr/leader-oath-keepers-and-oath-keepers-member-found-guilty-seditious-conspiracy-and-other.

653. "Leader of Proud Boys and Four Other Members Indicted in Federal Court for Seditious Conspiracy and Other Offenses Related to U.S. Capitol Breach," Department of Justice, (June 6, 2022), available at https://www.justice.gov/opa/pr/leader-proud-boys-and-four-other-members-indicted-federal-court-seditious-conspiracy-and.

654. *See supra*, Executive Summary.

655. Brian Naylor, "Read Trump's Jan. 6 Speech, A Key Part of Impeachment Trial," NPR, (Feb. 10, 2021), available at https://www.npr.org/2021/02/10/966396848/read-trumps-jan-6-speech-a-key-part-of-impeachment-trial.

656. Kristen Holmes, "Trump Calls for the Termination of the Constitution in Truth Social Post," CNN, (Dec. 4, 2022), available at https://www.cnn.com/2022/12/03/politics/trump-constitution-truth-social/index.html.

657. *See* Mariana Alfaro, "Trump Vows Pardons, Government Apology to Capitol Rioters if Elected," *Washington Post,* (Sept. 1, 2022), available at https://www.washingtonpost.com/national-security/2022/09/01/trump-jan-6-rioters-pardon/.

658. *See infra,* Chapter 7.

659. 167 Cong. Rec. H171-72 (daily ed. Jan. 13, 2021).

660. *See supra,* Executive Summary.

661. Select Committee to Investigate the January 6th Attack on the United States Capitol, Continued Interview of Cassidy Hutchinson, (June 20, 2022), pp. 84–87.

662. Documents on file with the Select Committee to Investigate the January 6th Attack on the United States Capitol (National Archives Production), 076P-R000008962_0009 (January 2, 2021, White House Presidential Call Log).

663. Documents on file with the Select Committee to Investigate the January 6th Attack on the United States Capitol (Mark Meadows Production), MM014864 (January 5, 2021, text message from Rep. Jim Jordan to Mark Meadows describing the Vice President's actions on January 6th).

664. *See* Documents on file with the Select Committee to Investigate the January 6th Attack on the United States Capitol (National Archives Production), P-R000255-259 (January 6, 2021, Presidential Daily Diary); Felicia Somnez, "Rep. Jim Jordan Tells House Panel He Can't Recall How Many Times He Spoke with Trump on Jan. 6," *Washington Post,* (Oct. 20, 2021), available at https://www.washingtonpost.com/politics/jordan-trump-calls-capitol-attack/2021/10/20/1a570d0e-31c7-11ec-9241-aad8e48f01ff_story.html.

665. Documents on file with the Select Committee to Investigate the January 6th Attack on the United States Capitol, (AT&T Production, Feb. 9, 2022).

666. Select Committee to Investigate the January 6th Attack on the United States Capitol, Deposition of Rudolph Giuliani, (May 20, 2022), pp. 205-07.

667. Select Committee to Investigate the January 6th Attack on the United States Capitol, Continued Interview of Cassidy Hutchinson, (May 17, 2022), p. 106.

668. Select Committee to Investigate the January 6th Attack on the United States Capitol, Transcribed Interview of Cassidy Hutchinson, (Feb. 23, 2022), pp. 72-73.

669. Select Committee to Investigate the January 6th Attack on the United States Capitol, Continued Interview of Cassidy Hutchinson, (Mar. 7, 2022), pp. 66-67.

670. Select Committee to Investigate the January 6th Attack on the United States Capitol, Continued Interview of Cassidy Hutchinson, (June 20, 2022), pp. 62–64.

671. *See* Sarah Lynch and David Shepardson, "Watchdog to Probe if Justice Dept. Officials Improperly Tried to Alter 2020 Election," *Reuters,* (Jan. 25, 2021), available at https://www.reuters.com/article/us-usa-trump-justice/watchdog-to-probe-if-justice-dept-officials-improperly-tried-to-alter-2020-election-idUSKBN29U21E ("'Throughout the past four years, I worked with Assistant Attorney General Clark on various legislative matters. When President Trump asked if I would make an introduction, I obliged,' Perry said in a statement.").

672. Select Committee to Investigate the January 6th Attack on the United States Capitol, Continued Interview of Cassidy Hutchinson, (June 20, 2022), p. 48.

673. Select Committee to Investigate the January 6th Attack on the United States Capitol, Transcribed Interview of Cassidy Hutchinson, (Feb. 23, 2022), p. 45.

674. Select Committee to Investigate the January 6th Attack on the United States Capitol, Continued Interview of Cassidy Hutchinson, (May 17, 2022), pp. 106–07.

675. Documents on file with the Select Committee to Investigate the January 6th Attack on the United States Capitol (Mark Meadows Production), MM011449.

676. Documents on file with the Select Committee to Investigate the January 6th Attack on the United States Capitol (Mark Meadows Production), MM011506, (November 2020 text messages from Rep. Andy Biggs to Mark Meadows).

677. Josh Kelety, "Congressman Andy Biggs Coordinated Efforts with Mark Finchem before Capitol Riot," *Phoenix New Times*, (Feb. 18, 2021), available at https://www.phoenixnewtimes.com/news/congressman-andy-biggs-coordinated-with-mark-finchem-before-capitol-riot-11532527.

678. Documents on file with the Select Committee to Investigate the January 6th Attack on the United States Capitol (Jim DeGraffenreid Production), DEGRAFFENREID 000554 (December 18, 2020, text messages between James DeGraffenreid, a Nevada fake elector for Trump, and another remarking that "Andy Biggs ... has reached out to NV to ask about our evidence").

679. Audrey Fahlberg, "January 6 Hearings Become Fundraising Fodder," *The Dispatch*, (July 7, 2022), available at https://thedispatch.com/p/january-6-hearings-become-fundraising; Archive of Political Emails, Jim Jordan, "The January 6th Committee Is After Me," June 9, 2022 12:41 p.m., available at https://politicalemails.org/messages/686023.

680. John Rowley III to the Honorable Bennie G. Thompson re: "Subpoena to Representative Scott Perry," (May 24, 2022), available at https://www.documentcloud.org/documents/22061774-scott-perry-j6-response.

681. Committee on Standards of Official Conduct, *House Ethics Manual*, p. 13 (2008).

682. Documents on file with the Select Committee to Investigate the January 6th Attack on the United States Capitol (National Archives Production), 076P-R001080 (December 21, 2020, WAVES records showing Representatives Babin, Biggs, Brooks, Gaetz, Gohmert, Gosar, Taylor Greene, Harris, Hice, Jordan, and Perry entering the White House).

683. *See* Select Committee to Investigate the January 6th Attack on the United States Capitol, Deposition of John Eastman, (Dec. 9, 2021); Select Committee to Investigate the January 6th Attack on the United States Capitol, Deposition of Roger Stone, (Dec. 17, 2021); Select Committee to Investigate the January 6th Attack on the United States Capitol, Deposition of Jeffrey Clark, (Feb. 2, 2022); Select Committee to Investigate the January 6th Attack on the United States Capitol, Deposition of Michael Flynn, (Mar. 10, 2022).

684. *Latif v. Obama*, 677 F.3d 1175, 1193 (D.C. Cir. 2012) (quoting *Mitchell v. United States*, 526 U.S. 314, 328 (1999)). Justice Scalia not only agreed with this principle, but he also reasoned that the Fifth Amendment does not prevent an adverse inference in even criminal cases. This is because the text of that Amendment does not require such a rule and applying an adverse inference to a refusal to testify is exactly in keeping with "normal evidentiary inferences." *See Mitchell*, 526 U.S. at 332 (Scalia, J., dissenting). Justice Thomas agreed with Justice Scalia. *See id.* at 341-42 (Thomas, J., dissenting).

685. Select Committee to Investigate the January 6th Attack on the United States Capitol, Deposition of Michael Flynn, (Mar. 10, 2022), p. 82.

686. *Trump v. Thompson*, 20 F.4th 10, 15-16 (D.C. Cir. 2021), *cert. denied*, 142 S.Ct. 1350 (2022).

687. *Trump v. Thompson*, 20 F.4th 10, 89 (D.C. Cir. 2021) (citation omitted), *cert. denied*, 142 S.Ct. 1350 (2022). Former President Trump also asked the United State Supreme Court to block the Select Committee from accessing his documents. The Supreme Court denied that request stating, "Because the Court of Appeals concluded that President Trump's claims would have failed even if he were the incumbent, his status as a former President necessarily made no difference to the court's decision." *Trump v. Thompson*, 142 S.Ct. 680, 680 (2022) (citation omitted).

688. H. Res. 851, 117th Cong., (2021); H. Rept. 117-216, Resolution Recommending that the House of Representatives Find Mark Randall Meadows in Contempt of Congress for Refusal to Comply with a Subpoena Duly Issued by the Select Committee to Investigate the January 6th Attack on the United States Capitol, 117th Cong., 1st Sess. (2021), available at https://www.congress.gov/117/crpt/hrpt216/CRPT-117hrpt216.pdf.

689. Statement of Interest of the United States at 9-10, *Meadows v. Pelosi et al.*, No. 1:21-cv-03217 (CJN) (D.D.C. July 15, 2022), ECF No. 42.

690. "Thompson & Cheney Statement on Justice Department Decisions on Contempt Referrals," Select Committee to Investigate the January 6th Attack on the United States Capitol, (June

3, 2022), available at https://january6th.house.gov/news/press-releases/thompson-cheney-statement-justice-department-decisions-contempt-referrals.

691. Dennis Aftergut, "Why the DOJ Did Not Indict Mark Meadows (and What It Should Do Next)," NBC News, (June 7, 2022), available at https://www.nbcnews.com/think/opinion/trump-lackey-mark-meadows-escaped-january-6-prosecution-peter-navarro-rcna32319.

692. H. Res. 1037, 117th Cong., (2022); H. Rept. 117-284, Resolution Recommending that the House of Representatives Find Peter K. Navarro and Daniel Scavino, Jr., in Contempt of Congress for Refusal to Comply with a Subpoena Duly Issued by the Select Committee to Investigate the January 6th Attack on the United States Capitol, 117th Cong., 2d Sess. (2022), available at https://www.congress.gov/117/crpt/hrpt284/CRPT-117hrpt284.pdf. In particular, Scavino may have further information on President Trump's advance knowledge from social media posts of the rioters' plans to invade the Capitol. See *supra* __.

693. H. Res. 730, 117th Cong., (2021); H. Rept. 117-152, Resolution Recommending that the House of Representatives Find Stephen K. Bannon in Contempt of Congress for Refusal to Comply with a Subpoena Duly Issued by the Select Committee to Investigate the January 6th Attack on the United States Capitol, 117th Cong., 1st Sess. (2021), available at https://www.congress.gov/117/crpt/hrpt152/CRPT-117hrpt152.pdf.

694. H. Res. 1037, 117th Cong., (2022); "Peter Navarro Indicted for Contempt of Congress," Department of Justice, (June 3, 2022), available at https://www.justice.gov/usao-dc/pr/peter-navarro-indicted-contempt-congress; H. Rept. 117-284, Resolution Recommending that the House of Representatives Find Peter K. Navarro and Daniel Scavino, Jr., in Contempt of Congress for Refusal to Comply with a Subpoena Duly Issued by the Select Committee to Investigate the January 6th Attack on the United States Capitol, 117th Cong., 2d Sess. (2022), available at https://www.congress.gov/117/crpt/hrpt284/CRPT-117hrpt284.pdf.

695. See *infra* 136.

696. Select Committee to Investigate the January 6th Attack on the United States Capitol, *Hearing on the January 6th Investigation*, 117th Cong., 2d sess., (July 12, 2022), at 2;14:00-2:14:50, available at https://youtu.be/rrUa0hfG6Lo.

697. Select Committee to Investigate the January 6th Attack on the United States Capitol, Deposition of John McEntee, (Mar. 28, 2022), pp. 153-55; Select Committee to Investigate the January 6th Attack on the United States Capitol, Transcribed Interview of Eric Herschmann, (Apr. 6, 2022), pp. 129-35; Select Committee to Investigate the January 6th Attack on the United States Capitol, Transcribed Interview of Pasquale Anthony "Pat" Cipollone, (July 8, 2022), pp. 176-77; Select Committee to Investigate the January 6th Attack on the United States Capitol, Continued Interview of Cassidy Hutchinson, (May 17, 2022), pp. 104-06.

698. Select Committee to Investigate the January 6th Attack on the United States Capitol, *Hearing on the January 6th Investigation*, 117th Cong., 2d sess., (June 23, 2022), at 2:22:05-2:23:41, available at https://www.youtube.com/live/Z4535-VW-bY?feature=share&t=8525.

699. Select Committee to Investigate the January 6th Attack on the United States Capitol, Deposition of John McEntee, (Mar. 28, 2022), pp. 153-55; Select Committee to Investigate the January 6th Attack on the United States Capitol, *Hearing on the January 6th Investigation*, 117th Cong., 2d sess., (June 23, 2022), at 2:23:41-2:24:42, available at https://www.youtube.com/watch?v=Z4535-VW-bY&t=8620s.

700. Select Committee to Investigate the January 6th Attack on the United States Capitol, Transcribed Interview of Eric Herschmann, (Apr. 6, 2022), pp. 129-35, esp. pp. 130-131; Select Committee to Investigate the January 6th Attack on the United States Capitol, *Hearing on the January 6th Investigation*, 117th Cong., 2d sess., (June 23, 2022), at 2:21:26-2:22:04, available at https://www.youtube.com/live/Z4535-VW-bY?feature=share&t=8486.

701. Select Committee to Investigate the January 6th Attack on the United States Capitol, Transcribed Interview of Eric Herschmann, (Apr. 6, 2022), p. 133.

702. Documents on file with the Select Committee to Investigate the January 6th Attack on the United States Capitol (National Archives Production), 076P-R000005854_0001 (January 11, 2021, email from Molly Michael to Rep. Mo Brooks, confirming receipt of email from Brooks

recommending pardons, including for "Every Congressman and Senator who voted to reject the electoral college vote submissions of Arizona and Pennsylvania"); Select Committee to Investigate the January 6th Attack on the United States Capitol, *Hearing on the January 6th Investigation*, 117th Cong., 2d sess., (June 23, 2022), at 2:20:52-2:21:12, available at https://www.youtube.com/live/Z4535-VW-bY?feature=share&t=8452.

703. Select Committee to Investigate the January 6th Attack on the United States Capitol, *Hearing on the January 6th Investigation*, 117th Cong., 2d sess., (June 28, 2022), available at https://www.govinfo.gov/committee/house-january6th.

704. The Committee has enormous respect for the U.S. Secret Service and recognized that the testimony regarding their work is sensitive for law enforcement, protectee security, and national security reasons. *See, e.g.*, Select Committee to Investigate the January 6th Attack on the United States Capitol, Transcribed Interview of USSS Employee "Driver", (Nov. 7, 2022), p. 4 (the Select Committee is not releasing the name of this individual); Select Committee to Investigate the January 6th Attack on the United States Capitol, Continued Interview of Anthony Ornato, (Nov. 28, 2022), p. 4; Select Committee to Investigate the January 6th Attack on the United States Capitol, Transcribed Interview of USSS Employee, (Nov. 21, 2022), p. 4; Select Committee to Investigate the January 6th Attack on the United States Capitol, Transcribed Interview of USSS Employee, (Nov. 18, 2022), p. 4 Select Committee to Investigate the January 6th Attack on the United States Capitol, Transcribed Interview of Robert Engel, (Nov. 17, 2022), p. 4.

705. Select Committee to Investigate the January 6th Attack on the United States Capitol, Transcribed Interview of USSS Employee, (Nov. 7, 2022), pp. 4, 86-87.

706. *See, e.g.*, Devlin Barrett, Jacqueline Alemany, Josh Dawsey, and Rosalind S. Heldeman, "The Justice Dept.'s Jan. 6 Investigation Is Looking at ... Everything," *Washington Post*, (Sept. 16, 2022), available at https://www.washingtonpost.com/national-security/2022/09/15/trump-january-6-subpoenas-meadows/; Josh Dawsey and Isaac Arnsdorf, "Prosecutors Seek Details from Trump's PAC in Expanding Jan. 6 Probe," *Washington Post*, (Sept. 8, 2022), available at https://www.washingtonpost.com/national-security/2022/09/08/trump-subpoenas-pac-jan-6/.

707. *See* Devlin Barrett, Josh Dawsey, and Isaac Stanley-Becker, "Trump's Committee Paying for Lawyers of Key Mar-a-Lago Witnesses," *Washington Post*, (Dec. 5, 2022), available at https://www.washingtonpost.com/national-security/2022/12/05/trump-witnesses-legal-bills-pac/.

708. The Committee sat for dozens of hours with Hutchinson and concluded that she is brave and earnest, and understood the intense backlash that would inevitably result from those who were enlisted to defend President Trump's behavior. [See *infra*, Chapter 7]. The thuggish behavior from President Trump's team, including efforts to intimidate described elsewhere in this report (*see e.g.* Chapter 3), gave rise to many concerns about Hutchinson's security, both in advance of and since her public testimony. (We note that multiple members of the Committee were regularly receiving threats of violence during this period.) Accordingly, the Committee attempted to take appropriate measures to help ensure her safety in advance of her testimony, including measures designed to minimize the risk of leaks that might put her safety at risk.

709. *See, e.g.*, Select Committee to Investigate the January 6th Attack on the United States Capitol, Transcribed Interview of Pasquale Anthony "Pat" Cipollone, (July 8, 2022), pp. 71-72 (noting that another witness reference may have been to Pat Philbin).

710. Select Committee to Investigate the January 6th Attack on the United States Capitol, Deposition of Kayleigh McEnany, (Jan. 12, 2022), pp. 264-65.

711. Select Committee to Investigate the January 6th Attack on the United States Capitol, Deposition of Kayleigh McEnany, (Jan. 12, 2022), pp. 52-57, 70-74, 282-88.

712. Select Committee to Investigate the January 6th Attack on the United States Capitol, Deposition of Kayleigh McEnany, (Jan. 12, 2022), pp. 142-45, 288-92. *See also* Select Committee to Investigate the January 6th Attack on the United States Capitol, Transcribed Interview of Sarah Matthews, (Feb. 8, 2022), pp. 12-15.

713. Select Committee to Investigate the January 6th Attack on the United States Capitol, Deposition of Kayleigh McEnany, (Jan. 12, 2022), pp. 183-86.

714. Select Committee to Investigate the January 6th Attack on the United States Capitol, Transcribed Interview of Sarah Matthews, (Feb. 8, 2022), pp. 39-41.

715. Select Committee to Investigate the January 6th Attack on the United States Capitol, Transcribed Interview of Sarah Matthews, (Feb. 8, 2022), p. 41.

716. Select Committee to Investigate the January 6th Attack on the United States Capitol, Transcribed Interview of Ivanka Trump, (Apr. 5, 2022), pp. 38-39, 120, 205, 210, 213-14.

717. Select Committee to Investigate the January 6th Attack on the United States Capitol, Transcribed Interview of Ivanka Trump, (Apr. 5, 2022), p. 27.

718. Select Committee to Investigate the January 6th Attack on the United States Capitol, Transcribed Interview of Julie Radford, (May 24, 2022), p. 19.

719. Select Committee to Investigate the January 6th Attack on the United States Capitol, Transcribed Interview of Ivanka Trump, (Apr. 5, 2022), p. 40.

720. Mark Meadows, *The Chief's Chief* (Ft. Lauderdale, FL: All Seasons Press, 2021).

721. Mark Meadows, *The Chief's Chief* (Ft. Lauderdale, FL: All Seasons Press, 2021), p. 259.

722. Mark Meadows, *The Chief's Chief* (Ft. Lauderdale, FL: All Seasons Press, 2021), p. 259.

723. Select Committee to Investigate the January 6th Attack on the United States Capitol, Continued Interview of Cassidy Hutchinson, (June 20, 2022), pp. 47-49.

724. Select Committee to Investigate the January 6th Attack on the United States Capitol, Transcribed Interview of Anthony Ornato, (Jan.y 28, 2022), pp. 76-77.

725. Select Committee to Investigate the January 6th Attack on the United States Capitol, Continued Interview of Anthony Ornato, (Mar. 29, 2022), pp. 46-47. Ornato was interviewed at length by the Select Committee in November 2022, after the Secret Service produced nearly a million new internal documents in August and September of this year.

726. Select Committee to Investigate the January 6th Attack on the United States Capitol, Continued Interview of Anthony Ornato, (Nov. 29, 2022), p. 92; *see also* Select Committee to Investigate the January 6th Attack on the United States Capitol, Continued Interview of Anthony Ornato, (Mar. 29, 2022), pp. 45-46 (stating that he had not heard about President Trump's instruction to others to ask Ornato about going to the Capitol).

727. Select Committee to Investigate the January 6th Attack on the United States Capitol, Interview of White House employee with national security responsibilities, (July 19, 2022), pp. 69-70; Select Committee to Investigate the January 6th Attack on the United States Capitol, Continued Interview of Cassidy Hutchinson, (June 20, 2022), pp. 4-6.

728. Select Committee to Investigate the January 6th Attack on the United States Capitol, Interview of White House employee with national security responsibilities, (July 19, 2022), pp. 69-70; Select Committee to Investigate the January 6th Attack on the United States Capitol, Continued Interview of Cassidy Hutchinson, (June 20, 2022), pp. 4-6.

729. Select Committee to Investigate the January 6th Attack on the United States Capitol, Transcribed Interview of White House employee with national security responsibilities, (July 19, 2022), pp. 69-70; Select Committee to Investigate the January 6th Attack on the United States Capitol, Continued Interview of Cassidy Hutchinson, (June 20, 2022), pp. 4-7; Select Committee to Investigate the January 6th Attack on the United States Capitol, Transcribed Interview of USSS Employee "Driver", (Nov. 7, 2022), pp. 77-80, 92-93; Select Committee to Investigate the January 6th Attack on the United States Capitol, Transcribed Interview of Mark Robinson, (July 7, 2022), pp. 17-18.

730. Select Committee to Investigate the January 6th Attack on the United States Capitol, Continued Interview of Anthony Ornato, (Nov. 29, 2022), pp. 104-105, 131-32, 135-36. *See also* Chapter 7.

731. *See, e.g.*, Select Committee to Investigate the January 6th Attack on the United States Capitol, Transcribed Interview of General Mark A. Milley, (Nov. 17, 2021), p. 199 (describing

another senior intelligence official worrying, ahead of January 6th, about violence at the Capitol); Select Committee to Investigate the January 6th Attack on the United States Capitol, Transcribed Interview of Donnell Harvin, (Jan. 24, 2022), pp. 22-23 (former Chief of Homeland Security and Intelligence for the District of Columbia describing the threat scene ahead of January 6th); Documents on file with the Select Committee to Investigate the January 6th Attack on the United States Capitol (Capitol Police Production), CTRL0000001532.0001, p.2 (January 5, 2021, FBI Situational Information Report).

732. Select Committee to Investigate the January 6th Attack on the United States Capitol, Continued Interview of Anthony Ornato, (Nov. 29, 2022), pp. 54-56.

733. Select Committee to Investigate the January 6th Attack on the United States Capitol, Continued Interview of Anthony Ornato, (Nov. 29, 2022), pp. 55-56.

734. See *supra* pp. 81-83. *See also* Select Committee to Investigate the January 6th Attack on the United States Capitol, Continued Interview of Anthony Ornato, (Nov. 29, 2022), p. 13 (Ornato confirming that one of his responsibilities was briefing the chief of staff and, through the chief of staff at times, the President on security-related issues).

735. "U.S. House of Representatives Debate on Impeachment of President Trump," C-SPAN, at 1:03:53 - 1:13:42, Jan. 13, 2021, available at https://www.c-span.org/video/?507879-4/debate-impeachment-president-trump; Tyler Moyer, "McCarthy: "President Bears Responsibility for Wednesday's Attack"," *Bakersfield Now*, (Jan. 13, 2021), available at https://bakersfieldnow.com/news/local/mccarthy-president-bears-responsibility-for-wednesdays-attack.

736. "House Minority Leader Weekly Briefing." C-SPAN, at 7:30 - 8:44, Jan. 21, 2021, available at https://www.c-span.org/video/?508185-1/minority-leader-mccarthy-backs-gop-conference-chair-liz-cheney; Rudy Talaka, "GOP Leader McCarthy Calls for Bipartisan Commission to Investigate Allegations of Members Helping Rioters," Mediaite, (Jan. 21, 2021), available at https://www.mediaite.com/news/gop-leader-mccarthy-calls-for-bipartisan-commission-to-investigate-allegations-of-members-helping-rioters/; "Rep. McCarthy Calls for Bipartisan Commission to Probe Capitol Riot," Newsmax, (Jan. 22, 2021), available at https://www.newsmax.com/politics/kevin-mccarthy-capitol-riot-boebert-probe/2021/01/21/id/1006648/.

737. Clare Foran, Ryan Nobles, and Annie Grayer, "Pelosi Announces Plans for '9/11-Type Commission' to Investigate Capitol Attack," CNN, (Feb. 15, 2021), available at https://www.cnn.com/2021/02/15/politics/pelosi-capitol-attack-commission/index.html.

738. "Letter to The Honorable Speaker Nancy Pelosi," House Republican Leader Kevin McCarthy, (Feb. 22, 2021), available at https://www.speaker.gov/sites/speaker.house.gov/files/Sharp%20MX-4141_20210518_081238.pdf.

739. "Letter to The Honorable Speaker Nancy Pelosi," House Republican Leader Kevin McCarthy, (Feb. 22, 2021), available at https://www.speaker.gov/sites/speaker.house.gov/files/Sharp%20MX-4141_20210518_081238.pdf.

740. "Letter to The Honorable Speaker Nancy Pelosi," House Republican Leader Kevin McCarthy, (Feb. 22, 2021), available at https://www.speaker.gov/sites/speaker.house.gov/files/Sharp%20MX-4141_20210518_081238.pdf.

741. Ryan Nobles, Annie Grayer, and Jeremy Herb, "Pelosi Concedes to Even Partisan Split on 1/6 Commission in Effort to Jumpstart Talks," CNN, (Apr. 20, 2021), available at https://www.cnn.com/2021/04/20/politics/nancy-pelosi-january-6-commission-talks/index.html; Ryan Nobles and Daniella Diaz, "Pelosi Makes Concession on Subpoenas for 9/11 Style Commission to Investigate Insurrection," CNN, (Apr. 22, 2021), available at https://www.cnn.com/2021/04/22/politics/nancy-pelosi-911-style-commission-insurrection-subpoenas/index.html.

742. John Bresnahan, Anna Palmer, and Jake Sherman, "Pelosi Taps Top Dem to Negotiate on Jan. 6 Commission," *Punchbowl News*, (May 11, 2021), available at https://punchbowl.news/archive/punchbowl-news-am-5-11/.

743. "Chairman Thompson Announces Bipartisan Agreement with Ranking Member Katko to Create Commission to Investigate the January 6 Attack on the Capitol," House Committee on Homeland Security, (May 14, 2021), available at https://homeland.house.gov/news/press-releases/chairman-thompson-announces-bipartisan-agreement-with-ranking-member-katko-to-create-commission-to-investigate-the-january-6-attack-on-the-capitol.

744. "McCarthy Statement on January 6 Commission Legislation," House Republican Leader Kevin McCarthy, (May 18, 2021), available at https://www.republicanleader.gov/mccarthy-statement-on-january-6-commission-legislation/.

745. "Pelosi Statement on McCarthy Opposition to January 6th Commission," Speaker of the House Nancy Pelosi, (May 18, 2021), available at https://www.speaker.gov/newsroom/51821.

746. "Pelosi Statement on McCarthy Opposition to January 6th Commission," Speaker of the House Nancy Pelosi, (May 18, 2021), available at https://www.speaker.gov/newsroom/51821; "Letter to The Honorable Speaker Nancy Pelosi," House Republican Leader Kevin McCarthy, (Feb. 22, 2021), available at https://www.speaker.gov/sites/speaker.house.gov/files/Sharp%20MX-4141_20210518_081238.pdf.

747. "Pelosi Statement on McCarthy Opposition to January 6th Commission," Speaker of the House Nancy Pelosi, (May 18, 2021), available at https://www.speaker.gov/newsroom/51821.

748. "U.S. House of Representatives House Session," C-SPAN, at 4:12:23-4:12:55, May 19, 2021, available at https://www.c-span.org/video/?511820-2/houses-passes-bill-create-january-6-commission-252-175.

749. "Roll Call 154 | Bill Number: H. R. 3233," Clerk of the U.S. House of Representatives, (May 19, 2021), available at https://clerk.house.gov/Votes/2021154?Page=1&Date=05%2F19%2F2021.

750. "Roll Call Vote 117th Congress - 1st Session," Question: On the Cloture Motion (Motion to Invoke Cloture Re: Motion to Proceed to H.R. 3233), H.R. 3233 - 117th Congress (2021): National Commission to Investigate the January 6 Attack on the United States Capitol Complex Act, H.R.3233, 117th Cong. (2021), available at https://www.senate.gov/legislative/LIS/roll_call_votes/vote1171/vote_117_1_00218.htm.

751. "House Speaker Nancy Pelosi Announces Select Committee on the January 6th Insurrection," C-SPAN, at 4:44-5:26, June 24, 2021, available at https://www.youtube.com/watch?v=guCcy9tUfn8.

752. Manu Raju and Clare Foran, "Officer Injured in Capitol Riot asks McCarthy to Denounce GOP January 6 Conspiracies," CNN, (June 25, 2021), available at https://www.cnn.com/2021/06/25/politics/michael-fanone-kevin-mccarthy-meeting/index.html.

753. Manu Raju and Clare Foran, "Officer Injured in Capitol Riot asks McCarthy to Denounce GOP January 6 Conspiracies," CNN, (June 25, 2021), available at https://www.cnn.com/2021/06/25/politics/michael-fanone-kevin-mccarthy-meeting/index.html.

754. "Roll Call 197 | Bill Number: H. Res. 503," Clerk of the U.S. House of Representatives, (June 30, 2021), available at https://clerk.house.gov/Votes/2021197.

755. "Pelosi Names Members to Select Committee to Investigate January 6th Attack on the U.S. Capitol," House Speaker Nancy Pelosi, (July 1, 2021), available at https://www.speaker.gov/newsroom/7121-0.

756. "McCarthy Names House Republicans to Serve on Select Committees," House Republican Leader Kevin McCarthy, (July 19, 2021), available at https://www.republicanleader.gov/mccarthy-names-house-republicans-to-serve-on-select-committees/.

757. "McCarthy Taps Banks to Lead Republicans on Jan 6 Committee," Congressman Jim Banks, (Jul. 19, 2021), available at https://banks.house.gov/news/documentsingle.aspx?DocumentID=1921.

758. "Pelosi Statement on Republican Recommendations to Serve on the Select Committee to Investigate the January 6th Attack on the U.S. Capitol," Speaker of the House Nancy Pelosi, (Jul. 21, 2021), available at https://www.speaker.gov/newsroom/72121-2.

759.   "Pelosi Statement on Republican Recommendations to Serve on the Select Committee to Investigate the January 6th Attack on the U.S. Capitol," Speaker of the House Nancy Pelosi, (Jul. 21, 2021), available at https://www.speaker.gov/newsroom/72121-2.

760.   "McCarthy Statement about Pelosi's Abuse of Power on January 6th Select Committee," Republican Leader Kevin McCarthy, (July 21, 2021), available at https://republicanleader.house.gov/mccarthy-statement-about-pelosis-abuse-of-power-on-january-6th-select-committee/; "McCarthy Pulls Republicans from Jan. 6 Select Committee after Pelosi Rejects Picks," *Axios*, (July 21, 2021), available at https://www.axios.com/2021/07/21/pelosi-jim-jordan-banks-select-committee.

761.   "Pelosi Announces Appointment of Congressman Adam Kinzinger to Select Committee to Investigate the January 6th Attack on the U.S. Capitol," House Speaker Nancy Pelosi, (July 25, 2021), available at https://www.speaker.gov/newsroom/72521; 167 Cong. Rec. H3885 (daily ed. July 26, 2021).

762.   *See, e.g., Eastman v. Thompson et al.*, No. 8:22-cv-99-DOC-DFM, 2022 U.S. Dist. LEXIS 25546, at *12-14 (C.D. Cal. Jan. 25, 2022); Memorandum Opinion, Republican National Committee v. Nancy Pelosi et al.. https://storage.courtlistener.com/recap/gov.uscourts.dcd.241102/gov.uscourts.dcd.241102.33.0.pdf.

1

THE BIG LIE

Late on election night 2020, President Donald J. Trump addressed the nation from the East Room of the White House. When Trump spoke, at 2:21 a.m. on November 4th, the President's re-election was very much in doubt. Fox News, a conservative media outlet, had correctly called Arizona for former Vice President Joseph R. Biden. Every Republican presidential candidate since 1996 had won Arizona. If the President lost the State, and in the days ahead it became clear that he had, then his campaign was in trouble. But as the votes continued to be counted, President Trump's apparent early lead in other key States—States he needed to win—steadily shrank. Soon, he would not be in the lead at all—he'd be losing.

So, the President of the United States did something he had planned to do long before election day: he lied.

"This is a fraud on the American public. This is an embarrassment to our country," President Trump said. "We were getting ready to win this election," the President continued. "Frankly, we did win this election. We did win this election." Trump claimed, without offering any evidence, that a "major fraud" was occurring "in our nation." [1]

Neither of President Trump's claims were true. He had no basis for claiming victory or that fraud was taking place. Millions of votes still had not been counted. The States were simply tabulating the ballots cast by the American people. Trump's own campaign advisors told him to wait—that it was far too early to declare victory.

As the evening progressed, President Trump called in his campaign team to discuss the results. Trump Campaign Manager William Stepien and other campaign experts advised him that the results of the election would not be known for some time, and that he could not truthfully declare victory. Stepien was of the view that, because ballots were going to be counted for days, "it was far too early to be making any proclamation [about having won the election]." Stepien told President Trump that his recommendation was to say, "votes are still being counted. It's...too early to call the race." [2]

Jason Miller, another senior Trump Campaign advisor, told the Select Committee that he argued in conversations with Stepien and others that night against declaring victory at the time as well, because "it was too early to say one way [or] the other" who had won. Miller recalled recommending that "we should not go and declare victory until we had a better sense of the numbers." [3]

According to testimony received by the Committee, the only advisor present who supported President Trump's inclination to declare victory was Rudy Giuliani, who, according to Miller, was "definitely intoxicated" that evening.[4]

President Trump's decision to declare victory falsely on election night and, unlawfully, to call for the vote counting to stop, was not a spontaneous decision. It was premeditated. The Committee has assembled a range of evidence of President Trump's preplanning for a false declaration of victory. This includes multiple written communications on October 31st and November 3, 2020, to the White House by Judicial Watch President Tom Fitton.[5] This evidence demonstrates that Fitton was in direct contact with President Trump and understood that he would falsely declare victory on election night and call for vote counting to stop. The evidence also includes an audio recording of President Trump's advisor Steve Bannon, who said this on October 31, 2020, to a group of his associates from China:

> And what Trump's going to do is just declare victory, right? He's gonna declare victory. But that doesn't mean he's the winner. He's just gonna say he's a winner....The Democrats, more of our people vote early that count. Their vote in mail. And so they're gonna have a natural disadvantage, and Trump's going to take advantage of it. That's our strategy. He's gonna declare himself a winner. So when you wake up Wednesday morning, it's going to be a firestorm....Also, if Trump, if Trump is losing, by ten or eleven o'clock at night, it's going to be even crazier. No, because he's gonna sit right there and say 'They stole it. I'm directing the Attorney General to shut down all ballot places in all 50 states. It's going to be, no, he's not going out easy. If Trump—if Biden's winning, Trump is going to do some crazy shit.[6]

Also in advance of the election, Roger Stone, another outside advisor to President Trump, made this statement:

I really do suspect it will still be up in the air. When that happens, the key thing to do is to claim victory. Possession is 9/10s of the law. No, we won. Fuck you, Sorry. Over. We won. You're wrong. Fuck you.[7]

In the days after the election, the President's own campaign team told him he had lost and there was no evidence of significant fraud. When his campaign staff wouldn't tell him what he wanted to hear, President Trump replaced them with what Attorney General William Barr described as a "clown car" of individuals willing to promote various conspiracy theories.[8]

But Donald Trump was no passive consumer of these lies. He actively propagated them. Time and again President Trump was informed that his election fraud claims were not true. He chose to spread them anyway. He did so even after they were legally tested and rejected in dozens of lawsuits. Not even the electoral college's certification of former Vice President Biden's victory on December 14, 2020, stopped the President from lying. Throughout, the Big Lie remained central to President Trump's efforts to block the peaceful transfer of power on January 6, 2021.

1.1   THE BIG LIE REFLECTED DELIBERATE EXPLOITATION OF THE "RED MIRAGE"

President Trump's "Big Lie" on election night was based on simple differences in how Americans vote. In 2020, it was well-known that Democrats were much more likely to vote via mail-in ballots than in person in 2020. On the other hand, Republicans generally preferred to vote in person on election day.[9] In key swing States with tight margins between the candidates, the election day votes would favor President Trump and disproportionately be counted first. Mail-in ballots, which would favor former Vice President Biden, would disproportionately be counted later. In some States it would take days to process the remaining mail-in ballots.

The timing of how votes are counted created the potential for what is known as a "Red Mirage"—or an illusion of a Republican (Red) victory in the early stages of vote counting. President Trump would appear to be in the lead on election night, but this was not the whole picture. Many mail-in votes for former Vice President Biden would not be counted on election day. Therefore, the actual winner would likely not be known on election night.

The "Red Mirage" phenomenon was widely known prior to the 2020 presidential election. Chris Stirewalt was the head of the Fox News elections desk that correctly called Arizona for Biden. Stirewalt and his team tried to warn viewers of the Red Mirage. He testified that over the past 40 or 50 years, "Americans have increasingly chosen to vote by mail or early or absentee," and that "Democrats prefer that method of voting more than

Photo by House Creative Services

Republicans do." [10] In nearly "every election," Stirewalt elaborated, "Republicans win Election Day and Democrats win the early vote, and then you wait and start counting." It "[h]appens every time." [11]

President Trump's campaign team made sure the President was briefed on the timing of vote tallying. Stepien, his campaign manager, told the Select Committee that President Trump was reminded on election day that large numbers of mail-in ballots would still remain to be counted over the coming days.[12] Stepien added that he personally reminded the President that while early returns may be favorable, the counting would continue: "I recounted back to 2016 when I had a very similar conversation with him on election day... I recounted back to that conversation with him in which I said, just like I said in 2016 was going to be a long night, I told him in 2020 that, you know, it was going to be a process again, as, you know, the early returns are going to be positive. Then we're going to, you know, be watching the returns of ballots as, you know, they rolled in thereafter." [13]

Ordinarily, the "Red Mirage" anomaly does not create problems in the election process because candidates wait for the votes to be tallied before declaring victory or conceding. As Stirewalt emphasized, prior to President Trump, "no candidate had ever tried to avail themselves of this quirk in the election counting system." [14]

President Trump, however, made a different choice. In an extraordinary breach of the American democratic process, he decided to exploit the potential for confusion about the staggered timing of vote counting to deceive the American public about the election results. He and his allies foreshadowed this decision in their statements in the months leading up to the November 2020 election.

1.2 TRUMP'S PRE-ELECTION PLANS TO DECLARE VICTORY

On Halloween, advisor Steve Bannon, who had served four years earlier as Donald Trump's 2016 campaign manager, laid out the election night plan. "What Trump's gonna do is just declare victory. Right? He's gonna declare victory. But that doesn't mean he's a winner," Bannon told a private audience. "He's just gonna *say* he's a winner." [15]

Bannon explained that the Democrats "[would] have a natural disadvantage" on election night, because more Democrats would vote by mail than Republicans and it would take time to count the mail-in ballots. This would give President Trump the illusion of a lead. "And Trump's going to take advantage of it," Bannon said. "That's our strategy. He's gonna declare himself a winner." [16]

In an interview on Fox News the morning of the election, Bannon insisted that President Trump needed to address the nation that night, to "provide the narrative engine for how we go forward." [17] During an episode of his podcast later that same day, Bannon clarified what he meant: President Trump is "going to claim victory. Right? He's going to claim victory." [18]

Tom Fitton drafted a victory statement for the President to read on election night.[19] On October 31st, he emailed the statement to President Trump's assistant, Molly Michael, and social media guru, Dan Scavino. Fitton wrote that election day, November 3rd, was the "deadline by which voters in states across the country *must* choose a president." Fitton argued that counting ballots that arrived after election day would be part of an effort by "partisans" to "overturn" the election results.[20]

Of course, that claim wasn't true—mail-in ballots are regularly processed after election day. Regardless, Fitton encouraged the President to pre-emptively declare victory. "We had an election today—and I won," Fitton wrote for President Trump.[21] Early in the evening on election day, Fitton emailed Michael again to say he had "[j]ust talked to him [President Trump] about the draft [statement]." [22] Later that evening, before President Trump made his election night remarks, Michael replied that she was "...redelivering to him [President Trump] now." [23]

October 31, 2020

He's just gonna say he's a winner!

Photo by Alex Wong/Getty Images

Roger Stone, President Trump's longtime political confidante, told several associates just prior to the election that Trump needed to declare victory—especially if the race wasn't called on election day. "Let's just hope we are celebrating" on election night, Stone said. "I really do suspect it will still be up in the air. When that happens, the key thing to do is claim victory." Stone elaborated with colorful language. "Possession is nine-tenths of the law. No, we won. Fuck you. Sorry. Over. We won. You're wrong. Fuck you." [24]

Indeed, published reports echoed these warnings about President Trump's election strategy. Two days before the election, Jonathan Swan of *Axios* reported that President Trump "has told confidants he'll declare victory on Tuesday night if it looks like he's 'ahead.'" [25] Swan added that "Trump's team is preparing to falsely claim that mail-in ballots counted after Nov. 3—a legitimate count expected to favor Democrats—are evidence of election fraud." [26] If the vote tally swung against Trump after election night in States such as Pennsylvania, then the Trump team would claim the Democrats had "stolen" the election.[27] Fox News election analysis Chris Stirewalt testified that he and his team "had gone to pains" to inform viewers that early votes would favor Republicans but the lead would be illusory "because the Trump campaign and the President had made it clear that they were going to try to exploit this anomaly." [28] Others warned that President Trump could exploit the Red Mirage as well.[29]

1.3 TRUMP'S PRE-ELECTION EFFORTS TO DELEGITIMIZE THE ELECTION PROCESS

President Trump also paved the way for his false election-night declaration of victory by blanketing voters with a blizzard of lies and statements delegitimizing mail-in voting in the middle of a deadly pandemic and consistently questioning the security of ballots. President Trump used the president's bully pulpit, including his heavily-trafficked Twitter feed, to tell one lie after another.

The Select Committee found dozens of instances in which President Trump claimed that mail-in voting would produce a "rigged" election. Trump repeatedly denounced mail-in voting on Twitter, during interviews, and even during the presidential debate. Here is a small sample of President Trump's attempts to delegitimize mail-in balloting.

On April 7, 2020, President Trump claimed:

Mail ballots are a very dangerous thing for this country, because they're cheaters. They go and collect them. They're fraudulent in many cases.... These mailed ballots come in. The mailed ballots are corrupt, in my opinion. And they collect them, and they get people to go in and sign them. And then they—they're forgeries in many cases. It's a horrible thing.[30]

The following day, April 8, President Trump tweeted:

Republicans should fight very hard when it comes to statewide mail-in voting. Democrats are clamoring for it. Tremendous potential for voter fraud, and for whatever reason, doesn't work out well for Republicans. @foxandfriends[31]

On May 24, President Trump tweeted:

The United States cannot have all Mail In Ballots. It will be the greatest Rigged Election in history. People grab them from mailboxes, print thousands of forgeries and "force" people to sign. Also, forge names. Some absentee OK, when necessary. Trying to use Covid for this Scam![32]

On September 17, President Trump falsely alleged that mail-in ballots were ripe for foreign interference:

@TrueTheVote There is a group of people (largely Radical Left Democrats) that want ELECTION MAYHEM. States must end this CRAZY mass

sending of Ballots. Also, a GIFT to foreign interference into our election!!! Stop it now, before it is too late.[33]

Before the election, as President Trump campaigned against mail-in voting, Bill Stepien sought an intercession. Along with House Minority Leader Kevin McCarthy, Stepien attempted to convince the President that mail-in voting was "not…a bad thing for his campaign."[34] They argued that President Trump's decision to discourage mail-in voting, while "urging [his] voters to vote only on election day leaves a lot to chance" and would fail to take advantage of a superior grassroots operation that could encourage Trump voters to return their ballots.[35] President Trump did not heed their warning. He continued to demonize mail-in voting. The Red Mirage was a key part of his "Big Lie."

Ominously, President Trump consistently refused to commit to accepting the outcome of the election. During an interview on Fox News in July, Chris Wallace asked: "Can you give a direct answer [if] you will accept the election?" President Trump responded: "I have to see. Look, you—I have to see. No, I'm not going to just say yes. I'm not going to say no, and I didn't last time either."[36]

On September 23, 2020, a reporter asked President Trump if he would commit to a "peaceful transferal of power after the election." The President refused, saying, "we're going to have to see what happens."[37] The President claimed, "the ballots are disaster," adding that if he could "get rid of the ballots…we'll have a very peaceful—there won't be a transfer, frankly; there'll be a continuation."[38] That is, according to President Trump, there would be a "continuation" of his presidency.

The following day, September 24, another reporter followed up by asking if the election would be legitimate only if President Trump won. The President again suggested there was something suspect about mail-in ballots, adding that he was "not sure" the election could be an honest one.[39]

1.4 PRESIDENT TRUMP'S LAUNCH OF THE BIG LIE

Consistent with the pre-election narrative planted by President Trump, within hours of polls closing, President Trump began pushing the claim that late-reported vote tallies were illegitimate.[40] Even though he had been reminded by his Campaign Manager that very day that a large number of mail-in ballots would not be counted for several hours or days,[41] President Trump claimed that Democrats were going to "find…ballots at four o'clock in the morning and add them to the list."[42] He also suggested that Democrats were continuing to vote after the polls had closed.[43]

Indeed, this is exactly what Steve Bannon described when he said President Trump would "take advantage" of the Democrats' "natural disadvantage" on election night.[44]

In the ensuing days and weeks, President Trump often referred to "dumps" of votes that were injected into the counting process.[45] His supporters latched onto these false claims.[46] There were no "dumps" of votes—just tallies of absentee ballots as they were reported by jurisdictions throughout the country in a fully transparent process.[47] These batches of ballots included votes for both Trump and Biden. The late-reported votes favored the former Vice President, just as President Trump's campaign advisors said they would, particularly in primarily Democratic cities.[48]

Attorney General Bill Barr recognized immediately that the "Red Mirage" was the basis for President Trump's erroneous claim of fraud. "[R]ight out of the box on election night, the President claimed that there was major fraud underway," Barr said. "I mean, this happened, as far as I could tell, before there was actually any potential of looking at evidence."[49] President Trump's claim "seemed to be based on the dynamic that, at the end of the evening, a lot of Democratic votes came in which changed the vote counts in certain states, and that seemed to be the basis for this broad claim that there was major fraud."[50]

President Trump knew about the Red Mirage. He chose to lie about it repeatedly—even after being directly informed that his claims were false. This was often the case in the post-election period. The President consciously disregarded facts that did not support his Big Lie.

1.5 POST-ELECTION: PRESIDENT TRUMP REPLACES HIS CAMPAIGN TEAM

President Trump's campaign leadership, including Bill Stepien (the campaign's manager) and Justin Clark (the campaign's deputy manager), supported President Trump, and were willing to pursue recounts and other standard post-election litigation, but they were not willing to promote baseless conspiracy theories.[51] Stepien and others characterized this group as "Team Normal."[52]

Less than two weeks after the election, President Trump pushed "Team Normal" aside because its members didn't tell him what he wanted to hear. In their place, Trump promoted Rudy Giuliani and his associates, men and women who spread baseless and extreme claims of election fraud. Giuliani, the former mayor of New York City, recruited several investigators and lawyers to assist him.[53] Giuliani's team included Jenna Ellis, Bernard Kerik, Boris Epshteyn, Katherine Friess, and Christina Bobb.[54] Ellis functioned as

Giuliani's deputy on the new Trump Campaign legal team.[55] Kerik, the former commissioner of the New York Police Department and a pardoned felon, served as Giuliani's chief investigator.[56] Other attorneys who collaborated with Giuliani's legal team included Sidney Powell, Cleta Mitchell, and John Eastman. As discussed elsewhere in this report, Eastman became a key player in President Trump's efforts to overturn the election.

1.6 PRESIDENT TRUMP'S CAMPAIGN TEAM TOLD HIM HE LOST THE ELECTION AND THERE WAS NO SIGNIFICANT FRAUD

President Trump's campaign team quickly realized that none of the significant fraud claims were real. Bill Stepien testified that, as of November 5th, the Trump Campaign had not found any proof of fraudulent activity. There were "allegations and reports," but "nothing hard [and] fast" that drew the results of the election into question.[57]

The Trump Campaign continued to investigate claims of fraud into the second week after the election. According to Stepien, as people shared "wild allegations" with the President, the campaign team was forced to review the facts and then serve as a "truth telling squad" to the President regarding why the claims "didn't prove to be true." [58] For example, Stepien recalled someone alleging that thousands of illegal votes had been cast in Arizona. That wasn't true. The votes had been submitted by overseas voters (such as military deployed or stationed abroad) who were obviously eligible to participate in the election.[59]

Alex Cannon was a lawyer for the Trump Campaign and previously worked for the Trump Organization. After the election, Cannon was tasked with looking into allegations of voter fraud in the 2020 election—including the claim that thousands of ineligible votes had been cast in Arizona.[60] Cannon recalled that Vice President Pence asked him what he was finding. "And I said that I didn't believe we were finding it, or I was not personally finding anything sufficient to alter the results of the election," Cannon responded. Vice President Pence thanked him.[61]

Cannon reported his assessment to Mark Meadows, the White House Chief of Staff, as well. In mid to late-November 2020, Meadows asked Cannon what his investigation had turned up. "And I remember sharing with him that we weren't finding anything that would be sufficient to change the results in any of the key states," Cannon told Meadows. "So there is no there, there?" Meadows replied.[62]

Jason Miller, a senior advisor to the Trump Campaign, pushed claims of election fraud in public. In private, however, Miller says that he told President Trump a different story, informing him numerous times that there was not enough election fraud to have changed the election:

> Miller: My understanding is that I think there are still very valid questions and concerns with the rules that were changed under the guise of COVID, but, specific to election day fraud and irregularities, there were not enough to overturn the election.
>
> Committee Staff: And did you give your opinion on that to the President?
>
> Miller: Yes.
>
> Committee Staff: What was his reaction when you told him that?
>
> Miller: "You haven't seen or heard"—I'm paraphrasing, but—"you haven't seen or heard all the different concerns and questions that have been raised."
>
> Committee Staff: How many times did you have this conversation with the President?
>
> Miller: Several. I couldn't put a specific number on it, though.
>
> Committee Staff: But more than one?
>
> Miller: Correct.[63]

Matthew Morgan, the Trump Campaign's top lawyer, came to a similar conclusion. Nearly two months after the election, on January 2nd, Morgan met with the Vice President's staff. According to Morgan, the consensus in the room was that even if all the claims of fraud and irregularities were "aggregated and read most favorably to the campaign...it was not sufficient to be outcome determinative."[64]

As far as the Trump Campaign's professional leadership was concerned, there was no evidence that the election had been "stolen" from President Trump. To the contrary, they had seen ample evidence that President Trump simply lost—and told the President so.

On November 6th, Jared Kushner arranged for the senior campaign staff to brief President Trump in the Oval Office on the state of the race.[65] Since election day, Matt Oczkowski, the Campaign's leading data expert, had tracked voting returns in the swing States to analyze the campaign's odds of success.[66] Miller texted such updates on data from key States to Meadows.[67] The Trump Campaign's data did not add up to victory. Oczkowski "delivered to the President in pretty blunt terms that he was going to lose"

Photo by Alex Wong/Getty Images

the election.[68] There were not enough outstanding votes in the battle-ground States for President Trump to overcome Biden's lead. President Trump disagreed and insisted that he would still prevail through legal challenges.[69]

But the data did not lie.

On November 7th, the *Associated Press* called Pennsylvania and the overall presidential election for former Vice President Biden.[70] At that point, a small team of the President's campaign advisors including Stepien met with the President and told him that his path to victory was virtually non-existent.[71] The campaign team conveyed to the President that his chance of success was only "5, maybe 10 percent," which Stepien explained to the Committee was a "very, very, very bleak" assessment.[72]

In retrospect, the campaign's estimate of a 5 to 10 percent chance of winning, as of November 7th, was far *too optimistic.* In one of the most favorable possible scenarios, for example, President Trump and his team would need to win recounts in Arizona and Georgia, while also prevailing in litigation challenging absentee or vote by mail ballots in Wisconsin, or possibly Michigan or Pennsylvania.[73] But the election wasn't even close enough to trigger automatic recounts in Arizona or Georgia.

The narrowest margin of total votes between the two candidates was in
Arizona, where former Vice President Biden won by more than 10,000 votes.
This may seem like a small number of votes, but it was more than enough
to avoid an automatic recount. As Benjamin Ginsberg, a longtime Republican elections lawyer, explained to the Select Committee, "the 2020 election
was not close." [74] Previous campaigns had successfully challenged vote dif-
ferentials in the hundreds—not thousands—of votes. [75] Ginsberg explained,
"you just don't make up those sorts of numbers in recounts." [76] Georgia
performed a hand recount of all the ballots anyway, confirming within
weeks of the election that Biden had won the State. [77] Also, by January 6th,
Arizona and New Mexico had conducted statutory post-election audits of
voting machines or randomly-selected, representative samples of ballots at
the State- or county-level that affirmed the accuracy of their election
results. [78]

Chris Stirewalt, who led the elections desk at Fox News at the time,
concurred with Ginsberg's analysis. Asked what President Trump's odds of
victory were as of November 7th, Stirewalt replied: "None." [79]

Meanwhile, the Trump Campaign continued to crunch the numbers. On
the morning of November 12th, Oczkowski circulated among top campaign
advisors a presentation describing what happened in each of the battleground States the campaign was monitoring. [80] This analysis by the data
team examined the turnout and margins on a county-by-county basis in a
dozen States while also analyzing demographic changes that impacted the
results. [81] Among the States were Arizona, Georgia, Michigan, Pennsylvania,
Nevada, and Wisconsin. [82] Oczkowski's team determined that President
Trump lost each of those six States because Biden had performed better
than President Trump in certain areas like population centers or suburbs. [83]
Yet, in the weeks that followed, President Trump and his new legal team—
the "clown car"—went to great lengths to challenge the results of the election in these six states, spreading multiple conspiracy theories.

The voting data told a clear story: President Trump lost. But, regardless
of the facts, the President had no intention of conceding defeat.

On election night, President Trump and Rudy Giuliani agreed that the
President should just declare victory—even though he had no basis for
doing so. Giuliani also told the Select Committee that President Trump
asked him on November 4th to take over his campaign's legal operation. [84]
Giuliani thought the only way that it would work would be for the President
to call the existing campaign team to announce Giuliani's takeover because,
in Giuliani's words, "they are going to be extraordinarily resentful, because
they don't like me already, and I don't trust them." [85] He said that the
President agreed. [86]

Although Giuliani wouldn't assume leadership of the Campaign's legal operations until mid-November, the former New York City mayor quickly began to butt heads with "Team Normal."

On November 6th, Giuliani and his team met with the Trump Campaign's leadership at its headquarters in Arlington, Virginia.[87]

"Team Normal" was not impressed. Stepien told the Select Committee the campaign team was concerned that Giuliani would be a distraction to them and to President Trump.[88] When Giuliani suggested traveling to Pennsylvania to assist in the campaign's efforts, the campaign team "didn't dissuade him from doing so."[89] After just 10 to 15 minutes in the conference room, Stepien and other staffers left the meeting.[90]

That same day, President Trump discussed the Campaign's legal strategy in the Oval Office with Giuliani, Clark, and Matt Morgan, the Trump Campaign's General Counsel.[91] Prior to the election, Morgan was responsible for the Campaign's litigation strategy.[92] Morgan and his team filed lawsuits challenging the changes States made to voting practices during the coronavirus pandemic.[93] Morgan also studied previous elections to determine the types of cases that were likely to succeed.[94] Clark described how the Campaign's original legal strategy was based on his general theory for election cases: "to look at what do you think, what do you know, and what can you prove" and then determine which cases to file from there.[95]

Giuliani had other ideas and advocated to President Trump that he be put in charge of the Campaign's legal operation so that he could pursue his preferred strategy.[96] "Mr. Giuliani didn't seem bound by those cases or by those precedents. He felt he could press forward on anything that he thought was wrong with the election and bring a strategy around that," Morgan explained.[97] "Rudy was just chasing ghosts," Clark said.[98] Morgan and Clark excused themselves from the meeting because it "was going nowhere."[99]

The next day, November 7th, Giuliani held a press conference at Four Seasons Total Landscaping in Philadelphia, Pennsylvania. He immediately began making outlandish claims, arguing that the Democrats had conspired to steal the election. "As you know from the very beginning, mail-in ballots were a source of some degree of skepticism, if not a lot of skepticism, as being innately prone to fraud," Giuliani said. "Those mail-in ballots could have been written the day before by the Democratic Party hacks that were all over the Convention Center."[100] Giuliani offered no evidence to support his shocking and baseless allegation. Echoes of President Trump's relentless campaign against mail-in balloting, and his decision to exploit the Red Mirage, were easy to hear.

Photo by Chris McGrath/Getty Images

On November 10th, Giuliani and Kerik met with President Trump in the Oval Office to discuss their investigation into voter fraud. White House Counsel Pat Cipollone and White House Senior Advisor Eric Herschmann were also in attendance. After Giuliani's presentation, President Trump asked Cipollone whether he had spoken to Attorney General Barr about the allegations of fraud.[101] One day before, Barr had issued a memorandum outlining a shift in DOJ policy that allowed Federal prosecutors to investigate claims of voting irregularities without waiting for the results to be certified.[102] President Trump's question was an early indication that he was going to pressure the DOJ to endorse his phony fraud claims.

Days later, Giuliani and Justin Clark engaged in a screaming match during a meeting in the Oval Office.[103] Giuliani was urging President Trump to file a lawsuit in Georgia, but Clark pointed out that a hand recount was already being conducted and argued it was better to wait.[104] Giuliani told President Trump that Clark was lying to him.[105] A formal changing of the guard would follow.

On November 14th, President Trump announced on Twitter that Giuliani was now the head of his campaign's legal team.[106] "Team Normal" saw drastic changes to their roles on the newly-structured campaign team—some self-imposed—and many outside law firms that had signed up to support the campaign's legal efforts disengaged completely.[107]

"I didn't think what was happening was necessarily honest or professional at that point in time," Stepien explained. "This wasn't a fight that I was comfortable with," he added.[108]

On the day the leadership change was announced, Giuliani participated in a "surrogate" briefing to coordinate messaging by Trump loyalists during their media appearances.[109] Giuliani announced that the messaging strategy should be "to go hard on Dominion/Smartmatic, bringing up Chavez and Maduro."[110] Giuliani claimed that additional lawsuits would soon be filed "to invalidate upwards of 1M ballots."[111]

Consistent with the messaging advanced by the new campaign team, President Trump in mid-November remained dug-in, still refusing to concede defeat. President Trump continued to insist that he was cheated out of victory, endorsing one wild conspiracy theory after another to deny the simple fact that he lost.

1.7   PRESIDENT TRUMP HAD HIS DAY IN COURT

"We've proven" the election was stolen, but "no judge, including the Supreme Court of the United States, has had the courage to allow it to be heard."[112] That was how President Trump described efforts to overturn the election in court one day before the electoral college met on December 14, 2020. That was false.

Judges across the nation *did* evaluate President Trump's claims that the election was stolen. As longtime Republican election attorney Benjamin Ginsberg testified before the Select Committee, the President's camp "did have their day in court," it's just that "in no instance did a court find that the charges of fraud were real."[113] In total, the Trump Campaign and allies of President Trump filed 62 separate lawsuits between November 4, 2020, and January 6, 2021, calling into question or seeking to overturn the election results.[114] Out of 62 cases, only one case resulted in a victory for the President Trump or his allies, which affected relatively few votes, did not vindicate any underlying claims of fraud, and would not have changed the outcome in Pennsylvania.[115] Thirty of the cases were dismissed by a judge *after* a hearing on the merits.[116]

In every State in which claims were brought, one or more judges specifically explained as part of their dismissal orders that they had evaluated the plaintiffs' allegations or supposed proof of widespread election fraud or other irregularities, and found the claims to be entirely unconvincing. In

62 CASES

9 states and D.C. are the sites of case filings between November 4, 2020 and January 6, 2021

61 losses, 1 win

22 judges appointed by Republican presidents oversaw cases

10 Trump appointed judges

3 All three Trump appointed Supreme Court justices rejected the fraud claims

Arizona, for example, the plaintiffs in *Bowyer v. Ducey* alleged that the election was tainted by the introduction of "hundreds of thousands of illegal, ineligible, duplicate or purely fictitious ballots."[117] A Federal judge dismissed their suit, finding it "void of plausible allegations" and "sorely wanting of relevant or reliable evidence."[118] Likewise, in *Ward v. Jackson*, an Arizona State-court judge dismissed a lawsuit by the State GOP chair following a two-day trial, finding no evidence of misconduct, fraud, or illegal votes.[119] This ruling was unanimously upheld by the State supreme court, where all seven justices were appointed by GOP governors.[120]

In Georgia, a State court dismissed *Boland v. Raffensperger*, which alleged that tens of thousands of illegal ballots were cast by out-of-State voters or with invalid signature matches.[121] The judge found that "the Complaint's factual allegations…rest on speculation rather than duly pled facts" and "do not support…a conclusion that sufficient illegal votes were cast to change or place in doubt the result of the election."[122] The judge who issued this decision had been appointed by a Republican governor, as had seven of the eight justices of the State supreme court who upheld her ruling.[123] Likewise, a Federal judge denied relief to the plaintiff in *Wood v. Raffensperger*, which alleged that new procedures for checking absentee ballot signatures spoiled the result by making it harder to reject illegal ballots, finding "no basis in fact or law to grant him the relief he seeks."[124]

The judge wrote that "[t]his argument is belied by the record" because absentee ballots were actually rejected for signature issues at the same rate as in 2018.[125]

In Michigan, a Federal judge found in *King v. Whitmer* that the plaintiffs' claims of "massive election fraud" were based on "nothing but speculation and conjecture that votes for President Trump were destroyed, discarded or switched to votes for Vice President Biden...."[126] Similarly, a State-court judge rejected plaintiffs' claims in two cases brought against Detroit and the surrounding county that accused them of systematic fraud in how absentee ballots were counted; the judge found that one group of plaintiffs "...offered no evidence to support their assertions,"[127] and that the other group's "interpretation of events is incorrect" and "decidedly contra-dicted" by "highly-respected" election experts.[128]

In Nevada, a State-court judge rejected a litany of claims of systematic election fraud in *Law v. Whitmer*, ruling that plaintiffs "did not prove under any standard of proof that illegal votes were cast and counted, or legal votes were not counted at all, due to voter fraud" or "for any other improper or illegal reason."[129] The ruling was unanimously upheld by the Nevada Supreme Court.[130]

In Pennsylvania, a Federal judge dismissed *Donald Trump for President v. Boockvar*, finding that the Trump Campaign had presented nothing but "strained legal arguments without merit and speculative accusations unpled in the operative complaint and unsupported by evidence."[131] The dismissal was upheld by the United States Court of Appeals for the Third Circuit, which held: "[C]alling an election unfair does not make it so. Charges require specific allegations and then proof. We have neither here."[132] That opinion was authored by another Trump appointee.[133]

Lastly, in Wisconsin, another judge dismissed a lawsuit accusing the Wisconsin Elections Commission of "constitutional violations" that "likely tainted more than 50,000 ballots."[134] The judge ruled: "This Court has allowed plaintiff the chance to make his case and he has lost on the mer-its," failing to show that the outcome was affected by Commission rules about drop boxes, ballot addresses, or individuals who claimed "indefinitely confined" status to vote from home.[135] The ruling was upheld by a three-judge panel of the United States Court of Appeals for the Seventh Circuit, all of whom were Republican appointees, including one appointed by President Trump himself.[136]

In all, the judges who heard these post-election cases included 22 Fed-eral judges appointed by Republican presidents.[137]

President Trump and his lawyers were well-aware that courts were consistently rejecting his claims. During a December 18th meeting in the

Oval Office with President Trump, Sidney Powell and others, White House Senior Advisor Eric Herschmann pointed out that President Trump's lawyers had their opportunity to prove their case in court, and failed. Powell fired back that "the judges are corrupt." Herschmann responded: "Every one? Every single case that you've done in the country you guys lost, every one of them is corrupt, even the ones we appointed?"[138]

President Trump was faced with another choice after having his day in court. He could accept that there was no real evidence of voter fraud, or he could continue to amplify conspiracy theories and lies. He chose the latter.

1.8 PRESIDENT TRUMP REPEATEDLY PROMOTED CONSPIRACY THEORIES

Instead of accepting his defeat, President Trump attempted to justify his Big Lie with a series of increasingly preposterous claims. The President was not simply led astray by those around him. The opposite was true. He actively promoted conspiracy theories and false election fraud claims even after being informed they were baseless. Millions of President Trump's supporters believed the election was stolen from him. Many of them still do, but President Trump knew the truth and chose to lie about it.

The power of the President's bully pulpit should not be underestimated, especially in the digital age.[139] President Trump's relentless lying sowed seeds of distrust in America's election system. Researchers who studied this election-denial phenomenon have noted: "President Trump didn't just prime his audience to be receptive to false narratives of election fraud—he inspired them to produce those narratives and then echoed those false claims back to them."[140] Social media played a prominent role in amplifying erroneous claims of election fraud. Shortly after election day, the "Stop the Steal" campaign, discussed more fully in Chapter 6, went viral. "Stop the Steal" influencers echoed President Trump's premature declaration of victory, asserting that he won the election, the Democrats stole it from him, and it was the responsibility of American "patriots" to combat this supposed injustice.[141]

This resulted in what Attorney General Barr has described as an "avalanche" of false claims, as President Trump's supporters attempted to justify his "Big Lie."[142] The post-election allegations of fraud or other malfeasance were "completely bogus," "silly" and "usually based on complete misinformation," Barr explained.[143] Nonetheless, many of President Trump's supporters wanted to believe them. The stolen election narrative has proven to be remarkably durable precisely because it is a matter of belief—not evidence, or reason. Each time a claim was debunked, more

Photo by Michael Ciaglo/Getty Images

claims emerged in its place. Barr later complained that this dynamic forced him and others to play "whack-a-mole." [144]

The United States Department of Justice, under Barr's leadership and then Acting Attorney General Jeffrey Rosen, was forced to knock down one lie after another. As discussed in Chapter 4, Barr took unprecedented steps to investigate the "avalanche" of lies. Claims of election fraud were referred to United States Attorney's offices and the FBI for investigation. Deputy Attorney General Richard Donoghue tracked dozens of investigations. None of them were found to have merit. [145] The top officials in President Trump's Justice Department personally told the President that the claims he was promoting were false. But that did not matter to the President. As Barr told the Select Committee, President Trump never showed any "indication of interest in what the actual facts were." [146]

For example, on December 27th, Rosen and Donoghue spent approximately two hours on the phone with President Trump. They debunked a litany of claims regarding the election, explaining that each had been investigated and found to be baseless. [147] According to Donoghue, President Trump "had this arsenal of allegations that he wanted to rely on." Donoghue thought it was necessary to explain to the President "based on actual investigations, actual witness interviews, actual reviews of documents, that these allegations simply had no merit." Donoghue wanted "to cut through the noise" and be "very blunt" with the President, making it clear "these allegations were simply not true."[148]

During their December 27th conversation with President Trump, Rosen and Donoghue rebutted false claims regarding: suitcases of ballots in Georgia, Dominion's voting machines in Antrim County, a truckload of ballots in Pennsylvania, ballots being scanned multiple times, people voting more than once, dead people voting, Native Americans being paid to vote, and more votes than voters in particular jurisdictions.[149] As the officials debunked each claim, President Trump "would just roll on to another one."[150] Donoghue told President Trump that Federal law enforcement officials had conducted dozens of investigations and hundreds of interviews, and they had concluded that the major allegations were not supported by the evidence developed.[151] Donoghue and Rosen told President Trump "flat out" that "much of the information he [was] getting [was] false and/or just not supported by the evidence."[152] President Trump responded: "You guys may not be following the internet the way I do."[153]

The Department of Justice was not alone in trying to contain the President's conspiracy-mongering. President Trump's lies were often debunked in real-time by State authorities, judges, experts, journalists, Federal officials, and even members of his own legal team. As discussed above, the President's campaign team found that there was no significant fraud in the election. So, the President pushed them aside. The courts rejected nearly every claim brought by the President's legal team. Even though courts rejected the claims as speculative, unsupported and meritless, President Trump, Rudy Giuliani, and others continued to assert them as truth to Trump's followers in speeches, tweets, and podcasts.[154]

The burden of refuting the false claims made by President Trump and his surrogates often fell on State and local officials. For example, in Michigan, the Secretary of State's office posted thorough and prompt responses to the claims of election fraud on a "Fact Check" page on its website.[155] In Georgia, the Secretary of State's office issued news releases and held frequent press conferences in the weeks following the election to respond to claims of fraud.[156] County clerks in the contested States also spoke out publicly to refute allegations. Even as the President undermined the public's confidence in how votes are cast and counted, these clerks assured voters that their elections were secure and they could have confidence in the results.[157] Outside experts also publicly denounced and dismantled the claims being raised and amplified by President Trump. This was done in the context of litigation, congressional hearings, and press releases.[158] President Trump simply ignored these authoritative sources and continued to promote false claims that had been soundly discredited.

Below, the Select Committee presents two case studies demonstrating how President Trump and his surrogates lied in the face of overwhelming evidence. The first case study deals with Dominion Voting Systems. President Trump repeatedly claimed that Dominion's software "switched votes" and "rigged" the election well after the leaders of campaign and Justice Department officials told him that these claims were baseless. The President's smear of Dominion was central to his "Big Lie."

The second case study examines video footage recorded in Fulton County on election night. President Trump and his representatives concocted a fictional narrative based on a deceptively edited version of the footage. After these two case studies, the Select Committee examines a variety of other claims the President repeatedly made. Once again, these claims had no basis in truth.

DOMINION VOTING SYSTEMS

Between election day and January 6th, President Trump repeatedly spread conspiracy theories about Dominion voting machines. The President tweeted or retweeted false claims about Dominion more than 30 times.[159] He also repeatedly lied about the company's software during his post-election speeches and interviews.[160] President Trump's own campaign staff, administration officials, and State officials, all told him the claims had no merit. Hand recounts confirmed the fidelity of the machines. But none of this overwhelming evidence mattered. President Trump demonstrated a conscious disregard for the facts and continued to maliciously smear Dominion.

President Trump's allies began spreading false claims regarding Dominion within days of the election. On November 8th, the day after networks called the election for Joe Biden, Sidney Powell claimed on Fox News that Dominion machines "were flipping votes in the computer system or adding votes that did not exist."[161] On November 12th, Rudy Giuliani appeared on Fox News to claim that Dominion was connected to Venezuelan dictator Hugo Chavez and its software was created "in order to fix elections."[162] The same day, President Trump retweeted a "REPORT" claiming that Dominion had "DELETED 2.7 MILLION TRUMP VOTES NATIONWIDE" and switched hundreds of thousands of votes in key swing states.[163]

By that time, the Trump Campaign team had looked into allegations regarding Dominion and its software and concluded that the claims were false. An internal campaign memo, dated November 12, said that Dominion's software "did not lead to improper vote counts" and cited reports concluding that, among other things, Dominion machines "Did Not Affect The Final Vote Count." [164] The memo also addressed various claims of foreign influence regarding Dominion.[165] Jason Miller told the Select Committee that by November 12th he had told President Trump the results of the analysis of the Dominion claims by the campaign's internal research team, specifically telling him "that the international allegations for Dominion were not valid." [166] Emails and text messages show that this same analysis was shared with Mark Meadows, President Trump's chief of staff.[167] White House Press Secretary Kayleigh McEnany told the Select Committee that she found herself "waving [President Trump] off of the Dominion theory," encouraging him to use more "fact-driven" arguments.[168] But it was to no avail.

Even though members of the Trump Campaign team reported that the result of the election was not compromised by any problems with Dominion machines, the President continued to assail Dominion on Twitter in the days that followed, for example retweeting a false claim that Dominion's machines were "engineered by China, Venezuela, [and] Cuba" and claiming that Dominion had "[r]igged" the election.[169]

Officials in the Trump administration also worked to debunk the false rumors about vote manipulation. The United States Department of Homeland Security's Cybersecurity & Infrastructure Security Agency (CISA) released a joint statement of election security officials on November 12, reassuring voters that the election was "the most secure in American history." CISA emphasized: "There is no evidence that any voting system deleted or lost votes, changed votes, or was in any way compromised." [170]

This was another decision point for the President. He could choose to endorse the findings of his administration's own cyber security experts, or he could continue to promote baseless fictions about Dominion. President Trump chose the lies. The President and his supporters never did produce any evidence showing that Dominion's machines affected the results of the election. But President Trump was undeterred by the facts. Indeed, the President and his supporters seized upon a simple human error in a small Michigan county as their initial pretense for these allegations as well as to keep the Dominion conspiracy theory alive.

During the early-morning hours of November 4th, Sheryl Guy, a clerk in Antrim County, Michigan, reported the *unofficial* results of the vote count.[171] Guy's online report was odd. It showed that former Vice President Biden had somehow won Antrim, a county that is majority-Republican and President Trump was expected to easily win. Trump's supporters quickly pointed to Biden's improbable win as evidence that Dominion had tampered with the votes.[172] That wasn't true. Guy had made a mistake in updating the election counting software after a late addition of a local candidate to the ballot in some of the county's precincts, which caused her unofficial counts to be off when she tallied the votes reported by the various precincts.[173] Guy, a Republican, was informed of the odd result and began to investigate immediately. The result was corrected, and President Trump won Antrim just as was expected.[174]

Within days, local and State officials in Michigan explained to the public what had happened. On November 7th, the Michigan Secretary of State's office issued a detailed description of Guy's error and assured the public that the *official* results were not impacted.[175] The Michigan Senate's Committee on Oversight, led by Republican Senator Ed McBroom, conducted its own comprehensive review of the claims related to Antrim County and confirmed that the initial reporting error was entirely attributable to an honest mistake by the county clerk.[176]

The mix-up in Antrim County was quickly corrected. A human erred—not the voting machines. But President Trump used it as a pretext to continue lying about Dominion.

On November 12th, the same day CISA released its statement on election security, President Trump asked Tim Walberg, a Republican Congressman from Michigan, to "check with key leadership in Michigan's Legislature as to how supportive they could be in regards to pushing back on election irregularities and potential fraud."[177] That night, President Trump asked his Acting Secretary of Homeland Security, Chad Wolf, to look into allegations of election irregularities in Michigan.[178] The next day, President Trump's assistant sent Wolf a letter from Michigan State legislators raising claims about the election, including an incorrect claim that flawed Dominion software had caused votes to be counted for the wrong candidate.[179]

Administration officials quickly knocked down the Dominion claim. Wolf forwarded the allegations to the leadership of CISA, including CISA Director Christopher Krebs.[180] Krebs provided Wolf with a press release from the Michigan Secretary of State that debunked the false claim about Antrim County and Dominion's software in detail.[181] Wolf shared an update about the information he received from Krebs with White House Chief of Staff Mark Meadows.[182]

On November 17th, Krebs tweeted out a statement issued by the nation's leading election scientists that dismissed claims that election systems had been manipulated as either "unsubstantiated" or "technically incoherent."[183] President Trump fired Krebs that same day.[184] President Trump claimed the statement released by Krebs was "highly inaccurate, in that there were massive improprieties and fraud."[185] The President had no evidence for his claim.

On November 19th, Rudy Giuliani, Sidney Powell, and Jenna Ellis held a press conference at the Republican National Committee (RNC) headquarters in Washington, DC. Powell asserted that there was "massive influence of communist money through Venezuela, Cuba, and likely China in the inter-ference with our elections here in the United States."[186] She pointed a fin-ger at Dominion, claiming its software was "created in Venezuela at the direction of Hugo Chavez to make sure he never lost an election," and Giu-liani echoed her claims.[187]

Hope Hicks told the Select Committee how that press conference was received in the White House. The day after the press conference, President Trump spoke by phone with Sidney Powell from the Oval Office. During the call, Powell repeated the same claims of foreign interference in the election she had made at the press conference. While she was speaking, the Presi-dent muted his speakerphone and laughed at Powell, telling the others in the room, "This does sound crazy, doesn't it?"[188]

A few days later, the Trump Campaign issued a statement claiming Powell was not part of the Trump Campaign's legal team.[189] But Powell's outlandish claims were no different from those President Trump was mak-ing himself. On November 19th, the same day as Powell's appearance at the RNC, President Trump tweeted and retweeted a link to a segment on One America News Network (OAN) that was captioned, "Dominion-izing the Vote."[190] The segment claimed that Dominion had switched votes from Trump to Biden. OAN featured a supposed cyber expert, Ron Watkins, a key figure in the QAnon conspiracy movement.[191] On his own Twitter account, Watkins celebrated and thanked his supporters just minutes after President Trump tweeted the clip, and President Trump went on to share the clip again several times in the days that followed.[192]

Officials inside the Trump administration continued to debunk the Dominion conspiracy theory, including during in-person meetings with President Trump. Attorney General Bill Barr met with President Trump face-to-face on three occasions after the election.[193] Barr told the Select Committee, "every time I was with the President, I raised the machines as sort of Exhibit A of how irresponsible this was."[194] During the first of these meetings, on November 23rd, Barr explained to the President that the con-spiracy theory about Dominion's voting machines had "zero basis," and was "one of the most disturbing allegations." Barr stressed that this was "crazy stuff" and was poisoning Americans' confidence in the voting sys-tem for no reason. This "complete nonsense" was "doing [a] great, great disservice to the country," Barr said.[195]

President Trump ignored Barr's grave concerns. On November 29th, President Trump was interviewed by Fox News' Maria Bartiromo. It was the

President's first interview since he lost his bid for reelection. He claimed the election was "rigged" and rife with "theft" and "a total fraud." [196] He repeated various conspiracy theories, leading with the claim that Dominion's voting machines had "glitches," which he alleged moved "thousands of votes from my account to Biden's account." [197] He claimed that there had been "big, massive dumps" of votes—a reference to the Red Mirage.[198] He rambled off various other, spurious allegations, including that dead people voted in significant numbers.[199] None of it was true.

On December 1st, Attorney General Barr met again with President Trump and told him that "the stuff his people were shoveling out to the public was bullshit." [200] Attorney General Barr specifically told President Trump that the claims about Dominion voting machines were "idiotic claims." [201] President Trump was still not dissuaded from continuing the lie. The day after his meeting with the Attorney General, President Trump released a video in which he repeated several claims of election fraud, including a claim that "votes had been wrongly switched from Trump to Biden" using Dominion voting machines.[202]

By early-December, courts had assessed and rejected claims that Dominion machines were manipulated to affect the outcome of the 2020 election. In Michigan, a Federal judge found that claims, including those related to fraud due to the use of Dominion voting machines, were based on "nothing but speculation and conjecture that votes were destroyed, discarded or switched...." [203] In Arizona, a Federal judge dismissed claims that Dominion machines had deleted, switched, or changed votes.[204] But President Trump and his supporters refused to accept denunciations of the fabricated Dominion claims.

Through December, President Trump and his legal team tried to echo the Dominion conspiracy theory by claiming to have found evidence that votes were switched in Antrim County. The clerk's unintentional error was fixed weeks earlier and there was no evidence showing that Dominion had altered the vote tally in Antrim, or anywhere else.[205] But President Trump's legal team used a case challenging a local marijuana ordinance that had passed by one vote to gain access to Dominion's voting machines. An Antrim County judge issued an order granting the plaintiff's experts access to the county's computer, Dominion voting machines, thumb drives and memory cards.[206] Although the purpose of the order was to allow the plaintiff to seek evidence related to his ordinance challenge, it soon became clear that President Trump's legal team was behind the effort.[207]

An organization named Allied Security Operations Group ("ASOG"), led by Russell Ramsland, conducted an analysis of Antrim County's voting machines and related systems. On December 13th, ASOG released a report on its findings. The inspection yielded no evidence of vote manipulation. Still, the report included an unsubstantiated assertion that the Dominion voting machines used in Antrim County and throughout Michigan were "purposefully designed with inherent error to create systemic fraud and influence election results" and that a malicious algorithm was used to manipulate the results of the 2020 election.[208] Documents obtained by the Select Committee show that President Trump and Vice President Mike Pence were briefed on ASOG's findings by Giuliani's team.[209] On December 14th, President Trump widely disseminated the ASOG report and accompanying talking points prepared by Giuliani's team.[210] He also trumpeted the report on Twitter, writing on December 14th: "WOW. This report shows massive fraud. Election changing result!"[211]

During a meeting with Attorney General Bill Barr that day, President Trump claimed the ASOG report was "absolute proof that the Dominion machines were rigged" and meant he was "going to have a second term."[212] Barr told the Select Committee that he believed the ASOG report was "very amateurish," its authors lacked "any real qualifications," and it failed to provide any supporting information for its sweeping conclusions about Dominion.[213] Barr told President Trump he would look into the report, but that the DOJ already had a good idea of what happened in Antrim County and it was human error, not a problem with the machines.[214] In any event, Barr promised President Trump they would have a definitive answer within a couple of days because a hand recount was being conducted.[215]

In the ensuing days, as Barr predicted, the ASOG report was swiftly and soundly criticized by experts within and outside the Trump Administration, including the Department of Justice and the Department of Homeland Security.[216] The initial analysis of election security experts at the Department of Homeland Security was that the ASOG report was "false and misleading" and "demonstrates a callous misunderstanding of the actual current voting certification process."[217] Subsequent analyses of the ASOG report and the underlying data from Antrim County were even more critical.[218] These thorough assessments of the Antrim County data and the ASOG report demonstrate that virtually every one of the claims that President Trump and his surrogates made about the report was false.[219] ASOG's inspection did not reveal any malicious software or algorithms or any other evidence that the voting machines had been compromised.[220]

Most importantly, as Attorney General Barr had promised President Trump, within days of the release of the ASOG report, a full hand recount of every ballot cast in Antrim County confirmed the results reported by the Dominion machines and refuted ASOG's assertion that an algorithm has manipulated the vote count.[221] Giuliani's chief investigator, Bernie Kerik, acknowledged that his team was not able to find any proof that a Dominion voting machine improperly switched, deleted, or injected votes during the 2020 election.[222]

President Trump was not swayed by these basic facts. The President continued to promote the ASOG report, hounding DOJ to investigate the matter further. He returned to ASOG's claims during a December 27th call with Acting Attorney General Rosen and Acting Deputy Attorney General Donoghue, citing the report's claimed error rate of 68 percent in Antrim County. Donoghue pointed out to the President that the difference between the computer and hand count was only one vote and that he "cannot and should not be relying on" ASOG's fraudulent claim, because it was simply "not true."[223]

President Trump's fixation on Dominion's voting machines and the baseless theory that the machines had manipulated votes led to a concerted effort to gain access to voting machines in States where President Trump was claiming election fraud. On the evening of December 18th, Powell, Lt. Gen. Michael Flynn (ret.) and Patrick Byrne met with the President at the White House. Over several hours, they argued that President Trump had the authority, under a 2018 executive order, to seize voting machines. Several administration officials joined the meeting and forcefully rejected this extreme proposal.[224] Multiple lawyers in the White House, including Eric Herschmann, Derek Lyons, and White House Counsel Pat Cipollone "pushed back strongly" against the idea of seizing voting machines. Cipollone told the Select Committee it was a "horrible idea," which had "no legal basis,"[225] and he emphasized that he had "seen no evidence of massive fraud in the election."[226] White House advisor Eric Herschmann similarly told the Select Committee that he "never saw any evidence whatsoever" to sustain the allegations against Dominion.[227] National Security Adviser Robert O'Brien phoned into the December 18th meeting and was asked if he had seen "any evidence of election fraud in the voting machines or foreign interference in our voting machines." O'Brien responded that his team had "looked into that, and there's no evidence of it."[228]

Around the same time, President Trump, Mark Meadows, and Rudy Giuliani were repeatedly asking the leadership of DHS whether the agency had authority to seize voting machines, and they were repeatedly told that DHS has no such unilateral authority.[229] Giuliani and Powell were also engaged in efforts to access voting machines in multiple States with the assistance of sympathetic local election officials.[230] Those efforts turned up no evidence of any vote manipulation by any Dominion machine, but President Trump continued to press this bogus claim.

On January 2, 2021, President Trump had a lengthy phone call with Georgia Secretary of State Brad Raffensperger. The President repeatedly brought up Dominion's voting machines, alleging that they were at the heart of a conspiracy against him.[231] Raffensperger was incredulous. "I don't believe that you're really questioning the Dominion machines," Raffensperger said. "Because we did a hand re-tally, a 100 percent re-tally of all the ballots, and compared them to what the machines said and came up with virtually the same result. Then we did the recount, and we got virtually the same result."[232] In other words, the story in Georgia was the same as the story in Antrim County, Michigan: Officials performed a hand recount to put to rest any allegations that Dominion's machines had manipulated the vote. But once again, President Trump consciously disregarded these basic facts and persisted with his lies.

During a January 4, 2021, speech in Dalton, Georgia, President Trump chose to ignore Secretary Raffensperger's straightforward observations. The President rhetorically attacked Dominion once again, claiming that a "crime" had been "committed in this state" and it was "immeasurable."[233] The President called for an "immediate forensic audit of an appropriate sampling of Dominion's voting machines and related equipment."[234] His allegations were both false and nonsensical. Georgia had already performed a statewide hand recount of all ballots.

President Trump and his allies have never provided any evidence showing that Dominion's voting software altered votes in the 2020 presidential election. In fact, some of the most vocal proponents of the Dominion claims harbored their own misgivings about the claims they were making in public. For example, Rudy Giuliani repeatedly claimed in public that Dominion voting machines stole the election, and that foreign countries had interfered in the election, but the evidence uncovered by the Select Committee reveals that he did not believe either of those things to be true. Giuliani testified that he did not believe that voting machines stole the election.[235] He also acknowledged that he had seen no evidence that foreign countries had interfered in the election or manipulated votes.[236]

This testimony is consistent with his lead investigator Bernie Kerik's acknowledgment that he had not come across proof that voting machines were used to switch, delete, or inject votes improperly.[237] Christina Bobb, an attorney who worked with Giuliani, similarly could not point to any evidence of wrongdoing by Dominion.[238] Even Sidney Powell, perhaps the most committed proponent of the Dominion falsehoods, was unable to provide the Select Committee with any evidence or expert report that demonstrated that the 2020 election outcome in any State had been altered through manipulation of voting machines.[239] And Powell defended herself in a defamation suit brought by Dominion by claiming that "no reasonable person would conclude that her statements were truly statements of fact." [240]

By January 6, 2021, President Trump's claims regarding Dominion had been debunked time and again. The President knew, or should have known, that he had no basis for alleging that Dominion's voting machines had cost him the election.

THE STATE FARM ARENA VIDEO

President Trump also recklessly promoted allegations that video footage from a ballot counting center in Fulton County, Georgia, was proof of major election fraud. He was repeatedly informed that these allegations were false, but he pressed them anyway.

On December 3rd, Rudy Giuliani presented State legislators with selectively edited footage of ballots being counted on Election Night at Fulton County's State Farm Arena.[241] Giuliani misrepresented the video as "a smoking gun" proving election fraud.[242] The President repeatedly claimed that he would have won Georgia, if not for a supposed conspiracy that unfolded on election night. President Trump and some of his supporters alleged that political operatives faked a water main rupture to expel Republican poll watchers.[243] These same operatives then supposedly took illegal ballots from suitcases hidden under tables and added those ballots to the official count multiple times over by scanning them more than once.[244] Not one of these allegations was true.

In a speech on December 5th, President Trump made the false claim about the State Farm Arena and claimed that "if you just take the crime of what those Democrat workers were doing...[t]hat's 10 times more than I need to win this state." [245] During a December 22nd speech, he played the same deceptive footage presented by Giuliani several weeks earlier.[246] President Trump also repeatedly scapegoated one of these Fulton County election workers during his January 2nd phone call with Georgia's Secretary of State, repeatedly referencing her by name and calling her "a professional vote scammer and hustler." [247] It was a malicious smear.

President Trump was directly notified *at least* four different times that the allegations he was making were false. On December 15th, then-Deputy Attorney General Jeffrey Rosen told him: "It wasn't a suitcase. It was a bin. That's what they use when they're counting ballots. It's benign." [248] Rosen's deputy, Richard Donoghue, also debunked this claim, including on a phone call on December 27th and in a meeting in the Oval Office on December 31st: "I told the President myself...several times, in several conversations, that these allegations about ballots being smuggled in in a suitcase and run through the machines several times, it was not true, that we had looked at it, we looked at the video, we interviewed the witnesses, and it was not true." [249]

Likewise, Georgia Secretary of State Brad Raffensperger told President Trump that his allegations about the video were false. During his January 2nd call with the President, Raffensperger explained that Giuliani's team "sliced and diced that video and took it out of context" and that "the events that transpired are nowhere near what was projected" once one looks at more complete footage. [250] Raffensperger also explained to the President that his team "did an audit of that, and we proved conclusively that they were not scanned three times." [251] Yet, when Raffensperger said he would send President Trump a link to the television segment, the President refused: "I don't care about the link. I don't need it." [252]

The actual evidence contradicted all of President Trump's claims about what the Fulton County video depicted. For example, the chief investigator for Raffensperger's office explained in a December 6th court filing that "there were no mystery ballots that were brought in from an unknown location and hidden under tables...." [253] As the investigator noted, the security footage showed there was nothing under the table when it was brought into the room. Hours later, with reporters and observers present, the "video shows ballots that had already been opened but not counted placed in the boxes, sealed up, [and] stored under the table." [254] This finding was affirmed by the FBI, DOJ, and the Georgia Bureau of Investigation, which interviewed witnesses and reviewed the full video footage and machine data from the site. [255]

The ballots in question were not double counted. This was confirmed by a full hand recount in November, as well as a subsequent review by investigators. [256] They found that although one of the workers was shown in the video scanning certain batches multiple times, this was for a valid reason: her scanner kept jamming. The investigators confirmed from scanner logs, as well as the footage, that she only hit the "accept" button once per batch. [257] Investigators also found that staff likely did not tell the observers to leave, let alone forcefully eject them from the facility. [258]

Despite this conclusive evidence and testimony, President Trump continued to point to the Fulton County video as evidence of a grand conspiracy. On January 5th, for instance, President Trump's executive assistant emailed a document "from POTUS" to Senator Josh Hawley (R-MO), Senator Ted Cruz (R-TX), and Representative Jim Jordan (R-OH) that cited "Suitcase Gate" among the "worst fraud incidents" in Georgia. [259]

During his January 6th speech, President Trump told the crowd that "in Fulton County, Republican poll watchers were ejected, in some cases, physically from the room under the false pretense of a pipe burst." The President continued:

> ...then election officials pull boxes, Democrats, and suitcases of ballots out from under a table. You all saw it on television, totally fraudulent. And illegally scanned them for nearly two hours, totally unsupervised. Tens of thousands of votes. This act coincided with a mysterious vote dump of up to 100,000 votes for Joe Biden, almost none for Donald Trump.[260]

No part of President Trump's story was true. He had already been informed that it was false.

In June 2021, when Giuliani's law license was revoked by a New York State appellate court, the court's ruling cited his statements about supposed suitcases of ballots in Georgia as one of its reasons for doing so. "If, as respondent claims, he reviewed the entire video, he could not have reasonably reached a conclusion that illegal votes were being counted," the court's ruling reads.[261]

President Trump's conspiracy-mongering endangered innocent public servants around the country, including in Fulton County. For example, during a December 10, 2020, appearance in Georgia, Giuliani falsely accused Ruby Freeman and Shaye Moss, two Black public servants shown in the Fulton County video, of "surreptitiously passing around USB ports as if they're vials of heroin or cocaine."[262] In fact, Moss had been given a ginger mint by her mother, Freeman.[263] As described in Chapter 2, baseless accusations like these forever changed the lives of election workers like Freeman and Moss. All in service of President Trump's Big Lie.

THE FAKE BALLOT MYTH

The Trump Campaign's distortion of the State Farm Arena video is just one example of the "fake ballots" lie. President Trump frequently claimed that "fake ballots" for Biden were injected into the vote-counting process. To hear the President tell it, there were truckloads of ballots delivered in the middle of the night to vote-counting centers and millions more votes were cast than there were registered voters. Judges, Trump administration officials, State authorities, and independent election experts found each iteration of the "fake ballot" claim to be just that: fake. The Trump Campaign and its surrogates brought nine cases that raised some version of a "fake ballots" claim. Every one of those cases was promptly dismissed.[264] For example, in *Costantino v. City of Detroit*, a Michigan court ruled that the plaintiff's claims regarding forged, backdated and double-counted votes in

Detroit were "incorrect and not credible" and "rife with speculation and guess-work about sinister motives." [265]

Many of the fake ballot claims were publicly raised and repeated by President Trump, but never included in any lawsuit. For example, a truck driver for the U.S. Postal Service claimed that he delivered hundreds of thousands of completed ballots from Bethpage, New York to Lancaster, Pennsylvania.[266] President Trump repeated this allegation numerous times.[267] The DOJ and FBI interviewed the relevant witnesses, including the truck driver, and reviewed the loading manifests. They determined that the allegation was not true.[268] Both Attorney General Barr and his successor, Jeffrey Rosen, told President Trump this claim was false. But that didn't stop the President from repeating it.

Another alleged "truckload of ballots" was supposedly delivered to the Detroit counting center at 4:30 a.m. on election night. This truck allegedly carried 100,000 ballots in garbage cans, wastepaper bins, cardboard boxes, and shopping baskets.[269] A widely circulated video purportedly showed an unmarked van dropping off ballots, which were then wheeled into the counting center on a wagon.[270] In fact, the only ballot delivery in Detroit after midnight on election night was an official delivery of 16,000 ballots, stacked in 45 well-organized trays of approximately 350 ballots each.[271] The wagon depicted in the video contained camera equipment being pulled by a reporter.[272] The claim of 100,000 fake ballots being smuggled into the counting center in the middle of the night is even more ridiculous in light of the fact that only 174,384 absent voter ballots were recorded in the City of Detroit in the 2020 election.[273] The addition of 100,000 fake ballots to approximately 74,000 legitimate ballots would certainly have been obvious to election officials.[274]

President Trump also repeatedly claimed that more votes were cast than there were registered voters in certain States, cities, or precincts. It was easy to fact-check these allegations and demonstrate they were false.

For example, in Pennsylvania, approximately nine million people were registered to vote and approximately 6.8 million votes were cast in the 2020 presidential election.[275] Nevertheless, President Trump and his allies made numerous "more votes than voters" claims in Pennsylvania. Citing 2020 mail-in voting data tweeted by Pennsylvania State Senator Doug Mastriano, President Trump claimed that 1.1 million ballots had been "created" and counted improperly.[276] In fact, there was no discrepancy in the actual numbers—Mastriano erroneously compared the 2.6 million mail-in ballots cast *in the November general* election to the 1.5 million ballots that were returned *in the June primary* election.[277]

President Trump also promoted a false claim by a different Pennsylvania legislator that Pennsylvania had 205,000 more votes than voters.[278] This claim was based on a flawed comparison by State Representative Frank Ryan of the votes recorded by State election authorities as having been cast and those reflected in a separate State registry.[279] In fact, the discrepancy was a result of some counties not yet uploading their official results to the registry.[280] In late-December 2020, Acting Deputy Attorney General Donoghue told President Trump that this allegation was baseless.[281] President Trump kept repeating it anyway.[282]

The President and his surrogates made similar false claims concerning excess votes in Michigan. Many of those claims originated with a grossly inaccurate affidavit submitted by Russell Ramsland, the person behind the "very amateurish" and "false and misleading" ASOG report regarding Dominion voting machines in Antrim County.[283] Ramsland claimed in a similar affidavit filed in Federal court in Georgia that 3,276 precincts in Michigan had turnout of between 84% and 350%, with 19 precincts reporting turnout in excess of 100%.[284] Ramsland's affidavit was widely ridiculed, in part, because he relied on data for dozens of precincts that are located in Minnesota, not Michigan.[285] Even after he corrected his affidavit to remove the Minnesota townships, his Michigan data remained wildly off-base.[286]

THE "MULTIPLE COUNTING OF BALLOTS" FICTION

The President and his surrogates repeatedly claimed that ballots for former Vice President Biden were counted multiple times.[287] These claims originated when some noticed election officials re-running stacks of ballots through counting machines. But the allegation is based on a fundamental misunderstanding of the vote-counting process—it is routine and appropriate for election officials to re-scan ballots if they are not properly scanned and tabulated in the initial effort. In *Costantino v. City of Detroit*, the court rejected the "incorrect and not credible" affidavits speculating that ballots were run through scanners and counted multiple times in favor of the "more accurate and persuasive explanation of activity" put forward by the "highly-respected" election official with 40 years of experience.[288]

As with other misguided claims of election fraud, the claim that ballots were counted multiple times disregards the safeguards in the voting process. In particular, as noted above, it would certainly have been apparent in the canvassing process if hundreds of ballots were counted multiple times in Detroit because the total number of ballots would greatly exceed the number of voters who voted. But that was not the case.

THE IMAGINARY "DEAD" AND "INELIGIBLE" VOTERS

In addition to their false claims regarding fake ballots, President Trump and his surrogates also relentlessly asserted that tens of thousands of ballots were cast by dead or otherwise ineligible voters. For example, President Trump and Giuliani frequently alleged that more than 66,000 unregistered juveniles voted in Georgia.[289] In fact, no underage people voted in Georgia.[290] Giuliani offered several different made-up figures of the number of non-citizens who supposedly voted in Arizona, but provided no evidence to substantiate his claims.[291] In fact, Arizona requires every new voter to provide proof of citizenship in order to register to vote—or to complete a Federal voter registration form that requires the individual to sign an attestation to citizenship status under penalty of perjury—and no person can vote without being registered.[292] By mid-November, Trump Campaign staff determined this allegation that thousands of non-citizens voted in Arizona was based on "highly unreliable" information, and it is one of the false claims that led to Giuliani losing his New York law license.[293] These "ineligible" voters did not exist.

Nor were thousands of votes cast in the names of dead Americans.

During his January 2nd, call with Georgia Secretary of State Raffensperger, the President claimed that "close to about 5,000 [dead] voters" cast ballots in the election. Raffensperger quickly informed the President this wasn't true.[294] But the "dead voter" lie wasn't limited to Georgia. President Trump wanted Americans to believe that "dead voters" contributed to his defeat in several battleground States.[295]

But even the Trump Campaign and its lawyers recognized early on that the claims regarding "dead voters" were grossly exaggerated, to say the least. By early November, Trump lawyers discovered that many people listed by the campaign as having died were actually alive and well.[296] In early December, Eric Herschmann advised Chief of Staff Meadows by text message that the Trump legal team had determined that the claim of more than 10,000 dead people voting in Georgia was not accurate.[297] The ensuing exchange makes clear that both men knew that Giuliani's claims were absurd:

> Herschmann: Just an FYI. Alex Cannon and his team verified that the 10k+ supposed dead people voting in GA is not accurate
>
> Meadows: I didn't hear that claim. It is not accurate. I think I found 22 if I remember correctly. Two of them died just days before the general
>
> Herschmann: It was alleged in Rudy's hearing today. Your number is much closer to what we can prove. I think it's 12

Meadows: My son found 12 obituaries and 6 other possibles depending on the Voter roll acuracy [sic]

Herschmann: That sounds more like it. Maybe he can help Rudy find the other 10k ??

Meadows: lol [298]

Shortly thereafter, a Georgia court dismissed the claim that there were tens of thousands of votes cast by ineligible voters, noting the claims "rest on speculation rather than duly pled facts." [299]

The Trump Campaign's own expert on the supposed "dead voters" admitted that the Campaign lacked the necessary data to make any conclusions about whether any (or how many) votes were cast in the name of a deceased person. [300] State officials *did* have such data, however, and were able to conduct the type of matching analysis required. These State authorities determined that there were only a handful of cases in which people voted on behalf of deceased individuals. [301]

Even in those cases where the person who voted actually did die, President Trump's lawyers knew that the vast majority of the voters included on their list of dead voters actually cast their votes before they passed. [302] In early-January 2021, just days before January 6th, Republican Senator Lindsey Graham asked several Trump lawyers to provide evidence to support the Campaign's claims regarding dead voters. [303] As Giuliani's team investigated, they concluded that they could not find evidence of dead voters anywhere near the number that Giuliani and President Trump were claiming publicly. After noting the shortcomings in their evidence, Katherine Friess, a lawyer working with the Giuliani legal team, warned that Senator Graham would "push back" on their evidence. [304] As predicted by Friess, Senator Graham was not impressed by the information provided by Giuliani's team. In his speech on the Senate floor on January 6th, Graham explained why he would not object to the certification of electoral votes. Senator Graham referred to the failure of the Trump attorneys to provide the evidence he requested:

They said there's 66,000 people in Georgia under 18 voted. How many people believe that? I asked, 'Give me 10.' Hadn't had one. They said 8,000 felons in prison in Arizona voted. Give me 10. Hadn't gotten one. Does that say there's—There's problems in every election. I don't buy this. Enough's enough. We've got to end it. [305]

Documents obtained by the Select Committee reveal that President Trump and his lawyers knew that the claims being made in court about dead or ineligible voters in Georgia were inaccurate, and the lawyers were concerned that if the President vouched for those claims in another court pleading he might be criminally prosecuted. On December 31st, as the lawyers rushed to file a Federal lawsuit in Georgia, some of the lawyers raised concerns about the President signing a "verification" under oath that the allegations regarding voter fraud in Georgia, including claims regarding dead people voting, were true. As Eastman noted in an email to his colleagues on December 31st:

> Although the President signed a verification [regarding the Georgia claims] back on Dec. 1, he has since been made aware that some of the allegations (and evidence proffered by the experts) has been inaccurate. For him to sign a new verification with that knowledge...would not be accurate. And I have no doubt that an aggressive DA or US Atty someplace will go after both the President and his lawyers once all the dust settles on this.[306]

Despite these concerns, President Trump and his attorneys filed a complaint that incorporated the same inaccurate numbers, and President Trump signed a verification swearing under oath that the inaccurate numbers were "true and correct" or "believed to be true and correct" to the best of his knowledge and belief.[307] A Federal judge reviewing the relevant emails and pleadings recently concluded:

> The emails show that President Trump knew that the specific numbers of voter fraud were wrong but continued to tout those numbers, both in court and to the public. The Court finds that these emails are sufficiently related to and in furtherance of a conspiracy to defraud the United States.[308]

1.9 PRESIDENT TRUMP'S JANUARY 6TH SPEECH

At noon on January 6, 2021, President Trump addressed thousands of his supporters at a rally just south of the White House. The election had been decided two months earlier. The courts found there was no evidence of significant fraud. The States certified their votes by mid-December. It was over—President Trump lost. But that's not what the President told those in attendance. He delivered an incendiary speech from beginning to end, arguing that nothing less than the fate of America was at stake.

"Our country has had enough," President Trump said. "We will not take it anymore and that's what this is all about."[309] He claimed that his followers had descended on Washington to "save our democracy" and "stop the

Photo by Samuel Corum/Getty Images

steal." [310] He refused, once again, to concede. And he proclaimed that "[t]oday I will lay out just some of the evidence proving that we won this election and we won it by a landslide." [311]

For months, President Trump had relentlessly promoted his Big Lie.[312] He and his associates manufactured one tale after another to justify it. For more than an hour on January 6th, the President wove these conspiracy theories and lies together.[313]

By the Select Committee's assessment, there were more than 100 times during his speech in which President Trump falsely claimed that either the election had been stolen from him, or falsely claimed that votes had been compromised by some specific act of fraud or major procedural violations. That day, President Trump repeated many of the same lies he had told for months—even after being informed that many of these claims were false. He lied about Dominion voting machines in Michigan, suitcases of ballots in Georgia, more votes than voters in Pennsylvania, votes cast by non-citizens in Arizona, and dozens of other false claims of election fraud.[314] None of those claims were true.

As explained in the chapters that follow, the Big Lie was central to President Trump's plan to stay in power. He used the Big Lie to pressure

State and local officials to undo the will of the people. His campaign convened fake electors on the baseless pretense that former Vice President Biden won several States due to fraud or other malfeasance. The President tried to subvert the Department of Justice by browbeating its leadership to endorse his election lies. And when the DOJ's senior personnel did not acquiesce, President Trump sought to install a loyalist who would.

When all those efforts failed, President Trump betrayed his own Vice President. He pressured Vice President Pence to obstruct the joint session of Congress on January 6th, falsely claiming that he had the power to refuse to count certain electoral votes. President Trump knew this was illegal but attempted to justify it with lies about the election.

On December 19, 2020, President Trump summoned a mob to Washington, DC on the same day that Congress was set to certify former Vice President Biden's victory by claiming the election was stolen and promising a "wild" protest.[315]

And the bogus stolen election claim was the focus of President Trump's speech on January 6th. The litany of lies he told riled up a mob that would march to the U.S. Capitol to intimidate Vice President Pence and Members of Congress.

"And we fight. We fight like hell. And if you don't fight like hell, you're not going to have a country anymore," President Trump told the crowd.[316] He incited them with these words just after praising his own election night lie—the Big Lie.

President Trump told his followers to "fight" to "save" their country from a bogus specter of supposed election fraud.[317] And many of them did.

ENDNOTES

1. "Donald Trump 2020 Election Night Speech Transcript," Rev, (Nov. 4, 2020), available at https://www.rev.com/blog/transcripts/donald-trump-2020-election-night-speech-transcript.

2. Select Committee to Investigate the January 6th Attack on the United States Capitol, Transcribed Interview of William Stepien, (Feb. 10, 2022), pp. 54, 60.

3. Select Committee to Investigate the January 6th Attack on the United States Capitol, Deposition of Jason Miller, (Feb. 3, 2022), pp. 74-75.

4. Select Committee to Investigate the January 6th Attack on the United States Capitol, Deposition of Jason Miller, (Feb. 3, 2022), pp. 75, 78.

5. Documents on file with the Select Committee to Investigate the January 6th Attack on the United States Capitol (National Archives Production), 076P-R000010020_0001 (Email chain between Tom Fitton and Molly Michael, starting on October 31, 2020, and ending on November 3, 2020, discussing a draft victory statement for President Trump).

6. We note that Bannon refused to testify and has been convicted of criminal contempt by a jury of his peers. *See* "Stephen K. Bannon Sentenced to Four Months in Prison on Two Counts of Contempt of Congress," Department of Justice, (Oct. 21, 2022), available at

https://www.justice.gov/usao-dc/pr/stephen-k-bannon-sentenced-four-months-prison-two-counts-contempt-congress; Dan Friedman, "Leaked Audio: Before Election Day, Bannon Said Trump Planned to Falsely Claim Victory," Mother Jones, (July 12, 2022), available at https://www.motherjones.com/politics/2022/07/leaked-audio-steve-bannon-trump-2020-election-declare-victory/.

7. At his interview, Stone invoked his Fifth Amendment Right not to incriminate himself, including to questions regarding his direct communications with Donald Trump and his role on January 6th. Select Committee to Investigate the January 6th Attack on the United States Capitol, *Business Meeting on the January 6th Investigation*, 117th Cong., 2d sess., (Oct. 13, 2022), at 39:15 - 39:33 available at https://www.youtube.com/watch?v=IQvuBoLBuC0.

8. Select Committee to Investigate the January 6th Attack on the United States Capitol, Transcribed Interview of William Barr, (June 2, 2022), p. 27.

9. Jennifer Agiesta and Marshall Cohen, "CNN Poll: Questions about Accuracy of Vote Counting Rise as Most Want to Vote before Election Day," CNN, (Aug. 18, 2020), available at https://www.cnn.com/2020/08/18/politics/cnn-poll-trump-biden-election-security-mail-in-voting/index.html; Mark Murray, "Biden Leads Trump by 10 points in Final Pre-Election NBC News/WSJ poll," NBC News, (Nov. 1, 2020, updated Nov. 2, 2020), available at https://www.nbcnews.com/politics/meet-the-press/biden-leads-trump-10-points-final-pre-election-nbc-news-n1245667.

10. Select Committee to Investigate the January 6th Attack on the United States Capitol, *Hearing on the January 6th Investigation*, 117th Cong., 2d sess., (June 13, 2022), available at https://www.govinfo.gov/committee/house-january6th.

11. Select Committee to Investigate the January 6th Attack on the United States Capitol, *Hearing on the January 6th Investigation*, 117th Cong., 2d sess., (June 13, 2022), available at https://www.govinfo.gov/committee/house-january6th.

12. Select Committee to Investigate the January 6th Attack on the United States Capitol, Transcribed Interview of William Stepien, (Feb. 10, 2022), p. 44.

13. Select Committee to Investigate the January 6th Attack on the United States Capitol, Transcribed Interview of William Stepien, (Feb. 10, 2022), pp. 44-45.

14. Select Committee to Investigate the January 6th Attack on the United States Capitol, *Hearing on the January 6th Investigation*, 117th Cong., 2d sess., (June 13, 2022), available at https://www.govinfo.gov/committee/house-january6th.

15. Dan Friedman, "Leaked Audio: Before Election Day, Bannon Said Trump Planned to Falsely Claim Victory," Mother Jones, (July 12, 2022), available at https://www.motherjones.com/politics/2022/07/leaked-audio-steve-bannon-trump-2020-election-declare-victory/. During our October 13 hearing, Robert Costa tweeted: "CBS News has confirmed that Oct. 31, 2020, was a key date in the pre-election maneuvers by Trump. Set off alarm with WH counsel and Herschmann, among others. I've seen texts from that night from some aides and they knew it was no joke; declaring victory was Trump's plan. Period." Maggie Haberman retweeted Costa, writing: "Trump told a conference call of a bunch of lawyers and informal advisers working for him earlier that month that he was going to go up and say he won, first reported by @jonathanvswan." Robert Costa (@costareports), Twitter, Oct. 13, 2022 1:29 p.m. ET, available at https://twitter.com/costareports/status/1580611586674151424?lang=en; *see also* Maggie Haberman (@maggieNYT), Twitter, Oct. 13, 2022 1:35 p.m. ET, available at https://twitter.com/maggienyt/status/1580613143637635072 ("Trump told a conference call of a bunch of lawyers and informal advisers working for him earlier that month that he was going to go up and say he won, first reported by @jonathanvswan").

16. Dan Friedman, "Leaked Audio: Before Election Day, Bannon Said Trump Planned to Falsely Claim Victory," Mother Jones, (July 12, 2022), available at https://www.motherjones.com/politics/2022/07/leaked-audio-steve-bannon-trump-2020-election-declare-victory/.

17. Fox Business, "Steve Bannon: Trump Won't Allow the Election to Be Stolen," YouTube, at 3:24, Nov. 3, 2020, available at https://www.youtube.com/watch?v=PDdxoyAUqoo.

18. "Steve Bannon: Donald Trump Will Claim Victory 'Right Before the 11 O'clock News'," Media Matters, (Nov. 3, 2020), available at https://www.mediamatters.org/steve-bannon/steve-bannon-donald-trump-will-claim-victory-right-11-oclock-news-0.

19. Documents on file with the Select Committee to Investigate the January 6th Attack on the United States Capitol (National Archives Production), 076P-R000010020_0001 (Email chain between Tom Fitton and Molly Michael, starting on October 31, 2020, and ending on November 3, 2020, discussing a draft victory statement for President Trump).

20. Documents on file with the Select Committee to Investigate the January 6th Attack on the United States Capitol (National Archives Production), 076P-R000010020_0001 (Email chain between Tom Fitton and Molly Michael, starting on October 31, 2020, and ending on November 3, 2020, discussing a draft victory statement for President Trump).

21. Documents on file with the Select Committee to Investigate the January 6th Attack on the United States Capitol (National Archives Production), 076P-R000010020_0001 (Email chain between Tom Fitton and Molly Michael, starting on October 31, 2020, and ending on November 3, 2020, discussing a draft victory statement for President Trump).

22. Documents on file with the Select Committee to Investigate the January 6th Attack on the United States Capitol (National Archives Production), 076P-R000010020_0001 (Email chain between Tom Fitton and Molly Michael, starting on October 31, 2020, and ending on November 3, 2020, discussing a draft victory statement for President Trump).

23. Documents on file with the Select Committee to Investigate the January 6th Attack on the United States Capitol (National Archives Production), 076P-R000010020_0001 (Email chain between Tom Fitton and Molly Michael, starting on October 31, 2020, and ending on November 3, 2020, discussing a draft victory statement for President Trump).

24. Select Committee to Investigate the January 6th Attack on the United States Capitol, *Business Meeting on the January 6th Investigation*, 117th Cong., 2d sess., (Oct. 13, 2022), at 38:18 - 39:32, available at https://www.youtube.com/watch?v=IQvuBoLBuC0.

25. Jonathan Swan, "Trump Plans to Declare Premature Victory If He Appears on Election Night," *Axios*, (Nov. 1, 2020), available at https://www.axios.com/2020/11/01/trump-claim-election-victory-ballots.

26. Jonathan Swan, "Trump Plans to Declare Premature Victory If He Appears on Election Night," *Axios*, (Nov. 1, 2020), available at https://www.axios.com/2020/11/01/trump-claim-election-victory-ballots.

27. Jonathan Swan, "Trump Plans to Declare Premature Victory If He Appears on Election Night," *Axios*, (Nov. 1, 2020), available at https://www.axios.com/2020/11/01/trump-claim-election-victory-ballots.

28. Select Committee to Investigate the January 6th Attack on the United States Capitol, *Hearing on the January 6th Investigation*, 117th Cong., 2d sess., (June 13, 2022), available at https://www.govinfo.gov/committee/house-january6th.

29. Months prior to the election, Josh Mendelsohn, the CEO of Hawkfish, a Democratic data and analytics firm, warned that President Trump would try to take advantage of the Red Mirage. *See* Margaret Talev, "Exclusive: Dem Group Warns of Apparent Trump Election Day Landslide," *Axios*, (Sept. 1, 2020), available at https://www.axios.com/2020/09/01/bloomberg-group-trump-election-night-scenarios. For other accounts warning that election night would see a Red Mirage, *see* Marshall Cohen, "Deciphering the 'Red Mirage,' the 'Blue Shift,' and the Uncertainty Surrounding Election Results This November," CNN, (Sept. 1, 2020), available at https://www.cnn.com/2020/09/01/politics/2020-election-count-red-mirage-blue-shift/index.html; Darragh Roche, "Trump Is Heading for a 'Red Mirage' Win on Election Night, Bloomberg-Funded Data Firm Says," *Newsweek*, (Sept. 1, 2020), available at https://www.newsweek.com/trump-phantom-win-election-1528948; Tom McCarthy, "'Red

Mirage': The 'Insidious' Scenario If Trump Declares Victory," *The Guardian*, (Oct. 31, 2020), available at https://www.theguardian.com/us-news/2020/oct/31/red-mirage-trump-election-scenario-victory.

30. "Remarks by President Trump, Vice President Pence, and Members of the Coronavirus Task Force in Press Briefing," White House, April 7, 2020, available at https://trumpwhitehouse.archives.gov/briefings-statements/remarks-president-trump-vice-president-pence-members-coronavirus-task-force-press-briefing-april-7-2020/.

31. Donald J. Trump (@realDonaldTrump), Twitter, Apr. 8, 2020 8:20 a.m. ET, available at http://web.archive.org/web/20201201162757/https://twitter.com/realDonaldTrump/status/1247861952736526336 (archived).

32. Donald J. Trump (@realDonaldTrump), Twitter, May 24, 2020 10:08 a.m. ET, available at http://web.archive.org/web/20200701075716/https://twitter.com/realDonaldTrump/status/1264558926021959680 (archived).

33. Donald J. Trump (@realDonaldTrump), Twitter, Sept. 17, 2020 7:56 a.m. ET, available at http://web.archive.org/web/20201115164217/https://twitter.com/realDonaldTrump/status/1306562791894122504 (archived).

34. Select Committee to Investigate the January 6th Attack on the United States Capitol, Transcribed Interview of William Stepien, (Feb. 10, 2022), p. 36; Documents on file with the Select Committee to Investigate the January 6th Attack on the United States Capitol, (National Archives Production), 076P-R000010941_0001-2, 076P-R000010940_0001-6 (July 23, 2020, emails regarding scheduling a meeting for the President with McCarthy, Stepien, and others).

35. Select Committee to Investigate the January 6th Attack on the United States Capitol, Transcribed Interview of William Stepien, (Feb. 10, 2022), p. 36.

36. Fox News, "President Trump Goes One-on-One with Chris Wallace," YouTube, July 19, 2020, available at https://www.youtube.com/watch?v=W6XdpDOH1JA; Pat Ward (@WardDPatrick), Twitter, July 19, 2020 10:15 a.m. ET, available at https://twitter.com/WardDPatrick/status/1284854318575878144.

37. "Remarks by President Trump in Press Briefing," White House, Sept. 23, 2020, available at https://trumpwhitehouse.archives.gov/briefings-statements/remarks-president-trump-press-briefing-092420/.

38. "Remarks by President Trump in Press Briefing," White House, Sept. 23, 2020, available at https://trumpwhitehouse.archives.gov/briefings-statements/remarks-president-trump-press-briefing-092420/.

39. Barbara Sprunt, "Trump Questions Election Again after White House Walked Back His Earlier Remarks," NPR, (Sept. 24, 2020), available at https://www.npr.org/2020/09/24/916440816/republican-leaders-reject-trump-hedging-on-transfer-of-power-amid-war-over-confi.

40. Donald J. Trump (@realDonaldTrump), Twitter, Nov. 4, 2020 12:49 a.m. ET, available at http://web.archive.org/web/20201105044240/https://twitter.com/realDonaldTrump/status/1323864823680126977 (archived); Donald J. Trump (@realDonaldTrump), Twitter, Nov. 4, 2020 10:04 a.m. ET, available at http://web.archive.org/web/20201104153504/https://twitter.com/realDonaldTrump/status/1324004491612618752 (archived).

41. Select Committee to Investigate the January 6th Attack on the United States Capitol, Transcribed Interview of William Stepien, (Feb. 10, 2022), pp. 44-45.

42. "Donald Trump 2020 Election Night Speech Transcript," Rev, (Nov. 4, 2020), available at https://www.rev.com/blog/transcripts/donald-trump-2020-election-night-speech-transcript.

43. *See* "Donald Trump 2020 Election Night Speech Transcript," Rev, (Nov. 4, 2020), available at https://www.rev.com/blog/transcripts/donald-trump-2020-election-night-speech-transcript; Donald J. Trump (@realDonaldTrump), Twitter, Nov. 4, 2020 12:49 a.m. ET, available at http://web.archive.org/web/20201104060648/https://twitter.com/realDonaldTrump/status/1323864823680126977 (archived).

44. Dan Friedman, "Leaked Audio: Before Election Day, Bannon Said Trump Planned to Falsely Claim Victory," Mother Jones, (July 12, 2022), available at https://www.motherjones.com/politics/2022/07/leaked-audio-steve-bannon-trump-2020-election-declare-victory/.

45. Factba.se, "Interview: Maria Bartiromo Interviews Donald Trump on Fox News - November 29, 2020," Vimeo, Nov. 29, 2020, at esp. 1:42-3:35, available at https://vimeo.com/485180163; Donald J. Trump (@realDonaldTrump), Twitter, Nov. 4, 2020 10:17 a.m. ET, available at https://media-cdn.factba.se/realdonaldtrump-twitter/1324007806694023169.jpg (archived); Donald J. Trump (@realDonaldTrump), Twitter, Nov. 4, 2020 10:04 a.m. ET, available at https://media-cdn.factba.se/realdonaldtrump-twitter/1324004491612618752.jpg (archived); Donald J. Trump (@realDonaldTrump), Twitter, Nov. 18, 2020 8:22 p.m. ET, available at https://media-cdn.factba.se/realdonaldtrump-twitter/1329233502139715586.jpg (archived); Donald J. Trump (@realDonaldTrump), Twitter, Nov. 19, 2020 8:49 p.m. ET, available at https://media-cdn.factba.se/realdonaldtrump-twitter/1329602736053252107.jpg (archived).

46. For example, one widely shared post claimed that, in the early-morning hours of November 4, hundreds of thousands of mail in ballots were "found" in Wisconsin, Michigan, and Pennsylvania, and all of the ballots were for Biden. Nick Adams (@NickAdamsinUSA), Twitter, Nov. 4, 2020 4:48 p.m., available at https://web.archive.org/web/20201110150437/https://twitter.com/NickAdamsinUSA/status/1324151663641448448 (archived).

47. In many metropolitan areas, absentee ballots are counted in centralized locations and reported in batches. For example, the ballots that were supposedly "found" in Wisconsin were absentee ballots reported by Milwaukee County when that county completed its tally. Of the approximately 181,000 votes reported between 3:26 and 3:44 a.m., Biden received approximately 83% of the votes and Trump received approximately 17%. *See* Eric Litke and Madeline Heim, "Fact check: Wisconsin Did Not 'Find' 100K Ballots around 4 a.m. the Morning after the Election, or Take Break from Counting Votes," *Milwaukee Journal Sentinel*, (Nov. 4, 2020), available at https://www.jsonline.com/story/news/politics/elections/2020/11/04/wisconsin-didnt-find-ballots-stop-count-voter-fraud-claims-untrue-politifact/6165435002/. In Michigan, no ballots were "found" between 3:30-5:00 a.m. Rather, approximately 200,000 votes were reported by Wayne County shortly after 6:00 a.m., the vast majority of which were for Biden. *See* Geoffrey Skelley, "Live Bog: 2020 Election Results Coverage: Michigan's Morning Update," FiveThirtyEight, (Nov. 4, 2020), available at https://fivethirtyeight.com/live-blog/2020-election-results-coverage/#294294. Overall, Biden won 68% of the vote in Wayne County, to 30% for Trump. However, among absentee voters, Biden won 75% to Trump's 23%. *See* "November 3, 2020 - General Election Results," Charter County of Wayne, Michigan, available at https://www.waynecounty.com/elected/clerk/november-3-2020-general-election-results.aspx.

48. Select Committee to Investigate the January 6th Attack on the United States Capitol, Transcribed Interview of William Stepien, (Feb. 10, 2022), p. 45; *See also* John Curiel, Charles Stewart III, and Jack Williams, *One Shift, Two Shifts, Red Shift, Blue Shifts: Reported Election Returns in the 2020 Election*, MIT Election Data and Science Lab, (July 9, 2021), p. 40, available at https://electionlab.mit.edu/sites/default/files/2021-07/curiel_stewart_williams_blue_shift_esra_final.pdf, (detailed analysis of timed reporting data shows that "smaller and more rural counties, which favored Trump, could report their ballots before the counties with hundreds of precincts and hundreds of thousands of voters").

49. Select Committee to Investigate the January 6th Attack on the United States Capitol, Transcribed Interview of William Barr, (June 2, 2022), p. 8.

50. Select Committee to Investigate the January 6th Attack on the United States Capitol, Transcribed Interview of William Barr, (June 2, 2022), p. 8.

51. Select Committee to Investigate the January 6th Attack on the United States Capitol, Transcribed Interview of William Stepien, (Feb. 10, 2022), p. 119, 124-26, 174.

52. Select Committee to Investigate the January 6th Attack on the United States Capitol, Transcribed Interview of William Stepien, (Feb. 10, 2022), p. 174.

53. Select Committee to Investigate the January 6th Attack on the United States Capitol, Deposition of Rudy Giuliani, (May 20, 2022), pp. 22–23.

54. Select Committee to Investigate the January 6th Attack on the United States Capitol, Deposition of Rudy Giuliani, (May 20, 2022), pp. 23, 26.

55. Select Committee to Investigate the January 6th Attack on the United States Capitol, Deposition of Rudy Giuliani, (May 20, 2022), p. 35 (describing Ellis as "a co-counsel" and "my number two person" so "generally, if you got an opinion from Jenna, it would be just like getting an opinion from me").

56. Select Committee to Investigate the January 6th Attack on the United States Capitol, Transcribed Interview of Bernard Kerik, (Jan. 13, 2022), pp. 10, 15–18.

57. Select Committee to Investigate the January 6th Attack on the United States Capitol, Transcribed Interview of William Stepien, (Feb. 10, 2022), p. 92.

58. Select Committee to Investigate the January 6th Attack on the United States Capitol, Transcribed Interview of William Stepien, (Feb. 10, 2022), pp. 111–112.

59. Select Committee to Investigate the January 6th Attack on the United States Capitol, Transcribed Interview of William Stepien, (Feb. 10, 2022), p. 134; Documents on file with the Select Committee to Investigate the January 6th Attack on the United States Capitol, (Mark Meadows Production), MM007288, (November 13, 2020, email from Bill Stepien to Mark Meadows, Justin Clark, and Jason Miller titled "Fwd: AZ Federal ID Voters").

60. Select Committee to Investigate the January 6th Attack on the United States Capitol, Transcribed Interview of Alex Cannon, (Apr. 13, 2022), pp. 19–23.

61. Select Committee to Investigate the January 6th Attack on the United States Capitol, Transcribed Interview of Alex Cannon, (Apr. 13, 2022), pp. 38–39.

62. Select Committee to Investigate the January 6th Attack on the United States Capitol, Transcribed Interview of Alex Cannon, (Apr. 13, 2022), pp. 33-34.

63. Select Committee to Investigate the January 6th Attack on the United States Capitol, Deposition of Jason Miller (Feb. 3, 2022), p. 119.

64. Select Committee to Investigate the January 6th Attack on the United States Capitol, Transcribed Interview of Matthew Morgan, (Apr. 25, 2022), pp. 117–18.

65. Select Committee to Investigate the January 6th Attack on the United States Capitol, Transcribed Interview of William Stepien, (Feb. 10, 2022), pp. 112–13.

66. Select Committee to Investigate the January 6th Attack on the United States Capitol, Deposition of Jason Miller (Feb. 3, 2022), p. 88–91.

67. Documents on file with the Select Committee to Investigate the January 6th Attack on the United States Capitol (Mark Meadows Production), MM010951-52 (November 3, 2020, Jason Miller text message to Mark Meadows at 10:27 pm); Documents on file with the Select Committee to Investigate the January 6th Attack on the United States Capitol (Mark Meadows Production), MM010972 (November 3, 2020, Jason Miller group text message to Mark Meadows and David Bossie at 11:53 pm); Documents on file with the Select Committee to Investigate the January 6th Attack on the United States Capitol (Mark Meadows Production), MM011343 (November 6, 2020, Jason Miller group text message to Mark Meadows, Ivanka Trump, Bill Stepien, Hope Hicks, Dan Scavino, and Jared Kushner at 11:10 am).

68. Select Committee to Investigate the January 6th Attack on the United States Capitol, Deposition of Jason Miller (Feb. 3, 2022), p. 91.

69. Select Committee to Investigate the January 6th Attack on the United States Capitol, Deposition of Jason Miller (Feb. 3, 2022), p. 91.

70. Select Committee to Investigate the January 6th Attack on the United States Capitol, Transcribed Interview of William Stepien, (Feb. 10, 2022), pp. 115–17; Brian Slodysko, "Explainer: Why AP Called Pennsylvania for Biden," Associated Press (Nov. 7, 2020), available at https://apnews.com/article/ap-called-pennsylvania-joe-biden-why-f7dba7b31bd21ec2819a7ac9d2b028d3.

71. Select Committee to Investigate the January 6th Attack on the United States Capitol, Transcribed Interview of William Stepien, (Feb. 10, 2022), pp. 115–20.

72. Select Committee to Investigate the January 6th Attack on the United States Capitol, Transcribed Interview of William Stepien, (Feb. 10, 2022), p. 118.

73. Select Committee to Investigate the January 6th Attack on the United States Capitol, Transcribed Interview of William Stepien, (Feb. 10, 2022), p. 119.

74. Select Committee to Investigate the January 6th Attack on the United States Capitol, *Hearing on the January 6th Investigation*, 117th Cong., 2d sess., (June 13, 2022), available at https://www.govinfo.gov/committee/house-january6th.

75. Select Committee to Investigate the January 6th Attack on the United States Capitol, *Hearing on the January 6th Investigation*, 117th Cong., 2d sess., (June 13, 2022), available at https://www.govinfo.gov/committee/house-january6th.; Federal Election Commission, "Federal Elections 2020 – Election Results for the U.S. President, the U.S. Senate and the U.S. House of Representatives," Oct. 2022, p. 12, available at https://www.fec.gov/resources/cms-content/documents/federalelections2020.pdf.

76. Select Committee to Investigate the January 6th Attack on the United States Capitol, *Hearing on the January 6th Investigation*, 117th Cong., 2d sess., (June 13, 2022), available at https://www.govinfo.gov/committee/house-january6th.

77. "Risk-Limiting Audit Report – Georgia Presidential Contest, November 2020," Georgia Secretary of State, (Nov. 19, 2020), available at https://sos.ga.gov/sites/default/files/2022-02/11.19_.20_risk_limiting_audit_report_memo_1.pdf.

78. *See* "Summary of Hand Count Audits – 2020 General Election," Arizona Secretary of State, (Nov. 17, 2020), available at https://azsos.gov/2020-general-election-hand-count-results; "Agreed Upon Procedures Report – Evaluation of the Accuracy of Voting Machine Tabulators Used for the 2020 General Elections Held on November 3, 2020 (Voting System Check)," New Mexico Secretary of State, (Dec. 15, 2020), available at https://api.realfile.rtsclients.com/PublicFiles/ee3072ab0d43456cb15a51f7d82c77a2/f740346c-7b6b-4479-acd6-068829382307/2020%20Post%20Election%20Voting%20System%20Check%20Audit%20Results.pdf. Similar audits conducted by Michigan, Pennsylvania, and Wisconsin also affirmed the results in those states, but their results are excluded from this list because in those instances their audit results were not available until after January 6th. Shortly after the election, Nevada also conducted some post-election checks that supported the validity of the results there too, including testing a sample of the voting machines to make sure votes were accurately recorded. Deposition of Joseph Gloria at 33, *Law v. Whitmer*, No. A-22-858609-W (Nev. Ct., Clark Cty. Dec. 1, 2020), p. 33, available at https://www.democracydocket.com/wp-content/uploads/2022/09/2022.10.31-NV-Poll-Worker-Response-to-Application-for-Mandamus-STAMPED.pdf; Rex Briggs, "Trump Supporters Asked me to Look into Voter Fraud in Nevada; What I found Debunked What They were Alleging," *Nevada Independent*, (Dec. 22, 2020), available at https://thenevadaindependent.com/article/trump-supporters-asked-me-to-look-into-voter-fraud-in-nevada-what-i-found-debunked-what-they-were-alleging.

79. Select Committee to Investigate the January 6th Attack on the United States Capitol, *Hearing on the January 6th Investigation*, 117th Cong., 2d sess., (June 13, 2022), available at https://www.govinfo.gov/committee/house-january6th.

80. Documents on file with the Select Committee to Investigate the January 6th Attack on the United States Capitol (Jared Kushner Production), JK_00115, JK00117-132 (November 12, 2020, email from Matt Oczkowski, and attached analysis of battleground states).

81. Documents on file with the Select Committee to Investigate the January 6th Attack on the United States Capitol (Jared Kushner Production), JK_00115, JK_00117-132 (November 12, 2020, email from Matt Oczkowski, and attached analysis of battleground states).

82. Documents on file with the Select Committee to Investigate the January 6th Attack on the United States Capitol (Jared Kushner Production), JK_00115, JK_00117-132 (November 12, 2020, email from Matt Oczkowski, and attached analysis of battleground states).

83. Documents on file with the Select Committee to Investigate the January 6th Attack on the United States Capitol (Jared Kushner Production), JK_00115, JK_00117-132 (November 12, 2020, email from Matt Oczkowski, and attached analysis of battleground states).

84. Select Committee to Investigate the January 6th Attack on the United States Capitol, Deposition of Rudolph Giuliani (May 20, 2022), pp. 22-23.

85. Select Committee to Investigate the January 6th Attack on the United States Capitol, Deposition of Rudolph Giuliani (May 20, 2022), pp. 22-23.

86. Select Committee to Investigate the January 6th Attack on the United States Capitol, Deposition of Rudolph Giuliani (May 20, 2022), pp. 22-23.

87. Select Committee to Investigate the January 6th Attack on the United States Capitol, Transcribed Interview of William Stepien, (Feb. 10, 2022), pp. 106-107. Sidney Powell and Jenna Ellis accompanied Giuliani. The campaign was represented by Jared Kushner, Bill Stepien, David Bossie (a former senior official on President Trump's 2016 campaign), Derek Lyons, and Justin Clark. *See* Select Committee to Investigate the January 6th Attack on the United States Capitol, Transcribed Interview of Jared Kushner, (Mar. 31, 2022), pp. 50-51; Select Committee to Investigate the January 6th Attack on the United States Capitol, Transcribed Interview of Derek Lyons, (Mar. 17, 2022), pp. 64-65. Eric Herschmann also arrived at the campaign headquarters as the meeting was underway. *See* Select Committee to Investigate the January 6th Attack on the United States Capitol, Transcribed Interview of Eric Herschmann, (Mar. 17, 2022), pp. 160-61.

88. Select Committee to Investigate the January 6th Attack on the United States Capitol, Transcribed Interview of William Stepien, (Feb. 10, 2022), p. 109.

89. Select Committee to Investigate the January 6th Attack on the United States Capitol, Transcribed Interview of William Stepien, (Feb. 10, 2022), p. 109.

90. Select Committee to Investigate the January 6th Attack on the United States Capitol, Transcribed Interview of William Stepien, (Feb. 10, 2022), p. 107.

91. Select Committee to Investigate the January 6th Attack on the United States Capitol, Transcribed Interview of Justin Clark, (May 17, 2022), p. 63; Select Committee to Investigate the January 6th Attack on the United States Capitol, Transcribed Interview of Matthew Morgan, (Apr. 25, 2022), pp. 34-35.

92. Select Committee to Investigate the January 6th Attack on the United States Capitol, Transcribed Interview of Matthew Morgan, (Apr. 25, 2022), pp. 14-16.

93. Select Committee to Investigate the January 6th Attack on the United States Capitol, Transcribed Interview of Matthew Morgan, (Apr. 25, 2022), p. 14-16.

94. Select Committee to Investigate the January 6th Attack on the United States Capitol, Transcribed Interview of Matthew Morgan, (Apr. 25, 2022), p. 41.

95. Select Committee to Investigate the January 6th Attack on the United States Capitol, Transcribed Interview of Justin Clark, (May 17, 2022), p. 63.

96. Select Committee to Investigate the January 6th Attack on the United States Capitol, Transcribed Interview of Matthew Morgan, (Apr. 25, 2022), pp. 34-35, 41-42.

97. Select Committee to Investigate the January 6th Attack on the United States Capitol, Transcribed Interview of Matthew Morgan, (Apr. 25, 2022), p. 41.

98. Select Committee to Investigate the January 6th Attack on the United States Capitol, Transcribed Interview of Justin Clark, (May 17, 2022), p. 63.

99.   Select Committee to Investigate the January 6th Attack on the United States Capitol, Transcribed Interview of Justin Clark, (May 17, 2022), p. 63.

100. "Rudy Giuliani Trump Campaign Philadelphia Press Conference at Four Seasons Total Landscaping," Rev, (Nov. 7, 2020), available at https://www.rev.com/blog/transcripts/rudy-giuliani-trump-campaign-philadelphia-press-conference-november-7.

101. Select Committee to Investigate the January 6th Attack on the United States Capitol, Transcribed Interview of Bernard Kerik, (Jan. 13, 2022), pp. 30-32.

102. "Memorandum from Attorney General William Barr on Post-Voting Election Irregularity Inquiries to the United States Attorneys, to the Assistant Attorneys General for the Criminal Division, Civil Rights Division, and National Security Division, and to the Director of the Federal Bureau of Investigation," Department of Justice, (Nov. 9, 2020), available at https://www.documentcloud.org/documents/20403358-william-barr-election-memo-november-9. Longstanding DOJ policy had been not to conduct such investigations prior to certification to avoid impacting election results. See Federal Prosecution of Election Offenses, 8th ed. Department of Justice, December 2017, at 84, available at https://www.justice.gov/criminal/file/1029066/download.

103. Select Committee to Investigate the January 6th Attack on the United States Capitol, Transcribed Interview of Justin Clark, (May 17, 2022), pp. 66-67; Mike Pence, So Help Me God, (New York: Simon & Schuster, 2022), at pp. 431-432.

104. Select Committee to Investigate the January 6th Attack on the United States Capitol, Transcribed Interview of Justin Clark, (May 17, 2022), pp. 66-67.

105. Select Committee to Investigate the January 6th Attack on the United States Capitol, Transcribed Interview of Justin Clark, (May 17, 2022), p. 67; Mike Pence, So Help Me God, (New York: Simon & Schuster, 2022), at pp. 431.

106. See Donald J. Trump (@realDonaldTrump), Twitter, Nov. 15, 2020 7:11 p.m. ET, available at http://web.archive.org/web/20201117115935/https://twitter.com/realDonaldTrump/status/1327811527123103746 (archived).

107. Select Committee to Investigate the January 6th Attack on the United States Capitol, Transcribed Interview of Matthew Morgan, (Apr. 25, 2022), pp. 37-38.

108. Select Committee to Investigate the January 6th Attack on the United States Capitol, Transcribed Interview of William Stepien, (Feb. 10, 2022), pp. 174-175.

109. Documents on file with the Select Committee to Investigate the January 6th Attack on the United States Capitol, (Mark Meadows Production), MM007112 (Nov. 14, 2020 email from Jason Miller to Bill Stepien, Justin Clark, David Bossie, Mark Meadows, and Jared Kushner describing Rudy Giuliani's surrogate briefing).

110. Documents on file with the Select Committee to Investigate the January 6th Attack on the United States Capitol, (Mark Meadows Production), MM007112 (Nov. 14, 2020 email from Jason Miller to Bill Stepien, Justin Clark, David Bossie, Mark Meadows, and Jared Kushner describing Rudy Giuliani's surrogate briefing).

111. Documents on file with the Select Committee to Investigate the January 6th Attack on the United States Capitol, (Mark Meadows Production), MM007112 (Nov. 14, 2020 email from Jason Miller to Bill Stepien, Justin Clark, David Bossie, Mark Meadows, and Jared Kushner describing Rudy Giuliani's surrogate briefing).

112. Factba.se, "Interview: Brian Kilmeade of Fox News Interviews Donald Trump - December 13, 2020," Vimeo, at 7:47, Dec. 13, 2020, available at https://vimeo.com/490517184.

113. Select Committee to Investigate the January 6th Attack on the United States Capitol, Hearing on the January 6th Investigation, 117th Cong., 2d sess., (June 13, 2022), available at https://www.govinfo.gov/committee/house-january6th.

114. Select Committee staff analyzed the lawsuits. See also, Brendan Williams, Did President Trump's 2020 Election Litigation Kill Rule 11?, 30 Pub. Interest L. J. 181, 189 (2021), available at https://www.bu.edu/pilj/files/2021/06/Williams.pdf.

115. The only case that involved a victory for the campaign was the Pennsylvania case of *Trump v. Boockvar*. In that case, the court found that the Pennsylvania Secretary of State could not extend the deadline for voters to cure their failure to provide proper identification for absentee ballots. This decision affected just a few thousand votes, which were not included in any tallies. *Trump v. Boockvar*, No. 602 MD 2020 (Pa. Commw. Ct. Nov. 12, 2020), available at https://www.democracydocket.com/wp-content/uploads/2020/11/602-MD-20-1.pdf.

116. *See* John Danforth, Benjamin Ginsberg, Thomas B. Griffith, et al., *Lost, Not Stolen: The Conservative Case that Trump Lost and Biden Won the 2020 Presidential Election*, (July 2022), p. 3, available at https://lostnotstolen.org/download/378/.

117. Complaint at 2, *Bowyer v. Ducey*, 506 F. Supp. 3d 699 (D. Ariz. Dec. 2, 2020) (No. 2:20-cv-02321), ECF No. 1.

118. *Bowyer v. Ducey*, 506 F. Supp. 3d 699, 706, 723 (D. Ariz. 2020).

119. Minute Entry and Order at 6-9, *Ward v. Jackson*, No. CV2020-015285 (Az. Sup. Ct. Dec. 4, 2020).

120. See *Ward v. Jackson*, No. CV-20-0343-AP, 2020 Ariz. LEXIS 313, at *6 (Ariz. 2020), also available at https://www.clerkofcourt.maricopa.gov/home/showpublisheddocument/1984/637437053596970000; Howard Fischer, "State Supreme Court rejects GOP bid to void election," *Arizona Capitol Times*, (Dec. 8, 2020), available at https://azcapitoltimes.com/news/2020/12/08/federal-judge-hears-arguments-in-election-challenge/; "Meet the Justices," Arizona Judicial Branch, (Dec. 8, 2020), available at http://web.archive.org/web/20201208032900/https://www.azcourts.gov/meetthejustices/ (archived); "Brutinel Elected as Next Arizona Supreme Court Chief Justice," *Associated Press*, (Nov. 20, 2018), available at https://apnews.com/article/27b725d44d384e2cb7a0e491ac82fe7f; Bob Christie, "Ducey Names 2 to New Arizona Supreme Court Seats," *Associated Press*, (Nov. 28, 2016), available at https://apnews.com/article/26fc7f154b0e4b4fb358987941ded8d0; "Arizona Governor Appoints New Supreme Court Justice," *Associated Press*, (Apr. 26, 2019), available at https://apnews.com/article/4ce4bf1d79724c03b1d4cf36f4b97cf1; Jonathan J. Cooper, "Ducey Appoints Montgomery to Arizona Supreme Court," *Associated Press*, (Sep. 4, 2019), available at https://apnews.com/article/bac43d42185c4b8bb9e8c465a59792c8.

121. Complaint at 1-2, *Boland v. Raffensperger*, No. 2020CV343018 (Ga. Super. Ct. Nov. 30, 2020), available at https://electioncases.osu.edu/wp-content/uploads/2020/11/Boland-v-Raffensperger-Complaint.pdf.

122. Final Order at 5-6, *Boland v. Raffensperger*, No. No. 2020CV343018 (Ga. Super. Ct. Dec. 8, 2020), available at https://electioncases.osu.edu/wp-content/uploads/2020/11/Boland-v-Raffensperger-Order-Dismissing-Complaint.pdf.

123. Order Denying Appeal, *Boland v. Raffensperger*, No. S21M0565 (Ga. Dec. 14, 2020), available at https://electioncases.osu.edu/wp-content/uploads/2020/11/Boland-v-Raffensperger-GA-SC-Order-Denying-Appeal.pdf; Jonathan Ringel, "Deal Picks Krause, Richardson for Fulton Superior," Law.com, (Dec. 28, 2018), available at https://www.law.com/dailyreportonline/2018/12/28/deal-picks-krause-richardson-for-fulton-superior/; "Chief Justice Harold D. Melton," Supreme Court of Georgia, (Oct. 16, 2020), available at http://web.archive.org/web/20201016174745/https://www.gasupreme.us/court-information/biographies/justice-harold-d-melton/ (archived); "Presiding Justice David E. Nahmias," Supreme Court of Georgia, (Nov. 20, 2020), available at http://web.archive.org/web/20201120204518/https://www.gasupreme.us/court-information/biographies/justice-david-e-nahmias/ (archived); "Chief Justice Michael P. Boggs," Supreme Court of Georgia, (last accessed Dec. 3, 2022), available at https://www.gasupreme.us/court-information/biographies/justice-michael-p-boggs/; "Presiding Justice Nels S.D. Peterson," Supreme Court of Georgia, (last accessed Dec. 3, 2022), available at https://www.gasupreme.us/court-information/biographies/justice-nels-s-d-peterson/; "Justice Sarah Hawkins Warren," Supreme Court of Georgia, (last accessed Dec. 3, 2022), available at https://www.gasupreme.us/court-information/biographies/justice-sarah-hawkins-warren/; "Justice Charles J. Bethel," Supreme Court of Georgia, (last accessed Dec. 3, 2022), available at

https://www.gasupreme.us/court-information/biographies/justice-charles-j-bethel/; "Justice Carla Wong McMillian," Supreme Court of Georgia, (last accessed Dec. 3, 2022), available at https://www.gasupreme.us/court-information/biographies/justice-carla-wong-mcmillian/.

124. *Wood v. Raffensperger*, 501 F. Supp. 3d 1310, 1317, 1327, 1331 (N.D. Ga. 2020).

125. *Wood v. Raffensperger*, 501 F. Supp. 3d 1310, 1327 (N.D. Ga. 2020).

126. Complaint for Declaratory, Emergency, and Permanent Injunctive Relief, *King v. Whitmer*, Case No. 2:20-cv-13134-LVP-RSW, (E.D. Mich. Nov. 25, 2020), ECF No. 1; *King v. Whitmer*, 505 F. Supp. 3d 720, 738 (E.D. Mich. 2020). In a subsequent decision, the judge called the case "a historic and profound abuse of the judicial process" and sanctioned the attorneys who filed the lawsuit *King v. Whitmer*, 556 F. Supp. 3d 680, 688-89 (E.D. Mich. 2021).

127. Opinion and Order at 1, 4, *Stoddard v. City Election Commission*, No. 20-014604-CZ, (Mich. Cty. Cir. Ct. Nov. 6, 2020), available at https://www.michigan.gov/-/media/Project/Websites/AG/releases/2020/november/Stoddard_et_al_v_City_Election_Commission_et_al_-_11-06-2020.pdf?rev=2fa32f93caa94365a1ee8c1c492a4e75.

128. Opinion and Order at 12-13, *Costantino v. Detroit*, No. 20-014780-AW, (Mich. Cty. Cir. Ct. Nov. 13, 2020), available at https://electioncases.osu.edu/wp-content/uploads/2020/11/Costantino-v-Detroit-Opinion-and-Order.pdf.

129. *Law v. Whitmer*, No. 10 OC 00163 1B, 2020 Nev. Unpub. LEXIS 1160, at *1, 29-31, 33, 48-49, 52, 54 (Nev. Dec. 8, 2020), available at https://casetext.com/case/law-v-whitmer-1 (attaching and affirming lower court decision).

130. *Law v. Whitmer*, No. 10 OC 00163 1B, 2020 Nev. Unpub. LEXIS 1160, at *3-4 (Nev. Dec. 8, 2020), available at https://casetext.com/case/law-v-whitmer-1 (attaching and affirming lower court decision).

131. *Donald J. Trump for President v. Boockvar*, 502 F. Supp. 3d 899, 906 (M.D. Pa. 2020).

132. *Donald J. Trump for President v. Boockvar*, 803 Fed. App'x. 377, 381 (M.D. Pa. 2020).

133. "Eleven Nominations Sent to the Senate Today," Trump White House Archives, (June 19, 2017), available at https://trumpwhitehouse.archives.gov/presidential-actions/eleven-nominations-sent-senate-today-3/.

134. Complaint at 72, *Trump v. Wisconsin Election Commission*, 506 F. Supp. 3d 620 (E.D. Wis. 2020) (No. 2:20-cv-01785), ECF No. 1; *Trump v. Wisconsin Election Commission*, 506 F. Supp. 3d 620, 625 (E.D. Wis. 2020) (dismissing case with prejudice).

135. *Trump v. Wisconsin Election Commission*, 506 F. Supp. 3d 620, 637-39 (E.D. Wis. 2020).

136. *Trump v. Wisconsin Election Commission*, 983 F.3d 919, 922 (7th Cir. 2020); Bill Glauber, "Federal Appeals Court Turns Down Donald Trump Push to Overturn Election Results in Wisconsin," *Milwaukee Journal Sentinel*, (Dec. 24, 2020), available at https://www.jsonline.com/story/news/politics/elections/2020/12/24/federal-appeals-court-rejects-trump-bid-overturn-wisconsin-results/4043650001/.

137. Select Committee to Investigate the January 6th Attack on the United States Capitol, *Hearing on the January 6th Investigation*, 117th Cong., 2d sess., (June 23, 2022), available at https://www.govinfo.gov/committee/house-january6th.

138. Select Committee to Investigate the January 6th Attack on the United States Capitol, Transcribed Interview of Eric Herschmann, (Apr. 6, 2022), pp. 170-71.

139. For example, Select Committee data analysts found that certain legacy media networks played a role in promoting false claims of voter fraud and other election conspiracies. *See* Staff Memorandum from Select Committee to Investigate the January 6th Attack on the United States Capitol Data Analysts, "Legacy Media Analysis," (Dec. 3, 2022).

140. Center for an Informed Public, Digital Forensic Research Lab, Graphika, & Stanford Internet Observatory, *The Long Fuse: Misinformation and the 2020 Election*, (Jun. 15, 2021), p. 173, available at https://stacks.stanford.edu/file/druid:tr171zs0069/EIP-Final-Report.pdf.

141. Center for an Informed Public, Digital Forensic Research Lab, Graphika, & Stanford Internet Observatory, *The Long Fuse: Misinformation and the 2020 Election*, (Jun. 15, 2021), p. 82, available at https://stacks.stanford.edu/file/druid:tr171zs0069/EIP-Final-Report.pdf.

142. Select Committee to Investigate the January 6th Attack on the United States Capitol, Transcribed Interview of William Barr, (June 2, 2022), p. 9.

143. Select Committee to Investigate the January 6th Attack on the United States Capitol, Transcribed Interview of William Barr, (June 2, 2022), p. 10.

144. Select Committee to Investigate the January 6th Attack on the United States Capitol, Transcribed Interview of William Barr, (June 2, 2022), p. 9; Select Committee to Investigate the January 6th Attack on the United States Capitol, Transcribed Interview of Richard Peter Donoghue, (Oct. 1, 2021), p. 67.

145. Select Committee to Investigate the January 6th Attack on the United States Capitol, Transcribed Interview of Richard Peter Donoghue, (Oct. 1, 2021) pp. 59-60.

146. Select Committee to Investigate the January 6th Attack on the United States Capitol, Transcribed Interview of William Barr, (June 2, 2022), pp. 36-37.

147. Select Committee to Investigate the January 6th Attack on the United States Capitol, *Hearing on the January 6th Investigation*, 117th Cong., 2d sess., (June 23, 2022), available at https://www.govinfo.gov/committee/house-january6th.

148. Select Committee to Investigate the January 6th Attack on the United States Capitol, *Hearing on the January 6th Investigation*, 117th Cong., 2d sess., (June 23, 2022), available at https://www.govinfo.gov/committee/house-january6th; *see also* Select Committee to Investigate the January 6th Attack on the United States Capitol, Transcribed Interview of Jeffrey Rosen, (Oct. 13, 2022), p. 60.

149. Select Committee to Investigate the January 6th Attack on the United States Capitol, Transcribed Interview of Richard Peter Donoghue, (Oct. 1, 2021), pp. 60-61, 63-64.

150. Select Committee to Investigate the January 6th Attack on the United States Capitol, Transcribed Interview of Richard Peter Donoghue, (Oct. 1, 2021), pp. 53, 67.

151. Select Committee to Investigate the January 6th Attack on the United States Capitol, Transcribed Interview of Richard Peter Donoghue, (Oct. 1, 2021), pp. 59-60.

152. Select Committee to Investigate the January 6th Attack on the United States Capitol, Transcribed Interview of Richard Peter Donoghue, (Oct. 1, 2021), pp. 61-62.

153. Select Committee to Investigate the January 6th Attack on the United States Capitol, Transcribed Interview of Richard Peter Donoghue, (Oct. 1, 2021), pp. 54-55.

154. *See, e.g.*, "Transcript of Trump's Speech at Rally Before US Capitol Riot," *Associated Press*, (Jan. 13, 2021), available at https://apnews.com/article/election-2020-joe-biden-donald-trump-capitol-siege-media-e79eb5164613d6718e9f4502eb471f27; *Law v. Whitmer*, No. 10 OC 00163 1B, 2020 Nev. Unpub. LEXIS 1160, at *3-4 (Nev. Dec. 8, 2020), available at https://casetext.com/case/law-v-whitmer-1 (attaching and affirming lower court decision); *Donald J. Trump for President v. Boockvar*, 502 F. Supp. 3d 899, 906 (M.D. Pa. 2020); *Wood v. Raffensperger*, 501 F. Supp. 3d 1310, 1317, 1327, 1331 (N.D. Ga. 2020); Donald J. Trump (@realDonaldTrump), Twitter, Dec. 26, 6:23 a.m. ET, available at http://web.archive.org/web/20201228020228/https://twitter.com/realDonaldTrump/status/1342974373632876545 (archived); Rudy Giuliani's Common Sense, "WATCH this BEFORE January 6th | Rudy Giuliani's Common Sense | Ep. 100," Rumble, at 29:30, available at https://rumble.com/embed/vcrv8j/?pub=4.

155. "Fact Checks," Michigan Department of State, (last accessed on Dec. 3, 2022), available at https://www.michigan.gov/sos/faqs/elections-and-campaign-finance/fact-checks.

156. *See, e.g.,* "Secretary of State's Office Debunks Ware County Voting Machine Story," Georgia Secretary of State, (Dec. 7, 2020), available at https://sos.ga.gov/news/secretary-states-office-debunks-ware-county-voting-machine-story; "News Conference on Georgia Vote Count," C-SPAN, Nov. 9, 2020, available at https://www.c-span.org/video/?477943-1/news-conference-georgia-vote-count; "Georgia Election Security," C-SPAN, Jan. 4, 2021, available at https://www.c-span.org/video/?507710-1/georgia-election-official-refutes-president-trumps-voter-fraud-allegations.

157. *See, e.g.,* PBS NewsHour, "WATCH: Wisconsin Elections Commission Gives Vote Counting Update," YouTube, Nov. 4, 2020, available at https://www.youtube.com/watch?v=Yg5liyyrObc.

158. *See, e.g.,* Declaration of Charles Stewart III, *Trump v. Raffensperger,* No. 2020CV33255 (Ga. Super. Ct. filed Dec. 14, 2020) (expert declaration of political scientist at MIT); *Examining Irregularities in the 2020 Election Before the S. Comm. on Homeland Security and Governmental Affairs,* 116th Cong. (Dec. 16, 2020) (statement of Chris Krebs, former Director of the Cybersecurity and Infrastructure Security Agency); "Scientists Say No Credible Evidence of Computer Fraud in the 2020 Election Outcome, But Policymakers Must Work with Experts to Improve Confidence," Matt Blaze's Exhaustive Search, (Nov. 16, 2020), available at https://www.mattblaze.org/blog/election-letter/.

159. Search results for "Dominion," Trump Twitter Archive V2, (last accessed Dec. 12, 2022), available at https://www.thetrumparchive.com/?searchbox=%22dominion%22.

160. *See, e.g.,* "Remarks by President Trump During Thanksgiving Video Teleconference with Members of the Military," Trump White House archives, (Nov. 27, 2020), available at https://trumpwhitehouse.archives.gov/briefings-statements/remarks-president-trump-thanksgiving-video-teleconference-members-military/; Factba.se, "Interview: Maria Bartiromo Interviews Donald Trump on Fox News – November 29, 2020," Vimeo, Nov. 29, 2020, available at https://factba.se/trump/transcript/donald-trump-interview-fox-news-sunday-morning-futures-maria-bartiromo-november-29-2020; "Donald Trump Speech on Election Fraud Claims Transcript December 2," Rev, (Dec. 2, 2020), available at https://www.rev.com/blog/transcripts/donald-trump-speech-on-election-fraud-claims-transcript-december-2; Factba.se, "Donald Trump Vlog: Contesting Election Results – December 22, 2020," (Dec. 22, 2020), available at https://factba.se/transcript/donald-trump-vlog-contesting-election-results-december-22-2020; "Donald Trump Rally Speech Transcript Dalton, Georgia: Senate Runoff Election," Rev, (Jan. 4, 2021), available at https://www.rev.com/blog/transcripts/donald-trump-rally-speech-transcript-dalton-georgia-senate-runoff-election; "Transcript of Trump's Speech at Rally Before US Capitol Riot," *Associated Press,* (Jan. 13, 2021), available at https://apnews.com/article/election-2020-joe-biden-donald-trump-capitol-siege-media-e79eb5164613d6718e9f4502eb471f27.

161. J.M. Rieger, "The False Claims from Fox News and Trump Allies Cited in Dominion's $1.6 Billion Lawsuit," *Washington Post,* (Mar. 26, 2021), available at https://www.washingtonpost.com/politics/2021/03/26/fox-trump-election-dominion/.

162. Elahe Izadi and Sarah Ellison, "Fox News Has Dropped 'Lou Dobbs Tonight,' Promoter of Trump's False Election Fraud Claims," *Washington Post,* (Feb. 5, 2021), available at https://www.washingtonpost.com/media/2021/02/05/lou-dobbs-canceled-fox/; 60 Minutes, "Dominion Voting Systems and the Baseless Conspiracy Theories about the 2020 Election | 60 Minutes," YouTube, at 2:12 – 3:20, (Oct. 23, 2022), at 2:12-2:51, available at https://youtu.be/492jILlPtlA?t=132.

163. Donald J. Trump (@realDonaldTrump), Twitter, Nov. 12, 2020 11:34 a.m. ET, available at http://web.archive.org/web/20201112163413/https://twitter.com/realDonaldTrump/status/1326926226888544256 (archived).

164. Documents on file with the Select Committee to Investigate the January 6th Attack on the United States Capitol (Zach Parkinson Production), Parkinson0388-0407 (Internal Trump Campaign memo dated November 12, 2020); Select Committee to Investigate the January 6th Attack on the United States Capitol, Deposition of Andrew Zachary "Zach" Parkinson, (May 18, 2022), pp. 46-47.

165. Documents on file with the Select Committee to Investigate the January 6th Attack on the
      United States Capitol (Zach Parkinson Production), Parkinson0388-0407 (Internal Trump
      Campaign memo dated November 12, 2020).

166. Select Committee to Investigate the January 6th Attack on the United States Capitol, Depo-
      sition of Jason Miller, (Feb. 3, 2022), pp. 117, 133.

167. Documents on file with the Select Committee to Investigate the January 6th Attack on the
      United States Capitol (Mark Meadows Production), MM007666, MM007669 (November 12,
      2020, email and attachment from Jason Miller to Mark Meadows transmitting abridged and
      full internal Trump Campaign memo); Documents on file with the Select Committee to
      Investigate the January 6th Attack on the United States Capitol (Mark Meadows Produc-
      tion), MM011902, MM011974 (Nov. 12 and 13, 2020 text messages from Jason Miller to Mark
      Meadows discussing the investigation into Dominion and the lack of evidence of foreign
      interference).

168. Select Committee to Investigate the January 6th Attack on the United States Capitol, Depo-
      sition of Kayleigh McEnany, (Jan. 12, 2022), pp. 143, 291.

169. Donald J. Trump (@realDonaldTrump), Twitter, Nov. 16, 2020 8:22 a.m. ET, available at
      https://www.thetrumparchive.com/?results=1&searchbox=%22engineered+by+china%22
      (archived); Donald J. Trump (@realDonaldTrump), Twitter, Nov. 16, 2020 8:26 a.m. ET, avail-
      able at http://web.archive.org/web/20201116132750/https://twitter.com/realdonaldtrump/
      status/1328328547598000130 (archived).

170. "Joint Statement from Elections Infrastructure Government Coordinating Council & the
      Election Infrastructure Sector Coordinating Executive Committees," Department of Home-
      land Security's Cybersecurity & Infrastructure Security Agency, (Nov. 12, 2020), available at
      https://www.cisa.gov/news/2020/11/12/joint-statement-elections-infrastructure-
      government-coordinating-council-election.

171. Mark Bowden and Matthew Teague, "How a County Clerk in Michigan Found Herself at the
      Center of Trump's Attempt to Overthrow the Election," *Time*, (Dec. 15, 2021), available at
      https://time.com/6128812/the-steal-antrim-county-michigan/; Emma Brown, Aaron C.
      Davis, Jon Swaine, and Josh Dawsey, "The Making of a Myth," *Washington Post*, (May 9,
      2021), available at https://www.washingtonpost.com/investigations/interactive/2021/
      trump-election-fraud-texas-businessman-ramsland-asog/.

172. Steven Nelson, "Michigan Republicans Claim Software Issue Undercounted Trump Votes,"
      New York Post, (Nov. 6, 2020), available at https://nypost.com/2020/11/06/michigan-gop-
      claims-software-issue-undercounted-trump-votes/.

173. "Isolated User Error in Antrim County Does Not Affect Election Results, Has No Impact on
      Other Counties or States," Michigan Secretary of State, (Nov. 7, 2020), available at https://
      www.michigan.gov/-/media/Project/Websites/sos/30lawens/Antrim_Fact_Check.pdf?rev=
      7a929e4d262e4532bbe574a3b82ddbcf; "Hand Audit of All Presidential Election Votes in
      Antrim County Confirms Previously Certified Results, Voting Machines Were Accurate,"
      Michigan Secretary of State, (Dec. 17, 2020), available at https://www.michigan.gov/sos/
      resources/news/2020/12/17/hand-audit-of-all-presidential-election-votes-in-antrim-
      county-confirms-previously-certified-result; J. Alex Halderman, *Analysis of the Antrim
      County, Michigan November 2020 Election Incident*, (Mar. 26, 2021), pp. 17-27, available at
      https://www.michigan.gov/-/media/Project/Websites/sos/30lawens/Antrim.pdf?rev=
      fbfe881cdc0043a9bb80b783d1bb5fe9; Michigan Senate Oversight Committee, *Report on the
      November 2020 Election in Michigan*, (June 23, 2021), pp. 14-19, 36-55, available at https://
      misenategopcdn.s3.us-east-1.amazonaws.com/99/doccuments/20210623/
      SMPO_2020ElectionReport_2.pdf.

174. Michigan Senate Oversight Committee, *Report on the November 2020 Election in Michigan*,
      (June 23, 2021), pp. 14-15, available at https://misenategopcdn.s3.us-east-
      1.amazonaws.com/99/doccuments/20210623/SMPO_2020ElectionReport_2.pdf.

175. "Isolated User Error in Antrim County Does Not Affect Election Results, Has No Impact on
      Other Counties or States," Michigan Secretary of State website, (Nov. 7, 2020), available at

https://www.michigan.gov/-/media/Project/Websites/sos/30lawens/
Antrim_Fact_Check.pdf?rev=7a929e4d262e4532bbe574a3b82ddbcf.

176. Michigan Senate Oversight Committee, *Report on the November 2020 Election in Michigan*, (June 23, 2021), pp. 14-19, available at https://misenategopcdn.s3.us-east-1.amazonaws.com/99/doccuments/20210623/SMPO_2020ElectionReport_2.pdf.

177. Documents on file with the Select Committee to Investigate the January 6th Attack on the United States Capitol (National Archives Production), 076P-R000010292_0001 (November 12, 2020, email from Tim Walberg to Molly Michel re: Additional Presidential Phone call follow up).

178. Select Committee to Investigate the January 6th Attack on the United States Capitol, Transcribed Interview of Chad Wolf, (Jan. 21, 2022), pp. 70-74; Documents on file with the Select Committee to Investigate the January 6th Attack on the United States Capitol, (Department of Homeland Security Production), CTRL0000033284, (Nov. 13, 2020, email from Molly Michael to Chad Wolf titled "Re: Michigan Letter").

179. Select Committee to Investigate the January 6th Attack on the United States Capitol, Transcribed Interview of Chad Wolf, (Jan. 21, 2022), pp. 72-74; Documents on file with the Select Committee to Investigate the January 6th Attack on the United States Capitol, (Department of Homeland Security Production), CTRL0000033284, (Nov. 13, 2020, email from Molly Michael to Chad Wolf titled "Re: Michigan Letter"); Select Committee to Investigate the January 6th Attack on the United States Capitol, Transcribed Interview of Chad Wolf, (Jan. 21, 2022), Exhibit 44, CTRL0000926977 (Nov. 13, 2020 letter to Michigan Secretary of State Jocelyn Benson from Michigan State Senators Lana Theis and Tom Barrett).

180. Select Committee to Investigate the January 6th Attack on the United States Capitol, Transcribed Interview of Chad Wolf, (Jan. 21, 2022), pp. 74-77 Select Committee to Investigate the January 6th Attack on the United States Capitol, Transcribed Interview of Chad Wolf (Jan. 21, 2022), Exhibit 45, CTRL0000926978, (Nov. 16, 2020 email from Christopher Krebs responding to Chad Wolf, Matthew Travis, and Brandon Wales entitled "RE: Allegations").

181. Select Committee to Investigate the January 6th Attack on the United States Capitol, Transcribed Interview of Chad Wolf, (Jan. 21, 2022), pp. 74-77; Select Committee to Investigate the January 6th Attack on the United States Capitol, Transcribed Interview of Chad Wolf (Jan. 21, 2022), Exhibit 45, CTRL0000926978, (Nov. 16, 2020 email from Christopher Krebs to Chad Wolf, Matthew Travis, and Brandon Wales entitled "RE: Allegations"); "Isolated User Error in Antrim County Does Not Affect Election Results, Has No Impact on Other Counties or States," Michigan Secretary of State, (Nov. 7, 2020), available at https://www.michigan.gov/-/media/Project/Websites/sos/30lawens/Antrim_Fact_Check.pdf?rev=7a929e4d262e4532bbe574a3b82ddbcf.

182. Select Committee to Investigate the January 6th Attack on the United States Capitol, Transcribed Interview of Chad Wolf, (Jan. 21, 2022), pp. 78-80. Even as the acting Secretary of DHS was providing Meadows information he received from his Director of CISA debunking the Dominion claims, the acting Assistant Secretary of DHS, Ken Cuccinelli, was providing back channel information to Meadows in a possible effort to promote the false Dominion claims. *See* Documents on file with the Select Committee to Investigate the January 6th Attack on the United States Capitol (National Archives Production), TEXT0000072, TEXT0000073, (Nov. 12, 2020 text messages from Ken Cuccinelli to Mark Meadows) (Cuccinelli: "I have the dominion list of everywhere the machines are deployed that we know of. [I]t is pretty extensive. It is in my DHS email account. Where do you want me to send it?" Meadows then provided Cuccinelli with his personal email address.)

183. Chris Krebs #Protect2020 (@CISAKrebs), Twitter, Nov. 17, 2020 11:45 a.m. ET, available at https://twitter.com/CISAKrebs/status/1328741106624901120.

184. Documents on file with the Select Committee to Investigate the January 6th Attack on the United States Capitol (National Archives Production), 076P-R000010360_0001, 076P-R000010361_0001, (November 17, 2020 email and attached letter to Christopher Krebs from White House Office of Presidential Personnel, stating respectively that "the President has

terminated your appointment" and that "Pursuant to the direction of the President, your appointment... is hereby terminated, effective immediately").

185.   Donald J. Trump (@realDonaldTrump), Twitter, Nov. 17, 2020 7:07 p.m. ET, available at http://web.archive.org/web/20201118040513/https://twitter.com/realdonaldtrump/status/1328852352787484677 (archived); Donald J. Trump (@realDonaldTrump), Twitter, Nov. 17, 2020 7:07 p.m. ET, available at http://web.archive.org/web/20201118040930/https://twitter.com/realDonaldTrump/status/1328852354049957888 (archived).

186.   "Rudy Giuliani Trump Campaign Press Conference Transcript November 19: Election Fraud Claims," Rev, (Nov. 19, 2020), available at https://www.rev.com/blog/transcripts/rudy-giuliani-trump-campaign-press-conference-transcript-november-19-election-fraud-claims.

187.   "Rudy Giuliani Trump Campaign Press Conference Transcript November 19: Election Fraud Claims," Rev, (Nov. 19, 2020), available at https://www.rev.com/blog/transcripts/rudy-giuliani-trump-campaign-press-conference-transcript-november-19-election-fraud-claims.

188.   Select Committee to Investigate the January 6th Attack on the United States Capitol, Transcribed Interview of Hope Hicks, (Oct. 25, 2022), pp. 88-91. *See also* Tucker Carlson: "Time for Sidney Powell to Show Us Her Evidence: We Asked the Trump Campaign Attorney for Proof of her Bombshell Claims. She Gave Us Nothing," Fox News, (Nov. 19, 2020), available at https://www.foxnews.com/opinion/tucker-carlson-rudy-giuliani-sidney-powell-election-fraud.

189.   Jenna Ellis (@JennaEllisEsq), Twitter, Nov. 22, 2020, 5:23 p.m. ET, available at https://twitter.com/JennaEllisEsq/status/1330638034619035655.

190.   Donald J. Trump, (@realDonaldTrump), Twitter, Nov. 19, 2020 12:41 a.m. ET and 3:47 p.m. ET, available at https://www.thetrumparchive.com/?searchbox=%22dominion-izing%22 (archived).

191.   One America News Network, "Cyber Analyst on Dominion Voting: Shocking Vulnerabilities," YouTube, at 0:41-1:14, 1:37-2:23, 2:42-3:36, Nov. 15, 2020, available at https://www.youtube.com/watch?v=eKcPoCNW8AA.

192.   Ron Watkins, (@codemonkeyz), Twitter, Nov. 19, 2020 12:45 a.m. ET, available at http://web.archive.org/web/20201121092200/https://twitter.com/CodeMonkeyZ/status/1329299640848584710 (archived); Ron Watkins, (@codemonkeyz), Twitter, Nov. 19, 2020 12:46 a.m. ET, available at http://web.archive.org/web/20201201175413/https://twitter.com/CodeMonkeyZ/status/1329300069623820289 (archived); Donald J. Trump, Twitter, Nov. 21, 2020 11:30 p.m. ET, Nov. 21, 2020, 11:31 p.m. ET, Nov. 21, 2020, 11:32 p.m. ET, Nov. 22, 2020, 3:35 p.m. ET, available at https://www.thetrumparchive.com/?searchbox=%22dominion-izing%22&dates=%5B%222020-11-20%22%2C%222020-11-24%22%5D (archived).

193.   Barr met with President Trump between election day and January 6th on November 23, December 1, and December 14. *See* Select Committee to Investigate the January 6th Attack on the United States Capitol, Transcribed Interview of William Barr, (Jun. 2, 2022), pp. 16, 22, 28.

194.   Select Committee to Investigate the January 6th Attack on the United States Capitol, Transcribed Interview of William Barr, (Jun. 2, 2022), pp. 25, 27, 50; William Barr, *One Damn Thing After Another: Memoirs of an Attorney General*, (New York: HarperCollins, 2022), at pp. 539, 554.

195.   Select Committee to Investigate the January 6th Attack on the United States Capitol, Transcribed Interview of William Barr, (Jun. 2, 2022), p. 19.

196.   Factba.se, "Interview: Maria Bartiromo Interviews Donald Trump on Fox News - November 29, 2020," Vimeo, Nov. 29, 2020, at. 1:00-1:43, 3:23-4:36, available at https://vimeo.com/485180163.

197.   Factba.se, "Interview: Maria Bartiromo Interviews Donald Trump on Fox News - November 29, 2020," Vimeo, at 1:00-1:43, Nov. 29, 2020, available at https://vimeo.com/485180163.

198. Factba.se, "Interview: Maria Bartiromo Interviews Donald Trump on Fox News - November 29, 2020," Vimeo, at 1:50–2:40, Nov. 29, 2020, available at https://vimeo.com/485180163.

199. Factba.se, "Interview: Maria Bartiromo Interviews Donald Trump on Fox News - November 29, 2020," Vimeo, at 3:50–4:24, 22:40–23:52, 24:26–24:50, Nov. 29, 2020, available at https://vimeo.com/485180163.

200. Select Committee to Investigate the January 6th Attack on the United States Capitol, Transcribed Interview of William Barr, (Jun. 2, 2022), pp. 22, 25–26.

201. Select Committee to Investigate the January 6th Attack on the United States Capitol, Transcribed Interview of William Barr, (Jun. 2, 2022), pp. 22, 25–26.

202. "Donald Trump Speech on Election Fraud Claims Transcript December 2," Rev, (Dec. 2, 2020), available at https://www.rev.com/blog/transcripts/donald-trump-speech-on-election-fraud-claims-transcript-december-2.

203. *King v. Whitmer*, 505 F. Supp. 3d 720, 738 (E.D. Mich. 2020)

204. *Bowyer v. Ducey*, 506 F. Supp. 3d 699, 723 (D. Ariz. 2020) (finding the complaint "void of plausible allegations that Dominion voting machines were hacked or compromised in Arizona during the 2020 General Election").

205. "Isolated User Error in Antrim County Does Not Affect Election Results, Has No Impact on Other Counties or States," Michigan Secretary of State, (Nov. 7, 2020), available at https://www.michigan.gov/-/media/Project/Websites/sos/30lawens/Antrim_Fact_Check.pdf?rev=7a929e4d262e4532bbe574a3b82ddbcf.

206. Decision and Order Granting Plaintiff's Motion for an Ex Parte Temporary Restraining Order, Show Cause Order and Preliminary Injunction, No. 2020009238CZ (Mich. Cty. Cir. Ct. Dec. 4, 2020).

207. Rudy W. Giuliani (@RudyGiuliani), Twitter, Dec. 4, 2020 7:12 p.m. ET, available at https://twitter.com/RudyGiuliani/status/1335014224532221952?s=20&t=20AZkk4gS2DeBo6q6QR-mw; Ronn Blitzer, "Trump Legal Team Celebrates after Michigan Judge Allows Probe of Dominion Voting Machines," Fox News, (Dec. 6, 2020), available at https://www.foxnews.com/politics/trump-legal-team-michigan-antrim-county-judge-order-dominion-machines; Select Committee to Investigate the January 6th Attack on the United States Capitol, Transcribed Interview of Bernard Kerik, (Jan. 13, 2022), pp. 19, 147.

208. Documents on file with the Select Committee to Investigate the January 6th Attack on the United States Capitol (National Archives Production), 076P-R000001368_00001, pp. 1, 6 (Allied Security Operations Group Antrim Michigan Forensics Report, dated Dec. 13, 2020).

209. Documents on file with the Select Committee to Investigate the January 6th Attack on the United States Capitol (National Archives Production), 076P-R00001254_00001 (December 14, 2020, email from Joanna Miller to Peter Navarro attaching the ASOG Report and noting that "POTUS and VPOTUS are briefed").

210. *See, e.g.,* Documents on file with the Select Committee to Investigate the January 6th Attack on the United States Capitol (Department of Justice Production), HouseSelect-Jan6-PartII-01132022-000798(December 14, 2020, email from Molly Michael re: From POTUS asking the AG to look at ASOG report); Documents on file with the Select Committee to Investigate the January 6th Attack on the United States Capitol (National Archives Production), 076P-R000001337_00001(December 14, 2020, email from Molly Michael to Acting Attorney General Jeffrey Rosen re: From POTUS attaching ASOG report); Documents on file with the Select Committee to Investigate the January 6th Attack on the United States Capitol (National Archives Production), 076P-R000001367_00001(December 14, 2020, email from Molly Michael to Michigan Senate Majority Leader Mike Shirkey re: From POTUS attaching ASOG report); Documents on file with the Select Committee to Investigate the January 6th Attack on the United States Capitol (National Archives Production) 076P-R000001361_00001(December 14, 2020, email from Molly Michael to Senator Kelly Loeffler re: From POTUS attaching ASOG report); Documents on file with the Select Committee to Investigate the January 6th Attack

on the United States Capitol (National Archives Production), 076P-
R000001358_00001(December 14, 2020, email from Molly Michael to Arizona Governor Doug
Ducey re: From POTUS attaching ASOG report); Documents on file with the Select Commit-
tee to Investigate the January 6th Attack on the United States Capitol (National Archives
Production), 076P-R000001370_00001 (December 14, 2020, email from Molly Michael to
Republican Party Chairwoman Ronna McDaniel re: From POTUS attaching ASOG report);
Documents on file with the Select Committee to Investigate the January 6th Attack on the
United States Capitol (National Archives Production), 076P-R000001378_00001 (December
14, 2020, email from Molly Michael to Pennsylvania State Senator Doug Mastriano re: From
POTUS attaching ASOG report).

211.   Donald J. Trump (@realDonaldTrump), Twitter, Dec. 14, 2020 2:59 p.m. ET, available at
        http://web.archive.org/web/20201214214435/https://twitter.com/realdonaldtrump/status/
        1338574268154646528 (archived).

212.   Select Committee to Investigate the January 6th Attack on the United States Capitol, Tran-
        scribed Interview of William Barr, (Jun. 2, 2022), pp. 28-29.

213.   Select Committee to Investigate the January 6th Attack on the United States Capitol, Tran-
        scribed Interview of William Barr, (Jun. 2, 2022), p. 29.

214.   Select Committee to Investigate the January 6th Attack on the United States Capitol, Tran-
        scribed Interview of William Barr, (Jun. 2, 2022), pp. 29-30.

215.   Select Committee to Investigate the January 6th Attack on the United States Capitol, Tran-
        scribed Interview of William Barr, (Jun. 2, 2022), pp. 29-30.

216.   *See, e.g.,* Select Committee to Investigate the January 6th Attack on the United States Capi-
        tol, Transcribed Interview of William Barr, (Jun. 2, 2022), pp. 29-30.

217.   *See* Documents on file with the Select Committee to Investigate the January 6th Attack on
        the United States Capitol (Department of Homeland Security Production) CTRL0000915111,
        CTRL0000915117-CTRL0000915118 (draft analyses of ASOG report). Notably, the final version
        of this review, which had been requested by the Attorney General, was edited by senior
        DHS officials to remove the language most critical of ASOG before being sent to the
        Department of Justice by Acting Assistant Secretary Ken Cuccinelli. *See* Documents on file
        with the Select Committee to Investigate the January 6th Attack on the United States Capi-
        tol (Department of Homeland Security Production) CTRL0000915120 (emails circulating
        draft analyses), CTRL0000926941 (noting report was "currently in the Secretary's office");
        Documents on file with the Select Committee to Investigate the January 6th Attack on the
        United States Capitol (Department of Justice Production) HCOR-Pre-CertificationEvents-
        07262021-000687-HCOR-Pre-CertificationEvents-07262021-000688 (email and report pro-
        vided to Donoghue by Cuccinelli); Select Committee to Investigate the January 6th Attack
        on the United States Capitol, Transcribed Interview of Richard Peter Donoghue, (Oct. 1,
        2021), pp. 29-31.

218.   *See* Michigan Senate Oversight Committee, *Report on the November 2020 Election in Michi-
        gan*, (June 23, 2021), p. 16, available at https://misenategopcdn.s3.us-east-
        1.amazonaws.com/99/doccuments/20210623/SMPO_2020ElectionReport_2.pdf; J. Alex
        Halderman, *Analysis of the Antrim County, Michigan November 2020 Election Incident*,"
        (Mar. 26, 2021), available at https://www.michigan.gov//media/Project/Websites/sos/
        30lawens/Antrim.pdf?rev=fbfe881cdc0043a9bb80b783d1bb5fe9.

219.   For example, President Trump and others frequently cited ASOG's finding that the Domin-
        ion machines had a "68% error rate," but that conclusion was based on a complete misun-
        derstanding of the scanner log files reviewed by ASOG. Their report also claimed that, due
        to these perceived "errors," a "staggering number of votes" were determined through an
        adjudication process that allowed for manipulation of votes, but no adjudication software
        was installed on the Dominion machines. J. Alex Halderman, *Analysis of the Antrim County,
        Michigan November 2020 Election Incident*, (Mar. 26, 2021), pp. 40-41, available at https://
        www.michigan.gov/-/media/Project/Websites/sos/30lawens/Antrim.pdf?rev=
        fbfe881cdc0043a9bb80b783d1bb5fe9.

220. Halderman concluded that "I am not aware of any credible evidence that any security problem was ever exploited against Antrim County's election system. As my analysis shows, the anomalies that occurred in the November 2020 results are fully explained by human error." J. Alex Halderman, *Analysis of the Antrim County, Michigan November 2020 Election Incident*, (Mar. 26, 2021), p. 46, available at https://www.michigan.gov/-/media/Project/Websites/sos/30lawens/Antrim.pdf?rev=fbfe881cdc0043a9bb80b783d1bb5fe9.

221. "Audits of the November 3, 2020 General Election," Michigan Secretary of State, (April 21, 2021), p. 32, available at https://www.michigan.gov/-/media/Project/Websites/sos/30lawens/BOE_2020_Post_Election_Audit_Report_04_21_21.pdf?rev=a3c7ee8c06984864870c540a266177f2.; "Hand Count Calculation Sheet (Office: President of the United States, County: Antrim)," Michigan Secretary of State, available at https://www.michigan.gov/-/media/Project/Websites/sos/30lawens/AntrimCounty_Presidential_Race_Full_Hand_Count_November2020.pdf?rev=0bf12f08c33444c59bd145fbcfbb3e40.

222. Select Committee to Investigate the January 6th Attack on the United States Capitol, Transcribed Interview of Bernard Kerik, (Jan. 13, 2022), p. 182.

223. Select Committee to Investigate the January 6th Attack on the United States Capitol, *Hearing on the January 6th Investigation*, 117th Cong., 2d sess., (June 23, 2022), available at https://www.govinfo.gov/committee/house-january6th.

224. Select Committee to Investigate the January 6th Attack on the United States Capitol, Transcribed Interview of Derek Lyons, (Mar. 17, 2022), pp. 21-22, 99; Select Committee to Investigate the January 6th Attack on the United States Capitol, Transcribed Interview of Pasquale Anthony "Pat" Cipollone, (Jul. 8, 2022), pp. 44-50.

225. Select Committee to Investigate the January 6th Attack on the United States Capitol, Transcribed Interview of Pasquale Anthony "Pat" Cipollone, (Jul. 8, 2022), pp. 42-43.

226. Select Committee to Investigate the January 6th Attack on the United States Capitol, Transcribed Interview of Pasquale Anthony "Pat" Cipollone, (Jul. 8, 2022), p. 50.

227. Select Committee to Investigate the January 6th Attack on the United States Capitol, Transcribed Interview of Eric Herschmann, (Apr. 6, 2022), p. 129.

228. Select Committee to Investigate the January 6th Attack on the United States Capitol, Transcribed Interview of Robert O'Brien, (Aug. 23, 2022), pp. 163-65.

229. Select Committee to Investigate the January 6th Attack on the United States Capitol, Transcribed Interview of Chad Wolf, (Jan. 21, 2022), pp. 97-98, 102-103; Select Committee to Investigate the January 6th Attack on the United States Capitol, Transcribed Interview of Ken Cuccinelli, (Dec. 7, 2021), pp. 49-54.

230. Select Committee to Investigate the January 6th Attack on the United States Capitol, Deposition of Rudolph Giuliani (May 20, 2022), pp. 157-59; Select Committee to Investigate the January 6th Attack on the United States Capitol, Deposition of Sidney Powell, (May 7, 2022), pp. 102-03; Documents on file with the Select Committee to Investigate the January 6th Attack on the United States Capitol, (Jenna Ellis Production), J.007465Ellis, J.007467Ellis (December 28-29, 2020, emails with Katherine Freiss, Doug Mastriano, Christina Bobb, Giuliani, and others about accessing voting machines); Emma Brown and Jon Swaine, "Inside the Secretive Effort by Trump Allies to Access Voting Machines," *Washington Post*, (Oct. 28, 2022), available at https://www.washingtonpost.com/investigations/2022/10/28/coffee-county-georgia-voting-trump/.

231. Brad Raffensperger, *Integrity Counts* (New York: Simon & Schuster, 2021), p. 191 (reproducing the call transcript);Amy Gardner and Paulina Firozi, "Here's the Full Transcript and Audio of the Call Between Trump and Raffensperger," *Washington Post*, (Jan. 5, 2021), available at https://www.washingtonpost.com/politics/trump-raffensperger-call-transcript-georgia-vote/2021/01/03/2768e0cc-4ddd-11eb-83e3-322644d82356_story.html.

232. Brad Raffensperger, *Integrity Counts* (New York: Simon & Schuster, 2021), p. 191 (reproducing the call transcript); Amy Gardner and Paulina Firozi, "Here's the Full Transcript and

Audio of the Call Between Trump and Raffensperger," *Washington Post*, (Jan. 5, 2021), available at https://www.washingtonpost.com/politics/trump-raffensperger-call-transcript-georgia-vote/2021/01/03/2768e0cc-4ddd-11eb-83e3-322644d82356_story.html.

233. "Donald Trump Rally Speech Transcript Dalton, Georgia: Senate Runoff Election," Rev, (Jan. 4, 2021), available at https://www.rev.com/blog/transcripts/donald-trump-rally-speech-transcript-dalton-georgia-senate-runoff-election.

234. "Donald Trump Rally Speech Transcript Dalton, Georgia: Senate Runoff Election," Rev, (Jan. 4, 2021), available at https://www.rev.com/blog/transcripts/donald-trump-rally-speech-transcript-dalton-georgia-senate-runoff-election.

235. Select Committee to Investigate the January 6th Attack on the United States Capitol, Deposition of Rudolph Giuliani, (May 20, 2022), p. 111.

236. Select Committee to Investigate the January 6th Attack on the United States Capitol, Deposition of Rudolph Giuliani, (May 20, 2022), p. 166.

237. Select Committee to Investigate the January 6th Attack on the United States Capitol, Transcribed Interview of Bernard Kerik (Jan. 13, 2022), p. 182. Kerik also emailed President Trump's chief of staff, Mark Meadows, on December 28, 2020, writing: "We can do all the investigations we want later, but if the president plans on winning, it's the legislators that have to be moved, and this will do just that." Document on file with the Select Committee (National Archives Production) 076P-R000004125_0001.

238. Select Committee to Investigate the January 6th Attack on the United States Capitol, Transcribed Interview of Christina Bobb, (Apr. 21, 2022), p. 46.

239. Select Committee to Investigate the January 6th Attack on the United States Capitol, Deposition of Sidney Powell, (May 7, 2022), pp. 89-96.

240. Defendant's Motion to Dismiss at 27-28, *U.S. Dominion, Inc. v. Powell*, No. 1:21-cv-00040 (D.D.C. filed Mar. 22, 2021), ECF No. 22-2.

241. Justin Gray, "Georgia Election Officials Show Frame-by-Frame What Happened in Fulton Surveillance Video," WSB-TV, (Dec. 4, 2020), https://www.wsbtv.com/news/politics/georgia-election-officials-show-frame-by-frame-what-really-happened-fulton-surveillance-video/T5M3PYIBYFHFFOD3CIB2ULDVDE/.

242. 11Alive, "Second Georgia Senate election hearing," YouTube, at 5:31:50-5:32:45, Dec. 3, 2020, available at https://www.youtube.com/watch?v=hRCXUNOwOjw.

243. *See, e.g.,* Donald J. Trump, (@realDonaldtrump), Twitter, Dec. 14, 2020 8:57 a.m. ET, available at http://web.archive.org/web/20201217181730/https://twitter.com/realDonaldTrump/status/1338483200046354434; Brad Raffensperger, *Integrity Counts* (New York: Simon & Schuster, 2021), p. 191 (reproducing the call transcript); Amy Gardner and Paulina Firozi, "Here's the Full Transcript and Audio of the Call Between Trump and Raffensperger," *Washington Post*, (Jan. 5, 2021), available at https://www.washingtonpost.com/politics/trump-raffensperger-call-transcript-georgia-vote/2021/01/03/2768e0cc-4ddd-11eb-83e3-322644d82356_story.html.

244. Brad Raffensperger, *Integrity Counts* (New York: Simon & Schuster, 2021), p. 191 (reproducing the call transcript); Amy Gardner and Paulina Firozi, "Here's the Full Transcript and Audio of the Call Between Trump and Raffensperger," *Washington Post*, (Jan. 5, 2021), available at https://www.washingtonpost.com/politics/trump-raffensperger-call-transcript-georgia-vote/2021/01/03/2768e0cc-4ddd-11eb-83e3-322644d82356_story.html.

245. Ryan Taylor, "Donald Trump Georgia Rally Transcript Before Senate Runoff Elections December 5," Rev, (Dec. 5, 2020), available at https://www.rev.com/blog/transcripts/donald-trump-georgia-rally-transcript-before-senate-runoff-elections-december-5.

246. "Donald Trump Vlog: Contesting Election Results—December 22, 2020," Factba.se, (Dec. 22, 2020), at 9:11 – 9:31, available at https://factba.se/transcript/donald-trump-vlog-contesting-election-results-december-22-2020.

247. Ryan Taylor, "Donald Trump Georgia Phone Call Transcript with Sec. of State Brad Raffens-
      perger: Says He Wants to 'Find' Votes," Rev, (Jan. 4, 2021), available at https://
      www.rev.com/blog/transcripts/donald-trump-georgia-phone-call-transcript-brad-
      raffensperger-recording.

248. U.S. Senate Committee on the Judiciary, Transcribed Interview of Jeffrey Rosen, (Aug. 7,
      2021), pp. 30-31, available at https://www.judiciary.senate.gov/imo/media/doc/
      Rosen%20Transcript.pdf.

249. Select Committee to Investigate the January 6th Attack on the United States Capitol, Tran-
      scribed Interview of Richard Peter Donoghue, (Oct. 1, 2021), pp. 42-43.

250. Brad Raffensperger, Integrity Counts (New York: Simon & Schuster, 2021), p. 191 (reproduc-
      ing the call transcript); Amy Gardner and Paulina Firozi, "Here's the Full Transcript and
      Audio of the Call Between Trump and Raffensperger," Washington Post, (Jan. 5, 2021), avail-
      able at https://www.washingtonpost.com/politics/trump-raffensperger-call-transcript-
      georgia-vote/2021/01/03/2768e0cc-4ddd-11eb-83e3-322644d82356_story.html.

251. Brad Raffensperger, Integrity Counts (New York: Simon & Schuster, 2021), p. 191 (reproduc-
      ing the call transcript); Amy Gardner and Paulina Firozi, "Here's the Full Transcript and
      Audio of the Call Between Trump and Raffensperger," Washington Post, (Jan. 5, 2021), avail-
      able at https://www.washingtonpost.com/politics/trump-raffensperger-call-transcript-
      georgia-vote/2021/01/03/2768e0cc-4ddd-11eb-83e3-322644d82356_story.html.

252. Brad Raffensperger, Integrity Counts (New York: Simon & Schuster, 2021), p. 191 (reproduc-
      ing the call transcript); Amy Gardner and Paulina Firozi, "Here's the Full Transcript and
      Audio of the Call Between Trump and Raffensperger," Washington Post, (Jan. 5, 2021), avail-
      able at https://www.washingtonpost.com/politics/trump-raffensperger-call-transcript-
      georgia-vote/2021/01/03/2768e0cc-4ddd-11eb-83e3-322644d82356_story.html.

253. Declaration of Frances Watson at 1-3, Pearson v. Kemp, 831 F. App'x. 467 (N.D. Ga. 2020) (No.
      1:20-cv-04809), ECF No. 72-1.

254. Declaration of Frances Watson at 1-3, Pearson v. Kemp, 831 F. App'x. 467 (N.D. Ga. 2020) (No.
      1:20-cv-04809), ECF No. 72-1.

255. U.S. Senate Judiciary Committee, Transcribed Interview of Byung J. "BJay" Pak, (Aug. 11,
      2021), pp. 14-25, available at https://www.judiciary.senate.gov/imo/media/doc/
      Pak%20Transcript.pdf; Response of the Georgia Secretary of State to the Court's Order of
      September 20, 2021 at 4-6, Favorito v. Wan, No. 2020CV343938 (Ga. Super. Ct. filed Oct. 12,
      2021).

256. "Georgia Election Officials Briefing Transcript December 7: Will Recertify Election Results
      Today," Rev, (December 7, 2020), available at https://www.rev.com/blog/transcripts/
      georgia-election-officials-briefing-transcript-december-7-will-recertify-election-results-
      today; Response of the Georgia Secretary of State to the Court's Order of September 20,
      2021 at 4-6, Favorito v. Wan, No. 2020CV343938 (Ga. Super. Ct. filed Oct. 12, 2021).

257. "Georgia Election Officials Briefing Transcript December 7: Will Recertify Election Results
      Today," Rev, (December 7, 2020), available at https://www.rev.com/blog/transcripts/
      georgia-election-officials-briefing-transcript-december-7-will-recertify-election-results-
      today; Response of the Georgia Secretary of State to the Court's Order of September 20,
      2021, at 4-6 and Exhibit A: Videotaped Deposition of James P. Callaway (Deputy Chief Inves-
      tigator of the Office of the Secretary of State) at 29-35, Favorito v. Wan, No. 2020CV343938
      (Ga. Super. Ct. filed Oct. 12, 2021) available at, https://s3.documentcloud.org/documents/
      21084096/favorito-sos-brief-in-response-to-order-of-92021-with-exs-a-and-b.pdf.

258. Declaration of Frances Watson at 2-3, Pearson v. Kemp, 831 F. App'x. 467 (N.D. Ga. 2020) (No.
      1:20-cv-04809), ECF No. 72-1; U.S. Senate Judiciary Committee, Transcribed Interview of
      Byung J. "BJay" Pak, (August 11, 2021), pp. 14-25, available at https://
      www.judiciary.senate.gov/imo/media/doc/Pak%20Transcript.pdf.

259. Documents on file with the Select Committee to Investigate the January 6th Attack on the United States Capitol, (National Archives Production), 076P-R000004670_0001-0013, 076P-R000004888_0001-0013, 076P-R000004948_0001-0013 (January 5, 2021, emails from Molly Michael re: "from POTUS" to Senators Josh Hawley and Ted Cruz and to Representative Jim Jordan attaching Background Briefing on 2020 Fraud).

260. "Transcript of Trump's Speech at Rally Before US Capitol Riot," *Associated Press*, (Jan. 13, 2021), available at https://apnews.com/article/election-2020-joe-biden-donald-trump-capitol-siege-media-e79eb5164613d6718e9f4502eb471f27.

261. *In the Matter of Rudolph W. Giuliani*, No. 2021-00506, slip op at *2, 22 (N.Y. App. Div. May 3, 2021), available at https://int.nyt.com/data/documenttools/giuliani-law-license-suspension/1ae5ad6007c0ebfa/full.pdf.

262. GA House Mobile Streaming, Governmental Affairs 12.10.20, Vimeo – Livestream, at 2:09:03 to - 2:13:10, available at https://livestream.com/accounts/25225474/events/9117221/videos/214677184.

263. Select Committee to Investigate the January 6th Attack on the United States Capitol, *Hearing on the January 6th Investigation*, 117th Cong., 2d sess., (June 21, 2022), available at https://www.govinfo.gov/committee/house-january6th.

264. *See* John Danforth, Benjamin Ginsberg, Thomas B. Griffith, et al., "Lost, Not Stolen: The Conservative Case that Trump Lost and Biden Won the 2020 Presidential Election," (July 2022), p. 3, available at https://lostnotstolen.org/download/378/.

265. Opinion and Order at *6, 13, *Costantino v. Detroit*, No. 20-014780-AW (Mich. Cty. Cir. Ct. filed Nov. 13, 2020), available at https://electioncases.osu.edu/wp-content/uploads/2020/11/Costantino-v-Detroit-Opinion-and-Order.pdf.

266. Complaint, Exhibit 2: Affidavit of Jesse Richard Morgan at 2, 10, *Mecalfe v. Wolf*, 2020 Pa. Commw. LEXIS 794 (Pa. Commw. Ct. 2020) (No. 636 MD 2020), available at https://www.pacourts.us/Storage/media/pdfs/20210603/212420-file-10836.pdf.

267. *See, e.g.*, Donald J. Trump (@realdonaldtrump), Twitter, Dec. 1, 2020 2:31 p.m. ET, available at http://web.archive.org/web/20201202014959/https://twitter.com/realdonaldtrump/status/1333856259662077954 (archived); Donald J. Trump (@realdonaldtrump), Twitter, Dec. 1, 2020 3:49 p.m. ET, available at http://web.archive.org/web/20201201221335/https://twitter.com/realDonaldTrump/status/1333875814585282567 (archived); Donald J. Trump (@realdonaldtrump), Twitter, Dec 2, 2020 6:42 p.m. ET, available at http://web.archive.org/web/20201203024425/https://twitter.com/realDonaldTrump/status/1334327204847775744 (archived).

268. Select Committee to Investigate the January 6th Attack on the United States Capitol, Transcribed Interview of Richard Peter Donoghue, (Oct. 1, 2021), p. 60; Select Committee to Investigate the January 6th Attack on the United States Capitol, Transcribed Interview of William Barr, (Jun. 2, 2022), pp. 45-46.

269. FOX News, "Sean Hannity," Nov. 19, 2020, available at https://archive.org/details/FOXNEWSW_20201120_060000_Hannity?start/1983.1.end/2077.5.

270. Brandon Waltens, "VIDEO: Wagons, Suitcases, and Coolers Roll into Detroit Voting Center at 4 AM [UPDATED]," *Texas Scorecard*, (Nov. 4, 2020), available at https://texasscorecard.com/federal/video-wagons-suitcases-and-coolers-roll-into-detroit-voting-center-at-4-am/; "Rudy Giuliani Trump Campaign Press Conference Transcript November 19: Election Fraud Claims," Rev, (Nov. 19, 2020), at 22:29-26:53, available at https://www.rev.com/blog/transcripts/rudy-giuliani-trump-campaign-press-conference-transcript-november-19-election-fraud-claims.

271. Affidavit of Christopher Thomas ¶ 18, *Texas v. Pennsylvania*, 592 U.S. ____ (2020) (describing ballot delivery), available at https://www.supremecourt.gov/DocketPDF/22/22O155/163387/20201210145418055_22O155%20MI%20APP.pdf; *see also* Opinion and Order at *6, 13, *Costantino v. Detroit*, No. 20-014780-AW (Mich. Cty. Cir. Ct. filed Nov. 13, 2020), available at

https://electioncases.osu.edu/wp-content/uploads/2020/11/Costantino-v-Detroit-Opinion-and-Order.pdf (relying on Christopher Thomas' affidavit to deny a petition for various relief related to allegations that the November 3, 2020 election in Michigan was fraudulent).

272. "How a WXYZ Wagon Sparked False Election Fraud Claims in Detroit," WXYZ, (Nov. 5, 2020), available at https://www.wxyz.com/news/how-a-wxyz-wagon-sparked-false-election-fraud-claims-in-detroit.

273. "Election Summary Report," City of Detroit, (Nov. 19, 2020), available at https://detroitmi.gov/document/november-3-2020-general-election-official-results.

274. A canvassing process in every State verifies that the number of voters indicated as having voted matches the number of ballots cast. If, as claimed, tens of thousands of illegitimate ballots were counted at the TCF Center in Detroit, the total number of ballots counted would be substantially higher than the total number of voters who voted, but in Detroit slightly fewer ballots were counted than voters who were listed as having voted. The net number of ballots for the City of Detroit counting boards was 21 more names than ballots, out of approximately 174,000 absentee votes cast. Michigan Secretary of State, "Audits of the November 3, 2020 General Election," (Apr. 21, 2021), p. 20, available at https://www.michigan.gov/-/media/Project/Websites/sos/30lawens/BOE_2020_Post_Election_Audit_Report_04_21_21.pdf?rev=a3c7ee8c06984864870c540a266177f2.

275. Approximately 4.2 million ballots were cast in-person on election day and 2.6 million mail and absentee ballots were cast. See "Pennsylvania's Election Stats," Pennsylvania Department of State, (accessed Dec. 4, 2022), available at https://www.dos.pa.gov/VotingElections/BEST/Pages/BEST-Election-Stats.aspx;"Official Returns – 2020 Presidential Election," Pennsylvania Department of State, (accessed Dec. 4, 2022), available at https://www.electionreturns.pa.gov/General/SummaryResults?ElectionID=83&ElectionType=G&IsActive=0.

276. Donald J. Trump, (@realDonaldTrump), Twitter, Nov. 28, 2020 12:09 a.m. ET, available at http://web.archive.org/web/20201128080915/https://twitter.com/realDonaldTrump/status/1332552283553476608 (archived), retweeting Senator Doug Mastriano (@SenMastriano), Twitter, Nov. 27, 2020, 1:59 p.m. ET, available at https://twitter.com/SenMastriano/status/1332398733401591808.

277. Jessica Calefati, "Fact-Checking False Claims about Pennsylvania's Presidential Election by Trump and His Allies," Philadelphia Inquirer, (Dec. 7, 2020), available at https://www.inquirer.com/politics/election/pennsylvania-election-results-trump-fraud-fact-check-20201206.html.

278. Donald J. Trump (@realDonaldTrump), Twitter, Dec. 28, 2020, 4:00 p.m. ET, available at http://web.archive.org/web/20201228211304/https://twitter.com/realdonaldtrump/status/1343663159085834248 (archived); Donald J. Trump (@realDonaldTrump), Twitter, Dec. 29, 2020, 8:59 a.m. ET, available at http://web.archive.org/web/20201229205204/https://twitter.com/realDonaldTrump/status/1343919651336712199 (archived); Donald J. Trump (@realDonaldTrump), Twitter, Dec. 29, 2020, 5:55 p.m. ET, available at http://web.archive.org/web/20201229225512/https://twitter.com/realdonaldtrump/status/1344054358418345985. Note that timestamps in archived tweets may reflect a time zone different from that where the tweet originated.

279. See Pennsylvania House Republican Caucus, "PA Lawmakers: Numbers Don't Add Up, Certification of Presidential Results Premature and In Error," (Dec. 28, 2020), available at https://www.pahousegop.com/News/18754/Latest-News/PA-Lawmakers-Numbers-Don%E2%80%99t-Add-Up,-Certification-of-Presidential-Results-Premature-and-In-Error. Representative Ryan also promoted the groundless claim of an unexplained discrepancy of 400,000 mail-in ballots in the state's database, which was based entirely on his ignorance of the fact that the database in question accounts for mail-in ballots and absentee ballots separately. Senate Committee on Homeland Security & Governmental Affairs, Examining Irregularities in the 2020 Election, (Dec. 16, 2020), Written Testimony of Pennsylvania State

Representative Frank Ryan, available at https://www.hsgac.senate.gov/imo/media/doc/ Testimony-Ryan-2020-12-16.pdf; Senate Committee on Homeland Security & Governmental Affairs, Examining Irregularities in the 2020 Election, (Dec. 16, 2020), Letter Submitted by Pennsylvania Secretary of the Commonwealth Kathy Boockvar, available at https:// www.dos.pa.gov/about-us/Documents/statements/2020-12-16-Senator-Johnson-and-Peters.pdf.

280. "Dept. of State: Republicans' Election Claims Are 'Repeatedly Debunked Conspiracy Theories'," WJAC-TV, (Dec. 29, 2020), available at https://wjactv.com/news/local/dept-of-state-republicans-election-claims-are-repeatedly-debunked-conspiracy-theories.

281. Senate Committee on the Judiciary, Transcribed Interview of Richard Donoghue, (Aug. 6, 2021), p. 156, available at https://www.judiciary.senate.gov/imo/media/doc/ Donoghue%20Transcript.pdf.

282. *See* "Donald Trump Rally Speech Transcript Dalton, Georgia: Senate Runoff Election," Rev, (Jan. 4, 2021), at 58:09, available at https://www.rev.com/blog/transcripts/donald-trump-rally-speech-transcript-dalton-georgia-senate-runoff-election; "Transcript of Trump's Speech at Rally Before US Capitol Riot," *Associated Press* (January 13, 2021), available at https://apnews.com/article/election-2020-joe-biden-donald-trump-capitol-siege-media-e79eb5164613d6718e9f4502eb471f27.

283. Select Committee to Investigate the January 6th Attack on the United States Capitol, Transcribed Interview of William Barr, (Jun. 2, 2022), p. 29; Affidavit of Russell James Ramsland, Jr., 556 F. Supp. 3d. 680, 724 (E.D. Mich. 2021), ECF 6-24, available at https:// www.courtlistener.com/docket/18693929/6/24/king-v-whitmer/. Ramsland submitted a similar affidavit in a case in Georgia. *See* Affidavit of Russell Ramsland, *Wood v. Raffensperger*, 501 F. Supp. 3d 1310 (N.D. Ga. 2020), ECF No. 7-1.

284. Affidavit of Russell Ramsland, *Wood v. Raffensperger*, 501 F. Supp. 3d 1310 (N.D. Ga. 2020), ECF No. 7-1.

285. Aaron Blake, "The Trump Campaign's Much-Hyped Affidavit Features a Big, Glaring Error," *Washington Post*, (Nov. 20, 2020), available at https://www.washingtonpost.com/politics/ 2020/11/20/trump-campaigns-much-hyped-affidavit-features-big-glaring-error/.

286. For example, Ramsland claimed 781.91% turnout in North Muskegon (actual turnout: 77.78%); 460.51% turnout in Zeeland Charter Township (actual turnout: 80.11%); and 139.29% turnout in Detroit (actual turnout: 50.88%). *See King v. Whitmer*, 556 F. Supp. 3d. 680, 724 (E.D. Mich. 2021); Michigan Senate Oversight Committee, *Report on the November 2020 Election in Michigan*, (June 23, 2021), available at https://misenategopcdn.s3.us-east-1.amazonaws.com/99/doccuments/20210623/SMPO_2020ElectionReport_2.pdf.

287. *See, e.g.*, "Transcript of Trump's Speech at Rally Before US Capitol Riot," *Associated Press*, (Jan. 13, 2021), available athttps://apnews.com/article/election-2020-joe-biden-donald-trump-capitol-siege-media-e79eb5164613d6718e9f4502eb471f27; "Donald Trump Speech on Election Fraud Claims Transcript December 2" Rev (Dec. 2, 2020), available at https:// www.rev.com/blog/transcripts/donald-trump-speech-on-election-fraud-claims-transcript-december-2; Donald J. Trump (@realDonaldTrump), Twitter, Dec. 3, 2020, 4:11 p.m. ET, available at http://web.archive.org/web/20201203211154/https://twitter.com/ realdonaldtrump/status/1334606278388277253 (archived); "Trump Lawyers Rudy Giuliani & Jenna Ellis Testify Before Michigan House Oversight Committee: Full Transcript," Rev, (Dec. 3, 2020), at 26:13, available at https://www.rev.com/blog/transcripts/trump-lawyers-rudy-giuliani-jenna-ellis-testify-before-michigan-house-oversight-committee-transcript; Affidavit of Mellissa A. Carone, *King v. Whitmer*, 505 F. Supp. 3d 720 (E.D. Mich. 2020), ECF No. 1-5, available at https://www.courtlistener.com/docket/18693929/1/5/king-v-whitmer/.

288. *See, e.g.*, Opinion and Order at *3, 12-13, *Costantino v. Detroit*, No. 20-014780-AW (Mich. Cty. Cir. Ct. filed Nov. 13, 2020), available at https://electioncases.osu.edu/wp-content/ uploads/2020/11/Costantino-v-Detroit-Opinion-and-Order.pdf; Affidavit of Christopher Thomas ¶¶ 2-18, *Texas v. Pennsylvania*, 592 U.S. ____ (2020) (describing his experience and

the process for tabulating votes), available at https://www.supremecourt.gov/DocketPDF/
22/22O155/163387/20201210145418055_22O155%20MI%20APP.pdf.

289. *See, e.g.,* "Transcript of Trump's Speech at Rally Before US Capitol Riot," *Associated Press*
(January 13, 2021), available at https://apnews.com/article/election-2020-joe-biden-
donald-trump-capitol-siege-media-e79eb5164613d6718e9f4502eb471f27; Rudy Giuliani's
Common Sense, "I CAN'T SAY THIS On National Television | Rudy Giuliani | Ep. 98," Rumble,
at 13:10 – 13:25, Dec. 30, 2020, available at https://rumble.com/vex72l-i-cant-say-this-on-
national-television-rudy-giuliani-ep.-98.html.

290. Right Side Broadcasting Network, "LIVE: Georgia House Hearing on Election Fraud, Brad
Raffensperger to Participate 12/23/20," YouTube, at 27:28, 43:02-43:28, Dec. 23, 2020, available at https://www.youtube.com/watch?v=R4cuakECmuA&t=2582s (Testimony of Ryan Germany, counsel to Georgia Secretary of State, before Georgia legislature stating: "The total
number of underage people who voted is zero. We were able to look at everyone who
voted and look at their birthdate in the voter registration system, and I think there was
four people who requested a ballot before they turned 18, and they all turned 18 prior to
November 3rd, which means they're allowed to vote.").

291. *See, e.g.* Bannon's War Room, "Episode 980 – The Border Tipping Point ... Peter Navarro on
the Stolen Election and Desperation in Del Rio," Rumble, May 27, 2021, available at https://
rumble.com/vhpam3-episode-980the-border-tipping-pointpeter-navarro-on-the-stolen-
election-and.html; Bannon's War Room, "Episode 979 – The HQ of the Runaway Train ...
Rachel Maddow's Anna Karenina Moment," Rumble, May 27, 2021, available at https://
rumble.com/vhp8yn-episode-979-the-hq-of-the-runaway-train-rachel-maddows-anna-
karenina-moment.html; Right Side Broadcasting Network, "LIVE: Arizona State Legislature
Holds Public Hearing on 2020 Election," YouTube, at 2:06:33-2:07:02, Nov. 30, 2020, available
at https://www.youtube.com/watch?v=rri6flxaXww.

292. "Proof of Citizenship Requirements," Arizona Secretary of State, (accessed Dec. 4, 2022),
available at https://azsos.gov/elections/voting-election/proof-citizenship-requirements.
In 2013, the Supreme Court struck down Arizona's "evidence-of-citizenship" requirement as
applied to federal elections. *See Arizona v. Inter Tribal Council of Arizona, Inc.,* 570 U.S. 1, 4,
19 (2013). Arizona law allows voters to register as "federal only" voters without proof of
citizenship, but those voters must provide a driver's license or Social Security Number,
which is then checked by election officials against immigration records before the person
is added to voter registration rolls. Daniel González, "Are Undocumented Immigrants Voting Illegally in Arizona?," *Arizona Republic,* (Oct. 27, 2016), available at https://
www.azcentral.com/story/news/politics/elections/2016/10/27/voter-fraud-undocumented-
immigrants-voting-illegally-arizona-donald-trump/91703916/.

293. Documents on file with the Select Committee to Investigate the January 6th Attack on the
United States Capitol, (Mark Meadows Production), MM007288, (November 13, 2020, email
from Bill Stepien to Mark Meadows, Justin Clark, and Jason Miller re: AZ Federal ID Voters);
In the Matter of Rudolph W. Giuliani, No. 2021-00506, slip op at *23-25 (N.Y. App. Div. May 3,
2021), available at https://int.nyt.com/data/documenttools/giuliani-law-license-
suspension/1ae5ad6007c0ebfa/full.pdf.

294. Brad Raffensperger, *Integrity Counts* (New York: Simon & Schuster, 2021), p. 191 (reproducing the call transcript); Amy Gardner and Paulina Firozi, "Here's the Full Transcript and
Audio of the Call Between Trump and Raffensperger," Washington Post, (Jan. 5, 2021), available at https://www.washingtonpost.com/politics/trump-raffensperger-call-transcript-
georgia-vote/2021/01/03/2768e0cc-4ddd-11eb-83e3-322644d82356_story.html.

295. For example, the President alleged in his January 6th speech that large numbers of ballots
were cast on behalf of dead people not just in Georgia but also in Michigan, Nevada, and
Pennsylvania. "Transcript of Trump's Speech at Rally Before US Capitol Riot," Associated
Press (January 13, 2021), https://apnews.com/article/election-2020-joe-biden-donald-
trump-capitol-siege-media-e79eb5164613d6718e9f4502eb471f27; *See also* Rudy Giuliani's
Common Sense, "I CAN'T SAY THIS On National Television | Rudy Giuliani | Ep. 98," Rumble,

at 15:10-15:46, (Dec. 30, 2020, reposted Mar. 22, 2021), available at https://rumble.com/ vex72l-i-cant-say-this-on-national-television-rudy-giuliani-ep.-98.html (making similar claims).

296. Documents on file with the Select Committee to Investigate the January 6th Attack on the United States Capitol, (Alex Cannon Production) AC-0013946, (November 12, 2020, email from Alex Cannon to Matt Wolking, Zach Parkinson, Tim Murtaugh, Ali Pardo, Matthew Morgan, and Andrew Clark titled "Re: dead voters"); Documents on file with the Select Committee to Investigate the January 6th Attack on the United States Capitol, (Tim Murtaugh Production) XXM-0009451 (November 8, 2020, email from Jason Miller to Zach Parkinson, Tim Murtaugh, and Matt Wolking re: PA Death Data stating that quality control checks will "significantly decrease[]" the number of "possible dead voters"), XXM-0009467 (November 8, 2020, email from Jason Miller to Zach Parkinson, Tim Murtaugh, and Matt Wolking re: GA Dead Voters), XXM-0009566 (November 9, 2020 email from Zach Parkinson to Jason Miller, Tim Murtaugh, and Matt Wolking re PA Death Data noting there "may be errors" with their data about people who were dead voters); Mark Niesse, "Alleged 'Dead' Georgia Voters Found Alive and Well after 2020 Election," *Atlanta Journal-Constitution*, (Dec. 27, 2021), available at https://www.ajc.com/politics/alleged-dead-georgia-voters-found-alive-and-well-after-2020-election/DAL3VY7NFNHL5OREMHD7QECOCA/.

297. Documents on file with the Select Committee to Investigate the January 6th Attack on the United States Capitol, (National Archives Production), TEXT0000198, (December 3, 2020, text message from Eric Herschmann to Mark Meadows).

298. Documents on file with the Select Committee to Investigate the January 6th Attack on the United States Capitol, (National Archives Production), TEXT0000198-203, (December 3, 2020, text messages between Eric Herschmann and Mark Meadows).

299. Final Order at 5-6, *Boland v. Raffensperger*, No.2020CV343018 (Ga. Super. Ct. filed Dec. 14 2020), available at https://electioncases.osu.edu/wp-content/uploads/2020/11/Boland-v-Raffensperger-Order-Dismissing-Complaint.pdf.

300. The expert, Bryan Geels, based his claims on a comparison of public voter information to public death records. *See* Documents on file with the Select Committee to Investigate the January 6th Attack on the U.S. Capitol (Christina Bobb Production), BOBB_CONG_00000683-84, 692-93, 706-07 (Affidavit of Bryan Geels dated Dec. 1, 2020, in *Trump v. Barron*, a case filed by the Trump Campaign in a Georgia Superior Court in Fulton County). However, the records reviewed included only name and year of birth for each individual listed. *Id.* at ¶ 28. Based on this limited information, it was impossible for Geels (or anyone else) to conclude that the person with a particular name and birth year was the same person listed in public death records with that name and birth year. *See id.*, at ¶ 50 (only the Secretary of State has the information to conduct a full analysis of this issue); *see also* Declaration of Charles Stewart III at 22, *Trump v. Raffensperger*, No. 2020CV33255 (Ga. Super. Ct. filed Dec. 14, 2020).

301. In Georgia, the Secretary of State found four cases where people voted in the names of deceased individuals. Mark Niesse, "Alleged 'Dead' Georgia Voters Found Alive and Well after 2020 Election," *Atlanta Journal-Constitution*, (Dec. 27, 2021), available at https:// www.ajc.com/politics/alleged-dead-georgia-voters-found-alive-and-well-after-2020-election/DAL3VY7NFNHL5OREMHD7QECOCA/; In Arizona, the Attorney General recently concluded its investigation into claims of supposed dead voters in the 2020 election and found only one instance in which a vote was cast on behalf of a person who died prior to the election. Mark Brnovich, Arizona Attorney General to The Honorable Karen Fann, Arizona Senate President, (Aug. 1, 2022), available at https://www.azag.gov/sites/default/ files/2022-08/Letter%20to%20Fann%20-%20EIU%20Update%20080122.pdf. In Michigan, the Senate Oversight Committee found only two instances in which votes were cast in the names of dead people: one was a clerical error (poll worker attributed vote to deceased father of person with same name residing at same address) and the other was a woman who died four days before the election but had sent in her absentee ballot before her death. Michigan Senate Oversight Committee, *Report on the November 2020 Election in*

Michigan, (June 23, 2021), available at https://misenategopcdn.s3.us-east-1.amazonaws.com/99/doccuments/20210623/SMPO_2020ElectionReport_2.pdf.

302. In an email obtained by the Select Committee, Katherine Friess, a lawyer who worked closely with Giuliani, shared this information with Giuliani and noted, "I don't think this makes a particularly strong case." Documents on file with the Select Committee to Investigate the January 6th Attack on the U.S. Capitol (Christina Bobb Production), BOBB-_CONG_00000621 (January 4, 2021, email from Katherine Friess re: Chairman Graham dead votes memo for your consideration).

303. Documents on file with the Select Committee to Investigate the January 6th Attack on the U.S. Capitol (Cleta Mitchell Production), CM00026036 (January 5, 2021 email from Cleta Mitchell to Richard Perry re: GA Data request by Senator Graham); Documents on file with the Select Committee to Investigate the January 6th Attack on the U.S. Capitol (Christina Bobb Production), BOBB_CONG_00000621 (January 4, 2021, email from Katherine Friess re: Chairman Graham dead votes memo for your consideration); Select Committee to Investigate the January 6th Attack on the United States Capitol, Transcribed Interview of Christina Bobb, (Apr. 21, 2022), pp. 141-42.

304. Documents on file with the Select Committee to Investigate the January 6th Attack on the U.S. Capitol (Christina Bobb Production), BOBB_CONG_00000621 (January 4, 2021, email from Katherine Friess re: Chairman Graham dead votes memo for your consideration).

305. ABC News, "Lindsey Graham Delivers Remarks on Capitol Breach," YouTube, at 3:05-3:30, Jan. 6, 2021, available at https://www.youtube.com/watch?v=JKHkYlRm_XM.

306. Documents on file with the Select Committee to Investigate the January 6th Attack on the United States Capitol, (Chapman University Production), Chapman060742, (Dec. 31, 2020 email from John Eastman to Alex Kaufman and Kurth Hibert); *see also* Documents on file with the Select Committee to Investigate the January 6th Attack on the United States Capitol, (National Archives Production), 076P-R000008384_0001 (December 31, 2020, email from Eric Herschmann to Cleta Mitchell and cc'ed to Mark Meadows and Molly Michael in which Herschmann wrote: "I was concerned about the President signing a verification about facts that may not be sustainable upon detailed scrutiny.").

307. Order Re Privilege of Remaining Documents at 17, *Eastman v. Thompson*, No. 8:22-cv-99-DOC_DFM, (Oct. 19, 2022), ECF no. 372, available at https://www.courtlistener.com/docket/62613089/372/john-c-eastman-v-bennie-g-thompson/.

308. Order Re Privilege of Remaining Documents at 17, *Eastman v. Thompson*, Case 8:22-cv-00099-DOC_DFM, (Oct. 19, 2022), ECF no. 372, available at https://www.courtlistener.com/docket/62613089/372/john-c-eastman-v-bennie-g-thompson/.

309. "Transcript of Trump's Speech at Rally Before US Capitol Riot," *Associated Press*, (Jan. 13, 2021), https://apnews.com/article/election-2020-joe-biden-donald-trump-capitol-siege-media-e79eb5164613d6718e9f4502eb471f27.

310. "Transcript of Trump's Speech at Rally Before US Capitol Riot," *Associated Press*, (Jan. 13, 2021), https://apnews.com/article/election-2020-joe-biden-donald-trump-capitol-siege-media-e79eb5164613d6718e9f4502eb471f27.

311. "Transcript of Trump's Speech at Rally Before US Capitol Riot," *Associated Press*, (Jan. 13, 2021), https://apnews.com/article/election-2020-joe-biden-donald-trump-capitol-siege-media-e79eb5164613d6718e9f4502eb471f27.

312. *See* "Donald Trump 2020 Election Night Speech Transcript," Rev, (Nov. 4, 2020), available at https://www.rev.com/blog/transcripts/donald-trump-2020-election-night-speech-transcript.

313. *See* "Donald Trump Speech 'Save America' Rally Transcript January 6," Rev, (Jan. 6, 2021), available at https://www.rev.com/blog/transcripts/donald-trump-speech-save-america-rally-transcript-january-6.

314. "Transcript of Trump's Speech at Rally Before US Capitol Riot," *Associated Press*, (Jan. 13,

2021), https://apnews.com/article/election-2020-joe-biden-donald-trump-capitol-siege-media-e79eb5164613d6718e9f4502eb471f27.

315. Donald J. Trump (@realDonaldTrump), Twitter, Dec. 19, 2020, 1:42 a.m. ET, available at https://www.thetrumparchive.com/?searchbox=%22wild+protest%22 (archived).

316. "Transcript of Trump's Speech at Rally Before US Capitol Riot," *Associated Press*, (Jan. 13, 2021), https://apnews.com/article/election-2020-joe-biden-donald-trump-capitol-siege-media-e79eb5164613d6718e9f4502eb471f27.

317. "Transcript of Trump's Speech at Rally Before US Capitol Riot," *Associated Press*, (Jan. 13, 2021), https://apnews.com/article/election-2020-joe-biden-donald-trump-capitol-siege-media-e79eb5164613d6718e9f4502eb471f27.

January 2, 2021

Look, we need only 11,000 votes.

Photo by Alex Wong/Getty Images

2

"I JUST WANT TO FIND 11,780 VOTES"

In a now infamous telephone call on January 2, 2021, President Trump pressured Georgia Secretary of State Brad Raffensperger for more than an hour. The President confronted him with multiple conspiracy theories about the election—none of which were true. Raffensperger and other Georgia officials debunked these allegations, one after another, during their call. Under Raffensperger's leadership, Georgia had, by that time, already conducted a statewide hand recount of all ballots. That recount and other post-election reviews proved that there was no widespread fraud, and that voting machines didn't alter the outcome of the election.[1] This should have put President Trump's allegations to rest. But, undeterred by the facts, the President badgered Raffensperger to overturn the Georgia results.

President Trump insisted that "the ballots are corrupt" and someone was "shredding" them.[2] He issued a thinly veiled threat, telling Raffensperger, "it is more illegal for you than it is for them because you know what they did and you're not reporting it."[3] Of course, the Georgia officials weren't doing anything "illegal," and there was nothing to "report." Even so, President Trump suggested that both Raffensperger and his general counsel, Ryan Germany, could face criminal jeopardy.[4] "That's a criminal, that's a criminal offense. And you can't let that happen," the President said.[5] "That's a big risk to you and to Ryan, your lawyer . . . I'm notifying you that you're letting it happen."[6]

And then the President made his demand. "So look. All I want to do is this. I just want to find 11,780 votes, which is one more than we have," President Trump told Raffensperger.[7]

It was a stunning moment. The President of the United States was asking a State's chief election officer to "find" enough votes to declare him the winner of an election he lost.

Raffensperger saw the President's warning to him on January 2nd as a threat. "I felt then—and I still believe today—that this was a threat," Raffensperger wrote in his book.[8] And this threat was multifaceted: first, the President "notifying" Raffensperger and his team of criminal activity could be understood as directing the law-enforcement power of the Federal Government against them. While Raffensperger did not know for certain whether President Trump was threatening such an investigation, he knew Trump had "positional power" as President and appeared to be promising to "make [my] life miserable." [9]

But the threat was also of a more insidious kind. As Raffensperger wrote in his book: "Others obviously thought [it was a threat], too, because some of Trump's more radical followers have responded as if it was their duty to carry out this threat." [10] Raffensperger's deputy held a press conference and publicly warned all Americans, including President Trump, that President Trump's rhetoric endangered innocent officials and private citizens, and fueled death threats against Georgia election workers, sexualized threats directed towards Raffensperger's wife, and harassment at the homes of Georgia election officials.[11] The January 2nd call promised more of the same. The upshot of President Trump's message to Raffensperger was: do what I ask, or you will pay.

President Trump's phone call with Secretary Raffensperger received widespread coverage after it was leaked. But Georgia was not the only State targeted by President Trump and his allies. The call was one element of a larger and more comprehensive effort—much of it unseen by and unknown to the general public—to overturn the votes cast by millions of American citizens across several States.

As Chapter 1 explained, the root of this effort was the "Big Lie": President Trump and his allies publicly claiming that the election was rife with fraud that could have changed the result, even though the President's own advisors, and the Department of Justice, told the President time and time again that this was not the case.[12] But in parallel with this strategy, President Trump and his allies zeroed in on key battleground States the President had lost, leaning on Republican State officials to overrule voters, disregard valid vote counts, and deliver the States' electoral votes to the losing candidate. Had this scheme worked, President Trump could have, for the first time in American history, subverted the results of a lawful election to stay in power. His was a deeply anti-democratic plan: to co-opt State legislatures—through appeals to debunked theories of election fraud, or pure partisan politics—to replace Biden electors with Trump electors, so President Trump would win the electoral vote count in the joint session of Congress on January 6th.

Had enough State officials gone along with President Trump's plot, his attempt to stay in power might have worked. It is fortunate that a critical mass of honorable officials withstood President Trump's pressure to participate in this scheme. They and others who stood up to him closed off avenues for thwarting the election so that, by noon on January 6th, President Trump was left with one desperate, final gambit for holding on to power: sending his armed, angry supporters to the U.S. Capitol.

2.1 THE ELECTORAL COLLEGE, AND PRESIDENT TRUMP'S ATTEMPT TO SUBVERT IT

When Americans vote for a presidential candidate on election day, they are actually casting votes for that candidate's proposed presidential electors to participate in the electoral college. After a State certifies its election results and announces a winner, it also issues a "certificate of ascertainment," which contains the names of the duly chosen electoral college electors. The electors whose names appear as having received the most votes on the certificate of ascertainment will go on to participate in the electoral college, while a losing candidate's proposed electors have no role to play and no standing to participate in the electoral college. This happens after every Presidential election, in each of the fifty States and the District of Columbia.

This process comes from a clause in the U.S. Constitution that gives States the power to choose electoral college electors according to State law.[13] That clause says that each State "shall appoint" electoral college electors "in such [m]anner as the Legislature thereof may direct." All 50 States have decreed that electors will be selected by popular vote.

Tuesday, November 3rd, was the day established by Federal law as election day in 2020. Each State's rules had been set—and courts had weighed in when certain rules were challenged. Polls opened around the country and votes came in, whether in person or via the mail, according to each State's laws.

Over 154 million voters cast votes according to the rules in place on election day.[14] President Trump lost. He and his supporters went to court, filing long-shot legal challenges to the election, but they failed in courts around the country, before judges appointed by executives of both parties (including President Trump himself), and, for those judges who were elected, that are members of both parties.

Rather than abiding by the rule of law and accepting the courts' rulings, President Trump and his advisors tried every which way to reverse the outcome at the State level. They pressured local and State elections officials to stop counting votes once it became clear that former Vice President Joseph Biden would prevail in the final count. They pressured Governors, secretaries of State, and local officials not to certify the popular vote in several swing States that former Vice-President Biden had won. And, when that did not work, they pressured State legislators to disregard the vote counts and instead appoint Trump electors to vote in the electoral college.

This fundamentally anti-democratic effort was premised on the incorrect theory that, because the Constitution assigns to State legislatures the role of directing how electoral college electors are chosen (which every State legislature had done *before* the election, giving that power to the people at the ballot boxes) then the State legislatures could simply choose Trump/Pence electors *after* seeing the election results. In effect, President Trump and his advisors pushed for the rules to be changed after the election—even if it meant disenfranchising millions of Americans.

2.2 THE PLAN EMERGES

More than a month before the Presidential election, the media reported that the Trump Campaign was already developing a fallback plan that would focus on overturning certain election results at the State level. An article published on September 23, 2020, in *The Atlantic* explained, "[a]ccording to sources in the Republican Party at the State and national levels, the Trump Campaign is discussing contingency plans to bypass election results and appoint loyal electors in battleground States where Republicans hold the legislative majority."[15] Ominously, the same reporting predicted, almost exactly, what would later come to pass: "With a justification based on claims of rampant fraud, Trump would ask State legislators to set aside the popular vote and exercise their power to choose a slate of electors directly."[16]

Numerous senior Trump Campaign advisors—including Campaign Manager William Stepien, Deputy Campaign Manager and Senior Counsel Justin Clark, and President Trump's lead attorney Rudolph Giuliani—all told the Select Committee that there was, indeed, a State-focused "strategy" or "track" to challenge the outcome of the election, which included pressing State legislators to challenge results in key States and to appoint new electoral college electors.[17]

"You know, in the days after election day, later in that first week, bleeding into the second, as our numbers and data looked bleaker, internally we knew that," Stepien told the Select Committee.[18] "As the AP [Associated Press] called the race, I think some surrounding the President were looking for different avenues to pursue." That's when Stepien remembered the concept first coming up.[19]

Those around President Trump were pushing this idea, and pushing it hard.

Just two days after the election, President Trump's son, Donald Trump, Jr., forwarded to White House Chief of Staff Mark Meadows a suggestion that "State Assemblies can step in and vote to put forward the electoral slate[,] Republicans control Pennsylvania, Wisconsin, Michigan, North Carolina, etc. we get Trump electors" and so "we either have a vote WE control and WE win OR it gets kicked to Congress 6 January . . ." [20] Chief of Staff Meadows responded: "Working on this for pa, ga and nc already." [21]

Within one week after the election, Meadows had also sent or received several other similar messages:

"The state legislature can take over the electoral process"—Mark Meadows's text to Georgia State Senator Marty Harbin. [22]

"Agreed"—Mark Meadows's text to a different sender, who suggested that the Trump Administration "should get that out there" if they were "seriously considering the state legislature strategy." [23]

"I will tell him"—Mark Meadows's text to a sender who suggested President Trump "[s]tart building momentum for the state legislatures." [24]

"I love it"—Mark Meadows's text to Representative Andy Biggs, who relayed what he acknowledged as a "highly controversial" idea to have "Republican legislature's (sic)" "appoint a look doors (sic) [electors]." [25]

". . . Why can't the states of GA NC PENN and other R controlled state houses declare this is BS (where conflicts and election not called that night) and just send their own electors . . . I wonder if POTUS knows this . . ."—former Secretary of Energy Rick Perry to Mark Meadows. [26]

Another White House official exploring such a plan less than a week after the election was Vince Haley, Deputy Assistant to the President for Policy, Strategy and Speechwriting. He suggested:

". . . Imagine if every red state legislature slated zero electors. It would reveal that we are a red country. To do this we would have to jack this to the nth degree as a battle of tribes . . . ." [27]

Haley pushed this strategy in several texts and emails, including to Assistant to the President and Director of Presidential Personnel Johnny McEntee, [28] an individual Haley characterized as "a very trusted lieutenant" for President Trump, "a direct conveyor to Boss with ideas," and "[a]t his side almost all the time." [29]

For Haley, however, purported election fraud was a way to justify President Trump-friendly legislatures changing the outcome of the election, but there were other reasons for doing so, too. Election fraud was "only one rationale for slating Trump electors," Haley told McEntee, and "[w]e should baldly assert" that State legislators "have the constitutional right to substitute their judgment for a certified majority of their constituents" if that prevents socialism.[30] Haley added, "[i]ndependent of the fraud—or really along with that argument—Harrisburg [Pennsylvania], Madison [Wisconsin], and Lansing [Michigan] do not have to sit idly by and submit themselves to rule by Beijing and Paris," proposing that radio hosts "rally the grassroots to apply pressure to the weak kneed legislators in those states . . ."[31]

McEntee replied "Yes!" and then: "Let's find the contact info for all these people now."[32] Hours later, Haley sent him names and—in most cases—cell phone numbers for top GOP legislators in six States, suggesting ". . . for POTUS to invite them down for a WH meeting . . ."[33] The President would later call several named in that message, including Rusty Bowers and Karen Fann in Arizona; Lee Chatfield and Mike Shirkey in Michigan; and Jake Corman in Pennsylvania.[34]

Others weighed in with the President about a State-focused plan, too. Some were already looking ahead to January 6th.

On November 8th, former Speaker of the House Newt Gingrich met President Trump at the White House.[35] Two days later, he sent a follow-up note to the President's executive assistant titled "please give to POTUS[,] newt."[36] It suggested that "[t]he only way Trump loses is rigged system" and added that President Trump could encourage "GOP legislatures elect not to send in electors," forcing a House vote by State delegations on January 6th that Gingrich expected President Trump would win.[37] Meadows replied: "Thanks Speaker."[38]

Newsmax CEO Christopher Ruddy had President Trump's ear and reportedly spoke with him by phone at least four times before December.[39] He forwarded a memo to other close advisors of the President recommending that the Trump team persuade one or more Republican-led chambers in Arizona, Georgia, Michigan, Pennsylvania, Wisconsin, and even Minnesota to "pick a separate competitive State slate of Electors," which the memo predicted might turn January 6th into "a cat-fight in Congress wherein VP Pence is Presiding."[40]

Attorney and conservative activist Cleta Mitchell was recruited by Mark Meadows immediately after the election to assist the Trump Campaign's legal work.[41] By November 5th, she emailed Dr. John Eastman of Chapman University,[42] who would later play an outsized role pushing a theory about

Photo by Alex Wong/Getty Images

what Vice President Pence could or couldn't do during the January 6th joint session of Congress that is detailed in Chapter 5 of this Report. In her email, Mitchell asked Eastman to write a memo justifying an idea that State legislators "reclaim" the power to pick electors and asked, rhetorically, "Am I crazy?"[43] Dr. Eastman wrote the memo, entitled "The Constitutional Authority of State Legislatures to Choose Electors," and sent it along for sharing "widely."[44]

According to the Office of Presidential Scheduling, President Trump was scheduled to meet in the Oval Office on November 10th with Morgan Warstler and John Robison, Texas entrepreneurs close to former Governor Rick Perry.[45] The next day, Warstler tweeted that he "[w]as in Oval yesterday,"[46] and months later wrote that "I told whole Trump team in Oval" that "State legislatures can choose the electors-no matter what current state law OR state courts say."[47]

After this apparent meeting, John Robison sent the White House an email entitled "URGENT follow up to our Tuesday Meeting with POTUS," that he asked be printed out for the President to "explain the move forward plan for what was discussed."[48] The email stated that "[President Trump] liked the plan we presented to use a parallel path of state legislators," and the attached memo proposed hundreds of briefings for State lawmakers by

President Trump's surrogates and members of the Freedom Caucus.[49] The email envisioned President Trump hosting "4+ MONSTER RALLY-TRIALS" with "[t]ens of thousands of Trump voters staring up at the GOP state legislators from their districts who ALONE control which slate of electors their state will submit," a proposal that seemed to foreshadow the State hearings that Rudolph Giuliani and President Trump championed less than a month later.[50]

Deputy White House Chief of Staff Dan Scavino called Robison's message "Bat. Shit. Crazy," but the President's executive assistant, who was asked to print it for the President, wrote "Printed," and may have shared it with the President anyway.[51]

By then, President Trump was engaged. According to Stepien, his Campaign Manager, the State-focused strategy came up in a November 11th meeting among close advisors as "something to consider." [52] At that point, the election had been called, but the President "was very interested in keeping pathways to victory open, so [Stepien] believe[d] [the President] found the concept intriguing." [53] Then, the plan "just started happening" even though it was something Stepien, "honestly, kind of dismissed at hand," characterizing it as one "of the crazy, crazier ideas that w[as] thrown out, in and around that time." [54]

But not everyone was convinced. On November 19th, the prior Republican Presidential nominee, Senator Mitt Romney (R-UT), issued a harsh public condemnation of President Trump's open and notorious efforts to overturn the election:

> Having failed to make even a plausible case of widespread fraud or conspiracy before a court of law, the President has now resorted to overt pressure on state and local officials to subvert the will of the people and overturn the election. It is difficult to imagine a worse, more undemocratic action by a sitting American President.[55]

Senator Romney was right to identify and decry President Trump's actions. And yet, in hindsight, it is clear that the effort to pressure State and local officials by the Trump team was only just getting started.

2.3 OUTREACH AND IMPLEMENTATION OF THE PLAN

Just one day after the State-focused plan came up in the Oval Office with the President and his top lieutenants, President Trump started taking concrete steps aimed at State legislators. And in the weeks that followed, the

President spearheaded outreach aimed at numerous officials in States he lost but that had GOP-led legislatures, including in Michigan, Pennsylvania, Georgia, and Arizona.

The Select Committee estimates that in the two months between the November election and the January 6th insurrection, President Trump or his inner circle engaged in at least 200 apparent acts of public or private outreach, pressure, or condemnation, targeting either State legislators or State or local election administrators, to overturn State election results. This included at least:

- 68 meetings, attempted or connected phone calls, or text messages, each aimed at one or more State or local officials;
- 18 instances of prominent public remarks, with language targeting one or more such officials;[56] and
- 125 social media posts by President Trump or senior aides targeting one or more such officials, either explicitly or implicitly, and mostly from his own account.[57]

Furthermore, these efforts by President Trump's team also involved two other initiatives that tried to enlist support from large numbers of State legislators all at once:

- The Trump Campaign contacted, or attempted to contact, nearly 200 State legislators from battleground States between November 30, 2020 and December 3, 2020, to solicit backing for possible Statehouse resolutions to overturn the election. At least some messages said they were "on behalf of the president."[58]
- Nearly 300 State legislators from battleground States reportedly participated in a private briefing with President Trump, Rudolph Giuliani, John Eastman, and others on January 2nd. The President reportedly urged them to exercise what he called "the real power" to choose electoral votes before January 6th, because, as President Trump said on the call, "I don't think the country is going to take it."[59]

It may be impossible to document each and every meeting, phone call, text message, or other contact that President Trump and his allies had with State and local officials in various battleground States. What follows is a summary that focuses on four States and that demonstrates the lengths to which President Trump would go in order to stay in power based on lies—the Big Lie—about the election.

PRESIDENT TRUMP'S EARLY PRESSURE ON PUBLIC SERVANTS

To carry out his plan, President Trump, Rudolph Giuliani, and other surrogates of President Trump publicly and privately sought assistance from State and local officials whom they assumed would help as Republicans on the same team with the "same goal." [60] Some helped. Others didn't.

On November 12th, U.S. Representative Tim Walberg (R-MI) sent an email to President Trump's Executive Assistant Molly Michael, describing a request he had received earlier that day:

> During my conversation with the President this morning he asked me to check with key leadership in Michigan's Legislature as to how supportive they could be in regards to pushing back on election irregularities and potential fraud. He wanted me to gauge their willingness to talk with him about efforts to bring about transparency and integrity in Michigan's election and report back to him. [61]

Representative Walberg added that he had already acted on this request: "I've had conversations with [Michigan] Speaker Lee Chatfield, Senate Majority Leader Mike Shirkey, and Senate President Pro Tempore Aric Nesbitt. They all assured me they would look forward to speaking with the President to report on their continuing efforts" related to overseeing the election "and receiving any suggestions from President Trump." [62] The President would soon host Chatfield, Shirkey, Nesbitt, and four other Michigan State lawmakers at the White House. [63]

In Arizona, on November 13, 2020, the day after officials finished counting ballots cast in Maricopa County, Chairwoman Kelli Ward, of the Arizona Republican Party, texted Mark Meadows that she had "[j]ust talked to POTUS" and that "[h]e may call the Chairman of the Maricopa Board of Supervisors," Clint Hickman. [64] Ward also left a message for Hickman that said, "I just talked to President Trump, and he would like me to talk to you and also see if he needs to give you a call to discuss what's happening on the ground in Maricopa. Give me a call back when you can." [65] According to Hickman, Ward was unusually active after the election, even for a party chair, and was the first person to pressure him. One of her first messages to Hickman before trying to connect him with President Trump was: "We need you to stop the counting." [66]

In Georgia, the President initially took a more public approach. After the Associated Press called the race there on November 12th, President Trump tweeted harsh criticisms of Governor Brian Kemp and Secretary of State Brad Raffensperger. [67] Often these tweets called for them to take specific actions that would have shifted the election results in his favor, such as rejecting a court settlement (which he referred to as a consent decree) that dictated the procedures for verifying signatures on absentee ballots. And he was relentless.

In November alone, President Trump tweeted that Raffensperger was "a so-called Republican (RINO)" and asked "Where is @BrianKempGA," [68] before suggesting that "They knew they were going to cheat." [69] He called to "Break the unconstitutional Consent Decree!" [70] and urged stricter signature matches with a demand to "Get it done! @BrianKempGA." [71] He called Kemp "hapless" and asked why he wouldn't use emergency powers to overrule Raffensperger on the signature-verification procedures, declaring that "Georgia Republicans are angry." [72] President Trump also retweeted posts asking, "Who needs Democrats when you have Republicans like Brian Kemp," and "why bother voting for Republicans if what you get is Ducey and Kemp?" [73]

Pennsylvania was an early, but not unique, example of how President Trump's State-pressure campaign affected the lives of the public servants running this country's elections.

On November 7th, Rudy Giuliani headlined a Philadelphia press conference in front of a landscaping business called Four Seasons Total Landscaping, near a crematorium and down the street from a sex shop.[74]

Standing in front of former New York Police Commissioner and recently-pardoned convicted felon, Bernard Kerik, Giuliani gave opening remarks and handed the podium over to his first supposed eyewitness to election fraud, who turned out to be a convicted sex offender.[75] Giuliani claimed "at least 600,000 ballots are in question" in Pennsylvania and falsely suggested that large numbers of ballots in the State had been cast for dead people, including boxer Joe Frazier and actor Will Smith's father.[76]

Within days, Republican Philadelphia City Commissioner Al Schmidt and others publicly debunked Giuliani's specific allegations of election fraud, including the claims about dead people voting in Pennsylvania elections.[77] In reaction, President Trump tweeted on the morning of November 11th that "[a] guy named Al Schmidt, a Philadelphia Commissioner and so-called Republican (RINO), is being used big time by the Fake News Media to explain how honest things were with respect to the Election in Philadelphia. He refuses to look at a mountain of corruption & dishonesty. We win!" [78]

That statement targeting Schmidt led to a deluge of threatening and harassing phone calls and emails by people who heard President Trump and falsely held out hope that Schmidt or someone else could overturn the results of Pennsylvania's election.[79]

As a public official, Schmidt was no stranger to threats. But being targeted by the President of the United States was different. In Schmidt's public testimony to the Select Committee, he described why. "[P]rior to that the threats were pretty general in nature. 'Corrupt election officials in Philadelphia are going to get what's coming to them'" and other similar threats.[80] "After the President tweeted at me by name, calling me out the way that he did," Schmidt explained, "the threats became much more specific, much more graphic, and included not just me by name but included members of my family by name, their ages, our address, pictures of our home. Just every bit of detail that you could imagine."[81]

As the President continued to push the Big Lie and vilify public officials, such threats multiplied.

EFFORTS TO PREVENT STATE AND LOCAL OFFICIALS FROM CERTIFYING THE ELECTION
Some of President Trump's early outreach was part of an effort to prevent State and local officials from certifying his loss. One example comes from Michigan, and the other from Arizona.

Wayne County, Michigan, includes Detroit and its surrounding areas. On November 17th, the county's Board of Canvassers met to certify election results, a process the Michigan Supreme Court described over a century ago as ministerial and clerical.[82]

The meeting started at 6:00 p.m. and lasted over three hours.[83] Its two Republican members, Board Chair Monica Palmer and Board Member William Hartmann, first voted to block the certification of the election.[84] After a brief break, Palmer and Hartmann returned, changed their votes, and certified the election results.[85] Just over twenty minutes later, Palmer and Hartmann received a call from President Trump and RNC Chair Ronna McDaniel.[86]

Palmer claimed that the call "was not pressure." Rather, she said, "[i]t was genuine concern for my safety" and "there were general comments about different States, but we really didn't discuss the details of the certification."[87]

The Select Committee doesn't know exactly what President Trump privately said on that phone call.[88] By the next evening, however, Palmer and Hartmann had each issued signed affidavits reassuming their earlier position that Wayne County's results should not be certified.[89] Palmer's affidavit even declared that "I rescind my prior vote," though rescinding wasn't possible and her statement had no legal effect.[90] And, President Trump apparently knew before it was public that Hartmann and Palmer would try to change their votes; almost eight hours *before* either of these affidavits were publicly released, President Trump tweeted that these "two harassed patriot Canvassers refuse to sign the papers!"[91]

Republicans in Arizona experienced similar treatment. In the most populous and electorally significant county in Arizona, Maricopa County's Board of Supervisors met on November 20th to certify the county's election results. Their Board, made up of four Republicans and one Democrat, carefully reviewed the official canvass, asked questions for approximately two hours, then unanimously voted to certify the results.[92]

Earlier that day, Kelli Ward contacted two of the board's members, Jack Sellers and Bill Gates, and asked them to delay the certification on the basis of supposed improprieties.[93] According to Sellers and Gates, however, Arizona law required certification that day and they had no information (neither then, nor ever) to doubt the county's election results.[94]

When Arizona certified its 2020 statewide election results on November 30th, it fell to Governor Doug Ducey, a Republican, to sign the certification. While on camera during the signing ceremony, Governor Ducey's phone played a ringtone for the song "Hail to the Chief," which he immediately silenced.[95]

The Governor later confirmed it had been President Trump calling and that he returned the President's call shortly afterwards, but declined to say what the two discussed other than saying that President Trump did not ask him to withhold certification.[96] The Select Committee does not know whether that is true, but that evening President Trump blasted Ducey on Twitter, accusing him of "rushing to put a Democrat in office," and warning that "Republicans will long remember!"[97] The President also retweeted posts bashing Ducey and his Georgia counterpart Brian Kemp, which asked "Who needs Democrats when you have Republicans like Brian Kemp and Doug Ducey?", "why bother voting for Republicans if what you get is Ducey and Kemp?", and "Brian Kemp: 'My state ran the most corrupt election in American history.' Doug Ducey: 'Hold my beer.'"[98] President Trump even commented "TRUE!" when retweeting a post that "Gov Ducey has betrayed the people of Arizona."[99]

Governor Ducey pushed back, writing on Twitter that, "I've been pretty outspoken about Arizona's election system, and bragged about it quite a bit, including in the Oval Office . . . In Arizona, we have some of the strongest election laws in the country . . . The problems that exist in other states simply don't apply here."[100] Governor Ducey explained the law for certifying elections in Arizona and pointed out that the certification now triggered a "5-day window for any elector to bring a credible challenge to the election results in court. If you want to contest the results, now is the time. Bring your challenges."[101] And, Governor Ducey referenced his oath of office:

Photo by Samuel Corum/Getty Images

"That's the law. I've sworn an oath to uphold it, and I take my responsibility seriously." [102] President Trump and his allies never brought a credible challenge and, instead, lost every case they brought challenging the results in Arizona.

EFFORTS TO REPLACE ELECTORAL COLLEGE ELECTORS AND OVERTURN THE ELECTION
Once counties and States certified the election, or when it was nearly certain that they would, President Trump and his team's focus largely shifted. President Trump and his team encouraged State legislators to meet in special sessions, if necessary, and choose electoral college electors who would vote for the Trump/Pence ticket. Ultimately, no State legislature took that step, but it was the basis for pressuring State officials from November through January 6, 2021.

MEETINGS WITH STATE LEGISLATORS—THE "HEARINGS"
The concept of State legislators appointing their own electors featured prominently in a series of hastily arranged official and unofficial "hearings" with State legislators that the Trump team announced on November 24, 2020.[103]

On November 25th, President Trump called in to an unofficial meeting with legislators in Gettysburg, Pennsylvania.[104] The meeting was set up to appear like an official hearing, but it was not. It took place in a hotel ballroom, and those presenting arguments or purported evidence, like Giuliani, Jenna Ellis, and others, were not placed under oath.[105] According to President *Pro Tempore* of the Pennsylvania Senate Jake Corman, he had initially been asked by State Senator Doug Mastriano to hold a hearing about the election. Corman responded that any formal hearing should be official, with sworn testimony, and open to both parties.[106] That was not what Senator Mastriano ultimately convened.

President Trump had originally made plans to attend the Pennsylvania gathering in person, but he cancelled after several advisors tested positive for COVID–19.[107] When President Trump called in and spoke to those gathered in the hotel ballroom, his false claims were met with cheers, and he made his purpose clear: "this election has to be turned around . . . Why wouldn't they overturn an election? Certainly overturn it in your State . . . We have to turn the election over." [108]

President Trump made the ask and Giuliani told the legislators how to carry it out. Giuliani told the assembled legislators that it was their "power" and "responsibility" to pick Pennsylvania's presidential electors and that "[they] have to convince the rest of [their] members, Republican and Democrat, they owe that to the people of" Pennsylvania.[109] Jenna Ellis told them that although Pennsylvania law dictates that electors are chosen by popular vote, "[y]ou can take that power back at any time. You don't need a court to tell you that." [110]

President Trump invited some of the lawmakers to come meet him at the White House that evening and, according to Giuliani, it was "a large group" that went.[111] Special Assistant to the President Cassidy Hutchinson's text messages with Kerik included the guest list and descriptions of the vehicles that would need access to the White House grounds.[112] Pennsylvania State Senator Doug Mastriano drove one car, a hired driver drove a van with most of the State legislators, and Kerik drove an SUV with attorney Katherine Friess and election-conspiracy proponent Phil Waldron.[113] Hutchinson estimated that at least 29 visitors traveled from Pennsylvania to the White House that day, and she explained that their conversation with the President touched on holding a special session of the State legislature to appoint Trump electors.[114]

Just a few days later, on November 30, 2020, President Trump also called into another one of Giuliani and Jenna Ellis's hotel "hearings," this time in Arizona. Several Arizona State lawmakers hosted the meeting at a Hyatt Regency in Phoenix after they did not receive permission to organize an official hearing at the State Capitol.[115] Before the hearing started, State GOP Representative Mark Finchem "promised information to show that the state's 11 electoral votes should not go to Democrat Joe Biden," and argued that "the U.S. Constitution empowers lawmakers to decide, on their own, whether the election was valid and, if not, to select the electors of their choice." [116]

Giuliani told the assembled legislators that the officials certifying Arizona's election results "have made no effort to find out" if the results of the election were accurate, "which seems to me gives the state legislature a perfect reason to take over the conduct of this election because it's being conducted irresponsibly and unfairly." [117] Likewise, Jenna Ellis said that it was "not just the choice, but the actual duty and obligation of the legislature to step in and to make sure that you don't certify false results." [118] During a recess, she also took to Twitter, writing, "[t]he certification of Arizona's FALSE results is unethical and knowingly participating in the corruption that has disenfranchised AZ voters. BUT, this in no way impacts the state legislature's ability to take back the proper selection of delegates." [119]

When it was President Trump's turn to address this handful of lawmakers over the phone, he called them "legends for taking this on," and used the opportunity to criticize Governor Ducey: "you'll have to figure out what's that all about with Ducey. He couldn't [certify] fast enough" and "Arizona will not forget what Ducey just did. We're not gonna forget." [120] That night Giuliani joined President Trump in criticizing Governor Ducey, while at the same time making baseless allegations about voting machines in Arizona and calling for a special legislative session to change the outcome of the election: "Governor Ducey of Arizona refuses to meet with me. He doesn't want to explain that he selected a foreign corrupt Voting Machine company to count the vote. I understand his reluctance, but [sic] just call a special session. Let's find out how crooked your election really was?" [121]

Michigan was next. Giuliani's team announced that the Michigan legislature would hold a hearing on December 1st, but the relevant committee chair excluded Giuliani because it was only open to witnesses "with first hand knowledge." [122] That chairman, Michigan State Senator Edward McBroom (R-Vulcan), had already held Senate Oversight hearings by then in an actual effort to evaluate claims of fraud in the 2020 election, which ultimately resulted in a comprehensive report that concluded that the Republican-led committee "found no evidence of widespread or systematic fraud" in Michigan's election. [123]

Michigan's House Oversight Committee, however, did allow Giuliani to testify in a hearing on December 2nd. Before the hearing, Giuliani joined the State's GOP chairwoman to give what was billed as a legal briefing. In the online presentation, Giuliani told the audience there's "nothing wrong with putting pressure on your state legislators" [124] to pick new electors and that "you have got to get them to remember that their oath to the Constitution sometimes requires being criticized. Sometimes it even requires being threatened." [125]

When Giuliani appeared for the hearing in Michigan, he was not placed under oath, used his time to refer to Michigan's election as a "con job," and urged legislators to "have the courage to say that certification that was done by your state is a complete phony." [126] The information presented was baseless—and sometimes racist—conspiracy theories. One witness brought to criticize Michigan's voter verification even said: "I think Chinese all look alike. So how would you tell? If some Chow shows up, you can be anybody and you can vote." [127] And, as he had promised in the legal briefing the day before, Giuliani then called on the legislators to do what the Trump Campaign had reportedly been discussing since before election day. He said that the State legislature could still singlehandedly decide the election result "anytime you want to. Anytime. You can take it back tonight. You can take it back the day before the electors go down to Washington." [128] Jenna Ellis also participated, insisting "no honest person can hear these citizens of your own state today . . . and can let this proceed. What the Constitution obligates you to do is to take back your plenary power." [129]

Finally, Georgia. There, Giuliani and others appeared in multiple hearings, the first of which was held on December 3, 2020. In that hearing, Giuliani was direct and called on Georgia legislators to overturn the election results—"you are the final arbiter of who the electors should be"—based on the false premise that "there is more than ample evidence to conclude that this election was a sham." [130] Then, at a separate hearing on December 10th, he told State legislators that Georgia's Governor, Lieutenant Governor, and secretary of State were engaged in a "cover up" of "a crime in plain sight," and that it fell to "the state legislature [ ] to vindicate the honor of the state." [131] And, Giuliani used yet another appearance, on December 30th, to call the 2020 election "the most crooked election, the most manipulated election in American history," and implore the Republican legislators to hold a special session to vote on appointing new electors, something he said that they could do "right up until the last moment" before January 6th.[132]

More perniciously, Giuliani also used these hearings to advance conspiracy theories that falsely accused Fulton County election workers of rigging Georgia's election results. His delegation to the December 3rd hearing played clips of election-night surveillance footage from the State Farm

Arena that showed election workers scanning ballots, sometimes after partisan poll watchers had gone home.[133] Although the poll watchers should have been there the entire time while election workers counted the votes, there was nothing nefarious about the circumstances and no question about the end result. In fact, the FBI, Department of Justice, and Georgia Bureau of Investigation would determine that these ballots were legitimate ballots, that observers were not illegally ejected, and that the ballots were scanned and counted properly, contrary to claims by President Trump and his attorneys.[134] And yet Giuliani baselessly declared at the December 3rd hearing that, to him, the video was a "powerful smoking gun" proving that "those votes are not legitimate votes."[135]

But Giuliani's claims took a more ominous turn during the December 10th hearing. There, he publicly named two of the election workers shown in the video, Ruby Freeman and her daughter, Wandrea ArShaye "Shaye" Moss, and accused them of vote-tampering and engaging in criminal conduct.[136] He seized on a clip of Freeman passing Moss a ginger mint, claiming that the two women, both Black, were smuggling USB drives "as if they're vials of heroin or cocaine." He also suggested that Freeman and Moss should be jailed and that they deserved to have their homes searched.[137] Not only were Giuliani's claims about Freeman and Moss reckless, racist, and false, they had real-world consequences that turned both women's lives upside down. And further heightening the personal impact of these baseless attacks, President Trump supported, and even repeated, them, as described later.

In the end, the hearings were widely panned. In Michigan alone, current and former Republican lawmakers publicly questioned the hearings and implored President Trump and his team to stop. U.S. Representative Paul Mitchell (R-Mich.) implored on Twitter "Please JUST STOP!" and "wondered why Republican leaders allowed testimony he said was 'driving the party into this ditch.'"[138] Similarly, former Michigan lawmaker Martin Howrylak (R-Oakland) said that he was "embarrassed" by the hearing, and former Michigan Senator Ken Sikkema (R-Grand Rapids) said that "the way the committee was run was atrocious."[139] Later, the President promoted a tweet calling a Democratic lawmaker a "#pos" for speaking out at the Michigan hearing.[140] Months later, Giuliani's license to practice law in New York was suspended for, among other reasons, the "false claims" he made on various dates, including during the hearings in Michigan, Pennsylvania, Arizona, and Georgia.[141]

THE TRUMP CAMPAIGN'S BARRAGE OF PHONE CALLS TO STATE LEGISLATORS

Not only was replacing electors a theme during the official and unofficial State hearings, it was also a critical component of President Trump's plan both before and after the hearings took place.

In fact, while the hearings were happening, the Trump Campaign set up an operation to contact hundreds of State legislators and ask them to support an effort to appoint electoral college electors for the Trump/Pence ticket in States that President Trump had lost.

On the same day as Giuliani's hearing in Michigan, Trump Campaign staff contacted dozens of Republicans in Michigan's State legislature. A Trump Campaign supervisor sent text messages to his team, directing them to reach out to lawmakers "to explain the process for legislative redress and tell them how to send representative[s] to th[e] electoral college." [142] He added: "We're gonna be lobbyists. Woot." [143]

According to a Campaign staffer's spreadsheet produced to the Select Committee, the Trump Campaign apparently tried contacting over 190 Republican State legislators in Arizona, Georgia, and Michigan, alone.[144]

One voicemail left as part of this initiative was leaked to the press on December 1, 2020. In it, a Trump Campaign staffer said, "I did want to personally reach out to you on behalf of the President." [145] Her main point came later in the message: "we want to know when there is a resolution in the House to appoint electors for Trump if the President can count on you to join in support." [146] Another message from this effort that reached reporters made the same ask and claimed that, "[a]fter a roundtable with the President, he asked us to reach out to you individually" to whip support for a "joint resolution from the State House and Senate" that would "allow Michigan to send electors for Donald J. Trump to the Electoral College and save our country." [147]

Soon after the voicemail leaked, the Campaign staffer who left this voicemail got a text message from one of her supervisors, who wrote: "Honest to god I'm so proud of this" because "[t]hey unwittingly just got your message out there." [148] He elaborated: "you used the awesome power of the presidency to scare a state rep into getting a statewide newspaper to deliver your talking points." [149]

OUTREACH BY PRESIDENT TRUMP AND SENIOR AIDES

While Campaign aides blanketed State officials with these calls, some State officials received more personalized outreach directly from President Trump, Giuliani, and their allies throughout the post-election period about this issue.

Michigan. As discussed earlier, Rep. Walberg reached out to State legislators in Michigan at the President's request in mid-November, including Senate Majority Leader Mike Shirkey and House Speaker Lee Chatfield. By November 18th, President Trump called Chatfield and Shirkey to invite them to what would become a meeting for a group of Michigan lawmakers in the Oval Office.[150] Although President Trump didn't tell Shirkey what the meeting would be about, the President was focused on the election and asked Shirkey what he and others were doing to investigate election fraud.[151] The meeting happened on November 20th.[152]

In Shirkey's words, there "wasn't a mystery" about why the group was at the White House once the meeting started.[153] When the President mentioned several baseless claims of election fraud in Wayne County, Shirkey told the President that he had lost the election and that it had nothing to do with Wayne County, where he had actually performed better than he had in 2016.[154]

From the President's body language, Shirkey concluded that wasn't what he wanted to hear. But the meeting continued, and the President dialed in Giuliani, who delivered a "long monologue," reciting a "litany" of allegations about supposed fraud that was short on substance.[155] Shirkey challenged Giuliani, asking "when are you going to . . . file a lawsuit in Michigan," which he said Giuliani did not answer.[156] Although Shirkey says he did not recall the President making any precise "ask," Chatfield recalled President Trump's more generic directive for the group to "have some backbone and do the right thing." [157] Chatfield understood that to mean they should investigate claims of fraud and overturn the election by naming electors for President Trump.[158] Shirkey told the President that he was not going to do anything that would violate Michigan law.[159]

After the meeting ended, Shirkey and Chatfield issued a joint statement: "We have not yet been made aware of any information that would change the outcome of the election in Michigan and as legislative leaders, we will follow the law and follow the normal process regarding Michigan's electors, just as we have said throughout this election." [160]

That was not the end, however. Chatfield and Shirkey received numerous calls from the President in the weeks following the election. Chatfield told the Select Committee that he received approximately five to ten phone calls from President Trump after the election, during which the President would usually ask him about various allegations of voter fraud.[161] Chatfield said that he repeatedly looked into the President's claims but never found anything persuasive that could have changed the outcome of the election.[162]

President Trump's calls were not enough, so he turned to the public. On January 3, 2021, the Trump Campaign posted a tweet that urged supporters

Photo by Rey Del Rio/Getty Images

to "Contact Speaker Lee Chatfield & Senate Majority Leader Mike Shirkey" to "Demand [a] vote on decertification."[163] Why President Trump thought the Michigan legislature would convene to decertify the election in a matter of hours when it had refused to do so since early November is not clear. But that didn't stop the President from making things personal. The President's January 3rd tweet included Shirkey's personal cellphone number as well as a number for Chatfield that turned out to be wrong. As a result, Shirkey said he received nearly 4,000 text messages, and another private citizen reported being inundated with calls and texts intended for Chatfield.[164]

Pennsylvania. On November 21st, Mark Meadows texted a number apparently belonging to Representative Scott Perry (R–PA) and asked: "Can you send me the number for the speaker and the leader of the PA Legislature. POTUS wants to chat with them."[165] Hours later, Meadows received a response of "Yes sir."[166] At the time, the leader of the Pennsylvania Senate was Jake Corman and the Speaker of the Pennsylvania House was Bryan Cutler.

Corman told the Select Committee that he received a call on Thanksgiving Day 2020 from Giuliani, urging him to call the legislature into a special session to replace Biden electors with Trump electors.[167] This idea wasn't new to Corman. President Trump and his allies had gone public about their intentions before then, including during the Pennsylvania hotel hearing, but Corman had braced himself for this even before the election. Before election day in 2020, a reporter from *The Atlantic* interviewed Corman and other prominent Republicans in Pennsylvania about the possibility that President Trump would try to circumvent the popular vote in swing States by asking the legislatures to appoint Trump/Pence electors. After the article, Corman drafted an op-ed, making it clear that the Pennsylvania legislature did not have the legal authority to appoint Trump/Pence electors in contravention of the popular vote, a position that he would generally maintain through the 2020 Presidential election cycle.[168]

During that call, Giuliani first tried "pumping [Corman] up as a patriot" before asking the Senator to call the Pennsylvania legislature into a special session. Corman told Giuliani that he did not have the authority to do that, a position with which his own lawyers agreed.[169] Giuliani's reply was that Corman must have bad lawyers. Corman said he offered to connect Giuliani with his legal team. His legal team spoke with Giuliani and a lawyer working with him, Jenna Ellis, the following day, reiterating their view that such a move by the legislature would be illegal.[170] That same day, or possibly the next, Giuliani and Ellis called him back to renew their request for a special legislative session and to demean Corman's attorneys, calling them "terrible," "bad," and "wrong."[171] Corman, however, held his ground and ended the call.[172]

While packing to return to Pennsylvania from his Thanksgiving visit to Florida, Corman says he received a call from an unknown number with a Washington, DC area code, which he let go to voicemail.[173] It turned out to be a White House operator calling on behalf of President Trump.[174]

Corman called back and spoke to President Trump, who insisted that he had won the election in Pennsylvania and said something to the effect of, "Jake, this is a big issue. We need your help."[175] Corman told the President that he couldn't do what the Trump team was asking; President Trump replied, "I'm not sure your attorneys are very good."[176] Corman wanted to end the call and offered to have his lawyers speak again with President Trump's, but they never had another call with the President's lawyers.[177]

Pennsylvania House Speaker Bryan Cutler was another main target for the President's team. He received voicemails in late November for four days in a row from Giuliani and/or Jenna Ellis, which he provided to the Select Committee.[178] Cutler explained that he did not feel comfortable talking with the President's team in case he ended up having to preside over a legislative session about the election, and he had his attorneys relay that to the President's team.[179] Giuliani received the message but continued to call Speaker Cutler nonetheless.[180]

In the first of these voicemails, on November 26th, Giuliani asked to "get together, quietly" to discuss "the amount of fraud that went on in your State," and said that Giuliani and Ellis had also just spoken to Pennsylvania House Majority Leader Kerry Benninghoff.[181] On November 27th, Ellis called and said in a second voicemail that they had just talked to Pennsylvania House Member Russ Diamond and were "very grateful" to the State's legislature "for doing your Article II duty."[182] On November 28th, Giuliani left a third voicemail and claimed to have "something important" that "really changes things," and said that "the president wanted me to make sure I got it to you."[183] And then on November 29th, Giuliani left a fourth message and said, "I understand that you don't want to talk to me now" but still sought "the courtesy of being able to talk to you as the president's lawyer" and a "fellow Republican" because "you're certifying what is a blatantly false statement . . . I can't imagine how that's in your interests or in the interests of our party."[184]

Giuliani and Ellis didn't get through, but the President did. "[I]f we wanted to do something, what were the options[?]" the President asked Cutler.[185] Cutler explained to President Trump that he could file a legal challenge contesting the election, and asked the President why his team had never requested a statewide recount.[186] Cutler was also clear about the "constitutional peculiarities" of Pennsylvania, where the State constitution specifically prohibits retroactive changes to how electors are chosen.[187]

Practically, President Trump's call achieved nothing. The President wasn't getting what he wanted in his calls to leaders in Pennsylvania: a special session of the legislature to appoint Trump/Pence electors.

Seemingly undeterred, President Trump invited several leaders of the Pennsylvania legislature to the White House for Christmas gatherings.[188] Senator Corman decided not to go, although Speaker Cutler did. President Trump spoke with Cutler on December 3rd, while Cutler, his chief of staff, and their wives were at that White House Christmas tour.[189] The issue of overturning the results of Pennsylvania's election came up again, as did the possibility of a special session of the State legislature to appoint Trump electors.[190] Cutler told the President that the State legislature could not reconvene without an order from the Governor and a petition from a supermajority of legislators, neither of which was likely to happen.[191] Cutler also told the President that they could not appoint new electors without a court order. In Cutler's opinion, President Trump "seemed to understand. And that was—that was clear."[192] The President's apparent understanding, however, did not result in any meaningful changes to his public rhetoric.

On December 3rd, the same day that Cutler met with President Trump, Cutler, Corman, House Majority Leader Benninghoff, and Senate Majority

Leader Kim Ward issued a three-page single-spaced joint statement asserting, in no uncertain terms, that Pennsylvania's General Assembly "lacks
the authority . . . to overturn the popular vote and appoint our own slate of
electors," since "[d]oing so would violate our Election Code and Constitution, particularly a provision that prohibits us from changing the rules for
election contests of the President after the election." [193] In response, President Trump retweeted a December 4th post by Bernard Kerik, which tagged
all four of these State legislators with the hashtag "Traitors," and declared
that "These are the four cowardice[sic] Pennsylvania legislators that intend
to allow the Democrat machine to #StealtheVote! #Cowards #Liars #Trai-
tors." [194]

But five days later, President Trump publicly thanked Cutler for signing
onto a December 4th letter that encouraged Members of Congress from
Pennsylvania to object to their State's electoral votes on January 6th. The
President tweeted: "Thank you to Speaker Cutler and all others in Pennsylvania and elsewhere who fully understand what went on in the 2020 election. It's called total corruption!" [195] When the Select Committee asked
Cutler about this apparent change in his position, he said that he signed on
to this letter not because of concerns that fraud or corruption meant the
results of the election Pennsylvania were wrong, but rather because of concerns about "programmatic changes or areas for improvement" related to
the election.[196] In fact, Cutler reiterated to the Committee that he "was not
personally aware of" any widespread election fraud that would have
changed the result of the election.[197]

The pressure facing State legislators during this period was significant.
On December 9th, the *New York Times* quoted Pennsylvania's Senate Majority Leader Kim Ward, revealing that she too had received a call from President Trump in which he pushed his election fraud narrative.[198] Ward told
the *Times* that she hadn't been given enough time to sign the same December 4th letter that Cutler did, but commented that if she had taken a stand
against it, "I'd get my house bombed tonight." [199]

Arizona. In late November, Arizona House Speaker Russell "Rusty" Bowers,
a longtime Republican who served 17 years in the State legislature, received
a call from President Trump and Giuliani.[200] Giuliani alleged that Arizona's
election results were skewed by illicit ballots, cast by non-citizens or on
behalf of dead people.[201] Bowers demanded proof for these audacious
claims on the call and President Trump told Giuliani to comply, but the evidence never came.[202] The point of the call, however, was different. Like in
Michigan and Pennsylvania, President Trump and his allies were working
the phones to get something. They wanted Bowers to hold a public hearing

Photo by House Creative Services

with the ultimate aim of replacing Presidential electors for former Vice President Joe Biden with electors for President Trump.[203]

Bowers had never heard of anything like that before, and Giuliani acknowledged that it had never been done. Where President Trump and Giuliani saw a potential opportunity, however, Bowers saw a fundamental problem.

As Bowers explained it, what they wanted him to do was "counter to my oath when I swore to the Constitution to uphold it." [204] And he said that to the President and Giuliani: "you are asking me to do something against my oath, and I will not break my oath." [205] Giuliani replied: "aren't we all Republicans here? I mean, I would think you would listen a little more open to my suggestions, that we're all Republicans." [206]

The pressure didn't stop with that call. On December 1st, Giuliani and Ellis got an audience with some of the most powerful Republican lawmakers in Arizona, including Bowers, Senate President Karen Fann, Senate President Pro Tempore Vince Leach, House Majority Leader and Senator-Elect Warren Petersen, Senate Majority Whip Sonny Borrelli, Senator Michelle Ugenti-Rita, and others.[207] The Select Committee was unable to get Giuliani and Ellis' perspective on this outreach because Giuliani claimed that his communications with Bowers—who was not his client nor part of

his legal team—were "privileged," while Ellis invoked her Fifth Amendment rights against self-incrimination.[208]

Bowers, on the other hand, told the Select Committee that Giuliani and
Ellis asked the lawmakers to deliver Arizona's electors for President Trump,
despite the certified popular vote count.[209] To bolster their request, Giuliani
and Ellis raised numerous allegations of election fraud at the meeting,
though they never produced evidence in support of their claims. In live testimony before the Committee, Bowers recalled Giuliani saying in this meeting that "we've got lots of theories, we just don't have the evidence."[210] At
the time, Bowers didn't know whether it was a gaffe or an example of Giuliani not thinking through what he had just said.[211] In any event, Bowers
said he and others in his group made particular note of that comment.[212]
And it was borne out; Bowers testified that "No one provided me, ever, such
evidence."[213]

In late December, in another phone call with President Trump, Bowers
reiterated that he would not do anything illegal for him.[214] Afterward, John
Eastman joined the chorus of Trump allies attempting to change his mind.
In a call on January 4th that included the Speaker's chief counsel as well as
Arizona House Majority Leader-Elect Ben Toma, Eastman urged Bowers to
hold a vote to decertify Arizona's Presidential electors.[215] When Bowers told
Eastman he couldn't unilaterally reconvene the legislature, Eastman urged
him to "just do it and let the court sort it out."[216] Bowers refused and the
Arizona legislature took no such action.

Many of President Trump's efforts in Arizona focused on State officials,
but his team also continued to reach out to the Board of Supervisors for
Maricopa County even after it certified the election. One focus was voting
machines. According to the *Arizona Republic*, Giuliani left a voicemail in
mid- to late-December for Board Member Steve Chucri that "I see we're
gonna get a chance to take a good look at those machines . . . give me a call
as soon as you get a chance. The president also wanted me to pass on a few
things to you, too."[217] On December 4th, Giuliani also left a message for the
Board's Chairman Clint Hickman: "I was very happy to see that there's
gonna be a forensic audit of the machines. And I really wanted to talk to you
about it a bit. The President wanted me to give you a call. All right? Thank
you. Give me a call back."[218] Hickman chose not to call back.[219]

Then, on Christmas Eve, Giuliani left voicemails for Board Members Bill
Gates and Jack Sellers, asking them to call him back. In his message for
Gates, Giuliani said:

> It's Giuliani, President Trump's lawyer. If you get a chance, would
> you please give me a call? I have a few things I'd like to talk over
> with you. Maybe we can get this thing fixed up. You know, I really

think it's a shame that Republicans sort of are both in this, kind of, situation. And I think there may be a nice way to resolve this for everybody.[220]

In his message for Sellers, Giuliani said "I'd like to see if there is a way that we can resolve this so that it comes out well for everyone. We're all Republicans, I think we all have the same goal. Let's see if . . . we can get this done outside of the court." [221] Like Hickman, neither Gates nor Sellers returned Giuliani's calls.[222]

So President Trump made the call himself. On December 31st, Board Chair Clint Hickman received a voicemail from the White House switch-board, asking him to call back for President Trump. Hickman said that he did not return the call, in part because the county was still facing litigation over the election.[223] Another call from the White House came through on January 3rd with a request that Hickman call back for the President. But, by then, the President's call with Georgia Secretary of State Brad Raffensperger, described below, had leaked, and Hickman "didn't want to walk into that space." [224]

Georgia. On December 5th, President Trump traveled to Georgia to headline a rally and mobilize voters in advance of a January Senate runoff. But the President's day started with a morning call to Governor Brian Kemp during which they discussed reconvening the legislature in a special session.[225] After the call, Kemp took to Twitter. He acknowledged that he had spoken to the President and that he told the President that he supported the idea of, and had already called for, a signature audit in Georgia.[226] President Trump responded later that night by complaining that Georgia had not yet done a signature-verification audit and instead insisted that the Governor should "[a]t least immediately ask for a Special Session of the Legislature." [227] The following day, Governor Kemp and Lieutenant Governor Geoff Duncan issued a definitive statement rejecting President Trump and his allies' calls to overturn the results in Georgia:

> While we understand four members of the Georgia Senate are requesting the convening of a special session of the General Assembly, doing this in order to select a separate slate of presidential electors is not an option that is allowed under state or federal law.

> State law is clear: the legislature could only direct an alternative method for choosing presidential electors if the election was not able to be held on the date set by federal law. In the 1960s, the General Assembly decided that Georgia's presidential electors will be determined by the winner of the State's popular vote. Any attempt

by the legislature to retroactively change that process for the November 3rd election would be unconstitutional and immediately enjoined by the courts, resulting in a long legal dispute and no short-term resolution.[228]

President Trump responded by directing his ire at Georgia officials and, throughout the month of December, President Trump grew even more relentless in his social media attacks against Kemp than he had been the previous month. He retweeted attorney Lin Wood calling on Georgians to call and urge the FBI to focus more on election fraud and "[t]ell them to also investigate @BrianKempGA @GeoffDuncanGA & @GaSecofState." [229] And he retweeted another post by Lin Wood that depicted Governor Kemp and Secretary Raffensperger wearing masks digitally altered to show the Chinese flag, and warned that they "will soon be going to jail." [230] Even without his many retweets, President Trump posted an average of about one tweet per day in December 2020 either criticizing Governor Kemp or pressuring him explicitly or implicitly to take actions to help overturn the election.[231]

President Trump seemed consumed with his plans to overturn the election and, based on documents obtained by the Select Committee, it appears that the President received input from many outside donors or advisors who had access to his staff's email addresses. On December 7th, a Trump donor named Bill White emailed senior Trump advisors, including Dan Scavino and Rudolph Giuliani, to say that he "[j]ust spoke to [Georgia State] Senator [William Burton] Jones [who] asked if Potus can R[e]T[weet] this now pls," along with a tweet by Senator Jones that read: "Georgia Patriot Call to Action...call your state Senate & House Reps & ask them to sign the petition for a special session." [232] President Trump and Giuliani each retweeted Senator Jones's tweet an hour later.[233]

Bill White also emailed Molly Michael, Dan Scavino, and Giuliani, on December 8th with information that he said "POTUS asked me last night" to send right away.[234] He recommended a Presidential tweet criticizing Georgia's Lt. Gov. Duncan as well as tweets to put pressure on Senate Majority Leader Mike Dugan and Senate President Pro Tempore Butch Miller.[235] He wrote that President Trump would be calling Dugan and Miller "to ask them to call special session and strategize with them why they are keeping this from happening." [236] Dugan later confirmed that he had received a call from President Trump's office but that the two of them were not able to connect.[237] And the following day, Steve Bannon revealed on his podcast that President Trump spoke to Georgia House Speaker Ralston and Speaker Pro Tempore Jan Jones.[238] Speaker Ralston confirmed that he spoke to President Trump on December 7th about the election, during which he told the President that Georgia law made a special legislative session "very much an uphill battle."²³⁹

2.4 AN OUTRIGHT REQUEST FOR VICTORY

Beyond asking State officials to not certify, to decertify, or to appoint Trump electors for consideration during the joint session, President Trump and some of his closest advisors inserted themselves directly into the counting of ballots and asked, outright, for enough votes to win.

White House Chief of Staff Mark Meadows did this. Not only did he place calls on behalf of the President to election officials in Georgia, Meadows traveled there to personally visit election officials and volunteers, coordinated with Members of Congress, and even suggested that the President send election workers Trump memorabilia like presidential challenge coins and autographed MAGA hats, a suggestion that his assistant Cassidy Hutchinson thought could be problematic and, ultimately, did not act on.²⁴⁰

When Meadows made a visit on short notice to examine the audit of absentee ballots in Cobb County, Georgia, he spoke to Deputy Secretary of State Jordan Fuchs and Frances Watson, the Secretary of State's chief investigator. Ultimately, Meadows connected Watson with the President, who claimed that he had won the election and pressed her to say that he had won. The Select Committee obtained a copy of their recorded call, which is detailed below.

The President told Watson that he had "won Georgia . . . by a lot," told her, "you have the most important job in the country right now," and suggested, "when the right answer comes out you'll be praised."²⁴¹ Four days later, Meadows texted Deputy Secretary of State Fuchs, in which he asked, "[i]s there a way to speed up Fulton county signature verification in order to have results before Jan 6 if the trump campaign assist[s] financially."²⁴² Fuchs wrote in response that she "Will answer ASAP."²⁴³

Meadows also played a central role in the lead up to the President's January 2, 2021, call with Georgia Secretary of State Brad Raffensperger. In fact, it was Meadows who originally sent text messages to Raffensperger and requested to speak: On November 19th, he texted "Mr Secretary. Mark Meadows here. If you could give me a brief call at your convenience. Thank you".²⁴⁴ And on December 5th, Meadows texted, "mr Secretary. Can you call the White House switchboard at [phone number]. For a call. Your voicemail is full."²⁴⁵ Then, on December 11th, Meadows texted, "Thanks so much" to a number that apparently belongs to United States Representative

Photo by House Creative Services

Jody Hice (R–GA) after Rep. Hice told him that he had just made a statement "regarding a recall on Raffensperger. If this is something Potus wants
to know and help push. . . ."[246]

All of that led to the remarkable January 2nd call between President
Trump and his advisors on one side, and Secretary of State Brad Raffensperger and his advisors on the other. By January 2nd, the President had
tried to speak by phone with Raffensperger at least 18 times.[247] Raffensperger, for his part, had avoided talking to the President because of ongoing
litigation with the President's Campaign.[248] Despite Raffensperger's reluctance, the two spoke, with their respective lawyers on the line. During the
call, President Trump went through his litany of false election-fraud claims
and then asked Raffensperger to deliver him a second term by "finding"
just enough votes to ensure victory. The President said, "I just want to find
11,780 votes, which is one more than we have because we won the
State."[249] He reiterated it several different ways: "fellas, I need 11,000
votes. Give me a break. You know, we have that in spades already. Or we can
keep going, but that's not fair to the voters of Georgia because they're
going to see what happened."[250]

When it was clear that Raffensperger and his advisors would not agree to the President's request, the President ramped up the pressure by accusing them of committing crimes: "the ballots are corrupt. And you are going to find that they are—which is totally illegal—it is more illegal for you than it is for them because, you know, what they did and you're not reporting it. That's a criminal, that's a criminal offense. And you can't let that happen. That's a big risk to you and to Ryan, your lawyer . . . I'm notifying you that you're letting it happen."[251]

The President would stop at nothing to win Georgia. Separate from asking Raffensperger to alter, without justification, the election results in Georgia, he also attacked election workers. In that call, President Trump mentioned Ruby Freeman's name 18 times, referred to her daughter Shaye Moss several of those times, and accused them of crimes.[252] Raffensperger and his aides rebutted President Trump's false claims of fraud on the call and explained why they were wrong, but they did not deliver the one thing President Trump wanted most: the 11,780 votes he asked for.[253]

The next day, President Trump tweeted about his phone call with Raffensperger, falsely claiming that "[Secretary Raffensperger] was unwilling, or unable, to answer questions such as the 'ballots under table' scam. . . . He has no clue!"[254] He added that Raffensperger, Governor Kemp, and Lt. Governor Duncan "are a disgrace" and "have done less than nothing" about rampant political corruption.[255]

Even though Raffensperger and his team repeatedly told the President why his specific allegations of election fraud in Georgia were wrong,[256] President Trump met the next day with the top leadership of the Justice Department in an effort to convince them to send a letter falsely claiming that the Department had "identified significant concerns" affecting the election results in Georgia and calling on Governor Kemp, Speaker Ralston, and Senate President Pro Tempore Miller to convene a special session.[257] It was only after a showdown in the Oval Office, described in Chapter 4 during which the White House Counsel and others threatened to resign that President Trump decided against replacing Department of Justice leadership and issuing that letter.

2.5 SOME OFFICIALS EAGERLY ASSISTED PRESIDENT TRUMP WITH HIS PLANS

While many State officials resisted President Trump's demands, some eagerly joined the President's efforts.

President Trump routinely coordinated with Pennsylvania State Senator Doug Mastriano, whose request led to the November 25, 2020, hotel "hearing" in Gettysburg, and who traveled to Washington to meet with the

Photo by Spencer Platt/Getty Images

President afterward.[258] Senator Mastriano, who would later charter and pay for buses to Washington for the President's "Stop the Steal" rally on January 6th and was near the Capitol during the attack, quickly rose to favor with the President.[259]

On November 30th, President Trump called Mastriano, interrupting him during a radio interview and telling listeners that "Doug is the absolute hero" and people are "really angry in Pennsylvania." [260]

On December 5th, Senator Mastriano sent an email to President Trump's executive assistant, Molly Michael, with a Supreme Court Amicus Brief for the President that the pair "discussed yesterday," related to a case brought by Representative Mike Kelly (R–PA) against his own State, which the Supreme Court rejected just a few days later.[261]

On December 14th, President Trump's executive assistant sent Mastriano an email "From POTUS" with talking points promoting a conspiracy theory about election machines.[262]

And on December 21st, Mastriano sent another email for President Trump, in which he wrote: "Dear Mr. President—attached please find the 'killer letter' on the Pennsylvania election that we discussed last night" that "I only just completed." [263] This letter recapped the Gettysburg hotel hearing on November 25th, and claimed that "there is rampant election

fraud in Pennsylvania that must be investigated, remedied and recti-
fied." [264] President Trump sent that letter to John Eastman, Acting Attorney
General Jeffrey Rosen, Acting Deputy Attorney General Richard Donoghue,
Rush Limbaugh, former Florida Attorney General Pam Bondi, Lou Dobbs,
and others.[265]

As January 6th approached, Senator Mastriano's involvement in
attempts to overturn the election only grew. On December 23rd, he led a
second group of Pennsylvania State senators for a meeting with President
Trump in the Oval Office, which Giuliani claimed "swayed about 20" of
them.[266] Neither Speaker Cutler nor Senate President Corman participated.

Mastriano also sent emails indicating that he spoke with President
Trump on December 27th, 28th, and 30th, along with files that President
Trump had requested or that he had promised to him.[267] One of these was a
pair of letters from State senators asking U.S. Senate Majority Leader Mitch
McConnell and House Minority Leader Kevin McCarthy to reject Pennsylvania's electoral votes on January 6th.[268] President Trump's executive assistant notified the White House's Director of Legislative Affairs that "[t]he
President would like the below attached letters to be sent to Mitch and
Kevin and all GOP house and senate members," but was told in reply,
"[g]iven the political nature of the letters, would you mind sending
them?" [269]

On January 5th, President Trump spoke again with Mastriano and then
notified the White House operator that Mastriano "will be calling in for the
Vice President" soon.[270] That evening Senator Mastriano sent two more
emails for the President. One was a letter addressed to Vice President Pence
on behalf of nearly 100 legislators from various States; the other was a letter directed to McConnell and McCarthy from Pennsylvania lawmakers, this
time asking Congress to postpone acting on the 6th.[271] President Trump
tweeted the letter that night, captioning it "BIG NEWS IN PENNSYLVANIA!"
and, after midnight, he retweeted that "Pennsylvania is going to Trump.
The legislators have spoken." [272] As described elsewhere in this report, that
letter, and letters like it, were used in the effort to convince Vice President
Pence that he could and should affect the outcome of the joint session of
Congress on January 6th.

The Select Committee subpoenaed Senator Mastriano to testify about
these interactions with President Trump and his advisors, among other
matters. Unlike numerous other witnesses who complied with subpoenas
and provided deposition testimony to the Select Committee, Mastriano did
not; he logged in to a virtual deposition at the appointed time but logged
out before answering any substantive questions or even taking the oath to
the tell the truth.[273]

The President apparently got what he wanted in State officials like Senator Mastriano, but not those who dared question or outright reject his anti-democratic efforts to overturn the election. In some cases, those who questioned him made the President and his advisors dig in and push harder. On January 1st, Campaign Senior Advisor Jason Miller asked for a "blast text and Twitter blast out" that would urge President Trump's supporters to "Contact House Speaker Bryan Cutler & Senate President Pro Tem Jake Corman!" to "Demand a vote on certification." [274] Senior Campaign attorneys, however, replied that this might violate Pennsylvania's "very stringent" lobbying laws and get them prosecuted or fined. [275] Instead, they agreed on a similar call to action aimed at Arizona Governor Doug Ducey and Arizona House Speaker Rusty Bowers rather than Speaker Cutler and President *Pro Tempore* Corman in Pennsylvania. [276]

2.6   THE FINAL OUTREACH TO STATE LEGISLATORS

The efforts to overturn the election through State legislatures continued throughout the final two weeks before the joint session of Congress on January 6th. Based on actual events and documents obtained by the Select Committee, President Trump's Campaign team, outside advisors, and motivated volunteers generally acted in accord with what was written down in a "Strategic Communications Plan" when engaging with, and sometimes demonizing, State officials. Activities that occurred thereafter were in accord with the plan.

The "Plan" was explained in a document that was presented to the White House. [277] The plan contemplated pressuring Republican legislators both in Congress and in six key swing States. The document itself purports to be the product of the "GIULIANI PRESIDENTIAL LEGAL DEFENSE TEAM" and declared that "We Have 10 Days to Execute This Plan & Certify President Trump!" [278]

Kerik told the Select Committee that pieces of the plan had been in place for some period of time before the document was actually created, and that he thought that the "catalyst" for actually memorializing the plan was the approaching deadline of January 6th. [279] In fact, the 10-day plan to help "certify president Trump" had been the subject of "continual discussions" for "6 weeks" and was "being discussed every day at some point prior to the 10 days that we're talking about. So it was a continuous thing that went on." [280]

Ultimately, the Giuliani team shared the Strategic Communications Plan and urged its implementation. Kerik sent the plan to Mark Meadows via email on December 28th with this note, in part:

There is only one thing that's going to move the needle and force the legislators to do what their [sic] constitutionally obligated to do, and that is apply pressure . . . . We can do all the investigations we want later, but if the president plans on winning, it's the legislators that have to be moved, and this will do just that. We're just running out of time.[281]

Neither Giuliani nor Kerik told the Select Committee that they recalled officially implementing the plan, and Giuliani said that he thought Meadows even rejected it, but there is no doubt that President Trump's team took certain actions consistent with it.[282]

The document described its goal as a "[n]ationwide communications outreach campaign to educate the public on the fraud numbers, and inspire citizens to call upon legislators and Members of Congress to disregard the fraudulent vote count and certify the duly-elected President Trump."[283] The "FOCUS of CAMPAIGN" was "SWING STATE REPUBLICAN SENATORS" in Arizona, Georgia, Michigan, Nevada, Pennsylvania, and Wisconsin, "REPULBICAN [sic] MEMBERS OF THE HOUSE" and "REPUBLICAN MEMBERS OF THE SENATE."[284] Among the steps that it recommended were "RALLIES AND PROTESTS" in six key swing States, including protests at "Governor's Mansions," "Lt. Governor's home[s]," "Secretary of State's homes," and "weak Members' homes."[285]

Although the plan did not mention specific individuals by name, an apparently related document produced to the Select Committee by Giuliani did, naming State legislative leaders as "TARGETS" under a header of "KEY TARGET STATE POINTS," including Arizona House Speaker Rusty Bowers, Arizona Senate President Karen Fann (incorrectly described as the State Senate's majority leader), Georgia House Speaker David Ralston, Georgia Senate Majority Leader Mike Dugan, Georgia Senate President Pro Tempore Butch Miller as a possible back up, Michigan House Speaker Lee Chatfield, Michigan Senate Majority leader Mike Shirkey, Pennsylvania House Speaker Brian Cutler, Pennsylvania House Majority Leader Kerry Benninghoff, Pennsylvania Senate President Pro Tempore Jake Corman, Pennsylvania Senate Majority Leader Kim Ward, Wisconsin State Assembly Speaker Robin Vos, and Wisconsin Senate Majority Leader Scott Fitzgerald.[286]

Consistent with these proposals, Giuliani appeared as a guest on Steve Bannon's podcast on New Year's Eve and told him that "we have a weak element to our party . . . a cowardly element"[287] and, "[n]ow I think every Republican knows—maybe this is worse—this election was stolen. Now the question is: can they live up to their oath of office? . . . We gotta start working on the leadership."[288] Giuliani also described President Trump's objective in this effort: "For the president, the way forward is really it's in the hands of the leaders of those legislatures and the Members of Congress, and what our people can do is let them know what they think, and that they're not gonna get away with pushing this aside. That the consequences of turning your back on a massive voter fraud are gonna be dire for them, and historically these people are gonna become enemies of the country." [289]

A key component of this plan was to call out Republican officials who rejected President Trump and his team's efforts or claims of fraud. Kerik and numerous other members of the Campaign's legal team did just that. On December 27th, Kerik suggested that Senator Pat Toomey (R-PA) was "corrupt" and said that "for any Pennsylvania official to certify their vote, it's malfeasance and criminal." [290] That was entirely consistent with Kerik's past tweets about the election, one of which apparently called public officials "who betrayed" President Trump "spineless disloyal maggots." [291] It wasn't just rhetoric, however, because, as described below, people showed up outside certain officials' home—sometimes menacingly—and, of course, showed up at the Capitol on January 6th.

The pressure in those final days did not stop with the types of activities outlined in the Strategic Communications Plan. January 2, 2021, was a busy day for a Saturday at the Trump White House. That was the day President Trump called on Georgia Secretary of State Raffensperger to find enough votes for victory in Georgia and participated in a call with Lindsay Graham and Members of the Freedom Caucus to plan for the joint session on January 6th. [292]

It was also the day that the President joined in a virtual briefing for nearly 300 Republican legislators from swing States. [293] The event was hosted by a short-lived organization called "Got Freedom?" that listed Jenna Ellis among its leadership team, [294] and included Giuliani, John Eastman, and Peter Navarro as the program's "featured speakers." [295] A press release by Got Freedom? said that the meeting was hosted by Phillip Kline, a former attorney general of Kansas, who was disbarred in 2013. [296] It indicated that purported proof of voter fraud "should serve as an important resource for state legislators as they make calls for state legislatures to meet to investigate the election and consider decertifying their state election results." [297]

According to the *Washington Examiner*, when President Trump joined the call he told the participants: "You know that we won the election, and you were also given false numbers to certify." It quoted him saying "[y]ou are the real power" because "[y]ou're more important than the courts. You're more important than anything because the courts keep referring to you, and you're the ones that are going to make the decision." When asked about that quote, specifically, Giuliani, who was on the call, said he didn't recall the exact words that the President used but told the Select Committee "that would be the sum or substance of what he had been saying and what he believed."[298] During the call, the President reportedly "referenced the planned protests in Washington" just days later on January 6th, and told the group "I don't think the country is going to take it."[299]

When reporting on the call, the *Washington Examiner* also provided details about what Giuliani told the assembled State legislators. Consistent with his team's "Strategic Communications Plan," Giuliani said, "[w]e need you to put excessive pressure on your leadership where the real weakness and cowardice is mostly located," and the report quoted Navarro telling them that "Your job, I believe, is to take action, action, action."[300] That evening, Navarro stated on *Fox News* that "these legislators—they are hot, they're angry, they want action," and "we explained exactly how the Democrat Party as a matter of strategy stole this election from Donald J. Trump."[301]

Organizers from Got Freedom? sent a follow-up email that evening to participants on behalf of Phill Kline, in which they described the event as "an important briefing for legislators who hold the power to decertify the results of their state elections."[302] It emphasized the following:

> As elected officials in the House and Senate of your respective States, Professor Eastman laid out the Constitutional imperatives for you:
> * Assert your plenary power
> * Demand that your laws be followed as written
> * Decertify tainted results unless and until your laws are followed
> * Insist on enough time to properly meet, investigate, and properly certify results to ensure that all lawful votes (but only lawful votes) are counted.[303]

The email also recommended that they ". . . sign on to a joint letter from state legislators to Vice President Mike Pence to demand that he call for a 12-day delay on ratifying the election . . ." on January 6th.[304] The letter ultimately garnered more than 100 signatures by State legislators from Arizona, Georgia, Michigan, Pennsylvania, and Wisconsin.[305] Doug Mastriano forwarded a copy of the letter via email to President Trump's executive assistant, and the National Archives produced to the Select Committee a printed version with a stamp at the top indicating, "THE PRESIDENT HAS SEEN."[306]

But this plan would fail to sway its intended audience. As discussed in Chapter 5, the Vice President rejected this and numerous other attempts to convince him to act unlawfully on January 6th. The election had been decided and certified by the States. It was the Vice President and Congress's job to open and count the legitimate electoral college votes.

And in the early morning hours of January 7th, after a day unlike any seen in American history, when a mob of angry insurrectionists attempted to violently upend a Presidential election, the Vice President and Members of Congress, shaken but steady, delayed but resolute, regrouped and reconvened and did their Constitutional duty to certify Joseph R. Biden as the next President of the United States.

President Trump's plot to pressure State legislators to overturn the vote of the electoral college failed—but only barely. Even so, the consequences of President Trump's efforts to overturn State election results were significant.

2.7 THE HARM CAUSED BY DEMONIZING PUBLIC SERVANTS

Many of the people who refused to be pushed into manipulating election results—governors, secretaries of State, State legislators, State and local election officials, and frontline election workers just doing their jobs— found themselves subjected to public demonization and subsequent spamming, doxing, harassment, intimidation, and violent threats. Some of the threats were sexualized or racist in nature and targeted family members. President Trump never discouraged or condemned these tactics, and in fact he was an active participant in directing his supporters, through tweets and speeches, to apply pressure to public servants who would not comply.

President Trump and his team were not above using incendiary rhetoric or threats to achieve their goal of overturning the election. Giuliani said so before the purported hearing in Michigan in December. Recall that he told an online audience, there's "nothin' wrong with putting pressure on your state legislators" [307] and "you have got to get them to remember that their oath to the Constitution sometimes requires being criticized. Sometimes it even requires being threatened." [308]

That pressure came privately and publicly in the post-election period.

Privately, for example, President Trump called Michigan Senate Majority Leader Mike Shirkey three times after their White House meeting: November 21st, November 25th, and December 14th.[309] Shirkey did not recall many specifics of those calls and claimed he did not remember the President applying any specific pressure.[310] The day after one of those calls, however, Shirkey tweeted that "our election process MUST be free of intimidation and threats," and "it's inappropriate for anyone to exert pressure on them." [311] From this and other public statements, it is clear that Shirkey was sensitive to outside forces pressuring people with roles in the

election. In fact, the same day that the electoral college met and voted former Vice President Joe Biden as the winner of the 2020 Presidential election, Shirkey received another call from President Trump and issued
another public statement. Shirkey's statement that day, December 14, 2020,
read: "Michigan's Democratic slate of electors should be able to proceed
with their duty, free from threats of violence and intimidation" and "[i]t is
our responsibility as leaders to follow the law . . . ."[312]

Publicly, President Trump used both Twitter posts and paid social
media and cable television ads to advance his pressure campaign.

In Arizona, for example, President Trump used social media to both
praise and criticize legislators. When Speaker Bowers and Senate President
Karen Fann requested an audit of Maricopa County's election software and
equipment, President Trump publicly commended them, retweeting a press
release about their announcement and commenting: "Thank you to Senate
President Karen Fann and House Speaker Russell Bowers—and all, for what
you are doing in Arizona. A fast check of signatures will easily give us the
state."[313] But just days later, President Trump assailed Bowers for opposing
a special session to appoint new electors. He retweeted a post by Campaign
lawyer Christina Bobb that accused Bowers of "intentionally misleading the
people of Arizona" and that included a demand by Stop-the-Steal organizer
Ali Alexander for 50,000 phone calls to Rusty Bowers "[r]ight the heck
now" to threaten him with a primary challenge.[314]

And, as his efforts to change the outcome of the election continued to
meet resistance, President Trump personally approved a series of advertisements that the Campaign ran on cable television and social media in
several important States. One advertisement in Arizona called for pressure
on Governor Ducey in particular, alleging, "The evidence is overwhelming.
Call Governor Ducey and your legislators. Demand they inspect the
machines and hear the evidence."[315] Another claimed that "illegal aliens
voted, and here in Arizona Trump votes were discarded. It's an outrage. Call
Governor Ducey and your legislators at 602–542–4331. Demand they
inspect the machines and hear the evidence. Call Governor Ducey, at 602–
542–4331. Stand up for President Trump. Call today. Paid for by Donald J.
Trump for President, Inc."[316]

Several days earlier, Trump Campaign Senior Advisor Jason Miller had
explained the intention for this round of advertisements in an email. He
wrote that, "the President and Mayor Giuliani want to get back up on TV
ASAP, and Jared [Kushner] has approved in budgetary concept, so here's
the gameplan" in order to "motivate the GOP base to put pressure on the
Republican Governors of Georgia and Arizona and the Republican-
controlled State legislatures in Wisconsin and Michigan to hear evidence of

voter fraud before January 6th." [317] Miller anticipated a budget of $5 million and asked for the messaging to follow an earlier round of advertisements, "but the endings need to be changed to include phone numbers and directions to call the local Governor or state legislature." [318] On December 22nd, Jason Miller texted Jared Kushner that "POTUS has approved the buy." [319]

References to anger and fighting were featured in some of the President's remarks during that period. After the Georgia Secretary of State's Chief Operating Officer, Gabriel Sterling, made an impassioned public plea and accurately warned that someone would die as a result of the threatening election-related rhetoric that President Trump failed to condemn, President Trump dismissively tweeted in response: "Rigged Election. Show signatures and envelopes. Expose the massive voter fraud in Georgia. What is Secretary of State and @BrianKempGA afraid of. They know what we'll find!!!" [320] The President also tweeted that, between Governor Ducey in Arizona and Governor Kemp in Georgia, "the Democrat Party could not be happier" because these Republicans "fight harder against us than do the Radical Left" and were singlehandedly responsible for losing him both States, something that "Republicans will NEVER forget[.]" [321] Regarding Kemp, he asked "What's wrong with this guy? What is he hiding?" [322] and he alleged that "RINOs" Governor Kemp, Lieutenant Governor Geoff Duncan, and Secretary Raffensperger "will be solely responsible" for Senators Loeffler and Perdue losing their senate runoff because they "[w]on't call a Special Session or check for Signature Verification! People are ANGRY!" [323]

President Trump's spoken remarks were not much different. After the President wrapped up a November 26th public phone call to wish U.S. service members a happy Thanksgiving, he answered a reporter's question about election integrity in Georgia by lashing out at Secretary Raffensperger in particular. President Trump made several baseless claims of election fraud in Georgia, declared that Raffensperger himself appeared to be complicit, and labeled the Georgia Secretary of State "an enemy of the people." [324]

President Trump and his team's practice of naming and viciously criticizing people had real consequences. Philadelphia City Commissioner Al Schmidt's story, recounted earlier, is just one of many examples. And the consequences weren't just limited to high-profile public figures. Schmidt's deputy, for example, Seth Bluestein faced threats after being demonized by a surrogate for President Trump, and many of the threats he received were anti-Semitic in nature. He received a Facebook message telling him that "EVERYONE WITH A GUN IS GOING TO BE AT YOUR HOUSE- AMERICANS LOOK AT THE NAME- ANOTHER JEW CAUGHT UP IN UNITED STATES

VOTER FRAUD." [325] Bluestein got a security detail at his home, and the experience gave his three-year-old daughter nightmares.[326]

Similarly, after President Trump promoted online accusations that Arizona House Speaker Rusty Bowers had been "intentionally misleading the people of Arizona . . ." [327] Bowers's personal cell phone and home address were published,[328] leading demonstrators to congregate at his home, honk horns and shout insults until police arrived.[329] Bowers told the Select Committee this was the first of at least nine protests at his home, sometimes with protesters shouting into bullhorns and calling him a pedophile.[330] One protestor who showed up at his home was armed and believed to be a member of an extremist militia.[331]

Sadly, those were not isolated incidents. Stories similar to Schmidt's and Bowers' proliferated after President Trump's loss in the election. Examples from each of the States discussed in this chapter are documented below, but this list is by no means exhaustive:

- *Arizona:* After Secretary of State Katie Hobbs's home address and son's phone number were publicly released, demonstrators congregated outside her home chanting "we are watching you." [332] A social media user at the time recommended: "Let's burn her house down and kill her family and teach these fraudsters a lesson." [333] Secretary Hobbs has continued to receive threats since then, reporting over 100 threats to the FBI in mid-2022, including a September 2021 voicemail message that "you should be hunted" and "will never be safe in Arizona again." [334]
- *Arizona:* Maricopa County Recorder Adrian Fontes testified before Congress that his family had "go-bags" packed in case they needed to evacuate and that, because of the threats, he had moved his children "out of the family home at least once for three days in the wake of serious threats to [his] family's safety." [335]
- *Arizona:* Paul Boyer, a Republican State senator, had to evacuate his family, get police protection, and change his phone number after he voted against jailing Maricopa's County Supervisors over election disputes.[336]
- *Arizona:* On January 5, 2021, a comment on a blog suggested some members of the Maricopa County Board of Supervisors "have earned a good old fashioned neck tie party" as "punishment for Treason." [337] According to Board member Clint Hickman, "the threats never abated." [338] And on January 6th, police convinced Hickman and his family to leave their home.[339]
- *Michigan:* Secretary of State Jocelyn Benson and her family were driven out of their home for several days after dozens of protestors with

bullhorns and firearms congregated outside "shouting obscenities and graphic threats into bullhorns"[340] while she spent time with her son and got him ready for bed.[341] Secretary Benson said that she only feels safe "sometimes" as a result of continuing threats.[342]

- *Michigan:* Several members of the Wayne County Board of Canvassers received threats, as did Aaron Van Langevelde, a Republican member of the State Board of Canvassers.[343] Van Langevelde was bombarded with communications and people began showing up at his family's home, forcing police to ensure his and his family's safety and escort him across the State after he voted to certify Michigan's election.[344]
- *Michigan:* Detroit City Clerk Janice Winfrey, a Democrat, and Rochester Hills City Clerk Tina Barton, a Republican, were both targeted. Barton had never before received a death threat in over a decade of work as an election official but, as a result of the 2020 Presidential election, was subject to "a torrent of threats and harassment," such as an anonymous caller who "repeatedly threatened to kill her and her family."[345] Winfrey was confronted outside her home by a man who indicated he had been surveilling her and that "You are going to pay dearly for your actions in this election!"[346] She started carrying a firearm because death threats against her continued.[347]
- *Michigan:* Michigan House Speaker Lee Chatfield confirmed that "I and my family have received numerous threats, along with members on both sides of the aisle."[348] This included the top Democrat on Michigan's House Oversight Committee, Rep. Cynthia Johnson, who was threatened with lynching after she challenged the witnesses that Giuliani offered to her committee.[349] One caller who allegedly threatened to kill Rep. Johnson and wipe out her family in December 2020 called the Capitol again on the morning of January 7, 2021, and said that "everyone better get out of the building because it'll fucking explode."[350]
- *Pennsylvania:* Secretary of the Commonwealth Kathy Boockvar said she received so many threats "I didn't feel comfortable walking the dog on the street."[351] This included a message in November 2020 threatening to murder her in her home at night, forcing her and her husband to flee for a week.[352] Another voicemail she received after certifying Pennsylvania's election results threatened: "You crooked f***ing bitch. You're done."[353]
- *Pennsylvania:* House Speaker Bryan Cutler told the Select Committee there were at least three protests outside either his district office or his home, and that his then-15-year-old son was home by himself for the first one.[354] Senate Jake Corman's spokesperson revealed in December 2020 that he, too, was being subjected to violent threats,[355] something

Senate Majority Leader Kim Ward also received.[356]

- *Pennsylvania:* Philadelphia City Commissioner Omar Sabir, spent several nights evacuated from his home and continued to receive death threats a year after the 2020 election, reflecting that, "I feel anxiety every time I walk outside of the house."[357] Commissioner Lisa Deeley, another City Commission colleague, also received death threats and said she suffers occasional anxiety attacks as a result.[358]

- *Georgia:* After Georgia Secretary of State Brad Raffensperger's email and phone number were published, he said that he and his wife received frequent hostile messages, some of which "typically came in sexualized attacks."[359] As a result, the Secretary's wife cancelled visits from their grandchildren out of fear for the kids' safety.[360] That was not an overreaction as that came after police found self-identified members of the Oath Keepers outside their home and after someone broke into their daughter-in-law's house.[361]

- *Georgia:* On January 5, 2021, Governor Kemp and Secretary Raffensperger were reportedly named in a Craigslist post encouraging people to "put an end to the lives of these traitors."[362]

- *Georgia:* Fulton County Elections Director Richard Barron was named and depicted on screen in the video President Trump played at his December 5th rally. He said that this incident led to a spike in death threats targeted at election workers, including himself.[363] His team's registration chief, Ralph Jones, received death threats following the election including one calling him a "n[igger] who should be shot," and another threatening "to kill him by dragging his body around with a truck."[364]

- *Georgia:* Election offices in ten Georgia counties received emailed threats of bombings that would "make the Boston bombings look like child's play" and that the "death and destruction" would continue "[u]ntil Trump is guaranteed to be POTUS . . . ."[365]

One of the most striking examples of the terror that President Trump and his allies caused came in Georgia, where election workers Ruby Freeman and Shaye Moss, mother and daughter, were besieged by incessant, terrifying harassment and threats that often evoked racial violence and lynching, instigated and incited by the President of the United States.

As described earlier, in a State legislative hearing in Georgia, Giuliani publicly—and baselessly—accused Freeman and Moss of engaging in criminal conduct. He showed a video of Freeman passing Moss a ginger mint before claiming that the two women, both Black, were smuggling USB drives "as if they're vials of heroin or cocaine."[366]

President Trump seemed fixated on Freeman and Moss, too. He played surveillance video showing them inside the State Farm Arena at a December 5th rally in Georgia,[367] and mentioned Freeman by name 18 times during the January 2nd call to Secretary of State Raffensperger in which he asked the Secretary to simply "find" enough votes to ensure victory.[368]

Freeman's and Moss's lives were forever changed. After their contact information was published, they were besieged by the President's supporters. In early December 2020, Freeman "told police she had received hundreds of threats at her home." [369] Moss's son also started receiving threatening phone calls, including one stating he "should hang alongside [his] nigger momma." [370]

In the wake of President Trump's December 5, 2020, rally, Freeman called 911 because strangers had come to her home trying to lure her out, sending threatening emails and text messages.[371] She pleaded with the 911 dispatcher for help after hearing loud banging on her door just before 10 p.m. "Lord Jesus, where's the police?" she asked the dispatcher. "I don't know who keeps coming to my door." "Please help me!" [372]

Ultimately, Freeman fled from her own home based on advice from the FBI.[373] She would not move back for months.[374]

In her testimony to the Select Committee, Freeman recounted how she had received "hundreds of racist, threatening, horrible calls and messages" and that now "[t]here is nowhere I feel safe—nowhere."[375] But it's not just a sense of security that the President and his followers took from Freeman. She told the Select Committee that she also lost her name and reputation:

> My name is Ruby Freeman. I've always believed it when God says that he'll make your name great, but this is not the way it was supposed to be. I could have never imagined the events that followed the Presidential election in 2020. For my entire professional life, I was Lady Ruby. My community in Georgia where I was born and lived my whole life knew me as Lady Ruby. . . . Now I won't even introduce myself by my name anymore. I get nervous when I bump into someone I know in the grocery store who says my name. I'm worried about who's listening. I get nervous when I have to give my name for food orders. I'm always concerned of who's around me. I've lost my name, and I've lost my reputation.

> I've lost my sense of security—all because a group of people, starting with Number 45 and his ally Rudy Giuliani, decided to scapegoat me and my daughter Shaye to push their own lies about how the presidential election was stolen.[376]

Freeman's sense of dread is well-founded. According to Federal prosecutors, a member of the Oath Keepers militia convicted of multiple offenses for his role in the January 6th insurrection had a document in his residence with the words "DEATH LIST" written across the top.[377]

His death list contained just two names: Ruby Freeman and Shaye Moss.[378]

ENDNOTES

1. *See, e.g.,* Stephen Fowler, "Risk-Limiting Audit Confirms Biden Won Georgia," GPB, (Nov. 19, 2020), available at https://www.gpb.org/news/2020/11/19/risk-limiting-audit-confirms-biden-won-georgia; Addie Haney, "Georgia Election Recount Results: Breaking Down Final Numbers," 11Alive, (Dec. 7, 2020), available at https://www.11alive.com/article/news/politics/elections/georgia-election-recount-results-final-numbers/85-cbaacd70-f7e0-40ae-8dfa-3bf18f318645.

2. Brad Raffensperger, *Integrity Counts* (New York: Simon & Schuster, 2021), p. 191 (reproducing the call transcript); Amy Gardner and Paulina Firozi, "Here's the Full Transcript and Audio of the Call Between Trump and Raffensperger," *Washington Post* (Jan. 5, 2021), available at https://www.washingtonpost.com/politics/trump-raffensperger-call-transcript-georgia-vote/2021/01/03/2768e0cc-4ddd-11eb-83e3-322644d82356_story.html.

3. Brad Raffensperger, *Integrity Counts* (New York: Simon & Schuster, 2021), p. 191 (reproducing the call transcript); Amy Gardner and Paulina Firozi, "Here's the Full Transcript and

Audio of the Call Between Trump and Raffensperger," *Washington Post* (Jan. 5, 2021), available at https://www.washingtonpost.com/politics/trump-raffensperger-call-transcript-georgia-vote/2021/01/03/2768e0cc-4ddd-11eb-83e3-322644d82356_story.html.

4. Brad Raffensperger, *Integrity Counts* (New York: Simon & Schuster, 2021), p. 191 (reproducing the call transcript); Amy Gardner and Paulina Firozi, "Here's the Full Transcript and Audio of the Call Between Trump and Raffensperger," *Washington Post* (Jan. 5, 2021), available at https://www.washingtonpost.com/politics/trump-raffensperger-call-transcript-georgia-vote/2021/01/03/2768e0cc-4ddd-11eb-83e3-322644d82356_story.html.

5. Brad Raffensperger, *Integrity Counts* (New York: Simon & Schuster, 2021), p. 191 (reproducing the call transcript); Amy Gardner and Paulina Firozi, "Here's the Full Transcript and Audio of the Call Between Trump and Raffensperger," *Washington Post* (Jan. 5, 2021), available at https://www.washingtonpost.com/politics/trump-raffensperger-call-transcript-georgia-vote/2021/01/03/2768e0cc-4ddd-11eb-83e3-322644d82356_story.html.

6. Brad Raffensperger, *Integrity Counts* (New York: Simon & Schuster, 2021), p. 191 (reproducing the call transcript); Amy Gardner and Paulina Firozi, "Here's the Full Transcript and Audio of the Call Between Trump and Raffensperger," *Washington Post* (Jan. 5, 2021), available at https://www.washingtonpost.com/politics/trump-raffensperger-call-transcript-georgia-vote/2021/01/03/2768e0cc-4ddd-11eb-83e3-322644d82356_story.html.

7. Brad Raffensperger, *Integrity Counts* (New York: Simon & Schuster, 2021), p. 191 (reproducing the call transcript); Amy Gardner and Paulina Firozi, "Here's the Full Transcript and Audio of the Call Between Trump and Raffensperger," *Washington Post* (Jan. 5, 2021), available at https://www.washingtonpost.com/politics/trump-raffensperger-call-transcript-georgia-vote/2021/01/03/2768e0cc-4ddd-11eb-83e3-322644d82356_story.html.

8. Brad Raffensperger, *Integrity Counts*, (New York: Simon & Schuster, 2021), at p. 194.

9. Select Committee to Investigate the January 6th Attack on the United States Capitol, Transcribed Interview of Brad Raffensperger, (Nov. 22, 2021), pp. 121-122, 126-27.

10. Brad Raffensperger, *Integrity Counts*, (New York: Simon & Schuster, 2021), at p. 194.

11. The Georgia Secretary of State's Chief Operating Officer, Gabriel Sterling, gave an impassioned public statement that included these points. "Georgia Election Official Gabriel Sterling: 'Someone's Going to Get Killed' Transcript," Rev, (Dec. 1, 2020), available at https://www.rev.com/blog/transcripts/georgia-election-official-gabriel-sterling-someones-going-to-get-killed-transcript. Shortly thereafter, President Trump fired back on Twitter in the form of a quote-tweet of a journalist's post that included the full footage of these parts of Sterling's remarks. Donald J. Trump (@realDonaldTrump), Twitter, Dec. 1, 2020 10:27 p.m. ET, available at http://web.archive.org/web/20201203173245/https://mobile.twitter.com/realDonaldTrump/status/1333975991518187521 (quoting Brendan Keefe (@BrendanKeefe), Twitter, Dec. 1, 2020 4:22 p.m. ET, available at https://twitter.com/BrendanKeefe/status/1333884246277189633).

12. See Chapter 1.

13. U.S. Const. art. II, §1, cl. 2 ("Each State shall appoint, in such Manner as the Legislature thereof may direct, a Number of Electors, equal to the whole Number of Senators and Representatives to which the State may be entitled in the Congress: but no Senator or Representative, or Person holding an Office of Trust or Profit under the United States, shall be appointed an Elector.").

14. *See* "Census Bureau Releases 2020 Presidential Election Voting Report," United States Census Bureau, (Feb. 17, 2022), available at https://www.census.gov/newsroom/press-releases/2022/2020-presidential-election-voting-report.html.

15. Barton Gellman, "The Election That Could Break America," *Atlantic*, (Sept. 23, 2020) available at https://www.theatlantic.com/magazine/archive/2020/11/what-if-trump-refuses-concede/616424/.

16.   Barton Gellman, "The Election That Could Break America," *Atlantic*, (Sept. 23, 2020) available at https://www.theatlantic.com/magazine/archive/2020/11/what-if-trump-refuses-concede/616424/.

17.   Select Committee to Investigate the January 6th Attack on the United States Capitol, Transcribed Interview of William Stepien, (Feb. 10, 2022), pp. 145-46, 148-53, 158; Select Committee to Investigate the January 6th Attack on the United States Capitol, Transcribed Interview of Justin Clark, (May 17, 2022), pp. 96, 98; Select Committee to Investigate the January 6th Attack on the United States Capitol, Deposition of Rudolph Giuliani, (May 20, 2022), p. 42. Although certain Select Committee witnesses confirmed the existence of this state-focused strategy, none testified that they knew about the strategy before the election.

18.   Select Committee to Investigate the January 6th Attack on the United States Capitol, Transcribed Interview of William Stepien, (Feb. 10, 2022), pp. 145-46.

19.   Select Committee to Investigate the January 6th Attack on the United States Capitol, Transcribed Interview of William Stepien, (Feb. 10, 2022), pp. 145-46.

20.   Documents on file with the Select Committee to Investigate the January 6th Attack on the United States Capitol (Mark Meadows Production), MM011213. Donald Trump Jr. publicly urged State legislators to help the same day. He called on Twitter for his father to "go to total war over this election" and retweeted a post by Fox News host Mark Levin urging Republican State legislatures to "GET READY TO DO YOUR CONSTITUTIONAL DUTY" by exercising "THE FINAL SAY OVER THE CHOOSING OF ELECTORS." David Knowles, "As Vote Count Swings Toward Biden, Trump's Backers Hit the Caps-Lock Key on Twitter," *Yahoo! News*, (Nov. 5, 2020), available at https://www.yahoo.com/video/as-vote-count-swings-toward-biden-trump-backers-hit-the-caps-lock-on-twitter-223931950.html.

21.   Documents on file with the Select Committee to Investigate the January 6th Attack on the United States Capitol (Mark Meadows Production), MM011318 (November 6, 2020, text message from Mark Meadows to Donald J. Trump, Jr.).

22.   Documents on file with the Select Committee to Investigate the January 6th Attack on the United States Capitol (Mark Meadows Production), MM011296 (November 5, 2020, text message from Mark Meadows to Marty Harbin).

23.   Documents on file with the Select Committee to Investigate the January 6th Attack on the United States Capitol (Mark Meadows Production), MM011686, MM011687 (November 9, 2020, text messages between Mark Meadows and Russell Vought).

24.   Documents on file with the Select Committee to Investigate the January 6th Attack on the United States Capitol (Mark Meadows Production), MM011560, MM011563 (November 7, 2020, text messages between Mark Meadows and Rep. Warren Davidson).

25.   Documents on file with the Select Committee to Investigate the January 6th Attack on the United States Capitol (Mark Meadows Production), MM011449, MM011451 (November 6, 2020, text messages between Mark Meadows and Rep. Andy Biggs).

26.   Documents on file with the Select Committee to Investigate the January 6th Attack on the United States Capitol (Mark Meadows Production), MM011087 (November 4, 2020, text message from Rick Perry to Mark Meadows).

27.   Documents on file with the Select Committee to Investigate the January 6th Attack on the United States Capitol (Vincent Haley Production), VMH-00004070, p. 44; *see also* Documents on file with the Select Committee to Investigate the January 6th Attack on the United States Capitol (Vincent Haley Production), VMH-00003041.

28.   Documents on file with the Select Committee to Investigate the January 6th Attack on the United States Capitol (Vincent Haley Production), VMH-00003543 (November 5, 2020, email from Vincent Haley to Johnny McEntee and Dan Huff re: State legislature plenary power under Constitution to state electoral college electors); Documents on file with the Select Committee to Investigate the January 6th Attack on the United States Capitol (Vincent Haley Production), VMH-00003559 (November 5, 2020, email from Vincent Haley to Johnny

McEntee and Dan Huff re: more notes on state legislature strategy); Documents on file with the Select Committee to Investigate the January 6th Attack on the United States Capitol (National Archives Production), 076P-R000010233_0001 (November 6, 2020, email chain between Vincent Haley, Johnny McEntee, and Daniel Huff re: Contact Info of key leaders in key States); Documents on file with the Select Committee to Investigate the January 6th Attack on the United States Capitol (National Archives Production), 076P-R000010198_0001 (November 6, 2020, email from Vincent Haley to Johnny McEntee and Daniel Huff re: Horowitz: How Republican-controlled state legislatures can rectify election fraud committed by courts and governors - TheBlaze); Documents on file with the Select Committee to Investigate the January 6th Attack on the United States Capitol (National Archives Production), 076P-R000010225_0001-10226_0001 (November 6, 2020, email from Vincent Haley to Johnny McEntee and Daniel Huff re: Contact info of key leaders in key States and attaching contact info); Documents on file with the Select Committee to Investigate the January 6th Attack on the United States Capitol (Vincent Haley Production), VMH-00004070, 4103-04, 4111-12, 4124-25 (various text messages between Vincent Haley, Johnny McEntee, and Daniel Huff discussing the state legislature plan).

29. Documents on file with the Select Committee to Investigate the January 6th Attack on the United States Capitol (Vincent Haley Production), VMH-00003009 (November 8, 2020, email chain between Vincent Haley and Newt Gingrich re: More of my exchange with John); Documents on file with the Select Committee to Investigate the January 6th Attack on the United States Capitol (Vincent Haley Production), VMH-00004103 (November 6, 2020, text message from Vincent Haley to Randy Evans).

30. Documents on file with the Select Committee to Investigate the January 6th Attack on the United States Capitol (Vincent Haley Production), VMH-00002107 (November 5, 2020, email chain between Vincent Haley, Daniel Huff, and Jonny McEntee re: more notes on the state legislature strategy).

31. Documents on file with the Select Committee to Investigate the January 6th Attack on the United States Capitol (Vincent Haley Production), VMH-00004103 (November 6, 2020, text message from Vincent Haley to Johnny McEntee).

32. Documents on file with the Select Committee to Investigate the January 6th Attack on the United States Capitol (Vincent Haley Production), VMH-00004104 (November 6, 2020, text message from Vincent Haley to Johnny McEntee).

33. Documents on file with the Select Committee to Investigate the January 6th Attack on the United States Capitol (National Archives Production), 076P-R000010225_0001 - 076P-R000010226_0001 (November 6, 2020, email from Vincent Haley to Johnny McEntee and Daniel Huff re: Contact info of key leaders in key States and attaching contact info); Documents on file with the Select Committee to Investigate the January 6th Attack on the United States Capitol (National Archives Production), 076P-R000010233_0001 (November 6, 2020, email chain between Vincent Haley, Johnny McEntee, and Daniel Huff re: Contact Info of key leaders in key States).

34. Documents on file with the Select Committee to Investigate the January 6th Attack on the United States Capitol (National Archives Production), 076P-R000010225_0001 - 076P-R000010226_0001 (November 6, 2020, email from Vincent Haley to Johnny McEntee and Daniel Huff re: Contact info of key leaders in key States and attaching contact info).

35. Documents on file with the Select Committee to Investigate the January 6th Attack on the United States Capitol (Vincent Haley Production), VMH-00004122-VMH-00004123 (November 8, 2020, text messages between Vincent Haley and Johnny McEntee).

36. Documents on file with the Select Committee to Investigate the January 6th Attack on the United States Capitol (National Archives Production), 076P-R000010533_0001 (November 10, 2020, email from Newt Gingrich to Molly Michael re: Only two options—please give to POTUS newt).

37. Documents on file with the Select Committee to Investigate the January 6th Attack on the United States Capitol (National Archives Production), 076P-R000010533_0001 (November 10, 2020, email from Newt Gingrich to Molly Michael re: Only two options—please give to POTUS newt).

38. Documents on file with the Select Committee to Investigate the January 6th Attack on the United States Capitol (National Archives Production), 076P-R000010586_0001 (November 10, 2020, email from Mark Meadows to Newt Gingrich re: Only two options—please give to POTUS newt).

39. Solange Reyner, "Newsmax CEO Ruddy: Trump 'Very Concerned' That Dems Will Steal Election," Newsmax, (Nov. 4, 2020), available at https://www.newsmax.com/newsmax-tv/chris-ruddy-2020-elections-democrats-white-house/2020/11/04/id/995386/; Christopher Ruddy (@ChrisRuddyNMX), Twitter, Nov. 12, 2020 4:43 p.m. ET, available at https://twitter.com/ChrisRuddyNMX/status/1327004111154319360; "Digest of Other White House Announcements (Administration of Donald J. Trump, 2020)," Government Publishing Office, p. 114, available at https://www.govinfo.gov/content/pkg/DCPD-2020DIGEST/pdf/DCPD-2020DIGEST.pdf; Michael M. Grynbaum and John Koblin,"Newsmax, Once a Right-Wing Also-Ran, Is Rising, and Trump Approves," New York Times, (Nov. 22, 2020), available at https://www.nytimes.com/2020/11/22/business/media/newsmax-trump-fox-news.html; Cordelia Lynch, "Trump Ally on President's Next Move after Thanksgiving Phone Call," Sky News, (Dec. 4, 2020), available at https://news.sky.com/story/trump-ally-on-presidents-next-move-after-thanksgiving-phone-call-12150612; Documents on file with the Select Committee to Investigate the January 6th Attack on the United States Capitol (National Archives Production), 076P-R000009409_0001 (December 2, 2020, email from John McLaughlin to Molly Michael re: Newsmax National Poll).

40. Documents on file with the Select Committee to Investigate the January 6th Attack on the United States Capitol (Mark Meadows Production), MM008861-MM008865 (November 7, 2020, email from John McLaughlin to Mark Meadows and Newt Gingrich re: "Gerald Brant's birthday party/ my Nov 7, 2020 memo on ON 'ELECTORAL L COUNT ACT OF 1887' AND REPUBLICAN PATHWAYS: [sic]," and attaching memo forwarded by Christopher Ruddy).

41. Select Committee to Investigate the January 6th Attack on the United States Capitol, Deposition of Cleta Mitchell, (May 18, 2022), pp. 14-15; Jeremy Herb and Sunlen Serfaty, "How GOP Lawyer Cleta Mitchell Joined Trump's 'Team Deplorables' Advancing His False Election Fraud Claims," CNN, (Oct. 13, 2021), available at https://www.cnn.com/2021/10/13/politics/trump-mitchell-georgia-election/index.html.

42. Select Committee to Investigate the January 6th Attack on the United States Capitol, Deposition of Cleta Mitchell, (May 18, 2022), pp. 74-75.

43. Documents on file with the Select Committee to Investigate the January 6th Attack on the United States Capitol (Chapman University Production), Chapman006671.

44. Documents on file with the Select Committee to Investigate the January 6th Attack on the United States Capitol (Chapman University Production), Chapman007670-Chapman007671, Chapman008087 (November 9, 2020, email chain between John Eastman, Lisa Nelson, Rep. Seth Grove, and Cleta Mitchell re: Connections for today! and attaching memo).

45. Documents on file with the Select Committee to Investigate the January 6th Attack on the United States Capitol (National Archives Production),076P-R000010584_0001 (November 10, 2020, email chain scheduling an external meeting with President Trump).

46. Break Up DC (@BreakItUp3), Twitter, Nov. 11, 2020, available at http://web.archive.org/web/20201111104529/https://twitter.com/BreakItUp3/status/1326475581005950976 ("Was in Oval yesterday. You are right."). For attribution of the account to Warstler, see The RSnake Show, "S01E10 - Morgan Warstler," YouTube, at 1:43:00 - 1:44:00, Apr. 20, 2022, available at https://www.youtube.com/watch?v=k-ojD3QAYfo; Break Up DC (@BreakItUp3), Twitter, June 16, 2022, available at http://web.archive.org/web/20220616124842/https://twitter.com/BreakItUp3/status/1537414050510000128 ("NO it is not. I went to the Oval right after election and spent an hour with Trump sitting at Resolute desk. I explain it all here: https://

youtu.be/k-ojD3QAYfo?t=2724 . . . Hint: the electoral count act is unconstitutional—there is only one slate of electors- whatever the state leg says").

47.   Break Up DC (@BreakItUp3), Twitter, June 15, 2022 7:40 p.m. ET, available at http://
       web.archive.org/web/20220615234134/https://twitter.com/BreakItUp3/status/
       1537218579225268225 (archived) ("She literally was advocating what I told whole Trump
       team in Oval- it's a fact - state legislatures can choose the electors- no matter what cur-
       rent state law OR state courts say . . . just ratify it amongst themselves That's WHY they
       call it a plenary power ever since Bush v. Gore.").

48.   Documents on file with the Select Committee to Investigate the January 6th Attack on the
       United States Capitol (National Archives Production), 076P-R000008528_0001 - 076P-
       R000008530_0001.

49.   Documents on file with the Select Committee to Investigate the January 6th Attack on the
       United States Capitol (National Archives Production), 076P-R000008528_0001-076P-
       R000008528_0003, 076P-R000008530_0001 - 076P-R000008530_0002.

50.   Documents on file with the Select Committee to Investigate the January 6th Attack on the
       United States Capitol (National Archives Production), 076P-R000008528_0001 - 076P-
       R000008528_0003, 076P-R000008530_0001 - 076P-R000008530_0002.

51.   Documents on file with the Select Committee to Investigate the January 6th Attack on the
       United States Capitol (National Archives Production), 076P-R000008531_0001, 076P-
       R000008257_0001.

52.   Select Committee to Investigate the January 6th Attack on the United States Capitol, Tran-
       scribed Interview of William Stepien, (Feb. 10, 2022), pp. 151-52.

53.   Select Committee to Investigate the January 6th Attack on the United States Capitol, Tran-
       scribed Interview of William Stepien, (Feb. 10, 2022), p. 153. This fits with several major
       news reports at the time. The *New York Times* reported that President Trump went into the
       meeting on the 11th with "something he wanted to discuss with his advisors," and
       "press[ed] them on whether Republican legislatures could pick pro-Trump electors in a
       handful of key states and deliver him the electoral votes he needs." Maggie Haberman,
       "Trump Floats Improbable Survival Scenarios as He Ponders His Future," *New York Times*,
       (Nov. 12, 2020, updated Nov. 23, 2020), available at https://www.nytimes.com/2020/11/12/
       us/politics/trump-future.html. Similarly, late on November 11th, the *Washington Post*
       reported that President Trump had "raised the idea of pressuring state legislators to pick
       electors favorable to him," and the *Wall Street Journal* also called the option of state legis-
       latures picking new electors "one potential strategy" discussed by his legal team. Philip
       Rucker, Josh Dawsey & Ashley Parker, "Trump Insists He'll Win, But Aides Say He Has No
       Real Plan to Overturn Results and Talks of 2024 Run," *Washington Post*, (Nov. 11, 2020),
       available at https://www.washingtonpost.com/politics/trump-election-results-strategy/
       2020/11/11/a32e2cba-244a-11eb-952e-0c475972cfc0_story.html; Rebecca Ballhaus, "What Is
       Trump's Legal Strategy? Try to Block Certification of Biden Victory in States," *Wall Street
       Journal*, (Nov. 11, 2020), available at https://www.wsj.com/articles/what-is-trumps-legal-
       strategy-try-to-block-certification-of-biden-victory-in-states-11605138852.

54.   Select Committee to Investigate the January 6th Attack on the United States Capitol, Tran-
       scribed Interview of William Stepien, (Feb. 10, 2022), p. 148-49.

55.   Senator Mitt Romney (@MittRomney), Twitter, Nov. 19, 2020 10:36 p.m. ET, available at
       https://twitter.com/MittRomney/status/1329629701447573504.

56.   This figure is almost certainly a significant undercount, since it only includes public
       remarks by President Trump, public testimony, or the most noteworthy interviews con-
       ducted by one of his subordinates, but it does not include a review of every single remark
       targeting State or local officials during this period by those presidential subordinates.

57.   This figure is also almost certainly an undercount, since it only includes those posts by
       President Trump's campaign or advisors when they covered new ground that was substan-
       tially different from social media posts that were already made by President Trump. Also,
       many of these posts were replicated across multiple platforms.

58. Jonathan Oosting, "Trump Campaign Lobbies Michigan Lawmakers to Ignore Vote, Give Him Electors," *Bridge Michigan*, (Dec. 2, 2020), available at https://www.bridgemi.com/michigan-government/trump-campaign-lobbies-michigan-lawmakers-ignore-vote-give-him-electors; MIRS Monday Podcast, "Call to Legislator From Someone Claiming to be with Trump Campaign (12/1/2020)," PodBean, Dec. 1, 2020, available at https://www.podbean.com/media/share/pb-iqskx-f3cfc6; Documents on file with the Select Committee to Investigate the January 6th Attack on the United States Capitol (Angela McCallum Production), McCallum_01_001570, (Undated Basic Script for calls to Representatives/Senators).

59. Paul Bedard, "Exclusive: Trump Urges State Legislators to Reject Electoral Votes, 'You Are the Real Power,'" *Washington Examiner*, (Jan. 3, 2021), available at https://www.washingtonexaminer.com/washington-secrets/exclusive-trump-urges-state-legislators-to-reject-electoral-votes-you-are-the-real-power.

60. Documents on file with the Select Committee to Investigate the January 6th Attack on the United States Capitol (Maricopa County Board of Supervisors Production), CTRL0000020072 (December 24, 2020, copy of voice message and a transcription) pp. 1–2); *see also* Yvonne Wingett Sanchez and Ronald J. Hansen, "'Asked to Do Something Huge': An Audacious Pitch to Reverse Arizona's Election Results," *AZ Central*, (Dec. 2, 2021), available at https://www.azcentral.com/in-depth/news/politics/elections/2021/11/18/arizona-audit-rudy-giuliani-failed-effort-replace-electors/6349795001/.

61. Documents on file with the Select Committee to Investigate the January 6th Attack on the United States Capitol (National Archives Production), 076P-R000010292_0001 (November 12, 2020, email from Rep. Tim Walberg to Molly Michael).

62. Documents on file with the Select Committee to Investigate the January 6th Attack on the United States Capitol (National Archives Production), 076P-R000010292_0001 (November 12, 2020, email from Rep. Tim Walberg to Molly Michael). The day after Representative Walberg's call with the President, President Trump's assistant forwarded to the Acting Secretary of the Department of Homeland Security a letter signed by two other Michigan legislators outlining claims of supposed election fraud. Documents on file with the Select Committee to Investigate the January 6th Attack on the United States Capitol, (Department of Homeland Security production), CTRL0000033284, (Nov. 13, 2020 email from Molly Michael to Chad Wolf titled "Re: Michigan Letter"); Documents on file with the Select Committee to Investigate the January 6th Attack on the United States Capitol, (no production listed, Ex. 44 from Chad Wolf interview), CTRL0000926977 (Nov. 13, 2020 letter to Michigan Secretary of State Jocelyn Benson from Michigan State Senators Lana Theis and Tom Barrett).

63. "Administration of Donald J. Trump, 2020, Digest of Other White House Announcements," Government Publishing Office, (Dec. 31, 2020), p. 115, available at https://www.govinfo.gov/content/pkg/DCPD-2020DIGEST/pdf/DCPD-2020DIGEST.pdf; Annie Grayer, Jeremy Herb & Kevin Liptak, "Trump Courts Michigan GOP Leaders in Bid to Overturn Election He Lost," CNN, (Nov. 19, 2020), available at https://www.cnn.com/2020/11/19/politics/gop-michigan-results-trump/.

64. Documents on file with the Select Committee to Investigate the January 6th Attack on the United States Capitol (Mark Meadows Production), MM012007 (text from Kelli Ward to Meadows).

65. Brahm Resnik, "'Stop the Counting': Records Show Trump and Allies Pressured Top Maricopa County Officials Over Election Results," 12News, (July 7, 2021), available at https://www.12news.com/article/news/politics/stop-the-counting-records-show-trump-and-allies-pressured-top-maricopa-county-officials-over-election-results/75-61a93e63-36c4-4137-b65e-d3f8bde846a7.

66. Select Committee to Investigation the January 6th Attack on the United States Capitol, Informal Interview with Clint Hickman, (Nov. 17, 2021); Documents on file with the Select Committee to Investigate the January 6th Attack on the United States Capitol (Maricopa County Board of Supervisors Production), CTRL0000020004.

67. Brian Slodysko, "EXPLAINER: Why AP called Georgia for Biden," *Associated Press*, (Nov. 13, 2020), available at https://apnews.com/article/why-ap-called-georgia-for-joe-biden-29c1fb0502efde50fdccb5e2c3611017.

68. Donald J. Trump (@realDonaldTrump), Twitter, Nov. 13, 2020 7:50 p.m. ET, available at https://media-cdn.factba.se/realdonaldtrump-twitter/1327413534901350400.jpg (archived).

69. Donald J. Trump (@realDonaldTrump), Twitter, Nov. 14, 2020 9:29 a.m. ET, available at https://media-cdn.factba.se/realdonaldtrump-twitter/1327619653020110850.jpg (archived).

70. Donald J. Trump (@realDonaldTrump), Twitter, Nov. 16, 2020 9:04 a.m. ET, available at https://media-cdn.factba.se/realdonaldtrump-twitter/1328338211284616193.jpg (archived).

71. Donald J. Trump (@realDonaldTrump), Twitter, Nov. 19, 2020 1:46 p.m. ET, available at https://media-cdn.factba.se/realdonaldtrump-twitter/1329420741553643522.jpg (archived).

72. Donald J. Trump (@realDonaldTrump), Twitter, Nov. 30, 2020 1:59 p.m. ET, available at https://media-cdn.factba.se/realdonaldtrump-twitter/1333410419554344964.jpg (archived).

73. President Donald J. Trump, "Tweets of November 30, 2020," The American Presidency Project, available at https://www.presidency.ucsb.edu/documents/tweets-november-30-2020; *see also* Fox 10 Staff, "Tweet mocking Arizona Gov. Doug Ducey and Georgia Gov. Brian Kemp Now on Billboard," Fox 10 News, (Dec. 9, 2020), available at https://www.fox10phoenix.com/news/tweet-mocking-arizona-gov-doug-ducey-and-georgia-gov-brian-kemp-now-on-billboard.

74. Miles Bryan, "From Obscure To Sold Out: The Story Of Four Seasons Total Landscaping In Just 4 Days," NPR, (Nov. 11, 2020), available at https://www.npr.org/2020/11/11/933635970/from-obscure-to-sold-out-the-story-of-four-seasons-total-landscaping-in-just-4-d.

75. Matt Friedman, "Man Featured at Giuliani Press Conference is a Convicted Sex Offender," *Politico*, (Nov. 9, 2020), available at https://www.politico.com/states/new-jersey/story/2020/11/09/man-featured-at-giuliani-press-conference-is-a-sex-offender-1335241.

76. McKenzie Sadeghi, "Fact Check: No Evidence Vote Was Cast in Joe Frazier's Name," *USA Today*, (Nov. 14, 2020), available at https://www.usatoday.com/story/news/factcheck/2020/11/14/fact-check-no-evidence-late-joe-frazier-voted-2020-election/6283956002/; Ledyard King and John Fritze, "Trump Attorney Rudy Giuliani Says Trump Won't Concede, Revives Baseless Claims of Voter Fraud," *USA Today*, (Nov. 7, 2020) available at https://www.usatoday.com/story/news/politics/elections/2020/11/07/joe-biden-victory-president-trump-claims-election-far-over/6202892002/.

77. Veronica Stracqualursi, "Republican Election Official in Philadelphia Says He's Seen No Evidence of Widespread Fraud," CNN, (Nov. 11, 2020), available at https://www.cnn.com/2020/11/11/politics/philadelphia-city-commissioner-2020-election-cnntv/index.html.

78. Donald Trump (@realDonaldTrump), Twitter, Nov. 11, 2020 9:03 a.m. ET, available at https://media-cdn.factba.se/realdonaldtrump-twitter/1326525851752656898.jpg (archived).

79. Select Committee to Investigate the January 6th Attack on the United States Capitol, *Hearing on the January 6th Investigation*, 117th Cong., 2d sess., (June 13, 2022), at 1:47:00 to 1:48:00, available at https://www.youtube.com/watch?v=pr5QUInmGI8.

80. Select Committee to Investigate the January 6th Attack on the United States Capitol, *Hearing on the January 6th Investigation*, 117th Cong., 2d sess., (June 13, 2022), at 1:47:00 to 1:48:00, available at https://www.youtube.com/watch?v=pr5QUInmGI8.

81. Select Committee to Investigate the January 6th Attack on the United States Capitol, *Hearing on the January 6th Investigation*, 117th Cong., 2d sess., (June 13, 2022), at 1:47:00 to 1:48:00, available at https://www.youtube.com/watch?v=pr5QUInmGI8.

82. *See McQuade v. Furgason*, 91 Mich. 438 (1892). The various Boards of Canvassers in Michigan know that the certification process is clerical because they are so instructed in the official "Michigan Boards of County Canvassers Manual." *See* "Procedures and Duties of the

Boards of County Canvassers," State of Michigan, (July 2022), pp. 18-19, available at https://www.michigan.gov/-/media/Project/Websites/sos/02lehman/BCC_Manual.pdf?rev=7270a5ddcefa465b8ab8b95930ef5890.

83. "Minutes of Meeting Wayne County Board of Canvassers, (Nov. 17, 2020), p. 1, available at https://www.waynecounty.com/elected/clerk/board-of-canvassers.aspx.

84. "Minutes of Meeting Wayne County Board of Canvassers, (Nov. 17, 2020), pp. 1-5, available at https://www.waynecounty.com/elected/clerk/board-of-canvassers.aspx.

85. "Minutes of Meeting Wayne County Board of Canvassers, (Nov. 17, 2020), p. 5, available at https://www.waynecounty.com/elected/clerk/board-of-canvassers.aspx.

86. Select Committee to Investigate the January 6th Attack on the United States Capitol, Informal Interview of Monica Palmer, (Sept. 28, 2021); Select Committee to Investigate the January 6th Attack on the United States Capitol, Informal Interview of Ronna Romney McDaniel, (Mar. 9, 2022); Phone records for Monica Palmer show calls from Ronna McDaniel at 9:53 PM and 10:04 PM. *See* Documents on file with the Select Committee to Investigate the January 6th Attack on the United States Capitol (Verizon Production, Feb. 9, 2022).

87. Annie Grayer, Jeremy Herb, and Kevin Liptak, "Trump Courts Michigan GOP Leaders in Bid to Overturn Election He Lost," CNN, (Nov. 19, 2020), https://www.cnn.com/2020/11/19/politics/gop-michigan-results-trump/.

88. Select Committee to Investigate the January 6th Attack on the United States Capitol, Informal Interview of Monica Palmer, (Sept. 28, 2021). Palmer told the Select Committee that she could not recall the exact words that President Trump used on the call, and she claimed that she could not even recall whether the President raised issues related to the election.

89. Kendall Karson, Katherine Faulders, and Will Steakin, "Republican Canvassers Ask to 'Rescind' Their Votes Certifying Michigan Election Results," ABC News, (Nov. 19, 2020), available at https://abcnews.go.com/US/wayne-county-republican-canvassers-rescind-votes-certifying-election/story?id=74290114; Krystle Holleman and Spencer Soicher, "Pair of Wayne Co. Board of Canvassers Members File Affidavits to Rescind Certification of Election Results," WILX10, (Nov. 19, 2020), available at https://www.wilx.com/2020/11/19/pair-of-wayne-county-board-of-canvassers-members-file-affidavits-to-rescind-certification-of-election-results/; Paul Egan, "GOP Members of Wayne County Board of Canvassers Say They Want to Rescind Votes to Certify," *Detroit Free Press*, (Nov. 19, 2020), available at https://www.freep.com/story/news/politics/elections/2020/11/19/wayne-county-board-of-canvassers-monica-palmer-william-hartmann/3775242001/.

90. Kendall Karson, Katherine Faulders, and Will Steakin, "Republican Canvassers Ask to 'Rescind' Their Votes Certifying Michigan Election Results," ABC News, (Nov. 19, 2020), available at https://abcnews.go.com/US/wayne-county-republican-canvassers-rescind-votes-certifying-election/story?id=74290114; Krystle Holleman and Spencer Soicher, "Pair of Wayne Co. Board of Canvassers Members File Affidavits to Rescind Certification of Election Results," WILX10, (Nov. 19, 2020), available at https://www.wilx.com/2020/11/19/pair-of-wayne-county-board-of-canvassers-members-file-affidavits-to-rescind-certification-of-election-results/; Paul Egan, "GOP Members of Wayne County Board of Canvassers Say They Want to Rescind Votes to Certify," *Detroit Free Press*, (Nov. 19, 2020), available at https://www.freep.com/story/news/politics/elections/2020/11/19/wayne-county-board-of-canvassers-monica-palmer-william-hartmann/3775242001/.

91. Donald Trump (@realDonaldTrump), Twitter, Nov. 18, 2020 10:38 a.m. ET, available at https://media-cdn.factba.se/realdonaldtrump-twitter/1329086548093014022.jpg (archived).

92. Select Committee to Investigate the January 6th Attack on the United States Capitol, Informal Interview of Jack Sellers and Bill Gates, (Oct. 6, 2021).

93. Select Committee to Investigate the January 6th Attack on the United States Capitol, Informal Interview of Jack Sellers and Bill Gates, (Oct. 6, 2021).

94. Select Committee to Investigate the January 6th Attack on the United States Capitol, Informal Interview of Jack Sellers and Bill Gates, (Oct. 6, 2021).

95. Jonathan J. Cooper, "Arizona Governor Silences Trump's Call, Certifies Election," *Associated Press*, (Dec. 2, 2020), available at https://apnews.com/article/election-2020-donald-trump-arizona-elections-doug-ducey-e2b8b0de5b809efcc9b1ad5d279023f4.

96. Jonathan J. Cooper, "Arizona Governor Silences Trump's Call, Certifies Election," *Associated Press*, (Dec. 2, 2020), available at https://apnews.com/article/election-2020-donald-trump-arizona-elections-doug-ducey-e2b8b0de5b809efcc9b1ad5d279023f4.

97. Donald Trump (@realDonaldTrump), Twitter, Nov. 30, 2020 3:39 p.m. ET, available at http://web.archive.org/web/20201201024920mp_/https:/twitter.com/realDonaldTrump/status/1333556242984431616 (archived).

98. President Donald J. Trump, "Tweets of November 30, 2020," The American Presidency Project, available at https://www.presidency.ucsb.edu/documents/tweets-november-30-2020; "Tweet Mocking Arizona Gov. Doug Ducey and Georgia Gov. Brian Kemp Now on Billboard," Fox 10 News, (Dec. 9, 2020), available at https://www.fox10phoenix.com/news/tweet-mocking-arizona-gov-doug-ducey-and-georgia-gov-brian-kemp-now-on-billboard.

99. Donald Trump (@realDonaldTrump), Twitter, Nov. 30, 2020 3:40 p.m. ET, available at http://web.archive.org/web/20201201022358/https:/twitter.com/realDonaldTrump/status/1333556458575818754 (archived).

100. Doug Ducey (@DougDucey), Twitter, Nov. 30, 2020 9:48 p.m. ET, available at https://twitter.com/dougducey/status/1333603735855976450.

101. Doug Ducey (@DougDucey), Twitter, Nov. 30, 2020 9:48 p.m. ET, available at https://twitter.com/dougducey/status/1333603735855976450.

102. Doug Ducey (@DougDucey), Twitter, Nov. 30, 2020 9:48 p.m. ET, available at https://twitter.com/dougducey/status/1333603735855976450.

103. "Pennsylvania, Arizona, Michigan Legislatures to Hold Public Hearings on 2020 Election,"" Donald J. Trump for President, (Nov. 24, 2020), available at http://web.archive.org/web/20201130045430/https://www.donaldjtrump.com/media/pennsylvania-arizona-michigan-legislatures-to-hold-public-hearings-on-2020-election/.

104. "Donald Trump Remarks Transcript: Pennsylvania Republican Hearing on 2020 Election," Rev, (Nov. 25, 2020), available at https://www.rev.com/blog/transcripts/donald-trump-remarks-transcript-pennsylvania-republican-hearing-on-2020-election.

105. Teresa Boeckel and J.D. Prose, "Pa. GOP Lawmakers Host Giuliani to Hear Election Concerns. Trump Visits Via Cell Phone," *York Daily Record*, (Nov. 25, 2020), available at https://www.ydr.com/story/news/politics/2020/11/25/pa-gop-lawmakers-host-rudy-giuliani-hear-election-concerns/6420319002/.

106. Select Committee to Investigate the January 6th Attack on the United States Capitol, Informal Interview of Jake Corman, (Jan. 25, 2022).

107. *See* Documents on file with the Select Committee to Investigate the January 6th Attack on the United States Capitol (National Archives Production), 076P-R000008474_0001 (November 25, 2020, email from Jared Small confirming that Trump will not be present in Gettysburg); Philip Rucker, Ashley Parker, Josh Dawsey, and Amy Gardner, "20 Days of Fantasy and Failure: Inside Trump's Quest to Overturn the Election," *Washington Post*, (Nov. 28, 2020), available at https://www.washingtonpost.com/politics/trump-election-overturn/2020/11/28/34f45226-2f47-11eb-96c2-aac3f162215d_story.html; Alayna Treene and Rebecca Falconer, "Trump Cancels Pennsylvania Trip for GOP Hearing on Voter Fraud Claims," *Axios*, (Nov. 25, 2020) available at https://www.axios.com/2020/11/25/trump-pennsylvania-gop-hearing-voter-fraud-claims. Apparently, White House Chief of Staff Mark Meadows also contemplated going to Pennsylvania for the hearing when the President couldn't attend.

Text messages between Cassidy Hutchinson and Meadows's Secret Service detail say, "U heard how mark is motorcading to gburg right[,] and potus isn't anymore." Documents on file with the Select Committee to Investigate the January 6th Attack on the United States Capitol (Cassidy Hutchinson production), CH-CTRL0000000080 (Nov. 25, 2020).

108. "Donald Trump Remarks Transcript: Pennsylvania Republican Hearing on 2020 Election," Rev, (Nov. 25, 2020), available at https://www.rev.com/blog/transcripts/donald-trump-remarks-transcript-pennsylvania-republican-hearing-on-2020-election.

109. "Pennsylvania Senate Republican Lawmaker Hearing Transcript on 2020 Election," Rev, (Nov. 26, 2020), available at https://www.rev.com/blog/transcripts/pennsylvania-senate-republican-lawmaker-hearing-transcript-on-2020-election.

110. "Pennsylvania Senate Republican Lawmaker Hearing Transcript on 2020 Election," Rev, (Nov. 26, 2020), available at https://www.rev.com/blog/transcripts/pennsylvania-senate-republican-lawmaker-hearing-transcript-on-2020-election.

111. Select Committee to Investigate the January 6th Attack on the United States Capitol, Deposition of Rudolph Giuliani, (May 20, 2022), pp. 65–66; Select Committee to Investigate the January 6th Attack on the United States Capitol, Deposition of Molly Michael, (Mar. 24, 2022), pp. 59–60, 62; "Administration of Donald J. Trump, 2020, Digest of Other White House Announcements," Government Publishing Office, (Dec. 31, 2020), p. 116, https://www.govinfo.gov/content/pkg/DCPD-2020DIGEST/pdf/DCPD-2020DIGEST.pdf.

112. Documents on file with the Select Committee to Investigate the January 6th Attack on the United States Capitol (Cassidy Hutchinson production), CH-CTRL0000000062 (Nov. 25, 2020, Cassidy Hutchinson's text messages with Bernie Kerik).

113. Documents on file with the Select Committee to Investigate the January 6th Attack on the United States Capitol (Cassidy Hutchinson production), CH-CTRL0000000062 (Nov. 25, 2020, Cassidy Hutchinson's text messages with Bernie Kerik).

114. Select Committee to Investigate the January 6th Attack on the United States Capitol, Continued Interview of Cassidy Hutchinson (Mar. 7, 2022), pp. 87, 91-92.

115. Howard Fischer, "GOP Officials Still Fighting Arizona's Vote Tally on Very Day Biden's Win Will Be Certified," Tuscon.com, (Nov. 30, 2020), available at https://tucson.com/news/local/gop-officials-still-fighting-arizonas-vote-tally-on-very-day-bidens-win-will-be-certified/article_021fbb5c-673f-549a-9cbb-900178c17079.html.

116. Howard Fischer, "GOP Officials Still Fighting Arizona's Vote Tally on Very Day Biden's Win Will Be Certified," Tuscon.com, (Nov. 30, 2020), available at https://tucson.com/news/local/gop-officials-still-fighting-arizonas-vote-tally-on-very-day-bidens-win-will-be-certified/article_021fbb5c-673f-549a-9cbb-900178c17079.html.

117. Right Side Broadcasting Network, "LIVE: Arizona State Legislature Holds Public Hearing on 2020 Election," YouTube, at 2:08:56, Nov. 30, 2020, available at https://www.youtube.com/watch?v=rri6flxaXww&t=7738s.

118. Right Side Broadcasting Network, "LIVE: Arizona State Legislature Holds Public Hearing on 2020 Election," YouTube, at 1:21:02, Nov. 30, 2020, available at https://www.youtube.com/watch?v=rri6flxaXww&t=4862s.

119. Jenna Ellis (@JennaEllisEsq), Twitter, Nov. 30, 2020 3:04 p.m. ET, available at https://twitter.com/jennaellisesq/status/1333502306176835588.

120. "Remarks: Donald Trump Calls in to Meeting of Arizona GOP Lawmakers on Election," Factbase, (Nov. 30, 2020), available at https://factba.se/transcript/donald-trump-remarks-arizona-gop-meeting-election-november-30-2020.

121. Rudy Giuliani (@RudyGiuliani), Twitter, Nov. 30, 2020 11:17 p.m. ET, available at https://twitter.com/RudyGiuliani/status/1333626364805533696.

122. "Pennsylvania, Arizona, Michigan Legislatures to Hold Public Hearings on 2020 Election," Donald J. Trump, (Nov. 24, 2020), available at http://web.archive.org/web/20201130045430/

https://www.donaldjtrump.com/media/pennsylvania-arizona-michigan-legislatures-to-hold-public-hearings-on-2020-election/; Jonathan Oosting (@jonathanoosting), Twitter, Nov. 24, 2020 5:35 p.m. ET, available at https://twitter.com/jonathanoosting/status/1331365885123178499; Jonathan Oosting (@jonathanoosting), Twitter, Nov. 30, 2020 3:42 p.m. ET, available at https://twitter.com/jonathanoosting/status/1333511772448370689.

123. *See* "Report on the November 2020 Election in Michigan," Michigan Senate Oversight Committee, (June 21, 2020), available at https://misenategopcdn.s3.us-east-1.amazonaws.com/99/doccuments/20210623/SMPO_2020ElectionReport_2.pdf.

124. Wood TV8, "Giuliani and Laura Cox Hold 'Legal Briefing' Before Giving Testimony Wednesday Evening," Facebook Watch, at 10:30-10:45, Dec. 2, 2020, available at https://www.facebook.com/woodtv/videos/rudy-giuliani-and-laura-cox-hold-legal-briefing-before-giving-testimony-wednesda/1996033023872394/.

125. Wood TV8, "Giuliani and Laura Cox Hold 'Legal Briefing' Before Giving Testimony Wednesday Evening," Facebook Watch, at 13:05-13:20, Dec. 2, 2020, available at https://www.facebook.com/woodtv/videos/rudy-giuliani-and-laura-cox-hold-legal-briefing-before-giving-testimony-wednesda/1996033023872394/.

126. Michigan House Oversight Committee, Public Hearing, (Dec. 12, 2020), at 4:03:13-4:04:22, 4:05:59-4:07:09, available at https://www.rev.com/tc-editor/shared/QQodU0TgHNW4ACZmBtqq6EbotJVTGos3UifEuLQA8ygjV7GrDDAeGJ6hdps86h_ywJAatI_KepUqEeZnloKHBiByyMI.

127. Edward-Isaac Dovere (@IsaacDovere), Twitter, Dec. 3, 2020 7:56 a.m. ET, available at https://twitter.com/IsaacDovere/status/1334481562193317888.

128. Michigan House Oversight Committee, Public Hearing, (Dec. 12, 2020), at 4:09:04, available at https://www.rev.com/tc-editor/shared/QQodU0TgHNW4ACZmBtqq6EbotJVTGos3UifEuLQA8ygjV7GrDDAeGJ6hdps86h_ywJAatI_KepUqEeZnloKHBiByyMI.

129. Michigan House Oversight Committee, Public Hearing, (Dec. 12, 2020), at 4:35:15, available at https://www.rev.com/tc-editor/shared/QQodU0TgHNW4ACZmBtqq6EbotJVTGos3UifEuLQA8ygjV7GrDDAeGJ6hdps86h_ywJAatI_KepUqEeZnloKHBiByyMI.

130. 11Alive, "Second Georgia Senate Election Hearing," YouTube, at 1:56:30 to 1:57:15, 5:29:20-5:32:45, Dec. 3, 2020, available at https://www.youtube.com/watch?v=hRCXUNOwOjw.

131. GA House Mobile Streaming, "Governmental Affairs 12.10.20," Vimeo – Livestream, at 1:51:55-1:52:55, available at https://livestream.com/accounts/25225474/events/9117221/videos/214677184.

132. Global TV Online, "#LIVE: Georgia State Senate Holds Meeting on 2020 Election . . . ," YouTube, at 3:08:00 to 3:09:30, 3:20:15 to 3:21:2, Dec. 30, 2020, available at https://youtu.be/D5c034r0RlU?t=12016.

133. 11Alive, "Second Georgia Senate Election Hearing," YouTube, at 0:33:30-0:58:00, December 3, 2020, available at https://www.youtube.com/watch?v=hRCXUNOwOjw.

134. Select Committee to Investigate the January 6th Attack on the United States Capitol, Transcribed Interview of Byung J. Pak, (May 19, 2022), pp. 10-23; United States Senate Judiciary Committee, Interview of Jeffrey Rosen, (August 7, 2021), pp. 30-31, available at https://www.judiciary.senate.gov/rosen-transcript-final; Declaration of Frances Watson at 1-3, *Pearson v. Kemp*, No. 1:20-cv-04809 (N.D. Ga., Dec. 6, 2020), ECF No. 72-1, available at https://www.documentcloud.org/documents/20420664-frances-watson-affidavit; Response of the Georgia Secretary of State to the Court's Order of September 20, 2021 at 5-7, 41-47, 53, 55, *Favorito v. Wan*, No. 2020CV343938 (Fulton County Sup. Ct., Ga., October 12, 2021), available at https://s3.documentcloud.org/documents/21084096/favorito-sos-brief-in-response-to-order-of-92021-with-exs-a-and-b.pdf; William P. Barr, *One Damn Thing After Another: Memoirs of an Attorney General* (Harper Collins, 2022), at pp. 541-42; "Georgia Election Officials Briefing Transcript December 7: Will Recertify Election Results Today,"

Rev, (December 7, 2020), available at https://www.rev.com/blog/transcripts/georgia-election-officials-briefing-transcript-december-7-will-recertify-election-results-today.

135. 11Alive, "Second Georgia Senate Election Hearing," YouTube, at 5:31:50-5:32:10, Dec. 3, 2020, available at https://www.youtube.com/watch?v=hRCXUNOwOjw.

136. GA House Mobile Streaming, "Governmental Affairs 12.10.20," Vimeo – Livestream, at 2:09:00-2:13:00, available at https://livestream.com/accounts/25225474/events/9117221/videos/214677184.

137. GA House Mobile Streaming, "Governmental Affairs 12.10.20," Vimeo – Livestream, at 2:09:00-2:13:00, available at https://livestream.com/accounts/25225474/events/9117221/videos/214677184.

138. Mike Wilkinson, "The Rudy Giuliani 'Circus' Has Left Lansing. The Reviews Are Bad," *Bridge Michigan*, (Dec. 3, 2020), available at https://www.bridgemi.com/michigan-government/rudy-giuliani-circus-has-left-lansing-reviews-are-bad.

139. Mike Wilkinson, "The Rudy Giuliani 'Circus' Has Left Lansing. The Reviews Are Bad," *Bridge Michigan*, (Dec. 3, 2020), available at https://www.bridgemi.com/michigan-government/rudy-giuliani-circus-has-left-lansing-reviews-are-bad.

140. Donald J. Trump (@realDonaldTrump), Twitter, Dec. 6, 2020 6:01 a.m. ET, https://media-cdn.factba.se/realdonaldtrump-twitter/1335464302766149632.jpg (archived)..

141. *In the Matter of Rudolph W. Giuliani*, No. 2021-00506, slip op at *2, 32 (N.Y. App. Div. May 3, 2021), available at https://int.nyt.com/data/documenttools/giuliani-law-license-suspension/1ae5ad6007c0ebfa/full.pdf.

142. Documents on file with the Select Committee to Investigate the January 6th Attack on the United States Capitol (Angela McCallum Production), McCallum_01_001501 (November 30, 2021, Michael Brown text message to group at 2:47 a.m.).

143. Documents on file with the Select Committee to Investigate the January 6th Attack on the United States Capitol (Angela McCallum Production), McCallum_01_001501 (November 30, 2021, Michael Brown text message to group at 2:47 a.m.).

144. Documents on file with the Select Committee to Investigate the January 6th Attack on the United States Capitol (Angela McCallum Production), McCallum_01_001528 - 1564 (Trump Campaign spreadsheet).

145. Mirs Monday Podcast, "Call to Legislator from Someone Claiming to Be With Trump Campaign (12/1/20)," *Podbean.com*, at 0:08, (Dec. 1, 2020), available at https://www.podbean.com/media/share/pb-iqskx-f3cfc6.

146. Mirs Monday Podcast, "Call to Legislator from Someone Claiming to Be With Trump Campaign (12/1/20)," *Podbean.com*, at 1:32, (Dec. 1, 2020), available at https://www.podbean.com/media/share/pb-iqskx-f3cfc6.

147. Jonathan Oosting, "Trump Campaign Lobbies Michigan Lawmakers to Ignore Vote, Give Him Electors," *Bridge Michigan*, (Dec. 2, 2020), available at https://www.bridgemi.com/michigan-government/trump-campaign-lobbies-michigan-lawmakers-ignore-vote-give-him-electors.

148. Documents on file with the Select Committee to Investigate the January 6th Attack on the United States Capitol (Angela McCallum production), McCallum_01_001523 (text messages with Michael Brown).

149. Documents on file with the Select Committee to Investigate the January 6th Attack on the United States Capitol (Angela McCallum production), McCallum_01_001523 (text messages with Michael Brown).

150. Select Committee to Investigate the January 6th Attack on the United States Capitol, Transcribed Interview of Michael Shirkey, (June 8, 2022), pp. 8-10; Senator Mike Shirkey (@SenMikeShirkey), Twitter, Nov. 20, 2020 6:13 p.m. ET, available at https://twitter.com/SenMikeShirkey/status/1329925843053899780.

151. Select Committee to Investigate the January 6th Attack on the United States Capitol, Transcribed Interview of Michael Shirkey, (June 8, 2022), p. 10.

152. "Administration of Donald J. Trump, 2020, Digest of Other White House Announcements," Government Publishing Office, (December 31, 2020), p. 115, available at https://www.govinfo.gov/content/pkg/DCPD-2020DIGEST/pdf/DCPD-2020DIGEST.pdf.

153. Select Committee to Investigate the January 6th Attack on the United States Capitol, Transcribed Interview of Michael Shirkey, (June 8, 2022), p. 16.

154. Select Committee to Investigate the January 6th Attack on the United States Capitol, Transcribed Interview of Michael Shirkey, (June 8, 2022), pp. 16-18.

155. Select Committee to Investigate the January 6th Attack on the United States Capitol, Transcribed Interview of Michael Shirkey, (June 8, 2022), pp. 21-22.

156. Select Committee to Investigate the January 6th Attack on the United States Capitol, Transcribed Interview of Michael Shirkey, (June 8, 2022), p. 22.

157. Select Committee to Investigate the January 6th Attack on the United States Capitol, Informal Interview of Lee Chatfield (Oct. 15, 2021). Leader Shirkey did not remember any specific "ask" from the President during the Oval Office meeting. Select Committee to Investigate the January 6th Attack on the United States Capitol, Transcribed Interview of Michael Shirkey, (June 8, 2022), p. 16 ("One thing I do remember is that he never, ever, to the best of my recollection, ever made a specific ask. It was always just general topics[.]").

158. Select Committee to Investigate the January 6th Attack on the United States Capitol, Informal Interview of Lee Chatfield (Oct. 15, 2021).

159. Select Committee to Investigate the January 6th Attack on the United States Capitol, Transcribed Interview of Michael Shirkey, (June 8, 2022), p. 57.

160. "Legislative Leaders Meet with President Trump," State Senator Mike Shirkey, (Nov. 20, 2020), available at https://www.senatormikeshirkey.com/legislative-leaders-meet-with-president-trump/.

161. Select Committee to Investigate the January 6th Attack on the United States Capitol, Informal Interview of Lee Chatfield, (Oct. 15, 2021).

162. Select Committee to Investigate the January 6th Attack on the United States Capitol, Informal Interview of Lee Chatfield, (Oct. 15, 2021).

163. Team Trump (Text TRUMP to 88022) (@TeamTrump), Twitter, Jan. 3, 2021 9:00 a.m. ET, available at http://web.archive.org/web/20210103170109/https://twitter.com/TeamTrump/status/1345776940196659201 (archived).

164. Select Committee to Investigate the January 6th Attack on the United States Capitol, Transcribed Interview of Michael Shirkey, (June 8, 2022), p. 52; Aaron Parseghian, "Former Michigan Resident Slammed with Calls after Trump Campaign Mistakenly Posts Number on Social Media," Fox 17 West Michigan, (Jan. 4, 2021), available at https://www.fox17online.com/news/politics/former-michigan-resident-slammed-with-calls-after-trump-campaign-mistakenly-posts-number-on-social-media.

165. Documents on file with the Select Committee to Investigate the January 6th Attack on the United States Capitol (Mark Meadows Production), MM012414 (text to Rep. Scott Perry from Meadows).

166. Documents on file with the Select Committee to Investigate the January 6th Attack on the United States Capitol (Mark Meadows Production), MM012445 (text to Meadows from Rep. Scott Perry).

167. Select Committee to Investigate the January 6th Attack on the United States Capitol, Informal Interview of Jake Corman, (Jan. 25, 2022); Jake Corman and Kerry Benninghoff, "Pa. Lawmakers Have No Role to Play in Deciding Presidential Election," *Centre Daily Times*, (Oct. 19, 2020), available at https://www.centredaily.com/opinion/article246527648.html.

168. Barton Gellman, "The Election That Could Break America," *The Atlantic*, (Sept. 23, 2020), available at https://www.theatlantic.com/magazine/archive/2020/11/what-if-trump-refuses-concede/616424/; Select Committee to Investigate the January 6th Attack on the United States Capitol, Informal Interview of Jake Corman, (Jan. 25, 2022); see Jake Corman, "Pa. Lawmakers Have No Role to Play in Deciding Presidential Election," *Centre Daily Times*, (Oct. 19, 2020) available at https://www.centredaily.com/opinion/article246527648.html. Senator Corman and other Pennsylvania lawmakers sent a letter to Congress in January that mentioned "numerous unlawful violations" of State law and asked that Congress "delay certification of the electoral college." Documents on file with the Select Committee to Investigate the January 6th Attack on the United States Capitol (National Archives Production), 076P-R000002160_00001. In his informal interview with the Select Committee, however, Senator Corman acknowledged that he signed the letter due to pressure he was receiving after the election, but explained that he believed fraud and these types of issues should be adjudicated in the courtroom, not the legislature, and, in any event, he said that he was never presented with credible evidence of voter fraud. *See* Select Committee to Investigate the January 6th Attack on the United States Capitol, Informal Interview of Jake Corman, (Jan. 25, 2022).

169. Select Committee to Investigate the January 6th Attack on the United States Capitol, Informal Interview of Jake Corman, (Jan. 25, 2022).

170. Select Committee to Investigate the January 6th Attack on the United States Capitol, Informal Interview of Jake Corman, (Jan. 25, 2022).

171. Select Committee to Investigate the January 6th Attack on the United States Capitol, Informal Interview of Jake Corman, (Jan. 25, 2022).

172. Select Committee to Investigate the January 6th Attack on the United States Capitol, Informal Interview of Jake Corman, (Jan. 25, 2022).

173. Select Committee to Investigate the January 6th Attack on the United States Capitol, Informal Interview of Jake Corman, (Jan. 25, 2022).

174. Select Committee to Investigate the January 6th Attack on the United States Capitol, Informal Interview of Jake Corman, (Jan. 25, 2022).

175. Select Committee to Investigate the January 6th Attack on the United States Capitol, Informal Interview of Jake Corman, (Jan. 25, 2022).

176. Select Committee to Investigate the January 6th Attack on the United States Capitol, Informal Interview of Jake Corman, (Jan. 25, 2022).

177. Select Committee to Investigate the January 6th Attack on the United States Capitol, Informal Interview of Jake Corman, (Jan. 25, 2022).

178. Documents on file with the Select Committee to Investigate the January 6th Attack on the United States Capitol (Bryan Cutler Production), B_CUTLER_0000131-0000134 (Giuliani and Ellis voicemails).

179. Select Committee to Investigate the January 6th Attack on the U.S. Capitol, Transcribed Interview of Bryan Cutler, (May 31, 2022), p. 21.

180. Select Committee to Investigate the January 6th Attack on the U.S. Capitol, Transcribed Interview of Bryan Cutler, (May 31, 2022), p. 21.

181. Documents on file with the Select Committee to Investigate the January 6th Attack on the United States Capitol (Bryan Cutler Production), B_CUTLER_0000131 (Giuliani and Ellis voicemail).

182. Documents on file with the Select Committee to Investigate the January 6th Attack on the United States Capitol (Bryan Cutler Production), B_CUTLER_0000132 (Jenna Ellis voicemail).

183. Documents on file with the Select Committee to Investigate the January 6th Attack on the United States Capitol (Bryan Cutler Production), B_CUTLER_0000133 (Giuliani voicemail).

184. Documents on file with the Select Committee to Investigate the January 6th Attack on the United States Capitol (Bryan Cutler Production), B_CUTLER_0000134 (Giuliani voicemail).

185. Select Committee to Investigate the January 6th Attack on the U.S. Capitol, Transcribed Interview of Bryan Cutler, (May 31, 2022), pp. 42-44, 46-47. The *New York Times* reported that Speaker Cutler spoke with President Trump twice by phone, Cutler told the Select Committee that this claim was incorrect and that he only spoke with the President by phone once, followed by their second conversation on December 3rd, which was in person. *See* Trip Gabriel, "Trump Asked Pennsylvania House Speaker about Overturning His Loss," *New York Times*, (Dec. 8, 2020), available at https://www.nytimes.com/2020/12/08/us/politics/trump-pennsylvania-house-speaker.html; *see also* Amy Gardner, Josh Dawsey and Rachael Bade, "Trump Asks Pennsylvania House Speaker for Help Overturning Election Results, Personally Intervening in a Third State," *Washington Post*, (Dec. 8, 2020), available at https://www.washingtonpost.com/politics/trump-pennsylvania-speaker-call/2020/12/07/d65fe8c4-38bf-11eb-98c4-25dc9f4987e8_story.html.

186. Select Committee to Investigate the January 6th Attack on the U.S. Capitol, Transcribed Interview of Bryan Cutler, (May 31, 2022), pp. 43-44.

187. Select Committee to Investigate the January 6th Attack on the U.S. Capitol, Transcribed Interview of Bryan Cutler, (May 31, 2022), pp. 26-27, 44.

188. Select Committee to Investigate the January 6th Attack on the U.S. Capitol, Transcribed Interview of Bryan Cutler, (May 31, 2022), pp. 49-57; Select Committee to Investigate the January 6th Attack on the United States Capitol, Informal Interview of Jake Corman, (Jan. 25, 2022).

189. Select Committee to Investigate the January 6th Attack on the U.S. Capitol, Transcribed Interview of Bryan Cutler, (May 31, 2022), p. 50.

190. Select Committee to Investigate the January 6th Attack on the U.S. Capitol, Transcribed Interview of Bryan Cutler, (May 31, 2022), pp. 50-55.

191. Select Committee to Investigate the January 6th Attack on the U.S. Capitol, Transcribed Interview of Bryan Cutler, (May 31, 2022), pp. 54-55.

192. Select Committee to Investigate the January 6th Attack on the U.S. Capitol, Transcribed Interview of Bryan Cutler, (May 31, 2022), pp. 56-57.

193. "Statement on Election Reform," Pennsylvania Senate GOP (Dec 3, 2020, accessed July 14, 2022), available at https://www.pasenategop.com/wp-content/uploads/2020/12/election-reform-120320.pdf.

194. Donald J. Trump (@realDonaldTrump), Twitter, Dec. 6, 2020 12:56 a.m. ET, available at https://media-cdn.factba.se/realdonaldtrump-twitter/1335463148137164802.jpg (archived).

195. Donald J. Trump (@realDonaldTrump), Twitter, Dec. 8, 2020 2:51 p.m. ET, available at https://media-cdn.factba.se/realdonaldtrump-twitter/1336322408970559495.jpg (archived); "Letter to Pennsylvania's Congressional Delegation," Pennsylvania State GOP, (Dec. 4, 2020, last accessed July 14, 2022), available at http://www.pahousegop.com/Display/SiteFiles/1/2020/120420CongressElection2020B.pdf.

196. Select Committee to Investigate the January 6th Attack on the U.S. Capitol, Transcribed Interview of Bryan Cutler, (May 31, 2022), pp. 60-61.

197. Select Committee to Investigate the January 6th Attack on the U.S. Capitol, Transcribed Interview of Bryan Cutler, (May 31, 2022), p. 61.

198. Trip Gabriel, "Even in Defeat, Trump Tightens Grip on State G.O.P. Lawmakers," *New York Times*, (Dec. 9, 2020), available at https://www.nytimes.com/2020/12/09/us/politics/trump-pennsylvania-electoral-college.html.

199. Trip Gabriel, "Even in Defeat, Trump Tightens Grip on State G.O.P. Lawmakers," *New York Times*, (Dec. 9, 2020), available at https://www.nytimes.com/2020/12/09/us/politics/trump-pennsylvania-electoral-college.html.

200. Select Committee to Investigate the January 6th Attack on the United States Capitol, *Hearing on the January 6th Investigation*, 117th Cong., 2d sess., (June 21, 2022), at 41:30-46:35, available at https://www.youtube.com/watch?v=xa43_z_82Og; Yvonne Wingett Sanchez and

Ronald J. Hansen, "White House Phone Calls, Baseless Fraud Charges: The Origins of the Arizona Election Review," *AZ Central*, (Nov. 17, 2021), available at https://www.azcentral.com/in-depth/news/politics/elections/2021/11/17/arizona-audit-trump-allies-pushed-to-undermine-2020-election/6045151001/.

201. Select Committee to Investigate the January 6th Attack on the United States Capitol, *Hearing on the January 6th Investigation*, 117th Cong., 2d sess., (June 21, 2022), at 41:30-46:35, available at https://www.youtube.com/watch?v=xa43_z_82Og; Yvonne Wingett Sanchez and Ronald J. Hansen, "White House Phone Calls, Baseless Fraud Charges: The Origins of the Arizona Election Review," *AZ Central*, (Nov. 17, 2021), available at https://www.azcentral.com/in-depth/news/politics/elections/2021/11/17/arizona-audit-trump-allies-pushed-to-undermine-2020-election/6045151001/.

202. Select Committee to Investigate the January 6th Attack on the United States Capitol, *Hearing on the January 6th Investigation*, 117th Cong., 2d sess., (June 21, 2022), at 41:30-46:35, available at https://www.youtube.com/watch?v=xa43_z_82Og; Yvonne Wingett Sanchez and Ronald J. Hansen, "White House Phone Calls, Baseless Fraud Charges: The Origins of the Arizona Election Review," *AZ Central*, (Nov. 17, 2021), available at https://www.azcentral.com/in-depth/news/politics/elections/2021/11/17/arizona-audit-trump-allies-pushed-to-undermine-2020-election/6045151001/.

203. Select Committee to Investigate the January 6th Attack on the United States Capitol, *Hearing on the January 6th Investigation*, 117th Cong., 2d sess., (June 21, 2022), at 41:30-46:35, available at https://www.youtube.com/watch?v=xa43_z_82Og; Yvonne Wingett Sanchez and Ronald J. Hansen, "White House Phone Calls, Baseless Fraud Charges: The Origins of the Arizona Election Review," *AZ Central*, (Nov. 17, 2021), available at https://www.azcentral.com/in-depth/news/politics/elections/2021/11/17/arizona-audit-trump-allies-pushed-to-undermine-2020-election/6045151001/.

204. Select Committee to Investigate the January 6th Attack on the United States Capitol, *Hearing on the January 6th Investigation*, 117th Cong., 2d sess., (June 21, 2022), at 41:30-46:35, available at https://www.youtube.com/watch?v=xa43_z_82Og.

205. Select Committee to Investigate the January 6th Attack on the United States Capitol, *Hearing on the January 6th Investigation*, 117th Cong., 2d sess., (June 21, 2022), at 41:30-46:35, available at https://www.youtube.com/watch?v=xa43_z_82Og.

206. Select Committee to Investigate the January 6th Attack on the United States Capitol, *Hearing on the January 6th Investigation*, 117th Cong., 2d sess., (June 21, 2022), at 41:30-46:35, available at https://www.youtube.com/watch?v=xa43_z_82Og. In his testimony to the Select Committee, Speaker Bowers said this appeal to party loyalty occurred in that call or in a later meeting, and that the President brought it up "more than once."

207. Dillon Rosenblatt and Julia Shumway, "Giuliani COVID-19 Diagnosis Closes Arizona Legislature," *Arizona Capitol Times*, (Dec. 6, 2020), available at https://azcapitoltimes.com/news/2020/12/06/giuliani-covid-19-diagnosis-closes-arizona-legislature/; Select Committee to Investigate the January 6th Attack on the United States Capitol, Informal Interview of Arizona House Speaker Rusty Bowers, (Nov. 17, 2021); Vince Leach (@VinceLeach), Twitter, Dec. 1, 2020 11:28 p.m. ET, available at https://twitter.com/VinceLeach/status/1333991317500727298. Speaker Bowers told the Committee that Giuliani and Ellis were accompanied by Katherine Friess, J. Philip Waldron, Bernard Kerik, and others. *See* Select Committee to Investigate the January 6th Attack on the United States Capitol, Informal Interview of Arizona House Speaker Rusty Bowers, (Nov. 17, 2021).

208. Select Committee to Investigate the January 6th Attack on the United States Capitol, Deposition of Rudolph Giuliani, (May 20, 2022), pp. 58-59; Select Committee to Investigate the January 6th Attack on the United States Capitol, Deposition of Jenna Ellis, (Mar. 8, 2022), pp. 50-51.

209. "Select Committee to Investigate the January 6th Attack on the U.S. Capitol, Transcribed Interview of Russel "Rusty" Bowers, (June 19, 2022), pp. 35-36; Select Committee to Investigate the January 6th Attack on the United States Capitol, Informal Interview of Arizona

House Speaker Rusty Bowers, (Nov. 17, 2021); "Speaker Bowers Addresses Calls for the Legislature to Overturn 2020 Certified Election Results," Arizona State Legislature, (Dec. 4, 2020), available at https://www.azleg.gov/press/house/54LEG/2R/201204STATEMENT.pdf

210. Select Committee to Investigate the January 6th Attack on the United States Capitol, *Hearing on the January 6th Investigation*, 117th Cong., 2d sess., (June 21, 2022), at 53:00-53:40, available at https://www.youtube.com/watch?v=xa43_z_82Og.

211. Select Committee to Investigate the January 6th Attack on the United States Capitol, *Hearing on the January 6th Investigation*, 117th Cong., 2d sess., (June 21, 2022), at 53:00-53:40, available at https://www.youtube.com/watch?v=xa43_z_82Og.

212. Select Committee to Investigate the January 6th Attack on the United States Capitol, *Hearing on the January 6th Investigation*, 117th Cong., 2d sess., (June 21, 2022), at 53:00-53:40, available at https://www.youtube.com/watch?v=xa43_z_82Og.

213. Select Committee to Investigate the January 6th Attack on the United States Capitol, *Hearing on the January 6th Investigation*, 117th Cong., 2d sess., (June 21, 2022), at 53:00-53:40, available at https://www.youtube.com/watch?v=xa43_z_82Og.

214. Select Committee to Investigate the January 6th Attack on the United States Capitol, *Hearing on the January 6th Investigation*, 117th Cong., 2d sess., (June 21, 2022), at 56:00-59:50, available at https://www.youtube.com/watch?v=xa43_z_82Og; Select Committee to Investigate the January 6th Attack on the United States Capitol, Transcribed Interview of Russell Bowers, (June 19, 2022), pp. 39-41.

215. Select Committee to Investigate the January 6th Attack on the United States Capitol, *Hearing on the January 6th Investigation*, 117th Cong., 2d sess., (June 21, 2022), at 56:00-59:50, available at https://www.youtube.com/watch?v=xa43_z_82Og.

216. Select Committee to Investigate the January 6th Attack on the United States Capitol, *Hearing on the January 6th Investigation*, 117th Cong., 2d sess., (June 21, 2022), at 56:00-59:50, available at https://www.youtube.com/watch?v=xa43_z_82Og.

217. "Trump Allies Leave Voicemail Messages for Maricopa County Supervisors," *AZ Central*, (July 2, 2021), available at https://www.azcentral.com/videos/news/politics/elections/2021/07/02/trump-allies-left-voicemail-messages-maricopa-county-supervisors-election-and-contested-results/7837919002/.

218. "Trump Allies Leave Voicemail Messages for Maricopa County Supervisors," *AZ Central*, (July 2, 2021), available at https://www.azcentral.com/videos/news/politics/elections/2021/07/02/trump-allies-left-voicemail-messages-maricopa-county-supervisors-election-and-contested-results/7837919002/.

219. *See* Select Committee to Investigate the January 6th Attack on the United States Capitol, Informal Interview of Clint Hickman, (Nov. 17, 2021); *see also* Yvonne Wingett Sanchez, "'We Need You to Stop the Counting': Records Detail Intense Efforts by Trump Allies to Pressure Maricopa County Supervisors," *AZ Central* (July 2, 2021), available at https://www.azcentral.com/story/news/politics/elections/2021/07/02/records-show-trump-allies-kelli-ward-rudy-giuliani-pressed-county-officials-over-election-results/7813304002/.

220. Yvonne Wingett Sanchez, "'Fighting for Democracy Here': Election Audit Pits Maricopa County Republicans vs. Arizona GOP," *AZ Central*, (May 23, 2021) available at https://www.azcentral.com/story/news/politics/elections/2021/05/23/election-audit-pits-maricopa-county-republicans-against-arizona-gop-senators/5186141001/; *see also* "Trump allies leave voicemail messages for Maricopa County supervisors," *AZ Central*, (July 2, 2021), available at https://www.azcentral.com/videos/news/politics/elections/2021/07/02/trump-allies-left-voicemail-messages-maricopa-county-supervisors-election-and-contested-results/7837919002/.

221. Documents on file with the Select Committee to Investigate the January 6th Attack on the United States Capitol (Maricopa County Board of Supervisors Production), CTRL0000020072, pp. 1-2 (December 24, 2020, copy of voice message and a transcription); *see also* Yvonne Wingett Sanchez and Ronald J. Hansen, "'Asked to Do Something Huge': An Audacious Pitch

to Reverse Arizona's Election Results," *AZ Central*, (Dec. 2, 2021), available at https://www.azcentral.com/in-depth/news/politics/elections/2021/11/18/arizona-audit-rudy-giuliani-failed-effort-replace-electors/6349795001/.

222.   Select Committee to Investigate the January 6th Attack on the United States Capitol, Informal Interview of Jack Sellers and Bill Gates, (Oct. 6, 2021).

223.   Yvonne Wingett Sanchez, "'We Need You to Stop the Counting': Records Detail Intense Efforts by Trump Allies to Pressure Maricopa County Supervisors," *AZ Central*, (July 2, 2021), available at https://www.azcentral.com/story/news/politics/elections/2021/07/02/records-show-trump-allies-kelli-ward-rudy-giuliani-pressed-county-officials-over-election-results/7813304002/.

224.   Yvonne Wingett Sanchez, "'We Need You to Stop the Counting': Records Detail Intense Efforts by Trump Allies to Pressure Maricopa County Supervisors," *AZ Central*, (July 2, 2021), available at https://www.azcentral.com/story/news/politics/elections/2021/07/02/records-show-trump-allies-kelli-ward-rudy-giuliani-pressed-county-officials-over-election-results/7813304002/.

225.   Document on file with the Select Committee to Investigate the January 6th Attack on the United States Capitol (Bill Stepien Production), WS00104-105 (December 5, 2021, email from Joshua Findlay to Matthew Morgan, Justin Clark, and Bill Stepien at 11:44 pm).

226.   Brian Kemp (@BrianKempGA), Twitter, Dec. 5, 2020 12:44 p.m., available at https://twitter.com/briankempga/status/1335278871630008324.

227.   Donald J. Trump (@realDonaldTrump), Twitter, Dec. 5, 2020 9:35 pm ET, available at https://media-cdn.factba.se/realdonaldtrump-twitter/1335336916582084614.jpg (archived). As detailed later in this report, the call for special sessions of legislatures in various States, including Georgia, never gained traction and, when all else failed, became a focus for two Department of Justice lawyers.

228.   Office of Governor Brian P. Kemp, "Gov. Kemp, Lt. Gov. Duncan Issue Statement on Request for Special Session of General Assembly," MadMimi.com, (Dec. 6, 2020), available at https://madmimi.com/p/50e7a11?pact=1301484-161142215-11561983238-b09ac0db7ff3f3c8bd594d6a33e7f63d0cf4c135.

229.   Donald J. Trump (@realDonaldTrump), Twitter, Dec. 8, 2020 3:07 p.m., available at http://web.archive.org/web/20201208200907/https://twitter.com/realdonaldtrump/status/1336401919422640128 (archived) (retweeting Lin Wood (@LLinWood), Twitter, Dec. 8, 2020, 11:22 a.m., available at http://web.archive.org/web/20201208200908/https://twitter.com/LLinWood/status/1336390712380813313 (archived)).

230.   Brett Samuels, "Trump Retweets Lawyer Who Said Republican Officials in Georgia Are 'Going to Jail'," *The Hill*, (Dec. 15, 2020), available at https://thehill.com/homenews/campaign/530250-trump-retweets-lawyer-who-says-republican-officials-in-georgia-are-going-to/.

231.   Search results for "'The Republican Governor of Georgia refuses' | 'As badly as we were treated in Georgia' | kemp | @briankempga," from November 30 to December 31, 2020, Trump Twitter Archive V2, (last accessed December 12, 2022), available at https://www.thetrumparchive.com/?searchbox=%22%5C%22The+Republican+Governor+of+Georgia+refuses%5C%22+%7C+%5C%22As+badly+as+we+were+treated+in+Georgia%5C%22+%7C+kemp+%7C+%40briankempga%22&dates=%5B%222020-11-30%22%2C%222020-12-30%22%5D&results=1.

232.   Document on file with the Select Committee to Investigate the January 6th Attack on the United States Capitol (National Archives Production), 076P-R000007750_0001, (December 7, 2020 email from Bill White to Dan Scavino and others) including screenshot of Burt Jones (@burtjonesforga), Twitter, Dec. 7, 2020 11:26 a.m., available at https://twitter.com/burtjonesforga/status/1335984150789173248), available at https://twitter.com/burtjonesforga/status/1335984150789173248).

233. Donald J. Trump (@realDonaldTrump), Twitter, Dec. 7, 2020 1:29 p.m. ET, available at https://factba.se/biden/topic/twitter?q=burtjonesforga&f= (archived); Rudy W. Giuliani (@RudyGiuliani), Twitter, Dec. 7, 2020 12:25 p.m., available at https://twitter.com/RudyGiuliani/status/1335998988101804035.

234. Documents on file with the Select Committee to Investigate the January 6th Attack on the United States Capitol (National Archives Production), 076P-R000007693_00001.

235. Documents on file with the Select Committee to Investigate the January 6th Attack on the United States Capitol (National Archives Production), 076P-R000007693_00001.

236. Documents on file with the Select Committee to Investigate the January 6th Attack on the United States Capitol (National Archives Production), 076P-R000007693_00001.

237. David Wickert and Greg Bluestein, "Inside the Campaign to Undermine Georgia's Election (Part I)," *Atlanta Journal-Constitution*, (Dec. 30, 2021), available at https://www.ajc.com/politics/election/georgia-2020-election-what-happened/.

238. Shepherd's Sling, "Steven K. Bannon - War Room Pandemic - Ep. #568/569 (Full 2hrs Podcast)," BitChute, at 16:50 - 18:00, Dec. 8, 2020, available at https://www.bitchute.com/video/KyK4QPP7Ngyt/; John Fredericks (@jfradioshow), Twitter, Dec. 7, 2020 5:30 p.m. ET, available at https://twitter.com/jfradioshow/status/1336075668090654724; Jim Hoft, "Developing: President Trump Speaks with Georgia House Speaker David Ralston and Speaker Pro-Tem Jan Jones on Endorsing Special Session," *Gateway Pundit*, (Dec. 7, 2020), available at https://www.thegatewaypundit.com/2020/12/developing-president-trump-speaks-georgia-house-speaker-david-ralston-speaker-pro-tem-jan-jones-endorsing-special-session/.

239. FYNTV FetchYourNews, "#BKP Has a Live Call-In with David Ralston," YouTube, at 2:30 - 3:12 (Dec. 8, 2020), available at http://web.archive.org/web/20201224164814/https://www.youtube.com/watch?v=ZdN5vNOl6F4&gl=US&hl=en (archived); Julie Carr, "Georgia Speaker of the House David Ralston Joins BKP Politics to Discuss His Call with President Trump and a Legal Path Forward," *Tennessee Star*, (Dec. 20, 2020), available at https://tennesseestar.com/2020/12/20/georgia-speaker-of-the-house-david-ralston-joins-bkp-politics-to-discuss-his-call-with-president-trump-and-a-legal-path-forward/.

240. Select Committee to Investigate the January 6th Attack on the United States Capitol, Continued Interview of Cassidy Hutchinson, (Mar. 7, 2022), pp. 162-67.

241. Documents on file with the Select Committee to Investigate the January 6th Attack on the United States Capitol (Georgia Secretary of State Production), GA SOS ORR (21-344) 005651 (Dec. 23, 2020 call between President Trump and Frances Watson); Select Committee to Investigate the January 6th Attack on the U.S. Capitol, Informal Interview with Frances Watson (Dec. 15, 2021); *see also* "Georgia Secretary of State Recording of Trump Phone Call to Election Investigator," American Oversight (Mar. 10, 2021), available at https://www.americanoversight.org/document/georgia-secretary-of-state-recording-of-trump-phone-call-to-election-investigator.

242. Documents on file with the Select Committee to Investigate the January 6th Attack on the United States Capitol (Mark Meadows Production), MM014152 (December 27, 2020 text message at 5:18 p.m. from Mark Meadows to Jordan Fuchs).

243. Documents on file with the Select Committee to Investigate the January 6th Attack on the United States Capitol (Mark Meadows Production), MM014153 (December 27, 2020 text message at 5:20 p.m. from Jordan Fuchs to Mark Meadows).

244. Documents on file with the Select Committee to Investigate the January 6th Attack on the United States Capitol (Mark Meadows Production), MM012317 (November 19, 2020 text message at 9:56 a.m. from Mark Meadows to Brad Raffensperger).

245. Documents on file with the Select Committee to Investigate the January 6th Attack on the United States Capitol (Mark Meadows Production), MM013362.

246. Documents on file with the Select Committee to Investigate the January 6th Attack on the United States Capitol (Mark Meadows Production), MM013632-33; *see also* Newsmax (@newsmax), Twitter, Dec. 11, 2020 9:45 p.m. ET, available at https://twitter.com/newsmax/status/1337589238078922752.

247. Philip Rucker, Ashley Parker, Josh Dawsey, and Seung Min Kim, "Trump Sabotaging GOP on His Way Out of Office with Push to Overturn Election," *Washington Post,* (Jan. 4, 2021), available at https://www.washingtonpost.com/politics/trump-sabotage-republicans/2021/01/04/df5d301e-4eb1-11eb-83e3-322644d82356_story.html.

248. "Georgia Sec. of State Discusses Phone Call with Trump About Election Results," Good Morning America, at 1:40 to 2:20, (Jan. 4, 2021), available at https://www.goodmorningamerica.com/news/video/georgia-sec-state-discusses-phone-call-trump-election-75032599.

249. Brad Raffensperger, Integrity Counts (New York: Simon & Schuster, 2021), p. 191 (reproducing the call transcript); Amy Gardner and Paulina Firozi, "Here's the Full Transcript and Audio of the Call Between Trump and Raffensperger," *Washington Post,* (Jan. 5, 2021), available at https://www.washingtonpost.com/politics/trump-raffensperger-call-transcript-georgia-vote/2021/01/03/2768e0cc-4ddd-11eb-83e3-322644d82356_story.html.

250. Amy Gardner and Paulina Firozi, "Here's the Full Transcript and Audio of the Call Between Trump and Raffensperger," *Washington Post,* (Jan. 5, 2021), available at https://www.washingtonpost.com/politics/trump-raffensperger-call-transcript-georgia-vote/2021/01/03/2768e0cc-4ddd-11eb-83e3-322644d82356_story.html.

251. Amy Gardner and Paulina Firozi, "Here's the Full Transcript and Audio of the Call Between Trump and Raffensperger," *Washington Post,* (Jan. 5, 2021), available at https://www.washingtonpost.com/politics/trump-raffensperger-call-transcript-georgia-vote/2021/01/03/2768e0cc-4ddd-11eb-83e3-322644d82356_story.html.

252. Brad Raffensperger, Integrity Counts (New York: Simon & Schuster, 2021), p. 191 (reproducing the call transcript); Amy Gardner and Paulina Firozi, "Here's the Full Transcript and Audio of the Call Between Trump and Raffensperger," *Washington Post,* (Jan. 5, 2021), available at https://www.washingtonpost.com/politics/trump-raffensperger-call-transcript-georgia-vote/2021/01/03/2768e0cc-4ddd-11eb-83e3-322644d82356_story.html (the Washington Post redacted Freeman's name and instead used "[name]" in the transcript); "Donald Trump Georgia Phone Call Transcript with Sec. of State Brad Raffensperger: Says He Wants to 'Find' Votes," Rev, (Jan. 4, 2021), available at https://www.rev.com/blog/transcripts/donald-trump-georgia-phone-call-transcript-brad-raffensperger-recording.

253. Amy Gardner and Paulina Firozi, "Here's the Full Transcript and Audio of the Call Between Trump and Raffensperger," *Washington Post,* (Jan. 5, 2021), available at https://www.washingtonpost.com/politics/trump-raffensperger-call-transcript-georgia-vote/2021/01/03/2768e0cc-4ddd-11eb-83e3-322644d82356_story.html.

254. Donald J. Trump (@realDonaldTrump), Twitter, Jan. 3, 2021 8:57 a.m. ET, available at https://media-cdn.factba.se/realdonaldtrump-twitter/1345731043861659650.jpg (archived). The archived image is in universal time.

255. Donald J. Trump (@realDonaldTrump), Twitter, Jan. 3, 2021 8:29 a.m. ET, available at https://media-cdn.factba.se/realdonaldtrump-twitter/1345723944654024706.jpg, (archived).

256. Select Committee to Investigate the January 6th Attack on the United States Capitol, *Hearing on the January 6th Investigation,* 117th Cong., 2d sess., (June 21, 2022), available at https://www.govinfo.gov/committee/house-january6th.

257. *See, e.g.,* Select Committee to Investigate the January 6th Attack on the United States Capitol, Transcribed Interview of Richard Donoghue, (Oct. 1, 2021), pp. 117-32; Documents on file with the Select Committee to Investigate the January 6th Attack on the United States Capitol (Department of Justice Production), HCOR-Pre-CertificationEvents-07262021-000698–000702 (Draft letter written by Jeffrey Clark).

258. "Senate Committee to Discuss Election Issues in Pennsylvania," Pennsylvania Senate GOP website (Nov. 24, 2020, last accessed on July 15, 2022), available at https://www.pasenategop.com/blog/senate-committee-to-discuss-election-issues-in-pennsylvania/; Select Committee to Investigate the January 6th Attack on the United States Capitol, Deposition of Rudolph Giuliani, (May 20, 2022), pp. 65-66. https://www.pasenategop.com/blog/senate-committee-to-discuss-election-issues-in-pennsylvania/.

259. Jeremy Roebuck and Andrew Seidman, "Pa. GOP lawmaker Doug Mastriano says he left the Capitol area before the riot. New videos say otherwise," Philadelphia Inquirer, (May 25, 2021), available at https://www.inquirer.com/news/doug-mastriano-capitol-riot-pennslyvania-video-20210525.html.

260. Eric Metaxas, "Interview: Eric Metaxas Interviews Donald Trump with Douglas Mastriano," Factba.se Archive, (Nov. 30, 2020), available at https://factba.se/transcript/donald-trump-interview-eric-metaxas-douglas-mastriano-november-30-2020; Senator Doug Mastriano (@SenMastriano), Twitter, Nov. 30, 2020 5:56 p.m. ET, available at https://twitter.com/senmastriano/status/1333545380965986307.

261. Documents on file with the Select Committee to Investigate the January 6th Attack on the United States Capitol (National Archives Production), 076P-R000008230_0001, 076P-R000008231_0001 (email and attachment from Mastriano to Molly Michael); see also Kelly v. Pennsylvania, 141 S. Ct. 950 (2020) (order denying application for injunctive relief presented to Justice Alito and denying referral to the full Court).

262. Documents on file with the Select Committee to Investigate the January 6th Attack on the United States Capitol (National Archives Production), 076P-R000001378_00001, 076P-R000001379_00001.

263. Documents on file with the Select Committee to Investigate the January 6th Attack on the United States Capitol (National Archives Production), 076P-R000003771_0001, 076P-R000003772_0001 (Dec. 21, 2020, email from Doug Mastriano to Molly Michael titled "Letter Requested by the President").

264. Documents on file with the Select Committee to Investigate the January 6th Attack on the United States Capitol (National Archives Production), 076P-R000003771_0001, 076P-R000003772_0001 (Dec. 21, 2020, email from Doug Mastriano to Molly Michael titled "Letter requested by the President").

265. See, e.g., Documents on file with the Select Committee to Investigate the January 6th Attack on the United States Capitol (National Archives Production), 076P-R000003748_0001, 076P-R000003749_0001, (Dec. 29, 2020, Doug Mastriano email to Molly Michael titled "Pennsylvania letter for AG Donoghue regarding election"; Documents on file with the Select Committee to Investigate the January 6th Attack on the United States Capitol, (National Archives Production), 076P-R000003753_0001, 076P-R000003754_0001, (Dec. 22, 2020, Molly Michael email to Rush Limbaugh titled "From POTUS"); Documents on file with the Select Committee to Investigate the January 6th Attack on the United States Capitol, (National Archives Production) 076P-R000003761_0001, 076P-R000003762_0001, (Dec. 22, 2020, Molly Michael email to Pam Bondi titled "From POTUS"); Documents on file with the Select Committee to Investigate the January 6th Attack on the United States Capitol, (National Archives Production) 076P-R000003766_0001, (Dec. 21, 2020, Molly Michael email to Lou Dobbs titled "2 attachments from POTUS"); Documents on file with the Select Committee to Investigate the January 6th Attack on the United States Capitol, (National Archives Production), 076P-R000008968_0001, (Jan. 1, 2021, Molly Michael email to Kevin McCarthy titled "From POTUS"); Documents on file with the Select Committee to Investigate the January 6th Attack on the United States Capitol, (National Archive Production) 076P-R000003759_0001, (Dec. 22, 2020, Molly Michael email to John Eastman, Justin Clark, and Michael Farris titled "From POTUS"); Documents on file with the Select Committee to Investigate the January 6th Attack on the United States Capitol, (National Archives Production) 076P-R000003763_0001, (December 21, 2020, email from Molly Michael to Christopher Michel re: From POTUS).

266. Charlotte Cuthbertson, "Trump 'Resolved, Determined' about Election, Says Pennsylvania Senator," *Epoch Times* (Dec. 24, 2020), available at https://www.theepochtimes.com/trump-resolved-determined-about-election-says-pennsylvania-senator_3632138.html; Marc Levy & Mark Scolforo, "White House Invites GOP Lawmakers in Pennsylvania to Lunch," *Associated Press*, (Dec. 23, 2020), available at https://apnews.com/article/donald-trump-pennsylvania-coronavirus-pandemic-c5b7f43af7794f01f6d339b7258b915a; Jan Murphy, "Pa. Senators Head to White House for Pre-Holiday Lunch with President Trump," *Penn Live – Patriot-News*, (Dec. 23, 2020), available at https://www.pennlive.com/news/2020/12/pa-senators-head-to-white-house-for-pre-holiday-lunch-with-president-trump.html; "Ep 608- Pandemic: Merry Christmas Eve Special Hour 1 (w/ Mayor Giuliani, Dr. Peter K. Navarro, Major Sgt. Scotty Neil, Former Navy Seal Tej Gill, Christopher Flannery)," War Room Podcast (Dec. 24, 2020), 25:17 to 25:25, available at https://warroom.org/2020/12/24/ep-608-pandemic-merry-christmas-eve-special-hour-1-w-dr-peter-k-navarro-major-sgt-scotty-neil-former-navy-seal-tej-gill-christopher-flannery/. Charlotte Cuthbertson, "Trump 'Resolved, Determined' about Election, Says Pennsylvania Senator," *Epoch Times* (Dec. 24, 2020), available at https://www.theepochtimes.com/trump-resolved-determined-about-election-says-pennsylvania-senator_3632138.html; Marc Levy & Mark Scolforo, "White House Invites GOP Lawmakers in Pennsylvania to Lunch," *Associated Press* (Dec. 23, 2020), available at https://apnews.com/article/donald-trump-pennsylvania-coronavirus-pandemic-c5b7f43af7794f01f6d339b7258b915a; Jan Murphy, "Pa. Senators Head to White House for Pre-Holiday Lunch with President Trump," *Penn Live – Patriot-News* (Dec. 23, 2020), available at https://www.pennlive.com/news/2020/12/pa-senators-head-to-white-house-for-pre-holiday-lunch-with-president-trump.html; "Ep 608- Pandemic: Merry Christmas Eve Special Hour 1 (w/ Mayor Giuliani, Dr. Peter K. Navarro, Major Sgt. Scotty Neil, Former Navy Seal Tej Gill, Christopher Flannery)", War Room Podcast (Dec.https://warroom.org/2020/12/24/ep-608-pandemic-merry-christmas-eve-special-hour-1-w-dr-peter-k-navarro-major-sgt-scotty-neil-former-navy-seal-tej-gill-christopher-flannery/.

267. *See, e.g.,* Documents on file with the Select Committee to Investigate the January 6th Attack on the United States Capitol (National Archives Production), 076P-R000008298_0001 (December 28, 2020, email from Molly Michael to Mark Meadows forwarding Senator Doug Mastriano info for the president), 076P-R000007593_0001 (December 28, 2020, email from Molly Michael to Scott Toland forwarding Senator Doug Mastriano info for the president), 076P-R000003748_0001, 076P-R000003749_0001 (December 29, 2020, email and attachments from Doug Mastriano to Molly Michael re: Pennsylvania letter for AG Donoghue regarding election), , 076P-R000003745_0001, 076P-R000003746_0001, 076P-R000003747_0001 (December 31, 2020, email from Doug Mastriano to Molly Michael re: Letters requested by President Trump and attachments).

268. *See* Documents on file with the Select Committee to Investigate the January 6th Attack on the United States Capitol (National Archives Production), 076P-R000003745_0001, 076P-R000003746_0001, 076P-R000003747_0001 (December 31, 2020, email from Doug Mastriano to Molly Michael re: Letters requested by President Trump and attachments).

269. Documents on file with the Select Committee to Investigate the January 6th Attack on the United States Capitol (National Archives Production), 076P-R000003732_0001(Email from Molly Michael to Amy Swonger, passing along information from Mastriano, 076P-R000008399_0001 (Email from Amy Swonger to Molly Michael responding)). According to the White House's Director of the Office of Legislative Affairs, Amy Swonger, the President repeatedly asked for her to distribute political materials after the election, which led her to seek advice from the White House Counsel's Office because fulfilling the President's request would likely violate the Hatch Act. *See* Select Committee to Investigate the January 6th Attack on the United States Capitol, Transcribed Interview of Amy Swonger, (Oct. 28, 2022), pp. 52-53.

270. Documents on file with the Select Committee to Investigate the January 6th Attack on the United States Capitol (National Archives Production), 076P-R000007439_0001 (White House switchboard call log from Jan. 5, 2022).

271. Documents on file with the Select Committee to Investigate the January 6th Attack on the United States Capitol (National Archives Production), 076P-R000004788_0001, 076P-R000004789_0001-0066 (January 5, 2021, email from Mastriano attaching letter for Vice President Pence signed by Pennsylvania legislators), 076P-R000004957_0001 (Molly Michael acknowledging receipt), 076P-R000005084_0001 (Molly Michael passing the letter along to Marc Short), 076P-R000007338_0001 (acknowledgment that the letter was printed for POTUS), 076P-R000004687_0001, 076P-R000004688_0001 (January 5, 2021, email and attached letter to Molly Michael re: Caucus Letter to Sen. McConnell and Rep. McCarthy).

272. Donald J. Trump (@realDonaldTrump), Twitter, Jan. 5, 2021 9:59 p.m. ET, available at https://www.thetrumparchive.com/?results=1&dates=%5B%222021-01-04%22%2C%222021-01-06%22%5D&searchbox=%22BIG+NEWS+IN+PENNSYLVANIA%21+https%3A%2F%2Ft.co%2F7JqTWYUgOr%22 (archived); Donald J. Trump (@realDonaldTrump), Twitter, Jan. 6, 2021 12:46 a.m. ET, available at https://www.thetrumparchive.com/?results=1&searchbox=%22pennsylvania+is+going+to+trump.+The+legislators%22 (archived).

273. Select Committee to Investigate the January 6th Attack on the United States Capitol, Deposition of Douglas Mastriano, (August 9, 2022), pp. 10-11.

274. Documents on file with the Select Committee to Investigate the January 6th Attack on the United States Capitol (Alex Cannon Production), AC-0000150 - 153(emails with Jason Miller re: emails to PA/AZ).

275. Documents on file with the Select Committee to Investigate the January 6th Attack on the United States Capitol (Alex Cannon Production), AC-0000150 - 153 (emails with Jason Miller re: emails to PA/AZ).

276. Documents on file with the Select Committee to Investigate the January 6th Attack on the United States Capitol (Alex Cannon Production), AC-0000150 - 153 (emails with Jason Miller re: emails to PA/AZ).

277. Select Committee to Investigate the January 6th Attack on the United States Capitol, Deposition of Rudolph Giuliani, (May 20, 2022), pp. 225-26; Select Committee to Investigate the January 6th Attack on the United States Capitol, Interview of Christina Bobb, (Apr. 21, 2022), pp. 128-34.

278. Documents on file with the Select Committee to Investigate the January 6th Attack on the United States Capitol (National Archives Production), 076P-R000001891_00001.

279. Select Committee to Investigate the January 6th Attack on the United States Capitol, Transcribed Interview of Bernard Kerik, (Jan. 13, 2022), pp. 138-39.

280. Select Committee to Investigate the January 6th Attack on the United States Capitol, Transcribed Interview of Bernard Kerik, (Jan. 13, 2022), pp. 136-37.

281. Documents on file with the Select Committee to Investigate the January 6th Attack on the United States Capitol (National Archives Production), 076P-R000001890_00001, 076P-R000001891_00001 (December 28, 2020, email with attachment from Bernard Kerik to Mark Meadows re: GIULIANI TEAM STRATEGIC COMMUNICATIONS PLAN - v1.pdf).

282. Select Committee to Investigate the January 6th Attack on the United States Capitol, Deposition of Rudolph Giuliani, (May 20, 2022), pp. 225-27; Select Committee to Investigate the January 6th Attack on the United States Capitol, Interview of Bernard Kerik, (Jan. 13, 2022), pp. 139-140.

283. Documents on file with the Select Committee to Investigate the January 6th Attack on the United States Capitol (National Archives Production), 076P-R000001891_00001.

284. Documents on file with the Select Committee to Investigate the January 6th Attack on the United States Capitol (National Archives Production), 076P-R000001891_00001.

285. Documents on file with the Select Committee to Investigate the January 6th Attack on the United States Capitol (National Archives Production), 076P-R000001891_00001.

286. Documents on file with the Select Committee to Investigate the January 6th Attack on the United States Capitol (Rudy Giuliani Production), RGGLOBAL_DOM_00008525.

287. Shepherd's Sling, "Steve Bannon's War Room, Episode 623," BitChute, at 13:20 - 13:29, Dec. 31, 2020, available at https://www.bitchute.com/video/KyK4QPP7Ngyt/.

288. Shepherd's Sling, "Steve Bannon's War Room, Episode 623," BitChute, at 17:07 - 18:17, Dec. 31, 2020, available at https://www.bitchute.com/video/KyK4QPP7Ngyt/.

289. Shepherd's Sling, "Steve Bannon's War Room, Episode 623," BitChute, at 24:49 - 25:14, Dec. 31, 2020, available at https://www.bitchute.com/video/KyK4QPP7Ngyt/.

290. Bernard B. Kerik (@BernardKerik), Twitter, Dec. 27, 2020 11:53 a.m. ET, available at https://twitter.com/bernardkerik/status/1343238609768501253.

291. Bernard B. Kerik (@BernardKerik), Twitter, Dec. 13, 2020 1:05 a.m. ET, available at https://twitter.com/bernardkerik/status/1338001989846888448.

292. Select Committee to Investigate the January 6th Attack on the United States Capitol, Transcribed Interview of Cassidy Hutchinson, (Feb. 23, 2022), pp. 43-45; Select Committee to Investigate the January 6th Attack on the United States Capitol, Continued Interview of Cassidy Hutchinson (Mar. 7, 2022), pp. 184-85; Select Committee to Investigate the January 6th Attack on the United States Capitol, Continued Interview of Cassidy Hutchinson (May 17, 2022), p. 74.

293. Documents on file with the Select Committee to Investigate the January 6th Attack on the United States Capitol (National Archives Production),076P-R000008962_0006 (January 2, 2021, White House Switchboard records); "Election Integrity Group Meets with Legislators from Contested States," *Cision PR Newswire*, (Jan. 2, 2021), available https://www.prnewswire.com/news-releases/election-integrity-group-meets-with-legislators-from-contested-states-301199902.html; Daniel Chaitin, "Navarro: Six-Person Team Briefed Hundreds of State Lawmakers, Showed 'Receipts' of 'Stolen' Election," *Washington Examiner*, (Jan. 2, 2021, updated Jan. 3, 2021), available at https://www.washingtonexaminer.com/news/navarro-6-person-team-briefed-hundreds-of-state-lawmakers-showed-receipts-of-stolen-election.

294. Team, Got Freedom?, available at http://web.archive.org/web/20201202221908/https:/got-freedom.org/team/ (archived).

295. Documents on file with the Select Committee to Investigate the January 6th Attack on the United States Capitol (Ed McBroom Production), M11-12 (January 2, 2021, email from Jillian Anderson, signed by Phil Kline re: BRIEFING FOLLOW UP: ELECTION 2020 | GOT FREEDOM?); "Election Integrity Group Meets with Legislators from Contested States," *Cision PR Newswire*, (Jan. 2, 2021), available https://www.prnewswire.com/news-releases/election-integrity-group-meets-with-legislators-from-contested-states-301199902.html.

296. Documents on file with the Select Committee to Investigate the January 6th Attack on the United States Capitol (Ed McBroom Production), M11-12 (January 2, 2021, email from Jillian Anderson, signed by Phil Kline re: BRIEFING FOLLOW UP: ELECTION 2020 | GOT FREEDOM?); "Election Integrity Group Meets with Legislators from Contested States," *Cision PR Newswire*, (Jan. 2, 2021), available https://www.prnewswire.com/news-releases/election-integrity-group-meets-with-legislators-from-contested-states-301199902.html.

297. "Election Integrity Group Meets with Legislators from Contested States," *Cision PR Newswire*, (Jan. 2, 2021), available https://www.prnewswire.com/news-releases/election-integrity-group-meets-with-legislators-from-contested-states-301199902.html.

298. Paul Bedard, "Exclusive: Trump Urges State Legislators to Reject Electoral Votes, 'You Are the Real Power'," *Washington Examiner*, (Jan. 3, 2021), available at https://www.washingtonexaminer.com/washington-secrets/exclusive-trump-urges-state-legislators-to-reject-electoral-votes-you-are-the-real-power; Select Committee to Investigate the January 6th Attack on the United States Capitol, Deposition of Rudolph Giuliani, (May 20, 2022), pp. 99-100.

299. Paul Bedard, "Exclusive: Trump Urges State Legislators to Reject Electoral Votes, 'You Are
      the Real Power'," *Washington Examiner*, (Jan. 3, 2021), available at https://
      www.washingtonexaminer.com/washington-secrets/exclusive-trump-urges-state-
      legislators-to-reject-electoral-votes-you-are-the-real-power.

300. Paul Bedard, "Exclusive: Trump Urges State Legislators to Reject Electoral Votes, 'You Are
      the Real Power'," *Washington Examiner*, (Jan. 3, 2021), available at https://
      www.washingtonexaminer.com/washington-secrets/exclusive-trump-urges-state-
      legislators-to-reject-electoral-votes-you-are-the-real-power.

301. Daniel Chaitan, "Navarro: Six-Person Team Briefed Hundreds of State Lawmakers Showed
      'Receipts' of 'Stolen' Election," *Washington Exam*iner, (Jan. 2, 2021), available at https://
      www.washingtonexaminer.com/news/navarro-6-person-team-briefed-hundreds-of-state-
      lawmakers-showed-receipts-of-stolen-election. The Select Committee attempted to ask
      Navarro about his participation in the call and other topics, but he ignored the Select
      Committee's subpoena and has been indicted by the Department of Justice.

302. Documents on file with the Select Committee to Investigate the January 6th Attack on the
      United States Capitol (Ed McBroom Production), M11-12 (January 2, 2021, email from Jillian
      Anderson, signed by Phil Kline re: BRIEFING FOLLOW UP: ELECTION 2020 | GOT FREEDOM?).

303. Documents on file with the Select Committee to Investigate the January 6th Attack on
      the United States Capitol (Ed McBroom Production), M11-12 (January 2, 2021, email
      from Jillian Anderson, signed by Phil Kline re: BRIEFING FOLLOW UP: ELECTION 2020 |
      GOT FREEDOM?)(quoted text bolded and italicized in original)

304. Documents on file with the Select Committee to Investigate the January 6th Attack on the
      United States Capitol (Ed McBroom Production), M11-12 (January 2, 2021, email from Jillian
      Anderson, signed by Phil Kline re: BRIEFING FOLLOW UP: ELECTION 2020 | GOT FREEDOM?).

305. Melanie Conklin, "These 15 State Legislators Asked Pence Not to Certify Election Results,"
      Wisconsin Examiner, (Jan. 14, 2021), available at https://wisconsinexaminer.com/2021/01/
      14/these-15-state-legislators-asked-pence-not-to-certify-election-results/.

306. Documents on file with the Select Committee to Investigate the January 6th Attack on the
      United States Capitol (National Archives Production Production), 076P-R000005084_0001
      (January 5, 2021, email from Doug Mastriano to Molly Michael re: Final letter to VP Pence,
      attaching the letter signed); Documents on file with the Select Committee to Investigate
      the January 6th Attack on the United States Capitol (National Archives Production Produc-
      tion), 076P-R000008735_0001 (January 5, 2021, letter to Vice President Pence signed by
      state legislators with "The President Has Seen" stamp).

307. Wood TV8, "Giuliani and Laura Cox Hold 'Legal Briefing' Before Giving Testimony Wednes-
      day Evening," Facebook Watch, at 10:30-10:45, Dec. 2, 2020, available at https://
      www.facebook.com/woodtv/videos/rudy-giuliani-and-laura-cox-hold-legal-briefing-before-
      giving-testimony-wednesda/1996033023872394/.

308. Wood TV8, "Giuliani and Laura Cox Hold 'Legal Briefing' Before Giving Testimony Wednes-
      day Evening," Facebook Watch, at 13:05-13:20, Dec. 2, 2020, available at https://
      www.facebook.com/woodtv/videos/rudy-giuliani-and-laura-cox-hold-legal-briefing-before-
      giving-testimony-wednesda/1996033023872394/.

309. Select Committee to Investigate the January 6th Attack on the United States Capitol, Tran-
      scribed Interview of Michael Shirkey, (June 8, 2022), pp. 33, 37, & 47-48. Documents on file
      with the Select Committee to Investigate the January 6th Attack on the United States Capi-
      tol, (AT&T Production, Feb. 9, 2022).

310. Select Committee to Investigate the January 6th Attack on the United States Capitol, Tran-
      scribed Interview of Michael Shirkey, (June 8, 2022), pp. 33-38.

311. Senator Mike Shirkey (@SenMikeShirkey), Twitter, Nov. 22, 2020 10:47 a.m. ET, available at
      https://twitter.com/SenMikeShirkey/status/1330538438723063815.

312. "Shirkey Issues Statement Regarding Election," Michigan Senate GOP, (from text, December 14, 2020), available at https://www.misenategop.com/shirkey-issues-statement-regarding-election/.

313. Donald Trump (@realDonaldTrump), Twitter, Dec. 4, 2020 2:49 p.m. ET, available at http://web.archive.org/web/20201211204139/https:/twitter.com/realDonaldTrump/status/1334993249082236931 (archived).

314. Donald J. Trump (@realDonaldTrump) RT of Christina Bobb (@christina_bobb) QT of Ali #StopTheSteal Alexander (@ali), Twitter, Dec. 6, 2020 12:53 a.m. ET, available at https://media-cdn.factba.se/realdonaldtrump-twitter/1335462365370994689.jpg (archived); "Tweets of December 6, 2020," The American Presidency Project at University of California Santa Barbara, https://www.presidency.ucsb.edu/documents/tweets-december-6-2020.

315. Team Trump, Facebook, Dec. 24, 2020 1:52 p.m., available at https://www.facebook.com/officialteamtrump/videos/arizona-contact-governor-ducey-and-your-legislators-todaydemand-they-hear-the-ev/303213471090533/.

316. Team Trump, Facebook, Dec. 26, 2020 5:36 p.m., available at https://www.facebook.com/officialteamtrump/videos/arizona-contact-governor-ducey-and-your-legislators-today/3496886293698026/.

317. Documents on file with the Select Committee to Investigate the January 6th Attack on the United States Capitol (Jamestown Associates Production), JTA000074-81 (Dec. 20, 2020, email chain from Jason Miller).

318. Documents on file with the Select Committee to Investigate the January 6th Attack on the United States Capitol (Jamestown Associates Production), JTA000074-81 (Dec. 20, 2020, email chain from Jason Miller).

319. Documents on file with the Select Committee to Investigate the January 6th Attack on the United States Capitol (Jared Kushner Production), JK_00423-436 (Dec. 22, 2020, text messages between Jason Miller and Jared Kushner, pp. 10-13).

320. Donald J. Trump (@realDonaldTrump), Twitter, , Dec. 1, 2020 10:27 p.m. ET, available at http://web.archive.org/web/20201203173245/https://mobile.twitter.com/realDonaldTrump/status/1333975991518187521 (archived).

321. Donald J. Trump (@realDonaldTrump), Twitter, Dec. 5, 2020 10:33 p.m. ET, available at https://media-cdn.factba.se/realdonaldtrump-twitter/1335351633459310593.jpg (archived).

322. Donald J. Trump (@realDonaldTrump), Twitter, Dec. 7, 2020 3:37 p.m. UTC, available at https://media-cdn.factba.se/realdonaldtrump-twitter/1335971721262796801.jpg (archived).

323. Donald J. Trump (@realDonaldTrump), Twitter, Dec. 7, 2020 7:50 p.m. ET, available at https://media-cdn.factba.se/realdonaldtrump-twitter/1336110929856040960.jpg (archived).

324. Donald Trump Thanksgiving Call to Troops Transcript 2020: Addresses Possibility of Conceding Election, Rev, (Nov. 26, 2020), available at https://www.rev.com/blog/transcripts/donald-trump-thanksgiving-call-to-troops-transcript-2020-addresses-possibility-of-conceding-election.

325. Linda So and Jason Szep, "Campaign of Fear: U.S. Election Workers Get Little Help from Law Enforcement as Terror Threats Mount," *Reuters*, (Sept. 8, 2021), available at https://www.reuters.com/investigates/special-report/usa-election-threats-law-enforcement/.

326. Fredreka Schouten, "Personal Threats, Election Lies and Punishing New Laws Rattle Election Officials, Raising Fears of a Mass Exodus," CNN, (July 21, 2021), available at https://www.cnn.com/2021/07/21/politics/election-officials-exodus/index.html.

327. Donald J. Trump (@realDonaldTrump) RT of Christina Bobb (@christina_bobb) QT of Ali #StopTheSteal Alexander (@ali), Twitter, Dec. 6, 2020 12:53 a.m. ET, available at https://media-cdn.factba.se/realdonaldtrump-twitter/1335462365370994689.jpg (archive); Donald J. Trump (@realDonaldTrump), Twitter, Dec. 6, 2020 12:53 a.m. ET, available at https://www.thetrumparchive.com/?searchbox=%22rusty+bowers%22&dates=%5B%222020-11-29%22%2C%222020-12-29%22%5D&results=1 (archived) (retweeting Christina Bobb).

328. Dennis Welch (@dennis_welch), Twitter, Dec. 8, 2020 11:23 p.m. ET, available at https://twitter.com/dennis_welch/status/1336526978640302080 (retweeting people who were posting Bowers's personal information); Dennis Welch (@dennis_welch), Twitter, Dec. 8, 2020 11:28 p.m. ET, available at https://twitter.com/dennis_welch/status/1336528029791604737.

329. Select Committee to Investigate the January 6th Attack on the U.S. Capitol, Transcribed Interview with Russel "Rusty" Bowers (June 19, 2022), pp. 50-52; Kelly Weill, "Arizona GOP Civil War Somehow Keeps Getting Weirder," *Daily Beast*, (Dec. 11, 2020), available at https://www.thedailybeast.com/arizona-republican-party-civil-war-somehow-keeps-getting-weirder; Yvonne Wingett Sanchez and Ronald J. Hansen, "'Asked to do Something Huge': An Audacious Pitch to Reserve Arizona's Election Results," *Arizona Republic*, (Nov. 18, 2021, updated Dec. 2, 2021), available at https://www.azcentral.com/in-depth/news/politics/elections/2021/11/18/arizona-audit-rudy-giuliani-failed-effort-replace-electors/6349795001/.

330. Select Committee to Investigate the January 6th Attack on the U.S. Capitol, Transcribed Interview with Russel "Rusty" Bowers (June 19, 2022), pp. 50-52.

331. House Select Committee to Investigate the January 6th Attack on the U.S. Capitol, Transcribed Interview with Russel "Rusty" Bowers (June 19, 2022), pp. 50-52.

332. Brahm Resnik, "VIDEO: Group chants 'We are watching you' outside Arizona Secretary of State Katie Hobbs' home," KPNX 12 News, (Nov. 18, 2020), available at https://www.12news.com/article/news/politics/video-group-chants-we-are-watching-you-outside-arizona-secretary-of-state-katie-hobbs-home/75-a569ae35-3b62-424e-88f8-f03ca8b89458; "Arizona Sec. of State Says She Hays Received Threats of Violence Following Election," Fox 10 Phoenix, (Nov. 18, 2020, updated Nov. 19, 2020), available at https://www.fox10phoenix.com/news/arizona-sec-of-state-says-she-has-received-threats-of-violence-following-election; Brahm Resnik, "Arizona Law Enforcement Investigating Social Media Threat against Top Elections Official," KPNX 12 News, (Nov. 18, 2020), available at https://www.12news.com/article/news/local/arizona/arizona-law-enforcement-investigating-social-media-threat-against-top-elections-official/75-486474ea-11c9-47ad-a325-8bbed6e3e231.

333. "Arizona Sec. of State Says She Hays Received Threats of Violence Following Election," Fox 10 Phoenix, (Nov. 18, 2020, updated Nov. 19, 2020), available at https://www.fox10phoenix.com/news/arizona-sec-of-state-says-she-has-received-threats-of-violence-following-election; Brahm Resnik, "Arizona Law Enforcement Investigating Social Media Threat against Top Elections Official," KPNX 12 News, (Nov. 18, 2020), available at https://www.12news.com/article/news/local/arizona/arizona-law-enforcement-investigating-social-media-threat-against-top-elections-official/75-486474ea-11c9-47ad-a325-8bbed6e3e231.

334. Isaac Dovere and Jeremy Herb, "'It's Absolutely Getting Worse': Secretaries of State Targeted by Trump Election Lies Live in Fear for their Safety and are Desperate for Protection," CNN, (Oct. 26, 2021), available at https://www.cnn.com/2021/10/26/politics/secretaries-of-state-personal-threats-trump-election-lies/index.html; Michael Wines and Eliza Fawcett, "Violent Threats to Election Workers are Common. Prosecutions are Not," *New York Times*, (June 27, 2022, updated July 1, 2022), available at https://www.nytimes.com/2022/06/27/us/election-workers-safety.html.

335. Committee on House Administration, Election Subversion: A Growing Threat to Election Integrity, Statement of Adrian Fontes Maricopa County Recorder (2016-2020), at *1, 6 (July 28, 2020), available at https://docs.house.gov/meetings/HA/HA00/20210728/113971/HHRG-117-HA00-Wstate-FontesA-20210728.pdf.

336. Bob Christie, "Months after Biden Win, Arizona Officials Still Face Threats," *Associated Press*, (Feb. 12, 2021), available at https://apnews.com/article/joe-biden-donald-trump-arizona-phoenix-elections-2bd2306acb2ae89c0ef37182fbb415b7.

337. Nicole Valdes, "Online Death Threats Target Maricopa County Board of Supervisors," ABC 15 Arizona, (Jan. 8, 2021, updated Jan. 9, 2021), available at https://www.abc15.com/news/state/enough-is-enough-online-death-threats-target-maricopa-county-board-of-supervisors.

338. *Washington Post*, "The Arizona election official who faced death threats for telling the truth," YouTube, at 0:21, Nov. 2, 2021, available at https://www.youtube.com/watch?v=6gAc47ivjYk.

339. Genesis Sandoval, "Hickman: A Year after 2020 Elections, Threats, Abuse Still Coming In," *Cronkite News Arizona PBS*, (Nov. 2, 2021), available at https://cronkitenews.azpbs.org/2021/11/02/hickman-a-year-after-2020-elections-threats-abuse-still-coming-in/.

340. United States Senate Committee on the Judiciary, Hearing on Protecting our Democracy's Frontline Workers (Aug. 3, 2022), Written testimony by Jocelyn Benson, available at https://www.judiciary.senate.gov/imo/media/doc/Testimony%20-%20Benson.pdf; Michigan Department of State, "Statement from Secretary of State Jocelyn Benson Concerning Threats against Her and Her Family," (Dec. 6, 2020), available at https://www.michigan.gov/sos/Resources/News/2020/12/06/statement-from-secretary-of-state-jocelyn-benson-concerning-threats-against-her-and-her-family; Select Committee to Investigate the January 6th Attack on the United States Capitol, Transcribed Interview of Jocelyn Benson, (June 2, 2022), pp. 35-39.

341. Michigan Department of State, "Statement from Secretary of State Jocelyn Benson Concerning Threats against Her and Her Family, (Dec. 6, 2020), available at https://www.michigan.gov/sos/Resources/News/2020/12/06/statement-from-secretary-of-state-jocelyn-benson-concerning-threats-against-her-and-her-family; Select Committee to Investigate the January 6th Attack on the United States Capitol, Transcribed Interview of Jocelyn Benson (June 2, 2022), pp. 35-39.

342. Isaac Dovere and Jeremy Herb, "'It's Absolutely Getting Worse': Secretaries of State Targeted by Trump Election Lies Live in Fear for their Safety and are Desperate for Protection," CNN, (Oct. 26, 2021), available at https://www.cnn.com/2021/10/26/politics/secretaries-of-state-personal-threats-trump-election-lies/index.html.

343. Select Committee to Investigate the January 6th Attack on the United States Capitol, Informal Interview of Aaron Van Langevelde and Adrianne Van Langevelde, (Oct. 21, 2021); Tim Alberta, "The Inside Story of Michigan's Fake Voter Fraud Scandal," *Politico*, (Nov. 24, 2020), available at https://www.politico.com/news/magazine/2020/11/24/michigan-election-trump-voter-fraud-democracy-440475; Rod Meloni and Natasha Dado, "Michigan AG Launches Investigation into Threats against Canvassers," *Click on Detroit*, (Nov. 24, 2020), available at https://www.clickondetroit.com/news/local/2020/11/24/michigan-ag-launches-investigation-into-threats-against-canvassers/.

344. Select Committee to Investigate the January 6th Attack on the United States Capitol, Informal Interview of Aaron Van Langevelde, (Oct. 21, 2021).

345. Trey Grayson, Matthew Masterson, Orion Danjuma, and Ben Berwick, "State and Local Solutions Are Integral to Protect Election Officials and Democracy," Just Security, (Feb. 9, 2022), available at https://www.justsecurity.org/80142/state-and-local-solutions-are-integral-to-protect-election-officials-and-democracy/; Stanford Internet Observatory, "Tina Barton – Aftermath – Death Threats," YouTube, (Sept. 20, 2021), available at https://www.youtube.com/watch?v=Xi5Y7bwvy-Y.

346. Melissa Nann Burke and George Hunter, "'I Feel Afraid': Detroit Clerk Winfrey Testifies to U.S. House Panel on Death Threats She Received," *Detroit News*, (July 28, 2021), available at https://www.detroitnews.com/story/news/politics/2021/07/28/winfrey-testifies-before-house-panel-threats-election-workers/5400419001/.

347. Linda So and Jason Szep, "Campaign of Fear: U.S. Election Workers Get Little Help from Law Enforcement as Terror Threats Mount," *Reuters*, (Sept. 8, 2021), available at https://www.reuters.com/investigates/special-report/usa-election-threats-law-enforcement/.

348. Dave Boucher, "Black Michigan Lawmaker Posts Voicemails Saying She Should be Lynched," *Detroit Free Press*, (Dec. 6, 2020), available at https://www.freep.com/story/news/politics/ elections/2020/12/06/michigan-lawmaker-posts-voicemails-saying-she-should-lynched/ 3849695001/.

349. Dave Boucher, "Black Michigan Lawmaker Posts Voicemails Saying She Should be Lynched," *Detroit Free Press*, (Dec. 6, 2020), available at https://www.freep.com/story/news/politics/ elections/2020/12/06/michigan-lawmaker-posts-voicemails-saying-she-should-lynched/ 3849695001/.

350. Kayla Clarke, "Man faces felony charges for bomb threat at Michigan Capitol Building, threats against state representative," *Click on Detroit*, (Jan. 8, 2021), available at https:// www.clickondetroit.com/news/local/2021/01/08/man-faces-felony-charges-for-bomb- threat-at-michigan-capitol-building-threats-against-state-representative/ (linking to affidavit).

351. Isaac Dovere and Jeremy Herb, "'It's Absolutely Getting Worse': Secretaries of State Tar- geted by Trump Election Lies Live in Fear for their Safety and are Desperate for Protec- tion," CNN, (Oct. 26, 2021), available at https://www.cnn.com/2021/10/26/politics/ secretaries-of-state-personal-threats-trump-election-lies/index.html; *see also* Select Committee to Investigate the January 6thAttack on the United States Capitol, Informal Interview of Kathy Boockvar, (Dec. 22, 2021).

352. Linda So and Jason Szep, "Campaign of Fear: U.S. Election Workers Get Little Help from Law Enforcement as Terror Threats Mount," *Reuters*, (Sept. 8, 2021), available at https:// www.reuters.com/investigates/special-report/usa-election-threats-law-enforcement/.

353. Isaac Dovere and Jeremy Herb, "'It's Absolutely Getting Worse': Secretaries of State Tar- geted by Trump Election Lies Live in Fear for their Safety and are Desperate for Protec- tion," CNN, (Oct. 26, 2021), available at https://www.cnn.com/2021/10/26/politics/ secretaries-of-state-personal-threats-trump-election-lies/index.html.

354. Select Committee to Investigate the January 6th Attack on the United States Capitol, Tran- scribed Interview of Bryan Cutler, (May 31, 2022), pp. 83-84.

355. Geoff Rushton, "Police Investigating Threat Made During State College Borough Council Meeting," *StateCollege.com*, (Dec. 8, 2020), available at https://www.statecollege.com/ police-investigating-threat-made-during-state-college-borough-council-meeting/.

356. Jan Murphy, "Meet Pa. Senate GOP Leader Kim Ward, the First Woman to Hold That Post: 'I Have To Do a Good Job'," *PennLive.com*, (Jan. 26, 2021), https://www.pennlive.com/news/ 2021/01/meet-pa-senate-gop-leader-kim-ward-the-first-woman-to-hold-that-post-i-have- to-do-a-good-job.html.

357. Matt Petrillo, "'We're Coming after You': Philadelphia Elections Officials Still Receiving Death Threats Following 2020 Presidential Election," CBS Philly 3, (Nov. 1, 2021), available at https://philadelphia.cbslocal.com/2021/11/01/philadelphia-election-officials-death-threat- donald-trump-joe-biden/; Linda So and Jason Szep, "Campaign of Fear: U.S. Election Work- ers Get Little Help from Law Enforcement as Terror Threats Mount," *Reuters*, (Sept. 8, 2021), available at https://www.reuters.com/investigates/special-report/usa-election-threats- law-enforcement/.

358. Linda So and Jason Szep, "Special Report: Terrorized U.S. Election Workers Get Little Help from Law Enforcement," *Reuters*, (Sept. 8, 2021), available at https://www.reuters.com/ legal/government/terrorized-us-election-workers-get-little-help-law-enforcement-2021-09- 08/.

359. Select Committee to Investigate the January 6th Attack on the United States Capitol, *Hear- ing on the January 6th Investigation*, 117th Cong., 2d sess., (June 21, 2022), at 2:10:00 to 2:11:00, available at https://www.youtube.com/watch?v=xa43_z_82Og.

360. Linda So, "Special Report: Trump-Inspired Death Threats are Terrorizing Election Workers," *Reuters*, (June 11, 2021), available at https://www.reuters.com/article/us-usa-trump-georgia-threats-special-rep/special-report-trump-inspired-death-threats-are-terrorizing-election-workers-idUSKCN2DN14M.

361. Select Committee to Investigate the January 6th Attack on the United States Capitol, *Hearing on the January 6th Investigation*, 117th Cong., 2d sess., (June 21, 2022), at 2:10:00 to 2:11:00, available at https://www.youtube.com/watch?v=xa43_z_82Og; Linda So, "Special Report: Trump-Inspired Death Threats are Terrorizing Election Workers," *Reuters*, (June 11, 2021), available at https://www.reuters.com/article/us-usa-trump-georgia-threats-special-rep/special-report-trump-inspired-death-threats-are-terrorizing-election-workers-idUSKCN2DN14M.

362. Jeff Pegues and Robert Legare, "Texas Man Charged with Making Election-Related Threats to Georgia Government Officials," CBS News, (Jan. 21, 2022), available at https://www.cbsnews.com/news/chad-christopher-stark-charged-election-related-threats-georgia-government-officials/.

363. Linda So, "Special Report: Trump-Inspired Death Threats are Terrorizing Election Workers," *Reuters*, (June 11, 2021), available at https://www.reuters.com/article/us-usa-trump-georgia-threats-special-rep/special-report-trump-inspired-death-threats-are-terrorizing-election-workers-idUSKCN2DN14M.

364. Linda So, "Special Report: Trump-Inspired Death Threats are Terrorizing Election Workers," *Reuters*, (June 11, 2021), available at https://www.reuters.com/article/us-usa-trump-georgia-threats-special-rep/special-report-trump-inspired-death-threats-are-terrorizing-election-workers-idUSKCN2DN14M.

365. Linda So, "Special Report: Trump-Inspired Death Threats are Terrorizing Election Workers," *Reuters* (June 11, 2021), available at https://www.reuters.com/article/us-usa-trump-georgia-threats-special-rep/special-report-trump-inspired-death-threats-are-terrorizing-election-workers-idUSKCN2DN14M.

366. GA House Mobile Streaming, "Governmental Affairs 12.10.20," Vimeo – Livestream, at 2:09:00-2:13:00, available at https://livestream.com/accounts/25225474/events/9117221/videos/214677184; Select Committee to Investigate the January 6th Attack on the United States Capitol, *Hearing on the January 6th investigation*, 117th Cong., 2d sess., (June 21, 2022), at 2:25:45 to 2:26:00, available at https://youtu.be/xa43_z_82Og?t=8745.

367. Donald Trump Georgia Rally Transcript Before Senate Runoff Elections December 5," Rev, (Dec. 5, 2020), available at https://www.rev.com/blog/transcripts/donald-trump-georgia-rally-transcript-before-senate-runoff-elections-december-5; Jason Szep and Linda So, "A Reuters Special Report: Trump Campaign Demonized Two Georgia Election Workers – and Death Threats Followed," *Reuters*, (Dec. 1, 2021), available at https://www.reuters.com/investigates/special-report/usa-election-threats-georgia/.

368. Brad Raffensperger, Integrity Counts (New York: Simon & Schuster, 2021), p. 191 (reproducing the call transcript); Amy Gardner and Paulina Firozi,Amy Gardner and Paulina Firozi, "Here's the Full Transcript and Audio of the Call Between Trump and Raffensperger," *Washington Post*, (Jan. 5, 2021), available at https://www.washingtonpost.com/politics/trump-raffensperger-call-transcript-georgia-vote/2021/01/03/2768e0cc-4ddd-11eb-83e3-322644d82356_story.html (the Washington Post redacted Freeman's name and instead used "[name]" in the transcript); "Donald Trump Georgia Phone Call Transcript with Sec. of State Brad Raffensperger: Says He Wants to 'Find' Votes," Rev, (Jan. 4, 2021), available at https://www.rev.com/blog/transcripts/donald-trump-georgia-phone-call-transcript-brad-raffensperger-recording.

369. Jason Szep and Linda So, "A Reuters Special Report: Trump Campaign Demonized Two Georgia Election Workers – and Death Threats Followed," *Reuters*, (Dec. 1, 2021), available at https://www.reuters.com/investigates/special-report/usa-election-threats-georgia/.

370. *Freeman v. Giuliani*, No. 21-cv-03354-BAH (D.D.C. filed May 10, 2022), ECF No. 22 (Amended Complaint at 52), available at https://www.courtlistener.com/docket/61642105/22/freeman-v-herring-networks-inc.

371. Jason Szep and Linda So, "A Reuters Special Report: Trump Campaign Demonized Two Georgia Election Workers – and Death Threats Followed," *Reuters*, (Dec. 1, 2021), available at https://www.reuters.com/investigates/special-report/usa-election-threats-georgia/.

372. Jason Szep and Linda So, "A Reuters Special Report: Trump Campaign Demonized Two Georgia Election Workers – and Death Threats Followed," *Reuters*, (Dec. 1, 2021), available at https://www.reuters.com/investigates/special-report/usa-election-threats-georgia/.

373. Amended Complaint at 52, *Freeman v. Giuliani*, No. 21-cv-03354-BAH (D.D.C. filed May 10, 2022), ECF No. 22, available at https://www.courtlistener.com/docket/61642105/22/freeman-v-herring-networks-inc.

374. Amended Complaint at 52, *Freeman v. Giuliani*, No. 21-cv-03354-BAH (D.D.C. filed May 10, 2022), ECF No. 22, available at https://www.courtlistener.com/docket/61642105/22/freeman-v-herring-networks-inc.

375. Select Committee to Investigate the January 6th Attack on the United States Capitol, Transcribed Interview of Ruby Freeman, (May 31, 2022), pp. 7-8.

376. Select Committee to Investigate the January 6th Attack on the United States Capitol, Transcribed Interview of Ruby Freeman, (May 31, 2022), pp. 7-8.

377. Government's Motion Regarding Anticipated Trial Evidence and Notice Pursuant to Federal Rule of Evidence 404(b) at 1-2, 24-26, *United States v. Rhodes, et al.*, No. 1:22-cr-15 (D.D.C. July 8, 2022), ECF No. 187; Brandi Buchman (@Brandi_Buchman), Twitter, Oct. 6, 2022 7:27 a.m. ET, available at https://twitter.com/Brandi_Buchman/status/1577983997711421441.

378. Hannah Rabinowitz and Holmes Lybrand, "Judge Says Oath Keepers Jury Won't See 'Death List'," CNN (Oct. 6, 2022), https://www.cnn.com/2022/10/06/politics/judge-says-oath-keepers-jury-wont-see-death-list-trial-day-3.

Georgia Electors cast their Electoral College votes
at the Georgia State Capitol on December 14, 2020.

3

FAKE ELECTORS AND THE "THE PRESIDENT OF THE SENATE STRATEGY"

On the morning of January 6th, in his speech at the Ellipse, President Trump exhorted his thousands of assembled supporters to march to the U.S. Capitol, explaining that "[w]e have come to demand that Congress do the right thing and only count the electors who have been lawfully slated, lawfully slated."[1] This was no off-the-cuff remark; it was the culmination of a carefully planned scheme many weeks in the making. This plea by the President turned the truth on its head. There was only one legitimate slate of electors from the battleground States of Arizona, Georgia, Michigan, Nevada, New Mexico, Pennsylvania, and Wisconsin, and Trump wanted them rejected. This scheme involved lawyers, such as Kenneth Chesebro and Rudy Giuliani, as well as Mark Meadows. It also was aided at key points by Chairwoman of the Republican National Committee Ronna McDaniel, Members of Congress, and Republican leaders across seven States—some of whom did not know exactly what they were being asked to do. President Trump oversaw it himself.

President Trump and his allies prepared their own fake slates of electoral college electors in seven States that President Trump lost: Arizona, Georgia, Michigan, Nevada, New Mexico, Pennsylvania, and Wisconsin. And on December 14, 2020—the date when true, certified electors were meeting to cast their electoral votes for the candidate who had won the popular vote in each of those States—these fake electors also met, ostensibly casting electoral votes for President Trump, the candidate who had lost.

There was no legitimate reason for Trump electors to meet, vote, and produce fake slates on December 14th in States that former Vice President Biden won. Instead, this effort was aimed directly at the President of the Senate (which, under the Constitution, is the Vice President) in his role at the joint session of Congress on January 6th. President Trump and his advisors wanted Vice President Pence to disregard real electoral college votes for former Vice President Biden, in favor of these fake competing electoral slates.

But there never were real, competing slates of electors. By the time the fake Trump electors met on December 14th, appropriate government officials in each of the seven States had already certified their State's official election results for former Vice President Biden. No court had issued an order reversing or calling into question those results, and most election-related litigation was over. And as detailed in Chapter 2, despite the illicit efforts of President Trump and his allies, no State legislature had agreed to the President's request to reverse the result of the election by appointing a different slate of electors.

Given all of this, these groups of Trump backers who called themselves Presidential electors were never actually electors, and the votes they purported to cast on December 14th were not valid. They were fake. They had no legal standing, and their fake votes could not have been used by Vice President Pence to disregard the real votes of electors chosen by the voters.

By January 6th, President Trump had been discouraged by his top lawyers from following through on this plan. The Trump Campaign's senior staff attorneys had concerns,[2] and several days before the joint session, the Acting Attorney General and the Deputy Attorney General blocked the sending of a letter indicating that there were "competing slates" of electors, including "in Georgia and several other States."[3] But this reasoning did nothing to change President Trump's rhetoric or plan. He continued to assert that there were "competing" or "dual" slates of electors to create an opportunity to stay in office on January 6th.[4]

These lawyers were right: President Trump's plan was illegal. In his June 7, 2022, opinion, Federal District Judge David Carter wrote that this initiative to "certify alternate slates of electors for President Trump" constituted a "critical objective of the January 6 plan."[5] This followed Judge Carter's earlier determination in March that "[t]he illegality of the plan was obvious," and "[e]very American—and certainly the President of the United States—knows that in a democracy, leaders are elected, not installed. With a plan this 'BOLD,' President Trump knowingly tried to subvert this fundamental principle. Based on the evidence the Court finds it more likely than not that President Trump corruptly attempted to obstruct the Joint Session of Congress on January 6, 2021."[6]

The fake elector effort was an unlawful, unprecedented and destructive break from the electoral college process that our country has used to select its President for generations.[7] It led directly to the violence that occurred on January 6th. To address the damage that it caused, it is important to understand how it transpired.

3.1 LAYING THE GROUNDWORK FOR THE FAKE ELECTOR PLAN: THE CHESEBRO MEMOS

The fake elector plan emerged from a series of legal memoranda written by an outside legal advisor to the Trump Campaign: Kenneth Chesebro. Although John Eastman would have a more prominent role in advising President Trump in the days immediately before January 6th, Chesebro—an attorney based in Boston and New York recruited to assist the Trump Campaign as a volunteer legal advisor—was central to the creation of the plan.[8] Memos by Chesebro on November 18th, December 9th, and December 13th, as discussed below, laid the plan's foundation.

Chesebro's first memo on November 18th suggested that the Trump Campaign could gain a few extra weeks for litigation to challenge Wisconsin's election results, so long as a Wisconsin slate of Republican nominees to the electoral college met on December 14th to cast placeholder electoral college votes on a contingent basis.[9] This memo acknowledged that "[i]t may seem odd that the electors pledged to Trump and Pence might meet and cast their votes on December 14 even if, at that juncture, the Trump-Pence ticket is behind in the vote count, and no certificate of election has been issued in favor of Trump and Pence."[10] However, Chesebro argued that if such a slate of alternate electors gathered to cast electoral votes on a contingent basis, this would preserve the Trump Campaign's options so "a court decision (or, perhaps, a state legislative determination) rendered after December 14 in favor of the Trump-Pence slate of electors should be timely."[11]

On December 9th, Chesebro penned a second memo, which suggested another purpose for fake electoral college votes on January 6th. It stated that unauthorized Trump electors in these States could be retroactively recognized "by a court, the state legislature, *or Congress*."[12] Under this theory, there would be no need for a court to decide that the election had been decided in error; instead, Congress itself could choose among dueling slates of purported electoral votes—and thereby decide the Presidential election—even though Article II of the Constitution grants that power to the electoral college via the States.[13]

Chesebro's contemporaneous communications make clear that the goal was having Congress act on the fake electoral votes. He emailed an organizer of the fake electors in Nevada that "the purpose of having the electoral votes sent in to Congress is to provide the opportunity to debate the election irregularities in Congress, and to keep alive the possibility that the votes could be flipped to Trump..."[14] And a legal advisor to the Arizona GOP reportedly described being told by Chesebro around this time that their supposed electors "would just be sending in 'fake' electoral votes to Pence so that 'someone' in Congress can make an objection when they start counting votes, and start arguing that the 'fake' votes should be counted."[15]

Many of the States contested by the Trump team had laws that specified requirements for electors to validly cast and transmit their votes—and the December 9, 2020, memo recognized that some of these criteria would be difficult, if not impossible, for the fake electors to fulfill. (As described later, most were not fulfilled.) For example, Nevada State law required that the secretary of state preside when Presidential electors meet,[16] and Nevada Secretary of State Barbara Cegavske, a Republican, had already signed a certificate ascertaining the Biden/Harris electors as the authorized, winning slate.[17] Several States also had rules requiring electors to cast their votes in the State capitol building, or rules governing the process for approving substitutes if any original proposed electors from the November ballot were unavailable. As a result, Chesebro's December 9, 2020, memo advised the Trump Campaign to abide by such rules, when possible, but also recognized that these slates could be "slightly problematic in Michigan," "somewhat dicey in Georgia and Pennsylvania," and "very problematic in Nevada."[18]

On December 13th, the fake elector scheme became even clearer in an email sent by Chesebro to Giuliani. His message was entitled "Brief notes on 'President of the Senate' strategy." It addressed how the fake electors meeting the next day, December 14th, could be exploited during the joint session of Congress on January 6th by the President of the Senate—a role that the Constitution grants to the Vice President of the United States.[19] Chesebro argued that, on January 6th, the President of the Senate could:

> ...firmly take the position that he, and he alone, is charged with the constitutional responsibility not just to open the votes, but to count them—including making judgments about what to do if there are conflicting votes...[20]

Chesebro's email suggested that the President of the Senate (which under the Constitution, is the Vice President) could toss out former Vice President Biden's actual electoral votes for any State where the Trump Campaign organized fake electors, simply "because there are two slates of votes." [21] Of course, there were never two slates of electoral votes, so this premise itself was fundamentally wrong. But he was arguing that even if votes by fake electors were never retroactively ratified under State law, their mere submission to Congress would be enough to allow the presiding officer to disregard valid votes for former Vice President Biden.[22] Chesebro suggested this might result in a second term for President Trump, or, at minimum, it would force a debate about purported election fraud—neither of which was a lawful, legitimate reason to organize and convene fake electors.[23]

As discussed below and in Chapter 5, John Eastman worked with Chesebro as January 6th approached and wrote two additional memos that built upon, and extended, the plan to use the fake electoral votes during the joint session.[24]

3.2 PRESIDENT TRUMP AND THE CAMPAIGN ADOPT THE FAKE ELECTOR SCHEME

In early December, the highest levels of the Trump Campaign took note of Chesebro's fake elector plan and began to operationalize it. On December 6th, White House Chief of Staff Mark Meadows forwarded a copy of Chesebro's November 18, 2020, memo to Trump Campaign Senior Advisor Jason Miller writing, "Let's have a discussion about this tomorrow." [25] Miller replied that he just engaged with reporters on the subject, to which Meadows wrote: "If you are on it then never mind the meeting. *We just need to have someone coordinating the electors for states.*" [26] Miller clarified that he had only been "working the PR angle" and they should still meet, to which Meadows answered: "Got it." [27] Later that week, Miller sent Meadows a spreadsheet that the Trump Campaign had compiled.[28] It listed contact information for nearly all of the 79 GOP nominees to the electoral college on the November ballot for Arizona, Georgia, Michigan, Nevada, Pennsylvania, and Wisconsin.[29] And on December 8th, Meadows received a text message from a former State legislator in Louisiana recommending that the proposed "Trump electors from AR [sic] MI GA PA WI NV all meet next Monday at their state capitols[,] [c]all themselves to order, elect officers, and cast their votes for the President.... Then they certify their votes and transmit that certificate to Washington." [30] Meadows replied: "We are." [31]

Cassidy Hutchinson, a Special Assistant to the President and an assistant to Chief of Staff Mark Meadows, confirmed Meadows's significant involvement in the plan. Hutchinson told the Select Committee that Meadows followed the progress of the fake elector effort closely and that she "remember[ed] him frequently having calls, meetings, and outreach with individuals and this just being a prominent topic of discussion in our office." When asked how many of his calls or meetings it came up in, she estimated "[d]ozens."[32]

The evidence indicates that by December 7th or 8th, President Trump had decided to pursue the fake elector plan and was driving it. Trump Campaign Associate General Counsel Joshua Findlay was tasked by the campaign's general counsel, Matthew Morgan, around December 7th or 8th with exploring the feasibility of assembling unrecognized slates of Trump electors in a handful of the States that President Trump had lost.[33] Findlay told the Select Committee "it was my understanding that the President made this decision...."[34] As recounted by Findlay, Morgan conveyed that the client—President Trump—directed the campaign lawyers to "look into electors in these potential litigation States[.]"[35]

President Trump personally called RNC Chairwoman Ronna Romney McDaniel days before December 14th to enlist the RNC's assistance in the scheme.[36] President Trump opened the call by introducing McDaniel to John Eastman, who described "the importance of the RNC helping the campaign to gather these contingent electors in case any of the legal challenges that were ongoing changed the results in any of the States."[37] According to McDaniel, she called President Trump back soon after the call ended, letting him know that she agreed to his request and that some RNC staffers were already assisting.[38]

On December 13th and 14th, President Trump worked with Rudolph Giuliani on the plan's implementation. On the 13th, Miller texted some of his colleagues to check in about the fake elector meetings scheduled for the following day. He let them know that Giuliani had told him "POTUS was aware" that they would be filing litigation in four States just "to keep the effort going"—which the Select Committee believes was to create a pretext to claim that it was still possible for the fake electors to be authorized retroactively.[39] (In subsequent litigation, a Federal district court found that President Trump "filed certain lawsuits not to obtain legal relief, but to disrupt or delay the January 6th congressional proceedings through the courts."[40]) The next day, Miller sent an email asking whether they were going to issue a press release about electors, and he was told the "Mayor [is] going to discuss with POTUS."[41]

3.3 THE CAMPAIGN LEGAL TEAM BOWS OUT, AND GIULIANI STEPS IN

Not everyone on the campaign was eager to pursue the fake elector plan. On December 11th, the U.S. Supreme Court rejected a high-profile lawsuit filed by the State of Texas challenging the election results in Pennsylvania,

Ronna McDaniel at the Republican National Convention on August 24, 2020.
(Photo by Chip Somodevilla/Getty Images)

Georgia, Michigan, and Wisconsin.[42] After that decision, the Trump Campaign's senior legal staffers said that they reduced their involvement in the fake elector effort, apparently because there was no longer a feasible scenario in which a court would determine that President Trump actually won

Rudy Giuliani speaks inside the Republican National Committee Headquarters in November about various lawsuits related to the 2020 election.

(Photo by Drew Angerer/Getty Images)

any of the States he contested.[43] Justin Clark, who oversaw the Trump Campaign's general counsel's office, said that he basically conveyed, "I'm out," and encouraged his colleagues on the legal team to do the same.[44] Findlay told the Select Committee that "we backed out of this thing," and Morgan, his boss, said he had Findlay pass off responsibility for the electors as "my way of taking that responsibility to zero."[45]

Clark told the Select Committee that "it never sat right with me that there was no...contingency whereby these votes would count."[46] "I had real problems with the process," Clark said, because "it morphed into something I didn't agree with."[47] In his view, the fake electors were "not necessarily duly nominated electors" despite being presented as such.[48] He said he believed he warned his colleagues that "unless we have litigation pending like in these States, like I don't think this is appropriate or, you know, this isn't the right thing to do."[49]

Morgan told the Select Committee that he saw no value in pushing slates of purported electors if they were not authorized by a State government's certificate of ascertainment. As he put it, "[M]y view was, as long as you didn't have a certificate of ascertainment, then the electors were, for lack of a better way of saying it, no good or not—not valid." [50] Findlay confirmed that Morgan told him after the Supreme Court ruling on December 11th that "there's not really anything left for us to do on this project" and that "it doesn't seem like a good idea for us to be involved in it." [51]

Campaign lawyers were not the only ones who doubted the legality of the fake elector plan. The Office of White House Counsel appears to have expressed concerns about it as well. In his testimony to the Select Committee, White House Counsel Pat Cipollone acknowledged his view that by mid-December, the electoral process was "done." Cipollone told the Select Committee that the White House Counsel's office "probably" had discussions about the electors plan and that his Deputy, Pat Philbin, would have been involved in evaluating the electors issue. [52] In an informal Committee interview, Philbin described the fake elector scheme as one of the "bad theories" that were like "Whac-A-Mole" in the White House during this period. [53] Mr. Cipollone agreed with this characterization. [54]

In her testimony, Cassidy Hutchinson testified that she heard at least one member of the White House Counsel's Office say that the plan was not legal:

> Committee Staff: ... to be clear, did you hear the White House Counsel's Office say that this plan to have alternate electors meet and cast votes for Donald Trump in States that he had lost was not legally sound?
>
> Hutchinson: Yes, sir. [55]

She also recalled a meeting that took place in or before mid-December during which this view was relayed to Giuliani and members of his team by lawyers in the White House Counsel's Office. [56]

By December 11th, Findlay emailed his main points of contact in six battleground States to say "[t]hank you for your work on the presidential elector project" and, in order to pass off his responsibilities, let them know that "Rudy's team has designated Kenneth Chesebro as the point person for the legal documents" going forward. [57]

While the campaign's core legal team stepped back from the fake elector effort on December 11th, it nonetheless went forward because "Rudy was in charge of [it]" and "[t]his is what he wanted to do," according to Findlay. [58] When Findlay was asked if this decision to let the effort proceed under Giuliani's direction "was coming from your client, the President," Findlay responded: "Yes, I believe so. I mean, he had made it clear that Rudy was in charge of this and that Rudy was executing what he wanted." [59] Findlay also recalled being told that Chesebro's elector memos had become "the justification for why Rudy and Ken were going to keep going forward with this stuff." [60] He explained that Giuliani "really bought into Ken's theory on this," and that the two of them "were kind of the main ones driving this" from that point forward.[61] Clark told the Select Committee that "...my understanding of who was driving the process...was Mayor Giuliani and his team." [62] On December 10th, when Kenneth Chesebro emailed one of the State party officials involved in organizing the fake elector effort in Nevada, he reported that "I spoke this evening with Mayor Giuliani [sic], who is focused on doing everything possible to ensure that that [sic] all the Trump-Pence electors vote on Dec. 14." [63]

In the days that followed this handoff, Chesebro would draft and distribute documents intended for use in the Trump team's fake elector ceremonies that were then shared with key contacts in Arizona,[64] Georgia,[65] Michigan,[66] Nevada,[67] New Mexico,[68] Pennsylvania,[69] and Wisconsin.[70] He also gave some of the groups step-by-step logistical guidance, such as when and where they should convene, how many copies each person would need to sign, and to send their fake votes to Congress via registered mail.[71] "Pretty Simple!" he commented in some of these emails.[72]

A campaign operative named Michael Roman was also tapped for a major operational role in the fake elector effort. When Findlay sent his email handing off certain responsibilities for the initiative, he also wrote that Giuliani's team had designated Roman "as the lead for executing the voting on Monday" December 14th.[73] Roman was the Trump Campaign's Director of Election Day Operations (EDO), with team members who specialized in political outreach and mobilization in battleground States where the Trump team now urgently needed the fake electors to meet on December 14th.

With help from his EDO staff, as well as Giuliani's team and RNC staffers working alongside the Campaign as part of the Trump Victory Committee, Roman ran an improvised "Electors Whip Operation." [74] For example, Roman sent an email on December 12th directing an aide to create "a tracker for the electors" with tabs for Arizona, Georgia, Michigan, Nevada, Pennsylvania, and Wisconsin, listing contact information, whether they had been contacted, whether they agreed to attend on December 14th, and names of "[s]ubstitute electors" to replace any reticent or unavailable participants as needed.[75] Roman referred to others on this email as the "WHIP TEAM" and directed them to fill out the spreadsheet, to update him on "what you have and what you need," and to plan on a call that evening.[76]

In the days that followed, this group focused on tracking which Republicans previously named as President Trump's nominees to the electoral college would be willing to show up for fake elector ceremonies, finding adequate substitutes for those who refused to attend, and actually coordinating the unrecognized elector signing ceremonies in seven States on December 14th.[77] In all seven States, these efforts to mobilize fake electors benefitted from support from the RNC, as well as the State Republican parties.[78] However, it was the Trump team who drove the process from start to finish, as one of the fake electors and later co-chair of the Michigan Republican party, Meshawn Maddock, told an audience in January 2022: "We fought to seat the electors. The Trump campaign asked us to do that." [79]

3.4   SOME OF THE PROPOSED FAKE ELECTORS EXPRESS CONCERNS ABOUT THE PLAN

The Trump team's fake elector plan raised concerns not just for several senior officials but also for some of the Republican activists being recruited to be the fake electors. Findlay told the Select Committee that "there were definitely electors in probably most of the States that had concerns about this process." [80] After being tasked with reaching out to the potential fake electors, Findlay notified his colleagues on December 10th that "a lot of questions are arising" from them.[81] He also noted that an RNC staffer seconded to the Trump Victory Committee "requested a call with the PA electors and/or leadership to address concerns," which "may be necessary to get people to appear." [82]

The Republican Party of Pennsylvania's general counsel relayed several specific concerns to the Trump Campaign via email on December 13th. Warning that "[w]e're all getting call [sic] from concerned Electors," he elaborated as follows:

> I'm told that on the call with the Electors they were told that the Ballot form would be conditioned upon ultimate certification by the Governor, indemnification by the campaign if someone gets sued or worse, (charged with something by the AG or someone else), and the receipt by the Electors of a legal opinion by a national firm and certified to be accurate by a Pa. lawyer.

> What was sent was a "memo" by Chesebro not addressed to the Electors, and no certification by a Pa. lawyer. To make it worse, Chesebro describes the Pa. plan as "dicey". And there's no indication by anyone with authority that there's any indemnification authorized by the campaign.[83]

> Pennsylvania GOP Chairman Lawrence Tabas informed the Select Committee that his State's fake electors never were indemnified by the Trump Campaign.[84]

When Wisconsin Republican Party Chairman Andrew Hitt was notified in late November that "the campaign wants to [sic] list of electors," he texted his executive director that "I am def concerned about their inquiry" and that "I hope they are not planning on asking us to do anything like try and say we are only the proper electors." [85] On December 12th, after Hitt received a message about a phone call with Giuliani to discuss the fake elector issue, he texted a colleague: "These guys are up to no good and its [sic] gonna fail miserably." [86] Despite such concerns, Hitt and many other fake electors participated anyway.[87]

Even so, 14 of the original Republicans who had been listed as electoral college nominees on the November ballot bowed out when the fake Trump electors gathered in December.[88] Former Michigan Secretary of State Terri Lynn Land declined to attend, which the State's GOP chair, Laura Cox, told the Select Committee was because "I think she just said she was uncomfortable with the whole thing" and that she "has her own beliefs." [89] A senior advisor for the Pennsylvania GOP said that Chairman Tabas "did not serve as an elector because Joe Biden won the election and it was Biden's electors that were certified." [90] Former U.S. Representative Tom Marino (R-PA) said he backed out because "I'm a constitutionalist," and "as a former prosecutor, when the attorney general says that he's not finding anything there, that's good enough for me." [91] The other eleven dropouts included a Georgia State lawmaker, a former State party chair from New Mexico, two former State party chairs from Pennsylvania, and Pennsylvania's RNC national committeewoman.[92]

Other participants asserted that they would have had much greater concerns if the Trump team had been more forthcoming about how the fake electoral votes would be used.[93] The Trump Campaign's director of election day operations in Georgia told the Select Committee that "I absolutely would not have" wanted to participate in organizing the Trump team's fake electors in Georgia "had I known that the three main lawyers for the campaign that I'd spoken to in the past and were leading up were not on board." [94] He said he felt "angry" because "no one really cared if—if people were potentially putting themselves in jeopardy" by doing this, and "we were just...useful idiots or rubes at that point." [95]

3.5 ON DECEMBER 14TH, THE FAKE ELECTORS MEET AND VOTE

On December 14th, using instructions provided by Chesebro, the fake Trump electors gathered and participated in signing ceremonies in all seven States. In five of these States—Arizona, Georgia, Michigan, Nevada, and Wisconsin—the certificates they signed used the language that falsely

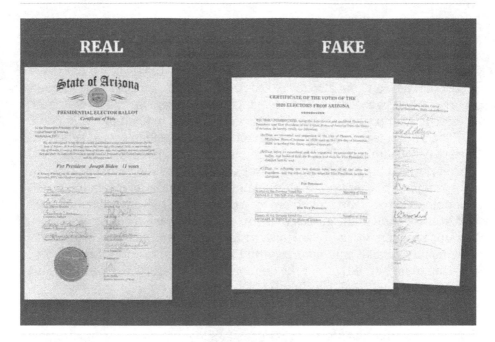

declared themselves to be "the duly elected and qualified Electors" from their State.[96] This declaration was false because none of the signatories had been granted that official status by their State government in the form of a certificate of ascertainment.

The paperwork signed by the fake Trump electors in two other States contained partial caveats. In New Mexico, the document they signed made clear that they were participating "on the understanding that it might later be determined that we are the duly elected and qualified Electors...." [97] In Pennsylvania, the document they signed indicated that they were participating "on the understanding that if, as a result of a final non-appealable Court Order or other proceeding prescribed by law, we are ultimately recognized as being the duly elected and qualified Electors...." [98]

All seven of these invalid sets of electoral votes were then transmitted to Washington, DC. Roman's team member in Georgia, for example, sent him an email on the afternoon of December 14th that affirmed the following: "All votes cast, paperwork complete, being mailed now. Ran pretty smoothly." [99] Likewise, Findlay updated Campaign Manager Bill Stepien and his bosses on the legal team that the Trump team's slate in Georgia was not able to satisfy all provisions of State law but still "voted as legally as possible under the circumstances" before transmitting their fake votes to Washington, DC, by mail.[100]

On the evening of December 14th, RNC Chairwoman McDaniel provided an update for President Trump on the status of the fake elector effort. She forwarded President Trump's executive assistant an "Elector Recap" email, which conveyed that "President Trump's electors voted" not just in "the states that he won" but also in six "contested states" (specifically, Arizona, Georgia, Michigan, Nevada, Pennsylvania, and Wisconsin).[101] Minutes later, President Trump's executive assistant replied: "It's in front of him!"[102]

The Trump team and the fake electors also engaged in acts of subterfuge to carry out their plans on December 14th. For instance, a campaign staffer notified the Georgia participants via email that he "must ask for your complete discretion."[103] He explained that their efforts required "complete secrecy," and told them to arrive at the State capitol building and "please state to the guards that you are attending a meeting with either Senator Brandon Beach or Senator Burt Jones."[104] Indeed, Greg Bluestein of the *Atlanta Journal-Constitution* reported that he tried to enter this group's meeting room but "[a] guy at the door called it an 'education meeting' and scrambled when I tried to walk in."[105]

Former Michigan GOP Chair Laura Cox told the Select Committee that an attorney who "said he was working with the President's Campaign" informed her that the Michigan slate for President Trump was "planning to meet in the capit[o]l and hide overnight so that they could fulfill the role of casting their vote in, per law, in the Michigan chambers."[106] She said that she "told him in no uncertain terms that that was insane and inappropriate," and that she warned Michigan's senate majority leader as a precaution.[107] Instead, the group of fake electors in Michigan signed their paperwork in the State GOP headquarters, where staff told them not to bring phones inside.[108]

3.6 THE FALLOUT FROM THE FAKE ELECTOR PLAN

In spite of the Trump Campaign's efforts to give the fake electors' votes the sheen of authenticity, they failed. The U.S. Senate Parliamentarian noted in correspondence by January 3rd that materials from the Trump team's supposed electors in Arizona, Georgia, Nevada, New Mexico, and Pennsylvania had "no seal of the state" and "no evidence votes were delivered by the executive of the state for signature by electors,"[109] and, as a result, these materials failed to meet requirements of federal law. Similarly, the Senate Parliamentarian noted that the Trump team's slates from Georgia, New Mexico, and Pennsylvania appeared to violate another statute which requires the approval of the Governor for the substitution of electors.[110]

Meanwhile, the documents from Michigan and Wisconsin did not even arrive to Congress on time, so they also had missed the required statutory deadline.[111]

Several of the Trump team's fake electoral slates also failed to follow State rules specifying where they were required to meet. In Georgia and Wisconsin, State lawmakers or their staff appear to have helped participants gather inside their State capitols.[112] But in Michigan, the fake Trump electors were blocked from entering the State capitol building.[113] Despite this, they still signed documents attesting that they "convened and organized in the State Capitol, in the City of Lansing, Michigan, and at 2:00 p.m.... performed the duties enjoined upon us."[114] That document had been signed earlier in the day off-site, and one of the signatories even told the Committee she didn't join their march to the State capitol building because she "didn't see a need to go."[115]

If the entire premise of the fake votes was not enough, these infirmities also meant that they had no legal relevance. In no way could they ever have been used by the Vice President to disregard the real votes of electors chosen by the voters.

In the weeks between December 14th and January 6th, President Trump's team continued to embrace the idea that the fake electoral votes had a purpose. Although Giuliani and White House speechwriter Stephen Miller made public comments on December 14th suggesting that the uncertified Trump votes were merely contingent, that pretense was dropped in short order.[116]

For example, on December 17th, White House Press Secretary Kayleigh McEnany said on Fox News that in numerous States "there has been an alternate slate of electors voted upon that Congress will decide in January."[117] On December 21st, President Trump and Vice President Pence each joined parts of a White House meeting in which Members of Congress from the Freedom Caucus encouraged the Vice President to reject Biden electors from one or more of the seven contested States.[118] And days later, Eastman cited the existence of the fake votes in an email to Boris Epshteyn, a member of the Giuliani legal team, writing, "[t]he fact that we have multiple slates of electors demonstrate[s] the uncertainty of either. That should be enough."[119]

As discussed further in Chapter 5, that email contained Eastman's 2-page memo proposing a strategy for January 6th based on the incorrect legal theory that Vice President Pence could assert some authority as President of the Senate to prevent or delay the election of former Vice President Biden during the joint session. Eastman's memo relied on the fake votes, which the memo featured in the very first line: "7 states have transmitted dual slates of electors."[120] When Eastman submitted his memo to Epshteyn, he also copied Chesebro, who had edited the memo and called it "[r]eally awesome."[121]

By that point, Chesebro and Eastman were coordinating their arguments about the fake-elector votes and how they should be used. On January 1, 2021, Chesebro sent an email to Eastman and Epshteyn that recommended that Vice President Pence derail the joint session of Congress. In it, he raised the idea of Vice President Pence declaring "that there are two competing slates of electoral votes" in several States, and taking the position that only he, or possibly Congress, could "resolve any disputes concerning them."[122]

Two days later, Eastman completed his second major memo advising President Trump and his team on strategies for January 6th, again arguing that there were "dual slates of electors from 7 states," and calling for Vice President Pence to assert power to act "[a]s the ultimate arbiter" to take steps that could overturn the election, either by sending the election back to State legislatures to reassess or by rejecting Biden's certified electoral votes from States in which there were also fake Trump electors.[123]

By early January, most of the fake elector votes had arrived in Washington, except those from Michigan and Wisconsin.[124] Undeterred, the Trump team arranged to fly them to Washington and hand deliver them to Congress for the Vice President himself. "Freaking trump idiots want someone to fly original elector papers to the senate President..." Wisconsin Republican Party official Mark Jefferson wrote to Party Chairman Hitt on January 4th.[125] Hitt responded, "Ok I see I have a missed call from [Mike] Roman and a text from someone else. Did you talk to them already? This is just nuts...."[126]

The next day, Trump Campaign Deputy Director for Election Day Operations G. Michael Brown sent a text message to other campaign staff suggesting that he was the person who delivered the fake votes to Congress.[127] After sending the group a photo of his face with the Capitol in the background, Brown said, "This has got to be the cover a book I write one day" and "I should probably buy [Mike] [R]oman a tie or something for sending me on this one. Hasn't been done since 1876 and it was only 3 states that did it."[128] The reference to 1876 alludes to a controversy during that election about certain States' electoral college votes.[129]

President Trump and his Campaign apparently had assistance from allies on Capitol Hill for this effort, including Senator Ron Johnson, his chief of staff, and the chief of staff to Representative Mike Kelly, although Senator Johnson has said that "[his] involvement in that attempt to

Senator Ron Johnson, February 12, 2021.

(Photo by Samuel Corum/Getty Images)

deliver" fake elector paperwork "spanned the course of a couple sec-onds."[130] On the morning of January 6th, Representative Kelly's then-chief of staff texted an aide to the Vice President, Chris Hodgson, about hand-delivering the fake elector votes to the Vice President's team before the joint session, a message that Hodgson ignored: "Just following up-any chance you or someone from your team can meet to take the Michigan and Wisconsin packets."[131]

According to the office of Senator Ron Johnson, Representative Kelly's chief of staff then had a phone call with Senator Johnson's chief of staff at 11:58 a.m. "about how Kelly's office could get us the electors [sic] because they had it."[132] Shortly after 11:30 a.m., the Trump Campaign's lead attor-ney in Wisconsin had texted Senator Johnson expressing a "[n]eed to get a document on Wisconsin electors to you [for] the VP immediately. Is there a staff person I can talk to immediately."[133] Senator Johnson then put his chief of staff in touch with the campaign to handle the issue.[134]

Shortly afterwards, Senator Johnson's chief of staff texted Hodgson: "[Sen.] Johnson needs to hand something to VPOTUS please advise."[135] When Hodgson asked what it was, the response he got was, "Alternate slate of electors for MI and WI because archivist didn't receive them."[136] Hodg-son did not mince words: "Do not give that to him [the Vice President].

Senator Mike Lee, April 28, 2016.

(Photo by Leigh Vogel/Getty Images)

He's about to walk over to preside over the joint session, those were supposed to come in through the mail." [137]

Those fake electoral votes, which the Trump team tried for weeks to manufacture and deliver, never made it to the Vice President. But they would have been invalid even if they did arrive on time. The Trump team's activities were based on the false pretense that these fake electoral votes had a decisive role to play at the joint session of Congress. And yet any such role that they could have played would have helped unlawfully obstruct an official proceeding that determines how our Nation carries out the peaceful transfer of power between Presidents.

Indeed, as the joint session approached, Senator Mike Lee had expressed grave concerns about the fake elector effort in a series of text messages to one of the Trump team's senior legal advisors. Although Senator Lee had spent a month encouraging the idea of having State legislatures endorse competing electors for Trump, he grew alarmed as it became clear that the Trump team wanted the fake electors' votes to be considered on January 6th even without authorization from any State government body. [138]

On December 30th, Senator Lee texted Trump advisor Cleta Mitchell that January 6th was "a dangerous idea," including "for the republic itself." [139] He explained that, "I don't think we have any valid basis for objecting to the electors" because "it cannot be true that we can object to any state's presidential electors simply because we don't think they handled their election well or suspect illegal activity."[140] Senator Lee even questioned her about the plan's dangerous long-term consequences: "[w]ill you please explain to me how this doesn't create a slippery slope problem for all future presidential elections?"[141]

ENDNOTES

1. "Transcript of Trump's Speech at Rally before US Capitol Riot," *Associated Press*, (Jan. 13, 2021), available at https://apnews.com/article/election-2020-joe-biden-donald-trump-capitol-siege-media-e79eb5164613d6718e9f4502eb471f27.

2. Documents on file with the Select Committee to Investigate the January 6th Attack on the United States Capitol, (Tim Murtaugh Production), XXM-0021349 (December 13, 2020, and December 14, 2020, text messages between Tim Murtaugh, Justin Clark, Jason Miller, and Eric Herschmann); Select Committee to Investigate the January 6th Attack on the United States Capitol, Transcribed Interview of Justin Clark, (May 17, 2022), p. 116; Select Committee to Investigate the January 6th Attack on the United States Capitol, Transcribed Interview of Matthew Morgan, (Apr. 25, 2022), pp. 70–72; Select Committee to Investigate the January 6th Attack on the United States Capitol, Transcribed Interview of Joshua Findlay, (May 25, 2022), pp. 38–43.

3. *See* Chapter 4; Senate Committee on the Judiciary Majority Staff Report, *Subverting Justice: How the Former President and His Allies Pressured DOJ to Overturn the 2020 Election*, (Oct. 7, 2021), pp. 20–39, 188, and Key Document H at pp. 185–191, available at https://www.judiciary.senate.gov/imo/media/doc/Interim%20Staff%20Report%20FINAL.pdf.

4. Documents on file with the Select Committee to Investigate the January 6th Attack on the United States Capitol (Chapman University Production), Chapman053475, Chapman053476 (December 23, 2020, email titled "PRIVILEGED AND CONFIDENTIAL—Dec 23 memo on Jan 6 scenario.docx" from John Eastman to Boris Epshteyn and Kenneth Chesebro, with attached memo titled "January 6 scenario"); Documents on file with the Select Committee to Investigate the January 6th Attack on the United States Capitol (Public Source), CTRL0000923050 (Jan. 3, 2021, John Eastman 6-page memo); John C. Eastman, "Privileged and Confidential– Jan 6 Scenario," (Jan. 3, 2021), available at https://www.scribd.com/document/528776994/Privileged-and-Confidential-Jan-3-Memo-on-Jan-6-Scenario; John C. Eastman, "Trying to Prevent Illegal Conduct from Deciding an Election is Not Endorsing a 'Coup'," American Greatness, (Sep. 30, 2021), available at https://amgreatness.com/2021/09/30/trying-to-prevent-illegal-conduct-from-deciding-an-election-is-not-endorsing-a-coup/ (embedded). *See also* Chapter 5.

5. Order Re Privilege of 599 Documents Dated November 3, 2020–January 20, 2021 at 23, *Eastman v. Thompson*, No. 8:22-cv-99 (C.D. Cal. June 7, 2022), ECF No. 356, available at https://storage.courtlistener.com/recap/gov.uscourts.cacd.841840/gov.uscourts.cacd.841840.356.0_1.pdf.

6. Order re Privilege of Documents Dated January 4–7, 2021 at 36, *Eastman v. Thompson*, 594 F. Supp. 3d 1156, (C.D. Cal. Mar. 28, 2022) (No. 8:22-cv-99-DOC-DFM), available at https://storage.courtlistener.com/recap/gov.uscourts.cacd.841840/gov.uscourts.cacd.841840.260.0_10.pdf.

7. The Trump team tried to justify its fake-elector scheme based in part on the 1960 Kennedy-Nixon election. At that time, following a close vote in Hawaii, Republican and Democratic electors each met and cast purported electoral college votes on the same day because there was ongoing litigation and a pending recount. Circumstances in 2020 were different, however, in part because there were no pending recounts. Kenneth Chesebro

reportedly recognized this difference in an email copied to Rudolph Giuliani that acknowledged certain concerns about their efforts could be "valid," because, as he put it, "in the Hawaii 1960 incident, when the Kennedy electors voted[,] there was a pending recount." Maggie Haberman and Luke Broadwater, "Arizona Officials Warned Fake Electors Plan Could 'Appear Treasonous'," *New York Times*, (Aug. 2, 2022), available at https://www.nytimes.com/2022/08/02/us/politics/arizona-trump-fake-electors.html.

8. David Thomas, "Lawyer Group Says Trump Attorney Broke Ethics Rules in Fake Elector Plan," *Reuters*, (Oct. 12, 2022), available at https://www.reuters.com/legal/legalindustry/lawyer-group-says-trump-attorney-broke-ethics-rules-fake-elector-plan-2022-10-12/; Select Committee to Investigate the January 6th Attack on the United States Capitol, *Hearing on the January 6th Investigation*, 117th Cong., 2d sess., (June 16, 2022), available at https://www.govinfo.gov/committee/house-january6th.

9. Documents on file with the Select Committee to Investigate the January 6th Attack on the United States Capitol (Chapman University Production), Chapman025125 (November 18, 2020, memo from Kenneth Chesebro titled "The Real Deadline for Settling a State's Electoral Votes"); Documents on file with the Select Committee to Investigate the January 6th Attack on the United States Capitol (Chapman University Production), Chapman025124 (December 7, 2020, email from Kenneth Chesebro with attachment "2020-11-20 Chesebro memo on real deadline2.pdf"); Documents on file with the Select Committee to Investigate the January 6th Attack on the United States Capitol (Joshua Findlay production), JF037 (November 18, 2020, memo from Kenneth Chesebro titled "The Real Deadline for Settling a State's Electoral Votes"). *See also* Alan Feuer, Maggie Haberman, and Luke Broadwater, "Memos Show Roots of Trump's Focus on Jan. 6 and Alternate Electors," *New York Times*, (Feb. 2, 2022), available at https://www.nytimes.com/2022/02/02/us/politics/trump-jan-6-memos.html.

10. Documents on file with the Select Committee to Investigate the January 6th Attack on the United States Capitol (Chapman University Production), Chapman025125 (November 18, 2020, memo from Kenneth Chesebro titled "The Real Deadline for Settling a State's Electoral Votes"); Documents on file with the Select Committee to Investigate the January 6th Attack on the United States Capitol (Chapman University Production), Chapman025124 (December 7, 2020, email from Kenneth Chesebro with attachment "2020-11-20 Chesebro memo on real deadline2.pdf"); Documents on file with the Select Committee to Investigate the January 6th Attack on the United States Capitol (Joshua Findlay Production), JF037 (Nov. 18, 2020, memo from Kenneth Chesebro titled "The Real Deadline for Settling a State's Electoral Votes"). *See also* Alan Feuer, Maggie Haberman, and Luke Broadwater, "Memos Show Roots of Trump's Focus on Jan. 6 and Alternate Electors," *New York Times*, (Feb. 2, 2022), available at https://www.nytimes.com/2022/02/02/us/politics/trump-jan-6-memos.html.

11. Documents on file with the Select Committee to Investigate the January 6th Attack on the United States Capitol (Chapman University Production), Chapman025125, (November 18, 2020, memo from Kenneth Chesebro titled "The Real Deadline for Settling a State's Electoral Votes") (underlining in original); Documents on file with the Select Committee to Investigate the January 6th Attack on the United States Capitol (Chapman University Production), Chapman025124, (December 7, 2020, email from Kenneth Chesebro with attachment "2020-11-20 Chesebro memo on real deadline2.pdf"); Documents on file with the Select Committee to Investigate the January 6th Attack on the United States Capitol (Joshua Findlay Production), CTRL0000082463_00009, (November 18, 2020, memo from Kenneth Chesebro titled "The Real Deadline for Settling a State's Electoral Votes"); Alan Feuer, Maggie Haberman, and Luke Broadwater, "Memos Show Roots of Trump's Focus on Jan. 6 and Alternate Electors," *New York Times*, (Feb. 2, 2022), available at https://www.nytimes.com/2022/02/02/us/politics/trump-jan-6-memos.html.

12. Emphasis added. Documents on file with the Select Committee to Investigate the January 6th Attack on the United States Capitol (Joshua Findlay Production), JF044, (December 9, 2020, memo from Kenneth Chesebro titled "Statutory Requirements for December 14 Electoral Votes"); Alan Feuer, Maggie Haberman, and Luke Broadwater, "Memos Show Roots of

Trump's Focus on Jan. 6 and Alternate Electors," *New York Times*, (Feb. 2, 2022), available at https://www.nytimes.com/2022/02/02/us/politics/trump-jan-6-memos.html.

13. U.S. Const., art. II, §. 1, cl. 2: ("Each State shall appoint, in such Manner as the Legislature thereof may direct, a Number of Electors, equal to the whole Number of Senators and Representatives to which the State may be entitled in the Congress: but no Senator or Representative, or Person holding an Office of Trust or Profit under the United States, shall be appointed an Elector.").

14. Documents on file with the Select Committee to Investigate the January 6th Attack on the United States Capitol (James DeGraffenreid Production), DEGRAFFENREID 000778, (December 11, 2020, email from Jim DeGraffenreid to Kenneth Chesebro with subject "URGENT—Trump-Pence campaign asked me to contact you to coordinate Dec. 14 voting by Nevada electors").

15. Maggie Haberman and Luke Broadwater, "'Kind of Wild/Creative': Emails Shed Light on Trump Fake Electors Plan," *New York Times*, (July 26, 2022), available at https://www.nytimes.com/2022/07/26/us/politics/trump-fake-electors-emails.html (emphasis in original). Although this alleged email described by the *New York Times* was not produced to the Select Committee, it matches certain information in a privilege log provided to the Select Committee by its reported sender. This includes the same reported sender (Jack Wilenchik), direct recipient (Boris Epshteyn), seven cc'ed recipients in the same order (Christina Bobb, Lee Miller, Dennis Wilenchik, Aaron Green, Josh Offenhartz, Christine Ferreira, and Victoria Stevens), title ("RE: [EXTERNAL]FW: petition for Cert and Motion for Expedited Consideration"), and date (12/8/2020), with only a negligible one-minute discrepancy in the time sent (4:27 p.m. versus 4:26 p.m.). *See* Documents on file with the Select Committee to Investigate the January 6th Attack on the United States Capitol, (Jack Wilenchik Production), CTRL0000922311, line 9 (Sept. 7, 2022, Jack Wilenchik Production 09_07_2022—PrivLog UPDATED).

16. "Nevada Revised Statutes," Title 24—Elections, Chapter 298—Presidential Electors and Elections, Nevada State Legislature, available at https://www.leg.state.nv.us/nrs/nrs-298.html#NRS298Sec065.

17. "Nevada Certificate of Ascertainment 2020," National Archives and Records Administration, (Dec. 2, 2020, also later updated Dec. 10, 2020), available at https://www.archives.gov/files/electoral-college/2020/ascertainment-nevada.pdf.

18. Documents on file with the Select Committee to Investigate the January 6th Attack on the United States Capitol (Joshua Findlay Production), JF044 (December 9, 2020, memo from Kenneth Chesebro titled "Statutory Requirements for December 14 Electoral Votes"). Where it wouldn't be possible to comply with State law, as in Nevada, Chesebro advised the so-called electors to proceed anyway, writing: "[T]hese technical aspects of state law are unlikely to matter much in the end." Documents on file with the Select Committee to Investigate the January 6th Attack on the United States Capitol (James DeGraffenreid Production), DEGRAFFENREID 000778, (December 11, 2020, email from Jim DeGraffenreid to Kenneth Chesebro with subject "URGENT—Trump-Pence campaign asked me to contact you to coordinate Dec. 14 voting by Nevada electors").

19. Documents on file with the Select Committee to Investigate the January 6th Attack on the United States Capitol (Chapman University Production), Chapman004708 (January 4, 2021, email from Kenneth Chesebro to John Eastman titled "Fwd: Draft 2, with edits", which includes in the chain a Dec. 13, 2020, email from Kenneth Chesebro to Rudy Giuliani titled "PRIVILEGED AND CONFIDENTIAL—Brief Notes on "President of the Senate" strategy").

20. Documents on file with the Select Committee to Investigate the January 6th Attack on the United States Capitol (Chapman University Production), Chapman004708 (January 4, 2021, email from Kenneth Chesebro to John Eastman titled "Fwd: Draft 2, with edits", which includes in the chain a Dec. 13, 2020, email from Kenneth Chesebro to Rudy Giuliani titled "PRIVILEGED AND CONFIDENTIAL—Brief Notes on "President of the Senate" strategy").

21. Documents on file with the Select Committee to Investigate the January 6th Attack on the United States Capitol (Chapman University Production), Chapman004708 (January 4, 2021, email from Kenneth Chesebro to John Eastman titled "Fwd: Draft 2, with edits", which includes in the chain a Dec. 13, 2020, email from Kenneth Chesebro to Rudy Giuliani titled "PRIVILEGED AND CONFIDENTIAL—Brief Notes on "President of the Senate" strategy").

22. Documents on file with the Select Committee to Investigate the January 6th Attack on the United States Capitol (Chapman University Production), Chapman004708 (January 4, 2021, email from Kenneth Chesebro to John Eastman titled "Fwd: Draft 2, with edits", which includes in the chain a Dec. 13, 2020, email from Kenneth Chesebro to Rudy Giuliani titled "PRIVILEGED AND CONFIDENTIAL—Brief Notes on "President of the Senate" strategy"). In his email, Mr. Chesebro argues that the President of the Senate should open "two envelopes" from the contested States including Arizona, "announce[ ] that he cannot and will not . . . count any electoral votes from [the contested State] because there are two slates of votes," and refuse to count them unless the election is "rerun," the courts engage in "adequate judicial review," or the State's legislature "appoint[s] electors." From this language, it is clear that Mr. Chesebro contemplated the fake votes being used in Congress without a court or State government adopting, ratifying, or otherwise selecting them as the proper electoral college votes from a contested State. To be fair, Chesebro concludes this email by telling Giuliani that "[m]any more points would need to be analyzed in making a complete argument that the President of the Senate possesses the sole power to count electoral votes, and anything to the contrary in the Electoral Count Act is unconstitutional." Despite that caution, the very next sentence advocates for a vigorous assertion of that power: "But at minimum this seems a defensible interpretation of the Twelfth Amendment, and one that ought to be asserted, vigorously, by whoever has the role of President of the Senate."

23. Documents on file with the Select Committee to Investigate the January 6th Attack on the United States Capitol (Chapman University Production), Chapman004708 (January 4, 2021, email from Kenneth Chesebro to John Eastman titled "Fwd: Draft 2, with edits", which includes in the chain a Dec. 13, 2020, email from Kenneth Chesebro to Rudy Giuliani titled "PRIVILEGED AND CONFIDENTIAL—Brief Notes on "President of the Senate" strategy").

24. Documents on file with the Select Committee to Investigate the January 6th Attack on the United States Capitol (Chapman University Production), Chapman053475, Chapman053476, (Dec. 23, 2020 email titled "PRIVILEGED AND CONFIDENTIAL—Dec 23 memo on Jan 6 scenario.docx" from John Eastman to Boris Epshteyn and Kenneth Chesebro, with attached memo titled "January 6 scenario"); Documents on file with the Select Committee to Investigate the January 6th Attack on the United States Capitol (Public Source), CTRL0000923050 (Jan. 3, 2021, John Eastman 6-page memo); John C. Eastman, "Privileged and Confidential–Jan 6 Scenario," (Jan. 3, 2021), available at https://www.scribd.com/document/528776994/Privileged-and-Confidential-Jan-3-Memo-on-Jan-6-Scenario and embedded at John C. Eastman, "Trying to Prevent Illegal Conduct from Deciding an Election is Not Endorsing a 'Coup'," American Greatness (Sep. 30, 2021), available at https://amgreatness.com/2021/09/30/trying-to-prevent-illegal-conduct-from-deciding-an-election-is-not-endorsing-a-coup/.

25. Documents on file with the Select Committee to Investigate the January 6th Attack on the United States Capitol (Mark Meadows Production), MM003771.

26. Documents on file with the Select Committee to Investigate the January 6th Attack on the United States Capitol (Mark Meadows Production), MM003771 (emphasis added).

27. Documents on file with the Select Committee to Investigate the January 6th Attack on the United States Capitol (Mark Meadows Production), MM003769.

28. Documents on file with the Select Committee to Investigate the January 6th Attack on the United States Capitol (Mark Meadows Production), MM010783, MM010784.

29. Documents on file with the Select Committee to Investigate the January 6th Attack on the United States Capitol (Mark Meadows Production), MM010783, MM010784.

30. Documents on file with the Select Committee to Investigate the January 6th Attack on the United States Capitol (Mark Meadows Production), MM013515.

31. Documents on file with the Select Committee to Investigate the January 6th Attack on the United States Capitol (Mark Meadows Production), MM013516.

32. Select Committee to Investigate the January 6th Attack on the United States Capitol, Continued Interview of Cassidy Hutchinson, (Mar. 7, 2022), pp. 54–55.

33. Select Committee to Investigate the January 6th Attack on the United States Capitol, Transcribed Interview of Joshua Findlay, (May 25, 2022), pp. 27–28.

34. Select Committee to Investigate the January 6th Attack on the United States Capitol, Transcribed Interview of Joshua Findlay, (May 25, 2022), p. 29.

35. Select Committee to Investigate the January 6th Attack on the United States Capitol, Transcribed Interview of Joshua Findlay, (May 25, 2022), pp. 86–87.

36. Select Committee to Investigate the January 6th Attack on the United States Capitol, Transcribed Interview of Ronna Romney McDaniel, (June 1, 2022), pp. 7–8. Ms. McDaniel didn't recall the exact date of the call, but thought it was at least "a few days before December 14th" and may have been sometime before the Supreme Court rejected the case *Texas v. Pennsylvania* on December 11th.

37. Select Committee to Investigate the January 6th Attack on the United States Capitol, Transcribed Interview of Ronna Romney McDaniel, (June 1, 2022), pp. 8–9.

38. Select Committee to Investigate the January 6th Attack on the United States Capitol, Transcribed Interview of Ronna Romney McDaniel, (June 1, 2022), pp. 9–13. McDaniel asserted to the Select Committee that even after December 14th she was under the impression that the seven slates of fake electors were strictly contingent in nature pending authorization by a court of law, and that she relayed this to several concerned Republican officials in the contested States. *See id.*, at 18. However, there is also no indication that she took action to condemn or block the misuse of these contingent elector slates by January 6th.

39. Documents on file with the Select Committee to Investigate the January 6th Attack on the United States Capitol (Tim Murtaugh Production), XXM-0021349, (December 13, 2020, text message from Jason Miller to Justin Clark and Eric Herschmann). For instance, on December 11th, Chesebro wrote to a lawyer working on litigation efforts in Arizona, asking him to file a petition that would keep the litigation alive through the 14th: "[C]an you get the cert. petition on file by Monday? Reason is that Kelli Ward & Kelly Townsend just spoke to the Mayor about the campaign's request that all electors vote Monday in all contested states. Ward and Townsend are concerned it could appear **treasonous** for the AZ electors to vote on Monday if there is no pending court proceeding that might, eventually, lead to the electors being ratified as the legitimate ones. Which is a valid point...." Maggie Haberman and Luke Broadwater, "Arizona Officials Warned Fake Electors Plan Could 'Appear Treasonous,'" *The New York Times*, (Aug. 2, 2022), available at https://www.nytimes.com/2022/08/02/us/politics/arizona-trump-fake-electors.html (emphasis in original).

40. Order re Privilege of Remaining Documents at 15, *Eastman v. Thompson et al., No. 8:22-cv-99-DOC-DFM* (C.D. Cal. Oct. 19, 2022), ECF No. 372.

41. Documents on file with the Select Committee to Investigate the January 6th Attack on the United States Capitol (Tim Murtaugh Production), XXM-0019417 (December 14, 2020, emails between Jason Miller and Boris Epshteyn).

42. Order Dismissing Bill of Complaint and Denying Certiorari, Texas v. Pennsylvania, 592 U.S. ___, (Dec. 11, 2020) (No. 155, Orig.), available at https://www.supremecourt.gov/orders/courtorders/121120zr_p860.pdf.

43. *See, e.g.*, Select Committee to Investigate the January 6th Attack on the United States Capitol, Transcribed Interview of Joshua Findlay, (May 25, 2022), pp. 87–88.

44. Select Committee to Investigate the January 6th Attack on the United States Capitol, Transcribed Interview of Justin Clark, (May 17, 2022), p. 116.

45. Select Committee to Investigate the January 6th Attack on the United States Capitol, Transcribed Interview of Joshua Findlay, (May 25, 2022), p. 69; Select Committee to Investigate the January 6th Attack on the United States Capitol, Transcribed Interview of Matthew Morgan, (Apr. 25, 2022), p. 74.

46. Select Committee to Investigate the January 6th Attack on the United States Capitol, Transcribed Interview of Justin Clark, (May 17, 2022), p. 118.

47. Select Committee to Investigate the January 6th Attack on the United States Capitol, Transcribed Interview of Justin Clark, (May 17, 2022), p. 114.

48. Select Committee to Investigate the January 6th Attack on the United States Capitol, Transcribed Interview of Justin Clark, (May 17, 2022), pp. 114, 116.

49. Select Committee to Investigate the January 6th Attack on the United States Capitol, Transcribed Interview of Justin Clark, (May 17, 2022), pp. 116, 118. However, Justin Clark's message in an email dated December 24th seems to potentially contradict his suggestions that the campaign legal team fully backed out: "In terms of political judgements on January 6 I know... that plans are being discussed and executed: alternate slates have been submitted, votes are being whipped, all of the arguments are in place and a not insignificant ad b[u]y was made highlighting the issues in the election." Documents on file with the Select Committee to Investigate the January 6th Attack on the United States Capitol (William Stepien Production), WS 00036.

50. Select Committee to Investigate the January 6th Attack on the United States Capitol, Transcribed Interview of Matthew Morgan, (Apr. 25, 2022), p. 70.

51. Select Committee to Investigate the January 6th Attack on the United States Capitol, Transcribed Interview of Joshua Findlay, (May 25, 2022), pp. 39–40.

52. Select Committee to Investigate the January 6th Attack on the United States Capitol, Transcribed Interview of Pasquale Anthony "Pat" Cipollone, (July 8, 2022), pp. 69–70, 73.

53. Select Committee to Investigate the January 6th Attack on the United States Capitol, Informal Interview of Patrick Philbin, (Apr. 13, 2022).

54. Select Committee to Investigate the January 6th Attack on the United States Capitol, Transcribed Interview of Pasquale Anthony "Pat" Cipollone, (July 8, 2022), pp. 75–76.

55. Select Committee to Investigate the January 6th Attack on the United States Capitol, Continued Interview of Cassidy Hutchinson, (Mar. 7, 2022), p. 64–65. (Hutchinson later clarified that she recalled hearing that from Pat Cipollone and, potentially, also Pat Philbin.)

56. Select Committee to Investigate the January 6th Attack on the United States Capitol, Continued Interview of Cassidy Hutchinson, (Mar. 7, 2022), pp. 64–65.

57. Documents on file with the Select Committee to Investigate the January 6th Attack on the United States Capitol (Joshua Findlay Production), JF052.

58. Select Committee to Investigate the January 6th Attack on the United States Capitol, Transcribed Interview of Joshua Findlay, (May 25, 2022), pp. 87–88.

59. Select Committee to Investigate the January 6th Attack on the United States Capitol, Transcribed Interview of Joshua Findlay, (May 25, 2022), pp. 87–88.

60. Select Committee to Investigate the January 6th Attack on the United States Capitol, Transcribed Interview of Joshua Findlay, (May 25, 2022), p. 44.

61. Select Committee to Investigate the January 6th Attack on the United States Capitol, Transcribed Interview of Joshua Findlay, (May 25, 2022), p. 30.

62. Select Committee to Investigate the January 6th Attack on the United States Capitol, Transcribed Interview of Justin Clark, (May 17, 2022), p. 125.

63. Documents on file with the Select Committee to Investigate the January 6th Attack on the United States Capitol (James DeGraffenreid Production), CTRL0000044010_00031 (Dec. 10, 2020 email from Kenneth Chesebro to James DeGraffenreid and others).

64. Documents on file with the Select Committee to Investigate the January 6th Attack on the United States Capitol (Joshua Findlay Production), JF051, JF054.

65. Documents on file with the Select Committee to investigate the January 6th Attack on the United States Capitol (David Shafer Production), 108751.0001_000004, 108751.0001_000019, 108751.0001_000020, 108751.0001_000021, 108751.0001_000024.

66. Documents on file with the Select Committee to Investigate the January 6th Attack on the United States Capitol (Joshua Findlay Production), JF049.

67. Documents on file with the Select Committee to Investigate the January 6th Attack on the United States Capitol (James DeGraffenreid Production), DEGRAFFENREID 000786; Documents on file with the Select Committee to investigate the January 6th Attack on the United States Capitol (Michael McDonald Production), MCDONALD 000789.

68. Documents on file with the Select Committee to Investigate the January 6th Attack on the United States Capitol (Joshua Findlay Production), JF061.

69. Documents on file with the Select Committee to Investigate the January 6th Attack on the United States Capitol (Lawrence Tabas Production), CTRL0000061077.

70. Documents on file with the Select Committee to Investigate the January 6th Attack on the United States Capitol (Andrew Hitt Production), Hitt000011.

71. Documents on file with the Select Committee to Investigate the January 6th Attack on the United States Capitol (Andrew Hitt Production), Hitt000011.

72. Documents on file with the Select Committee to Investigate the January 6th Attack on the United States Capitol (Andrew Hitt Production), Hitt000011; Documents on file with the Select Committee to Investigate the January 6th Attack on the United States Capitol (David Shafer Production), 108751.0001 000004; Documents on file with the Select Committee to Investigate the January 6th Attack on the United States Capitol (Lawrence Tabas Production), CTRL0000061077; Documents on file with the Select Committee to Investigate the January 6th Attack on the United States Capitol (James DeGraffenreid Production), DEGRAFFENREID 000786; Documents on file with the Select Committee to Investigate the January 6th Attack on the United States Capitol (Kenneth Chesebro Production), KC_Elector_Correspondence_000211, KC_Elector_Correspondence_000215.

73. Documents on file with the Select Committee to Investigate the January 6th Attack on the United States Capitol (Joshua Findlay Production), JF052.

74. Documents on file with the Select Committee to Investigate the January 6th Attack on the United States Capitol (Robert Sinners Production), CTRL0000083897, CTRL0000083898.

75. Documents on file with the Select Committee to Investigate the January 6th Attack on the United States Capitol (Robert Sinners Production), CTRL0000083897.

76. Documents on file with the Select Committee to Investigate the January 6th Attack on the United States Capitol (Robert Sinners Production), CTRL0000083897. Members of this team appear to have included Trump Victory Committee or Trump Campaign EDO State or regional directors for relevant States, including Arizona and New Mexico (Thomas Lane), Georgia (Robert Sinners), Michigan (Shawn Flynn), Nevada (Jesse Law and Valerie McConahay), Pennsylvania (James Fitzpatrick), and Wisconsin (Ryan Terrill, who had originally worked on North Carolina issues but later shifted to Wisconsin), as well as Mr. Roman's deputy (G. Michael Brown). *See* Documents on file with the Select Committee to Investigate the January 6th Attack on the United States Capitol (Laura Cox Production), Laura Cox 000339; Documents on file with the Select Committee to Investigate the January 6th Attack on the United States Capitol (Rudy Giuliani Production), RGGLOBAL_DOM_00001373; Documents on file with the Select Committee to Investigate the January 6th Attack on the United States Capitol (Tim Murtaugh Production) XXM-0010338, XXM-0008776, XXM-0011867; Richard Ruelas, "Trump Campaign Official Subpoenaed by FBI Appears to Be at Meeting of Fake Arizona Electors," *Arizona Republic*, (June 23, 2022), available at https://www.azcentral.com/story/news/politics/arizona/2022/06/23/fbi-subpoenas-thomas-lane-trump-campaign-arizona/7708133001/; Jonathan Oosting, "Trump Fake Elector Probe into

2020 Race Expands with Michigan Subpoenas," *Bridge Michigan*, (June 23, 2022), available at https://www.bridgemi.com/michigan-government/trump-fake-elector-probe-2020-race-expands-michigan-subpoenas; Zach Montellaro and Holly Otterbein, "Trump Calls for Poll Watchers. Election Officials Call for Calm," *Politico*, (Sept. 30, 2020), available at https://www.politico.com/news/2020/09/30/trump-poll-watchers-election-423996; Luke Broadwater, "Jan. 6 Inquiry Subpoenas 6 Tied to False Pro-Trump Elector Effort," *New York Times*, (Feb. 15, 2022), available at https://www.nytimes.com/2022/02/15/us/politics/jan-6-subpoenas-trump.html.

77. Documents on file with the Select Committee to Investigate the January 6th Attack on the United States Capitol (Robert Sinners Production), CTRL0000083898.

78. David Shafer (@DavidShafer), Twitter, Dec. 14, 2020 12:51 p.m. ET, available at https://twitter.com/DavidShafer/status/1338542161932021762; David Shafer (@DavidShafer), Twitter, Dec. 14, 2020 1:07 p.m. ET, available at https://twitter.com/DavidShafer/status/1338546066346676224; "Republican Electors Cast Procedural Vote, Seek to Preserve Trump Campaign Legal Challenge," Pennsylvania Republican Party website, (Dec. 14, 2020), available at https://pagop.org/2020/12/14/republican-electors-cast-procedural-vote/; "Statement on Republican Electors Meeting," Republican Party of Wisconsin, (Dec. 14, 2020), available at https://wisgop.org/republican-electors-2020/; Republican Party of Arizona (@AZGOP), Twitter, Dec. 14, 2020 5:13 p.m. ET, available at https://twitter.com/AZGOP/status/1338608056985239554.

79. Marshall Cohen, Zachary Cohen, and Dan Merica, "Trump Campaign Officials, Led by Rudy Giuliani, Oversaw Fake Electors Plot in 7 States," CNN, (Jan. 20, 2022), available at https://www.cnn.com/2022/01/20/politics/trump-campaign-officials-rudy-giuliani-fake-electors/index.html.

80. Select Committee to Investigate the January 6th Attack on the United States Capitol, Transcribed Interview of Joshua Findlay, (May 25, 2022), p. 58.

81. Documents on file with the Select Committee to Investigate the January 6th Attack on the United States Capitol (Tim Murtaugh Production), XXM-0016071 (December 10, 2020, email from Joshua Findlay to Nick Trainer and Matt Morgan re: Presidential Elector Issues).

82. Documents on file with the Select Committee to Investigate the January 6th Attack on the United States Capitol (Tim Murtaugh Production), XXM-0016071 (December 10, 2020, email from Joshua Findlay to Nick Trainer and Matt Morgan re: Presidential Elector Issues); Select Committee to Investigate the January 6th Attack on the United States Capitol, Transcribed Interview of Joshua Findlay, (May 25, 2022), pp. 55–59; Michael C. Bender, "Republicans Hire Nine Regional Directors for Trump 2020 Election," *Wall Street Journal*, (May 8, 2019), available at https://www.wsj.com/articles/trump-campaign-hires-nine-regional-directors-for-2020-election-11557355628.

83. Documents on file with the Select Committee to Investigate the January 6th Attack on the United States Capitol (Lawrence Tabas Production), CTRL0000061085 (December 13, 2020, email chain between Thomas King III and James Fitzpatrick re: Pa. Electors).

84. Select Committee to Investigate the January 6th Attack on the United States Capitol, Informal Interview of Lawrence Tabas, (Apr. 11, 2022).

85. Documents on file with the Select Committee to Investigate the January 6th Attack on the United States Capitol (Andrew Hitt Production), Hitt000076 (December 4, 2020, Text messages between Andrew Hitt and Mark Jefferson); Select Committee to Investigate the January 6th Attack on the United States Capitol, Deposition of Andrew Hitt, (Feb. 28, 2022), p. 8.

86. Documents on file with the Select Committee to Investigate the January 6th Attack on the United States Capitol (Andrew Hitt Production), Hitt000083 (December 12, 2020, Text messages between Andrew Hitt and Mark Jefferson).

87. Documents on file with the Select Committee to Investigate the January 6th Attack on the United States Capitol (National Archives Production), CTRL0000037949 (December 14, 2020, memorandum from purported electors in Wisconsin).

88. Kira Lerner, "UPDATED Trump's Fake Electors: Here's the Full List," *News from the States*, (June 29, 2022), available at https://www.newsfromthestates.com/article/updated-trumps-fake-electors-heres-full-list; Documents on file with the Select Committee to Investigate the January 6th Attack on the United States Capitol (National Archives Production), CTRL0000037568, CTRL0000037944, CTRL0000037945, CTRL0000037946, CTRL0000037947, CTRL0000037948, CTRL0000037949 (December 14, 2020, memoranda from slates of purported electors in Arizona, Georgia, Michigan, New Mexico, Nevada, Pennsylvania, and Wisconsin).

89. Select Committee to Investigate the January 6th Attack on the United States Capitol, Deposition of Laura Cox, (May 3, 2022), pp. 77–78.

90. Beth Reinhard, Amy Gardner, Josh Dawsey, Emma Brown, and Rosalind S. Helderman, "As Giuliani Coordinated Plan for Trump Electoral Votes in States Biden Won, Some Electors Balked," *Washington Post*, (Jan. 20, 2022), available at https://www.washingtonpost.com/investigations/electors-giuliani-trump-electoral-college/2022/01/20/687e3698-7587-11ec-8b0a-bcfab800c430_story.html.

91. Beth Reinhard, Amy Gardner, Josh Dawsey, Emma Brown, and Rosalind S. Helderman, "As Giuliani Coordinated Plan for Trump Electoral Votes in States Biden Won, Some Electors Balked," *Washington Post*, (Jan. 20, 2022), available at https://www.washingtonpost.com/investigations/electors-giuliani-trump-electoral-college/2022/01/20/687e3698-7587-11ec-8b0a-bcfab800c430_story.html.

92. Kira Lerner, "UPDATED Trump's fake electors: Here's the full list," *News from the States*, (June 29, 2022), available at https://www.newsfromthestates.com/article/updated-trumps-fake-electors-heres-full-list.

93. *See, e.g.*, Select Committee to Investigate the January 6th Attack on the United States Capitol, Deposition of Andrew Hitt, (Feb. 28, 2022), pp. 50–51.

94. Select Committee to Investigate the January 6th Attack on the United States Capitol, Transcribed Interview of Robert Sinners, (June 15, 2022), pp. 18–19.

95. Select Committee to Investigate the January 6th Attack on the United States Capitol, Transcribed Interview of Robert Sinners, (June 15, 2022), pp. 37–38.

96. Documents on file with the Select Committee to Investigate the January 6th Attack on the United States Capitol (National Archives Production), CTRL0000037568, CTRL0000037944, CTRL0000037945 CTRL0000037946, CTRL0000037947, CTRL0000037948, CTRL0000037949 (December 14, 2020, memoranda from slates of purported electors in Arizona, Georgia, Michigan, Nevada, and Wisconsin).

97. Documents on file with the Select Committee to Investigate the January 6th Attack on the United States Capitol (National Archives Production), CTRL0000037946 (December 14, 2020, memorandum from purported electors in New Mexico).

98. Documents on file with the Select Committee to Investigate the January 6th Attack on the United States Capitol (National Archives Production), CTRL0000037948 (December 14, 2020, memorandum from purported electors in Pennsylvania).

99. Documents on file with the Select Committee to Investigate the January 6th Attack on the United States Capitol (Robert Sinners Production), CTRL0000083893 (December 14, 2020, email chain from Robert Sinners to Mike Roman and others re: Whip Update).

100. Documents on file with the Select Committee to Investigate the January 6th Attack on the United States Capitol (William Stepien Production), WS 00095, WS 00096 (December 14, 2020, email from Joshua Findlay to Matt Morgan, Justin Clark, and cc'ing Bill Stepien re: Georgia Update).

101. Documents on file with the Select Committee to Investigate the January 6th Attack on the United States Capitol (National Archives Production), 076P-R000009527_0001, (December 14, 2020, forwarded email from Ronna McDaniel to Molly Michael with the subject line: "FWD: Electors Recap—Final").

102. Documents on file with the Select Committee to Investigate the January 6th Attack on the United States Capitol (National Archives Production), 076P-R000009527_0001, (December 14, 2020, forwarded email from Ronna McDaniel to Molly Michael with the subject line: "FWD: Electors Recap—Final").

103. Documents on file with the Select Committee to Investigate the January 6th Attack on the United States Capitol (Shawn Still Production), CTRL0000042623_00018 (December 13, 2020, email from Shawn Still to Dana Pagan subject: "Fwd: Information on Duties of Presidential Electors—Monday, December 14th").

104. Documents on file with the Select Committee to Investigate the January 6th Attack on the United States Capitol (Shawn Still Production), CTRL0000042623_00018 (December 13, 2020, email from Shawn Still to Dana Pagan subject: "Fwd: Information on Duties of Presidential Electors—Monday, December 14th").

105. Greg Bluestein (@bluestein), Twitter, Dec. 14, 2020 11:32 a.m. ET, available at https://twitter.com/bluestein/status/1338522299360800771; Select Committee to Investigate the January 6th Attack on the United States Capitol, Deposition of Shawn Still, (Feb. 25, 2022), pp. 41–48; Michael Isikoff and Daniel Klaidman, "Exclusive: Fulton County DA Sends 'Target' Letters to Trump Allies in Georgia Investigation," Yahoo! News, (July 15, 2022), available at https://news.yahoo.com/exclusive-fulton-county-da-sends-target-letters-to-trump-allies-in-georgia-investigation-152517469.html.

106. Select Committee to Investigate the January 6th Attack on the United States Capitol, Deposition of Laura Cox, (May 3, 2022), pp. 53–54.

107. Select Committee to Investigate the January 6th Attack on the United States Capitol, Deposition of Laura Cox, (May 3, 2022), pp. 53–54.

108. Select Committee to Investigate the January 6th Attack on the United States Capitol, Deposition of Mayra Rodriguez, (Feb. 22, 2022), pp. 14–18.

109. Documents on file with the Select Committee to Investigate the January 6th Attack on the United States Capitol (National Archives Production), VP-R0000417_0001, VP-R0000418_0001 (January 3, 2021, email from Elizabeth MacDonough, subject "RE: COV tracker" with attachment); Documents on file with the Select Committee to Investigate the January 6th Attack on the United States Capitol (Chris Hodgson Production), 00094 (Attachment to email from Elizabeth MacDonough, subject "RE: COV tracker").

110. Documents on file with the Select Committee to Investigate the January 6th Attack on the United States Capitol (National Archives Production), VP-R0000417_0001, VP-R0000418_0001 (January 3, 2021, email from Elizabeth MacDonough, subject "RE: COV tracker" with attachment); Documents on file with the Select Committee to Investigate the January 6th Attack on the United States Capitol (Chris Hodgson Production), 00094 (Attachment to email from Elizabeth MacDonough, subject "RE: COV tracker").

111. Select Committee to Investigate the January 6th Attack on the United States Capitol, Deposition of Chris Hodgson, (Mar. 30, 2022), pp. 144–45, 206–07.

112. In Wisconsin they were able to enter with apparent help from the chief of staff for then majority leader of the Wisconsin State Senate, Scott Fitzgerald, who now represents Wisconsin in the U.S. House of Representatives. In Georgia, a freelance reporter who has testified to the Fulton County grand jury claims to have found that the room in which the fake electors met was reserved by the office of Georgia House Speaker David Ralston, which is consistent with what Georgia GOP Chairman David Shafer told the Select Committee. See "Open Records Regarding Wisconsin's Fake Electors Suggest Congressman Scott Fitzgerald Played Significant Role in Trying to Overturn a Free and Fair Election," Office of Wisconsin State Senator Chris Larson, (Jan. 25, 2022), available at https://legis.wisconsin.gov/senate/07/Larson/media/2056/1-25-22-fitzgerald-electors-pr.pdf; Letter from Cyrus Anderson, Deputy Sergeant at Arms, Wisconsin State Senate to State Sen. Chris Larson, attaching documents, Jan. 24, 2022, available at https://legis.wisconsin.gov/senate/07/Larson/media/2052/12-14-20-open-records-request-results-short.pdf; Select Committee to Investigate the January 6th Attack on the United States Capitol, Deposition of David Shafer, (Feb.

25, 2022), pp. 93–94, 106; Michael Isikoff and Daniel Kladman, "Exclusive: Fulton County DA Sends 'Target' Letters to Trump Allies in Georgia Investigation," *Yahoo! News*, (July 15, 2022), available at https://news.yahoo.com/exclusive-fulton-county-da-sends-target-letters-to-trump-allies-in-georgia-investigation-152517469.html; George Chidi, "Bearing Witness," The Atlanta Objective with George Chidi, (June 29, 2022), available at https://theatlantaobjective.substack.com/p/bearing-witness; Documents on file with the Select Committee to Investigate the January 6th Attack on the United States Capitol (Shawn Still Production), 108755.0001_000009 (December 13, 2020, email from Shawn Still to Dana Pagan re: "Fwd: Information of Duties of Presidential Electors—Monday Dec. 14th").

113.   Daniel Villareal, "Michigan Republicans Tried to Submit Fake Electoral Votes to Capitol," *Newsweek*, (Dec. 15, 2020), available at https://www.newsweek.com/michigan-republicans-tried-submit-fake-electoral-votes-capitol-1555028.

114.   Documents on file with the Select Committee to Investigate the January 6th Attack on the United States Capitol (National Archives Production), CTRL0000037945, p. 2 (December 14, 2020, memorandum of purported Michigan electors for Donald J. Trump).

115.   Select Committee to Investigate the January 6th Attack on the United States Capitol, Deposition of Mayra Rodriguez, (Feb. 22, 2022), pp. 18, 21; Laina G. Stebbins, "Feds Serve Subpoenas to Pro-Trump Fake Electors in Michigan," *Michigan Advance* (June 23, 2022), available at https://michiganadvance.com/blog/feds-serve-subpoenas-to-pro-trump-fake-electors-in-michigan/.

116.   Brett Samuels, "Stephen Miller: 'Alternate' Electors Will Keep Trump Election Challenge Alive," *The Hill*, (Dec. 14, 2020), available at https://thehill.com/homenews/campaign/530092-stephen-miller-alternate-electors-will-keep-trump-challenge-alive-post/; Steve Bannon's War Room Radio, "STEVE BANNON'S WAR ROOM RADIO SPECIAL EPISODE582," *BitChute*, (aired on Dec. 14, 2020, reposted on BitChute Aug. 22, 2021), at 10:30–13:00, available at https://www.bitchute.com/video/v889V3Thxgcj/.

117.   Mike Wereschagin, "Pa. Republicans' Hedged Language May Have Saved Them from Prosecution over Electoral Vote Scheme," *Lancaster Online*, (Jan. 17, 2022), available at https://lancasteronline.com/news/politics/pa-republicans-hedged-language-may-have-saved-them-from-prosecution-over-electoral-vote-scheme/article_849d4f7e-7589-11ec-8881-6383a823557d.html.

118.   Select Committee to Investigate the January 6th Attack on the United States Capitol, Continued Interview of Cassidy Hutchinson, (Mar. 7, 2022), pp. 143–48.

119.   Documents on file with the Select Committee to Investigate the January 6th Attack on the United States Capitol (Chapman University Production), Chapman053475 (December 23, 2020, John Eastman email to Boris Epshteyn and Ken Chesebro).

120.   Documents on file with the Select Committee to Investigate the January 6th Attack on the United States Capitol (Chapman University Production), Chapman053476 (Word Document, "PRIVILEGED AND CONFIDENTIAL January 6 Scenario," attached in Dec. 23, 2020, John Eastman email to Boris Epshteyn and Ken Chesebro).

121.   Documents on file with the Select Committee to Investigate the January 6th Attack on the United States Capitol (Chapman University Production), Chapman053475 (December 23, 2020, John Eastman email to Boris Epshteyn and Ken Chesebro).

122.   Documents on file with the Select Committee to Investigate the January 6th Attack on the United States Capitol (Chapman University Production), Chapman061863 (January 1, 2021, Kenneth Chesebro email to John Eastman and Boris Epshteyn at 10:26 p.m.).

123.   Both of Dr. Eastman's memos described here are discussed at length in the chapter addressing President Trump's pressure on the Vice President. *See* Chapter 5. *See also* Documents on file with the Select Committee to Investigate the January 6th Attack on the United States Capitol (Chapman University Production), Chapman053475, Chapman053476, (Dec. 23, 2020 email titled "PRIVILEGED AND CONFIDENTIAL—Dec 23 memo on Jan 6 scenario.docx" from John Eastman to Boris Epshteyn and Kenneth Chesebro, with attached memo titled "January 6 scenario"); Documents on file with the Select Committee

to Investigate the January 6th Attack on the United States Capitol (Public Source), CTRL0000923050 (Jan. 3, 2021, John Eastman 6-page memo); John C. Eastman, "Privileged and Confidential–Jan 6 Scenario," (Jan. 3, 2021), available at https://www.scribd.com/document/528776994/Privileged-and-Confidential-Jan-3-Memo-on-Jan-6-Scenario and embedded at John C. Eastman, "Trying to Prevent Illegal Conduct from Deciding an Election is Not Endorsing a 'Coup'," American Greatness (Sep. 30, 2021), available at https://amgreatness.com/2021/09/30/trying-to-prevent-illegal-conduct-from-deciding-an-election-is-not-endorsing-a-coup/

124. Documents on file with the Select Committee to Investigate the January 6th Attack on the United States Capitol (National Archives Production), VP-R0000417_0001, VP-R0000418_0001 (January 3, 2021 email and attachment from Senate Parliamentarian to Office of the Vice President); Documents on file with the Select Committee to Investigate the January 6th Attack on the United States Capitol (Chris Hodgson Production) 00094 (additional copy of same attachment sent from Senate Parliamentarian to Office of the Vice President).

125. Documents on file with the Select Committee to Investigate the January 6th Attack on the United States Capitol (Andrew Hitt Production), Hitt000089 (January 4, 2021, Andrew Hitt text message to Mark Jefferson at 9:02 p.m.).

126. Documents on file with the Select Committee to Investigate the January 6th Attack on the United States Capitol (Andrew Hitt Production), Hitt000089 (January 4, 2021, Andrew Hitt text message to Mark Jefferson at 9:02 p.m.).

127. Documents on file with the Select Committee to Investigate the January 6th Attack on the United States Capitol (Angela McCallum Production), McCallum_01_001576, McCallum_01_001577 (Michael Brown text message to Angela McCallum at undetermined time); Select Committee to Investigate the January 6th Attack on the United States Capitol, Deposition of Angela McCallum (Dec. 8, 2021), p. 122.

128. Documents on file with the Select Committee to Investigate the January 6th Attack on the United States Capitol (Angela McCallum Production), McCallum_01_001576, McCallum_01_001577 (Michael Brown text message to Angela McCallum at undetermined time); Select Committee to Investigate the January 6th Attack on the United States Capitol, Deposition of Angela McCallum (Dec. 8, 2021), p. 122.

129. The Select Committee does not know where Brown delivered the fake votes. The Select Committee attempted to contact Brown multiple ways, including by subpoena, but servers could not locate him and he never responded to outreach. The Select Committee served Mike Roman with a subpoena, but he asserted his Fifth Amendment rights and did not answer any substantive questions about the fake-elector scheme. What the Select Committee has determined, however, is that Brown likely delivered the fake electoral eollege votes to at least one of President Trump's allies in Congress. *See* Select Committee to Investigate the January 6th Attack on the United States Capitol, Deposition of Michael Roman, (Aug. 10, 2022), p. 40.

130. Jason Lemon, "Johnson Says Involvement With 1/6 Fake Electors Plan Only 'Lasted Seconds'," *Newsweek*, (Aug. 21, 2022), available at https://www.newsweek.com/johnson-says-involvement-1-6-fake-electors-plan-only-lasted-seconds-1735486; Documents on file with the Select Committee to Investigate the January 6th Attack on the United States Capitol (Chris Hodgson Production), CTRL0000056548_00007 (January 6, 2021, text message at 8:41 a.m. ET from Matt Stroia to Chris Hodgson); Documents on file with the Select Committee to Investigate the January 6th Attack on the United States Capitol (Chris Hodgson Production), CTRL0000056548_000035 (Jan. 6, 2021, text message around 12:37 p.m. ET from Sean Riley to Chris Hodgson) ("Johnson needs to hand something to VPOTUS please advise . . . Alternate slate of electors for MI and WI because archivist didn't receive them . . .").

131. Documents on file with the Select Committee to Investigate the January 6th Attack on the United States Capitol (Chris Hodgson Production), CTRL0000056548_00007 (January 6, 2021, Matt Stroia text message to Chris Hodgson at 8:41 a.m. ET).

132. Lawrence Andrea, "Pennsylvania Congressman Concludes Internal Investigation with Few Answers After Ron Johnson's Claims About False Electors," *Milwaukee Journal Sentinel*, (July 14, 2022), available at https://www.jsonline.com/story/news/politics/2022/07/14/few-answers-mike-kellys-probe-into-false-electors-ron-johnson-pennsylvania-wisconsin/10059776002/.

133. "The Vicki McKenna Show—Keep and Bear Arms," iHeart Radio, June 23, 2022, at 9:30–15:00, available at https://www.iheart.com/podcast/139-vicki-mckenna-27246267/episode/the-vicki-mckenna-show-keep-98666092/?position=570&embed=true; John Solomon, "Jan. 6 Panel's Ron Johnson Narrative Exposes Ills of One-Sided Hearing," *Just The News*, (June 23, 2022), available at https://justthenews.com/government/jan-6-panels-ron-johnson-narrative-exposes-ills-one-sided-hearing (linking to image of text message available at https://justthenews.com/sites/default/files/2022-06/TroupisJohnson1.pdf).

134. "The Vicki McKenna Show—Keep and Bear Arms," iHeart Radio, June 23, 2022, at 9:30–15:00, available at https://www.iheart.com/podcast/139-vicki-mckenna-27246267/episode/the-vicki-mckenna-show-keep-98666092/?position=570&embed=true; John Solomon, "Jan. 6 Panel's Ron Johnson Narrative Exposes Ills of One-Sided Hearing," *Just The News*, (June 23, 2022), available at https://justthenews.com/government/jan-6-panels-ron-johnson-narrative-exposes-ills-one-sided-hearing (linking to image of text message available at https://justthenews.com/sites/default/files/2022-06/JohnsonTroupis2Redacted.pdf).

135. Documents on file with the Select Committee to Investigate the January 6th Attack on the United States Capitol (Chris Hodgson Production), CTRL0000056548_00035 (January 6, 2021, Sean Riley text message to Chris Hodgson at 12:37 p.m. ET).

136. Documents on file with the Select Committee to Investigate the January 6th Attack on the United States Capitol (Chris Hodgson Production), CTRL0000056548_00035 (January 6, 2021, Sean Riley text message to Chris Hodgson at 12:37 p.m. ET).

137. Documents on file with the Select Committee to Investigate the January 6th Attack on the United States Capitol (Chris Hodgson Production), CTRL0000056548_00035 (January 6, 2021, Sean Riley text message to Chris Hodgson at 12:37 p.m. ET).

138. Documents on file with the Select Committee to Investigate the January 6th Attack on the United States Capitol (Mark Meadows Production), MM013494, MM014589, MM014592, MM014595, MM014598, MM014722 (Mark Meadows text messages with Sen. Mike Lee on December 8, 2020, January 3, 2021, and January 4, 2021); Documents on file with the Select Committee to Investigate the January 6th Attack on the United States Capitol (Cleta Mitchell Production), CM00015452, CM00015477 (Cleta Mitchell text messages with Sen. Mike Lee on December 9, 2020 and December 30, 2020).

139. Documents on file with the Select Committee to Investigate the January 6th Attack on the United States Capitol (Cleta Mitchell Production), CM00015477.

140. Documents on file with the Select Committee to Investigate the January 6th Attack on the United States Capitol (Cleta Mitchell Production), CM00015477.

141. Documents on file with the Select Committee to Investigate the January 6th Attack on the United States Capitol (Cleta Mitchell Production), CM00015477.

4

"JUST CALL IT CORRUPT AND LEAVE THE REST TO ME"

4.1 THE DOJ FOUND NO SIGNIFICANT EVIDENCE OF FRAUD

U.S. Attorney General William Barr knew there would be trouble before all the votes had been counted. "So, right out of the box on election night, the President claimed that there was major fraud underway," Barr explained. "I mean, this happened, as far as I could tell, before there was actually any potential of looking at evidence."[1] President Trump was quick to claim, "there was major fraud" based solely on the phenomenon known as the "Red Mirage."[2]

As explained elsewhere in this report, Democrats were more inclined to vote via mail-in ballot during the 2020 Presidential election than Republicans, who were more likely to vote in-person on election day. This was widely known, and partly a result of, President Trump's own public statements criticizing mail-in balloting. It also created a gap in the timing of how votes were tallied. The early vote tally favored Republicans on election night because the mail-in ballots, which skewed toward Democrats, were not yet fully counted. This occurred not just in 2020, but also in previous elections.[3] The President knew of this phenomenon but exploited it on election night, nonetheless, as he and his allies had planned to do.[4]

President Trump exploited this timing gap and used it as "the basis for this broad claim that there was major fraud," Barr said.[5] But the Attorney General "didn't think much of that." People "had been talking for weeks and everyone understood for weeks that that was going to be what happened on election night," Barr explained.[6] Cities with Democratic majorities in the battleground States wouldn't have their votes fully counted until "the end of the cycle," with "a lot of Democratic votes coming in at the end."[7] This was not some well-guarded secret, as "everyone understood that the dynamic of election night in many States would be whether or not the Democratic votes at the end of the day would overcome the election day votes."[8]

Within days of the election, the President made an "avalanche" of fraud allegations. It "was like playing Whac-A-Mole," Barr explained, "because something would come out one day and the next day it would be another issue."[9] Barr told his "staff very soon after the election" that he "didn't think the President would ever admit that he lost the election, and he would blame it on fraud, and then he would blame the actions and evidence on the Department of Justice."[10]

Barr soon took steps to investigate claims of fraud in the 2020 Presidential election, even in the absence of evidence. The Department of Justice's (DOJ) longstanding policy had been to avoid any substantive investigations until after the election's results were certified.[11] As the country's premier Federal law enforcement agency, DOJ is justifiably concerned that its substantial power can influence the outcome of an election, and it has enacted policies to mitigate this possibility.[12]

On November 7, 2020, the media declared former Vice President Biden the winner of the Presidential election. Two days later, on November 9th, Attorney General Barr authorized wider investigations into claims of election fraud.[13] Barr instructed DOJ and FBI personnel "to pursue substantial allegations of voting and vote tabulation irregularities prior to the certification of elections in your jurisdictions in certain cases."[14] Barr noted that nothing in his memo "should be taken as any indication that the Department has concluded that voting irregularities have impacted the outcome of any election."[15]

4.2 NOVEMBER 23, 2020: BARR CHALLENGES PRESIDENT TRUMP'S ELECTION LIES

As Barr predicted, the President did call on him for information about alleged election fraud. Trump challenged him with a blizzard of conspiracy theories in three face-to-face meetings after the election. The first such meeting occurred on November 23, 2020.

On November 23rd, the Attorney General spoke with White House Counsel Pat Cipollone, who said that it was important for him come to the White House and speak to President Trump.[16] Barr had not seen the President since before the election in late October, and the White House counsel believed that it was important that the Attorney General explain what the Department of Justice was doing related to claims of election fraud.[17]

"The President said there had been major fraud and that, as soon as the facts were out, the results of the election would be reversed," Barr recalled.

U.S. Attorney General William Barr at the Department of Justice on December 21, 2020.
(Photo by Michael Reynolds-Pool/Getty Images)

Trump continued "for quite a while," and Barr was "expecting" what came next.[18] President Trump alleged that "the Department of Justice doesn't think it has a role looking into these fraud claims."[19] Barr anticipated this line of attack because the President's counsel, Rudolph Giuliani, was making all sorts of wild, unsubstantiated claims.[20] And Giuliani wanted to blame DOJ for the fact that no one had come up with any real evidence of fraud.[21] Of course, by the time of this meeting, U.S. Attorneys' Offices had been explicitly authorized to investigate substantial claims for 2 weeks and had yet to find any evidence of significant voter fraud.[22]

Barr explained to the President why he was wrong. DOJ, was willing to investigate any "specific and credible allegations of fraud."[23] The fact of the matter was that the claims being made were "just not meritorious" and were "not panning out."[24] Barr emphasized to the President that DOJ "doesn't take sides in elections" and "is not an extension of your legal team."[25]

During the November 23rd meeting, Barr also challenged one of President Trump's central lies. He "specifically raised the Dominion voting machines, which I found to be one of the most disturbing allegations."[26] "Disturbing," Barr explained, because there was "absolutely zero basis for the allegations," which were being "made in such a sensational way that they obviously were influencing a lot of people, members of the public." [27] Americans were being deceived into thinking "that there was this systematic corruption in the system and that their votes didn't count and that these machines, controlled by somebody else, were actually determining it, which was complete nonsense." [28] Barr stressed to the President that this was "crazy stuff," arguing that not only was the conspiracy theory a waste of time, but it was also "doing [a] great, great disservice to the country." [29]

As Attorney General Barr left the meeting, he talked with Mark Meadows, the White House Chief of Staff, and Jared Kushner, President Trump's son-in-law.[30] "I think he's become more realistic and knows that there's a limit to how far he can take this," Meadows said, according to Barr.[31] Kushner reassured Barr, "we're working on this, we're working on it." [32] Barr was hopeful that the President was beginning to accept reality.[33] The opposite happened.

"I felt that things continued to deteriorate between the 23rd and the weekend of the 29th," Barr recalled.[34] Barr was concerned because President Trump began meeting with delegations of State legislators, and it appeared to him that "there was maneuvering going on." [35] Barr had "no problem" with challenging an election "through the appropriate process," but "worried" that he "didn't have any visibility into what was going on" and that the "President was digging in." [36]

4.3 DECEMBER 1, 2020: PRESIDENT TRUMP IS IRATE AFTER BARR SAYS THERE IS NO SIGNIFICANT FRAUD

Attorney General Barr had been clear that DOJ was investigating claims of fraud. The Department simply was not turning up any real evidence of malfeasance, and certainly nothing that would overturn the election. Just as Barr feared, the President turned on DOJ anyway.

On November 29, 2020, Fox News's Maria Bartiromo interviewed President Trump. It was his first TV interview since he lost his bid for reelection. The President claimed the election was "rigged" and rife with "fraud." [37] President Trump repeated various conspiracy theories, leading with the claim that Dominion's voting machines had "glitches," which moved "thousands of votes from my account to Biden's account." [38] President Trump pointed to "dumps of votes,"a reference to the batches of mail-in ballots that had been tabulated later in the counting process.[39] He rambled off various other, spurious allegations, including that dead people voted in significant numbers.[40]

"This is total fraud," the President said.[41] "And how the FBI and Department of Justice—I don't know—maybe they're involved, but how people are getting away with this stuff—it's unbelievable. This election was rigged. This election was a total fraud."[42]

"Where is the DOJ and the FBI in all of this, Mr. President?" Bartiromo asked.[43] "You have laid out some serious charges here. Shouldn't this be something that the FBI is investigating? Are they? Is the DOJ investigating?" Bartiromo asked incredulously.[44]

"Missing in action," the President replied, "can't tell you where they are."[45] He conceded that when he asked if DOJ and FBI were investigating, "everyone says yes, they're looking at it."[46] But he didn't leave it there. "You would think if you're in the FBI or Department of Justice, this is, this is the biggest thing you could be looking at," President Trump said. "Where are they? I've not seen anything. I mean, just keep moving along. They go onto the next President."[47] He claimed the FBI was not even investigating Dominion, adding that votes processed in its machines "are counted in foreign countries."[48]

None of this was true. Just 6 days earlier, Attorney General Barr had explained to President Trump how DOJ and FBI were investigating fraud claims. Barr also made it a point to emphasize that the Dominion claims were nonsense. The President simply lied. The "crazy stuff," as Barr put it, was all Trump could cite.

Attorney General Barr then decided to speak out. He invited Michael Balsamo, an *Associated Press (AP)* reporter, to lunch on December 1st. Barr told the journalist that "to date, we have not seen fraud on a scale that could have effected a different outcome in the election."[49]

That made the President irate.

Later that evening, Attorney General Barr met with President Trump at the White House. It was their second face-to-face meeting after the November election.[50] At first, President Trump didn't even look at Attorney General Barr.[51] The President "was as mad as I've ever seen him, and he was trying to control himself," Barr said.[52] The President finally "shoved a newspaper" with the *AP* quote in Barr's face.[53]

"Well, this is, you know, killing me. You didn't have to say this. You must've said this because you hate Trump—you hate Trump," Barr remembered him saying.[54] "No, I don't hate you, Mr. President," Barr replied. "You know, I came in at a low time in your administration. I've tried to help your administration. I certainly don't hate you."[55]

President Trump peppered him with unsupported conspiracy theories.[56] Because he had authorized DOJ and FBI to investigate fraud claims, Attorney General Barr was familiar with the conspiracy theories raised by the President. The "big ones" he investigated included claims such as: Dominion voting machines switched votes, votes had been "dumped at the end of

the night in Milwaukee and Detroit," non-residents voted in Nevada, the
number of ballots counted in Pennsylvania exceeded the number of votes
cast, as well as a story about a truck driver supposedly driving thousands of
pre-filled ballots from New York to Pennsylvania, among others.[57] Under
Attorney General Barr, DOJ would also investigate a false claim that a video
feed in Fulton County captured multiple runs of ballots for former Vice
President Biden. As explained in detail in Chapter 1 of this report, there was
no truth to any of these allegations, but that didn't stop President Trump
from repeatedly citing these fictional accounts.

"And I told him that the stuff that his people were shoveling out to the
public was bullshit, I mean, that the claims of fraud were bullshit," Barr
recalled about the December 1st meeting.[58] "And, you know, he was indig-
nant about that. And I reiterated that they wasted a whole month of these
claims on the Dominion voting machines and they were idiotic claims." [59]

President Trump repeated that there had been a "big vote dump" in
Detroit.[60] But Attorney General Barr quickly parried this claim.[61] There was
nothing suspicious in how the votes flowed into a central location, Barr
explained, because that is how votes are always counted in Wayne County.[62]
Moreover, Barr pointed out that the President performed *better* in Detroit in
2020 than he had in 2016. "I mean, there's no indication of fraud in
Detroit," Barr said.[63] Barr explained that the "thing about the truck driver
is complete, you know, nonsense." [64] DOJ and FBI had investigated the
matter, including by interviewing the relevant witnesses.[65] There was no
truck filled with ballots.

Nothing that Attorney General Barr said during that meeting could satisfy President Trump. So, the President shifted the focus to Barr. He complained that the Attorney General hadn't indicted former FBI Director
James Comey and that U.S. Attorney John Durham's investigation into the
origins of the FBI's Crossfire Hurricane investigation hadn't made more
progress.[66] "Look, I know that you're dissatisfied with me," Barr said, "and
I'm glad to offer my resignation." [67] President Trump pounded the table in
front of him with his fist and said, "Accepted." [68]

White House lawyers Pat Cipollone and Eric Herschmann tracked Barr
down in the parking lot after he left.[69] They convinced Barr to stay in the
administration.[70] But his days as Attorney General were numbered. President Trump was not going to stop spreading conspiracy theories. Nor would
the President cease in his effort to co-opt DOJ for his own corrupt political
purposes.

President Trump released a video on Facebook the very next day.[71] He
repeated many of the same lies, including the conspiracy theory about
Dominion voting machines switching votes. The President also offered

charts, falsely claiming that fraudulent "vote dumps" had swung the election against him.[72] Among the examples he cited was the supposed "vote dump" in Detroit, Michigan.[73] In fact, Barr had already debunked this and other claims.

On December 3, 2020, Rudolph Giuliani appeared before the Georgia Senate Government Oversight Committee to allege that massive cheating had occurred during the election.[74] Giuliani offered a video recorded on election night at the State Farm Arena in Atlanta, Georgia, as a key piece of evidence.[75] Giuliani alleged that the video showed a secret suitcase of ballots being double- and triple-counted after Republican poll watchers had been inappropriately dismissed.[76] The video was selectively edited and showed nothing of the sort. The Georgia Secretary of State's Office investigated and immediately debunked the claim, finding that the secret suitcase was just a secure box and nothing nefarious had occurred.[77] President Trump, Giuliani and others continued to push the lie anyway.

On December 4th, Attorney General Barr asked Byung J. ("BJay") Pak, who was then the U.S. Attorney for the Northern District of Georgia, to independently investigate the State Farm claim. Barr told Pak that this was a "priority," because "he was going to go to the White House for a meeting" and the "issue might come up." Barr asked Pak to "try to substantiate the allegation made by Mr. Giuliani." [78]

Pak watched the video from State Farm Arena and asked the FBI to investigate the matter further. Pak told the Select Committee that FBI agents "interviewed the individuals" shown in the video who were supposedly "double, triple counting" the ballots, and "determined that nothing irregular happened in the counting and the allegations made by Mr. Giuliani were false." [79] And, as noted above, the supposed "suitcase" was a secure storage container used to store ballots. With this evidence in hand, Pak told Attorney General Barr that there was no substance to the allegations.[80]

4.4 DECEMBER 14, 2020: BARR SUBMITS HIS RESIGNATION

Finally, Attorney General Barr had had enough. He submitted his resignation on December 14, 2020.[81] During an interview with the Select Committee, former Attorney General Barr reflected on his face-to-face encounters with President Trump in November and December 2020:

> And, in that context, I made clear I did not agree with the idea of saying the election was stolen and putting out this stuff which I told the President was bullshit. And, you know, I didn't want to be part of it. And that's one of the reasons that went into me deciding to leave when I did.

Former Acting Attorney General Jeffrey Rosen testifies before the Select Committee on June 23, 2022.

(Photo by House Creative Services)

I observed, I think it was on December 1st, that—you know, I believe you can't live in a world where the incumbent administration stays in power based on its view, unsupported by specific evidence, that the election—that there was fraud in the election.[82]

Around mid-day on December 14th, Attorney General Barr met with President Trump and Meadows in the Oval Office to discuss his resignation.[83] When he arrived, and even before Barr could mention his resignation, President Trump began speaking at length about the recently released Allied Security Operations Group (ASOG) report on Dominion voting machines in Antrim County, Michigan.[84] While the Attorney General had been briefed on the allegations in Antrim County and did not find them credible, he promised the President that he would have DOJ investigate them.[85] The Attorney General then told President Trump that he had come for a separate reason and wished to speak to the President privately, so Meadows left.[86]

Barr told President Trump that it was clear the President was dissatisfied with him as Attorney General and that he had decided to resign.[87] President Trump accepted his resignation and asked Barr who would replace him; Attorney General Barr recommended Jeffrey A. Rosen as Acting Attorney General and Richard Donoghue as his deputy.[88] Although President Trump called Donoghue to discuss the possibility of appointing him Acting Attorney General, Donoghue advised that normal procedures be followed and Rosen be named Acting Attorney General.[89] President Trump followed this advice, and upon Barr's departure, Rosen became Acting Attorney General while Donoghue would function as his deputy.

4.5 ACTING ATTORNEY GENERAL JEFFREY ROSEN AND ACTING DEPUTY ATTORNEY GENERAL RICHARD DONOGHUE HOLD THE LINE

Barr felt that he was leaving the Department in the hands of two trusted lieutenants. But President Trump immediately began to pressure Rosen and Donoghue, just as he had Barr.

On December 14, 2020, the day Barr resigned, Molly Michael, Special Assistant to the President and Oval Office Coordinator, sent an email to Acting Attorney General Jeffrey Rosen. The email had two documents attached, both of which were labeled "From POTUS."[90] The first was a set of talking points focused on false allegations of voter fraud in Antrim County, Michigan. The second document was the same ASOG report the President had given Barr.[91]

The next day, President Trump held a meeting in the White House with Acting Attorney General Rosen, Acting Deputy Attorney Donoghue, Cipollone, Meadows, Acting Deputy Secretary of Homeland Security Ken Cuccinelli, and Acting General Counsel of the Department of Homeland Security Chad Mizelle.[92] Barr did not attend, even though he was not scheduled to leave DOJ until the following week. The timing of the meeting was notable, as the previous day the electoral college had met and cast their votes in favor of former Vice President Biden.

During testimony before the Select Committee, Donoghue explained that the December 15th, meeting "was largely focused on" the ASOG report.[93] According to Donoghue, the President "was adamant that the report must be accurate, that it proved that the election was defective, that he in fact won the election, and the [D]epartment should be using that report to basically tell the American people that the results were not trustworthy."[94] President Trump discussed "other theories as well," including erroneous allegations of voter fraud in Georgia and Pennsylvania, but "the bulk of that conversation on December 15th focused on Antrim County, Michigan."[95] President Trump asked why DOJ wasn't "doing more to look at this" and whether the Department was "going to do its job."[96]

Former Acting Deputy Attorney General Richard Donoghue testifies before the Select Committee on June 23, 2022.

(Photo by House Creative Services)

The Department of Justice *was* doing its job. In fact, Attorney General Barr had ordered unprecedented investigations into the many specious claims of voter fraud. The President simply didn't want to hear the truth—that DOJ found that not one of the bogus claims was true. As explained in Chapter 1, the original vote totals in Antrim County were the result of a human error that had since been corrected, not the result of any problem with Dominion machines or software. There was no evidence of fraud.

4.6 PRESIDENT TRUMP IS INTRODUCED TO JEFFREY CLARK

On December 21, 2020, 11 House Republicans met with President Trump at the White House to discuss their plans for objecting to the certification of the electoral college vote on January 6th.[97] After the meeting, Mark Meadows tweeted: "Several members of Congress just finished a meeting in the Oval Office with @realDonaldTrump preparing to fight back against mounting evidence of voter fraud. Stay tuned."[98] Among those in attendance was Congressman Scott Perry, a Republican from Pennsylvania.[99]

By the next day, Representative Perry had introduced a little-known DOJ official named Jeffrey Clark to the President.[100] At the time, Clark was

Former Assistant Attorney General Jeffrey Clark appears on a screen during a Select Committee hearing on June 23, 2022.

(Photo by Mandel Ngan-Pool/Getty Images)

the Acting Head of the Civil Division and Head of the Environmental and Natural Resources Division at the Department of Justice.[101] Clark had no experience in, or responsibilities related to, investigating allegations of election fraud.

President Trump called Acting Attorney General Rosen "virtually every day" between December 23rd and January 3rd.[102] The President usually discussed his "dissatisfaction" with DOJ, claiming the Department was not doing enough to investigate election fraud.[103] On Christmas Eve, Trump brought up Jeffrey Clark's name. Rosen found it "peculiar," telling the Select Committee: "I was quizzical as to how does the President even know Mr. Clark?"[104]

Rosen then spoke directly with Clark on December 26th.[105] Clark revealed that he had met with the President in the Oval Office several days prior.[106] Clark had told the President that if he were to change the leadership at the Department of Justice, "then the Department might be able to do more" to support the President's claims that the election had been stolen from him.[107]

In his discussion with Acting Attorney General Rosen, Clark was "defensive" and "apologetic," claiming that the meeting with President

Trump was "inadvertent and it would not happen again, and that if anyone asked him to go to such a meeting, he would notify Rich Donoghue and me [Rosen]." [108] Of course, Clark had good reasons to be defensive. His meeting with President Trump and Representative Perry on December 22nd was a clear violation of Department policy, which limits interactions between the White House and the Department's staff. As Steven Engel, former Assistant Attorney General for the Office of Legal Counsel, explained to the Select Committee, "it's critical that the Department of Justice conducts its criminal investigations free from either the reality or any appearance of political interference." [109] For that reason, the Department has longstanding polices in place, across administrations, to "keep these communications as infrequent and at the highest levels as possible, just to make sure that people who are less careful about it, who don't really understand these implications, such as Mr. Clark, don't run afoul of the of those contact policies." [110] Rosen added that only the Attorney General or Deputy Attorney General "can have conversations about criminal matters with the White House," or they can "authorize" someone from within DOJ to do so.[111] Clark had no such authorization.

Representative Perry continued to advocate on Clark's behalf. The Congressman texted Meadows on December 26th, writing: "Mark, just checking in as time continues to count down. 11 days to 1/6 and 25 days to inauguration. We gotta get going!" [112] Representative Perry followed up: "Mark, you should call Jeff. I just got off the phone with him and he explained to me why the principal deputy [position] won't work especially with the FBI. They will view it as not having the authority to enforce what needs to be done." [113] Meadows responded: "I got it. I think I understand. Let me work on the deputy position." [114] Representative Perry then sent additional texts: "Roger. Just sent you something on Signal", "Just sent you an updated file", and "Did you call Jeff Clark?" [115]

4.7 DECEMBER 27TH PHONE CALL

On December 27, 2020, President Trump called Acting Attorney General Rosen once again. At some point during the lengthy call, Rosen asked that Acting Deputy Attorney General Donoghue be conferenced in.[116] According to Donoghue's contemporaneous notes, Trump referenced three Republican politicians, all of whom had supported the President's election lies and the "Stop the Steal" campaign.[117] One was Representative Scott Perry. Another was Doug Mastriano, a State senator from Pennsylvania who would later be on the grounds of the U.S. Capitol during the January 6th attack.[118] President Trump also referenced Representative Jim Jordan from Ohio, praising him as a "fighter." [119] Representatives Perry and Jordan had often teamed up to spread lies about the election. The two spoke at a "Stop the Steal" rally in front of the Pennsylvania State capitol in Harrisburg, just days after the November election.[120] The pair also pressed their conspiratorial case during interviews with friendly media outlets.[121]

President Trump made a "stream of allegations" during the December 27th call.[122] As reflected in his notes, Donoghue considered the call to be an "escalation of the earlier conversations," with the President becoming more adamant that "we weren't doing our job." [123] President Trump trafficked in "conspiracy theories" he had heard from others, and Donoghue sought to "make it clear to the President these allegations were simply not true." [124] Donoghue sought to "correct" President Trump "in a serial fashion as he moved from one theory to another." [125]

The President returned to the discredited ASOG report, which former Attorney General Barr had already dismissed as complete nonsense. ASOG had claimed—based on no evidence—that the Dominion voting machines in Antrim County, Michigan had suffered from a 68 percent error rate. As noted above and in Chapter 1, that was not close to being true.

Bipartisan election officials in Antrim County completed a hand recount of all machine-processed ballots on December 17, 2020, which should have ended the lies about Dominion's voting machines.[126] The net difference between the machine count and the hand recount was only 12 out of 15,718 total votes.[127] The machines counted just one vote more for former Vice President Biden than was tallied during the hand recount.[128] Donoghue informed the President that he "cannot and should not be relying on" ASOG's claim, because it was "simply not true." [129] This did not stop the President from later repeating the debunked allegation multiple times, including during his January 6th speech at the Ellipse.[130]

Acting Deputy Attorney General Donoghue debunked a "series" of other conspiracy theories offered by President Trump during the December 27th call as well. One story involved a truck driver "who claimed to have moved an entire tractor trailer of ballots from New York to Pennsylvania." [131] There was no truth to the story. The FBI "interviewed witnesses at the front end and the back end of" the truck's transit route, "looked at loading manifests," questioned the truck driver, and concluded that there were no ballots in the truck.[132]

President Trump then returned to the conspiracy theory about voting in Detroit. Former Attorney General Barr had already debunked the claim that a massive number of illegal votes had been dumped during the middle of the night, but the President would not let it go. President Trump alleged that someone "threw the poll watchers out," and "you don't even need to look at the illegal aliens voting—don't need to. It's so obvious."[133] The President complained that the "FBI will always say there's nothing there," because while the Special Agents ("the line guys") supported him, the Bureau's leadership supposedly did not.[134] This was inconsistent with Donoghue's view.[135] But President Trump complained that he had "made some bad decisions on leadership" at the FBI.[136]

President Trump also "wanted to talk a great deal about Georgia, [and] the State Farm Arena video," claiming it was "fraud staring you right in the face."[137] President Trump smeared Ruby Freeman, a Georgia election worker who was merely doing her job, as a "Huckster" and an "Election scammer."[138] President Trump said the "networks," meaning the television networks, had "magnified the tape and saw them running them [ballots] through repeatedly."[139] The President repeated the lie that Democrats had "[c]losed the facility and then came back with hidden ballots under the table."[140] He suggested that both Rosen and Donoghue "go to Fulton County and do a signature verification." They would "see how illegal it is" and "find tens of thousands" of illegal ballots.[141]

President Trump "kept fixating" on the supposed suitcase in the video.[142] But Acting Deputy Attorney General Donoghue debunked the President's obsession. "There is no suitcase," Donoghue made clear.[143] Donoghue explained that the DOJ had looked at the video and interviewed multiple witnesses. The "suitcase" was an official lock box filled with genuine votes.[144] And election workers simply did not scan ballots for former Vice President Biden multiple times.[145] All of this was recorded by security cameras.[146]

In response to what President Trump was saying during the conversation, Rosen and Donoghue tried to make clear that the claims the President made weren't supported by the evidence. "You guys must not be following the internet the way I do," the President remarked.[147] But President Trump was not finished peddling wild conspiracy theories.

The President pushed the claim that Pennsylvania had reported 205,000 more votes than there were voters in the state.[148] "We'll look at whether we have more ballots in Pennsylvania than registered voters," Acting Attorney General Rosen replied, according to Donoghue. They "[s]hould be able to check that out quickly."[149] But Rosen wanted President Trump to "understand that the DOJ can't and won't snap its fingers and change the outcome of the election. It doesn't work that way."[150]

"I don't expect you to do that," President Trump responded. "Just say the election was corrupt and leave the rest to me and the Republican Congressmen."[151]

Donoghue explained this "is an exact quote from the President."[152]

"We have an obligation to tell people that this was an illegal, corrupt election," President Trump told the DOJ team at another point in the call.[153] President Trump insisted this was DOJ's "obligation," even though Rosen and Donoghue kept telling him there was no evidence of fraud sufficient to overturn the outcome of the election. "We are doing our job," Donoghue informed the President. "Much of the info you're getting is false."[154]

The call on December 27th was contentious for additional reasons. President Trump did not want to accept that the Department of Justice was not an arm of his election campaign. He wanted to know why the Department did not assist in his campaign's civil suits against States. There was a simple answer: There was no evidence to support the campaign's claims of fraud.[155]

Donoghue and Rosen also "tried to explain to the President on this occasion and on several other occasions that the Justice Department has a very important, very specific, but very limited role in these elections."[156] The States "run their elections" and DOJ is not "quality control for the States."[157] DOJ has "a mission that relates to criminal conduct in relation to federal elections" and also has "related civil rights responsibilities."[158] But DOJ cannot simply intervene to alter the outcome of an election or support a civil suit.[159]

When President Trump made these demands on December 27th, it was already crystal clear that the Department of Justice had found no evidence of systemic fraud.[160] The Department simply had no reason to assert that the 2020 Presidential contest was "an illegal corrupt election."[161]

"People tell me Jeff Clark is great" and that "I should put him in," President Trump said on the call. "People want me to replace the DOJ leadership."[162] Donoghue responded "[S]ir, that's fine, you should have the leadership you want, but understand, changing the leadership in the Department won't change anything."[163]

The President did not really care what facts had been uncovered by the Department of Justice. President Trump just wanted the Department to say the election was corrupt, so he and the Republican Congressmen could exploit the statement in the days to come, including on January 6th. And when Rosen and Donoghue resisted the President's entreaties, he openly mused about replacing Rosen with someone who would do the President's bidding.

4.8 CONGRESSMAN SCOTT PERRY CALLS DONOGHUE

Toward the end of the December 27th call, President Trump asked Donoghue for his cell number.[164] Later that day, Representative Perry called

Representative Scott Perry, November 14, 2022.

(Photo by Anna Moneymaker/Getty Images)

Donoghue to press the President's case.[165] Representative Perry was one of President Trump's key congressional allies in the effort to overturn the election's results. Representative Perry was an early supporter of the "Stop the Steal" campaign and, as noted above, addressed the crowd at one such event outside the Pennsylvania State capitol in Harrisburg on November 5, 2020.[166] Representative Perry was also one of 27 Republican Congressmen who signed a letter requesting that President Trump "direct Attorney General Barr to appoint a Special Counsel to investigate irregularities in the 2020 election." The letter was dated December 9, 2020—more than 1 week after Barr told the press there was no evidence of significant fraud.[167] There was no reason to think that a Special Counsel was warranted. Representative Perry and the other congressmen advocated for one to be appointed anyway.

Representative Perry attended the December 21st Oval Office meeting along with at least 10 other congressional Republicans to discuss the strategy for objecting to the electoral college votes on January 6th. Along with 125 other Republican Members of Congress. Representative Perry also supported Texas's lawsuit against Pennsylvania and three other states.[168] That is, Representative Perry supported Texas's effort to nullify the certified electoral college vote from four states, including his own home state.

Donoghue took notes during his conversation with Representative Perry and provided those notes to the Select Committee.[169] The notes reflect that when Representative Perry called Donoghue on December 27th, Representative Perry explained that President Trump asked him to call and that he, Representative Perry, did not think DOJ had been doing its job on the election.[170] Representative Perry brought up other, unrelated matters and argued that the "FBI doesn't always do the right thing in all instances."[171] Representative Perry also brought up Jeff Clark. He said he liked him and thought that Clark "would do something about this," meaning the election fraud allegations.[172]

On the evening of December 27th, Representative Perry emailed Donoghue a set of documents alleging significant voting fraud had occurred in Pennsylvania.[173] One document asserted that election authorities had counted 205,000 more votes than had been cast.[174] Representative Perry also shared this same claim on Twitter the following day.[175] President Trump kept raising the same claim. Sometimes there was an alleged discrepancy of 205,000 votes, other times it was supposedly 250,000 votes.[176] Either way, it was not true.

Acting Deputy Attorney General Donoghue forwarded Representative Perry's email to Scott Brady, who was the U.S. Attorney for the Western District of Pennsylvania at the time.[177] As Brady soon discovered, there was no discrepancy.[178] President Trump's supporters came up with the claim by comparing the Pennsylvania Secretary of State's website, which reported the total number of votes as 5.25 million, to a separate State election registry, which showed only 5 million votes cast.[179] The problem was simple: Pennsylvania's election site had not been updated.[180] The totals for four counties had not yet been reported on the election site. Once those votes were counted on the site, the totals matched. This was simply not an example of fraud, as President Trump, Representative Perry and others would have it.

4.9 DECEMBER 28, 2020: THE CLARK LETTER

On December 28, 2020, Clark sent a 5-page draft letter to Donoghue and Rosen.[181] The letter was addressed to three Georgia State officials: Governor Brian Kemp, Speaker of the House David Ralston, and President *Pro Tempore* of the Senate Butch Miller. It contained places for Rosen and Donoghue to affix their signatures, which they steadfastly refused to do.[182] The letter, if signed and sent, may very well have provoked a constitutional crisis.[183]

The letter was attached to an email from Clark, in which he requested authorization to attend a classified briefing by the Office of the Director of

National Intelligence (ODNI) "led by DNI Ratcliffe on foreign election interference issues." [184] ODNI did not find any foreign interference in the voting
process or counting,[185] but Clark apparently believed some of the conspiracy theories that had been floated. Specifically, Clark claimed that
"hackers have evidence (in the public domain) that a Dominion machine
accessed the internet through a smart thermostat with a net connection
trail leading back to China." Clark added: "ODNI may have additional classified evidence." [186] This crackpot claim had been shared by other Trump
officials and associates as well.[187] Ultimately, after Clark received the ODNI
briefing, "he acknowledged [to Donoghue] that there was nothing in that
briefing that would have supported his earlier suspicion about foreign
involvement." [188]

Clark intended to send the letter to officials in Georgia and several other
contested States that President Trump needed to flip if he was going to
overturn the election results. "The Department of Justice is investigating
various irregularities in the 2020 election for President of the United
States," Clark wrote.[189] Clark continued: "The Department will update you
as we are able on investigatory progress, but at this time we have identified
significant concerns that may have impacted the outcome of the election in
multiple States, including the State of Georgia." [190]

Clark continued by arguing that Georgia's State legislature should call a
special session. "In light of these developments, the Department recommends that the Georgia General Assembly should convene in special session
so that its legislators are in a special position to take additional testimony,
receive new evidence, and deliberate on the matter consistent with its
duties under the U.S. Constitution," Clark wrote.[191] Clark referenced the fake
electors that the President and his campaign organized and argued that
there were two competing slates of electors, both of which were legitimate.[192] "The Department believes that in Georgia and several other States,
both a slate of electors supporting Joseph R. Biden, Jr., and a separate slate
of electors supporting Donald J. Trump, gathered on [December 14, 2020] at
the proper location to cast their ballots, and that both sets of those ballots
have been transmitted to Washington, D.C., to be opened by Vice President
Pence," Clark wrote.[193]

The letter was a lie. Senior DOJ officials—Barr, Rosen and Donoghue—
had repeatedly stated the opposite. They found no evidence of fraud that
would have impacted the election's results—none. But since mid-
November, the Trump Campaign's legal team under Giuliani attempted to
execute its dual-track strategy of both filing lawsuits and convincing state
legislatures in contested states to appoint separate slates of Presidential
electors for President Trump.[194] By late December, however, the dual-track

approach had largely failed, and no legislatures had sent a second lawful slate of electors for Trump to Congress. Clearly, President Trump and his campaign team could not get the job done. So, the President and those around him sought to use the hefty imprimatur of the U.S. Department of Justice to achieve the same thing. No doubt, a letter coming from the Department of Justice is different from a meandering call from Giuliani or one of his associates. And, because it was December 28th and there was little more than a week until the January 6th joint session of Congress, President Trump needed more, and soon. Clark's letter, which laid out a plan that was almost identical to what President Trump and his team had pressured State officials to carry out virtually since election day, could have been just what President Trump needed.

Several examples demonstrate the parallels between President Trump's and Rudolph Giuliani's approach to overturning the election in November and December, and what Clark proposed in this letter. First, the letter sought to have the Georgia State legislature convene a special session to focus on allegations of fraud in the election.[195] Giuliani and his team had been making calls to State legislatures and telling them in both official and unofficial State legislature committee hearings that State legislatures should convene in special sessions.[196] They also argued that State legislatures had the authority to convene a special session themselves, despite limitations in State law requiring such a session to be convened by the governor.[197] Clark included the same argument in his draft letter.[198]

Additionally, the draft letter recommended that the Georgia legislature consider choosing the alternate—fake—slate of electoral college electors that sent fake electoral college votes to Congress and Vice President Pence.[199] Having State legislatures choose Trump electors in States where President Trump lost was one of the Trump team's early goals immediately after the election, but it didn't work.[200] When no State legislature appointed its own set of electors before December 14th, the Trump Campaign arranged for electors to meet in contested States anyway and cast fake electoral college votes.[201] This letter, with the Department of Justice seal at the top, was just one more way that President Trump and those close to him could pressure State officials to send competing electoral college votes to Congress for consideration during the joint session, despite former Vice President Biden's certified victory in each of the contested States.

Despite the similarities between the requests in Clark's proposed letter and the requests that President Trump and his team made to State officials for nearly 2 months, the extent to which Clark directly coordinated his actions with the Trump Campaign and its outside advisors is unclear. Clark asserted his Fifth Amendment rights and various other privileges to avoid answering the Select Committee's questions about these and other top-ics.[202] When Giuliani was asked during his Select Committee deposition whether he remembered discussing DOJ issuing a letter like Clark's, Giu-liani refused to answer because it implicated attorney-client privilege with President Trump, but when asked if he recalled ever recommending that Clark be given election-related responsibilities at DOJ, Giuliani said, "I do recall saying to people that somebody should be put in charge of the Justice Department who isn't frightened of what's going to be done to their repu-tation, because the Justice Department was filled with people like that."[203] And the investigation has also revealed that Clark and John Eastman were in communication throughout this period.[204]

One person who had worked with Eastman and others in his circle was a lawyer installed to work with Clark at the Department of Justice in mid-December—the final weeks of the Trump administration—named Ken Klu-kowski.[205] Klukowski was a Trump administration political appointee serving as a senior counsel under Clark in DOJ's Civil Division.[206] After serving as a lawyer in the Office and Management and Budget (OMB) for more than a year and volunteering as a lawyer for the Trump Campaign after election day, Klukowski only joined the Department when the admin-istration's personnel staff "expedite[d]" his appointment because the White House's Presidential Personnel Office "want[ed] him in soon."[207]

On the morning of December 28th, Clark asked Klukowski to draft the Georgia letter for him.[208] Clark dictated the substantive key points of the letter to Klukowski and told him exactly what to include.[209] After several meetings with Clark throughout the day to update him on progress, Klu-kowski turned in his assignment and gave the letter to Clark, which Clark sent along to Acting Attorney General Rosen and Acting Deputy Attorney General Donoghue, as described above.[210]

Donoghue quickly responded to Clark's email, stating "there is no chance that I would sign this letter or anything remotely like this."[211] The plan set forth by Clark was "not even within the realm of possibility."[212] Donoghue warned that if they sent Clark's letter, it "would be a grave step for the Department to take and it could have tremendous Constitutional, political and social ramifications for the country."[213] Contrary to President Trump's and Clark's wild claims about the election, Donoghue stressed that DOJ's ongoing investigations related to matters of such a "small scale that they simply would not impact the outcome of the Presidential Election."[214] Clark's assertion to the contrary was baseless.

Donoghue and Rosen reaffirmed their strong opposition to the draft letter in a "contentious" meeting with Clark on December 28th.[215] "What you are doing is nothing less than the United States Justice Department meddling in the outcome of a presidential election," Donoghue admonished Clark, to which Clark indignantly responded, "I think a lot of people have meddled in this election." [216]

Under questioning by Rosen and Donoghue, Clark eventually also revealed that he had been in a meeting in the Oval Office with President Trump. Donoghue demanded to know, "Why the hell are we hearing your name from the President of the United States and a Congressman?" [217] When Clark was reminded that meeting the President without authorization or informing his superiors was a clear violation of the White House contacts policy, he retorted, "It's a policy, there's a lot more at stake here than a policy." [218] In fact, the contacts policy was designed for situations just like this where political figures might try to influence criminal investigations or legal actions taken by the Department of Justice, as President Trump attempting to do.[219]

In the days that followed, Clark called witnesses, got a briefing from ODNI and pursued his own investigations. Acting Deputy Attorney General Donoghue was "shocked" to learn that Clark did not cease his efforts even after learning there was "no foreign interference." [220] Instead of adhering to the facts, Clark "doubled down." During a follow-up meeting on January 2nd, Clark acknowledged he had received the ODNI briefing, and he acknowledged that there was nothing in the briefing that would have supported his earlier suspicion about foreign involvement, but he nevertheless "spewed out some of these theories, some of which we'd heard from the President, but others which were floating around the internet and media, and just kept insisting that the Department needed to act and needed to send those letters." [221]

4.10 DECEMBER 29TH MEETING

The next day, Rosen, Donoghue, and Engel had a meeting with Mark Meadows, Pat Cipollone, and Cipollone's deputy, Pat Philbin, in the White House Chief of Staff's office.[222] While the meeting dealt primarily with the Presidential transition, the group discussed a draft civil complaint modeled after *Texas v. Pennsylvania* that the President wanted the Department of Justice to file challenging the results of the Presidential election, tentatively called *United States v. Pennsylvania*.[223] The DOJ officials said that they had not had time to thoroughly review the proposed suit, but initially indicated that it appeared to be flawed and did not seem "viable" for DOJ to file.[224] Meadows suggested that the DOJ leadership meet with William Olson and Kurt Olsen, the two attorneys affiliated with the Trump Campaign that had been working on the proposed suit, and added that Eastman and a retired judge from North Carolina named Mark Martin both had views about the lawsuit.[225]

In this meeting, Meadows also raised a new and outrageous allegation of election fraud: that an Italian company had been involved in changing votes in the Presidential election.[226] According to Meadows, there was a man, whom Donoghue later learned was in an Italian prison, who claimed to have information supporting the allegation and that CIA officers stationed in Rome were either aware of the plot to interfere in the election or had participated in it.[227] Donoghue described how it was apparent that Meadows was not clear on the specifics of the allegation but passed them along to DOJ to investigate, nonetheless.[228] Following the meeting Donoghue provided the information to the FBI, which quickly determined that the allegations were not credible.[229] Meadows and other senior officials in the Trump administration, however, pressed DOJ to investigate every allegation of fraud regardless of how absurd or specious.

In the days after the December 29th meeting with Meadows, the senior DOJ officials more closely examined the proposed *United States v. Pennsylvania* lawsuit and determined that DOJ could not file it.[230] Engel was principally tasked with examining the veracity of the suit and summarized his analysis in a series of talking points that he provided to Donoghue on December 31st.[231] Engel concluded that for multiple reasons, the proposed lawsuit lacked merit. First, the U.S. Government did not have standing to challenge how a State administered its election.[232] Such a challenge could only be brought by President Trump as a candidate and his campaign, or, possibly, an aggrieved electoral college elector.[233] Second, there was no identified precedent in the history of the Supreme Court establishing that such a lawsuit could be filed by the U.S. Government.[234] Third, by late December, States had already certified the results of their elections and the electoral college had met, so suing States by this point would not impact the results of the election.[235] Finally, unlike *Texas v. Pennsylvania*, which was one State suing another State, this lawsuit would not automatically be heard by the Supreme Court, so it should have been filed in a Federal district court months prior—if at all—to have any possibility of impacting the outcome of the election.[236]

When asked about it during his interview with the Select Committee, Engel described *United States v. Pennsylvania* as "a meritless lawsuit" and said, "there was never a question" about whether "the Department was going to file" it.[237] As senior DOJ officials had already explained to President Trump multiple times in November and December 2020, the Department of Justice was strictly limited in what election-related actions it could

Steven Engel testifies before the Select Committee on June 23, 2022.
(Photo by House Creative Services)

take. It could not oversee States' actions in administering their elections, and it could not support litigation filed by President Trump's campaign.[238] Nonetheless, President Trump continued to push DOJ to file this lawsuit over the following days and essentially act as an arm of his political campaign.

4.11 ROSEN'S DECEMBER 30TH CALL WITH PRESIDENT TRUMP

Even after the December 29th meeting, President Trump and those working on his behalf still wanted DOJ leadership to file *United States* v. *Pennsylvania*. On December 30th, Acting Attorney General Rosen had a phone call with President Trump that included a discussion about the lawsuit.[239] During the call, Rosen clearly explained to the President that DOJ could not file the lawsuit.[240] Rosen said, "This doesn't work. There's multiple problems with it. And the Department of Justice is not going to be able to do it." [241] According to Rosen, President Trump accepted what he said without argument.[242] Yet President Trump and his allies continued pressuring the Department to file the lawsuit.

4.12   DECEMBER 31ST MEETING

On December 31st, 2020, President Trump suddenly returned to Washington, DC, from Florida, where he had been celebrating Christmas. Shortly after Air Force One landed, Rosen and Donoghue were summoned to the Oval Office once again. They met with the President that afternoon. President Trump "was a little more agitated than he had been in the meeting on the 15th," according to Donoghue.[243] The President remained "adamant that the election has been stolen, that he won, that the American people were being harmed by fraud, and that he believed the Justice Department should be doing something about it."[244]

The President once again raised the prospect of naming Clark the Acting Attorney General.[245] Donoghue and Rosen repeated what they had told the President previously—that he "should have the leaders that" he wanted, "but it's really not going to change anything."[246]

President Trump again asked why DOJ would not file a complaint with the Supreme Court, alleging that the election was fraudulent. Rosen and Donoghue explained, once more, that the DOJ did not have standing.[247] DOJ represents the Federal government, not the American people. President Trump was incredulous and became "very animated."[248] The President kept repeating the same questions, "How is that possible? How can that possibly be?"[249]

President Trump also floated the prospect of naming a special counsel, suggesting Ken Cuccinelli from the Department of Homeland Security as a possible candidate.[250] "This sounds like the kind of thing that would warrant appointment of a special counsel," Donoghue recalled the President saying.[251] The President did not order the DOJ to name a special counsel, but he was clearly still thinking about it. Donoghue and Rosen "didn't say a lot" in response, but simply pointed out that there was no evidence to support the many individual allegations that had been made, so there was "no evidence that would warrant appointing a special counsel."[252]

President Trump again raised the Antrim County, Michigan allegations.[253] As mentioned above, bipartisan election officials in Antrim County completed a hand recount of all ballots on December 17th.[254] This should have resolved the matter once and for all. There was simply no evidence that Dominion's machines had manipulated the result. But President Trump would not accept this reality.

During the December 31st meeting, the President also raised the prospect of seizing the voting machines. "Why don't you guys seize machines?" he asked.[255] "You guys should seize machines because there will be evidence," Donoghue recalled President Trump saying.[256] Rosen pushed back, saying the DOJ had no basis to seize voting machines from the States. They needed a search warrant, but there was no evidence to justify one.[257] Rosen explained to President Trump again that the DOJ has no responsibility for oversight, as the States conduct the elections. Rosen added that to the extent that any Federal agency is involved, it is the Department of Homeland Security, which ensures "software selection and quality control."[258] At that point, the President called Ken Cuccinelli.[259] Donoghue recalled the President saying something along the lines of, "Ken, the Acting Attorney General is telling me it's your job to seize machines."[260] Rosen had said nothing of the sort, but Cuccinelli quickly shot down the President's line of inquiry, making it clear that the Department of Homeland Security had no such authority.[261] White House Counsel Pat Cipollone was also in attendance and supported the DOJ leadership throughout the meeting.[262]

When Rosen spoke to Clark by phone on December 31st or January 1st, Clark revealed that he had spoken to the President again, despite previously promising Rosen and Donoghue that he would inform them of any other contact that he received from the White House.[263] Clark told Rosen that President Trump had offered Clark the position of Acting Attorney General and asked him to respond by Monday, January 4th. Clark, however, said that he needed to do some "due diligence" related to claims of election fraud before deciding whether he would accept the President's offer.[264]

4.13 JANUARY 2, 2021: ROSEN AND DONOGHUE CONFRONT CLARK AGAIN

On Saturday, January 2nd, Rosen and Donoghue attempted, once again, to persuade Clark to stand down. The two reiterated that Clark should stop meeting with the President.[265] Donoghue reprimanded Clark, emphasizing that he was the boss and that Clark's ongoing contacts with the President were a violation of DOJ's White House contact policy.[266] Clark acknowledged that he had been briefed by the ODNI, as he had requested, and "that there was nothing in that briefing that would have supported his earlier suspicion about foreign involvement."[267] Nevertheless, Clark still wanted to send his letter to Georgia and other contested States alleging voter fraud.[268]

During the conversation, Clark confirmed President Trump had offered him the position of Acting Attorney General.[269] Clark told Rosen that he would decline the offer—if Rosen and Donoghue signed his dishonest letter to officials in Georgia.[270] The two refused once again, making it clear "that there was no way we were going to sign that letter."[271] Rosen reiterated his decision in an email on the night of January 2nd, writing: "I confirmed again today that I am not prepared to sign such a letter."[272]

That same day, President Trump attempted to coerce Georgia Secretary of State Brad Raffensperger into manufacturing enough votes to steal the election in that State. That call is discussed in Chapter 2 of this report. But one part of it deserves mention here. During that same call, President Trump brought up BJay Pak, whom President Trump had appointed as the U.S. Attorney for the Northern District of Georgia. President Trump referred to Pak as "your never-Trumper U.S. attorney there." [273] The implication was that Pak was not doing enough to validate President Trump's fictitious claims of voter fraud. President Trump's mention of Pak proved to be ominous.

4.14 JANUARY 3, 2021: CLARK INFORMS DOJ LEADERSHIP THAT HE WILL ACCEPT PRESIDENT TRUMP'S OFFER

On January 3rd, Clark informed Rosen that he had decided to accept the President's offer to serve as the Acting Attorney General. Clark offered Rosen the position of his deputy.[274] Rosen thought that Clark's offer was "preposterous" and "nonsensical." [275] Rosen told the Select Committee that "there was no universe where I was going to do that to stay on and support someone else doing things that were not consistent with what I thought should be done." [276] Donoghue believed it was a done deal, and Clark would become the head of DOJ. But Pat Cipollone told Rosen that it was "not a done deal and that we should fight this out at the White House." [277]

White House call logs from January 3rd show that President Trump and Clark spoke four times that day starting at 6:59 a.m.[278] The first three calls of the day, two in the morning and one in the early afternoon, show that the President spoke with "Mr. Jeffrey Clark." [279] The final call between the two of them, from 4:19 to 4:22 p.m., however, shows that President Trump spoke to "Acting Attorney General Jeffrey Clark," suggesting that Clark had, in fact, accepted the President's offer.[280]

Acting Attorney General Rosen told the Select Committee that he would have felt comfortable being replaced by either Donoghue or Engel, but he did not "want for the Department of Justice to be put in a posture where it would be doing things that were not consistent with the truth, were not consistent with its own appropriate role, or were not consistent with the Constitution." [281]

As a result, Rosen took four immediate steps to try and prevent Clark's ascension to Attorney General. First, he called Meadows and asked him to set up a meeting for that evening with President Trump.[282] Second, he

PAT CIPOLLONE

DONALD TRUMP

JEFFREY CLARK

JEFFREY ROSEN

PAT PHILBIN

STEVEN ENGEL

RICHARD DONOGHUE

ERIC HERSCHMANN

Select Committee graphic

spoke to Cipollone, who told Rosen that Clark's appointment was not inevitable and that he would also be at the meeting that evening to support Rosen and Donoghue.[283] Third, Rosen called Engel and asked him to come to DOJ headquarters so he could attend the White House meeting.[284] Finally, Rosen asked Donoghue and another senior Department attorney named Patrick Hovakimian to convene a meeting of the rest of the Department's leadership to describe the situation to them and hear how they would react to Clark's appointment.[285]

Hovakimian set up a conference call. Although some of the Assistant Attorneys General were not able to participate in the call, all of those who did agreed that they would resign if Rosen were removed from office.[286] Pat Hovakimian drafted a resignation letter that read:

> This evening, after Acting Attorney General Jeff Rosen over the course of the last week repeatedly refused the President's direct instructions to utilize the Department of Justice's law enforcement powers for improper ends, the President removed Jeff from the Department. PADAG Rich Donoghue and I resign from the Department, effectively immediately.[287]

Hovakimian never sent the letter because the threat of mass resignations dissuaded President Trump from replacing Rosen. Regardless, the letter stated a plain truth: President Trump was trying to use DOJ for his own "improper ends."

THE JANUARY 3, 2021, OVAL OFFICE MEETING

At Rosen's request, White House Chief of Staff Mark Meadows arranged a meeting with the President at 6:15 p.m. that evening.[288]

We should pause to reflect on the timing and purpose of the meeting. Congress was set to meet in a joint session in less than 72 hours. The States had already certified their electors. Former Vice President Biden was going to be certified as the winner of the 2020 Presidential election. There was no material dispute over Biden's victory. Trump and his lawyers had not produced any evidence of significant fraud. Instead, they presented one nonsensical conspiracy theory after another. The DOJ and FBI were forced to debunk these claims—and they did.

None of this stopped President Trump's effort to subvert DOJ. Quite the opposite. The President pushed forward with a plan to install Jeff Clark as the Acting Attorney General, apparently to attempt to interfere with the certification of the electoral college vote on January 6th. It is for this reason Rosen requested an emergency meeting on January 3rd.

Before heading into the Oval Office, Rosen and Donoghue discussed the possible leadership change with Cipollone and Pat Philbin. "They were completely opposed to it," Donoghue explained.[289] In fact, no one who attended the Oval Office meeting supported the leadership change—other than Jeff Clark.[290] Donoghue didn't initially join the meeting, but the President soon called him in.[291]

During the meeting, Clark attempted to defend the last-minute move to make him Acting Attorney General. Clark said he would "conduct real investigations that would, in his view, uncover widespread fraud."[292] Clark declared that this was the "last opportunity to sort of set things straight with this defective election," and he had the "intelligence," the "will," and "desire" to "pursue these matters in the way that the President thought most appropriate."[293] Everyone else quickly disagreed.[294]

President Trump asked Donoghue and Engel what they would do, and both confirmed they would resign.[295] Donoghue added that theirs would not be the only resignations. "You should understand that your entire Department leadership will resign," Donoghue recalled saying.[296] This included every Assistant Attorney General. "Mr. President, these aren't bureaucratic leftovers from another administration," Donoghue continued.[297] "You picked them. This is your leadership team. You sent every one of them to the Senate; you got them confirmed."[298] Donoghue argued that the President would look bad in the wake of the mass resignations. "What is that going to say about you, when we all walk out at the same time?"[299] Donoghue recalled asking the President. "And what happens if, within 48 hours, we have hundreds of resignations from your Justice Department because of your actions? What does that say about your leadership?" [300] Steve Engel reinforced Donoghue's point, saying that Clark would be leading a "grave-yard." [301]

White House Counsel Pat Cipollone threatened to resign as well, describing Clark's letter as a "murder-suicide pact." [302] Cipollone warned that the letter would "damage everyone who touches it" and no one should have anything to do with it.[303]

Some of the participants in the meeting argued that Clark was the wrong person for the job of Attorney General. Clark attempted to defend his credentials, arguing that he had been involved in complicated civil and environmental litigation.[304] "That's right. You're an environmental law-yer," Donoghue fired back.[305] "How about you go back to your office, and we'll call you when there's an oil spill." [306]

The meeting lasted approximately 3 hours.[307] Only toward the end of the contentious affair did President Trump decide to reverse his earlier decision to make Clark the Acting Assistant Attorney General. Donoghue recalled President Trump addressing Clark along the following lines:

> I appreciate your willingness to do it. I appreciate you being willing to suffer the abuse. But the reality is, you're not going to get any-thing done. These guys are going to quit. Everyone else is going to resign. It's going to be a disaster. The bureaucracy will eat you alive. And no matter how you want to get things done in the next few weeks, you won't be able to get it done, and it's not going to be worth the breakage.[308]

Clark tried to change President Trump's mind, saying "history is call-ing, this our opportunity" and "we can get this done." [309] But the President was clearly rattled by the threat of mass defections and reiterated that the change would not happen. President Trump then wondered what would happen to Clark, and if Donoghue was going to fire him. Donoghue explained that only the President had that authority. That was the end of the matter. "And we all got up and walked out of the Oval Office," Dono-ghue recalled.[310]

But for one DOJ employee, the matter was not entirely settled. During the January 3rd meeting in the Oval Office, President Trump complained bitterly about BJay Pak, the U.S. Attorney for the Northern District of Geor-gia.[311] Barr had tasked Pak with investigating the State Farm Arena video in early December 2020. Like the FBI and Georgia State officials, Pak con-cluded that nothing nefarious had occurred. President Trump was dissatis-fied.[312]

"No wonder nothing's been found in Atlanta, because the U.S. attorney there is a Never Trumper," Donoghue recalled the President saying.[313]

Donoghue objected, saying Pak had "been doing his job." [314] But the President insisted, pointing out that Pak criticized him years earlier. "This guy is a Never Trumper," the President reiterated. [315] "He should never have been in my administration to begin with. How did this guy end up in my administration?" [316] The President threatened to fire Pak. [317] When Donoghue pointed out that Pak was already planning to resign the next day, a Monday, President Trump insisted that it be Pak's last day on the job. [318] Pak later confirmed to Donoghue that he would be leaving the next day. [319]

President Trump asked if those in attendance at the Oval Office meeting knew Bobby Christine, who was the U.S. Attorney for the Southern District of Georgia. [320] Even though Pak had a first assistant, who was next in line for Pak's job upon his resignation, President Trump wanted Christine to take the role. [321] Christine did take over for Pak, but he did not find any evidence of fraud either. It was Donoghue's impression that Christine "concluded that the election matters...were handled appropriately." [322]

Later in the evening of January 3rd, President Trump called Donoghue to pass along yet another conspiracy theory. [323] The President had heard that an ICE agent outside of Atlanta was in custody of a truck filled with shredded ballots. [324] Donoghue explained that ICE agents are part of the Department of Homeland Security, so the matter would be under that Department's purview. President Trump asked Donoghue to inform Ken Cuccinelli. [325] That story—like all the others—turned out to be fiction when DOJ investigators evaluated the claim. The truck *was* carrying shredded ballots, but they were from a *previous* election. The old ballots had been shredded to make room for storing ballots from the 2020 election. [326]

4.15   PRESIDENT TRUMP'S UNPRECEDENTED ATTEMPT TO SUBVERT THE DOJ

The most senior DOJ officials at the end of President Trump's term stopped him from co-opting America's leading law enforcement agency for his own corrupt purposes. Recall that Attorney General Barr commented "you can't live in a world where the incumbent administration stays in power based on its view, unsupported by specific evidence, that the election—that there was fraud in the election. [327]

Richard Donoghue concluded that Jeffrey Clark's letter "may very well have spiraled us into a constitutional crisis." [328]

Jeffrey Rosen summed up his short time as the Acting Attorney General like this:

[D]uring my tenure, we appointed no special prosecutors, we sent no letters to States or State legislators disputing the election out‐come; we made no public statements saying the election was cor‐rupt and should be overturned; we initiated no Supreme Court actions, nor filed or joined any other lawsuits calling into question the legitimacy of our election and institutions.[329]

President Trump attempted to get DOJ to do each of those things.

ENDNOTES

1. Select Committee to Investigate the January 6th Attack on the United States Capitol, Tran‐scribed Interview of William Barr, (June 2, 2022), p. 8. The Select Committee recognizes and appreciates the investigation conducted by the Senate Committee on the Judiciary and the report it issued about this Chapter's topic. *See* Senate Committee on the Judiciary, 117th Cong. 1st sess., *Subverting Justice: How the Former President and His Allies Pressured DOJ to Overturn the 2020 Election,* (Oct. 7, 2021), available at https://www.judiciary.senate.gov/imo/media/doc/Interim%20Staff%20Report%20FINAL.pdf.

2. Select Committee to Investigate the January 6th Attack on the United States Capitol, Tran‐scribed Interview of William Barr, (June 2, 2022), p. 8; *See* Margaret Talev, "Exclusive: Dem Group Warns of Apparent Trump Election Day Landslide," *Axios,* (Sept. 1, 2020), available at https://www.axios.com/2020/09/01/bloomberg-group-trump-election-night-scenarios.

3. *See* Chapter 1.

4. *See* Chapter 1.

5. Select Committee to Investigate the January 6th Attack on the United States Capitol, Tran‐scribed Interview of William Barr, (June 2, 2022), pp. 8–9.

6. Select Committee to Investigate the January 6th Attack on the United States Capitol, Tran‐scribed Interview of William Barr, (June 2, 2022), pp. 8–9.

7. Select Committee to Investigate the January 6th Attack on the United States Capitol, Tran‐scribed Interview of William Barr, (June 2, 2022), pp. 8–9.

8. Select Committee to Investigate the January 6th Attack on the United States Capitol, Tran‐scribed Interview of William Barr, (June 2, 2022), pp. 8–9.

9. Select Committee to Investigate the January 6th Attack on the United States Capitol, Tran‐scribed Interview of William Barr, (June 2, 2022), p. 9.

10. Select Committee to Investigate the January 6th Attack on the United States Capitol, Tran‐scribed Interview of William Barr, (June 2, 2022), p. 23.

11. Richard C. Pilger, ed., "Federal Prosecution of Election Offenses: Eighth Edition," Depart‐ment of Justice (December 2017), p. 84, available at https://www.justice.gov/criminal/file/1029066/download.

12. Richard C. Pilger, ed., "Federal Prosecution of Election Offenses: Eighth Edition," Depart‐ment of Justice (December 2017), p. 84 available at https://www.justice.gov/criminal/file/1029066/download. The DOJ further advises that "federal law enforcement personnel should carefully evaluate whether an investigative step under consideration has the potential to affect the election itself." The department's concern is that "[s]tarting a public criminal investigation of alleged election fraud before the election to which the allega‐tions pertain has been concluded runs the obvious risk of chilling legitimate voting and campaign activities." Moreover, "[i]t also runs the significant risk of interjecting the investi‐gation itself as an issue, both in the campaign and in the adjudication of any ensuing election contest." *Id.*

13. Documents on file with the Select Committee to Investigate the January 6th Attack on the United States Capitol (Department of Justice Production), HouseSelect-Jan6-PartII-01132022-000616-617 (November 9, 2020, memorandum from Attorney General Barr).

14. Documents on file with the Select Committee to Investigate the January 6th Attack on the United States Capitol (Department of Justice Production), HouseSelect-Jan6-PartII-01132022-000616-617 (November 9, 2020, memorandum from Attorney General Barr).

15. Documents on file with the Select Committee to Investigate the January 6th Attack on the United States Capitol (Department of Justice Production), HouseSelect-Jan6-PartII-01132022-000616-617 (November 9, 2020, memorandum from Attorney General Barr).

16. Select Committee to Investigate the January 6th Attack on the United States Capitol, Transcribed Interview of William Barr, (June 2, 2022), p. 18.

17. Select Committee to Investigate the January 6th Attack on the United States Capitol, Transcribed Interview of William Barr, (June 2, 2022), p. 18.

18. Select Committee to Investigate the January 6th Attack on the United States Capitol, Transcribed Interview of William Barr, (June 2, 2022), p. 18.

19. Select Committee to Investigate the January 6th Attack on the United States Capitol, Transcribed Interview of William Barr, (June 2, 2022), p. 18.

20. Select Committee to Investigate the January 6th Attack on the United States Capitol, Transcribed Interview of William Barr, (June 2, 2022), p. 18.

21. Select Committee to Investigate the January 6th Attack on the United States Capitol, Transcribed Interview of William Barr, (June 2, 2022), p. 18.

22. Select Committee to Investigate the January 6th Attack on the United States Capitol, Transcribed Interview of William Barr, (June 2, 2022), pp. 18-19.

23. Select Committee to Investigate the January 6th Attack on the United States Capitol, Transcribed Interview of William Barr, (June 2, 2022), p. 18.

24. Select Committee to Investigate the January 6th Attack on the United States Capitol, Transcribed Interview of William Barr, (June 2, 2022), p. 18.

25. Select Committee to Investigate the January 6th Attack on the United States Capitol, Transcribed Interview of William Barr, (June 2, 2022), p. 18.

26. Select Committee to Investigate the January 6th Attack on the United States Capitol, Transcribed Interview of William Barr, (June 2, 2022), p. 19.

27. Select Committee to Investigate the January 6th Attack on the United States Capitol, Transcribed Interview of William Barr, (June 2, 2022), p. 19.

28. Select Committee to Investigate the January 6th Attack on the United States Capitol, Transcribed Interview of William Barr, (June 2, 2022), p. 19.

29. Select Committee to Investigate the January 6th Attack on the United States Capitol, Transcribed Interview of William Barr, (June 2, 2022), p. 19.

30. Select Committee to Investigate the January 6th Attack on the United States Capitol, Transcribed Interview of William Barr, (June 2, 2022), p. 19

31. Select Committee to Investigate the January 6th Attack on the United States Capitol, Transcribed Interview of William Barr, (June 2, 2022), p. 19.

32. Select Committee to Investigate the January 6th Attack on the United States Capitol, Transcribed Interview of William Barr, (June 2, 2022), pp. 19-20.

33. Select Committee to Investigate the January 6th Attack on the United States Capitol, Transcribed Interview of William Barr, (June 2, 2022), p. 20.

34. Select Committee to Investigate the January 6th Attack on the United States Capitol, Transcribed Interview of William Barr, (June 2, 2022), p. 22.

35. Select Committee to Investigate the January 6th Attack on the United States Capitol, Transcribed Interview of William Barr, (June 2, 2022), pp. 22-23.

36. Select Committee to Investigate the January 6th Attack on the United States Capitol, Transcribed Interview of William Barr, (June 2, 2022), pp. 22-23.

37. Factba.se, "Interview: Maria Bartiromo Interviews Donald Trump on Fox News - November 29, 2020," Vimeo, Nov. 29, 2020, available at https://vimeo.com/485180163; Fox News, "Trump Asks, 'Where's Durham?' During First Interview Since the Election," YouTube, Nov. 29, 2020, available at https://www.youtube.com/watch?v=szStcNBIL68; *see also* Alexis Benveniste, "Fox News' Maria Bartiromo Gave Trump His First TV Interview Since the Election. It Was Filled with Lies," CNN (Nov. 29, 2020), available at https://www.cnn.com/2020/11/29/media/bartiromo-trump-interview.

38. Factba.se, "Interview: Maria Bartiromo Interviews Donald Trump on Fox News - November 29, 2020," Vimeo, Nov. 29, 2020, available at https://vimeo.com/485180163; Fox News, "Trump Asks, 'Where's Durham?' During First Interview Since the Election," YouTube, Nov. 29, 2020, available at https://www.youtube.com/watch?v=szStcNBIL68; *see also* Alexis Benveniste, "Fox News' Maria Bartiromo Gave Trump His First TV Interview Since the Election. It Was Filled with Lies," CNN (Nov. 29, 2020), available at https://www.cnn.com/2020/11/29/media/bartiromo-trump-interview.

39. Factba.se, "Interview: Maria Bartiromo Interviews Donald Trump on Fox News - November 29, 2020," Vimeo, Nov. 29, 2020, available at https://vimeo.com/485180163; Fox News, "Trump Asks, 'Where's Durham?' During First Interview Since the Election," YouTube, Nov. 29, 2020, available at https://www.youtube.com/watch?v=szStcNBIL68; *see also* Alexis Benveniste, "Fox News' Maria Bartiromo Gave Trump His First TV Interview Since the Election. It Was Filled with Lies," CNN (Nov. 29, 2020), available at https://www.cnn.com/2020/11/29/media/bartiromo-trump-interview.

40. Factba.se, "Interview: Maria Bartiromo Interviews Donald Trump on Fox News - November 29, 2020," Vimeo, Nov. 29, 2020, available at https://vimeo.com/485180163; Fox News, "Trump Asks, 'Where's Durham?' During First Interview Since the Election," YouTube, Nov. 29, 2020, available at https://www.youtube.com/watch?v=szStcNBIL68; *see also* Alexis Benveniste, "Fox News' Maria Bartiromo Gave Trump His First TV Interview Since the Election. It Was Filled with Lies," CNN (Nov. 29, 2020), available at https://www.cnn.com/2020/11/29/media/bartiromo-trump-interview.

41. Factba.se, "Interview: Maria Bartiromo Interviews Donald Trump on Fox News - November 29, 2020," Vimeo, at 4:20, Nov. 29, 2020, available at https://vimeo.com/485180163; Fox News, "Trump Asks, 'Where's Durham?' During First Interview Since the Election," YouTube, Nov. 29, 2020, available at https://www.youtube.com/watch?v=szStcNBIL68; *see also* Alexis Benveniste, "Fox News' Maria Bartiromo Gave Trump His First TV Interview Since the Election. It Was Filled with Lies," CNN (Nov. 29, 2020), available at https://www.cnn.com/2020/11/29/media/bartiromo-trump-interview.

42. "Interview: Maria Bartiromo Interviews Donald Trump on Fox News - November 29, 2020," Vimeo, at 4:25, Nov. 29, 2020, available at https://vimeo.com/485180163; Fox News, "Trump Asks, 'Where's Durham?' During First Interview Since the Election," YouTube, Nov. 29, 2020, available at https://www.youtube.com/watch?v=szStcNBIL68; *see also* Alexis Benveniste, "Fox News' Maria Bartiromo Gave Trump His First TV Interview Since the Election. It Was Filled with Lies," CNN (Nov. 29, 2020), available at https://www.cnn.com/2020/11/29/media/bartiromo-trump-interview.

43. Factba.se, "Interview: Maria Bartiromo Interviews Donald Trump on Fox News - November 29, 2020," Vimeo, Nov. 29, 2020, available at https://vimeo.com/485180163; Fox News, "Trump Asks, 'Where's Durham?' During First Interview Since the Election," YouTube, Nov. 29, 2020, available at https://www.youtube.com/watch?v=szStcNBIL68; *see also* Alexis Benveniste, "Fox News' Maria Bartiromo Gave Trump His First TV Interview Since the Election. It Was Filled with Lies," CNN (Nov. 29, 2020), available at https://www.cnn.com/2020/11/29/media/bartiromo-trump-interview.

44. Factba.se, "Interview: Maria Bartiromo Interviews Donald Trump on Fox News - November 29, 2020," Vimeo, Nov. 29, 2020, available at https://vimeo.com/485180163; Fox News, "Trump Asks, 'Where's Durham?' During First Interview Since the Election," YouTube, Nov.

29, 2020, available at https://www.youtube.com/watch?v=szStcNBIL68; *see also* Alexis Benveniste, "Fox News' Maria Bartiromo Gave Trump His First TV Interview Since the Election. It Was Filled with Lies," CNN (Nov. 29, 2020), available at https://www.cnn.com/2020/11/29/media/bartiromo-trump-interview.

45. Factba.se, "Interview: Maria Bartiromo Interviews Donald Trump on Fox News - November 29, 2020," Vimeo, Nov. 29, 2020, available at https://vimeo.com/485180163; Fox News, "Trump Asks, 'Where's Durham?' During First Interview Since the Election," YouTube, Nov. 29, 2020, available at https://www.youtube.com/watch?v=szStcNBIL68; *see also* Alexis Benveniste, "Fox News' Maria Bartiromo Gave Trump His First TV Interview Since the Election. It Was Filled with Lies," CNN (Nov. 29, 2020), available at https://www.cnn.com/2020/11/29/media/bartiromo-trump-interview.

46. Factba.se, "Interview: Maria Bartiromo Interviews Donald Trump on Fox News - November 29, 2020," Vimeo, Nov. 29, 2020, available at https://vimeo.com/485180163; Fox News, "Trump Asks, 'Where's Durham?' During First Interview Since the Election," YouTube, Nov. 29, 2020, available at https://www.youtube.com/watch?v=szStcNBIL68; *see also* Alexis Benveniste, "Fox News' Maria Bartiromo Gave Trump His First TV Interview Since the Election. It Was Filled with Lies," CNN (Nov. 29, 2020), available at https://www.cnn.com/2020/11/29/media/bartiromo-trump-interview.

47. Factba.se, "Interview: Maria Bartiromo Interviews Donald Trump on Fox News - November 29, 2020," Vimeo, Nov. 29, 2020, available at https://vimeo.com/485180163; Fox News, "Trump Asks, 'Where's Durham?' During First Interview Since the Election," YouTube, Nov. 29, 2020, available at https://www.youtube.com/watch?v=szStcNBIL68; *see also* Alexis Benveniste, "Fox News' Maria Bartiromo Gave Trump His First TV Interview Since the Election. It Was Filled with Lies," CNN (Nov. 29, 2020), available at https://www.cnn.com/2020/11/29/media/bartiromo-trump-interview.

48. Fox News, "Trump Asks, 'Where's Durham?' During First Interview Since the Election," YouTube, Nov. 29, 2020, available at https://www.youtube.com/watch?v=szStcNBIL68; "Interview: Maria Bartiromo Interviews Donald Trump on Fox News - November 29, 2020," Vimeo, Nov. 29, 2020, available at ; Fox News, "Trump Asks, 'Where's Durham?' During First Interview Since the Election," YouTube, Nov. 29, 2020, available at https://www.youtube.com/watch?v=szStcNBIL68; *see also* Alexis Benveniste, "Fox News' Maria Bartiromo Gave Trump His First TV Interview Since the Election. It Was Filled with Lies," CNN (Nov. 29, 2020), available at https://www.cnn.com/2020/11/29/media/bartiromo-trump-interview. https://vimeo.com/485180163; *see also* Alexis Benveniste, "Fox News' Maria Bartiromo Gave Trump His First TV Interview Since the Election. It Was Filled with Lies," CNN (Nov. 29, 2020), available at https://www.cnn.com/2020/11/29/media/bartiromo-trump-interview.

49. Michael Balsamo, "Disputing Trump, Barr Says No Widespread Election Fraud," *Associated Press*, (Dec. 1, 2020, updated June 28, 2022), available at https://apnews.com/article/barr-no-widespread-election-fraud-b1f1488796c9a98c4b1a9061a6c7f49d.

50. Select Committee to Investigate the January 6th Attack on the United States Capitol, Transcribed Interview of William Barr, (June 2, 2022), pp. 23-24. Also attending the meeting were Pat Cipollone (Chief White House Counsel to the President), Pat Philbin (Deputy White House Counsel to the President), Eric Herschmann, and Barr's chief of staff, Will Levi. *Id.*

51. Select Committee to Investigate the January 6th Attack on the United States Capitol, Transcribed Interview of William Barr, (June 2, 2022), pp. 23-24.

52. Select Committee to Investigate the January 6th Attack on the United States Capitol, Transcribed Interview of William Barr, (June 2, 2022), pp. 23-24.

53. Select Committee to Investigate the January 6th Attack on the United States Capitol, Transcribed Interview of William Barr, (June 2, 2022), pp. 23-24.

54. Select Committee to Investigate the January 6th Attack on the United States Capitol, Transcribed Interview of William Barr, (June 2, 2022), pp. 23-24.

55. Select Committee to Investigate the January 6th Attack on the United States Capitol, Transcribed Interview of William Barr, (June 2, 2022), pp. 24-25.

56. Select Committee to Investigate the January 6th Attack on the United States Capitol, Transcribed Interview of William Barr, (June 2, 2022), pp. 25-26.

57. Select Committee to Investigate the January 6th Attack on the United States Capitol, Transcribed Interview of William Barr, (June 2, 2022), pp. 11, 25-26.

58. Select Committee to Investigate the January 6th Attack on the United States Capitol, Transcribed Interview of William Barr, (June 2, 2022), p. 25.

59. Select Committee to Investigate the January 6th Attack on the United States Capitol, Transcribed Interview of William Barr, (June 2, 2022), p. 25.

60. Select Committee to Investigate the January 6th Attack on the United States Capitol, Transcribed Interview of William Barr, (June 2, 2022), p. 25.

61. Select Committee to Investigate the January 6th Attack on the United States Capitol, Transcribed Interview of William Barr, (June 2, 2022), p. 25.

62. Select Committee to Investigate the January 6th Attack on the United States Capitol, Transcribed Interview of William Barr, (June 2, 2022), p. 25.

63. Select Committee to Investigate the January 6th Attack on the United States Capitol, Transcribed Interview of William Barr, (June 2, 2022), pp. 25-26.

64. Select Committee to Investigate the January 6th Attack on the United States Capitol, Transcribed Interview of William Barr, (June 2, 2022), pp. 25-26.

65. Select Committee to Investigate the January 6th Attack on the United States Capitol, Transcribed Interview of William Barr, (June 2, 2022), p. 26.

66. Select Committee to Investigate the January 6th Attack on the United States Capitol, Transcribed Interview of William Barr, (June 2, 2022), p. 26.

67. Select Committee to Investigate the January 6th Attack on the United States Capitol, Transcribed Interview of William Barr, (June 2, 2022), p. 26.

68. Select Committee to Investigate the January 6th Attack on the United States Capitol, Transcribed Interview of William Barr, (June 2, 2022), p. 26.

69. Select Committee to Investigate the January 6th Attack on the United States Capitol, Transcribed Interview of William Barr, (June 2, 2022), p. 26.

70. Select Committee to Investigate the January 6th Attack on the United States Capitol, Transcribed Interview of William Barr, (June 2, 2022), pp. 26-28.

71. "Campaign 2020: President Trump Statement on 2020 Election Results," C-SPAN, Dec. 2, 2020, available at https://www.c-span.org/video/?506975-1/president-trump-statement-2020-election-results; "Donald Trump Speech on Election Fraud Claims Transcript December 2," Rev, (Dec. 2, 2020), available at https://www.rev.com/blog/transcripts/donald-trump-speech-on-election-fraud-claims-transcript-december-2.

72. "Campaign 2020: President Trump Statement on 2020 Election Results," C-SPAN, Dec. 2, 2020, available at https://www.c-span.org/video/?506975-1/president-trump-statement-2020-election-results; "Donald Trump Speech on Election Fraud Claims Transcript December 2," Rev, (Dec. 2, 2020), available at https://www.rev.com/blog/transcripts/donald-trump-speech-on-election-fraud-claims-transcript-december-2.

73. "Campaign 2020: President Trump Statement on 2020 Election Results," C-SPAN, Dec. 2, 2020, available at https://www.c-span.org/video/?506975-1/president-trump-statement-2020-election-results; "Donald Trump Speech on Election Fraud Claims Transcript December 2," Rev, (Dec. 2, 2020), available at https://www.rev.com/blog/transcripts/donald-trump-speech-on-election-fraud-claims-transcript-december-2. Trump said: "Here's an example. This is Michigan. At 6:31 in the morning, a vote dump of 149,772 votes came in unexpectedly. We were winning by a lot. That batch was received in horror. We have a company that's very suspect. Its name is Dominion. With the turn of a dial or the change of a chip, you can press a button for Trump and the vote goes to Biden. What kind of a system is this?" Id.

74. 11Alive, "Second Georgia Senate Election Hearing," YouTube, at 1:56:30 - 1:57:15, 5:29:20 - 5:32:45, Dec. 3, 2020, available at https://www.youtube.com/watch?v=hRCXUNOwOjw.

75. 11Alive, "Second Georgia Senate Election Hearing," YouTube, at 1:56:30 - 1:57:15, 5:29:20 - 5:32:45, Dec. 3, 2020, available at https://www.youtube.com/watch?v=hRCXUNOwOjw.

76. 11Alive, "Second Georgia Senate Election Hearing," YouTube, at 0:33:30 - 0:58:00, Dec. 3, 2020, available at https://www.youtube.com/watch?v=hRCXUNOwOjw. The Trump campaign also shared the video online. Donald J Trump, "Video from GA Shows Suitcases Filled with Ballots Pulled from Under a Table AFTER Poll Workers Left," YouTube, Dec. 3, 2020, available at https://www.youtube.com/watch?v=nVP_60Hm4P8.

77. Gabriel Sterling (@GabrielSterling), Twitter, Dec. 4, 2020 6:41 a.m. ET, available at https://twitter.com/GabrielSterling/status/1334825233610633217?ref_src=twsrc%5Etfw%7Ctwcamp%5Etweetembed%7Ctwterm%5E1334825233610633217%7Ctwgr%5E%7Ctwcon%5Es1_&ref_url=https%3A%2F%2Fwww.gpb.org%2Fnews%2F2020%2F12%2F04%2Ffact-checking-rudy-giulianis-grandiose-georgia-election-fraud-claim. At the time, Gabe Sterling was the Chief Operating Officer in the Georgia Secretary of State's Office.

78. Select Committee to Investigate the January 6th Attack on the United States Capitol, *Hearing on the January 6th Investigation*, 117th Cong., 2d sess., (June 13, 2022), available at https://www.govinfo.gov/committee/house-january6th.

79. Select Committee to Investigate the January 6th Attack on the United States Capitol, *Hearing on the January 6th Investigation*, 117th Cong., 2d sess., (June 13, 2022), available at https://www.govinfo.gov/committee/house-january6th.

80. Select Committee to Investigate the January 6th Attack on the United States Capitol, Transcribed Interview of Byung Jin Pak, (May 19, 2022), p. 19.

81. "Read William Barr's Resignation Letter to President Trump," *Washington Post*, (Dec. 14, 2020), available at https://www.washingtonpost.com/context/read-william-barr-s-resignation-letter-to-president-trump/2b0820cb-3890-498a-bd46-c1b248049c70/?itid=lk_inline_manual_4.

82. Select Committee to Investigate the January 6th Attack on the United States Capitol, Transcribed Interview of William Barr, (June 2, 2022), pp. 65-66.

83. Select Committee to Investigate the January 6th Attack on the United States Capitol, Transcribed Interview of William Barr, (June 2, 2022), p. 28.

84. Select Committee to Investigate the January 6th Attack on the United States Capitol, Transcribed Interview of William Barr, (June 2, 2022), p. 28.

85. Select Committee to Investigate the January 6th Attack on the United States Capitol, Transcribed Interview of William Barr, (June 2, 2022), pp. 28-30.

86. Select Committee to Investigate the January 6th Attack on the United States Capitol, Transcribed Interview of William Barr, (June 2, 2022), p. 30.

87. Select Committee to Investigate the January 6th Attack on the United States Capitol, Transcribed Interview of William Barr, (June 2, 2022), p. 32.

88. Select Committee to Investigate the January 6th Attack on the United States Capitol, Transcribed Interview of William Barr, (June 2, 2022), p. 32.

89. Select Committee to Investigate the January 6th Attack on the United States Capitol, Transcribed Interview of Richard Peter Donoghue, (Oct. 1, 2021), pp. 39-40.

90. Documents on file with the Select Committee to Investigate the January 6th Attack on the United States Capitol (Department of Justice Production), HCOR-Pre-CertificationEvents-06032021-000425, HCOR-Pre-CertificationEvents-06032021-000426, HCOR-Pre-CertificationEvents-06032021-000429 (December 14, 2020, email from Molly Michael to Jeffrey Rosen subject "From POTUS" with two attachments).

91. Documents on file with the Select Committee to Investigate the January 6th Attack on the United States Capitol (Department of Justice Production), HCOR-Pre-CertificationEvents-06032021-000425, HCOR-Pre-CertificationEvents-06032021-000426, HCOR-Pre-CertificationEvents-06032021-000429 (December 14, 2020, email from Molly Michael to Jeffrey Rosen subject "From POTUS" with two attachments).

92. Select Committee to Investigate the January 6th Attack on the United States Capitol, Transcribed Interview of Richard Peter Donoghue, (Oct. 1, 2021), pp. 32-33.

93. Select Committee to Investigate the January 6th Attack on the United States Capitol, *Hearing on the January 6th Investigation*, 117th Cong., 2d sess., (June 23, 2022), available at https://www.govinfo.gov/committee/house-january6th.

94. Select Committee to Investigate the January 6th Attack on the United States Capitol, *Hearing on the January 6th Investigation*, 117th Cong., 2d sess., (June 23, 2022), available at https://www.govinfo.gov/committee/house-january6th.

95. Select Committee to Investigate the January 6th Attack on the United States Capitol, *Hearing on the January 6th Investigation*, 117th Cong., 2d sess., (June 23, 2022), available at https://www.govinfo.gov/committee/house-january6th.

96. U.S. Senate Committee on the Judiciary, Transcribed Interview of Jeffrey Rosen, (Aug. 7, 2021), at p. 34, available at https://www.judiciary.senate.gov/imo/media/doc/Rosen%20Transcript.pdf.

97. Documents on file with the Select Committee to Investigate the January 6th Attack on the United States Capitol (National Archives Production), 076P-R001080 (December 21, 2020, WAVES visitor records).

98. Mark Meadows (@MarkMeadows), Twitter, Dec. 21, 2020 6:03 pm, available at https://twitter.com/MarkMeadows/status/1341157317451124745.

99. Documents on file with the Select Committee to Investigate the January 6th Attack on the United States Capitol (National Archives Production), 076P-R001080 (WAVES visitor records for December 21, 2020).

100. Select Committee to Investigate the January 6th Attack on the United States Capitol, Deposition of Molly Michael, (March 24, 2022), pp. 205-06; Documents on file with the Select Committee to Investigate the January 6th Attack on the United States Capitol (National Archives Production), 076P-R000009364_0001 (December 21 and 22, 2020 email chain between Molly Michael and Jeffrey Clark discussing a December 22, 2020 meeting at the White House); Documents on file with the Select Committee to Investigate the January 6th Attack on the United States Capitol (National Archives Production), 076P-R000009365_0001 (December 22, 2020 email from Molly Michael to staff regarding a meeting at 6 p.m. in the Yellow Oval with Jeffrey Clark and another guest); Jonathan Tamari & Chris Brennan, "Pa. Congressman Scott Perry Acknowledges Introducing Trump to Lawyer at the Center of Election Plot," *Philadelphia Inquirer*, (Jan. 25, 2021), available at https://www.inquirer.com/politics/pennsylvania/scott-perry-trump-georgia-election-results-20210125.html.

101. Select Committee to Investigate the January 6th Attack on the United States Capitol, Transcribed Interview of Jeffrey Rosen, (Oct. 13, 2021), pp. 52-53.

102. Select Committee to Investigate the January 6th Attack on the United States Capitol, *Hearing on the January 6th Investigation*, 117th Cong., 2d sess., (June 23, 2022), available at https://www.govinfo.gov/committee/house-january6th.

103. Select Committee to Investigate the January 6th Attack on the United States Capitol, *Hearing on the January 6th Investigation*, 117th Cong., 2d sess., (June 23, 2022), available at https://www.govinfo.gov/committee/house-january6th.

104. Select Committee to Investigate the January 6th Attack on the United States Capitol, *Hearing on the January 6th Investigation*, 117th Cong., 117th sess., (June 23, 2022), available at https://www.govinfo.gov/committee/house-january6th.

105. Select Committee to Investigate the January 6th Attack on the United States Capitol, Transcribed Interview of Jeffrey Rosen, (Oct. 13, 2021), pp. 55-56, 78.

106. Select Committee to Investigate the January 6th Attack on the United States Capitol, Transcribed Interview of Jeffrey Rosen, (Oct. 13, 2021), pp. 55-56.

107. Select Committee to Investigate the January 6th Attack on the United States Capitol, Deposition of Kenneth Klukowski, (Dec. 15, 2021), pp. 53-55.

108. Select Committee to Investigate the January 6th Attack on the United States Capitol, *Hearing on the January 6th Investigation*, 117th Cong., 2d sess., (June 23, 2022), available at https://www.govinfo.gov/committee/house-january6th.

109. Select Committee to Investigate the January 6th Attack on the United States Capitol, *Hearing on the January 6th Investigation*, 117th Cong., 2d sess., (June 23, 2022), available at https://www.govinfo.gov/committee/house-january6th.

110. Select Committee to Investigate the January 6th Attack on the United States Capitol, *Hearing on the January 6th Investigation*, 117th Cong., 2d sess., (June 23, 2022), available at https://www.govinfo.gov/committee/house-january6th.

111. Select Committee to Investigate the January 6th Attack on the United States Capitol, *Hearing on the January 6th Investigation*, 117th Cong., 2d sess., (June 23, 2022), available at https://www.govinfo.gov/committee/house-january6th ; Documents on file with the Select Committee to Investigate the January 6th Attack on the United States Capitol (Department of Justice Production), HCOR-Pre-CertificationEvents-07262021-000681 (May 11, 2009, memorandum laying out the policy for "Communications with the White House and Congress").

112. Documents on file with the Select Committee to Investigate the January 6th Attack on the United States Capitol (Mark Meadows Production), MM014099 (December 26, 2020, text message from Rep. Perry to Mark Meadows).

113. Documents on file with the Select Committee to Investigate the January 6th Attack on the United States Capitol (Mark Meadows Production), MM0140100 (December 26, 2020, text message from Rep. Perry to Mark Meadows).

114. Documents on file with the Select Committee to Investigate the January 6th Attack on the United States Capitol (Mark Meadows Production), MM014101 (December 26, 2020, text message from Mark Meadows to Rep. Perry).

115. Documents on file with the Select Committee to Investigate the January 6th Attack on the United States Capitol (Mark Meadows Production), MM014102-014103, MM014178.

116. Select Committee to Investigate the January 6th Attack on the United States Capitol, Transcribed Interview of Richard Peter Donoghue, (Oct. 1, 2021), pp. 47-48.

117. Documents on file with the Select Committee to Investigate the January 6th Attack on the United States Capitol (Department of Justice Production), HCOR-Pre-Certification-Events-07282021-000735.

118. Documents on file with the Select Committee to Investigate the January 6th Attack on the United States Capitol (Department of Justice Production), HCOR-Pre-Certification-Events-07282021-000735; Ryan Deto, "Sen. Mastriano and Former State Rep. Saccone among Trump Supporters who Occupied U.S. Capitol," *Pittsburgh City Paper*, (Jan. 6, 2021), available at https://www.pghcitypaper.com/pittsburgh/sen-mastriano-and-former-state-rep-saccone-among-trump-supporters-who-occupied-us-capitol/Content?oid=18690728; Erin Bamer, "Mastriano Defends Protest Appearance; Other GOP Lawmakers Say Little," York Dispatch, (Jan. 7, 2021), available at https://www.yorkdispatch.com/story/news/2021/01/07/mastriano-at-no-point-did-he-storm-us-capitol/6579049002/.

119. Select Committee to Investigate the January 6th Attack on the United States Capitol, Transcribed Interview of Richard Peter Donoghue, (Oct. 1, 2021), pp. 47-50; *see also* Documents on file with the Select Committee to Investigate the January 6th Attack on the United States Capitol (Department of Justice Production), HCOR-Pre-Certification-Events-07282021-000735.

120. Dan Geiter, "Rally to 'Stop the Steal' of the 2020 Election" *PennLive*, (Nov. 5, 2020) available at https://www.pennlive.com/galleries/J3FJ24LCKVCT5OW3U2TJ6BV4RE/.

121. *See, e.g.*, Scott Perry for Congress, "#StopTheSteal," Facebook, November 6, 2020, available at https://www.facebook.com/watch/?v=406418637058079.

122. Select Committee to Investigate the January 6th Attack on the United States Capitol, Transcribed Interview of Richard Peter Donoghue, (Oct. 1, 2021), pp. 47-48, 53.

123. Select Committee to Investigate the January 6th Attack on the United States Capitol, *Hearing on the January 6th Investigation*, 117th Cong., 2d sess., (June 23, 2022), available at https://www.govinfo.gov/committee/house-january6thSelect; Documents on file with the Select Committee to Investigate the January 6th Attack on the United States Capitol (Department of Justice Production), HCOR-Pre-Certification-Events-07282021-000739 (December 27, 2020, handwritten notes from Richard Donoghue about call with President Trump).

124. Select Committee to Investigate the January 6th Attack on the United States Capitol, *Hearing on the January 6th Investigation*, 117th Cong., 2d sess., (June 23, 2022), available at https://www.govinfo.gov/committee/house-january6thSelect; Documents on file with the Select Committee to Investigate the January 6th Attack on the United States Capitol (Department of Justice Production), HCOR-Pre-Certification-Events-07282021-000739 (December 27, 2020, handwritten notes from Richard Donoghue about call with President Trump).

125. Select Committee to Investigate the January 6th Attack on the United States Capitol, *Hearing on the January 6th Investigation*, 117th Cong., 2d sess., (June 23, 2022), available at https://www.govinfo.gov/committee/house-january6thSelect; Documents on file with the Select Committee to Investigate the January 6th Attack on the United States Capitol (Department of Justice Production), HCOR-Pre-Certification-Events-07282021-000739 (December 27, 2020, handwritten notes from Richard Donoghue about call with President Trump).

126. "Hand Audit of All Presidential Election Votes in Antrim County Confirms Previously Certified Results, Voting Machines Were Accurate," Michigan Secretary of State, (Dec. 17, 2020), available at https://www.michigan.gov/sos/resources/news/2020/12/17/hand-audit-of-all-presidential-election-votes-in-antrim-county-confirms-previously-certified-result.

127. "Hand Audit of All Presidential Election Votes in Antrim County Confirms Previously Certified Results, Voting Machines Were Accurate," Michigan Secretary of State, (Dec. 17, 2020), available at https://www.michigan.gov/sos/resources/news/2020/12/17/hand-audit-of-all-presidential-election-votes-in-antrim-county-confirms-previously-certified-result.

128. "Hand Audit of All Presidential Election Votes in Antrim County Confirms Previously Certified Results, Voting Machines Were Accurate," Michigan Secretary of State, (Dec. 17, 2020), available at https://www.michigan.gov/sos/resources/news/2020/12/17/hand-audit-of-all-presidential-election-votes-in-antrim-county-confirms-previously-certified-result.

129. Select Committee to Investigate the January 6th Attack on the United States Capitol, *Hearing on the January 6th Investigation*, 117th Cong., 2d sess., (June 23, 2022), available at https://www.govinfo.gov/committee/house-january6thSelect; Select Committee to Investigate the January 6th Attack on the United States Capitol, Transcribed Interview of Richard Peter Donoghue, (Oct. 1, 2021), p. 60; Documents on file with the Select Committee to Investigate the January 6th Attack on the United States Capitol (Department of Justice Production), HCOR-Pre-Certification-Events-07282021-000739 (December 27, 2020, handwritten notes from Richard Donoghue about call with President Trump).

130. Select Committee to Investigate the January 6th Attack on the United States Capitol, *Hearing on the January 6th Investigation*, 117th Cong., 2d sess., (June 23, 2022), available at https://www.govinfo.gov/committee/house-january6th?path=/browsecommittee/chamber/house/committee/january6th.

131. Select Committee to Investigate the January 6th Attack on the United States Capitol, *Hearing on the January 6th Investigation*, 117th Cong., 2d sess., (June 23, 2022), available at

https://www.govinfo.gov/committee/house-january6thSelect; Select Committee to Investigate the January 6th Attack on the United States Capitol, Transcribed Interview of Richard Peter Donoghue, (Oct. 1, 2021), p. 60.

132. Select Committee to Investigate the January 6th Attack on the United States Capitol, *Hearing on the January 6th Investigation*, 117th Cong., 2d sess., (June 23, 2022), available at https://www.govinfo.gov/committee/house-january6thSelect; Select Committee to Investigate the January 6th Attack on the United States Capitol, Transcribed Interview of Richard Peter Donoghue, (Oct. 1, 2021), p. 60; Documents on file with the Select Committee to Investigate the January 6th Attack on the United States Capitol (Department of Justice Production), HCOR-Pre-Certification-Events-07282021-000739 (December 27, 2020, handwritten notes from Richard Donoghue about call with President Trump).

133. Select Committee to Investigate the January 6th Attack on the United States Capitol, Transcribed Interview of Richard Peter Donoghue, (Oct. 1, 2021), p. 55; Documents on file with the Select Committee to Investigate the January 6th Attack on the United States Capitol (Department of Justice Production), HCOR-Pre-Certification-Events-07282021-000737 (December 27, 2020, handwritten notes from Richard Donoghue about call with President Trump).

134. Select Committee to Investigate the January 6th Attack on the United States Capitol, Transcribed Interview of Richard Peter Donoghue, (Oct. 1, 2021), p. 55; Documents on file with the Select Committee to Investigate the January 6th Attack on the United States Capitol (Department of Justice Production), HCOR-Pre-Certification-Events-07282021-000737 (December 27, 2020, handwritten notes from Richard Donoghue about call with President Trump).

135. Select Committee to Investigate the January 6th Attack on the United States Capitol, Transcribed Interview of Richard Peter Donoghue, (Oct. 1, 2021), p. 55.

136. Select Committee to Investigate the January 6th Attack on the United States Capitol, Transcribed Interview of Richard Peter Donoghue, (Oct. 1, 2021), pp. 55-56; Documents on file with the Select Committee to Investigate the January 6th Attack on the United States Capitol (Department of Justice Production), HCOR-Pre-Certification-Events-07282021-000739 (December 27, 2020, handwritten notes from Richard Donoghue about call with President Trump).

137. Select Committee to Investigate the January 6th Attack on the United States Capitol, *Hearing on the January 6th Investigation*, 117th Cong., 2d sess., (June 23, 2022), available at https://www.govinfo.gov/committee/house-january6thSelect.

138. Select Committee to Investigate the January 6th Attack on the United States Capitol, Transcribed Interview of Richard Peter Donoghue, (Oct. 1, 2021), p. 54; Documents on file with the Select Committee to Investigate the January 6th Attack on the United States Capitol (Department of Justice Production), HCOR-Pre-Certification-Events-07282021-000739 (December 27, 2020, handwritten notes from Richard Donoghue about call with President Trump).

139. Select Committee to Investigate the January 6th Attack on the United States Capitol, Transcribed Interview of Richard Peter Donoghue, (Oct. 1, 2021), p. 54; Documents on file with the Select Committee to Investigate the January 6th Attack on the United States Capitol (Department of Justice Production), HCOR-Pre-Certification-Events-07282021-000739 (December 27, 2020, handwritten notes from Richard Donoghue about call with President Trump).

140. Select Committee to Investigate the January 6th Attack on the United States Capitol, Transcribed Interview of Richard Peter Donoghue, (Oct. 1, 2021), p. 54; Documents on file with the Select Committee to Investigate the January 6th Attack on the United States Capitol (Department of Justice Production), HCOR-Pre-Certification-Events-07282021-000739 (December 27, 2020, handwritten notes from Richard Donoghue about call with President Trump).

141. Select Committee to Investigate the January 6th Attack on the United States Capitol, Transcribed Interview of Richard Peter Donoghue, (Oct. 1, 2021), p. 64; Documents on file with the Select Committee to Investigate the January 6th Attack on the United States Capitol (Department of Justice Production), HCOR-Pre-Certification-Events-07282021-000741 (December 27, 2020, handwritten notes from Richard Donoghue about call with President Trump).

142. Select Committee to Investigate the January 6th Attack on the United States Capitol, Transcribed Interview of Richard Peter Donoghue, (Oct. 1, 2021), p. 60.

143. Select Committee to Investigate the January 6th Attack on the United States Capitol, Transcribed Interview of Richard Peter Donoghue, (Oct. 1, 2021), p. 60.

144. Select Committee to Investigate the January 6th Attack on the United States Capitol, Transcribed Interview of Richard Peter Donoghue, (Oct. 1, 2021), pp. 60-61.

145. Select Committee to Investigate the January 6th Attack on the United States Capitol, Transcribed Interview of Richard Peter Donoghue, (Oct. 1, 2021), pp. 60-61.

146. Select Committee to Investigate the January 6th Attack on the United States Capitol, Transcribed Interview of Richard Peter Donoghue, (Oct. 1, 2021), pp. 60-61.

147. Select Committee to Investigate the January 6th Attack on the United States Capitol, Transcribed Interview of Richard Peter Donoghue, (Oct. 1, 2021), pp. 54-55; Documents on file with the Select Committee to Investigate the January 6th Attack on the United States Capitol (Department of Justice Production), HCOR-Pre-Certification-Events-07282021-000737 (December 27, 2020, handwritten notes from Richard Donoghue about call with President Trump).

148. Select Committee to Investigate the January 6th Attack on the United States Capitol, Transcribed Interview of Richard Peter Donoghue, (Oct. 1, 2021), pp. 54, 58; Documents on file with the Select Committee to Investigate the January 6th Attack on the United States Capitol (Department of Justice Production), HCOR-Pre-Certification-Events-07282021-000737, HCOR-Pre-Certification-Events-07282021-000738 (December 27, 2020, handwritten notes from Richard Donoghue about call with President Trump).

149. Select Committee to Investigate the January 6th Attack on the United States Capitol, Transcribed Interview of Richard Peter Donoghue, (Oct. 1, 2021), pp. 54, 58; Documents on file with the Select Committee to Investigate the January 6th Attack on the United States Capitol (Department of Justice Production), HCOR-Pre-Certification-Events-07282021-000737, HCOR-Pre-Certification-Events-07282021-000738 (December 27, 2020, handwritten notes from Richard Donoghue about call with President Trump).

150. Select Committee to Investigate the January 6th Attack on the United States Capitol, Transcribed Interview of Richard Peter Donoghue, (Oct. 1, 2021), pp. 54, 58; Documents on file with the Select Committee to Investigate the January 6th Attack on the United States Capitol (Department of Justice Production), HCOR-Pre-Certification-Events-07282021-000737, HCOR-Pre-Certification-Events-07282021-000738 (December 27, 2020, handwritten notes from Richard Donoghue about call with President Trump).

151. Select Committee to Investigate the January 6th Attack on the United States Capitol, Transcribed Interview of Richard Peter Donoghue, (Oct. 1, 2021), p. 58; Documents on file with the Select Committee to Investigate the January 6th Attack on the United States Capitol (Department of Justice Production), HCOR-Pre-Certification-Events-07282021-000738, HCOR-Pre-Certification-Events-07282021-000739 (December 27, 2020, handwritten notes from Richard Donoghue about call with President Trump).

152. Select Committee to Investigate the January 6th Attack on the United States Capitol, Transcribed Interview of Richard Peter Donoghue, (Oct. 1, 2021), p. 58. Trump also mentioned the possibility of the DOJ saying the "election is corrupt or suspect or not reliable" during a public press conference. "We told him we were not going to do that," Donoghue explained. *Id.* at p. 59.

153. Select Committee to Investigate the January 6th Attack on the United States Capitol, Transcribed Interview of Richard Peter Donoghue, (Oct. 1, 2021), p. 62; Documents on file with the Select Committee to Investigate the January 6th Attack on the United States Capitol (Department of Justice Production), HCOR-Pre-Certification-Events-07282021-000740 (December 27, 2020, handwritten notes from Richard Donoghue about call with President Trump).

154. Select Committee to Investigate the January 6th Attack on the United States Capitol, Transcribed Interview of Richard Peter Donoghue, (Oct. 1, 2021), p. 60; Documents on file with the Select Committee to Investigate the January 6th Attack on the United States Capitol (Department of Justice Production), HCOR-Pre-Certification-Events-07282021-000739, HCOR-Pre-Certification-Events-07282021-000740 (December 27, 2020, handwritten notes from Richard Donoghue about call with President Trump).

155. Select Committee to Investigate the January 6th Attack on the United States Capitol, Transcribed Interview of Richard Peter Donoghue, (Oct. 1, 2021), p. 61.

156. Select Committee to Investigate the January 6th Attack on the United States Capitol, *Hearing on the January 6th Investigation*, 117th Cong., 2d sess., (June 23, 2022), available at https://www.govinfo.gov/committee/house-january6thSelect.

157. Select Committee to Investigate the January 6th Attack on the United States Capitol, *Hearing on the January 6th Investigation*, 117th Cong., 2d sess., (June 23, 2022), available at https://www.govinfo.gov/committee/house-january6thSelect.

158. Select Committee to Investigate the January 6th Attack on the United States Capitol, *Hearing on the January 6th Investigation*, 117th Cong., 2d sess., (June 23, 2022), available at https://www.govinfo.gov/committee/house-january6thSelect.

159. Select Committee to Investigate the January 6th Attack on the United States Capitol, *Hearing on the January 6th Investigation*, 117th Cong., 2d sess., (June 23, 2022), available at https://www.govinfo.gov/committee/house-january6thSelect.

160. Donoghue testified before the Select Committee: "There were isolated instances of fraud. None of them came close to calling into question the outcome of the election in any individual state." Select Committee to Investigate the January 6th Attack on the United States Capitol, *Hearing on the January 6th Investigation*, 117th Cong., 2d sess., (June 23, 2022), available at https://www.govinfo.gov/committee/house-january6thSelect.

161. Select Committee to Investigate the January 6th Attack on the United States Capitol, Transcribed Interview of Richard Peter Donoghue, (Oct. 1, 2021), p. 62; Documents on file with the Select Committee to Investigate the January 6th Attack on the United States Capitol (Department of Justice Production), HCOR-Pre-Certification-Events-07282021-000740 (December 27, 2020, handwritten notes from Richard Donoghue about call with President Trump).

162. Select Committee to Investigate the January 6th Attack on the United States Capitol, Transcribed Interview of Richard Peter Donoghue, (Oct. 1, 2021), p. 62.

163. Select Committee to Investigate the January 6th Attack on the United States Capitol, Transcribed Interview of Richard Peter Donoghue, (Oct. 1, 2021), p. 62.

164. Select Committee to Investigate the January 6th Attack on the United States Capitol, Transcribed Interview of Richard Peter Donoghue, (Oct. 1, 2021), p. 65.

165. Select Committee to Investigate the January 6th Attack on the United States Capitol, Transcribed Interview of Richard Peter Donoghue, (Oct. 1, 2021), pp. 72-75.

166. Dan Gleiter, "Rally to 'Stop the Steal' of the 2020 Election," *Penn Live*, (Nov. 5, 2020), available at https://www.pennlive.com/galleries/J3FJ24LCKVCT5OW3U2TJ6BV4RE/.

167. Letter from the Office of Rep. Lance Gooden and Signed by 26 other Members of Congress to the President of the United States, Dec. 9, 2020, available at https://www.politico.com/f/?id=00000176-4701-d52c-ad7e-d7fdbfe50000.

168. Motion for Leave to File Amicus Brief by U.S. Representative Mike Johnson and 125 other Members, *Texas v. Pennsylvania*, 592 U.S. ____ (Dec. 10, 2020) (No. 155, Orig.), available at https://www.supremecourt.gov/DocketPDF/22/22O155/163550/20201211132250339_Texas%20v.%20Pennsylvania%20Amicus%20Brief%20of%20126%20Representatives%20--%20corrected.pdf.

169. Select Committee to Investigate the January 6th Attack on the United States Capitol, Transcribed Interview of Richard Peter Donoghue, (Oct. 1, 2021), pp. 72-73; Documents on file with the Select Committee to Investigate the January 6th Attack on the United States Capitol (Department of Justice Production), HCOR-Pre-CertificationEvents-07262021-000705, HCOR-Pre-CertificationEvents-07262021-000706, (Dec. 27, 2020, handwritten notes). Donoghue's handwritten notes from the call are dated Dec. 28, 2020, but he confirmed the call took place on Dec. 27.

170. Select Committee to Investigate the January 6th Attack on the United States Capitol, Transcribed Interview of Richard Peter Donoghue, (Oct. 1, 2021), pp. 72-73; Documents on file with the Select Committee to Investigate the January 6th Attack on the United States Capitol (Department of Justice Production), HCOR-Pre-CertificationEvents-07262021-000705, HCOR-Pre-CertificationEvents-07262021-000706, (Dec. 27, 2020, handwritten notes).

171. Select Committee to Investigate the January 6th Attack on the United States Capitol, Transcribed Interview of Richard Peter Donoghue, (Oct. 1, 2021), pp. 72-73; Documents on file with the Select Committee to Investigate the January 6th Attack on the United States Capitol (Department of Justice Production), HCOR-Pre-CertificationEvents-07262021-000705, HCOR-Pre-CertificationEvents-07262021-000705, (Dec. 27, 2020, handwritten notes).

172. Select Committee to Investigate the January 6th Attack on the United States Capitol, Transcribed Interview of Richard Peter Donoghue, (Oct. 1, 2021), p. 73; Documents on file with the Select Committee to Investigate the January 6th Attack on the United States Capitol (Department of Justice Production), HCOR-Pre-CertificationEvents-07262021-000705, HCOR-Pre-CertificationEvents-07262021-000706, (Dec. 27, 2020, handwritten notes).

173. Documents on file with the Select Committee to Investigate the January 6th Attack on the United States Capitol (Department of Justice Production), HCOR Pre CertificationEvents 06032021-000001 - HCOR-Pre-CertificationEvents-06032021-000018.

174. Documents on file with the Select Committee to Investigate the January 6th Attack on the United States Capitol (Department of Justice Production), HCOR-Pre-CertificationEvents-06032021-000008.

175. RepScottPerry (@RepScotPerry), Twitter, Dec. 28, 2020 6:01 p.m. ET, available at https://twitter.com/RepScottPerry/status/1343693703664308225.

176. *See* Chapter 1.

177. Select Committee to Investigate the January 6th Attack on the United States Capitol, Transcribed Interview of Richard Peter Donoghue, (Oct. 1, 2021), pp. 74-75.

178. Select Committee to Investigate the January 6th Attack on the United States Capitol, Transcribed Interview of Richard Peter Donoghue, (Oct. 1, 2021), pp. 75-76.

179. Select Committee to Investigate the January 6th Attack on the United States Capitol, Transcribed Interview of Richard Peter Donoghue, (Oct. 1, 2021), pp. 75-76.

180. Select Committee to Investigate the January 6th Attack on the United States Capitol, Transcribed Interview of Richard Peter Donoghue, (Oct. 1, 2021), pp. 75-76.

181. Documents on file with the Select Committee to Investigate the January 6th Attack on the United States Capitol (Department of Justice Production), HCOR-Pre-CertificationEvents-07262021-000697 – HCOR-Pre-CertificationEvents-07262021-000702.

182. Documents on file with the Select Committee to Investigate the January 6th Attack on the United States Capitol (Department of Justice Production), HCOR-Pre-CertificationEvents-07262021-000697 – HCOR-Pre-CertificationEvents-07262021-000702.; Documents on file with the Select Committee to Investigate the January 6th Attack on the United States Capitol

(Department of Justice Production), HCOR-Pre-CertificationEvents-06032021-000200 (December 28, 2020, email from Richard Donoghue to Jeffrey Clark, cc'ing Jeffrey Rosen, including Rosen's reply to Donoghue; Select Committee to Investigate the January 6th Attack on the United States Capitol, *Hearing on the January 6th Investigation*, 117th Cong., 2d sess., (June 23, 2022), available at https://www.govinfo.gov/committee/house-january6th.

183.   Select Committee to Investigate the January 6th Attack on the United States Capitol, *Hearing on the January 6th Investigation*, 117th Cong., 2d sess., (June 23, 2022), available at https://www.govinfo.gov/committee/house-january6th.

184.   Documents on file with the Select Committee to Investigate the January 6th Attack on the United States Capitol (Department of Justice Production), HCOR-Pre-CertificationEvents-07262021-000697 – HCOR-Pre-CertificationEvents-07262021-000702.

185.   *See* National Intelligence Council, *Intelligence Community Assessment: Foreign Threats to the 2020 US Federal Elections*, (Mar. 10, 2021), available at https://www.dni.gov/index.php/newsroom/reports-publications/reports-publications-2021/item/2192-intelligence-community-assessment-on-foreign-threats-to-the-2020-u-s-federal-elections (declassified version of a January 7, 2021, report to President Trump, senior Executive Branch officials, and Congressional leadership). The report concluded, among other things, "We have no indications that any foreign actor attempted to alter any technical aspect of the voting process in the 2020 US elections, including voter registration, casting ballots, vote tabulation, or reporting results."

186.   Documents on file with the Select Committee to Investigate the January 6th Attack on the United States Capitol (Department of Justice Production), HCOR-Pre-CertificationEvents-07262021-000697 – HCOR-Pre-CertificationEvents-07262021-000702.

187.   Zachary Cohen & Sara Murray, "New Details Shed Light on Ways Mark Meadows Pushed Federal Agencies to Pursue Dubious Election Claims," CNN, (Dec. 2, 2021), available at https://www.cnn.com/2021/12/02/politics/mark-meadows-election-fraud-liaison/index.html; Select Committee to Investigate the January 6th Attack on the United States Capitol, Transcribed Interview of Eric Herschmann, (Apr. 6, 2022) at pp. 168-69.

188.   Select Committee to Investigate the January 6th Attack on the United States Capitol, Transcribed Interview of Richard Peter Donoghue, (Oct. 1, 2021), p. 113.

189.   Documents on file with the Select Committee to Investigate the January 6th Attack on the United States Capitol (Department of Justice Production), HCOR-Pre-CertificationEvents-07262021-000697 – HCOR-Pre-CertificationEvents-07262021-000702.

190.   Documents on file with the Select Committee to Investigate the January 6th Attack on the United States Capitol (Department of Justice Production), HCOR-Pre-CertificationEvents-07262021-000697 – HCOR-Pre-CertificationEvents-07262021-000702.

191.   Documents on file with the Select Committee to Investigate the January 6th Attack on the United States Capitol (Department of Justice Production), HCOR-Pre-CertificationEvents-07262021-000697 – HCOR-Pre-CertificationEvents-07262021-000702.

192.   Documents on file with the Select Committee to Investigate the January 6th Attack on the United States Capitol (Department of Justice Production), HCOR-Pre-CertificationEvents-07262021-000697 – HCOR-Pre-CertificationEvents-07262021-000702.

193.   Documents on file with the Select Committee to Investigate the January 6th Attack on the United States Capitol (Department of Justice Production), HCOR-Pre-CertificationEvents-07262021-000697 – HCOR-Pre-CertificationEvents-07262021-000702.

194.   *See* Chapters 2 and 3 regarding the Trump Campaign's efforts to overturn the results of the election in contested states and have fake Electoral College electors submit fake votes to Congress.

195.   Documents on file with the Select Committee to Investigate the January 6th Attack on the United States Capitol (Department of Justice Production), HCOR-Pre-CertificationEvents-07262021-000697 – HCOR-Pre-CertificationEvents-07262021-000702.

196. *See* Chapter 2 for additional information on these hearings.

197. *See* Chapter 2; *see also* Ga. Const., art. V, § 2, ¶ VII.

198. Documents on file with the Select Committee to Investigate the January 6th Attack on the United States Capitol (Department of Justice Production), HCOR-Pre-CertificationEvents-07262021-000697 – HCOR-Pre-CertificationEvents-07262021-000702.

199. Documents on file with the Select Committee to Investigate the January 6th Attack on the United States Capitol (Department of Justice Production), HCOR-Pre-CertificationEvents-07262021-000698 – HCOR-Pre-CertificationEvents-07262021-000702.

200. *See* Chapter 2.

201. *See* Chapter 3.

202. Select Committee to Investigate the January 6th Attack on the United States Capitol, Deposition of Jeffrey Clark, (Feb 2, 2022), pp. 24-27.

203. Select Committee to Investigate the January 6th Attack on the United States Capitol, Deposition of Rudolph Giuliani, (May 20, 2022), pp. 101-03.

204. Documents on file with the Select Committee to Investigate the January 6th Attack on the United States Capitol (Chapman production), Chapman061893 (January 1, 2021, emails between Jeffrey Clark and John Eastman); *see* Documents on file with the Select Committee to Investigate the January 6th Attack on the United States Capitol (Verizon Production, July 1, 2022) (showing five calls between John Eastman and Jeffrey Clark from January 1, 2021, through January 8, 2021)

205. *See, e.g.*, Select Committee to Investigate the January 6th Attack on the United States Capitol, Deposition of Kenneth Klukowski (Dec. 15, 2021), p. 182. The Select Committee questioned, and sought documents from, Klukowski about his interactions with Eastman and others related to the 2020 election and the January 6th joint session of Congress. Klukowski, however, objected to certain questions, and withheld a number of relevant communications, on the basis of attorney-client privilege, work product, or the First Amendment, including communications that he had with Eastman. For example, on December 9th, before Klukowski joined the Department of Justice, he sent an email to Eastman with an attachment of draft talking points arguing that state legislators in states where Biden won could disregard the election results and appoint electors for Trump. *See* Documents on file with the Select Committee to Investigate the January 6th Attack on the United States Capitol (Chapman University Production), Chapman028219, Chapman028220 (December 9, 2020, email from Klukowski to Eastman, attaching memo). Those same talking points were circulated the same day among Ken Blackwell, Ed Meese, John Eastman, Jason Miller, Alan Dershowitz, and Chief of Staff Mark Meadows with Blackwell's comment, "A constitutional road map to victory and DJT's reelection! It's a matter of political will and courage to do the right thing." *See* Documents on file with the Select Committee to Investigate the January 6th Attack on the United States Capitol (Chapman University Production), Chapman027943, Chapman027944 (Klukowski was not included on the email from Blackwell, but his talking points were attached). During his deposition with the Select Committee, Klukowski said that the document containing the talking points looked like a document he had drafted, but asserted attorney-client privilege when asked certain questions asked about the document. *See* Select Committee to Investigate the January 6th Attack on the United States Capitol, Continued Deposition of Kenneth Klukowski, (June 10, 2022), pp. 27-29. The Select Committee also obtained from a source other than Klukowski an email sent to him, Eastman, Rep. Louis Gohmert's Chief of Staff, and others on December 28th with the subject line "VP Briefing on 1/6/21 Meeting" and a message from Edward Corrigan that said, "I believe the VP and his staff would benefit greatly from a briefing by John and Ken" but cautioned to "make sure we don't overexpose Ken given his new position." *See* Documents on file with the Select Committee to Investigate the January 6th Attack on the United States Capitol (Chapman University Production), Chapman056164 (December 28, 2020, email to Klukowski and others). Klukowski said he never participated in such a briefing, but Eastman did in the days leading up to January 6th and encouraged

the Vice President to prevent or delay the certification of the presidential election during the joint session of Congress. *See* Select Committee to Investigate the January 6th Attack on the United States Capitol, Deposition of Kenneth Klukowski, (June 10, 2022), pp. 50-57; *see also* Chapter 5 about Eastman and his communications with the Vice President. As described here, Klukowski drafted the letter for Clark that included discussions about state legislatures, Electoral College electors, and the joint session of Congress.

206. Select Committee to Investigate the January 6th Attack on the United States Capitol, Deposition of Kenneth Klukowski (Dec. 15, 2021), p. 17.

207. Select Committee to Investigate the January 6th Attack on the United States Capitol, Deposition of Kenneth Klukowski, (Dec. 15, 2021), p. 23; Documents on file with the Select Committee to Investigate the January 6th Attack on the United States Capitol (Department of Justice Production), HouseSelect-Jan6-PartII-12142021-000104. Klukowski's first day on the job was December 15th. When asked why he would be willing to start a job on December 15th that would end by January 20th, Klukowski said that he had been trying to get to the Department of Justice for several months, he was "hopeful" that he could "get as many medals on my chest as possible during that short period of time," and "given that it was going to cross the New Year's dateline, [he] figured [his] resume would say Department of Justice 2020 and 2021," enabling him to get into an interview for future jobs before a future employer "would find out how few of days in each of those calendar years we were actually talking about." Select Committee to Investigate the January 6th Attack on the United States Capitol, Deposition of Kenneth Klukowski, (Dec. 15, 2021), pp. 30, 41.

208. Select Committee to Investigate the January 6th Attack on the United States Capitol, Deposition of Kenneth Klukowski, (Dec. 15, 2021), pp. 65-66.

209. Select Committee to Investigate the January 6th Attack on the United States Capitol, Deposition of Kenneth Klukowski, (Dec. 15, 2021), pp. 71-73.

210. Select Committee to Investigate the January 6th Attack on the United States Capitol, Deposition of Kenneth Klukowski, (Dec. 15, 2021), pp. 66, 75-76.

211. Documents on file with the Select Committee to Investigate the January 6th Attack on the United States Capitol (Department of Justice Production), HCOR-Pre-CertificationEvents-06032021-000200 (December 28, 2020, email from Richard Donoghue to Jeffrey Clark, cc'ing Jeffrey Rosen, including Rosen's reply to Donoghue).

212. Documents on file with the Select Committee to Investigate the January 6th Attack on the United States Capitol (Department of Justice Production), HCOR-Pre-CertificationEvents-06032021-000200 (December 28, 2020, email from Richard Donoghue to Jeffrey Clark, cc'ing Jeffrey Rosen, including Rosen's reply to Donoghue).

213. Documents on file with the Select Committee to Investigate the January 6th Attack on the United States Capitol (Department of Justice Production), HCOR-Pre-CertificationEvents-06032021-000200 (December 28, 2020, email from Richard Donoghue to Jeffrey Clark, cc'ing Jeffrey Rosen, including Rosen's reply to Donoghue).

214. Documents on file with the Select Committee to Investigate the January 6th Attack on the United States Capitol (Department of Justice Production), HCOR-Pre-CertificationEvents-06032021-000200 (December 28, 2020, email from Richard Donoghue to Jeffrey Clark, cc'ing Jeffrey Rosen, including Rosen's reply to Donoghue).

215. Select Committee to Investigate the January 6th Attack on the United States Capitol, Transcribed Interview of Richard Peter Donoghue, (Oct. 1, 2021), pp. 81-82.

216. Select Committee to Investigate the January 6th Attack on the United States Capitol, Transcribed Interview of Richard Peter Donoghue, (Oct. 1, 2021), p. 82.

217. Select Committee to Investigate the January 6th Attack on the United States Capitol, Transcribed Interview of Richard Peter Donoghue, (Oct. 1, 2021), p. 83.

218. Select Committee to Investigate the January 6th Attack on the United States Capitol, Transcribed Interview of Richard Peter Donoghue, (Oct. 1, 2021), p. 82.

219. Documents on file with the Select Committee to Investigate the January 6th Attack on the United States Capitol (Department of Justice Production), HCOR-Pre-CertificationEvents-07262021-000681 (Department of Justice policy), HCOR-Pre-CertificationEvents-07262021-000685 (White House policy).

220. Select Committee to Investigate the January 6th Attack on the United States Capitol, *Hearing on the January 6th Investigation*, 117th Cong., 2d sess., (June 23, 2022), available at https://www.govinfo.gov/committee/house-january6th.

221. Select Committee to Investigate the January 6th Attack on the United States Capitol, *Hearing on the January 6th Investigation*, 117th Cong., 2d sess., (June 23, 2022), available at https://www.govinfo.gov/committee/house-january6th.

222. Select Committee to Investigate the January 6th Attack on the United States Capitol, Transcribed Interview of Steven Engel, (Jan. 13, 2022), pp. 27-28.

223. Select Committee to Investigate the January 6th Attack on the United States Capitol, Transcribed Interview of Richard Peter Donoghue, (Oct. 1, 2021), pp. 86-87; Select Committee to Investigate the January 6th Attack on the United States Capitol, Transcribed Interview of Jeffrey Rosen, (Oct. 13, 2021), pp. 79-80, 91-92, 132-33.

224. Select Committee to Investigate the January 6th Attack on the United States Capitol, Transcribed Interview of Jeffrey Rosen, (Oct. 13, 2021), pp. 91-93, 132-33.

225. Select Committee to Investigate the January 6th Attack on the United States Capitol, Transcribed Interview of Richard Peter Donoghue, (Oct. 1, 2021), p. 87; Select Committee to Investigate the January 6th Attack on the United States Capitol, Transcribed Interview of Jeffrey Rosen, (Oct. 13, 2021), pp. 91-93, 132-33.

226. Select Committee to Investigate the January 6th Attack on the United States Capitol, Transcribed Interview of Richard Peter Donoghue, (Oct. 1, 2021), pp. 88-89; Documents on file with the Select Committee to Investigate the January 6th Attack on the United States Capitol (Department of Justice Production), HCOR-Pre-CertificationEvents-06032021-000678 (January 1, 2021, email from Mark Meadows to Jeffrey Rosen with link to YouTube video); Brad Johnson, "Rome, Satellites, Servers: an Update," YouTube, available at https://web.archive.org/web/20210102201919/https://www.youtube.com/watch?v=YwtbK5XXAMk&feature=youtu.be (archived) (showing the conspiracy Meadows asked DOJ to investigate).

227. Select Committee to Investigate the January 6th Attack on the United States Capitol, Transcribed Interview of Richard Peter Donoghue, (Oct. 1, 2021), pp. 88-90.

228. Select Committee to Investigate the January 6th Attack on the United States Capitol, Transcribed Interview of Richard Peter Donoghue, (Oct. 1, 2021), p. 89.

229. Select Committee to Investigate the January 6th Attack on the United States Capitol, Transcribed Interview of Richard Peter Donoghue, (Oct. 1, 2021), pp. 90-91.

230. Select Committee to Investigate the January 6th Attack on the United States Capitol, Transcribed Interview of Richard Peter Donoghue, (Oct. 1, 2021), pp. 87, 91-92; Documents on file with the Select Committee to Investigate the January 6th Attack on the United States Capitol (Department of Justice Production), HCOR-Pre-CertificationEvents-07262021-000708 (December 31, 2020, email from Steven Engel to Richard Donoghue attaching "U.S. v. Penn OJ suit").

231. Documents on file with the Select Committee to Investigate the January 6th Attack on the United States Capitol (Department of Justice Production), HCOR-Pre-CertificationEvents-07262021-000708 - HCOR-Pre-CertificationEvents-07262021-000709 (December 31, 2020, email from Steven Engel to Richard Donoghue attaching "U.S. v. Penn OJ suit" re: one pager, with document titled "Evaluation of Potential Original-Jurisdiction Suit in the Supreme Court"); Select Committee to Investigate the January 6th Attack on the United States Capitol, Transcribed Interview of Richard Peter Donoghue, (Oct. 1, 2021), pp. 91-92.

232. Documents on file with the Select Committee to Investigate the January 6th Attack on the United States Capitol (Department of Justice Production), HCOR-Pre-CertificationEvents-07262021-000709 (Document titled "Evaluation of Potential Original-Jurisdiction Suit in the Supreme Court").

233. Documents on file with the Select Committee to Investigate the January 6th Attack on the United States Capitol (Department of Justice Production), HCOR-Pre-CertificationEvents-07262021-000709 (Document titled "Evaluation of Potential Original-Jurisdiction Suit in the Supreme Court").

234. Documents on file with the Select Committee to Investigate the January 6th Attack on the United States Capitol (Department of Justice Production), HCOR-Pre-CertificationEvents-07262021-000709 (Document titled "Evaluation of Potential Original-Jurisdiction Suit in the Supreme Court").

235. Documents on file with the Select Committee to Investigate the January 6th Attack on the United States Capitol (Department of Justice Production), HCOR-Pre-Certificationevents-07262021-000709 (Document titled "Evaluation of Potential Original-Jurisdiction Suit in the Supreme Court").

236. Documents on file with the Select Committee to Investigate the January 6th Attack on the United States Capitol (Department of Justice Production), HCOR-Pre-Certificationevents-07262021-000709 (Document titled "Evaluation of Potential Original-Jurisdiction Suit in the Supreme Court"). The memo cites *United States v. Texas* although it likely refers to the case filed by Texas and rejected by the Supreme Court, *Texas v. Pennsylvania*. *See* Order Dismissing Bill of Complaint and Denying Certiorari, *Texas v. Pennsylvania*, 592 U.S. ___, (Dec. 11, 2020) (No. 155, Orig.), available at https://www.supremecourt.gov/orders/courtorders/121120zr_p860.pdf.

237. Select Committee to Investigate the January 6th Attack on the United States Capitol, Transcribed Interview of Steven Engel, (Jan. 13, 2022), p. 33.

238. Select Committee to Investigate the January 6th Attack on the United States Capitol, Transcribed Interview of Richard Peter Donoghue, (Oct. 1, 2021), pp. 87, 91-92 (noting the Department's limited authority relative to *United States v. Pennsylvania*); Select Committee to Investigate the January 6th Attack on the United States Capitol, *Hearing on the January 6th Investigation*, 117th Cong., 2d sess., (June 23, 2022), available at https://www.govinfo.gov/committee/house-january6th (summarizing the many times Department officials told the President about the limited authority to take actions related to the election).

239. Select Committee to Investigate the January 6th Attack on the United States Capitol, Transcribed Interview of Jeffrey Rosen, (Oct. 13, 2021), pp. 96-97.

240. Select Committee to Investigate the January 6th Attack on the United States Capitol, Transcribed Interview of Jeffrey Rosen, (Oct. 13, 2021), pp. 96-97.

241. Select Committee to Investigate the January 6th Attack on the United States Capitol, Transcribed Interview of Jeffrey Rosen, (Oct. 13, 2021), pp. 96-97.

242. Select Committee to Investigate the January 6th Attack on the United States Capitol, Transcribed Interview of Jeffrey Rosen, (Oct. 13, 2021), pp. 96-97.

243. Select Committee to Investigate the January 6th Attack on the United States Capitol, Transcribed Interview of Richard Peter Donoghue, (Oct. 1, 2021), p. 106.

244. Select Committee to Investigate the January 6th Attack on the United States Capitol, Transcribed Interview of Richard Peter Donoghue, (Oct. 1, 2021), p. 106.

245. Select Committee to Investigate the January 6th Attack on the United States Capitol, Transcribed Interview of Richard Peter Donoghue, (Oct. 1, 2021), p. 107.

246. Select Committee to Investigate the January 6th Attack on the United States Capitol, Transcribed Interview of Richard Peter Donoghue, (Oct. 1, 2021), p. 107.

247. Select Committee to Investigate the January 6th Attack on the United States Capitol, Transcribed Interview of Richard Peter Donoghue, (Oct. 1, 2021), pp. 107-08.

248. Select Committee to Investigate the January 6th Attack on the United States Capitol, Transcribed Interview of Richard Peter Donoghue, (Oct. 1, 2021), p. 108.

249. Select Committee to Investigate the January 6th Attack on the United States Capitol, Transcribed Interview of Richard Peter Donoghue, (Oct. 1, 2021), p. 108.

250. Select Committee to Investigate the January 6th Attack on the United States Capitol, Transcribed Interview of Richard Peter Donoghue, (Oct. 1, 2021), p. 108.

251. Select Committee to Investigate the January 6th Attack on the United States Capitol, Transcribed Interview of Richard Peter Donoghue, (Oct. 1, 2021), p. 108.

252. Select Committee to Investigate the January 6th Attack on the United States Capitol, Transcribed Interview of Richard Peter Donoghue, (Oct. 1, 2021), pp. 108-09.

253. Select Committee to Investigate the January 6th Attack on the United States Capitol, Transcribed Interview of Richard Peter Donoghue, (Oct. 1, 2021), pp. 108-09.

254. "Hand Audit of All Presidential Election Votes in Antrim County Confirms Previously Certified Results, Voting Machines Were Accurate," Michigan Secretary of State, (Dec. 17, 2020), available at https://www.michigan.gov/sos/resources/news/2020/12/17/hand-audit-of-all-presidential-election-votes-in-antrim-county-confirms-previously-certified-result.

255. Select Committee to Investigate the January 6th Attack on the United States Capitol, Transcribed Interview of Richard Peter Donoghue, (Oct. 1, 2021), p. 109.

256. Select Committee to Investigate the January 6th Attack on the United States Capitol, Transcribed Interview of Richard Peter Donoghue, (Oct. 1, 2021), p. 109.

257. Select Committee to Investigate the January 6th Attack on the United States Capitol, Transcribed Interview of Richard Peter Donoghue, (Oct. 1, 2021), p. 109.

258. Select Committee to Investigate the January 6th Attack on the United States Capitol, Transcribed Interview of Richard Peter Donoghue, (Oct. 1, 2021), pp. 109-10.

259. Select Committee to Investigate the January 6th Attack on the United States Capitol, Transcribed Interview of Richard Peter Donoghue, (Oct. 1, 2021), p. 110.

260. Select Committee to Investigate the January 6th Attack on the United States Capitol, Transcribed Interview of Richard Peter Donoghue, (Oct. 1, 2021), p. 110.

261. Select Committee to Investigate the January 6th Attack on the United States Capitol, Transcribed Interview of Richard Peter Donoghue, (Oct. 1, 2021), pp. 109-10.

262. Select Committee to Investigate the January 6th Attack on the United States Capitol, Transcribed Interview of Richard Peter Donoghue, (Oct. 1, 2021), pp. 109-11.

263. Select Committee to Investigate the January 6th Attack on the United States Capitol, *Hearing on the January 6th Investigation*, 117th Cong., 2d sess., (June 23, 2022), available at https://www.govinfo.gov/committee/house-january6th; Select Committee to Investigate the January 6th Attack on the United States Capitol, Transcribed Interview of Jeffrey Rosen, (Oct. 13, 2021), pp. 72-73.

264. Select Committee to Investigate the January 6th Attack on the United States Capitol, *Hearing on the January 6th Investigation*, 117th Cong., 2d sess., (June 23, 2022), available at https://www.govinfo.gov/committee/house-january6th; Select Committee to Investigate the January 6th Attack on the United States Capitol, Transcribed Interview of Jeffrey Rosen, (Oct. 13, 2021), pp. 72-73.

265. Select Committee to Investigate the January 6th Attack on the United States Capitol, Transcribed Interview of Richard Peter Donoghue, (Oct. 1, 2021), p. 114.

266. Select Committee to Investigate the January 6th Attack on the United States Capitol, Transcribed Interview of Richard Peter Donoghue, (Oct. 1, 2021), pp. 113-14.

267. Select Committee to Investigate the January 6th Attack on the United States Capitol, Transcribed Interview of Richard Peter Donoghue, (Oct. 1, 2021), p. 113.

268. Select Committee to Investigate the January 6th Attack on the United States Capitol, Transcribed Interview of Richard Peter Donoghue, (Oct. 1, 2021), p. 113.

269. Select Committee to Investigate the January 6th Attack on the United States Capitol, Transcribed Interview of Richard Peter Donoghue, (Oct. 1, 2021), pp. 111-15.

270. Rosen confirmed this during testimony before the Select Committee. "ADAM KINZINGER: So in that meeting did Mr. Clark say he would turn down the President's offer if you reversed your position and signed the letter? JEFFREY A. ROSEN: Yes." Select Committee to Investigate the January 6th Attack on the United States Capitol, *Hearing on the January 6th Investigation*, 117th Cong., 2d sess., (June 23, 2022), available at https://www.govinfo.gov/committee/house-january6th

271. Select Committee to Investigate the January 6th Attack on the United States Capitol, *Hearing on the January 6th Investigation*, 117th Cong., 2d sess., (June 23, 2022), available at https://www.govinfo.gov/committee/house-january6th.

272. Documents on file with the Select Committee to Investigate the January 6th Attack on the United States Capitol (Department of Justice Production), HCOR-Pre-CertificationEvents-06032021-000200 (January 2, 2021, email from Jeffrey Rosen to Richard Donoghue re: Two Urgent Action Items).

273. Brad Raffensperger, *Integrity Counts* (New York: Simon & Schuster, 2021), p. 191 (reproducing the call transcript); Amy Gardner and Paulina Firozi, "Here's the Full Transcript and Audio of the Call between Trump and Raffensperger," *Washington Post*, (Jan. 5, 2021), available at https://www.washingtonpost.com/politics/trump-raffensperger-call-transcript-georgia-vote/2021/01/03/2768e0cc-4ddd-11eb-83e3-322644d82356_story.html.

274. Select Committee to Investigate the January 6th Attack on the United States Capitol, Transcribed Interview of Richard Peter Donoghue, (Oct. 1, 2021), pp. 117-18; Select Committee to Investigate the January 6th Attack on the United States Capitol, *Hearing on the January 6th Investigation*, 117th Cong., 2d sess., (June 23, 2022), available at https://www.govinfo.gov/committee/house-january6th.

275. Select Committee to Investigate the January 6th Attack on the United States Capitol, Transcribed Interview of Richard Peter Donoghue, (Oct. 1, 2021), pp. 117-18; Select Committee to Investigate the January 6th Attack on the United States Capitol, *Hearing on the January 6th Investigation*, 117th Cong., 2d sess., (June 23, 2022), available at https://www.govinfo.gov/committee/house-january6th.

276. Select Committee to Investigate the January 6th Attack on the United States Capitol, Transcribed Interview of Richard Peter Donoghue, (Oct. 1, 2021), pp. 117-18; Select Committee to Investigate the January 6th Attack on the United States Capitol, *Hearing on the January 6th Investigation*, 117th Cong., 2d sess., (June 23, 2022), available at https://www.govinfo.gov/committee/house-january6th.

277. Select Committee to Investigate the January 6th Attack on the United States Capitol, Transcribed Interview of Richard Peter Donoghue, (Oct. 1, 2021), p. 118.

278. Documents on file with the Select Committee to Investigate the January 6th Attack on the United States Capitol (National Archives Production), 076P-R000007891_0001 - 076P-R000007891_0009 (January 3, 2021, White House Presidential Call Log).

279. Documents on file with the Select Committee to Investigate the January 6th Attack on the United States Capitol (National Archives Production), 076P-R000007891_0001 - 076P-R000007891_0009 (January 3, 2021, White House Presidential Call Log).

280. Documents on file with the Select Committee to Investigate the January 6th Attack on the United States Capitol (National Archives Production), 076P-R000007891_0001 – 076P-R000007891_0009 (January 3, 2021, White House Presidential Call Log).

281. Select Committee to Investigate the January 6th Attack on the United States Capitol, *Hearing on the January 6th Investigation*, 117th Cong., 2d sess., (June 23, 2022), available at https://www.govinfo.gov/committee/house-january6th.

282. Select Committee to Investigate the January 6th Attack on the United States Capitol, *Hearing on the January 6th Investigation*, 117th Cong., 2d sess., (June 23, 2022), available at https://www.govinfo.gov/committee/house-january6th.

283. Select Committee to Investigate the January 6th Attack on the United States Capitol, Transcribed Interview of Richard Peter Donoghue, (Oct. 1, 2021), p. 118; Select Committee to Investigate the January 6th Attack on the United States Capitol, *Hearing on the January 6th Investigation*, 117th Cong., 2d sess., (June 23, 2022), available at https://www.govinfo.gov/committee/house-january6th.

284. Select Committee to Investigate the January 6th Attack on the United States Capitol, *Hearing on the January 6th Investigation*, 117th Cong., 2d sess., (June 23, 2022), available at https://www.govinfo.gov/committee/house-january6th.

285. Select Committee to Investigate the January 6th Attack on the United States Capitol, *Hearing on the January 6th Investigation*, 117th Cong., 2d sess., (June 23, 2022), available at https://www.govinfo.gov/committee/house-january6th.

286. Select Committee to Investigate the January 6th Attack on the United States Capitol, *Hearing on the January 6th Investigation*, 117th Cong., 2d sess., (June 23, 2022), available at https://www.govinfo.gov/committee/house-january6th ("And so it was unanimous; everyone was going to resign if Jeff Rosen was removed from the seat," Donoghue explained). The only exception was John Demers, the Assistant Attorney General for the National Security Division. Donohue encouraged Demers to stay on because he didn't want to further jeopardize national security. *See* Select Committee to Investigate the January 6th Attack on the United States Capitol, Transcribed Interview of Richard Peter Donoghue, (Oct. 1, 2021), pp. 119-20.

287. Documents on file with the Select Committee to Investigate the January 6th Attack on the United States Capitol (Department of Justice Production), HCOR-Pre-CertificationEvents-07262021-000729 (January 3, 2021, Resignation Letter by Patrick Hovakimian).

288. Select Committee to Investigate the January 6th Attack on the United States Capitol, Transcribed Interview of Richard Peter Donoghue, (Oct. 1, 2021), pp. 121-22; Select Committee to Investigate the January 6th Attack on the United States Capitol, *Hearing on the January 6th Investigation*, 117th Cong., 2d sess., (June 23, 2022), available at https://www.govinfo.gov/committee/house-january6th.

289. Select Committee to Investigate the January 6th Attack on the United States Capitol, Transcribed Interview of Richard Peter Donoghue, (Oct. 1, 2021), p. 122.

290. Select Committee to Investigate the January 6th Attack on the United States Capitol, Transcribed Interview of Richard Peter Donoghue, (Oct. 1, 2021), p. 127. "It was definitely a consensus. We were all on the same page except for Jeff Clark," Donoghue said. *Id.* The Oval Office meeting attendees include Jeffrey Rosen, Richard Donoghue, Pat Cipollone, Pat Philbin, Eric Herschmann, Steve Engel, Jeff Clark and President Trump. *See id.*, at 123.

291. Select Committee to Investigate the January 6th Attack on the United States Capitol, Transcribed Interview of Richard Peter Donoghue, (Oct. 1, 2021), p. 122.

292. Select Committee to Investigate the January 6th Attack on the United States Capitol, Transcribed Interview of Richard Peter Donoghue, (Oct. 1, 2021), p. 124.

293. Select Committee to Investigate the January 6th Attack on the United States Capitol, Transcribed Interview of Richard Peter Donoghue, (Oct. 1, 2021), p. 124.

294. Select Committee to Investigate the January 6th Attack on the United States Capitol, Transcribed Interview of Richard Peter Donoghue, (Oct. 1, 2021), pp. 124-25.

295. Select Committee to Investigate the January 6th Attack on the United States Capitol, Transcribed Interview of Richard Peter Donoghue, (Oct. 1, 2021), p. 125.

296. Select Committee to Investigate the January 6th Attack on the United States Capitol, Transcribed Interview of Richard Peter Donoghue, (Oct. 1, 2021), p. 125.

297. Select Committee to Investigate the January 6th Attack on the United States Capitol, Transcribed Interview of Richard Peter Donoghue, (Oct. 1, 2021), p. 125.

298. Select Committee to Investigate the January 6th Attack on the United States Capitol, Transcribed Interview of Richard Peter Donoghue, (Oct. 1, 2021), p. 125.

299. Select Committee to Investigate the January 6th Attack on the United States Capitol, Transcribed Interview of Richard Peter Donoghue, (Oct. 1, 2021), p. 125.

300. Select Committee to Investigate the January 6th Attack on the United States Capitol, Transcribed Interview of Richard Peter Donoghue, (Oct. 1, 2021), p. 125.

301. Select Committee to Investigate the January 6th Attack on the United States Capitol, Transcribed Interview of Richard Peter Donoghue, (Oct. 1, 2021), p. 125.

302. Select Committee to Investigate the January 6th Attack on the United States Capitol, Transcribed Interview of Richard Peter Donoghue, (Oct. 1, 2021), p. 126.

303. Select Committee to Investigate the January 6th Attack on the United States Capitol, Transcribed Interview of Richard Peter Donoghue, (Oct. 1, 2021), pp. 126-27.

304. Select Committee to Investigate the January 6th Attack on the United States Capitol, Transcribed Interview of Richard Peter Donoghue, (Oct. 1, 2021), p. 126.

305. Select Committee to Investigate the January 6th Attack on the United States Capitol, Transcribed Interview of Richard Peter Donoghue, (Oct. 1, 2021), p. 126.

306. Select Committee to Investigate the January 6th Attack on the United States Capitol, Transcribed Interview of Richard Peter Donoghue, (Oct. 1, 2021), p. 126.

307. Select Committee to Investigate the January 6th Attack on the United States Capitol, Transcribed Interview of Richard Peter Donoghue, (Oct. 1, 2021), p. 133.

308. Select Committee to Investigate the January 6th Attack on the United States Capitol, Transcribed Interview of Richard Peter Donoghue, (Oct. 1, 2021), pp. 131-32.

309. Select Committee to Investigate the January 6th Attack on the United States Capitol, Transcribed Interview of Richard Peter Donoghue, (Oct. 1, 2021), p. 132.

310. Select Committee to Investigate the January 6th Attack on the United States Capitol, Transcribed Interview of Richard Peter Donoghue, (Oct. 1, 2021), p. 132.

311. Select Committee to Investigate the January 6th Attack on the United States Capitol, Transcribed Interview of Richard Peter Donoghue, (Oct. 1, 2021), pp. 129-31.

312. Select Committee to Investigate the January 6th Attack on the United States Capitol, Transcribed Interview of Byung Jin Pak, (May 19, 2022), pp. 11-19.

313. Select Committee to Investigate the January 6th Attack on the United States Capitol, Transcribed Interview of Richard Peter Donoghue, (Oct. 1, 2021), p. 129.

314. Select Committee to Investigate the January 6th Attack on the United States Capitol, Transcribed Interview of Richard Peter Donoghue, (Oct. 1, 2021), p. 129.

315. Select Committee to Investigate the January 6th Attack on the United States Capitol, Transcribed Interview of Richard Peter Donoghue, (Oct. 1, 2021), p. 129.

316. Select Committee to Investigate the January 6th Attack on the United States Capitol, Transcribed Interview of Richard Peter Donoghue, (Oct. 1, 2021), p. 129.

317. Select Committee to Investigate the January 6th Attack on the United States Capitol, Transcribed Interview of Richard Peter Donoghue, (Oct. 1, 2021), p. 129.

318. Select Committee to Investigate the January 6th Attack on the United States Capitol, Transcribed Interview of Richard Peter Donoghue, (Oct. 1, 2021), p. 129-30.

319. Select Committee to Investigate the January 6th Attack on the United States Capitol, Transcribed Interview of Richard Peter Donoghue, (Oct. 1, 2021), pp. 134-35.

320. Select Committee to Investigate the January 6th Attack on the United States Capitol, Transcribed Interview of Richard Peter Donoghue, (Oct. 1, 2021), p. 130.

321. Select Committee to Investigate the January 6th Attack on the United States Capitol, Transcribed Interview of Richard Peter Donoghue, (Oct. 1, 2021), p. 130.

322. Select Committee to Investigate the January 6th Attack on the United States Capitol, Transcribed Interview of Richard Peter Donoghue, (Oct. 1, 2021), pp. 135-36.

323. Select Committee to Investigate the January 6th Attack on the United States Capitol, Transcribed Interview of Richard Peter Donoghue, (Oct. 1, 2021), pp. 133-34.

324. Select Committee to Investigate the January 6th Attack on the United States Capitol, Transcribed Interview of Richard Peter Donoghue, (Oct. 1, 2021), pp. 133-34.

325. Select Committee to Investigate the January 6th Attack on the United States Capitol, Transcribed Interview of Richard Peter Donoghue, (Oct. 1, 2021), p. 134.

326. Select Committee to Investigate the January 6th Attack on the United States Capitol, Transcribed Interview of Richard Peter Donoghue, (Oct. 1, 2021), pp. 134-37.

327. Select Committee to Investigate the January 6th Attack on the United States Capitol, Transcribed Interview of William Barr, (June 2, 2022), p. 66.

328. Select Committee to Investigate the January 6th Attack on the United States Capitol, *Hearing on the January 6th Investigation*, 117th Cong., 2d sess., (June 23, 2022), available at https://www.govinfo.gov/committee/house-january6th.

329. Select Committee to Investigate the January 6th Attack on the United States Capitol, Transcribed Interview of Jeffrey Rosen, (Oct. 13, 2021), pp. 8-9.

5

"A COUP IN SEARCH OF A LEGAL THEORY"

On the morning of January 6, 2021, Vice President Michael R. Pence gathered his staff to pray. Vice President Pence and his closest advisors knew the day ahead "would be a challenging one." [1] They asked God for "guidance and wisdom" in the hours to come. [2] No Republican had been more loyal to President Donald J. Trump throughout his turbulent presidency than Vice President Pence. The Vice President rarely, if ever, criticized his boss. But as January 6th approached, President Trump turned on his own Vice President.

President Trump was desperate. As described in the previous chapters, the President was searching for a way to stay in power. He had lost the election to former Vice President Biden. He had run out of legal options to overturn the election weeks earlier, when his lawyers lost nearly every court challenge they filed.

The President pursued other means as well. President Trump and his lawyers tried to convince State and local officials to overturn the election, but they met resistance. Those same officials would not break the law or violate their oath to the Constitution. President Trump and his associates tried to convince State legislatures to replace the legitimate electors won by former Vice President Biden with Trump electors. The Trump Campaign even convened their own fake electors who submitted false electoral votes to Washington. But those efforts failed, too.

President Trump also attempted to use the Department of Justice (DOJ) for his own corrupt political purposes. President Trump offered the job of Acting Attorney General to a loyalist. He wanted this same DOJ official, Jeffrey Clark, to send a letter to several States suggesting that they should certify the fake electors convened by the Trump Campaign. President Trump's effort to subvert the DOJ came to a head on January 3rd, when the Department's senior personnel and lawyers in the White House Counsel's Office threatened mass resignations if Clark was installed.

At that point, theories about a role the Vice President could play at the joint session had been circulating in certain corners of the internet and among Trump-supporting attorneys.[3] President Trump focused his attention on the man who had loyally served by his side for four years.

On January 4, 2021, President Trump summoned Vice President Pence to a meeting in the Oval Office with John Eastman, a law professor representing President Trump in litigation challenging the election result. Eastman argued, on President Trump's behalf, that the Vice President could take matters into his own hands during the joint session on January 6th. Eastman offered Vice President Pence two options. First, the Vice President could unilaterally reject the certified electors from several States won by former Vice President Biden, thereby handing the presidency to President Trump. Or, according to Eastman, Vice President Pence could delay the joint session to give State legislatures the opportunity to certify new electors loyal to the President. Eastman admitted, in front of the president, that both options violated the Electoral Count Act of 1887, the statute that sets forth the process for counting and disputing electoral votes during the joint session.[4] Eastman admitted as much in a subsequent conversation with the Vice President's staff as well.[5]

Therefore, President Trump knew, or should have known, that this scheme was illegal—in fact, it violated the Electoral Count Act and the U.S. Constitution. President Trump repeatedly demanded that Vice President Pence go through with it anyway.

Vice President Pence rejected President Trump's demands "many times" on January 4th and in the days that followed.[6] Vice President Pence correctly pointed out that he had no power to take any action other than counting the certified electoral votes. America's founders could not possibly have contemplated a scenario in which the Vice President could unilaterally reject electoral votes and decide the outcome of a Presidential election. However, instead of backing down, President Trump ratcheted up the pressure even further, relentlessly harassing Vice President Pence both in public and in private.

President Trump used his bully pulpit, at rallies and on Twitter, to lie to his supporters. President Trump told them that Vice President Pence had the power to deliver another 4 years in the White House. It was not true. President Trump's campaign of coercion became so intense that Marc Short, Vice President Pence's Chief of Staff, alerted the head of the Vice President's Secret Service detail to the impending danger. On January 5th, Short warned that as the "disagreements" between President Trump and Vice President Pence "became more public, that the president would lash out in some way." [7]

Indeed, President Trump did. And those around him recognized that his lashing out at the Vice President could have disastrous consequences. On the morning of January 6th, an agent in the Secret Service's intelligence division was alerted to online chatter "regarding the VP being a dead man walking if he doesn't do the right thing." [8] A few minutes later, another agent made a comment that turned out to be an ominous prediction: "I saw several other alerts saying they will storm the [C]apitol if he [the Vice President] doesn't do the right thing etc." [9]

During his speech at the Ellipse on January 6th, President Trump repeatedly pointed his finger at Vice President Pence. President Trump insisted that "if Mike Pence does the right thing, we win the election." [10] President Trump added: "And Mike Pence is going to have to come through for us, and if he doesn't, that will be a, a sad day for our country because you're sworn to uphold our Constitution." [11]

President Trump's scheme required Vice President Pence to *break* his oath to the Constitution, not uphold it. By the time President Trump spoke at the Ellipse, he also knew that Vice President Pence had no intention of overturning the election.

President Trump then sent a mob to the U.S. Capitol. He did so even after being informed by the Secret Service that people in the crowd possessed weapons. He wanted his supporters to intimidate Vice President Pence and any other Republican who refused his demands. The President told the crowd assembled before him to march down Pennsylvania Avenue, to "our Republicans, the weak ones" at the U.S. Capitol, "to try and give them the kind of pride and boldness that they need to take back our country." [12]

The mob overran the U.S. Capitol in short order. At 2:24 p.m., while the attack was well underway, President Trump tweeted:

> *Mike Pence didn't have the courage to do what should have been done to protect our Country and our Constitution, giving States a chance to certify a corrected set of facts, not the fraudulent or inaccurate ones which they were asked to previously certify. USA demands the truth!* [13]

Again, the opposite was true. Vice President Pence showed courage on January 6th. The Vice President refused to be intimidated by President Trump's mob, even as chants of "Hang Mike Pence!" echoed throughout the halls of the U.S. Capitol and a makeshift gallows was constructed on the Capitol grounds. [14]

It is no mystery why the mob turned on Vice President Pence. President Trump told his supporters that the election was stolen, and that Vice President Pence had the power, but lacked the courage, to fix it. None of this was true.

President Trump and Vice President Pence have both reflected on the events of January 6th in the months since then. Vice President Pence has described President Trump's demands as "un-American."[15] President Trump has since insisted that Vice President Pence "could have overturned the Election!"[16] Asked about the calls to hang the Vice President, President Trump said it was "common sense."[17]

In early 2022, U.S. District Judge David Carter evaluated the Trump-Eastman scheme to pressure the Vice President. Judge Carter described it as "a campaign to overturn a democratic election, an action unprecedented in American history."[18] It was "a coup in search of a legal theory," Judge Carter found, that likely violated at least two Federal laws.[19] The Trump-Eastman scheme was not a feature of the U.S. Constitution, as President Trump told his supporters. Instead, it "would have permanently ended the peaceful transition of power, undermining American democracy and the Constitution."[20]

And it all began because President Trump refused to accept the result of the election, expressed through the votes of 81 million Americans.

5.1 PRESIDENT TRUMP AND HIS ALLIES EMBARK ON A DESPERATE GAMBIT TO BLOCK CERTIFICATION OF THE 2020 PRESIDENTIAL ELECTION.

THE INTELLECTUAL FRAMEWORK FOR THE THEORY THAT THE VICE PRESIDENT COULD CHANGE THE OUTCOME OF THE ELECTION AT THE JOINT SESSION EMERGED FROM DISCUSSIONS AMONG THE LAWYERS WORKING WITH THE TRUMP CAMPAIGN AFTER THE 2020 ELECTION.

When the electoral college met to cast votes for the certified winner in each State on December 14, 2020, any possibility of President Trump reversing his defeat came to an end. The contest was decided well before then, but December 14th marked what should have been the formal end of the Trump campaign. Former Vice President Biden had won the election and his victory was cemented by the States' electoral votes. Instead of bowing to this reality, some pro-Trump lawyers had already begun scheming ways to deny the inevitable. Over the course of the post-election period, as their other plans each failed, the importance of January 6th and the need to pressure Vice President Pence increased. These same lawyers concluded that the Vice President could help President Trump subvert the election on January 6th, but they would need Vice President Pence to set aside history and the law to do so. They'd need him to violate the Electoral Count Act of 1887 ("the ECA"). The ECA had governed the joint session for 130 years, but it was an inconvenient barrier for President Trump's plan to stay in office.

KENNETH CHESEBRO ARTICULATED A "PRESIDENT OF THE SENATE" STRATEGY IN EARLY DECEMBER, WHEN THE TRUMP CAMPAIGN WAS CONVENING "ALTERNATE" ELECTORS IN KEY STATES PRESIDENT TRUMP LOST.

On December 13, 2020, Kenneth Chesebro, a pro-Trump lawyer, sent a memo to Rudolph Giuliani, the President's lead outside counsel, upon request from Trump Campaign official Boris Epshteyn.[21] Chesebro laid out a "'President of the Senate' strategy," arguing that the "President of the Senate" ("he, and he alone") is charged with "making judgments about what to do if there are conflicting votes."[22] Chesebro argued that when the joint session met on January 6th, the President of the Senate should not count Arizona's electoral college votes for former Vice President Biden, "[b]ecause there are two slates of votes."[23] Of course, there were not two legitimate "slates of votes" from Arizona. There were the official electors, certified by the State, and a group of fake electors convened by the Trump campaign.

Chesebro's memo set President Trump's pressure campaign on a course to target the Vice President on January 6.[24] Judge Carter found that the "draft memo pushed a strategy that knowingly violated the Electoral Count Act" and "is both intimately related to and clearly advanced the plan to obstruct the Joint Session of Congress on January 6, 2021."[25] That plan was also advanced by John Eastman.[26]

ON DECEMBER 23, JOHN EASTMAN DRAFTED THE FIRST OF HIS TWO "JANUARY 6TH SCENARIO" MEMOS, ARTICULATING THE ARGUMENT THAT UNDER THE CONSTITUTION THE VICE PRESIDENT IS THE "ULTIMATE ARBITER."

On December 23, 2020, Eastman wrote a two-page memo summarizing ways to ensure that "President Trump is re-elected."[27] Eastman suggested that Vice President Pence could refuse to count the electoral college votes from seven States: Arizona, Georgia, Michigan, Nevada, New Mexico, Pennsylvania, and Wisconsin. According to Eastman, Vice President Pence could simply reject these States' electoral college votes. At that point, President Trump would have 232 electoral college votes compared to former Vice President Biden's 222. This was sufficient, in Eastman's view, to guarantee President Trump's victory, because he would have a majority of the electoral college votes. "Pence then gavels President Trump as re-elected," Eastman wrote.

Eastman considered the possibility that Democrats in Congress would object, stating the plain truth that 270 electoral college votes are necessary to win. In that event, according to Eastman, the election could be sent to the House of Representatives.[28] The Republican-majority of delegations in the House would then re-elect Trump as president. Eastman concluded: "The main thing here is that Pence should do this without asking for permission—either from a vote of the joint session or from the Court.... The fact is that the Constitution assigns this power to the Vice President as the ultimate arbiter. We should take all of our actions with that in mind." [29]

From the start, President Trump was looped in on Eastman's proposal. The same day Eastman started preparing the memo, he sent an email to President Trump's assistant Molly Michael, at 1:32 p.m.: "Is the President available for a very quick call today at some point? Just want to update him on our overall strategic thinking." [30] Only five minutes later, Eastman received a call from the White House switchboard; according to his phone records, the conversation lasted for almost 23 minutes.[31]

EASTMAN CHANGED HIS EVALUATION OF THE 12TH AMENDMENT, AND THE ROLE OF THE VICE PRESIDENT, AFTER PRESIDENT TRUMP LOST THE ELECTION.

In Eastman's theory, which was the foundation of President Trump's January 6th plot, the Vice President of the United States is the "ultimate arbiter" and could unilaterally decide the victor of the 2020 Presidential election.[32] However, just before the 2020 presidential election, Eastman had acknowledged in writing that the Vice President had no such expansive power.

In the course of a lengthy exchange of ideas and emails throughout the pre- and post-election period with an individual named Bruce Colbert, Eastman provided comments on a letter Colbert was drafting to President Trump.[33] The draft letter purported to provide recommendations of "crucial legal actions" for the Trump Campaign to take "to help secure your election victory as President of the United States." [34] One of the draft letter's recommendations was that "the President of the Senate decides authoritatively what 'certificates' from the states to 'open.'" In response, Eastman wrote on October 17, 2020, "I don't agree with this" and continued, "[t]he 12th Amendment only says that the President of the Senate opens the ballots in the joint session and then, in the passive voice, that the votes shall then be counted. 3 USC § 12 says merely that he is the presiding officer, and then it spells out specific procedures, presumptions, and default rules for which slates will be counted. *Nowhere does it suggest that the President of the Senate gets to make the determination on his own.* § 15 doesn't, either." [35]

By the first week of December, Eastman's correspondence with this same individual illustrates that he was open to advocating for the very point he had rejected before the election—that is, that "the 12th Amendment confers dispositive authority on the President of the Senate to decide which slate to count." [36] And on December 5, 2020, Eastman wrote to Colbert, "I have spoken directly with folks at the top of the chain of command on this. They are now aware of the issues." [37]

The emails also signaled another idea that Eastman would continue to repeat in the coming weeks: that the Vice President could act without getting permission from a court. Specifically, he argued that they could take the position that the Vice President's authority was a "non-justiciable political question"—in other words, that Vice President Pence could just act, and no court would have jurisdiction to rule on the issue.[38] As Eastman's emails later in the month make clear, he thought there was an important reason to keep this issue out of the courts—they would rule that the theory was unlawful.

EASTMAN'S "JANUARY 6 SCENARIO" CLEARLY REQUIRED THE VICE PRESIDENT TO VIOLATE THE ELECTORAL COUNT ACT, THE FEDERAL LAW GOVERNING THE CERTIFICATION OF PRESIDENTIAL ELECTIONS.

There are other parts of Eastman's two-page December 23rd memo worthy of attention. Eastman wrote that Vice President Pence could recuse himself from presiding over the joint session of Congress on January 6th. In that event, the session would be overseen by the Senate President *Pro Tempore*, Senator Charles Grassley. Eastman was clearly arguing that Vice President Pence (or Senator Grassley) *should violate the Electoral Count Act.* "When he gets to Arizona, he announces that he has multiple slates of electors, and so is going to defer decision on that until finishing the other States," Eastman wrote.[39] "This would be the first break with the procedure set out in the Act."[40] This "break" with "procedure" that Eastman's memo was openly advocating for was in other words the Vice President breaking the law. When Chesebro read Eastman's memo, he commented favorably, declaring it "[r]eally awesome."[41]

At this point, Eastman continued, Congress would likely follow the "process" set forth in the Electoral Count Act, and "the two houses [would] break into their separate chambers" for debate.[42] But Eastman advised "we should not allow the Electoral Count Act constraint on debate to control" and the Trump team "should demand normal rules (which includes the filibuster)."[43] Eastman thought this would create a "stalemate," giving "the state legislatures more time to weigh in to formally support the alternate slate of electors, if they had not already done so."[44] As discussed previously in this report, at the time he drafted this memo—and throughout the post-election period—Eastman, Giuliani, President Trump and others were simultaneously working to replace certified electors for former Vice President Biden in certain States. Eastman, Giuliani, and President Trump all pressured State legislators to name their own separate electors or to certify the campaign's fake electors.

EASTMAN'S THEORY WAS—IN THE WORDS OF PRESIDENT TRUMP'S SENIOR WHITE HOUSE AND CAMPAIGN OFFICIALS—"INSANE," "CRAZY," "NUTTY" AND IT WOULD NEVER PRACTICALLY WORK.

Eric Herschmann, an attorney working for President Trump in the White House, met with Eastman to discuss his memo. Herschmann thought Eastman's plan was "crazy." Herschmann summarized the conversation to the Select Committee:

> And I said to him, hold on a second, I want to understand what you're saying. You're saying you believe the Vice President, acting as President of the Senate, can be the sole decisionmaker as to, under your theory, who becomes the next President of the United States? And he said, yes. And I said, are you out of your F'ing mind, right? And that was pretty blunt. I said, you're completely crazy. You're going to turn around and tell 78 plus million people in this country that your theory is, this is how you're going to invalidate their votes because you think the election was stolen? I said, they're not going to tolerate that. I said, you're going to cause riots in the streets. And he said words to the effect of there's been violence in this history of our country to protect the democracy or to protect the [R]epublic.[45]

As recounted by Herschmann, Eastman was shockingly unconcerned with the prospect of violence should Vice President Pence follow his and President Trump's recommended course.

Herschmann asked a straightforward question—if the States wanted to recertify their electors, then why weren't they doing it themselves? "Why aren't they already coming into session and saying, we want to change the [S]tates, and why do you need the VP to go down this path[?]"[46] Eastman had no response. In addition to being "crazy," Herschmann "didn't think there was any chance in the world" that Eastman's plan "could work."[47]

Herschmann pressed Eastman further, asking if he had "any precedent at all for the VP or anyone acting in the capacity as the President of the Senate declaring some statute invalid."[48] Eastman replied "no," but argued that "these are unprecedented times."[49] Herschmann was unimpressed, calling this a "ridiculous" answer.[50]

White House Counsel Pasquale Anthony "Pat" Cipollone thought the Eastman plan was "nutty."[51] Trump Campaign official Jason Miller testified that the Campaign's General Counsel, Matt Morgan, and Deputy Campaign Manager, Justin Clark, thought Eastman was "crazy," understood that there was "no validity to [his theory] in any way, shape, or form," and shared their views with "anyone who would listen."[52]

THE VICE PRESIDENT'S CONCLUSION THAT HE DID NOT HAVE THE ABILITY TO AFFECT THE OUTCOME OF THE ELECTION

Vice President Pence's counsel, Greg Jacob, was simultaneously researching the role of the Vice President during the joint session. The Office of the Vice President produced a preliminary staff memo on the subject on October 26, 2020.[53] Jacob then discussed the matter with Marc Short on election day or the day before.

This wasn't the first time Jacob would be required to write a memo about the Vice President's role in the electoral process. Before the election, Short explained to him that some in the White House were encouraging President Trump to prematurely declare victory on election night.[54] Of course, that is exactly what President Trump did. Jacob and Short wanted to avoid the Vice President getting drawn in to any such declarations, and Jacob pointed to his role in presiding over the counting of the electoral votes on January 6th as a reason not to. Jacob sent a memo to Short on election day reflecting this advice.[55]

Then, on December 7, 2020, the Lincoln Project aired a provocative ad taunting President Trump, saying that Vice President Pence "Will Put the Nail in Your Political Coffin" during the joint session on January 6th.[56] This prompted a discussion between Jacob and Vice President Pence.[57] Jacob authored another memo, dated December 8, 2020.[58] Jacob continued researching the Vice President's role during the joint session into early January. Jacob told the Select Committee that his view of the matter was not fully formed until then.[59]

Jacob did extensive research on and historical analysis of both the Electoral Count Act of 1887 and the 12th Amendment to the U.S. Constitution.[60] The 12th Amendment contains a single relevant line: "The President of the Senate shall, in the Presence of the Senate and House of Representatives, open all the Certificates, and the Votes shall then be counted." [61] Though Jacob concluded that this line was "inartfully drafted," it said nothing about resolving disputes over electoral votes.[62]

Jacob concluded that the Vice President must adhere to the Electoral Count Act.[63] The ECA has been followed for 130 years and "every single time that there has been any objection to electors, it has been resolved in accordance with the Electoral Count Act procedures," Jacob testified.[64] After reviewing the history and relevant cases, Jacob found that "[t]here is no justifiable basis to conclude that the Vice President has that kind of authority" to affect the outcome of the presidential election.[65] Jacob stated that his "review of text, history, and, frankly, just common sense" all confirmed that the Vice President had no such power.[66]

Greg Jacob testifies before the Select Committee on June 16, 2022.
Photo by House Creative Services

PRESIDENT TRUMP'S ALLIES FILED LAWSUITS SEEKING A COURT ORDER DIRECTING VICE PRESIDENT PENCE NOT TO COUNT CERTAIN ELECTORAL VOTES.

One of President Trump's congressional allies, Representative Louie Gohmert (R–TX), pushed a version of Eastman's theory in the courts. On December 27, 2020, Representative Gohmert and several of the Trump Campaign's fake electors for the State of Arizona (including Republican Party Chair Kelli Ward) filed suit against Vice President Pence in the U.S. District Court for the Eastern District of Texas.[67] As Ward explained to Marc Short in a phone call the day the suit was filed, President Trump was aware of the lawsuit and had signed off on it: "We wouldn't have done that without the president telling us it was okay," she told him.[68]

In the suit, the Plaintiffs alleged that there were "competing slates" of electors from five States.[69] They asked the court to rule that portions of the Electoral Count Act of 1887 were unconstitutional and that "the Twelfth Amendment contains the exclusive dispute resolution mechanisms" for determining an objection raised by a Member of Congress to the electors submitted by any State.[70] Essentially, Representative Gohmert was asking the court to tell Vice President Pence that he was prohibited from following the procedures set forth in the Electoral Count Act. Much like Eastman's

Representative Louie Gohmert outside the Capitol on March 17, 2021.
(Photo by Chip Somodevilla/Getty Images)

theory, the *Gohmert* plaintiffs asserted that the Vice President has the "exclusive authority and sole discretion" to determine which electoral votes to count.[71]

Although the *Gohmert* suit was premised on the same theory Eastman advocated, Eastman did not agree with the decision to file suit. Eastman argued that filing a suit against the Vice President had "close[ ] to zero" chance of succeeding, and there was a "very high" risk that the court would issue an opinion stating that "Pence has no authority to reject the Biden-certified ballots."[72] As highlighted by Judge Carter, Eastman's theory was that Vice President Pence should take this action "without asking for permission" from Congress or the courts.[73] Another attorney, Bill Olson, stated that getting a judicial determination "that Pence is constrained by [the Electoral Count Act]" could "completely tank the January 6 strategy."[74] Those who were advocating to press on with the Eastman scheme did not want to bring it before a Federal judge because of the high risk that a court's determination that the scheme was illegal would stop the plan to overturn the election dead in its tracks.

Eastman himself pushed this cavalier attitude towards the courts and compliance with the law during a call with Arizona House Speaker Rusty

John McEntee, February 28, 2020.

(Photo by Alex Wong/Getty Images)

Bowers on January 4th. During this call, just two days before the joint session, Eastman pressed Speaker Bowers to bring the Arizona House into session to certify Trump electors or decertify the Biden electors.[75] Speaker Bowers responded as he had previously responded to similar entreaties by Giuliani and President Trump: by explaining that doing so would require him to violate his oaths to the U.S. and Arizona Constitutions and that he "wasn't going to take such an action."[76] Undeterred, Eastman still pushed Speaker Bowers to "just do it and let the courts sort it through."[77]

Ultimately, Representative Gohmert's legal gambit failed; a U.S. district judge dismissed the case quickly.[78] The judge's ruling was upheld by the Supreme Court, which rejected Gohmert's appeal without further consideration.[79]

**OTHER INDIVIDUALS ADVISING PRESIDENT TRUMP AND HIS CAMPAIGN ALSO ADVO-
CATED FOR A ROLE FOR THE VICE PRESIDENT AT THE JOINT SESSION.**
Other individuals inside and outside the White House also advanced ver-
sions of the theory that the Vice President had agency in the joint session.
The issue of Vice President Pence's role came up during a December meet-
ing in the Oval Office. Either President Trump or his chief of staff, Mark
Meadows, tasked John McEntee, the director of the Presidential Personnel
Office, with researching the matter further.[80] Though McEntee was one of
President Trump's close advisors, he was not a lawyer and had no relevant
experience. Yet, he wrote a one-page memo claiming that "the VP has sub-
stantial discretion to address issues with the electoral process." [81]

This wasn't the only one-page analysis drafted by McEntee before
January 6th.[82] He later proposed a "middle path" in which he envisioned
the Vice President accepting *only half* the electoral votes from six disputed
States (specifically, Wisconsin, Michigan, Pennsylvania, Georgia, Arizona
and Nevada).[83] McEntee portrayed this as a way to avoid "disenfranchis-
[ing]" States while still achieving the desired result: delivering a second
term to President Trump. McEntee conveyed this memo to the President
with a cover note reading, "This is probably our only realistic option
because it would give Pence an out." [84] McEntee told the Select Committee
that this judgment was based on his assessment that "it was, like, pretty
obvious [the Vice President] wasn't going to just reject...the electors or
whatever was being asked of him at that time." [85]

Another advocate of a plan for the Vice President to play a role in the
joint session was Jenna Ellis, a lawyer working for the Trump Campaign.
She argued in two memos that Vice President Pence had the power to delay
the counting of certified electoral votes. In the first memo, addressed to
President Trump and dated December 31, 2020, Ellis advised that Vice
President Pence should "not open any of the votes" from six States that
"currently have electoral delegates in dispute." [86] Ellis asserted that this
"dispute" provided "sufficient rational and legal basis to question whether
the [S]tate law and Constitution was followed." Ellis proposed a delay of ten
days, as the Vice President and Congress awaited a "response from the
[S]tate legislatures, which would then need to meet in an emergency electoral session." If any of the State legislatures "fails to provide a timely
response, no electoral votes can be opened and counted from that [S]tate."
Ellis claimed that Vice President Pence would not be "exercising discretion
nor establishing new precedent," but instead "simply asking for clarifica-
tion from the constitutionally appointed authority." [87]

Ellis sent the substance of this memorandum in an email to Fox News
host Jeanine Pirro on January 1, 2021, under the subject line "Constitutional

Jenna Ellis on December 2, 2020 in Lansing, Michigan.

(Photo by Rey Del Rio/Getty Images)

option."[88] And, on January 4, 2021, she sent the same substance to Fox News contributor John Solomon under the subject line "Pence option."[89]

Ellis addressed a second memo, dated January 5, 2021, to Jay Sekulow, an outside attorney who represented President Trump during his first impeachment proceedings and in other litigation.[90] Ellis again claimed that Vice President Pence had the power to delay the certification of the vote. Ellis recommended that the Vice President should, when he arrived at the first contested State (Arizona), "simply stop the count" on the basis that the States had not made a "final determination of ascertainment of electors." "The [S]tates would therefore have to act."[91]

Sekulow clearly disagreed. "Some have speculated that the Vice President could simply say, 'I'm not going to accept these electors,' that he has the authority to do that under the Constitution," Sekulow said during an episode of his radio show.[92] "I actually don't think that's what the Constitution has in mind." Sekulow added that the Vice President serves a merely "ministerial, procedural function."[93]

In addition, Herschmann discussed this memo with Sekulow. They agreed that Ellis did not have the "qualifications or the experience to be giving advice on this" or to be "litigating the challenges" that President

Trump's team was filing in court.[94] Herschmann did not think that Sekulow shared the memo with the President.[95]

5.2 PRESIDENT TRUMP AND HIS ALLIES EXERT INTENSE PUBLIC AND PRIVATE PRESSURE ON THE VICE PRESIDENT IN ADVANCE OF THE JOINT SESSION OF CONGRESS ON JANUARY 6TH

JANUARY 2, 2021: THE VICE PRESIDENT MEETS WITH HIS ADVISORS, CEMENTING HIS INTENDED PATH FOR THE JOINT SESSION.

On January 2, 2021, Vice President Pence met with his counsel Greg Jacob, Chief of Staff Marc Short, and Matt Morgan to discuss the joint session.[96] Morgan was the Trump Campaign's General Counsel and had previously served as counsel to Vice President Pence. At this point, the Vice President already had a clear understanding of what his role would be in the electoral count.[97] Vice President Pence was concerned that most people did not understand how the certification of the electoral votes worked. So Jacob began drafting a statement for the Vice President to issue on January 6th. The statement was intended to provide a "civic education" on the joint session, explaining to the American people his actions, including why the Vice President "didn't have the authorities that others had suggested that he might."[98]

The men discussed the various points of pressure being applied to the Vice President, including Eastman's theories, the *Gohmert* suit, Ellis's arguments, as well as how the electoral count process should work. They also discussed allegations of irregularities and maladministration of the election, concluding that none of the allegations raised was sufficient to reverse President Trump's defeat.[99]

While Vice President Pence recognized Congress's authority under the Electoral Count Act to raise objections to the certification, neither he nor his staff were aware of any evidence of fraud that would have had a material effect on the outcome of the election in any State.[100] Because of President Trump's repetition of election fraud allegations, Jacob and the Vice President's staff conducted their own evaluation of these claims. Jacob asked Morgan to send the campaign's best evidence of election "fraud, maladministration, irregularities, [and] abuses in the system."[101] The Vice President's legal staff memorialized the review they conducted of these materials in a memo to Vice President Pence, which concluded: "most allegations of substantive voter fraud—defined to mean the casting of illegal ballots in violation of prevailing election laws—are either relatively small in number, or cannot be verified."[102]

Vice President Pence also discussed the Trump Campaign's fake electors with his advisors. Both Jacob and Morgan assured Vice President Pence that there were not dual slates of electors. The electors organized by the Trump Campaign were not valid.[103] Morgan had already written a memo on the topic in December, concluding that the "alternate" electors—that is, fake—lacked a certificate of ascertainment issued by the State.[104] Without such an ascertainment, the Trump Campaign's fake electors had no standing during the joint session. Jacob had also prepared a "flow chart" memo outlining each of the legal provisions implicated in the joint session on January 6th.[105] Jacob advised Vice President Pence that "none of the slates that had been sent in would qualify as an alternate slate within the meaning of the Electoral Count Act."[106] Vice President Pence was still worried that the fake elector issue was sowing confusion, so he wanted his statement on January 6th to be as transparent as possible.[107]

That same day, January 2nd, Marc Short released a brief statement on behalf of the Vice President. "Vice President Pence shares the concerns of millions of Americans about voter fraud and irregularities in the last election," the statement read. "The vice president welcomes the efforts of members of the House and Senate to use the authority they have under the law to raise objections and bring forward evidence before the Congress and the American people on January 6th."[108] Short testified that the statement was consistent with the Vice President's view that he did not have the power to reject electors.[109] Short issued this statement because of the "swirl" regarding the question of "where [Vice President Pence] stood."[110]

Steve Bannon's podcast, *War Room: Pandemic*, was one of the primary sources of this swirl.

JANUARY 2, 2021: EASTMAN AND BANNON QUESTION THE "COURAGE AND SPINE" OF VICE PRESIDENT PENCE.

Steve Bannon's podcast, *War Room: Pandemic*, was one of the primary sources of this swirl. Eastman was a guest on a January 2nd episode of Bannon's show. Much of their conversation focused on Vice President Pence, and the belief that he had the power to overturn the election.

"[W]e are entering into one of the most, um, important constitutional crisis [*sic*] the country's ever had," Bannon said.[111] Bannon complained that Vice President Pence had "spit the bit," meaning he had given up on efforts to keep President Trump in power.[112] Eastman claimed that the election had been "illegally conducted," and so the certified votes now "devolved back to the [S]tate legislature[s], and the only other place where it devolved back to is to Congress and particularly the Vice President, who will sit in presiding over a Joint Session of Congress beginning on January 6 to count the ballots."[113] Eastman claimed that the Vice President (and Congress) had the power to reject the certified electors from several States out-of-hand. "[T]hey've got multiple slates of ballots from seven states," Eastman said. "And they've gotta decide [ ] which is the valid slate to count...I think they have that authority to make that determination on their own." [114]

Bannon claimed the Vice President of the United States is "hardwired in," and an "actual decisionmaker." [115] The Vice President's role is not "ministerial," Bannon declared. [116] Eastman agreed. [117] "Are we to assume that this is going to be a climactic battle that's going to take place this week about the very question of the constitutionality of the Electoral Count Act of 1887?" Bannon asked. [118]

Eastman replied, "I think a lot of that depends on the courage and the spine of the individuals involved." Bannon asked Eastman if he meant Vice President Mike Pence. "Yes," Eastman answered. [119]

JANUARY 3, 2021: EASTMAN DRAFTS ANOTHER "JANUARY 6 SCENARIO" MEMO "WAR GAMING" THE WAYS THAT VICE PRESIDENT PENCE COULD CHANGE THE OUTCOME OF THE ELECTION.

The next day, January 3, 2021, Eastman drafted a six-page memo that imagined several scenarios for January 6th, only some of which led to President Trump's victory. [120] In a section titled, "War Gaming the Alternatives," Eastman set forth the ways he thought President Trump could remain in power. [121] Importantly, Eastman concluded that President Trump could remain president if—and only if—Vice President Pence followed Eastman's illegal advice and determined which electoral college ballots were "valid." [122] In another scenario, Eastman imagined that President Trump may somehow win re-election in January 2021 if Vice President Pence remanded the electoral votes to State legislatures, such that they could have ten days to investigate President Trump's baseless claims of fraud. In that case, Eastman allowed that former Vice President Biden may still win, should the State legislatures determine that the evidence was "insufficient to alter the results of the election." [123]

Eastman Knew that there Were No Valid "Alternate" Slates, But He Nonetheless Predicated His Advice to the Vice President and President on this Claim. In his six-page memo, consistent with the earlier two-page memo, Eastman states that "the Trump electors" met and transmitted votes, finding that "[t]here are thus dual slates of electors from 7 [S]tates." [124] Even since January 6th, Eastman has continued to affirm and defend his assertion that there were dual slates of electors, writing: "Trump electors from seven [S]tates in which election challenges were still pending met (albeit of their own accord) on the date designated by Congress, cast their votes, and transmitted those votes to Congress." [125]

Eastman used these slates as a premise for his argument that the result of the election was disputed. However, Eastman acknowledged on multiple occasions—both before and after January 6th—that these "dual slates" had no legal significance. In an email sent on December 19, 2020, Eastman wrote that the seven Trump/Pence slates of electors "will be dead on arrival in Congress" "unless those electors get a certification from their State Legislators."[126] Of course, this certification never came and there was no basis for any action on the "dual slates."[127]

Nevertheless, on December 23, 2020, Eastman used the existence of these slates as a justification for the Vice President to act, in an email to Boris Epshteyn, a Trump Campaign lawyer. "The fact that we have multiple slates of electors demonstrates the uncertainty of either. That should be enough."[128]

Again after January 6th, Eastman acknowledged in an email that the fake electors' documents were invalid and irrelevant.[129] "Alas," he said, "[T]hey had no authority" because "[n]o legislature certified them."[130]

Eastman concluded his memo by asserting that his plan was "BOLD, Certainly," but he attempted to justify it, arguing that "this Election was Stolen by a strategic Democrat plan to systematically flout existing election laws for partisan advantage; we're no longer playing by Queensbury Rules, therefore."[131]

Eastman repeated what he wrote in his earlier, shorter memo, claiming that Vice President Pence should act "without asking for permission—either from a vote of the joint session or from the Court."[132] Eastman claimed "that the Constitution assigns this power to the Vice President as the ultimate arbiter."[133] Eastman ended on an especially hyperbolic note. If the election's results were not upended, "then the sovereign people no longer control the direction of their government, and we will have ceased to be a self-governing people. The stakes could not be higher."[134]

January 4, 2021: President Trump and Eastman Meet with Pence and His Staff in the Oval Office.

Eastman Argues in an Oval Office Meeting that the Vice President can Reject Electoral Votes or that He Can Delay the Certification, Sending the Electoral Votes Back to the States. Late in the afternoon of January 4, 2021, President Trump summoned Vice President Pence to the Oval Office for a showdown.[135] President Trump and Eastman sought to convince the Vice President that he had the power to refuse to count the certified electors from several States won by former Vice President Biden.

Short and Jacob attended with the Vice President.[136] Trump's chief of staff, Mark Meadows, was only briefly present, leaving as the meeting started.[137]

The White House Counsel is Excluded from the Meeting. One key lawyer was conspicuously absent: Pat Cipollone, the White House Counsel. Cipollone and his deputy, Pat Philbin, were shooting down a series of "terrible" proposals at the time.[138] Philbin told the Select Committee that he considered resigning every day from approximately November 15 until the end of the administration.[139] Philbin had researched the Vice President's role in the January 6th joint session and concluded that Vice President Pence had no power to affect the outcome.[140] Cipollone agreed and informed Short and Jacob that this was the opinion of White House Counsel's Office.[141]

Mark Meadows invited Cipollone to speak with Eastman prior to the Oval Office meeting.[142] Cipollone told Eastman that his scheme was "not something that is consistent with the appropriate reading of the law." [143] After delivering this assessment directly to Eastman in Meadows' office, Cipollone walked to the Oval Office with the intent to attend the meeting. However, by the time the Vice President and his staff arrived, Cipollone was gone.[144]

Cipollone declined to testify as to what he told President Trump or why he did not attend the Oval Office meeting, but he was clear that he didn't end up attending the meeting because of something that happened after he walked into the Oval Office.[145] Whatever happened, Cipollone maintained, was protected by executive privilege, suggesting that he was asked to leave by the President.[146] What is clear, however, is that Cipollone had already shared his view directly with Meadows and Eastman, i.e., that the proposal President Trump and Eastman were about to advocate to the Vice President was illegal.[147]

During this Oval Office Meeting, Eastman Admits that Both Paths are Based on the Same Legal Theory and Concedes His Plan Violates the Electoral Count Act. During the Oval Office meeting, Eastman claimed that there were two legally viable options.[148] First, Vice President Pence could reject outright the certified electors submitted by several States, and second, he could suspend the joint session and send the "disputed" electoral votes back to the States.[149] Eastman advised that the Vice President had the "raw authority to determine objections himself," according to Jacob.[150] However, by the end of the meeting Eastman was emphasizing the second option that he argued would be "more politically palatable" than the "more aggressive" option of the Vice President rejecting electoral votes outright.[151] If Vice President Pence did not want to reject the electors, Eastman claimed, then the Vice President could send the certified electoral votes back to the States for further deliberation.

Eastman later conceded that both actions were based on the same underlying legal theory of the Vice President's power.[152] Eastman also

Pat Cipollone is seen on a screen during a Select Committee hearing on July 12, 2022.
(Photo by Sarah Silbiger-Pool/Getty Images)

admitted—during this meeting with the President and Vice President—that his proposal violated the Electoral Count Act.[153] Moreover, Eastman eventually acknowledged that the concept of the Vice President unilaterally rejecting electors was not supported by precedent and that the Supreme Court would never endorse it.[154]

Jacob recorded his reflections on the January 4th meeting in a contemporaneous memo to the Vice President.[155] Jacob's memo confirms that Eastman admitted that his proposal violated the law in the presence of President Trump.

First, Jacob wrote, Eastman acknowledged that "his proposal violates several provisions of statutory law"—namely, the Electoral Count Act of 1887.[156] Jacob's memo explains that the Electoral Count Act calls for all vote certificates to be "acted upon," and any objections to a State's certificates be "finally disposed of." However, as Jacob wrote, Eastman was proposing instead that "no action be taken" on the certificates from the States Eastman asserted were "contested." And, according to the Electoral Count Act, the Vice President (as President of the Senate) is to "call for objections." But Eastman did not want the Vice President to "call for objections" for these States. As Jacob noted, this would have deprived Congress of the ability under the Act to make, debate, and vote on objections.[157]

Additionally, the Electoral Count Act contains a provision that requires any "competing slates of electors" to be "submitted to the Senate and House for debate and disposition." As Jacob noted, Eastman conceded that the "alternate" (fake) electors' votes were not proper. But Eastman's proposal still would have refused to count the real electors' votes from those States and instead referred both the real and fake electors' votes to State legislatures "for disposition." Finally, in order for State legislatures to take action to determine which of the slates should be counted, Eastman's proposal called for "an extended recess of the joint session." But this too would have violated the Electoral Count Act, which provides only for very short delays.[158]

There was another foundational problem with Eastman's plan. There were no legitimate "competing" or "alternate" slates of electors. President Trump, Eastman and others had manufactured the conditions they needed in order to claim that the election result was "disputed" by convening fake electors who sent fake documents to Washington before January 6th. And their efforts to convince State legislatures to certify Trump electors had already failed.

Jacob noted in his memo that in the Oval Office meeting, Eastman conceded "no legislature has appointed or certified any alternate slate of electors" and that the purported "alternate slates" (fake electors) were illegitimate without what Jacob described as "the imprimatur of approval by a State legislature."[159] Moreover, Eastman acknowledged that "no Republican-controlled legislative majority in any disputed States has expressed an intention to designate an alternate slate of electors."[160] In other words, Eastman acknowledged that the fake votes were invalid, that no State legislature had approved them, and no State legislature *would* approve them.[161] But President Trump and Eastman still pressed this unlawful scheme on the Vice President. Although Eastman started the January 4th Oval Office meeting maintaining that Vice President Pence had unilateral authority to reject electors, by the end of the meeting he conceded that he would "not recommend that the Vice President assert that he has the authority unilaterally to decide which of the competing slates of electors should be counted."[162]

Jacob ended his memo with a scathing summary. "If the Vice President implemented Professor Eastman's proposal, he would likely lose in court," Jacob wrote. "In a best-case scenario in which the courts refused to get involved, the Vice President would likely find himself in an isolated standoff against both houses of Congress, as well as most or all of the applicable State legislatures, with no neutral arbiter to break the impasse."[163]

Following the Oval Office meeting, during the evening of January 4, 2021, Jacob invited Eastman to send along "any written materials on electoral vote counting issues," including a law review article by Laurence Tribe that Eastman had cited in the Oval Office meeting that day, for Jacob to review on the Vice President's behalf.[164] Jacob reviewed everything that Eastman submitted; nothing changed the analysis he had already done for the Vice President, indeed much of it did not even support Eastman's own arguments.[165]

The Vice President was Not Persuaded by Eastman's Theory and Remained Convinced That His Role at the Joint Session would be Merely Ceremonial. Pence did not relent on January 4th, or at any point during the harrowing two days that followed. "[F]rom my very first conversation with the Vice President on the subject, his immediate instinct was that there is no way that one person could be entrusted by the Framers to exercise that authority," Jacob testified. "And never once did I see him budge from that view, and the legal advice that I provided him merely reinforced it. So, everything that he said or did during [the January 4th meeting in the Oval Office] was consistent with his first instincts on this question."[166]

JANUARY 4, 2021: PRESIDENT TRUMP PUBLICLY PRESSURES THE VICE PRESIDENT DURING A RALLY SPEECH IN GEORGIA.
President Trump did not relent either. His instinct was to increase public pressure on Vice President Pence, despite the Vice President's consistent message to President Trump about the limits of his authority. That evening, during a Senate campaign rally in Dalton, Georgia, President Trump made it

seem as if the Presidential election hadn't already been decided and pro-jected his unhinged ambitions onto his opponents.[167] President Trump claimed that "there's nothing the radical Democrats will not do to get power that they so desperately crave," including "the outright stealing of elections, like they're trying to do with us."[168]

"We're not going to let it happen," President Trump said, adding, "I hope Mike Pence comes through for us, I have to tell you." President Trump called Vice President Pence a "great vice president," a "great guy," as well as a "wonderful" and "smart man." But he alluded to the Vice President's role, "he's going to have a lot to say about it," and added an ominous note. "Of course, if he doesn't come through, I won't like him quite as much," President Trump said.[169]

JANUARY 5, 2021: EASTMAN PRESSURES PENCE'S STAFF IN A PRIVATE MEETING WHILE PRESIDENT TRUMP TWEETS.

In a Reversal of Where the Oval Office Meeting Ended the Day Before, Eastman Argues that Pence Should Reject Electors Outright. Eastman met with Jacob and Short again the following day.[170] During the Oval Office meeting the Vice President had made clear that he would not unilaterally reject electors, and, by pivoting to recommend the Vice President send the electors back to the States, Eastman seemed to recognize this. But the following morning, Eastman returned to pressing for the more "aggressive" path.[171]

Jacob recorded Eastman's request on January 5, 2021, in a handwritten note: "Requesting VP reject."[172] Jacob later summarized Eastman's remarks as follows: "I'm here asking you to reject the electors."[173] This overnight reversal surprised Jacob because Eastman was returning to the more aggressive position he had seemed to abandon in the Oval Office meeting the day before.[174] President Trump's tweets that morning may explain Eastman's reversal. While Eastman was meeting with the Vice President's staff, his client, President Trump, was pressing the argument publicly.

At 11:06 a.m. on the morning of January 5th, President Trump tweeted: "The Vice President has the power to reject fraudulently chosen electors." As his tweet made clear, President Trump would not be persuaded by reason—or the law. The President made this public statement despite the Vice President's clear and consistent rejection of this theory including dur-ing an in-person meeting the day before. During that same meeting, East-man conceded that this "aggressive" path of rejecting electors was not advisable.

Herschmann briefly participated in the January 5th meeting, seeing it as "an opportunity . . . to just chew [Eastman] out."[175] Herschmann had already pushed back "brutal[ly]" on Eastman's theory regarding the Vice

President. In this conversation, he emphasized the need to fact check dubious claims of election fraud.[176] Herschmann told Eastman that "someone better make sure" that the allegations Eastman provided to members of Congress were accurate before they objected to the certification of the vote the next day.[177] "[N]othing should come out of someone's mouth that [isn't] independently verified and [ ] reliable."[178]

At the End of the Morning Meeting, Eastman Concedes to Pence's Counsel That His Theory Has No Historical Support. Jacob then had his own "Socratic" debate with Eastman over the legal merits of his position. According to Jacob, Eastman conceded much ground by the end of the session. Eastman "all but admitted that it [his plan] didn't work."[179]

For example, Eastman had previously claimed to have found historical support in the actions of John Adams and Thomas Jefferson, who both presided over the counting of electoral votes when they were Vice President. Not so. Jacob told the Select Committee that Eastman conceded in private that the cases of Jefferson and Adams did not serve "as examples for the proposition that he was trying to support of a Vice Presidential assertion of authority to decide disputes[,] because no dispute was raised in either case during the joint session." Jacob added: "And, moreover, there was no [question] as to the outcomes in those States."[180]

Eastman conceded that there was no historical support for the role that he and President Trump were pushing Vice President Pence to play. No Vice President—before or after the adoption of the Electoral Count Act—had ever exercised such authority. This included then-Vice President Richard Nixon's handling of the electoral votes of Hawaii following the 1960 election. Though Eastman and other Trump lawyers used this Hawaii example to justify the theory that the Vice President could unilaterally choose which electors to count, Eastman admitted to Jacob that Vice President Nixon had not in fact done what Eastman was recommending Vice President Pence do.[181]

Eastman also admitted that he would not grant the expansive powers he advocated for Vice President Pence to any other Vice President. Eastman did not think that Vice President Kamala Harris should have such power in 2025, nor did he think that Vice President Al Gore should have had such authority in 2001.[182] He also acknowledged that his theory would lose 9–0 at the Supreme Court.[183]

According to Jacob, Eastman "acknowledged by the end that, first of all, no reasonable person would actually want that clause [of the 12th Amendment] read that way because if indeed it did mean that the Vice President

Judge J. Michael Luttig testifies before the Select Committee on June 16, 2022.
Photo by House Creative Services

had such authority, you could never have a party switch thereafter." If politicians followed Eastman's advice, "[y]ou would just have the same party win continuously if indeed a Vice President had the authority to just declare the winner of every State."[184]

The Vice President's office was unmoved by Eastman's specious reasoning. As he left Marc Short's office, Eastman was thinking of his client's reaction. "They're going to be really disappointed that I wasn't able to persuade you," Eastman said.[185]

Former Republican Officials with Executive, Legislative, and Judicial Experience All Agreed with Vice President Pence's Conclusion about His Limited Role at the Joint Session. As President Trump's pressure campaign intensified, the Vice President's outside counsel, Richard Cullen, turned for support to John Michael Luttig, a conservative former judge of the U.S. Court of Appeals for the Fourth Circuit.[186] Eastman had clerked for Luttig—a man with impeccable legal and conservative credentials—more than two decades prior. Luttig rejected Eastman's so-called legal analysis of the Vice President's role in no uncertain terms. In a series of tweets, posted at 9:53 a.m. on January 5th, Luttig set forth his legal conclusions.

"The only responsibility and power of the Vice President under the Constitution is to faithfully count the electoral college votes as they have been cast," Judge Luttig wrote. "The Constitution does not empower the Vice President to alter in any way the votes that have been cast, either by rejecting certain of them or otherwise." [187]

Confusion in the media about where the Vice President stood on this issue prompted former Speaker of the House Paul Ryan to reach out to the Vice President to share his belief that the Vice President had no unilateral authority.[188] Short also spoke with former Speaker Ryan and as he testified to the Select Committee, "I said to him, Mr. Speaker, you know Mike...you know he recognizes that. And we sort of laughed about it, and he said, I get it." [189]

The Vice President also consulted with former Vice President Dan Quayle, who reinforced and affirmed Vice President Pence's consistent understanding of his role.[190]

JANUARY 5, 2021: PRESIDENT TRUMP AGAIN PRESSURES VICE PRESIDENT PENCE IN A ONE-ON-ONE MEETING AT THE WHITE HOUSE AND ANOTHER PHONE CALL WITH EASTMAN.

President Trump demanded to see Vice President Pence again that same day. Vice President Pence had canceled a planned lunch with President Trump, intending to work on the statement he planned to issue on January 6th to explain publicly why he wouldn't bow to the President's pressure.[191] But Pence couldn't avoid Trump. Vice President Pence had to delay a Coronavirus Task Force meeting later that same day when he was called to the Oval Office to meet with the President.[192]

The two men met alone, without staff present. While we have not developed direct evidence of what was discussed during this one-on-one meeting between the President and Vice President, it did not change the fundamental disagreement between them about the limits of the Vice President's authority during the joint session. Jacob said the Vice President left the meeting "determined." [193] Vice President Pence did tell Marc Short what transpired during the meeting, but Short refused to tell the Select Committee what was said.[194] Short described Vice President Pence's demeanor as "steady." [195] Short testified that the below excerpt from the book *Peril* may have been sensationalized but was generally consistent with Short's understanding of the discussion:

> "If these people say you have the power, wouldn't you want to?"
> Trump asked.
>
> "I wouldn't want any one person to have that authority," Pence said.

"But wouldn't it almost be cool to have that power?" Trump asked.

"No," Pence said. "Look, I've read this, and I don't see a way to do it. We've exhausted every option. I've done everything I could and then some to find a way around this. It's simply not possible. My interpretation is: No....

"No, no, no!" Trump shouted. "You don't understand, Mike. You can do this. I don't want to be your friend anymore if you don't do this."[196]

Later that day, Jacob and Short were both present for a call between President Trump and Vice President Pence.[197] Eastman and at least one other lawyer were with President Trump on the call as well.[198]

Eastman recognized that Vice President Pence was not going to change his mind on rejecting electors outright, but he still asked if the Vice President would consider sending the electors back to the States.[199] "I don't see it," Vice President Pence responded, "but my counsel will hear out whatever Mr. Eastman has to say."[200]

Jacob received other calls from Eastman on January 5th.[201] Jacob told the Select Committee that he had a detailed discussion with Eastman concerning the ways his proposal would violate the Electoral Count Act.[202] Eastman resorted to a ridiculous argument—comparing their current situation to the crisis that faced President Abraham Lincoln during the Civil War. Eastman invoked President Lincoln's suspension of the writ of habeas corpus.[203] He also told Jacob to "stay tuned" because "we" were trying to get some letters from State legislators indicating that they were interested in the Vice President sending the electors back to the States.[204]

JANUARY 5, 2021: AN ACCURATE NEW YORK TIMES ARTICLE ABOUT THE VICE PRESIDENT PROMPTS A FALSE STATEMENT IN RESPONSE BY PRESIDENT TRUMP.
On the evening of January 5th, *The New York Times* published an article titled, "Pence Said to Have Told Trump He Lacks Power to Change Election Result."[205] The *Times* reported on the tension brewing within the White House, citing "people briefed on the conversation" between President Trump and Vice President Pence that had taken place in the Oval Office the previous day. "Vice President Mike Pence told President Trump on Tuesday [January 4th] that he did not believe he had the power to block congressional certification of Joseph R. Biden, Jr.'s victory in the presidential election despite Mr. Trump's baseless insistence that he did," the *Times* reported.[206]

The *Times'* report was published at approximately 7:36 that evening.[207] Jason Miller called President Trump to make sure he had seen it.[208] President Trump spoke to Miller at least twice, once at 8:18 p.m. and a second time at 9:22 p.m.[209] Immediately after concluding his second call with Jason

Miller, President Trump asked to speak to the Vice President; President Trump and Vice President Pence spoke from 9:33 to 9:41 p.m.[210] President Trump also spoke with Steve Bannon and Eastman, among others.[211]

At 9:58 p.m. on January 5th, President Trump issued a statement that he had dictated to Jason Miller disputing the *Times'* account.[212] President Trump lied—repeatedly—in his short statement.[213] The President claimed the article was "fake news." It wasn't. President Trump claimed he and Vice President Pence were "in total agreement that the Vice President has the power to act." They weren't. President Trump claimed the election "was illegal." It wasn't. President Trump then laid out Vice President Pence's options for the next day, summarizing Eastman's theory:

> Our Vice President has several options under the U.S. Constitution. He can decertify the results or send them back to the [S]tates for change and certification. He can also decertify the illegal and corrupt results and send them to the House of Representatives for the one vote for one [S]tate tabulation.[214]

This was also a blatant attempt to mischaracterize the Vice President's position in the hope that public opinion would somehow sway the resolute Vice President. President Trump knew full well at the time that he and Vice President Pence were *not* "in total agreement." The Vice President's counsel, Greg Jacob, was shocked by the statement.[215] "[T]he Vice President was not in agreement that the Vice President had the power to take the actions that were being asked of him that day," Jacob later told the Select Committee.[216] Marc Short was furious as well and called Jason Miller to forcefully "express [his] displeasure that a statement could have gone out that misrepresented the Vice President's viewpoint without consultation."[217]

The Vice President was "obviously irritated that a statement putting words in his mouth" was issued by the President and considered issuing his own statement contradicting President Trump's.[218] Ultimately, Pence and Short concluded that it was not worthwhile since it was already late in the evening and they expected the question to be resolved by Vice President Pence's "Dear Colleague" letter the next day.[219]

JANUARY 5, 2021: BANNON PUBLICLY AMPLIFIES THE PRESSURE ON VICE PRESIDENT PENCE.

While President Trump misrepresented the Vice President's agreement with Eastman's theory, his on-again, off-again political advisor, Steve Bannon, pressed President Trump's campaign against Vice President Pence in public. Bannon echoed the public pressure on Pence that the President continued to propagate by talking about his purported authority. The Select Committee learned from phone records that Bannon spoke to President Trump at least twice on January 5th.[220]

During a January 5, 2021, episode of *War Room: Pandemic*, Bannon and his guests openly berated Vice President Pence. Bannon cited an erroneous news report claiming that Senator Grassley would preside over the certification of the electoral college vote—instead of Vice President Pence.[221] Bannon's cohost, Raheem Kassam, took credit for the public pressure placed on Vice President Pence. "I want to remind people who has been sitting here, saying 'Light Pence Up' for the last couple of weeks. Right? That would be Raheem Kassam." They then discussed President Trump's speech in Georgia the previous evening. "I think the President of the United States took your advice last night, wrote a line in there," Bannon said. To which Kasseem responded: "...and yours...hold the line."

Jack Posobiec, an alt-right personality with a large Twitter following, chimed in quoting a member of their audience as saying that "Pence will betray Donald Trump." [222] In response, Bannon stated: "Call the play. Run the play." [223]

The "play" was Bannon's version of the "Green Bay Sweep"—a plan to subvert the transfer of power on January 6th named for a brutally effective power running play developed in the National Football League (NFL) in the 1960's. Steve Bannon's political version of the sweep was intended to undermine the legitimate results of the 2020 presidential election.

One account of Bannon's "Green Bay Sweep" comes from Peter Navarro, Director of the White House Office of Trade and Manufacturing Policy. Navarro refused to cooperate with the Select Committee and was subsequently indicted for contempt of Congress. Although he doesn't fully explain in his book, *In Trump Time: A Journal of America's Plague Year*, how Bannon's sweep was intended to work, Navarro writes that Vice President Pence was envisioned as the "quarterback" who would "assert his constitutional power" to delay certification.[224] Navarro writes that his own role was to "carefully document the fraud and myriad election irregularities," while Bannon's "role was to figure out how to use this information—what he called the 'receipts.'" [225]

Navarro's account helps explain why Trump and his loyalists became so fixated on Vice President Pence. They saw Vice President Pence as their last hope for keeping President Trump in office. Navarro writes of Pence's supposed "betrayal." [226] In a telling sentence, Navarro likens Vice President Pence to Brutus, a Roman politician and the most famous assassin of Julius Caesar. Navarro writes:

On this cold, momentous day, I shiver as I think to myself, "January 6
will be either Mike Pence's finest hour or the traitorous 'Et tu, Brute?'
end of both his and Donald Trump's political careers." [227]

The goal of these Trump allies was clear: to overturn the election result. [228] Statements by participants in this effort indicate there were several different endgame strategies in mind. One was to get the Vice President to unilaterally reject the Electoral College votes of Arizona, Georgia, Pennsylvania, and other States, then simply declare that Trump had won a majority of the electors actually submitted. The other major possibility was to reject or "return" the Electoral College votes of these States and then declare there was no majority in the Electoral College process, thereby triggering a so-called contingent election under the 12th Amendment. [229] This would have meant that the House of Representatives had chosen the president not on the basis of one-member-one-vote, but on the basis of one-State-one-vote, pursuant to the 12th Amendment. Donald Trump's strategists emphasized repeatedly that the GOP had a 27-to-22 margin in control of the States' Congressional delegations, with Pennsylvania being tied at 9-to-9, therefore presumably a non-factor.

5.3 PRESIDENT TRUMP AND HIS ALLIES CONTINUE TO PRESSURE THE VICE PRESIDENT ON JANUARY 6TH, THREATENING HIS LIFE AND OUR DEMOCRACY.

JANUARY 6, 2021: PRESIDENT TRUMP CONTINUED TO FALSELY ASSERT IN MULTIPLE TWEETS POSTED THE MORNING OF JANUARY 6TH THAT THE VICE PRESIDENT HAD A ROLE TO PLAY IN THE OUTCOME OF THE ELECTION.

Despite the public pressure initiated by the President and amplified by Bannon, Navarro and others, there was no ambiguity in the Vice President's decision. By January 6th, President Trump had been told multiple times that Vice President Pence was not going to reject the certified electors from any State. Nor was Vice President Pence going to move for a delay and send the electors back to the States. Either move would have been illegal, requiring Vice President Pence to break the law, violating his oath to the U.S. Constitution. Pence made his decision clear "[m]any times" to President Trump, and he was "very consistent" in rejecting the President's demands. [230] President Trump continued to publicly pressure the Vice President anyway.

At 1:00 a.m. on January 6th, President Trump tweeted:

If Vice President @Mike_Pence comes through for us, we will win
the Presidency. Many States want to decertify the mistake they

made in certifying incorrect & even fraudulent numbers in a process NOT approved by their State Legislatures (which it must be). Mike can send it back![231]

Later that morning, at 8:17 a.m., President Trump tweeted again:

States want to correct their votes, which they now know were based on irregularities and fraud, plus corrupt process never received legislative approval. All Mike Pence has to do is send them back to the States, AND WE WIN. Do it Mike, this is a time for extreme courage![232]

And, at 8:22 a.m., President Trump tweeted again, making a pitch for Congress to choose him, as if people's votes on election day and the electoral college didn't matter:

THE REPUBLICAN PARTY AND, MORE IMPORTANTLY, OUR COUNTRY, NEEDS THE PRESIDENCY MORE THAN EVER BEFORE—THE POWER OF THE VETO. STAY STRONG![233]

President Trump's tweets made it clear that he thought the Republican State legislatures would simply deliver him victory. President Trump emphasized this point, writing twice that if Vice President Pence gave in, "we win." However, there was no sign of a change in the Vice President's position. A moment of truth was looming.

January 6, 2021: President Trump Has a "[H]eated" Conversation with Vice President Pence Before his Rally on the Ellipse. President Trump tried to reach Vice President Pence by phone early that morning.[234] He finally talked to his Vice President at approximately 11:20 a.m.[235] The exchange quickly became contentious.

Eric Herschmann, a lawyer in the White House Counsel's Office, overheard the conversation. Members of President Trump's family and other White House officials were present as well.[236] Herschmann recalled that "it started off as a calmer tone, everything, and then it became heated."[237] Ivanka Trump also described the call as "pretty heated."[238] Ivanka Trump elaborated: "It was a different tone than I'd heard him take with the Vice President before."[239] Ivanka Trump told her Chief of Staff, Julie Radford, that "her dad had just had an upsetting conversation with the Vice President."[240] President Trump had even called Vice President Pence the "P Word."[241]

Nick Luna, President Trump's personal assistant (commonly known as the "body man"), was also in the Oval Office during the conversation. Luna told the Select Committee that President Trump called Vice President Pence

President Trump on the phone in the Oval Office.
Photo provided to the Select Committee by the National Archives and Records Administration.

a "wimp" on the call, with President Trump adding that he "made the wrong decision" in choosing Pence as his running mate.[242]

Keith Kellogg, Vice President Pence's National Security Advisor, also heard the conversation. President Trump "told the Vice President that, you know, he has legal authority to send these folks [the electors] back to the respective States," Kellogg told the Select Committee.[243] President Trump insisted that Vice President Pence had the "constitutional authority to" reject certain electoral college votes.[244] When Vice President Pence would not budge, President Trump told him "you're not tough enough to make the call." [245]

But Vice President Pence would not be bullied. The Vice President, who was at his residence at the time, had been meeting with Greg Jacob to finalize the statement he would be releasing later that day. When the President called, Pence stepped away to answer the phone. According to Jacob, when Pence returned, he did not say anything about the call—but he looked "steely, determined, [and] grim," as he reentered the room.[246]

c. January 6, 2021: Trump, Eastman and Giuliani Continue to Pressure Vice President Pence at the Ellipse Rally. Despite the Vice President's unwavering stance, the President and his outside counsel continued to turn up the heat of public pressure.

At President Trump's urging, thousands had gathered on the morning of January 6th to hear the President and others speak at a rally held at the Ellipse, a park just south of the White House. Before President Trump spoke, Eastman took the stage alongside Giuliani. Both would further amplify the President's public pressure on the Vice President, but when Giuliani spoke on the Ellipse, he already knew that what Eastman had outlined would never practically happen.

At 9:31 a.m. that morning, Giuliani called Eric Herschmann "out of the blue" to ask him for his view and analysis of the practical implications of Eastman's theory.[247] According to Herschmann, after an "intellectual discussion about…the VP's role," Giuliani agreed that the "practical implication of [what Eastman had proposed] would be almost impossible." [248] Immediately after this 5½ minute conversation with Herschmann, Giuliani had two calls with the White House, at 9:41 a.m. and 9:53 a.m.[249]

Giuliani recognized Eastman who joined him on stage, claiming that he was "one of the preeminent constitutional scholars in the United States." [250]

Giuliani said Vice President Pence could either "decide on the validity of these crooked ballots, or he can send it back to the legislat[ures], give them five to 10 days to finally finish the work." [251] He added that that they had "letters from five legislat[ures] begging us to do that." [252] This was not true. At most, what Giuliani, Eastman and other allies of President Trump had managed to procure were letters from individual State legislators or groups of State legislators. None of the letters came from a majority of any State's legislative chamber, let alone a majority of an entire State legislature.[253]

For instance, a letter that Eastman described to Jacob as a "[m]ajor new development" on the evening of January 5th contained the signatures of 21 members of the Pennsylvania Senate.[254] Eastman claimed that it "now looks like PA Legislature will vote to recertify its electors if Vice President Pence implements the plan we discussed," but the letter asked only for a "delay" in certification to "allow for due process." [255] The Select Committee learned from the most senior Pennsylvania Senate Republican that he signed the letter because of pressure he was feeling due to the voluminous post-election outreach from President Trump, Trump allies, and the public.[256] And, he only agreed to sign a letter directed to Congressional leaders—not the Vice President—after raising in a conversation with Vice President Pence's brother, Congressman Greg Pence, his desire to avoid pressuring the Vice President.[257]

Moreover, as Jacob explained, "what any of the State legislatures said they did or did not want to do had no impact on the legal analysis of what the Vice President's authorities were."[258] There was simply no legal path to send any votes back to the States on January 6th.

On the stage at the President's rally on the Ellipse, Giuliani repeated a conspiracy theory about the "crooked Dominion machines...deliberately" changing votes via an algorithm.[259] He explained that the 10-day delay in the certification would be used "to see the machines that are crooked" and "to find criminality there"—demonstrating that his repeated assertions of a stolen election were not based on any real proof, or even evidence, of actual widespread fraud or criminality.[260]

"Let's have trial by combat," Giuliani told the crowd.[261]

Eastman came to the microphone following Giuliani, and he proceeded to repeat proven falsehoods regarding voting machines. He then issued his "demand":

> And all we are demanding of Vice President Pence is this afternoon, at 1:00, he let the legislatures of the state look into this so we get to the bottom of it, and the American people know whether we have control of the direction of our government, or not. We no longer live in a self-governing republic if we can't get the answer to this question. This is bigger than President Trump. It is a very essence of our republican form of government, and it has to be done. And anybody that is not willing to stand up to do it, does not deserve to be in the office. It is that simple.[262]

Eastman told the assembled crowd that nothing less than the fate of the American Republic was in Vice President Pence's hands.

President Trump Directs the Angry Mob at the Capitol to Pressure Vice President Pence.

When President Trump later took the stage at the Ellipse, he heaped praise on Giuliani and Eastman. "He's got guts, unlike a lot of people in the Republican Party," President Trump said of Giuliani. "He's got guts. He fights, he fights."[263] President Trump described Eastman as "one of the most brilliant lawyers in the country."[264] President Trump claimed that Eastman had looked at the election and said, "What an absolute disgrace that this can be happening to our Constitution."[265] Trump falsely argued that the keys to the election were in Vice President Pence's hands, saying:

*And he [Eastman] looked at Mike Pence, and I hope Mike is going to do
the right thing. I hope so. I hope so. Because if Mike Pence does the right
thing, we win the election.... [T]his is from the number one, or certainly
one of the top, Constitutional lawyers in our country. He has the absolute right to do it.*[266]

President Trump repeatedly lied, claiming that several States wanted to
overturn former Vice President Biden's victory:

*States want to revote. The States got defrauded. They were given false
information. They voted on it. Now they want to recertify. They want it
back. All Vice President Pence has to do is send it back to the States to
recertify and we become president and you are the happiest people.*[267]

Contrary to the statement President Trump dictated the night before, he
all but admitted that Vice President Pence did not agree with him:

*And I actually, I just spoke to Mike. I said: "Mike, that doesn't take cour-
age. What takes courage is to do nothing. That takes courage." And then
we're stuck with a president who lost the election by a lot and we have
to live with that for four more years. We're just not going to let that
happen.*[268]

Later in his speech at the Ellipse, President Trump repeated:

*So, I hope Mike has the courage to do what he has to do. And I hope he
doesn't listen to the RINOs and the stupid people that he's listening
to.*[269]

This was nothing less than a direct appeal to the large angry crowd to
pressure Vice President Mike Pence to change his settled and oft-repeated
conclusion about the limits of his authority. It was a shocking attempt to
use public opinion to change the Vice President's position. President Trump
launched a mob toward the Capitol with the false hope that there was a scenario in which Vice President Pence would do what Eastman and President
Trump had asked him to do, preventing the transfer of authority to
President-elect Biden.

VICE PRESIDENT PENCE FULFILLED HIS DUTY ON JANUARY 6TH

**The Vice President Waited to Release His Statement Out of Deference to Presi-
dent Trump, Who Was Still Speaking on the Ellipse, and Ultimately Released It
Just Minutes Before the Joint Session Convened at 1:00 p.m.** President Trump's
speech began late and ran long. He didn't finish speaking until approximately 1:10 p.m.—after the joint session had begun at 1:00 p.m. Minutes
before he gaveled the joint session into order, Vice President Mike Pence
released the "Dear Colleague" letter he had been working on for days with

his staff.[270] There was never any ambiguity in Vice President Pence's understanding of his role and authority, but he wanted to make it clear for everyone to see. "This may be the most important thing I ever say," Vice President Pence remarked.[271]

"Today it will be my duty to preside when the Congress convenes in Joint Session to count the votes of the Electoral College, and I will do so to the best of my ability," Vice President Pence wrote. Vice President Pence explained that his "role as presiding officer is largely ceremonial" and dismissed the arguments that he could take unilateral action as contrary to his oath to support and defend the Constitution:

> As a student of history who loves the Constitution and reveres its Framers, I do not believe that the Founders of our country intended to invest the Vice President with unilateral authority to decide which electoral votes should be counted during the Joint Session of Congress, and no Vice President in American history has ever asserted such authority. Instead, Vice Presidents presiding over Joint Sessions have uniformly followed the Electoral Count Act, conducting the proceedings in an orderly manner even where the count resulted in the defeat of their party or their own candidacy.[272]

Vice President Pence Adheres to the U.S. Constitution and Complies with the Law Governing the Certification of the Presidential Election. When Vice President Pence gaveled the opening of the joint session, he knew that many of his Republican colleagues planned to challenge the election's results based on fictitious claims of fraud. The Vice President took steps to ensure that those objections adhered to the process set forth in the Electoral Count Act.

Every four years, on January 6th, vice presidents read from a script that remains essentially unchanged. Eastman's theory of the Vice President's power and the Trump Campaign's scheme to convene and submit the slates of "alternate" (fake) electors motivated Vice President Pence and his advisors to alter the script and to make sure they were prepared to respond to any unexpected actions in the joint session.[273]

Vice President Pence met with the Senate Parliamentarian on January 3rd to discuss the joint session and revised the joint session scripts in consultation with her office.[274] Vice President Pence and the Parliamentarian agreed that the Vice President's role is ministerial.[275]

The Vice President knew that the fake slates of electors organized by the Trump Campaign were not certified by the States and thus were not valid; he revised the script for the joint session to be transparent with the American people about what the Vice President would—and wouldn't—be doing during the joint session.[276]

Vice President Pence during the Joint Session of Congress.
(Photo by Win McNamee/Getty Images)

One of the most noticeable and important changes to the script was directed specifically at thwarting the fake electors scheme. The Vice President knew, informed by the research and analysis of his staff, that absent certification of the electoral votes by a State authority, the purported "alternate" slates were "not consequential" and would play no role in the certification of the Presidential election at the joint session.[277] The Senate Parliamentarian confirmed this understanding.[278]

For decades, Vice Presidents read a similar simple passage concerning the ascertainment of the vote. Most recently, Vice President Joseph Biden read this passage aloud in 2017, as did his most recent predecessors:

> After ascertainment has been had that the certificates are authentic and correct in form, the tellers will count and make a list of the votes cast by the electors of the several States.

On January 6, 2021, Vice President Pence read from a revised script (emphasis added):

> After ascertaining that the certificates are regular in form and authentic, tellers will announce the votes cast by the electors for each state, beginning with Alabama, which the parliamentarians

advise me is the only certificate of vote from that State and purports to be a return from the State that has annexed to it a certificate from an authority of that State purporting to appoint or ascertain electors.[279]

Vice President Pence used the same phrasing for each of the 50 States counted.

The Vice President's attention to this issue was warranted. Trump's allies pushed the fake electors scheme until the very end. Although the Trump Campaign had taken pains to direct the fake electors to send their documents to the appropriate authorities immediately after voting on December 14th, and though the Senate Parliamentarian's and Vice President's offices had been tracking the receipt by mail of both the legitimate and fake certificates, the Trump Campaign apparently became concerned that two States' documents had not been received before the joint session.[280]

On January 4th, the Trump campaign asked Republican Party officials in Wisconsin to fly their fake electors' documents to Washington, DC.[281] Shortly after, staffers for Representative Mike Kelly (R–PA) and Senator Ron Johnson (R–WI) reached out to Vice President Pence's Director of Legislative Affairs, apparently seeking to deliver the fake certificates.[282] A message from Senator Johnson's staffer was sent just minutes before the beginning of the joint session. This staffer stated that Senator Johnson wished to hand-deliver to the Vice President the fake electors' certificates from Michigan and Wisconsin. The Vice President's aide unambiguously turned him away.[283]

Vice President Pence made certain to call for objections as well, in compliance with the Electoral Count Act. After the tellers read off the votes cast for each State, he asked: "Are there any objections to counting the certificate of vote of the state … that the teller has verified, appears to be regular in form and authentic?"[284]

For most States, there were no objections. Republicans only rose to object to the States that President Trump contested. The first such state was Arizona. At approximately 1:46 p.m., Congressman Paul Gosar (R–AZ) announced his objection.[285] "I rise for myself and 60 of my colleagues to object to the counting of the electoral ballots from Arizona," Gosar said.[286]

Vice President Pence then asked: "Is the objection in writing and Signed by a senator?" It was. Senator Ted Cruz endorsed the unfounded challenge to Arizona's electoral votes.[287] Because the objections complied with the law, Vice President Pence directed the House and Senate to withdraw from the joint session so that the House and Senate could separately debate and vote on the objection.[288]

When the joint session finally resumed after the attack on the Capitol, the clerks announced the results of each chamber's vote. Just six U.S. Senators voted for the objection to the counting of Arizona's electoral college votes. The objection was also defeated in the House, though 121 Republican Members voted to reject Arizona's legitimate electors.[289] Pennsylvania was the only other State the chambers debated, after the House's objection was signed by Senator Josh Hawley (R–Mo.).[290]

5.4 PRESIDENT TRUMP ENDANGERS PENCE'S LIFE, CAUSING THE VICE PRESIDENT, HIS FAMILY, AND STAFF TO NARROWLY MISS THE RIOTERS AS THEY FLEE THE MOB ATTACKING THE CAPITOL.

As the debate over Arizona's legitimate electors took place on the Senate floor, the Vice President's staff could see trouble brewing outside.[291] From inside the Vice President's ceremonial office, staffers witnessed the crowds swelling on the east side of the Capitol. Then, the rioters broke through security barriers.[292] Jacob told young staffers that they should stand back from the windows, because the Vice President's office was not "the most popular office on the block right now."[293]

The Vice President was presiding over the Senate debate on the Arizona objection when the noise from the rioters became audible and those in the Senate Chamber realized the rioters had entered the Capitol.[294] The Secret Service evacuated Vice President Pence from the Senate floor at 2:12 p.m.[295] Twelve minutes later, at 2:24 p.m., President Trump tweeted that Vice President Pence "didn't have the courage to do what should have been done to protect our country and our Constitution."[296] By that time, the Secret Service had moved the Vice President to his ceremonial office across the hall.[297] But the situation was spiraling out of control—and they wouldn't stay there long. As Sarah Matthews, the Deputy White House Press Secretary, later explained: President Trump's tweet was like "pouring gasoline on the fire."[298]

Thirty seconds after President Trump's tweet, rioters who were already inside the Capitol opened the East Rotunda door just down the hall. A mere thirty seconds later, rioters breached the crypt one floor below the Vice President.

Though the Vice President refused the Secret Service's first two attempts to evacuate him from his ceremonial office, the situation quickly became untenable and the Vice President was told that the Secret Service could no longer protect him in this office in the Capitol that was quickly being overrun.[299] Marc Short recalls Tim Giebels, the head of the Vice President's Secret Service protective detail, saying, "At this point, I can't protect you behind these glass doors, and so I need to move you." [300] This time, the third, the Secret Service was not asking the Vice President to move; they were stating the fact that the Vice President must be moved.[301] At 2:20 p.m., NSC staff monitoring radio communications reported that the second floor of the Capitol and the door to the Senate Chamber "ha[ve] now been breached." [302]

At 2:25 p.m., the Secret Service rushed the Vice President, his family, and his senior staff down a flight of stairs, through a series of hallways and tunnels to a secure location.[303] The Vice President and his team stayed in that same location for the next four and a half hours.

The angry mob had come within 40 feet of the Vice President as he was evacuated.[304] President Trump never called to check on Vice President Pence's safety, so Marc Short called Mark Meadows to tell him they were safe and secure.[305] Short himself became *persona non grata* with President Trump. The President directed staff to revoke Short's access to the White House after Vice President Pence refused to betray his oath to the Constitution.[306] Marc Short never spoke with President Trump again.[307]

After arriving at the secure location, the head of the Vice President's Secret Service detail wanted to move the Vice President away from the Capitol, and staff hurried into the waiting vehicles. But the Vice President refused to get in the car.[308] As Greg Jacob explained in his testimony to the Select Committee:

> The Vice President wouldn't get in his car.... [H]e was determined that unless there was imminent danger to bodily safety that he was not going to abandon the Capitol and let the rioters have a victory of having made the Vice President flee or made it difficult to restart the process later that day.[309]

It was an unprecedented scene in American history. The President of the United States had riled up a mob that hunted his own Vice President.

The Vice President's staff came to believe that the theory "pushed and sold" to the public that the Vice President had a role to play in the joint session was a cause of the attack on the Capitol. "The reason that the Capitol was assaulted was that the people who were breaching the Capitol believed that... the election [outcome] had not yet been determined, and, instead, there was some action that was supposed to take place in Washington, D.C., to determine it," Jacob said.[310] "I do think [the violence] was the result of that position being continuously pushed and sold to people who ended up believing that with all their hearts." [311] The people had been "told that the Vice President had the authority" to determine the outcome of the election during the joint session.[312]

Photo provided to the Select Committee by the National Archives and Records Administration.

Of course, that was President Trump's and John Eastman's plan all along—to convince people that the election had been stolen, and that Vice President Pence could take action to change the outcome during the joint session on January 6th.

Jacob was writing an email to Eastman when the Capitol was breached.[313] At 2:14 p.m., just before being evacuated, Jacob hurriedly hit send on his email, but not before adding the following: "thanks to your bullshit, we are now under siege." [314]

Eastman quickly replied to Jacob's email and, incredibly, blamed Vice President Pence and Jacob for the attack. "The 'siege' is because YOU and your boss did not do what was necessary to allow this to be aired in a public way so the American people can see for themselves what happened," Eastman wrote.[315] Naturally, Jacob was "somewhere between aghast and livid." [316] It was "ridiculous" to blame Vice President Pence for the attack, when he simply followed the law.[317]

THE JOINT SESSION RECONVENES: "LET'S GET BACK TO WORK."
The Senate reconvened at approximately 8:06 p.m.[318] Congressional leadership and the Vice President insisted on finishing the work of the people. "Today was a dark day in the history of the United States Capitol," Vice President Pence said. "But thanks to the swift efforts of U.S. Capitol Police,

Photo provided to the Select Committee by the National Archives and Records Administration.

federal, state and local law enforcement, the violence was quelled. The
Capitol is secured, and the people's work continues." The Vice President
addressed "those who wreaked havoc in our Capitol today," saying "you did
not win." Vice President Pence continued:

> *Violence never wins. Freedom wins. And this is still the people's house.*
> *And as we reconvene in this chamber, the world will again witness the*
> *resilience and strength of our democracy, for even in the wake of*
> *unprecedented violence and vandalism at this Capitol, the elected repre-*
> *sentatives of the people of the United States have assembled again on*
> *the very same day to support and defend the Constitution of the United*
> *States.*

"Let's get back to work," Vice President Pence concluded.[319]

Despite the violence that had unfolded at the Capitol, Eastman kept agi-
tating for further delay. At 11:44 p.m. on January 6th, Eastman sent yet
another email to Greg Jacob.[320] In a shockingly tone-deaf manner, Eastman
claimed that the Electoral Count Act had been violated already, by allowing
debate beyond two hours, so—he argued—Vice President Pence should no
longer be concerned that what President Trump and Eastman had pressured

him to do also would violate it.[321] "Of course," as Jacob pointed out, the debate couldn't have been completed in two hours due to the "intervening riot of several hours."[322]

Eastman argued that Vice President Pence should "adjourn for 10 days to allow the legislatures to finish their investigations, as well as to allow a full forensic audit of the massive amount of illegal activity that has occurred here."[323] Eastman described this—a delay in the certification of the vote and the peaceful transfer of power with no legal or historical precedent or support, based on entirely specious and disproven allegations of election fraud, following on a violent attack on the seat of American democracy—as a "relatively minor violation."[324]

Vice President Pence later described Eastman's email as "rubber room stuff," meaning it was certifiably crazy.[325]

5.5   AFTERMATH OF THE ATTACK.

Eastman called Herschmann on January 7th to discuss litigation on behalf of the Trump Campaign in Georgia.[326] This gave Herschmann another opportunity to lay into Eastman. "[Are] you out of your F'ing mind?" Herschmann asked. "I only want to hear two words coming out of your mouth from now on: orderly transition." Herschmann said. After some berating, Eastman repeated after Herschmann: "Orderly transition." "Now I'm going to give you the best free legal advice you're ever getting in your life," Herschmann said. "Get a great F'ing criminal defense lawyer, you're going to need it."[327] Days afterward, Eastman sent an email to Giuliani, making a request that tacitly acknowledged just how much trouble he was in: "I've decided that I should be on the pardon list, if that is still in the works."[328]

Vice President Pence and his team never bowed to President Trump's relentless pressure. They began January 6, 2021, with a prayer. The attack on the U.S. Capitol delayed the peaceful transfer of power. The joint session did not end until early in the morning on January 7th.

At 3:50 a.m. that morning, Short texted Vice President Pence a passage from Second Timothy, chapter 4, verse 7: "I fought the good fight. I finished the race. I have kept the faith."[329]

ENDNOTES

1. Select Committee to Investigate the January 6th Attack on the United States Capitol, Deposition of Marc Short, (Jan. 26, 2022), pp. 10–11.

2. Select Committee to Investigate the January 6th Attack on the United States Capitol, Deposition of Marc Short, (Jan. 26, 2022), pp. 10–11.

3. *See, e.g.,* Ivan E. Raiklin (Former Green Beret Commander) (@Raiklin), Twitter, Dec. 22, 2020, available at https://web.archive.org/web/20201222232155/https://twitter.com/Raiklin/

status/1341520753984942081 (archived) ("America, @VP @Mike_Pence MUST do this, tomorrow!"); Donald J. Trump (@realDonaldTrump), Twitter, Dec. 23, 2020 7:40:30 p.m. ET, available at https://web.archive.org/web/20201224033528/http://twitter.com/realDonaldTrump (archived).

4. Select Committee to Investigate the January 6th Attack on the United States Capitol, Deposition of Greg Jacob, (Feb. 1, 2022), pp. 95, ("[T]he Vice President mostly asked a series of questions in that meeting of Mr. Eastman"), 130 (Q: "Did John Eastman ever admit, as far as you know, in front of the President that his proposal would violate the Electoral Count Act?" A: "I believe he did on the 4th." Q: "Okay. And can you tell us what the President's reaction was?" A: "A I can't."); Documents on file with the Select Committee to Investigate the January 6th Attack on the United States Capitol (National Archives Production), VP-R0000107 (Greg Jacob memo to Vice President Pence, titled "Analysis of Professor Eastman's Proposals").

5. Select Committee to Investigate the January 6th Attack on the United States Capitol, Deposition of Greg Jacob, (Feb. 1, 2022), p. 96 (Eastman acknowledging that the legal basis for his proposed paths was the same and, as recounted by Greg Jacob, "[y]ou couldn't get there either way unless you . . . set aside a number of the positions of the Electoral Count Act").

6. Select Committee to Investigate the January 6th Attack on the United States Capitol, Deposition of Marc Short, (Jan. 26, 2022), pp. 26–27 ("But just to pick up on that, Mr. Short, was it your impression that the Vice President had directly conveyed his position on these issues to the President, not just to the world through a Dear Colleague Letter, but directly to President Trump?" A: "Many times." Q: "And had been consistent in conveying his position to the President?" A: "Very consistent.").

7. Select Committee to Investigate the January 6th Attack on the United States Capitol, Deposition of Marc Short, (Jan. 26, 2022), pp. 18–20.

8. Documents on file with the Select Committee to Investigate the January 6th Attack on the United States Capitol (U.S. Secret Service Production), CTRL0000092958 (January 6, 2021, message at 10:39 a.m. ET).

9. Documents on file with the Select Committee to Investigate the January 6th Attack on the United States Capitol (US Secret Service Production), CTRL0000092978 (January 6, 2021, message at 10:43 a.m. ET).

10. "Transcript of Trump's Speech at Rally Before US Capitol Riot," *Associated Press*, (Jan. 13, 2021), available at https://apnews.com/article/election-2020-joe-biden-donald-trump-capitol-siege-media-e79eb5164613d6718e9f4502eb471f27.

11. "Transcript of Trump's Speech at Rally Before US Capitol Riot," *Associated Press*, (Jan. 13, 2021), available at https://apnews.com/article/election-2020-joe-biden-donald-trump-capitol-siege-media-e79eb5164613d6718e9f4502eb471f27.

12. "Transcript of Trump's Speech at Rally Before US Capitol Riot," *Associated Press*, (Jan. 13, 2021), available at https://apnews.com/article/election-2020-joe-biden-donald-trump-capitol-siege-media-e79eb5164613d6718e9f4502eb471f27.

13. Donald J. Trump (@realDonaldTrump), Twitter, Jan. 6, 2021 2:24 p.m. ET, available at https://web.archive.org/web/20210106192450/https://twitter.com/realdonaldtrump/status/1346900434540240897 (archived).

14. Select Committee to Investigate the January 6th Attack on the United States Capitol, *Hearing on the January 6th Investigation*, 117th Cong., 2d sess., (June 16, 2022), available at https://www.govinfo.gov/committee/house-january6th; Rebecca Shabad, "Noose Appears Near Capitol; Protesters Seen Carrying Confederate Flags," NBC News, (Jan. 6, 2021), available at https://www.nbcnews.com/politics/congress/live-blog/electoral-college-certification-updates-n1252864/ncrd1253129#blogHeader.

15. *See* Quint Forgey, " 'Almost No Idea More Un-American': Pence Breaks with Trump on Jan. 6," *Politico*, (June 25, 2021), available at https://www.politico.com/news/2021/06/25/pence-trump-jan-6-496237.

16. Statement by Donald J. Trump, 45th President of the United States of America, Jan. 30, 2022, available at https://web.archive.org/web/20220131171840/https://www.donaldjtrump.com/news/news-8nkdvatd7g1481 (archived) ("If the Vice President (Mike Pence) had 'absolutely no right' to change the Presidential Election results in the Senate, despite fraud and many other irregularities, how come the Democrats and RINO Republicans, like Wacky Susan Collins, are desperately trying to pass legislation that will not allow the Vice President to change the results of the election? Actually, what they are saying, is that Mike Pence did have the right to change the outcome, and they now want to take that right away. Unfortunately, he didn't exercise that power, he could have overturned the Election!") (emphasis added).

17. Mike Allen, "Exclusive Audio: Trump Defends Threats to 'Hang' Pence," *Axios*, (Nov. 12, 2021), available at available at https://www.axios.com/2021/11/12/trump-hang-mike-pence-january-6-audio ("Jonathan Karl: 'Were you worried about him during that siege? Were you worried about his safety?' Trump: 'No, I thought he was well-rotected, and I had heard that he was in good shape. No. Because I had heard he was in very good shape. But, but, no, I think—' Karl: 'Because you heard those chants—that was terrible. I mean—' Trump: 'He could have—well, the people were very angry.' Karl: *They were saying 'hang Mike Pence.'* Trump: *'Because it's common sense,* Jon. It's common sense that you're supposed to protect. How can you—if you know a vote is fraudulent, right?—how can you pass on a fraudulent vote to Congress? How can you do that?') (emphasis added).

18. Order Re Privilege of Documents Dated January 4-7, 2021 at 44, *Eastman v. Thompson et al.*, 594 F. Supp. 3d 1156, (C.D. Cal. Mar. 28, 2022) (No. 8:22-cv-99-DOC-DFM).

19. Order Re Privilege of Documents Dated January 4-7, 2021 at 36, 40, 44, *Eastman v. Thompson et al.*, 594 F. Supp. 3d 1156, (C.D. Cal. Mar. 28, 2022) (No. 8:22-cv-99-DOC-DFM) ("Based on the evidence, the Court finds that it is more likely than not that President Trump and Eastman dishonestly conspired to obstruct the Joint Session of Congress on January 6, 2021.").

20. Order Re Privilege of Documents Dated January 4-7, 2021 at 44, *Eastman v. Thompson et al.*, 594 F. Supp. 3d 1156, (C.D. Cal. Mar. 28, 2022) (No. 8:22-cv-99-DOC-DFM).

21. Documents on file with the Select Committee to Investigate the January 6th Attack on the United States Capitol (Chapman University Production), Chapman004708. This document was ordered to be produced to the Select Committee by Judge Carter over Eastman's assertion of attorney-client privilege and upon a finding that the crime-fraud exception to the attorney-client privilege applied. Order Re Privilege of Documents Dated January 4-7, 2021 at 41-42, *Eastman v. Thompson et al.*, 594 F. Supp. 3d 1156, (C.D. Cal. Mar. 28, 2022) (No. 8:22-cv-99-DOC-DFM).

22. Documents on file with the Select Committee to Investigate the January 6th Attack on the United States Capitol (Chapman University Production), Chapman004708.

23. Documents on file with the Select Committee to Investigate the January 6th Attack on the United States Capitol (Chapman University Production), Chapman004708.

24. Neither Eastman nor Chesebro provided substantive answers in response to the Select Committee's questions about the development of this strategy. *See* Select Committee to Investigate the January 6th Attack on the United States Capitol, Deposition of John Eastman, (Dec. 9, 2021); Select Committee to Investigate the January 6th Attack on the United States Capitol, Deposition of Kenneth Chesebro, (Oct. 25, 2022). It is thus difficult to determine who first suggested this concept. Evidence obtained by the Select Committee suggests that key players like Eastman, Giuliani, and Epshteyn were starting to discuss the Vice President's role at the joint session in late November or early December. *See, e.g.*, Select Committee to Investigate the January 6th Attack on the United States Capitol, Transcribed Interview of Cassidy Hutchinson, (Feb. 23, 2022), pp. 71–73 (discussing conversations

involving Mark Meadows, Rudolph Giuliani's legal team, and Members of Congress in late November or early December); Documents on file with the Select Committee to Investigate the January 6th Attack on the United States Capitol (Chapman University Production), Chapman023534 (December 5, 2020 email from John Eastman remarking that "folks at the top of the chain of command on this...are now aware of the issues"). *See also* Michael Wolff, *Landslide: The Final Days of the Trump Presidency* (New York: Henry Holt and Company, 2021), p. 135 (describing post-Thanksgiving outreach from Boris Epshteyn to the White House regarding the Vice President theory).

25. Order Re Privilege of Documents Dated January 4-7, 2021 at 41-42, *Eastman v. Thompson et al.*, 594 F. Supp. 3d 1156, (C.D. Cal. Mar. 28, 2022) (No. 8:22-cv-99-DOC-DFM) ("Because the memo likely furthered the crimes of obstruction of an official proceeding and conspiracy to defraud the United States, it is subject to the crime-fraud exception and the Court ORDERS it to be disclosed.").

26. The Select Committee's investigation found that Eastman was communicating about the joint session with Kenneth Chesebro in December 2020. *See e.g.*, Documents on file with the Select Committee to Investigate the January 6th Attack on the United States Capitol (Chapman University Production), Chapman053460, Chapman053475 (December 23, 2020, emails between John Eastman, Kenneth Chesebro, and Boris Epshteyn regarding procedural proposals for joint session).

27. Documents on file with the Select Committee to Investigate the January 6th Attack on the United States Capitol (Chapman University Production), Chapman052976. This memo was originally obtained by the *Washington Post*'s Bob Woodward and Robert Costa and subsequently published by CNN. "READ: Trump Lawyer's Memo on Six-Step Plan for Pence to Overturn the Election," CNN, (Sept. 21, 2021), available at https://www.cnn.com/2021/09/21/politics/read-eastman-memo/index.html.

28. Under the Constitution, if no candidate receives a majority of electoral college votes, this triggers a process where the House of Representatives decides the president. When that happens, each State gets one vote for President, chosen by the Representatives from that state. The candidate who receives a majority of the 50 State votes becomes the president. At the time, there were more Republicans than Democrats in 26 of the 50 State House delegations, leading Eastman to predict that "President Trump [would be] re-elected" under that scenario. *See* Documents on file with the Select Committee to Investigate the January 6th Attack on the United States Capitol (Chapman University Production), Chapman052976.

29. Documents on file with the Select Committee to Investigate the January 6th Attack on the United States Capitol (Chapman University Production), Chapman052976. Note that Eastman has acknowledged the authenticity of a publicly disclosed version of this document, describing it as "a preliminary, incomplete draft" of "the legal memo [he] wrote in January." John C. Eastman, "Trying to Prevent Illegal Conduct from Deciding an Election Is Not Endorsing a 'Coup'," *American Greatness*, (Sept. 30, 2021), available at https://amgreatness.com/2021/09/30/trying-to-prevent-illegal-conduct-from-deciding-an-election-is-not-endorsing-a-coup/ (linking to two-page document titled "PRIVILEGED AND CONFIDENTIAL, January 6 scenario, available at http://cdn.cnn.com/cnn/2021/images/09/20/eastman.memo.pdf).

30. Documents on file with the Select Committee to Investigate the January 6th Attack on the United States Capitol (Chapman University Production), Chapman053561 (December 23, 2020, email from John Eastman to Molly Michael).

31. Documents on file with the Select Committee to Investigate the January 6th Attack on the United States Capitol, (Verizon Production, July 11, 2022) (Dec. 23, 2020 cellular data records from John Eastman). The morning that Eastman began preparing the memo, he received a call from Boris Epshteyn at 8:58 am. Eleven minutes later, Eastman called Chesebro, and the two spoke for over 41 minutes. Eastman continued to trade calls with Epshteyn and Chesebro throughout the day. *See* Documents on file with the Select Committee to Investigate the January 6th Attack on the United States Capitol, (Verizon Production, July 11, 2022) (December 23, 2020, phone records for John Eastman)

32. Documents on file with the Select Committee to Investigate the January 6th Attack on the United States Capitol (Chapman University Production), Chapman052976, p. 2 (Memo regarding January 6 scenario).

33. Documents on file with the Select Committee to Investigate the January 6th Attack on the United States Capitol (Chapman University Production), Chapman003226.

34. Documents on file with the Select Committee to Investigate the January 6th Attack on the United States Capitol (Chapman University Production), Chapman003228. Note that this letter refers to, and purports to supplement, the recommendations of what Eastman described in his correspondence with Mr. Colbert as "a major war game simulation" that he claimed—on October 24, 2020—was "already before the President and his team." Documents on file with the Select Committee to Investigate the January 6th Attack on the United States Capitol (Chapman University Production), Chapman031983. The war game exercise in which Eastman participated is reflected in a report issued by the Claremont Institute and the Texas Public Policy Foundation. "79 Days Report", (Oct. 20, 2020), available at https://www.texaspolicy.com/79-days-to-inauguration-taskforce-report/.

35. Documents on file with the Select Committee to Investigate the January 6th Attack on the United States Capitol (Chapman University Production), Chapman003228 (emphasis added).

36. Documents on file with the Select Committee to Investigate the January 6th Attack on the United States Capitol (Chapman University Production), Chapman031983.

37. Documents on file with the Select Committee to Investigate the January 6th Attack on the United States Capitol (Chapman University Production), Chapman023534.

38. Documents on file with the Select Committee to Investigate the January 6th Attack on the United States Capitol (Chapman University Production), Chapman031983.

39. Documents on file with the Select Committee to Investigate the January 6th Attack on the United States Capitol (Chapman University Production), Chapman052976 (memo regarding January 6 scenarios).

40. Documents on file with the Select Committee to Investigate the January 6th Attack on the United States Capitol (Chapman University Production), Chapman052976 (memo regarding January 6 scenarios).

41. Documents on file with the Select Committee to Investigate the January 6th Attack on the United States Capitol (Chapman University Production), Chapman052966 (December 23, 2020, email from Kenneth Chesebro).

42. Documents on file with the Select Committee to Investigate the January 6th Attack on the United States Capitol (Chapman University Production), Chapman052976 (memo regarding January 6 scenarios).

43. Documents on file with the Select Committee to Investigate the January 6th Attack on the United States Capitol (Chapman University Production), Chapman052976 (memo regarding January 6 scenarios).

44. Documents on file with the Select Committee to Investigate the January 6th Attack on the United States Capitol (Chapman University Production), Chapman052976 (memo regarding January 6).

45. Select Committee to Investigate the January 6th Attack on the United States Capitol, Transcribed Interview of Eric Herschmann, (Apr. 6, 2022), p. 26; see also id., at 36-377 (stating that he did not understand Eastman's statement to be suggesting that violence would be justified to keep President Trump in office).

46. Select Committee to Investigate the January 6th Attack on the United States Capitol, Transcribed Interview of Eric Herschmann, (Apr. 6, 2022), p. 28.

47. Select Committee to Investigate the January 6th Attack on the United States Capitol, Transcribed Interview of Eric Herschmann, (Apr. 6, 2022), pp. 26, 28-29.

48. Select Committee to Investigate the January 6th Attack on the United States Capitol, Transcribed Interview of Eric Herschmann, (Apr. 6, 2022), p. 29.

49. Select Committee to Investigate the January 6th Attack on the United States Capitol, Transcribed Interview of Eric Herschmann, (Apr. 6, 2022), p. 29.

50. Select Committee to Investigate the January 6th Attack on the United States Capitol, Transcribed Interview of Eric Herschmann, (Apr. 6, 2022), p. 29.

51. Select Committee to Investigate the January 6th Attack on the United States Capitol, Deposition of Jason Miller, (Feb. 3, 2022), p. 157.

52. Select Committee to Investigate the January 6th Attack on the United States Capitol, Deposition of Jason Miller, (Feb. 3, 2022), pp. 142, 152.

53. Documents on file with the Select Committee to Investigate the January 6th Attack on the United States Capitol (National Archives Production), 079P-R0000731. Neither this memo, nor a December 8, 2020, memo that followed, reflects the full advice that Greg Jacob ultimately gave to the Vice President regarding the joint session. *See* Select Committee to Investigate the January 6th Attack on the United States Capitol, Deposition of Greg Jacob, (Feb. 1, 2022), pp. 10–11, 32. The OVP Legal Staff memo, dated October 26, 2020, is titled "The Unconstitutionality of the Electoral Count Act." This memo adopts certain legal academics' criticism of the Electoral Count Act and introduces several concepts that would later be cited by proponents of the theory of an expansive view of the Vice President's power. Greg Jacob's legal memo to the Vice President, dated December 8, 2020, notes that the Electoral Count Act prescribes the process for counting electoral votes "to the extent it is constitutional" and seems to allow for the possibility of the Vice President "assert[ing] a constitutional privilege." Documents on file with the Select Committee to Investigate the January 6th Attack on the United States Capitol (National Archives Production), 079P-R0000785. Through his extensive research and analysis, Greg Jacob's understanding developed both as to the legal and historical precedent for the joint session and ultimately led him to the unavoidable conclusions that, one, the Electoral Count Act governed the joint session and, two, its procedures had never been deviated from since it was passed.

54. Select Committee to Investigate the January 6th Attack on the United States Capitol, Deposition of Greg Jacob Deposition, (Feb. 1, 2022), pp. 11–13, 25–26 (noting that Marc Short didn't "name names" of the people he was concerned would encourage the President to prematurely declare victory).

55. Documents on file with the Select Committee to Investigate the January 6th Attack on the United States Capitol (National Archives Production), 079VP-R000011579_0001, 079VP-R000011579_0002 (November 3, 2020, Greg Jacob memo to Marc Short, titled "Electoral Vote Count"). The Election Day memo identifies the 12th Amendment and the Electoral Count Act as the relevant legal framework, but leaves open "whether it is the Vice President, or Congress, that has ultimate constitutional authority to decide electoral vote disputes." It also represents an incomplete understanding of the factual precedents, describing then-Vice President Nixon's conduct in January 1961 as "single-handedly resolv[ing] a dispute over competing slates of electors that were submitted by the State of Hawaii." (In fact, after additional research Jacob concluded the opposite was true.) As addressed elsewhere in this chapter, this memo does not reflect Greg Jacob's full legal analysis or ultimate advice, nor the Vice President's conclusion, about the authority of the Vice President at the joint session.

56. Daniel Villarreal, "Lincoln Project Ad Tells Trump That Pence 'Will Put the Nail in Your Political Coffin'," *Newsweek*, (Dec. 8, 2020), available at https://www.newsweek.com/lincoln—project-ad-tells-trump-that-pence-will-put-nail-your-political-coffin-1553331.

57. Select Committee to Investigate the January 6th Attack on the United States Capitol, Deposition of Greg Jacob, (Feb. 1, 2022), p. 13; Select Committee to Investigate the January 6th Attack on the United States Capitol, *Hearing on the January 6th Investigation*, 117th Cong., 2d sess., (Jun. 16, 2022), available at https://www.govinfo.gov/committee/house-january6th; Select Committee to Investigate the January 6th Attack on the United States Capitol, Deposition of Marc Short, (Jan. 26, 2022), pp. 135–36 (noting the ad buy was limited to "D.C. and Palm Beach").

58. Documents on file with the Select Committee to Investigate the January 6th Attack on the United States Capitol (National Archives Production), 079P-R0000785_0001, 079P-R0000785_0002, 079P-R0000785_0003, 079P-R0000785_0004 (December 8, 2020, Greg Jacob memo to Vice President Pence, titled "January 6 Process for Electoral Vote Count"); see also, Select Committee to Investigate the January 6th Attack on the United States Capitol, Deposition of Greg Jacob, (Feb. 1, 2022), p. 32. This December 8, 2020, memo reflects Jacob's more detailed understanding of the mechanics of "modern practice" under the Electoral Count Act, including the process by which the House and Senate separate to debate a member of the House's objection if it is signed by a Senator, but not the full analysis of the precedent that Jacob would ultimately do before January 6, 2021.

59. Select Committee to Investigate the January 6th Attack on the United States Capitol, Deposition of Greg Jacob, (Feb. 1, 2022), p. 102.

60. Select Committee to Investigate the January 6th Attack on the United States Capitol, Deposition of Greg Jacob, (Feb. 1, 2022), pp. 33, 102.

61. U.S. Const. art. II, § 1, cl 3; U.S. Const., Amend. XII.

62. Select Committee to Investigate the January 6th Attack on the United States Capitol, Hearing on the January 6th Investigation, 117th Cong., 2d sess., (June 16, 2022), available at https://www.govinfo.gov/committee/house-january6th.

63. Select Committee to Investigate the January 6th Attack on the United States Capitol, Deposition of Greg Jacob, (Feb. 1, 2022), pp. 14–16.

64. Select Committee to Investigate the January 6th Attack on the United States Capitol, Deposition of Greg Jacob, (Feb. 1, 2022), pp. 14–16.

65. Select Committee to Investigate the January 6th Attack on the United States Capitol, Hearing on the January 6th Investigation, 117th Cong., 2d sess., (June 16, 2022), available at https://www.govinfo.gov/committee/house-january6th. In testimony given at a Select Committee hearing, Judge Luttig disagreed with Jacob's characterization of the sentence carried through from the Constitution to the 12th Amendment, describing it instead as "pristine[ly] clear," but the witnesses were in agreement that there was "no basis in the Constitution or laws of the United States at all for the theory espoused by Mr. Eastman." Id.; see Select Committee to Investigate the January 6th Attack on the United States Capitol, Hearing on the January 6th Investigation, 117th Cong., 2d sess., (June 16, 2022), available at https://www.govinfo.gov/committee/house-january6th. ("I am in complete agreement with Judge Luttig; it is unambiguous that the Vice President does not have the authority to reject electors."). Note that Vice President Pence apparently agreed with Jacob regarding the clarity of the Constitutional language, as Jacob testified that he joked, "I can't wait to go to heaven and meet the Framers and tell them, 'The work that you did in putting together our Constitution is a work of genius. Thank you. It was divinely inspired. There is one sentence that I would like to talk to you a little bit about.'" Id.

66. Select Committee to Investigate the January 6th Attack on the United States Capitol, Hearing on the January 6th Investigation, 117th Cong., 2d sess., (June 16, 2022), available at https://www.govinfo.gov/committee/house-january6th.

67. Complaint, Gohmert et al. v. Pence, 510 F. Supp. 3d 435, (No. 6:20-cv-0660), (E.D. Tex. Dec. 27, 2020), ECF No. 1.

68. Mike Pence, So Help Me God (New York: Simon & Schuster, 2022), p. 443.

69. Complaint, Gohmert et al. v. Pence, 510 F. Supp. 3d 435, (No. 6:20-cv-0660), (E.D. Tex. Dec. 27, 2020), ECF No. 1.

70. Complaint, Gohmert et al. v. Pence, 510 F. Supp. 3d 435, (No. 6:20-cv-0660), (E.D. Tex. Dec. 27, 2020), ECF No. 1.

71. Complaint, Gohmert et al. v. Pence, 510 F. Supp. 3d 435, (No. 6:20-cv-0660), (E.D. Tex. Dec. 27, 2020), ECF No. 1.

72. Documents on file with the Select Committee to Investigate the January 6th Attack on the United States Capitol (Chapman University Production), Chapman055337 (December 22, 2020, John Eastman email to William Olson, Larry Joseph, Mark Martin, Kurt Olson, Kris Kobach, Phillip Jauregui, Pat McSweeney, and Don Brown, titled "Re: Draft Complaint").

73. Order Re Privilege of Documents Dated January 4-7, 2021 at 6, *Eastman v. Thompson et al.*, 594 F. Supp. 3d 1156 (C.D. Cal. 2022) (No. 8:22-cv-99-DOC-DFM).

74. Documents on file with the Select Committee to Investigate the January 6th Attack on the United States Capitol (Chapman University Production), Chapman055337 (December 22, 2020, William Olson email to Larry Joseph, Mark Martin, Kurt Olson, Kris Kobach, John Eastman, Phillip Jauregui, Pat McSweeney, and Don Brown, titled "Re: Draft Complaint").

75. Select Committee to Investigate the January 6th Attack on the United States Capitol, Transcribed Interview of Russell "Rusty" Bowers, (June 19, 2022), pp. 42–45; Documents on file with the Select Committee to Investigate the January 6th Attack on the United States Capitol (Chapman University Production), Chapman003584, (January 4, 2021, emails between John Eastman and Andrew Pappas, coordinating the call between Eastman and Speaker Bowers). Eastman also asked Speaker Bowers to sign a letter drafted by Arizona Rep. Mark Finchem directed to Vice President Pence asking him not to certify the election on January 6th; Bowers refused. Select Committee to Investigate the January 6th Attack on the United States Capitol, Transcribed Interview of Russell "Rusty" Bowers, (June 19, 2022), at p. 45–46.

76. Select Committee to Investigate the January 6th Attack on the United States Capitol, Transcribed Interview of Russell "Rusty" Bowers, (June 19, 2022), at p. 46. Speaker Bowers had already addressed publicly both the pressure he was receiving to overturn the result of the election as well as his firm belief that doing so would violate his oath of office. Documents on file with the Select Committee to Investigate the January 6th Attack on the United States Capitol (Rusty Bowers Production), CTRL0000062389 (Nov. 18, 2020, Dear Colleague letter with attached "Post-Election Frequently Asked Questions"), Documents on file with the Select Committee to Investigate the January 6th Attack on the United States Capitol (Rusty Bowers Production), CTRL0000071098_00069 (December 4, 2020, Press Release titled "Speaker Bowers Addresses Calls for the Legislature to Overturn 2020 Certified Election Results).

77. Select Committee to Investigate the January 6th Attack on the United States Capitol, Transcribed Interview of Russell "Rusty" Bowers, (June 19, 2022), at p. 46. Speaker Bowers also received a call on the morning of January 6th from Representative Andy Biggs in which Rep. Biggs asked Speaker Bowers to sign a letter being sent by other Arizona legislators and/or to support decertification of Arizona's electors; Speaker Bowers again refused. Select Committee to Investigate the January 6th Attack on the United States Capitol, *Hearing on the January 6th Investigation*, 117th Cong., 2d sess., (June 21, 2022), available at https://www.govinfo.gov/committee/house-january6th.

78. *Gohmert et al. v. Pence*, 510 F. Supp. 3d 435, 443 (E.D. Tx. 2021).

79. *Gohmert et al. v. Pence*, 141 S. Ct. 972 (2021).

80. Select Committee to Investigate the January 6th Attack on the United States Capitol, Deposition of John McEntee, (Mar. 28, 2022), pp. 132–34.

81. Documents on file with the Select Committee to Investigate the January 6th Attack on the United States Capitol (John McEntee Production), McEntee0001 (document titled "JEFFERSON USED HIS POSITION AS VP TO WIN").

82. Documents on file with the Select Committee to Investigate the January 6th Attack on the United States Capitol (National Archives Production), P-R000236-000238 (John McEntee note and drafted analysis, titled "PENCE CAN LET THE STATES DECIDE"). Note that the Select Committee received both documents from the National Archives in a format consistent with the documents having been torn apart and taped back together.

83. Documents on file with the Select Committee to Investigate the January 6th Attack on the United States Capitol (National Archives Production), P-R000236-237 (John McEntee note and drafted analysis, titled "PENCE CAN LET THE STATES DECIDE").

84. Documents on file with the Select Committee to Investigate the January 6th Attack on the United States Capitol (National Archives Production), P-R000237; Select Committee to Investigate the January 6th Attack on the United States Capitol, Deposition of John McEntee, (Mar. 28, 2022), p. 147.

85. Select Committee to Investigate the January 6th Attack on the United States Capitol, Deposition of John McEntee, (Mar. 28, 2022), pp. 147-48.

86. Documents on file with the Select Committee to Investigate the January 6th Attack on the United States Capitol (Short production), J6C-TSM-0001, J6C-TSM-0002. Note that the file name of the document ("MEMO_POTUS_January6VPAction.pdf") is visible in an email in which Marc Short forwards to Greg Jacob the memo received from Mark Meadows. Documents on file with the Select Committee to Investigate the January 6th Attack on the United States Capitol (National Archives Production), VP-R0000033, VP-R0000034.

87. Documents on file with the Select Committee to Investigate the January 6th Attack on the United States Capitol (National Archives Production), VP-R0000034.

88. Documents on file with the Select Committee to Investigate the January 6th Attack on the United States Capitol (Jenna Ellis Production), J.007206Ellis.

89. Documents on file with the Select Committee to Investigate the January 6th Attack on the United States Capitol (Jenna Ellis Production), J.007472Ellis.

90. Documents on file with the Select Committee to Investigate the January 6th Attack on the United States Capitol (Jenna Ellis Production), CTRL0000916457_00002, (January 5, 2021, memo from Jenna Ellis to Jay Sekulow). This document was published by *Politico* on December 10, 2021. Betsy Woodruff Swan and Kyle Cheney, "Trump Campaign Lawyer Authored 2 Memos Claiming Pence Could Halt Biden's Victory," *Politico*, (Dec. 10, 2021), available at https://www.politico.com/news/2021/12/10/trump-lawyer-pence-biden-524088. In response to a Select Committee subpoena, Ellis produced a privilege log reflecting several communications from Ellis to Sekulow on January 5 and 6, 2021, each of which was described as "[e]mail discussion of internal legal strategy for possible pending litigation."

91. Documents on file with the Select Committee to Investigate the January 6th Attack on the United States Capitol (Jenna Ellis Production), CTRL0000916457_00002 (January 5, 2021, memo from Ellis to Jay Sekulow).

92. Politico (@politico), Twitter, Jan. 5, 2021 2:31 p.m. ET, available at https://twitter.com/politico/status/1346539955724681221 ("'I actually don't think that's what the Constitution has in mind,' Jay Sekulow, the chief counsel of the American Center for Law & Justice, says about the possibility of Pence rejecting the Electoral College results").

93. Politico (@politico), Twitter, Jan. 5, 2021 2:31 p.m. ET, available at https://twitter.com/politico/status/1346539955724681221.

94. Select Committee to Investigate the January 6th Attack on the United States Capitol, Transcribed Interview of Eric Herschmann, (Apr. 6, 2022), p. 208.

95. Select Committee to Investigate the January 6th Attack on the United States Capitol, Transcribed Interview of Eric Herschmann, (Apr. 6, 2022), p. 208.

96. Select Committee to Investigate the January 6th Attack on the United States Capitol, Deposition of Greg Jacob, (Feb. 1, 2022), p. 68; Select Committee to Investigate the January 6th Attack on the United States Capitol, Transcribed of Matt Morgan, (Apr. 25, 2022), pp. 19, 113. Matt Morgan was at the time a lawyer with Elections, LLC serving as General Counsel of the Trump Campaign and also acting as counsel to Vice President Pence's leadership PAC.

97. Select Committee to Investigate the January 6th Attack on the United States Capitol, Transcribed Interview of Matthew Morgan, (Apr. 25, 2022), pp. 117, 125 ("I had no question about what he was going to do on January 6th.").

98. Select Committee to Investigate the January 6th Attack on the United States Capitol, Deposition of Greg Jacob, (Feb. 1, 2022), p. 68. *See also* Select Committee to Investigate the January 6th Attack on the United States Capitol, Deposition of Chris Hodgson, (Mar. 30, 2022), p. 179 (stating that the reasons why Vice President Pence wanted to issue a public statement included the public discourse, letters from State legislators, and reporting about communications between the President and Vice President).

99. Select Committee to Investigate the January 6th Attack on the United States Capitol, Transcribed Interview of Matthew Morgan, (Apr. 25, 2022), pp. 114, 116.

100. Select Committee to Investigate the January 6th Attack on the United States Capitol, Deposition of Marc Short, (Jan. 26, 2022), pp. 166-68 ("I'm not aware of any evidence that the campaign had, and I'm not aware of any evidence the campaign shared with our office that would have again provided specific evidence of theft or fraud that would have had a material change in any of the States.").

101. Select Committee to Investigate the January 6th Attack on the United States Capitol, Transcribed Interview of Matt Morgan, (Apr. 25, 2022), pp. 99–00; Select Committee to Investigate the January 6th Attack on the United States Capitol, Deposition of Greg Jacob, (Feb. 1, 2022), pp. 36-37.

102. Documents on file with the Select Committee to Investigate the January 6th Attack on the United States Capitol (National Archives Production), 079P-R0000745; *see also* Select Committee to Investigate the January 6th Attack on the United States Capitol, Deposition of Greg Jacob, (Feb. 1, 2022), p. 38. Following the meeting on January 2, 2021, Greg Jacob shared the following memo with Matt Morgan. *See* Documents on file with the Select Committee to Investigate the January 6th Attack, (Matt Morgan Production), AGSC16-000103.

103. Select Committee to Investigate the January 6th Attack on the United States Capitol, Deposition of Greg Jacob, (Feb. 1, 2022), pp. 61-62.

104. Documents on file with the Select Committee to Investigate the January 6th Attack on the United States Capitol (Matt Morgan Production), AGSC16-000066; Select Committee to Investigate the January 6th Attack on the United States Capitol, Transcribed Interview of Matt Morgan, (Apr. 25, 2022), p. 74 ("My view, for an electoral count vote to count, you need a certificate of ascertainment and then the vote of the elector itself, that the vote of an elector without a certificate of ascertainment would not be validly submitted.").

105. Documents on file with the Select Committee to Investigate the January 6th Attack on the United States Capitol (National Archives Production), 079P-R0000698; *see also* Documents on file with the Select Committee to Investigate the January 6th Attack on the United States Capitol (Chris Hodgson Production),00131; Select Committee to Investigate the January 6th Attack on the United States Capitol, Deposition of Chris Hodgson, (Mar. 30, 2022), p. 128 (stating that as of the date of this memo, January 2, 2021, "there were no open questions at that point that I'm aware of.").

106. Select Committee to Investigate the January 6th Attack on the United States Capitol, Deposition of Greg Jacob, (Feb. 1, 2022), p. 52.

107. Select Committee to Investigate the January 6th Attack on the United States Capitol, Deposition of Greg Jacob, (Feb. 1, 2022), pp. 68-69. Jacob shared a draft version of the statement with Matt Morgan. *See* Select Committee to Investigate the January 6th Attack on the United States Capitol, Transcribed Interview of Matt Morgan, (Apr. 25, 2022), pp. 119-120. This draft version clearly set forth Vice President Pence's position, "I Preside, Congress Decides." The draft statement read: I cannot believe that the Framers, who above all else feared the concentrated power of a Caesar, intended to appoint a single individual, often directly interested in the outcome, to unilaterally determine the validity of electoral votes. In the wrong hands, such a power would be the undoing of the Republic." Documents on file with the Select Committee to Investigate the January 6th Attack on the United States Capitol (Matt Morgan Production), AGSC16-000149.

108. Philip Rucker, Josh Dawsey, "Growing Number of Trump Loyalists in the Senate Vow to Challenge Biden's Victory," *Washington Post*, (Jan. 2, 2021), available at https://www.washingtonpost.com/politics/senators-challenge-election/2021/01/02/81a4e5c4-4c7d-11eb-a9d9-1e3ec4a928b9_story.html.

109. Select Committee to Investigate the January 6th Attack on the United States Capitol, Deposition of Marc Short, (Jan. 26, 2022), pp. 166–68.

110. Select Committee to Investigate the January 6th Attack on the United States Capitol, Deposition of Marc Short, (Jan. 26, 2022), pp. 165-66.

111. Documents on file with the Select Committee to Investigate the January 6th Attack on the United States Capitol (Select Committee Transcription), CTRL0000082311, p. 7 (January 2, 2021, Steve Bannon War Room Transcript).

112. Documents on file with the Select Committee to Investigate the January 6th Attack on the United States Capitol (Select Committee Transcription), CTRL0000082311, p. 3 (January 2, 2021, Steve Bannon War Room Transcript).

113. Documents on file with the Select Committee to Investigate the January 6th Attack on the United States Capitol (Select Committee Transcription), CTRL0000082311, p. 6 (January 2, 2021, Steve Bannon War Room Transcript).

114. Documents on file with the Select Committee to Investigate the January 6th Attack on the United States Capitol (Select Committee Transcription), CTRL0000082311, p. 7 (January 2, 2021, Steve Bannon War Room Transcript).

115. Documents on file with the Select Committee to Investigate the January 6th Attack on the United States Capitol (Select Committee Transcription), CTRL0000082311, p. 7 (January 2, 2021, Steve Bannon War Room Transcript).

116. Documents on file with the Select Committee to Investigate the January 6th Attack on the United States Capitol (Select Committee Transcription), CTRL0000082311, p. 7 (January 2, 2021, Steve Bannon War Room Transcript).

117. Documents on file with the Select Committee to Investigate the January 6th Attack on the United States Capitol (Select Committee Transcription), CTRL0000082311, p. 8 (January 2, 2021, Steve Bannon War Room Transcript).

118. Documents on file with the Select Committee to Investigate the January 6th Attack on the United States Capitol (Select Committee Transcription), CTRL0000082311, p. 7 (January 2, 2021, Steve Bannon War Room Transcript).

119. Andrew Kaczynski, Em Steck, "Trump Lawyer John Eastman Said 'Courage and the Spine' Would Help Pence Send Election to the House in Comments before January 6," CNN, (Oct. 30, 2021), available at https://www.cnn.com/2021/10/30/politics/kfile-john-eastman-said-pence-could-throw-election-to-house/index.html.

120. Documents on file with the Select Committee to Investigate the January 6th Attack on the United States Capitol (Public Source), CTRL0000923171 (January 3, 2021, 6-page Eastman memo). Note that Eastman publicly disclosed this document, describing it as "the final version of [his] memo" and embedding it with a filename "Jan 3 Memo on Jan 6 Scenario." John C. Eastman, "Trying to Prevent Illegal Conduct From Deciding an Election Is Not Endorsing a 'Coup'," *American Greatness*, (Sept. 30, 2021), available at https://amgreatness.com/2021/09/30/trying-to-prevent-illegal-conduct-from-deciding-an-election-is-not-endorsing-a-coup/. Eastman has also tried to rewrite history with regard to this memo, arguing that it noted that Congress has the power to make the final determination regarding electoral votes, even though the memo concludes, "[t]he fact is that the Constitution assigns this power to the Vice President as the ultimate arbiter. We should take all of our actions with that in mind." *See* John McCormack, "John Eastman vs. the Eastman Memo," *National Review*, (Oct. 22, 2021), available at https://www.nationalreview.com/2021/10/john-eastman-vs-the-eastman-memo (emphasis added).

121. Documents on file with the Select Committee to Investigate the January 6th Attack on the
      United States Capitol (Public Source) CTRL0000923171, pp. 4-5 (January 3, 2021, 6-page East-
      man memo).

122. Documents on file with the Select Committee to Investigate the January 6th Attack on the
      United States Capitol (Public Source) CTRL0000923171, (January 3, 2021, 6-page Eastman
      memo) (describing the majority of the "TRUMP WINS" scenarios as resulting from the Vice
      President unilaterally determining "which" electoral slate from a State is valid, after
      "asserting that the authority to make that determination under the 12th Amendment . . . is
      his alone (and anything in the Electoral Count Act to the contrary is therefore unconstitu-
      tional).").

123. Documents on file with the Select Committee to Investigate the January 6th Attack on the
      United States Capitol (Public Source) CTRL0000923171, (January 3, 2021, 6-page Eastman
      memo) p. 5.

124. Documents on file with the Select Committee to Investigate the January 6th Attack on the
      United States Capitol (Public Source) CTRL0000923171, (January 3, 2021, 6-page Eastman
      memo) p. 2; Documents on file with the Select Committee to Investigate the January 6th
      Attack on the United States Capitol (Chapman University Production), Chapman052976
      (December 23, 2020, 2-page Eastman memo).

125. John C. Eastman, "Constitutional Statesmanship," Claremont Review of Books, (Fall 2021)
      available at https://claremontreviewofbooks.com/constitutional-statesmanship/.

126. Documents on file with the Select Committee to Investigate the January 6th Attack on the
      United States Capitol (Chapman University Production), Chapman043035 (December 19,
      2020, email from John Eastman to Bruce Colbert, re: Latest draft). It is not clear what rela-
      tionship or connection existed between John Eastman and Bruce Colbert before the elec-
      tion; documents produced to the Select Committee demonstrate that Eastman and Mr.
      Colbert exchanged dozens of emails during the time period covered by the Select Commit-
      tee's subpoena to Chapman University (November 3, 2020, to January 20, 2021).

127. Select Committee to Investigate the January 6th Attack on the United States Capitol, *Hear-
      ing on the January 6th Investigation*, 117th Cong., 2d sess., (Jun. 16, 2022), available at
      [https://www.govinfo.gov/committee/house-january6th.] (Judge Luttig testifying, "[T]here
      was no support whatsoever in either the Constitution of the United States nor the laws of
      the United States for the Vice President, frankly, ever to count alternative electoral slates
      from the States that had not been officially certified by the designated State official in the
      Electoral Count Act of 1887.").

128. Documents on file with the Select Committee to Investigate the January 6th Attack on the
      United States Capitol (Chapman University Production), Chapman053475, (December 23,
      2020, email from John Eastman to Boris Epshteyn and Kenneth Chesebro, "FW: Draft 2, with
      edits"); Documents on file with the Select Committee to Investigate the January 6th Attack
      on the United States Capitol (Chapman University Production), Chapman053476 (December
      23, 2020, 2-page Eastman memo).

129. Documents on file with the Select Committee to Investigate the January 6th Attack on the
      United States Capitol (Chapman University Production), Chapman063984 (January 10, 2021,
      email from John Eastman to Valerie Moon, re: Tell us in layman's language, what the heck
      happened with the dual electors? Please?). This email appears to be a response by East-
      man to an unsolicited email from a member of the public.

130. Documents on file with the Select Committee to Investigate the January 6th Attack on the
      United States Capitol (Chapman University Production), Chapman063984 (January 10, 2021,
      email from John Eastman to Valerie Moon, re: Tell us in layman's language, what the heck
      happened with the dual electors? Please?).

131. Documents on file with the Select Committee to Investigate the January 6th Attack on the
      United States Capitol (Public Source) CTRL0000923171, p. 5 (January 3, 2021, 6-page Eastman
      memo).

132. Documents on file with the Select Committee to Investigate the January 6th Attack on the United States Capitol (Public Source), CTRL0000923171, p. 5 (January 3, 2021, 6-page Eastman memo).

133. Documents on file with the Select Committee to Investigate the January 6th Attack on the United States Capitol (Public Source), CTRL0000923171, p. 5 (January 3, 2021, 6-page Eastman memo).

134. Documents on file with the Select Committee to Investigate the January 6th Attack on the United States Capitol (Public Source), CTRL0000923171, p. 5 (January 3, 2021, 6-page Eastman memo).

135. The pressure placed on the Vice President by the President was a "multiweek campaign" that reached a crescendo in the days before January 6th. Select Committee to Investigate the January 6th Attack on the United States Capitol, Deposition of Greg Jacob, (Feb. 1, 2022), p. 33. The Vice President's Chief of Staff, Marc Short, saw the separation between the President and the Vice President building for weeks. Select Committee to Investigate the January 6th Attack on the United States Capitol, Deposition of Marc Short, (Jan. 26, 2022), pp. 34–35, 216-17.

136. Select Committee to Investigate the January 6th Attack on the United States Capitol, Deposition of Marc Short, (Jan. 26, 2022), pp. 191, 204-05; Select Committee to Investigate the January 6th Attack on the United States Capitol, Deposition of Greg Jacob, (Feb. 1, 2022), p. 82; Select Committee to Investigate the January 6th Attack on the United States Capitol, *Hearing on the January 6th Investigation*, 117th Cong., 2d sess., (June 16, 2022), available at https://www.govinfo.gov/committee/house-january6th.

137. Select Committee to Investigate the January 6th Attack on the United States Capitol, Deposition of Marc Short, (Jan. 26, 2022), pp. 191, 204-05.

138. Select Committee to Investigate the January 6th Attack on the United States Capitol, Transcribed Interview of Pasquale Antony "Pat" Cipollone, (July 8, 2022), pp. 49 (regarding the declaration of martial law), 56 (regarding the appointment of Sidney Powell as special counsel), 58–59, 66 (regarding the seizure of voting machines), 110 (regarding the elevation of Jeff Clark to Acting Attorney General).

139. Select Committee to Investigate the January 6th Attack on the United States Capitol, Informal Interview of Patrick Philbin, (Apr. 13, 2022), p. 5. Philbin told the Select Committee that in the end he decided not to resign out of a sense of obligation: "All of the pilots can't jump off the plane because there's still a lot of passengers in the back and we need to land the plane."

140. Select Committee to Investigate the January 6th Attack on the United States Capitol, Informal Interview of Patrick Philbin, (Apr. 13, 2022).

141. Select Committee to Investigate the January 6th Attack on the United States Capitol, Transcribed Interview of Pasquale Antony "Pat" Cipollone, (July 8, 2022), pp. 79 ("My view was that the Vice President didn't have the legal authority to do anything except what he did."), 81 (testifying that his views on the role of the Vice President were "extremely aligned" with the Vice President's staff), 88 ("I thought that the Vice President did not have the authority to do what was being suggested under a proper reading of the law."); *See also* Select Committee to Investigate the January 6th Attack on the United States Capitol, Informal Interview of Patrick Philbin, (Apr. 13, 2022).

142. Select Committee to Investigate the January 6th Attack on the United States Capitol, Transcribed Interview of Pasquale Antony "Pat" Cipollone, (July 8, 2022), pp. 85–86.

143. Select Committee to Investigate the January 6th Attack on the United States Capitol, Transcribed Interview of Pasquale Antony "Pat" Cipollone, (July 8, 2022), p. 85.

144. Select Committee to Investigate the January 6th Attack on the United States Capitol, Transcribed Interview of Pasquale Antony "Pat" Cipollone, (July 8, 2022), p. 94 (testifying that

the privileged interaction that resulted in his exclusion from the meeting took place in the presence of Meadows and Eastman, but before the Vice President, Short, and Jacob arrived).

145.   Select Committee to Investigate the January 6th Attack on the United States Capitol, Transcribed Interview of Pasquale Antony "Pat" Cipollone, (July 8, 2022), pp. 85–86 ("I did walk to that meeting and I did go into the Oval Office with the idea of attending that meeting, and then I ultimately did not attend the meeting.").

146.   Select Committee to Investigate the January 6th Attack on the United States Capitol, Transcribed Interview of Pasquale Antony "Pat" Cipollone, (July 8, 2022), pp. 86, 94. Cipollone refused to describe further why he didn't attend the meeting—"[t]he reasons for that are privileged"—and would not tell the Select Committee whether he voluntarily decided not to attend or was told not to.

147.   Select Committee to Investigate the January 6th Attack on the United States Capitol, Transcribed Interview of Pasquale Antony "Pat" Cipollone, (July 8, 2022), pp. 85, 88.

148.   Select Committee to Investigate the January 6th Attack on the United States Capitol, Deposition of Greg Jacob, (Feb. 1, 2022), pp. 88–89 ("[A]t the meeting on the 4th, Eastman expressed the view that both paths were legally viable.").

149.   Select Committee to Investigate the January 6th Attack on the United States Capitol, *Hearing on the January 6th Investigation*, 117th Cong., 2d sess., (June 16, 2022), available at https://www.govinfo.gov/committee/house-january6th.

150.   Select Committee to Investigate the January 6th Attack on the United States Capitol, Deposition of Greg Jacob, (Feb. 1, 2022), p. 89. *See also* Select Committee to Investigate the January 6th Attack on the United States Capitol, Deposition of Greg Jacob, (Feb. 1, 2022), pp. 90 ("I think that was threaded throughout, that, again, both were legally viable but that the preferred course would be to send it back to the States."), 91 (". . . he [Eastman] thought that the more prudent course was a procedural send it back to the States, rather than reject electors."), 93 ("On the 4th, I think that he said that both were legally viable options. But I do think that he said that he was not saying that that was the one that the Vice President should do.").

151.   Select Committee to Investigate the January 6th Attack on the United States Capitol, Deposition of Greg Jacob, (Feb. 1, 2022), pp. 89, 91 ("[H]e thought that the more prudent course was a procedural send it back to the states, rather than reject electors"), 96 ("[M]y impression was he was thinking more acceptance [by] the country of the action taken"). *See also* Select Committee to Investigate the January 6th Attack on the United States Capitol, *Hearings on the January 6th Investigation*, 117th Cong., 2d sess., (June 16, 2022), available at https://www.govinfo.gov/committee/house-january6th.

152.   Select Committee to Investigate the January 6th Attack on the United States Capitol, Deposition of Greg Jacob, (Feb. 1, 2022), p. 96; Select Committee to Investigate the January 6th Attack on the United States Capitol, *Hearing on the January 6th Investigation*, 117th Cong., 2d sess., (June 16, 2022), available at https://www.govinfo.gov/committee/house-january6th.

153.   Select Committee to Investigate the January 6th Attack on the United States Capitol, Deposition of Greg Jacob, (Feb. 1, 2022), pp. 95, 130 (Q: "Did John Eastman ever admit, as far as you know, in front of the President that his proposal would violate the Electoral Count Act?" A: "I believe he did on the 4th." Q: "Okay. And can you tell us what the President's reaction was?" A: "A I can't."); Documents on file with the Select Committee to Investigate the January 6th Attack on the United States Capitol (National Archives Production), VP-R0000107 (Greg Jacob writing after the Oval Office meeting on January 4th, "Professor Eastman acknowledges that his proposal violates several provisions of statutory law.").

154.   Select Committee to Investigate the January 6th Attack on the United States Capitol, Deposition of Marc Short, (Jan. 26, 2022), pp. 202–03.

155. Documents on file with the Select Committee to Investigate the January 6th Attack on the United States Capitol (National Archives Production), VP-R0000107. Select Committee to Investigate the January 6th Attack on the United States Capitol, Deposition of Greg Jacob, (Feb. 1, 2022), p. 127.

156. Documents on file with the Select Committee to Investigate the January 6th Attack on the United States Capitol (National Archives Production), VP-R0000107 ("Professor Eastman acknowledges that his proposal violates several provisions of statutory law"); Select Committee to Investigate the January 6th Attack on the United States Capitol, Deposition of Greg Jacob, (Feb. 1, 2022), pp. 127–28.

157. Documents on file with the Select Committee to Investigate the January 6th Attack on the United States Capitol (National Archives Production), VP-R0000107.

158. Documents on file with the Select Committee to Investigate the January 6th Attack on the United States Capitol, (National Archives Production), VP-R0000107. Jacob notes in his memo that Eastman's proposal also "contradicted the opinion authored by Republican Supreme Court Justice Joseph Bradley as the decided vote on the Electoral Commission of 1877." Whereas Eastman wanted the Vice President to refer the manufactured dispute over slates of electors back to the State legislatures, Justice Bradley wrote that the President of the Senate (the Vice President) "is not invested with any authority for making any investigation outside of the joint meeting of the two Houses."

159. Documents on file with the Select Committee to Investigate the January 6th Attack on the United States Capitol (National Archives Production), VP-R0000107 ("[Professor Eastman] stated that in his view, the imprimatur of approval by a State legislature is important to the legitimacy of counting any slate of electors other than the one initially certified by the State's executive.").

160. Documents on file with the Select Committee to Investigate the January 6th Attack on the United States Capitol (National Archives Production), VP-R0000107.

161. When pressed by Eric Herschmann on whether states really wanted to certify an alternate slate, and why they hadn't taken steps to do so on their own, Eastman had no explanation or response. Select Committee to Investigate the January 6th Attack on the United States Capitol, Transcribed Interview of Eric Herschmann, (Apr. 6, 2022), pp. 28–29.

162. Documents on file with the Select Committee to Investigate the January 6th Attack on the United States Capitol (National Archives Production), VP-R0000107 ("Professor Eastman does not recommend that the Vice President assert that he has the authority unilaterally to decide which of the competing slates of electors should be counted"); Select Committee to Investigate the January 6th Attack on the United States Capitol, Deposition of Greg Jacob, (Feb. 1, 2022), p. 127.

163. Documents on file with the Select Committee to Investigate the January 6th Attack on the United States Capitol (National Archives Production), VP-R0000107.

164. Documents on file with the Select Committee to Investigate the January 6th Attack on the United States Capitol (National Archives Production), VP-R0000085.

165. Documents on file with the Select Committee to Investigate the January 6th Attack on the United States Capitol (National Archives Production), VP-R0000182, VP-R0000183, VP-R0000180, VP-R0000181; Select Committee to Investigate the January 6th Attack on the United States Capitol, Deposition of Greg Jacob, (Feb. 1, 2022), pp. 102–03 ("[I]n fact, there were no materials, new materials that were actually presented to me by Mr. Eastman . . . I was open to receiving anything that anybody wanted to give me that might bear on that question . . . But I also correctly was of the view that I had already looked at everything and that we knew [ ] where we stood.").

166. Select Committee to Investigate the January 6th Attack on the United States Capitol, Deposition of Greg Jacob, (Feb. 1, 2022), p. 95.

167. "Donald Trump Rally Speech Transcript Dalton, Georgia: Senate Runoff Election," Rev, (Jan. 4, 2021), available at https://perma.cc/VAD2-TWVQ ("Hello, Georgia, by the way. There's no

way we lost Georgia. There's no way. That was a rigged election, but we're still fighting it and you'll see what's going to happen. We'll talk about it.").

168.   "Donald Trump Rally Speech Transcript Dalton, Georgia: Senate Runoff Election," Rev, (Jan. 4, 2021), available at https://perma.cc/VAD2-TWVQ.

169.   "Donald Trump Rally Speech Transcript Dalton, Georgia: Senate Runoff Election," Rev, (Jan. 4, 2021), available at https://perma.cc/VAD2-TWVQ.

170.   Select Committee to Investigate the January 6th Attack on the United States Capitol, Deposition of Greg Jacob, (Feb. 1, 2022), pp. 96, 105; Select Committee to Investigate the January 6th Attack on the United States Capitol, Deposition of Marc Short, (Jan. 26, 2022), p. 201; Documents on file with the Select Committee to Investigate the January 6th Attack on the United States Capitol (National Archives Production), VP-R0000182.

171.   Select Committee to Investigate the January 6th Attack on the United States Capitol, Deposition of Marc Short Deposition (Jan. 26, 2022) p. 201; see also, Select Committee to Investigate the January 6th Attack on the United States Capitol, Deposition of Greg Jacob (Feb. 1, 2022) pp. 92, 94, 106; Select Committee to Investigate the January 6th Attack on the United States Capitol, Hearing on the January 6th Investigation, 117th Cong., 2d sess., (Jun. 16, 2022), available at https://www.govinfo.gov/committee/house-january6th.

172.   Documents on file with the Select Committee to Investigate the January 6th Attack on the United States Capitol (Greg Jacobs Production), CTRL0000070421, p. 1 (Jan. 5, 2021, Greg Jacob handwritten notes).

173.   Select Committee to Investigate the January 6th Attack on the United States Capitol, Hearing on the January 6th Investigation, 117th Cong., 2d sess., (June 16, 2022), available at https://www.govinfo.gov/committee/house-january6th; See also Select Committee to Investigate the January 6th Attack on the United States Capitol, Deposition of Greg Jacob, (Feb. 1, 2022), pp. 92 ("He, again, came into the meeting saying, 'What I'm here to ask you to do is to reject the electors.'").

174.   Select Committee to Investigate the January 6th Attack on the United States Capitol, Deposition of Greg Jacob, (Feb. 1, 2022), pp. 93–95. Eastman acknowledged to Jacob that the previous day's discussions had included the "send it back to the states" path, but he reaffirmed that the ask on the morning of January 5th was to reject electors outright. Select Committee to Investigate the January 6th Attack on the United States Capitol, Deposition of Greg Jacob, (Feb. 1, 2022), p. 105; Select Committee to Investigate the January 6th Attack on the United States Capitol, Hearing on the January 6th Investigation, 117th Cong., 2d sess., (June 16, 2022), available at https://www.govinfo.gov/committee/house-january6th ("So on the 4th, that had been the path that he had said, 'I am not recommending that you do that,' but on the 5th, he came in and expressly requested that.").

175.   Select Committee to Investigate the January 6th Attack on the United States Capitol, Transcribed Interview of Eric Herschmann, (Apr. 6, 2022), pp. 24-25.

176.   Select Committee to Investigate the January 6th Attack on the United States Capitol, Transcribed Interview of Eric Herschmann, (Apr. 6, 2022), pp. 26-27.

177.   Select Committee to Investigate the January 6th Attack on the United States Capitol, Transcribed Interview of Eric Herschmann, (Apr. 6, 2022), p. 24.

178.   Select Committee to Investigate the January 6th Attack on the United States Capitol, Transcribed Interview of Eric Herschmann, (Apr. 6, 2022), p. 24.

179.   Select Committee to Investigate the January 6th Attack on the United States Capitol, Deposition of Greg Jacob, (Feb. 1, 2022), pp. 107, 117.

180.   Select Committee to Investigate the January 6th Attack on the United States Capitol, Deposition of Greg Jacob, (Feb. 1, 2022), pp. 107–08. Jacob debated with Eastman all of the historical examples, concluding that in "the 130 years of practice" the Electoral Count Act had been followed "every single time"; Select Committee to Investigate the January 6th Attack on the United States Capitol, Deposition of Greg Jacob, (Feb. 1, 2022), pp. 109-10.

181. Select Committee to Investigate the January 6th Attack on the United States Capitol, Deposition of Greg Jacob, (Feb. 1, 2022), p. 108. What Jacob found when he looked into the Nixon example is that first, there were no competing slates of electors from Hawaii. In fact, a Republican slate was originally certified by the outgoing Governor, but after a judicially ordered recount, it was clear that the Democratic candidate had won, and the incoming Governor certified a new slate consistent with the outcome of the election after the recount. Then-Vice President Nixon, when he arrived at Hawaii in the joint session, "magnanimously" acknowledged that it was clear that Hawaii's votes for Kennedy were the correct votes and called for objections (of which there were none). This precedent was therefore an example of the Vice President complying with the Electoral Count Act's procedures regarding objections to electors. *See* Select Committee to Investigate the January 6th Attack on the United States Capitol, Deposition of Greg Jacob, (Feb. 1, 2022), pp. 15-16.

182. Select Committee to Investigate the January 6th Attack on the United States Capitol, Deposition of Greg Jacob, (Feb. 1, 2022), p. 110.

183. Select Committee to Investigate the January 6th Attack on the United States Capitol, Deposition of Greg Jacob, (Feb. 1, 2022), p. 110 ("[H]e ultimately acknowledged that none of [the Justices] would actually back this position when you took into account the fact that what you have is a mildly ambiguous [constitutional provision], a nonsensical result that has all kinds of terrible policy implications, and uniform historical practice against it").

184. Select Committee to Investigate the January 6th Attack on the United States Capitol, Deposition of Greg Jacob, (Feb. 1, 2022), p. 110.

185. Select Committee to Investigate the January 6th Attack on the United States Capitol, Deposition of Greg Jacob, (Feb. 1, 2022), p. 111. Jacob told the Select Committee he did not know to whom Eastman was referring when he indicated "they" would be disappointed that Vice President Pence had not been convinced it was appropriate to reject electors.

186. Select Committee to Investigate the January 6th Attack on the United States Capitol, Deposition of Marc Short, (Jan. 26, 2022), pp. 95–96, 210–11.

187. J. Michael Luttig (@judgeluttig), Twitter, Jan. 5, 2021 9:53 a.m. ET, *et seq.*, available at https://twitter.com/judgeluttig/status/1346469787329646592 ("The only responsibility and power of the Vice President under the Constitution is to faithfully count the electoral college votes as they have been cast,").

188. Select Committee to Investigate the January 6th Attack on the United States Capitol, Deposition of Marc Short, (Jan. 26, 2022), pp. 151-52.

189. Select Committee to Investigate the January 6th Attack on the United States Capitol, Deposition of Marc Short, (Jan. 26, 2022), pp. 151-52.

190. Select Committee to Investigate the January 6th Attack on the United States Capitol, Deposition of Marc Short, (Jan. 26, 2022), pp. 152, 209; *see also* Tom Hamburger, Josh Dawsey, and Jacqueline Alemany, "Jan. 6 Panel Grapples with How to Secure Testimony from Lawmakers, Pence," *Washington Post*, (Jan. 15, 2022), available at https://www.washingtonpost.com/politics/2022/01/15/jan-6-subpoenas-committee ("'I did not notice any hesitation on his part,' Quayle said of his conversation with Pence. 'I interpreted his questions as looking for confirmation that what he was going to do was right and that he had no flexibility. That's the way I read it. Given the pressure he was under, I thought it was perfectly normal, very smart on his part to call me.'").

191. Select Committee to Investigate the January 6th Attack on the United States Capitol, Deposition of Greg Jacob, (Feb. 1, 2022), p. 157.

192. Select Committee to Investigate the January 6th Attack on the United States Capitol, Deposition of Greg Jacob, (Feb. 1, 2022), p. 158; Select Committee to Investigate the January 6th Attack on the United States Capitol, Deposition of Marc Short, (Jan. 26, 2022), pp. 215-17.

193. Select Committee to Investigate the January 6th Attack on the United States Capitol, Deposition of Greg Jacob, (Feb. 1, 2022), pp. 157-58.

194. Select Committee to Investigate the January 6th Attack on the United States Capitol, Deposition of Marc Short, (Jan. 26, 2022), p. 215.

195. Select Committee to Investigate the January 6th Attack on the United States Capitol, Deposition of Marc Short, (Jan. 26, 2022), p. 216.

196. Bob Woodward and Robert Costa, *Peril*, (New York: Simon & Schuster, 2021), p. 229; Select Committee to Investigate the January 6th Attack on the United States Capitol, Deposition of Marc Short, (Jan. 26, 2022), pp. 215-16.

197. Select Committee to Investigate the January 6th Attack on the United States Capitol, Deposition of Greg Jacob, (Feb. 1, 2022), p. 160.

198. Select Committee to Investigate the January 6th Attack on the United States Capitol, Deposition of Marc Short, (Jan. 26, 2022), pp. 220-22; Select Committee to Investigate the January 6th Attack on the United States Capitol, Deposition of Greg Jacob, (Feb. 1, 2022), pp. 116, 120. Note that Marc Short recalled that it was this afternoon phone call that led to the in-person meeting between Eastman and Jacob, however, documents received by the Select Committee and Jacob's more detailed recollection of his interactions with Eastman establishes that the in-person meeting occurred in the morning of January 5, 2021.

199. Select Committee to Investigate the January 6th Attack on the United States Capitol, *Hearing on the January 6th Investigation*, 117th Cong., 2d sess., (June 16, 2022), available at https://www.govinfo.gov/committee/house-january6th. (describing the message on this phone call between the Vice President and President Trump with Eastman's participation as, "Well, we hear you loud and clear, you are not going to reject. But remember last night, I said that there was this more prudent course where you could just send it back to the States? Would you be willing to do that[?]"); *see also* Select Committee to Investigate the January 6th Attack on the United States Capitol, Deposition of Greg Jacob, (Feb. 1, 2022), pp. 96-97, 120.

200. Select Committee to Investigate the January 6th Attack on the United States Capitol, Deposition of Greg Jacob, (Feb. 1, 2022), p. 121.

201. Select Committee to Investigate the January 6th Attack on the United States Capitol, Deposition of Greg Jacob, (Feb. 1, 2022), pp. 121-22 (describing calls from Eastman and at least one other lawyer (likely either Kurt Olsen or Bill Olson)).

202. Select Committee to Investigate the January 6th Attack on the United States Capitol, Deposition of Greg Jacob, (Feb. 1, 2022), pp. 122-23.

203. Select Committee to Investigate the January 6th Attack on the United States Capitol, Deposition of Greg Jacob, (Feb. 1, 2022), p. 123 (recounting Eastman's argument that election fraud was resulting in the Constitution being "shredded across all these different states" and comparing it to the Civil War).

204. Select Committee to Investigate the January 6th Attack on the United States Capitol, Deposition of Greg Jacob, (Feb. 1, 2022), pp. 122-24.

205. Maggie Haberman and Annie Karni, "Pence Said to Have Told Trump He Lacks Power to Change Election Result," *New York Times*, (Jan. 5, 2021), available at https://web.archive.org/web/20210106003845/https://www.nytimes.com/2021/01/05/us/politics/pence-trump-election-results.html. The same *Times* reporters had also published on January 4th an article again accurately reporting that President Trump "had directly pressed Mr. Pence to find an alternative to certifying Mr. Biden's win." Annie Karni and Maggie Haberman, "Pence's Choice: Side with the Constitution or His Boss," *New York Times*, (Jan. 4, 2021), available at https://www.nytimes.com/2021/01/04/us/politics/pence-trump.html.

206. Maggie Haberman and Annie Karni, "Pence Said to Have Told Trump He Lacks Power to Change Election Result," *New York Times*, (Jan. 5, 2021), available at https://www.nytimes.com/2021/01/05/us/politics/pence-trump-election-results.html.

207. Maggie Haberman and Anne Karni, "Pence Said to Have Told Trump He Lacks Power to Change Election Result," *New York Times*, (Jan. 5, 2021), available at https://

web.archive.org/web/20210106003845/https://www.nytimes.com/2021/01/05/us/politics/pence-trump-election-results.html (archived version showing original publication date of Jan. 5, 2021, at 7:36 p.m. ET).

208. Select Committee to Investigate the January 6th Attack on the United States Capitol, Deposition of Jason Miller, (Feb. 3, 2022), pp. 169-70.

209. Documents on file with the Select Committee to Investigate the January 6th Attack on the United States Capitol (National Archives Production), 076P-R000007439, (CTRL0000082597) (January 5, 2021, White House Presidential call log).

210. Documents on file with the Select Committee to Investigate the January 6th Attack on the United States Capitol (National Archives Production), 076P-R000007439, (CTRL0000082597) (January 5, 2021, White House Presidential call log).

211. Documents on file with the Select Committee to Investigate the January 6th Attack on the United States Capitol (National Archives Production), 076P-R000007439, (CTRL0000082597) (January 5, 2021, White House Presidential call log).

212. Meredith Lee (@meredithllee), Twitter, Jan. 5, 2021, 9:58 p.m. ET, available at https://twitter.com/meredithllee/status/1346652403605647367?lang=en (emphasis added); Select Committee to Investigate the January 6th Attack on the United States Capitol, Deposition of Jason Miller, (Feb. 3, 2022), p. 175 ("[T]ypically on these, I might have a couple of wording suggestions . . . ultimately the way this came out was the way he wanted [it] to."); see id at 174-76.

213. Select Committee to Investigate the January 6th Attack on the United States Capitol, Hearing on the January 6th Investigation, 117th Cong., 2d sess., (June 16, 2022), available at https://www.govinfo.gov/committee/house-january6th; Select Committee to Investigate the January 6th Attack on the United States Capitol, Deposition of Marc Short, (Jan. 26, 2022), p. 224; Select Committee to Investigate the January 6th Attack on the United States Capitol, Deposition of Chris Hodgson, (Mar. 30, 2022), pp. 184-85.

214. Meredith Lee (@meredithllee), Twitter, Jan. 5, 2021, 9:58 p.m. ET, available at https://twitter.com/meredithllee/status/1346652403605647367?lang=en.

215. Select Committee to Investigate the January 6th Attack on the United States Capitol, Deposition of Greg Jacob, (Feb. 1, 2022), p. 161 ("[W]hoever drafted the statement it was not accurate.").

216. Select Committee to Investigate the January 6th Attack on the United States Capitol, Deposition of Greg Jacob, (Feb. 1, 2022), p. 161.

217. Select Committee to Investigate the January 6th Attack on the United States Capitol, Deposition of Marc Short, (Jan. 26, 2022), p. 224; Select Committee to Investigate the January 6th Attack on the United States Capitol, Deposition of Greg Jacob, (Feb. 1, 2022), p. 163.

218. Select Committee to Investigate the January 6th Attack on the United States Capitol, Deposition of Marc Short, (Jan. 26, 2022), p. 223.

219. Select Committee to Investigate the January 6th Attack on the United States Capitol, Deposition of Marc Short, (Jan. 26, 2022), p. 223.

220. Documents on file with the Select Committee to Investigate the January 6th Attack on the United States Capitol (National Archives Production), CTRL0000082597, (reflecting calls with Mr. Stephen Bannon on Jan. 5, 2021, from 8:57 a.m. to 9:08 a.m. and from 9:46 p.m. to 9:52 p.m.).

221. Documents on file with the Select Committee to Investigate the January 6th Attack on the United States Capitol (Select Committee Transcription), CTRL0000082317 (Jan. 5, 2021, Steve Bannon War Room Transcript) (Bannon: "All hell is going to break loose tomorrow. Just understand this: All hell is going to break loose tomorrow. It's going to be quick . . . It's the fog of war." Bannon discussed putting Sen. Grassley's number on the screen, and suggested they encourage users at TheDonald.win to contact the Senator. (At the time, users at TheDonald.win were openly planning for violence and to surround the U.S. Capitol on

January 6. *See* Chapter 6.) Bannon told his audience. "I'll tell you this, it's not going to happen like you think it's going to happen, Ok? It's going to be quite extraordinarily different. And all I can say is strap in.").

222.   Documents on file with the Select Committee to Investigate the January 6th Attack on the United States Capitol (Select Committee Transcription) CTRL0000082317, (Jan. 5, 2021) (Steve Bannon War Room Transcript).

223.   Documents on file with the Select Committee to Investigate the January 6th Attack on the United States Capitol (Select Committee Transcription) CTRL0000082317, (Jan. 5, 2021) (Steve Bannon War Room Transcript).

224.   Peter Navarro, *In Trump Time: A Journal of America's Plague Year* (St. Petersburg, FL: All Seasons Press, 2021), p. 252.

225.   Peter Navarro, *In Trump Time: A Journal of America's Plague Year* (St. Petersburg, FL: All Seasons Press, 2021), p. 263.

226.   Peter Navarro, *In Trump Time: A Journal of America's Plague Year* (St. Petersburg, FL: All Seasons Press, 2021), p. 271.

227.   Peter Navarro, *In Trump Time: A Journal of America's Plague Year* (St. Petersburg, FL: All Seasons Press, 2021), p. 252.

228.   Peter Navarro, *In Trump Time: A Journal of America's Plague Year* (St. Petersburg, FL: All Seasons Press, 2021), p. 263.

229.   *See e.g.*, Documents on file with the Select Committee to Investigate the January 6th Attack on the United States Capitol (Chapman University Production), Chapman052976.

230.   Select Committee to Investigate the January 6th Attack on the United States Capitol, Deposition of Marc Short, (Jan. 26, 2022), pp. 26-27 ("But just to pick up on that, Mr. Short, was it your impression that the Vice President had directly conveyed his position on these issues to the President, not just to the world through a Dear Colleague Letter, but directly to President Trump?" A: "Many times." Q: "And had been consistent in conveying his position to the President?" A: "Very consistent."); *see also* Select Committee to Investigate the January 6th Attack on the United States Capitol, Deposition of Greg Jacob, (Feb. 1, 2022), p. 102 ("[T]hat's where the Vice President started. That's where he stayed the entire way."); Select Committee to Investigate the January 6th Attack on the United States Capitol, Deposition of Chris Hodgson, (Mar. 30, 2022), p. 181 ("I believe that the Vice President was consistent in his understanding of the law and the precedent and his belief as to what his authority was and was not on January 6th.").

231.   Donald J. Trump (@realDonaldTrump), Twitter, Jan. 6, 2021 1:00 a.m. ET, available at https://web.archive.org/web/20210106072109/https://twitter.com/realdonaldtrump/status/1346698217304584192 (archived).

232.   Donald J. Trump (@realDonaldTrump), Twitter, Jan. 6, 2021 8:17 a.m. ET, available at https://web.archive.org/web/20210106131747/https://twitter.com/realdonaldtrump/status/1346808075626426371 (archived).

233.   Donald J. Trump (@realDonaldTrump), Twitter, Jan. 6, 2021 8:22 a.m. ET, available at https://web.archive.org/web/20210106132244/https://twitter.com/realdonaldtrump/status/1346809349214248962 (archived).

234.   At 9:02 a.m., President Trump instructed the White House operator to call back with the Vice President; the operator instead informed the President at 9:15 a.m. that a message was left for the Vice President. Documents on file with the Select Committee to Investigate the January 6th Attack on the United States Capitol (National Archives Production), P-R000261 (Presidential Call Log, White House Switchboard), P-R000255 (Daily Diary).

235.   Documents on file with the Select Committee to Investigate the January 6th Attack on the United States Capitol (National Archives Production), P-R000285 ("11:20 –c w/ VPOTUS"); Documents on file with the Select Committee to Investigate the January 6th Attack on the United States Capitol (National Archives Production), P-R000255 ("The President talked on

a phone call to an unidentified person"); *see also* Select Committee to Investigate the January 6th Attack on the United States Capitol, Deposition of Marc Short, (Jan. 26, 2022), p. 12 (stating that a military aide interrupted Pence's meeting with staff to inform the Vice President that the President was holding to speak with him).

236. Present in the Oval Office during the call with the Vice President were Melania Trump, Donald Trump, Jr., Ivanka Trump, Eric Trump, Kimberly Guilfoyle, and Lara Trump, as well as Mark Meadows, Stephen Miller, Eric Herschmann, and Gen. Keith Kellogg. *See* Select Committee to Investigate the January 6th Attack on the United States Capitol, Transcribed Interview of Ivanka Trump, (Apr. 5, 2022), pp. 30-32, 37.

237. Select Committee to Investigate the January 6th Attack on the United States Capitol, Transcribed Interview of Eric Herschmann, (Apr. 6, 2022), p. 47.

238. Select Committee to Investigate the January 6th Attack on the United States Capitol, Transcribed Interview of Ivanka Trump, (Apr. 5, 2022), p. 39.

239. Select Committee to Investigate the January 6th Attack on the United States Capitol, Transcribed Interview of Ivanka Trump, (Apr. 5, 2022), p. 41.

240. Select Committee to Investigate the January 6th Attack on the United States Capitol, Deposition of Julie Radford, (May 24, 2022), pp. 17-18.

241. Select Committee to Investigate the January 6th Attack on the United States Capitol, Deposition of Julie Radford, (May 24, 2022), p. 19 ("And the word that she relayed to you that the President called the Vice President—apologize for being impolite—but do you remember what she said her father called him?" "The 'P'word."). *See also* Peter Baker, Maggie Haberman, and Annie Karni, "Pence Reached His Limit with Trump. It Wasn't Pretty," *New York Times*, (Jan. 12, 2021), available at https://www.nytimes.com/2021/01/12/us/politics/mike-pence-trump.html; Jonathan Karl, *Betrayal: The Final Act of the Trump Show*, (New York: Dutton, 2021), at pp. 273–74 ("[Y]ou said, 'You can be a patriot or you can be a pussy.' Did you really say that or is that an incorrect report? 'I wouldn't dispute it,' [President Trump] answered.").

242. Select Committee to Investigate the January 6th Attack on the United States Capitol, Transcribed Interview of Nicholas Luna, (Mar. 21, 2022), p. 127.

243. Select Committee to Investigate the January 6th Attack on the United States Capitol, Deposition of Keith Kellogg, (Dec. 14, 2021), p. 90; *see also* Select Committee to Investigate the January 6th Attack on the United States Capitol, Transcribed Interview of Donald J. Trump, Jr., (May 3, 2022), p. 84 ("I know the line of questioning was about sending it back to the States, but that's about the extent of my recollection.").

244. Select Committee to Investigate the January 6th Attack on the United States Capitol, Deposition of Keith Kellogg, (Dec. 14, 2021), p. 91 ("Q: [Y]ou said he told the Vice President that he has the legal authority to reject certain votes. Is that what you said? A: That he had the constitutional authority to do that, yes."); *see also* Select Committee to Investigate the January 6th Attack on the United States Capitol, Transcribed Interview of Eric Herschmann (Apr. 6, 2022), p. 48 (describing it as "a general discussion about the legal and constitutional authority of the VP").

245. Select Committee to Investigate the January 6th Attack on the United States Capitol, Deposition of Keith Kellogg, (Dec. 14, 2021), p. 92.

246. Select Committee to Investigate the January 6th Attack on the United States Capitol, Hearing on the January 6th Investigation, 117th Cong., 2d sess., (June 16, 2022), available at https://www.govinfo.gov/committee/house-january6th; Select Committee to Investigate the January 6th Attack on the United States Capitol, Deposition of Greg Jacob, (Feb. 1, 2022), p. 169.

247. Select Committee to Investigate the January 6th Attack on the United States Capitol, Transcribed Interview of Eric Herschmann, (Apr. 6, 2022), p. 40; Documents on file with the Select Committee to Investigate the January 6th Attack on the United States Capitol, (AT&T Production, Feb. 9, 2022).

248. Select Committee to Investigate the January 6th Attack on the United States Capitol, Transcribed Interview of Eric Herschmann, (Apr. 6, 2022), pp. 40–41.

249. Documents on file with the Select Committee to Investigate the January 6th Attack on the United States Capitol, (AT&T Production, Feb. 9, 2022).

250. "Rudy Giuliani Speech Transcript at Trump's Washington, D.C. Rally: Wants 'Trial by Combat,'" Rev, (Jan. 6, 2021), available at https://www.rev.com/blog/transcripts/rudy-giuliani-speech-transcript-at-trumps-washington-d-c-rally-wants-trial-by-combat.

251. "Rudy Giuliani Speech Transcript at Trump's Washington, D.C. Rally: Wants 'Trial by Combat,'" Rev, (Jan. 6, 2021), available at https://www.rev.com/blog/transcripts/rudy-giuliani-speech-transcript-at-trumps-washington-d-c-rally-wants-trial-by-combat.

252. "Rudy Giuliani Speech Transcript at Trump's Washington, D.C. Rally: Wants 'Trial by Combat,'" Rev, (Jan. 6, 2021), available at https://www.rev.com/blog/transcripts/rudy-giuliani-speech-transcript-at-trumps-washington-d-c-rally-wants-trial-by-combat ("We now have letters from five legislators begging us to do that. They're asking us. Georgia, Pennsylvania, Arizona, Wisconsin, and one other coming in.").

253. *See, e.g.*, Documents on file with the Select Committee to Investigate the January 6th Attack on the United States Capitol (Marc Short Production), J6C-TSM-0003, J6C-TSM-0004, (January 6, 2021, email from Molly Michael to March Short containing subject line "2057Rayburn_20210106_002040.pdf" and an attached letter). The letter bore the signatures of 19 of the 60 members of the Arizona House and 4 of the 30 members of the Arizona Senate.

254. Documents on file with the Select Committee to Investigate the January 6th Attack on the United States Capitol (Chapman University Production), Chapman005235, Chapman005236, (January 5, 2021, email from John Eastman to Greg Jacob with an attached letter dated January 4, 2021). In an interview given after January 6th, Eastman argued that the Vice President still should have acted on the basis of the statement of a minority of the Pennsylvania legislature because "it was over Christmas, and they were having trouble getting ahold of people to sign the letter." John McCormack, "John Eastman vs. the Eastman Memo," *National Review*, (Oct. 22, 2021), available at https://www.nationalreview.com/2021/10/john-eastman-vs-the-eastman-memo/.

255. Documents on file with the Select Committee to Investigate the January 6th Attack on the United States Capitol (Chapman University Production), Chapman005235, Chapman005236.

256. Select Committee to Investigate the January 6th Attack on the United States Capitol, Informal Interview of Jake Corman, (Jan. 25, 2022).

257. Select Committee to Investigate the January 6th Attack on the United States Capitol, Informal Interview of Jake Corman, (Jan. 25, 2022). Corman told the Select Committee that he understood the Vice President's role at the joint session was not substantive.

258. Select Committee to Investigate the January 6th Attack on the United States Capitol, Deposition of Greg Jacob, (Feb. 1, 2022), pp. 167-68; *see also* Select Committee to Investigate the January 6th Attack on the United States Capitol, Deposition of Marc Short, (Jan. 26, 2022), p. 14; Select Committee to Investigate the January 6th Attack on the United States Capitol, Deposition of Chris Hodgson, (Mar. 30, 2022), pp. 166-67.

259. "Rudy Giuliani Speech Transcript at Trump's Washington, D.C. Rally: Wants 'Trial by Combat'," Rev, (Jan. 6, 2021), available at https://www.rev.com/blog/transcripts/rudy-giuliani-speech-transcript-at-trumps-washington-d-c-rally-wants-trial-by-combat.

260. "Rudy Giuliani Speech Transcript at Trump's Washington, D.C. Rally: Wants 'Trial by Combat'," Rev, (Jan. 6, 2021), available at https://www.rev.com/blog/transcripts/rudy-giuliani-speech-transcript-at-trumps-washington-d-c-rally-wants-trial-by-combat.

261. "Rudy Giuliani Speech Transcript at Trump's Washington, D.C. Rally: Wants 'Trial by Combat'," Rev, (Jan. 6, 2021), available at https://www.rev.com/blog/transcripts/rudy-giuliani-speech-transcript-at-trumps-washington-d-c-rally-wants-trial-by-combat.

262. "Rudy Giuliani Speech Transcript at Trump's Washington, D.C. Rally: Wants 'Trial by Combat'," Rev, (Jan. 6, 2021), available at https://www.rev.com/blog/transcripts/rudy-giuliani-speech-transcript-at-trumps-washington-d-c-rally-wants-trial-by-combat (emphasis added). Note in particular Eastman's assertions regarding voting machines, for example, "They put those ballots in a secret folder in the machines. Sitting there waiting until they know how many they need." Eastman would later describe what he was calling on the Vice President to do as merely "to pause the proceedings." John C. Eastman, "Setting the Record Straight on the POTUS 'Ask'," *The American Mind*, (Jan. 18, 2021), available at https://americanmind.org/memo/setting-the-record-straight-on-the-potus-ask/.

263. Brian Naylor, "Read Trump's Jan. 6 Speech, A Key Part of Impeachment Trial," NPR, (Feb. 10, 2021), available at https://www.npr.org/2021/02/10/966396848/read-trumps-jan-6-speech-a-key-part-of-impeachment-trial.

264. Brian Naylor, "Read Trump's Jan. 6 Speech, A Key Part of Impeachment Trial," NPR, (Feb. 10, 2021), available at https://www.npr.org/2021/02/10/966396848/read-trumps-jan-6-speech-a-key-part-of-impeachment-trial.

265. Brian Naylor, "Read Trump's Jan. 6 Speech, A Key Part of Impeachment Trial," NPR, (Feb. 10, 2021), available at https://www.npr.org/2021/02/10/966396848/read-trumps-jan-6-speech-a-key-part-of-impeachment-trial.

266. Brian Naylor, "Read Trump's Jan. 6 Speech, A Key Part of Impeachment Trial," NPR, (Feb. 10, 2021), available at https://www.npr.org/2021/02/10/966396848/read-trumps-jan-6-speech-a-key-part-of-impeachment-trial.

267. Brian Naylor, "Read Trump's Jan. 6 Speech, A Key Part of Impeachment Trial," NPR, (Feb. 10, 2021), available at https://www.npr.org/2021/02/10/966396848/read-trumps-jan-6-speech-a-key-part-of-impeachment-trial.

268. Brian Naylor, "Read Trump's Jan. 6 Speech, A Key Part of Impeachment Trial," NPR, (Feb. 10, 2021), available at https://www.npr.org/2021/02/10/966396848/read-trumps-jan-6-speech-a-key-part-of-impeachment-trial.

269. Brian Naylor, "Read Trump's Jan. 6 Speech, A Key Part of Impeachment Trial," NPR, (Feb. 10, 2021), available at https://www.npr.org/2021/02/10/966396848/read-trumps-jan-6-speech-a-key-part-of-impeachment-trial.

270. Mike Pence (@Mike_Pence), Twitter, Jan. 6, 2021 1:02 p.m. ET, available at https://twitter.com/Mike_Pence/status/1346879811151605762. Between 12:45 and 1:00 p.m., Vice President Pence processed with the Senate to the House Chamber. *See* Select Committee to Investigate the January 6th Attack on the United States Capitol, Deposition of Chris Hodgson, (Mar. 30, 2022), pp. 202-03. The Vice President's statement was issued publicly and distributed on the House floor before the Vice President convened the joint session at approximately 1:05 p.m. *See* Select Committee to Investigate the January 6th Attack on the United States Capitol, Deposition of Greg Jacob, (Feb. 1, 2022), p. 173; *see also* Donna Cassata and Felicia Sonmez, "Congress Meets in Joint Session to Confirm Biden's Win, Over the Objections of Dozens of Republicans," *Washington Post*, (Jan. 6, 2021), available at https://www.washingtonpost.com/politics/2021/01/06/congress-electoral-college-vote-live-updates/#link-DUX3QUF3TVDNZDEGO7KIK2JSYE.

271. Select Committee to Investigate the January 6th Attack on the United States Capitol, Deposition of Greg Jacob, (Feb. 1, 2022), p. 164.

272. Mike Pence (@Mike_Pence), Twitter, Jan. 6, 2021 1:02 p.m. ET, available at https://twitter.com/Mike_Pence/status/1346879811151605762; *see also* Documents on file with the Select Committee to Investigate the January 6th Attack on the United States Capitol (National Archives Production), VP-R0000121, (January 6, 2021, Dear Colleague letter issued by Vice President Pence).

273. Select Committee to Investigate the January 6th Attack on the United States Capitol, Deposition of Marc Short, (Jan. 26, 2022), pp. 27-28 (testifying that, in consultation with the Senate Parliamentarian, the Vice President purposefully revised the standard language used by previous vice presidents at the joint session of Congress because of efforts by the

Trump Campaign and allies to create the public perception that there were "other slates of electors that were being considered or [ ] being put forward.").

274. Select Committee to Investigate the January 6th Attack on the United States Capitol, Deposition of Marc Short, (Jan. 26, 2022), pp. 186-88; Select Committee to Investigate the January 6th Attack on the United States Capitol, Deposition of Greg Jacob, (Feb. 1, 2022), pp. 53-54; Select Committee to Investigate the January 6th Attack on the United States Capitol, Deposition of Chris Hodgson, (Mar. 30, 2022), pp. 50-51. The Senate Parliamentarian offers advice and guidance on compliance with the Senate's rules. *See* CRS Report, The Office of the Parliamentarian in the House and Senate, (Nov. 28, 2018) RS20544. The Office of the Secretary of the Senate, on behalf of the Senate Parliamentarian and her staff, declined requests for information about this topic, as well as other January 6-related topics, from the Select Committee citing the independent relationship of the Senate and House as well as "historical congressional norms."

275. Select Committee to Investigate the January 6th Attack on the United States Capitol, Deposition of Greg Jacob, (Feb. 1, 2022), p. 64; Select Committee to Investigate the January 6th Attack on the United States Capitol, Deposition of Chris Hodgson, (Mar. 30, 2022), pp. 54-56 (testifying that the Vice President's understanding of his role as explained in the Dear Colleague letter he released on January 6th was set as of his meeting with the Parliamentarian on January 3rd).

276. Select Committee to Investigate the January 6th Attack on the United States Capitol, Deposition of Greg Jacob, (Feb. 1, 2022), pp. 68-70; Select Committee to Investigate the January 6th Attack on the United States Capitol, Deposition of Marc Short, (Jan. 26, 2022), pp. 2728; Documents on file with the Select Committee to Investigate the January 6th Attack on the United States Capitol (Chris Hodgson Production), 00163, (Vice President Superscript for Joint Session to Count Electoral Ballots January 6, 2021), 00181, (Response to Submissions NOT Certified by a State); Documents on file with the Select Committee to Investigate the January 6th Attack on the United States Capitol (National Archives Production), VP-R0000103_0001 (Pence joint session scripted responses).

277. Select Committee to Investigate the January 6th Attack on the United States Capitol, Deposition of Marc Short, (Jan. 26, 2022), p. 42. Jacob learned through the media that Trump electors had met and purported to cast electoral votes but, seeing no indication that any of the groups that met had "an imprimatur of State authority," he concluded that they would not qualify as competing slates under the Electoral Count Act. *See* Select Committee to Investigate the January 6th Attack on the United States Capitol, Deposition of Greg Jacob, (Feb. 1, 2022), p. 51; *see also* Select Committee to Investigate the January 6th Attack on the United States Capitol, Deposition of Greg Jacob, (Feb. 1, 2022), p. 54 ("I'm sure I, either in my oral conversation with Elizabeth [MacDonough] or in looking at this spreadsheet, confirmed my conclusion that none of these had the requisite State authority.").

278. The Senate Parliamentarian and her staff tracked the receipt of legitimate electoral votes from the states as well as the private citizen submissions (including the fake slates submitted by Trump electors) and identified the many deficiencies of the fake documents. Documents on file with the Select Committee to Investigate the January 6th Attack on the United States Capitol (National Archives Production), VP R0000323_0001 (Jan. 3, 2021 email exchange with Senate Parliamentarian), VP R0000417_0001 (Jan. 2 and 3, 2021 email exchange with Senate Parliamentarian), VP R0000418_0001 (list of deficiencies in alternate elector slates); Documents on file with the Select Committee to Investigate the January 6th Attack on the United States Capitol (Chris Hodgson Production), 00094, (list of deficiencies in alternate elector slates). The Senate Parliamentarian reviewed each purported slate of electoral votes to separate those in regular form and authorized by a State from those submitted by private citizens—the Trump Campaign's fake electors fell into this latter category. *See* Select Committee to Investigate the January 6th Attack on the United States Capitol, Deposition of Greg Jacob, (Feb. 1, 2022), pp. 53—54; *see also* Select Committee to Investigate the January 6th Attack on the United States Capitol, Deposition of Chris Hodgson, (Mar. 30, 2022), pp. 44-45.

279. "House Chamber During Joint Session," C-SPAN, at 11:07–11:37, Jan. 6, 2021, available at https://www.c-span.org/video/?507748-1/house-chamber-joint-session (emphasis added).

280. Select Committee to Investigate the January 6th Attack on the United States Capitol, Deposition of Andrew Hitt, (Feb. 28, 2022), pp. 94-95. *See also* Documents on file with the Select Committee to Investigate the January 6th Attack on the United States Capitol (National Archives Production), VP-R0000076, VP-R0000417, VP-R0000418, (January 3, 2021, emails and spreadsheet showing OVP staff tracking the arrival of fake electors' certificates).

281. Documents on file with the Select Committee to Investigate the January 6th Attack on the United States Capitol (Andrew Hitt Production), Hitt000090 (text messages exchanged between Republican officials in Wisconsin, including statement that "[f]reaking trump idiots want someone to fly original elector papers to the Senate President.").

282. Documents on file with the Select Committee to Investigate the January 6th Attack on the United States Capitol (Chris Hodgson Production), 00012, (message from Rep. Kelly's Chief of Staff, Matt Stroia, to Chris Hodgson on Jan. 6, 2021, at 8:41 am), 00058, (messages from Senator Johnson's Chief of Staff, Sean Riley, to Chris Hodgson on Jan. 6, 2021, around 12:37 pm).

283. Documents on file with the Select Committee to Investigate the January 6th Attack on the United States Capitol (Chris Hodgson Production), 00058 (Chris Hodgson responding to Sean Riley, "Do not give that to him. He's about to walk over to preside over the joint session, those were supposed to come in through the mail[.]" And, "The VP absolutely should not receive any mail that hasn't been screened.").

284. *See, e.g.*, "House Chamber During Joint Session," C-SPAN, at 15:33–15:59, Jan. 6, 2021, available at https://www.c-span.org/video/?507748-1/house-chamber-joint-session.

285. Karoun Demirjian, "GOP Members Object to Arizona's Electoral Votes for Biden," *Washington Post*, (Jan. 6, 2021), available at https://www.washingtonpost.com/politics/2021/01/06/congress-electoral-college-vote-live-updates/#link-TSWL74F2SVHBHET7GQR5IEP6FI .

286. "House Chamber During Joint Session," C-SPAN, at 15:59–17:16, Jan. 6, 2021, available at https://www.c-span.org/video/?507740-1/house-chamber-joint-session.

287. "House Chamber During Joint Session," C-SPAN, at 17:16–18:01, Jan. 6, 2021, available at https://www.c-span.org/video/?507748-1/house-chamber-joint-session.

288. Select Committee to Investigate the January 6th Attack on the United States Capitol, Deposition of Marc Short, (Jan. 26, 2022), p. 29.

289. House vote on Arizona (Roll No. 10): 167 Cong. Rec. H93 (daily ed. Jan. 6, 2021): 121-303; House vote on PA (Roll No. 11): 167 Cong. Rec. H112 (daily ed. Jan. 6, 2021): 138-282; Senate vote on Arizona (Rollcall Vote No. 1 Leg.): 167 Cong. Rec. S31-32 (daily ed. Jan. 6, 2021): 6-93; Senate vote on PA (Rollcall Vote. No. 2 Leg.): 167 Cong. Rec. S38 (daily ed. Jan. 6, 2021): 7-92.

290. Katie Meyer, "Congress Certifies Pa. Results, Biden's Victory After Chaotic Day of Violent Insurrection," WHYY, (Jan. 6, 2021), available at https://whyy.org/articles/casey-fitzpatrick-condemn-violent-insurrection-as-congress-moves-toward-certifying-biden/.

291. Select Committee to Investigate the January 6th Attack on the United States Capitol, Deposition of Greg Jacob, (Feb. 1, 2022), pp. 173-74.

292. Select Committee to Investigate the January 6th Attack on the United States Capitol, Deposition of Greg Jacob, (Feb. 1, 2022), pp. 173-75.

293. Select Committee to Investigate the January 6th Attack on the United States Capitol, Deposition of Greg Jacob, (Feb. 1, 2022), p. 193.

294. Select Committee to Investigate the January 6th Attack on the United States Capitol, Deposition of Chris Hodgson, (Mar. 30, 2022), pp. 208-09.

295. Select Committee to Investigate the January 6th Attack on the United States Capitol, Deposition of Chris Hodgson, (Mar. 30, 2022), pp. 208-10; Documents on file with the Select Committee to Investigate the January 6th Attack on the United States Capitol (National Archives Production), P-R001019–P-R001020 (Jan. 6, 2021, NSC Chat Log).

296. Donald J. Trump (@realDonaldTrump), Twitter, Jan. 6, 2021 2:24 p.m. ET, available at https://web.archive.org/web/20210106192450/https://twitter.com/realdonaldtrump/status/1346900434540240897.

297. Documents on file with the Select Committee to Investigate the January 6th Attack on the United States Capitol (National Archives Production), P-R001019–P-R001020 (NSC Chat Log).

298. Select Committee to Investigate the January 6th Attack on the United States Capitol, Transcribed Interview of Sarah Matthews, (Feb. 8, 2022), pp. 37-38.

299. Select Committee to Investigate the January 6th Attack on the United States Capitol, Deposition of Marc Short, (Jan. 26, 2022), pp. 30-31.

300. Select Committee to Investigate the January 6th Attack on the United States Capitol, Deposition of Marc Short, (Jan. 26, 2022), pp. 30-31.

301. Select Committee to Investigate the January 6th Attack on the United States Capitol, Deposition of Marc Short, (Jan. 26, 2022), pp. 30-31.

302. Documents on file with the Select Committee to Investigate the January 6th Attack on the United States Capitol (National Archives Production), P-R001019–P-R001020 (NSC Chat Log).

303. See Chapter 8; see also Select Committee to Investigate the January 6th Attack on the United States Capitol, Deposition of Marc Short, (Jan. 26, 2022), pp. 31-32.

304. Select Committee to Investigate the January 6th Attack on the United States Capitol, Hearing on the January 6th Investigation, 117th Cong., 2d sess., (June 16, 2022), available at https://www.govinfo.gov/committee/house-january6th.

305. Select Committee to Investigate the January 6th Attack on the United States Capitol, Deposition of Marc Short, (Jan. 26, 2022), pp. 63-65.

306. On the evening of January 6, 2021, the President's Military Aide told the Vice President's Military Aide (who relayed it to the Secret Service) that Marc Short's access to the White House complex had been cancelled. Documents on file with the Select Committee to Investigate the January 6th Attack on the United States Capitol (Secret Service Production), CTRL0000513149 (January 6-7, 2021), CTRL0000673145 (January 6, 2021). Several people relayed to Marc Short that "some who instigated the President"—possibly Peter Navarro— suggested to the President that "Marc was responsible for leading the Vice President on the path he took," which resulted in the President exclaiming that Mr. Short should be locked out of the White House. Select Committee to Investigate the January 6th Attack on the United States Capitol, Deposition of Marc Short, (Jan. 26, 2022), pp. 236-37; see also Biba Adams, "Pence's Chief of Staff Denied Entry into WH: Trump 'Blaming Me'," Yahoo News, (Jan. 7, 2021), available at https://www.yahoo.com/video/pence-chief-staff-denied-entry-173848235.html.

307. Select Committee to Investigate the January 6th Attack on the United States Capitol, Deposition of Marc Short, (Jan. 26, 2022), p. 238.

308. Select Committee to Investigate the January 6th Attack on the United States Capitol, Deposition of Marc Short, (Jan. 26, 2022), p. 31, 45 ("The reason was he felt like, for the world's greatest democracy, to see a motorcade, a 15-car motorcade fleeing the Capitol would send all the wrong signals. So he was adamant to say: I want to stay here in the Capitol."); see also Select Committee to Investigate the January 6th Attack on the United States Capitol, Hearing on the January 6th Investigation, 117th Cong., 2d sess., (June 16, 2022), available at https://www.govinfo.gov/committee/house-january6th.

309. Select Committee to Investigate the January 6th Attack on the United States Capitol, Deposition of Marc Short, (Jan. 26, 2022), pp. 29-31, 44-45; Select Committee to Investigate the January 6th Attack on the United States Capitol, Deposition of Greg Jacob, (Feb. 1, 2022), pp. 176-77; Select Committee to Investigate the January 6th Attack on the United States Capitol, Hearing on the January 6th Investigation, 117th Cong., 2d sess., (June 16, 2022), available at https://www.govinfo.gov/committee/house-january6th.

310. Select Committee to Investigate the January 6th Attack on the United States Capitol, Deposition of Greg Jacob, (Feb. 1, 2022), p. 198.

311. Select Committee to Investigate the January 6th Attack on the United States Capitol, Deposition of Greg Jacob, (Feb. 1, 2022), pp. 198-99.

312. Select Committee to Investigate the January 6th Attack on the United States Capitol, Deposition of Greg Jacob, (Feb. 1, 2022), pp. 198-99.

313. Jacob told the Select Committee that he recognized that January 6 was going to be "an historically important day" and he wanted to memorialize exactly what he thought of the arguments made by Eastman on January 5th, to supplement the memo he wrote to Vice President Pence reflecting the arguments Eastman made on January 4th. Select Committee to Investigate the January 6th Attack on the United States Capitol, Deposition of Greg Jacob, (Feb. 1, 2022), pp. 200-01.

314. Documents on file with the Select Committee to Investigate the January 6th Attack on the United States Capitol (Chapman University Production), Chapman005370 (January 6, 2021, emails between Greg Jacob and John Eastman).

315. Documents on file with the Select Committee to Investigate the January 6th Attack on the United States Capitol (Chapman University Production), Chapman005379 (January 6, 2021, emails between Greg Jacob and John Eastman).

316. Select Committee to Investigate the January 6th Attack on the United States Capitol, Deposition of Greg Jacob, (Feb. 1, 2022), p. 200.

317. Select Committee to Investigate the January 6th Attack on the United States Capitol, Deposition of Greg Jacob, (Feb. 1, 2022), p. 200.

318. Select Committee to Investigate the January 6th Attack on the United States Capitol, Deposition of Chris Hodgson, (Mar. 30, 2022), pp. 246-47.

319. "READ: Mike Pence's Statement to the Senate on the Storming of the Capitol," *U.S. News*, (Jan. 6, 2021), available at https://www.usnews.com/news/elections/articles/2021-01-06/read-mike-pences-statement-to-the-senate-on-the-storming-of-the-capitol; *see also* Select Committee to Investigate the January 6th Attack on the United States Capitol, Deposition of Chris Hodgson, (Mar. 30, 2022), p. 246 (testifying that the Vice President wrote his remarks himself in his ceremonial office after the Capitol was cleared).

320. Documents on file with the Select Committee to Investigate the January 6th Attack on the United States Capitol (National Archives Production), VP-R0000155, (January 6, 2021, emails between Greg Jacob and John Eastman).

321. Documents on file with the Select Committee to Investigate the January 6th Attack on the United States Capitol, (National Archives Production), VP-R0000155, p. 1, (January 6, 2021, emails between Greg Jacob and John Eastman).

322. Select Committee to Investigate the January 6th Attack on the United States Capitol, Hearing on the January 6th Investigation, 117th Cong., 2d sess., (June 16, 2022), available at https://www.govinfo.gov/committee/house-january6th.

323. Documents on file with the Select Committee to Investigate the January 6th Attack on the United States Capitol (National Archives Production), VP-R0000155, (January 6, 2021, emails between Greg Jacob and John Eastman). Note that Greg Jacob's testimony establishes that this email was likely received on January 6, 2021, at 11:44 p.m., not at 4:44 a.m. the following morning as shown on the face of this document as produced. Select Committee to Investigate the January 6th Attack on the United States Capitol, Deposition of Greg Jacob, (Feb. 1, 2022), p. 205. As noted in the Executive Summary, the Select Committee also received certain documents in UTC time, which is five hours ahead of EST.

324. Documents on file with the Select Committee to Investigate the January 6th Attack on the United States Capitol (Chapman University Production), Chapman005479 (January 6, 2021, emails between Greg Jacob and John Eastman). This email represents John Eastman again encouraging, in writing and just after the violent attack on the Capitol had been quelled,

that the Vice President use this as a justification for a further and much more serious violation of the law—delaying the certification. Select Committee to Investigate the January 6th Attack on the United States Capitol, *Hearing on the January 6th Investigation*, 117th Cong., 2d sess., (June 16, 2022), available at https://www.govinfo.gov/committee/house-january6th. Eastman attempted to minimize what he was doing by calling the Electoral Count Act a "minor procedural statute." Select Committee to Investigate the January 6th Attack on the United States Capitol, Deposition of Greg Jacob, (Feb. 1, 2022), p. 133. In an email sent at 1:33 p.m., just before the Capitol was breached, Eastman wrote, "I'm sorry Greg, but this is small minded. You're sticking with minor procedural statutes while the Constitution is being shredded." Documents on file with the Select Committee to Investigate the January 6th Attack on the United States Capitol (National Archives Production), VP-R0000166.

325.   Select Committee to Investigate the January 6th Attack on the United States Capitol, *Hearing on the January 6th Investigation*, 117th Cong., 2d sess., (June 16, 2022), available at https://www.govinfo.gov/committee/house-january6th.

326.   Select Committee to Investigate the January 6th Attack on the United States Capitol, Transcribed Interview of Eric Herschmann, (Apr. 6, 2022), pp. 43-44.

327.   Select Committee to Investigate the January 6th Attack on the United States Capitol, Transcribed Interview of Eric Herschmann, (Apr. 6, 2022), pp. 43-44.

328.   Documents on file with the Select Committee to Investigate the January 6th Attack on the United States Capitol (Chapman University Production), Chapman0064047, (January 11, 2021, email from John Eastman to Rudy Giuliani).

329.   Select Committee to Investigate the January 6th Attack on the United States Capitol, Deposition of Marc Short, (Jan. 26, 2022), pp. 35-36.

6

"BE THERE, WILL BE WILD!"

On December 14, 2020, electors around the country met to cast their Electoral College votes. Their vote ensured former Vice President Joe Biden's victory and cemented President Donald J. Trump's defeat. The people, and the States, had spoken. Members of President Trump's own Cabinet knew the election was over. Attorney General William Barr viewed it as "the end of the matter."[1] Secretary of State Mike Pompeo and Secretary of Labor Eugene Scalia concurred.[2] That same day, Scalia told President Trump directly that he should concede defeat.[3]

President Trump had no intention of conceding. As he plotted ways to stay in power, the President summoned a mob for help.

At 1:42 a.m., on December 19th, President Trump tweeted: "Big protest in D.C. on January 6th. Be there, will be wild!"[4]

The President's tweet galvanized tens of thousands of his supporters around the country. President Trump had been lying to them since election day, claiming he won, and that the Democrats had stolen victory from him. Now, with a single tweet, the President focused his supporters' anger on the joint session of Congress in Washington, DC on January 6th.

Anika Navaroli, the longest-tenured member of Twitter's Trust and Safety Policy team, monitored the reaction to President Trump's "be wild" tweet. She told the Select Committee that the President was "essentially staking a flag in DC ... for his supporters to come and rally."[5] The tweet created a "fire hose" of calls to overthrow the U.S. Government. President Trump's supporters had a new sense of urgency because they felt "as if their Commander in Chief" had summoned them.[6]

For many extremists and conspiracy theorists, the President's announcement was a call to arms.[7]

For the Proud Boys—described in more detail below—and their leader, Henry "Enrique" Tarrio, President Trump's tweet set in motion a chain of events that led directly to the attack on the U.S. Capitol. In the days that followed, the Proud Boys reorganized their hierarchy, imposed a stricter

Tarrio's video appears on a screen during a Select Committee hearing on June 09, 2022.
Photo by Drew Angerer/Getty Images

chain-of-command, and instructed followers to go "incognito" on January 6th.[8] The Proud Boys had made their presence known at previous pro-Trump events, including "Stop the Steal" rallies, where they brandished their black and yellow apparel and engaged in street brawls.[9] Suddenly, they did not want to stand out from the crowd. They wanted to blend in. They were planning something big.[10]

Tarrio allegedly used encrypted messages to plot the January 6, 2021, attack. On January 4, 2021, Tarrio told his men that they should "storm the Capitol." [11] While the attack was underway, Tarrio claimed credit in a private chat, writing: "We did this." [12] And on the evening of January 6th, Tarrio released a video of a man, presumably Tarrio himself, dressed in an odd costume standing in front of the U.S. Capitol. The eerie production had been recorded prior to the events of that day. Tarrio—who was not in Washington, DC on January 6th[13]—titled it, "Premonition." [14]

The Oath Keepers, a far-right, anti-government militia movement—also described in more detail below—began planning for January 6th after the President's tweet as well. Stewart Rhodes, the group's leader, had agitated against the U.S. Government for years.[15] Immediately following the 2020 presidential election, Rhodes and others schemed to stop the peaceful transfer of power. They stored weapons outside of Washington, DC,[16] hoping that President Trump would deputize them as his own militia.[17] An Oath Keeper leader, Kelly Meggs, read President Trump's December 19th tweet and commented in a Facebook message: "He called us all to the Capitol and wants us to make it wild!!! Sir Yes Sir!!!"[18] The Oath Keepers formed two military "stacks" and marched up the steps of the U.S. Capitol on January 6th. Meggs led one of them.[19]

Members of both the Proud Boys and Oath Keepers have been charged with "seditious conspiracy" and other serious crimes, including conspiracy to interfere with a Federal proceeding; some, including Stewart Rhodes, have been convicted.[20] U.S. law defines seditious conspiracy as plotting "to overthrow," or "to oppose by force," or to use "force to prevent, hinder, or delay the execution of any law of the United States."[21] Some of the two groups' members have already admitted that this is what they intended to do.[22]

Other extremists and conspiracy theorists mobilized after President Trump's tweet as well. These movements are described in more detail in subsequent sections. Three Percenter militias—another far-right, anti-government movement—shared "#OccupyCongress" memes[23] and planned for violence at the U.S. Capitol.[24] Nick Fuentes, leader of the white nationalist "Groypers," rallied his followers for January 6th.[25] Fuentes bragged afterwards that the "Capitol siege was fucking awesome."[26] Users on TheDonald.win, a website populated by some of President Trump's most ardent fans, openly discussed surrounding and occupying the U.S. Capitol.[27]

Adherents of QAnon, a bizarre and dangerous conspiracy cult, believed January 6th would bring the prophesied "Storm"—a violent purge of Democrats and government officials promised by the mysterious online personality known only as "Q."[28] QAnon's devotees flocked to Washington, DC because of the President's tweet and subsequent rhetoric. They shared a digital banner, "Operation Occupy the Capitol," which depicted the U.S. Capitol being torn in two.[29]

One especially notorious conspiracy theorist, Alex Jones, repeatedly told his *InfoWars*' viewers that January 6th would be a day of reckoning.[30] Jones is known for his outlandish conspiracy-mongering, including his baseless claim that the massacre of school children at Sandy Hook Elementary School was really a "false flag" operation staged by the U.S. Government. Of course, his vicious lie was disproven in court, but Jones is obsessed with "deep state" conspiracy theories and often propagates them.[31] After the 2020 presidential election, Jones argued that President Trump should use the power of the Government to impose martial law on American citizens.[32] Along with his *InfoWars* co-hosts, Jones amplified President Trump's "Big

Lie" and relentlessly promoted President Trump's "wild" protest. One of Jones' co-hosts floated the idea of "storming right into the Capitol."[33] Jones himself marched to the Capitol January 6th.[34]

Jones's influence helped shape the planning for January 6th behind the scenes as well. The Select Committee investigated how event organizers and the White House staff planned President Trump's rally at the Ellipse, a park south of the White House. This event was intended to rile up the President's supporters just prior to the joint session of Congress. A wealthy heiress paid for the event after listening to Jones' *InfoWars* rant about the importance of President Trump's tweet. She spent $3 million with the goal to "get as many people there as possible."[35] It worked—Americans who believed the election was stolen flocked to the Nation's capital.

By January 5th, President Trump's supporters—a large, angry crowd ready for instructions—had assembled in Washington. That evening, he could hear his raucous supporters at a rally not far from the White House. The President knew his supporters were "angry,"[36] and he planned to call on them to march on the U.S. Capitol.[37] He even wanted to join them on the march.[38] It was all part of President Trump's plan to intimidate officials and obstruct the joint session of Congress.

"We fight like hell," President Trump told the crowd assembled at the Ellipse on January 6, 2021. "And if you don't fight like hell, you're not going to have a country anymore."[39] Some of those in attendance, as well as else-where in Washington that day, were already prepared to fight. They had begun preparing two and a half weeks earlier—when President Trump told them it would "be wild!"

6.1 HOW FAR-RIGHT EXTREMISTS AND CONSPIRACY THEORISTS PLANNED FOR JANUARY 6TH

THE "STOP THE STEAL" COALITION

President Trump's "be wild" tweet immediately mobilized extremists and conspiracy theorists in the "Stop the Steal" coalition. The phrase "Stop the Steal" was originally coined in early 2016 by President Trump's longtime political advisor, Roger Stone.[40] At the time, Stone alleged first that Candidate Trump's Republican rivals were attempting to steal Candidate Trump's nomination.[41] After Trump became the nominee, Stone repurposed the saying to claim that former Secretary of State Hillary Clinton would steal the presidency.[42] When President Trump won the 2016 election, "Stop the Steal" was rendered moot—and did not become a significant political movement until President Trump's defeat on election night in 2020.[43] As early as November 5, 2020, Stone advised associates that he intended to reconstitute "Stop the Steal" by building an army of lawyers and suing "like there's no tomorrow."[44]

Ali Alexander, a rightwing provocateur who has worked closely with Stone,[45] quickly organized a new "Stop the Steal" campaign. On November 10, 2020, Alexander established "Stop the Steal" as an entity incorporated in Alabama.[46] Alexander added a bank account and various websites.[47]

One of Alexander's key allies in the "Stop the Steal" movement was Alex Jones. Prior to January 6th, Jones riled up crowds both in-person and online with incendiary rhetoric about the election. Jones' *InfoWars* was also a platform for others in the election-denial coalition. For instance, both Enrique Tarrio and Stewart Rhodes made multiple appearances on *InfoWars*, including between election day 2020 and January 6, 2021.[48]

Another frequent guest on *InfoWars* was Roger Stone—a nexus character in the "Stop the Steal" coalition.[49] Stone recommended that then Presidential Candidate Donald Trump appear on Jones's show in December 2015.[50] Trump accepted the invitation and praised Jones at length during his appearance.[51] The significance of Trump's interview with Jones should not be underestimated. Donald Trump was a leading presidential contender at the time and would go on to win the election. His appearance with Jones normalized *InfoWars*, welcoming its conspiracy-minded audience into Trump's base.[52] Trump did not appear on *InfoWars* again. However, Stone continued to make regular guest appearances.[53]

After election day 2020, Alexander Jones, and other "Stop the Steal" organizers, held rallies around the country to protest fictional claims of voter fraud. These events provided an opportunity for radicals and extremists to coalesce. The Proud Boys, Oath Keepers, and Three Percenters were all attendees. QAnon adherents were well-represented. So, too, were the white nationalist Groypers and their leader, Nick Fuentes.

"Stop the Steal" events and other protests throughout 2020 helped build the momentum for January 6th. The Select Committee collected data on 85 right-wing events between January 1, 2020, and January 20, 2021, which were inspired by opposition to COVID-19 lockdown measures, racial justice protests, and, later, the perceived theft of President Trump's victory.[54] Far-right extremists protested at or inside State capitols, or at other government buildings, in at least 68 instances.[55] Of those, 49 occurred during the period after the election through January 6th.[56] In the year leading up to January 6th, there were at least nine events at which far-right actors entered State capitols.[57] At least four of these capitol incursions—in Michigan,[58] Idaho,[59] Arizona,[60] and Oregon[61]—involved identifiable individuals who later participated in the attack on the U.S. Capitol.

Alex Jones and Ali Alexander inside the Georgia State Capitol during a "Stop the Steal" rally on November 18, 2020 in Atlanta, Georgia.

Photo by Elijah Nouvelage/Getty Images

Consider, for example, the protests held in Atlanta between November 18 and 21, 2020. Leaders and rank-and-file members of the Proud Boys, Oath Keepers, and Groypers, gathered outside the State capitol and the governor's mansion for nonstop events, including armed protests. Enrique Tarrio[62] and Stewart Rhodes[63] personally led contingents of the Proud Boys and Oath Keepers, respectively.

Jones first announced the Atlanta events on InfoWars on November 16th. In his announcement, Jones teased that he would be joined by Roger Stone and also called on listeners to "surround the governor's mansion" in order to prevent the election results from being certified.[64] Fuentes advertised that he would be speaking at the capitol every day at noon.[65] In fiery speeches across Atlanta, Fuentes spread election lies as well as wink-and-nod hints at intimidation and violence.[66]

Alexander, standing alongside Jones and Fuentes outside the State capitol on November 18th, exhorted the crowd to "storm the capitol" with them.[67] The three men led a crowd into the State capitol building. On November 20th, Roger Stone gave a speech outside the Georgia capitol. Speaking through a telephone held up by Alexander, Stone advanced election lies, and finished with a provocative rallying cry: "Victory or death!"[68]

That same day, Fuentes told the crowd, "Look, we've been in front of the State capitol, maybe we've been trying the wrong approach." [69] Days earlier, at a nighttime event outside the governor's mansion, Alexander, again flanked by Jones and Fuentes, goaded the crowd: "We'll light the whole shit on fire." [70]

While the crowd did not turn violent, the "Stop the Steal" protests in Atlanta, Georgia, prefigured January 6th in important respects. "Stop the Steal" organizers tried to use the mob they had assembled—including extremists from the Proud Boys, Oath Keepers, Three Percenters and Groypers—to intimidate lawmakers and overturn the election results in Georgia, which was required to certify former Vice President Biden's victory in the State by the end of that week.[71] They implored their followers to "storm the capitol." [72] As discussed in Chapter 8, this same coalition of radicals did just that on January 6, 2021.

Other "Stop the Steal" events helped pave the way for the events of January 6th. Two rallies in Washington D.C.—on November 14 and December 12, 2020—were critically important. Alexander's "Stop the Steal" was not the only protest organization present at these events. Both were called "Million MAGA Marches" and drew in other rally organizers. One of these other protests was called the "Jericho March" prayer rally.[73] Regardless, the same constellation of actors that appeared in Atlanta also incited Trump supporters in Washington.

For instance, during the Jericho March rally on December 12th, Stewart Rhodes called on President Trump to invoke the Insurrection Act as part of a desperate gambit to remain in power. In Rhodes' vision, he would lead militiamen on behalf of President Trump when others tried to remove him from office.[74] If President Trump did not invoke the Insurrection Act, Rhodes warned the crowd, then they would be forced to wage a "much more desperate [and] much more bloody war." Alex Jones also gave an incendiary speech at the Jericho March event, declaring: "I don't know who is going to the White House in 38 days, but I sure know this, Joe Biden is a globalist, and Joe Biden will be removed, one way or another!" [75]

As the crowds gathered in Washington on December 12th, President Trump was publicly lobbying the Supreme Court to hear his fictious claims of election fraud. The President assailed the Supreme Court on Twitter throughout the day.[76] The "Stop the Steal" coalition was eager to help. After the Jericho March event ended, Jones, his InfoWars co-host Owen Shroyer, and Ali Alexander led a march on the Supreme Court. Once there, the crowd chanted slogans such as "Stop the Steal!"; "1776!!"; "Our revolution!"; and "The fight has just begun!!" [77]

"Million MAGA March" protest on November 14, 2020 in Washington, DC.
Photo by Tasos Katopodis/Getty Images

President Trump made sure to let the protestors in Washington know that he personally approved of their mission. During the November rally, President Trump waved to the crowd from his presidential motorcade.[78] Then, on the morning of December 12th, President Trump tweeted: "Wow! Thousands of people forming in Washington (D.C.) for Stop the Steal. Didn't know about this, but I'll be seeing them! #MAGA."[79] Later that day, President Trump flew over the protestors in Marine One.[80]

When President Trump tweeted one week later that there would be a "wild" protest in Washington on January 6th, the "Stop the Steal" coalition immediately began to mobilize. Jones posted an article on the *InfoWars* website asking readers if they would "answer President Trump's call to defend the Republic?"[81] The next day, December 20th, Jones devoted much of his *InfoWars* show to the President's announcement. Jones told his audience several times that if 10 million Americans came to Washington, DC on January 6th, Congress would have to listen to them.[82] He repeated this idea over the course of the episode, saying things such as, "He's calling *you*, he needs your help, we need your help, we need 10 million people there," "[w]e need martial law and have to prevent the police state of foreigners from taking over." Jones added: "It's literally in our hands. It's literally up to us."[83]

Other *InfoWars* hosts promoted the "wild" protest as well. In late December, Matt Bracken told InfoWars viewers that it may be necessary to storm the U.S. Capitol. "We're going to only be saved by millions of Americans moving to Washington, occupying the entire area, if—if necessary storming right into the Capitol," Bracken said. "You know, they're—we know the rules of engagement. If you have enough people, you can push down any kind of a fence or a wall." [84]

Far-right extremists planned to do just that.

6.2 THE PROUD BOYS: "[Y]OU WANT TO STORM THE CAPITOL"

From the Proud Boys' founding in 2016, violence was intrinsic to their mission. "We will kill you. That's the Proud Boys in a nutshell," their founder said.[85] New recruits pledge an oath, established in the group's bylaws, identifying themselves as unapologetic "Western chauvinists," [86] promoting an exclusionary, hyper-masculine interpretation of Western culture.[87] They find common ground in an embrace of misogyny and hate for their perceived enemies.[88] The group is somewhat ethnically diverse, but their public and private messages fester with toxic white supremacist, xenophobic, and anti-Semitic slurs.[89]

The Proud Boys have participated in, or instigated, protests since their founding.[90] They've long been known as street brawlers looking for a fight.[91] But 2020 was a watershed year for the group. As protests spread around the country, the Proud Boys deputized themselves as agents of law and order—vigilantes against perceived threats.[92] More often, they played the role of instigators.[93] They portrayed themselves as counter-protestors and identified their targets as Black Lives Matter and Antifa—though they were hard-pressed to define their organizational enemies.[94]

During the presidential debate on September 29, 2020, President Trump was asked to disavow far-right extremists, including the Proud Boys. The President did not explicitly condemn the group. Instead, he seemingly endorsed their mission. "Stand back and stand by," President Trump told the Proud Boys, before adding, "but I'll tell you what … somebody's got to do something about Antifa and the left." [95] The President's words electrified the group, injecting new life into their recruitment and activities. According to Nick Quested, a filmmaker who spent significant time with the group and testified before the Select Committee, the Proud Boys had found their "savior" in President Trump.[96]

Joseph Biggs, a senior Proud Boy, immediately trumpeted President Trump's debate statement on Parler,[97] a fringe social media platform. Biggs made it clear that the Proud Boys were ready to fight Antifa.[98] The group's

A Proud Boy during a "Stop the Steal" rally on November 7, 2020 in Salem, Oregon.
Photo by Nathan Howard/Getty Images

size "tripled" in response to President Trump's apparent endorsement, according to Jeremy Bertino, a Proud Boys leader who has pleaded guilty to seditious conspiracy in relation to January 6th.[99] Similarly, Enrique Tarrio and another Proud Boys member, George Meza, testified to the Select Committee that the President's comment was a pivotal, energizing moment.[100] The group started selling merchandise with their new "stand back and stand by" slogan the very same night.[101]

As the presidential votes were tallied, the Proud Boys became agitated at the prospect that President Trump would lose. On November 5, 2020, Biggs posted on social media, "It's time for fucking war if they steal this shit."[102] As former Vice President Joe Biden's victory became apparent, Proud Boys leaders directed their ire toward others in the Government. Biggs, speaking on a Proud Boys livestream show with Tarrio and others, warned that government officials are "evil scum, and they all deserve to die a traitor's death." Ethan Nordean—another Proud Boys leader who allegedly helped lead the attack at the Capitol—responded, "Yup, Day of the Rope,"[103] referring to a day of mass lynching of "race traitors" in the white supremacist novel *The Turner Diaries*.[104]

THE PROUD BOYS IN WASHINGTON PRIOR TO JANUARY 6TH

Within days of the election, dozens of "Stop the Steal" protests were organized around the country.[105] The Proud Boys participated alongside other right-wing extremist groups in some of them, including a November 7, 2020, protest outside of the Pennsylvania State capitol in Harrisburg.[106] The two events in Washington, DC—on November 14, 2020, and the other on December 12, 2020—proved to be especially important for the group's evolution.

The daytime events on both dates passed by without violence or major unrest, but as the sun set, bouts of violence erupted,[107] driven by clashes between far-right extremist groups—chiefly the Proud Boys—and counter-protestors.[108] Among far-right extremists, the Proud Boys had the largest showing in both November and December,[109] with roughly 200 to 300 Proud Boys at the November 14th rally, and the same number or more in December.[110] As discussed in Chapter 8, they mustered about the same contingent for the attack on the U.S. Capitol.

The gathering on November 14th provided a chance for Tarrio to socialize with rally leaders and far-right celebrities. In fact, his travel to DC by private jet appears to have been paid for by Patrick Byrne, a businessman who had President Trump's ear in the last weeks of his presidency and encouraged the President to authorize the seizure of voting machines in a December 18th meeting.[111] Tarrio's testimony and photographs from the day show that he met with "Stop the Steal" organizer Ali Alexander that evening, and the pair toasted each other.[112] Tarrio described the event as a "historic" meeting of Trump supporters and celebrated the opportunity to share that platform with Alexander, Jones, and Jones' *InfoWars* co-host, Owen Shroyer.[113] Shroyer would later be charged with crimes committed during the January 6th attack.[114]

A month later, the Proud Boys returned to the Nation's capital. On the evening of December 11th, hundreds of Proud Boys and friends gathered in downtown Washington, DC to listen to an impromptu bullhorn speech by Tarrio and Nordean, along with Roger Stone and Shroyer.[115] Stone implored the crowd to "fight to the bitter end."[116]

The next day, as the Proud Boys marched in force on the streets, Tarrio teased in a social media post that he had a meeting in the White House.[117] The visit, which was only a public White House tour, appears to have been facilitated by a friend, Bianca Gracia, the head of Latinos for Trump.[118] As the rallies concluded the next day, the Proud Boys took to the streets again. Two key events occurred that evening.

First, members of the Proud Boys tore down a Black Lives Matter banner from a historically Black church in downtown Washington, DC.[119] They filmed themselves burning it.[120] Tarrio was eventually charged with destruction of property.[121] He was arrested on January 4, 2021, and banned from Washington, DC, barring him from joining the group at the Capitol.[122] As explained in Chapter 8, however, Tarrio's arrest did not stop him from conspiring with his men on January 6th.

Minutes after the flag burning, a man wearing black clothes walked into a crowd of Proud Boys.[123] Assuming he was associated with Antifa, they began pushing and harassing him, and he drew a knife in response.[124] In the ensuing melee, four Proud Boys suffered stab wounds, including Bertino, a confidant to Tarrio.[125] Bertino's wounds were severe and life-threatening, preventing him from joining the group on January 6th.[126]

STORMING THE WINTER PALACE

The Proud Boys began to reorient and formalize their operations to focus on January 6th after President Trump's December 19th tweet. Inspired, in part, by Bertino's stabbing, the Proud Boys centered their new hierarchy in group chats that used terms such as "Ministry of Self Defense" (MOSD).[127] However, the words "Self Defense" were misleading: Enrique Tarrio and others would soon go on the offense. And the MOSD served as their organizational scaffolding for the January 6, 2021, attack.

On December 20, 2020, Tarrio established a "national rally planning committee" and created an encrypted MOSD chat to organize their activities.[128] Tarrio added Proud Boys leaders from across the country, including several who played lead roles in the violence on January 6th.[129] In the ensuing weeks, the Proud Boys traded equipment recommendations, shared maps marked with law enforcement positions, and established command and control structures.[130] A separate encrypted chat, named "Boots on the Ground," was established for foot soldiers who would be in Washington, DC on January 6th.[131]

The Proud Boys' planning for January 6th was a significant step in the group's evolution. Previously, they were loosely organized. The MOSD was created to enforce a "top down structure" with a defined leadership.[132] Tarrio stressed the command structure by telling members that they needed to "[f]it in [] or fuck off."[133]

From the start, it was clear that MOSD chat members were intensely interested in disrupting the electoral count on January 6th. On December 20, 2020, one MOSD leader stated, "I assume most of the protest will be at the capital [sic] building given what's going on inside."[134] On December 29, 2020, in a group message to the MOSD, a member wrote, "I know most of the events will be centered around freedom plaza...." Tarrio responded, "Negative. They're centered around the Capitol."[135]

On December 30, 2020, Tarrio received an intriguing document titled, "1776 Returns."[136] The document was apparently sent to him by cryptocurrency investors in South Florida.[137] The file's author(s) divided their plan into five parts, "Infiltrate, Execution, Distract, Occupy and Sit-In," with the goal of overrunning several Federal buildings around the U.S. Capitol. The plan specifically mentioned House and Senate office buildings, setting forth steps for occupying them. The author(s) called for "the masses to rush the building[s]," distract law enforcement in the area by pulling fire alarms around the city, target specific Senators' offices, and disguise participants' identities with COVID masks.[138]

One proposal mentioned in the document is titled, "Storm the Winter Palace."[139] This is a reference to a dramatic reenactment of the 1917 Bolshevik Revolution, during which Vladimir Lenin ordered his forces to take over the Romanovs' residence in Petrograd. The "Winter Palace" was the seat of the provisional government, which had held out against the Bolshevik revolutionaries. The Proud Boys would frame their actions on January 6th as part of the American Revolution. But the "1776 Returns" document shows their inspiration came at least in part from the Communist Revolution, which led to 70-plus years of totalitarian rule. No historical event has been less American.

The Proud Boys did not adopt the "1776 Returns" plan in full. Several Proud Boys testified that they were unaware of the document before it became public.[140] But the document does appear to have been significantly edited while in the Proud Boys' hands.[141] The person who sent it to Tarrio—his ex-girlfriend, Eryka Gemma Flores—commented, "The revolution is [more] important than anything." To which Tarrio responded: "That's what every waking moment consists of … I'm not playing games."[142]

On January 3rd, Tarrio posted a conspicuous question on Telegram: "What if we invade it?" The first response to his post read: "January 6th is D day [sic] in America."[143] In private, on the Proud Boys' leadership group message, planning continued. One MOSD leader, John Stewart, floated a plan that centered around "the front entrance to the Capitol building."[144] At 7:10 p.m. on January 3rd, Stewart wrote to the MOSD leaders:

> I mean the main operating theater should be out in front of the house of representatives. It should be out in front of the Capitol building. That's where the vote is taking place and all of the objections. So, we can ignore the rest of these stages and all that shit and plan the operations based around the front entrance to the Capitol building. I strongly recommend you use the national mall and not Pennsylvania avenue though. It's wide-open space, you can see everything coming from all angles.[145]

Early the next morning, on January 4th, Tarrio sent a voice memo to the same group of MOSD leaders stating, "I didn't hear this voice until now, you want to storm the Capitol." [146]

One of Tarrio's comrades in the Proud Boys' leadership, Charles Donohoe—who pleaded guilty to conspiracy to obstruct an official proceeding and assaulting, resisting, or impeding certain officers[147]—later told authorities that by January 4th he "was aware that members of MOSD leadership were discussing the possibility of storming the Capitol." [148] Donohoe "believed that storming the Capitol would achieve the group's goal of stopping the government from carrying out the transfer of presidential power" and "understood that storming the Capitol would be illegal." [149] By the following evening, January 5th, Tarrio was discussing with other Proud Boy leaders a "tactical plan" for the following day. Their "objective" was "to obstruct, impede, or interfere with the certification of the Electoral College vote." [150] Moreover, Donohoe understood that the Proud Boys "would pursue this through the use of force and violence, in order to show Congress that 'we the people' were in charge." [151] On January 6th, Charles Donohoe understood that two of his fellow Proud Boys' leaders—Ethan Nordean and Joe Biggs—"were searching for an opportunity to storm the Capitol." [152]

Jeremy Bertino, the Proud Boys leader who was stabbed on the night of December 12th, later told authorities that his fellow extremists plotted to stop the peaceful transfer of power. In October 2022, Bertino pleaded guilty to "seditious conspiracy" and other crimes.[153] Bertino admitted that the Proud Boys traveled to Washington, DC on January 6, 2021, "to stop the certification of the Electoral College Vote." They "were willing to do whatever it would take, including using force against police and others, to achieve that objective." [154]

In testimony before the Select Committee, Bertino recalled a telling text exchange with Tarrio on the evening of January 6th. "I was like, 'holy shit,' or something like that I said to him," Bertino recalled. "And I was like, 'I can't believe this is happening,' or something like that, and '1776.' " [155]

Tarrio replied to Bertino: "Winter Palace." [156]

6.3   THE OATH KEEPERS: "HE CALLED US ALL TO THE CAPITOL AND WANTS US TO MAKE IT WILD!!!"

The Oath Keepers, founded in 2009 by Elmer Stewart Rhodes, is a far-right anti-government organization. The group targets former and current military and law enforcement for recruitment. Their name refers to the oath taken by public servants to support and defend the U.S. Constitution. The Oath Keepers' claimed fealty to the U.S. Constitution is belied by their obsession with conspiracy theories about alleged evil-intentioned elites in the Government.[157] Rhodes has often spouted these conspiracy theories on *InfoWars*.[158]

Over the summer of 2020, the Oath Keepers organized armed groups, ostensibly to serve as volunteer, self-appointed security at protests around the country. The Oath Keepers used the protests to draw in new recruits.[159] They also built muscle memory by coordinating for these events. For example, the Oath Keepers hired Michael Greene, who later coordinated Oath Keepers' activities on January 5th and 6th, to lead security operations in multiple cities around the country.[160] In the early part of 2020, protests against COVID-related lockdowns served as additional growth and networking opportunities. Kellye SoRelle, a lawyer for the Oath Keepers, met the Oath Keepers at a lockdown protest in Austin, Texas in early 2020. SoRelle saw these COVID events as a "coalescing moment" for different far-right groups.[161]

The "Stop the Steal" movement created another opportunity for the Oath Keepers to grow their influence. Rhodes repeatedly amplified the stolen election conspiracy theory. On November 10, 2020, he posted a "Call to Action!" on the Oath Keepers website, alleging the election was "stolen" and exhorting his followers to "refuse to EVER recognize this as a legitimate election, and refuse to recognize Biden as a legitimate winner."[162] Under a section entitled "What We the People Must Do," Rhodes quoted a "patriot from Serbia, who also loves America." The Serbian author described how his fellow countrymen fomented a political revolution. Parts of the statement presaged the attack on the U.S. Capitol:

> … Millions gathered in our capital [sic]. There were no barricades strong enough to stop them, nor the police determined enough to stop them. Police and Military aligned with the people after few hours of fist-fight [sic]. We stormed the Parliament. And burned down fake state Television! WE WON![163]

The Oath Keepers were obsessed with the Insurrection Act—seeing it as a way for President Trump to cling to power. Rhodes believed that the President could empower militias like the Oath Keepers to enforce law and order after other Americans refused to accept President Trump's rule.[164] Indeed, President Trump had been intensely interested in the Insurrection Act as a potential tool to quell the protests in summer 2020.[165] Rhodes wished the Act had been invoked then, but he did not give up on the fantasy.[166] As mentioned above, Rhodes called for President Trump to invoke the Insurrection Act during his speech in Washington on December 12, 2020.[167]

That day, Rhodes also coordinated with Jericho March organizers to provide security.[168] He coordinated with a paramilitary group known as 1st

Amendment Praetorian (1AP), to guard VIPs, including retired Lieutenant General Michael Flynn and Patrick Byrne.[169] Rhodes indicated that the Oath Keepers would be "working closely" with them for the event.[170]

The Oath Keepers continued to call for President Trump to invoke the Insurrection Act throughout December 2020, arguing that the President needed to do so to "Stop the Steal."[171] This fantasy reflected a warped sense of reality. Rhodes testified that President Trump could have mobilized "unorganized militia," including the Oath Keepers, to suppress an insurrection if he attempted to stay in power after losing the election.[172] But the Oath Keepers themselves were the ones contemplating insurrection. On December 10, 2020, Rhodes messaged others: "Either Trump gets off his ass and uses the Insurrection Act to defeat the Chicom puppet coup or we will have to rise up in insurrection (rebellion) against the ChiCom puppet Biden. Take your pick."[173] Rhodes was blunt in other messages to the Oath Keepers, writing: "We need to push Tump [sic] to do his duty. If he doesn't, we will do ours. Declare Independence. Defy[,] Resist[,] Defend[,] Conquer or Die. This needs to be our attitude."[174]

6.4 "TRUMP SAID IT'S GONNA BE WILD!!!!!!! IT'S GONNA BE WILD!!!!!!!"

As the Proud Boys began their plans for January 6th, Kelly Meggs, the leader of the Florida chapter of the Oath Keepers, reached out. In the past, the Proud Boys and the Oath Keepers had their differences, deriding each other's tactics and ethos during the summer 2020 protests.[175] But President Trump's tweet on December 19th conveyed a sense of urgency which provided the two extremist rivals the opportunity to work together for a common goal.

After President Trump's tweet, Meggs called Enrique Tarrio. They spoke for 3 minutes and 26 seconds.[176] Meggs also sent a message on Facebook, bragging about an alliance he had formed among the Oath Keepers, the Florida Three Percenters, and the Proud Boys: "We have decided to work together and shut this shit down."[177] The Oath Keepers were making plans of their own, too.

"Oath Keepers president [Rhodes] is pretty disheartened," Roberto Minuta, one of Rhodes' men, messaged someone on December 19th. "He feels like it's go time, the time for peaceful protest is over in his eyes. I was talking with him last night."[178] Minuta has been charged with "seditious conspiracy" and other crimes.[179]

In the days that followed, the Oath Keepers planned for violence. They used encrypted chats on Signal to discuss travel plans, trade tips on tactical equipment to bring, and develop their plans for once they were on the ground in the DC area.[180] On December 21st, 2020, Joshua James messaged the group, stating, "SE region is creating a NATIONAL CALL TO ACTION FOR DC JAN 6TH. ... 4 states are mobilizing[.]"[181] Meggs, Rhodes, and others created several different chat groups to coordinate for January 6th.[182]

On December 22nd, Meggs echoed President Trump's tweet in a Facebook message to someone else:

> Trump said It's gonna be wild!!!!!!! It's gonna be wild!!!!!!! He wants us to make it WILD that's what he's saying. He called us all to the Capitol and wants us to make it wild!!! Sir Yes Sir!!! Gentlemen we are heading to DC pack your shit!!"[183]

Meggs also wrote that the Oath Keepers would have 50–100 members in Washington, DC on January 6th.[184]

The Oath Keepers hosted periodic group video meetings to discuss plans for January 6th. Richard Dockery, a former Oath Keepers member, testified to the Select Committee about a video call that took place around December 31st, and related specifically to planning for January 6th.[185] During the call, Oath Keepers' leadership announced plans to provide security for far-right celebrities like Roger Stone.[186] If there were any problems while they were providing security, "there was a quick reaction force in Virginia that would come help them out ... and that they would have firearms."[187]

Rhodes announced during an episode of *InfoWars* in November 2020 that the Oath Keepers had established a "Quick Reaction Force" (QRF) outside of Washington, DC.[188] After President Trump announced the "wild" protest, the group's advanced coordination largely focused on planning related to their QRF, as well as the various security details for VIPs and stage areas on January 5th and 6th.[189] Oath Keepers from North Carolina, Florida, South Carolina, and Arizona converged on the Comfort Inn in Ballston, Virginia, and used the location to store their cache of weapons for January 6th.[190] Oath Keepers leaders communicated actively about the QRF for January 6th.[191] Rhodes and another contingent of Oath Keepers stayed at the Hilton Garden Inn in Vienna, Virginia, and stored weapons there as well.[192]

Rhodes amassed an arsenal of military-grade assault weapons and equipment in the days leading up to January 6th. On December 30th, Rhodes spent approximately $7,000 on two night-vision devices and a weapon sight and shipped them to Marsha Lessard, a rally organizer who lived near Washington, DC and who had previously been in contact with the organizers of the Ellipse rally.[193] On January 1st and 2nd, Rhodes purchased additional weapons and accessories at a cost of approximately $5,000.[194] The following day, January 3rd, Rhodes and Kellye SoRelle departed Texas for Washington, DC. While traveling, Rhodes spent an additional $6,000 on an AR-style rifle and firearms attachments.[195] Making one final shopping trip in Mississippi, Rhodes purchased $4,500 of firearms equipment including more sights, magazines, and weapons parts on January 4th.[196]

On the morning of January 6th, with weapons stockpiled, Rhodes messaged the Signal group of Oath Keepers leaders:

> We have several well equipped [sic] QRFs outside DC. And there are many, many others, from other groups, who will be watching and waiting on the outside in case of worst case [sic] scenarios.[197]

6.5 "READY TO STEP IN AND DO WHAT IS NEEDED"

Stewart Rhodes's and Oath Keepers' lawyer Kellye SoRelle arrived in Washington on the afternoon of January 5th.[198] They immediately went to Freedom Plaza, where President Trump had instructed rally organizers to give some of his most extreme supporters time to speak.[199] As a small group of Oath Keepers patrolled Freedom Plaza, they were able to see the results of President Trump's call to mobilize.[200] SoRelle testified that there were Oath Keepers, Proud Boys, and "Alex Jones people" mingling together in the crowd, with "just a small distinction between them." [201]

The Oath Keepers later found themselves at the Phoenix Park Hotel,[202] where they ate and drank with a motley coalition of far-right political activists who were united in their shared belief in President Trump's Big Lie.[203] Among them were: Proud Boys-linked Bianca Gracia of Latinos for Trump; Joshua Macias, leader of Vets for Trump;[204] and Amanda Chase, a Virginia State senator.[205] In a livestream discussion moderated by Chase, they promoted false election fraud claims. Macias and Rhodes encouraged President Trump to invoke the Insurrection Act and call up combat veterans who are "ready to step in and do what is needed." [206]

SoRelle later told the Select Committee that there was discussion of going to "storm the Capitol," although she claimed that this was "normal" discussion and supposedly did not indicate violence or "any of that type of stuff." [207]

That same evening, Gracia asked SoRelle and Rhodes to follow her to a garage where she was supposed to meet Proud Boys leader Enrique Tarrio,[208] who had just been released from custody and ordered to leave the DC area.[209] Instead of immediately leaving Washington, DC, Tarrio instead made his way to a garage near the hotel where the others gathered.[210] Portions of the ensuing meeting were captured on video by documentary filmmaker Nick Quested and his camera crew. SoRelle claims that she was asked to attend to discuss Tarrio's legal woes,[211] but there is evidence indicating that the conversation turned tactical.

Tarrio discussed the court's order, informing the group he was going north to Maryland, so he could "stay close just to make sure my guys are ok."[212] Tarrio discussed his confiscated phone with Gracia. He told her that "they couldn't get in there," apparently referencing the two-factor authentication enabled on his phone.[213] Tarrio also appeared familiar with another attendee, Vets for Trump leader Macias, who rested his hand on Tarrio's shoulder at various points.[214] Rhodes and Tarrio shook hands.[215]

Much of the substantive conversation between Rhodes, Tarrio, and the others cannot be heard because Tarrio asked Quested's camera crew to stop recording.[216] However, some of the conversation is audible from afar and Rhodes can be heard telling Tarrio that he "has three groups in Tyson's Corner,"[217] a reference to the QRFs that he had mustered in the event that President Trump called the Oath Keepers into service.

Tarrio later expressed appreciation for Rhodes's presence at the garage meeting and underscored that their two organizations needed to stand together on January 6th. Tarrio explained that the Proud Boys and Oath Keepers are "just two different groups" and that he and Rhodes "don't get along," but said that "for situations like this where there is a need to unite regardless of our differences ... what he did today was commendable."[218] Tarrio added that Rhodes's presence at the garage meeting was "thoughtful" because Rhodes had "quickly provided security" for the meeting and "seemed concerned" about Tarrio's legal situation.[219] In a likely nod to prior coordination between Proud Boys and Oath Keepers at other post-election events, Tarrio further explained that "my guys have helped him [Rhodes] out in the past," and that he and Rhodes have "mutual respect" for one another.[220] Tarrio then traveled north to a hotel near Baltimore, Maryland, where he stayed through the events of the next day.[221]

6.6 "FRIENDS OF STONE"

As explained above, a constellation of far-right characters came together in late 2020 as part of the "Stop the Steal" cause. Among them was Roger Stone, a right-wing political operative whose career as a self-trumpeted dirty trickster stretched back decades. Stone is arguably President Trump's oldest political advisor.[222] For example, he worked for Donald Trump's independent presidential bid during the 2000 campaign.[223] In addition to his political connections, Stone cultivated relationships with far-right extremists, including the two groups charged with seditious conspiracy: the Oath Keepers and the Proud Boys.

The Select Committee found that at least seven members of the Oath Keepers provided security for Stone, or were seen with him, in the weeks

Roger Stone in front of the Supreme Court on January 5, 2021 in Washington, DC.
Photo by Tasos Katopodis/Getty Images

immediately preceding the attack on the U.S. Capitol.[224] Text messages released by Edward Vallejo, an Oath Keeper charged with seditious conspiracy and other crimes, show that Stewart Rhodes and Kelly Meggs discussed providing security for Stone.[225] Some of these Oath Keepers guarded Stone during an event at Freedom Plaza in Washington, DC on the night of January 5th.[226] Stone was also flanked by Oath Keepers outside of the Willard Hotel on the morning of January 6th.[227] One of the Oath Keepers who provided security for Stone was Joshua James, who pleaded guilty to seditious conspiracy, obstruction of Congress and other charges in March 2022.[228] James was also reportedly seen in Stone's hotel room at the Willard hours before the attack on the U.S. Capitol.[229]

Stone has a longstanding, close relationship with the Proud Boys. Stone has taken the Proud Boys oath[230] and repeatedly defended the group.[231] Danish documentarians filmed him working with Proud Boys for years.[232] In one scene, filmed in 2019, Stone warmly greets Joe Biggs, a Proud Boys leader central to the Capitol violence. Stone says of Biggs: "My guy, right here."[233] In a 2019 court case, Stone identified Enrique Tarrio as one of his volunteers, explaining that Tarrio had access to his phone and could post to Stone's Instagram account from it.[234]

As mentioned above, Stone, Tarrio and another Proud Boy leader, Ethan Nordean, addressed an impromptu rally in Washington, DC on the night of December 11, 2020. Owen Shroyer, an *InfoWars* host, was also with them.[235] "We will fight to the bitter end for an honest count of the 2020 election," Stone told the crowd. "Never give up, never quit, never surrender, and fight for America!"[236] A few weeks later, on January 2, 2021, Tarrio led a Proud Boys protest outside of Senator Marco Rubio's home in Florida. The Proud Boys wanted to convince Rubio to vote against certification of the vote on January 6th.[237] Stone reportedly called into the event to speak to Tarrio's crowd.[238]

One way in which Stone maintained these contacts was through a Signal chat group named "F.O.S."—or Friends of Stone.[239] Two days after the election, Stone sent a text: "We provide information several times a day. So please monitor the F.O.S. feed so you can act in a timely fashion."[240] Ali Alexander and Stone continued to coordinate about Stop the Steal strategy and events between the election and January 6th.[241] In addition to Alexander, Stone's "Friends" on the Signal chat included Rhodes and Tarrio.[242]

In July 2020, President Trump granted Stone clemency after he was convicted of lying to Congress and other charges.[243] Then, on December 23rd, President Trump pardoned Stone.[244] Several days later, at a dinner on the evening of December 27th, Stone thanked President Trump. In a post on Parler, Stone wrote that he "thanked President Trump in person tonight for pardoning me" and also recommended to the President that he "appoint a special counsel" to stop "those who are attempting to steal the 2020 election through voter fraud." Stone also wrote that he wanted "to ensure that Donald Trump continues as our president."[245] Finally, he added: "#StopTheSteal" and "#rogerstonedidnothingwrong."[246] The Select Committee has learned that Stone discussed the January 6th event with the President, likely at this same dinner on December 27th.[247] The President told Stone he "was thinking of speaking."[248]

The Select Committee sought to question Roger Stone about his relationships with President Trump and far-right extremists, as well as other issues. During his deposition, Stone invoked his Fifth Amendment right nearly 90 times.[249] Stone has publicly stated that he committed no wrongdoing and that he encouraged a peaceful protest.[250]

6.7 WHITE NATIONALISTS: "THE CAPITOL SIEGE WAS FUCKING AWESOME..."

Nick Fuentes is an online provocateur who leads a white nationalist movement known as "America First," or the "Groypers." Fuentes immediately responded to President Trump's "be wild" tweet. On December 19, 2020,

Fuentes wrote on Twitter: "I will return to Washington DC to rally for President Trump on January 6th!" [251] Fuentes and his Groypers did return to Washington, DC for the joint session. As the attack was underway, Fuentes incited followers from his perch immediately outside of the U.S. Capitol. Some of his followers joined the attack inside, with one even sitting in Vice President Pence's seat on the Senate dais.[252]

Fuentes and a fellow Groyper leader, Patrick Casey, rose to prominence in 2017 after rallying at the Charlottesville "Unite the Right" event.[253] For years, the Groypers have repeatedly promoted white supremacist and Christian nationalist beliefs, often cloaked in wink-and-nod humor, puns, or religion, and they regularly gin up public opposition to other right-wing organizations or politicians whom they deem insufficiently conservative.[254]

Fuentes was a key voice for "Stop the Steal" conspiracy theories leading up to January 6th. He spent 2 months leading rallies in State capitals across the country,[255] spreading the Big Lie and livestreaming coded calls to violence.[256] He also used his livestream to raise significant funds between November 2020 and January 2021.[257]

On November 9, 2020, Fuentes promised, "GROYPERS ARE GOING TO STOP THIS COUP!" [258] Two days later, Fuentes organized a "Stop the Steal" rally at the Michigan State Capitol. He told the crowd that they should be "more feral" in their tactics to overturn the election, suggesting that they target lawmakers in their homes.[259] On November 14th, Fuentes rallied a crowd of his followers at the Million MAGA March in Washington, DC, pushing "Stop the Steal" conspiracies, calling for President Trump to rule for life, and exhorting his followers to "storm every State capitol until January 20, 2021, until President Trump is inaugurated for 4 more years." [260]

As discussed above, Fuentes was a prominent figure at the "Stop the Steal" rally in Atlanta, Georgia, in November 2020.[261] He promoted election conspiracies, criticized the Republican Party, joked about the Holocaust, and denounced former Vice President Biden as illegitimate.[262] Fuentes also suggested his followers intimidate politicians in their homes.[263]

On December 12th, Fuentes again rallied a crowd of supporters at the "Stop the Steal" events in Washington, DC, calling for the destruction of the Republican Party because it had failed to overturn the election.[264] As others spoke at the Jericho March rally, Fuentes headlined a "Stop the Steal" protest just a few blocks away.[265]

On January 4th, Fuentes suggested that his followers kill State legislators who don't support efforts to overturn the 2020 election. As discussed in Chapter 2, President Trump and his surrogates were pressuring State legislators at the time to do just that. Fuentes complained that his side "had

no leverage." Fuentes then asked: "What can you and I do to a state legislator, besides kill them?" He then quickly added: "Although we should not do
that. I am not advising that, but I mean, what else can you do, right?[266]

On January 5th, Casey advertised the marches in Washington, DC on his
Telegram channel and provided repeated updates on the logistics of getting
into the city. Casey also spoke to his followers about the next day's rally on
a livestream on DLive.[267] As discussed in Chapter 8, the Groypers clearly
played a role in the January 6th attack. They even planted their flag in the
inner chambers of the U.S. Capitol.[268] Fuentes crowed about the attack the
day after, tweeting: "The Capitol Siege was fucking awesome and I'm not
going to pretend it wasn't." [269] In another tweet on January 7th, Fuentes
wrote: "For a brief time yesterday the US Capital [sic] was once again occupied by The American People, before the regime wrested back control." [270]

Despite his boasts on Twitter, Fuentes exercised his Fifth Amendment
privilege against self-incrimination and refused to provide information
about his organizing activities to the Select Committee.[271]

6.8 THE THREE (III%) PERCENTERS: "#OCCUPYCONGRESS"

The Oath Keepers were not the only anti-government extremists who
viewed President Trump's December 19th, tweet as a call to arms. Militias
around the country were similarly inspired to act. "People were retweeting
it right and left. ... I saw people retweeting it, talking about, yeah, it's going
to be crazy, going to be a huge crowd," Michael Lee Wells, a militia leader
in North Carolina, told the Select Committee.[272] Members of militias known
as the "Three Percenters" were electrified.

The Three Percenters believe that three percent of American colonists
successfully overthrew the British during the American Revolution.[273] This
is not true. Far more than a tiny fraction of the colonial population fought
in or supported the Revolutionary War.[274] Regardless, this ahistorical belief
has become an organizing myth for militias around modern-day America.

As with the Oath Keepers, many Three Percenters have turned against
the U.S. Government, such that they equate it with the British monarchy
and believe it should be overthrown.[275] The movement does not have one,
centralized hierarchy. Instead, semi-autonomous branches organize and
run themselves.[276] The Three Percenter cause was growing prior to the
attack on the U.S. Capitol. Jeremy Liggett, a militia leader in Florida, told
the Select Committee it was "trendy" in far-right circles to identify with
the Three Percenter movement in the months leading up to January 6th.[277]

President Trump tapped into this well of anti-government extremism.
The President's repeated insistence that the election had been stolen resonated with militia members who were already inclined to believe in shady

political conspiracies. The President's December 19th tweet mobilized Three Percenters around the country. Suddenly, they had a focal point for their anti-government beliefs: the joint session of Congress on January 6th. Court filings and other evidence reveal that Three Percenters immediately began planning for violence after President Trump's "be wild" announcement.

For example, Lucas Denney and Donald Hazard led a militia affiliated with the Three Percenter movement called the "Patriot Boys of North Texas." Both Denney and Hazard were charged with assaulting officers on January 6th.[278] Denney pleaded guilty and has been sentenced to 52 months in prison.[279] After President Trump's tweet, they discussed travel plans, as well as the need to procure body armor, helmets, knuckle gloves and pepper spray.[280] But they did not plan to act alone. Instead, they saw themselves as part of a coalition. In multiple messages, both Denney and Hazard claimed they were also affiliated with Proud Boys and intended to work with them on or before January 6th.[281]

Denney repeatedly cited President Trump's tweet. "Trump himself is calling for a big protest in DC on January 6th. I'm not going to miss this one," Denney told Hazard on December 21st.[282] On December 30th, Denney wrote in a Facebook message:

> Trump has called this himself. For everyone to come. It's the day the electoral college is suppose to be certified by congress to offi-cially elect Biden. But, Pence is in charge of this and he's going to throw out all the votes from States that were proved to have fraud. There's so much more going on behind the scenes though. That's why he's called this rally for support. ... Trump will stay President ...[283]

As this message indicates, Denney was well-aware of President Trump's multi-part plan to disrupt the transfer of power. He thought that Vice President Pence had the power to "throw out" electoral votes, just as the President demanded. In other messages, Denney claimed that President Trump wanted militias to descend on Washington, DC so they could serve as a security force against a perceived threat from Antifa and Black Lives Matter on January 6th.[284]

Additional messages between the two reveal their intent to march on the U.S. Capitol. For instance, Denney attempted to post two banners on Facebook that advertised events on January 6th.[285] Both banners contained the hashtag "#OccupyCongress." The pictures contained images of the U.S. Capitol and referenced "The Great Betrayal." One of them read "If They Won't Hear Us" and "They Will Fear Us." In another post, Denney wrote: "I can't wait to be in the middle of it on the front line on the 6th."[286]

Curiously, Denney had also heard a "rumor" that President Trump would march with them. On January 4, 2021, he stated in a Facebook message:

> Things are going to be happening here. Trump is going to be speaking to everyone Wed [January 6] before everyone marches to the capital [sic]. Rumour [sic] has it that he may march with us. I'll tell you more when you get here on where to be wed and what time so you have the best seats.[287]

On or about January 6th, Denney sent another message via Facebook, writing: "Trump speaking to us around 11 am then we march to the capital and after that we have special plans that I can't say right now over Facebook. But keep an eye out for live feed tomorrow from me. Tomorrow will be historic."[288] Later on January 6th, during the attack, Hazard was captured on video bragging: "We have stormed our nation's capitol."[289]

The Patriot Boys of North Texas were not the only Three Percenter group that mobilized after President Trump's tweet. The Department of Justice has alleged that multiple other cadres of Three Percenter militiamen prepared for violence on January 6th and then took part in the attack on the U.S. Capitol.

In Florida, a Three Percenter organization known as the "Guardians of Freedom" established a "B-squad" for January 6th because they allegedly wanted to avoid being called a "militia."[290] These men were led by Jeremy Liggett, mentioned above.[291]

On December 24, 2020, the B-squad sent out a flyer, "CALLING ALL PATRIOTS!" to Washington, D.C.[292] The flyer read: "The Guardians of Freedom III% are responding to the call from President Donald J. Trump to assist in the security, protection, and support of the people as we all protest the fraudulent election and re-establish liberty for our nation. JOIN US & Thousands of other Patriots!"[293] The B-Squad claimed it was the "right & duty of the people to alter or to abolish" the Government.[294] Its members discussed bringing tactical gear to Washington, DC.[295]

On December 30th, Liggett posted a meme to Facebook stating that "3% Will Show In Record Numbers In DC."[296] When the Select Committee asked about this post, Liggett downplayed its significance or disclaimed any knowledge about other Three Percenter groups that might "show in record numbers."[297] However, on January 3, 2021, Liggett posted a "safety video" on Facebook in which he and others dressed in military gear. Liggett instructed listeners about self-defense and the tools they (like him) could bring to Washington, DC, including "an expandable metal baton, a walking cane and a folding knife."[298] He advised "all of you Patriots going to

Washington, D.C. ... to support Trump," and to "keep up the fight."[299] Several "B-squad" members have been charged with civil disorder and disorderly and disruptive conduct, which took place while rioters nearby were assaulting officers in the tunnel area of the Capitol's Lower West Terrace on January 6th.[300]

In California, another group of men associated with the Three Percenter movement quickly began plotting their next moves after President Trump's tweet. Alan Hostetter and Russell Taylor ran a non-profit known as the American Phoenix Project, which protested COVID-19 lockdowns and the 2020 election results, while also promoting violence ahead of January 6th.[301] Ahead of the joint session, Hostetter and Taylor organized a small group in an encrypted chat they named "The California Patriots—DC Brigade."[302]

On December 19th, Taylor linked to President Trump's "will be wild" tweet and asked members of the chat "Who is going?"[303] The same day, Hostetter posted a message to his Instagram account, explaining he was traveling to Washington, DC on January 6th because President Trump "tweeted that all patriots should descend on Washington DC" and that day "is the date of the Joint Session of Congress in which they will either accept or reject the fake/phony/stolen electoral college votes."[304] The next day, Taylor renamed the Telegram chat as "The California Patriots-Answer the Call Jan 6."[305] On December 29th, Taylor posted to that chat: "I personally want to be on the front steps and be one of the first ones to breach the doors!"[306]

Between December 19th and January 6th, Hostetter, Taylor and their alleged co-conspirators exchanged messages about bringing weapons, such as hatchets, bats, or large metal flashlights, as well as possibly firearms, with them to Washington, DC.[307] They were "ready and willing to fight."[308] In one message, Hostetter predicted that January 6th would be similar to the "War of Independence" because "[t]here will likely be 3% of us again that will commit fully to this battle, but just as in 1776 patriots will prevail."[309]

There are additional examples of how President Trump's "be wild" tweet led Three Percenters to descend on the U.S. Capitol. One Three Percenter group issued an open letter on December 16, 2020, announcing that they "stand ready and are standing by to answer the call from our President should the need arise that We The People are needed to take back our country from the pure evil that is conspiring to steal our country away from the American people.... We will not act unless we are told to."[310] In late December, after the President's tweet, The Three Percenters Original (TTPO) issued a letter to its members announcing that "this organization will be answering that call!"[311]

There is also additional evidence showing that militia groups like the Three Percenters coordinated with other groups both before and on January 6th. Josh Ellis, the owner of the MyMilitia website, testified that he used Zello (a walkie-talkie app) when he was in Washington, DC on January 6th. The Proud Boys, Oath Keepers, other militia members, and "regular patri- ots" all used these Zello channels in the leadup to January 6th and in response to President Trump's December 19th tweet. They used these chan- nels to share intelligence.[312]

6.9 QANON: "OPERATION OCCUPY THE CAPITOL"

Shortly after the January 6th attack, a video of a bearded man in a "Q" shirt chasing U.S. Capitol Police Officer Ryan Goodman through the halls of the U.S. Capitol went viral.[313] That man was Doug Jensen, a QAnon believer.[314] After Jensen's arrest, FBI agents asked him why he traveled from Iowa to Washington, DC in the first place. "Trump posted make sure you're there, January 6 for the rally in Washington, D.C.," Jensen responded.[315]

Jensen was not the only QAnon believer to attack the U.S. Capitol on January 6th. The letter "Q" and related slogans, such as "Where We Go One, We Go All," were ubiquitous among the rioters. They were visible on shirts, signs, and flags throughout the crowd. What was once a marginal digital movement had become a bricks-and-mortar force powerful enough to help obstruct a joint session of Congress.

QAnon is a bizarre and dangerous cult that gained popularity in 2017, when a person known only as "Q" began posting on 4chan, an anonymous message board.[316] The poster supposedly held a "Q" security clearance at the Department of Energy. QAnon adherents believe that President Trump is a messianic figure battling the forces of the "deep state" and a Satanic pedophile ring operated by leading Democrats and the American elite.[317] Q's first post in October 2017 predicted that former Secretary of State Hillary Clinton would be arrested in short order.[318] Although that prophecy did not come to pass, the conspiracy theory evolved and grew over time, spreading across social media platforms and eventually finding a home in 8kun, another anonymous message board known for trafficking in conspiracy theories and hate.[319]

President Trump was given multiple opportunities to disavow QAnon. Instead, he essentially endorsed its core tenets. During an August 19, 2020, press briefing, President Trump was asked what he thought about the QAnon belief that he was fighting a Satanic cabal. "I mean, you know, if I can help save the world from problems, I'm willing to do it. I'm willing to put myself out there," he replied.[320] During a townhall on NBC News two weeks prior to the election, President Trump first claimed he "knew nothing" about QAnon, but he then praised its believers for being "very strongly against pedophilia." The President emphasized: "And I agree with that. I mean, I do agree with that." [321]

In 2020, QAnon played a significant role in spreading various election conspiracy theories. After the election, QAnon accounts amplified the claim that Dominion Voting System's software had altered votes. [322] On November 19th, President Trump tweeted and retweeted a link to a segment on One America News Network (OAN) that was captioned, "Dominion-izing the Vote." [323] The segment claimed that Dominion had switched votes from President Trump to former Vice President Biden. OAN featured a supposed cyber expert, Ron Watkins, a key figure in the QAnon conspiracy movement. [324] Watkins's father, Jim, owned the 8kun site that "Q" called home, and Ron helped oversee its message boards. [325]

After promoting the OAN segment, President Trump retweeted Ron Watkins's account on several other occasions. On December 15, 2020, President Trump retweeted a post in which Watkins spread false claims of foreign influence in the election. [326] Then, on January 3rd, President Trump retweeted Ron Watkins's account four more times. [327]

QAnon's adherents were clearly paying attention to President Trump's words—and tweets. The President's "be wild" tweet was widely heard as a clarion call. Jim Watkins told the Select Committee that "thousands and thousands of people probably" agreed that the President's December 19th tweet was a call for them to come to Washington, DC. [328] Jim Watkins himself marched in Washington, DC on January 6th because of the President's call, but he has not been charged with any crime. [329]

Other QAnon adherents flocked to Washington, DC in response to the President's call to action. "POTUS HAS REQUESTED YOUR ATTENDANCE Washington DC JANUARY 6TH 2021," Thomas Munn, a QAnon believer, posted on Facebook. Munn added: "Our President has only asked two things from us, so far...#1 Vote #2 January 6, 2021." [330] Jacob Chansley, better known as the QAnon Shaman, told the FBI that he traveled from Arizona because President Trump had requested that all "patriots" come to Washington, DC on January 6th. [331]

During the investigation, the Select Committee learned that the QAnon conspiracy theory often overlaps with other extremist beliefs. Stewart Rhodes of the Oath Keepers testified to the Select Committee that he's "not a Q-tard" and "not a follower of Q at all." [332] However, Rhodes cynically exploited QAnon for his own purposes. The Oath Keepers' website and text messages were littered with QAnon phrases. [333] Nick Quested, a filmmaker who shadowed the Proud Boys, often heard QAnon themes in the Proud Boys' private discussions. [334]

As January 6th drew closer, multiple posts on the QAnon-linked website 8kun indicated that violence was imminent. "You can go to Washington on Jan 6 and help storm the Capitol," one user wrote. This same user continued: "As many Patriots as can be. We will storm the government buildings, kill cops, kill security guards, kill federal employees and agents, and demand a recount."[335] Other posts on 8kun debated the politicians that users should target once they got inside the Capitol.[336]

A QAnon-inspired banner was also widely shared by groups planning events for January 5th and 6th. The top of the image read: "Operation Occupy the Capitol." The central image showed the U.S. Capitol being torn in two. In the lower left corner, there appeared a QAnon phrase: "#WeAreTheStorm."[337]

6.10 THEDONALD.WIN: "OCCUPY THE CAPITOL"

Within three minutes of President Trump's tweet, a user on TheDonald.win message board posted: "Trump Tweet. Daddy Says Be In DC on Jan. 6th."[338] Moderators pinned the post to the top of the board from December 19th until January 6th. It garnered nearly 6,000 comments and more than 24,000 upvotes during that time.[339] Many of the site's users quickly interpreted President Trump's tweet as a call for violence. For example, one user wrote, "[Trump] can't exactly openly tell you to revolt. This is the closest he'll ever get."[340] Jody Williams, the site's then-owner, testified that while users had been talking about traveling to Washington, DC since the election, after the tweet "anything else was kind of shut out, and it just was going to be the 6th."[341]

In the days that followed, users on TheDonald.win discussed: surrounding and occupying the U.S. Capitol; cutting off access tunnels used by Members of Congress; the types of weapons they should bring; and even how to build a hangman's gallows.[342] The parallels to what transpired on January 6th are obvious.

TheDonald.win and its predecessor site was a website for some of its namesake's most ardent fans. Even before President Trump was elected, his social media team monitored and interacted with the site's users. In the summer of 2016, then-candidate Trump himself engaged in a written question and answer session on TheDonald, which at the time was a forum on Reddit.[343] This online community, which had upwards of 790,000 users, was banned by Reddit in mid-2020.[344] However, the site's users migrated to another online location, becoming TheDonald.win.[345]

Dan Scavino, the President's social media guru, amplified content from this website. During the 2016 presidential campaign, "a team in the war

White House social media director Dan Scavino Jr.

Photo by Chip Somodevilla/Getty Images

room at Trump Tower was monitoring social media trends, including TheDonald subreddit ... and privately communicating with the most active users to seed new trends." [346] "Campaign staffers monitored Twitter and TheDonald subreddit, and pushed any promising trends up to social media director Dan Scavino, who might give them a boost with a tweet." [347] In 2017, President Trump tweeted a video of himself attacking CNN. [348] The video had appeared on The Donald four days earlier. [349] In 2019, *Politico* reported that Scavino "regularly monitors Reddit, with a particular focus on the pro-Trump /r/The_Donald channel." [350]

The Select Committee sought to question Scavino about how he and others on President Trump's social media team interacted with The Donald subreddit and then TheDonald.win. But Scavino refused to cooperate with the committee's subpoena. [351]

After President Trump's December 19th tweet, users on the site posted simple maps of the U.S. Capitol and telegraphed their intent to invade the building. [352] "If we occupy the capitol building, there will be no vote," one user wrote. [353] "The media will call us evil if we have to occupy the Capitol Building on January 6th. Let them," another post read. [354] One user argued the goal should be to "surround the enemy" and "create [a] perimeter" around the Capitol on January 6th, such that no one was allowed to leave until President Trump was "re-admitted for another 4 years." [355] This same user posted a diagram of the U.S. Capitol's perimeter with arrows indicating where the "Capitol Access Tunnels" were located.

On January 5th, another user on TheDonald.win encouraged President Trump's supporters to "be prepared to secure the capitol building," claiming that "there will be plenty of ex military to guide you." [356] Multiple other posts made it clear that the U.S. Capitol was the target on January 6th, with one poster writing that people should bring "handcuffs and zip ties to DC," so they could enact "citizen's arrests" of those officials who certified the election's results. [357] Another post highlighted the "most important map for January 6th. Form a TRUE LINE around the Capitol and the tunnels." [358] That "post included a detailed schematic of Capitol Hill with the tunnels surrounding the complex highlighted." [359]

Other posts on TheDonald.win included specific plans to build gallows outside the U.S. Capitol. "Gallows are simpler and more cost effective, plus they're an American old west tradition too," one user wrote on December 22, 2020. [360] A week later, another wrote: "Let's construct a Gallows outside the Capitol building next Wednesday so the Congressmen watching from their office windows shit their pants." [361] Another said that "building a hanging platform in front of Congress on the 6 should send a strong message." [362] The site hosted a diagram showing how to tie a hangman's knot, [363] with one site member writing that they should build gallows "so the traitors know the stakes." [364] On January 5, 2021, hours before the attack began, a user posted an image of gallows and titled it, "Election Fraud Repair Kit." [365]

Text messages between Trump Campaign Senior Advisor Jason Miller and White House Chief of Staff Mark Meadows show that these kinds of posts reached deep into the President's inner circle. Miller sent Meadows a text on December 30th, declaring, "I got the base FIRED UP." [366] The thread contained a link to a TheDonald.win comment thread filled with reactions to a post by Miller promoting January 6th. [367] Users in the thread made comments such as "gallows don't require electricity," and that millions will "bust in through the doors if they try to stop Pence from declaring Trump the winner," all in response to Miller. [368]

On December 19, 2020, the same day President Trump posted his inflammatory "be wild" tweet, he also tweeted a noteworthy video. The short clip was titled, "FIGHT FOR TRUMP!—SAVE AMERICA—SAVE THE WORLD." [369] The video reportedly appeared on TheDonald.win two days earlier. [370] As with so much else on TheDonald.win, this refrain featured prominently on the day of the attack on the Capitol. During his speech at the Ellipse south of the White House on January 6th, the crowd broke out into a chant of "Fight for Trump! Fight for Trump!" President Trump thanked those in attendance. [371]

In the two and a half weeks since he first announced the January 6th "protest," extremists and conspiracy theorists plotted to make the unprecedented, presidentially announced protest against the peaceful transfer of power "wild" indeed. Meanwhile, event organizers and White House staffers prepared for the final rally of President Trump's term.

6.11   HOW THE WHITE HOUSE AND RALLY ORGANIZERS PREPARED FOR JANUARY 6TH

In the days following President Trump's tweet, rally organizers secured permits for about one dozen events in Washington, DC on January 5th and 6th.[372] At 7:12 a.m., not even 6 hours after President Trump's tweet, Cindy Chafian, an executive at Women for America First (WFAF), emailed the National Park Service (NPS) about an event that had been planned to coincide with President-elect Biden's inauguration on January 20, 2021.[373] Chafian's ask was simple: "Can I change the date to January 6th?"[374]

WFAF was founded in 2019 by Amy and Kylie Kremer, a mother-daughter pair who were longtime supporters of the President.[375] WFAF became a significant player in the "Stop the Steal" movement.[376] The Kremers started a "Stop the Steal" Facebook group that gathered some 365,000 members in less than 24 hours.[377] Their online organizing coincided with their on-the-ground mobilization activities. The Kremers organized a bus tour to promote the Big Lie, in addition to events in Washington, DC on November 14, 2020, and December 12, 2020.[378] After President Trump's December 19th tweet, the Kremers focused on January 6th. Kylie Kremer proudly declared their support on Twitter: "The calvary [sic] is coming, President! JANUARY 6th | Washington, DC TrumpMarch.com #MarchForTrump #StopTheSteal."[379] After the date of their permit was revised, WFAF ultimately provided President Trump the stage on the Ellipse where he would direct the crowd to march on the Capitol.[380]

The Kremers were not alone in responding quickly to the President's tweet. Ali Alexander, the founder of Stop the Steal, LLC,[381] was eager to get ahead of other organizers. On the morning of December 19th, Alexander told his event planner, "Everyone is trying to get the jump on us so I'd like to get the court side of the capitol (lawn) and I'd like to get capitol steps and court."[382] Alexander told his event planner to "grab whatever we can. All of it."[383] Alexander's team did just that: they registered and launched a new website, WildProtest.com,[384] which advertised planned events for January 6th under a banner that read: "President Trump Wants You in DC January 6."[385]

Still other organizers were quick to seize on the President's tweet. Arina Grossu and Robert Weaver, co-founders of the self-proclaimed "Judeo-Christian" Jericho March organization,[386] held a rally in Washington, DC on

December 12, 2020. Oath Keepers leader Stewart Rhodes, Flynn, Jones, Alexander, and others shared a stage at that event.[387] Grossu and Weaver exchanged emails just a few hours after President Trump's first mention of January 6th. In an email on the morning of December 19th, Weaver told Grossu to "enjoy the peace before the storm" and said, "Trump has called for a protest on 1/6, FYI." [388] The Jericho March's website used President Trump's "Be there, will be wild!" language to advertise additional events between January 2nd and January 6, 2021.[389]

Marsha Lessard, the leader of a vaccine-skeptic group, Virginia Freedom Keepers, worked to stage an event with Bianca Gracia, the leader of Latinos for Trump on January 6th.[390] The women had ties to the Oath Keepers[391] and Proud Boys,[392] respectively—two groups central to the violence on January 6. Latinos for Trump reportedly advertised their January 6th event with the same QAnon-inspired banner, "Operation Occupy the Capitol." [393] Another conservative group, Moms for America, worked with Alexander before securing a permit for an event on January 5th.[394]

6.12 "HE'S CALLING ON *YOU*, HE NEEDS YOUR HELP"

As discussed above, Alex Jones was one of the loudest supporters of the "Stop the Steal" movement. Jones dedicated much of the December 20th episode of his *InfoWars* show to President Trump's "be wild" tweet, telling his listeners that nothing less than the fate of the American Republic was at stake. "He's calling *you*, he needs your help, we need your help," Jones told his audience.[395] The Select Committee has learned that, between the time of the President's tweet and Jones's December 20th show, Jones's staff had several calls with Chafian, who had just procured a new permit for WFAF's event on the Ellipse.[396] The two parties apparently discussed whether this newly hatched January 6th event was an opportunity to work together.[397]

Jones's broadcast also led to an influx of funds for the January 6th event at the Ellipse. Julie Fancelli is the billionaire heiress to the Publix supermarket fortune and a longtime supporter of President Trump.[398] Fancelli had recently become a donor to Jones's *InfoWars* site.[399] She listened to Jones's December 20th show,[400] and decided she wanted to back the cause.

Inspired by Jones and the fervor that continued to surround the President's tweet, Fancelli called Caroline Wren, a Republican fundraiser linked to the Trump Campaign, the next day.[401] According to Wren, Fancelli said that "she wanted to see a lot of people there in DC, so how much would that cost?" [402] Fancelli spoke with Jones's staff and they recommended that she connect with Chafian, who was organizing the Ellipse rally.[403] In the waning days of 2020, Fancelli and Jones spoke several times.[404]

Fancelli worked with Wren to create a multimillion-dollar budget to convene as many supporters of President Trump as possible.[405] To ensure that Fancelli's dollars made maximum impact, Wren contacted some of the major players who were rallying supporters for January 6th. Wren emailed Kylie Kremer[406] and exchanged texts with Jones[407] and Chafian.[408] Fancelli's goal was clear: she wanted to spend $3 million to "get as many people there as possible."[409] The resulting budget allocated $500,000 to a busing program and a centralized ad campaign by the Tea Party Express to promote the event.[410] Another $500,000 went to assisting WFAF and Jones in their organizational efforts.[411]

Caroline Wren also connected with Ali Alexander. On December 29th, Wren told the Stop the Steal leader, "I can pay for the buses and I have my team looking for available companies, so let me know what cities you need them in!"[412] Wren's offer came in response to a tweet from Alexander earlier that day: "Coalition of us working on 25 new charter buses to bring people FOR FREE to #JAN6 #STOPTHESTEAL for President Trump. If you have money for more buses or have a company, let me know. We will list our buses sometime in the next 72 hours. STAND BACK & STAND BY!"[413]

The final words of Alexander's tweet directly echoed President Trump's command to the Proud Boys during the September 29, 2020, presidential debate.[414] Alexander's word choice was apt. The Proud Boys were already planning to show up in force, and to ensure that the crowd would be "wild."

6.13   "TRUMP IS SUPPOSED TO ORDER US TO THE CAPITOL"

On the evening of December 27th, President Trump boosted the upcoming event on Twitter: "See you in Washington, DC, on January 6th. Don't miss it. Information to follow!"[415] The Select Committee learned that this tweet came after the White House spoke with a former Trump staffer, Justin Caporale, who was asked to help produce the Ellipse rally.[416] That same evening, the President had dinner with Donald Trump, Jr., and his girlfriend Kimberly Guilfoyle,[417] who spoke with rally organizer Caroline Wren during the meal.[418] Wren also texted Guilfoyle talking points that described her ambitions for the event, saying that "buses of people are coming in from all over the country to support you. It's going to be huge, we are also adding in programming the night of January 5th."[419]

After Guilfoyle's call with Wren, there was a series of calls among the senior White House staff,[420] likely underscoring the seriousness of the White House's interest in the event.

Within a few days, the White House began to take a more direct role in coordinating the rally at the Ellipse.[421] In a December 29th text to Wren, Caporale wrote that after the President's planned speech there "maybe [sic] a call to action to march to the [C]apitol and make noise."[422]

This is the earliest indication uncovered by the Select Committee that the President planned to call on his supporters to march on the U.S. Capitol. But it wasn't the last. On January 2nd, rally organizer Katrina Pierson informed Wren that President Trump's Chief of Staff, Mark Meadows, had said the President was going to "call on everyone to march to the [C]apitol."[423]

Inside the White House, the President's intent was well-known. Cassidy Hutchinson, an aide to Meadows, recalled in her testimony that she over-heard discussions to this effect toward the end of December or early January. One such discussion included an exchange between Meadows and Rudolph Giuliani that occurred on January 2nd.[424] Hutchinson understood that President Trump wanted to have a crowd at the Capitol in connection with what was happening inside—the certification of the electoral count.[425] Hutchinson also recalled that President Trump's allies in Congress were aware of the plan. During a call with members of the House Freedom Caucus, the idea of telling people to go to the Capitol was discussed as a way to encourage Congress to delay the electoral college certification and send it back to the States.[426]

On January 4th, WFAF's Kylie Kremer informed Mike Lindell, the CEO of MyPillow and an ally of President Trump, that "POTUS is going to have us march there [the Supreme Court]/the Capitol" but emphasized that the plan "stays only between us."[427]

The "Stop the Steal" coalition was aware of the President's intent. On January 5th, Ali Alexander sent a text to a journalist saying: "Ellipse then US capitol [sic]. Trump is supposed to order us to the capitol [sic] at the end of his speech but we will see."[428]

6.14 "WELL, I SHOULD WALK WITH THE PEOPLE."

President Trump wanted to personally accompany his supporters on the march from the Ellipse to the U.S. Capitol. During a January 4th meeting with staffers and event organizer Katrina Pierson, President Trump empha-sized his desire to march with his supporters.[429] "Well, I should walk with the people," Pierson recalled President Trump saying.[430] Though Pierson said that she did not take him "seriously," she knew that "he would abso-lutely want to be with the people."[431] Pierson pointed out that President Trump "did the drive-by the first time and the flyover the second time"—a reference to the November and December 2020 protests in Washington, DC.[432] During these previous events, President Trump made cameo appearances to fire up his supporters. Now, as January 6th approached, the President again wanted to be there, on the ground, as his supporters marched on the U.S. Capitol.

The President's advisors tried to talk him out of it. White House Senior Advisor Max Miller "shot it down immediately" because of concerns about the President's safety.[433] Pierson agreed.[434] But President Trump was persistent, and he floated the idea of having 10,000 National Guardsmen deployed to protect him and his supporters from any supposed threats by leftwing counter-protestors.[435] Miller again rejected the President's idea, saying that the National Guard was not necessary for the event. Miller testified that there was no further conversation on the matter.[436] After the meeting, Miller texted Pierson, "Just glad we killed the national guard and a procession." [437] That is, President Trump briefly considered having the National Guard oversee his procession to the U.S. Capitol. The President did not order the National Guard to protect the U.S. Capitol, or to secure the joint session proceedings.

Although his advisors tried to talk the President out of personally going, they understood that his supporters would be marching.[438] Pierson's agenda for the meeting reflected the President's plan for protestors to go to the U.S. Capitol after the rally.[439] But President Trump did not give up on the idea of personally joining his supporters on their march, as discussed further in Chapter 7.

6.15 "POTUS...LIKES THE CRAZIES."

As Katrina Pierson helped plan the Ellipse rally, she faced another complication. The "Stop the Steal" movement played an outsized role in promoting January 6th. And now, as the day approached, its leading voices wanted prime speaking gigs—perhaps even on the same stage as President Trump. Roger Stone, Alex Jones and Ali Alexander were all angling for significant stage time. Pierson knew they were trouble.

In her testimony before the Select Committee, Pierson cited several concerns, including that Jones and Alexander had played a prominent role in the November 2020 protest in Atlanta, Georgia. This was no ordinary protest. Jones and Alexander "had gone into the Georgia Capitol with some inflammatory rhetoric," Pierson explained.[440] When Pierson was asked if Jones and Alexander "surrounding the governor's mansion" and "going into the Capitol" were the "kind of thing" that gave her pause, she responded: "Absolutely." [441] After the Georgia protest, Pierson explained,

Photos of Roger Stone, Alex Jones and Ali Alexander appear on a screen during a Select Committee hearing on July 12, 2022.

Photo by Anna Moneymaker/Getty Images

the Kremers—who had helped organize "Stop the Steal" activities—distanced themselves from Jones and Alexander.[442]

But there was an additional problem. President Trump wanted to include the "Stop the Steal" leaders in the January 6th event. As Pierson put it in a text message to Kylie Kremer: "POTUS ... likes the crazies."[443] Pierson said that she believed this was the case because President Trump "loved people who viciously defended him in public."[444] But their "vicious" defenses of the President clearly troubled Pierson.

Pierson tried to trim the speaker lineup—which still included the "Stop the Steal" trio of Stone, Jones, and Alexander. She was initially vetoed by the White House after Deputy Chief of Staff for Communications Dan Scavino,[445] who had approved the "original psycho list."[446] At one point, she texted Scavino's boss, Mark Meadows, saying: "Things have gotten crazy and I desperately need some direction."[447] She was concerned by the possibility of "crazy people" being included in the event, their incendiary role in Georgia, and the fact that people coming to Washington, DC were planning to protest at the U.S. Capitol.[448]

Meadows told Pierson that she should take control of the situation and remove the possibility of controversial speakers.[449] Pierson agreed to do so.[450] But the President remained an obstacle. During their January 4th meeting, Pierson tried to convince President Trump to minimize the role of these potentially explosive figures at the Ellipse. She offered to place them at a planned event the night before in Freedom Plaza or on other stages in DC on January 6th. She told the President to "[k]eep the fringe on the fringe"[451] and advised him to "[e]liminate convicted felons that could damage other speakers."[452]

President Trump was still unwilling to remove them from the lineup entirely. The President instructed Pierson to give Stone a speaking slot on January 5th and asked for more information about Ali Alexander.[453] After discussing the matter with Scavino, President Trump also requested that Alexander be given a speaking slot. President Trump "brought up Ali [Alexander] … just keep him on stage not associated with POTUS or main event," Scavino wrote.[454]

In the end, the "Stop the Steal" leaders—Stone, Jones and Alexander — did not appear on the stage at the Ellipse on January 6th, although they did speak at other planned events, consistent with the President's request about Alexander. "POTUS expectations are [to have something] intimate and then send everyone over to the Capitol," Pierson explained in a text message to Justin Caporale and Taylor Budowich.[455] Caporale redacted this text and others in his early production of documents to the Select Committee, and he only revealed them after they had already been produced by other witnesses.[456]

However, other incendiary voices—in addition to President Trump's — were given time on the Ellipse stage. The Select Committee learned that President Trump's aides warned him against the inclusion of figures like John Eastman[457] and Rudolph Giuliani,[458] given their false claims about election fraud.[459] Both men, of course, ended up sharing a stage with him on January 6th.[460] Meadows himself directed that they be allowed to speak.[461]

6.16 JANUARY 5, 2021: "FORT TRUMP"

While the "Stop the Steal" coalition was not given speaking slots on the Ellipse stage on January 6th, its leaders had plenty of opportunities to speak the day before. And they used their platforms to rile up the crowd in Washington, DC in advance of the joint session.

Ali Alexander spoke at an event sponsored by Moms for America in front of the U.S. Capitol. Alexander claimed that he was honored to be sharing the same stage with President Trump the following day, even though behind the scenes his appearance had been nixed.[462]

"We must rebel," Alexander told rallygoers. "I'm not even sure if I'm going to leave D.C. We might make this 'Fort Trump,' right?" Alexander said, while standing in front of the U.S. Capitol. "We're going to keep fighting for you, Mr. President."[463] On his Twitter account, Alexander also spread the idea that President Trump's supporters should occupy areas of Washington, DC, using the phrases and hashtags such as "Fort Trump" and "#OccupyDC".[464]

Alex Jones and Roger Stone spoke at a separate event hosted by Virginia Women for Trump in front of the Supreme Court.[465] The event, named the "One Nation Under God" prayer rally, was cohosted by the American Phoenix Project—the Three Percenter-linked group run by Alan Hostetter and Russel Taylor, discussed above, which is charged with conspiracy to obstruct an official proceeding.[466]

Jones repeated his claims about the election being stolen, claiming that those in attendance stood against a "Satanic world government."[467] Stone led a "Stop the Steal" chant, claiming the "evidence of election fraud is not only growing, it is overwhelming, and it is compelling." President Trump "won the majority of the legal votes cast" and President Trump "won this election," Stone said. Nothing less than the fate of Western Civilization was at stake, according to Stone:

> Let's be very clear. This is not fight between Republicans and
> Democrats. This is not a fight between liberals and conservatives.
> This is a fight for the future the United States of America. It is a
> fight for the future of Western Civilization as we know it. It's a fight
> between dark and light. It's a fight between the godly and the god-
> less. It's a fight between good and evil. And we dare not fail, or we
> will step out into one thousand years of darkness.[468]

Stone claimed that they "renounce violence" and those on "the left … are the violent ones." But he insisted that "nothing is over until we say it is," and "Victory will be ours."[469]

Both Taylor and Hostetter spoke as well. Hostetter told the crowd, "We are at war."[470] Taylor promised to "fight" and "bleed," vowing that "Patriot[s]" would "not return to our peaceful way of life until this election is made right."[471]

A long rally was also hosted at Freedom Plaza, an open-air space on Pennsylvania Avenue in Washington, DC. It is a symbolic protest site, standing in the direct line between the White House and the U.S. Capitol. Stone, Jones and Alexander all appeared at Freedom Plaza on the evening of January 5th. Their remarks were incendiary.

Stone repeated his apocalyptic language from earlier in the day, claiming that rallygoers were embroiled in "an epic struggle for the future of this country between dark and light."[472] "I want them to know that 1776 is always an option," Ali Alexander said. "These degenerates in the deep state are going to give us what we want, or we are going to shut this country down."[473] When Alex Jones took to the stage, he screamed at the crowd: "*It's 1776!*"[474]

Another speaker that evening was Lt. Gen. Michael Flynn (ret.). "Tomorrow, tomorrow, trust me, the American people that are standing on the soil that we are standing on tonight, and they're going to be standing on this soil tomorrow, this is soil that we have fought over, fought for, and we will fight for in the future," Flynn also told the crowd. Flynn addressed Members of Congress, saying "those of you who are feeling weak tonight, those of you that don't have the moral fiber in your body, get some tonight because tomorrow, we the people are going to be here, and we want you to know that we will not stand for a lie. We will not stand for a lie."[475]

6.17 "TOGETHER, WE WILL STOP THE STEAL."

On the evening of January 5th, the President edited the speech he would deliver the next day at the Ellipse. The President's speechwriting team had only started working on his remarks the day before.[476] Despite concerns from the speechwriting team, unfounded claims coming from Giuliani and others made their way into the draft.[477]

The initial draft circulated on January 5th emphasized that the crowd would march to the U.S. Capitol.[478] Based on what they had heard from others in the White House, the speechwriting team expected President Trump to use his address to tell people to go to the Capitol.[479]

That evening, President Trump convened an impromptu gathering in the Oval Office with members of his staff, primarily his press team[480] and White House Deputy Chief of Staff Dan Scavino, who was in charge of President Trump's personal Twitter account.[481] Despite the bitter cold, the President ordered his staff to keep the door to the Rose Garden open so he could hear the music and cheering from his supporters at Freedom Plaza.[482] The music playing at Freedom Plaza was so loud "you could feel it shaking in the Oval."[483]

As President Trump listened, he was tweeting, at one point telling his supporters he could hear them from the Oval Office.[484] His speechwriters incorporated those tweets into a second draft of the speech that was circulated later that evening.[485] The following appeared in both tweet form[486] and was adapted into the speech:

> "All of us here today do not want to see our election victory stolen by emboldened Radical Left Democrats. Our Country has had enough, they won't take it anymore! Together, we will STOP THE STEAL."[487]

President Trump and members of his staff in the Oval Office on the evening of January 5, 2021.
Photo provided to the Select Committee by the National Archives and Records Administration.

In speaking with staff, he still seemed optimistic that "Congress would take some sort of action in his favor."[488] The White House photographer, who was also in attendance, recalled that President Trump again remarked that he should go to the Capitol the next day, and even asked about the best route to get there.[489] The President peppered staff for ideas concerning how "we could make the RINOs do the right thing" and make the next day "big."[490] Deputy Press Secretary Sarah Matthews, who was present in the Oval Office that evening, understood that President Trump wanted to get Republican Members of Congress to send the electoral votes back to the States, rather than certify the election.[491] Matthews recalled that initially no one spoke up in response, since they were trying to "process" what he had said.[492]

Eventually, Deere suggested that President Trump should focus his speech on his administration's accomplishments, rather than on his claim that the election had been stolen.[493] But the President told Deere that while they had accomplished a lot, the crowd was going to be "fired up" and "angry" the next day because they believed the election had been stolen and was rigged.[494] President Trump knew the crowd was angry because he could hear them.[495] Of course, President Trump was responsible, more than any other party, for ginning up their anger.

President Trump ended the evening by asking an aide how many people were going to be at the rally. The aide responded that he was not sure but told President Trump that he saw videos on Twitter of "pro-trump people chanting on planes heading to DC," which he asked to be shared with Scavino.[496]

"We will not let them silence your voices," the President told the crowd from the podium at the Ellipse. "We're not going to let it happen, I'm not going to let it happen."[497] His supporters started chanting, "fight for Trump!" The President thanked them.[498]

President Trump knew not only that his supporters were angry, but also that some of them were armed.[499] At times, he ad-libbed, deliberately stoking their rage even more. At one point he said: "And we fight. We fight like hell. And if you don't fight like hell, you're not going to have a country anymore."[500] The word "fight," or a variation thereof, appeared only twice in the prepared text.[501] President Trump would go on to utter the word twenty times during his speech at the Ellipse.[502]

President Trump had summoned a mob, including armed extremists and conspiracy theorists, to Washington, DC on the day the joint session of Congress was to meet. He then told that same mob to march on the U.S. Capitol and "fight." They clearly got the message.

ENDNOTES

1. Select Committee to Investigate the January 6th Attack on the United States Capitol, Transcribed Interview of William Barr, (June 2, 2022), p. 62.

2. Select Committee to Investigate the January 6th Attack on the United States Capitol, Transcribed Interview of William Barr, (June 2, 2022), pp. 27,62; Select Committee to Investigate the January 6th Attack on the United States Capitol, Transcribed Interview of Michael Pompeo, (Aug. 9, 2022), p. 30; Select Committee to Investigate the January 6th Attack on the United States Capitol, Transcribed Interview of Eugene Scalia, (June 30, 2022), p. 11.

3. Select Committee to Investigate the January 6th Attack on the United States Capitol, Transcribed Interview of Eugene Scalia, (June 30, 2022), p. 11. Others throughout the White House similarly recognized that December 14 was a milestone in America's constitutional process, and it was time for the President to move on. But it was not just members of President Trump's Cabinet who viewed that the election was over, and that President Trump had lost by December 14—President Trump's top advisors at the White House came to similar conclusions. For example, White House Counsel Pat Cipollone agreed with Senator McConnell's December 15th comments on the Senate floor and viewed the process for challenging the election as "done." *See* Select Committee to Investigate the January 6th Attack on the United States Capitol, Transcribed Interview of Pasquale Anthony "Pat" Cipollone, (July 8, 2022), p. 73. White House Deputy Press Secretary and Deputy Assistant to the President Judd Deere also recognized the significance of the electoral college vote in determining the president and vice president and conveyed this to President Trump. He also advised him to concede. *See* Select Committee to Investigate the January 6th Attack on the United States Capitol, Deposition of Judson P. Deere, (Mar. 3, 2022), pp. 23-25. White House Advisor Ivanka Trump viewed the electoral college vote as important and had already started planning for leaving the administration prior to then. *See* Select Committee to Investigate the January 6th Attack on the United States Capitol, Transcribed Interview of Ivanka Trump, (Apr. 5, 2022), p. 193. White House Advisor Jared Kushner similarly viewed that day as "significant." Select Committee to Investigate the January 6th Attack on the United States Capitol, Transcribed Interview of Jared Kushner, (Mar. 31, 2022), p. 107.

4. President Trump's full tweet read: "Peter Navarro releases 36-page report alleging election fraud 'more than sufficient' to swing victory to Trump https://t.co/D8KrMHnFdK. A great report by Peter. Statistically impossible to have lost the 2020 Election. Big protest in D.C. on January 6th. Be there, will be wild!" President Donald J. Trump: Tweets of December 19, 2020, The American Presidency Project, available at https://www.presidency.ucsb.edu/documents/tweets-december-19-2020.

5. Select Committee to Investigate the January 6th Attack on the United States Capitol, Deposition of J. Smith, (May 9, 2022), p. 79. Navaroli appeared for two deposition session with the Select Committee, the first of which was conducted anonymously to protect her identity. In this deposition session, she was called "J. Smith." She later agreed to put her name in the record and sat for another round of questioning. Testimony from that second session is referred to as "Deposition of Anika Navaroli."

6. Select Committee to Investigate the January 6th Attack on the United States Capitol, Deposition of Anika Navaroli, (Sept. 1, 2022), pp. 66-67. She went on to characterize the tweet as an "RSVP card" that became a "rallying point" for the President's supporters, one that prompted violent responses from users that were highly suggestive of the coming violence targeting DC on January 6th. *Id.*, at p. 64. Another former Twitter employee, whose deposition was also conducted anonymously, testified that the tweet "in many ways kind of crystallized the plans" for violence and that, after that point, supporters of President Trump began tweeting about movements to D.C. Select Committee to Investigate the January 6th Attack on the United States Capitol, Deposition of J. Johnson, (Sept. 7, 2022), p. 55.

7. The President's call to action quickly reverberated beyond Twitter and spread across the internet. On one social networking site, Discord, a forum called "DonaldsArmy.US" erupted in the hours after the tweet, with users seeing it as a "call to action" and beginning to organize travel plans to D.C., including by discussing how and whether to evade DC gun restrictions and bring firearms into the city. *See* Summary Memorandum from Select Committee to Investigate the January 6th Attack on the United States Capitol. Briefing with Discord, (July 29, 2022); *see also* Documents on file with the Select Committee to Investigate the January 6th Attack on the United States Capitol (Discord Production), JAN6C_DIS_000269 (Memo from Discord titled "DonaldsArmy.US and BASEDMedia.").

8. Second Superseding Indictment at ¶ 28, *United States v. Nordean et al.*, No. 1:1:21-cr-175 (D.D.C. Mar. 7, 2022), ECF No. 305.

9. *See, e.g.*, Ian Ward, "How a D.C. Bar Became the 'Haven' for the Proud Boys," *Politico*, (Dec. 14, 2020), available at https://www.politico.com/news/magazine/2020/12/14/harrys-bar-proud-boys-washington-dc-445015.

10. Second Superseding Indictment at ¶37, *United States v. Nordean et al.*, No. 1:21-cr-175 (D.D.C. Mar. 7, 2022), ECF No. 305 (citing Tarrio's message to the Proud Boys on December 29, 2020, that they would "not be wearing our traditional Black and Yellow" on January 6th; they would "be incognito.").

11. Second Superseding Indictment at ¶ 50, *United States v. Nordean et al.*, No. 1:1:21-cr-175 (D.D.C. Mar. 7, 2022), ECF No. 305.

12. Second Superseding Indictment at ¶ 100, *United States v. Nordean et al.*, No. 1:1:21-cr-175 (D.D.C. Mar. 7, 2022), ECF No. 305.

13. Select Committee to Investigate the January 6th Attack on the United States Capitol, Deposition of Henry Tarrio, (Feb. 4, 2022), pp. 83-84.

14. Second Superseding Indictment at ¶ 107, *United States v. Nordean et al.*, No. 1:21-cr-175 (D.D.C. Mar. 7, 2022), ECF No. 305.

15. *See, e.g.*, Mike Levine, "How A Standoff in Nevada Years Ago Set The Militia Movement on A Crash Course with The US Capitol," ABC News, (Jan. 5, 2022), available at https://abcnews.go.com/US/standoff-nevada-years-ago-set-militia-movement-crash/story?id=82051940.

16. Indictment at ¶¶ 67, 68, *United States v. Rhodes, III, et al.*, No. 22-cr-15 (D.D.C. June 22, 2022), ECF No. 167.

17. *See* Select Committee to Investigate the January 6th Attack on the United States Capitol, Deposition of Elmer Stewart Rhodes, (Feb. 22, 2022), pp. 132,134; Stewart Rhodes and Kellye SoRelle, "Open Letter to President Trump: You Must Use the Insurrection Act to 'Stop the Steal' and Defeat the Coup," Oathkeepers.org, (Dec. 14, 2020), available at https:// web.archive.org/web/20210123133022/https:/oathkeepers.org/2020/12/open-letter-to-president-trump-you-must-use-insurrection-act-to-stop-the-steal-and-defeat-the-coup/ (archived). Jason Van Tatenhove, the former spokesman of the Oath Keepers described how he suspected that Rhodes saw the Insurrection Act as a blank check: "He could pretty much do whatever he wanted, and [President Trump] could install Stewart and the Oath Keepers as some sort of security force that would bring them real legitimacy and political power." Select Committee to Investigate the January 6th Attack on the United States Capitol, Transcribed Interview of Jason Van Tatenhove, (Mar. 9, 2022), p. 73.

18. Third Superseding Indictment at ¶ 37, *United States v. Crowl et al.*, No. 1:21-cr-28 (D.D.C., Mar. 31, 2021), ECF No. 127.

19. Third Superseding Indictment at ¶ 95-99, *United States v. Crowl et al.*, No. 1:21-cr-28 (D.D.C., Mar. 31, 2021), ECF No. 127.

20. Trial Transcript at 10502-508, *United States v. Rhodes et al.*, No. 1:22-cr-15 (D.D.C. Nov. 29, 2022); Alan Feuer and Zach Montague, "Oath Keepers Leader Convicted of Sedition in Land-mark Jan. 6 Case," *New York Times*, (Nov. 29, 2022), available at https://www.nytimes.com/ 2022/11/29/us/politics/oath-keepers-trial-verdict-jan-6.html.

21. 18 U.S.C. § 2384.

22. For example, one Proud Boy, Jeremy Bertino, pleaded guilty to "seditious conspiracy" and other crimes in October 2022. Bertino admitted to authorities that the Proud Boys traveled to Washington on January 6, 2021, "to stop the certification of the Electoral College Vote." They "were willing to do whatever it would take, including using force against police and others, to achieve that objective." *See* "Former Leader of Proud Boys Pleads Guilty to Sedi-tious Conspiracy for Efforts to Stop Transfer of Power Following 2020 Presidential Elec-tion," Department of Justice, (Oct. 6, 2022), available at https://www.justice.gov/opa/pr/ former-leader-proud-boys-pleads-guilty-seditious-conspiracy-efforts-stop-transfer-power.

23. Criminal Complaint at 10-11, *United States v. Hazard*, No. 1:21-mj-868 (D.D.C. Dec. 7, 2021), ECF No. 1.

24. *See, e.g.*, Indictment at ¶¶ 34-37, *United States v. Hostetter et al.*, No. 1:21-cr-392 (D.D.C. June 9, 2021), ECF No. 1.

25. Malachi Barrett, "Far-Right Activist Who Encouraged U.S. Capitol Occupation Also Organized 'Stop the Steal' Rally in Michigan," *Mlive*, (Jan. 7, 2021), available at https://www.mlive.com/ politics/2021/01/far-right-activist-who-encouraged-us-capitol-occupation-also-organized-stop-the-steal-rally-in-michigan.html.

26. Nicholas J. Fuentes (@NickJFuentes), Twitter, Jan. 7, 2021 10:56 p.m. ET, available at https:// web.archive.org/web/20210107185745/https://twitter.com/NickJFuentes/status/ 1347255833516765185 (archived).

27. Ken Dilanian and Ben Collins, "There Are Hundreds of Posts About Plans to Attack the Capitol. Why Hasn't This Evidence Been Used in Court?," NBC News, (Apr. 20, 2021), avail-able at https://www.nbcnews.com/politics/justice-department/we-found-hundreds-posts-about-plans-attack-capitol-why-aren-n1264291.

28. Statement of Mike Rothschild, (Mar. 23, 2022), at pp. 3-6.

29. *See*, "NCRI Assessment of The Capitol Riots," Rutgers Miller Center for Community Protec-tion and Resilience," Network Contagion Research Institute, (Jan. 9, 2021) available at https://millercenter.rutgers.edu/wp-content/uploads/2021/01/NCRI-Assessment-of-the-Capitol-Riots-1.pdf.

30. "Breaking: Trump Calls for Americans to March on DC January 6 to Stop Foreign Takeover," InfoWars, (Dec. 19, 2020), (archived) available at https://web.archive.org/web/20201219175757/https://www.infowars.com/posts/breaking-trump-calls-for-americans-to-march-on-dc-january-6-to-stop-foreign-takeover/.

31. Jacob Knutson, "Jury Orders Alex Jones to Pay Nearly $1 Billion in Sandy Hook Defamation Trial," Axios, (Oct. 12, 2022), available at https://www.axios.com/2022/10/12/alex-jones-sandy-hook-defamation-trial.

32. "The Alex Jones Show," Prison Planet TV, at 21:53, Dec. 20, 2020, available at http://tv.infowars.com/index/display/id/11151.

33. Jones's promotion of the January 6th event began almost immediately after the President's tweet. See The Alex Jones Show, "January 6th Will Be a Turning Point in American History," Banned.Video, at 16:29, Dec. 31, 2020, available at https://banned.video/watch?id=5fee715284a7b6210e12a2f7.

34. See, Lena V. Groeger, Jeff Kao, Al Shaw, Moiz Syed, and Maya Eliahou, "What Parler Saw During the Attack on the Capitol," Pro Publica, (Jan. 17, 2021), available at https://projects.propublica.org/parler-capitol-videos/?id=5OCkdwJRD0a3 (showing Alex Jones marching down Pennsylvania Avenue at 1:10 p.m.).

35. Select Committee to Investigate the January 6th Attack on the United States Capitol, Deposition of Caroline Wren, (Dec. 17, 2021), pp. 50, 70-71.

36. Select Committee to Investigate the January 6th Attack on the United States Capitol, Deposition of Judson P. Deere, (Mar. 3, 2022), p. 86.

37. Select Committee to Investigate the January 6th Attack on the United States Capitol, Transcribed Interview of Cassidy Hutchinson, (Feb. 23, 2022), pp. 32-33, 41; Select Committee to Investigate the January 6th Attack on the United States Capitol, Continued Interview of Cassidy Hutchinson, (June 20, 2022), pp. 107-108, 135.

38. Select Committee to Investigate the January 6th Attack on the United States Capitol, Deposition of Judson P. Deere, (Mar. 3, 2022), pp. 70-71.

39. Senate Committee on Homeland Security and Governmental Affairs and Committee on Rules and Administration, 117th Congress, "Examining the U.S. Capitol Attack: A Review of the Security, Planning, and Response Failures on January 6" (Staff Report), (June 8, 2021), p. B-22.

40. Rob Kuznia, Curt Devine, Nelli Black, and Drew Grin, "Stop the Steal's Massive Disinformation Campaign Connected to Roger Stone and Steve Bannon," CNN Business, (Nov. 14, 2020), available at https://www.cnn.com/2020/11/13/business/stop-the-steal-disinformation-campaign-invs/index.html.

41. Charles Homans, "How 'Stop the Steal' Captured the American Right," New York Times, (July 19, 2022), available at https://www.nytimes.com/2022/07/19/magazine/stop-the-steal.html. ("During his time as a Trump campaign adviser, Stone urged the candidate to run on immigration, and now he linked these views to the plots that he claimed were afoot to deny Trump the nomination. In the Republican primaries, Trump was 'a nationalist in a field of globalists,' Stone said in an interview that April with Stefan Molyneux, a Canadian alt-right podcaster. If the globalists failed to steal the primaries outright, there would be a 'naked attempt to steal this from Donald Trump' at the Republican National Convention in Cleveland, Stone declared. 'The fix is in.'")

42. Rob Kuznia, Curt Devine, Nelli Black, and Drew Grin, "Stop the Steal's Massive Disinformation Campaign Connected to Roger Stone and Steve Bannon," CNN Business, (Nov. 14, 2020), available at https://www.cnn.com/2020/11/13/business/stop-the-steal-disinformation-campaign-invs/index.html.

43. Rob Kuznia, Curt Devine, Nelli Black, and Drew Grin, "Stop the Steal's Massive Disinformation Campaign Connected to Roger Stone and Steve Bannon," CNN Business, (Nov. 14,

2020), available at https://www.cnn.com/2020/11/13/business/stop-the-steal-disinformation-campaign-invs/index.html.

44. Documents on file with the Select Committee to Investigate the January 6th Attack on the United States Capitol (Christoffer Guldbrandsen Production), Video file 201105.

45. *See,* Hugo Lowell, "Film Offers Inside Look at Roger Stone's 'Stop the Steal' Efforts before January 6," *The Guardian,* (July 8, 2022), available at https://www.theguardian.com/us-news/2022/jul/07/roger-stone-ali-alexander-film-jan-6-stop-the-steal.

46. Select Committee to Investigate the January 6th Attack on the United States Capitol, Deposition of Ali Alexander, (Jan. 9, 2021), p. 18.

47. Select Committee to Investigate the January 6th Attack on the United States Capitol, Deposition of Ali Alexander, (Dec. 9, 2021), pp. 199-200.

48. *See, e.g.,* WillfulWarrior, "Hispanic Proud Boys Leader: 'We Fought Off Antifa Terrorists for 12 Hrs'," BitChute, Nov. 19, 2020, available at https://www.bitchute.com/video/if5u7EuD7NU3/; Infowars: War Room, "Enrique Tarrio Spat on While Flying to Austin Texas," BitChute, Dec. 2, 2020, available at https://www.bitchute.com/video/yKijHk6m25RL/; BNN, "Full Show: Witnesses Testify on Michigan Voter Fraud; Thousands of Illegal Votes Counted for Biden," BitChute, Dec. 2, 2020, available at https://www.bitchute.com/video/74N0WNHOjiRy/; Jan 6th Protest and Save America March (2020-2H), "Patriots Plot Their Recapture of America in D.C. This Weekend," Banned.Video, Nov. 9, 2020, available at https://archive.org/details/banned.video_-_jan_6th_protest_and_save_america_march_2020-2h/2020-11-11T02%3A07.148Z+-+Patriots+Plot+Their+Recapture+Of+America+In+D.C.+This+Weekend/2020-11-11T02%3A19%3A07.148Z+-+%20Patriots+Plot+Their+Recapture+Of+America+In+D.C.+This+Weekend.mp4 (archived); The Alex Jones Show, "Oathkeepers Founder: Americans Need to Overcome Their Fears And Join The March on DC," Banned-.Video, Nov. 10, 2020, available at https://freeworldnews.tv/watch?id=5fab1b880ad7422090a8242f.

49. Kellye SoRelle, a lawyer for the Oath Keepers, described Stone (along with Alexander) as among the key players who were the "midpoint," "the ones who tr[ied] to orchestrate" joint efforts in the post-election period. *See* Select Committee to Investigate the January 6th Attack on the United States Capitol, Deposition of Kellye SoRelle, (Apr. 13, 2022), pp. 60-66.

50. Frontline, "Alex Jones and Donald Trump: How the Candidate Echoed the Conspiracy Theorist on the Campaign Trail," PBS, (July 28, 2020), available at https://www.pbs.org/wgbh/frontline/article/alex-jones-and-donald-trump-how-the-candidate-echoed-the-conspiracy-theorist-on-the-campaign-trail/.

51. Eric Bradner, "Trump Praises 9/11 Truther's 'Amazing' Reputation," CNN, (Dec. 2, 2015), available at https://www.cnn.com/2015/12/02/politics/donald-trump-praises-9-11-truther-alex-jones.

52. *See* Elizabeth Williamson, "Alex Jones and Donald Trump: A Fateful Alliance Draws Scrutiny," *New York Times,* (Mar. 7, 2022), available at https://www.nytimes.com/2022/03/07/us/politics/alex-jones-jan-6-trump.html ("Infowars grossed more than $50 million annually during the Trump presidency by selling diet supplements, body armor, and other products on its website.").

53. *See, e.g.,* Joshua Zitser, "Roger Stone Makes Donation Plea for Alex Jones After Verdict Says He Must Pay $49m for Sandy Hook 'Hoax' Claims," *Business Insider,* (Aug. 7, 2022), available at https://www.businessinsider.com/video-roger-stone-asks-donations-infowars-alex-jones-sandy-hook-2022-8.

54. *See* AirTable Collection from Select Committee to Investigate the January 6th Attack on the United States Capitol, "Images of State Protests before January 6, 2021."

55. *See* AirTable Collection from Select Committee to Investigate the January 6th Attack on the United States Capitol, "Images of State Protests before January 6, 2021."

56. *See* AirTable Collection from Select Committee to Investigate the January 6th Attack on the United States Capitol, "Images of State Protests before January 6, 2021."

57. See AirTable Collection from Select Committee to Investigate the January 6th Attack on the United States Capitol, "Images of State Protests before January 6, 2021."

58. Jonathan Oosting, "FBI arrests Ryan Kelley, Michigan GOP Governor Candidate, over Capitol Riots," *Bridge Michigan*, (June 9, 2022), available at https://www.bridgemi.com/michigan-government/fbi-arrests-ryan-kelley-michigan-gop-governor-candidate-over-capitol-riots.

59. James Dawson, "Unmasked Protesters Push Past Police into Idaho Lawmakers' Session," NPR, (Apr. 25, 2022), available at https://www.npr.org/2020/08/25/905785548/unmasked-protesters-push-past-police-into-idaho-lawmakers-session; Jeremy Stiles, "Boise Woman Sentenced for Role in U.S. Capitol Riot," KTVB, (May 24, 2022), available at https://www.ktvb.com/article/news/crime/boise-woman-sentenced-for-role-in-us-capitol-riot-pamela-hemphill-january-6-2021/277-3aa12194-5a54-4abe-88a2-d644cf5043aa.

60. Documents on file with the Select Committee to Investigate the January 6th Attack on the United States Capitol (Sergeant at Arms for the Arizona House of Representatives Production), CTRL0000930907, CTRL0000930908 (December 4, 2020, surveillance footage from the Arizona House of Representatives). available at https://house.app.box.com/folder/183317506767.

61. Sergio Olmos and Conrad Wilson, "At Least 3 Men from Oregon Protest Appear to Have Joined Insurrection at U.S. Capitol," Oregon Public Broadcasting, (Jan. 10, 2021), available at https://www.opb.org/article/2021/01/10/oregon-washington-protest-insurrection-david-anthony-medina-tim-davis/.

62. Brendan Guttenschwager (@BGOnTheScene), Twitter, Nov. 19, 2020 1:03 p.m. ET, available at https://twitter.com/BGOnTheScene/status/1329485442165706752.

63. Justwanna Grill, "Oathkeepers leader GROYPED in Atlanta," YouTube, Nov. 4, 2020, available at https://www.youtube.com/watch?v=V_rDOm5oKu0.

64. Timothy Johnson, "Alex Jones Calls on Supporters to 'Surround' the Georgia Governor's Mansion to Prevent Election Results from Being Certified," Media Matters, (Nov. 17, 2020), available at https://www.mediamatters.org/alex-jones/alex-jones-calls-supporters-surround-georgia-governors-mansion-prevent-election-results.

65. Nicholas J. Fuentes (@NickJFuentes), Twitter, Nov. 17, 2020, available at https://web.archive.org/web/20201120061341/https://twitter.com/NickJFuentes (archived).

66. *See, e.g.*, Aquarium Groyper, "Nick Fuentes Georgia State Capitol 11/20/2020," YouTube, Nov. 20, 2020, available at https://www.youtube.com/watch?v=OS1f—Tkn1M.

67. Jacqueline Alemany et al., "Red Flags," *Washington Post*, (Oct. 31, 2021), https://www.washingtonpost.com/politics/interactive/2021/warnings-jan-6-insurrection/.

68. Derrick Mullins, "'Stop the Steal' Connected 2 Roger Stone-Roger Stone Calls Ali Anderson in Front of Atlanta GA Crowd," YouTube Nov. 24, 2020, available at https://perma.cc/MWS3-HNGD.

69. Brendan Gutenschwager (@BGOnTheScene), Twitter, Nov. 20, 2022 12:38 p.m. ET, available at https://twitter.com/BGOnTheScene/status/1329841457377800198.

70. Zach D. Roberts (@zdroberts), Twitter, Jan. 14, 2022 11:38 p.m. ET, available at https://twitter.com/zdroberts/status/1482210446769807360.

71. Alexandra Hurtzler, "Alex Jones Leads 'Stop the Steal' Rally at Georgia's Capitol to Protest Election Results," *Newsweek*, (Nov. 18, 2020), available at https://www.newsweek.com/alex-jones-leads-stop-steal-rally-georgias-capitol-protest-election-results-1548533.

72. Jacqueline Alemany et al., "Red Flags," *Washington Post*, (Oct. 31, 2021), https://www.washingtonpost.com/politics/interactive/2021/warnings-jan-6-insurrection/.

73. Statement of Andrew Seidel, (Mar. 18, 2022), at p. 9.

74. Mike Giglio, "The Oath Keepers' Radical Legal Defense of January 6th," *New Yorker*, (Oct. 1, 2022), available at https://www.newyorker.com/news/news-desk/the-oath-keepers-radical-legal-defense-of-january-6th.

75. "Pro-Trump Rallies in DC Attract Extremists & Erupt into Violence," Anti-Defamation League, (Dec. 13, 2020), available at https://www.adl.org/blog/pro-trump-rallies-in-dc-attract-extremists-erupt-into-violence. Despite this, one of the organizers of the Jericho March maintained that the "tone" of the rally was supposed to be "prayerful, spirit-filled, peaceful, joyful, and vibrant, a unified celebration." *See* Select Committee to Investigate the January 6th Attack on the United States Capitol, Transcribed Interview of Arina Grossu, (Apr. 29, 2022), p. 40.

76. *See* President Donald J. Trump: Tweets of December 12, 2020, The American Presidency Project, available at https://www.presidency.ucsb.edu/documents/tweets-december-19-2020.

77. "Pro-Trump Rallies in DC Attract Extremists & Erupt into Violence," Anti-Defamation League, (Dec. 13, 2020), available at http://www.adl.org/blog/pro-trump-rallies-in-DC-attract-extremists-erupt-into-violence.

78. Grace Segers, "Trump's Motorcade Passes Supporters Gathered for 'Million MAGA March'," CBS News, (Nov. 14, 2020), available at https://www.cbsnews.com/news/million-maga-march-washington-dc-trumps-motorcade-passes-supporters/.

79. Donald J. Trump (@realdonaldtrump), Twitter, Dec. 12, 2020 9:59 a.m. ET, available at https://www.thetrumparchive.com/?searchbox=%22Wow%21+Thousands+of+people+forming%22 (archived).

80. Ashraf Khalil, "Marine One Buzzes Trump Supporters Rallying for President's Bid to Stay in Office in Washington," *Chicago Tribune*, (Dec. 12, 2020), available at https://www.chicagotribune.com/election-2020/ct-trump-election-20201212-z4zwtovupzhsppphzrlfhj3i3a-story.html.

81. "Breaking: Trump Calls for Americans to March on DC January 6 to Stop Foreign Takeover," InfoWars, (Dec. 19, 2020), available at https://web.archive.org/web/20201219175757/https://www.infowars.com/posts/breaking-trump-calls-for-americans-to-march-on-dc-january-6-to-stop-foreign-takeover/ (archived).

82. "The Alex Jones Show," Prison Planet TV, Dec. 20, 2020, available at http://tv.infowars.com/index/display/id/11151.

83. "The Alex Jones Show," Prison Planet TV, Dec. 20, 2020, at 1:27:13, available at http://tv.infowars.com/index/display/id/11151.

84. The Alex Jones Show, "January 6th Will Be a Turning Point in American History," Banned.Video, at 16:29, Dec. 31, 2020, available at https://banned.video/watch?id=5fee715284a7b6210e12a2f7.

85. "Proud Boys," Anti-Defamation League, (Jan. 23, 2020), available at https://www.adl.org/proudboys.

86. Documents on file with the Select Committee to Investigate the January 6th Attack on the United States Capitol (Proud Boys International Production), PBI 12 (The Constitution and Bylaws of Proud Boys International L.L.C., revised November 24, 2018).

87. "Proud Boys," Stanford University Center for International Security and Cooperation, (January 2022), available at https://cisac.fsi.stanford.edu/mappingmilitants/profiles/proud-boys.

88. "Proud Boys," Stanford University Center for International Security and Cooperation, (January 2022), available at https://cisac.fsi.stanford.edu/mappingmilitants/profiles/proud-boys.

89. *See, e.g.*, Documents on file with the Select Committee to Investigate the January 6th Attack on the United States Capitol (Jay Thaxton Production), CTRL0000055644, (December 27-28, 2020, "Ministry of Self Defense," Telegram messages from 7:43 p.m.-1:53 a.m.); "Proud

Boys," Stanford University Center for International Security and Cooperation, (January 2022), available at https://cisac.fsi.stanford.edu/mappingmilitants/profiles/proud-boys.

90. *See, e.g.*, Jason Wilson, "Portland Rally: Proud Boys Vow to March Each Month after Biggest Protest of Trump Era," *The Guardian*, (Aug. 17, 2019), available at https://www.theguardian.com/us-news/2019/aug/17/portland-oregon-far-right-rally-proud-boys-antifa.

91. *See* Statement of Heidi L. Beirich, Ph.D., (Mar. 22, 2022), at p.1.

92. *See, e.g.*, Select Committee to Investigate the January 6th Attack on the United States Capitol, Deposition of George Meza, (Mar. 16, 2022), p. 155.

93. *See, e.g.*, Cleve R. Wootson Jr., "Thousands of Proud Boys Plan to Rally in Portland, Setting Up Another Clash in a Combustible City," *Washington Post*, (Sept. 25, 2020), available at https://www.washingtonpost.com/nation/2020/09/25/portland-oregon-proud-boys-rally/; *see also*, Aaron Wolfson and Hampton Stall, "Actor Profile: Proud Boys," Armed Conflict Location & Event Data Project, (Apr. 22, 2021), available at https://acleddata.com/2021/04/22/actor-profile-proud-boys/ (noting the "percentage of events with counter-demonstrators in which Proud Boys members participated was more than 10 times the rate at which others engaged with counter-demonstrators.").

94. Nick Quested, a filmmaker who followed the Proud Boys through January 6th, described how Proud Boys couldn't define Black Lives Matter or Antifa—and that, in person, Proud Boys simply identified them as "people of color and people with progressive values." Select Committee to Investigate the January 6th Attack on the United States Capitol, Transcribed Interview of Nick Quested, (Apr. 5, 2022), p. 78.

95. Kathleen Ronayne and Michael Kunzelman, "Trump to Far-Right Extremists: 'Stand Back and Stand By,'" *Associated Press*, (Sept. 30, 2020), available at https://apnews.com/article/election-2020-joe-biden-race-and-ethnicity-donald-trump-chris-wallace-0b32339da25fbc9e8b7c7c7066a1db0f.

96. Select Committee to Investigate the January 6th Attack on the United States Capitol, Transcribed Interview of Nick Quested, (Apr. 5, 2022), p. 117.

97. Emails obtained by the Select Committee show that Parler featured alarmingly violent and specific posts that in some cases advocated for civil war. *See, e.g.*, Documents on file with the Select Committee to Investigate the January 6th Attack on the United States Capitol (Parler Production), PARLER_00000006 (December 24, 2020, email forwarded to the FBI, "We need to mass an armed force of American Patriots 150,000 on the Virginia side of the Potomac prepared to react to the congressional events of January 6th"). In a January 2, 2021, email, a Parler employee wrote that they were "concerned about Wednesday," which would be January 6th. *See* Documents on file with the Select Committee to Investigate the January 6th Attack on the United States Capitol (Parler Production), PARLER_00000009 (January 2, 2021, email forwarded to the FBI, "One more from same account. More where came from. Concerned about Wednesday...").

98. Atlantic Council's DFRLab, "#StopTheSteal: Timeline of Social Media and Extremist Activities Leading to 1/6 Insurrection," Just Security, (Feb. 10, 2021), available at https://www.justsecurity.org/74622/stopthesteal-timeline-of-social-media-and-extremist-activities-leading-to-1-6-insurrection/.

99. Select Committee to Investigate the January 6th Attack on the United States Capitol, Deposition of Jeremy Bertino, (Apr. 26, 2022), p. 38; *see also* "Former Leader of Proud Boys Pleads Guilty to Seditious Conspiracy for Efforts to Stop Transfer of Power Following 2020 Presidential Election," Department of Justice, (Oct. 6, 2022), available at https://www.justice.gov/opa/pr/former-leader-proud-boys-pleads-guilty-seditious-conspiracy-efforts-stop-transfer-power.mer-leader-proud-boys-pleads-guilty-seditious-conspiracy-efforts-stop-transfer-power.

100. Select Committee to Investigate the January 6th Attack on the United States Capitol, Deposition of Henry Tarrio, (Feb. 4, 2022), pp. 50-51, 221-22; Select Committee to Investigate the January 6th Attack on the United States Capitol, Deposition of George Meza, (Mar. 16, 2022), pp. 21-22.

101. Select Committee to Investigate the January 6th Attack on the United States Capitol, Deposition of Henry Tarrio, (Feb. 4, 2022), p. 221.

102. Tom Dreisbach, "Conspiracy Charges Bring Proud Boys' History Of Violence into Spotlight," NPR, (Apr. 9, 2021), available at https://www.npr.org/2021/04/09/985104612/conspiracy-charges-bring-proud-boys-history-of-violence-into-spotlight.

103. Tom Dreisbach, "Conspiracy Charges Bring Proud Boys' History Of Violence into Spotlight," NPR, (Apr. 9, 2021), available at https://www.npr.org/2021/04/09/985104612/conspiracy-charges-bring-proud-boys-history-of-violence-into-spotlight.

104. "Day of the Rope," Anti-Defamation League, available at https://www.adl.org/resources/hate-symbol/day-rope.

105. "Contested States," #StopTheSteal, (Nov. 7, 2020), available at http://archive.ph/C9lwN (archived).

106. Christopher Mathias, "After Trump's Defeat, His Supporters Held a Heavily Armed Pity Party," Huff Post, (Nov. 7, 2020), available at https://www.huffpost.com/entry/harrisburg-trump-rally-defeat-extremists-proud-boys-armed-militias_n_5fa756ddc5b67c3259afbc42.

107. Select Committee to Investigate the January 6th Attack on the United States Capitol, Transcribed Interview of Robert Glover, (May 2, 2022), p. 10.

108. Select Committee to Investigate the January 6th Attack on the United States Capitol, Transcribed Interview of Robert Glover, (May 2, 2022), p. 10.

109. Select Committee to Investigate the January 6th Attack on the United States Capitol, Deposition of Michael Simmons, (Feb. 10, 2022), p. 71; Select Committee to Investigate the January 6th Attack on the United States Capitol, Deposition of George Douglas Smith, Jr., (Apr. 28, 2022), p. 47.

110. Select Committee to Investigate the January 6th Attack on the United States Capitol, Deposition of Jeremy Bertino, (Apr. 26, 2022), pp. 81-82; Select Committee to Investigate the January 6th Attack on the United States Capitol, Transcribed Interview of Robert Glover, (May 2, 2022), p. 19; Select Committee to Investigate the January 6th Attack on the United States Capitol, Transcribed Interview of Nick Quested, (Apr. 5, 2022), p. 26.

111. Select Committee to Investigate the January 6th Attack on the United States Capitol, Transcribed Interview of Patrick Byrne, (July 15, 2022), pp. 151-52.

112. Select Committee to Investigate the January 6th Attack on the United States Capitol, Deposition of Henry Tarrio, (Feb. 4, 2022), pp. 107-09; Luke O'Brien, "How Republican Politics (And Twitter) Created Ali Alexander, The Man Behind 'Stop the Steal'," Huff Post, (Mar. 7, 2021), available at https://www.huffpost.com/entry/republicans-twitter-ali-alexander-stop-the-steal_n_6026fb26c5b6f88289fbab57.

113. Select Committee to Investigate the January 6th Attack on the United States Capitol, Deposition of Henry Tarrio, (Feb. 4, 2022), pp. 107-09.

114. Criminal Complaint, United States v. Shroyer, No. 1:21-mj-572 (D.D.C. Aug. 19, 2021), ECF No. 1, available at https://www.justice.gov/usao-dc/case-multi-defendant/file/1428181/download.

115. Select Committee to Investigate the January 6th Attack on the United States Capitol, Transcribed Interview of Nick Quested, (Apr. 5, 2022), pp. 17-19; Ryan Goodman, Justin Hendrix, Just Security, "Exclusive: New Video of Roger Stone with Proud Boys Leaders Who May Have Planned for Capitol Attack," (Feb. 6, 2021), available at https://www.justsecurity.org/74579/exclusive-new-video-of-roger-stone-with-proud-boys-leaders-who-may-have-planned-for-capitol-attack/.

116. Ryan Goodman & Justin Hendrix, "EXCLUSIVE: New Video of Roger Stone with Proud Boys Leaders Who May Have Planned for Capitol Attack," Just Security, (Feb. 6, 2021), available at https://www.justsecurity.org/74579/exclusive-new-video-of-roger-stone-with-proud-boys-leaders-who-may-have-planned-for-capitol-attack/.

117. Will Carless, "How a Trump Booster Group Helped the Head of Extremist Proud Boys Gain Access to the White House," *USA Today*, (Dec. 19, 2020), available at https://www.usatoday.com/story/news/nation/2020/12/19/latinos-trump-group-tied-proud-boys-leader-enrique-tarrio/3931868001/.

118. Select Committee to Investigate the January 6th Attack on the United States Capitol, Deposition of Henry Tarrio, (Feb. 4, 2022), p. 117.

119. Select Committee to Investigate the January 6th Attack on the United States Capitol, Deposition of Jeremy Bertino, (Apr. 26, 2022), pp. 125-27; Affidavit in Support of Arrest Warrant, *United States v. Tarrio*, No. 2020 CRWSLD 5553, (D.C. Super. Ct. Dec. 30, 2020).

120. Select Committee to Investigate the January 6th Attack on the United States Capitol, Deposition of Jeremy Bertino, (Apr. 26, 2022), p. 127.

121. Affidavit in Support of Arrest Warrant, *United States v. Tarrio*, No. 2020 CRWSLD 5553, (D.C. Super. Ct. Dec. 30, 2020).

122. Peter Herman and Martin Weil, "Proud Boys Leader Arrested in the Burning of Church's Black Lives Matter Banner, D.C. Police Say," *Washington Post*, (Jan. 4, 2021), available at https://www.washingtonpost.com/local/public-safety/proud-boys-enrique-tarrio-arrest/2021/01/04/8642a76a-4edf-11eb-b96e-0e54447b23a1_story.html; Laura Wamsley, "Proud Boys Leader Released from Police Custody and Ordered to Leave D.C.," NPR, (Jan. 5, 2021), available at https://www.npr.org/2021/01/05/953685035/proud-boys-leader-released-from-police-custody-and-ordered-to-leave-d-c.

123. Select Committee to Investigate the January 6th Attack on the United States Capitol, Transcribed Interview of Robert Glover, (May 2, 2022), p. 16.

124. Elizabeth Elizalde, "Proud Boys Surround Man with Knife at Violent DC Trump Rally," *New York Post*, (Dec. 13, 2020), available at https://nypost.com/2020/12/13/one-person-stabbed-during-massive-proud-boys-brawl-in-dc/.

125. Select Committee to Investigate the January 6th Attack on the United States Capitol, Deposition of Jeremy Bertino, (Apr. 26, 2022), pp. 128-29.

126. Select Committee to Investigate the January 6th Attack on the United States Capitol, Deposition of Jeremy Bertino, (Apr. 26, 2022), p. 129.

127. Select Committee to Investigate the January 6th Attack on the United States Capitol, Deposition of Jeremy Bertino, (Apr. 26, 2022), pp. 130-131.

128. Second Superseding Indictment at ¶ 30, *United States v. Nordean, et al.*, No. 1:21-cr-175 (D.D.C. Mar. 7, 2022), ECF No. 305.

129. Second Superseding Indictment at ¶ 32, *United States v. Nordean, et al.*, No. 1:21-cr-175 (D.D.C. Mar. 7, 2022), ECF No. 305; *see also* Documents on file with the Select Committee to Investigate the January 6th Attack on the United States Capitol (Jay Thaxton Production), CTRL0000055644, (December 27-28, 2020, "Ministry of Self Defense," Telegram messages from 7:43 p.m.-1:53 a.m.).

130. *See*, Documents on file with the Select Committee to Investigate the January 6th Attack on the United States Capitol (Jay Thaxton Production), CTRL0000055644, (December 27-28, 2020, "Ministry of Self Defense," Telegram messages from 7:43 p.m.-1:53 a.m.).

131. Second Superseding Indictment at ¶ 55, *United States v. Nordean, et al.*, No. 1:21-cr-175 (D.D.C. Mar. 7, 2022), ECF No. 305.

132. Third Superseding Indictment at ¶ 38, *United States v. Nordean, et al.*, No. 1:21-cr-175 (D.D.C. June 6, 2022), ECF No. 380; Documents on file with the Select Committee to Investigate the January 6th Attack on the United States Capitol (Jay Thaxton Production),

CTRL0000055644, (December 27-28, 2020, "Ministry of Self Defense," Telegram messages from 7:43 p.m.-1:53 a.m.).

133. Second Superseding Indictment at ¶ 33, *United States v. Nordean, et al.*, No. 1:21-cr-175 (D.D.C. Mar. 7, 2022), ECF No. 305.

134. Second Superseding Indictment at ¶ 31, *United States v. Nordean, et al.*, No. 1:21-cr-175 (D.D.C Mar. 7, 2022), ECF No. 305; *see also* Carter Walker, "Carlisle Proud Boy Member Targeted in Search Warrant Tied to Jan. 6 Plot," *Lancaster Online* (Mar. 12, 2022), available at https://lancasteronline.com/news/politics/carlisle-proud-boy-member-targeted-in-search-warrant-tied-to-jan-6-plot/article_c2596928-a258-11ec-a6bb-c79ff2e0e8a7.html (identifying John Stewart as Person-3 in Second Superseding Indictment).

135. Documents on file with the Select Committee to Investigate the January 6th Attack on the United States Capitol, (Jay Thaxton Production), CTRL0000055644, (December 29, 2020, "Ministry of Self Defense," Telegram message at 11:09 a.m.).

136. Second Superseding Indictment at ¶ 41, *United States v. Nordean, et al.*, No. 1:21-cr-175 (D.D.C. Mar. 7, 2022) ECF No. 305.

137. Select Committee to Investigate the January 6th Attack on the United States Capitol, Transcribed Interview of Samuel Armes, (July 18, 2022), p. 10-14 (describing Armes' role in drafting a prior version of the document, which he then shared with Eryka Gemma Flores, another cryptocurrency investor who shared the document with Tarrio); Select Committee to Investigate the January 6th Attack on the United States Capitol, Informal Interview of Eryka Gemma Flores, (July 1, 2022).

138. Zachary Rehl's Motion to Reopen Detention Hearing and Request for a Hearing, Exhibit 1: "1776 Returns," *United States v. Nordean, et al.*, No. 1:21-cr-175 (D.D.C. June 15, 2022) ECF No. 401-1, available at https://s3.documentcloud.org/documents/22060615/1776-returns.pdf.

139. Zachary Rehl's Motion to Reopen Detention Hearing and Request for a Hearing, Exhibit 1: "1776 Returns," *United States v. Nordean, et al.*, No. 1:21-cr-175 (D.D.C. June 15, 2022) ECF No. 401-1, available at https://s3.documentcloud.org/documents/22060615/1776-returns.pdf.

140. Select Committee to Investigate the January 6th Attack on the United States Capitol, Deposition of Matthew Thomas Walter, (Mar. 9, 2022), pp. 70-71; Select Committee to Investigate the January 6th Attack on the United States Capitol, Deposition of Christopher Barcenas, (Mar. 10, 2022), p. 98; Select Committee to Investigate the January 6th Attack on the United States Capitol, Deposition of George Meza, (Mar. 16, 2022), p. 118; Select Committee to Investigate the January 6th Attack on the United States Capitol, Deposition of Jeremy Bertino, (Apr. 26, 2022), p. 23.

141. Select Committee to Investigate the January 6th Attack on the United States Capitol, Transcribed Interview of Samuel Armes, (July 18, 2022), p. 14.

142. Second Superseding Indictment at ¶ 41, *United States v. Nordean, et al.*, No. 1:21-cr-175 (D.D.C. Mar. 7, 2022), ECF No. 305.

143. Georgia Wells, Rebecca Ballhaus, and Keach Hagey, "Proud Boys, Seizing Trump's Call to Washington, Helped Lead Capitol Attack," *Wall Street Journal*, (Jan. 17, 2021), available at https://www.wsj.com/articles/proud-boys-seizing-trumps-call-to-washington-helped-lead-capitol-attack-11610911596.

144. Second Superseding Indictment at ¶ 49, *United States v. Nordean, et al.*, No. 1:21-cr-175 (D.D.C. Mar. 7, 2022), ECF No. 305; Carter Walker, "Carlisle Proud Boy Member Targeted in Search Warrant Tied to Jan. 6 Plot," *Lancaster Online* (Mar. 12, 2022), available at https://lancasteronline.com/news/politics/carlisle-proud-boy-member-targeted-in-search-warrant-tied-to-jan-6-plot/article_c2596928-a258-11ec-a6bb-c79ff2e0e8a7.html (identifying John Stewart as Person-3 in Second Superseding Indictment).

145. Second Superseding Indictment at ¶ 49, *United States v. Nordean, et al.*, No. 1:21-cr-175 (D.D.C. Mar. 7, 2022), ECF No. 305; Carter Walker, "Carlisle Proud Boy Member Targeted in Search Warrant Tied to Jan. 6 Plot," *Lancaster Online* (Mar. 12, 2022), available at https://lancasteronline.com/news/politics/carlisle-proud-boy-member-targeted-in-search-

warrant-tied-to-jan-6-plot/article_c2596928-a258-11ec-a6bb-c79ff2e0e8a7.html (identifying John Stewart as Person-3 in Second Superseding Indictment).

146.   Second Superseding Indictment at ¶ 50, *United States v. Nordean et al.*, No. 1:21-cr-175 (D.D.C. Mar. 7, 2022) ECF No. 305.

147.   Plea Agreement at 1, *United States v. Donohoe*, No. 1:21-cr-175 (D.D.C. Apr. 8, 2022), ECF No. 335.

148.   Statement of Offense at 4, *United States v. Donohoe*, No. 1:21-cr-00175-4-TJK (D.D.C. Apr. 8, 2022).

149.   Statement of Offense at 4, *United States v. Donohoe*, No. 1:21-cr-00175-4-TJK (D.D.C. Apr. 8, 2022).

150.   Statement of Offense at 6, *United States v. Donohoe*, No. 1:21-cr-00175-4-TJK (D.D.C. Apr. 8, 2022).

151.   Statement of Offense at 6, *United States v. Donohoe*, No. 1:21-cr-00175-4-TJK (D.D.C. Apr. 8, 2022).

152.   Statement of Offense at 8, *United States v. Donohoe*, No. 1:21-cr-00175-4-TJK (D.D.C. Apr. 8, 2022).

153.   "Former Leader of Proud Boys Pleads Guilty to Seditious Conspiracy for Efforts to Stop Transfer of Power Following 2020 Presidential Election," Department of Justice, (Oct. 6, 2022), available at http://www.justice.gov/opa/pr/former-leader-proud-boys-pleads-guilty-seditious-conspiracy-efforts-stop-transfer-power.

154.   "Former Leader of Proud Boys Pleads Guilty to Seditious Conspiracy for Efforts to Stop Transfer of Power Following 2020 Presidential Election," Department of Justice, (Oct. 22, 2022), available at https://www.justice.gov/opa/pr/former-leader-proud-boys-pleads-guilty-seditious-conspiracy-efforts-stop-transfer-power.

155.   Select Committee to Investigate the January 6th Attack on the United States Capitol, Deposition of Jeremy Bertino, (Apr. 26, 2022), p. 156.

156.   Select Committee to Investigate the January 6th Attack on the United States Capitol, Deposition of Jeremy Bertino, (Apr. 26, 2022), p. 156.

157.   *Statement of Sam Jackson, Ph.D., (Mar. 30, 2022), at p. 2.*

158.   Zachary Cohen, "Oath Keepers Leader Spewed Anti-government Hate for More than a Decade. Alex Jones Gave Him the Audience," CNN, (Jan. 14, 2022), available at https://www.cnn.com/2022/01/14/politics/oath-keepers-stewart-rhodes-alex-jones-invs/index.html.

159.   The Select Committee found that the idea that violence loomed from the left was a powerful draw for people to join the Oath Keepers. Richard Dockery, a former Oath Keepers member from Florida, decried "all the riots and stuff I was seeing on the news all over the country" and expressed concern about Antifa and Black Lives Matter activity in his area of Florida, a prospect that he called "nerve-wracking." Select Committee to Investigate the January 6th Attack on the United States Capitol, Deposition of Richard Dockery, (Feb. 2, 2022), pp. 10, 31. Because of this, he said that the Oath Keepers "seemed like a really good organization to support" in order to keep communities safe. *Id.*, at p. 9. Similarly, Jeff Morelock told the Select Committee that joining the Oath Keepers "would give me a chance to do something to help instead of just sitting on the couch," referring to watching protests on television. Select Committee to Investigate the January 6th Attack on the United States Capitol, Deposition of Jeffrey Lawrence Morelock, (Jan. 26, 2022), pp. 87-88. Jason Van Tatenhove, a former spokesman for the Oath Keepers and confidant to Rhodes who has since publicly denounced the group, described how the Oath Keepers tried to deliberately leverage this dynamic to increase their clout. Select Committee to Investigate the January 6th Attack on the United States Capitol, Transcribed Interview of Jason Van Tatenhove, (Mar. 9, 2022), pp. 54-55.

160.   Select Committee to Investigate the January 6th Attack on the United States Capitol, Deposition of Elmer Stewart Rhodes, (Feb. 2, 2022), pp. 103-104.

161. Select Committee to Investigate the January 6th Attack on the United States Capitol, Deposition of Kellye SoRelle, (Apr. 13, 2022), pp. 9-10.

162. Stewart Rhodes, "Call to Action! March on DC, Stop the Steal, Defend the President, & Defeat the Deep State," Oath Keepers, (Nov. 10, 2020), available at https://oathkeepers.org/2020/11/call-to-action-march-on-dc-stop-the-steal-defend-the-president-defeat-the-deep-state/.

163. Stewart Rhodes, "Call to Action! March on DC, Stop the Steal, Defend the President, & Defeat the Deep State," Oath Keepers, (Nov. 10, 2020), available at https://oathkeepers.org/2020/11/call-to-action-march-on-dc-stop-the-steal-defend-the-president-defeat-the-deep-state/.

164. Stewart Rhodes and Kellye SoRelle, "Open Letter to President Trump: You Must Use the Insurrection Act to 'Stop the Steal' and Defeat the Coup," Oath Keepers, (Dec. 14, 2020), available at https://web.archive.org/web/20210123133022/https:/oathkeepers.org/2020/12/open-letter-to-president-trump-you-must-use-insurrection-act-to-stop-the-steal-and-defeat-the-coup/.

165. Michael S. Schmidt and Maggie Haberman, "Trump Aides Prepared Insurrection Act Order During Debate Over Protests," *New York Times*, (June 25, 2021), available at https://www.nytimes.com/2021/06/25/us/politics/trump-insurrection-act-protests.html.

166. Select Committee to Investigate the January 6th Attack on the United States Capitol, Deposition of Elmer Stewart Rhodes, (Feb. 2, 2022), p. 131.

167. "Pro-Trump Rallies in DC Attract Extremists & Erupt into Violence," Anti-Defamation League, (Dec. 13, 2020), available at https://www.adl.org/blog/pro-trump-rallies-in-dc-attract-extremists-erupt-into-violence.

168. In texts between Rhodes and Rob Weaver, one of the organizers of the Jericho March, Weaver instructed his associate to work with Rhodes "on extra security." Documents on file with the Select Committee to Investigate the January 6th Attack on the United States Capitol (Robert Weaver Production), Weaver J6 Prod. (S. Rhodes)0001 (December 11, 2020, text from Rob Weaver at 1:39 p.m.).

169. Documents on file with the Select Committee to Investigate the January 6th Attack on the United States Capitol, (Thomas Speciale Production), CTRL0000050180, pp. 1-6, 26-28 (Signal Chat Titled Dec 12 DC Security/Leadership); Documents on file with the Select Committee to Investigate the January 6th Attack on the United States Capitol (Robert Weaver Production), Weaver J6 Production) Prod. (S. Rhodes)0039 (Signal Chat Titled Dec 12 DC Security/Leadership).; Superseding Indictment at 12, *United States v. Rhodes et al.*, No. 1:22-cr-15 (D.D.C. June 22, 2022), ECF No. 167 (noting that on December 11, 2020, Rhodes "sent a message to an invitation-only Signal group chat titled, 'Dec 12 DC Security/Leadership,' which included James, MINUTA, and others. RHODES stated that if President-Elect Biden were to assume the presidency, 'It will be a bloody and desperate fight. We are going to have a fight. That can't be avoided.' ").

170. Documents on file with the Select Committee to Investigate the January 6th Attack on the United States Capitol (Robert Weaver Production), Weaver J6 Prod. (S. Rhodes) 0045 (December 10, 2020, Stewart Rhodes chat with Dec. 12 DC Security/Leadership at 10:17p.m.).

171. Stewart Rhodes and Kellye SoRelle, "Open Letter to President Trump: You Must Use the Insurrection Act to 'Stop the Steal' and Defeat the Coup," Oath Keepers, (Dec. 14, 2020), available at https://web.archive.org/web/20210123133022/https:/oathkeepers.org/2020/12/open-letter-to-president-trump-you-must-use-insurrection-act-to-stop-the-steal-and-defeat-the-coup/.

172. Select Committee to Investigate the January 6th Attack on the United States Capitol, Deposition of Elmer Stewart Rhodes, (Feb. 2, 2022), pp. 132, 134.

173. Trial Exhibit 6748, *United States v. Rhodes et al.*, No. 1:22-cr-15 (D.D.C. Oct. 20, 2022); Kyle Cheney, "Prosecutors Detail Oath Keepers' Mounting Frustration with Trump as Jan. 6 Approached," *Politico*, (Oct. 20, 2022), available at https://www.politico.com/news/2022/10/20/oath-keepers-trump-jan-6-00062779.

174. Documents on file with the Select Committee to Investigate the January 6th Attack on the United States Capitol (Alondra Propes Production), CTRL0000029585, p.1 (Stewart Rhodes writing in 'OKFL Hangout' chat).

175. Stewart Rhodes and Alondra Propes characterized the Proud Boys as street brawlers in contrast to the Oath Keepers' discipline. *See* Select Committee to Investigate the January 6th Attack on the United States Capitol, Deposition of Elmer Stewart Rhodes, (Feb. 22, 2022), pp. 40, 43; Select Committee to Investigate the January 6th Attack on the United States Capitol, Transcribed Interview of Alondra Propes, (Jan. 31, 2022), pp. 42-43, 136. Kellye SoRelle described the Proud Boys as extreme white supremacists. *See* Select Committee to Investigate the January 6th Attack on the United States Capitol, Deposition of Kellye SoRelle, (Apr. 13, 2022), p. 63-64. Enrique Tarrio characterized the Oath Keepers as "oath breakers" and embarrassing. *See* Select Committee to Investigate the January 6th Attack on the United States Capitol, Deposition of Henry Tarrio, (Feb. 4, 2022), pp. 77, 193-94.

176. Documents on file with the Select Committee to Investigate the January 6th Attack on the United States Capitol (Google Voice Production, Feb. 25, 2022).

177. Government's Opposition to Defendant's Renewed Request for Pretrial Release at 7, *United States v. Meggs*, No. 1:21-cr-28 (D.D.C. Mar. 23, 2021). Select Committee to Investigate the January 6th Attack on the United States Capitol, Deposition of Henry Tarrio, (Feb. 4, 2022), p. 125.

178. Superseding Indictment at ¶ 28, *United States v. Rhodes et al.*, No. 1:22-cr-25 (D.D.C. June 22, 2022), ECF No. 167.

179. "Leader of Oath Keepers and 10 Other Individuals Indicted in Federal Court for Seditious Conspiracy and Other Offenses Related to U.S. Capitol Breach," Department of Justice, (Jan. 13, 2022), available at https://www.justice.gov/usao-dc/pr/leader-oath-keepers-and-10-other-individuals-indicted-federal-court-seditious-conspiracy.

180. *See* Superseding Indictment at ¶ 17, *United States v. Rhodes et al.*, No. 1:22-cr-25 (D.D.C. June 22, 2022), ECF No. 167; Select Committee to Investigate the January 6th Attack on the United States Capitol, Transcribed Interview of Landon Bentley, (May 12, 2022), p. 11 (discussing use of Signal as an encrypted chat).

181. Superseding Indictment at ¶ 29, *United States v. Rhodes, et al.*, No. 1:22-cr-15 (D.D.C. June 22, 2022), ECF No. 167.

182. Superseding Indictment at ¶¶ 38, 39, *United States v. Rhodes et al.*, No. 1:22-cr-15 (D.D.C. June 22, 2022), ECF No. 167.

183. Third Superseding Indictment at ¶ 37, *United States v. Crowl et al.*, No. 1:21-cr-28 (D.D.C., Mar. 31, 2021), ECF No. 127.

184. Third Superseding Indictment at ¶ 37, *United States v. Crowl et al.*, No. 1:21-cr-28 (D.D.C., Mar. 31, 2021), ECF No. 127.

185. Select Committee to Investigate the January 6th Attack on the United States Capitol, Deposition of Richard Dockery, (Feb. 2, 2022), pp. 48-52.

186. Select Committee to Investigate the January 6th Attack on the United States Capitol, Deposition of Richard Dockery, (Feb. 2, 2022), p. 49.

187. Select Committee to Investigate the January 6th Attack on the United States Capitol, Deposition of Richard Dockery, (Feb. 2, 2022), p. 51.

188. Infowars Army, "Alex Jones Show—DOJ Launches National Probe of Election Fraud," BitChute, Nov. 10, 2020, available at https://www.bitchute.com/video/NoELuXs06RzX/.

189.   *See, e.g.,* Documents on file with the Select Committee to Investigate the January 6th
        Attack on the United States Capitol, (Robert Weaver Production), Weaver J6 Prod. (S.
        Rhodes) 0011 (January 1, 2021, Stewart Rhodes chat with Jan 5/6 DC OK Security/VIP Chat at
        7:58-8:00 pm).

190.   Superseding Indictment at ¶ 45, *United States v. Rhodes et al.,* No. 1:22-cr-15 (D.D.C. June
        22, 2022), ECF No. 167; Select Committee to Investigate the January 6th Attack on the United
        States Capitol, Transcribed Interview of Frank Marchisella, (Apr. 29, 2022), p. 34.

191.   Superseding Indictment at ¶ 44, *United States v. Rhodes et al.,* No. 1:22-cr-15 (D.D.C. June
        22, 2022), ECF No. 167.

192.   Superseding Indictment at ¶ 68, *United States v. Rhodes et al.,* No. 1:22-cr-15 (D.D.C. June
        22, 2022), ECF No. 167. Documents filed with the Select Committee to Investigate the Janu-
        ary 6th Attack on the United States Capitol (Hilton Garden Inn Production), MHG000049-103
        (January 2-8, 2021, Hilton Garden Inn invoices).

193.   Superseding Indictment at ¶ 37, *United States v. Rhodes et al.,* No. 1:22-cr-15 (D.D.C. June
        22, 2022), ECF No. 167; Select Committee to Investigate the January 6th Attack on the United
        States Capitol, Deposition of Kellye SoRelle, (Apr. 13, 2022), p. 180.

194.   Superseding Indictment at ¶ 47, *United States v. Rhodes et al.,* No. 1:22-cr-15 (D.D.C. June
        22, 2022) ECF No. 167.

195.   Superseding Indictment at ¶ 57, *United States v. Rhodes et al.,* No. 1:22-cr-15 (D.D.C. June
        22, 2022), ECF No. 167.

196.   Superseding Indictment at ¶ 61, *United States v. Rhodes, et al.,* No. 1:22-cr-15 (D.D.C. June
        22, 2022), ECF No. 167.

197.   Superseding Indictment at ¶ 70, *United States v. Rhodes et al.,* No. 1:22-cr-15 (D.D.C. June
        22, 2022), ECF No. 167.

198.   Select Committee to Investigate the January 6th Attack on the United States Capitol, Tran-
        scribed Interview of Frank Marchisella, (Apr. 29, 2022), p. 39.

199.   Select Committee to Investigate the January 6th Attack on the United States Capitol, Depo-
        sition of Kellye SoRelle, (Apr. 13, 2022), p. 196.

200.   Select Committee to Investigate the January 6th Attack on the United States Capitol, Tran-
        scribed Interview of Frank Marchisella, (Apr. 29, 2022), p. 40.

201.   Select Committee to Investigate the January 6th Attack on the United States Capitol, Depo-
        sition of Kellye SoRelle, (Apr. 13, 2022), p. 196.

202.   Select Comittee to Investigate the January 6th Attack on the United States Capitol, Tran-
        scribed Interview of Frank Marchisella, (Apr. 29, 2022), pp. 40-42.

203.   Select Committee to Investigate the January 6th Attack on the United States Capitol, Tran-
        scribed Interview of Frank Marchisella, (Apr. 29, 2022), pp. 45-47.

204.   Macias had traveled to DC after his arrest for bringing weapons to a vote-counting center
        in Philadelphia while votes were being counted in November 2020. Claudia Lauer, "Philly
        DA Seeks Contempt Charge for Vets for Trump Cofounder," *AP News,* (June 13, 2022), avail-
        able at https://apnews.com/article/capitol-siege-pennsylvania-riots-philadelphia-virginia-
        d74b05c01aebde1ca26a9c080a5022d8.

205.   Documents on file with the Select Committee to Investigate the January 6th Attack on the
        United States Capitol (Frank Marchiseall Production), CTRL0000040442 (January 5, 2021,
        Frank Marchisella video of Facebook live stream).

206.   Documents on file with the Select Committee to Investigate the January 6th Attack on the
        United States Capitol (Frank Marchisealla Production), CTRL0000040442, (January 5, 2021,
        Frank Marchisella video of Facebook live stream) at 0:36.

207.   Select Committee to Investigate the January 6th Attack on the United States Capitol, Depo-
        sition of Kellye SoRelle, (Apr. 13, 2022), pp. 207-08.

208. Select Committee to Investigate the January 6th Attack on the United States Capitol, Deposition of Kellye SoRelle, (Apr. 13, 2022), p. 197.

209. Select Committee to Investigate the January 6th Attack on the United States Capitol, Deposition of Kellye SoRelle, (Apr. 13, 2022), p. 197.

210. Second Superseding Indictment at ¶ 23, *United States v. Nordean, et al.*, No. 1:21-cr-175 (D.D.C. Mar. 7, 2022), ECF No. 305.

211. Select Committee to Investigate the January 6th Attack on the United States Capitol, Deposition of Kellye SoRelle, (Apr. 13, 2022), p. 197.

212. Documents on file with the Select Committee to Investigate the January 6th Attack on the United States Capitol, (Nick Quested Production), Video file ML_DC_20210105_Sony_FS7-GC_1859.mov, at 0:50 (Jan. 5, 2021).

213. Documents on file with the Select Committee to Investigate the January 6th Attack on the United States Capitol, (Nick Quested Production), Video file ML_DC_20210105_Sony_FS7-GC_1859.mov, at 1:31 (Jan. 5, 2021).

214. Documents on file with the Select Committee to Investigate the January 6th Attack on the United States Capitol, (Nick Quested Production), Video file ML_DC_20210105_Sony_FS7-GC_1859.mov, at 1:00 (Jan. 5, 2021).

215. Select Committee to Investigate the January 6th Attack on the United States Capitol, Deposition of Kellye SoRelle, (Apr. 13, 2022), p. 202.

216. Spencer S. Hsu, "Video Released of Garage Meeting of Proud Boys, Oath Keepers Leaders," *Washington Post*, embedded video at 3:20, (May 24, 2022), available at https://www.washingtonpost.com/dc-md-va/2022/05/24/tarrio-rhodes-video/.

217. Documents on file with the Select Committee to Investigate the January 6th Attack on the United States Capitol (Nick Quested Production), Video file ML_DC_20210105_Sony_FS7-GC_1864.mov, at 0:14 (Jan. 5, 2021).

218. Documents on file with the Select Committee to Investigate the January 6th Attack on the United States Capitol (Nick Quested Production), Video file ML_DC_20210105_Sony_FS5_Clip0042.mov, at 2:32-3:38 (Jan. 5, 2021).

219. Documents on file with the Select Committee to Investigate the January 6th Attack on the United States Capitol (Nick Quested Production), Video file ML_DC_20210105_Sony_FS5_Clip0042.mov, at 2:32-3:38 (Jan. 5, 2021).

220. Documents on file with the Select Committee to Investigate the January 6th Attack on the United States Capitol (Nick Quested Production), Video file ML_DC_20210105_Sony_FS5_Clip0042.mov, at 2:32-3:38 (Jan. 5, 2021).

221. Select Committee to Investigate the January 6th Attack on the United States Capitol, Deposition of Henry Tarrio, (Feb. 4, 2022), pp. 83-84.

222. *See In re Stone*, 940 F.3d 1332, 1334 (D.C. Cir. 2019); *United States v. Stone*, 394 F. Supp. 3d 1, 7-8 (D.D.C. 2019).

223. David Freedlander, "An Oral History of Donald Trump's Almost-Run for President in 2000," *Intelligencer*, (Oct. 11, 2018), available at https://nymag.com/intelligencer/2018/10/trumps-almost-run-for-president-in-2000-an-oral-history.html.

224. *See* Trial Transcript at 3806, *United States v. Rhodes et al.*, No. 1:22-cr-15 (D.D.C. Oct. 17, 2022) (testimony and exhibits showing Kelly Meggs and Jessica Watkins discussed providing security for Roger Stone); Dalton Bennett and Jon Swaine, "The Roger Stone Tapes," *Washington Post*, available at https://www.washingtonpost.com/investigations/interactive/2022/roger-stone-documentary-capitol-riot-trump-election/; Matthew Mosk, Olivia Rubin, Ali Dukakis, and Fergal Gallagher, "Video Surfaces Showing Trump Ally Roger Stone Flanked by Oath Keepers on Morning of Jan. 6," ABC News, (Feb. 5, 2021), available at https://abcnews.go.com/US/video-surfaces-showing-trump-ally-roger-stone-flanked/story?id=75706765; Christiaan Triebert (@trbrtc), Twitter, Feb. 19, 2021 4:35 p.m., available at https://twitter.com/trbrtc/status/1362878609334165505 (Kelly Meggs with Roger Stone); Spencer S.

Hsu, Manuel Roig-Franzia, and Devlin Barrett, "Roger Stone Keeps Appearing in Capitol Breach Investigation Court Filings," *Washington Post*, (Mar. 22, 2021), available at https://www.washingtonpost.com/local/public-safety/roger-stone-court-filings-capitol-riot/2021/03/22/c689a77c-87f8-11eb-82bc-e58213caa38e_story.html (Mark Grods with Roger Stone); Andrew Smrecek (@combat_art_training), Instagram, Dec. 15, 2020, available at https://www.instagram.com/p/CI0g8dlhEyG/ (Connie Meggs and Jason Dolan with Roger Stone) (last accessed Dec. 11, 2022).

225.   Motion for Bond, Exhibit 1 at 76, 90, 96, 98, *United States v. Rhodes et al.*, No. 1:22-cr-15 (D.D.C. Jan. 12, 2022), ECF No. 102-1.

226.   Christiaan Triebert, Ben Decker, Derek Watkins, Arielle Ray, and Stella Cooper, "First They Guarded Roger Stone. Then They Joined the Capitol Attack," *New York Times*, (Feb. 14, 2021), available at https://www.nytimes.com/interactive/2021/02/14/us/roger-stone-capitol-riot.html.

227.   Matthew Mosk, Olivia Rubin, Ali Dukakis, and Fergal Gallagher, "Video Surfaces Showing Trump Ally Roger Stone Flanked by Oath Keepers on Morning of Jan. 6," ABC News, (Feb. 5, 2021), available at https://abcnews.go.com/US/video-surfaces-showing-trump-ally-roger-stone-flanked/story?id=75706765.

228.   "Leader of Alabama Chapter of Oath Keepers Pleads Guilty to Seditious Conspiracy and Obstruction of Congress for Efforts to Stop Transfer of Power Following 2020 Presidential Election," Department of Justice Office of Public Affairs, (Mar. 2, 2022), available at https://www.justice.gov/opa/pr/leader-alabama-chapter-oath-keepers-pleads-guilty-seditious-conspiracy-and-obstruction.

229.   Dalton Bennett and Jon Swaine, "The Roger Stone Tapes," *Washington Post*, (Mar. 4, 2022), available at https://www.washingtonpost.com/investigations/interactive/2022/roger-stone-documentary-capitol-riot-trump-election/.

230.   Kelly Weill, "How the Proud Boys Became Roger Stone's Personal Army," *Daily Beast*, (Jan. 29, 2019), available at https://www.thedailybeast.com/how-the-proud-boys-became-roger-stones-personal-army-6.

231.   *See, e.g.*, Andy Campbell, "EXCLUSIVE: Roger Stone Admits He's Been Advising The Proud Boys For Years," *Huff Post*, (Sept. 22, 2022), available at https://www.huffpost.com/entry/roger-stone-we-are-proud-boys_n_632c57ebe4b09d8701bd02e2.

232.   *See, e.g.*, Documents on file with the Select Committee to Investigate the January 6th Attack on the United States Capitol (Christoffer Guldbrandsen Production), Video files 190926 I bil + fondraiser, 191003 Stone dag 3 backstage fundraiser 2 onstage, 200220.

233.   Documents on file with the Select Committee to Investigate the January 6th Attack on the United States Capitol (Christoffer Guldbrandsen Production), Video file 190926 i bil + fond-raiser.

234.   Ryan Goodman and Justin Hendrix, "EXCLUSIVE: New Video of Roger Stone with Proud Boys Leaders Who May Have Planned for Capitol Attack," Just Security, (Feb. 6, 2021), available at https://www.justsecurity.org/74579/exclusive-new-video-of-roger-stone-with-proud-boys-leaders-who-may-have-planned-for-capitol-attack/.

235.   Ryan Goodman and Justin Hendrix, "EXCLUSIVE: New Video of Roger Stone with Proud Boys Leaders Who May Have Planned for Capitol Attack," Just Security, (Feb. 6, 2021), available at https://www.justsecurity.org/74579/exclusive-new-video-of-roger-stone-with-proud-boys-leaders-who-may-have-planned-for-capitol-attack/.

236.   Ryan Goodman and Justin Hendrix, "EXCLUSIVE: New Video of Roger Stone with Proud Boys Leaders Who May Have Planned for Capitol Attack," Just Security, (Feb. 6, 2021), available at https://www.justsecurity.org/74579/exclusive-new-video-of-roger-stone-with-proud-boys-leaders-who-may-have-planned-for-capitol-attack/.

237. Georgia Wells, Rebecca Ballhaus, and Keach Hagey, " Proud Boys, Seizing Trump's Call to Washington, Helped Lead Capitol Attack," *Wall Street Journal*, (Jan. 17, 2021), available at https://www.wsj.com/articles/proud-boys-seizing-trumps-call-to-washington-helped-lead-capitol-attack-11610911596.

238. Georgia Wells, Rebecca Ballhaus, and Keach Hagey, " Proud Boys, Seizing Trump's Call to Washington, Helped Lead Capitol Attack," *Wall Street Journal*, (Jan. 17, 2021), available at https://www.wsj.com/articles/proud-boys-seizing-trumps-call-to-washington-helped-lead-capitol-attack-11610911596.

239. Documents on file with the Select Committee to Investigate the January 6th Attack on the United States Capitol (Kellye SoRelle Production), CTRL0000060762 - CTRL0000060858 (screenshotting messages in the Friends of Stone chat); Dalton Bennett and Jon Swaine, "The Roger Stone Tapes," *Washington Post*, available at https://www.washingtonpost.com/investigations/interactive/2022/roger-stone-documentary-capitol-riot-trump-election/; Documents on file with the Select Committee to Investigate the January 6th Attack on the United States Capitol (Christoffer Guldbrandsen Production), Video file 200705.

240. Documents on file with the Select Committee to Investigate the January 6th Attack on the United States Capitol (Christoffer Guldbrandsen Production), Video file 201105.

241. Hugo Lowell, "Film Offers Inside Look at Roger Stone's 'Stop the Steal' Efforts Before January 6," *The Guardian*, (July 8, 2022), available at https://www.theguardian.com/us-news/2022/jul/07/roger-stone-ali-alexander-film-jan-6-stop-the-steal.

242. Document on file with the Select Committee to Investigate the January 6th Attack on the United States Capitol (Kellye SoRelle Production), CTRL0000060802, CTRL0000060798 (screenshots from the Friends of Stone chat).

243. "Executive Grant of Clemency for Roger Jason Stone, Jr.," Department of Justice, (July 10, 2020), available at https://www.justice.gov/pardon/page/file/1293796/download.

244. Amita Kelly, Ryan Lucas, and Vanessa Romo, "Trump Pardons Roger Stone, Paul Manafort And Charles Kushner," NPR, (Dec. 23, 2020), available at https://www.npr.org/2020/12/23/949820820/trump-pardons-roger-stone-paul-manafort-and-charles-kushner.

245. PatriotTakes[American flag] (@PatriotTakes), Twitter, Dec. 28, 2020 3:50 a.m. ET, available at https://twitter.com/patriottakes/status/1343479434376974336.

246. PatriotTakes[American flag] (@PatriotTakes), Twitter, Dec. 28, 2020 3:50 a.m. ET, available at https://twitter.com/patriottakes/status/1343479434376974336; *See also* Ali Dukakis, "Roger Stone Thanks President Trump for Pardon in Person," ABC News, (Dec. 28, 2020), available at https://abcnews.go.com/Politics/roger-stone-president-trump-pardon-person/story?id=74940512.

247. Select Committee to Investigate the January 6th Attack on the United States Capitol, Transcribed Interview of Kristin Davis, (August 2, 2022), p. 41; Documents on file with Select Committee to Investigate the January 6th Attack on the United States Capitol, (Kristin Davis Production), CTRL0000928609, p. 7 (December 30, 2020, text message from Kristin Davis to Chris Lippe at 6:05 p.m.).

248. Documents on file with Select Committee to Investigate the January 6th Attack on the United States Capitol (Kristin Davis Production), CTRL0000928609, p. 7 (December 30, 2020, text message from Kristin Davis to Chris Lippe at 6:05 p.m.).

249. Select Committee to Investigate the January 6th Attack on the United States Capitol, Deposition of Roger Stone, (Dec. 17, 2021).

250. Will Steakin, Matthew Mosk, James Gordon Meek, and Ali Dukakis, "Longtime Trump Advisers Connected to Groups Behind Rally that Led to Capitol Attack," ABC News, (Jan. 15, 2021), available at https://abcnews.go.com/US/longtime-trump-advisers-connected-groups-rally-led-capitol/story?id=75261028.

251. "Nicholas J. Fuentes: Five Things to Know," Anti-Defamation League, (July 9, 2021, updated Nov. 30, 2022), available at https://www.adl.org/resources/blog/nicholas-j-fuentes-five-things-know?gclid=EAIaIQobChMI4iTXgYH6-wIVaUpyCh08sgxaEAAYASAAEgLGNPD_BwE; Nicholas J. Fuentes (@NickJFuentes), Twitter, Dec. 18, 2020 11:26 p.m. ET, available at https://web.archive.org/web/20201219072617/https:/twitter.com/NickJFuentes/status/1340196694571540490 (archived). As noted in the Executive Summary, this tweet, like others, was likely sent from or archived in a separate time zone, which explains why it shows a sent date of December 18, 2020, while President Trump issued his tweet at 1:42 a.m. on December 19, 2020.

252. "California Man Sentenced to 42 Months in Prison for Actions During Jan. 6 Capitol Breach," Department of Justice, (Oct. 19, 2022), available at https://www.justice.gov/usao-dc/pr/california-man-sentenced-prison-actions-during-jan-6-capitol-breach; Tom Dreisbach, Allison Mollenkamp, "A Former UCLA Student Was Sentenced to over Three Years in Prison for Capitol Riot," NPR, (Oct. 19, 2022), available at https://www.npr.org/2022/10/19/1129912913/a-former-ucla-student-was-sentenced-to-over-three-years-in-prison-for-capitol-ri.

253. "Student Who Attended Charlottesville White Supremacist Rally Leaves Boston University After Backlash," Time, (Aug. 17, 2017), https://time.com/4905939/nicholas-fuentes-white-supremacist-rally-charlottesville/; "Neo-Nazi Hipsters Identity Evropa Exposed In Discord Chat Leak," Unicorn Riot, (Mar. 6, 2019), https://unicornriot.ninja/2019/neo-nazi-hipsters-identity-evropa-exposed-in-discord-chat-leak/.

254. See Statement of Oren Segal, Marilyn Mayo and Morgan Moon, (Mar. 31, 2022); "Groypers Army and 'America First'," Anti-Defamation League, (Mar. 17, 2020), available at https://www.adl.org/reources/backgrounders/groyper-army-and-america-first.

255. See, e.g., Malachi Barrett, "Far-right Activist Who Encouraged U.S. Capitol Occupation also Organized 'Stop the Steal' Rally in Michigan," MLive, (Jan. 7, 2021), available at https://www.mlive.com/politics/2021/01/far-right-activist-who-encouraged-us-capitol-occupation-also-organized-stop-the-steal-rally-in-michigan.html; Studio IKN, "Nick Fuentes at Stop the Steal Phoenix," YouTube, Nov. 29, 2020, available at https://www.youtube.com/watch?v=U_vjzjMDenk.

256. Megan Squire (@MeganSquire0), Twitter, Jan. 5, 2021 10:27 a.m. ET, available at https://twitter.com/MeganSquire0/status/1346478478523125767?s=20.

257. Fuentes personally earned $50,000 from his livestreams between November 3, 2020, and January 19, 2021. He raised his highest-ever total the day after the 2020 election, and he raised similarly high figures on January 5, 2021. Some of Fuentes' proceeds were refunded to customers following Fuentes' ban from DLive. See Statement of Michael Edison Hayden, Megan Squire, Ph.D., Hannah Gais, and Susan Corke, (Apr. 7, 2022), at 6-7.

258. See, Statement of Oren Segal, Marilyn Mayo, and Morgan Moon, (Mar. 31, 2022), at 12.

259. Malachi Barrett, "Far-Right Activist Who Encouraged U.S. Capitol Occupation Also Organized 'Stop the Steal' Rally in Michigan," MLive, (Jan. 7, 2021), available at https://www.mlive.com/politics/2021/01/far-right-activist-who-encouraged-us-capitol-occupation-also-organized-stop-the-steal-rally-in-michigan.html.

260. Chuck Tanner, "Deciphering Nick Fuentes' 'Stop the Steal' Speeches," Institute for Research and Education on Human Rights, (Nov. 24, 2020), available at https://www.justsecurity.org/74622/stopthesteal-timeline-of-social-media-and-extremist-activities-leading-to-1-6-insurrection/.

261. "#StopTheSteal: Timeline of Social Media and Extremist Activities Leading to 1/6 Insurrection," Just Security (Feb. 10, 2021), available at https://www.justsecurity.org/74622/stopthesteal-timeline-of-social-media-and-extremist-activities-leading-to-1-6-insurrection/.

262. Chuck Tanner, "White Nationalists Prominent at 'Stop the Steal' Mobilization in Georgia," Institute for Research and Education on Human Rights," (Nov. 24, 2020), available at

https://www.irehr.org/2020/11/24/white-nationalists-prominent-at-stop-the-steal-mobilization-in-georgia/.

263. Aquarium Groyper, "Nick Fuentes Georgia State Capitol 11/20/2020," YouTube, at 1:38, Nov. 20, 2020, available at https://www.youtube.com/watch?v=OS1f--Tkn1M.

264. Peter White, "MAGA Protestors Chant 'Destroy the GOP' at Pro-Trump Rally," *Rolling Stone*, (Dec. 12, 2020), available at https://www.rollingstone.com/politics/politics-news/protesters-chant-destroy-the-gop-at-pro-trump-rally-1102967/.

265. "Pro-Trump Rallies in DC Attract Extremists & Erupt into Violence," Anti-Defamation League, (Dec. 13, 2020), available at https://www.adl.org/blog/pro-trump-rallies-in-dc-attract-extremists-erupt-into-violence.

266. Megan Squire (@MeganSquire0), Twitter, Jan. 5, 2021 10:27 a.m. ET, available at https://twitter.com/MeganSquire0/status/1346478478523125767?s=20.

267. Patrick Casey (@Patrickcaseyusa), Telegram, Jan. 5, 2021 6:20 p.m.; Documents on file with the Select Committee to Investigate the January 6th Attack on the United States Capitol (Public Source), CTRL0000930909 - CTRL0000930912 (collection of Patrick Casey telegram posts).

268. Mallory Simon and Sara Sidner, "Decoding the Extremist Symbols and Groups at the Capitol Hill Insurrection," CNN, (Jan. 11, 2021), available at https://www.cnn.com/2021/01/09/us/capitol-hill-insurrection-extremist-flags-soh/index.html.

269. Nicholas J. Fuentes (@NickJFuentes), Twitter, Jan. 7, 2021 10:56 a.m. ET, available at https://web.archive.org/web/20210107185745/https://twitter.com/NickJFuentes/status/1347255833516765185 (archived).

270. Nicholas J. Fuentes (@NickJFuentes), Twitter, Jan. 7, 2021 1:03 p.m. ET, available at https://web.archive.org/web/20210107210736/https://twitter.com/NickJFuentes/status/1347287851629764610 (archived).

271. *See* Select Committee to Investigate the January 6th Attack on the United States Capitol, Deposition of Nicholas J. Fuentes, (Feb. 16, 2022).

272. Select Committee to Investigate the January 6th Attack on the United States Capitol, Deposition of Michael Lee Wells, (Apr. 14, 2022), p. 72.

273. Alejandro J. Beutel, Daryl Johnson, "The Three Percenters: A Look Inside an Anti-Government Militia," Newlines Institute for Strategy and Policy, (Feb. 2021), at 8, available at https://newlinesinstitute.org/wp-content/uploads/20210225-Three-Percenter-PR-NISAP-rev051021.pdf; "Three Percenters," Southern Poverty Law Center, available at https://www.splcenter.org/fighting-hate/extremist-files/group/three-percenters.

274. Statement of Oren Segal, Marilyn Mayo, and Morgan Moon, (Mar. 31, 2022), at 12-13.

275. Statement of Oren Segal, Marilyn Mayo, and Morgan Moon, (Mar. 31, 2022), at 13.

276. Statement of Oren Segal, Marilyn Mayo, and Morgan Moon, (Mar. 31, 2022), at 13.

277. Select Committee to Investigate the January 6th Attack on the United States Capitol, Deposition of Jeremy Liggett, (May 17, 2022), pp. 6-7.

278. "Two Texas Men Charged with Assault on Law Enforcement During Jan. 6 Capitol Breach," Department of Justice, (Dec. 14, 2021), available at https://www.justice.gov/usao-dc/pr/two-texas-men-charged-assault-law-enforcement-during-jan-6-capitol-breach.

279. "Texas Man Sentenced to 52 Months in Prison For Assaulting Law Enforcement Officers During Jan. 6 Capitol Breach," Department of Justice, (Sept. 28, 2022), available at https://www.justice.gov/usao-dc/pr/texas-man-sentenced-prison-assaulting-law-enforcement-officers-during-jan-6-capitol.

280. Criminal Complaint at 9, 13, *United States v. Hazard*, No. 1:21-mj-868 (D.D.C. Dec. 7, 2021), ECF No. 1.

281. Criminal Complaint at 8-12, *United States. v. Hazard*, No. 1:21-mj-868 (D.D.C. Dec. 7, 2021), ECF No. 1. For example, Denney told Hazard that they "will need linking up with the proud

boys." *Id.*, at 8. Denney described the hotel he booked as "the same place everyone else is getting in the Proud Boys crew and other militia's until it gets full." *Id.*, at 9. In a separate post on Facebook, Denney stated that the Patriot Boys of North Texas were "allied with the Patriot Prayer and the Proud Boys." *Id.*, at 9. In another Facebook message on December 29, Denney wrote: "We are linking up with thousands of Proud Boys and other militia that will be there. This is going to be huge. And it's going to be a fight." *Id.*, at 10. Similarly, Hazard wrote on Facebook: "I belong to a militia group that's affiliated with the proud boys" and "We're affiliated with the proud boys which have folks of all races as there's several thousand members." *Id.*, at 12.

282. Criminal Complaint at 8, *United States. v. Hazard*, No. 1:21-mj-868 (D.D.C. Dec. 7, 2021), ECF No. 1.

283. Criminal Complaint at 10, *United States. v. Hazard*, No. 1:21-mj-868 (D.D.C. Dec. 7, 2021), ECF No. 1.

284. Criminal Complaint at 11, *United States. v. Hazard*, No. 1:21-mj-868 (D.D.C. Dec. 7, 2021), ECF No. 1. Hazard also echoed this idea. *Id.*, at 14.

285. Criminal Complaint at 10-11, *United States. v. Hazard*, No. 1:21-mj-868 (D.D.C. Dec. 7, 2021), ECF No. 1.

286. Criminal Complaint at 10, *United States. v. Hazard*, No. 1:21-mj-868 (D.D.C. Dec. 7, 2021), ECF No. 1.

287. Criminal Complaint at 12, *United States. v. Hazard*, No. 1:21-mj-868 (D.D.C. Dec. 7, 2021), ECF No. 1.

288. Criminal Complaint at 12, *United States. v. Hazard*, No. 1:21-mj-868 (D.D.C. Dec. 7, 2021), ECF No. 1.

289. Criminal Complaint at 16, *United States. v. Hazard*, No. 1:21-mj-868 (D.D.C. Dec. 7, 2021), ECF No. 1.

290. Statement of Facts at 2, *United States v. Cole et al.*, No. 1:22-mj-184-RMM (D.D.C. Aug, 29, 2022), ECF No. 5-1

291. Statement of Facts at 2, *United States v. Cole et al.*, No. 1:22-mj-184, (D.D.C. Aug. 29, 2022), ECF No. 5-1.

292. Statement of Facts at 4, *United States v. Cole et al.*, No. 1:22-mj-184, (D.D.C. Aug. 29, 2022), ECF No. 5-1.

293. Statement of Facts at 4, *United States v. Cole et al.*, No. 1:22-mj-184, (D.D.C. Aug. 29, 2022), ECF No. 5-1.

294. Statement of Facts at 4, *United States v. Cole et al.*, No. 1:22-mj-184, (D.D.C. Aug. 29, 2022), ECF No. 5-1.

295. Statement of Facts at 28, *United States v. Cole et al.*, No. 1:22-mj-184, (D.D.C. Aug. 29, 2022), ECF No. 5-1.

296. Statement of Facts at 5, *United States v. Cole et al.*, No. 1:22-mj-184, (D.D.C. Aug. 29, 2022), ECF No. 5-1.

297. Select Committee to Investigate the January 6th Attack on the United States Capitol, Deposition of Jeremy Liggett, (May 17, 2022), pp. 50-51.

298. Statement of Facts at 28, *United States v. Cole et al.*, No. 1:22-mj-184, (D.D.C. Aug. 29, 2022), ECF No. 5-1; #SeditionHunters (@SeditionHunters), Twitter, June 7, 2021 2:11 p.m. ET, available at https://twitter.com/SeditionHunters/status/1401965056980627458.

299. Statement of Facts at 5-6, *United States v. Cole et al.*, No. 1:22-mj-184, (D.D.C. Aug. 29, 2022), ECF No. 5-1; #SeditionHunters (@SeditionHunters), Twitter, June 7, 2021 2:11 p.m. ET, available at https://twitter.com/SeditionHunters/status/1401965056980627458.

300. "Five Florida Men Arrested on Charges for Actions During Jan. 6 Capitol Breach," United States Department of Justice, (Aug. 24, 2022) available at https://www.justice.gov/usao-dc/pr/five-florida-men-arrested-charges-actions-during-jan-6-capitol-breach.

301. Indictment Dated June 9, 2021 at 1, *United States v. Hostetter et. al.*, No. 1:1:21-cr-392 (D.D.C. June 9, 2021); Michael Kunzelman, "Capitol Rioter Used Charity to Promote Violence, Feds Say," *Associated Press*, (June 16, 2021), available at https://apnews.com/article/donald-trump-joe-biden-riots-health-coronavirus-pandemic-71a7b8121b6f70016f7cab601021a989.

302. Indictment at ¶ 38, *United States v. Hostetter et al.*, No. 1:21-cr-392 (D.D.C. June 9, 2021), ECF No. 1.

303. *Indictment at 7, United States v. Hostetter et al.*, No. 1:21-cr-392 (D.D.C. June 9, 2021), ECF No. 1.

304. Indictment at 7, *United States v. Hostetter et al.*, No. 1:21-cr-392 (D.D.C. June 9, 2021), ECF No. 1.

305. Indictment at 8, *United States v. Hostetter et al.*, No. 1:21-cr-392 (D.D.C. June 9, 2021), ECF No. 1.

306. Indictment at 9, *United States v. Hostetter et al.*, No. 1:21-cr-392 (D.D.C. June 9, 2021), ECF No. 1.

307. Indictment at 8-11, *United States v. Hostetter et al.*, No. 1:21-cr-392 (D.D.C. June 9, 2021), ECF No. 1.

308. Indictment at 8-11, *United States v. Hostetter et al.*, No. 1:21-cr-392 (D.D.C. June 9, 2021), ECF No. 1.

309. Indictment at 12, *United States v. Hostetter et al.*, No. 1:21-cr-392 (D.D.C. June 9, 2021), ECF No. 1.

310. The National Council and The Three Percenters - Original, "TTPO Stance on Election Fraud," Dec. 16, 2020, available at http://archive.ph/YemCC (archived).

311. *See* post by username @hatdonuts2, patriots.win, December 29, 2020, 7:56 p.m. ET, available at https://patriots.win/p/11RO2hdyR2/x/c/4DrwV8RcV1s; Statement of Facts at 7-8, *United States v. Buxton*, No. 1:21-cr-739 (D.D.C. Dec. 8, 2021), ECF No. 1-1.

312. Select Committee to Investigate the January 6th Attack on the United States Capitol, Deposition of Josh Ellis, (May 19, 2022), p. 38.

313. "Lone Capitol Police Officer Eugene Goodman Diverts Capitol Rioters," *Washington Post*, (Jan. 11, 2021). available at https://www.washingtonpost.com/video/national/lone-capitol-police-officer-eugene-goodman-diverts-capitol-rioters/2021/01/11/ba67a5e8-5f9b-4a9a-a7b7-93549f6a81b3_video.html

314. Scott MacFarlane and Gillian Morley, "QAnon Follower Doug Jensen Convicted on All Jan. 6 Charges," CBS News, (Sept. 23, 2022), available at https://www.cbsnews.com/news/qanon-follower-doug-jensen-convicted-on-all-jan-6-charges/.

315. Interview of: Douglas Austin Jensen Dated Jan. 8, 2021 at 19, *United States v. Jensen*, No. 1:21-cr-6 (D.D.C., Apr. 8, 2022), ECF No. 69-1.

316. Statement of Mike Rothschild, (Mar. 23, 2022), at 12.

317. Statement of Mike Rothschild, (Mar. 23, 2022), at 2-3.

318. "QAnon," Anti-Defamation League, (May 4, 2020), available at https://www.adl.org/resources/backgrounder/qanon.

319. Kelly Weill, "QAnon's Home 8kun is Imploding - and Q Has Gone Silent," *Daily Beast*, (Nov. 13, 2020), available at https://www.thedailybeast.com/qanons-home-8kun-is-implodingand-q-has-gone-silent?ref=scroll.

320. "Remarks by President Trump in Press Briefing," White House, (Aug. 19, 2020), available at https://trumpwhitehouse.archives.gov/briefings-statements/remarks-president-trump-press-briefing-august-19-2020/.

321. NBC News, "Trump Denounces White Supremacy, Sidesteps Question on QAnon," YouTube, at 1:32, 2:34, Oct. 15, 2020, available at https://youtu.be/3hybkzCWb_w.

322.   Ben Collins, "QAnon's Dominion Voter Fraud Conspiracy Theory Reaches the President,"
       NBC News, (Nov. 13, 2020), available at https://www.nbcnews.com/tech/tech-news/q-
       fades-qanon-s-dominion-voter-fraud-conspiracy-theory-reaches-n1247780; National Conta-
       gion Research Institute, "The QAnon Conspiracy: Destroying Families, Dividing
       Communities, Undermining Democracy," p. 20, available at https://networkcontagion.us/
       wp-content/uploads/NCRI-%E2%80%93-The-QAnon-Conspiracy-FINAL.pdf.

323.   Donald J. Trump (@realdonaldtrump), Twitter, Nov. 19, 2020 12:41 a.m. ET and 3:47 p.m. ET,
       available at https://www.thetrumparchive.com/?searchbox=%22Dominion-
       izing+the+Vote%22 (archived).

324.   One America News Network, "Cyber Analyst on Dominion Voting: Shocking Vulnerabilities,"
       YouTube, at 0:45, Nov. 15, 2020, available at https://youtu.be/eKcPoCNW8AA.

325.   Select Committee to Investigate the January 6th Attack on the United States Capitol, Depo-
       sition of James Watkins, (June 6, 2022), p. 11. Watkins denied under oath that either he or
       his son Ron are "Q." Id., at 38, 122.

326.   Donald J. Trump (@realdonaldtrump), Twitter, Dec. 15, 2020 12:32 a.m. ET, available at
       https://www.thetrumparchive.com/?searchbox=%22Soon-to-be+AG+Rosen+recently+
       wrote+an+essay+on+foreign+influence+in+US+elections.+foreign+actors+are+covertly+
       trying+to%22 (archived).

327.   President Donald J. Trump, "Tweets of January 3, 2021," The American Presidency Project,
       available at, available at https://www.presidency.ucsb.edu/documents/tweets-january-3-
       2021 (archived).

328.   Select Committee to Investigate the January 6th Attack on the United States Capitol, Depo-
       sition of James Watkins, (June 6, 2022), p. 77; Select Committee to Investigate the January
       6th Attack on the United States Capitol, Deposition of Jody Williams, (June 7, 2022), p. 67
       (noting, as the then-owner of TheDonald.win, that President Trump's December 19th tweet
       was "everywhere," including with "Q people.").

329.   Select Committee to Investigate the January 6th Attack on the United States Capitol, Depo-
       sition of James Watkins, (June 6, 2022), pp. 74, 76.

330.   Statement of Offense at 3, United States v. Munn, No. 1:21-cr-474 (D.D.C. May 13, 2022), ECF
       No. 78.

331.   Statement of Facts at 3, United States v. Chansley, No. 1:21-cr-3 (D.D.C. Jan. 8, 2021), ECF No.
       1-1.

332.   Select Committee to Investigate the January 6th Attack on the United States Capitol, Depo-
       sition of Elmer Stewart Rhodes, (Feb. 2, 2022), p. 162.

333.   See, e.g., Trial Exhibit 6860 (1.S.656.9257), United States v. Rhodes et al., No. 1:22-cr-15
       (D.D.C. Oct. 13, 2022) (Rhodes messaging an Oath Keepers chat that "Let's adopt the Q slo-
       gan of WWG1WGA. Where We Go One, We Go All. We nullify TOGETHER We defy TOGETHER.
       We resist TOGETHER We defend TOGETHER. They come for one of us, they come for all of
       us. When they come for us, we go for them. When they strike at our leaders, we strike at
       their leaders. This is the path of the Founders. It's what they did."); Trial Exhibit 4064,
       United States v. Rhodes et al., No. 1:22-cr-15 (D.D.C. Oct. 6, 2022) (printout of December 23,
       2020, open letter to President Trump posted by Stewart Rhodes on the Oath Keeper web-
       site, imploring the President to invoke the Insurrection Act to prevent a communist take-
       over of the United States through the inauguration of Joe Biden).

334.   Select Committee to Investigate the January 6th Attack on the United States Capitol, Tran-
       scribed Interview of Nick Quested, (Apr. 5, 2022), p. 53.

335.   Ben Collins and Brandy Zadrozny, "Extremists Made Little Secret of Ambitions to 'Occupy'
       Capitol in Weeks Before Attack," NBC News, (Jan. 8, 2021), available at https://
       www.nbcnews.com/tech/internet/extremists-made-little-secret-ambitions-occupy-capital-
       weeks-attack-n1253499.

336. Kari Paul, Luke Harding and Severin Carrell, "Far-Right Website 8kun Again Loses Internet Service Protection Following Capitol Attack," *The Guardian*, (Jan. 15, 2021), available at https://www.theguardian.com/technology/2021/jan/15/8kun-8chan-capitol-breach-violence-isp.

337. Ben Collins and Brandy Zadrozny, "Extremists Made Little Secret of Ambitions to 'Occupy' Capitol in Weeks Before Attack," NBC News, (Jan. 8, 2021), available at https://www.nbcnews.com/tech/internet/extremists-made-little-secret-ambitions-occupy-capital-weeks-attack-n1253499.

338. Post by username r3deleven, "Trump Tweet. Daddy Says Be In DC On Jan. 6th," Patriots.Win, Dec. 19, 2020, available at https://web.archive.org/web/20210105024826/https://thedonald.win/p/11R4q2aptJ/trump-tweet-daddy-says-be-in-dc-/c/ (archived).

339. "How a Trump Tweet Sparked Plots, Strategizing to 'Storm and Occupy' Capitol with 'Hand-cuffs and Zip Ties'," SITE Intelligence Group, (Jan. 9, 2021), available at https://ent.siteintelgroup.com/Far-Right-/-Far-Left-Threat/how-a-trump-tweet-sparked-plots-strategizing-to-storm-and-occupy-capitol-with-handcuffs-and-zip-ties.html.

340. "How a Trump Tweet Sparked Plots, Strategizing to 'Storm and Occupy' Capitol with 'Hand-cuffs and Zip Ties'," SITE Intelligence Group, (Jan. 9, 2021), available at https://ent.siteintelgroup.com/Far-Right-/-Far-Left-Threat/how-a-trump-tweet-sparked-plots-strategizing-to-storm-and-occupy-capitol-with-handcuffs-and-zip-ties.html.

341. Select Committee to Investigate the January 6th Attack on the United States Capitol, Deposition of Jody Williams, (June 7, 2022), p. 72.

342. Ryan Goodman and Justin Hendrix, "The Absence of 'The Donald'," Just Security, (Dec. 6, 2021), available at https://www.justsecurity.org/79446/the-absence-of-the-donald/.

343. Amrita Khalid, "Donald Trump Participated in a Reddit AMA, but not Much of Anything was Revealed," *Daily Dot*, (July 27, 2016), available at https://www.dailydot.com/debug/donald-trump-reddit-ama-fail/.

344. Memorandum from Select Committee to Investigate the January 6th Attack on the United States Capitol, Briefing with Reddit, (May 19, 2022); Mike Isaac, "Reddit, Acting Against Hate Speech, Bans 'The_Donald' Subreddit," *New York Times*, (Jan. 29, 2020, Updated Jan. 27, 2021), available at https://www.nytimes.com/2020/06/29/technology/reddit-hate-speech.html.

345. Select Committee to Investigate the January 6th Attack on the United States Capitol, Deposition of Jody Williams, (June 7, 2022), pp. 31-32. In fact, Williams testified that he and other moderators had the opportunity to advertise the new website on Reddit for months. *See id.*, at 32-33. This gave TheDonald.win "immediate" access to "hundreds of thousands of people" who used the Reddit forum. *See id.*, at 33.

346. Ben Schreckinger, "World War Meme: How a Group of Anonymous Keyboard Commandos Conquered the Internet for Donald Trump and Plans to Deliver Europe to the Far Right," *Politico Magazine*, (Mar./Apr. 2017), available at https://www.politico.com/magazine/story/2017/03/memes-4chan-trump-supporters-trolls-internet-214856/.

347. Ben Schreckinger, "World War Meme: How a Group of Anonymous Keyboard Commandos Conquered the Internet for Donald Trump and Plans to Deliver Europe to the Far Right," *Politico Magazine*, (Mar./Apr. 2017), available at https://www.politico.com/magazine/story/2017/03/memes-4chan-trump-supporters-trolls-internet-214856/.

348. Daniella Silva, "President Trump Tweets Wrestling Video of Himself Attacking 'CNN'," NBC News, (July 2, 2017), available at https://www.nbcnews.com/politics/donald-trump/president-trump-tweets-wwe-video-himself-attacking-cnn-n779031.

349. Justin Hendrix, "TheDonald.win and President Trump's Foreknowledge of the Attack on the Capitol," Just Security, (Jan. 12, 2021), available at https://www.justsecurity.org/79813/thedonald-win-and-president-trumps-foreknowledge-of-the-attack-on-the-capitol/.

350. Andrew Restuccia, Daniel Lippman, and Eliana Johnson, "'Get Scavino in Here': Trump's Twitter Guru is the Ultimate Insider," *Politico*, (May 16, 2019), available at https://www.politico.com/story/2019/05/16/trump-scavino-1327921.

351. H. Rept. 117-284, Resolution Recommending that the House of Representatives Find Peter K. Navarro and Daniel Scavino, Jr., in Contempt of Congress for Refusal to Comply with a Subpoena Duly Issued by the Select Committee to Investigate the January 6th Attack on the United States Capitol, 117th Cong., 2d Sess. (2022), available at https://www.congress.gov/117/crpt/hrpt284/CRPT-117hrpt284.pdf.

352. Justin Hendrix, "TheDonald.win and President Trump's Foreknowledge of the Attack on the Capitol," Just Security, (Jan. 12, 2021), available at https://www.justsecurity.org/79813/thedonald-win-and-president-trumps-foreknowledge-of-the-attack-on-the-capitol/.

353. Post, "If we occupy the capitol building, there will be no vote," Patriots.Win, available at https://patriots.win/p/11Rh1RiP9l/if-we-occupy-the-capitol-buildin/.

354. Post by username REDMARAUDER, "The media will call us evil if we have to occupy the Capitol Building on January 6th. Let them," Patriots.Win, Jan. 2, 2021, available at https://patriots.win/p/11ROC9U7EM/the-media-will-call-us-evil-if-w/.

355. Post by username Sharker, "THIS IS NOT A RALLY OR PROTEST. We are all here for the sole purpose of correcting this ILLEGAL election. Surround the enemy and do NOT LET THEM LEAVE until this mess is cleaned up with Trump being re-admitted for 4 more years. SACK UP PATRIOTS." Patriots.Win, Jan. 5, 2021, available at https://patriots.win/p/11Rh1WGo3K/this-is-not-a-rally-or-protest-w/c/.

356. Ben Schreckinger, "World War Meme: How a Group of Anonymous Keyboard Commandos Conquered the Internet for Donald Trump—and Plans to Deliver Europe to the Far Right," *Politico Magazine*, (March/April 2017) available at https://www.politico.com/magazine/story/2017/03/memes-4chan-trump-supporters-trolls-internet-214856.

357. "How a Trump Tweet Sparked Plots, Strategizing to 'Storm and Occupy' Capitol with 'Handcuffs and Zip Ties'," SITE Intelligence Group, (Jan. 9, 2021), available at https://ent.siteintelgroup.com/Far-Right-/-Far-Left-Threat/how-a-trump-tweet-sparked-plots-strategizing-to-storm-and-occupy-capitol-with-handcuffs-and-zip-ties.html.

358. Alex Thomas, "Team Trump Was in Bed With Online Insurrectionists before He Was Even Elected," *Daily Dot*, (Jan. 15, 2021), available at https://www.dailydot.com/debug/dan-scavino-reddit-donald-trump-disinformation/.

359. Alex Jones, "Team Trump Was in Bed With Online Insurrectionists before He Was Even Elected," *Daily Dot*, (Jan. 15, 2021), available at https://www.dailydot.com/debug/dan-scavino-reddit-donald-trump-disinformation/.

360. Post by username wartooth6, "Gallows are simpler and more cost effective, plus they're an American old west tradition too," Patriots.Win, Dec. 22, 2020, available at https://patriots.win/p/11RNfN5v3p/gallows-are-simpler-and-more-cos/c/.

361. Post by username psybrnaut, "Builder Pedes…Let's construct a Gallows outside the Capitol Building next Wednesday so the Congressmen watching from their office windows shit their Pants…," Patriots.Win, Dec. 30, 2020, available at https://patriots.win/p/11RO2pYG2P/builder-pedes-lets-construct-a-g/c/.

362. Post by username TacticalGeorge, "Building a hanging platform in front of Congress on the 6 should send a strong message," Patriots.Win, Dec. 30, 2020, available at https://patriots.win/p/11RO2oQy77/building-a-hanging-platform-in-f/.

363. Post by username Krunchi, "The One Thing You Must Know Before Going To DC on The 6th…," Patriots.Win, Jan. 3, 2021, available at https://web.archive.org/web/20210105080829/https://thedonald.win/p/11ROGmlHG5/the-one-thing-you-must-know-befo/ (archived).

364. Post by username Badradness, "We will be building a gallows right in front of the Capitol so the traitors know the stakes. I'm driving up in a sedan but if a patriot with a pickup will assist I'm down to spend from my credit line at Home Depot for all of the supplies needed

for this. Driving up Monday night or early Tuesday.," Patriots.Win, Jan. 3, 2021, available at https://patriots.win/p/11ROGrJPVQ/we-will-be-building-a-gallows-ri/c/.

365. Post by username AFLP, "Gallows on the Capitol Lawn," Patriots.Win, Jan. 5, 2021, available at https://patriots.win/p/11RhArKEQ3/gallows-on-the-capitol-lawn/.

366. Documents on File with the Select Committee to Investigate the January 6th Attack on the United States Capitol, (Mark Meadows Production), MM014441; Select Committee to Investigate the January 6th Attack on the United States Capitol, Deposition of Jason Miller, (Feb. 3, 2022), pp. 209.

367. See Select Committee to Investigate the January 6th Attack on the United States Capitol, Deposition of Jason Miller, (Feb. 3, 2022), Exhibit 45, pp. 4, 13. In his testimony to the Select Committee, Miller denied reading such comments and claimed not to recall whether Meadows had followed up with him about the thread. However, Miller did say that "sometimes" he would "click and see what people are saying" on sites like TheDonald.win, if he received a Google alert about himself. Select Committee to Investigate the January 6th Attack on the United States Capitol, Deposition of Jason Miller, (Feb. 3, 2022), pp. 209, 212, 214.

368. Select Committee to Investigate the January 6th Attack on the United States Attack on the United States Capitol, Deposition of Jason Miller, (Feb. 3, 2022), p. 209, Exhibit 47.

369. Donald J. Trump (@realDonaldTrump), Twitter, Dec. 19, 2020 1:24 p.m. ET, available at https://twitter.com/realDonaldTrump/status/1340362336390004737.

370. Justin Hendrix, "TheDonald.win and President Trumps Foreknowledge of the Attack on the Capitol," Just Security, (Jan. 12, 2021), available at https://www.justsecurity.org/79813/thedonald-win-and-president-trumps-foreknowledge-of-the-attack-on-the-capitol/.

371. Lena V. Groeger, Jeff Kao, Al Shaw, Moiz Syed, and Maya Eliahou, "What Parler Saw During the Attack on the Capitol," Pro Publica, at 12:05 p.m. ET at 0:30, Jan. 17, 2021, available, https://projects.propublica.org/parler-capitol-videos/; Statement of Catherine A. Sanderson, Ph.D., (June 3, 2022), at 5.

372. Through review of public records, the Select Committee identified organizers for about a dozen events scheduled for January 5th or 6th secured permits from either the U.S. Capitol Police (USCP) or National Park Service (NPS). Except for two events—one unrelated to January 6th and the other put on by a group that regularly held demonstrations around D.C.— all of the applications were submitted after President Trump's December 19th tweet. The three most important events were: Cindy Chafian's January 5th event at Freedom Plaza (using the group name "The Eighty Percent Coalition"); WFAF's January 6th event at the Ellipse; and Ali Alexander's January 6th event on the Capitol grounds (under the "One Nation Under God" moniker). In addition to the permits issued to WFAF, Cindy Chafian, and Ali Alexander (under the "One Nation Under God" moniker), at least nine additional permits were issued by USCP or NPS for events in Washington, D.C., on January 5, 2021 or January 6, 2021.

373. Documents on file with the Select Committee to Investigate the January 6th Attack on the United States Capitol (Department of the Interior Production), DOI_46000428_00005162 (Dec. 19, 2020, Cindy Chafian email Re: Status of application - Women for America First at 7:12 AM).

374. Documents on file with the Select Committee to Investigate the January 6th Attack on the United States Capitol (Department of the Interior Production), DOI_46000428_00005162 (Dec. 19, 2020, Cindy Chafian email Re: Status of application - Women for America First at 7:12 AM).

375. Select Committee to Investigate the January 6th Attack on the United States Capitol, Transcribed Interview of Kylie Kremer, (Jan. 12, 2022), p. 5.

376. Select Committee to Investigate the January 6th Attack on the United States Capitol, Transcribed Interview of Amy Kremer, (Feb. 18, 2022), pp. 8-10.

377. Select Committee to Investigate the January 6th Attack on the United States Capitol, Transcribed Interview of Amy Kremer, (Feb. 18, 2022), pp. 8-10.

378. Women for America First, "March for Trump Bus Tour," trumpmarch.com, available at https://web.archive.org/web/20201226001527/https://trumpmarch.com/..

379. Kylie Jane Kremer (@KylieJaneKremer), Twitter, Dec. 19, 2020 3:50 p.m. ET, available at https://twitter.com/kyliejanekremer/status/1340399063875895296?lang=en.

380. Women For America First Ellipse Public Gathering Permit, National Park Service, available at https://www.nps.gov/aboutus/foia/upload/21-0278-Women-for-America-First-Ellispse-permit_REDACTED.pdf.

381. Select Committee to Investigate the January 6th Attack on the United States Capitol, Deposition of Ali Alexander, (Dec. 9, 2021), p. 15.

382. Documents on file with the Select Committee to Investigate the January 6th Attack on the United States Capitol (Resource Group Production), CTRL0000010113 (Dec. 19, 2020, Ali Alexandra text message to Stephen Brown at 10:49 a.m.).

383. Documents on file with the Select Committee to Investigate the January 6th Attack on the United States Capitol (Resource Group Production), CTRL0000010113 (Dec. 19, 2020, Ali Alexandra text message to Stephen Brown at 10:49 a.m.).

384. "Valuation and Analysis," WildProtest.com, (Jan. 14, 2021 (last updated)), available at https://wildprotest.com.siteindices.com/.

385. "President Trump Wants You in DC January 6," WildProtest.com, (Dec 19.2020), available at https://web.archive.org/web/20201223062953/http://wildprotest.com/ (archived).

386. Select Committee to Investigate the January 6th Attack on the United States Capitol, Transcribed Interview of Arina Grossu, (Apr. 29, 2022), p. 40.

387. Statement of Andrew J. Seidel, (Mar. 18, 2022), at 11, 13.

388. Documents on file with the Select Committee to Investigate the January 6th Attack on the United States Capitol (Arina Grossu Production), Grossu_01_002721 (Dec. 19, 2020, Rob Weaver email message to Arina Grossu at 8:20 a.m. CT).

389. Documents on file with the Select Committee to Investigate the January 6th Attack on the United States Capitol, (Arina Grossu Production), Arina Grossu Exhibit 20 (Jericho March Rally registration page).

390. Select Committee to Investigate the January 6th Attack on the United States Capitol, Informal Interview of Marsha Lessard, (Dec. 10, 2021); *see also* Documents on file with the Select Committee to Investigate the January 6th Attack on the United States Capitol (Capitol Police Production), CTRL0000001834 (Permit Relating to Demonstration Activities on United States Capitol Grounds for Virginia Freedom Keepers, No. 20-12-25).

391. . *See* Superseding Indictment at ¶ 37, *United States v. Rhodes et al.*, No. 1:22-cr-15 (D.D.C. June 22, 2022) (noting that Stewart Rhodes, President of the Oath Keepers, shipped weapons to Lessard's home in Virginia before his arrival in DC for January 6th); Select Committee to Investigate the January 6th Attack on the United States Capitol, Deposition of Kellye SoRelle, (Apr. 13, 2022), p. 180.

392. *See* Select Committee to Investigate the January 6th Attack on the United States Capitol, Deposition of Henry Tarrio, (Feb. 4, 2021), p. 117 (testifying that Gracia arranged a White House tour for him in December 2020).

393. Latinos for Trump (@Officiallft2021), Twitter, Dec. 27, 2020 7:58 p.m., available at https://twitter.com/i/web/status/1343360740313321474.

394. Documents on file with the Select Committee to Investigate the January 6th Attack on the United States Capitol, (Nathan Martin Production), NMartin0318 (December 30, 2020, email from Kimberly Fletcher of Moms for America to Ali Alexander and Nathan Martin re: MFA VIP list for White House); Documents on file with the Select Committee to Investigate the January 6th Attack on the United States Capitol (Resource Group Production),

CTRL0000010100 (December 27, 2020, text messages between Nathan Martin, Stephen Martin, Kimberly Fletcher, and Ali Alexander discussing permitting); Documents on file with the Select Committee to Investigate the January 6th Attack on the United States Capitol (Capitol Police Production), CTRL0000000086, CTRL0000000086.0001 (December 23, 2020, Special Event Assessment identifying Fletcher as a speaker at the "Wild Protest" event during the same time as MFA's permitted event in a different area).

395. "The Alex Jones Show," Prison Planet TV, at 10:07, Dec. 20, 2020, available at http://tv.infowars.com/index/display/id/11151.

396. Documents on file with the Select Committee to Investigate the January 6th Attack on the United States Capitol, (T-Mobile Production, Nov. 19, 2021).

397. Select Committee to Investigate the January 6th Attack on the United States Capitol, Informal Interview of Cynthia "Cindy" Chafian (Nov. 1-2, 2021).

398. *See*, Beth Reinhard, Jaqueline Alemany, and Josh Dawsey, "Low-Profile Heiress Who 'Played a Strong Role' in Financing Jan. 6 Rally is Thrust Into Spotlight," *Washington Post*, (Dec. 8, 2021), available at https://www.washingtonpost.com/investigations/publix-heiress-capitol-insurrection-fancelli/2021/12/08/5144fe1c-5219-11ec-8ad5-b5c50c1fb4d9_story.html.

399. Documents on File with the Select Committee to Investigate the January 6th Attack on the United States Capitol (Julia Fancelli Production), REL0000000994, (Bank Statements for Julia Fancelli at the Bank of Central Florida from December 10, 2020, to January 10, 2021).

400. Select Committee to Investigate the January 6th Attack on the United States Capitol, Deposition of Caroline Wren, (Dec. 17, 2021), p. 58.

401. Documents on file with the Select Committee to Investigate the January 6th Attack on the United States Capitol, (Verizon Production, Feb. 9, 2022).

402. Select Committee to Investigate the January 6th Attack on the United States Capitol, Deposition of Caroline Wren, (Dec. 17, 2021), pp. 45-46.

403. Select Committee to Investigate the January 6th Attack on the United States Capitol, Deposition of Caroline Wren, (Dec. 17, 2021), p. 71.

404. Documents on file with the Select Committee to Investigate the January 6th Attack on the United States Capitol, (Verizon Production, Feb. 9, 2022).

405. Documents on file with the Select Committee to Investigate the January 6th Attack on the United States Capitol (Caroline Wren Production), REVU_000014 (January 4 - 6, 2021, Fancelli Budget & Trip Plan).

406. Documents on file with the Select Committee to Investigate the January 6th Attack on the United States Capitol (Caroline Wren Production), REVU_000005 (December 27, 2020, Kylie Kremer e-mail to Caroline Wren at 11:25 am).

407. Documents on file with the Select Committee to Investigate the January 6th Attack on the United States Capitol (Caroline Wren Production), REVU_000468 (December 27, 2020, Caroline Wren text message thread with Alex Jones).

408. Documents on file with the Select Committee to Investigate the January 6th Attack on the United States Capitol (Caroline Wren Production), REVU_000550 (Dec. 27, 2020, Caroline Wren text messages with Cindy Chafian).

409. Select Committee to Investigate the January 6th Attack on the United States Capitol, Deposition of Caroline Wren, (Dec. 17, 2021), pp. 50, 70-71.

410. Documents on file with the Select Committee to Investigate the January 6th Attack on the United States Capitol (Caroline Wren Production), REVU_000014 (January 4 - 6, 2021, Fancelli Budget & Trip Plan

411. Documents on file with the Select Committee to Investigate the January 6th Attack on the United States Capitol (Caroline Wren Production), REVU_000014 (January 4 - 6, 2021, Fancelli Budget & Trip Plan

412. Documents on file with the Select Committee to Investigate the January 6th Attack on the United States Capitol (Caroline Wren Production), REVU_000482 (December 29, 2020, Caroline Wren text message to Ali Alexander at 4:19 p.m.).

413. Documents on file with the Select Committee to Investigate the January 6th Attack on the United States Capitol (Caroline Wren Production), REVU_000482 (December 29, 2020, Caroline Wren text message to Ali Alexander at 4:19 pm).

414. Kathleen Ronayne and Michael Kunzelman, "Trump to Far-Right Extremists: `Stand Back and Stand By,'" *Associated Press*, (Sept. 30, 2020), available at https://apnews.com/article/ election-2020-joe-biden-race-and-ethnicity-donald-trump-chris-wallace- 0b32339da25fbc9e8b7c7c7066a1db0f.

415. Donald J. Trump (@realDonaldTrump), Twitter, Dec. 27, 2020 5:51 p.m. ET, available at https://www.thetrumparchive.com (archived).

416. Select Committee to Investigate the January 6th Attack on the United States Capitol, Deposition of Justin Caporale, (Mar. 1, 2022), pp. 20-21.

417. *See* Select Committee to Investigate the January 6th Attack on the United States Capitol, Transcribed Interview of Donald Trump, Jr., (May 3, 2022), p.30; Anthony Man, "At Trump Golf Club in West Palm Beach, Roger Stone Thanks President for Pardon," *Orlando Sun Sentinel*, (Dec. 28, 2020), available at https://www.sun-sentinel.com/news/politics/ elections/fl-ne-roger-stone-thanks-trump-pardon-20201228-2ejqzv6e7vhyvf26cxz6e6jysa- story.html.

418. Documents on file with the Select Committee to Investigate the January 6th Attack on the United States Capitol, (AT&T Production, Dec. 17, 2021).

419. Documents on file with the Select Committee to Investigate the January 6th Attack on the United States Capitol (Caroline Wren Production), REVU_000444, pp. 1-3 (December 27, 2020, text message from Caroline Wren to Kimberly Guilfoyle at 7:10 p.m.).

420. As revealed in the phone records for the personal cell phones of Max Miller and Anthony Ornato. *See* Documents on file with the Select Committee to Investigate the January 6th Attack on the United States Capitol, (Verizon Production, Dec. 17, 2021); Documents on file with the Select Committee to Investigate the January 6th Attack on the United States Capitol (Verizon Production, Sep. 23, 2022). The Select Committee also subpoenaed the phone records for the personal cell phones of Robert Peede, Mark Meadows, Dan Scavino, and Justin Caporale. They each filed lawsuits to block the respective phone companies' production of the phone records, which were still pending at the time of writing. Thus, there may have been additional relevant phone calls among or involving these four of which the Select Committee is not aware.

421. Select Committee to Investigate the January 6th Attack on the United States Capitol, Deposition of Max Miller, (Jan. 20, 2022), pp. 36-37.

422. Select Committee to Investigate the January 6th Attack on the United States Capitol, Deposition of Justin Caporale, (Mar. 1, 2020), p. 44; Documents on file with the Select Committee to Investigate the January 6th Attack on the United States Capitol (Caroline Wren Production), REVU_0644 (December 29, 2020, text messages with Justin Caporale).

423. Select Committee to Investigate the January 6th Attack on the United States Capitol, Transcribed Interview of Katrina Pierson, (Mar. 25, 2022), pp. 79-82; Documents on file with the Select Committee to Investigate the January 6th Attack on the United States Capitol (Caroline Wren Production), REVU_0181 (January 2nd email from Katrina Pierson to Caroline Wren and Taylor Budowich).

424. Select Committee to Investigate the January 6th Attack on the United States Capitol, Transcribed Interview of Cassidy Hutchinson, (Feb. 23, 2022), pp. 32-33, 41; Select Committee to Investigate the January 6th Attack on the United States Capitol, Continued Interview of Cassidy Hutchinson, (June 20, 2022), pp. 107-08, 135.

425. Select Committee to Investigate the January 6th Attack on the United States Capitol, Transcribed Interview of Cassidy Hutchinson, (Feb. 23, 2022), p. 42.

426. Select Committee to Investigate the January 6th Attack on the United States Capitol, Transcribed Interview of Cassidy Hutchinson, (Feb. 23, 2022), pp. 44-45, 47, 52-54; Select Committee to Investigate the January 6th Attack on the United States Capitol, Continued Interview of Cassidy Hutchinson, (June 20, 2022), p. 87.

427. Documents on file with the Select Committee to Investigate the January 6th Attack on the United States Capitol (Kylie Kremer Production), KKremer5447, p. 3 (January 4, 2021, text message from Kylie Kremer to Mike Lindell at 9:32 a.m.).

428. Documents on file with the Select Committee to Investigate the January 6th Attack on the United States Capitol (Ali Alexander Production), CTRL0000017718, p. 41 (January 5, 2021 text message with Liz Willis at 7:19 a.m.).

429. *See* Select Committee to Investigate the January 6th Attack on the United States Capitol, Transcribed Interview of Katrina Pierson, (Mar. 25, 2022), pp. 120-21.

430. Select Committee to Investigate the January 6th Attack on the United States Capitol, Transcribed Interview of Katrina Pierson, (Mar. 25, 2022), p. 121.

431. Select Committee to Investigate the January 6th Attack on the United States Capitol, Transcribed Interview of Katrina Pierson, (Mar. 25, 2022), p. 121.

432. Select Committee to Investigate the January 6th Attack on the United States Capitol, Transcribed Interview of Katrina Pierson, (Mar. 25, 2022), p. 121.

433. Select Committee to Investigate the January 6th Attack on the United States Capitol, Deposition of Max Miller, (Jan. 20, 2022), pp. 91-92.

434. Select Committee to Investigate the January 6th Attack on the United States Capitol, Transcribed Interview of Katrina Pierson, (Mar. 25, 2022), p. 123.

435. Select Committee to Investigate the January 6th Attack on the United States Capitol, Transcribed Interview of Katrina Pierson, (Mar. 25, 2022), pp. 121-26.

436. Select Committee to Investigate the January 6th Attack on the United States Capitol, Deposition of Max Miller, (Jan. 20, 2022), pp. 98-99.

437. Documents on file with the Select Committee to Investigate the January 6th Attack on the United States Capitol, (Max Miller Production) Miller Production 0001, p. 1 (January 4, 2021, text message from Max Miller to Katrina Pierson).

438. Select Committee to Investigate the January 6th Attack on the United States Capitol, Transcribed Interview of Katrina Pierson, (Mar. 25, 2022), p. 121.

439. Select Committee to Investigate the January 6th Attack on the United States Capitol, Transcribed Interview of Katrina Pierson, (Mar. 25, 2022), p. 95; Documents on file with the Select Committee to Investigate the January 6th Attack on the United States Capitol (Katrina Pierson Production), KPierson0180, at 180, 196-97 (January 4, 2021, President Trump Meeting Agenda).

440. Select Committee to Investigate the January 6th Attack on the United States Capitol, Transcribed Interview of Katrina Pierson, (Mar. 25, 2022), p. 41.

441. Select Committee to Investigate the January 6th Attack on the United States Capitol, Transcribed Interview of Katrina Pierson, (Mar. 25, 2022), p. 42.

442. Select Committee to Investigate the January 6th Attack on the United States Capitol, Transcribed Interview of Katrina Pierson, (Mar. 25, 2022), pp. 42-43.

443. Documents on file with the Select Committee to Investigate the January 6th Attack on the United States Capitol (Katrina Pierson Production), KPierson0374 (December 30, 2020, Katrina Pierson text message to Kylie Kremer); Select Committee to Investigate the January 6th Attack on the United States Capitol, Transcribed Interview of Katrina Pierson, (Mar. 25, 2022), p. 4.

444. Select Committee to Investigate the January 6th Attack on the United States Capitol, Transcribed Interview of Katrina Pierson, (Mar. 25, 2022), p. 86.

445. Select Committee to Investigate the January 6th Attack on the United States Capitol, Transcribed Interview of Katrina Pierson, (Mar. 25, 2022), pp. 62-63.

446. Select Committee to Investigate the January 6th Attack on the United States Capitol, Transcribed Interview of Katrina Pierson, (Mar. 25, 2022), p. 84; Documents on file with the Select Committee to Investigate the January 6th Attack on the United States Capitol, (Katrina Pierson Production), KPierson0924 (January 2, 2021, Katrina Pierson text message to Mark Meadows at 1:39 p.m. and 1:40 p.m.)

447. Select Committee to Investigate the January 6th Attack on the United States Capitol, Transcribed Interview of Katrina Pierson, (March 25, 2022), p. 74; Documents on file with the Select Committee to Investigate the January 6th Attack on the United States Capitol (Katrina Pierson Production), KPierson0921, (January 2, 2021, Katrina Pierson text message to Mark Meadows at 5:16 p.m.).

448. Select Committee to Investigate the January 6th Attack on the United States Capitol, Transcribed Interview of Katrina Pierson, (Mar. 25, 2022), pp. 76-77, 80-81.

449. Select Committee to Investigate the January 6th Attack on the United States Capitol, Transcribed Interview of Katrina Pierson, (Mar. 25, 2022), pp. 75-77.

450. Documents on file with the Select Committee to Investigate the January 6th Attack on the United States Capitol (Katrina Pierson Production), KPierson0924 (January 2, 2021 Katrina Pierson text message to Mark Meadows at 5:49 p.m.).

451. Select Committee to Investigate the January 6th Attack on the United States Capitol, Transcribed Interview of Katrina Pierson, (Mar. 25, 2022), p. 108; Documents on file with the Select Committee to Investigate the January 6th Attack on the United States Capitol, (Katrina Pierson Production), KPierson180 (January 4, 2021, agenda for meeting with President Trump at 1:21 p.m.).

452. Select Committee to Investigate the January 6th Attack on the United States Capitol, Transcribed Interview of Katrina Pierson, (Mar. 25, 2022), pp. 107-08; Documents on file with the Select Committee to Investigate the January 6th Attack on the United States Capitol, (Katrina Pierson Production), KPierson0196 (Document titled: "Meeting w/ POTUS - January 4th 2021 at 3:30pm ET").

453. Select Committee to Investigate the January 6th Attack on the United States Capitol, Transcribed Interview of Katrina Pierson, (Mar. 25, 2022), pp. 116-18.

454. Documents on file with the Select Committee to Investigate the January 6th Attack on the United States Capitol, (Katrina Pierson Production), KPierson0906 (January 5, 2021, text message from Dan Scavino to Katrina Pierson at 4:23 a.m.).

455. Documents on file with the Select Committee to Investigate the January 6th Attack on the United States Capitol (Justin Caporale Production), Caporale_05_003987, (Jan. 3, 2021, Katrina Pierson text message to Justin Caporale and Taylor Budowich); *see also* Select Committee to Investigate the January 6th Attack on the United States Capitol, Transcribed Interview of Katrina Pierson, (Mar. 25, 2022), p. 79; Documents on file with the Select Committee to Investigate the January 6th Attack on the United States Capitol (Taylor Budowich Production), Budo-00714 (January 2, 2021, Katrina Pierson email to Caroline Wren and Taylor Budowich at 10:49 p.m.).

456. Documents on file with the Select Committee to Investigate the January 6th Attack on the United States Capitol (Justin Caporale Production), Caporale_02_000673-88, (Jan. 3, 2021, Justin Caporale text message to Katrina Pierson, redacted).

457. Select Committee to Investigate the January 6th Attack on the United States Capitol, Deposition of Max Miller, (Jan. 20, 2022), pp. 81-83. Miller testified that he had not been involved in or paying attention to the conversation until the President directly addressed him about Giuliani. Miller's testimony was not credible on this point. Miller said he did not take notes, yet in communications with people after the fact he recounted details about the President's decision regarding speakers other than Giuliani, Eastman, Powell, Wood, and Flynn. *See* Select Committee to Investigate the January 6th Attack on the United States

Capitol, Deposition of Max Miller, (Jan. 20, 2022), p. 85 (stating that neither he nor Peede took notes); *id.* at p. 107 (confirming that he told Megan Powers on January 5th that President Trump cut Paxton from the list).

458. In the January 4 meeting with Pierson and Miller, President Trump initially indicated that Giuliani would not be able to speak at the Ellipse because he needed to be working on lobbying Members of Congress to block certification of the electoral college vote, yet another sign that the President intended January 6th to be a full-fledged effort to stay in power. Select Committee to Investigate the January 6th Attack on the United States Capitol, Transcribed Interview of Katrina Pierson, (Mar. 25, 2022), p. 117.

459. Select Committee to Investigate the January 6th Attack on the United States Capitol, Deposition of Max Miller, (Jan. 20, 2022), pp. 81-83, 129-30.

460. User-Generated Clip, "John Eastman at January 6 Rally," CSPAN, Mar. 24, 2021, available at https://www.c-span.org/video/?c4953961/user-clip-john-eastman-january-6-rally.

461. Select Committee to Investigate the January 6th Attack on the United States Capitol, Deposition of Max Miller, (Jan. 20, 2022), pp. 115-116.

462. It appears that Alexander was given front row seating for the Ellipse rally. He tweeted a picture in front of the Ellipse stage, writing: "Nice seats! Thank you @realdonaldtrump!" Ali [Orange Square] #StopTheSteal (@Ali), Twitter, Jan. 6, 2021, available at https://web.archive.org/web/20210107094927/https:/twitter.com/ali (archived)

463. Moms for America, "Save the Republic: Ali Alexander," Rumble, at 2:24, Jan. 29, 2021, available at https://rumble.com/vdepmx-save-the-republic-ali-alexander.html.

464. Ali [Orange Square] #StopTheSteal (@Ali), Twitter, Jan. 5, 2021, available at https://web.archive.org/web/20210107094927/https:/twitter.com/ali (archived).

465. NTD Television, "'Virginia Women for Trump' Rally at Supreme Court," Facebook Live, Jan. 5, 2021, available at https://www.facebook.com/NTDTelevision/videos/220171109588984.

466. Radley Balko, "Meet the Police Chief Turned Yoga Instructor Prodding Wealthy Suburbanites to Civil War," *Washington Post*, (Jan. 27, 2021), available at https://www.washingtonpost.com/opinions/2021/01/27/alan-hostetter-capitol-riot-police-chief-yoga-instructor/.

467. NTD Television, "'Virginia Women for Trump' Rally at Supreme Court," Facebook Live, at 20:10, Jan. 5, 2021, available at https://www.facebook.com/NTDTelevision/videos/220171109588984.

468. NTD Television, "'Virginia Women for Trump' Rally at Supreme Court," Facebook Live, at 1:44:14 -1:45:54, Jan. 5, 2021, available at https://www.facebook.com/NTDTelevision/videos/220171109588984.

469. NTD Television, "'Virginia Women for Trump' Rally at Supreme Court," Facebook Live, at1:46:04 – 1:49:40, Jan. 5, 2021, available at https://www.facebook.com/NTDTelevision/videos/220171109588984.

470. Radley Balko, "Meet the Police Chief Turned Yoga Instructor Prodding Wealthy Suburbanites to Civil War," *Washington Post*, (Jan. 27, 2021), available at https://www.washingtonpost.com/opinions/2021/01/27/alan-hostetter-capitol-riot-police-chief-yoga-instructor/.

471. Indictment at ¶ 56, *United States v. Hostetter et al.*, No. 1:21-cr-392 (D.D.C., June 9, 2021), ECF No. 1.

472. EpiqEpoch, "Roger Stone January 5, 2021 Freedom Plaza," Rumble, at 8:09, Jan. 6, 2021, available at https://rumble.com/vchgtl-roger-stone-january-5-2021-freedom-plaza.html.

473. Project Truth Beam, "Jan 5th Freedom Plaza: Ali Alexander," Rumble, at 1:58-2:21, Jan.16, 2021, available at https://rumble.com/vcx1mt-jan-5th-freedom-plaza-ali-alexander.html.

474. EpiqEpoch, "Alex Jones January 5, 2021 Freedom Plaza," Rumble, at 1:24, Jan. 6, 2021, available at https://rumble.com/vchguz-alex-jones-january-5-2021-freedom-plaza.html.

475. EpiqEpoch, "Gen. Michael Flynn, January 5, 2021 Freedom Plaza," Rumble, at 5:28, Jan. 6, 2021, available at https://rumble.com/vchisz-gen.-michael-flynn-january-5-2021-freedom-plaza.html.

476. Select Committee to Investigate the January 6th Attack on the United States Capitol, Deposition of Ross Worthington, (Feb. 15, 2022), p. 112.

477. Select Committee to Investigate the January 6th Attack on the United States Capitol, Transcribed Interview of William Bock IV, (Apr. 15, 2022), pp. 23, 32; Documents on file with the Select Committee to Investigate the January 6th Attacks on the United States Capitol (National Archives Production), 076P-R000002884_00001, (January 5, 2021, email from Worthington to Staff Secretary at 7:46 p.m., attaching a draft speech). In the final hours before the speech, White House lawyers would insist that the speech needed fact-checking and were most worried about the claims about Dominion Voting. *See* Documents on file with the Select Committee to Investigate the January 6th Attack on the United States Capitol, (National Archives Production) 076P-R000007308_0001 (January 5, 2021, email from Worthington to Staff Secretary at 7:46 p.m.). But President Trump would deliver the speech with the allegations intact. *See* Senate Committee on Homeland Security and Governmental Affairs and Committee on Rules and Administration, 117th Congress, "Examining the U.S. Capitol Attack: A Review of the Security, Planning, and Response Failures on January 6" (Staff Report), p. B-18, (June 8, 2021).

478. Documents on file with the Select Committee to Investigate the January 6th Attack on the United States Capitol, (Vincent Haley Production), VMH-00002701-02 (Draft Speech, "Stop the Steal Rally").

479. Select Committee to Investigate the January 6th Attack on the United States Capitol, Deposition of Stephen Miller (Apr. 14, 2022), p. 125-26; Select Committee to Investigate the January 6th Attack on the United States Capitol, Transcribed Interview of Ross Worthington (Feb. 15, 2022), p. 124.

480. Select Committee to Investigate the January 6th Attack on the United States Capitol, Transcribed Interview of Sarah Matthews, (Feb. 8, 2022), pp. 15-16.

481. Select Committee to Investigate the January 6th Attack on the United States Capitol, Transcribed Interview of Sarah Matthews, (Feb. 8, 2022), p. 16; *see also* Documents on file with the Select Committee to Investigate the January 6th Attack on the United States Capitol, (National Archives Production), Photo files 69c1_x032_555c_7, 0d9d_x039_557d_7 (January 5, 2021, photos of the meeting).

482. Select Committee to Investigate the January 6th Attack on the United States Capitol, Deposition of Nicholas Luna, (Mar. 21, 2022), pp. 76-77; Select Committee to Investigate the January 6th Attack on the United States Capitol, Transcribed Interview of Sarah Matthews, (Feb. 8, 2022), pp. 17, 19-20; Select Committee to Investigate the January 6th Attack on the United States Capitol, Deposition of Judson P. Deere, (Mar. 3, 2022), p. 84; Select Committee to Investigate the January 6th Attack on the United States Capitol, Transcribed Interview of Madison Fox Porter, (May 5, 2022), p. 19.

483. Select Committee to Investigate the January 6th Attack on the United States Capitol, Transcribed Interview of Sarah Matthews, (Feb. 8, 2022), pp. 16-17; Select Committee to Investigate the January 6th Attack on the United States Capitol, Deposition of Judson Deere, (Mar. 3, 2022), pp. 83-84.

484. Donald J. Trump (@RealDonaldTrump), Twitter, Jan. 5, 2021 5:05 p.m. ET, available at https://www.thetrumparchive.com/?searchbox=%22Washington+is+being+inundated%22 (archived). ("Washington is being inundated with people who don't want to see an election victory stolen by emboldened Radical Left Democrats. Our Country has had enough, they won't take it anymore! We hear you (and love you) from the Oval Office. MAKE AMERICA GREAT AGAIN!").

485. The Select Committee has obtained two drafts of the speech from January 5th, one of which was circulated at approximately 3:30 p.m. and another at 7:40 p.m. *See* Documents on file with the Select Committee to Investigate the January 6th Attack on the United

States Capitol (Vincent Haley Production), VMH-00002700, VMH-00002708 (January 5, 2021, email from Ross Worthington to Stephen Miller circulating draft speech at 3:30 p.m.); Documents on file with the Select Committee to Investigate the January 6th Attack on the United States Capitol, (National Archives Production), 076P-R000002878_00001, 076P-R000002879_00001, (January 5, 2021, email from Ross Worthington to Stephen Miller circulating draft speech at 7:40 p.m.).

486. Donald J. Trump (@RealDonaldTrump), Twitter, Jan. 5, 2021 5:05 p.m. ET, available at https://www.thetrumparchive.com (archived). ("Washington is being inundated with people who don't want to see an election victory stolen by emboldened Radical Left Democrats. Our Country has had enough, they won't take it anymore! We hear you (and love you) from the Oval Office. MAKE AMERICA GREAT AGAIN!").

487. Documents on file with the Select Committee to Investigate the January 6th Attack on the United States Capitol, (National Archives Production), 076P-R000002879_00001 (Draft of Jan. 6, 2021 speech by President Donald Trump).

488. Select Committee to Investigate the January 6th Attack on the United States Capitol, Deposition of Judson P. Deere, (Mar. 3, 2022), pp. 91-92.

489. Select Committee to Investigate the January 6th Attack on the United States Capitol, Deposition of Shealah Craighead, (June 8, 2022), pp. 32-33. Craighead believed that she later shared this with Ornato. *See id.*, at 33.

490. Select Committee to Investigate the January 6th Attack on the United States Capitol, Transcribed Interview of Sarah Matthews, (Feb. 8, 2022), p. 17; Select Committee to Investigate the January 6th Attack on the United States Capitol, Deposition of Judson P. Deere, (Mar. 3, 2022), p. 99.

491. Select Committee to Investigate the January 6th Attack on the United States Capitol, Transcribed Interview of Sarah Matthews, (Feb. 8, 2022), p. 17. Deere did not recall this specific question nor responding to it, but did remember advising President Trump that he should focus on his administration's accomplishments during his January 6th Ellipse rally speech rather than his stolen election claims. Deere recalled President Trump asking about which Members of Congress would be with him the next day and vote against certifying the election. Select Committee to Investigate the January 6th Attack on the United States Capitol, Deposition of Judson Deere, (Mar. 3, 2022), pp. 88-90, 92, 99-100.

492. Select Committee to Investigate the January 6th Attack on the United States Capitol, Transcribed Interview of Sarah Matthews, (Feb. 8, 2022), p. 17.

493. Select Committee to Investigate the January 6th Attack on the United States Capitol, Transcribed Interview of Sarah Matthews, (Feb. 8, 2022), p. 17; Select Committee to Investigate the January 6th Attack on the United States Capitol, Deposition of Judson Deere, (Mar. 3, 2022), pp. 85-86.

494. Select Committee to Investigate the January 6th Attack on the United States Capitol, Deposition of Judson P. Deere, (Mar. 3, 2022), pp. 86-87, 99.

495. Select Committee to Investigate the January 6th Attack on the United States Capitol, Deposition of Judson P. Deere, (Mar. 3, 2022), p. 86.

496. Documents on file with the Select Committee to Investigate the January 6th Attack on the United States Capitol, 076P-R000007361_0001 (January 5, 2021, email from Austin Ferrer to Dan Scavino at 10:16 p.m.).

497. Senate Committee on Homeland Security and Governmental Affairs and Committee on Rules and Administration, 117th Congress, "Examining the U.S. Capitol Attack: A Review of the Security, Planning, and Response Failures on January 6" (Staff Report), p. B-2, (June 8, 2021); Statement of Catherine A. Sanderson, Ph.D., (June 3, 2022), at 5.

498. Lena V. Groeger, Jeff Kao, Al Shaw, Moiz Syed, and Maya Eliahou, "What Parler Saw During the Attack on the Capitol," *Pro Publica*, at 12:05 p.m. ET at 0:30, Jan. 17, 2021, available, https://projects.propublica.org/parler-capitol-videos/; Statement of Catherine A. Sanderson, Ph.D., (June 3, 2022), at 5.

499. Select Committee to Investigate the January 6th Attack on the United States Capitol, Continued Interview of Cassidy Hutchinson, (June 20, 2022), pp. 11-19.

500. Senate Committee on Homeland Security and Governmental Affairs and Committee on Rules and Administration, 117th Congress, "Examining the U.S. Capitol Attack: A Review of the Security, Planning, and Response Failures on January 6" (Staff Report), pp. B-22, 23, (June 8, 2021).

501. Documents on file with the Select Committee to Investigate the January 6th Attack on the United States Capitol (National Archives Production), 076P-R000002911_00001, 076P-R000002912_00001 (January 6, 2021, email from Robert Gabriel Jr. to Dan Scavino at 1:25 p.m. re: Final draft attached with attachment '210106 Save America March.doc'); Statement of Jennifer Mercieca, (Mar. 31, 2022), at 18.

502. Statement of Jennifer Mercieca, (Mar. 31, 2022), at 18.

President Trump speaks at the January 6th Ellipse rally.

Photo by Tasos Katopodis/Getty Images

7

187 MINUTES OF DERELICTION

At 1:10 p.m. on January 6th, President Trump concluded his speech at the Ellipse. By that time, the attack on the U.S. Capitol had already begun. But it was about to get much worse. The President told thousands of people in attendance to march down Pennsylvania Avenue to the Capitol. He told them to "fight like hell" because if they didn't, they were "not going to have a country anymore." Not everyone who left the Ellipse did as the Commander-in-Chief ordered, but many of them did. The fighting intensified during the hours that followed.[1]

By 1:21 p.m., President Trump was informed that the Capitol was under attack. He could have interceded immediately. But the President chose not to do so. It was not until 4:17 p.m. that President Trump finally tweeted a video in which he told the rioters to go home.

The 187 minutes between the end of President Trump's speech and when he finally told the mob to leave the U.S. Capitol was a dereliction of duty. In the U.S. military, a service member is deemed to be "derelict in the performance of duties when that person willfully or negligently fails to perform that person's duties or when that person performs them in a culpably inefficient manner." [2] As Commander-in-Chief, President Trump had the power—more than any other American—to muster the U.S. Government's resources and end the attack on the U.S. Capitol. He willfully remained idle even as others, including his own Vice President, acted.

President Trump could have called top officials at the Department of Justice, the Department of Homeland Security, the Department of Defense, the F.B.I., the Capitol Police Department, or the DC Mayor's Office to ensure that they quelled the violence. He made no such calls. Instead, President Trump reached out to Rudolph Giuliani and friendly Members of Congress, seeking their assistance in delaying the joint session of Congress. And the President tweeted at 2:24 p.m., at the height of the violence, that his own Vice President lacked the "courage" to act—a statement that could only further enrage the mob. Meanwhile, Vice President Michael Pence assumed the duties of the President, requesting the assistance of top officials, even though he was not in the chain of command and had no constitutional power to issue orders.

In testimony before the Select Committee, Chairman of the Joint Chiefs of Staff General Mark Milley explained that President Trump did "[n]othing," "[z]ero" to marshal the Government's resources during the assault on the U.S. Capitol.[3] In contrast, Vice President Pence had "two or three calls" with General Milley and other military officials—even as the mob hunted him. During those calls, Vice President Pence was "very animated" and "issued very explicit, very direct, unambiguous orders." The Vice President told Acting Secretary of Defense Chris Miller to "get the military down here, get the [National] [G]uard down here," and "put down this situation."[4] President Trump could have made those same demands. He chose not to do so—a damning fact that President Trump's own Chief of Staff, Mark Meadows, quickly tried to cover up.

"We have to kill the narrative that the Vice President is making all the decisions," General Milley recalled Meadows as saying. "We need to establish the narrative, you know, that the President is still in charge and that things are steady or stable," Meadows said, which General Milley described as a "[r]ed flag."[5] In his testimony, General Milley also reflected on what it meant for a President not to be taking action in a time of crisis:

> You know, you're the Commander in Chief. You've got an assault going on on the Capitol of the United States of America, and there's nothing? No call? Nothing? Zero? And it's not my place to, you know, pass judgment or—I'm the, you know—but no attempt to call the Secretary of Defense? No attempt to call the Vice President of the United States of America, who's down on the scene? To my knowledge, it wasn't—I just noted it.[6]

President Trump's closest advisors—both inside and out of the White House—implored him to act sooner. Earlier in the week, two of the President's most trusted aides, Eric Herschmann and Hope Hicks, both wanted President Trump to emphasize that January 6th would be a peaceful protest. President Trump refused.[7]

On the 6th, as the riot began to escalate, a colleague texted Hicks and wrote, "Hey, I know you're seeing this. But he really should tweet something about Being NON-violent."[8] "I'm not there," Hicks replied. "I suggested it several times Monday and Tuesday and he refused."[9]

Once the attack was underway, President Trump initially ignored the counsel of his own family, members of his administration, Republican elected officials, and friendly Fox News personalities. Both Ivanka Trump and Donald Trump, Jr. wanted their father to tell the rioters to go home sooner. The President delayed. At 2:38 p.m., President Trump sent this tweet: "Please support our Capitol Police and Law Enforcement. They are truly on the side of our Country. Stay peaceful!"[10] Sarah Matthews, the White House Deputy Press Secretary, told the Select Committee that President Trump resisted using the word "peaceful." The President added the words "Stay peaceful!" only after Ivanka Trump suggested the phrase.[11] Trump, Jr. quickly recognized that his father's tweet was insufficient. "He's got to condem [sic] this shit. Asap. The captiol [sic] police tweet is not enough," Trump, Jr. wrote in a text to White House Chief of Staff Mark Meadows.[12] President Trump did not tell the rioters to disperse in either his 2:38 p.m. tweet, or another tweet at 3:13 p.m.[13]

Multiple witnesses told the Select Committee that Minority Leader Kevin McCarthy contacted the President and others around him, desperately trying to get him to act. McCarthy's entreaties led nowhere. "I guess they're just more upset about the election theft than you are," President Trump told McCarthy.[14] Top lawyers in the White House Counsel's Office attempted to intercede. Two Fox News primetime personalities, always so obsequious, begged those around the President to get him to do more. But President Trump was unmoved.

There's no question that President Trump had the power to end the insurrection. He was not only the Commander-in-Chief of the U.S. military, but also of the rioters.

One member of the mob, Stephen Ayres, told the Select Committee that he and others quickly complied as soon as President Trump finally told them to go home. "[W]e literally left right after [President Trump's 4:17 p.m. video] come out. You know, to me if he would have done that earlier in the day, 1:30 [p.m.] . . . maybe we wouldn't be in this bad of a situation or something," Ayres said.[15] Another rioter, Jacob Chansley, commonly referred to as the "QAnon Shaman," was one of the first 30 rioters to enter the U.S. Capitol. Chansley told a reporter that he left the building because "Trump asked everybody to go home."[16] At 4:25 p.m., just eight minutes after President Trump tweeted his video, an Oath Keeper named Ed Vallejo messaged other members of his group, a fair number of whom were at the Capitol: "Gentleman [sic], Our Commander-in-Chief has just ordered us to go home. Comments?"[17]

Even then, President Trump did not disavow the rioters. He endorsed their cause, openly sympathized with them, and repeated his Big Lie once again. "I know your pain, I know you're hurt. We had an election that was stolen from us," President Trump said at the beginning of his 4:17 p.m. video. "It was a landslide election, and everyone knows it, especially the other side. But you have to go home now. We have to have peace. We have

President Trump appears on a monitor in the White House briefing room depicting a video he released instructing rioters to go home.

(Photo by Joshua Roberts/Getty Images)

to have law and order. We have to respect our great people in law and order. We don't want anybody hurt." The President portrayed the violence as something his political foes would use against him, saying: "This was a fraudulent election, but we can't play into the hands of these people."[18]

The President concluded his short video by again praising the men and women who had overrun the U.S. Capitol. "We have to have peace. So go home. We love you. You're very special," President Trump said. "You've seen what happens. You see the way others are treated that are so bad and so evil. I know how you feel, but go home, and go home in peace."[19]

Just after 6:00 p.m. on January 6th, President Trump issued his final tweet of the day, again lauding the rioters and justifying their cause. President Trump made excuses for the riot, saying this is what happens "when a sacred landslide election victory is so unceremoniously & viciously stripped away from great patriots who have been badly & unfairly treated for so long." The President added: "Go home with love & in peace. Remember this day forever!"[20]

The following day, President Trump's advisors encouraged him to deliver a short speech denouncing the attack on the U.S. Capitol. The President struggled to deliver his prepared remarks. According to Cassidy

Hutchinson, President Trump wanted to say that he would pardon the rioters. Lawyers in the White House Counsel's Office objected, so this language
was not included.[21] John McEntee, the Director of the White House Presidential Personnel Office, also testified that in the days following the attack,
he heard President Trump mention the possibility of a "blanket pardon" for
all those involved in the events of January 6th.[22]

President Trump never did give up on the prospect. Since leaving office,
the now former President has said he would consider "full pardons with an
apology to many" of the January 6th defendants if he is reelected.[23]

7.1 "REINSERT THE MIKE PENCE LINES"

President Trump tweeted three times on the morning of January 6th,
repeating a false claim of election fraud at 8:06 a.m.,[24] pressuring Vice
President Pence to delay the electoral count at 8:17 a.m.,[25] and urging
Republican party officials to do the same at 8:22 a.m.[26] He made calls to his
Republican allies in Congress, many of whom were already committed to
objecting to the electoral count.[27] And he dialed his lawyers and advisors—
including Steve Bannon and Rudolph Giuliani (twice), both of whom had
been counseling the President on how to stay in power.[28]

There was one person—critical to his plan—whom President Trump
tried to reach but couldn't. At 9:02 a.m., he asked the switchboard operator
to call his Vice President. Vice President Pence did not answer the call.[29]

Instead, between 9:52 a.m. and 10:18 a.m., the President spoke with his
speechwriter, Stephen Miller, about the words he would deliver at the Save
America Rally just hours later.[30] The former President's speech had come
together over the course of 36 hours, going from a screed aimed at encouraging congressional objections to one that would ultimately incite mob violence.[31]

Only four minutes after the call concluded, at 10:22 a.m., Miller emailed
revisions to the speechwriters, instructing them to "[s]tart inputting these
changes asap" that included "red highlights marking POTUS edits."[32] The
President had made some cosmetic additions, like peppering in the word
"corrupt" throughout,[33] but there was one substantive edit—a new
target—that would focus the crowd's anger on one man.

None of the preceding drafts mentioned Vice President Pence whatsoever. But now, at the very last minute, President Trump slipped in the following sentences calling the Vice President out by name:

> Today, we will see whether Republicans stand strong for the integ-
> rity of our elections. And we will see whether Mike Pence enters
> history as a truly great and courageous leader. All he has to do is

President Trump speaks with speechwriter Stephen Miller about his Ellipse speech in the Oval Office on the morning of January 6, 2021.
(Photo provided to the Select Committee by the National Archives and Records Administration)

refer the illegally-submitted electoral votes back to the states that were given false and fraudulent information where they want to recertify. With only 3 of the 7 states in question we win and become President and have the power of the veto.[34]

No one on the speechwriting team could explain why President Trump added these lines just 30 minutes before he was originally scheduled to speak at 11:00 a.m.[35] But by 10:49 a.m., Vincent Haley, a speechwriter who was helping load the teleprompter at the Ellipse, was told to hold off and delete the mention of the Vice President—for now.[36] Miller said that Eric Herschmann, a lawyer who was one of the President's senior advisors, asked him in a "brief sidebar" that morning to omit reference to the Vice President and his role in the certification process because he "didn't concur with the legal analysis" and that it "wouldn't advance the ball" but would be "counterproductive" instead.[37] As detailed in Chapter 5, Herschmann and others in the White House were vocal critics of Dr. John Eastman's theory, which claimed that the Vice President had the unilateral power to reject electors during the joint session of Congress. President Trump repeatedly pressured Pence to either reject certified electors, or delay the

President Trump on a phone call with Vice President Mike Pence in the Oval Office on the morning of January 6, 2021.
(Photo provided to the Select Committee by the National Archives and Records Administration)

electoral count based on Eastman's unconstitutional and illegal theory. Vice President Pence would not budge. The Vice President consistently rejected President Trump's demands.

After tweeting four more times that morning—all of them spreading lies about the election[38]—the President apparently thought he had one last chance to convince his number two to overrule the will of the American people.

As recounted in Chapter 5, President Trump called Vice President Pence at 11:17 a.m.[39] The call between the two men—during which the President soon grew "frustrat[ed] or heated,"[40] visibly upset,[41] and "angry"[42]— lasted nearly 20 minutes.[43] And President Trump insulted Vice President Pence when he refused to obstruct or delay the joint session.

After that call, General Keith Kellogg said that the people in the room immediately went back to editing the Ellipse speech.[44] At 11:30 a.m., Miller emailed his assistant, Robert Gabriel, with no text in the body but the sub- ject line: "insert—stand by for phone call."[45] At 11:33 a.m., Gabriel emailed the speechwriting team: "REINSERT THE MIKE PENCE LINES. Confirm receipt."[46] One minute later, speechwriter Ross Worthington confirmed

President Trump looks backstage at the crowd gathered at the Ellipse.
(Photo provided to the Select Committee by the National Archives and Records Administration)

that he had reached Vincent Haley by phone.[47] Haley corroborated that he added one "tough sentence about the Vice President" while he was at the teleprompter.[48]

The final written draft had the following Pence reference: "And we will see whether Mike Pence enters history as a truly great and courageous leader."[49] Haley wasn't confident that line was what he reinserted, but email traffic and teleprompter drafts produced by the National Archives and Records Administration (NARA) indicate that he was mistaken.[50]

After defying President Trump's pressure, Vice President Pence—and the ire of the President he inspired—was back in the speech.

After the heated call, President Trump's personal assistant Nicholas Luna handed him a message on White House card stock and the President departed for the Ellipse to give his speech.[51] Preserved by NARA, the message read: "THEY ARE READY FOR YOU WHEN YOU ARE."[52] When it finally came time for him to speak, President Trump repeatedly directed his anger at Vice President Pence—often ad-libbing lines that were not included in the draft text.

7.2 "I'LL BE THERE WITH YOU"

From a tent backstage at the Ellipse, President Trump looked out at the crowd of approximately 53,000 supporters and became enraged. Just under half of those gathered—a sizeable stretch of about 25,000 people[53]— refused to walk through the magnetometers and be screened for weapons,[54] leaving the venue looking half-empty to the television audience at home.

According to testimony received by the Committee, earlier that morning at the White House, the President was told that the onlookers were unwilling to pass through the magnetometers because they were armed. "We have enough space, sir. They don't want to come in right now," Deputy Chief of Staff Tony Ornato reportedly told President Trump. "They have weapons that they don't want confiscated by the Secret Service." [55]

So, when President Trump got to the rally site and could see the crowd for himself, "[h]e was fucking furious," as Cassidy Hutchinson later texted Ornato.[56] Hutchinson testified that just minutes before addressing the crowd, President Trump shouted to his advance team: "I don't [fucking] care that they have weapons. They're not here to hurt *me*. Take the [fucking] mags away. Let my people in. They can march to the Capitol from here. Take the [fucking] mags away." [57]

By noon, President Trump took to the stage at the Ellipse.[58] The President wanted all of those in attendance, including those who hadn't passed through the magnetometers, to come closer to the stage. "And I'd love to have if those tens of thousands of people would be allowed," President Trump said. "But I'd love it if they could be allowed to come up here with us. Is that possible? Can you just let [them] come up, please?" [59]

President Trump repeatedly made it clear to those around him in the days before January 6th that he wanted to march to the Capitol alongside his supporters. That is, President Trump wanted to join his supporters in what the Secret Service refers to as an "off-the-record" movement (OTR).

While the President spoke, Hutchinson texted Ornato, "He also kept mentioning OTR to Capitol before he took the stage." [60] Minutes before the President stepped out, Chief of Staff Mark Meadows assured the President he was working on it.[61]

President Trump's plan to march appeared once in an early draft of the script, then a later revision was made to add the word "building" after "Capitol," making it clear exactly where the crowd should go.[62] And the President repeatedly told the crowd that he would join them.

"[A]fter this, we're going to walk down, and I'll be there with you, we're going to walk down, we're going to walk down," he said to the crowd. "[W]e're going to walk down to the Capitol, and we're going to cheer on our brave senators and congressmen and women, and we're probably not going to be cheering so much for some of them." [63]

President Trump used the phrase scripted for him by his White House speechwriters, "peacefully and patriotically" once, about 20 minutes into his speech.[64] Then he spent the next 50-or-so minutes amping up his crowd with lies about the election, attacking his own Vice President and Republican Members of Congress, and exhorting the crowd to fight. "And we fight. We fight like hell" the President said to a crowd that had already spent the day chanting, "Fight for Trump! Fight for Trump!," and that would keep up the chorus when storming the Capitol.[65]

Finally, he told the crowd where to go to "take back our country": "So we're going to, we're going to walk down Pennsylvania Avenue. I love Pennsylvania Avenue. And we're going to the Capitol, and we're going to try and give . . . we're going to try and give our Republicans, the weak ones because the strong ones don't need any of our help. We're going to try and give them the kind of pride and boldness that they need to take back our country. So let's walk down Pennsylvania Avenue." [66]

When the President announced his intentions from the microphone, people listened.

House Republican Leader Representative. Kevin McCarthy called Hutchinson mid-speech: [67]

"Do you guys think you're coming to my office[?]" he asked her.[68]
She assured him that they weren't coming at all.[69]

"Figure it out. Don't come up here," he replied.[70]

The announcement from the stage put the Secret Service on alert, prompting agents to designate over email a last-minute response team "to filter in with the crowds" on the President's "walk/motorcade over" to the Capitol and establish an emergency plan "if things go south." [71] White House security officials were monitoring the situation in real time, remarking that President Trump was "going to the Capitol" and that "they are finding the best route now." [72] Nonetheless, these staffers were in "a state of shock," [73] because they knew—particularly if the President joined—this would "no longer [be] a rally." [74]

"[W]e all knew . . . that this was going to move to something else if he physically walked to the Capitol," an employee said. "I don't know if you want to use the word 'insurrection,' 'coup,' whatever. We all knew that this would move from a normal democratic . . . public event into something else." [75]

But the logistics made the move all but impossible.

It was complicated for the Secret Service to coordinate a presidential movement even on a normal day. But today was not a normal day. Tens of thousands of President Trump's supporters had flooded into downtown DC in the days before the rally, and the Secret Service would have to account for that unpredictability. By the end of the President's speech, it was clear that the crowd at the Capitol was growing violent.

At 1:19 p.m., a Secret Service agent wrote to Bobby Engel, the head of President Trump's Secret Service detail: "FYSA . . . [Capitol Police] having serious challenges securing [the Capitol]. Nine priority breach attempts at this time. OTR to anywhere near there is not advisable. Give me a call when free. Front Office concerned about OTR to [the Capitol]." [76]

7.3   THE PRESIDENT'S ANGER WHEN HE COULD NOT MARCH TO THE CAPITOL

President Trump concluded his remarks at 1:10 p.m. Luna heard the President mention his intention to join the march to the Capitol "after he finished his remarks." [77] Just before the President got into his vehicle, Meadows told him, "We're going to work on it, sir." [78] President Trump was seated in his motorcade vehicle by 1:17 p.m.[79]

The Committee received information informally from current and former members of the Secret Service and former White House staff relevant to what happened next—what a number of witnesses have described as an "angry," "irate," or "furious" interaction in the Presidential vehicle between the President and the Secret Service.[80] That initial information, received informally, shaped the Committee's questioning of witnesses. The Committee's principal concern was that the President *actually intended* to participate personally in the January 6th efforts at the Capitol, leading the effort to overturn the election either from inside the Chamber or from a stage outside the Capitol. The Committee regarded those facts as important because they are relevant to President Trump's intent on January 6th. But a book published by Mark Meadows in November 2021 made the categorical claim that the President *never* intended to travel to the Capitol that day.[81] Because the Meadows book conflicted sharply with information that was being received by the Committee, the Committee became increasingly wary that witnesses might intentionally conceal what happened.

In our initial informal discussion with the lead of the President's detail, Robert Engel confirmed that President Trump did wish to travel to the Capitol from the Ellipse, but stated that he did not recall many other details.[82] But the Committee also received information from Kayleigh McEnany and Cassidy Hutchinson that also directly contradicted Mark Meadows's book and provided considerably more detail. McEnany testified that

President Trump did indeed wish to travel to the Capitol on January 6th, and continued to have that goal even after returning from the Ellipse to the White House.[83] McEnany, who spoke with President Trump shortly after he returned to the White House, recalls him expressing a desire to go to the Capitol: "I recall him . . . saying that he wanted to physically walk and be a part of the march and then saying that he would ride the Beast if he needed to, ride in the Presidential limo." [84] When asked, McEnany confirmed that "yes, he did seem sincere about wanting to do that." [85] Hutchinson's testimony was generally consistent with the information the Select Committee was receiving informally. Like McEnany, Hutchinson confirmed that the President did ask to be transported to Capitol Hill.[86] Many other White House witnesses would ultimately confirm that President Trump wished to travel to the Capitol on January 6th, comprehensively rebutting the false statements in Meadows's book.[87]

Part of Hutchinson's account was a second-hand description of what occurred in the Presidential vehicle, which built upon and was consistent with information the Committee has received informally.

Hutchinson testified that, when she returned from the Ellipse, Ornato was standing outside his office door when he "waved me down," Hutchinson said. The two of them walked into Ornato's office, and he shut the door behind them.[88] Engel was already there, sitting in a chair "looking down, kind of looking a little lost and kind of discombobulated." [89]

According to Hutchinson, Ornato then recounted a struggle in the President's car.[90] At no point during Ornato's telling—or at any point thereafter—did Engel indicate that what Ornato relayed was untrue.[91]

Another witness, a White House employee with national security responsibilities, provided the Committee with a similar description: Ornato related the "irate" interaction in the presidential vehicle to this individual in Ornato's White House office with Engel present.[92] And just as Hutchinson testified, this employee told the Select Committee that Engel listened to Ornato's retelling of the episode and did not dispute it: "I don't remember his specific body language, but . . . [h]e did not deny the fact that the President was irate." [93] Engel testified that he does not recall either the conversation with Hutchinson or the similar conversation with the White House employee with national security responsibilities.[94]

The Committee regarded both Hutchinson and the corroborating testimony by the White House employee with national security responsibilities national security official as earnest and has no reason to conclude that either had a reason to invent their accounts. A different Secret Service

Cassidy Hutchinson describes a story relayed to her by Tony Ornato about President Trump's desire to go to the Capitol after the Ellipse speech on January 6th during a January 6th Select Committee hearing.

(Photo by Brandon Bell/Getty Images)

agent, who served on a protective detail at the White House and was present in the presidential motorcade at the Ellipse, provided this view:

> Committee Staff: Just a couple of additional questions. Ms. Hutchinson has suggested to the Committee that you sympathized with her after her testimony, and believed her account. Is that accurate?

> Witness: I have no—yeah, that's accurate. I have no reason—I mean, we—we became friends. We worked—I worked every day with her for 6 months. Yeah, she became a friend of mine. We had a good working relationship. I have no reason—she's never done me wrong. She's never lied that I know of. I don't have any reason—I don't—I don't distrust Ms. Hutchinson.[95]

Also, the White House employee with national security responsibilities indicated that knowledge of the angry altercation in the Presidential vehicle was known within the White House—and was "[water] cooler talk." [96] In addition, Hutchinson has provided testimony to the Committee about efforts by her prior counsel, who was apparently paid by a Trump-funded organization, to suggest that Hutchinson did not need to testify about the issue in the presidential vehicle, could suggest that she "did not recall" it, or should downplay it.[97]

To further corroborate the accounts received of President Trump's intent to travel to the Capitol, the Committee interviewed a member of the Metropolitan Police who was also present in the motorcade, Officer Mark Robinson. Officer Robinson confirmed that he was aware contemporaneously of the "heated discussion" that took place in the Presidential vehicle:

> Committee Staff: And was there any description of what was occurring in the car?
>
> Mr. Robinson: No. Only that—the only description I received was that the President was upset and that he was adamant about going to the Capitol, and there was a heated discussion about that.
>
> Committee Staff: When you say "heated," is that your word, or is that the word that was described by the TS agent?
>
> Mr. Robinson: No. The word described by the TS agent meaning that the President was upset, and he was saying there was a heated argument or discussion about going to the Capitol.
>
> . . . .
>
> Mr. Schiff: So about how many times would you say you've been part of that motorcade with the President?
>
> Mr. Robinson: Probably over a hundred times.
>
> Mr. Schiff: And, in that hundred times, have you ever witnessed another discussion of an argument or a heated discussion with the President where the President was contradicting where he was supposed to go or what the Secret Service believed was safe?
>
> Mr. Robinson: No.[98]

The Committee also interviewed the Secret Service agent who was in the same car as Officer Robinson. That person shared a similar account, and confirmed that he did not take issue with Officer Robinson's testimony: "[The driver of the Presidential car] said something to the effect of, 'The President is pretty adamant that he wants to go to the Capitol,'" the agent said, recalling what he had heard on the 6th.[99]

In addition, the Committee interviewed the USSS Press Secretary, who communicated with both Engel and with the driver in the presidential vehicle after Hutchinson appeared publicly. That witness indicated that Engel's account of the events confirmed that the President was indeed angry, or furious.[100] In fact, when asked about a reporter's tweet indicating that sources within the Secret Service confirmed that "Trump was furious about not being [able] to go to [the] Capitol with his supporters," the Press Secretary said he "certainly corroborated it" with the reporter because "that's what I had been told, you know, that [the President] was upset, he was agitated, about not being able to go[.]"[101]

In addition to the testimony above, the Committee has reviewed hundreds of thousands of new Secret Service documents, including many demonstrating that the Secret Service had been informed of potential violence at the Capitol before the Ellipse rally on January 6th. (These documents were critical to our understanding of what the Secret Service and White House knew about the threat to the Capitol on January 6th.) The Committee has also more recently conducted additional interviews with Engel and Ornato, and has also interviewed the driver of the Presidential vehicle.

Both Engel and the driver[102] testified that, within 30 seconds of getting into the vehicle, the President asked if he could travel to the Capitol.[103] This again is directly inconsistent with the account of events in Meadows's book. According to Engel, he told the President immediately that the move wasn't happening.[104] The President was unhappy with Engel's response and began "pushing pretty hard to go."[105] The President repeatedly asked why he could not go to the Capitol.[106] Engel replied that the Secret Service "didn't have any people at the Capitol" to provide the President with appropriate security.[107] The President responded angrily, telling Engel and the driver "I'm the President and I'll decide where I get to go."[108] He reassured Engel that "it would essentially be fine and that the people there [meaning the people who were marching from the Ellipse to the Capitol at President Trump's instruction] were [Trump] supporters or something to that effect,"[109] According to the Secret Service agent driving the vehicle, the President was "animated and irritated" about not going to the Capitol.[110]

According to Mr. Engel, he ultimately told the President that they would "assess what our options were and wait until we can get a plan in place before we went down there."[111] We note that the driver's account acknowledged President Trump's anger to a greater degree than either Engel's initial account in Spring 2022, or his more recent account in November 2022. Engel did not characterize the exchange in the vehicle the way Hutchinson described the account she heard from Ornato, and indicated that he did not recall President Trump gesturing toward him.[112] Engel did not recall being present when Ornato gave either Hutchinson or the White House employee with national security responsibilities an accounting of the events.[113] The driver testified that he did not recall seeing what President Trump was doing and did not recall whether there was movement.[114]

The Select Committee has great respect for the men and women of the Secret Service. That said, it is difficult to fully reconcile the accounts of several of the witnesses who provided information with what we heard from Engel and Ornato.[115] But the principal factual point here is clear and undisputed: President Trump specifically and repeatedly requested to be taken to the Capitol. He was insistent and angry, and continued to push to travel to the Capitol even after returning to the White House.

The motorcade didn't disband upon arriving to the White House, as they usually do. Instead, they were instructed to stand by in case the President's move to the Capitol did indeed happen.[116] The Select Committee received a document from the Secret Service that reflects that at 1:25 p.m., "PPD IS ADVISING THAT [THE PRESIDENT] IS PLANNING ON HOLDING AT THE WHITE HOUSE FOR THE NEXT APPROXIMATE TWO HOURS, THEN MOVING TO THE CAPITOL." [117] "They had not made a decision whether or not we were going to transport the President to the Capitol," Robinson was told.[118]

Engel testified that he went to Ornato's office when he returned to the West Wing in order to discuss a possible move to the Capitol by President Trump.[119] Given the deteriorating security conditions at the Capitol, it was quickly determined that they could not safely transport the President there.[120] The motorcade waited on West Executive Drive approximately 40 minutes before finally receiving word from the Secret Service that the move had been officially nixed. Internal Secret Service communications bear this out: Not until 1:55 p.m. did Engel notify other agents via email that "[w]e are not doing an OTR to [the Capitol]." [121]

7.4 "WE'RE GOING TO TRY TO GET THE PRESIDENT TO PUT OUT A STATEMENT"

Minutes after arriving back at the White House, the President ran into a member of the White House staff and asked whether he or she watched his speech on television.[122]

"Sir, they cut it off because they're rioting down at the Capitol," the employee said.

The President asked what he or she meant by that.

"[T]hey're rioting down there at the Capitol," the employee repeated.

"Oh really?" the President asked. "All right, let's go see." [123]

A photograph taken by the White House photographer—the last one permitted until later in the day—captures the moment the President heard the news from the employee at 1:21 p.m.[124] By that time, if not sooner, he had been made aware of the violent riot at the Capitol.

President Trump walked through the corridor from the Oval Office into the Presidential Dining Room and sat down at the table with the television remote and a Diet Coke close at hand.[125] For the rest of the afternoon—as his country faced an hours-long attack—he hunkered down in or around the dining room, watching television.[126] He left only for a few minutes— from 4:03 p.m. to 4:07 p.m.—to film a video in the Rose Garden, only a few steps away, after hours of arm-twisting.[127] But otherwise, the President remained in the dining room until 6:27 p.m., when he returned to his private residence.[128]

What happened during the 187 minutes from 1:10 p.m. to 4:17 p.m., when President Trump finally told the rioters to go home, is—from an official standpoint—undocumented.

For instance, the Presidential Daily Diary—the schedule that tracks every meeting and phone call in which the President partakes—is inexplicably blank between 1:21 p.m. and 4:03 p.m.[129] When asked to explain the gap in record-keeping on and around January 6th, White House officials in charge of its maintenance provided no credible explanation, including: "I don't recall a specific reason."[130]

The men who spent most of the afternoon in that room with the President, Mark Meadows and Dan Scavino, both refused to comply with lawful subpoenas from the Select Committee.[131] Others in the dining room appeared before the Select Committee but cited executive privilege to avoid answering questions about their direct communications with President Trump.[132] Others who worked just outside of the Oval Office, like the President's personal secretaries Molly Michael and Austin Ferrer Piran Basauldo, claimed not to remember nearly anything from one of the most memorable days in recent American history.[133]

The White House photographer, Shealah Craighead, had been granted access to photograph the President during his January 6th speech, but once she got to the White House—and it became clear that an attack was unfolding on the Capitol's steps—she was turned away.[134]

"The President [didn't] want any photos," she was told.[135]

Here's what President Trump did during the 187 minutes between the end of his speech and when he finally told rioters to go home: For hours, he watched the attack from his TV screen.[136] His channel of choice was Fox News.[137] He issued a few tweets, some on his own inclination and some only at the repeated behest of his daughter and other trusted advisors.[138] He made several phone calls, some to his personal lawyer Rudolph Giuliani, some to Members of Congress about continuing their objections to the electoral certification, even though the attack was well underway.[139]

Here's what President Trump did not do: He did not call any relevant law enforcement agency to ensure they were working to quell the violence. He did not call the Secretary of Defense; he did not call the Attorney General; he did not call the Secretary of Homeland Security.[140] And for hours on end, he refused the repeated requests—from nearly everyone who talked to him—to simply tell the mob to go home.[141]

Throughout the afternoon, senior staff regularly entered the room to give him updates on what was happening at the Capitol.[142] And, of course, President Trump used Twitter, where information is shared on an instantaneous basis.

Shortly after President Trump entered the dining room, White House Press Secretary Kayleigh McEnany swung by to "check in with him" about the letter Vice President Pence released around 1:00 p.m. announcing that he would not, in fact, overturn the will of the voters.

The President, once again, brought up going to the Capitol.[143] McEnany recorded what he said in her notes, certain of which she later produced to the Select Committee: "POTUS wanted to walk to [sic] capital. Physically walk. He said fine ride beast," referring to the nickname for the presidential vehicle. "Meadows said not safe enough[.]"[144]

Meadows told Hutchinson at some point in the day that "the President wasn't happy that Bobby [Engel] didn't pull it off for him," meaning the trip to the Capitol, "and that Mark didn't work hard enough to get the movement on the books."[145]

Despite the turmoil just outside its walls, the proceedings in the joint session—which had begun at 1:00 p.m.—were still ongoing, and the President was watching them on the television.[146] He was eager to know which senators were lodging objections on his behalf.[147] "Back there and he wants list of senators," McEnany's notes read. "Who [sic] objecting to what. He's calling them one by one."[148]

The Select Committee subpoenaed several Members of Congress who reportedly spoke with President Trump during the afternoon.[149] None of them complied.[150]

Cellular records obtained by the Select Committee suggest that President Trump was on the phone with his lawyer Rudolph Giuliani at least twice during this period. Giuliani's phone connected with the White House switchboard for 3 minutes and 53 seconds at 1:39 p.m. and again for more than 8 minutes at 2:03 p.m.[151] Between the two calls, at 1:49 p.m., President Trump tweeted a link to a video of his speech from the Ellipse.[152]

Before 1:57 p.m., Herschmann phoned Senior Advisor to the President Jared Kushner—who was on a plane travelling home from overseas—advising him that "people are trying to break into the Capitol" and that "this is getting pretty ugly." [153]

"We're going to see what we can do here," Herschmann said. "We're going to try to get the President to put out a statement." [154]

7.5 "HE DOESN'T WANT TO DO ANYTHING"

Throughout the afternoon, the President's advisors tried to get him to tell the mob to leave the Capitol, but to no avail.

Ben Williamson, the White House Acting Director of Communications, watched on the news as officers and rioters pepper sprayed each other and crowds used bicycle barricades to push against officers holding the line.[155] He and Sarah Matthews, the Deputy Press Secretary, devised a plan: He would go to Meadows and she would go to McEnany to urge that the President issue a statement.[156] Williamson first texted Meadows:

"Would recommend POTUS put out a tweet about respecting the police over at the Capitol." [157]

Minutes later, around 2:05 p.m., Hutchinson found Meadows seated in his office on the couch, absorbed by his cell phone screen.[158]

"Are you watching the TV, chief?" she asked. He indicated he was.

"Have you talked to the President?" she asked.

"No," he replied. "He wants to be alone right now." [159]

Rioters broke into the west side of the Capitol building around 2:13 p.m.[160] Just a few minutes later, Hutchinson saw Cipollone "barreling down the hallway" and—after looking at Hutchinson and shaking his head—opened the door to Meadows's office unannounced.[161] Meadows was right where she left him, "still sitting on his phone." [162]

"The rioters have gotten to the Capitol, Mark. We need to go down and see the President now," she heard Cipollone say.[163] Cipollone would not confirm or deny any of this exchange, citing executive privilege.[164]

"He doesn't want to do anything, Pat," Meadows said, peering up from his phone.[165]

"Mark something needs to be done, or people are going to die and the blood's gonna be on your [fucking] hands," Cipollone said. "This is getting out of control. I'm going down there." [166]

Meadows finally stood up from the couch and walked with Cipollone toward the dining room to meet with the President.[167]

7.6 "HE THINKS MIKE DESERVES IT"

At exactly 2:24 p.m., President Trump made his first public statement during the attack on the Capitol by tweet. It read nothing like the statement his advisors had envisioned. It read:

> Mike Pence didn't have the courage to do what should have been done to protect our Country and our Constitution, giving States a chance to certify a corrected set of facts, not the fraudulent or inaccurate ones which they were asked to previously certify. USA demands the truth! [168]

Minutes later, Meadows and Cipollone returned from their talk with the President.[169] No statement was forthcoming.

"Mark, we need to do something more. They're literally calling for the Vice President to be [fucking] hung," Hutchinson heard Cipollone say.[170]

"You heard him, Pat," Meadows replied. "He thinks Mike deserves it. He doesn't think they're doing anything wrong." [171]

"This is [fucking] crazy. We need to be doing something more," Cipollone said.[172]

Cipollone told the Select Committee that "there needed to be an immediate and forceful response, statement, public statement, that people need to leave the Capitol now." [173] He said he was "pretty clear" about his view in the White House that day, and he made that view known as soon as he became aware of the unrest.[174] He would not comment on how the President responded, or on this conversation with Meadows, citing executive privilege.[175] He did indicate that everyone in the White House—except President Trump—agreed that people needed to leave the Capitol:

> Vice Chair Cheney: And who on the staff did not want people to leave the Capitol?
>
> Mr. Cipollone: On the staff?
>
> Vice Chair Cheney: In the White House.
>
> Mr. Cipollone: I can't think of anybody on that day who didn't want people to get out of the Capitol once the—particularly once the violence started. No. I mean—
>
> Mr. Schiff: What about the President?
>
> Vice Chair Cheney: Yeah.
>
> Mr. Cipollone: Well, she said the staff. So I answered.
>
> Vice Chair Cheney: No. I said in the White House.

Noose set up outside of the Capitol on January 6, 2021.

(Photo by Drew Angerer/Getty Images)

Mr. Cipollone: Oh, I'm sorry. I apologize. I thought you said who else on the staff. [*Pauses to confer with counsel*] Yeah. I can't reveal communications. But obviously I think, you know—yeah.[176]

What the President *did* tweet—a broadside at his Vice President— enlarged the target on Vice President Pence's back. A Secret Service agent in the Protective Intelligence Division, tasked with monitoring threats against protectees in part by scouring social media, told his colleagues the tweet was "probably not going to be good for Pence."[177]

A second agent in reply noted that it had garnered "[o]ver 24K likes in under 2 mins."[178]

7.7 "I GUESS THEY'RE JUST MORE UPSET ABOUT THE ELECTION THEFT THAN YOU ARE"

Minutes after drawing increased attention to his besieged Vice President, the President called newly elected Senator Tommy Tuberville of Alabama at 2:26 p.m.[179] He misdialed, calling Senator Mike Lee of Utah instead, but one passed the phone to the other in short order.[180]

President Trump wanted to talk objections to the electoral count. But Senator Tuberville—along with every other elected official trapped and surrounded in the building—had other things on his mind.[181]

"I said, 'Mr. President, they've taken the Vice President out. They want me to get off the phone, I gotta go,'" Senator Tuberville told reporters.[182] "'[W]e're not doing much work here right now.'"[183]

In the next half hour, between 2:26 p.m. and 3:06 p.m., President Trump spoke with House Leader Kevin McCarthy.[184]

Leader McCarthy told the public in a live interview with CBS News, while he and his colleagues were sheltering at a secure location,[185] that he was "very clear" in telling President Trump "to talk to the nation to tell them to stop this."[186]

Leader McCarthy later recounted his conversation to a number of people, including Representative Jaime Herrera Beutler, a Republican congresswoman from Washington State.[187] "You have got to get on TV, you've got to get on Twitter, you've got to call these people off," he said he told the President.[188]

"[These] aren't my people, you know, these are—these are Antifa," President Trump insisted, against all evidence.[189] "They're your people. They literally just came through my office windows, and my staff are running for cover. I mean, they're running for their lives. You need to call them off," Leader McCarthy told him.[190]

What President Trump said next was "chilling," in Representative Herrera Beutler's words.[191]

"Well, Kevin, I guess they're just more upset about the election theft than you are," the President said.[192]

The call then devolved into a swearing match.[193]

Mick Mulvaney, former Chief of Staff to President Trump, had a similar call with Leader McCarthy in the days after the attack. McCarthy told Mulvaney that he urged the President to get the rioters to stop, and the President replied, "Kevin, maybe these people are just more angry about this than you are."[194]

Marc Short, the Vice President's Chief of Staff, spoke with Leader McCarthy later that afternoon.[195] Leader McCarthy told Short that he had spoken with President Trump and that he was "frustrat[ed]" that the White House was "not taking the circumstance as seriously as they should at that moment."[196] The administration was demonstrating a "lack of response or lack of responsibility," Leader McCarthy told Short.[197]

At 2:49 p.m.—as the violence escalated—President Trump's speechwriter Gabriel Robert texted someone: "Potus im sure is loving this."[198]

7.8 "STAY PEACEFUL!"

No one was getting through to the President.

So Herschmann went to Ivanka Trump's office, hoping she would come to the dining room and be "a calming influence" on her father.[199] Herschmann "just sort of barged in" and told her to turn on the television.[200] After taking in a few of the violent scenes together, Herschmann and Ivanka Trump left the room and walked to the dining room, where her father was holed up.[201]

At 2:38 p.m., the President issued a tweet: [202]

Please support our Capitol Police and Law Enforcement. They are truly on the side of our Country. Stay peaceful! [203]

Ivanka Trump told the Select Committee that the President "did not push back on [her] suggestion" to issue the tweet, and that it was either she or President Trump himself who suggested the last line, "Stay peaceful!" [204] She confirmed there may have been some tweaking of the wording.[205] McEnany, who was in the room at the time, wrote in her notes that "I say add 'we support PEACEFUL protest.' Ivanka add stay peaceful! Instead." [206] To the Select Committee, McEnany echoed Ivanka Trump that the President wasn't resistant in any way to putting out the message.[207]

But in private, McEnany told a different story to her deputy Sarah Matthews.

Back in the White House press office, Matthews told McEnany that the tweet did not go far enough in condemning the violence.[208] McEnany— noting that other staffers in the room were distracted—said "in a hushed tone . . . that the President did not want to include any sort of mention of peace in that tweet." [209]

That took "some convincing on their part," McEnany said, and "it wasn't until Ivanka Trump suggested the phrase 'Stay peaceful!' that he finally agreed to include it." [210]

Ivanka Trump repeatedly returned to the dining room to counsel her father throughout the day. It has been reported that each time Ivanka Trump "thought she had made headway" with her father, Meadows would call her "to say the [P]resident still needed more persuading"—a cycle that repeated itself over "several hours" that afternoon.[211] After one such trip, Ivanka Trump told the Select Committee she went to her husband's office next door because she needed to "regroup" and collect herself.[212]

Several witnesses corroborated pieces of this account. General Kellogg said he saw Ivanka Trump coming and going from the dining room at least twice that afternoon.[213] Hutchinson said that it was "several times." [214] Once, Ivanka Trump reportedly left her father with a look on her face as if

Sarah Matthews testifies at a January 6th Select Committee hearing.
(Photo by House Creative Services)

"[s]he had just had a tough conversation."[215] Radford, Ivanka Trump's Chief of Staff, saw that she was "[v]isibly upset" but continued going "down there when people were asking her to be down there and trying to get action taken."[216]

Radford told the Select Committee that Ivanka Trump believed that "[s]omething should be said or put out that was even stronger."[217]

Hutchinson, too, recalled Ivanka Trump dropping by Meadows's office alongside Cipollone and talking about trying to convince her father to say something "more direct than he had wanted to at that time and throughout the afternoon."[218]

"I remember her saying at various points," Hutchinson said, "she wanted her dad to send them home. She wanted her dad to tell them to go home peacefully, and she wanted to include language that he necessarily wasn't on board with at the time."[219]

7.9 "THE PRESIDENT NEEDS TO STOP THIS ASAP"

President Trump's 2:38 p.m. tweet did not condemn the violence at the Capitol. It did not tell rioters to leave the building.

Testimony footage of former White House Press Secretary Kayleigh McEnany is played during a January 6th Select Committee hearing.

(Photo by Pool/Getty Images)

In the minutes before the tweet, Fox News—on the President's screen—relayed that the Capitol was on lockdown;[220] that Capitol police officers were injured; that rioters were in the building and "just feet from the House chamber."[221] In the minutes afterward, networks would report there was tear gas in the Capitol, forcing Members of Congress to evacuate in protective masks.[222] At 2:39 p.m., Secret Service agents reported that "[m]ore just got in."[223]

"I don't know how they're gonna retake the Capitol building back at this point," one agent wrote to others two minutes later.[224]

At 2:44 p.m., a Capitol police officer shot a rioter named Ashli Bab- bitt.[225] A handwritten note—dashed off onto a White House pocket card and preserved by the National Archives—read: "1x civilian gunshot wound to chest @ door of House cha[m]ber."[226] One White House employee saw the note on the dining table in front of President Trump.[227]

A barrage of text messages inundated Meadows's phone with a consis- tent plea.[228] Everyone from conservative media personalities to Republican allies in Congress—and even the President's own family—urged the Presi- dent to do more:

Representative Marjorie Taylor Greene, 2:28 p.m.: "Mark I was just told there is an active shooter on the first floor of the Capitol Please tell the President to calm people[.] This isn't the way to solve anything."[229]

Laura Ingraham, 2:32 p.m.: "Hey Mark, The [sic] president needs to tell people in the Capitol to go home." "This is hurting all of us." "He is destroying his legacy and playing into every stereotype . . . we lose all credibility against the BLM/Antifa crowd if things go South." "You can tell him I said this."[230]

Mick Mulvaney, 2:35 p.m.: "Mark: he needs to stop this, now. Can I do anything to help?"[231]

Representative Barry Loudermilk, 2:44 p.m.: "It's really bad up here on the hill." "They have breached the Capitol."[232] At 2:48 p.m., Meadows responded: "POTUS is engaging."[233] At 2:49 p.m., Loudermilk responded: "Thanks. This doesn't help our cause."[234]

Representative William Timmons, 2:46 p.m.: "The president needs to stop this ASAP."[235] At 2:49 p.m., Meadows responded: "We are doing it."[236]

Donald Trump, Jr., 2:53 p.m.: "He's got to condem [sic] this shit. Asap. The captiol [sic] police tweet is not enough."[237] Meadows responded: "I am pushing it hard. I agree."[238] Later, Trump, Jr., continued: "This his [sic] one you go to the mattresses on. They will try to fuck his entire legacy on this if it gets worse."[239]

White House staff discussed issuing yet another, stronger statement to address the ongoing—and escalating—violence. Around 3:00 p.m., one proposal was written in block capital letters on a pocket card from the chief of staff's office:

ANYONE WHO ENTERED THE CAPITOL ILLEGALLY WITHOUT PROPER AUTHORITY SHOULD LEAVE IMMEDIATELY[.][240]

The handwriting appears to have been scrawled quickly and somewhat messily. Hutchinson recalled Meadows returning from the dining room with the note in hand and placing it on her desk.[241] The word "illegally" had been newly crossed out.[242]

But there would be no further action, Meadows told her.[243]

At 3:13 p.m., 35 minutes after his last tweet, the President issued another tweet. Rather than coming out with a stronger statement, the 3:13 p.m. tweet largely parroted the one preceding it:

Guns are drawn in the House Chamber on January 6th as rioters attempt to break in.
(Photo by Drew Angerer/Getty Images)

I am asking for everyone at the U.S. Capitol to remain peaceful. No violence! Remember, WE are the Party of Law & Order—respect the Law and our great men and women in Blue. Thank you! [244]

Ivanka Trump—who was in the room when her father published the message—told the Select Committee that "the gravity of the situation" made her feel "that it would be helpful to tweet again." [245] "The [earlier] tweet didn't stop the violence," Herschmann said. [246]

This tweet—like the last one—didn't tell the rioters to go home. It suggested that they "remain" at the Capitol, albeit peacefully.

7.10 "WE LOVE YOU. YOU'RE VERY SPECIAL"

The President's tweets were not tamping down on the violence, and White House staff knew it. [247] By 3:17 p.m., Fox News was reporting gunshots on Capitol Hill. Law enforcement officers could be seen in the House chamber, pointing guns over the barricaded door: The chyron blared "Guns Drawn on House Floor." [248] Between 3:29 p.m. and 3:42 p.m., the network was flashing images of a protestor in the presiding officer's chair, right where Vice

President Pence had been sitting 90 minutes earlier.[249] Other images showed Members of Congress trapped in the House gallery, crouching below the balcony for cover.[250]

Allies continued to text Meadows, begging the President to order the mob to go home and indicating that it was time the American people hear from the President directly:

Unknown, 3:04 p.m.: "Are you with potus right now? Hearing he is in the dining room watching this on TV . . ." "Is he going to say anything to de-escalate apart from that Tweet?"[251]

Reince Priebus, 3:09 p.m.: "TELL THEM TO GO HOME !!!"[252]

Unknown, 3:13 p.m.: "POTUS should go on air and defuse this. Extremely important."[253]

Alyssa Farah, 3:13 p.m.: "Potus has to come out firmly and tell protestors to dissipate. Someone is going to get killed . . ."[254]

Representative Chip Roy, 3:25 p.m.: "Fix this now."[255] Meadows responded: "We are."[256]

Sean Hannity (Fox News), 3:31 p.m.: "Can he make a statement. I saw the tweet. Ask people to peacefully leave the capital [sic]."[257] Meadows responded: "On it."[258]

Katrina Pierson, 3:40 p.m.: "Note: I was able to keep the crazies off the stage. I stripped all branding of those nutty groups and removed videos of all of the psychos. Glad it [sic] fought it."[259]

Unknown, 3:42 p.m.: "Pls have POTUS call this off at the Capitol. Urge rioters to disperse. I pray to you."[260]

Unknown, 3:57 p.m.: "Is he coming out?" "He has to right?"[261]

Brian Kilmeade, 3:58 p.m. (Fox News): "Please get him on tv. Destroying every thing you guys have accomplished."[262]

Donald Trump, Jr., 4:05 p.m.: "We need an oval address. He has to lead now. It's gone too far and gotten out of hand."[263]

At any moment in the afternoon, it would have been easy for President Trump to get before cameras and call off the attack. The White House Press Briefing Room is just down the hallway from the Oval Office, past the Cabinet Room and around the corner to the right. It would have taken less than 60 seconds for the President to get there.[264] The space, moreover, is outfitted with cameras that are constantly "hot," meaning that they are on and ready to go live at a moment's notice.[265] The White House press corps is

also situated in the West Wing, right by the briefing room.[266] The whole affair could have been assembled in minutes.[267]

However, it was not until nearly 3 hours after the violence began that President Trump finally agreed to tell the mob to go home.[268]

The Presidential Daily Diary notes that President Trump left the dining room to shoot the video at 4:03 p.m.[269] By this point—per Fox News coverage playing continually in the dining room—more law enforcement officers had arrived at the Capitol to resist the violent mob.[270]

The video shoot took place in the Rose Garden, the outdoor space that borders the Oval Office and the West Wing.[271] The setup was not ornate, just a camera and a microphone. Luna made sure that the background and lighting looked good, and that President Trump's hair and tie were in place.[272] President Trump delivered his remarks in one take, more or less, although he stopped and restarted at one point.[273] In all, the video took less than 4 minutes to shoot, and the President was back in the dining room by 4:07 p.m.[274]

"I would stick to this script . . . ," McEnany told President Trump before he stepped out to film.[275]

He didn't.

Kushner and others had drafted a statement, but President Trump spoke entirely off the cuff.[276] Here's what he said:

> I know your pain. I know you're hurt. We had an election that was stolen from us. It was a landslide election and everyone knows it, especially the other side. But you have to go home now. We have to have peace. We have to have law and order. We have to respect our great people in law and order. We don't want anybody hurt. It's a very tough period of time. There's never been a time like this where such a thing happened where they could take it away from all of us, from me, from you, from our country. This was a fraudulent election. But we can't play into the hands of these people. We have to have peace. So go home, we love you. You're very special. You've seen what happens. You see the way others are treated that are so bad and so evil. I know how you feel, but go home and go home in peace.[277]

A photo obtained from the National Archives shows President Trump and Herschmann huddled next to each other, watching a completed take through the monitor on the video camera.[278]

"There needs to be a more direct statement" telling the rioters to leave the Capitol, Luna heard Herschmann—yet again—tell the President.[279] Herschmann testified that he did not recall this exchange.[280]

But according to Luna, President Trump rejected the note.

"These people are in pain," he said in reply.[281]

Down at the Capitol, the video began streaming onto rioters' phones, and by all accounts including video footage taken by other rioters, they listened to President Trump's command.

"Donald Trump has asked everybody to go home," one rioter shouted as he "deliver[ed] the President's message." "That's our order," another rioter responded. Others watching the video responded: "He says, go home."[282]

The crowd afterward began to disperse.[283] The video made clear what had been evident to many, including those closest to him: The President could have called off the rioters far earlier and at any point that day.[284] But he chose not to do so.[285]

It was not until it was obvious that the riot would fail to stop the certification of the vote that the President finally relented and released a video statement made public at 4:17 p.m.[286]

President Trump huddles with aides, watching a completed take of a video through the monitor of the video camera.
(Photo provided to the Select Committee by the National Archives and Records Administration)

7.11 "REMEMBER THIS DAY FOREVER!"

After leaving the Rose Garden, the President returned to the dining room. At 6:01 p.m., he issued another tweet, the last of the day:

> These are the things and events that happen when a sacred land-slide election victory is so unceremoniously & viciously stripped away from great patriots who have been badly & unfairly treated for so long. Go home with love & in peace. Remember this day for-ever! [287]

He retired to his residence for the evening at 6:27 p.m.[288] A White House photographer captured the President walking back to the residence with an employee in tow, carrying personal items President Trump wished to bring home with him for the night.[289] In the employee's hands are the gloves the President was wearing while addressing the crowd at the Ellipse.[290]

The President had one parting comment to the employee—the thing that was evidently occupying his mind even after an afternoon of violence—before he retired to his home.

"Mike Pence let me down," the President concluded.[291]

7.12 PRESIDENT TRUMP STILL SOUGHT TO DELAY THE JOINT SESSION

Even after President Trump finally told the rioters to go home, he and his lead attorney, Rudolph Giuliani, continued to seek to delay the joint session of Congress.

Giuliani began frantically calling the White House line the very minute that the President's video went up on Twitter.[292] Failing to get through, he called back, once every minute—4:17 p.m., 4:18 p.m., 4:19 p.m., 4:20 p.m.[293] He managed to get through, briefly, to Mark Meadows at 4:21 p.m., and then kept calling the White House line: at 4:22 p.m., three times on two different phones at 4:23 p.m., 4:24 p.m., and once more at 5:05 p.m.[294] He finally managed to speak with President Trump at 5:07 p.m., and the two spoke for almost 12 minutes.[295]

After he spoke with President Trump, Giuliani's phone calls went nearly without fail to Members of Congress: Senator Marsha Blackburn, and then Senator Mike Lee.[296] He made three calls to Senator Bill Hagerty, then two to Representative Jim Jordan.[297] He called Senator Lindsey Graham,[298] Senator Josh Hawley,[299] and Senator Ted Cruz.[300] Giuliani had two calls with Senator Dan Sullivan over the course of the evening.[301] There were another three calls to Representative Jordan, none of which connected.[302] After 8:06 p.m., when the joint session resumed, the calls to Members of Congress finally stopped.[303] Shortly afterward, at 8:39 p.m., Giuliani had one final call of 9 minutes with the President.[304]

When asked about these calls during his deposition before the Select Committee, Giuliani initially refused to answer. Giuliani insisted his calls to Members of Congress—none of whom were his client—were all attorney-client privileged.[305] But Giuliani eventually relented.

"I was probably calling to see any—if anything could be done," he said. "About the vote—the vote." [306]

We know definitively what Giuliani was up to because he left a voice message for Senator Tuberville—inadvertently on Senator Lee's phone—recording his request.[307] He wanted for "you, our Republican friends to try to just slow it down," referring to the electoral count, and delay the joint session.[308] Here are his own words:

> The only strategy we can follow is to object to numerous States and raise issues so that we get ourselves into tomorrow—ideally until the end of tomorrow. So if you could object to every State and, along with a congressman, get a hearing for every State, I know we would delay you a lot, but it would give us the opportunity to get the legislators who are very, very close to pulling their vote.[309]

Mike Pence reopens the joint session of Congress and resumes counting electoral votes.
(Photo by Will McNamee/Getty Images)

The President, too, was at home, but he remained focused on his goal. Between 6:54 p.m. and 11:23 p.m., he spoke with 13 people, some more than once.[310] Of the 13, six ignored or expressly refused to comply with Select Committee requests for their testimony.[311] Two agreed to appear but refused to answer questions about their phone calls with the President, citing executive privilege.[312] Two more refused to answer questions, claiming attorney-client privilege.[313]

Of the 13, five were President Trump's attorneys or lawyers who worked with him on efforts to reverse the outcome of the election. With one exception, each of these calls took place before 8:06 p.m., when Vice President Pence reopened the joint session of Congress and resumed counting the electoral votes.[314] The President spoke with White House Counsel Pat Cipollone for 7 minutes at 7:01 p.m.[315] He spoke with Kurt Olsen and Mark Martin, lawyers who both advised him on the Vice President's role in the joint session:[316] He spoke with Martin for 9 minutes at 7:30 p.m., and Olsen twice, for 11 minutes at 7:17 p.m. and for another 10 minutes at 7:40 p.m.[317] He spoke with Cleta Mitchell, the lawyer leading his election challenges in Georgia, for 2 minutes at 7:53 p.m.[318] The President spoke with Herschmann for 5 minutes at 10:50 p.m.[319]

Another five of the people who spoke with President Trump that night were employees or outside advisors who counseled him on communications issues. These calls, by contrast, predominantly took place after the joint session resumed.[320] He spoke with his communications director, Scavino, twice: for 7 minutes at 7:08 p.m. and for 15 minutes at 9:55 p.m.[321] He spoke with McEnany for 11 minutes at 9:42 p.m.[322] He took calls from Steve Bannon, for 7 minutes at 10:19 p.m., and Sean Hannity, for 8 minutes at 11:08 p.m.[323]

At 9:23 p.m., President Trump spoke with Jason Miller, his Campaign Communications Director, for 18 minutes.[324]

Of his own initiative, Miller had drafted a statement for the President assuring the nation that the transfer of power—despite the day's events— would, indeed, take place.[325] On their call, the President pushed back on the phrasing.

The President wanted the statement to promise a "peaceful transition" of power, rather than just an "orderly" one.[326]

Miller rejected the change and told him why rather bluntly.

"[T]hat ship's kind of already sailed," he said, "so we're going to say 'orderly transition.' "[327]

7.13 HE "JUST DIDN'T WANT TO TALK ABOUT IT ANYMORE"

The President did not, by any account, express grief or regret for what happened at the Capitol. Neither did he appear to grasp the gravity of what he had set in motion.

In his last phone call of the night, the President spoke with Johnny McEntee, his Director of Personnel.[328]

"[T]his is a crazy day," the President told him. McEntee said his tone was one of "[l]ike, wow, can you believe this shit . . .?"[329]

Did he express sadness over the violence visited upon the Capitol?

"No," McEntee said. "I mean, I think he was shocked by, you know, it getting a little out of control, but I don't remember sadness, specifically."[330]

President Trump didn't make any other phone calls for the rest of the night.[331] The President didn't call Vice President Pence. In fact, President Trump never called to check on his Vice President's safety that day. He didn't call the heads of any of the Federal law enforcement agencies. He didn't call the leadership—neither Republican nor Democrat—of the legislative branch of government that had just been overrun by a mob.[332]

Only two days after the riot, by January 8th, the President was over the whole thing.

He "just didn't want to talk about it anymore," he told his press aides. "[H]e was tired of talking about it." [333]

Ivanka Trump claimed to the Select Committee that her father was "disappointed and surprised" by the attack, but she could not name a specific instance of him expressly saying it.

"He—I just felt that," she said. "I know him really well." [334]

Here's what she could definitively say:

Committee Staff: Has he ever expressed to you any sentiment that he did or did not do the right thing in how he responded on the day of the 6th?

Ms. Trump: No.

Committee Staff: Has he ever expressed any sentiment about something that he wished he had done on the day of the 6th?

Ms. Trump: No.

Committee Staff: Has he ever said anything to you about the people who were injured or who died that day?

Ms. Trump: No.

Committee Staff: Has he ever said anything to you about whether he should or should not continue to talk about the 2020 Presidential election after the events on the 6th?

Ms. Trump: No. [335]

7.14 PRESIDENT TRUMP'S "RHETORIC KILLED SOMEONE"

The President may not have expressed regret over his behavior, but some of his most loyal supporters made the connection between his words and the violence.

A member of the speechwriting team, Patrick MacDonnell, conceded the next day in a text that "maybe the rhetoric could have been better." [336] As the riot was in full throttle, even steadfast supporter Ali Alexander of "Stop the Steal" texted, "POTUS is not ignorant of what his words will do." [337]

"We all look like domestic terrorists now," Hope Hicks texted Julie Radford. [338]

Separately, Hicks texted Herschmann, "So predictable and so sad."

"I know," he replied. "Tragic."

"I'm so upset. Everything we worked for wiped away," she continued.

"I agree. Totally self-inflicted," he wrote. [339]

Brad Parscale, Trump's Former Campaign Manager, texted Katrina Pierson at 7:21 p.m. on January 6th, saying the day's events were the result of a "sitting president asking for civil war." [340]

"This week I feel guilty for helping him win . . . a woman is dead," Parscale added.

"You do realize this was going to happen," Pierson answered.

"Yeah. If I was trump [sic] and knew my rhetoric killed someone," he said.

"It wasn't the rhetoric," she said.

Parscale's reply: "Yes it was." [341]

ENDNOTES

1. As explained in Chapter 8, the Proud Boys and other extremists initiated the attack shortly before the joint session of Congress was set to begin at 1:00 p.m. The rioters who streamed down Pennsylvania to the U.S. Capitol from the Ellipse then provided crucial momentum for the attack.

2. "Manual for Courts-Martial United States," Department of Defense, (2019), at 334, available at https://jsc.defense.gov/Portals/99/Documents/2019%20MCM%20(Final)%20(20190108).pdf?ver=2019-01-11-115724-610.

3. Select Committee to Investigate the January 6th Attack on the United States Capitol, Transcribed Interview of General Mark. A. Milley, (Nov. 17, 2021), p. 268.

4. Select Committee to Investigate the January 6th Attack on the United States Capitol, Transcribed Interview of General Mark. A. Milley, (Nov. 17, 2021), p. 83.

5. Select Committee to Investigate the January 6th Attack on the United States Capitol, Transcribed Interview of General Mark. A. Milley, (Nov. 17, 2021), p. 296.

6. Select Committee to Investigate the January 6th Attack on the United States Capitol, Transcribed Interview of General Mark. A. Milley, (Nov. 17, 2021), p. 268.

7. Select Committee to Investigate the January 6th Attack on the United States Capitol, Transcribed Interview of Hope Hicks, (October 25, 2022), pp. 108-110; Documents on file with the Select Committee to Investigate the January 6th Attack on the United States Capitol (Hope Hicks Production), SC_HH_033 (Jan. 6, 2021, Hogan Gidley text message to Hope Hicks at 2:19 p.m. EST).

8. Documents on file with the Select Committee to Investigate the January 6th Attack on the United States Capitol (Hope Hicks Production), SC_HH_033 (Jan. 6, 2021, Hogan Gidley text message to Hope Hicks at 2:19 p.m. EST).

9. Documents on file with the Select Committee to Investigate the January 6th Attack on the United States Capitol (Hope Hicks Production), SC_HH_033 (Jan. 6, 2021, Hogan Gidley text message to Hope Hicks at 2:19 p.m. EST).

10. Donald J. Trump (@realDonaldTrump), Twitter, Jan. 6, 2021 2:38 p.m. ET, available at https://media-cdn.factba.se/realdonaldtrump-twitter/1346904110969315332.jpg (archived).

11. Select Committee to Investigate the January 6th Attack on the United States Capitol, Transcribed Interview of Sarah Matthews (Feb. 8, 2022), pp. 39–41.

12. Documents on file with the Select Committee to Investigate the January 6th Attack on the United States Capitol (Mark Meadows Production), MM014925 (January 6, 2021, Donald Trump Jr. text message to Mark Meadows at 2:53 p.m. ET).

13. At 3:13 p.m., President Trump tweeted: "I am asking for everyone at the U.S. Capitol to remain peaceful. No violence! Remember, WE are the Party of Law & Order—respect the Law and our great men and women in Blue. Thank you!" Donald J. Trump (@realDonaldTrump), Twitter, Jan. 6, 2021 3:13 p.m. ET, available at https://media-cdn.factba.se/realdonaldtrump-twitter/1346912780700577792.jpg (archived).

14. Tommy Christopher, "WATCH: GOP Rep Reveals Details of Trump's Bombshell Call with McCarthy Refusing to Call off Capitol Rioters," Mediaite, (Feb. 13, 2021), available at https://www.mediaite.com/news/watch-gop-rep-reveals-details-of-trumps-bombshell-call-with-mccarthy-refusing-to-call-off-capitol-rioters/.

15. Select Committee to Investigate the January 6th Attack on the United States Capitol, Hearing on the January 6th Investigation, 117th Cong., 2d sess., (July 12, 2022), available at https://www.govinfo.gov/committee/house-january6th.

16. "New Video of Capitol Rioter: 'Trump is Still Our President,'" CNN Business, at 0:37, Feb. 6, 2021, available at https://www.cnn.com/videos/media/2021/02/06/qanon-capitol-rioter-video-trump-still-president-sot-nr-vpx.cnn.

17. Trial Exhibit 6732 (1.S.159.1165-67, 84), *United States v. Rhodes et al.*, No. 1:22-cr-15 (D.D.C Nov. 1, 2022). Vallejo was manning the quick reaction force at a hotel in Arlington, Virginia, awaiting word to bring in a cache of weaponry; he was not at the Capitol on January 6th. Trial Exhibit 6731, *United States v. Rhodes et al.*, No. 1:22-cr-15 (D.D.C. Oct. 20, 2022) (Vallejo messaged his group in the afternoon "QRF standing by at hotel. Just say the word"); Trial Transcript at 2728, *United States v. Rhodes et al.*, No. 1:22-cr-15 (D.D.C. Oct. 12, 2022) (Oath Keeper Terry Cummings testified that "I had not seen that many weapons in one location since I was in the military" when he arrived at the Arlington hotel).

18. "Trump Video Telling Protesters at Capitol Building to Go Home: Transcript," Rev, (Jan. 6, 2021), available at https://www.rev.com/blog/transcripts/trump-video-telling-protesters-at-capitol-building-to-go-home-transcript.

19. "Trump Video Telling Protesters at Capitol Building to Go Home: Transcript," Rev, (Jan. 6, 2021), available at https://www.rev.com/blog/transcripts/trump-video-telling-protesters-at-capitol-building-to-go-home-transcript.

20. Donald J. Trump (@realdonaldtrump), Twitter, Jan. 6, 2021 6:01 ET, available at https://www.presidency.ucsb.edu/documents/tweets-january-6-2021 (archived).

21. Select Committee to Investigate the January 6th Attack on the United States Capitol, Hearing on the January 6th Investigation, 117th Cong., 2d sess., (June 28, 2022), available at https://www.govinfo.gov/committee/house-january6th; Select Committee to Investigate the January 6th Attack on the United States Capitol, Continued Interview of Cassidy Hutchinson, (June 20, 2022), p. 125.

22. Select Committee to Investigate the January 6th Attack on the United States Capitol, Deposition of John McEntee, (Mar. 28, 2022), p. 157.

23. Mariana Alfaro, "Trump Vows Pardon, Government Apology to Capitol Rioters if Elected," *Washington Post*, (Sept. 1, 2022), available at https://www.washingtonpost.com/national-security/2022/09/01/trump-jan-6-rioters-pardon/.

24. Donald J. Trump (@realdonaldtrump), Twitter, Jan. 6, 2021 8:06 a.m. ET, available at https://www.thetrumparchive.com/?searchbox=%22Sleepy+Eyes+Chuck+Todd+is+so+happy%22 (archived).

25. Donald J. Trump (@realdonaldtrump), Twitter, Jan. 6, 2021 8:17 a.m. ET, available at https://www.thetrumparchive.com/?searchbox=%22All+Mike+Pence+has+to+do+is%22 (archived).

26. Donald J. Trump (@realdonaldtrump), Twitter, Jan. 6, 2021 8:22 a.m. ET, available at https://www.thetrumparchive.com/?results=1 (archived).

27. Documents with file with the Select Committee to Investigate the January 6th Attack on the United States Capitol (National Archives Production), P-R000255 (January 6, 2021, The Daily Diary of President Donald J. Trump at 8:23 a.m. ET).

28. Documents on file with the Select Committee to Investigate the January 6th Attack on the United States Capitol (National Archives Production), P-R000255 (January 6, 2021, The Daily Diary of President Donald J. Trump at 8:23 a.m. ET). The Select Committee issued subpoenas to Bannon, Olson, and Giuliani in order to learn more about these telephone conversations, among other things. Bannon refused to comply with his subpoena, leading to his referral and ultimate conviction for criminal contempt of Congress. Olson sued to block the Select Committee from enforcing his subpoena. Giuliani spoke with the Select Committee but asserted attorney-client privilege with respect to all of his telephone conversations with President Trump on January 6th. Select Committee to Investigate the January 6th Attack on the United States Capitol, Deposition of Rudolph Giuliani, (May 20, 2022), p. 198.

29. Documents on file with the Select Committee to Investigate the January 6th Attack on the United States Capitol (National Archives Production), P-R000255 (January 6, 2021, The Daily Diary of President Donald J. Trump at 9:02 a.m. ET); Select Committee to Investigate the January 6th Attack on the United States Capitol, Deposition of Marc Short, (Jan. 26, 2022), p. 12.

30. Select Committee to Investigate the January 6th Attack on the United States Capitol, Deposition of Stephen Miller, (Apr. 14, 2022), p. 145.

31. Select Committee to Investigate the January 6th Attack on the United States Capitol, Deposition of Ross Worthington, (Feb. 15, 2022), p. 112; Documents on file with the Select Committee to Investigate the January 6th Attack on the United States Capitol (Ross Worthington Production), RW_0002633 (Jan. 4, 2021, email at 10:00 p.m. from Ross Worthington to Patrick MacDonnell asking for research related to the January 6th speech).

32. Documents on file with the Select Committee to Investigate the January 6th Attack on the United States Capitol (Ross Worthington Production), RW_0002341–RW_0002351 (Jan. 6, 2021, Stephen Miller emails to Ross Worthington, Vincent Haley and Robert Gabriel, Jr. at 10:22 and 10:23 a.m. ET, attaching draft speech).

33. Documents on file with the Select Committee to Investigate the January 6th Attacks on the United States Capitol (Ross Worthington Production), RW_0002341–2344 (Jan. 6, 2021, email from Stephen Miller to Ross Worthington, Vincent Haley, and Robert Gabriel, re: EDITS, attaching draft Save America March speech with edits and comments).

34. Documents on file with the Select Committee to Investigate the January 6th Attacks on the United States Capitol (Ross Worthington Production), RW_0002341–2343 (Jan. 6, 2021, email from Stephen Miller to Ross Worthington, Vincent Haley, and Robert Gabriel, re: EDITS, attaching draft Save America March speech with edits and comments).

35. Select Committee to Investigate the January 6th Attack on the United States Capitol, Deposition of Ross Worthington, (Feb. 15, 2022), p. 164. Select Committee to Investigate the January 6th Attack on the United States Capitol, Deposition of Vincent Haley, (April 12, 2022), pp. 88–89; Select Committee to Investigate the January 6th Attack on the United States Capitol, Transcribed Interview of Sarah Miller, (April 14, 2022), p. 148.

36. Documents on file with the Select Committee to Investigate the January 6th Attack on the United States Capitol (National Archives Production), 076P-R000007430_0001 (Jan. 6, 2021, Ross Worthington email to Vincent M. Haley at 10:49 a.m. ET).

37. Select Committee to Investigate the January 6th Attack on the United States Capitol, Deposition of Stephen Miller, (Apr. 14, 2022), p. 154.

38. Donald Trump (@realDonaldTrump), Twitter, Jan. 6, 2021 9:00 a.m. ET, available at https://www.thetrumparchive.com/?results=1&searchbox=%22they+just+happened+to+find%22 (archived); Donald Trump (@realDonaldTrump), Twitter, Jan. 6, 2021 9:15 a.m. ET, available at https://www.thetrumparchive.com/?results=1&searchbox=%22they+states+want+to+redo%22 (archived); Donald Trump (@realDonaldTrump), Twitter, Jan. 6, 2021 9:16 a.m. ET, available at https://www.thetrumparchive.com/?results=1&searchbox=%22even+Mexico%22 (archived); Donald Trump (@realDonaldTrump), Twitter, Jan. 6, 2021 10:44 a.m. ET, available at https://www.thetrumparchive.com/?results=1&searchbox=%22these+scoundrels+are+only+toying%22 (archived).

39. Documents on file with the Select Committee to Investigate the January 6th Attack on the Capitol, (National Archives Production), P-R000285 (January 6, 2021, Schedule marked private with handwritten notes at 11:22 a.m. ET); Select Committee to Investigate the January 6th Attack on the United States Capitol, Deposition of Keith Kellogg, Jr., (Dec. 14, 2021) pp. 90–93; Select Committee to Investigate the January 6th Attack on the United States Capitol, Deposition of Nicholas Luna, (Mar. 21, 2021), p. 126.

40. Select Committee to Investigate the January 6th Attack on the United States Capitol, Transcribed Interview of Eric Herschmann, (Apr. 6, 2022), pp. 48–49; *see also* Select Committee to Investigate the January 6th Attack on the United States Capitol, Transcribed Interview of White House Employee, (June 10, 2022), p. 22 ("I could just tell in his voice when he was talking to the Vice President that he was disappointed and frustrated.").

41. Select Committee to Investigate the January 6th Attack on the United States Capitol, Transcribed Interview of Eric Herschmann, (Apr. 6, 2022), p. 4.

42. Select Committee to Investigate the January 6th Attack on the United States Capitol, Deposition of Julie Radford, (May 24, 2020), p. 18.

43. *Compare* Documents on file with the Select Committee to Investigate the January 6th Attack on the United States Capitol (National Archives Production), P-R000285 (January 6, 2021, schedule with handwritten notes about the meeting); *with* Documents on file with the Select Committee to Investigate the January 6th Attack on the United States Capitol (Secret Service Production), CTRL0000100198 (communication noting "Mogul" en route to the Ellipse at 11:39 a.m.).

44. Select Committee to Investigate the January 6th Attack on the United States Capitol, Deposition of Keith Kellogg, Jr., (Dec. 14, 2021), p. 93.

45. Documents on file with the Select Committee to Investigate the January 6th Attack on the United States Capitol (National Archives Production), 076P_R000007558_0001 (Jan. 6, 2021, Stephen Miller email to Robert Gabriel Jr.).

46. Documents on file with the Select Committee to Investigate the January 6th Attack on the United States Capitol (National Archives Production), 076P-R000007531_0001 (Jan. 6, 2021, Robert Gabriel Jr. email to Ross Worthington at 11:33 a.m. ET).

47. Documents on file with the Select Committee to Investigate the January 6th Attack on the United States Capitol (National Archives Production), 076P_R000007531_0001 (Jan. 6, 2021, Ross Worthington email to Robert Gabriel Jr. at 11:34 a.m. ET).

48. Select Committee to Investigate the January 6th Attack on the United States Capitol, Deposition of Vincent Haley, (Apr. 12, 2022), p. 95.

49. Documents on file with the Select Committee to Investigate the January 6th Attacks on the United States Capitol (Ross Worthington Production), RW_0002341–2343 (January 6, 2021, email from Stephen Miller to Ross Worthington, Vincent Haley, and Robert Gabriel, re: EDITS, attaching draft Save America March speech with edits and comments).

50. *See* Select Committee to Investigate the January 6th Attack on the United States Capitol, Deposition of Vincent Haley, (Apr. 12, 2022), p. 95; Document on file with the Select Committee (National Archives Production), 076P-R000007557_0001, 076P-R000007557_0034, 076P-R000002896_00001, 076P-R000002896_00025, 076P-R000002984_0001, 076P-R000002984_00304 (various drafts, including teleprompter inputs, of the speech).

51. Select Committee to Investigate the January 6th Attack on the United States Capitol, Deposition of Nicholas Luna, (Mar. 21, 2022), p. 126.

52. Documents on file with the Select Committee to Investigate the January 6th Attack on the United States Capitol (National Archives Production), P-R000286 (January 6, 2021, note from Nicholas Luna to President Trump).

53. Documents on file with the Select Committee to Investigate the January 6th Attack on the United States Capitol (Secret Service Production), CTRL0000111236 (January. 6, 2021, Email Re: CSD Activity Log #2 at 2:49 p.m. ET).

54. Select Committee to Investigate the January 6th Attack on the United States Capitol, Transcribed Interview of Cassidy Hutchinson, (Feb. 23, 2022), pp. 87–88; Documents on file with the Select Committee to Investigate the January 6th Attack on the United States Capitol, (National Archives Production), 076P-R000005179_0001–0002 (January 6, 2021 email reporting on the status of people going through the magnetometers and noting "[s]everal thousand on the mall watching but not in line.").

55. Select Committee to Investigate the January 6th Attack on the United States Capitol, Continued Interview of Cassidy Hutchinson, (June 20, 2022), pp. 12–13.

56. Documents on file with the Select Committee to Investigate the January 6th Attack on the United States Capitol (Cassidy Hutchinson Production), CH-0000000069, (January 6, 2021, Cassidy Hutchinson text message to Tony Ornato at 12:45 p.m. ET).

57. Select Committee to Investigate the January 6th Attack on the United States Capitol, Continued Interview of Cassidy Hutchinson, (June 20, 2022), pp. 15–16; *see also* Select Committee to Investigate the January 6th Attack on the United States Capitol, *Hearing on the January 6th Investigation*, 117th Cong., 2d sess., (June 28, 2022), available at https://www.govinfo.gov/committee/house-january6th ("[W]e were standing towards the front of the tent with the TVs really close to where he would walk out to go on to the stage. The—these conversations happened two to three minutes before he took the stage that morning").

58. Documents on file with the Select Committee to Investigate the January 6th Attack on the United States Capitol (National Archives Production), P-R000255 (Jan. 6, 2021, Daily Diary of President Donald J. Trump at 11:55 a.m. ET).

59. "Donald Trump Speech 'Save America' Rally Transcript January 6," Rev, (Jan. 6, 2021), available at https://www.rev.com/blog/transcripts/donald-trump-speech-save-america-rally-transcript-january-6 (time-stamping the speech).

60. Documents on file with the Select Committee to Investigate the January 6th Attack on the United States Capitol (Cassidy Hutchinson Production), CH-0000000069 (January 6, 2021, Cassidy Hutchinson text message to Tony Ornato at 12:45 p.m. ET).

61. Select Committee to Investigate the January 6th Attack on the United States Capitol, Continued Interview of Cassidy Hutchinson, (June 20, 2022), p. 8.

62. Documents on file with the Select Committee to Investigate the January 6th Attack on the United States Capitol (National Archives Production), 076P-R000002879_00001 ("Save America March" speech early draft); Select Committee to Investigate the January 6th Attack on the United States Capitol, Deposition of Ross Worthington, (Feb. 15, 2022), p. 157.

63. Brian Naylor, "Read Trump's Jan. 6 Speech, A Key Part of Impeachment Trial," *NPR*, (Feb. 10, 2021), available at https://www.npr.org/2021/02/10/966396848/read-trumps-jan-6-speech-a-key-part-of-impeachment-trial.

64. "Donald Trump Speech 'Save America' Rally Transcript January 6," Rev, (Jan. 6, 2021), available at https://www.rev.com/blog/transcripts/donald-trump-speech-save-america-rally-transcript-january-6 (timestamping the speech).

65. "Donald Trump Speech 'Save America' Rally Transcript January 6," Rev, (Jan. 6, 2021), available at https://www.rev.com/blog/transcripts/donald-trump-speech-save-america-rally-transcript-january-6 (time-stamping the speech); Documents on file with the Select Committee to Investigate the January 6th Attack on the United States Capitol (Alex Holder Production) Video file Clip 45DAY32CAMB0050.mov at 3:10–3:40 (capturing "fight for Trump" chants during Donald Trump, Jr.'s speech); Lena V. Groeger, Jeff Kao, Al Shaw, Moiz Syed, and Maya Eliahou, "What Parler Saw During the Attack on the Capitol," ProPublica, at 12:01 pm at 3:33 and at 12:05 pm at 0:30 (Jan. 17, 2021), available at https://projects.propublica.org/parler-capitol-videos/ (capturing "fight for Trump" chants droning out the President after he told the crowd "we will not let them silence your voices"); FORMER WAGIE, "FULL FOOTAGE: Patriots STORM U.S. Capitol," YouTube, at 59:00, Jan. 6, 2021, posted Jan. 8, 2021, available at https://www.youtube.com/watch?v=iNFcdpZdkh0.

66. Brian Naylor, "Read Trump's Jan. 6 Speech, A Key Part of Impeachment Trial," *NPR*, (Feb. 10, 2021), available at https://www.npr.org/2021/02/10/966396848/read-trumps-jan-6-speech-a-key-part-of-impeachment-trial.

67. Select Committee to Investigate the January 6th Attack on the United States Capitol, *Hearing on the January 6th Investigation*, 117th Cong., 2d sess., (June 28, 2022), available at https://www.govinfo.gov/committee/house-january6th. *But see* Select Committee to Investigate the January 6th Attack on the United States Capitol, Transcribed Interview of Cassidy Hutchinson, (Feb. 23, 2022), p. 129 ("It wasn't—he didn't give me an impressions that he was frustrated or angry at the prospect of what the President had said on the stage. It was more of him trying to rush to get insight on what our plans were and wanted to have insight and be read in on that in case we had been planning to go up to the Capitol.").

68. Documents on file with the Select Committee to Investigate the January 6th Attack on the United States Capitol (Cassidy Hutchinson Production), CH-0000000069.

69. Select Committee to Investigate the January 6th Attack on the United States Capitol, Transcribed Interview of Cassidy Hutchinson, (Feb. 23, 2022), pp.128–29; Select Committee to Investigate the January 6th Attack on the United States Capitol, *Hearing on the January 6th Investigation*, 117th Cong., 2d sess., (June 28, 2022), available at https://www.govinfo.gov/committee/house-january6th.

70. Select Committee to Investigate the January 6th Attack on the United States Capitol, *Hearing on the January 6th Investigation*, 117th Cong., 2d sess., (June 28, 2022), available at https://www.govinfo.gov/committee/house-january6th.

71. Documents on file with the Select Committee to Investigate the January 6th Attack on the United States Capitol (Secret Service Production), USSS0000176702.

72. Documents on file with the Select Committee to Investigate the January 6th Attack on the United States Capitol (National Archives Production), P-R001005-1026 (January 6, 2021, National Security Council staff chat logs); *See* Select Committee to Investigate the January 6th Attack on the United States Capitol, Transcribed Interview White House Security Official, (July 11, 2022), p. 47 (discussing clearing a route to the Capitol for "Mogul").

73. Select Committee to Investigate the January 6th Attack on the United States Capitol, Transcribed Interview of White House Security Official, (July 11, 2022), p. 45.

74. Select Committee to Investigate the January 6th Attack on the United States Capitol, Transcribed Interview of White House Security Official, (July 11, 2022), p. 45.

75. Select Committee to Investigate the January 6th Attack on the United States Capitol, Transcribed Interview of White House Security Official , (July 11, 2022), p. 45.

76. Documents on file with the Select Committee to Investigate the January 6th Attack on the United States Capitol (Secret Service Production), CTRL0000208061 (January 6, 2021, email to Robert Engel at 1:19 p.m. ET). Despite the fact that the prospect of an OTR to the Capitol was raised at the highest levels within the Secret Service, some of its highest-ranking agents insisted to the Select Committee that they did not recall any such discussions on the day of January 6th. Select Committee to Investigate the January 6th Attack on the United States Capitol, Transcribed Interview of Robert Engel, (Mar. 4. 2022), p. 77. When presented with his text messages with Cassidy Hutchinson in which she referred to an "OTR to Capitol," Tony Ornato insisted that he didn't "recall ever talking about this with her." Select Committee to Investigate the January 6th Attack on the United States Capitol, Transcribed Interview of Anthony Ornato, (Mar. 29, 2022), p. 62.

77. Select Committee to Investigate the January 6th Attack on the United States Capitol, Deposition of Nicholas Luna, (Mar. 21, 2022), p. 117.

78. Select Committee to Investigate the January 6th Attack on the United States Capitol, Continued Interview of Cassidy Hutchinson, (June 20, 2022), p. 8.

79. Documents on file with the Select Committee to Investigate the January 6th Attack on the United States Capitol (National Archives Production), P-R000257 (January 6, 2021, Presidential Daily Diary).

80. *See, e.g.,* Select Committee to Investigate the January 6th Attack on the United States Capi-
     tol, Transcribed Interview of United States Secret Service Employee "Press Secretary,"
     (October 31, 2022), pp. 49–51 (the word "furious" was "consistent with what was described
     to me that occurred—you know, agitated, furious, upset, angry, whatever adjective").

81. Mark Meadows, *The Chief's Chief,* (St. Petersburg: All Seasons Press, 2021), at p. 250 ("When
     he got offstage, President Trump let me know that he had been speaking metaphorically
     about the walk to the Capitol. . . . It was clear the whole time that he didn't actually intent
     to walk down Pennsylvania Avenue with the crowd.").

82. Select Committee to Investigate the January 6th Attack on the United States Capitol, Infor-
     mal Interview of Robert Engel, (Mar. 4, 2022).

83. Select Committee to Investigate the January 6th Attack on the United States Capitol, Depo-
     sition of Kayleigh McEnany, (Jan. 12, 2022), pp. 158–62.

84. Select Committee to Investigate the January 6th Attack on the United States Capitol, Depo-
     sition of Kayleigh McEnany, (Jan. 12, 2022), p. 159.

85. Select Committee to Investigate the January 6th Attack on the United States Capitol, Depo-
     sition of Kayleigh McEnany, (Jan. 12, 2022), p. 160.

86. *See, e.g.,* Select Committee to Investigate the January 6th Attack on the United States Capi-
     tol, Continued Interview of Cassidy Hutchinson, (June 20, 2022), pp. 5–8.

87. *See, e.g.,* Select Committee to Investigate the January 6th Attack on the United States Capi-
     tol, Deposition of Max Miller, (Jan. 20, 2022), p. 90; Select Committee to Investigate the
     January 6th Attack on the United States Capitol, Deposition of Judson P. Deere, (Mar. 3,
     2022), p. 71; Select Committee to Investigate the January 6th Attack on the United States
     Capitol, Deposition of Nicholas Luna, (Mar. 21, 2022) p. 118; Select Committee to Investigate
     the January 6th Attack on the United States Capitol, Transcribed Interview of White House
     Security Official, (July 11, 2022) pp. 35–36.

88. Select Committee to Investigate the January 6th Attack on the United States Capitol, Con-
     tinued Interview of Cassidy Hutchinson, (June 20, 2022), p. 5.

89. Select Committee to Investigate the January 6th Attack on the United States Capitol, Con-
     tinued Interview of Cassidy Hutchinson, (June 20, 2022), p. 5.

90. Select Committee to Investigate the January 6th Attack on the United States Capitol, *Hear-
     ing on the January 6th Investigation*, 117th Cong., 2d sess., (June 28, 2022), available at
     https://www.govinfo.gov/committee/house-january6th.

91. Select Committee to Investigate the January 6th Attack on the United States Capitol, Con-
     tinued Interview of Cassidy Hutchinson, (June 20, 2022), pp. 6–7.

92. Select Committee to Investigate the January 6th Attack on the United States Capitol, Tran-
     scribed Interview of White House Employee with National Security Responsibilities, (July 19,
     2022), pp. 69–71.

93. Select Committee to Investigate the January 6th Attack on the United States Capitol, Tran-
     scribed Interview of White House Employee with National Security Responsibilities, (July 19,
     2022), p. 71.

94. Select Committee to Investigate the January 6th Attack on the United States Capitol, Con-
     tinued Interview of Robert Engel, (Nov. 17, 2022), pp. 143–44, 147-48.

95. Select Committee to Investigate the January 6th Attack on the United States Capitol, Tran-
     scribed Interview of United States Secret Service Employee, (Nov. 21, 2022), pp. 92–93.

96. Select Committee to Investigate the January 6th Attack on the United States Capitol, Tran-
     scribed Interview of White House Employee with National Security Responsibilities (July 19,
     2022), p. 73 ("In the days following that, I do remember, you know, again, hearing again
     how angry the President was when, you know, they were in the limo.")

97. Select Committee to Investigate the January 6th Attack on the United States Capitol, Con-
     tinued Interview of Cassidy Hutchinson, (Sep. 14, 2022), pp. 34, 36, 37–38, 55.

98. Select Committee to Investigate the January 6th Attack on the United States Capitol, Transcribed Interview of Mark Robinson, (July 7, 2022), pp. 18, 23.

99. Select Committee to Investigate the January 6th Attack on the United States Capitol, Transcribed Interview of United States Secret Service Employee, (Nov. 4, 2022), pp. 99–100.

100. Select Committee to Investigate the January 6th Attack on the United States Capitol, Transcribed Interview of United States Secret Service Employee "Press Secretary," (Oct. 31, 2022), pp. 46, 50.

101. Select Committee to Investigate the January 6th Attack on the United States Capitol, Transcribed Interview of United States Secret Service Employee "Press Secretary," (Oct. 31, 2022), p. 50; see also Carol Leonnig (@CarolLeonnig), Twitter, June 28, 2022 7:46 p.m. ET, available at https://twitter.com/CarolLeonnig/status/1541931078184845312. The press secretary confirmed that he or she confirmed this information to the reporter because "that's what I had been told." "[Engel] did indicate—you know, kind of outlined . . . that the President did want to go to the Capitol, and Mr. Engel advised that we cannot go," the press secretary testified. "And you know, [President Trump] was agitated, but Mr. Engel advised that—you know, it was kind of a non-issue. It was agitated verbally, and they proceeded to the White House." Select Committee to Investigate the January 6th Attack on the United States Capitol, Transcribed Interview of United States Secret Service Employee "Press Secretary," (Oct. 31, 2022), pp. 46, 50.

102. The Select Committee has agreed not to name the Secret Service agent who was driving the vehicle to protect his privacy. We will refer to him in this report as "the driver."

103. See Select Committee to Investigate the January 6th Attack on the United States Capitol, Transcribed Interview of Secret Service Employee "Driver," (Nov. 7, 2022), p. 77; Select Committee to Investigate the January 6th Attack on the United States Capitol, Continued Interview of Robert Engel, (Nov. 17, 2022), pp. 100–01.

104. Select Committee to Investigate the January 6th Attack on the United States Capitol, Continued Interview of Robert Engel, (Nov. 17, 2022), pp. 100–01.

105. Select Committee to Investigate the January 6th Attack on the United States Capitol, Transcribed Interview of Secret Service Employee "Driver," (Nov. 7, 2022), p. 77.

106. Select Committee to Investigate the January 6th Attack on the United States Capitol, Transcribed Interview of Secret Service Employee "Driver," (Nov. 7, 2022), p. 77.

107. Select Committee to Investigate the January 6th Attack on the United States Capitol, Transcribed Interview of Secret Service Employee "Driver," (Nov. 7, 2022), p. 78.

108. Select Committee to Investigate the January 6th Attack on the United States Capitol, Transcribed Interview of Secret Service Employee "Driver," (Nov. 7, 2022), p. 79.

109. Select Committee to Investigate the January 6th Attack on the United States Capitol, Transcribed Interview of Secret Service Employee "Driver," (Nov. 7, 2022), p. 78. This recollection of the President's phrasing seems very similar to Hutchinson's testimony about President Trump's statement before he took the stage at the Ellipse: "I'm the President. Take the F'ing mags away. They're not here to hurt me." Select Committee to Investigate the January 6th Attack on the United States Capitol, Continued Interview of Cassidy Hutchinson, (June 20, 2022), pp. 11–12.

110. Select Committee to Investigate the January 6th Attack on the United States Capitol, Transcribed Interview of United States Secret Service Employee, (Nov. 7, 2022), pp. 78, 92.

111. Select Committee to Investigate the January 6th Attack on the United States Capitol, Transcribed Interview of United States Secret Service Employee, (Nov. 7, 2022), p. 78.

112. Select Committee to Investigate the January 6th Attack on the United States Capitol, Continued Interview of Robert Engel, (Nov. 17, 2022), p. 102. Mr. Engel also did not recall another occasion where testimony indicates that the incident in the presidential vehicle was mentioned. Mr. Engel's counsel has asked the Committee not to make certain evidence relating to that occasion public.

113. Select Committee to Investigate the January 6th Attack on the United States Capitol, Continued Interview of Robert Engel, (Nov. 17, 2022), pp. 143–44, 147–48.

114. Select Committee to Investigate the January 6th Attack on the United States Capitol, Transcribed Interview of Secret Service Employee "Driver," (Nov. 7, 2022), p. 80.

115. The Justice Department will have all of the relevant information and can make decisions about whether and how to proceed based upon this evidence.

116. Select Committee to Investigate the January 6th Attack on the United States Capitol, Continued Interview of Robert Engel, (Nov. 17, 2022), p. 121.

117. Documents on file with the Select Committee to Investigate the January 6th Attack on the United States Capitol (Secret Service Production), CTRL0000882478 at p. 4 (January 6, 2021, PID update at 1:25 p.m.).

118. Select Committee to Investigate the January 6th Attack on the United States Capitol, Transcribed Interview of Mark Robinson, (July 7, 2022), pp. 18–19.

119. Select Committee to Investigate the January 6th Attack on the United States Capitol, Continued Interview of Robert Engel, (Nov. 17, 2022), p. 121.

120. Select Committee to Investigate the January 6th Attack on the United States Capitol, Continued Interview of Robert Engel, (Nov. 17, 2022), p. 125.

121. Documents on file with the Select Committee to Investigate the January 6th Attack on the United States Capitol (Secret Service Production), CTRL0000208061 (January 6 2021, email from Robert Engel at 1:55 p.m.).

122. Select Committee to Investigate the January 6th Attack on the United States Capitol, Transcribed Interview of White House Employee, (June 10, 2022), p. 27.

123. Select Committee Interview Investigate the January 6th Attack on the United States Capitol, Transcribed Interview of White House Employee, (June 10, 2022), p. 27.

124. Documents on file with the Select Committee to Investigate the January 6th Attack on the United States Capitol (National Archives Production), Photo file 40a8_hi_j0087_0bea.

125. Select Committee Interview Investigate the January 6th Attack on the United States Capitol, Transcribed Interview of White House Employee, (June 10, 2022), pp. 27–28.

126. Documents on file with the Select Committee to Investigate the January 6th Attack on the United States Capitol (National Archives Production), P-R000255 (Jan. 6, 2021, Daily Diary of President Donald J. Trump).

127. Documents on file with the Select Committee to Investigate the January 6th Attack on the United States Capitol (National Archives Production), P-R000255 (Jan. 6, 2021, Daily Diary of President Donald J. Trump).

128. Documents on file with the Select Committee to Investigate the January 6th Attack on the United States Capitol (National Archives Production), P-R000255 (Jan. 6, 2021, Daily Diary of President Donald J. Trump).

129. Documents on file with the Select Committee to Investigate the January 6th Attack on the United States Capitol (National Archives Production), P-R000255 (Jan. 6, 2021, Daily Diary of President Donald J. Trump). *See also* Documents on file with the Select Committee to Investigate the January 6th Attack on the United States Capitol (National Archives Production), P-R000028 (Memorandum from White House Diarist confirming that "[t]he Oval Log for January 6, 2021 was not received").

130. Select Committee to Investigate the January 6th Attack on the United States Capitol, Deposition of Molly Michael, (Mar. 24, 2022), p 29 ("Why did that change, that you were not taking any records?" "I don't recall a specific reason."); Select Committee to Investigate the January 6th Attack on the United States Capitol, Transcribed Interview of Eric Herschmann, (Apr. 6, 2022), p. 111–12 (attributing the lack of recordkeeping to Michael's absence in the

White House, though she was present in the Outer Oval during the afternoon); Select Committee to Investigate the January 6th Attack on the United States Capitol, Deposition of Austin Ferrer Piran Basualdo, (Apr. 8, 2022), p. 86.

131. H. Rept. 117-216, Resolution Recommending that the House of Representatives Find Mark Randall Meadows in Contempt of Congress for Refusal to Comply with a Subpoena Duly Issued by the Select Committee to Investigate the January 6th Attack on the United States Capitol, 117th Cong., 1st Ssess. (2021), available at https://www.congress.gov/117/crpt/hrpt216/CRPT-117hrpt216.pdf; H. Rept. 117-284, Resolution Recommending that the House of Representatives Find Peter K. Navarro and Daniel Scavino, Jr., in Contempt of Congress for Refusal to Comply with a Subpoena Duly Issued by the Select Committee to Investigate the January 6th Attack on the United States Capitol, 117th Cong., 2d sess. (2022), available at https://www.congress.gov/117/crpt/hrpt284/CRPT-117hrpt284.pdf.

132. *See, e.g.*, Select Committee to Investigate the January 6th Attack on the United States Capitol, Transcribed Interview of Eric Herschmann, (Apr. 6, 2022), p. 118; Select Committee to Investigate the January 6th Attack on the United States Capitol, Transcribed Interview of Pasquale Anthony "Pat" Cipollone, (July 8, 2022), pp. 155–57.

133. *See, e.g.*, Select Committee to Investigate the January 6th Attack on the United States Capitol, Deposition of Molly Michael, (Mar. 24, 2022), p. 136 ("The phones were ringing. A lot was happening. I don't recall."); Select Committee to Investigate the January 6th Attack on the United States Capitol, Deposition of Austin Ferrer Piran Basualdo, (Apr. 8, 2022), pp. 109–10 ("I don't remember where I was that afternoon." "Do you remember being at the White House that afternoon, even if you don't remember where exactly you were in the White House?" "No, I do not." "Do you remember being home, wherever home is for you, on the afternoon of January 6th, as opposed to being at the White House?" "No, I don't." "So you don't remember whether you were at home or at the White House in the afternoon of January 6th, 2021?" "Again, that day was very blurry.").

134. Select Committee to Investigate the January 6th Attack on the United States Capitol, Deposition of Shealah Craighead, (June 8, 2022), p. 46.

135. Select Committee to Investigate the January 6th Attack on the United States Capitol, Deposition of Shealah Craighead, (June 8, 2022), p. 46. It is the standard practice of the White House photographers to cover the President from the moment he steps out of the residence until he returns there at the end of the day. *Id.* at 7. Craighead pushed back, telling Michael that the White House would want to document the day for historical purposes, but Michael did not relent. *Id.* at p. 28.

136. *See, e.g.*, Select Committee to Investigate the January 6th Attack on the United States Capitol, Deposition of Keith Kellogg, Jr., (Dec. 14, 2021), p. 115 ("Well, I saw the President watching TV.").

137. Select Committee Interview Investigate the January 6th Attack on the United States Capitol, Transcribed Interview of White House Employee, (June 10, 2022), p. 23.

138. *See, e.g.*, Select Committee to Investigate the January 6th Attack on the United States Capitol, Transcribed Interview of Ivanka Trump, (Apr. 5, 2022), p. 64 ("I recall walking in and saying, 'You have to put out a strong statement condemning violence and asking for peace to be restored.").

139. *See, e.g.*, Documents on file with the Select Committee to Investigate the January 6th Attack on the United States Capitol (AT&T Production, Feb. 9, 2022); *See also* Jonathan Karl, *Betrayal: The Final Act of the Trump* Show, (New York: Dutton, 2021), p. 287.

140. *See, e.g.*, Select Committee to Investigate the January 6th Attack on the United States Capitol, Transcribed Interview of Pasquale Anthony "Pat" Cipollone, (July 8, 2022), p. 174; Select Committee to Investigate the January 6th Attack on the United States Capitol, Deposition of Keith Kellogg, Jr., (Dec. 14, 2021), pp. 126–27.

141. Select Committee to Investigate the January 6th Attack on the United States Capitol, Continued Interview of Cassidy Hutchinson, (June 20, 2022), p. 129.

142. Select Committee to Investigate the January 6th Attack on the United States Capitol, Deposition of Kayleigh McEnany, (Jan. 12, 2022), pp. 169–70.

143. Select Committee to Investigate the January 6th Attack on the United States Capitol, Deposition of Kayleigh McEnany, (Jan. 12, 2022), pp. 159–60.

144. Documents on file with the Select Committee to Investigate the January 6th Attack on the United States Capitol (Kayleigh McEnany Production), KMC_000000724 (Jan. 6, 2021, Kayleigh McEnany notes).

145. Select Committee to Investigate the January 6th Attack on the United States Capitol, Continued Interview of Cassidy Hutchinson, (June 20, 2022), p. 8.

146. Select Committee to Investigate the January 6th Attack on the United States Capitol, Deposition of Kayleigh McEnany, (Jan. 12, 2022), p. 164.

147. Select Committee to Investigate the January 6th Attack on the United States Capitol, Deposition of Kayleigh McEnany, (Jan. 12, 2022), p. 164.

148. Documents on file with the Select Committee to Investigate the January 6th Attack on the United States Capitol (Kayleigh McEnany Production), KMC_000000724 (Jan. 6, 2021, Kayleigh McEnany notes).

149. *See, e.g.*, Select Committee to Investigate the January 6th Attack on the United States Capitol, Subpoena to Honorable Kevin McCarthy, (May 12, 2022), available at https://january6th.house.gov/sites/democrats.january6th.house.gov/files/2022-05-12-Subpoena-for%20OGC-McCarthy%20Kevin%20%28002%29.pdf; Select Committee to Investigate the January 6th Attack on the United States Capitol, Subpoena to Representative Jim Jordan, (May 12, 2022), available at https://january6th.house.gov/sites/democrats.january6th.house.gov/files/2022-05-12-Subpoena-for%20OGC-Jordan%20Jim%20%28002%29.pdf.

150. *See, e.g.*, Select Committee to Investigate the January 6th Attack on the United States Capitol, Subpoena to Honorable Kevin McCarthy, (May 12, 2022), available at https://january6th.house.gov/sites/democrats.january6th.house.gov/files/2022-05-12-Subpoena-for%20OGC-McCarthy%20Kevin%20%28002%29.pdf; Select Committee to Investigate the January 6th Attack on the United States Capitol, Subpoena to Representative Jim Jordan, (May 12, 2022), available at https://january6th.house.gov/sites/democrats.january6th.house.gov/files/2022-05-12-Subpoena-for%20OGC-Jordan%20Jim%20%28002%29.pdf.

151. Documents on file with the Select Committee to Investigate the January 6th Attack on the United States Capitol (AT&T Production, Feb. 9, 2022).

152. Donald J. Trump (@realDonaldTrump), Twitter, Jan. 6, 2020 1:49 p.m. ET, available at https://www.thetrumparchive.com/?searchbox=%22https%3A%2F%2Ft.co%2FizItBeFE6G%22 (archived).

153. Select Committee to Investigate the January 6th Attack on the United States Capitol, Transcribed Interview of Jared Kushner, (Mar. 31, 2022), p. 144.

154. Select Committee to Investigate the January 6th Attack on the United States Capitol, Transcribed Interview of Jared Kushner, (Mar. 31, 2022), p. 145.

155. Select Committee to Investigate the January 6th Attack on the United States Capitol, Deposition of Benjamin Williamson, (Jan. 25, 2022) p. 60. Live feeds of the Capitol began showing pepper spray exchanges between officers and rioters around 1:29 p.m. See Documents on file with the Select Committee to Investigate the January 6th Attack on the United States Capitol (Secret Service Production), CTRL0000094153; Documents on file with the Select Committee to Investigate the Attack on the United States Capitol (Secret Service Production), CTRL0000094192; Select Committee to Investigate the January 6th Attack on the United States Capitol, *Hearing on the January 6th Investigation*, 117th Cong., 2d sess., (July 21, 2022), at 40:00, available at https://www.govinfo.gov/committee/house-january6th.

156. Select Committee to Investigate the January 6th Attack on the United States Capitol, Transcribed Interview of Sarah Matthews, (Feb. 8, 2022), pp. 36–37.

157. Documents on file with the Select Committee to Investigate the January 6th Attack on the United States Capitol (Benjamin Williamson Production), CTRL0000034784 (Jan. 6, 2021, Benjamin Williamson text message to Mark Meadows at 2:02 p.m. EST); Select Committee to Investigate the January 6th Attack on the United States Capitol, Deposition of Benjamin Williamson (Jan. 25, 2022), p. 64.

158. Select Committee to Investigate the January 6th Attack on the United States Capitol, Continued Interview of Cassidy Hutchinson, (June 20, 2022), p. 24 ("I saw that he was sitting on his couch on his cell phone, same as the morning, where he was just kind of scrolling and typing.").

159. Select Committee to Investigate the January 6th Attack on the United States Capitol, Continued Interview of Cassidy Hutchinson, (June 20, 2022), p. 24.

160. The Select Committee's review of U.S. Capitol Police surveillance footage showed that Proud Boy Dominic Pezzola smashed a Senate Wing window at 2:13 p.m. and rioters entered through that window, as well as an adjacent door, shortly thereafter. *See also* Third Superseding Indictment at 21, *United States v. Nordean et al.*, No. 1:21-cr-175 (D.D.C. June 6, 2022), ECF No. 380 (noting that Dominic Pezzola "used [a] riot shield . . . to break a window of the Capitol" at "2:13 p.m." and that "[t]he first members of the mob entered the Capitol through this broken window"); 167 Cong. Rec. S634 (daily ed. Feb. 10, 2021), available at https://www.congress.gov/117/crec/2021/02/10/CREC-2021-02-10-pt1-PgS615-4.pdf.

161. Select Committee to Investigate the January 6th Attack on the United States Capitol, Continued Interview of Cassidy Hutchinson, (June 20, 2022), p. 25. Cipollone confirmed that he first went to the dining room when he saw that "people had breached the Capitol, they had gotten into the Capitol." Select Committee to Investigate the January 6th Attack on the United States Capitol, Transcribed Interview of Pasquale Anthony "Pat" Cipollone, (July 8, 2022), p. 149.

162. Select Committee to Investigate the January 6th Attack on the United States Capitol, Continued Interview of Cassidy Hutchinson, (June 20, 2022), p. 26.

163. Select Committee to Investigate the January 6th Attack on the United States Capitol, Continued Interview of Cassidy Hutchinson, (June 20, 2022), p. 26.

164. Select Committee to Investigate the January 6th Attack on the United States Capitol, Transcribed Interview of Pasquale Anthony "Pat" Cipollone, (July 8, 2022), p. 150.

165. Select Committee to Investigate the January 6th Attack on the United States Capitol, Continued Interview of Cassidy Hutchinson, (June 20, 2022), p. 26.

166. Select Committee to Investigate the January 6th Attack on the United States Capitol, Continued Interview of Cassidy Hutchinson, (June 20, 2022), p. 26. Cipollone did not elaborate but testified generally that he was "very upset about what was happening" at the Capitol and wanted "action to be taken related to that." Select Committee to Investigate the January 6th Attack on the United States Capitol, Transcribed Interview of Pasquale Anthony "Pat" Cipollone, (July 8, 2022), p. 149.

167. Select Committee to Investigate the January 6th Attack on the United States Capitol, Continued Interview of Cassidy Hutchinson, (June 20, 2022), p. 26.

168. Donald J. Trump (@realDonaldTrump), Twitter, Jan. 6, 2021 2:24 p.m. ET, available at https://www.thetrumparchive.com/?searchbox=%22Mike+Pence+didn%E2%80%99t+have+%22 (archived).

169. Select Committee to Investigate the January 6th Attack on the United States Capitol, Continued Interview of Cassidy Hutchinson, (June 20, 2022), p. 27.

170. Select Committee to Investigate the January 6th Attack on the United States Capitol, Continued Interview of Cassidy Hutchinson, (June 20, 2022), p. 27.

171. Select Committee to Investigate the January 6th Attack on the United States Capitol, Continued Interview of Cassidy Hutchinson, (June 20, 2022), p. 27. President Trump himself has defended publicly the rioters who chanted "Hang Mike Pence!" In an interview, journalist Jonathan Karl asked President Trump about the chants. "Well, the people were very angry," he responded. The President continued: "Because it's common sense . . . . How can you—if you know a vote is fraudulent, how can you pass a fraudulent vote to Congress? How can you do it?" Jonathan Karl, *Betrayal: The Final Act of the Trump Show*, (New York: Dutton, 2021), p. 340.

172. Select Committee to Investigate the January 6th Attack on the United States Capitol, Continued Interview of Cassidy Hutchinson, (June 20, 2022), p. 27. Hutchinson recalled one other thing that Meadows said, referring to the tweet attacking Vice President Pence: "[T]his is the best we're going to get for now." Select Committee to Investigate the January 6th Attack on the United States Capitol, Continued Interview of Cassidy Hutchinson, (May 17, 2022), p. 17. Hutchinson believes that this conversation took place after the 2:24 p.m. tweet, but the context suggests that it may have taken place after the 2:38 p.m. or 3:13 p.m. tweets.

173. Select Committee to Investigate the January 6th Attack on the United States Capitol, Transcribed Interview of Pasquale Anthony "Pat" Cipollone, (July 8, 2022), p. 150.

174. Select Committee to Investigate the January 6th Attack on the United States Capitol, Transcribed Interview of Pasquale Anthony "Pat" Cipollone, (July 8, 2022), p. 150.

175. Select Committee to Investigate the January 6th Attack on the United States Capitol, Transcribed Interview of Pasquale Anthony "Pat" Cipollone, (July 8, 2022), p. 161.

176. Select Committee to Investigate the January 6th Attack on the United States Capitol, Transcribed Interview of Pasquale Anthony "Pat" Cipollone, (July 8, 2022), p. 161; Select Committee to Investigate the January 6th Attack on the United States Capitol, *Hearing on the January 6th Investigation*, 117th Cong., 2d sess., (July 21, 2022), at 1:29:45–1:31:50, available at https://www.youtube.com/watch?v=pbRVqWbHGuo.

177. Documents on file with the Select Committee to Investigate the January 6th Attack on the United States Capitol (Secret Service Production), CTRL0000095185.

178. Documents on file with the Select Committee to Investigate the January 6th Attack on the United States Capitol (Secret Service Production), CTRL0000095247.

179. Lauren Fox and Clare Foran, "GOP Sen. Mike Lee Hands Over Phone Records to House Impeachment Managers," CNN, (Feb. 13, 2021), available at https://www.cnn.com/2021/02/13/politics/mike-lee-phone-records-impeachment-trial/index.html.

180. Mike Lillis, "Tuberville Defends Account of Trump Call During Capitol Riot," *The Hill*, (Feb. 12, 2021), available at https://thehill.com/homenews/senate/538704-tuberville-defends-account-of-trump-call-during-capitol-riot/. Sen. Tuberville stated publicly that the originating number was identified as "White House" on Sen. Lee's phone, suggesting that the call came through the White House Switchboard. *Id.*

181. Jonathan Karl, *Betrayal: The Final Act of the Trump Show*, (New York: Dutton, 2021), at p. 287.

182. Jonathan Karl, *Betrayal: The Final Act of the Trump Show*, (New York: Dutton, 2021), at p. 287.

183. Eddie Burkhalter, "Tuberville Says He Attended Jan. 5 Fundraiser at Trump's Washington Hotel," *Alabama Political Reporter*, (Feb. 19, 2021), available at https://www.alreporter.com/2021/02/19/tuberville-says-he-attended-jan-5-fundraiser-at-trumps-washington-hotel/.

184. The call likely happened after the evacuation of the House chamber starting at approximately 2:38 p.m., and Rep. McCarthy spoke about it to CBS News's Norah O'Donnell by phone between approximately 3:00 to 3:15 p.m. CBS News, "House Minority Leader Kevin McCarthy: I Completely Condemn the Violence in the Capitol," YouTube, Jan. 6, 2021, available at https://www.youtube.com/watch?v=MpBbpqO5qgU. Molly Michael testified that she

recalls receiving the incoming call from Leader McCarthy on Dan Scavino's landline and transferring it to a landline in the dining room. She does not recall when the call took place, nor did she hear anything about what was discussed. Select Committee to Investigate the January 6th Attack on the United States Capitol, Deposition of Molly Michael, (Mar. 24, 2022), pp. 131–32.

185. "House Minority Leader Kevin McCarthy: 'I Completely Condemn the Violence in the Capitol,'" CBS News, (Jan. 6, 2021), available at https://www.cbsnews.com/video/house-minority-leader-kevin-mccarthy-condemn-the-violence/#x.

186. "House Minority Leader Kevin McCarthy: 'I Completely Condemn the Violence in the Capitol,'" CBS News, (Jan. 6, 2021), available at https://www.cbsnews.com/video/house-minority-leader-kevin-mccarthy-condemn-the-violence/#x.

187. Tommy Christopher, "WATCH: GOP Rep Reveals Details of Trump's Bombshell Call with McCarthy Refusing to Call off Capitol Rioters," Mediaite, (Feb. 13, 2021), available at https://www.mediaite.com/news/watch-gop-rep-reveals-details-of-trumps-bombshell-call-with-mccarthy-refusing-to-call-off-capitol-rioters/.

188. Tommy Christopher, "WATCH: GOP Rep Reveals Details of Trump's Bombshell Call with McCarthy Refusing to Call off Capitol Rioters," Mediaite, (Feb. 13, 2021), available at https://www.mediaite.com/news/watch-gop-rep-reveals-details-of-trumps-bombshell-call-with-mccarthy-refusing-to-call-off-capitol-rioters/.

189. Tommy Christopher, "WATCH: GOP Rep Reveals Details of Trump's Bombshell Call with McCarthy Refusing to Call off Capitol Rioters," Mediaite, (Feb. 13, 2021), available at https://www.mediaite.com/news/watch-gop-rep-reveals-details-of-trumps-bombshell-call-with-mccarthy-refusing-to-call-off-capitol-rioters/.

190. Tommy Christopher, "WATCH: GOP Rep Reveals Details of Trump's Bombshell Call with McCarthy Refusing to Call off Capitol Rioters," Mediaite, (Feb. 13, 2021), available at https://www.mediaite.com/news/watch-gop-rep-reveals-details-of-trumps-bombshell-call-with-mccarthy-refusing-to-call-off-capitol-rioters/.

191. Tommy Christopher, "WATCH: GOP Rep Reveals Details of Trump's Bombshell Call with McCarthy Refusing to Call off Capitol Rioters," Mediaite, (Feb. 13, 2021), available at https://www.mediaite.com/news/watch-gop-rep-reveals-details-of-trumps-bombshell-call-with-mccarthy-refusing-to-call-off-capitol-rioters/.

192. Tommy Christopher, "WATCH: GOP Rep Reveals Details of Trump's Bombshell Call with McCarthy Refusing to Call off Capitol Rioters," Mediaite, (Feb. 13, 2021), available at https://www.mediaite.com/news/watch-gop-rep-reveals-details-of-trumps-bombshell-call-with-mccarthy-refusing-to-call-off-capitol-rioters/.

193. Tommy Christopher, "WATCH: GOP Rep Reveals Details of Trump's Bombshell Call with McCarthy Refusing to Call off Capitol Rioters," Mediaite, (Feb. 13, 2021), available at https://www.mediaite.com/news/watch-gop-rep-reveals-details-of-trumps-bombshell-call-with-mccarthy-refusing-to-call-off-capitol-rioters/.

194. Select Committee to Investigate the January 6th Attack on the United States Capitol, Transcribed Interview of John Michael "Mick" Mulvaney, (July 28, 2022), p. 43.

195. Select Committee to Investigate the January 6th Attack on the United States Capitol, Deposition of Marc Short, (Jan. 26, 2022), p. 46.

196. Select Committee to Investigate the January 6th Attack on the United States Capitol, Deposition of Marc Short, (Jan. 26, 2022), p. 46.

197. Select Committee to Investigate the January 6th Attack on the United States Capitol, Deposition of Marc Short, (Jan. 26, 2022), p. 47.

198. Documents on file with the Select Committee to Investigate the January 6th Attack on the United States Capitol (Ross Worthington Production), RW_0002307 (Jan. 6, 2021, Gabriel Roberts text message at 2:49 p.m.).

199. Select Committee to Investigate the January 6th Attack on the United States Capitol, Transcribed Interview of Eric Herschmann, (Apr. 6, 2022), p. 72.

200. Select Committee to Investigate the January 6th Attack on the United States Capitol, Transcribed Interview of Ivanka Trump, (Apr. 5, 2022), p. 68; *see also* Select Committee to Investigate the January 6th Attack on the United States Capitol, Transcribed Interview of Eric Herschmann, (Apr. 6, 2022), pp. 68–69.

201. Select Committee to Investigate the January 6th Attack on the United States Capitol, Transcribed Interview of Ivanka Trump, (Apr. 5, 2022), p. 70.

202. Select Committee to Investigate the January 6th Attack on the United States Capitol, Transcribed Interview of Eric Herschmann, (Apr. 6, 2022), p. 69 ("And she was in there for a few minutes, and then came out and he had issued a tweet."); Select Committee to Investigate the January 6th Attack on the United States Capitol, Transcribed Interview of Ivanka Trump, (Apr. 5, 2022), p. 64 ("Within, I believe, a few minutes he had issued that—he put out that tweet, a version of that tweet.").

203. Donald J. Trump (@realDonaldTrump), Twitter, Jan. 6, 2021 2:38 p.m. ET, available at https://www.thetrumparchive.com/?searchbox=%22please+support+our%22 (archived).

204. Select Committee to Investigate the January 6th Attack on the United States Capitol, Transcribed Interview of Ivanka Trump, (Apr. 5, 2022), pp. 87–89.

205. Select Committee to Investigate the January 6th Attack on the United States Capitol, Transcribed Interview of Ivanka Trump, (Apr. 5, 2022), p. 88.

206. Documents on file with the Select Committee to Investigate the January 6th Attack on the United States Capitol (Kayleigh McEnany Production), KMC_000000724, (January 6, 2021, Kayleigh McEnany Notes); Select Committee to Investigate the January 6th Attack on the United States Capitol, Deposition of Kayleigh McEnany, (Jan. 12, 2022), p. 185.

207. Select Committee to Investigate the January 6th Attack on the United States Capitol, Transcribed Interview of Ivanka Trump, (Apr. 5, 2022), pp. 88–89; Select Committee to Investigate the January 6th Attack on the United States Capitol, Deposition of Kayleigh McEnany, (Jan. 12, 2022), p. 185.

208. Select Committee to Investigate the January 6th Attack on the United States Capitol, *Hearing on the January 6th Investigation*, 117th Cong., 2d sess., (July 21, 2022), available at https://www.govinfo.gov/committee/house-january6th.

209. Select Committee to Investigate the January 6th Attack on the United States Capitol, *Hearing on the January 6th Investigation*, 117th Cong., 2d sess., (July 21, 2022), available at https://www.govinfo.gov/committee/house-january6th.

210. Select Committee to Investigate the January 6th Attack on the United States Capitol, *Hearing on the January 6th Investigation*, 117th Cong., 2d sess., (July 21, 2022), available at https://www.govinfo.gov/committee/house-january6th.

211. Carol Leonnig and Philip Rucker, *I Alone Can Fix It: Donald J. Trump's Catastrophic Final Year* (New York: Penguin, 2021), p. 474.

212. Select Committee to Investigate the January 6th Attack on the United States Capitol, Transcribed Interview of Ivanka Trump, (Apr. 5, 2022), p. 91.

213. Select Committee to Investigate the January 6th Attack on the United States Capitol, Deposition of Keith Kellogg, Jr., (Dec. 14, 2021), p 141.

214. Select Committee to Investigate the January 6th Attack on the United States Capitol, Transcribed Interview of Cassidy Hutchinson, (Feb. 23, 2022), p. 170.

215. Bob Woodward and Robert Costa, *Peril*, (New York: Simon & Schuster, 2021), p. 248.

216. Select Committee to Investigate the January 6th Attack on the United States Capitol, Deposition of Julie Radford, (May 24, 2022), p. 32.

217. Select Committee to Investigate the January 6th Attack on the United States Capitol, Deposition of Julie Radford, (May 24, 2022), p. 30.

218. Select Committee to Investigate the January 6th Attack on the United States Capitol, Continued Interview of Cassidy Hutchinson, (June 20, 2022), p. 37; Hutchinson recalls that Meadows, Herschmann, Ivanka Trump, and others would come and go from the Chief of Staff's office at intervals throughout the afternoon. "I don't know if it was for a breather or to have a conversation away from the dining room," she said. *Id.*, at 31.

219. Select Committee to Investigate the January 6th Attack on the United States Capitol, Continued Interview of Cassidy Hutchinson, (June 20, 2022), p. 38.

220. Fox News, "U.S. Capitol on Lockdown as Protests Threaten Security," YouTube, Jan. 6, 2021, available at https://www.youtube.com/watch?v=oFWGBnJ0rQA.

221. Fox News, "Breaking News: Protestors Now inside U.S. Capitol," YouTube, at 2:40, Jan. 6, 2021, available at https://www.fox29.com/video/887421.

222. Fox News, "Pro-Trump Protestors Storm U.S. Capitol," YouTube, Jan. 6, 2021, available at https://www.youtube.com/watch?v=tVPSYr-xG6s.

223. Documents on file with the Select Committee to Investigate the January 6th Attack on the United States Capitol (Secret Service Production), CTRL0000095389.

224. Documents on file with the Select Committee to Investigate the January 6th Attack on the United States Capitol (Secret Service Production), CTRL0000095393 (Jan. 6, 2021, text between Secret Service agents at 2:41 p.m. EST).

225. Marshall Cohen and Avery Lotz, "The January 6 Insurrection: Minute-by-Minute," CNN, (July 29, 2022), available at https://www.cnn.com/2022/07/10/politics/jan-6-us-capitol-riot-timeline/index.html.

226. Documents on file with the Select Committee to Investigate the January 6th Attack on the United States Capitol (National Archives Production), P-R000241 (Jan. 6, 2021, Note to President Trump).

227. Select Committee Interview Investigate the January 6th Attack on the United States Capitol, Transcribed Interview of White House Employee, (June 10, 2022), pp. 46–47.

228. *See, e.g.,* Documents on file with the Select Committee to Investigate the January 6th Attack on the United States Capitol (Mark Meadows Production), MM014921, MM014923, MM014926.

229. Documents on file with the Select Committee to Investigate the January 6th Attack on the United States Capitol (Mark Meadows Production), MM014906. Recently, Representative Greene has qualified her stance on armed rioters at the Capitol. At a Young Republicans event in New York, she said: "I got to tell you something, if Steve Bannon and I had oganized [January 6th], we would have won. Not to mention, it would've been armed." She claims she was joking. Aaron Blake, "Analysis: Marjorie Taylor Greene's Jan. 6 'Joke' Has Been Building for a Long Time," *Washington Post*, (Dec. 12, 2022), available at https://www.washingtonpost.com/politics/2022/12/12/greene-january-6-punchline/.

230. Documents on file with the Select Committee to Investigate the January 6th Attack on the United States Capitol (Mark Meadows Production), MM014907, MM014908, MM014909, (Jan. 6, 2021, Laura Ingraham text message to Mark Meadows at 2:32 pm); Documents on file with the Select Committee to Investigate the Jan. 6th Attack on the United States Capitol (Mark Meadows Production), MM014911 (Jan. 6, 2021, Laura Ingraham text message to Mark Meadows at 2:32 p.m.).

231. Documents on file with the Select Committee to Investigate the January 6th Attack on the United States Capitol (Mark Meadows Production), MM014912.

232. Documents on File with the Select Committee to Investigate the January 6th Attack on the United States Capitol (Mark Meadows Production), MM014914, MM014915.

233. Documents on file with the Select Committee to Investigate the January 6th Attack on the United States Capitol (Mark Meadows Production), MM014921.

234. Documents on file with the Select Committee to Investigate the January 6th Attack on the United States Capitol (Mark Meadows Production), MM014922.

235. Documents on file with the Select Committee to Investigate the January 6th Attack on the United States Capitol (Mark Meadows Production), MM014919.

236. Documents on file with the Select Committee to Investigate the January 6th Attack on the United States Capitol (Mark Meadows Production), MM014923.

237. Documents on file with the Select Committee to Investigate the January 6th Attack on the United States Capitol (Mark Meadows Production), MM014925.

238. Documents on file with the Select Committee to Investigate the January 6th Attack on the United States Capitol (Mark Meadows Production), MM014926.

239. Documents on file with the Select Committee to Investigate the January 6th Attack on the United States Capitol (Mark Meadows Production), MM014928.

240. Documents on file with the Select Committee to Investigate the January 6th Attack on the United States Capitol (National Archives Production), P-R000240 (January 6, 2021 proposed statement).

241. Select Committee to Investigate the January 6th Attack on the United States Capitol, *Hearing on the January 6th Investigation*, 117th Cong., 2d sess., (June 28, 2022), available at https://www.govinfo.gov/committee/house-january6th.

242. Select Committee to Investigate the January 6th Attack on the United States Capitol, *Hearing on the January 6th Investigation*, 117th Cong., 2d sess., (June 28, 2022), available at https://www.govinfo.gov/committee/house-january6th.

243. Select Committee to Investigate the January 6th Attack on the United States Capitol, *Hearing on the January 6th Investigation*, 117th Cong., 2d sess., (June 28, 2022), available at https://www.govinfo.gov/committee/house-january6th.

244. Donald Trump (@realDonaldTrump), Twitter, Jan. 6, 2021 3:13 p.m. EST, available at https://www.thetrumparchive.com/?searchbox=%22remain+peaceful%22 (archived).

245. Select Committee to Investigate the January 6th Attack on the United States Capitol, Transcribed Interview of Ivanka Trump, (Apr. 5, 2022), p. 119.

246. Select Committee to Investigate the January 6th Attack at the United States Capitol, Transcribed Interview of Eric Herschmann, (Apr. 6, 2022), p. 88.

247. *See, e.g.*, Select Committee to Investigate the January 6th Attack on the United States Capitol, Transcribed Interview of Eric Herschmann, (Apr. 6, 2022), p. 88; Select Committee to Investigate the January 6th Attack on the United States Capitol, Deposition of Kayleigh McEnany, (Jan. 12, 2022), p. 172; Select Committee to Investigate the January 6th Attack on the United States Capitol, Transcribed Interview of Pasquale Anthony "Pat" Cipollone, (July 8, 2022), p. 155.

248. "Pergram: Most Significant Breach of Government Institution Since 1814," Fox News, Jan. 6, 2021, available at https://www.foxnews.com/video/6220760122001#sp=show-clips.

249. Fox News, "Individual Shot in U.S. Capitol," YouTube, at 1:59, Jan. 6, 2021, available at https://www.youtube.com/watch?v=oL-M0LuE3Hk.

250. "Andy McCarthy Blasts Pro-Trump Protesters after Breach at Capitol," Fox News, at 1:28, Jan. 6, 2021, available at https://www.foxnews.com/video/6220757649001#sp=show-clips.

251. Documents on File with the Select Committee to Investigate the January 6th Attack on the United States Capitol (Mark Meadows Production), MM014932, MM014934.

252. Documents on File with the Select Committee to Investigate the January 6th Attack on the United States Capitol (Mark Meadows Production), MM014935. This was sent from a phone number associated with Priebus's family member.

253. Documents on File with the Select Committee to Investigate the January 6th Attack on the United States Capitol (Mark Meadows Production), MM014936.

254. Documents on File with the Select Committee to Investigate the January 6th Attack on the United States Capitol (Mark Meadows Production), MM014937.

255. Documents on File with the Select Committee to Investigate the January 6th Attack on the United States Capitol (Mark Meadows Production), MM014939.

256. Documents on File with the Select Committee to Investigate the January 6th Attack on the United States Capitol (Mark Meadows Production), MM014943.

257. Documents on File with the Select Committee to Investigate the January 6th Attack on the United States Capitol (Mark Meadows Production), MM014944.

258. Documents on file with the Select Committee to Investigate the January 6th Attack on the United States Capitol (Mark Meadows Production), MM014947.

259. Documents on File with the Select Committee to Investigate the January 6th Attack on the United States Capitol (Mark Meadows Production), MM014948.

260. Document on File with the Select Committee to Investigate the January 6th Attack on the United States Capitol (Mark Meadows Production), MM014949.

261. Documents on file with the Select Committee to Investigate the January 6th Attack on the United States Capitol (Mark Meadows Production), MM014956, MM014957.

262. Document on File with the Select Committee to Investigate the January 6th Attack on the United States Capitol (Mark Meadows Production), MM014961.

263. Document on File with the Select Committee to Investigate the January 6th Attack on the United States Capitol (Mark Meadows Production), MM014964.

264. Select Committee to Investigate the January 6th Attack on the United States Capitol, *Hearing on the January 6th Investigation*, 117th Cong., 2d sess., (July 21, 2022), available at https://www.govinfo.gov/committee/house-january6th.

265. Select Committee to Investigate the January 6th Attack on the United States Capitol, *Hearing on the January 6th Investigation*, 117th Cong., 2d sess., (July 21, 2022), available at https://www.govinfo.gov/committee/house-january6th; *see also* CBS News, "House Minority Leader Kevin McCarthy: 'I completely condemn the violence in the Capitol,'" YouTube, Jan. 6, 2021, available at https://www.youtube.com/watch?v=MpBbpqO5qgU.

266. Select Committee to Investigate the January 6th Attack on the United States Capitol, *Hearing on the January 6th Investigation*, 117th Cong., 2d sess., (July 21, 2022), available at https://www.govinfo.gov/committee/house-january6th.

267. Select Committee to Investigate the January 6th Attack on the United States Capitol, *Hearing on the January 6th Investigation*, 117th Cong., 2d sess., (July 22, 2022), available at https://www.govinfo.gov/committee/house-january6th; Select Committee to Investigate the January 6th Attack on the United States Capitol, Transcribed Interview of Pasquale Anthony "Pat" Cipollone, (July 8, 2022), p. 163.

268. Donald Trump (@realDonaldTrump), Twitter, Jan. 6, 2021 4:17 p.m. ET, available at https://www.thetrumparchive.com/?searchbox=%22https%3A%2F%2Ft.co%2FPm2PKV0Fp3%22 (archived).

269. Documents on file with the Select Committee to Investigate the January 6th Attack on the United States Capitol (National Archives Production), P-R000255 (Jan. 6, 2021, Daily Diary of President Donald J. Trump).

270. "Bill Hemmer Reports," Fox News, at 3:56 p.m. ET, available at https://archive.org/details/FOXNEWSW_20210106_200000_Bill_Hemmer_Reports/start/3360/end/3420 (archived).

271. Select Committee to Investigate the January 6th Attack on the United States Capitol, Deposition of Nicholas Luna, (Mar. 21, 2022), pp. 162–63.

272. Select Committee to Investigate the January 6th Attack on the United States Capitol, Deposition of Nicholas Luna, (Mar. 21, 2022), p. 162.

273. Documents on file with the Select Committee to Investigate the January 6th Attack on the United States Capitol (National Archives Production), Video file 40983.

274.   Documents on file with the Select Committee to Investigate the January 6th Attack on the United States Capitol (National Archives Production), P-R000255 (Jan. 6, 2021, Daily Diary of President Donald J. Trump).

275.   Select Committee to Investigate the January 6th Attack on the United States Capitol, Deposition of Kayleigh McEnany, (Jan. 12, 2022), p. 234. President Trump did not react to her suggestion, McEnany said. *See id.*

276.   Select Committee to Investigate the January 6th Attack on the United States Capitol, Deposition of Nicholas Luna, (Mar. 21, 2022), p. 161; Select Committee to Investigate the January 6th Attack on the United States Capitol, Transcribed Interview of Eric Herschmann, (Apr. 6, 2022), pp. 97–99.

277.   Donald Trump (@realDonaldTrump), Twitter, Jan. 6, 2021 4:17 p.m. ET, available at https://www.thetrumparchive.com/?searchbox=%22https%3A%2F%2Ft.co%2FPm2PKV0Fp3%22 (archived).

278.   Documents on file with the Select Committee to Investigate the January 6th Attack on the United States Capitol (National Archives Production), Photo file 4243_hi_j0233_61ae.

279.   Select Committee to Investigate the January 6th Attack on the United States Capitol, Deposition of Nicholas Luna, (Mar. 21, 2022), p. 182. See Select Committee to Investigate the January 6th Attack on the United States Capitol, Interview of White House Employee, (June 10, 2022), pp. 49–50 (remembering that someone in the Rose Garden told the President something along the lines "that he needed to use stronger, more forceful" language in the video).

280.   Select Committee to Investigate the January 6th Attack on the United States Capitol, Transcribed Interview of Eric Herschmann, (Apr. 6, 2022), p. 99.

281.   Select Committee to Investigate the January 6th Attack on the United States Capitol, Deposition of Nicholas Luna, (Mar. 21, 2022), p. 181.

282.   Select Committee to Investigate the January 6th Attack on the United States Capitol, *Hearing on the January 6th Investigation*, 117th Cong., 2d sess., (July 21, 2022), at 1:58:30, available at https://www.youtube.com/watch?v=pbRVqWbHGuo.

283.   Select Committee to Investigate the January 6th Attack on the United States Capitol, *Hearing on the January 6th Investigation*, 117th Cong., 2d sess., (July 12, 2022), available at https://www.govinfo.gov/committee/house-january6th. ("[A]s soon as that come out, everybody started talking about it and that's—it seemed like it started to disperse.").

284.   Select Committee to Investigate the January 6th Attack on the United States Capitol, *Hearing on the January 6h Investigation*, 117th Cong., 2d sess., (July 12, 2022), available at https://www.govinfo.gov/committee/house-january6th ("Basically, when President Trump put his tweet out. We literally left right after that [had] come out.").

285.   Select Committee to Investigate the January 6th Attack on the United States Capitol, Hearing on the January 6th Investigation, 117th Cong., 2d sess., (July 12, 2022), available at https://www.govinfo.gov/committee/house-january6th. ("[I]f he would have done that earlier in the day, 1:30, I—you know, we wouldn't be in this—maybe we wouldn't be in this bad of a situation or something.").

286.   "Bill Hemmer Reports," Fox News, Jan. 6, 2021, available at https://archive.org/details/FOXNEWSW_20210106_200000_Bill_Hemmer_Reports/start/780/end/840.

287.   Donald J. Trump (@realDonaldTrump), Twitter, Jan. 6, 2020 6:01 p.m. ET, available at https://www.thetrumparchive.com/?searchbox=%22these+are+the+things+and+events%22 (archived).

288.   T, available at https://www.thetrumparchive.com/?searchbox=%22these+are+the+things+and+events%22 (archived).

289.   *See* Select Committee to Investigate the January 6th Attack on the United States Capitol, Interview of White House Employee, (June 10, 2022), p. 53.

290. Documents on file with the Select Committee to Investigate the January 6th Attack on the United States Capitol (National Archives production), Photo file 364c_hi_j0246_2fa8.

291. See Select Committee to Investigate the January 6th Attack on the United States Capitol, Interview of White House Employee, (June 10, 2022), p. 53.

292. Documents on file with the Select Committee to Investigate the January 6th Attack on the United States Capitol (AT&T Production, Feb. 9, 2022).

293. Documents on file with the Select Committee to Investigate the January 6th Attack on the United States Capitol (AT&T Production, Feb. 9, 2022).

294. Documents on file with the Select Committee to Investigate the January 6th Attack on the United States Capitol (AT&T Production, Feb. 9, 2022).

295. Documents on file with the Select Committee to Investigate the January 6th Attack on the United States Capitol (AT&T Production, Feb. 9, 2022).

296. Documents on file with the Select Committee to Investigate the January 6th Attack on the United States Capitol (Rudolph Giuliani Production, Mar. 11, 2022).

297. Documents on file with the Select Committee to Investigate the January 6th Attack on the United States Capitol (Rudolph Giuliani Production, Mar. 11, 2022); Documents on file with the Select Committee to Investigate the January 6th Attack on the United States Capitol (AT&T Production, Feb. 9, 2022).

298. Documents on file with the Select Committee to Investigate the January 6th Attack on the United States Capitol (AT&T Production, Feb. 9, 2022).

299. Documents on file with the Select Committee to Investigate the January 6th Attack on the United States Capitol (Rudolph Giuliani Production, Mar. 11, 2022).

300. Documents on file with the Select Committee to Investigate the January 6th Attack on the United States Capitol (Rudolph Giuliani Production, Mar. 11, 2022).

301. Documents on file with the Select Committee to Investigate the January 6th Attack on the United States Capitol (Rudolph Giuliani Production, Mar. 11, 2022).

302. Documents on file with the Select Committee to Investigate the January 6th Attack on the United States Capitol (AT&T Production, Feb. 9, 2022).

303. Documents on file with the Select Committee to Investigate the January 6th Attack on the United States Capitol (Rudolph Giuliani Production, Mar. 11, 2022); Documents on file with the Select Committee to Investigate the January 6th Attack on the United States Capitol (AT&T Production, Feb. 9, 2022).

304. Documents on file with the Select Committee to Investigate the January 6th Attack on the United States Capitol (National Archives Production), P-R000255 (Jan. 6, 2021, Daily Diary of President Donald J. Trump); Documents on file with the Select Committee to Investigate the January 6th Attack on the United States Capitol (AT&T Production, Feb. 9, 2022).

305. Select Committee to Investigate the January 6th Attack on the United States Capitol, Deposition of Rudolph Giuliani, (May 20, 2022), p. 206. ("You were leaving messages or having phone calls with United States Senators about the joint session of Congress. How could that possibly be [a] privileged conversation?" "Because the conversation is about the theory of the case, and my representation of the client.").

306. Select Committee to Investigate the January 6th Attack on the United States Capitol, Deposition of Rudolph Giuliani, (May 20, 2022), p. 207.

307. Select Committee to Investigate the January 6th Attack on the United States Capitol, Deposition of Rudolph Giuliani, (May 20, 2022), p. 206; Documents on file with the Select Committee to Investigate the January 6th Attack on the United States Capitol (Robert O'Brien Production), NSA 0040 (January 6, 2021, text message from Sen. Mike Lee to Robert O'Brien at 10:55 p.m. EST reading, "You can't make this up. I just got this voice message [from] Rudy Giuliani, who apparently thought he was calling Senator Tuberville." "You've got to listen to that message. Rudy is walking malpractice.").

308. Steve Hayes, "Giuliani to Senator: 'Try to Just Slow it Down,'" *The Dispatch*, (Jan. 6, 2021), available at https://thedispatch.com/p/giuliani-to-senator-try-to-just-slow.

309. Steve Hayes, "Giuliani to Senator: 'Try to Just Slow it Down,'" *The Dispatch*, (Jan. 6, 2021), available at https://thedispatch.com/p/giuliani-to-senator-try-to-just-slow.

310. Those 13 people are Pat Cipollone, Dan Scavino, Kurt Olsen, Mark Martin, Cleta Mitchell, Rudy Giuliani, Kayleigh McEnany, Jason Miller, Mark Meadows, Steve Bannon, Eric Herschmann, Sean Hannity, and John McEntee. *See* Documents on file with the Select Committee to Investigate the January 6th Attack on the United States Capitol (National Archives Production), P-R000255 (Jan. 6, 2021, Daily Diary of President Donald J. Trump); Documents on file with the Select Committee to Investigate the January 6th Attack on the United States Capitol (National Archives Production), P-R000261 (Jan. 6, 2021, the Presidential Call Log).

311. H. Rept. 117-152, Resolution Recommending that the House of Representatives Find Stephen K. Bannon in Contempt of Congress for Refusal to Comply with a Subpoena Duly Issued by the Select Committee to Investigate the January 6th Attack on the United States Capitol, 117th Cong., 1st sess. (2021), available at https://www.congress.gov/117/crpt/hrpt152/CRPT-117hrpt152.pdf; H. Rept. 117–216, Resolution Recommending that the House of Representatives Find Mark Randall Meadows in Contempt of Congress for Refusal to Comply with a Subpoena Duly Issued by the Select Committee to Investigate the January 6th Attack on the United States Capitol, 117th Cong., 1st sess. (2021), available at https://www.congress.gov/117/crpt/hrpt216/CRPT-117hrpt216.pdf; H. Rept. 117–284, Resolution Recommending that the House of Representatives Find Peter K. Navarro and Daniel Scavino, Jr., in Contempt of Congress for Refusal to Comply with a Subpoena Duly Issued by the Select Committee to Investigate the January 6th Attack on the United States Capitol, 117th Cong., 2d sess. (2022), available at https://www.congress.gov/117/crpt/hrpt284/CRPT-117hrpt284.pdf; Erik Larson, "Lawyer Who Talked to Trump on Day of Capitol Riot Sues over Subpoena," *Bloomberg*, (Mar. 25, 2022), available at https://www.bloomberg.com/news/articles/2022-03-25/lawyer-who-talked-to-trump-on-day-of-mob-riot-sues-over-subpoena (discussing Kurt Olsen); Caleb Ecarma, "Sean Hannity Wants the January 6 Committee to Believe He's a Journalist," *Vanity Fair*, (Jan. 5, 2022), available at https://www.vanityfair.com/news/2022/01/sean-hannity-january-6-committee-journalist.

312. Select Committee to Investigate the January 6th Attack on the United States Capitol, Transcribed Interview of Eric Herschmann, (Apr. 6, 2022), p. 118; Select Committee to Investigate the January 6th Attack on the United States Capitol, Transcribed Interview of Pasquale Anthony "Pat" Cipollone, (July 8, 2022), p. 195.

313. Select Committee to Investigate the January 6th Attack on the United States Capitol, Deposition of Cleta Mitchell, (May 18, 2022), p. 131; Select Committee to Investigate the January 6th Attack on the United States Capitol, Deposition of Rudolph Giuliani, (May 20, 2022), p. 211.

314. Documents on file with the Select Committee to Investigate the January 6th Attack on the United States Capitol (National Archives Production), P-R000255 (Jan. 6, 2021, Daily Diary of President Donald J. Trump); "WATCH: 'Let's Get Back to Work,' Pence Urges Senate," PBS, (Jan. 6, 2021), available at https://www.pbs.org/newshour/politics/watch-lets-get-back-to-work-pence-urges-senate.

315. Documents on file with the Select Committee to Investigate the January 6th Attack on the United States Capitol (National Archives Production), P-R000255 (Jan. 6, 2021, Daily Diary of President Donald J. Trump).

316. Olsen authored a memo urging Vice President Pence to adjourn the joint session of Congress without counting electoral votes. *See* Documents on file with the Select Committee on the January 6th Attack on the United States Capitol (Chapman University Production) Chapman004979 (Jan. 2, 2021, Kurt Olsen Draft Memorandum Entitled, "The Role of the Vice President in Receiving Votes from the Electoral College.") Martin advised President Trump that Vice President Pence possessed the constitutional authority to impede the electoral

count. *See* Nicholas Fandos, Peter Baker, and Maggie Haberman, "House Moves to Force Trump Out, Vowing Impeachment if Pence Won't Act," *New York Times*, (Jan. 10, 2021), available at https://www.nytimes.com/2021/01/10/us/politics/trump-impeachment.html. Both corresponded with John Eastman and others regarding plans to convene alternate electors in states won by Joe Biden. *See* Documents on file with the Select Committee to Investigate the January 6th Attack on the United States Capitol (Chapman University Production), Chapman023998 (Dec. 6, 2020, Michael Farris email forwarding an email concerning the "Importance of Republican Electors in AZ, GA, MI, NV, PA and WI Voting on Dec 14" at 1:54 p.m. ET). President Trump asked to speak with Mr. Olsen and Mr. Martin before he left the dining room. *See* Documents on file with the Select Committee to Investigate the January 6th Attack on the United States Capitol (National Archives Production), 076P-R000007401_00001 (Jan. 6, 2021, Molly Michael email to MBX WHO MA Joint White House Switchboard at 11:28 p.m. ET).

317.   Documents on file with the Select Committee to Investigate the January 6th Attack on the United States Capitol (National Archives Production), P-R000255 (Jan. 6, 2021, Daily Diary of President Donald J. Trump).

318.   Documents on file with the Select Committee to Investigate the January 6th Attack on the United States Capitol (National Archives Production), P-R000255 (Jan. 6, 2021, Daily Diary of President Donald J. Trump). Mitchell declined to discuss her conversations with President Trump on attorney-client privilege grounds. She did, however, acknowledge that following the phone call, she took steps to dismiss the President's pending election suit in Georgia. *See* Select Committee to Investigate the January 6th Attack on the United States Capitol, Deposition of Cleta Mitchell, (May 18, 2022), p. 131.

319.   Documents on file with the Select Committee to Investigate the January 6th Attack on the United States Capitol (National Archives Production), P-R000259 (Jan. 6, 2021, Daily Diary of the President Donald J. Trump); Select Committee to Investigate the January 6th Attack on the United States Capitol, Transcribed Interview of Eric Herschmann, (Apr. 6, 2022), p. 118 (Herschmann refused to answer questions about the phone call, citing executive privilege).

320.   Documents on file with the Select Committee to Investigate the January 6th Attack on the United States Capitol (National Archives Production), P-R000255–P-R000259 (Jan. 6, 2021, Daily Diary of President Donald J. Trump).

321.   Documents on file with the Select Committee to Investigate the January 6th Attack on the United States Capitol (National Archives Production), P-R000255–P-R000259 (Jan. 6, 2021, Daily Diary of President Donald J. Trump).

322.   Documents on file with the Select Committee to Investigate the January 6th Attack on the United States Capitol (National Archives Production), P-R000255–P-R000259 (Jan. 6, 2021, Daily Diary of President Donald J. Trump).

323.   Documents on file with the Select Committee to Investigate the January 6th Attack on the United States Capitol (National Archives Production), P-R000255–P-R000259 (Jan. 6, 2021, Daily Diary of President Donald J. Trump).

324.   Documents on file with the Select Committee to Investigate the January 6th Attack on the United States Capitol (National Archives Production), P-R000255–P-R000259 (Jan. 6, 2021, Daily Diary of President Donald J. Trump).

325.   Select Committee to Investigate the January 6th Attack on the United States Capitol, Deposition of Jason Miller, (Feb. 3, 2022), pp. 258–59.

326.   Select Committee to Investigate the January 6th Attack on the United States Capitol, Deposition of Jason Miller, (Feb. 3, 2022), p. 258.

327.   Select Committee to Investigate the January 6th Attack on the United States Capitol, Deposition of Jason Miller, (Feb. 3, 2022), p. 258.

328. Select Committee to Investigate the January 6th Attack on the United States Capitol, Deposition of John McEntee (Mar. 28, 2022), pp. 160–61; Documents on file with the Select Committee to Investigate the January 6th Attack on the United States Capitol (National Archives Production), P-R000259 (Jan. 6, 2021, Daily Diary of the President Donald J. Trump).

329. Select Committee to Investigate the January 6th Attack on the United States Capitol, Deposition of John McEntee, (Mar. 28, 2022), p. 161.

330. Select Committee to Investigate the January 6th Attack on the United States Capitol, Deposition of John McEntee, (Mar. 28, 2022), p. 161.

331. Insert: Documents on file with the Select Committee (National Archives Production), P-R000259 (Jan. 6, 2021, Daily Diary of the President Donald J. Trump).

332. Documents with file with the Select Committee to Investigate the January 6th Attack on the United States Capitol (National Archives Production), P-R000255 (Jan. 6, 2021, The Daily Diary of President Donald J. Trump).

333. Select Committee to Investigate the January 6th Attack on the United States Capitol, Deposition of Judson P. Deere, (Mar. 3, 2022), pp. 42–43.

334. Select Committee to Investigate the January 6th Attack on the United States Capitol, Transcribed Interview of Ivanka Trump, (Apr. 5, 2022), pp. 179–80.

335. Select Committee to Investigate the January 6th Attack on the United States Capitol, Transcribed Interview of Ivanka Trump, (Apr. 5, 2022), p. 180.

336. Documents on file with the Select Committee to Investigate the January 6th Attack on the United States Capitol (Patrick MacDonnell Production), PM000158 (Jan. 7, 2021, Patrick Mac-Donnell text message to personal contact at 9:46 p.m. EST).

337. Documents on file with the Select Committee to Investigate the January 6th Attack on the United States Capitol (Ali Alexander Production), CTRL0000017719, p. 3; Select Committee to Investigate the January 6th Attack on the United States Capitol, Deposition of Ali Alexander, (Dec. 9, 2021), p. 57.

338. Documents on file with the Select Committee to Investigate the January 6th Attack on the United States Capitol (Hope Hicks Production), SC_HH_042.

339. Documents on file with the Select Committee to Investigate the January 6th Attack on the United States Capitol (Hope Hicks Production), SC_HH_040.

340. Documents on file with the Select Committee to Investigate the January 6th Attack on the United States Capitol (Katrina Pierson Production), KPierson0717 (Jan. 6, 2021, Brad Parscale text message to Katrina Pierson at 7:14 p.m. ET).

341. Documents on file with the Select Committee to Investigate the January 6th Attack on the United States Capitol (Katrina Pierson Production), KPierson0718– KPierson20 (Jan. 6, 2021, Brad Parscale text message to Katrina Pierson at 7:22 p.m. ET).

8

ANALYSIS OF THE ATTACK

Late in the evening on January 6, 2021, Henry "Enrique" Tarrio, the head of the Proud Boys, posted a video on his Parler account. The brief footage showed a masked man, wearing a black cape, standing in front of the U.S. Capitol Building. Tarrio titled the 18-second video, set to ominous music, "Premonition." He offered no further explanation. The clear implication of the brief footage, recorded sometime prior to January 6th, was that Tarrio had foreknowledge of the events that transpired earlier that same day.[1]

Indeed, Tarrio cheered on his fellow Proud Boys as they attacked the U.S. Capitol. He had been arrested and ordered to leave Washington, DC two days earlier. Although Tarrio was not physically present, he continued to monitor and communicate with his men via encrypted chats and social media. At 2:36 p.m. on January 6th, Tarrio wrote on Parler that he was "enjoying the show," adding: "Do what must be done" and "#WeTheP-eople."[2] Two minutes later, Tarrio wrote: "Don't fucking leave." Several minutes after that, Tarrio messaged his Proud Boys: "Make no mistake..." and "We did this..."[3]

Law enforcement officials subsequently uncovered significant evidence showing that Tarrio and his lieutenants planned to storm the U.S. Capitol. In June 2022, Tarrio and four other Proud Boys were charged with seditious conspiracy and other crimes related to their alleged responsibility for the assault.[4] The U.S. Department of Justice (DOJ) has alleged that they "conspired to prevent, hinder and delay the certification of the Electoral College vote, and to oppose by force the authority of the government of the United States."[5] On January 6, 2021, the Proud Boys "directed, mobilized and led members of the crowd onto the Capitol grounds and into the Capitol, leading to dismantling of metal barricades, destruction of property, breaching of the Capitol building, and assaults on law enforcement."[6]

The Select Committee's analysis corroborates the DOJ's findings and allegations. The Select Committee reviewed extensive footage of the attack, including that recorded by the U.S. Capitol Police's (USCP) surveillance cameras, the Metropolitan Police Department's (MPD) body-worn cameras, publicly available videos, as well as on-the-ground film produced by an embedded documentarian. The Select Committee interviewed rioters, law enforcement officers, and witnesses that were present on January 6th, while also consulting thousands of court filings. Using these sources of information, the Select Committee developed a timeline of events to understand how the unprecedented attack on the U.S. Capitol unfolded.

As explained below, the Proud Boys marched from the Washington Monument to the U.S. Capitol on the morning of January 6th. While tens of thousands of President Trump's supporters gathered at a rally at the Ellipse near the White House, the Proud Boys prepared to attack. Shortly before the joint session of Congress was set to begin at 1:00 p.m., the Proud Boys instigated an assault on outmanned law enforcement at the Peace Circle, a key location. They quickly overran security barriers and made their way onto the U.S. Capitol's restricted grounds. Throughout the next several hours, members of the Proud Boys led the attack at key breach points, preventing law enforcement from gaining crowd control and inciting others to press forward.

President Trump finished his speech at the Ellipse at approximately 1:10 p.m. Toward the end of his remarks, the President directed his supporters to march down Pennsylvania Avenue to the Capitol. Their natural path took them through the Peace Circle, which had already been cleared out by the Proud Boys and their associates. Thousands of rioters and protestors streamed onto the Capitol's restricted grounds in short order.

The Proud Boys were not solely responsible for attacking the U.S. Capitol. As explained in Chapter 6, other far-right extremists and conspiracy theorists prepared for violence after President Trump summoned them to Washington for a "wild" protest on January 6th. And they joined in the assault as well. Three Percenters, QAnon adherents, and other radicals were on the frontlines, pressing the charge. The Oath Keepers attacked the Capitol, forming two military-style "stacks" to push their way into the building. The white nationalist Groypers were present as their leader gave an inflammatory speech from the same Peace Circle where the attack was launched. Like members of the Proud Boys, Oath Keepers, and Three Percenters, some of the Groypers have been charged for their actions on January 6th.

Unaffiliated Americans enraged by President Trump's lies rioted as well. The January 6th, attack has often been described as a riot—and that is partly true. Some of those who trespassed on the Capitol's grounds or entered the building did not plan to do so beforehand. But it is also true that extremists, conspiracy theorists and others were prepared to fight. That is

Trump supporters from around the country gather at the Washington Monument on the morning of January 6, 2021.

Photo by Brent Stirton/Getty Images

an insurrection. They answered President Trump's call to action. Some, like the Proud Boys, deliberately harnessed the mob's anger to overrun the Capitol.

8.1 THE MOB ASSEMBLES IN WASHINGTON

During the early morning hours of January 6th, tens of thousands of Americans from around the country began to gather at the Ellipse and the Washington Monument. They had come to hear President Trump speak and, more importantly, for his "wild" protest.

Nick Quested, a documentary filmmaker, captured the mood that morning. Jacob Chansley (a.k.a. the QAnon Shaman) proclaimed "this is our 1776," vowing "Joe Biden is never getting in."[7] An unnamed woman from Georgia, who said she hosted a podcast dedicated to a new so-called Patriot Party, also proclaimed January 6th to be the new 1776. She added an ominous warning. "I'm not allowed to say what's going to happen today because everyone's just going to have to watch. Something's gonna happen, one way or the other."[8]

The Secret Service set up magnetometers to screen for weapons and other contraband, but many rally-goers chose to avoid the screening altogether.

At 6:29 a.m., Stewart Rhodes, the leader of the Oath Keepers, reminded his group's members that DC prohibited blades over "3 inches" and encouraged them to "[k]eep [the knives] low profile."[9] Others were thinking along the same lines. At 7:25 a.m., the National Park Service reported that a significant number of attendees ditched their bags in trees, rather than have them inspected.[10] Cassidy Hutchinson told the Select Committee she heard that thousands of people refused to walk through magnetometers to enter the Ellipse because they did not want to be screened for weapons.[11] According to Hutchinson, the Deputy Chief of Staff for Operations whose responsibilities included security-related issues, Tony Ornato, told the President that the onlookers "don't want to come in right now. They—they have weapons that they don't want confiscated by the Secret Service."[12] When he arrived at the Ellipse that morning, President Trump angrily said: "I don't [fucking] care that they have weapons. They're not here to hurt *me*. They can march to the Capitol from here."[13]

Approximately 28,000 rally-goers did pass through the magnetometers. The Secret Service confiscated a significant number of prohibited items from these people, including: 269 knives or blades, 242 cannisters of pepper spray, 18 brass knuckles, 18 tasers, 6 pieces of body armor, 3 gas masks, 30 batons or blunt instruments, and 17 miscellaneous items like scissors, needles, or screwdrivers.[14]

At 8:07 a.m., Secret Service countersurveillance agents reported that "members of the crowd are wearing ballistic helmets, body armor and carrying radio equipment and military grade backpacks."[15] By 9:45 a.m., the Secret Service noted people openly carrying pepper spray as they strolled the streets.[16]

President Trump's mob was itching for a fight. National Park Service officers arrested a man who had entered the restricted area around the Washington Monument. Immediately, about 100 people started forming a circle around the officer, "threaten[ing] law enforcement," as the officer later recounted.[17] The officer retreated into the Washington Monument with the man in custody.[18] The crowd responded angrily, punching the Monument's glass windows and continuing to threaten officers.[19] Law enforcement around the Washington Monument felt so unsafe that they "locked themselves in a security box by the mall."[20] Rioters nevertheless "scaled the sides of the security box and climbed on top of the structure."[21] It was a harbinger of things to come.

MPD monitored and responded to a stream of threats that morning. Three men in fatigues from Broward County, Florida brandished AR-15s in front of MPD officers on 14th Street and Independence Avenue.[22] MPD advised over the radio that one individual was possibly armed with a "Glock" at Fourteenth Street and Constitution Avenue, and another was possibly armed with a "rifle" at Fifteenth Street and Constitution Avenue around 11:23 a.m.[23] The National Park Service detained an individual with a rifle between 12:00 and 1:00 p.m.[24]

Far-right extremists brought guns into Washington or the surrounding area. Christopher Kuehne, a member of the Proud Boys, met up with friends on January 5th to discuss their plans for the following day. One person in attendance said he did not travel to Washington just to "march around" and asked, "do we have patriots here willing to take it by force?"[25] Kuehne told them he had guns, and he was ready to go.[26] During the attack, Kuehne helped prop open Capitol blast doors as besieged law enforcement retreated inside.[27] Guy Reffitt, a Three Percenter from Texas, attended the rally at the Ellipse, and then carried a loaded firearm onto Capitol grounds.[28] Jerod Thomas Bargar lost his gun—that he'd carried from the Ellipse in a 'We the People' holster[29]—while scuffling with police on the west side of the Capitol around 2:30 p.m.[30] Bargar wanted to be armed, he said, when he went into the "belly of the beast." [31]

Mark Andre Mazza drove from Indiana, bringing a Taurus revolver, a .45-caliber weapon that he loaded with both shotgun and hollow-point rounds.[32] After assaulting a police officer, he lost the weapon,[33] dropping it or losing it on the steps of the lower West Plaza leading to the Capitol's West Front Terrace.[34] The Select Committee reviewed Mazza's social media accounts before they were taken down, finding that he shared multiple conspiracy theories, including QAnon material.[35] Mazza later indicated that he intended to target House Speaker Nancy Pelosi, telling authorities that "you'd be here for another reason" if he had found the Speaker inside the Capitol.[36]

Lonnie Leroy Coffman from Falkville, Alabama, parked by the Capitol building before walking nearly 2 miles to the Ellipse to hear the President speak.[37] In his car, he had stocked a handgun, a rifle, a shotgun, hundreds of rounds of ammunition, large-capacity ammunition-feeding devices, machetes, camouflage smoke devices, a bow and arrow, and 11 Mason jars filled with gasoline and styrofoam, as well as rags and a lighter (tools needed to make Molotov cocktails).[38] Police found two more handguns on Coffman when he was arrested later that day.[39]

Many in attendance were aware of Washington's prohibition on carrying a concealed weapon and made plans accordingly. The Oath Keepers left their guns stowed away in their cars or across State lines for easy access should they be needed.[40] The group staged a "quick reaction force" across the river in Virginia, amassing an arsenal to come to DC "by land" or "by sea," as Florida State-chapter lead—and defendant convicted of seditious conspiracy—Kelly Meggs said.[41] Oath Keeper Jason Dolan testified at the seditious conspiracy trial that the "quick reaction force [was] ready to go get our firearms in order to stop the election from being certified within Congress."[42] Dolan further testified that the Oath Keepers came to Washington, DC "to stop the certification of the election.... [b]y any means necessary. That's why we brought our firearms."[43]

Garret Miller—a January 6th defendant who traveled from Richardson, Texas—posted on Facebook that "he was bringing guns with him but 'might just keep 1 hidden one and store the rest in Virginia'" after learning about the DC law.[44] He also threatened to assassinate Congresswoman Alexandria Ocasio-Cortez and predicted a "civil war could start."[45]

Many members of the crowd decided against bringing firearms into the nation's capital, and armed themselves in other ways. Alex Kirk Harkrider from Carthage, Texas, and his co-defendant, Ryan Nichols, left guns in a parked car just outside the district before attending the rally.[46] Harkrider still brought a tomahawk axe.[47] During the march to the Capitol, he yelled "[c]ut their fucking heads off!"[48] One rioter told the Select Committee he saw another carrying a "pitchfork."[49]

Members of the mob carried flags and turned the flagpoles into weapons. Michael Foy, from Wixom, Michigan, carried a hockey stick to the Ellipse—he draped a Trump flag over it.[50] Just hours later, Foy used that hockey stick to repeatedly beat police officers at the inaugural tunnel.[51] Former New York City police officer Thomas Webster carried a Marine flag, which he later used to attack an officer holding the rioters back at the lower West Plaza.[52] Another individual, Danny Hamilton, carried a flag with a sharpened tip, which he said was "for a certain person," to which Trevor Hallgren(who had traveled with Hamilton to Washington, DC) responded: "it has begun." Later, Hallgren commented that "[t]here's no escape Pelosi, Schumer, Nadler. We're coming for you.... Even you AOC. We're coming to take you out. To pull you out by your hairs." On January 5th, Hallgren took a tour of the Capitol with Representative Barry Loudermilk, during which he took pictures of hallways and staircases.[53]

The mob President Trump summoned to Washington, DC, on January 6th, was prepared to fight.

8.2 MARCH OF THE PROUD BOYS

While tens of thousands of President Trump's supporters attended the rally at the Ellipse, the Proud Boys had other plans. On the morning of January

6th, they gathered at the Washington Monument. At 10:30 a.m., the Proud Boys started their march down the National Mall towards the U.S. Capitol. In total, there were approximately 200–300 Proud Boys, as well as their associates, in the group.[54]

Enrique Tarrio, the chairman of the Proud Boys, was not in attendance. As explained in Chapter 6, Tarrio had been arrested two days earlier and ordered to leave Washington. However, Tarrio continued to monitor events remotely from Baltimore, communicating with his men throughout the day. With Tarrio offsite, the Proud Boys were led by three other senior members of the group: Ethan Nordean, Joseph Biggs, and Zachary Rehl.

Ethan Nordean (a.k.a. "Rufio Panman") was a member of the Proud Boys' Elders chapter and president of his local chapter in Seattle, Washington.[55] Nordean was regarded as the leader for January 6th after Tarrio was arrested.[56] In the days leading up to January 6th, Nordean made ominous comments on social media. In conversations with his fellow Proud Boys, he argued that the Presidential election was tainted by fraud and violence was a necessary remedy. For example, on January 4th, Nordean posted a video on social media with the title: "Let them remember the day they decided to make war with us." [57] In another social media post on January 5th, Nordean warned "we are coming for them." [58] He added a telling line: "You've chosen your side, black and yellow teamed with red, white and blue against everyone else." [59] The "black and yellow" is a reference to the Proud Boys. And when Nordean wrote the "red, white and blue," he likely meant the Trump supporters who would be in attendance for January 6th.

Joseph Biggs (a.k.a. "Sergeant Biggs") was a senior Proud Boys member and served as an event "organizer" for the group.[60] Biggs previously worked with Alex Jones and InfoWars.[61] In late December 2020, Biggs posted a message on Parler in which he explained that the Proud Boys "will not be attending DC in colors." [62] That is, unlike at previous events, the Proud Boys would not wear their branded, black and yellow clothing, but instead seek to be inconspicuous. Biggs continued:

> We will be blending in as one of you. You won't see us. You'll even think we are you…We are going to smell like you, move like you, and look like you. The only thing we'll do that's us is think like us! Jan 6th is gonna be epic.[63]

Tarrio posted a similar message, saying the Proud Boys would go "incognito" on January 6th.[64] Consistent with this decision, Biggs was dressed in a plaid shirt, glasses, and dark hat as he led the march from the Washington Monument.[65] Other Proud Boys dressed in a similar fashion.

Protestors, including a group of Proud Boys, gather at the Capitol on January 6, 2021.
Photo by Jon Cherry/Getty Images

Zachary Rehl (a.k.a. "Captain Trump") was president of the local Philadelphia, Pennsylvania Proud Boys chapter.[66] Like his comrades, Rehl believed President Trump's Big Lie about the 2020 Presidential election.[67] He raised more than $5,500 in funds for January 6th. Like Nordean, Biggs and others, Rehl was dressed "incognito" as he helped lead the group from the Washington Monument.[68]

Shortly after 11:00 a.m., the Proud Boys arrived at the west side of the Capitol, near a reflecting pool. From there, they marched to the east front of the Capitol. Surveillance footage shows the Proud Boys passing Garfield Circle on the southwest corner of the Capitol at 11:15 a.m.[69] They walked north towards the Peace Circle next, and surveillance cameras captured them on video there at approximately 11:21 a.m.[70] There was just one USCP officer standing guard at the Peace Circle fence at the time.[71]

As the Proud Boys paraded around the Capitol grounds, Nick Quested, a documentary filmmaker who spent time with the group, recalled them taunting USCP officers. One Proud Boy told the officers to "[r]emember your oath," "[c]hoose a side," and "[b]e on the right side of history."[72] By 11:41 a.m., the Proud Boys made their way around to the east side of the Capitol, crossing along Constitution Avenue.[73] While on the east front, they posed for pictures with members of their Arizona delegation, who were clearly identifiable by their orange caps.[74] They then walked back across the north side of the Capitol towards the National Mall, where they stopped to eat at food trucks.[75] The Proud Boys stayed by the food trucks until they returned to the Peace Circle at approximately 12:49 p.m.[76]

8.3 THE INITIAL ATTACK

Within minutes of arriving at the Peace Circle, the Proud Boys and their associates launched the attack on the U.S. Capitol. The circle is the site of the Peace Monument, a statue erected from 1877 to 1878 to commemorate naval deaths at sea during the Civil War with "two classically robed" women—one woman representing "grief," covering her face, and the other woman representing "history." The woman standing in for "history" holds a tablet that reads, "They died that their country might live." [77]

The Peace Circle's geographical location is crucially important for understanding how the January 6th, attack unfolded. It sits at the end of Pennsylvania Avenue, just in front of the U.S. Capitol. At the conclusion of his speech at the Ellipse, President Trump directed rally attendees to march down Pennsylvania Avenue to the U.S. Capitol. Their shortest natural path would lead them right to the Peace Circle and to the northwest side of the Capitol grounds, also known as the West Plaza. By the time rally-goers arrived, the Proud Boys and their allies had already removed the fencing that stood in the crowd's way. As a result, thousands of people streamed into the restricted Capitol grounds with relative ease.

When the Proud Boys arrived back at the Peace Circle at 12:49 p.m., they still had about 200 to 300 members and many other protestors had joined them.[78] Shortly after arriving, the Proud Boys incited the crowd with antagonistic chants such as "1776."[79] Officer Caroline Edwards, who was standing guard, explained to the Select Committee that the Proud Boys asked her and the other USCP officers if they could walk past the fencing and talk to the officers. "No," she replied. The Proud Boys and others immediately turned on Edwards and her fellow officers, referring to them as "Nancy Pelosi's dogs" and shouting.[80]

At approximately 12:51 p.m., Quested captured a rioter named Ryan Samsel with his arm around Proud Boys leader Joe Biggs, who led the chants.[81] Samsel subsequently claimed that Biggs encouraged him to push through the barricades and, when Samsel hesitated to follow through, Biggs "flashed a gun, questioned his manhood and repeated his demand" to move to the front and "challenge the police." [82] Biggs has contested Samsel's version of events.[83] After speaking with Biggs, Samsel breached the outer fencing of the Peace Circle at 12:53 p.m.[84] The first set of fencing at the

Peace Circle was staged on 1st Street Northwest, with the second set of fencing not far behind. Once Samsel breached the outer fencing, USCP officers, including Officer Edwards, moved from their posts to meet Samsel and other rioters.[85]

In less than a minute, at 12:54 p.m., the rioters pushed USCP officers to the ground, removed the fencing, and quickly stormed east towards the U.S. Capitol building.[86] Officer Edwards was thrown to the ground, causing her to hit her head on concrete steps.[87]

Two Proud Boys from New York, Dominic Pezzola and William Pepe, were among those leading the march to the next line of security barriers.[88] Pepe, an employee of the Metropolitan Transportation Authority in upstate New York, took sick leave to travel to Washington for the January 6th events.[89] Pepe dragged part of the fence away at the next security barrier, ensuring that USCP officers were left defenseless.[90] The Proud Boys' actions were not spontaneous. Jeffrey Finley, a Proud Boys leader from West Virginia, later admitted "there appeared to be a coordinated effort to pull the barricades apart."[91] Proud Boy Jeremy Bertino admitted to similar facts when pleading guilty to seditious conspiracy, stating stated that he "believed...that the purpose of traveling to Washington, DC, on January 6, 2021, was to stop the certification of the Electoral College Vote, and that the MOSD leaders were willing to do whatever it would take, including using force against police and others, to achieve that objective." Based on discussions he and other Proud Boys leaders had in the leadup to January 6th, he "believed that storming the Capitol would achieve the group's goal of stopping Congress from certifying the Electoral College Vote. Bertino understood that storming the Capitol or its grounds would be illegal and would require using force against police or other government officials."[92]

Parallel to the Peace Circle, at the Garfield Circle walkway located at the southeast corner of the Capitol grounds, rioters breached the fencing at 12:55 p.m. and began rushing the West Plaza where they would converge with others from the Peace Circle.[93]

By 12:58 p.m., the crowd filled the lower West Plaza of the Capitol just below the inauguration stage that had been built for the ceremony scheduled two weeks later. After the initial breaches, the USCP was able to deploy enough officers to stop the rioters from advancing past the base of the inauguration stage. More importantly, rioter momentum was further halted when the first group of MPD officers arrived on scene at 1:11 p.m.,[94] almost precisely as President Trump finished his Ellipse speech. The MPD officers initially pushed back the rioters on the West Plaza, slowing them down before they would later breach the Capitol.[95]

A stalemate ensued on the West Plaza before rioters were able to make any further progress. Rally-goers arriving from the Ellipse provided crucial momentum.

8.4 PRESIDENT TRUMP'S MOB DESCENDS ON THE U.S. CAPITOL

Toward the end of his speech at the Ellipse, President Trump made sure an already angry crowd of his supporters stayed enraged. "We fight like hell[,] and if you don't fight like hell, you're not going to have a country anymore," the President told the tens of thousands of people who had assembled at the Ellipse, or in the vicinity. About one minute later, President Trump directed those in attendance "to walk down Pennsylvania Avenue ... to the Capitol." The President told the people they were "going to try and give" Republicans, including his own Vice President, "the kind of pride and boldness that they need to take back our country." [96]

"There's enough people here to storm the Capitol," a member of the crowd said at 1:06 p.m., just as the President was concluding his remarks.[97] Ronald Sandlin, who pleaded guilty to and has been sentenced for felonies committed on January 6th, including telling officers in the Capitol that "[y]ou're going to die," watched the President's speech from a nearby restaurant and live-streamed a video in which he encouraged "other patriots" to "take the Capitol." [98] Sandlin repeated the phrase "freedom is paid for with blood" several times during his video.[99]

"We're getting ready to go march on Capitol Hill. We're gonna go fuck some shit up," Cody Mattice, another January 6th defendant who pleaded guilty and has been sentenced,[100] said while walking to the Capitol. Mattice later added: "We're getting up front, and we're taking this shit." [101] Ryan Nichols, who was charged with eight felonies, livestreamed a diatribe as he marched towards the Capitol at 1:40 p.m. Nichols echoed the President's unconstitutional claim that Vice President Pence had the power to decide the election himself. "I'm hearing that Pence just caved.... I'm telling you if Pence caved, we're gonna drag motherfuckers through the streets," Nichols said.[102] "Cut their heads off!" Nichols yelled with his codefendant Harkrider, before encouraging others to join "Republican protestors [who] are trying to enter the House right now." [103]

On the way to the Capitol, Oath Keeper Jessica Watkins chatted with others in a Zello group named "Stop the Steal J6." Watkins said that "100%" of the Ellipse crowd was "marching on the Capitol," because "it has spread like wildfire that Pence has betrayed us." [104] As she approached the Capitol with a contingent of Oath Keepers, Watkins said: "I'm probably gonna go silent when I get there 'cause I'm a be a little busy.[105] Donald

Hazard, a Three Percenter from Texas who claimed to be allied with Proud Boys on January 6th, told a *Washington Post* reporter that he wanted his face recorded on video as he marched to the Capitol. "I want the enemy to know exactly who is coming after them," Hazard explained.[106]

Leaders of the "Stop the Steal" movement continued to incite the crowd during the march as well. Alex Jones of InfoWars arrived at the Ellipse shortly before 9:00 a.m. on the morning of January 6th.[107] After some initial difficulty gaining access to the event area, Jones was seated in the VIP section.[108] While Jones stayed to listen to a portion of President Trump's speech, planning for the crowd's march to the Capitol was already under-way and Jones intended to leave the Ellipse early to lead the march. The origins of the plan to have Jones lead the march are unclear. Jones has pub-licly stated that "the White House told me three days before, we are going to have you lead the March." [109] Stop the Steal's Ali Alexander also believed "the White House" wanted him to lead a march to the Capitol.[110] It is likely that both got that idea from Caroline Wren, a Republican fundraiser who helped organize the Ellipse event.[111] Jones texted Wren at 12:27 p.m., asking when he should leave the Ellipse and begin the march.[112]

While Wren originally expected Jones, Roger Stone, and retired Lt. Gen. Michael Flynn to march to the Capitol, Stone did not attend the Ellipse rally and so he was not present to accompany Jones on the march as planned.[113] Additionally, while President Trump was delivering his speech, Wren asked Flynn if he was going to march with Jones. Flynn responded, "Hell, no. It's freezing." [114]

While Stone and Flynn did not march, Jones and Alexander led others to the Capitol, though it is not clear how many people followed them.[115] Jones and Alexander gathered with Jones's camera and security crew just outside the event perimeter, near Freedom Plaza, to discuss their plans.[116] The dis-cussion, recorded by Alex Jones's film crew, sheds some light on what Jones and Alexander knew about the President's plans and what they intended for the march. The group, which included InfoWars host Owen Shroyer, huddled outside the Ellipse security perimeter to discuss how best to pro-ceed. They tried to predict the Presidential motorcade's route to the Capitol. The video shows Alex Jones telling his crew, "I think the Wren lady, where's she at? She knows what they said they were going to do. Everything she's said has been accurate, so we need to call her real quick." [117] They then decided to walk down Pennsylvania Avenue, as the President had directed in his speech.

Shroyer recommended the group wait for President Trump to finish speaking, and they agreed to at least delay their departure from Freedom Plaza to allow Jones to gather a crowd. [118] Jones began speaking from his

Alex Jones uses a bullhorn to speak to crowd on January 6, 2021.
Photo by Jon Cherry/Getty Images

bullhorn, imploring people to gather and walk down Pennsylvania Avenue.[119] While using the bullhorn, Jones told the crowd that they were experiencing "the second American revolution,"[120] and stated, "[l]et's go take our country back. Trump is only minutes away. Let's start marching to the Capitol, peacefully."[121]

Proud Boys were among the crowd Jones gathered during his march. Matthew Walter, president of a Tennessee chapter of the organization,[122] was near the National Mall with two other Proud Boys from Tennessee and decided to join Jones.[123] Other, more prominent members of the Proud Boys appear to have been in contact with Jones and Shroyer about the events of January 6th and on that day. Records for Enrique Tarrio's phone show that while the attack on the Capitol was ongoing, he texted with Jones three times and Shroyer five times.[124] Ethan Nordean's phone records reflect that he exchanged 23 text messages with Shroyer between January 4th and 5th, and that he had one call with him on each of those days.[125] Records of Joseph Biggs's communications show that he texted with Shroyer eight times on January 4th and called him at approximately 11:15 a.m. on January 6th, while Biggs and his fellow Proud Boys were marching at and around the Capitol.[126]

Once they had marched the length of Pennsylvania Avenue and reached the west side of the Capitol, Jones and Alexander used a bullhorn to continue directing those around them to the east side, making further references to President Trump's alleged imminent arrival. A video recorded by a rallygoer at 1:51 p.m. shows Jones and Alexander standing together as Jones encourages the crowd to proceed to the east side of the Capitol. He tells those listening that "we've got a permit on the other side, it's great that this happened, but Trump's not going to come when we've taken this over. We are not Antifa, we are not BLM." [127]

Jones has repeatedly claimed that he tried to calm the crowd, but his actions also coincided with two police line breaches and one breach of the Capitol building itself. At 1:57 p.m., minutes after Jones encouraged rally goers to move east, newly arrived protestors breached the bike rack fencing used to keep the crowd away from the east side steps. [128] After the breach, police retreated to the base of the large set of steps behind them and the crowd moved forward to meet the newly established police line. [129]

Jones followed shortly behind the crowd that led the initial east fence breach, and his arrival coincided with the next breach up the east stairs. Publicly available video shows Jones already departed from the west side, rounding the north side of the Capitol on the way to the east side at 2:00 p.m. [130] As he was walking, Jones told his group, "those fucking cops need to fucking back off man." [131] He was then asked about Vice President Pence, to which Jones responded: "he floundered and was neutral, he passed the ball." [132] At the conclusion of the video, one of Jones's camera crew can be heard saying, "let's take a break here. Let me talk to this cop to see if I can get Alex up there to deescalate the situation." Other video released by Jones shows one of his camera crew interacting with USCP officers and asking how Jones can help deescalate the situation. [133] The Select Committee's review of the evidence showed that Jones simultaneously called on the crowd to "fight" and start a "revolution," while occasionally peppering his rhetoric with the word "peacefully."

Minutes after Jones's arrival on the scene, at approximately 2:06 p.m., rioters breached the new police line and stormed up the stairs towards the Columbus Doors (also known as the Rotunda Doors). [134] The crowd's cheers and celebration as they move up the steps can be heard while Jones's camera crew negotiates with USCP officers nearby. [135] As explained below, the rioters broke through another key breach point with Jones and Alexander on the scene just minutes later.

Rioters clash with police at the Capitol on January 6, 2021.

Photo by Brent Stirton/Getty Images

8.5 THE MOB SURGES

Far-right extremists continued to lead the charge as protestors streamed onto the U.S. Capitol's restricted grounds. On the north side of the West Plaza, there was a scaffold with stairs used by construction workers to build the inauguration stage. Law enforcement officers were stationed at the base of the stairs, preventing rioters from climbing to the upper West Plaza, where doors to the Capitol building itself were located. At 1:49 p.m., MPD declared a riot at the Capitol.[136]

Shortly before 1:50 p.m., rioters gathered in front of this scaffold on the northwest corner of the Capitol. The rioters included Proud Boys and other extremists. One rioter, Guy Reffitt, belonged to a Three Percenter group from Texas.[137] By approximately 1:50 p.m., he stood at the front of the pack near the scaffold, carrying a pistol and flexicuffs.[138] He wore body armor under a blue jacket and a helmet with a mounted body camera.[139]

Reffitt advanced on the police line, absorbing rubber bullets and pushing through chemical spray.[140] As he recounted shortly after the attack, Reffitt got "everything started moving forward."[141] He "started the fire" and the presence of law enforcement was not going to prevent Reffitt's advance.[142] According to Reffitt:

> [T]here was no reason for me to give up because I had come so far to do what I wanted, what we wanted and needed to do. And I had a mindset. I didn't mean to actually be the first guy up there. I didn't even mean to do that. I just, the adrenaline and knowing that I can't let my country fall.[143]

Reffitt had indeed planned for violence on January 6th, noting on December 28, 2020, that he would "be in full battle rattle."[144] While driving to Washington, DC on January 5th, Reffitt expressed his desire to "drag[ ] those people out of the Capitol by their ankles" and "install[ ] a new government."[145] On the morning of January 6th, Reffitt clarified the target, telling "other members of his militia group and those gathered around him" at the Ellipse that "I'm taking the Capitol with everybody fucking else"and that "[w]e're all going to drag them mother fuckers out kicking and screaming....I just want to see Pelosi's head hit every fucking stair on the way out...And Mitch McConnell too. Fuck' em all."[146] Reffitt was convicted and ultimately sentenced to 7 years in prison for his conduct.[147]

A member of the Proud Boys, Daniel Scott, helped lead the charge up the scaffolding stairs.[148] Scott, also known as Milkshake, had marched with the Proud Boys from the Washington Monument to the Capitol. During the march, Scott was recorded in a video yelling, "Let's take the fucking Capitol!"[149] Someone else responded, "Let's not fucking yell that, alright?" And then Nordean added: "It was Milkshake, man, you know...idiot." Scott had apparently blurted out the Proud Boys' plan. At the scaffolding, Scott then helped others "take" the U.S. Capitol. While wearing a blue cap with white lettering that read, "Gods, Guns & Trump," he pushed police officers backwards, clearing a path for the rioters. Another Proud Boy, Chris Worrell, was also nearby.[150] As rioters massed under the scaffold, Worrell sprayed officers with OC (or pepper) spray.[151] Other Proud Boys were present at the scaffold, including Micajah Jackson[152] and Matthew Greene.[153]

The attack at and in the vicinity of the scaffolding cleared a path for a wave of rioters who forced their way up the stairs and to the U.S. Capitol building itself.[154] As the rioters rushed up the stairs, another January 6th defendant, Ryan Kelley, climbed up the scaffolding around 1:51 p.m.[155] In the ensuing minutes he waved people on, encouraging them to follow.[156] Kelley—who ran in the Republican primary to be the governor of Michigan in 2022—denied to the Select Committee that he had climbed the scaffolding to wave people on.[157] The FBI arrested Kelley a few months after his deposition.[158]

By 2:00 p.m., rioters at the top of the scaffolding stairs were only feet away from Capitol building doors and windows.

8.6 THE UNITED STATES CAPITOL IS BREACHED

Incited by President Trump, over the course of the next hour, extremists, conspiracy theorists and others breached the U.S. Capitol building at several locations. They probed for weaknesses in the building's defenses, battling law enforcement personnel who stood in their way. Once again, the Proud Boys and other extremists played conspicuous roles.

THE SENATE WING IS BREACHED AT 2:13 P.M.

At 2:13 p.m., Dominic Pezzola, a Proud Boy from New York, smashed a window on the Senate wing.[159] This was the first breach of the Capitol building. Pezzola used a riot shield he stole from a law enforcement officer to break through the window. After climbing through, rioters were able to easily open a nearby Senate wing door from the inside—giving them unfettered passage into the building at 2:14 p.m. Two minutes later, at approximately 2:16 p.m., rioters pushed opened a second door, the Senate fire door, from the inside.[160] Just as the building was being breached, Vice President Pence and Speaker Pelosi were ushered off the Senate and House floors, respectively.[161]

The first person to enter the Capitol building was a Kentucky native named Michael Sparks. Sparks had expressed his desire to kill people after watching protests in the summer of 2020.[162] Following one of President Trump's calls to Washington, DC on December 30, 2020, Sparks answered that he would "be there."[163]

As Pezzola entered the building, he was joined by other noteworthy extremists and conspiracy theorists. Robert Gieswein, an individual from Colorado affiliated with Three Percenters who espoused conspiracy beliefs, climbed through the Senate wing window.[164] Doug Jensen, a QAnon adherent, was part of this first cadre of people to enter the Capitol as well.[165] Jensen wore a brazen "Q" shirt. Jensen later told authorities that he "intentionally positioned himself to be among the first people inside the United States Capitol because…he wanted to have his t-shirt seen on video so that 'Q' could 'get the credit.'"[166] Another prominent QAnon believer, Jacob Chansley (a.k.a. the "QAnon Shaman"), also entered through the Senate wing door at approximately 2:14 p.m.[167]

White supremacists and Confederate-sympathizers were among the first rioters to enter the U.S. Capitol. Kevin Seefried and his son, Hunter, entered the building at approximately 2:13 p.m. through the Senate wing window smashed by Proud Boy Dominic Pezzola.[168] Kevin Seefried carried a

Doug Jensen and rioters confront police after storming the Capitol.
(Photo by Win McNamee/Getty Images)

Confederate Battle Flag with him and unfurled it inside the building. According to some historians, while the Confederate Flag has appeared in the building before, it was the first time that an insurrectionist ever carried the banner inside the U.S. Capitol.[169] According to court filings, Hunter Seefried helped punch out the Senate wing window and then clear the broken glass before he, his father and others entered the Capitol.[170] Kevin Seefried was found guilty of obstructing an official proceeding, which is a felony offense, as well as four misdemeanors.[171] The Department of Justice has alleged that at 2:16 p.m., just 3 minutes after the Senate wing was first breached, five individuals associated with the Nick Fuentes's white nationalist "America First" movement entered the U.S. Capitol.[172] The five, all of whom are in their 20s, have been identified as: Joseph Brody, Thomas Carey, Gabriel Chase, Jon Lizak, and Paul Lovley.[173] Four of the five "initially met at an America First event and attended subsequent events together."[174] Nick Fuentes and other America First leaders espouse "a belief that they are defending against the demographic and cultural changes in America."[175] Online researchers say that Brody is the masked man seen in a photo wearing a MAGA hat and holding a rifle in front of a Nazi flag.[176] (The photo was not taken on January 6th.) As discussed in Chapter 6, members of the America First movement, commonly known as

"Groypers," were well-represented at "Stop the Steal" events in late 2020 and these rallies helped pave the road to January 6th. Indeed, at least three members of the group—Lovley, Lizak and Chase—attended the "Stop the Steal, March for Trump" rally in Washington, DC on November 14, 2020.[177]

On January 6th, Brody and his America First associates made their way to various points inside and outside of the Capitol after the initial breach, including House Speaker Nancy Pelosi's conference room and office, as well as the U.S. Senate Chamber.[178] After exiting the Capitol, the group went to the north side of the building. One of the five, Brody, and another rioter allegedly used a "metal barricade" to assault a law enforcement officer who was defending the North Door.[179] (The attack on the North Door is discussed below.) Brody and Chase also allegedly helped others destroy media equipment.[180] Still another America First associate, Riley Williams, directed rioters up a staircase to Speaker Pelosi's office and was accused of aiding and abetting the theft of a laptop found there.[181] Other white supremacists were among the first rioters to enter the U.S. Capitol. Timothy Hale-Cusanelli, an Army Reservist from New Jersey who was identified by a confidential source to law enforcement as an "an avowed white supremacist and Nazi sympathizer," entered through the Senate wing breach around 2:14 p.m.[182] Hale-Cusanelli "[u]sed tactical hand signals" to direct other members of the mob, and he commanded them to "'advance' on the Capitol."[183] Afterwards, he bragged to a friend that January 6th was "exhilarating," that he hoped "for a 'civil war,' and that the 'tree of liberty must be refreshed with the blood of patriots and tyrants.'"[184] Robert Packer was also among the first rioters to enter the Capitol, and he made his way into the Crypt by 2:25 p.m.[185] Packer was wearing a "Camp Auschwitz" sweatshirt, a "symbol of Nazi hate ideology," at the time.[186]

After breaking in, some of the first rioters headed north toward the Senate chambers.[187] Officer Eugene Goodman, a USCP officer, intercepted them before they headed up the stairs leading to the chambers. Immediately after entering, a rioter asked Officer Goodman, "Where are the [M]embers at?" and "where are they counting the votes?"[188] Jensen, Gieswein, Sparks, and others stalked Officer Goodman through the halls of the Senate.[189] Jensen demanded that Officer Goodman and other USCP officers arrest Vice President Pence.[190] Sparks chanted, "This is our America!"[191] Other rioters who entered through the Senate wing door clashed with police offices at the Senate carriage door located on the northeast side of the Capitol.[192] When the rioters followed Officer Goodman up the stairs to the Senate Chamber, they were stopped by a line of USCP officers outside the Ohio Clock Tower.[193]

Joe Biggs of the Proud Boys entered the Capitol shortly after the first breach. At 2:14 p.m., Biggs walked through the senate wing door and moved north. Part of his route was captured in videos posted on Parler, a right-wing social media site.[194] Someone recorded the Proud Boys leader shortly after he entered the Capitol and asked him, "Hey Biggs what do you gotta say?"[195] Smiling, Biggs replied: "this is awesome!"[196] Other Proud Boys were seen with Biggs, or near him, as he entered the Capitol. One of them is Paul Rae, a Proud Boys member from Florida, who appears to have communicated directly with Biggs after they entered through the door.[197] Another Proud Boy from Florida, Arthur Jackman, was seen with his hand on Biggs's right shoulder. Jackman "became involved in the Proud Boys to support Donald Trump," was in Washington on January 6th "to support President Trump and to stop the steal" and "believe[d] the election was stolen." Still another, Joshua Pruitt, who was clad in a Punisher shirt, entered the Capitol through the Senate wing door around this time.[198] At approximately 2:17 p.m., 3 minutes after entering the U.S. Capitol for the first time, Biggs exited through another door.[199]

At 2:43 p.m., law enforcement was able to regain control of the Senate wing door, forcing all the rioters out. But their success lasted for only 5 minutes. At 2:48 p.m., rioters again breached the Senate wing door, pushing law enforcement out of the way.[200] The second breach was one of the more violent breaches of the day, with the mob forcefully pushing law enforcement backwards until the pathway was clear for them to enter.

THE COLUMBUS DOORS (EAST ROTUNDA DOORS) ARE BREACHED AT 2:24 P.M. AND 2:38 P.M.

While the Proud Boys and other extremists were overwhelming law enforcement at the West Plaza scaffolding, another group led the attack on security barriers on the East Plaza. At 2:06 p.m., a crowd broke through security barriers and charged a set of doors just outside the Rotunda.[201] The mob's surge occurred just minutes after Alex Jones arrived on the scene.[202] The crowd's cheers and celebration as they move up the steps can be heard while Jones's camera crew negotiates with USCP officers nearby.[203]

Once rioters had filled the Rotunda stairs, Jones and his team, along with the Proud Boy Walter, ascended the stairs. They moved into the thick of the crowd at the top of the stairs, where Jones began calling for peace but also revolution, leading the crowd in chants of "1776" and other bellicose rhetoric.[204] Publicly available video shows that Jones reached the top of the stairs at 2:18 p.m.[205] Walter told the Select Committee that he thought Jones was successful in getting some people down, "but I also think that may have created enough space for people to be able to move, whereas before you couldn't move."[206] Apparently, Jones's security team also realized he was not successfully controlling the crowd, as one of his security guards reportedly told him, "Alex, they're going to blame this all on you, we got to get out of here as fast as possible." [207] By approximately 2:21 p.m., Jones began descending the stairs.[208] Despite claiming to make attempts to calm the crowd, Jones further incited the mob as he departed, loudly proclaiming "we will never submit to the new world order" and then leading the crowd in the chant "fight for Trump." [209]

At 2:24 p.m., rioters gained entrance to the Capitol through the doors leading into the Rotunda,[210] an entrance that was only a few feet directly behind Jones as he was speaking. As the Rotunda was breached by rioters, Jones and Alexander left the area and decided to leave the Capitol complex area altogether.[211]

Law enforcement officials were able to thwart the initial breach of the doors leading into the Rotunda. By 2:28 p.m., they temporarily regained control and stopped rioters from entering.[212] But their success was short-lived. Within ten minutes, the doors were breached once again.[213] And two members of the Proud Boys—Ronald Loehrke and James Haffner—helped lead the attack.[214]

Loehrke was allegedly recruited by Nordean, the Proud Boys leader, for January 6th. In late December 2020, Nordean asked Loehrke via text message if he was coming to "DC." [215] After Loehrke indicated he was, Nordean said he wanted Loehrke "on the front line" with him.[216] Loehrke replied, "Sounds good man." [217] Loehrke and Haffner marched with the Proud Boys from the Washington Monument to the Capitol grounds and were present during the breach at the Peace Circle.[218] The pair made their way to the east side of the Capitol, where they began removing the security barriers and resisting USCP officers. [219] Other members of the crowd joined. Eventually, the rioters breached these barriers too, allowing them to reach the doors of the Rotunda.

When the rioters reached the Columbus Doors, they were again stopped by USCP officers. But as the officers explained to the Select Committee, the rioters pushed them against the doors and sprayed them with OC spray (commonly known as pepper spray), making it impossible to defend the Capitol.[220] James Haffner was one of the rioters who allegedly sprayed the officers.[221]

Shortly after Haffner and others assaulted the USCP officers, they were able to breach the Columbus Doors at approximately 2:38 p.m. A Proud Boys contingent—including Haffner, Loehrke, and Joe Biggs—then entered the Capitol.[222] It was the second time that Biggs entered the U.S. Capitol that day.

A military-style "stack" of Oath Keepers entered through the Columbus Doors as well. The Oath Keeper members attended the Ellipse rally, where they were provided personal security details for VIPs in attendance.[223] Afterwards, they marched to the Capitol, as directed by President Trump.

Stewart Rhodes, the leader of the Oath Keepers, monitored the attack on the Capitol from just outside, including during the assault on the Columbus Doors. At 2:28 p.m., Rhodes texted members of the F.O.S., or Friends of Stone, (FOS) Signal chat—which included Roger Stone, the Proud Boys' Enrique Tarrio, Ali Alexander, Alex Jones, and others[224]—that he was at the "Back door of the U.S. Capitol." [225] Rhodes followed up at 2:30 p.m. by texting members of another chat that there was "Pounding on the doors" of the Capitol.[226]

At 2:32 p.m., Rhodes held a three-way call with two other Oath Keepers, Kelly Meggs and Michael Green.[227] Three minutes later, Meggs's group ("Stack 1") started pushing through the rioters amassed on the East Plaza steps in a military-stack formation, with each person placing a hand on the shoulder of the person in front.[228] This stack entered the Capitol around 2:40 p.m.[229]

One minute later, Rhodes was caught on camera on the Upper West Terrace responding to a rioter who said the Members of Congress must be "shitting their pants inside." Rhodes replied: "Amen They need to shit their fucking pants. Sic semper tyrannis." [230]

Once inside, Stack 1 moved through the Rotunda. At 2:44 p.m., Stack 1 pushed into the Senate hallway, which was filled with officers blocking the way. "Push, push, push. Get in there. They can't hold us," Watkins implored the others. However, the officers repelled their attack, pushing them back into the Rotunda.[231]

Other Oath Keepers made their way to the Capitol as Stack 1 tried to advance. Joshua James and another group of Oath Keepers ("Stack 2") pushed through the Columbus Doors at approximately 3:15 p.m.[232] "This is my fucking Capitol. This is not yours. This is my building," James shouted at officers inside the Rotunda who were trying to push the rioters out of the Capitol.[233]

ADDITIONAL BREACH POINTS

In addition to the breaches discussed above, rioters opened other entry points into the U.S. Capitol. The Upper West Terrace door, which leads directly into the Rotunda, was breached at 2:33 p.m. when rioters opened it from the inside.[234]

Inside the Capitol, rioters broke through the police lines, such as in the Crypt, a space located directly underneath the Rotunda. The Crypt is anchored by a marble "compass stone," marking the center of the building, and is lined with 13 statues representing the original American colonies.[235] The rioters quickly moved towards the House Chambers and, by 2:40 p.m., started to crowd the main doors outside the Chambers, moving to the east side near the Speaker's lobby. As they moved to the east side, rioters opened the east House doors from the inside at 2:41 p.m., allowing rioters from the northeast side of the Capitol to enter.[236]

The north doors were the last Capitol doors breached. At 3:10 p.m., rioters entered through the north doors where they were quickly met by USCP.[237] Within a minute, the hallway just inside the doors was filled with rioters. At 3:12 p.m., a combination of USCP and MPD officers forcefully pushed the rioters out of the doors.[238] However, rioters continued to attack just outside the north doors throughout the afternoon and evening.

The north doors have an outer entranceway that is separated by a vestibule from a set of inner doors that lead directly into the Capitol. Rioters threw bricks at the doors and forcefully tried to stop police officers from clearing the area.[239] Law enforcement officers briefly opened the inner doors to spray a chemical irritant that was intended to disperse the mob.[240] But the rioters continued to fight. For instance, as the crowd held the outer doors open, John Thomas Gordon of West Virginia repeatedly threw a heavy projectile at the inner doors, while swearing at the officers.[241] Another rioter gave Gordon, who came to Washington to attend the "Stop the Steal" rally, a pair of goggles so he would withstand the chemical spray. Gordon kicked the inner doors as he and others desperately tried to enter the Capitol.[242] Law enforcement held the doors, withstanding the mob's best efforts to break in.

As law enforcement officers started to clear the building, rioters continued to fight police officers at the tunnel on the West Plaza. Rioters violently struck officers, including MPD Officer Daniel Hodges, and sprayed them with OC spray. Although rioters did not break through the police line at the tunnel, they were able to successfully break a window just north of it. There is no surveillance coverage for this area, so Select Committee staff was unable to determine the precise time of the breach. According to open-source videos, however, the breach appears to occur at approximately 4:15 p.m.[243]

8.7 PRESIDENT TRUMP POURS FUEL ON THE FIRE

After Dominic Pezzola and others breached the Capitol at 2:13 p.m., a mob quickly entered and headed towards the Senate and House Chambers, where Members were meeting.[244] As the crowd moved through the Capitol, they chanted "Fight for Trump" and "Stop the Steal!" They also chanted

"Nancy, Nancy" as they searched for Speaker Pelosi.[245] At 2:18 p.m., the House went into recess as hundreds of rioters confronted USCP officers inside the Crypt, which is a short distance from the first breach point.[246]

USCP officers formed a line across the Crypt in an attempt to stop the mob's advance.[247] By 2:21 p.m., the rioters had tried to break through police lines, but they were temporarily unsuccessful.[248]

As USCP officers held the line inside the Crypt, President Trump poured fuel on the fire, tweeting at 2:24 p.m.:

> "Mike Pence didn't have the courage to do what should have been done to protect our Country and our Constitution, giving states a chance to certify a corrected set of facts, not the fraudulent or inaccurate ones which they were asked to previously certify. USA demands the truth!" [249]

One minute later, the mob violently pushed through the USCP officers in the Crypt and continued moving south towards the House Chamber.[250] Joshua Pruitt, the Proud Boy dressed in a Punisher shirt, was at the front of the line as rioters broke through in the Crypt.[251] Officer David Millard told the Select Committee that rioters in the Crypt claimed they were in the Capitol because their "boss" told them to be there—meaning President Trump.[252] Officer Millard also recalled members of the mob telling him they were there to stop the steal.[253]

After breaking through the police line in the Crypt, the mob pursued USCP officers as they retreated to the U.S. Capitol Visitor's Center (CVC). Pruitt was among the rioters who advanced into the CVC, where he came close to Senator Chuck Schumer.[254] When the USCP officers attempted to lower metal barriers to halt the crowd's momentum, another small group of Proud Boys immediately interceded to prevent the barricades from coming down.[255] The Proud Boy contingent included three men from the Kansas City, Kansas area: William Chrestman,[256] Chris Kuehne,[257] and Louis Colon.[258] Felicia Konold and Cory Konold, two Proud Boy associates from Arizona, joined the Kansas City group while marching from the Washington Monument to the Capitol earlier in the day and were on the scene.[259] Two other Proud Boys, Nicholas Ochs and Nicholas DeCarlo, filmed the incident.[260]

Surveillance footage shows Chrestman using a wooden club, or modified axe handle, to prevent the barrier from being lowered to the floor.[261] Colon later admitted to authorities that he purchased and modified an axe handle "to be used as both a walking stick and an improvised weapon" on January 6th.[262] Colon also told authorities that he attended a meeting with Chrestman and others on the night of January 5th, during which someone

Rioters enter the Senate Chamber.

Photo by Win McNamee/Getty Images

asked, "do we have patriots here willing to take it by force?" Colon understood that the individual meant that they should use "force against the
government." This same individual commented that they should "go in
there and take over." [263]

At 2:36 p.m., the mob pushed through a line of USCP officers guarding
the House Chamber.[264] Rioters also entered the Senate Chamber.[265] Within
minutes, Jacob Chansley (a.k.a. the QAnon Shaman) entered the Senate
Chamber, making his way to the Senate dais, where Vice President Pence
had been presiding over the joint session. An officer asked Chansley to
vacate the dais, but instead he shouted, "Mike Pence is a fucking traitor."
Chansley also left a note that read: "It's Only a Matter of Time. Justice is
Coming!" [266] Surrounded by others, Chansley held a conspiracy-laden
prayer session, saying: "Thank you for allowing the United States of
America to be reborn. Thank you for allowing us to get rid of the commu-
nists, the globalists, and the traitors within our government." [267] Other
extremists, including at least one associate of the white nationalist
"America First" movement, also sat in the Vice President's seat.[268]

While law enforcement fought to contain the mob inside the Capitol,
the fighting raged outside as well. Key agitators continued to fire up the

crowd. Nick Fuentes, the leader of the "America First" movement, amplified President Trump's rhetoric aimed at Vice President Pence, including the President's 2:24 p.m. tweet.[269] Speaking through a bullhorn while standing on the Peace Monument, Fuentes shouted:

> We just heard that Mike Pence is not going to reject any fraudulent elector votes! That's right, you heard it here first: Mike Pence has betrayed the United States of America. Mike Pence has betrayed the President and he has betrayed the people of the United States of America—and we will never ever forget![270]

As rioters flowed through the halls and offices inside the Capitol, others broke through the defensive lines of USCP and MPD officers on the lower West Plaza at 2:28 p.m., allowing them to take over the inauguration stage.[271] According to MPD Officer Michael Fanone, MPD officers were then forced to conduct the "first fighting withdrawal" in the history of the force, with law enforcement seeking to "reestablish defensive lines" to prevent the "crowd that had swelled to approximately 20,000 from storming the U.S. Capitol." [272]

After surging through the West Plaza, rioters quickly headed towards the West Plaza tunnel. The violence that escalated at 2:28 p.m. on the lower West Plaza continued as rioters reached the tunnel. By 2:41 p.m., law enforcement retreated inside the tunnel, allowing rioters to slowly fill in.[273] Just ten minutes later, the mob jammed the tunnel, desperately trying to break through the police lines.[274] The fighting in and immediately outside of the tunnel raged for over two hours.[275]

Throughout the afternoon, members of the mob struck officers with weapons, shot them with OC (or pepper) spray, and dragged officers from the tunnel into the crowd. Lucas Denney, a Three Percenter from Texas who carried a baton on January 6th, pushed a riot shield into and on top of police officers at the tunnel. The crowd chanted "heave-ho!" as Denney did so.[276] Jeffrey Scott Brown sprayed a chemical or pepper spray at officers and pushed the front of the line in the tunnel.[277] Kyle Young, a January 6th defendant with a long prior criminal history, participated in multiple assaults and violence at the tunnel, including using a pole to jab at police officers.

Young's 16-year-old son was present during the fighting.[278] Robert Morss, a former Army Ranger who wore a military-style vest, participated in a heave-ho effort in the tunnel where he and rioters had created a shield wall.[279] Peter Schwartz and another rioter passed a large cannister of spray back and forth before Schwartz's companion sprayed officers and then the two joined in the heave-ho.[280]

Rioters assault police officers at a tunnel to the Capitol.

Photo by Brent Stirton/Getty Images

One of the most brutal attacks of the day occurred outside the tunnel when rioters dragged MPD Officer Michael Fanone into the crowd, and then tased, beat, and robbed him while a Blue Lives Matter flag fluttered above him. Albuquerque Head, a rioter from Tennessee, grabbed Officer Fanone around the neck and pulled him into the mob.[281] "I got one!" Head shouted.[282] Lucas Denney, the Three Percenter, "swung his arm and fist" at Officer Fanone, grabbed him, and pulled him down the stairs.[283] Daniel Rodriguez then tased him in the neck. Kyle Young lunged towards Officer Fanone, restraining the officer's wrist.[284] While Young held him, still another rioter, Thomas Sibick, reached towards him and forcibly removed his police badge and radio.[285] Officer Fanone feared they were after his gun. Members of the crowd yelled: "Kill him!," "Get his gun!" and "Kill him with his own gun!"[286]

In an interview with FBI agents, Daniel Rodriguez admitted his role in the attack on Officer Fanone.[287] During that same interview, Rodriguez discussed the influences that led him down the path to January 6th. Rodriguez was a fan of Alex Jones's InfoWars and told FBI agents that he became active at rallies after watching the conspiracy show.[288] Rodriguez was motivated by Jones's decision to support then candidate Trump in 2015.[289] He also began to affiliate himself with the Three Percenter movement, which he learned about by watching InfoWars.[290] And when President Trump called for a "wild" protest in Washington on January 6th, Rodriguez thought it was necessary to respond. "Trump called us. Trump called us to DC," Rodriguez told interviewing agents.[291] "If he's the commander in chief and the leader of our country, and he's calling for help—I thought he was calling for help," Rodriguez explained. "I thought he was—I thought we were doing the right thing." [292]

Rodriguez and another January 6th defendant, Edward Badalian, began preparing for violence after President Trump's December 19th tweet. They gathered weapons and tactical gear[293] and discussed their plans in a Signal chat named, "Patriots 45 MAGA Gang."

"Congress can hang. I'll do it," Rodriguez posted to the chat. Please let us get these people dear God." [294]

Badalian also posted a flyer titled "MAGA_CAVALRY," which showed rally points for "patriot caravans" to connect with the "Stop The Steal" movement in DC.[295] The same flyer was popular among Three Percenters and other self-described "patriot" groups. It also garnered the attention of law enforcement. The FBI's Norfolk, Virginia division noted in a January 5th intelligence assessment that the flyer was accompanied by another image, titled "Create Perimeter," which depicted the U.S. Capitol and other buildings being surrounded by the same caravans.[296]

8.8   THE EVACUATION

When rioters surrounded the perimeter of the Capitol, and reached the Senate and House Chambers, Members were forced to evacuate for safety. USCP officers responded to both Chambers and served as escorts. By the time the Capitol was breached, the Senate and House had split from the joint session, with Senators returning to their Chamber to debate the objection to Arizona's electoral vote. The House remained in its Chamber to debate the objection.[297]

Starting in the Senate, Vice President Pence was escorted off the floor at 2:12 p.m. and was taken to his Senate office. Between 2:12 p.m. and 2:25 p.m., Secret Service agents worked to identify potential threats and a route that could be used to transport Vice President Pence.[298] One of the issues for Vice President Pence's evacuation was that the rioters were outside the Ohio Clock Tower, which was just feet away from the staircase that Vice President Pence could descend to evacuate.[299] Eventually, after the mob started filling the entire Capitol, the Secret Service made the decision to move Vice President Pence, and he was escorted from the Senate at 2:25 p.m.[300] By 2:27 p.m., the Vice President can be seen moving toward a secure

Members of Congress are evacuated from the House Chamber.
(Photo by Drew Angerer/Getty Images)

location connected to the Capitol. The Vice President arrived at the secure location at 2:29 p.m.[301] Following the Vice President's evacuation, Senators were evacuated at 2:30 p.m.[302]

On the House side, Speaker Pelosi, House Majority Leader Steny Hoyer, and House Majority Whip James Clyburn were removed from the House floor at the same time as Vice President Pence. By 2:18 p.m., USCP surveillance showed Speaker Pelosi in the basement hallway headed towards the garage.[303] The surveillance footage also showed Leader Hoyer and Whip Clyburn in the same basement as Speaker Pelosi. At 2:23 p.m., Speaker Pelosi and Whip Clyburn were moved to an undisclosed location.[304]

Minority Leader Kevin McCarthy was evacuated just after Speaker Pelosi left the Capitol. At 2:25 p.m., as rioters were moving through the Crypt and breaking through the east Rotunda door, Leader McCarthy and his staff hurriedly evacuated his office.[305] At approximately 2:38 p.m., the Members of Congress on the House floor began their evacuation.[306] Members of Congress can be seen evacuating through the Speaker's Lobby when a USCP officer fatally shot Ashli Babbitt at 2:44 p.m.[307] Members and staffers were just feet away when Babbitt attempted to climb through a shattered glass door. USCP officers had barricaded the door with furniture to prevent the rioters from gaining direct access to elected officials.

The congressional Members in the House Gallery were evacuated after the Members on the House floor. Congressional Members in the Gallery had to wait to be evacuated because rioters were still roaming the hallways right outside the Chamber. At 2:49 p.m., as Members were trying to evacuate the House Gallery, the USCP emergency response team cleared the hallways with long rifles so that the Members could be escorted to safety.[308] USCP surveillance footage shows several rioters lying on the ground, with long rifles pointed at them, as Members evacuate in the background.[309] By 3:00 p.m., the area had been cleared and Members were evacuated from the House gallery to a secure location. [310]

8.9 CLEARING THE U.S. CAPITOL BUILDING AND RESTRICTED GROUNDS

Shortly after law enforcement officers evacuated the House and Senate Members, they started to clear rioters out of the Capitol and off the grounds. Starting before 3:00 p.m., law enforcement spent approximately three hours pushing rioters out of the Capitol building and off the East and West Plazas. In general, law enforcement cleared rioters out of the Capitol through three doors: (1) the House side door located on the northeast side of the Capitol; (2) the Columbus Doors (East Rotunda Doors); and (3) the Senate wing door, which was next to the first breach point. As discussed above, the Proud Boys and other extremists led the charge at the latter two locations during the early stages of the attack.

Outside the Capitol, law enforcement pushed the mob from the upper West Plaza towards the East Plaza, crossing the north doors. Eventually, these rioters were forced to exit the Capitol grounds on the east side. The last point where rioters were removed was the lower West Plaza—the scene of some of the most intense hand-to-hand fighting that day. After law enforcement cleared the tunnel, where violence had raged for hours, police officers corralled rioters to the west and away from the Capitol building.[311]

After rioters first breached the Senate wing door on the first floor, they immediately moved south towards the House Chamber. This route took them to the Crypt—with the mob filling this room by 2:24 p.m. This was also one of the first rooms that law enforcement cleared as they started to secure the building. By 2:49 p.m., law enforcement officers cleared the Crypt by pushing towards the Senate wing door and up the stairs to the Rotunda.[312]

Around the same time that police officers cleared the Crypt, they also removed rioters from hallways immediately adjacent to the House and Senate Chambers. On the House side, rioters were pushed out shortly before 3:00 p.m. The House hallway immediately in front of the House Chamber's door was cleared at 2:56 p.m.[313] The mob outside of the Speaker's lobby was pushed out of the House side door at 2:57 p.m.[314]

USCP officers were able to quickly clear out the Senate Chamber, which was initially breached at 2:42 p.m.[315] Rioters were cleared from the hallways outside the Senate by 3:09 p.m.[316] Surveillance shows officers checking the Senate Gallery and hallways for rioters; there are no people on camera by this time.[317]

The Rotunda served as a key point where the mob settled during the Capitol attack. For example, at 2:45 p.m., hundreds of people can be seen standing in the Rotunda.[318] It appears law enforcement officers funneled rioters from other parts of the Capitol into the Rotunda. Once they had President Trump's supporters herded there, law enforcement started to push them towards the east doors shortly after 3:00 p.m. At 3:25 p.m., law enforcement successfully pushed rioters out of the Rotunda and closed the doors so that the room could remain secure.[319] By 3:43 p.m., just 18 minutes after the Rotunda doors were closed, law enforcement successfully pushed the rioters out of the east doors of the Capitol.[320]

The last rioters in the Capitol building were cleared out of the Senate wing door—the same location where rioters first breached the building at 2:13 p.m. Like the other locations inside the Capitol, law enforcement began forcing rioters out of the Senate wing door after 3:00 p.m. By 3:40 p.m., law enforcement had successfully pushed many of the rioters out of the door and onto the upper West Plaza.[321] However, officers were unable to close the doors because some rioters remained in the doorway and attempted to re-enter the building. At 4:23 p.m., a combination of USCP and MPD officers forced these people out of the doorway and successfully secured the door.[322]

After clearing the inside of the Capitol, law enforcement officers proceeded to sweep the perimeter adjacent to the building, starting with the upper West Plaza. After pushing the last rioter out of the Senate wing door, officers started to clear the upper West Plaza, which is located just outside this same doorway. Law enforcement officers in riot gear formed a line and marshalled the crowd north from the upper West Plaza. By 4:31 p.m., 8 minutes after closing the Senate wing door, rioters were cleared from the upper West Plaza.[323]

Many of these same officers started to secure the north side of the Capitol as they pushed rioters from the upper West Plaza towards the East Plaza. By approximately 4:32 p.m., law enforcement officers walked out of the North Doors, forming additional lines to push rioters eastward. As discussed earlier, the North Doors had been the location of violent fighting throughout much of the afternoon. By 4:46 p.m., law enforcement had

Police officers form line to push rioters away from the Capitol building.
(Photo by Spencer Platt/Getty Images)

successfully pushed the rioters from the north side of the Capitol to the
East Plaza.[324]

Law enforcement cleared the East Plaza next. By 4:59 p.m., officers had
swept all the remaining rioters from the east stairs of the Capitol.[325] At this
point, the mob that had overrun the upper West Plaza, the north side of the
Capitol, and the East Plaza had been moved off the grounds adjacent to the
Capitol.

The last areas of the Capitol grounds to get cleared were the tunnel and
the lower West Plaza. Thousands of rioters had packed into the West Plaza
just after the initial invasion, led by the Proud Boys and their associates.
The tunnel was the location of the day's most violent fighting and the conflict extended until late in the day.

After 5:00 p.m., it appears that law enforcement directed their attention
to clearing the lower West Plaza, including the tunnel. At 5:04 p.m., police
officers in the tunnel shot smoke bombs to get the remaining rioters to
back away from the doors.[326] By 5:05 p.m., the rioters had all retreated and
the police officers inside the tunnel moved out and started clearing out the
area.[327]

At 5:13 p.m., on the opposite side of the lower West Plaza, officers
pushed the mob down the scaffold stairs and to the lower West Plaza.[328]

Vice President Pence and Speaker Pelosi preside over the joint session of Congress.
Photo by Erin Schaff–Pool/Getty Images

These are the same stairs that rioters, led by the Proud Boys and other extremists, had previously climbed before reaching the Senate wing door.

Once the rioters from the tunnel and the scaffold were all situated on the lower West Plaza, officers formed another line and started walking the mob back towards the grass—which was away from the actual Capitol building. The line appears to have been fully formed at 5:19 p.m., and the officers started their sweep at 5:30 p.m.[329] By 5:37 p.m., police officers pushed rioters back to the grassy area away from the Capitol. It was at this time that in or around the Capitol building.[330] At 6:56 p.m., a little more than an hour after the Capitol grounds were cleared, Vice President Pence returned to the Capitol from the loading dock.[331] Vice President Pence walked up the stairs in the basement of the Capitol to his office in the Senate at 7:00 p.m.[332]

Shortly after 8:00 p.m., the joint session of Congress resumed, with Vice President Pence saying: "Let's get back to work." [333] At 3:32 a.m., the Congress completed the counting of the votes and certified the election of Joseph R. Biden, Jr. as the 46th President of the United States.

ENDNOTES

1. Enrique Tarrio (@NobleLead), Parler, Jan. 6, 2021 11:16 p.m. ET, available at https://
   twitter.com/ryanjreilly/status/1533921251743391745 (Ryan J. Reilly (@ryanjreilly), Twitter,
   June 6, 2022 5:18 p.m. ET (retweeting the Premonition video)).

2. Third Superseding Indictment at 22, *United States v. Nordean et al.*, No. 1:21-cr-175 (D.D.C.
   June 6, 2022), ECF No. 380.

3. Third Superseding Indictment at 22, *United States v. Nordean et al.*, No. 1:21-cr-175 (D.D.C.
   June 6, 2022), ECF No. 380.

4. "Leader of Proud Boys and Four Other Members Indicted in Federal Court for Seditious
   Conspiracy and Other Offenses Related to U.S. Capitol Breach," Department of Justice,
   (June 6, 2022), available at https://www.justice.gov/opa/pr/leader-proud-boys-and-four-
   other-members-indicted-federal-court-seditious-conspiracy-and.

5. "Leader of Proud Boys and Four Other Members Indicted in Federal Court for Seditious
   Conspiracy and Other Offenses Related to U.S. Capitol Breach," Department of Justice,
   (June 6, 2022), available at https://www.justice.gov/opa/pr/leader-proud-boys-and-four-
   other-members-indicted-federal-court-seditious-conspiracy-and.

6. "Leader of Proud Boys and Four Other Members Indicted in Federal Court for Seditious
   Conspiracy and Other Offenses Related to U.S. Capitol Breach," Department of Justice,
   (June 6, 2022), available at https://www.justice.gov/opa/pr/leader-proud-boys-and-four-
   other-members-indicted-federal-court-seditious-conspiracy-and.

7. Documents on file with the Select Committee to Investigate the January 6th Attack on the
   United States Capitol (Nick Quested Production), Video file
   ML_DC_20210106_Sony_FS5_Clip0065_1, at 0:04 and 1:14 (Jacob Chansley being interviewed
   the morning of the 6th).

8. Documents on file with the Select Committee to Investigate the January 6th Attack on the
   United States Capitol (Nick Quested Production), Video file
   ML_DC_20210106_Sony_FS5_Clip0067_1, at 11:43 (an unnamed woman being interviewed the
   morning of the 6th).

9. Trial Transcript at 4542 and Trial Exhibit No. 6370, *United States v. Rhodes et al.*, No. 1:22-
   cr-15 (D.D.C. Oct. 20, 2022).

10. Documents on file with the Select Committee to Investigate the January 6th Attack on the
    United States Capitol (Secret Service Production), CTRL0000882478, p. 1 (event summary of
    January 6th rally).

11. *See, e.g.*, Select Committee to Investigate the January 6th Attack on the United States Capi-
    tol, Transcribed Interview of Cassidy Hutchinson, (Feb. 23, 2022), pp. 87–88; Select Commit-
    tee to Investigate the January 6th Attack on the United States Capitol, Continued Interview
    of Cassidy Hutchinson, (June 20, 2022), pp. 12–13.

12. Select Committee to Investigate the January 6th Attack on the United States Capitol, Con-
    tinued Interview of Cassidy Hutchinson, (June 20, 2022), pp. 12–13.

13. Select Committee to Investigate the January 6th Attack on the United States Capitol, Con-
    tinued Interview of Cassidy Hutchinson, (June 20, 2022), pp. 11–12.

14. Documents on file with the Select Committee to Investigate the January 6th Attack on the
    United States Capitol (Secret Service Production), CTRL0000086772, (Coordinated Response
    to a Request for Information from the Select Committee, Nov. 18, 2021).

15. Documents on file with the Select Committee to Investigate the January 6th Attack on the
    United States Capitol (Secret Service Production), CTRL0000882478 (event summary of
    January 6th rally).

16. Documents on file with the Select Committee to Investigate the January 6th Attack on the United
    States Capitol (Secret Service Production), CTRL0000882478 (event summary of January 6th rally).

17. Documents on file with the Select Committee to Investigate the January 6th Attack on the United States Capitol (Department of Interior Production), DOI_46003146_00005053, (general arrest report at the Washington Monument on the morning of January 6th).

18. Documents on file with the Select Committee to Investigate the January 6th Attack on the United States Capitol (Department of Interior Production), DOI_46003146_00005053, (general arrest report at the Washington Monument on the morning of January 6th).

19. Documents on file with the Select Committee to Investigate the January 6th Attack on the United States Capitol (Department of Interior Production), DOI_46003146_00005053, (general arrest report at the Washington Monument on the morning of January 6th).

20. Select Committee to Investigate the January 6th Attack on the United States Capitol, Informal Interview of National Parks Service Staff, (Oct. 27–28, 2021), p. 6.

21. Select Committee to Investigate the January 6th Attack on the United States Capitol, Informal Interview of National Parks Service Staff, (Oct. 27–28, 2021), p. 6.

22. Tom Jackman, Rachel Weiner, and Spencer S. Hsu, "Evidence of Firearms in Jan. 6 Crowd Grows as Arrests and Trials Mount," *Washington Post*, (July 8, 2022), available at https://www.washingtonpost.com/dc-md-va/2022/07/08/jan6-defendants-guns/.

23. Documents on file with the Select Committee to Investigate the January 6th Attack on the United States Capitol (Secret Service Production), CTRL0000882478 (event summary of Jan 6 rally).

24. Documents on file with the Select Committee to Investigate the January 6th Attack on the United States Capitol (District of Columbia Production), MPD 73–78 (District of Columbia, Metropolitan Police Department, Transcript of Radio Calls, January 6, 2021); Documents on file with the Select Committee to Investigate the January 6th Attack on the United States Capitol (District of Columbia Production), CTRL0000070375, at 3:40 (District of Columbia, Metropolitan Police Department, audio file of radio traffic from Jan. 6, 2021, from 12:00–13:00).

25. Statement of Offense at 4, *United States v. Colon*, No. 1:21-cr-160, (D.D.C. Apr. 27, 2022), ECF 143.

26. Statement of Offense at 4, *United States v. Colon*, No. 1:21-cr-160, (D.D.C. Apr. 27, 2022), ECF 143.

27. Affidavit in Support of Criminal Complaint and Arrest Warrant at 21–23, *United States v. Kuehne*, No. 1:21-cr-160, (D.D.C. Feb. 10, 2021), available at https://www.justice.gov/usao-dc/case-multi-defendant/file/1366446/download.

28. See Spencer S. Hsu and Tom Jackman, "First Jan. 6 Defendant Convicted at Trial Receives Longest Sentence of 7 Years," *Washington Post*, (Aug. 1, 2022), available at https://www.washingtonpost.com/dc-md-va/2022/08/01/reffitt-sentence-jan6/.

29. Statement of Facts at 3, 5, *United States v. Bargar*, No. 1:22-mj-169, (D.D.C. July 29, 2022), ECF No. 1-1. *See* Documents on file with the Select Committee to Investigate the January 6th Attack on the United States Capitol, (District of Columbia Production, Axon Body 3 X6039BLAL, at 14:30:03 (MPD body camera footage).

30. Statement of Facts at 5, *United States v. Bargar*, No. 1:22-mj-169, (D.D.C. July 29, 2022), ECF No. 1-1.

31. Statement of Facts at 5, *United States v. Bargar*, No. 1:22-mj-169, (D.D.C. July 29, 2022), ECF No. 1-1.

32. Statement of Offense at 3, *United States v. Mazza*, No. 1:21-cr-736, (D.D.C. June 17, 2022), ECF No. 25.

33. Statement of Offense at 3-4, *United States v. Mazza*, No. 1:21-cr-736, (D.D.C. June 17, 2022), ECF No. 25; Statement of Facts at 2, *United States v. Mazza*, No. 1:21-cr-736, (D.D.C. Nov. 12, 2021), ECF No. 1-1.

34. Government's Sentencing Memorandum at 9–10, *United States v. Mazza*, No. 1:21-cr-736 (D.D.C. Sept. 23, 2022), ECF No. 30.

35. For example, on November 13, 2020, Mazza (@MarkNunzios64) tweeted at President Trump: "Can you unseal obama's birth certificate and college transcripts?" On Facebook, Mazza shared a Q "drop" titled "The Armor of God," a 9/11 Truther video, and multiple posts dedicated to lies about the 2020 Presidential election. Screenshots on file with the Select Committee.

36. Hannah Rabinowitz and Holmes Lybrand, "Armed US Capitol Rioter Tells Investigators if He Had Found Pelosi, 'You'd be Here for Another Reason,'" CNN, (Nov. 23, 2021), available at https://www.cnn.com/2021/11/22/politics/loaded-firearm-january-6-charged-mark-mazza/index.html.

37. Government's Memorandum in Aid of Sentencing at 3, *United States v. Coffman*, No. 1:21-cr-4, (Mar. 2, 2022), ECF 28.

38. Government's Memorandum in Aid of Sentencing at 3, *United States v. Coffman*, No. 1:21-cr-4, (Mar. 2, 2022), ECF 28.

39. Government's Memorandum in Aid of Sentencing at 4, *United States v. Coffman*, No. 1:21-cr-4, (Mar. 2, 2022), ECF 28.

40. Select Committee to Investigate the January 6th Attack on the United States Capitol, Deposition of Jeffrey Lawrence Morelock, (Jan. 26, 2022), p. 81.

41. Trial Exhibit 1.S.159.524, *United States v. Rhodes et al.*, No. 1:22-cr-15, (D.D.C Oct. 4, 2022); Trial Transcript at 10502-08, *United States v. Rhodes et al.*, No. 1:22-cr-15 (D.D.C. Nov. 29, 2022)

42. Trial Transcript at 4109, *United States v. Rhodes et al.*, No. 1:22-cr-15, (D.D.C. Oct. 18, 2022).

43. Trial Transcript at 4106-08, *United States v. Rhodes et al.*, No. 1:22-cr-15 (D.D.C. Oct. 18, 2022)

44. Government's Opposition to Defendant's Motion to Revoke Magistrate Judge's Detention Order at 4, *United States v. Miller*, No. 1:21-cr-119, (D.D.C. Mar. 29, 2021), ECF No. 16.

45. Statement of Facts at 2, 9, *United States v. Miller*, No. 1:21-cr-119 (D.D.C. Jan. 19, 2021), ECF No. 1-1.

46. Government's Opposition to Defendant's Motion to Modify Release Conditions at 3, *United States v. Harkrider*, No. 1:21-cr-117, (D.D.C. July 8, 2021), ECF No. 40.

47. Government's Opposition to Defendant's Motion to Modify Release Conditions at 3, *United States v. Harkrider*, No. 1:21-cr-117, (D.D.C. July 8, 2021), ECF No. 40.

48. Dylan Stableford, "New Video Shows Alleged Jan. 6 Capitol Rioters Threatening Pence," Yahoo! News (Feb. 7, 2022), available at https://news.yahoo.com/new-video-jan-6-capitol-riot-pence-threat-drag-through-streets-195249884.html.

49. Select Committee to Investigate the January 6th Attack on the United States Capitol, Transcribed Interview of Eric Barber, (Mar. 16, 2022), p. 41.

50. Statement of Facts at 3–4, *United States v. Foy*, No. 1:21-cr-108 (D.D.C. Jan. 20, 2021), ECF No. 1-1.

51. Statement of Facts at 3–4, *United States v. Foy*, No. 1:21-cr-108 (D.D.C. Jan. 20, 2021), ECF No. 1-1; Government's Opposition to Defendant's Emergency Bond Review Motion at 5 n.3, *United States v. Foy*, No. 1:21-cr-108 (D.D.C. Mar. 12, 2021), ECF No. 11.

52. Statement of Facts at 2–4, *United States v. Webster*, No. 1:21-cr-208 (D.D.C. Feb. 19, 2021), ECF No. 1-1. *See also* Holmes Lybrand, "Former NYPD Officer Sentenced to 10 Years in Prison for Assaulting a Police Officer on January 6," CNN (Sept. 1, 2022), available at https://www.cnn.com/2022/09/01/politics/nypd-officer-january-6-sentencing/index.html.

53. January 6th Committee, "Loudermilk Footage," YouTube, June 5, 2022, available at https://www.youtube.com/watch?v=G9RNJ1tx4zw.

54. Select Committee to Investigate the January 6th Attack on the United States Capitol, Transcribed Interview of Nick Quested, (Apr. 5, 2022), pp. 123–25.

55. First Superseding Indictment at 3, *United States v. Nordean et al.*, No. 1:21-cr-175 (D.D.C. Mar. 10, 2021), ECF No. 26; "Auburn, Washington Member of Proud Boys Charged with Obstructing an Official Proceeding, Other Charges Related to the Jan. 6 Riots," Department of Justice, (Feb. 3, 2021), available at https://www.justice.gov/usao-wdwa/pr/auburn-washington-member-proud-boys-charged-obstructing-official-proceeding-other.

56. Third Superseding Indictment at 16, *United States v. Nordean et al.*, No. 21-cr-175 (TJK) (D.D.C. June 6, 2022), ECF No. 380, available at https://www.justice.gov/usao-dc/case-multi-defendant/file/1510971/download; Statement of Offense at 4, *United States v. Finley*, No. 1:21-cr-526 (D.D.C. March 8, 2022), available at https://www.justice.gov/usao-dc/case-multi-defendant/file/1492396/download.

57. "Auburn, Washington Member of Proud Boys Charged with Obstructing an Official Proceeding, Other Charges Related to the Jan. 6 Riots," Department of Justice, (Feb. 3, 2021), available at https://www.justice.gov/usao-wdwa/pr/auburn-washington-member-proud-boys-charged-obstructing-official-proceeding-other.

58. "Auburn, Washington Member of Proud Boys Charged with Obstructing an Official Proceeding, Other Charges Related to the Jan. 6 Riots," Department of Justice, (Feb. 3, 2021), available at https://www.justice.gov/usao-wdwa/pr/auburn-washington-member-proud-boys-charged-obstructing-official-proceeding-other.

59. "Auburn, Washington Member of Proud Boys Charged with Obstructing an Official Proceeding, Other Charges Related to the Jan. 6 Riots," Department of Justice, (Feb. 3, 2021), available at https://www.justice.gov/usao-wdwa/pr/auburn-washington-member-proud-boys-charged-obstructing-official-proceeding-other.

60. Third Superseding Indictment at 16, *United States v. Nordean et al.*, No. 1:21-cr-175 (D.D.C. June 6, 2022), ECF No. 380, available at https://www.justice.gov/usao-dc/case-multi-defendant/file/1510971/download.

61. *See* "War Room - 2019-AUG 09, Friday - Joe Biggs and Owen Shroyer Talk Internet Censorship and Democrat Party Terrorism," Spreaker.com, (Aug. 9, 2019), available at https://www.spreaker.com/user/realalexjones/08-09-19-warroom; Alexandra Garrett, "Joe Biggs, Proud Boys Leader and Former Infowars Staffer, Arrested Over Capitol Riot," *Newsweek*, (Jan. 20, 2021), available at https://www.newsweek.com/joe-biggs-proud-boys-leader-former-infowars-staffer-arrested-over-capitol-riot-1563181.

62. Affidavit in Support of Criminal Complaint at 4, *United States v. Biggs*, No. 1:21-cr-175 (D.D.C. Jan. 19, 2021), available at https://www.justice.gov/opa/page/file/1357251/download.

63. Affidavit in Support of Criminal Complaint at 4, *United States v. Biggs*, No. 1:21-cr-175 (D.D.C. Jan. 19, 2021), available at https://www.justice.gov/opa/page/file/1357251/download.

64. Affidavit in Support of Criminal Complaint at 4, *United States v. Biggs*, No. 1:21-cr-175 (D.D.C. Jan. 19, 2021), available at https://www.justice.gov/opa/page/file/1357251/download.

65. Affidavit in Support of Criminal Complaint at 4, *United States v. Biggs*, No. 1:21-cr-175 (D.D.C. Jan. 19, 2021), available at https://www.justice.gov/opa/page/file/1357251/download.

66. Statement of Offense at 4, *United States v. Finley*, No. 1:21-cr-526 (D.D.C. Apr. 6, 2022), ECF No. 38, available at https://www.justice.gov/usao-dc/case-multi-defendant/file/1492396/download; First Superseding Indictment at 3, *United States v. Nordean et al.*, No. 1:21-cr-175 (D.D.C. Mar. 10, 2021), ECF No. 26, available at https://www.justice.gov/usao-dc/case-multi-defendant/file/1377586/download.

67. First Superseding Indictment at 3, *United States v. Nordean et al.*, No. 1:21-cr-175 (D.D.C. Mar. 10, 2021), ECF No. 26, available at https://www.justice.gov/usao-dc/case-multi-defendant/file/1377586/download.

68. First Superseding Indictment at 8–9, 12, *United States v. Nordean et al.*, No. 1:21-cr-175 (D.D.C. Mar. 10, 2021), ECF No. 26, available at https://www.justice.gov/usao-dc/case-multi-defendant/file/1377586/download.

69. U.S. Capitol Police Camera U.S. Capitol Police Camera 9004.

70. U.S. Capitol Police Camera 3187.

71. Documents on file with the Select Committee to Investigate the January 6th Attack on the United States Capitol (Nick Quested Production), Video file Iphone_Nick_DC_20210106_IMG_1081_1_1.mov, at 0:14; Select Committee to Investigate the January 6th Attack on the United States Capitol, Transcribed Interview of Nick Quested, (Apr. 5, 2022), pp. 139–40.

72. Select Committee to Investigate the January 6th Attack on the United States Capitol, Transcribed Interview of Nick Quested, (Apr. 5, 2022), p. 138.

73. Select Committee to Investigate the January 6th Attack on the United States Capitol, Transcribed Interview of Nick Quested, (Apr. 5, 2022), pp. 130–31.

74. Select Committee to Investigate the January 6th Attack on the United States Capitol, Transcribed Interview of Nick Quested, (Apr. 5, 2022), p. 134; Documents on file with the Select Committee to Investigate the January 6th Attack on the United States Capitol (Nick Quested Production), Video file M_DC_20210106_Sony_GC280A_0486.mov.

75. Select Committee to Investigate the January 6th Attack on the United States Capitol, Transcribed Interview of Nick Quested, (Apr. 5, 2022), pp. 132, 143.

76. U.S. Capitol Police Camera 946.

77. "Peace Monument," Architect of the Capitol, available at https://www.aoc.gov/explore-capitol-campus/art/peace-monument.

78. U.S. Capitol Police Cameras 946, 3187.

79. Documents on file with the Select Committee to Investigate the January 6th Attack on the United States Capitol (Nick Quested Production), Video file ML_DC_20210106_Sony_GC280A_0498.mov, at 0:00–0:30.

80. Select Committee to Investigate the January 6th Attack on the United States Capitol, Transcribed Interview of Caroline Elizabeth Edwards, (Apr. 18, 2022), pp. 33–38; Documents on file with the Select Committee to Investigate the January 6th Attack on the United States Capitol (Nick Quested Production), Video file ML_DC_20210106_Sony_GC280A_0498 2022-05-15 15.00.38 at 1:15.

81. Documents on file with the Select Committee to Investigate the January 6th Attack on the United States Capitol (Nick Quested Production), Video file Iphone_Nick_DC_20210106_IMG_1116_1.mov.

82. Alan Feuer, "Dispute over Claim that Proud Boys Leader Urged Attack at Capitol," *New York Times*, (Oct. 7, 2021), available at https://www.nytimes.com/2021/10/07/us/politics/proud-boys-capitol-riot.html.

83. Alan Feuer, "Dispute over Claim that Proud Boys Leader Urged Attack at Capitol," *New York Times*, (Oct. 7, 2021), available at https://www.nytimes.com/2021/10/07/us/politics/proud-boys-capitol-riot.html.

84. U.S. Capitol Police Camera 946.

85. Select Committee to Investigate the January 6th Attack on the United States Capitol, Transcribed Interview of Caroline Elizabeth Edwards, (Apr. 18, 2022), pp. 41–42.

86. U.S. Capitol Police Cameras 945, 946, and 3187; Documents on file with the Select Committee to Investigate the January 6th Attack on the United States Capitol (Nick Quested Production), Video files Iphone_Nick_DC_20210106_IMG_1127_1.mov, Iphone_Nick_DC_20210106_IMG_1127 2_1.mov; Elijah Schaffer (@ElijahSchaffer), Twitter, Jan.

6, 2021 6:46 p.m. ET, available at https://twitter.com/ElijahSchaffer/status/1346966514990149639.

87. Select Committee to Investigate the January 6th Attack on the United States Capitol, Transcribed Interview of Caroline Elizabeth Edwards, (Apr. 18, 2022), pp. 44; Video files Iphone_Nick_DC_20210106_IMG_1127_1.mov, Iphone_Nick_DC_20210106_IMG_1127 2_1.mov; Elijah Schaffer (@ElijahSchaffer), Twitter, Jan. 6, 2021 6:46 p.m. ET, available at https://twitter.com/ElijahSchaffer/status/1346966514990149639.

88. Affidavit in Support of Criminal Complaint and Arrest Warrant at 6–8, *United States v. Jackman*, No. 1:21-cr-378 (D.D.C. Mar. 26, 2021), ECF No. 1-1.

89. Statement of Facts at 1–2, *United States v. Pepe*, No. 1:21-cr-52 (D.D.C. Jan. 11, 2021), ECF No. 1-1.

90. Affidavit in Support of Criminal Complaint and Arrest Warrant at 7, *United States v. Jackman*, No. 1:21-cr-378 (D.D.C. Mar. 26, 2021), ECF No. 1-1.

91. Statement of Offense at 5, *United States v. Finley*, No. 1:21-cr-526 (D.D.C. Apr. 6, 2022), ECF No. 38.

92. Statement of Offense at 2–5, *United States v. Bertino*, No. 1:22-cr-329 (D.D.C. Oct. 6, 2022), ECF No. 5.

93. U.S. Capitol Police Camera 908.

94. U.S. Capitol Police Camera 944.

95. U.S. Capitol Police Camera 944; Trial Exhibit 1515.1, *United States v. Rhodes et al.*, No. 1:22-cr-15 (D.D.C. Oct. 18, 2022); Trial Exhibit 6757, *United States v. Rhodes et al.*, No. 1:22-cr-15 (D.D.C. Nov. 1, 2022) (showing timelapse of security footage outside the Capitol).

96. "Donald Trump Speech 'Save America' Rally Transcript January 6," Rev, (Jan. 6, 2021), available at https://www.rev.com/blog/transcripts/donald-trump-speech-save-america-rally-transcript-january-6.

97. Documents on file with the Select Committee to Investigate the January 6th Attack on the United States Capitol (Alex Holder Production), Video file 45DAY32CAMB0059.mov, at 2:11 (using audio track 4 to hear the statement clearly from someone off camera).

98. "Tennessee Man Pleads Guilty to Felony Charges for Actions During Jan. 6 Capitol Breach," Department of Justice, (Sep. 30, 2022), available at https://www.justice.gov/usao-dc/pr/tennessee-man-pleads-guilty-felony-charges-actions-during-jan-6-capitol-breach.

99. "Tennessee Man Pleads Guilty to Felony Charges for Actions During Jan. 6 Capitol Breach," Department of Justice, (Sep. 30, 2022), available at https://www.justice.gov/usao-dc/pr/tennessee-man-pleads-guilty-felony-charges-actions-during-jan-6-capitol-breach.

100. "Two Men Sentenced to 44 Months in Prison for Assaulting Law Enforcement Officers During Jan. 6 Capitol Breach," Department of Justice, (July 15, 2022), available at https://www.justice.gov/usao-dc/pr/two-men-sentenced-prison-assaulting-law-enforcement-officers-during-jan-6-capitol-breach.

101. Statement of Offense at 4, *United States v. Mattice*, No. 1:21-cr-657 (D.D.C. Apr. 22, 2022), ECF No. 44.

102. Government's Opposition to Defendant's Motion for Release from Pretrial Detention at 10–11, *United States v. Nichols*, No. 1:21-cr-117 (D.D.C. Nov. 29, 2021), ECF No. 61; Tom Dreisbach (@TomDreisbach), Twitter, Feb. 4, 2022, 7:40 p.m. ET, available at https://twitter.com/TomDreisbach/status/1489763508459687937?ref_src=twsrc%5Etfw%7Ctwcamp%5Etweetembed%7Ctwterm%5E1489763508459687937%7Ctwgr%5E%7Ctwcon%5Es1_&ref_url=; Select Committee to Investigate the January 6th Attack on the United States Capitol, Public Hearing, (June 16, 2022), at 0:14:11–0:15:00, https://youtu.be/vBjUWVKuDj0?t=851; Hearing on Motion to Modify Conditions of Release, Exhibit 07 at 7:43–8:00, *United States v. Nichols*, No. 1:21-cr-117 (D.D.C. Dec. 20, 2021). Nichols had made similarly violent statements since the November 2020 election, with increasing references to fighting on January 6th following President Trump's December 19th tweet. *See* Government's Opposition to Defendant's

Motion for Release from Pretrial Detention at 4–8, *United States v. Nichols*, No. 1:21-cr-117 (D.D.C. Nov. 29, 2021), ECF No. 61 (documenting the many communications Nichols had with his codefendant planning for violence).

103. Government's Opposition to Defendant's Motion for Release from Pretrial Detention at 10–11, *United States v. Nichols*, No. 1:21-cr-117 (D.D.C. Nov. 29, 2021), ECF No. 61; Tom Dreisbach (@TomDreisbach), Twitter, Feb. 4, 2022, 7:40 p.m. ET, available at: https://twitter.com/TomDreisbach/status/1489763508459687937?ref_src=twsrc%5Etfw%7Ctwcamp%5Etweetembed%7Ctwterm%5E1489763508459687937%7Ctwgr%5E%7Ctwcon%5Es1_&ref_url=; Select Committee to Investigate the January 6th Attack on the United States Capitol, Public Hearing, (June 16, 2022), at 0:14:11–0:15:00, https://youtu.be/vBjUWVKuDj0?t=851; Hearing on Motion to Modify Conditions of Release, Exhibit 07 at 7:43–8:00, *United States v. Nichols*, No. 1:21-cr-117 (D.D.C. Dec. 20, 2021).

104. On the Media, "Jessica Watkins on 'Stop The Steal J6' Zello Channel (Unedited)," Sound-Cloud, at 4:00–4:12, Mar. 8, 2021, available at https://soundcloud.com/user-403747081/jessica-watkins-on-stop-the-steal-j6-zello-channel-unedited.

105. On the Media, "Jessica Watkins on 'Stop The Steal J6' Zello Channel (Unedited)," Sound-Cloud, at 5:30–5:34, Mar. 8, 2021, available at https://soundcloud.com/user-403747081/jessica-watkins-on-stop-the-steal-j6-zello-channel-unedited.

106. Statement of Facts at 13, *United States v. Hazard*, No. 1:22-cr-70 (D.D.C. Dec. 7, 2021), ECF No. 1-1; Joy Sharon Yi and Kate Woodsome, "How the Capitol Attack Unfolded, from Inside Trump's Rally to the Riot | Opinion," *The Washington Post*, at 1:32–1:42, (Jan. 12, 2021), available at https://www.washingtonpost.com/video/opinions/how-the-capitol-attack-unfolded-from-inside-trumps-rally-to-the-riot-opinion/2021/01/12/a7146251-b076-426e-a2e3-8b503692c89d_video.html.

107. Documents on file with the Select Committee to Investigate the January 6th Attack on the United States Capitol (Caroline Wren Production), REVU_000474 (Jan. 6, 2021, Alex Jones text message to Caroline Wren).

108. Documents on file with the Select Committee to Investigate the January 6th Attack on the United States Capitol (Caroline Wren Production), REVU_000474 (Jan. 6, 2021, Alex Jones text message to Caroline Wren).

109. Select Committee to Investigate the January 6th Attack on the United States Capitol, Deposition of Alexander Jones, (Jan. 24, 2022), Exhibit 13 at 0:29 (excerpt from The Alex Jones Show on Jan. 7, 2022).

110. Select Committee to Investigate the January 6th Attack on the United States Capitol, Deposition of Caroline Wren, (Dec. 17, 2021), pp. 260–61.

111. Select Committee to Investigate the January 6th Attack on the United States Capitol, Deposition of Caroline Wren, (Dec. 17, 2021), pp. 260–61; *See generally* The Alex Jones Show, "Humanity is Carrying Out its Own Great Reset Against Planet's Corrupt Elite - FULL SHOW 1/24/22," Banned.Video, at 37:00, Jan. 24, 2022, available at https://banned.video/watch?id=61ef3e9d186875155e97ece8&list=5d81058ce2ea200013c01580.

112. Select Committee to Investigate the January 6th Attack on the United States Capitol, Deposition of Alexander Jones, (Jan. 24, 2022), Ex. 13 at 0:29 (Excerpt from The Alex Jones Show on Jan. 7, 2022); Documents on file with the Select Committee to Investigate the January 6th Attack on the United States Capitol (Caroline Wren Production), REVU_000475 (Jan. 6, 2021, Alex Jones text message to Caroline Wren); Documents on file with the Select Committee to Investigate the January 6th Attack on the United States Capitol (Caroline Wren Production), REVU_000484 (Jan. 5, 2021, Tim Enlow text message to Caroline Wren).

113. Select Committee to Investigate the January 6th Attack on the United States Capitol, Deposition of Caroline Wren, (Dec. 17, 2021), p. 244.

114. Select Committee to Investigate the January 6th Attack on the United States Capitol, Deposition of Caroline Wren, (Dec. 17, 2021), p. 244.

115. Select Committee to Investigate the January 6th Attack on the United States Capitol, Deposition of Caroline Wren, (Dec. 17, 2021), p. 244.

116. The Alex Jones Show, "Humanity is Carrying Out its Own Great Reset Against Planet's Corrupt Elite - FULL SHOW 1/24/22," Banned.Video, at 37:00, Jan. 24, 2022, available at https://banned.video/watch?id=61ef3e9d186875155e97ece8&list=5d81058ce2ea200013c01580.

117. The Alex Jones Show, "Humanity is Carrying Out its Own Great Reset Against Planet's Corrupt Elite - FULL SHOW 1/24/22," Banned.Video, at 37:44, Jan. 24, 2022, available at https://banned.video/watch?id=61ef3e9d186875155e97ece8&list=5d81058ce2ea200013c01580.

118. The Alex Jones Show, "Humanity is Carrying Out its Own Great Reset Against Planet's Corrupt Elite - FULL SHOW 1/24/22," Banned.Video, at 37:26, Jan. 24, 2022, available at https://banned.video/watch?id=61ef3e9d186875155e97ece8&list=5d81058ce2ea200013c01580.

119. The Alex Jones Show, "Humanity is Carrying Out its Own Great Reset Against Planet's Corrupt Elite - FULL SHOW 1/24/22," Banned.Video, at 37:58, Jan. 24, 2022, available at https://banned.video/watch?id=61ef3e9d186875155e97ece8&list=5d81058ce2ea200013c01580.

120. The Alex Jones Show, "Humanity is Carrying Out its Own Great Reset Against Planet's Corrupt Elite - FULL SHOW 1/24/22," Banned.Video, at 38:00, Jan. 24, 2022, available at https://banned.video/watch?id=61ef3e9d186875155e97ece8&list=5d81058ce2ea200013c01580.

121. The Alex Jones Show, "Humanity is Carrying Out its Own Great Reset Against Planet's Corrupt Elite - FULL SHOW 1/24/22," Banned.Video, at 38:16, Jan. 24, 2022, available at https://banned.video/watch?id=61ef3e9d186875155e97ece8&list=5d81058ce2ea200013c01580 .

122. Select Committee to Investigate the January 6th Attack on the United States Capitol, Deposition of Matthew Walter, (Mar. 9, 2022), p. 78.

123. Select Committee to Investigate the January 6th Attack on the United States Capitol, Deposition of Matthew Walter, (Mar. 9, 2022), p. 75.

124. Documents on file with the Select Committee to Investigate the January 6th Attack on the United States Capitol (Google Voice Production, Feb. 25, 2022).

125. Documents on file with the Select Committee to Investigate the January 6th Attack on the United States Capitol (Verizon Production, Nov. 19, 2021).

126. Documents on file with the Select Committee to Investigate the January 6th Attack on the United States Capitol (AT&T Production, Nov. 24, 2021).

127. Select Committee to Investigate the January 6th Attack on the United States Capitol, Deposition of Alexander Jones, (Jan. 24, 2022), Exhibit 12 at 0:20.

128. Lena Groeger, Jeff Kao, Al Shaw, Moiz Syed and Maya Eliahou, "What Parler Saw During the Attack on the Capitol," ProPublica, (Jan. 17, 2021), available at https://projects.propublica.org/parler-capitol-videos/?id=HS34fpbzqg2b.

129. Lena Groeger, Jeff Kao, Al Shaw, Moiz Syed and Maya Eliahou, "What Parler Saw During the Attack on the Capitol," ProPublica, (Jan. 17, 2021), available at https://projects.propublica.org/parler-capitol-videos/?id=Qo3hom0Qb1at.

130. Lena Groeger, Jeff Kao, Al Shaw, Moiz Syed and Maya Eliahou, "What Parler Saw During the Attack on the Capitol," ProPublica, (Jan. 17, 2021), available at https://projects.propublica.org/parler-capitol-videos/?id=QgPXUnbdhx3q.

131. Lena Groeger, Jeff Kao, Al Shaw, Moiz Syed and Maya Eliahou, "What Parler Saw During the Attack on the Capitol," ProPublica, (Jan. 17, 2021), available at https://projects.propublica.org/parler-capitol-videos/?id=QgPXUnbdhx3q.

132. Lena Groeger, Jeff Kao, Al Shaw, Moiz Syed and Maya Eliahou, "What Parler Saw During the Attack on the Capitol," ProPublica, (Jan. 17, 2021), available at https://projects.propublica.org/parler-capitol-videos/?id=QgPXUnbdhx3q.

133. Jan. 6th Protest and Save America March, "Raw BodyCam: Watch As Alex Jones Works With Capitol Police To Try And Quell The Riot," Banned.Video, at 8:45, Jan. 12, 2021, available at https://banned.video/watch?id=5ffe25bc0d763c3dca0c4da1.

134. Lena Groeger, Jeff Kao, Al Shaw, Moiz Syed and Maya Eliahou, "What Parler Saw During the Attack on the Capitol," ProPublica, (Jan. 17, 2021), available at https://projects.propublica.org/parler-capitol-videos/?id=a8lp9oooOT3m.

135. Jan. 6th Protest and Save America March, "Raw BodyCam: Watch as Alex Jones Works with Capitol Police To Try And Quell The Riot," Banned.Video, at 15:10, Jan. 12, 2021, available at https://Banned.Video/watch?id=5ffe25bc0d763c3dca0c4da1.

136. Documents on file with the Select Committee to Investigate the January 6th Attack on the United States Capitol (District of Columbia Production), MPD 125–MPD 126 (District of Columbia, Metropolitan Police Department, Transcript of Radio Calls, January 6, 2021)

137. Government's Memorandum in Support of Pretrial Detention of Defendant Guy Wesley Reffitt at 4, *United States v. Reffitt*, No. 1:21-cr-32 (D.D.C. Mar. 13, 2021), ECF No. 10.

138. *See* Government's Memorandum in Support of Pretrial Detention of Defendant Guy Wesley Reffitt at 4–5, *United States v. Reffitt*, No. 1:21-cr-00032 (D.D.C. Mar. 13, 2021), ECF No. 10.

139. *See* Government's Memorandum in Support of Pretrial Detention of Defendant Guy Wesley Reffitt at 4–5, *United States v. Reffitt*, No. 1:21-cr-00032 (D.D.C. Mar. 13, 2021), ECF No. 10.

140. *See* Government's Memorandum in Support of Pretrial Detention of Defendant Guy Wesley Reffitt at 5, *United States v. Reffitt*, No. 1:21-cr-00032 (D.D.C. Mar. 13, 2021), ECF No. 10.

141. *See* Government's Memorandum in Support of Pretrial Detention of Defendant Guy Wesley Reffitt at 5, *United States v. Reffitt*, No. 1:21-cr-00032 (D.D.C. Mar. 13, 2021), ECF No. 10.

142. *See* Government's Memorandum in Support of Pretrial Detention of Defendant Guy Wesley Reffitt at 5, *United States v. Reffitt*, No. 1:21-cr-00032 (D.D.C. Mar. 13, 2021), ECF No. 10.

143. *See* Government's Memorandum in Support of Pretrial Detention of Defendant Guy Wesley Reffitt at 6, *United States v. Reffitt*, No. 1:21-cr-00032 (D.D.C. Mar. 13, 2021), ECF No. 10.

144. *See* Government's Memorandum in Support of Pretrial Detention of Defendant Guy Wesley Reffitt at 12, *United States v. Reffitt*, No. 1:21-cr-00032 (D.D.C. Mar. 13, 2021), ECF No. 10.

145. *See* Government's Memorandum in Support of Pretrial Detention of Defendant Guy Wesley Reffitt at 4, *United States v. Reffitt*, No. 1:21-cr-32 (D.D.C. Mar. 13, 2021), ECF No. 10.

146. Government's Sentencing Memorandum, *United States v. Reffitt*, No. 1:21-cr-32 (D.D.C. July 15, 2022), ECF No. 158.

147. *See* Spencer S. Hsu and Tom Jackman, "First Jan. 6 Defendant Convicted at Trial Receives Longest Sentence of 7 Years," *Washington Post*, (Aug. 1, 2022), available at https://www.washingtonpost.com/dc-md-va/2022/08/01/reffitt-sentence-jan6/.

148. *See* Statement of Facts at ¶¶ 14, 20, *United States v. Scott*, No. 1:21-mj-411 (D.D.C. April 29, 2021), ECF No. 1-1, available at https://www.justice.gov/usao-dc/case-multi-defendant/file/1395876/download.

149. *See* Statement of Facts at ¶ 16, *United States v. Scott*, No. 1:21-mj-411 (D.D.C. April 29, 2021), ECF No. 1-1, available at https://www.justice.gov/usao-dc/case-multi-defendant/file/1395876/download.

150. Statement of Facts at 9, *United States v. Worrell*, No. 1:21-mj-296 (D.D.C. Mar. 10, 2021), ECF No. 1-1, available at https://www.justice.gov/usao-dc/case-multi-defendant/file/1379556/download.

151. Statement of Facts at 10–11, *United States v. Worrell*, No. 1:21-mj-296 (D.D.C. Mar. 10, 2021), ECF No. 1-1, available at https://www.justice.gov/usao-dc/case-multi-defendant/file/1379556/download.

152. Statement of Offense at ¶ 9, *United States v. Jackson*, No. 1:21-cr-484 (D.D.C. Nov. 22, 2021), ECF No. 19, available at https://www.justice.gov/usao-dc/case-multi-defendant/file/1452291/download.

153. Statement of Offense at ¶¶ 1, 25, *United States v. Greene*, No. 1:21-cr-52-33 (D.D.C. Dec. 22, 2021), ECF No. 105, available at https://www.justice.gov/usao-dc/press-release/file/1458266/download.

154. Lena Groeger, Jeff Kao, Al Shaw, Moiz Syed and Maya Eliahou, "What Parler Saw During the Attack on the Capitol," ProPublica, (Jan. 17, 2021), available at https://projects.propublica.org/parler-capitol-videos/?id=zOZ8CgfNU1SY.

155. Statement of Facts at 5, *United States v. Kelley*, No. 1:22-cr-222 (D.D.C. June 8, 2022), ECF No. 1.

156. Statement of Facts at 6, *United States v. Kelley*, No. 1:22-cr-222 (D.D.C. June 8, 2022), ECF No. 1.

157. *See* Select Committee to Investigate the January 6th Attack on the United States Capitol, Deposition of Ryan Kelley, (Apr. 21, 2022), pp. 7, 70–71, 79–80, and Exhibit 15.

158. Arrest Warrant at 1, *United States v. Kelley*, No. 1:22-cr-222 (D.D.C. June 9, 2022), ECF No. 5.

159. U.S. Capitol Police Camera 102; Third Superseding Indictment at 21, *United States v. Nordean et al.*, No. 1:21-cr-175 (D.D.C. June 6, 2022), ECF No. 380 (noting that Dominic Pezzola "used [a] riot shield . . . to break a window of the Capitol" at "2:13 p.m." and that "[t]he first members of the mob entered the Capitol through this broken window"); 167 Cong. Rec. S634 (daily ed. Feb. 10, 2021), available at https://www.congress.gov/117/crec/2021/02/10/CREC-2021-02-10-pt1-PgS615-4.pdf.

160. U.S. Capitol Police Camera 689; Third Superseding Indictment at 21, *United States v. Nordean et al.*, No. 1:21-cr-175 (D.D.C. June 6, 2022), ECF No. 380 (noting that Dominic Pezzola "used [a] riot shield . . . to break a window of the Capitol" at "2:13 p.m." and that "[t]he first members of the mob entered the Capitol through this broken window."); 167 Cong. Rec. S634 (daily ed. Feb. 10, 2021), available at https://www.congress.gov/117/crec/2021/02/10/CREC-2021-02-10-pt1-PgS615-4.pdf.

161. Third Superseding Indictment at 21, *United States v. Nordean et al.*, No. 1:21-cr-175 (D.D.C. June 6, 2022), ECF No. 380 (noting that Dominic Pezzola "used [a] riot shield . . . to break a window of the Capitol" at "2:13 p.m." and that "[t]he first members of the mob entered the Capitol through this broken window"); 167 Cong. Rec. S634 (daily ed. Feb. 10, 2021), available at https://www.congress.gov/117/crec/2021/02/10/CREC-2021-02-10-pt1-PgS615-4.pdf. *See also* Ashley Parker, Carol D. Leonnig, Paul Kane, and Emma Brown, "How the Rioters Who Stormed the Capitol Came Dangerously Close to Pence," *Washington Post*, (Jan. 15, 2021), available at https://www.washingtonpost.com/politics/pence-rioters-capitol-attack/2021/01/15/ab62e434-567c-11eb-a08b-f1381ef3d207_story.html; Kat Lonsdorf, Courtney Dorning, Amy Isackson, Mary Louise Kelly, and Aeilsa Chang, "A Timeline of How The Jan. 6 Attack Unfolded—Including Who Said What and When," NPR, (June 9, 2022), available at https://www.npr.org/2022/01/05/1069977469/a-timeline-of-how-the-jan-6-attack-unfolded-including-who-said-what-and-when.

162. Peter Manseau, "His Pastors Tried to Steer Him Away from Social Media Rage. He Stormed the Capitol Anyway," *Washington Post*, (Feb. 19, 2021), available at https://www.washingtonpost.com/religion/2021/02/19/michael-sparks-capitol-siege-jan-6-christian/.

163. Statement of Facts at 9, *United States v. Sparks*, No. 1:21-cr-87 (D.D.C. Jan. 19, 2021), ECF No. 1.

164. Complaint and Affidavit at 9–10, *United States v. Gieswein*, No. 1:21-cr-24 (D.D.C. Jan. 16, 2021), ECF No. 1. As an example of his conspiracy beliefs, Gieswein claimed that American politicians "have completely destroyed our country and sold them to the Rothschilds and Rockefellers." This is a standard anti-Semitic trope. *See* Complaint and Affidavit at 11, *United States v. Gieswein*, No. 1:21-cr-24 (D.D.C. Jan. 16, 2021), ECF No. 1. Gieswein also denied that he was a Three Percenter as of January 6, 2021, even though he affiliated with an apparent Three Percenter group at previous times. *See* Mr. Gieswein's Motion for Hearing & Revocation of Detention Order at 2–3, 18–19, 25, *United States v. Gieswein*, No. 1:21-cr-24 (D.D.C. June 8, 2021), ECF No. 18. When the FBI arrested Gieswein, the criminal complaint noted that he "appears to be affiliated with the radical militia group known as the Three Percenters." Criminal Complaint at 5, *United States v. Gieswein*, No. 1:21-cr-24 (D.D.C. Jan. 16, 2021), available at https://www.justice.gov/opa/page/file/1360831/

download. *See also* Adam Rawnsley (@arawnsley), Twitter, Jan. 17, 2021 9:13 p.m. ET, available at https://twitter.com/arawnsley/status/1350989535954530315 (highlighting photos of Gieswein flashing a Three Percenter symbol).

165. Statement of Facts at 1–2, *United States v. Jensen*, No. 1:21-cr-6 (D.D.C. Jan. 8, 2021), ECF No. 1.

166. Statement of Facts at 2, *United States v. Jensen*, No. 1:21-cr-6 (D.D.C. Jan. 8, 2021), ECF No. 1.

167. "Arizona Man Sentenced to 41 Months in Prison On Felony Charge in Jan. 6 Capitol Breach," Department of Justice, (Nov. 17, 2021), available at https://www.justice.gov/usao-dc/pr/arizona-man-sentenced-41-months-prison-felony-charge-jan-6-capitol-breach.

168. Statement of Facts at 2, *United States v. Seefried*, No. 1:21-mj-46 (D.D.C. Jan. 13, 2021), available at: https://www.justice.gov/usao-dc/press-release/file/1354306/download.

169. Statement of Facts at 2, *United States v. Seefried*, No. 1:21-mj-46 (D.D.C. Jan. 13, 2021), available at https://www.justice.gov/usao-dc/press-release/file/1354306/download; Maria Cramer, "Confederate Flag an Unnerving Sight in the Capitol," *New York Times*, (Jan. 9, 2021), available at https://www.nytimes.com/2021/01/09/us/politics/confederate-flag-capitol.html.

170. Statement of Facts at 2, 5, *United States v. Seefried*, No. 1:21-mj-46 (D.D.C. Jan. 13, 2021), available at https://www.justice.gov/usao-dc/press-release/file/1354306/download.

171. "Delaware Man Sentenced to 24 Months in Prison for Actions Related to Capitol Breach," Department of Justice, (Oct. 24, 2022), available at https://www.justice.gov/usao-dc/pr/delaware-man-sentenced-24-months-prison-actions-related-capitol-breach.

172. "Virginia Man Arrested on Felony and Misdemeanor Charges for Actions During Jan. 6 Capitol Breach," Department of Justice, (Sep. 20, 2022), available at https://www.justice.gov/usao-dc/pr/virginia-man-arrested-felony-and-misdemeanor-charges-actions-during-jan-6-capitol-breach; Statement of Facts at 44, *United States v. Brody, et al.*, No. 1:22-mj-203 (D.D.C. Sep. 12, 2022), available at https://www.justice.gov/usao-dc/press-release/file/1536736/download.

173. "Virginia Man Arrested on Felony and Misdemeanor Charges for Actions During Jan. 6 Capitol Breach," Department of Justice, (Sep. 20, 2022), available at https://www.justice.gov/usao-dc/pr/virginia-man-arrested-felony-and-misdemeanor-charges-actions-during-jan-6-capitol-breach.

174. Statement of Facts at 44, *United States v. Brody, et al.*, No. 1:22-mj-203 (D.D.C. Sep. 12, 2022), available at https://www.justice.gov/usao-dc/press-release/file/1536736/download.

175. Statement of Facts at 44, *United States v. Brody, et al.*, No. 1:22-mj-203 (D.D.C. Sep. 12, 2022), available at https://www.justice.gov/usao-dc/press-release/file/1536736/download.

176. Neil Vigdor and Alan Feuer, "A Jan. 6 Defendant Coordinated Volunteers to Help Youngkin's Campaign," *New York Times*, (Oct. 6, 2022), available at https://www.nytimes.com/2022/10/06/us/politics/joseph-brody-jan-6-youngkin.html.

177. Statement of Facts at 43, *United States v. Brody, et al.*, No. 1:22-mj-203 (D.D.C. Sept. 12, 2022), available at https://www.justice.gov/usao-dc/press-release/file/1536736/download.

178. "Virginia Man Arrested on Felony and Misdemeanor Charges for Actions During Jan. 6 Capitol Breach," Department of Justice, (Sep. 20, 2022), available at https://www.justice.gov/usao-dc/pr/virginia-man-arrested-felony-and-misdemeanor-charges-actions-during-jan-6-capitol-breach.

179. "Virginia Man Arrested on Felony and Misdemeanor Charges for Actions During Jan. 6 Capitol Breach," Department of Justice, (Sep. 20, 2022), available at https://www.justice.gov/usao-dc/pr/virginia-man-arrested-felony-and-misdemeanor-charges-actions-during-jan-6-capitol-breach.

180. "Virginia Man Arrested on Felony and Misdemeanor Charges for Actions During Jan. 6 Capitol Breach," Department of Justice (Sep. 20, 2022), available at https://www.justice.gov/

usao-dc/pr/virginia-man-arrested-felony-and-misdemeanor-charges-actions-during-jan-6-capitol-breach; Statement of Facts at 40–43, *United States v. Brody, et al.,* No. 1:22-mj-203 (D.D.C. Sep. 12, 2022), available at https://www.justice.gov/usao-dc/press-release/file/1536736/download.

181. Statement of Facts at 2–3, 6–7, *United States v. Williams,* No. 1:21-cr-618 (D.D.C. Jan. 17, 2021), available at https://www.justice.gov/opa/page/file/1357051/download. A jury found Williams guilty of certain felony and misdemeanor charges, but could not reach a verdict on other charges, including the aiding and abetting charge. *See* "Pennsylvania Woman Found Guilty of Felony and Misdemeanor Charges Related to Capitol Breach," Department of Justice, (Nov. 21, 2022), available at https://www.justice.gov/usao-dc/pr/pennsylvania-woman-found-guilty-felony-and-misdemeanor-charges-related-capitol-breach.

182. Government's Sentencing Memorandum at 12, *United States v. Hale-Cusanelli,* No. 1:21-cr-37 (D.D.C. Sep. 15, 2022), ECF No. 110; "New Jersey Man Sentenced to 48 Months in Prison for Actions Related to Capitol Breach," Department of Justice, (Sep. 22, 2022), available at https://www.justice.gov/usao-dc/pr/new-jersey-man-sentenced-prison-actions-related-capitol-breach; Statement of Facts at 2, *United States v. Hale-Cusanelli,* No. 1:21-cr-37, (D.D.C. Jan. 15, 2021), available at https://www.justice.gov/opa/page/file/1356066/download. Pictures available online depict Hale-Cusanelli with a Hitler-style mustache. *See* Holmes Lybrand and Andrew Millman, "U.S. Capitol Rioter and Alleged Nazi Sympathizer Sentenced to 4 Years in Prison," CNN, (Sep. 22, 2022), available at https://www.cnn.com/2022/09/22/politics/timothy-hale-cusanelli-stephen-ayres-capitol-riot/index.html.

183. "New Jersey Man Sentenced to 48 Months in Prison for Actions Related to Capitol Breach," Department of Justice, (Sep. 22, 2022), available at https://www.justice.gov/usao-dc/pr/new-jersey-man-sentenced-prison-actions-related-capitol-breach.

184. "New Jersey Man Sentenced to 48 Months in Prison for Actions Related to Capitol Breach," Department of Justice, (Sep. 22, 2022), available at https://www.justice.gov/usao-dc/pr/new-jersey-man-sentenced-prison-actions-related-capitol-breach.

185. Statement of Offense at 3, *United States v. Packer,* No. 1:21-cr-103 (D.D.C. Jan. 13, 2021), available at https://www.justice.gov/usao-dc/case-multi-defendant/file/1469561/download.

186. Affidavit in Support of Criminal Complaint and Arrest Warrant at 4–5, *United States v. Packer,* No. 1:21-cr-103, (D.D.C. Jan. 13, 2021), available at https://www.justice.gov/usao-dc/press-release/file/1353201/download.

187. U.S. Capitol Police Cameras 102, 123.

188. Igor Bobic (@igorbobic), Twitter, Jan. 6, 2021 3:09 p.m. ET, available at https://twitter.com/igorbobic/status/1346911809274478594; Spencer S. Hsu, "Officer Describes How Jan. 6 Rioters Pursued Him through Capitol," *Washington Post,* (June 15, 2022), available at https://www.washingtonpost.com/dc-md-va/2022/06/13/eugene-goodman-capitol-police-testimony/.

189. Igor Bobic (@igorbobic), Twitter, Jan. 6, 2021 3:09 p.m. ET, available at https://twitter.com/igorbobic/status/1346911809274478594; Peter Manseau, "His Pastors Tried to Steer Him Away from Social Media Rage. He Stormed the Capitol Anyway," *Washington Post,* (Feb. 19, 2021), available at https://www.washingtonpost.com/religion/2021/02/19/michael-sparks-capitol-siege-jan-6-christian/; Government's Opposition to Defendant's Motion for Hearing & Revocation of Detention Order at 8, *United States v. Robert Gieswein,* No. 1:21-cr-24 (EGS) (D.D.C. June 15, 2021), available at https://extremism.gwu.edu/sites/g/files/zaxdzs2191/f/Robert%20Gieswein%20Government%20Opposition%20to%20Motion%20for%20Hearing%20and%20Revocation%20of%20Detention%20Order.pdf.

190. "Iowa Man Found Guilty of Felony and Misdemeanor Charges Related to Capitol Breach," Department of Justice, (Sep. 23, 2022), https://www.justice.gov/usao-dc/pr/iowa-man-found-guilty-felony-and-misdemeanor-charges-related-capitol-breach.

191. Peter Manseau, "His Pastors Tried to Steer Him Away from Social Media Rage. He Stormed the Capitol Anyway," Washington Post, (Feb. 19, 2021), available at https://www.washingtonpost.com/religion/2021/02/19/michael-sparks-capitol-siege-jan-6-christian/.

192. U.S. Capitol Police Cameras 113, 114.

193. U.S. Capitol Police Camera 213; Igor Bobic (@igorbobic), Twitter, Jan. 6, 2021 3:09 p.m. ET, available at https://twitter.com/igorbobic/status/1346911809274478594.

194. Lena Groeger, Jeff Kao, Al Shaw, Moiz Syed and Maya Eliahou, "What Parler Saw During the Attack on the Capitol," ProPublica, (Jan. 17, 2021), available at https://projects.propublica.org/parler-capitol-videos/?id=s8XNlAskWNvi.

195. Lena Groeger, Jeff Kao, Al Shaw, Moiz Syed and Maya Eliahou, "What Parler Saw During the Attack on the Capitol," ProPublica, (Jan. 17, 2021), available at https://projects.propublica.org/parler-capitol-videos/?id=s8XNlAskWNvi.

196. Lena Groeger, Jeff Kao, Al Shaw, Moiz Syed and Maya Eliahou, "What Parler Saw During the Attack on the Capitol," ProPublica, (Jan. 17, 2021), available at https://projects.propublica.org/parler-capitol-videos/?id=s8XNlAskWNvi.

197. Affidavit in Support of Criminal Complaint and Arrest Warrant at 12, *United States v. Rae*, No. 1:21-cr-378 (D.D.C. Mar. 23, 2021), ECF No. 1.

198. Statement of Offense at 4, United States v. Pruitt, No. 1:21-cr-23 (D.D.C. June 3, 2022), ECF No. 61, available at https://www.justice.gov/usao-dc/case-multi-defendant/file/1510401/download.

199. U.S. Capitol Police Cameras 113, 114.

200. U.S. Capitol Police Camera 102.

201. U.S. Capitol Police Cameras 932, 933.

202. Lena Groeger, Jeff Kao, Al Shaw, Moiz Syed and Maya Eliahou, "What Parler Saw During the Attack on the Capitol," ProPublica, (Jan. 17, 2021), available at https://projects.propublica.org/parler-capitol-videos/?id=a8lp9oooOT3m.

203. Jan. 6th Protest and Save America March, "Raw BodyCam: Watch as Alex Jones Works with Capitol Police to Try and Quell the Riot," Banned.Video, at 15:10, posted Jan. 12, 2021, available at https://banned.video/watch?id=5ffe25bc0d763c3dca0c4da1

204. CNN Business, "Alex Jones' Influence on January 6," CNN, Feb. 26, 2022, available at https://www.cnn.com/videos/media/2022/02/26/alex-jones-influence-january-6-documentary.cnnbusiness.

205. Hunting Insurrectionists, "East Main 'Columbus' Doors 1:45-4:45pm - 56 video sync - Jan 6th Capitol Attack Footage," YouTube, at 31:53, Mar. 12, 2021, available at https://www.youtube.com/watch?v=z1gODZvbhqs&t=1901s.

206. Select Committee to Investigate the January 6th Attack on the United States Capitol, Deposition of Matthew Thomas Walter, (Mar. 9, 2022), p. 79.

207. Select Committee to Investigate the January 6th Attack on the United States Capitol, Deposition of Matthew Thomas Walter, (Mar. 9, 2022), p. 79.

208. Hunting Insurrectionists, "East Main 'Columbus' Doors 1:45-4:45pm - 56 video sync - Jan 6th Capitol Attack Footage," YouTube, at 36:15, Mar. 12, 2021, available at https://www.youtube.com/watch?v=z1gODZvbhqs&t=1901s

209. CNN Business, "Alex Jones' Influence on January 6," CNN, at 2:20–2:28, Feb. 26, 2022, available at https://www.cnn.com/videos/media/2022/02/26/alex-jones-influence-january-6-documentary.cnnbusiness.

210. Hunting Insurrectionists, "East Main 'Columbus' Doors 1:45-4:45pm - 56 video sync - Jan 6th Capitol Attack Footage," YouTube, at 39:19, Mar. 12, 2021, available at https://www.youtube.com/watch?v=z1gODZvbhqs&t=1901s.

211. Select Committee to Investigate the January 6th Attack on the United States Capitol, Deposition of Ali Alexander, (Dec. 9, 2021), pp. 64–66.

212. U.S. Capitol Police Cameras 7029, 7216.

213. U.S. Capitol Police Camera 7029.

214. Complaint with Arrest Warrant at 16–19, *United States v. Loehrke*, No. 1:21-mj-672 (D.D.C. Nov. 30, 2021), ECF No. 1, available at https://www.justice.gov/usao-dc/case-multi-defendant/file/1459171/download.

215. Complaint with Arrest Warrant at 12, *United States v. Loehrke*, No. 1:21-mj-672 (D.D.C. Nov. 30, 2021), ECF No. 1, available at https://www.justice.gov/usao-dc/case-multi-defendant/file/1459171/download.

216. Complaint with Arrest Warrant at 12, *United States v. Loehrke*, No. 1:21-mj-672 (D.D.C. Nov. 30, 2021), ECF No. 1, available at https://www.justice.gov/usao-dc/case-multi-defendant/file/1459171/download.

217. Complaint with Arrest Warrant at 12, *United States v. Loehrke*, No. 1:21-mj-672 (D.D.C. Nov. 30, 2021), ECF No. 1, available at https://www.justice.gov/usao-dc/case-multi-defendant/file/1459171/download.

218. Complaint with Arrest Warrant at 14–19, *United States v. Loehrke*, No. 1:21-mj-672 (D.D.C. Nov. 30, 2021), ECF No. 1, available at https://www.justice.gov/usao-dc/case-multi-defendant/file/1459171/download; "Two Men Charged with Obstructing Law Enforcement During Jan. 6 Capitol Breach," Department of Justice, (Dec. 3, 2021), available at https://www.justice.gov/usao-dc/pr/two-men-charged-obstructing-law-enforcement-during-jan-6-capitol-breach.

219. Complaint with Arrest Warrant at 24–29, *United States v. Loehrke*, No. 1:21-mj-672 (D.D.C. Nov. 30, 2021), ECF No. 1, available at https://www.justice.gov/usao-dc/case-multi-defendant/file/1459171/download.

220. Select Committee to Investigate the January 6th Attack on the United States Capitol, Informal Interview of Brian Adams and Marc Carrion, (Apr. 20, 2022).

221. "Two Men Charged with Obstructing Law Enforcement During Jan. 6 Capitol Breach," Department of Justice, (Dec. 3, 2021), available at https://www.justice.gov/usao-dc/pr/two-men-charged-obstructing-law-enforcement-during-jan-6-capitol-breach.

222. U.S. Capitol Police Camera 7029.

223. *See* Chapter 6.

224. Trial Transcript at 4532:20–4534:9, *United States v. Rhodes et al.*, No. 1:22-cr-15 (D.D.C. Oct. 20, 2022).

225. Trial Transcript at 4642:24–4643:6 and Trial Exhibit 6731, United States v. Rhodes et al., No. 1:22-cr-15 (D.D.C. Oct. 20, 2022).

226. Trial Transcript at 4643:22–4644:4 and Trial Exhibit 6731, United States v. Rhodes et al., No. 1:22-cr-15 (D.D.C. Oct. 20, 2022).

227. Trial Transcript at 4520:9–4521:5, 4744:20–4745:21, Trial Exhibits 1503, 6740, *United States v. Rhodes et al.*, No. 1:22-cr-15 (D.D.C. Oct. 20, 2022).

228. Seventh Superseding Indictment at 21–22, *United States v. Crowl et al.*, No. 21-cr-28 (D.D.C. Jan. 12, 2022), available at https://www.justice.gov/opa/press-release/file/1462476/download.

229. Seventh Superseding Indictment at 22, *United States v. Crowl et al.*, No. 21-cr-28 (D.D.C. Jan. 12, 2022), available at https://www.justice.gov/opa/press-release/file/1462476/download.

230. Trial Transcript at 4724:8–15 and Trial Exhibit 1500 at 13:02–13:25, *United States v. Rhodes et al.*, No. 1:22-cr-15 (D.D.C. Oct. 20, 2022).

231. Trial Transcript at 4779:1–4790:3 and Trial Exhibit 1505, *United States v. Rhodes et al.*, No. 1:22-cr-15 (D.D.C. Oct. 20, 2022).

232. U.S. Capitol Police Camera 7029; "Leader of Alabama Chapter of Oath Keepers Pleads Guilty to Seditious Conspiracy and Obstruction of Congress for Efforts to Stop Transfer of Power Following 2020 Presidential Election," Department of Justice, (Mar. 2, 2022), available at https://www.justice.gov/opa/pr/leader-alabama-chapter-oath-keepers-pleads-guilty-seditious-conspiracy-and-obstruction#:~:text=Joshua%20James%2C%2034%2C%20of%20Arab,with%20the%20government's%20ongoing%20investigation; Statement of Offense at 8, *United States v. James*, No. 1:22-cr-15 (D.D.C. Mar. 2, 2022), ECF No. 60, available at https://www.justice.gov/opa/press-release/file/1479551/download.

233. Trial Transcript at 4803:10–4804:23 and Trial Exhibit 1089.1, *United States v. Rhodes et al.*, No. 1:22-cr-15 (D.D.C. Oct. 20, 2022).

234. U.S. Capitol Police Camera 912.

235. "Crypt," Architect of the Capitol, available at https://www.aoc.gov/explore-capitol-campus/buildings-grounds/capitol-building/crypt.

236. U.S. Capitol Police Camera 267.

237. U.S. Capitol Police Cameras 123, 124.

238. U.S. Capitol Police Cameras 123, 124.

239. Watchers Guild, "Rioters Fight with Police at Capitol Building - Washington D.C. - JAN/6/2020," YouTube, Jan. 6, 2020, available at https://www.youtube.com/watch?v=U7DiLh2Pbl4; News2Share, "January 6 United States Capitol Attack," YouTube, June 4, 2021, available at https://www.youtube.com/watch?v=9TshRdxXi9c.

240. Statement of Offense at 4, *United States v. Gordon*, No. 1:22-cr-343 (D.D.C. Oct. 28, 2022), ECF No. 26, available at http://www.justice.gov/usao-dc/press-release/file/1547751/download.

241. Statement of Offense at 4, *United States v. Gordon*, No. 1:22-cr-343 (D.D.C. Oct. 28, 2022), ECF No. 26, available at http://www.justice.gov/usao-dc/press-release/file/1547751/download.

242. Statement of Offense at 4, *United States v. Gordon*, No. 1:22-cr-343 (D.D.C. Oct. 28, 2022), ECF No. 26, available at http://www.justice.gov/usao-dc/press-release/file/1547751/download.

243. Hunting Insurrectionists, "West Terrace 'Tunnel' - 3:50 - 4:21 pm - Jan 6th," YouTube, Mar. 12, 2021, available at https://www.youtube.com/watch?v=Yil1JemYMM0&t=1405s.

244. U.S. Capitol Police Camera 102.

245. Documents on file with the Select Committee to Investigate the January 6th Attack on the United States Capitol (Nick Quested Production), Video file Inside Capitol.mov at 23:01–23:35.

246. U.S. Capitol Police Cameras 178, 402.

247. Documents on file with the Select Committee to Investigate the January 6th Attack on the United States Capitol (Nick Quested Production), Video file Inside Capitol.mov at 13:10–15:47.

248. U.S. Capitol Police Cameras 178, 402.

249. Jake Tapper (@jaketapper), Twitter, Feb. 10, 2021 5:50 p.m. ET, available at https://twitter.com/jaketapper/status/1359635955389509638 (screenshotting Donald J. Trump (@realDonaldTrump), Twitter, Jan. 6, 2021 2:24 p.m. ET, available at https://www.thetrumparchive.com/?searchbox=%22usa+demands+the+truth%22).

250. U.S. Capitol Police Cameras 178, 402.

251. U.S. Capitol Police Cameras 178, 402.

252. *See* Select Committee to Investigate the January 6th Attack on the United States Capitol, Transcribed Interview of David Millard, (Apr. 18, 2022), p. 28.

253.	*See* Select Committee to Investigate the January 6th Attack on the United States Capitol, Transcribed Interview of David Millard, (Apr. 18, 2022), p. 28.

254.	Plea Agreement at 5, *United States v. Pruitt*, No. 1:21-cr-23 (D.D.C. June 3, 2022), ECF No. 61.

255.	Complaint at 34–38, *United States v. Chrestman*, No. 1:21-cr-160 (D.D.C. Feb. 10, 2021), available at https://www.justice.gov/usao-dc/case-multi-defendant/file/1366441/download; Ryan J. Reilly (@ryanjreilly), Twitter, Nov. 26, 2022 1:00 p.m. ET, available at https://twitter.com/ryanjreilly/status/1596564571371749378 (showing video Proud Boy Nicholas DeCarlo filmed while inside the Capitol).

256.	Complaint at 34–38, *United States v. Chrestman*, No. 1:21-cr-160, (D.D.C. Feb. 10, 2021), available at https://www.justice.gov/usao-dc/case-multi-defendant/file/1366441/download.

257.	Indictment at 5, 8–9, *United States v. Kuehne et al.*, No. 1:21-cr-160 (D.D.C. Feb. 26, 2021), ECF No. 29.

258.	Statement of Offense at 3, *United States v. Colon*, No. 1:21-cr-160 (D.D.C. Apr. 27, 2022), ECF No. 143.

259.	Indictment at 5, 8–9, *United States v. Kuehne et al.*, No. 1:21-cr-160 (D.D.C. Feb. 26, 2021), ECF No. 29.

260.	Complaint at 36, *United States v. Chrestman*, No. 1:21-cr-160, (D.D.C. Feb. 10, 2021), available at https://www.justice.gov/usao-dc/case-multi-defendant/file/1366441/download; Ryan J. Reilly (@ryanjreilly), Twitter, Nov. 26, 2022 1:00 p.m. ET, available at https://twitter.com/ryanjreilly/status/1596564571371749378 (showing video Proud Boy Nicholas DeCarlo filmed while inside the Capitol).

261.	Complaint at 36, *United States v. Chrestman*, No. 1:21-cr-160, (D.D.C. Feb. 10, 2021), available at https://www.justice.gov/usao-dc/case-multi-defendant/file/1366441/download.

262.	Statement of Offense at 4, *United States v. Colon*, No. 1:21-cr-160, (D.D.C. Apr. 27, 2022), ECF No. 143.

263.	Statement of Offense at 4, *United States v. Colon*, No. 1:21-cr-160, (D.D.C. Apr. 27, 2022), ECF No. 143.

264.	U.S. Capitol Police Camera 251.

265.	Lena Groeger, Jeff Kao, Al Shaw, Moiz Syed and Maya Eliahou, "What Parler Saw During the Attack on the Capitol," ProPublica, (Jan. 17, 2021), available at https://projects.propublica.org/parler-capitol-videos/?id=sbGOy4rN0ue4.

266.	Statement of Offense at 12–14, *United States v. Chansley*, No. 1:21-cr-3 (D.D.C. Sep. 3, 2021), ECF No. 70.

267.	Statement of Offense at 15, *United States v. Chansley*, No. 1:21-cr-3 (D.D.C. Sep. 3, 2021), ECF No. 70.

268.	Christian Secor, a young Groyper, sat in the Vice President's seat. *See* "California Man Sentenced to 42 Months in Prison for Actions During Jan. 6 Capitol Breach," Department of Justice, (Oct. 19, 2022), available at https://www.justice.gov/usao-dc/pr/california-man-sentenced-prison-actions-during-jan-6-capitol-breach; Complaint at 6, 14–15, *United States v. Secor*, No. 1:21-mj-232 (D.D.C. Feb 13, 2021), ECF No. 1.

269.	Other agitators, such as Vets 4 Trump founder Joshua Macias (who was with Stewart Rhodes and Enrique Tarrio on January 5th), also attacked Vice President Pence outside the Capitol. *See* Select Committee to Investigate the January 6th Attack on the United States Capitol, Deposition of Joshua Macias, (May 2, 2022), pp. 27–28, and Exhibit 14; capitolhunters (@capitolhunters), Twitter, May 27, 2021 8:36 p.m. ET, available at https://twitter.com/capitolhunters/status/1398075750482337792 (video of Macias calling Vice President Pence a "Benedict Arnold" outside of the Capitol on January 6th).

270.	Reagan Battalion (@ReaganBattalion), Twitter, Jan. 7, 2021 5:03 a.m. ET, available at https://twitter.com/ReaganBattalion/status/1347121703823044608.

271.	U.S. Capitol Police Camera 944.

272. Sentencing Transcript at 19, *United States v. Young*, No. 1:21-cr-291 (D.D.C. Sep. 27, 2022), ECF No. 170.

273. U.S. Capitol Police Camera 74.

274. U.S. Capitol Police Camera 74.

275. Government's Sentencing Memorandum at 4–8, *United States v. Head*, No. 1:21-cr-291 (D.D.C. Oct. 19, 2022), ECF No. 159.

276. Statement of Facts at 5, 29–31, 39, *United States v. Denney*, No. 1:22-cr-70 (D.D.C. Dec. 7, 2021), ECF No. 1-1; Status Coup News, "UNBELIEVABLE Footage | Trump Supporters Battle Cops Inside the Capitol," YouTube, at 24:09, Jan. 7, 2021, available at https://www.youtube.com/watch?v=cJOgGsC0G9U.

277. Statement of Facts at 2, 6–7, *United States v. Brown*, No. 1:21-cr-178 (D.D.C. Aug. 16, 2021), ECF No. 1-1; Storyful Viral, "Scenes of Chaos Captures Inside US Capitol as Crowd Challenges Police," YouTube, at 20:05, 21:03, Jan. 7, 2021, available at https://www.youtube.com/watch?v=qc0U755-uiM.

278. Government's Sentencing Memorandum at 25–28, 55, *United States v. Young*, No. 1:21-cr-291 (D.D.C. Sep. 13, 2022), ECF No. 140; Status Coup News, "UNBELIEVABLE Footage | Trump Supporters Battle Cops Inside the Capitol," YouTube, at 9:45–9:56, Jan. 7, 2021, available at https://www.youtube.com/watch?v=cJOgGsC0G9U.

279. Statement of Facts for Stipulated Trial at 6–9, *United States v. Morss*, No. 1:21-cr-40 (D.D.C. Aug. 23, 2022), ECF No. 430; Torsten Ove, "Former Army Ranger Charged with Assaulting Cops during Capitol Riot Faces DC Bench Trial," *Pittsburgh Post-Gazette*, (Aug. 17, 2022), available at: https://www.post-gazette.com/news/crime-courts/2022/08/17/robert-morss-pittsburgh-glenshaw-army-ranger-charged-assaulting-police-capitol-riot-insurrection-january-6-bench-trial/stories/202208170094.

280. Government's Opposition to Defendant's Motion to Set Bond and Conditions of Release at 6–7, *United States v. Schwartz*, No. 1:21-cr-178 (D.D.C. June 15, 2021), ECF No. 26.

281. Statement of Offense at 4, *United States v. Head*, No. 1:21-cr-291 (D.D.C. May 6, 2022), ECF No. 124; Government's Sentencing Memorandum at 1–4, 18, 25, *United States v. Head*, No. 1:21-cr-291 (D.D.C. Oct. 19, 2022), ECF No. 159; Documents on file with the Select Committee to Investigate the January 6th Attack on the United States Capitol (District of Columbia Production), Axon Body 3 No. X6039B9N0, at 15:17–15:20 (MPD body camera footage); "Tennessee Man Sentenced to 90 Months in Prison for Assaulting Law Enforcement Officer During Capitol Breach," Department of Justice, (Oct. 27, 2022), available at https://www.justice.gov/usao-dc/pr/tennessee-man-sentenced-prison-assaulting-law-enforcement-officer-during-capitol-breach.

282. Government's Sentencing Memorandum at 1–4, 18, 25, *United States v. Head*, No. 1:21-cr-291 (D.D.C. Oct. 19, 2022).

283. Statement of Facts at 33–34, *United States v. Denney*, No. 1:22-cr-70 (D.D.C. Dec. 7, 2021), ECF No. 1-1.

284. Government's Sentencing Memorandum at 2, 30–31, *United States v. Young*, No. 1:21-cr-291 (D.D.C. Sept. 13, 2022), ECF No. 140.

285. Statement of Facts at 4–11, *United States v. Sibick*, No. 1:21-cr-291 (D.D.C. Mar. 10, 2021), ECF No. 1-1 (noting that Sibick told the FBI he was trying to help Officer Fanone while other rioters attempted to get the officer's gun).

286. Documents on file with the Select Committee to Investigate the January 6th Attack on the United States Capitol (District of Columbia Production), (Axon Body 3 No. X6039B9N0), at 15:18:51–15:21:12 (MPD body camera footage); Government's Sentencing Memorandum at 27-28, *United States v. Young*, No. 1:21-cr-291 (D.D.C. Sept. 13, 2022), ECF No. 140.

287. Motion to Suppress by Daniel Rodriguez, Exhibit A at 38–39, 43–45, 70–71, *United States v. Rodriguez*, No. 1:21-cr-246 (D.D.C. Oct. 25, 2021), ECF No. 38-1.

288. Motion to Suppress by Daniel Rodriguez, Exhibit A at 17–18, *United States v. Rodriguez*, No. 1:21-cr-246 (D.D.C. Oct. 25, 2021), ECF No. 38-1.

289. Motion to Suppress by Daniel Rodriguez, Exhibit A at 118, *United States v. Rodriguez*, No. 1:21-cr-246 (D.D.C. Oct. 25, 2021), ECF No. 38-1 (quoting Rodriguez saying: "And I was already—Trump was already, like—this is 2015, and I was already into InfoWars and Alex Jones, and he's backing up Trump. And I'm like, all right, man. This is it. I'm going to—this is—I'm going to fight for this. I'm going to do—I want to do this.").

290. Motion to Suppress by Daniel Rodriguez, Exhibit A at 131, *United States v. Rodriguez*, No. 1:21-cr-246 (D.D.C. Oct. 25, 2021), ECF No. 38-1.

291. Motion to Suppress by Daniel Rodriguez, Exhibit A at 34, *United States v. Rodriguez*, No. 1:21-cr-246 (D.D.C. Oct. 25, 2021), ECF No. 38-1.

292. Motion to Suppress by Daniel Rodriguez, Exhibit A at 34, *United States v. Rodriguez*, No. 1:21-cr-246 (D.D.C. Oct. 25, 2021), ECF No. 38-1.

293. Indictment at 2, 5–7, *United States v. Rodriguez et al.*, No. 1:21-cr-246 (D.D.C. Nov. 19, 2021), ECF No. 65.

294. Indictment at 2, 5–7, *United States v. Rodriguez et al.*, No. 1:21-cr-246 (D.D.C. Nov. 19, 2021), ECF No. 65.

295. Indictment at 2, 5–7, *United States v. Rodriguez et al.*, No. 1:21-cr-246 (D.D.C. Nov. 19, 2021), ECF No. 65.

296. Documents on file with the Select Committee to Investigate the January 6th Attack on the United States Capitol (Capitol Police Production), CTRL0000001532.0001 (Jan. 5, 2021, FBI Situational Information Report); *see also* Statement of Facts at 11, 39, *United States v. Denney*, No. 1:22-cr-70 (D.D.C. Dec. 7, 2021), ECF No. 1-1 (noting that Denney, a Three Percenter, posted similar messages about occupying Congress on Facebook).

297. *See* 167 Cong. Rec. S633-38 (daily ed. Feb. 10, 2021), available at https://www.congress.gov/117/crec/2021/02/10/CREC-2021-02-10-pt1-PgS615-4.pdf; Marshall Cohen and Avery Lotz, "The January 6 Insurrection: Minute-by-Minute," CNN, (July 29, 2022), available at https://www.cnn.com/2022/07/10/politics/jan-6-us-capitol-riot-timeline/index.html.

298. United States Secret Service Radio Tango Frequency at 14:14–14:25. Select Committee staff reviewed recordings of this radio frequency. *See also*, U.S. Capitol Police Camera 462.

299. U.S. Capitol Police Camera 961.

300. United States Secret Service Radio Tango Frequency at 14:14–14:25. Select Committee staff reviewed recordings of this radio frequency. *See also* U.S. Capitol Police Camera 462.

301. U.S. Capitol Police Camera 7023.

302. U.S. Capitol Police Camera 461.

303. U.S. Capitol Police Camera 077.

304. U.S. Capitol Police Cameras 3062, 6059, 6146.

305. U.S. Capitol Police Camera 269.

306. Select Committee staff analyzed thousands of hours of surveillance footage from the United States Capitol. There is no camera that captured the evacuation because CSPAN cameras focus on the dais (so they miss the activity on the floor), and there are no CCTV cameras around the floor. The staff first identified Members appearing in the basement of the Capitol at exactly 2:40 p.m. ET. Based on knowledge of the Capitol and judging the distance traveled, staff have estimated that it took Members approximately 2 minutes from leaving the floor to getting to the basement, which puts the evacuation at approximately 2:38 p.m. This time is consistent with informal contemporaneous accounts provided by Members and law enforcement officers who were there. *See* U.S. Capitol Police Camera 0077.

307. U.S. Capitol Police Camera 0077.

308. U.S. Capitol Police Camera 360.

309. U.S. Capitol Police Camera 360.
310. U.S. Capitol Police Camera 360.
311. U.S. Capitol Police Camera 944.
312. U.S. Capitol Police Camera 403.
313. U.S. Capitol Police Camera 251.
314. U.S. Capitol Police Camera 267.
315. U.S. Capitol Police Camera 304.
316. U.S. Capitol Police Cameras 202, 303, 461, 462.
317. U.S. Capitol Police Cameras 202, 303, 461, 462.
318. U.S. Capitol Police Camera 960.
319. U.S. Capitol Police Camera 960.
320. U.S. Capitol Police Camera 7029.
321. U.S. Capitol Police Camera 102.
322. U.S. Capitol Police Camera 102.
323. U.S. Capitol Police Camera 926.
324. U.S. Capitol Police Cameras 927, 928, 929.
325. U.S. Capitol Police Camera 933.
326. U.S. Capitol Police Cameras 074, 944.
327. U.S. Capitol Police Camera 074.
328. U.S. Capitol Police Camera 924.
329. U.S. Capitol Police Camera 944.
330. U.S. Capitol Police Camera 944.
331. U.S. Capitol Police Camera 7032.
332. U.S. Capitol Police Camera 011.
333. "WATCH: 'Let's Get Back to Work,' Pence Urges Senate," PBS, (Jan. 6, 2021), available at
      https://www.pbs.org/newshour/politics/watch-lets-get-back-to-work-pence-urges-senate.

1. Electoral Count Act.

As our Report describes, Donald J. Trump, John Eastman, and others corruptly attempted to violate the Electoral Count Act of 1887 in an effort to overturn the 2020 Presidential Election. To deter other future attempts to overturn Presidential Elections, the House of Representatives has passed H.R. 8873, "The Presidential Election Reform Act," and the Senate should act promptly to send a bill with these principles to the President. H.R. 8873 reaffirms that a Vice President has no authority or discretion to reject an official electoral slate submitted by the Governor of a state. It also reforms Congress's counting rules to help ensure that objections in the joint session conform to Congress's narrow constitutional role under Article II and the Twelfth Amendment. It provides that presidential candidates may sue in federal court to ensure that Congress receives the state's lawful certification, and leaves no doubt that the manner for selecting presidential electors cannot be changed retroactively after the election is over.

2. Accountability.

The Select Committee has made criminal referrals to the Department of Justice, and both the Department of Justice and other prosecutorial authorities will now make their determinations on whether to prosecute individuals involved in the events resulting in an attack on the United States Congress on January 6, 2021. Additional steps may also be appropriate to ensure criminal or civil accountability for anyone engaging in misconduct described in this Report. Those courts and bar disciplinary bodies responsible for overseeing the legal profession in the states and the District of Columbia should continue to evaluate the conduct of attorneys described in this Report. Attorneys should not have the discretion to use their law licenses to undermine the constitutional and statutory process for peacefully transferring power in our government. The Department of Justice should also take appropriate action to prevent its attorneys from participating in campaign-related activities, or (as described in this report) activities aimed at subverting the rule of law and overturning a lawful election. This report also identifies specific attorney conflicts of interest for the Department to evaluate.

3. Violent Extremism.

Federal Agencies with intelligence and security missions, including the Secret Service, should (a) move forward on whole-of-government strategies to combat the threat of violent activity posed by all extremist groups, including white nationalist groups and violent anti-government groups while respecting the civil rights and First Amendment civil liberties of all citizens; and (b) review their intelligence sharing protocols to ensure that threat intelligence is properly prioritized and shared with other responsible intelligence and security agencies on a timely basis in order to combat the threat of violent activity targeting legislative institutions, government operations, and minority groups.

4. Fourteenth Amendment, Section 3.

Under Section 3 of the Constitution's Fourteenth Amendment, an individual who previously took an oath to support the Constitution of the United States, but who has "engaged in an insurrection" against the same, or given "aid or comfort to the enemies of the Constitution" can be disqualified from holding future federal or state office. The Select Committee has referred Donald Trump and others for possible prosecution under 18 U.S.C. 2383, including for assisting and providing aid and comfort to an insurrection. The Committee also notes that Donald J. Trump was impeached by a majority of the House of Representatives for Incitement of an Insurrection, and there were 57 votes in the Senate for his conviction. Congressional committees of jurisdiction should consider creating a formal mechanism for evaluating whether to bar those individuals identified in this Report under Section 3 of the 14th Amendment from holding future federal or state office. The Committee believes that those who took an oath to protect and defend the Constitution and then, on January 6th, engaged in insurrection can appropriately be disqualified and barred from holding government office—whether federal or state, civilian or military—absent at least two-thirds of Congress acting to remove the disability pursuant to Section 3 of the Fourteenth Amendment. The Committee notes that Ms. Wasserman Schultz and Mr. Raskin have introduced H. Con. Res. 93 to declare the January 6 assault an insurrection and H.R. 7906 to establish specific procedures and standards for disqualification under section 3 of the Fourteenth Amendment in the United States district court for the District of Columbia.

5. National Special Security Event.

Until January 6th, 2021, the joint session of Congress for counting electoral votes was not understood to pose the same types of security risks as other major events on Capitol Hill. Both the inaugural and the State of the Union have long been designated as National Special Security Events, requiring specific security measures and significant advance planning and preparation. Given what occurred in 2021, Congress and the Executive Branch should work together to designate the joint session of Congress occurring on January 6th as a National Special Security Event.

6. To the extent needed, consider reforming certain criminal statutes, including to add more severe penalties.

As indicated in the Report, the Committee believes that 18 U.S.C. § 1512(c)2 and other existing provisions of law can be applied to efforts to obstruct, influence, or impede the joint session on January 6th, including to related planning efforts to overturn the lawful election results on that date. To the extent that any court or any other prosecutorial authorities ultimately reach any differing conclusion, Congress should amend those statutes to cover such conduct. Congress should also consider whether the severity of penalties under those statutes is sufficient to deter unlawful conduct threatening the peaceful transfer of power.

7. House of Representatives Civil Subpoena Enforcement Authority.

The current authority of the House of Representatives to enforce its subpoenas through civil litigation is unclear. Congressional committees of jurisdiction should develop legislation to create a cause of action for the House of Representatives to enforce its subpoenas in federal court, either following the statutory authority that exists for the Senate in 2 U.S.C. § 288d and 28 U.S.C. § 1365 or adopting a broad approach to facilitate timely oversight of the executive branch.

8. Threats to Election Workers.

Congressional committees of jurisdiction should consider enhancing federal penalties for certain types of threats against persons involved in the election process and expanding protections for personally identifiable information of election workers.

9. Capitol Police Oversight.

Congressional committees of jurisdiction should continue regular and rigorous oversight of the United States Capitol Police as it improves its planning, training, equipping, and intelligence processes and practices its critical incident response protocols, both internally and with law enforcement partners. Joint hearings with testimony from the Capitol Police Board should take place. Full funding for critical security measures should be assured.[1]

10. Role of the Media.

The Committee's investigation has identified many individuals involved in January 6th who were provoked to act by false information about the 2020 election repeatedly reinforced by legacy and social media. The Committee agrees that individuals remain responsible for their own actions, including their own criminal actions. But congressional committees of jurisdiction should continue to evaluate policies of media companies that have had the effect of radicalizing their consumers, including by provoking people to attack their own country.

11. Discussion of the Insurrection Act.

The Committee has been troubled by evidence that President Trump's possible use of the Insurrection Act was discussed by individuals identified in this Report. Congressional Committees of jurisdiction should further evaluate all such evidence, and consider risks posed for future elections.

ENDNOTE

1.   The Select Committee has shared concerns about two specific areas of security with the Committee on House Administration.

EPILOGUE

We Must Fight for Democracy Itself

By Representative Jamie Raskin
(Democrat of Maryland)

We have it within our power to begin the world over again.

—THOMAS PAINE

What now, dear America?

Well, the fight of our lives continues, and may this book in your hands become a powerful new weapon for truth in the coming battles to strengthen American democracy and protect American freedom.

I take pride in the work of our bipartisan committee and excellent staff, now embodied by this report. After over a year and a half we were able to pierce the thick, moving fog of "Big Lie" propaganda and make plain to America how Donald Trump masterminded and mobilized successive attempts to overthrow the 2020 presidential election and, finally, on January 6, 2021, provoked and unleashed dangerous, insurrectionary violence at the United States Capitol, the purpose of which was the undoing of our constitutional order and the seizure of the presidency in a coup.

We could have lost it all on that day and been plunged into authoritarianism, mass violence, even civil war. We had some luck on our side at crucial moments, along with extraordinary valor and courage from our police officers and patriotism from a lot of election officials along the way. But we can't count on good luck anymore.

What we're facing today is a full-scale frontal assault on democracy—not just in the mob that forced members of the House and Senate, along with the vice president, to flee running from the joint session, but in the form of more systematic threats to majority rule. Those threats have included massive voter suppression, gerrymandering of state and federal legislative districts, the use of the filibuster to block protection of voting rights, and right-wing judicial activism to undermine the Voting Rights Act and other pro-democracy laws adopted by Congress.

What we need in response is a determined public effort, not just to guarantee that there's individual criminal accountability and justice done for the people who leveled this assault on our institutions, but to ensure that we take collective responsibility for addressing the kind of thoroughgoing assault on democratic elections that begins every election year long before the votes are counted. We need a plan to fortify American democratic institutions against future coups, insurrections, political violence, and electoral subversion.

As I saw the mob approach the Capitol the day of the insurrection, I remembered a quote from Voltaire that seemed to capture for me the madness unfolding in Trump's party: "Anyone who can make you believe absurdities can make you commit atrocities."

Donald Trump's Big Lies, Q-Anon conspiracy theories, Fox News disinformation, Putin's propaganda—these are the interlocking enemies of truth and democratic freedom in America. Truth and democracy are inextricably bound together. As my father, Marcus Raskin, once explained: "Democracy must have a ground to stand on, and that ground is the truth."

But even if fighting zealously for the truth about particular attacks on democracy is urgently necessary today—and has been the animating ethos of our committee—it is also radically insufficient. The last two years have shown that it is far easier to identify and prosecute criminal acts that form part of an insurrection or coup than it is to identify and confront the institutional dynamics and structural conditions that set the stage for insurrectionist violence and outbreaks of extremist politics in the first place.

So that is our task in the days ahead. We must fight for democracy itself. We must insist that government be the instrument of the common good rather than a money-making operation for those who can capture high office. We must debunk the "insurrectionary" theory of the Constitution advanced by right-wing forces contending that self-proclaimed private militias have the right to forcibly overthrow the government. We need to defend the democratic culture of truth and facts against the disinformation and conspiracy theory propounded by democracy's enemies online.

When people praise our committee by saying that we are "defending democracy," my colleagues and I are grateful because this is a project of which we are justly proud. But this framing leaves the misimpression that democracy is a static thing, a collection of regular institutions and practices.

Democracy is partly that, but it is also much more. It is a continuing project, the always unfinished quest of linking the people with the power. Democracy is a dynamic process, not a destination but a journey.

It has always been the American journey. Lincoln spoke in lawyerlike terms of "government of the people, by the people, and for the people," but he knew that we began as a slave republic of propertied white males. It has only been through successive waves of momentous social, political, and constitutional struggle that we have come closer to realizing Lincoln's tantalizing and elusive vision.

If you read the Constitution the way I do, most of the seventeen constitutional amendments we have added since the original Bill of Rights are *democratizing* amendments that have transformed us from a slave republic into a democratic one by banning slavery (the 13th amendment), constitutionalizing equal protection and due process (the 14th amendment), forbidding race discrimination in voting (the 15th amendment), shifting the mode of election of U.S. Senators from the legislatures to the people (the 17th amendment), enfranchising women (the 19th amendment), granting people in Washington, D.C., voting rights in presidential elections (the 23rd amendment), ending poll taxes (the 24th amendment), creating stability and order in the peaceful transfer of power (the 25th amendment), and lowering the voting age to 18 (the 26th amendment).

The struggle for a "more perfect Union" has always been a seesaw battle. Alexis de Tocqueville observed in *Democracy in America* that political democracy and voting rights in our country are always either shrinking and contracting or growing and expanding.

We have been in a decidedly contractionary period. Lincoln's anti-slavery, pro-freedom, and pro-immigrant Republican Party, which worked to protect the Union, has become Donald Trump's authoritarian and paranoid cult of personality, which works to subvert the constitutional order and depress democratic participation.

Although it is a minority and a shrinking minority, Trump's party remains a potent threat because it has one important thing going for it—a bag of sinister tricks that all work the same way: *to thwart democracy.* Some of the tricks, like the voter suppression now ubiquitous in red states, choke off popular participation. Some of them, like legislative gerrymandering of state and federal districts, blockade the popular will, fracturing and dissolving political majorities and enthroning political minorities decade after decade.

Other tricks—the use of the filibuster to block voting rights legislation or the right-wing judicial activism that dismembered the Voting Rights Act in cases like *Shelby County v. Holder)*—obstruct the workings of legislative democracy and dismantle basic legislative framework statutes that are the foundation of democratic inclusion.

And the final and most dangerous trick is the unleashing of violent extremism and sabotage against public institutions at all levels when nothing else works to stop the political expression of majority rule.

Our country is in a struggle between the will of the majority and the reactionary determination of the minority to impose the kind of structural choke holds that deprive democracy of oxygen. Many of these chokeholds, like gerrymandering and the filibuster, are not built into the Constitution but are rather improvised political practices deeply antithetical to constitutional values.

The filibuster, for example, is just part of a Senate rule, and it is a tool already riddled with more than 100 exceptions, including in the Budget Reconciliation Act, the Trade Adjustment Act and judicial nominations. If the pro-democracy party can build an effective majority in the Senate, it could carve out another exception to the filibuster for legislation affecting voting rights and democratic participation.

Of course, other anti-democratic institutions are built directly into the Constitution, like the antiquated and obsolete Electoral College, which has produced presidents who lost the popular vote at least five times in our history, twice in this new century alone.

Designed at a time before all the people's right to vote was even a serious idea, much less a reality, and before communications and transportation technology made a national vote for president feasible, the Electoral College is not only profoundly anti-democratic in essence. It also depresses turnout and political action by consigning the vast majority of Americans to "safe" blue or red states that become flyover country for presidential candidates in a winner-take-all system where it is perfectly clear who is going to win in the vast majority of states long before Election Day.

Surely it is time for America to leave the Electoral College behind in the same way we cast aside other anti-democratic filters in the original design, like state legislatures choosing United States senators, the disenfranchisement of women, or poll taxes as a condition for voting. We spend hundreds of millions of dollars every year promoting American political democracy to other nations, remaking their electoral institutions, and they never tell us how impressed they are by our electoral college system or how eager they are to emulate it.

The 2020 election also showed that this undemocratic and arbitrary system is dangerous because bad faith actors have learned how to strategically plant booby traps in every dark corner of its obsolete and complicated architecture. Attendance at the symbolic counting of electoral votes in the joint session of Congress, the quaint ceremony that was disrupted by a rampaging mob on January 6th, can now get you killed.

It's time to elect the president the way we elect mayors, governors, senators, members of Congress, and everyone else: every vote counts and each one counts equally, and whoever gets the most votes wins.

The best way to accomplish that, a mechanism that will lead eventually to a constitutional amendment, is the National Popular Vote Interstate Compact, an agreement among participating states and the District of Columbia to award their electoral votes to whichever presidential candidate wins the nationwide popular vote.

Most pro-democracy constitutional amendments have built on prior state-based efforts like this, such as states granting women the right to vote before the 19th Amendment or states delegating the power to choose senators to the people even before passage of the 17th Amendment. As I write, the movement for the National Popular Vote has already signed up 15 states and the District of Columbia in a coalition containing 195 electoral votes or 72% of the 270 votes needed to activate the compact.

A pro-democracy push must work to revive another lost but critical mechanism of moving disenfranchised populations into the circle of democratic membership and equality by admitting new states to the union.

Nearly three-quarters of the 50 states today entered the Union after it was created, the most recent, Hawaii and Alaska, in 1959. Reviving that process begins with the 713,000 citizens of Washington, D.C., the only residents of a national capital on earth locked out of their own national legislature. Unlike Trump's mob which descended with bloodthirsty rage upon our police officers and interrupted the constitutional transfer of power for the first time in American history, the vastly larger community of citizens living in Washington has a real political grievance, not an imaginary one.

Statehood is also necessary for enfranchising and empowering more than 3.5 million American citizens in Puerto Rico. People there have tasted the bitter fruits of colonial disenfranchisement with Hurricane Maria and other natural disasters, where they have been cheated out of millions of dollars in aid. The House has passed legislation creating a binding plebiscite so Puerto Ricans can choose among three different status alternatives, and it is time for Congress to elevate Puerto Rico's status to a pressing agenda item for the future of democracy in America.

New statehood admissions will help create a more fully responsive and inclusive Congress and government. But how to break out of the GOP's matrix of democracy suppression is a brainteaser that can be solved only by a mass movement pressing on every lever of power against the enemies of democratic progress and inclusion. But we will find our right way on the path if we take to heart the philosopher John Dewey's profound insight that the only solution to the ills of democracy is more democracy.

The Democratic Party—the only major party in America today still standing by free and fair elections and defending the Constitution—will obviously be the political home for pro-democracy Americans for the foreseeable future. But it will have friends and allies across the political spectrum, including Republicans like Liz Cheney and Adam Kinzinger, true Libertarians, Greens, and the tens of millions of Independents who plan to keep the Constitution, the Bill of Rights, and the pragmatic common sense of the people close to their hearts.

More important, American civil society—the universities, the businesses, the labor unions, cities and towns, the free press and media, the churches and nonprofit sector—has been showing an eagerness to pick up the banner of democracy and freedom in America and to resist tyranny when it comes calling.

My father used to say that "when everything looks hopeless, you are the hope." And so you are and so am I. Democracy is each of us pulling together. Most Americans passionately favor democracy, both as a set of existing practices and as a continuing pragmatic experiment in finding ways to link the people with the power. Most Americans reject MAGA appeals, whether direct or coded, to racism, anti-semitism, misogyny, and immigrant-bashing.

This has been an especially hard time for young people who have little memory of any other political reality than the grim one recorded in these pages. They have been confined by Covid-19 and haunted by climate change. And they are surrounded by the politics and culture of right-wing authoritarianism.

Go and organize with them, and tell them about the great changes we have seen in our lives. Tell them that prior generations of patriots have faced daunting odds and crisis in their own times. Those generations fought for democracy and freedom and they prevailed. So will we.

9 781250 877529